S0-BRT-606

Environmental Psychology

Principles and Practice

FIFTH EDITION

Robert Gifford

UNIVERSITY OF VICTORIA

ℰ Optimal Books

COPYRIGHT © 2014 OPTIMAL BOOKS

http://optimalenvironments.com

Distributed by Hermit Distributing
2665 Bodie Mountain Road, Colville, WA 99114

All rights reserved. No part of the material protected by this copyright notice may be reproduced or utilized in any form or by any means, electronic or manual, including photocopying, scanning, recording, or by any storage and retrieval system, without the written permission of the copyright owner.

Printed on recycled, chlorine-free paper

CATALOGUING INFORMATION

Gifford, Robert.
Environmental psychology: Principles and practice / Robert Gifford—5th ed.
Includes bibliographical references and indexes.
ISBN 978-0-9937719-0-3

1. Environmental psychology. I. Title
  [BF353.G54   2014]

Printed in Canada

You are holding a first printing of this book. Read the back cover.

Source credits on pages 557-560 constitute an extension of this copyright page.

This edition is for Robert Sommer— scientist, artist, and inspiration.

Contents

TABLE OF CONTENTS PHOTOS:

1. Bob Friesen. Blueberry farm, Mission, BC.‡

2. TJ Watt. A (former) ancient red cedar in the Klanawa
Valley on southwestern Vancouver Island, BC.

3. Kent Kallberg. Night dining in White Rock, BC.‡

4. Phil Best. Night in Slocan, BC.‡

5. Ryan Jensen. Wet'suwet'en fisherman, Smithers, BC.‡

PHOTO CREDITS for other images in this text appear in
the credits section of this book, pages 557–560.

‡ Indicates use courtesy of the Union of British Columbia
Municipalities and the Picture BC initiative.

ENVIRONMENTAL BENEFITS STATEMENT

Optimal Books saved the following resources by printing the pages of this book on chlorine-free paper made with 10% post-consumer waste.

TREES	WATER	ENERGY	SOLID WASTE	GREENHOUSE GASES
11	5,442	6	364	1,004
FULLY GROWN	GALLONS	MILLION BTUs	POUNDS	POUNDS

 Environmental impact estimates were made using the Environmental Paper Network Paper Calculator 3.2. For more information visit www.papercalculator.org.

Preface

AS I HAVE SAID IN PAST PREFACES, EVERY AUTHOR, BUT ESPECIALLY AN ENVIRONMENTAL PSYCHOLOGIST, SHOULD THINK TWICE ABOUT INKING WORDS ONTO PROCESSED TREES— even using recycled paper, as this book does—and three times about producing another version of the same book. Why have I done it for the fifth time?

The simple answer is that environmental psychologists and their kindred spirits have produced an amazing body of work in the last seven years. *The Journal of Environmental Psychology*, which I have had the honour to edit for the last 12 years, has experienced another doubling of submitted manuscripts in the last few years, that is, four times as many per year as when I began. I have reviewed hundreds of articles, chapters, and books in the course of this fifth revision, and once again, hundreds of new publications enrich and update what is known about what I only half-jokingly called in a previous preface the "multifarious personal and environmental outcomes [that] are the mediated and moderated products of multifaceted individuals engaged in many different behaviors and psychological processes as they influence and are influenced by multiform settings." Now the book includes, for the better I hope, over 4,400 citations.

As always, I happily plead guilty to failing to simplify the incredible diversity of theory and research that has emerged in this field. As I have said before, I cannot in good conscience reduce the glorious diversity of ideas and findings that have sprung from the fertile minds of environmental psychologists to simplified statements that obfuscate the complex reality of our transactions with our environments. However, I have struggled to do this in as clear prose as possible. This is why I have committed the cardinal sin, in the eyes of some, of using the superscript system instead of authors' names in parentheses as in APA style. I am quite certain that you would be less interested in reading the book if you saw those thousands of names in the main text pages. All the authors' names may be found in the notes at the end of each chapter and in name index. That being said, students, know that in your papers you should use the parenthetical APA style when you cite the work of authors! (For examples, see the Suggested Readings and References for each chapter).

THE BOOK HAS EVOLVED A LITTLE since the fourth edition, although I have kept the order of the chapters and their themes intact for the most part. Although I think that the social and interpersonal aspects of environmental psychology are fascinating, far less research is being conducted on them now. Perhaps it is because funding agencies are much more focused on supporting "big problems" than "interesting phenomena" today, not that the former cannot also be the latter. Therefore, I have combined the chapters on personal space and territoriality into a single chapter, and the chapters on crowding and privacy into another single chapter. This leaves space for two new chapters, if the book is to retain the overall number of chapters that suits most courses in environmental psychology. Over the last seven years, two topics have become much more important for environmental psychologists: place attachment and climate change. I have asked two people whose knowledge and ability I greatly respect to be the lead authors of these chapters. Leila Scannell's work on place attachment has led to one of the most-cited *Journal of Environmental Psychology* articles in recent years. Reuven Sussman's brave and admirable efforts to combine good science with important applications in climate-related behaviors made him an easy choice for the climate chapter.

Each chapter is arranged, for the most part, in five sections, as in earlier editions. In general, the topic is introduced, the research methods appropriate to that topic are introduced, existing knowledge in the area is surveyed, relevant theories are described, and case studies that used the concepts conclude each chapter. Rather than use a Glossary, which to me requires attention-distracting searches away from one's place in the text, I have endeavored to place each key term in bold (sometimes in italics) and to define it in plain English, in context.

ONLY ONE NAME APPEARS ON THE TITLE PAGE, but this book could not have been written without the help of many persons. As always, and forever, I wish to thank the spirits of my parents Robert and Dorothy, whose support and encouragement got me started ("Hey, Mom, I can ride this thing!"), and Robert Sommer, for the start he gave a slightly lost soul before the field we now call environmental psychology even had a name.

AS FOR DIRECT EFFORT ON THIS EDITION, a succession of brave souls struggled with the endless details that comprise a work like this, and I am grateful to each. No one has worked harder or longer on the book than my wonderful sister, Coe Gifford. But others contributed in important ways: Marc Christensen created the modern, colorful,

atmospheric design. Eva Gifford served in several valuable roles: literature researcher, chapter editor, author photographer, and much-loved nightly correspondent. Lindsay McCunn, Reuven Sussman, Christine Kormos, Angel Chen, Karine Lacroix, and Geoff Stevenson contributed to the refinement of the book's final form. Gerhard Aichelberger cheerfully answered many questions about production. Special gratitude goes to Cécile Lacombe, for her forbearance, support, and love during all these long months.

MY SINCERE THANKS TO THE INSTRUCTORS WHO ADOPTED THE EARLIER EDITIONS, particularly those who have offered their views and suggestions over the years, but also to those who are adopting this edition for the first time. Students: welcome to the fascinating and (at least to me!) crucial scientific and practice-oriented field of study that examines how environments and individuals work together, and struggle against each other.

YES, FOR THOSE WHO NOTICE SUCH THINGS, Joe Lyons' secret maxim did work again.

INSTRUCTORS AND STUDENTS, please feel free to contact me with questions, comments, or suggestions at any of the addresses below.

Robert Gifford
Department of Psychology and School of Environmental Studies
University of Victoria
Victoria, BC   V8W 3P5
Canada

email: rgifford@uvic.ca
http://web.uvic.ca/psyc/gifford/
Fax: 250-721-8929
Telephone: 250-721-7532

The Nature and Scope of Environmental Psychology

Perhaps one of the outstanding weaknesses of contemporary psychological theory is the relative neglect of the environment by many of the most influential theoretical viewpoints.

—ISIDOR CHEIN[1]

What Is Environmental Psychology?

ENVIRONMENTAL PSYCHOLOGY is the study of transactions between individuals and their physical settings. In these transactions, individuals change the environment, and their behavior and experiences are changed by the environment. Environmental psychology includes theory, research, and practice aimed at improving our relationship with the natural environment and making buildings more humane (See Figures 1-1 and 1-2).

As a recognized and named field, environmental psychology is less than 50 years old, but some social scientists have worked on these issues for decades more. In the early days of psychology, most researchers concentrated on processes *within persons.* Later, the emphasis was extended to interactions *between persons.* Yet, considering the enormous cost of misusing nature and natural resources and the huge investment society makes in the construction and maintenance of the physical environment (including buildings, parks, streets, the atmosphere, and bodies of water), the long delay before *person-environment relations* received adequate attention seems almost tragic.

Fortunately, since then thousands of studies have dealt with the major topics discussed in this book. Much of this work has been stimulated by the recognition of environmental problems such as sustainability, climate change, pollution, energy shortages, and unsuitable buildings. Other research is motivated by pure curiosity about how and why humans act and feel in their built and natural settings. Many mysteries remain about the intricacies of person-environment transactions, but we have begun to understand a great number of them.

This chapter describes the main issues and topics of environmental psychology. Its dual goals of discovery and application are emphasized. The origins and present status of the field are discussed, along with overviews of its major theoretical approaches and some observations on research methods. Comments on the

FIGURE 1–1 Environmental psychology investigates persons–in–relation–to–nature.

international dimensions and future prospects of environmental psychology close the chapter.

The Issues

THE SIMPLE DEFINITION that opens this chapter does not convey the fascinating variety of topics that environmental psychologists study. Each of the following actual headlines alludes to a problem that will be discussed in this book:

- Is the Climate Problem in Our Heads?
- Violence: A Fact of Life in Overcrowded Jails
- Working in an Office Is Dangerous to Your Health
- Sanctuary Now Battlefield as Neighbors Fight Fence
- Crazy Summer Days Goad Child Abuse
- Will My Place Attachment Make Me a NIMBY?
- We're All Climate-Change Idiots
- When Kids Crave Privacy
- Quotas Slashed in Attempt to Help Troubled Herring Fishery
- What's Wrong With High-rises?
- Designers Modify Open Office to Meet Complaints of Workers
- The Noise Pollution Toll

HEADLINES ARE MERELY MARKERS, but each one is based on a serious problem in the real world. Each problem involves not just the environment but some *transaction* between individuals and their physical settings (see Figure 1-3). The term **environment**, in this book, means natural settings, natural resources, national parks, wilderness, wildlife and their penned-up cousins, the climate, and built settings such as homes, offices, schools and streets. On the human side of the transaction, environmental psychologists usually focus on the behavior and experience of individuals and small groups (householders, office workers, pedestrians, pupils, extraverts, shoppers, neighbors, hikers, dormitory residents, burglars, architects, commuters, and other everyday people), and less often to large aggregates of people (e.g., "society" or "humankind").

Environmental psychologists recognize the need to accomplish two related goals: to understand person-environment transactions and to use this knowledge to help solve a wide variety of problems. The subtitle of this book,

FIGURE 1–2 This uncompleted building could serve as a symbol of environmental psychology's task in the built environment. It will have important effects on people who will use it for perhaps a hundred years or even more. To what extent did the architects consider the needs of its users when they designed it? Environmental psychologist specialize in bridging the often-large gap between building designers and the people who will work, study, or live in their buildings.

Principles and Practice, was chosen quite deliberately: environmental psychology distinctly includes both science and application. As individuals, of course, environmental psychologists have only enough energy to work on a few of the topics described in the book. Some feel more comfortable working on the *principles*; others feel more comfortable with the *practice*. The situation is similar to that in medicine, where some physicians go into family practice while others conduct research in a laboratory. Nevertheless, every environmental psychologist supports the need for theory, research, *and* practice that may help to solve the many ecological and architectural problems in the world.[2]

Finding the Principles

TO EASE A REAL-WORLD PROBLEM, one must have knowledge to apply. Two forms of knowledge are *theory* and *research findings*. Theory guides both research and practice by

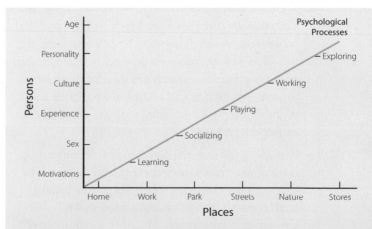

FIGURE 1–3 Environmental psychology's three dimensions: persons, processes, and places. All human activity occurs in this three-dimensional space. The fourth dimension, time, is also examined by some environmental psychologists.

providing a coherent framework for understanding problematic human-environment transactions. In environmental psychology, theories do not themselves provide answers to specific problems. Instead, their job is to provide directions toward solutions.

Many theories will be described in the following chapters. Their number and variety illustrate the ferment and enthusiasm to be found in environmental psychology. A sorting-out process may eventually reduce their number, but to seek a single, all-inclusive theory probably is unwise. Even in working on a single problem, multiple viewpoints are helpful in enabling one to see more of the problem's ramifications. Seven major theoretical approaches will be briefly described later in this chapter, but most theories are described in the chapter where they are most relevant.

The second form of knowledge that may be applied to a problem is that gained from research. This book is crammed with the findings of studies on dozens of topics, perhaps too many for some readers. However, reality is complex, and I would feel very uncomfortable telling half a story when I am aware that we know more than a simplistic account would suggest. On the other hand, readers sometimes are surprised that the published research in environmental psychology does *not* yet contain answers to certain questions. We're working on it! (Might you be willing to help out someday?)

Why *should* you read about all these studies, then?

1. Despite the complexities, some results *do* appear time after time. Certain findings have been confirmed repeatedly, and now have the status of principles of which we can be quite sure.

2. Previous research provides guidance for future study. Occasionally it reveals a dead end: let's not go there! More often, research not only finds "something," it provokes new questions by producing unanticipated outcomes. Future research can then be more sophisticated: Researchers can avoid known pitfalls and be aware of important issues that were unknown to earlier researchers.

3. Knowledge of research serves to correct misconceptions about person-environment transactions. The following are only a few examples of conclusions from research that go against conventional beliefs: Crowding is *not* strongly related to the number of other persons around; human territoriality is *not* primarily associated with aggression; paper cups

are *not* environmentally superior to Styrofoam cups, and full-spectrum lighting is *not* necessarily better for people. In each of these cases, other personal or environmental factors are more important. One basic message I hope to convey is that every person-environment transaction is governed by a multiplicity of influences. No single factor shapes human experience or behavior.

The Principles in Practice

WHILE RECOGNIZING THE VALUE of theory and research, some environmental psychologists nevertheless prefer to *apply* knowledge. Instead of working in an academic setting, where most researchers work, they venture into private practice or work for governments. After appropriate graduate training, they operate as consultants or civil servants. The practicing environmental psychologist makes good use of research findings to develop policy or to assist a specific client. Some are primarily geared to improving the built environment,[3] which is important because even environmental activists spend the vast majority of their time in buildings, and others are dedicated to overcoming sustainability problems in the natural and global ecosystems,[4] which must be solved if our quality of life, and that of the other species with which we share this planet, is to be optimized.

IN SUM *Environmental psychology is a relatively young but vital discipline that pursues both scientific principles and practical application as it seeks to ameliorate a wide variety of problems in the natural and built environments that arise from person-environment transactions. Much is known, but much is still unknown, too, and this challenge of the unknown is what motivates many science-minded environmental psychologists. Practicing environmental psychologists are motivated by the conviction that they can improve the way people interact with nature and natural resources or help create more humane buildings and communities by employing the hard-earned knowledge garnered by their research-oriented colleagues.*

ENVIRONMENTAL PSYCHOLOGY MAY SEEM at first to be indistinguishable from the main core of psychology because most psychologists examine the relations between environmental stimuli and human responses in one way or another. However, what sets environmental psychology apart is its commitment to research and practice that subscribe to the following goals and principles:

- Improve our stewardship of natural resources and the built environment.

- Study everyday settings (or close simulations of them).

- Consider the person and the setting to be a holistic entity.

- Recognize that individuals actively cope with, and shape, environments; they do not passively respond to environmental forces.

- Work in conjunction with other disciplines.[5]

Although environmental psychology's origins may be traced almost as far back as the rest of scientific psychology, it has always been on the edge of psychology—in two senses.

1. It still is not part of the central core of psychology. It is not taught in every university or college, nor can it claim as many researchers as some other areas of psychology.

2. The main concern of environmental psychology—the physical environment—has rarely received serious attention in psychology, as the quotation that opens this chapter points out.

Although the major processes and topics in mainstream psychology—development, cognition, learning, social relations, abnormal behavior—occur in everyday physical settings, only environmental psychology systematically investigates the physical settings in which these processes occur. To offer just one example, learning ultimately and intimately relates to classrooms, yet relatively few studies of learning in other areas of psychology are conducted *in* classrooms.

That environmental psychology has deep roots within the field and is at the same time at the edge of the discipline

is illustrated in the theoretical work of Egon Brunswik and Kurt Lewin, two great precursors of the field. Egon Brunswik (1903-1955) was born in Budapest, trained in Vienna, and emigrated to the United States in the 1930s. Brunswik originally concentrated on the basic process of perception (to be discussed in Chapter 2), but his ideas have been extended far beyond that. In calling for a more detailed analysis of the way that physical environment factors affect behavior, Brunswik probably was first to use the term *environmental psychology*, back in 1943, although his vision of it at that time was not quite the same as its current meaning.[6]

Brunswik also strongly advocated **representative design**, the idea that research designs should include a much wider array of environmental stimuli than psychologists of the day typically employed. These stimuli, he said, should be more representative of the real world of the persons we are trying to understand. Brunswik and others[7] believed that the physical environment *can* affect people without their knowing. For example, the hum of a fluorescent light fixture might affect an office worker's satisfaction with work or productivity even though the office worker is unaware of the hum. Brunswik believed that if such factors truly can affect us psychologically, they must be studied systematically.

Kurt Lewin (1890-1947), the other great precursor in this field, was born in Prussia and trained in Germany. He, too, emigrated to the United States in the 1930s. His **field theory** was one of the

EGON BRUNSWIK *was the first person to use the term* environmental psychology *in print. His lens model is a very useful tool for understanding how people perceive and comprehend physical environments.*

KURT LEWIN *was an inspired theorist, and inspiring teacher, and the founder of action research, an important element in environmental psychology's problem-solving goal.*

ROGER BARKER *was a student of Kurt Lewin and the founder of behavioral ecology and behaviour setting theory.*

first to give active consideration to the molar physical environment. Lewin's idea of **action research** was perhaps the first major push in psychology toward linking scientific research with real social change. Lewin's influence, through these two ideas, has been very strong in environmental psychology. Lewin proposed that this field of inquiry be called "psychological ecology."

Despite their influential ideas, however, neither Brunswik nor Lewin performed studies that today would be called environmental psychology. Brunswik had few students, and for many years his ideas had little influence on psychology; that is one reason why his ideas, although important, remain on the edge of psychology. Lewin, on the other hand, has had a strong influence in psychology. A dynamic and charismatic person, he inspired many students who, in turn, have profoundly shaped the direction of social science. However, most of Lewin's students interpreted his ideas to mean that the *social* environment was crucial; the physical environment was not stressed.

However, two of Lewin's students, Roger Barker and Herbert Wright, did take the physical environment more seriously and pursued psychological ecology, but later changing the name to **ecological psychology**. This term did not refer to nature, as it might today, but to what might be called human ecology. They began a large-scale and long-lasting research project in 1947 that studied **behavior settings**, small ecological units enclosing everyday human behavior.[8] Behavior settings include both the social rules *and* the physical-spatial aspects of our daily lives. The classroom, the sports event, the concert, the restaurant, and the council meeting are examples. Barker and his colleagues worked hard to describe the social and physical characteristics of these and other identifiable behavior settings for entire small towns. In reflecting on the origins of his research, Barker later said,

> The awful truth dawned upon me that although I was well informed about the behavior of children when confronted with tests and experiments devised by scientific investigators, I knew no more than a lay person about the situations and conditions the towns provided their children and how the children behaved.[9]

The ideas of Brunswik and Lewin helped create the intellectual basis for environmental psychology as a formal discipline, but its empirical roots began much earlier. Before 1920, psychologists had studied the effect of noise[10] and heat[11] on work performance. A study of where students sat in classrooms in relation to the grades they earned was published in 1921,[12] and the famous Hawthorne studies of the effect of lighting level on work performance began in 1924.[13] However, these studies were almost atheoretical; the researchers were looking for simple, deterministic effects of the environment on work performance.

By the 1950s, other pioneers in environmental psychology were at work, even before the field had a name. For example, in 1956 researchers showed that the same photos of people were rated more positively when the ratings were done in a beautiful room than when they were done in an average or ugly room, even though the aesthetics of the room were never mentioned to the raters.[14] In the middle 1950s, Robert Sommer and Humphrey Osmond began to systematically alter the physical elements of buildings in Saskatchewan and to monitor the effects of these changes on behavior.[15, 16] By rearranging furniture and redesigning wards in a geriatric hospital, they found they could increase communication among the elderly women in the hospital. At the same time, Sommer began his famous studies of personal space.[17] In New York another team, headed by William Ittelson and Harold Proshansky, read about Sommer and Osmond's research and began to map the behavior of patients on a mental hospital ward.[18]

The first conferences specifically devoted to what was then called architectural psychology were held at the University of Utah in 1961 and 1966. The first Ph.D. program in environmental psychology was established at the City University of New York (CUNY) in 1968. One marker of environmental psychology's relative youth is that the first Ph.D. in the CUNY program was earned in 1975, whereas the first American Ph.D. in psychology was granted over a hundred years earlier, in 1861.

By the late 1960s, the first professional journals devoted to the field were established; the most prominent of these today are the *Journal of Environmental Psychology* and *Environment and Behavior*. In 1968 the largest environment-behavior organization, the Environmental Design Research Association (EDRA), was formed; it has held annual meetings since 1969. The International Association of People-Environment Studies (IAPS) also had its origins in the late 1960s, and became a formal organization in 1981. Most of the large national and international psychology organizations have a section or division devoted to environmental psychology. Many of these organizations, journals, and graduate schools are listed in the Appendix, if you are interested.

IN SUM *Whisperings of an environmental psychology began in the 1910s, some early theoretical work was done in the 1930s and 1940s, followed by a trickle of activity in the 1950s, which began in the late 1960s to grow into a torrent by the 1970s, and that continues today.*

THEORIES AND APPROACHES IN BRIEF

AS NOTED EARLIER, NO SINGLE THEORY applies to all the topics in environmental psychology. Competing theories still jostle one another to explain person-environment events. If the future is like the brief past, new theories will evolve and there will be mergers, takeovers, bankruptcies, and spin-offs among the current theories.

This is normal in all of science. The tidy picture we learn about in school overlooks the messy actual history of competing and dead theories in order to save time and to present what appears to be a logical sequence of new ideas and discoveries. Remember the ancient story about three blind sages who encounter a being unknown to them (an elephant). One sage, grasping the animal's tail, described the being as ropelike. Another, holding its trunk, claimed that the being was like a hose. A third, arms wrapped around a stout leg, could not believe the others were unable to

realize that the being resembles a tree. Similarly, each of today's theories in environmental psychology probably is an accurate but partial explanation of human behavior in physical contexts. Developing theory within the field is a crucial part of its development.[19]

Eight broad theoretical approaches to environmental psychology will be described briefly, after I first present an overall organizing framework that describes the scope of the field. This should allow you to begin thinking about how the research findings you will soon be reading about fit into the big picture.

An Organizing Model

Figure 1-4 broadly depicts the scope of environmental psychology. It includes the main elements of the field without making specific theoretical propositions. Within a political, economic, cultural, and historical context[20] (not shown in the figure), a person enters a natural or built environment, which has a multitude of objective features. In conducting research about this person-environment transaction, the environmental psychologist selects some of these features for study; not all of them can be examined in any one study. The consequences for the person and for the environment are partly determined by that broad context, which suggest a script (that is, an ordinary or normal set of behaviors for that place and time). The person's plans upon entering the environment, if any, usually reflect this script, but not everyone follows the script. The person's behavior, thoughts, and emotions are also influenced by the person's own talents, dispositions, and past experiences. Consciously or not, the person is influenced by the setting

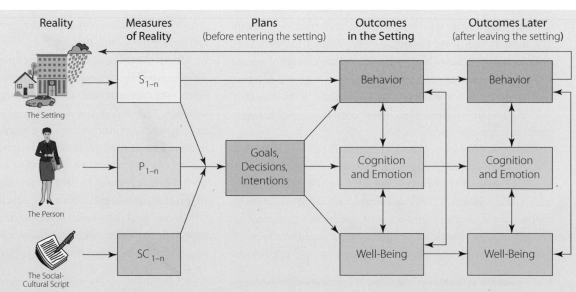

FIGURE 1–4
A comprehensive overview of environmental psychology. What we see, do, think, plan, and feel are partly a function of the various natural and built settings surrounding us. Our well-being and that of the environment depends on mutual transactions between ourselves and the settings in which we live, work, study, and visit.

and influences it. These transactions between person and environment often have important outcomes both for the person's actions, thoughts, and well-being, and for the well-being of the environment. Some outcomes are immediate; others are delayed. The twin goals of most environmental psychologists are to understand these transactions and to improve outcomes for both persons and environments.

One of the most important functions of a theory is to provide generalizations that give order and meaning to specific observations about person-environment relations. We turn now to eight theoretical approaches that help organize thinking about person-environment transactions.

Stimulation Theories

The stimulation theories emphasize the fundamental influence of the physical environment as a crucial source of sensory information.[21] This stimulation includes relatively simple stimuli such as noise, light, temperature, and color, but also more complex stimuli such as forests, classrooms, offices, residences, and other people. In environmental psychology, the stimulus is not some artificial display of lines, dots, or words on a computer screen, but information from or about the real world in which we live.

Environmental stimulation can vary in amount and meaning. In terms of *amount*, it varies in such obvious dimensions as intensity, duration, frequency, and number of sources. The *meaning* of stimulation refers to each person's integration and interpretation of the stimulus information that arrives. These are related: changing the amount of stimulation can change its meaning.

Among these stimulation-oriented theories are adaptation-level theory, overload theory, restricted environmental stimulation theory, stress theory, and phenomenology. The **adaptation-level theory,** developed by Harry Helson, maintains that individuals adapt to certain levels of stimulation in certain contexts; no particular amount of stimulation is good for everyone at all times.[22] It asserts that stimulation that differs from one's adaptation level changes one's perceptions and behavior.

Other stimulation-based theories focus on how psychologically or physiologically aroused we are by stimuli.[23, 24] **Overload theory** concentrates on the effects of too much stimulation.[25-27] Considerable research in environmental psychology originates with problems that may be viewed from an overload perspective, such as the effects of noise, heat, cold, and crowding. However, we sometimes find ourselves in settings that offer too little stimulation. According to **restricted environmental stimulation theory** (REST), too little stimulation causes problems for us in some circumstances, as you might expect, but in others it yields surprisingly positive results.[28] The performance of easy cognitive tasks, for example, is improved under low stimulation conditions.[29]

Stress theories, another stimulation-based approach, have become important in recent years. Environmental psychologists use them to help explain the behavioral and health effects that occur when environmental stimulation exceeds an individual's adaptive resources.[30, 31, 32] Stress theories have been applied in a wide variety of everyday contexts. Suspected stressors include high population density, air pollution, hospitals, offices, extreme temperatures, traffic, noise, and disasters. We distinguish *acute stressors* (negative, intense, relatively short impacts that are in the forefront of consciousness) from *ambient stressors* (negative, chronic, global environmental conditions that usually remain in the background of consciousness and seem hard to alter) and *daily hassles* (negative, non-urgent, recurrent stressors)[33]

One basic stress model emphasizes physiological responses, and another emphasizes psychological responses.[34] On the physiological side, Hans Selye first described the general adaptation syndrome, a pattern of bodily reactions that remains similar even when the specific source of the stress varies. The pituitary and adrenal glands respond to stressors in a particular sequence: first alarm, then resistance, then exhaustion from the cumulative effort of much resistance. The psychological side of stress emphasizes the role of cognitive appraisal—that is, our efforts to assess the seriousness of the situation and to cope with the stressor. Thus, the *meaning* of the stressor is an important factor in psychological stress.[35]

Other theorists emphasize the meaning of stimulation even more. The bestowal of meaning—together with our selection, construction, modification, and destruction of settings—is among the ways we shape the environment during our continuous series of transactions with it. The personal meanings given to a place by a person are essential to our *experience* of an environment.[36] The meaning of the environment, in this sense, has been the province of **phenomenology**, a form of careful contemplation in which one goal is to understand what a setting truly means, especially to those who regularly spend time in the setting.[37] As we become increasingly familiar with a setting, we create meaning for it. This meaning may be positive or negative in tone, similar or different from the meanings attached to it by others, weak or strong. Places without meaning affect us differently than places with meaning; we treat places without meaning differently than we treat meaningful places.

Control Theories

A SECOND GENERAL SET OF THEORIES IN ENVIRONMENTAL PSYCHOLOGY FOCUSES ON THE NOTION OF CONTROL. We may adapt to a certain level of stimulation and sometimes be faced with too little or too much of it, but another obviously important consideration is how much control we *actually* have (or *think* we have, or *want* to have) over environments and the stimulation they present. Clearly, those who have much control over the amount and kind of stimulation that comes their way generally are better off than those who have little control. We may have considerable control in some settings, such as at home, and very little in others, such as in traffic jams.

Theories of **personal control** have been developed to account for the effects of being able or unable to influence stimulation patterns.[38] In everyday social transactions, we attempt to achieve personal control through several **boundary regulation mechanisms**, such as personal space and territoriality.[39]

The lack of control often leads to **psychological reactance**, the attempt to regain the freedom one has lost.[40] Individuals who conclude that control is difficult or impossible to regain may succumb to **learned helplessness**, the conviction that no amount of effort can succeed in overcoming an unpleasant or painful situation.[41]

Behavior Setting Theory

A third major theoretical construct is **behavior setting theory**, which is a central part of Roger Barker's ecological psychology, mentioned earlier.[42, 43] A central tenet of behavior setting theory is that consistent, prescribed patterns of behavior, called **programs,** are found in many places. If you enter a classroom, a sporting event, or even a political protest, you are likely to see recurrent activities, regularly carried out by persons holding specific roles. For example, every basketball game features two teams of players who run, pass, and score, officials who monitor rule violations,

fans who cheer and boo, and vendors offering food and drink.

Variations in the actions of individuals do occur, of course, but traditional behavior setting theorists pay less attention to psychological processes and individual differences among participants than do the stimulation and control theorists. They are impressed by the *uniformity* in the actions of those who occupy a given role, especially in contrast to the behavior of those occupying other roles. Consider, for example, the differences in behavior of players, officials, and fans in a basketball game. Behavior setting theorists tend to explain person-environment relations primarily in terms of the social features of a setting, such as its rules, customs and typical activities, and its physical features.

One key concept in behavior setting theory is the level of **staffing**.[44] For a variety of reasons, a given behavior setting may attract many or few who wish to participate in its activities. When there are too many individuals around (and the behavior setting fails to find a way to exclude extras), overstaffing results. When too few are attracted, understaffing results. You can probably recall instances of both overstaffed and understaffed behavior settings in your experience. What were the consequences for individuals in these settings?

Others have extended the behavior setting concept in time.[45,46] Behavior settings are not static entities; they are born, they struggle, adapt, thrive, and they die. (Can you think of a behavior setting that once was common but is dying out? Another that is quite new and becoming common?).

Decision-making Theories

The fourth group of theories emphasizes that we make decisions that have environmental consequences. When we choose to drive, take an airplane flight, choose organic foods, or reduce the water we use, we affect the local and the global environment. Often these choices reflect a dilemma in which we must choose between our own interests (flying home to see our families during a vacation) and those of the environment (not using a form of transportation that is among the worst for the climate).

One framework for understanding why and when we make which decisions is the **human interdependence paradigm**.[47] Its proponents assert that we make choices without knowing with any certainty what the outcome for us or the environment will be, or when the outcome will manifest itself. It also recognizes that your decisions affect me, and mine affect yours, and in fact that all our decisions affect all of us. This important area of environmental psychology will be discussed at length later, when sustainability, resource management, and commons dilemmas are discussed. Ecological issues are also the subject of other theories that have decision-making at their core.

One might argue that many choices are made by many people without any thought or consideration for the environment. In other words, that people usually do not make conscious decisions. Out of habit, we hop in the car, make our plane reservations, or have a nice long hot shower. The reply from these theoreticians is that even non-conscious choices do represent decisions. The obvious solution to problems caused by this mindlessness is to make ourselves and others more aware of the non-conscious decisions we make that degrade the environment.

Attitude-Behavior Theories

A fifth broad approach places heavy emphasis on attitudes, which are mental constructs that include cognitive, affective (emotional), and conative (intention) elements. The various attitude theories employ constructs that represent some or all of these elements to predict behavior. Theories of this type claim most of the attention in modern environmental psychology. They typically include such constructs as beliefs, values, norms, perceived control, goals, worldviews, perceived equity, and stated intentions.

The popularity of attitude-behavior theories may lie in the relative ease of testing their usefulness, compared to that of other broad theoretical approaches. Proponents of the other approaches may argue that popularity should not necessarily be equated with value as tools for understanding human-environment transactions.

Integral Theories

A SIXTH GROUP OF THEORETICIANS HAVE SEARCHED for a model that captures the full complexity of everyday person-environment relations. The term *integral* characterizes these four approaches. Perhaps the earliest explicit theory of environmental psychology was proposed by Isidor Chein.[48] He called it a description of the "geo-behavioral environment," although when his proposal was published in 1954, environmental psychology as we know it did not

yet exist. Chein's integral framework consisted of five major elements:

1. Instigators: Environmental stimuli that trigger particular behaviors.[49]
2. Goal objects and noxients: Situations that can satisfy needs or produce pain or unpleasantness.
3. Supports and constraints: Aspects of the physical environment that facilitate (lights, desks, roads) or restrict (fences, locks, trackless wilderness) our actions.
4. Directors: Features of the environment that tell us what to do or where to go.
5. Global environment: Generalized characteristics of an environment (e.g., the Arctic is "harsh," jungles are "wet," and high-rises are "made of steel and glass").

In broad terms, if one understands a person's environments in terms of Chein's five elements, one probably will be able to understand that person's behavior quite well.

A second form of integral theory is **interactionism** (see Figure 1-5). It represents an advance over older deterministic theories that attributed most or all of the causes of human behavior *either* to the person *or* to the environment. In interactionism, persons and environments are considered to be separate entities, but they are continually engaged in a series of interactions.

A third form, called **transactionalism**, emphasizes that person and environment are part of one inclusive entity.[50] This means that neither individuals nor settings can be adequately defined without reference to the other, and that activities of one necessarily influence the other.[51] We influence environments and environments influence us.

Finally, **organismic theories** emphasize the dynamic interplay of social, societal, and individual factors in a mutual, complex system.[52] Behavior is viewed as part of many possible developmental equilibria that have both short-term and long-term goals, and contextual changes that may occur rapidly or gradually.[53] This trend toward including more distant influences on human behavior includes a more recent attempt to diagram the dynamic and revolving influences from and back to the natural, political, and technological domains.[54,55]

These latter integral theories represent the highest, most encompassing dreams of environmental psychologists. They probably do describe "the way it really is." However, a persistent problem for integral theories is a gap between their attractive themes and the reality of current research methods. Few methods have yet been developed that are capable of adequately testing integral theories, and some argue that a theory that cannot be tested is not worthy of the name. Nevertheless, integral theories are valuable, at minimum, as reminders for scientists and policy-makers of the many influences at work in our daily transactions with our environments.

The Operant Approach

A seventh theoretical perspective is the **operant** approach,[56] which goes far in the opposite direction, focusing very specifically on some particular behavior and its immediate reinforcers. Its goal within environmental psychology usually is to modify the behavior of individuals whose actions are contributing to some environmental problem. Specific problematic behaviors are identified, then appropriate positive reinforcements are delivered when individuals engage in more beneficial behavior. Some prime examples of problems that have been attacked with the operant approach are recycling, littering, and residential energy wastage.

Environment-Centered and Mental Health-Oriented Approaches

THE EIGHTH GENERAL THEORETICAL DIRECTION might be termed the environment-centered approach. Three such approaches, without ignoring people, pay special attention to the state or quality of the environment. The first contrasts **instrumental** versus **spiritual** views of the environment: Should the environment be viewed as a tool for supporting human goals, such as productivity, or as a context in which important human values can be cultivated?[57]

Other approaches contrast person-centered theories with approaches that concentrate on preserving, conserving, and helping the natural environment.[58, 59] **Conservation psychology**[60] is a recent proposal modeled on conservation biology that is largely redundant with the long-held concerns of environmental psychologists who study ecological problems, but it adds some needed emphasis on the relationship between people and wild animals.[61] For example, a recent conservation psychology conference was designed for professionals in zoos, museums, and nature centers.

Another approach, **ecopsychology**, focuses on mental health or spiritual aspects of human-environment transactions. Adherents often think of the bond between individuals and the Earth in terms of ecological unconsciousness, denial, addiction, and mental health.[62] The first English use of the term in this sense appears to have occurred in 1986.[63] Ecopsychology was popularized in a 1992 book by Theodore Roszak, a history professor, who claimed that the Earth was crying out for rescue from the heavy weight of industrialism.[64] He wrote that the needs of the Earth and the needs of each person were a continuum, that both were suffering from related causes, and that Earth is a kind of living being, embodied by the goddess Gaia.

Ecopsychologists view the Earth as sacred[65] but victimized.[66] This damage to the Earth is thought, in turn, to cause individuals "psychological destruction,"[67] which, in their view, is a leading cause of human pain.[68] The solutions to this problem include developing an ecological self through the spiritual inspiration that is said to come from wilderness,[69] from living more sustainably, as ecopsychologists seem to believe that peoples in less-developed areas of the world do,[70] through understanding the ideas of "deep ecology,"[71] and from developing a new understanding of self in relation to the planet through counseling or nature experiences.

Although environmental psychologists agree that many individuals could lead more environmentally responsible lives, many are uneasy with the unscientific approach of ecopsychology. The themes and claims of ecopsychology are attractive, but most are difficult to evaluate scientifically. Some environmental psychologists

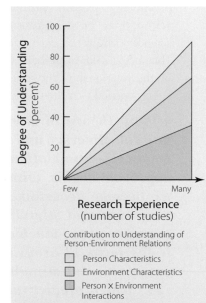

FIGURE 1–5 The growth of knowledge about person–environment transactions. In general, our understanding of outcomes (such as behaviors, cognitions, and well-being) grows with the number of quality scientific investigations. Some outcomes can be primarily explained by knowing key information about the *person*, and others primarily by knowing key information about the *setting*. Finally, some outcomes require an explanation based on knowing which kind of person is in which kind of setting: an *interaction* between person and setting.

consider ecopsychology to be a well-meaning but misguided quasi-religious movement.

However, a few researchers have adopted the basic attitude of ecopsychology but try to conduct scientific research. One team showed, for example, that natural landscaping in housing projects encourages more use of outdoor areas and more social interaction.[72] Another examined the roots of environmental activism and found that it appears to begin with nature experiences in early childhood, and that models within the activist's family are important.[73] Experiencing nature as a spiritual inspiration may be facilitated by social interaction combined with wilderness immersion.[74] Other research suggests that various kinds of contact with nature promote health.[75]

Ecopsychology and environmental psychology, according to some authors, may be able to offer each other useful ideas and techniques, and, therefore, to create a powerful synthesis for understanding and change.[76] That is, ecopsychology's passion without environmental psychology's science may be dangerous; environmental psychology's science without ecopsychology's passion may be irrelevant. That being said, in perhaps the most eloquent discussion of the relationship between the two approaches, Joseph Reser worried that the two may simply be incompatible.[77]

IN SUM *Theory in environmental psychology is vital, diverse, and still developing. Some emphasize stimulation. The adaptation-level approach begins with the assumption that we become accustomed to a certain level of environmental stimulation. The common occurrence of too much or too little stimulation is the focus of arousal, overload, restricted environmental stimulation, and stress theories, which predict that a wide range of behaviors and experiences will be affected. A second type of theory emphasizes the importance of an individual's real, perceived, or desired control over stimulation, as in personal control, boundary regulation, learned helplessness, and reactance. Third, ecological psychology asserts the importance of behavior settings, naturally occurring small-scale social-physical units consisting of regular patterns of person-environment behavior. A fourth group of theories, including the human interdependence paradigm, emphasizes that we make decisions, consciously or not, to use or overuse natural resource, and that these decisions have profound effects on the environment and ourselves. Fifth, the popular attitude-behavior theories use beliefs, perceived norms, goals, values, intentions, and similar constructs to predict pro-environmental actions. Sixth, integral approaches such as interactionism, transactionalism, and organismic theory attempt to describe the full, complex interrelationship of persons and setting, including political, economic, cultural, and technological influences. Seventh, the operant approach downplays abstract constructs, instead adopting a direct problem-solving strategy that employs behavior modification techniques. Eighth, environment-centered and mental health-influenced theories such as the instrumental-spiritual model, conservation psychology, and ecopsychology raise the issue of the environment's own welfare and its ability to support our well-being.*

RESEARCH METHODS IN ENVIRONMENTAL PSYCHOLOGY

ENVIRONMENTAL PSYCHOLOGISTS, with their diversity of theoretical approaches, use a wide variety of methods in their work within these very different paradigms. Because each of these methods is best described in the chapter covering the topic in which it is primarily used, I will not undertake a detailed examination of particular research methods here. For those who are keen to learn more research methods in environmental psychology, entire books are available.[78-80] However, research methods are important, so an overview at this point is worthwhile.

Environmental psychology is a **multiple-paradigm field.**[81] This means that different researchers may employ not only different methods, but entirely different *kinds* of methods, based on different philosophies of science. Research methods vary not merely in their procedures, but in the underlying beliefs and values of the investigators who use them. One example would be the stark contrast between the reinforcement strategies of the operant approach and the experiential strategies of the phenomenologists.

However, paradigms need not conflict with each other; they can represent alternative, complementary visions of the same phenomena at different levels of analysis. The word *paradigm* also means something broader than research methods: it is an overall perspective about what a discipline as a whole is all about. For example, one view is that environmental psychology consists of three broad paradigms. [82] The **adaptation paradigm** sees biological and psychological survival as the key process. Perception, cognition, coping with stress, and assessment of physical environments are all viewed as processes aimed at helping us to survive as a species. Second, the **opportunity structure paradigm** considers the environment as a place for us to actively fulfill goals, as opposed to merely reacting to the environment's threats and demands. We plan and use the environment—or at least try to—in order to achieve our goals. Third, the **sociocultural paradigm** recognizes that environmental psychology is nested within other contexts and disciplines: history and culture, as well as economic and societal forces, cannot be ignored as we seek to understand person-environment relations. [83]

Environmental psychologists generally advocate the use of multiple methods and approaches to gain knowledge. They recognize that each method has strengths and weaknesses. Researchers cannot include all methods in any one study, so the findings of any single study must be treated as one piece of knowledge to be integrated with the findings of other studies before firm conclusions may be drawn. Researchers must be very cautious about drawing strong conclusions from single studies, which are likely to have one or more limitations. Responsible researchers search for patterns of results in a cumulative *series* of studies. Multiple methods, multiple paradigms, and multiple studies are necessary for full understanding.

On the other hand, not just any method will do for answering a particular question. Once that question is identified—and it is essential to have a *clear* question or hypothesis—some research methods become much better choices than others. However, in order to select the *best* method, researchers must be aware of the many possibilities.

Researchers cannot select the best method if they have never heard of it!

Some methods employed by environmental psychologists are standard social science techniques, such as interviews, rating scales, and laboratory experiments. However, many other methods—including some of the ways to study personal space, cognitive maps, and movement through buildings—are unique to environmental psychology.

A central concern of environmental psychology is **external validity**, the degree to which results of a study apply in contexts beyond the setting where they were obtained. This concern has led to a widespread suspicion of laboratory research: How sure are we that whatever occurs in a lab will occur in an everyday setting? However, some studies (particularly those in which the specific purpose is to definitively test a theory) are best conducted in laboratories. Lab studies *do* have a place in environmental psychology, especially when experimental control of hypothesized influences is necessary.

Nevertheless, concern with external validity naturally leads to a preference for **field studies** when the study's results are to be immediately applied. In this case, the study should be conducted in the very setting that is under consideration, or in one as similar as possible. Of course, some studies cannot be conducted in the setting for which the results are intended. For example, research on the performance or satisfaction of employees who will work in a *proposed* office complex is impossible. Yet if the research waits until the complex is built, it will be too late to use the results in the design of the complex. One solution is to simulate the building before it is constructed. Sophisticated facilities have been built to simulate offices (in Irvine, California), regional landscapes (in Berkeley, California), and residences (in Lausanne, Switzerland), and now proposed buildings can be very well simulated as virtual worlds using computers.

However, field studies usually cannot provide critical tests of theories or reach conclusions about the causal nature of events in the setting. This is because, in real settings, many influences other than those of interest to the investigator are at work and may influence the outcomes. Thus, the ideal research method for many purposes is the **field experiment**. This kind of study is conducted in the actual field setting of interest, but the researcher is able to randomly assign participants to different conditions and to control all the major independent variables or presumed influences on behavior or well-being.

In a field experiment, researchers can claim external validity automatically, because the investigation occurs in the very setting to which they wish to generalize their findings, *and* they can draw causal conclusions because other influences have been controlled through random assignment and other features of the scientific method. Unfortunately, as you might have guessed, opportunities to conduct field experiments are quite rare; researchers are rarely granted the kind of full control over a field setting that is needed for a field experiment. Therefore, in the normal course of research, investigators forge ahead with laboratory experiments and field studies, and seek the truth from considering the results found in a series of investigations that use both types of methods.

A compromise between field studies and true experiments is the **quasi-experimental design**. True experiments require the random assignment of participants to different conditions and experimenter control of the variables hypothesized to affect behavior or thinking. Quasi-experimental designs might, for example, include real classrooms but accept the limitation that the experimenter is unable to randomly assign pupils to the classrooms. Or, in a study of outdoor heat on aggression, rates of violent acts on hot versus normal days might be compared even though the investigator could not control the day's temperature. In short, quasi-experimental designs resemble true experimental designs, but cannot manage to satisfy some of the criteria required for true experiments.

IN SUM *Environmental psychologists fully accept that person-environment transactions are influenced by many different factors, which has led to multiple paradigms for studying them. A wide variety of research methods are employed. Some are standard in social science, but many others have been devised especially for environmental psychology. A strong preference for performing research in the everyday world means that field studies are common. Sometimes simulated settings are necessary, but they are used primarily when a field study is not possible. True experiments are desirable when a researcher seeks to isolate particular causes and effects, and* *laboratories are used for this purpose. Field experiments are the best route to external validity, but they are rarely feasible. Quasi-experimental research designs that fulfill some of the elements of experiment and field studies are a common compromise.*

ENVIRONMENTAL PSYCHOLOGY TODAY

Environmental psychology got its formal start in the late 1960s and has steadily developed since then. The 1980s saw the establishment of a major new international journal, the *Journal of Environmental Psychology* (1981) and the publication of comprehensive handbooks in 1987,[84] 2002,[85] and 2012.[86] Nevertheless, it remains one of the smaller areas of psychology; not every university or college teaches it (kudos to your school for including it!). This is strange and unfortunate because opinion polls often show that the general public's concern for the environment is very strong, sometimes even its greatest concern.

Nevertheless, environmental psychologists strongly believe in their mission and often persist in conducting their studies and applying them in the everyday world without adequate funding. A search of the psychology research database found, for example, that the absolute number and proportion of articles related to environmental issues and attitudes doubled in the 1990s. The number of articles submitted to the *Journal of Environmental Psychology* doubled from 2002 to 2006, and doubled once again from 2006 to 2012. Interest by members of the public—once they have heard of it—is very strong, but so far societal institutions in some countries, even some wealthy ones, have not rewarded this interest with as much support as the field deserves. You can gauge the average person's interest by simply mentioning that you are taking this course, and checking the reaction. I can almost guarantee that the person will show some interest.

Over the years, scientific interest in the various areas of environmental psychology has shifted and developed. Interest in our transactions with the built environment has been stable, and interest in sustainability and ecological issues has greatly increased.[87] As we move into a world of increasing social and technological change, environmental psychology will be called upon to help with our attempts to cope with a very demanding and always-evolving virtual world.[88] Are you experiencing what I call Change Overload Disorder?

Three Levels of Inquiry

Environmental psychology is studied at three levels of analysis that increase in breadth or complexity; these three levels are reflected in the structure of this book. At the most basic level (the first third of the book) are studies of fundamental psychological processes like perception, cognition, attitudes, and personality as they filter and structure our experiences of the physical environment. At the next level (the middle third of the book) comes the management of social space: interpersonal distancing (or personal space), territoriality, crowding, and privacy. At the third level (the last third of the book) are the physical setting aspects of our transactions with complex everyday physical settings— workplaces, schools, residences, urban places, place attachment, our troubled relationship with nature, sustainability, climate change, and the psychology of environmental design and architecture.

The entire enterprise of environmental psychology is difficult to comprehend in its entirety, even for professionals. This book is based on several thousand articles and books. Yet even this represents only a fraction of all the published work in environmental psychology. Even these thousands of studies do not provide final answers to the theoretical issues and practical problems environmental psychologists try to solve.

Simple, clear conclusions are very attractive, but they are not realistic. Therefore, try to enjoy the *diversity* of viewpoints and findings you will encounter in the following chapters. Be aware that compared to the long histories of disciplines like medicine, physics, or mathematics, these are still the early days of environmental psychology, when most studies uncover previously unknown territory as much as they further our knowledge of the known terrain. Think of yourself as riding along with the pioneers—because you are!

International, Space, and Polar Dimensions

FROM ITS FIRST STIRRINGS, before it had a name, environmental psychology is almost 100 years old. The oldest scientific study that might be called environmental psychology may be an examination of the effect of heat on tin-plate workers in England in 1919.[89] In Germany, Willy Hellpach explored some concepts in the field during the 1920s.[90] Lighting in English dwellings was studied in the 1930s.[91]

In Japan, Tetsuro Watsuji considered environment-behavior relations throughout the 1930s[92] and a strong movement has developed in Japan since then,[93] beginning with an early book on architectural psychology.[94] In Canada, the effects of restricted environmental stimulation were first investigated in McGill University laboratories in the middle 1950s.[95] The first research on personal space and the first explicit use of environmental psychology to design buildings occurred in Saskatchewan about the same time.[96]

Sweden has long been at the forefront of environmental psychology,[97] with a particular early emphasis on the visual perception of architecture,[98, 99] and ecological concern has spurred considerable research into air and noise pollution.[100, 101] Cold outdoor environments have produced much work directed towards creating quality indoor environments[102] and understanding the very meaning of the environment.[103, 104] The Netherlands has been a very strong source of research, particularly in transportation and energy issues.[105] In the United States, some research began in the late 1950s, and some of the major organizations in the field were first begun in the US.

Research in environmental psychology is also well-established in Italy,[106] Australia,[107] Israel,[108] and in Estonia.[109] In other countries, environmental psychology has developed more slowly. Nevertheless, devoted groups of researchers exist in France,[110] Turkey,[111] Venezuela,[112] Mexico,[113, 114] other countries of Latin America,[115] Saudi Arabia,[116] South Africa,[117] and Finland.[118] In recent years, regular international conferences have helped to knit the worldwide community of environmental psychology. A census I undertook in 2007 found about 600 researchers who consider their professional role to be, all or in part, an environmental psychologist. A second census completed in 2011 saw that number increase to over 1000.

Environmental psychologists are also at work above and below the surface of the earth, at its top and bottom,

FIGURE 1–6 Environmental psychologists have studied environments in space as well as on Earth. The International Space Station was designed in part by environmental psychologists.

and in all sorts of extreme environments.[119] Environmental psychologists have researched the ability of submarine crews to orient themselves in their watery abodes, investigated the design of living and working quarters on space stations,[120-122] in all sorts of capsules[123] and examined environment-behavior transactions in both the Arctic and Antarctic[124,125] (see Figure 1-6).

IN SUM *Environmental psychology has taken root in many countries as well as under the sea, at both poles, and above the earth. To some extent, the field has a unique character in different places because each country has distinct environmental problems and philosophies. Links among environmental psychologists have been increasing, with more international conferences and exchanges of views in prominent scientific journals.*

Challenges and Future Prospects

Environmental psychology is a vigorous young discipline; it will be increasingly influential as cries for a more realistic psychology that solves problems of everyday living in the real world by most or all people are heard. Some experts even see it as a blueprint for the future of psychology as a whole.[126] Already, signs of the influence of the environmental psychology perspective may be seen in many other areas of psychology. Environmental psychology has been described as the leader in a revolution of relevance that is sweeping such other areas as developmental and cognitive psychology.[127] However, four challenges for the field also exist.

1. *Translating research into practice.* Translating research into practice has been a recognized difficulty since the beginning of the field. In this book, many successful applications are described. Nevertheless, each new project seems to raise its own peculiar obstacles to be overcome. Some think the field and its practitioners will have to become much more political in order to have greater impact.[128]

2. *Further integrating and developing theory.* Theoretical diversity is stimulating and productive, but further integration and development of theory is necessary.[129] More efforts like those of thinkers who have explored the relations between environmental psychology and psychophysics,[130] for example, or behavior setting theory and the operant approach,[131] are necessary.

3. *Discovering more powerful research methods.* Environmental psychology has come of age in its advocacy of more complex types of theory. However, the need exists for research methods that can do justice to the complexity of the more inclusive theories.[132]

4. *Achieving a more coherent core.*[133] When fields of inquiry are mere collections of topics that are not linked together, they can be absorbed into other fields and disappear. Some authors worry that as environmental psychology's influence expands, it could lose its own identity,[134] while others are certain that will not happen because the field deals with an absolutely fundamental and essential unit of analysis: persons-in-their-environments.[135] Several perspectives that explore the wholeness and distinctiveness of environmental psychology are now appearing,[136-141] but more are needed; the field's boundaries are still growing and changing. A chief goal of this book is to reveal the natural coherence of environmental psychology even as it evolves.

SUMMARY

Environmental psychology is a relatively new area of psychology, but its roots are deep in the history of the discipline. It seeks understanding of person-environment transactions (principles) and the application of that understanding to solve real-world problems that most or even all people face (practice). Some environmental psychologists work more on the principles, while others work more on the practice. Several complementary but distinct paradigms are used—some contemplative, some experimental, and some consultative.

Around the world, the face of environmental psychology varies with national and regional concerns, but it retains a fundamental commitment to understanding and improving relations between humans and their environments. Environmental psychology is at the forefront of a general movement to make psychology as a whole more relevant to everyday life, but it is still challenged to find more ways to turn knowledge into practice, to devise methods that are better able to accomplish its goals, to reach greater consensus on what constitutes its central core, and to develop more comprehensive theories reflecting and embodying that core. However, the field is vigorous and it *will* meet these challenges. As the title of a 2014 review article in psychology's highest-impact journal says, "Environmental psychology matters!"[142]

Suggested Supplementary Readings

Bechtel, R.. & Churchman, A. (Eds.)(2002). *Handbook of environmental psychology*. New York: Wiley.

Clayton, S. (Ed.)(2012). *Handbook of environmental and conservation psychology*. New York: Cambridge University Press.

Gifford, R. (2009). Environmental psychology: Manifold visions, unity of purpose. *Journal of Environmental Psychology, 29,* 387-389.

Gifford, R., Steg, L., & Reser, J. P. (2011). Environmental psychology. In Martin, P., Cheung, F., Kyrios, M., Littlefield, L., Knowles, M., Overmier, B., & Prieto, J. P. (Eds.). *IAAP Handbook of Applied Psychology* (pp. 440-471). New York: Oxford.

Gifford, R. (2014). Environmental psychology matters. *Annual Review of Psychology, 65,* 541-580.

The most central journal in the field: *Journal of Environmental Psychology*

Another very central journal: *Environment and Behavior*

References

1. Chein, I. (1954). The environment as a determinant of behavior. *Journal of Social Psychology, 39,* 115-127.

2. Gifford, R. (2009). Environmental psychology: Manifold visions, unity of purpose. *Journal of Environmental Psychology, 29,* 387-389.

3. Preiser, W. F. E., Vischer, J. C., & White, E. T. (Eds.). (1991). *Design intervention: Toward a more humane architecture.* New York: Van Nostrand Reinhold.

4. Nickerson, R. S. (2003). *Psychology and environmental change.* Mahwah, NJ: Erlbaum.

5. Hobson, K. (2006). Environmental psychology and the geographies of ethical and sustainable consumption: aligning, triangulating, challenging? *Area, 38,* 292-300.

6. Brunswik, E. (1943). Organismic achievement and environmental probability. *Psychological Review, 50,* 255-272.

7. Chein, I. (1954). The environment as a determinant of behavior. *Journal of Social Psychology, 39,* 115-127.

8. Barker, R. G., & Wright, H. (1955). *Midwest and its children.* New York: Row and Peterson.

9. This weeks' citation classic. (1980). *Current Contents, 12*(26), 10.

10. Morgan, J. J. (1916). The overcoming of distraction and other resistances, *Archives of Psychology, No. 35, 24,* 1-84.

11. Vernon, H. M. (1919). *The influence of hours of work and of ventilation on output in tinplate manufacture.* Industrial Fatigue Research Board, Report No. 1. London, UK: HMSO.

12. Griffith, C. R. (1921). A comment upon the psychology of the audience. *Psychological Monographs, 30*(136), 36-47.

13. Snow, C. E. (1927). Research on industrial illumination. *The Tech Engineering News, 8,* 257-282.

14. Maslow, A. H., & Mintz, N. L.(1956).Effects of esthetic surroundings: Initial effects of three esthetic conditions upon perceiving "energy and "well- being" in faces. *Journal of Psychology, 41,* 247-254.

15. Sommer, R. (1969). *Personal space: The behavioral basis of design.* Englewood Cliffs, NJ: Prentice Hall.

16. Osmond, H. (1957). Function as the basis of psychiatric ward design. *Mental Hospitals* (Architectural Supplement), *8,* 23-30.

17. Sommer, R. (1959). Studies in personal space. *Sociometry, 22,* 247-260.

18. Ittelson, W. H., Proshansky, H. M., & Rivlin, L. (1970). The environmental psychology of the psychiatric ward. In H. M. Proshansky, L. G. Rivlin, & W. H. Ittelson (Eds.), *Environmental psychology: Man and his physical setting.* New York: Holt, Rinehart, and Winston.

19. Bonnes, M., Lee, T., & Boniauto, M. (Eds.). (2003). *Psychological theories for environmentalissues.* Aldershot, UK: Aldgate.

20. Uzzell, D., & Räthzel, N. (2009). Transforming environmental psychology. *Journal of Environmental Psychology, 29,* 340-350.

21. Wohlwill, J. F. (1966). The physical environment: A problem for a psychology of stimulation. *Journal of Social Issues, 22,* 29-38.

22. Helson, H. (1964). *Adaptation-level theory.* New York: Harper and Row.

23. Berlyne, D. E. (1960). *Conflict, arousal and curiosity.* New York: McGraw-Hill.

24. Mehrabian, A., & Russell, J. A. (1974). *An approach to environmental psychology.* Cambridge, MA: MIT Press.

25. Cohen, S. (1978). Environmental load and the allocation of attention. In A. Baum, J. E. Singer,& S. Valins (Eds.), *Advances in environmental psychology* (Vol. 1). Hillsdale, NJ: Erlbaum.

26. Milgram, S. (1970). The experience of living in cities. *Science, 167,* 1461-1468.

27. Shalini, M., & Stokols, D. (2012). Psychological and Health Outcomes of Perceived Information Overload. *Environment and Behavior, 44,* 737-759.

28. Suedfeld, P. (1980). *Restricted environmental stimulation: Research and clinical applications.* New York: Wiley.

29. Suedfeld, P. (1980), Landon, P. B., & Ballard, E. J. (1983). Effects of reduced stimulation on divergent and convergent thinking. *Environment and Behavior, 15,* 727-738.

30. Selye, H. (1976). *Stress in health and disease.* Wobern, MA: Butterworth.

31. Stokols, D. (1979). A congruence analysis of human stress. In I. Sarason & C. Spielberger (Eds.), *Stress and anxiety.* Washington, DC: Hemisphere Press.

32. Evans, G. W. (1999). *Measurement of the physical environment as stressor.* In S. L. Friedman, &T. D. Wachs, (Eds.), *Measuring environment across the life span: Emerging methods and concepts.* Washington, DC: American Psychological Association.

33. Campbell, J. M. (1983). Ambient stressors. *Environment and Behavior, 15,* 355-380.

34. Evans, G. W. (Ed.). (1982). *Environmental stress.* New York: Cambridge University Press.

35. Lazarus, R. (1966). *Psychological stress and the coping process.* New York: McGraw-Hill.

36. Buttimer, A., & Seamon, D. (Eds.). (1980). *The human experience of space and place.* London: Croom Helm.

37. Graumann, C. F. (2002). The phenomenological approach to people-environment studies. In R. B. Bechtel, & A. Churchman (Eds.), *Handbook of environmental psychology* (pp. 95-113). New York: Wiley.

38. Barnes, R. D. (1981). Perceived freedom and control in the built environment. In J. H. Harvey (Ed.), *Cognition, social behavior and the environment.* Hillsdale, NJ: Erlbaum.

39. Altman, I. (1975). *The environment and social behavior: Privacy, personal space, territoriality and crowding.* Monterey, CA: Brooks/Cole.

40. Brehm, J. W. (1966). *A theory of psychological reactance.* New York: Academic Press.

41. Seligman, M. E. P. (1975). *Helplessness.* San Francisco: Freeman.

42. Barker, R. G. (1968). *Ecological psychology: Concepts and methods for studying the environment of human behavior.* Stanford, CA: Stanford University Press.

43. Wicker, A. W. (1979). *An introduction to ecological psychology.* Monterey, CA: Brooks/Cole.

44. Wicker, A. W. (1979). *An introduction to ecological psychology.* Monterey, CA: Brooks/Cole.

45. Wicker, A. W. (1987). Behavior settings reconsidered: Temporal stages, resources, internal dynamics, context. In D. Stokols & I. Altman (Eds.), *Handbook of environmental psychology.* New York: Wiley.

46. Georgiou, D., Carspecken, P. F., & Willems, E. P. (1996). An expansion of Roger Barker's behavior setting survey for an ethno-ecological approach to person-environment interactions. *Journal of Environmental Psychology, 16,* 319-333.

47. Gärling, T., Biel, A.,&Gustafsson, M. (2002). The new environmental psychology: The human interdependence paradigm. In Bechtel, R. B. & Churchman, A., *Handbook of environmental psychology,* pp. 85-94. Hoboken, NJ: Wiley.

48. Chein, I. (1954). The environment as a determinant of behavior. *Journal of Social Psychology, 39,* 115-127.

49. de Rivera, J. (1986). The "objective-behavioral" environment of Isidor Chein: In memory of a humanistic scientist. *Environment and Behavior, 18,* 95-108.

50. Stokols, D., & Shumaker, S. A. (1981). People in places: A transactional view of settings. In J. H. Harvey (Ed.), *Cognition, social behavior and the environment.* Hillsdale, NJ: Erlbaum.

51. Altman, I., & Rogoff, B. (1987). World views in psychology and environmental psychology: Trait, interactional, organismic and transactional perspectives. In I. Altman & D. Stokols (Eds.), *Handbook of environmental psychology,* New York: Wiley.

52. Wapner, S. (1981). Transactions of persons-in-environments: Some critical transitions. *Journal of Environmental Psychology, 1,* 223-239.

53. Clitheroe, H. C., Jr., Stokols, D., & Zmuidzinas, M. (1998). Conceptualizing the context of environment and behavior. *Journal of Environmental Psychology, 18,* 103-112.

54. Gifford, R. (2006). A general model of social dilemmas. *International Journal of Ecological Economics and Statistics, 5,* 23-40.

55. Gifford, R. (2008). Toward a comprehensive model of social dilemmas. In A. Biel, D. Eek, T. Gärling, & M. Gustafsson (Eds.). *New issues and paradigms in research on social dilemmas.* New York: Springer.

56. Geller, E. S. (1987). Environmental psychology and applied behavior analysis: From strange bedfellows to a productive marriage. In D. Stokols & I. Altman (Eds.), *Handbook of environmental psychology,* New York: Wiley.

57. Stokols, D. (1990). Instrumental and spiritual views of people-environment relations. *American Psychologist, 45,* 641-646.

58. Demick, J., & Wapner, S., (1990). Role of psychological science in promoting environmental quality. *American Psychologist, 45*, 631-632.

59. Strathman, A., Baker, S., & Kost, K. (1991). Distinguishing the psychologies of the sociophysical and the natural environment. *American Psychologist, 46*, 164-165.

60. Clayton, S., & Brook, A. (2005). Can psychology help save the world? A model for conservation psychology. *Analyses of Social Issues and Public Policy, 5*, 87-102.

61. Saunders, C. D., Brook, A., and Myers, O. E., Jr. (2006) Using psychology to save biodiversity and human well-being. *Conservation Biology, 20*, 702-705.

62. Reser, J. P. (1995). Whither environmental psychology? The transpersonal ecopsychology crossroads. *Journal of Environmental Psychology, 15*, 1-23.

63. De Weiss, S. P., & Diaz-Loving, R. (1986). Applied psychology in Mexico. *Applied Psychology: An International Review, 35*, 577-598.

64. Roszak, T. (1992). *The voice of the earth.* New York: Simon and Schuster.

65. Becker, C. B. (1999). Ethics for the coming century. In C.B. Becker (Ed.), *Asian and Jungian Views of Ethics* (pp. 113-134). Westport: Greenwood Press/Greenwood.

66. Cock, P. (1996). Toward an ecopsychology for sustainable development. In S. C. Carr & J. F. Schumaker (Eds.), *Psychology and the Developing World* (pp. 191-198). Westport: Praeger Publishers/Greenwood.

67. Petri, H. (1991). Zur psychoanalyse der vergifteten kindheit. / Psychoanalysis of poisoned childhood. *Psychotherapie Psychosomatik Medizinische Psychologie, 41*, 155-165.

68. Howard, G. S. (1997). *Ecological psychology: Creating a more earth-friendly human nature.* Notre Dame: University of Notre Dame Press.

69. Frederickson, L. M., Anderson, D. H. (1999). A qualitative exploration of the wilderness experience as a source of spiritual inspiration. *Journal of Environmental Studies, 19*, 21-39.

70. Cock, P. (1996). Toward an ecopsychology for sustainable development. In S. C. Carr & J. F. Schumaker (Eds.), *Psychology and the developing world* (pp. 191-198). Westport: Praeger Publishers/Greenwood.

71. Bragg, E. A. (1996). Towards ecological self: Deep ecology meets constructionalist self-theory. *Journal of Environmental Psychology, 16*, 93-108.

72. Coley, R. L., Kuo, F. E., & Sullivan, W. C. (1997). Where does community grow? The social context created by nature in urban public housing. *Environment and Behavior, 29*, 468-494.

73. Horwitz, W. A. (1996). Developmental origins of environmental ethics: The life experiences of activists. *Ethics and Behavior, 6*, 29-54.

74. Frederickson, L. M., Anderson, D. H. (1999). A qualitative exploration of the wilderness experience as a source of spiritual inspiration. *Journal of Environmental Studies, 19*, 21-39.

75. Frumkin, H. (2001). Beyond toxicity: Human health and the environment. *American Journal of Preventive Medicine, 20*, 234-240.

76. Bragg, E. A. (1996). Towards ecological self: Deep ecology meets constructionalist self-theory. *Journal of Environmental Psychology, 16*, 93-108.

77. Reser, J. P. (1995). Whither environmental psychology? The transpersonal ecopsychology crossroads. *Journal of Environmental Psychology, 15*, 1-23.

78. Zeisel, J. (1981). *Inquiry by design: Tools for environment-behavior research.* Monterey, CA: Brooks/Cole.

79. Bechtel, R. B., Marans, R. W., & Michelson, W. (1987). *Methods in environmental and behavioral research.* New York: Van Nostrand.

80. Gifford, R. (Ed.) (forthcoming). *Research methods for environmental psychology.* New York: Wiley.

81. Craik, K. H. (1977). Multiple scientific paradigms in environmental psychology. *International Journal of Psychology, 12*, 147-157.

82. Saegert, S., & Winkel, G. H. (1990). Environmental psychology. *Annual Review of Psychology, 41*, 441-447.

83. Uzzell, D., & Räthzel, N. (2009). Transforming environmental psychology. *Journal of Environmental Psychology, 29*, 340-350.

84. D. Stokols & I. Altman (Eds.). (1987). *Handbook of environmental psychology,* New York: Wiley.

85. Bechtel, R.. & Churchman, A. (Eds.)(2002). *Handbook of environmental psychology.* New York: Wiley.

86. Clayton, S. (Ed.)(2012) *Handbook of environmental and conservation psychology.* New York: Cambridge University Press.

87. Giuliani, M. V., & Scopelliti, M. (2009). Empirical research in environmental psychology: Past, present, and future. *Journal of Environmental Psychology, 29*, 375-386.

88. Stokols, D., Misra, S., Runnerstrom, M. G., & Hipp, J. A. (2009). Psychology in an age of ecological crisis: From personal angst to collective action. *American Psychologist, 64*, 181-193.

89. Vernon, H. M. (1919). *The influence of hours of work and of ventilation on output in tinplate manufacture.*

90. Fuhrer, U. (1983). Oekopsychologie: Some general implications from a particular literature. *Journal of Environmental Psychology, 3*, 239-252.

91. Chapman, D., & Thomas, G. (1944). Lighting in dwellings. In *The lighting of buildings (Post war building studies, No. 12).* London: HMSO.

92. Yamamoto, T. (1984). *Current trends in Japanese psychology.* Paper presented at the annual meetings of the American Psychological Association, Toronto, August.

93. Inui, M. (1982). Environmental psychology in Japan. *Journal of Environmental Psychology, 2*, 313-321.

94. Kobayashi, S. (1961). *An introduction to architectural psychology.* Tokyo: Shokokusha Publishing.

95. Heron, W., Doane, B. K., & Scott, T. H. (1956). Visual disturbances after prolonged perceptual isolation. *Canadian Journal of Psychology, 10*, 13-18.

96. Sommer, R., & Ross, H. (1958). Social interaction on a geriatrics ward. *International Journal of Social Psychiatry, 4*, 128-133.

97. Gärling, T. (1982). Swedish environmental psychology. *Journal of Environmental Psychology, 2*, 233-251.

98. Gärling, T. (1969). Studies in visual perception of architectural spaces and rooms. *Scandinavian Journal of Psychology, 10*, 250-256.

99. Hesselgren, S. (1967). *The language of architecture.* Lund: Studentlitteratur.

100. Berglund, B., Berglund, U., & Lindvall, T. (1976). Psychological processing of odor mixtures. *Psychological Review, 83*, 432-441.

101. Berglund, B., Berglund, U., & Lindvall, T. (1976). Scaling loudness, noisiness, and annoyance of community noises. *Journal of Acoustical Society of America, 60*, 1119-1125.

102. Wyon, D. P., Lofberg, H. A., & Lofstedt, B. (1975). Environmental research at the climate laboratory of the National Swedish Institute of Building Research. *Man-Environment Systems, 5*, 107-200.

103. Acking, C. A., & Sorte, G. (1973). How do we verbalize what we see? *Landscape Architecture, 64*, 470-475.

104. Kuller, R. (1972). *A semantic model for describing perceived environment* (sic). Unpublished doctoral dissertation, Lund Institute of Technology, Lund, Sweden.

105. Kremer, A., & Stringer, M. (1987). Environmental psychology in the Netherlands. In D. Stokols & I. Altman (Eds.), *Handbook of environmental psychology,* New York: Wiley.

106. Perussia, F. (1983). A critical approach to environmental psychology in Italy. *Journal of Environmental Psychology, 3*, 263-277.

107. Thorne, R., & Hall, R. (1987). Environmental psychology in Australia. In D. Stokols & I. Altman (Eds.), *Handbook of environmental psychology.* New York: Wiley.

108. Churchman, A. (1984). *Environmental psychology in Israel.* Paper presented at a symposium on "International Developments in Environmental Psychology," annual meetings of the American Psychological Association, Toronto, August.

109. Niit, T., Kruusval, J., & Heidmets, M. (1981). Environmental psychology in the Soviet Union. *Journal of Environmental Psychology, 1*, 157-177.

110. Jodelet, D. (1987). Environmental psychology in France. In D. Stokols & I. Altman (Eds.), *Handbook of environmental psychology.* New York: Wiley.

111. Pamir, A. H. (1981). An overview of Turkish research and education in environmental social science. *Journal of Environmental Psychology, 1*, 315-328.

112. Sanchez, E., Wiesenfeld, E., & Cronick, K. (1983). Environmental psychology in Venezuela. *Journal of Environmental Psychology, 3*, 161-172.

113. Diaz-Guerrero, R. (1984). Contemporary psychology in Mexico. *Annual Review of Psychology, 35*, 83-112.

114. Montero-Y-Lopez, M. (1997). Scientific productivity in environmental psychology in Mexico: A bibliometric analysis. *Environment and Behavior, 29*, 169-197.

115. Corral-Verdugo, V. (1997). Environmental psychology in Latin America: Efforts in critical situations. *Environment and Behavior, 29*, 163-168.

116. Al-Soliman, T. M. (1991). Societal values and their effect on the built environment in Saudi Arabia: A recent account. *Journal of Architectural and Planning Research, 8*, 235-254.

117. van Staden, F. J. (1987). A decade of environmental psychology in South Africa. *South African Journal of Psychology, 17*, 72-75.

118. Setala, M., & Syvaneen, M. (1988). Environmental psychology in Finland. *Journal Environmental Psychology, 8*, 315-323.

119. Suedfeld, P. (1990). Groups in isolation and confinement: Environments and experiences. In A. H. Harrison, Y. A. Clearwater, & C. P. McKay (Eds.), *From Antarctica to outer space: Life in isolation and confinement*. New York: Springer-Verlag.

120. Clearwater, Y. (1985). A human place in outer space. *Psychology Today, 19*(7), 34-43.

121. Harrison, A. A., Struthers, N. J., & Putz, B. J. (1991). Mission destination, mission duration, gender, and student perceptions of space habitat acceptability. *Environment and Behavior, 23*, 221-232.

122. Gifford, R., & Lacombe, C. (2006). *The habitability of spacecraft: Assessments of a virtual reality simulation of the ISS across cultural, personality, and individual differences*. Report to the Canadian Space Agency.

123. Suedfeld, P., & Steel, G. D. (2000). The environmental psychology of capsule habitats. *Annual Review of Psychology, 51*, 227-253.

124. Rothblum, E. D. (1990). Psychological factors in the Antarctic. *Journal of Psychology, 124*, 253-273.

125. Leon, G. R., Sandal, G. M., & Larsen, E. (2011). Human performance in polar environments. *Journal of Environmental Psychology, 31*, 353-360.

126. Ellis, P. (1980). Review of Designing for therapeutic environments. *Bulletin of the British Psychological Society, 33*, 325-326.

127. Altman, I. (1981). Reflections on environmental psychology: 1981. *Human Environments, 2*, 5-7.

128. Philip, D. (1996). The practical failure of architectural psychology. *Journal of Environmental Psychology, 16*, 277- 284.

129. Bonnes, M., Lee, T., & Boniauto, M. (Eds.). (2003). *Psychological theories for environmentalissues*. Aldershot, UK: Aldgate.

130. Baird, J. C., & Berglund, B. (1989). Thesis for environmental psychophysics. *Journal of Environmental Psychology,9*, 345-356.

131. Willems, E. P. (1974). Behavioral technology and behavioral ecology. *Journal of Applied Behavior Analysis, 7*, 151-164.

132. Stokols, D. (1982). Environmental psychology: A coming of age. In A. Kraut (Ed.), *The G. Stanley Hall LectureSeries* (Vol. 2), Washington, DC: American Psychological Association.

133. Canter, D. V., & Craik, K. H. (1981). Environmental psychology. *Journal of Environmental Psychology, 1*, 1-11.

134. Stokols, D. (1995). The paradox of environmental psychology. *American Psychologist, 50*, 821-837.

135. Craik, K. H. (1996). Environmental psychology: A core field within psychological science. *American Psychologist, 51*, 1186-1187.

136. Winkel, G., Saegert, S., & Evans, G. W. (2009). An ecological perspective on theory, methods, and analysis in environmental psychology: Advances and challenges. *Journal of Environmental Psychology, 29*, 318-328.

137. Kaplan, S., & Kaplan, R. (2009). Creating a larger role for environmental psychology: The reasonable person model as an integrative framework. *Journal of Environmental Psychology, 29*, 329-339.

138. Pelletier, L., Lavergne, K., & Sharp, E. (2008). Environmental psychology and sustainability: Comments on topics important for our future. *Canadian Psychology/Psychologie canadienne, 49*, 304-308.

139. Günther, H. (2009). The environmental psychology of research. *Journal of Environmental Psychology, 29*, 358-365.

140. Gifford, R. (2007). Environmental psychology and sustainable development: Expansion, maturation, and challenges. *Journal of Social Issues, 63*, 199-212.

141. Uzzell, D., & Räthzel, N. (2009). Transforming environmental psychology. *Journal of Environmental Psychology, 29*, 340-350.

142. Gifford, R. (2014). Environmental psychology matters. *Annual Review of Psychology, 65*, 541-580.

CHAPTER 2:

Environmental Perception and Cognition

We know a great deal about the perception of a one-eyed man with his head in a clamp watching glowing lights in a dark room, but surprisingly little about his perceptual abilities in a real-life situation.

—HELEN ROSS[1]

THE LONG WEEKEND LOOKED VERY PROMISING *except for the fog that clung to the valley, enveloping the town. Tom had asked Jane, whom he had recently met, to go camping in the mountains. As they made their way out of town through Friday afternoon traffic, the snail's pace made the sights along the city streets somehow more vivid. The glaring yellow motel and fast-food restaurant signs along the strip seemed larger and closer than usual.*

"How far is it to the campsite?" Jane asked as they cleared town and the fog.

"Right over there," said Tom. "See that jagged peak just to the left? Guess how far it is."

"I'd say about an hour," said Jane. "How far is it?"

"I don't know for sure," Tom replied, "but I would guess it's closer than that, maybe 40 minutes." After they had driven through landscapes that gradually changed from dry golden grasses and green oaks to evergreen shrubs and slender pines for about an hour and a half, the jagged peak did look quite a bit closer, but it was still some distance away.

When they finally entered the park, Tom tried to recall where that great campsite from last year was. Jane spotted a "You are here" map just inside the gates, but they could not orient themselves from it. They could not decide whether the map was too vague to be useful or if too many exams had burned out their map-reading circuits.

Tom finally was able to conjure up a mental image of the park; he remembered that the roads were arranged in a unique system of concentric circles. Now it came back: the good site was just near that giant fir on the third ring road.

As Friday evening settled into utter peace, Tom and Jane sat on a ridge watching the sun sink into a distant range of snowy peaks. The pleasing thunder of a waterfall could be heard, and a deep, dark mountain lake lay before them. The meadow wildflowers around them gathered dew and began to fold their petals.

IF YOU AND I LOOKED UP AND DOWN A STREET, WOULD WE SEE THE SAME THING? How would our thoughts about what we see differ? Would you and I have the same mental map of the streets surrounding this one? Environmental psychology begins with the basic processes involved as we come to know our surroundings. This chapter and the next one cover several closely connected psychological processes that occur as we perceive and comprehend natural and built environments.[2]

Environmental perception is the initial gathering of information. We are primarily visual beings,[3] but environmental perception includes the ways and means by which we collect information through all our senses. The term environmental perception sometimes is used more broadly to include aspects of how we appraise and assess environments, but in this chapter it will refer to the initial information-gathering and "first impressions" phase of the process; how we reach secondary conclusions such as whether we prefer or like a scene is discussed in the next chapter.

The topics in the first half of this chapter include the nature and measurement of environmental perception, what influences it, theories about how it works, and some of its applications to design and planning. In the course of this discussion, basic awareness of our immediate surroundings and perceptual adaptation are also examined.

The second half of the chapter is about **environmental cognition**, that is, how we think about places. Much of the research *within* that umbrella term is concerned with **spatial cognition**, which is about how we acquire, store, organize, and recall information about locations, distances, and arrangements in buildings, streets, and the great outdoors. Through experience, for example, we develop an extensive body of knowledge about the buildings, streets, and communities around us. These topics include cognitive mapping, spatial knowledge, memory for environments, and orientation in built and natural settings. Methods of investigating environmental cognition—as well as influences on it, theories about it, and its application to environmental design—are discussed.

ENVIRONMENTAL PERCEPTION

Wherever you are, take a just a moment to look around. Then *really* look around, conscious that you are perceiving the environment. Experience may suggest that perception is simple and automatic, but it is not. We are so familiar with the act of perceiving that the wondrous complexity of the process emerges only when we deliberately turn our perceptual talents back on themselves to observe what is going on as we see, hear, smell, taste, and touch the world. Perception of the everyday world is an exceedingly complicated phenomenon.

Distinctions and Variations

CONTRASTS WITH TRADITIONAL PERCEPTION RESEARCH. When psychologists long ago began to study perception, they quickly realized the complexity of the task facing them. Many decided that in order to learn about the process, the complexity of everyday perception would have to be reduced, for example by presenting the perceiver with a simple stimulus in the laboratory, where maximum control over all possible extraneous influences may be exerted.

Environmental psychologists, in contrast, embrace and even celebrate the complexity of the environmental displays they choose to study (e.g., buildings, cities, landscapes, roads while driving). The older approach has been called **object perception**, in contrast to **environmental perception**[4,5,6] (see Figure 2-1). In object perception research, the emphasis is on the properties of simple stimuli, such as their brightness, color, depth, perceptual constancy, form, and apparent movement. In environmental perception, the emphasis is on large-scale scenes, treated as whole entities. The difference between the two approaches is not merely in the size and complexity of the stimulus presented; the role of the perceiver is also different. In environmental perception studies, the participants often move in and around the scene; they are *part* of the scene. Moving through the environmental display means that the perceiver experiences it from multiple perspectives. The perceiver often is *connected* to the environmental display by a clear goal or purpose. For example, we scan a wilderness area for a clean campsite; while driving, we watch signs and lights to avoid being in an accident; we look over the restaurant for a private table, and so on.

An important challenge for environmental perception research, of course, is to account for the myriad of personal and physical influences on the perception of these complex and dynamic scenes.

AWARENESS AND ADAPTATION. The environment constantly offers many more pieces of information than we can possibly handle. We are always selecting for our attention a relatively small, manageable portion of the available information. We may focus intensely or minimally on environmental displays ranging in size from architectural details to

FIGURE 2–1 Traditional perception researchers usually examine how simple displays, such as the Gestalt figure (top) are seen. Environmental psychologists study real scenes (bottom).

vast panoramic landscapes that range in distance from very near to very distant.

We may actively scrutinize the environment (e.g., when we evaluate an apartment as a possible place to rent) or we may adapt or habituate to some environmental displays so that we really do not *see* them at all (e.g., a street you walk along every day). An unfortunate example of this **habituation** is the way some people adapt to air pollution. It is noticed when it is new, such as when a person moves to a smoggy place, or when there is a sudden increase in smoke. Basing his observations on a principle of psychophysics called the **Weber-Fechner law**, Robert Sommer pointed out that as the amount of air pollution increases, larger and larger increments of *new* air pollution are needed

before people notice that pollution is becoming worse.[7] The same amount of smoke that would have outraged a community when it had little air pollution is barely noticed after the community becomes heavily polluted. The problem is that the new amount is just as damaging as the original amount.

We sometimes pay very little attention to our physical surroundings even when they cause some discomfort, a state I have called **environmental numbness**.[8] This numbness, or lack of awareness of our surroundings, often arises when more lively aspects of the world—such as the attentions of a friend, absorption in a book, or daydreaming—command our attention. Environmental numbness can cause us to overlook major problems, such as pollution, or expose us to minor hazards, such as bumping into a cupboard door, or major hazards while driving[9] or absent-mindedly walking across a street.

On the positive side, we are capable of greatly enhancing our awareness and appreciation of the environment. Herbert Leff provided an elaborate description of ways we might consciously direct our perceptions and cognitions to obtain richer environmental experiences.[10] Here are some of Leff's exercises for getting more out of any particular scene:

- Rapidly switch your visual focus from one point in the scene to another while forming a vivid impression of each view.

- Look for views in the scene that would make personally relevant photographs.

- Imagine what it would be like to be one of the objects in the scene.

- See inanimate objects as if they were alive.

The mental gymnastics involved in these exercises can produce very positive feelings while increasing your environmental awareness.

IN SUM *Environmental psychologists usually study the perception of whole, everyday scenes. In doing so, they sometimes must sacrifice a degree of experimental control, but in return they are able to investigate the perception of real, complex settings as perceivers move through them. Awareness and adaptation mean that we select a few cues from scenes and ignore most others. Unfortunately,* *ignoring some cues (environmental numbness) can be harmful. Fortunately, some ways to perceive everyday settings in ways that result in positive experiences have been developed.*

Research Methods

How can environmental perception be studied? This question may be answered in terms of how the environment is presented to the perceiver or in terms of how we measure a person's perception.

PRESENTING THE ENVIRONMENT TO THE PERCEIVER. As noted above, environmental psychologists prefer to study the perception of whole, complex, everyday scenes. Ideally, this means showing real (live) scenes to subjects, and this is often done. For my own doctoral dissertation, I took groups of people from building to building on a "magical mystery tour."[11] However, this is not always possible. For example, what if you want to know how people will perceive a building that has not yet been constructed, or a real landscape that is far away? Real scenes change—weather conditions and lighting, for example—which mean that if researchers wish to present the *same* scene to many perceivers over the course of several sessions, they cannot rely on live presentations.

Thus, sometimes—if necessary—virtual reality, photos, videos, sketches, or models of everyday scenes are used.[12] A typical study might compare responses to a wild river based on video pictures plus sound, video pictures with no sound, and still photos with no sound.[13] Some laboratories have enabled people to simulate travel through entire miniaturized regions[14,15] (see Figure 2-2). Simulations do have shortcomings, such as the inability of the perceiver to be *in* the actual scene, but some are surprisingly good at producing the same perceptual responses elicited by the real setting.[16] Some researchers focus on which aspect of the scene is simulated best by which type of simulation.[17] A simple sequence of color slides or videos often is quite good,[18-20] but the newer virtual reality presentations probably are even better.[21]

STUDYING THE PROCESS OF PERCEPTION. Turning to the second question, how can we measure a person's perception? After all, perception is a private experience. Because researchers do not have direct access to others' experienc-

FIGURE 2–2 This environmental simulation laboratory at the University of California's Berkeley campus was used to assess how different plans for the development of the region affect landscape quality in the eyes of local residents. A tiny camera at the point of the mobile apparatus at the left produced a video image on the monitor that is similar to the view that would be seen by a motorist passing through the region.

es, perception is usually measured indirectly. Five general methods of doing so are used.

1. The most common method is simply to ask perceivers what they see (or hear, smell, touch, taste). These **self-report methods** include questionnaires, interviews, checklists, and free descriptions. An obvious shortcoming of these methods is that perceivers may produce inaccurate reports of their own perceptions. They may not pay careful attention to their own perceptions of a moment ago, they may incorrectly recall or entirely forget perceptions from the past, or they may report what they think the experimenter wishes to hear. Finally, perception is filtered through language.[22] Self-report methods nevertheless are useful as reasonably accurate, economical ways to study environmental perception.

2. A second way of studying what perceivers in everyday situations attend to, **time-sampling**, was suggested long ago by Brunswik[23] and revived later by others.[24,25] The idea is simple: Ask observers to move through a setting and to report, at certain intervals, exactly what they are looking at, listening to, etc. This is another form of self-report, but it adds value in the sense of being an "on-line" method that can be used to discover what perceivers are paying attention to without relying on their memory, and whether these elements are moving or stationary, large or small, near or far, straight ahead or to one side, and so on.[26]

3. A third method is used to infer something about perception from the perceiver's behavior. This **behavior-inference method** has been used, for

example, in studies of museums and art galleries. The length of time museum visitors spend looking at a painting or a science exhibit has been used as an index of their interest in that display.

4. Environmental perception can be investigated with the **psychophysical method.** Psychophysicists know that people can reliably adjust some physical variable (e.g., the heaviness of a weight) in direct proportion to the perception of a psychological construct (e.g., the seriousness of a crime).[27] These magnitude estimations allow for the calculation of equations called power functions that express a psychological variable in terms of a known physical scale. In one example of this, subjects adjusted the brightness of a light to correspond to their perception of how architecturally complex different houses seemed to them.[28]

5. In the **phenomenological approach**, which will be discussed later in more detail, the researcher usually is also the perceiver. Rather than employ many subjects, the goal is to use a single very careful trained observer whose goal is to perceive the essence of a setting in a qualitative way.

IN SUM *Environmental psychologists present real settings to perceivers whenever they can, but sometimes they must use simulations. Some simulations produce responses that are very similar to those elicited by real environments. Five general methods of studying environmental perception are self-reports, time-sampling, behavior inference, psychophysical, and phenomenology. Because each method has strengths and weaknesses, multiple methods are used whenever possible. Multiple methods allow the researcher to more fully understand environmental perception.*

Influences on Environmental Perception

HAVE YOU EVER DISAGREED WITH SOMEONE about the distance to a place, the temperature in a room, or the beauty of a scene? If so, you already know that perceptions of the environment can differ. What accounts for these differences? Some can be attributed to the nature of our species, some to differences among perceivers (e.g., differences associated

with perceptual ability or training), some to cultural differences, and others have been explained by physical variations among environmental displays (e.g., architectural style, level of maintenance, or degree of visual complexity).

Personal Influences. Which characteristics of observers themselves are associated with different perceptions of the environment? Obviously, variability in perceptual ability is one factor. Impaired sight or hearing produces a restricted or fuzzy image of one's surroundings. For example, veteran factory workers and rock music performers often hear less well than others.[29] But personal characteristics—such as being human (evolutionary bases), gender, education or training, experience with a setting, and whether a person likes the setting—also affect environmental perception.

To some extent, the way we see the world must be founded on our early history as a species. We "grew up" on the plains of Africa. Do we prefer scenes that remind us of this "home"? Indeed, some studies suggest that we prefer savanna or savanna-like landscapes to other landscapes,[30] but others find that although we do like nature scenes, and this appears to be supported by brain-imaging studies,[31] we prefer lush green landscapes with water and familiar landscapes to savanna.[32] Other work by Robert Sommer suggests that our preferences for tree shapes, one important component of the landscape, appears to be driven both by evolution (the shape of acacia trees, typical of the savanna, are preferred in many cultures) and by one's own familiar trees, the ones one grew up with, with evolution perhaps being a stronger influence.[33]

Men and women may perceive distances differently, on average.[34] For example, men seem to perceive distances to visible buildings as significantly less than distances to hidden buildings, but women do not perceive the distances differently.[35] Attitudes also matter: whether people see a forest as a commodity to be utilized (or not) importantly influences their preferences for forest scenes.[36]

Another important difference in perception is based on education or training. Along with the basic knowledge we acquire as we earn our job qualifications, we seem to learn a *way of seeing* that is characteristic of our chosen profession. Civil engineers see roads and dams where only slopes, streams, and valleys exist; architects see form, light, and color where the rest of us see walls, floors, and doors. Many studies have found differences between the appraisals made by design professionals versus nonprofessionals, and even between different groups of design professionals.[37,38]

To understand this better, some researchers examine the particular *ways* that architects' perceptions differ from those of others. For example, landscape architects and others may not differ in the *quantitative* features of backyards (e.g., the number of different plants and activity areas), but landscape architects see them differently in *qualitative* ways (e.g., how "defined" the landscape is).[39] To the extent that such discrepancies represent differences in the original perceptions of these professionals (before the information is interpreted), and some physiological evidence suggests that they do,[40] their education as professionals seems to be the cause of these differences in environmental perception.[41]

One's experience with, and evaluation of, the setting also affects environmental perception. Even small differences in familiarity can affect perception in interesting ways. For example, people who had been in a room for only half an hour saw it as smaller than did those who had just entered it.[42] Buildings with which perceivers are more familiar are judged to be closer to them than are less familiar buildings.[43] Finally, individuals perceive the distance to buildings they find pleasing more accurately than they judge distances to buildings they find less pleasing.[44]

Cultural and Social Influences. The cultural context in which individuals are raised can lead to quite different ways of seeing the world. The anthropologist Colin Turnbull, for example, described his experiences with the Mbuti people in the Congo.[45] The Mbuti live in dense rainforest and rarely experience vistas that extend for more than 30 meters. Once Turnbull took his Mbuti guide out of the forest to a broad plain where a herd of buffalo could be seen several kilometers away. The guide asked, "What sort of insects are those?" Turnbull explained that they were plains buffalo, animals about twice as large as the rainforest buffalo with which the Mbuti are familiar. The guide laughed and told Turnbull not to tell such stupid stories. Turnbull drove his guide closer to the herd. As they approached, the buffalo seemed, to the guide, to be growing in size, and he was convinced that witchcraft was at work. His lack of experience with distance vision interfered with **size constancy**—the learned tendency to stabilize *perceived* size despite changes in objective distance and the size of the image on our retinas.

This is one example of what has been called the **carpentered-world hypothesis**, which attributes certain differences in perception to the striking discrepancies among the perceptual environments of various societies. Urban settings, with their high frequency of rectangular objects and straight lines, produce different perceptual experiences than un-carpentered settings, simple rural places where curved, rounded lines characterize the houses and landscape.[46]

Perceptions are also influenced by the environment that is the focus of the perception. Perhaps unfortunately, physical neighborhoods are judged in part by the sort of people believed to live in them; if people that one considers "good" live in it, the evaluation of the area itself is likely to be positive, and if the residents are deemed "bad" the area itself will be perceived negatively.[47]

Physical Influences. Environmental perception also depends, of course, on the scene being perceived. No one would confuse the Eiffel Tower with the Rocky Mountains. However, for relatively similar scenes, some controversy exists about the relative importance of person-based and environment-based influences on perception. Some emphasize the considerable processing of visual information that occurs by sensory receptors and the brain, involving both physiology and learning. Others point to obvious physical differences in the settings being perceived. Holders of this point of view would reply, "Yes, but will anyone claim that an open sewer looks the same as a wild river?" This perspective was expressed in the title of a presentation by an early environmental psychologist: "The Environment is *Not* in the Head!"[48] One resolution of this controversy is the proposition that the more scenes differ, the stronger the influence of the environment; the more scenes are similar, the greater the influence of personal factors.

Which physical features of a scene affect our perceptions of it? This is a vast topic, but I will offer a few examples. What makes rooms look larger or smaller? You may have heard that light-colored rooms appear larger than dark-colored rooms; this is one way to make a room look larger, but it's not the only way. The type and placement of light also can affect the perceived spaciousness of a room.[49] For example, when light illuminates only its walls, a room looks larger than when light illuminates the middle of the room, but not its walls. Rooms with windows look larger than those without, and those with more furniture look smaller than those with less furniture.[50] Perhaps counterintuitively, lower ceilings increase perceived spaciousness.[51]

What makes one room look more open or enclosed than another? One obvious ("duh!") answer is that greater

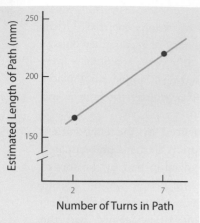

FIGURE 2–3 Distances are perceived as longer when the route has more turns in it.

enclosedness (less openness) is perceived when a room has walls, floors, and ceilings, which "establish space."[52,53] Less obvious is that enclosure is also related to how light or dark the scene is, the depth of view, and the number of its boundaries (sides) that are open at the front of the scene,[54] its floor area,[55] and the pictorial format, if the room is presented as an image.[56]

One might ask whether which of these elements is most important in establishing the room's degree of enclosedness, whether the elements each contribute to the perception, or do they work only as combinations? Apparently, ceilings are three times as important in establishing the perception of enclosedness as floors, and that walls are twice as important.[57] Although walls, floors, and ceilings each make their own independent contribution to the perception, they apparently do not *combine* to enhance the perception of enclosedness.[58]

In a fascinating book, Helen Ross described many perceptual illusions that occur in natural settings.[59] Fog, for example, makes features of the environment such as trees or hills appear to be farther away and larger than they actually are. The same effects occur when objects are viewed under water, especially as the water grows murkier. Other work suggests that fog creates a feeling of danger.[60] This is because fog tends to make a place look more open, but we feel safer in places with more perceived enclosure.

The **terrestrial saucer effect** leads mountain climbers to believe that neighboring mountain peaks equal in altitude to their own are much higher than their own. The same effect also influences the perception of roads so that, under certain conditions, slopes that are actually uphill appear to be downhill, and vice versa.

Similarly, when people walk a path that is either uphill or downhill, they tend to overestimate its length; when a trail is winding, they err about the direction it is taking them in favor of the direction of the vanishing point (the direction implied by the last point of the trail that can be seen).[61] Among other known perceptual effects caused by physical influences, the estimated length of a path grows as a function of the number of turns in the path[62,63] and the number of intersections along the path,[64] rectangular rooms appear larger than square rooms of equal size,[65] and distances *to* landmarks are estimated as smaller than distances *from* landmarks[66,67] (see Figure 2-3).

As perceivers, we tend to subjectively cluster locations that show no particular physical pattern, and these clusterings affect our distance judgments. In particular, we underestimate distances between locations *within* these clusters, but overestimate the distances between locations across *separate* clusters.[68]

All these effects in natural and built settings may be illusions or distortions, but that certainly does not mean they are unimportant. For instance, the very lives of drivers and divers are at stake in the case of the fog, road, and underwater effects. The path and room size distortions may affect perceptions of crowding, status, confinement, and other psychologically important aspects of building interiors.[69] Perceptions on city streets and in nature are also affected by the physical context, with potentially serious consequences. When pedestrians are subjected to more traffic noise, their perceptual field narrows.[70] They look straight ahead more, missing much information from the periphery of their paths, which could be fatal to a pedestrian who steps off a curb, or to a cyclist.

IN SUM *The available evidence suggests that environmental perceptions such as length, distance, spaciousness, and size largely depend on which physical elements are in the scene and how they are arranged. However, personal factors (e.g., familiarity with the place), culture (e.g., being raised in a carpentered world), and training (e.g., in architecture) also influence the way we see the world.*

Theories of Environmental Perception

Environmental perception, like the rest of environmental psychology, needs models, theories, and frameworks to provide a guiding, overall picture of the environment perception process and to generate testable hypotheses for research. No single theory of environmental perception is universally accepted, but the following theories, or a combination of them, may someday yield a valuable, encompassing, widely accepted theory.

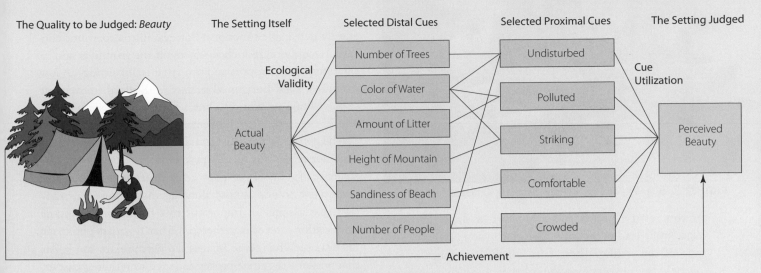

FIGURE 2-4 Brunswik's lens model applied to environmental perception. Qualities of the setting itself are not perceived directly. Rather, they are manifested in **distal cues** (objectively measurable characteristics of the setting). **Proximal cues** are the observer's subjective impressions of these distal cues. Perceived beauty will closely approximate actual beauty (i.e., there will be high **achievement**) if (a) actual beauty truly is manifested in the distal cues (i.e., high **ecological validity**), (b) proximal cues are closely related to distal cues, and (c) proximal cues are closely related to observers' **judgments** of beauty (i.e., observers have excellent cue utilization).

EGON BRUNSWIK: PROBABILISTIC FUNCTIONALISM. One influential approach to environmental perception is based on the work of Egon Brunswik, who was introduced in Chapter 1 and whose theory may be described best by reference to his **lens model**[71] (see Figure 2-4). Brunswik's importance derives from his view that both the perceiver and the environment are important: "Both the organism and the environment will have to be seen as systems, each with properties of their own...As much as psychology must be concerned with the texture of the organism...it must also be concerned with the texture of the environment" (p. 5).[72]

Brunswik observed (pun intended!) that the environment offers a multitude of cues; the perceiver must make sense of the most important ones to function effectively in a setting; this is why Brunswik is a **functionalist**. Usually, only a small number of cues in a given scene are useful to the perceiver. Therefore, many cues are given little attention while close attention is paid to a few others. Infants, or anyone cast suddenly into a new setting, may be perceptually confused because they are overwhelmed with cues and have not yet learned to sort the important cues from the unimportant ones. Think of the last time you entered a setting that was completely new to you.

The theory's **probabilism** refers to Brunswik's belief that no single cue is either a perfectly reliable or perfectly unreliable clue to the true nature of the environment, but rather has a certain *probability* of being accurate. Some cues are considerably less certain or accurate than others.

Ecological validity refers to the degree of "truth" in the probabilistic relations between the environment and each of the cues. It represents the odds that cues would lead to effective perception of the setting, if they exist, and if the perceiver uses them. **Cue utilization** is the probabilistic weight given to each cue by the perceiver, whether the cue is valid or not. Of course, we do not usually assign these weights as a conscious cue-by-cue process; we gradually learn what to look for in a given setting, and gradually learn which cues are most important. When perceivers use the cues in a manner that matches the way the cues are truly related to the environment, they will accurately perceive the scene. That is, when cue utilization closely matches ecological validity, **achievement** will be high (i.e., when the perceiver's reading of the environment closely matches the actual environment).

Brunswik believed that perception is our active attempt to extract a *useful* image of the environment from the mass of potentially confusing cues. He viewed perceivers as intentionally seeking useful images of the environment to assist them as they make their way through the world. After we have repeatedly sampled settings as "intuitive scientists," we become familiar with them. In Brunswik's terms, we have learned which cues are important and how to use them. Perceptual problems arise in new or strange settings, especially those that offer patterns of cues which do not bear a resemblance to those in our familiar settings. Such problems (recall Helen Ross' climbers and divers, as well

FIGURE 2-5 James Gibson would say that these surfaces **afford** seating.

as your own experience as a bicyclist or driver in a new place) may lead us to draw false conclusions about the nature of the setting. These false conclusions range in seriousness from misjudging the color of a wall to misjudging a curve on the highway under foggy conditions.

Brunswik's approach can usefully guide environmental psychology research aimed at identifying *which* setting cues reveal actual conditions that may not be directly visible. One such condition might be objective crime and fear of crime in a residential neighborhood. Which of the many observable features of a residential street are highly correlated with crime?[73] For example, is the presence versus absence of litter on a street (as just one cue) a valid cue to crime rates? Half the task is to discover how strong the relation truly is between the presence of street litter and objective crime rates. This is represented by the left half of the lens model. On the right side of the lens model, the task is to determine the extent to which residents *interpret* the presence versus absence of street litter as an indicator of crime. A perceiver can err either by overestimating or underestimating the true connection between the presence of street lamps and crime rates. High achievement occurs when the perceiver weights a pattern of cues that might include the street-litter cue (right side of the lens model) the same way they are actually weighted (left side of the lens model). To be successful, perceivers must accurately "read" their environments.

JAMES GIBSON: AFFORDANCES. Gibson's approach to environmental perception differs from Brunswik's in that Gibson believed certain arrangements of cues give the perceiver *direct, immediate* perceptions of the environment.[74,75] Gibson believed that the world could be usefully conceptualized as being composed of **substances** (such as wood, steel, glass) and **surfaces** (such as floors, walls, ceilings). The arrangements of these substances and surfaces (called **layouts**) provide what Gibson called **affordances**, or in-

stantly detectable functions. For example, a solid horizontal surface about 18 inches/45 cm off the ground is said to offer or "afford" support and rest (that is, for sitting). A low, extended, solid horizontal surface will "afford" movement (e.g., walking or skating), but a vertical solid surface will "afford" the stopping of movement[76] (see Figure 2-5).

The perception of such affordances, Gibson maintained, does not require us to interpret sensory information, construct reality, or weight cues, as in Brunswik's theory. His perspective stands almost alone against a powerful tradition that assigns an important role to the processing of information after it is gathered. Other theorists point out, for example, that some images we perceive are so similar that without cognitive processes (such as recalling past experiences or attending to neighboring contextual cues), we could not be sure what we are seeing.[77]

Nevertheless, Gibson's ideas have served to help refocus attention on the environment itself, particularly on the everyday environment, as a crucial element in perception. The relevance of Gibson's ideas to environmental psychology and the design professions also lies in his insistence that perception is *not* composed of elemental building blocks of perception such as color, form, and shape. Traditional architectural education, drawing on the traditions of visual arts such as painting and sculpture, emphasizes these very building blocks as the "basis" of design. Architecture students are taught to see form and shape. Gibson argued that this is exactly what architects should *not* be taught.[78] He argued that we, the users of the built environment, do not see form and shape when we see a place; instead, we perceive affordances—what the place can *do* for us. A recent study developed ways to measure the affordances in the community for two needs of adolescents: places for social interaction and places to retreat.[79]

DANIEL BERLYNE: COLLATIVE PROPERTIES. Berlyne contributed a different set of important insights about environmental perception.[80,81] His ideas straddle the distinction between perception and cognition, which is somewhat artificial anyway. In the next chapter we will move further across this bridge, from this chapter's emphasis on "what we see" (environmental perception) to "our judgments about what we see" (environmental appraisal), such as whether the scene is beautiful or preferred. Berlyne's view was that environmental scenes have several **collative properties**, that is, characteristics that cause the perceiver to pay attention, investigate further, and compare. These collative properties include **novelty** (newness to the perceiver), **incongruity** (the perception that something is out of place), **complexity** (a large variety of elements in the display), and **surprisingness** (unexpected elements).

Berlyne believed that these collative properties influence the perceiver's aesthetic judgments of, and desire to explore, environmental "displays," that is, landscapes or buildings one encounters. He proposed that collative properties do so via two psychological dimensions, **hedonic tone** (that is, the amount of beauty or pleasure experienced) and **uncertainty-arousal**. For one kind of "display" (paintings), these relations are fairly clear: images of moderate complexity, novelty, incongruity, and surprisingness are perceived as more beautiful than are images that are either very high or very low on these collative properties.

The implications of Berlyne's theory for environmental design have inspired some designers to suggest that buildings ought to be designed in accordance with his ideas. For example, certain designers argued back in the 1960s that modern architecture built recently at that time should have more complexity because most urban buildings were too simple in their exterior lines.[82,83] Since then, new building facades have indeed become more complex.

However, although scenes of built environments show the predicted results (buildings of moderate complexity are most preferred), responses to landscapes do not always.[84] Perhaps the relations between beauty and the collative properties are more varied than Berlyne thought. Research on collative properties other than complexity has found, for example, a straight-line relation between the property and rated beauty or preference, for example, rather than the inverted-U shape relation predicted by Berlyne, with the greatest preference found at moderate levels of the property.[85]

Nevertheless, Berlyne's ideas have stimulated researchers to search for properties of environmental displays that reliably lead to certain perceptions. Subsequent researchers have, for example, suggested some additions to the list of collative properties. One such addition is **fittingness**, or how well a certain environmental element (for example, a house) suits a certain setting (for example, the wilderness).[86] Because collative properties are very relevant to our judgments *about* what we perceive, they will appear again in the next chapter.

PHENOMENOLOGY. The fourth theory of environment perception we shall consider is phenomenology. This theory has its roots in philosophy. Martin Heidegger, for example, discussed *dwelling* as a "process of existence" through which a mere place becomes a dear home.[87] Phenomenology's value for environmental psychology has been advocated since the early 1980s.[88,89]

The phenomenological approach ultimately results in a self-report, but these self-reports differ in important ways from those discussed earlier.

1. The emphasis is on the perceptions of an individual, or at least one individual at a time, rather than on group averages.

2. Like Gibson, but in sharp contrast to Brunswik, phenomenologists try to overcome or erase the distinction between the setting and the perceiver.

3. The researcher usually is also the perceiver, although sometimes the researcher asks perceivers who live or work in the setting, or are visiting it, to help by carefully reporting their impressions.

4. Phenomenologists try to understand the unique and holistic meaning of a place qualitatively, as revealed *by* the place, rather than by resorting to external concepts or ideas. Because of its emphasis on each unique setting, the phenomenology of place has produced penetrating portraits of particular locations, such as homes,[90] cities,[91] and marketplaces,[92] as well as particular experiences, such as **topophilia** (emotional attachment to a place)[93] and **existential outsideness** (alienation from a place).[94]

The phenomenological approach has been accused of certain inconsistencies,[95,96] but its advocates believe these critics do not understand the discipline of phenomenology.[97] The critics may be judging this psychological form of phenomenology as if it were a philosophy, when its goals in this field are more practical: to gain insight into the ways that people *in* settings view them, and to understand the meaning and relevance of a place to those who know the place best. In this way, phenomenological environmental psychology can make valuable contributions to the design of settings by eliciting the meaning of places to those who will have to live or work in them. Phenomenology appeals to a different sort of researcher than to those who are enamored of the experimental methods. Even its critics agree that it is a valuable complement to the other approaches to environmental psychology.

IN SUM *The theories of Brunswik, Gibson, Berlyne, and phenomenology each have had a major impact on current thinking and research in environmental perception. Each began as a traditional (non-environmental) theory, but each contained important seeds that made it fruitful for environmental psychology. The theories that have stimulated considerable pure research (i.e., attempting to understand how people perceive the environment, with little concern for practice or application), have also been extended into the practical domains of planning and architecture.*

Environmental Perception and Design

Many of the findings reported above can be used to create rooms, buildings, and streetscapes that look larger, smaller, more open or enclosed, simple or complex, instantly functional or desirably mysterious. But let's consider a somewhat different design question next.

WHAT DOES THE "TYPICAL" LOCAL BUILDING LOOK LIKE? If an old building in your community is facing the wrecking ball, some people will try to save it. One reason for saving heritage buildings is that they preserve the architectural character of the community or region. But how do we know just what that architectural character of the region actually looks like?

Researchers wanted to answer this question for classic farmhouses in a rural area of Pennsylvania.[98] They showed residents a series of drawings in which building elements such as window shape and roof slant varied. The residents judged each scene according to how "typical" it seemed of local farmhouses. Through these ratings, the researchers were able to identify which architectural features made a farmhouse look most like a *typical* farmhouse to residents of that area.

In this way, environmental psychologists can discover the essence of architectural character for a city, town, or region. The knowledge that residents used to make their ratings was buried in their experience; they hardly realized that their lifetime of perceiving these buildings had resulted in a particular image of how a typical local farmhouse looks.

HAVE A LITTLE DAYDREAM. Transport yourself back to your all-time favorite place, whether that is your childhood home, street, neighborhood, town, or campground, farm, or wilderness. Conjure the place up in as much colorful detail as you can. What do you think about it? Can you recall how to find your way around it? What important elements were in it and where they were placed? Its size and where it is located relative to other nearby places? You are engaged in environmental cognition.

Distinctions and Definitions

ENVIRONMENTAL COGNITION AND SPATIAL COGNITION. Environmental cognition is the general term for how we think about environments. Because one aspect of environmental cognition, spatial cognition, has been studied so much, it will be discussed on its own. Spatial cognition is how we acquire, store, organize, and recall information about locations, distances, and arrangements in buildings, streets, and the great outdoors. It includes wayfinding, the thinking processes that help us navigate through an environment, estimate distances, recognize routes, and read maps, and it is reflected in cognitive maps, the pictorial and semantic images in our heads related to how places are arranged.[99] If you look around, evidence of cognitive mapping is extremely widespread, from public transport maps, to you-are-here maps, to every person's memory and thinking about the spatial relations between every place in his or her life.[100]

Influences on Environmental Cognition

HOW DO WE THINK ABOUT PLACES? In many ways! Some examples of environmental cognition are how people conceptualize natural environments,[101] the mental models held by citizens of developed countries that cause unsustainable behaviors,[102] the mental models of hazards held by everyday people,[103] how farmers think about droughts,[104] attributions we make about the causes of, responsibility for, and likely future disease rates following toxic spills,[105] how people mentally categorize different kinds of restaurants,[106] or how we imagine more versus less pleasant places.[107]

PERSONAL INFLUENCES. Environmental cognition also includes the various forms of limited thinking or biases people engage in when they consider environmental issues.[108] Some of these include the fixed-pie bias, pseudo-sacredness, egocentrism, overconfidence, unrealistic optimism, feelings of endowment,[109] different kinds of memory for places,[110] and which nations they include is they sketch a map of the world.[111] Researchers have also examined how familiarity with[112] or renovations to[113] buildings affect memories for them, or which outdoor scenes are remembered after hiking.[114]

PHYSICAL INFLUENCES. How does the environment affect environmental cognition? Joachim Wohlwill introduced the concept of an **optimal level of stimulation**, based on the Harry Helson's adaptation-level theory.[115,116] The idea is that for any given activity, one may be either over or under-stimulated, leading to a decrease in satisfaction. Each of us adapts to a certain level of stimulation, which might be relatively high or low in objective terms, depending on our circumstances. As the level of stimulation we experience in a given setting moves a little away from this adaptation level, our pleasure is hypothesized to increase. The change is stimulating, if you will pardon the choice of words. However, as the level of stimulation changes further in the same direction, it becomes too much or too little stimulation to enjoy, and pleasure declines. Thus, when a setting is too novel, complex, or fast-moving for our usual adaptation level, we find it overstimulating or stressful; our pleasure, and perhaps our performance, may suffer. The same outcome may occur when we find a setting understimulating—that is, too familiar, simple, slow-moving, or just plain boring.

The cognitive outcomes of low-level stimulation have been studied experimentally by Peter Suedfeld and others, using the **restricted environmental stimulation technique**, or REST. The results do not always agree with the adaptation-level theory prediction that large changes in stimulation have negative consequences. In one study, volunteers spent 24 hours in a dark and silent chamber.[117] Control group volunteers (imagine being among them!) were confined to a small room, but were allowed stimulation (a phone and any activity they chose except leaving the room). Earlier research had shown that drastic stimulus reduction can *improve* performance on simple cognitive tasks. Suedfeld and colleagues wanted to know the effects of REST on complex and difficult tasks, and they selected

tasks that varied in both complexity and difficulty. The restricted stimulation group performed worse than the control group on complex tasks, but not on difficult tasks. However, these results may depend on just what the task is. In another study, with a different kind of task, the performance of low-stimulation participants suffered with increases in both task complexity and task difficulty.[118]

These environmental cognition questions are important, and they deserve more research, but so far most research has focused on spatial cognition rather than on these forms of environmental cognition. We turn now to that topic.

KEVIN LYNCH introduced key *concepts in spatial cognition, including path, edge, node, district, and landmark.*

Spatial Cognition

YOU ARE NOT A COMPASS. A cardinal principle of spatial cognition is that, as in environmental perception, we do not process information about the environment the way machines do.[119] Our cognitive processing, from a mechanical point of view, is full of errors, and it varies from one person to the next. Yet, as a species, we are remarkably successful. These deviations (from objective reality and from one another), together with our success as a species, suggest that we must entertain two ideas: First, that spatial cognition must be determined in part by differences in our individual backgrounds, and second, that our imperfect images must nevertheless be quite useful to us.

Our cognitive maps help us solve spatial problems, such as how to infer the way from one place to another when we have never directly traversed that particular route, and where to find needed resources of all kinds, from the closest all-night grocery store to the best place to find truffles in the forest. They also simplify and facilitate communication. We absorb into these images the distinctive monuments, symbols, and arrangements of streets and we are able conjure them up in order to recognize and enjoy places we have known. In sum, we make mistakes, but most of us nevertheless still do quite well most of the time.

LEGIBILITY. Understanding of the peculiar ways that humans think about their environments may be used to design better settings. The central concept in this applied area is **legibility**, the ease with which a setting may be recognized and organized by people. The concept was established by Kevin Lynch in his classic book *The Image of the City*.[120] Some cities, for example, are much more legible than others. But what makes a city legible? Lynch suggested five elements of cities that contribute to legibility (you might find it useful to think of examples of each element where you live):

1. **PATHS.** The routes along which people travel. Typically, paths are roads, walkways, and public transit routes.

2. **EDGES.** Lines not primarily designed for travel, such as cliffs, or escarpments, or the shores of rivers, lakes, or oceans.

3. **DISTRICTS.** Moderate-sized areas that city residents identify as having a particular character.

4. **NODES.** Well-known points that people travel to and from, often at the junctures of important paths, such as key intersections, transit terminals, and popular plazas or squares.

5. **LANDMARKS.** Easily viewed elements, either on a grand scale (e.g., the tallest building in town) or on a smaller scale (e.g., a statue or unique storefront).

These five elements were suggested by Lynch speculatively, without much formal research. Their validity, however, has been confirmed by more experimental methods.[121,122] In these studies, the elements in maps drawn by everyday people were subjected to a sophisticated statistical technique called cluster analysis. Five distinct clusters of map elements emerged, and these were very similar to the elements Lynch hypothesized. Subsequent studies show that legible university campuses, for example, have distinct landmarks and clear networks of paths.[123] Lynch's list has been augmented by the interesting idea that places vary in **social legibility**, that is, that the *meaning* of environmental elements varies in different cultures, which results in the same place having different legibility for different people.[124]

The term **cognitive map** is so intuitively attractive that it is easy to oversimplify both its meaning and its role in our daily activities.[125,126] A cognitive map is not a folded piece of paper in the cranium; no miniature navigator sits inside our heads poring over intricacies of the map by the light of our ideas. In fact, some psychologists doubt that spatial knowledge is represented at all like a map in the head.[127] They feel that maps contain far too much information to be conjured up all at once. Instead, they believe we sequentially retrieve small parts of our information base when we draw maps or give directions. Nevertheless, we clearly possess huge stores of spatial information, both pictorial and verbal, about the paths, edges, nodes, districts, and landmarks of places we know.

Spatial cognition research is concerned with our memory for, orientation in, and knowledge about distances and locations in physical settings. The next sections describe how and why some features of the environment are remembered while others are forgotten, the processes involved in getting lost and getting found, and how we organize (and sometimes incorrectly organize) the physical features of our homes, cities, countries, and even the world as a whole.

IN SUM *We do not acquire, store, and recall information about locations, distances, and arrangements mechanically. Yet our ways of doing so usually are effective and non-random. The study of cognitive maps reveals some human strategies for processing environmental information. Legible places are easier to comprehend: they have clear paths and distinct edges, districts, nodes, and landmarks.*

Research Methods for Spatial Cognition

Spatial cognition must be studied indirectly; we cannot see what is going on in people's heads. The research goal is to extract an accurate representation of the individual's spatial knowledge. The most common way of approaching this problem has been to ask individuals to sketch a map, construct a scale model, or estimate distances between pairs of places. Other methods of studying spatial cognition are available.[128] For example, some researchers have actually tested children and adults in mazes.[129] Others have created virtual environments for their research participants to find their way around in.[130-134] Perhaps the least-used method, despite its great potential, is naturalistic observation of people in the midst of everyday wayfinding.[135,136] However, none of these methods yields the individual's actual spatial knowledge. For example, a **sketch map** is not a cognitive map; it is a representation of what is stored in the head and therefore is limited in its accuracy by such factors as the person's drawing ability, stage of development, memory, and problems with translating a place onto a piece of paper.

Evidence on the accuracy of these methods is mixed.[137] Sometimes the methods are **reliable** (yield similar results from one measurement to the next),[138] and sometimes they are not.[139] Their **validity** (the results truly represent an individual's cognitive map) is a challenge for most spatial cognition methods. For example, in a study of North American aboriginal people, paper-and-pencil measures of spatial cognition bore little relation to their ability to wayfind in the real environment,[140] although in another study, sketch maps did represent the actual movements of individuals around a setting,[141] and in two others, spatial decision-making was similar whether the experimenters used simulations or actual wayfinding.[142,143]

One way to establish whether a computer simulation method of studying spatial cognition is valid is to replicate studies that were previously conducted in actual settings to determine whether the same results are obtained, and this has been successful.[144] A different approach is to ask people to estimate the distances between numerous places, and to analyze the estimations using a sophisticated statistical procedure called **multidimensional scaling**.[145]

Nevertheless, some researchers believe that *any* translation from cognitive distance to physical distance will be extremely difficult.[146] Given the uncertainty of these measures, and the reality that wayfinding itself involves a number of different cognitive tasks and processes,[147] the best approach is to employ multiple measures of spatial cognition,[148,149] or at least to be certain the measure used is truly appropriate to the particular form of spatial cognition being studied.

IN SUM *Spatial cognition measurement techniques include sketch maps, model construction or manipulation, distance estimation, virtual environments, and naturalistic observation in mazes or everyday settings. Evidence for their usefulness is mixed. Once again, the best solution to the problem of imperfect methods is to employ multiple methods, so as to gain complementary perspectives on the truth, and to carefully select the most appropriate methods for the particular investigation being undertaken.[150]*

Influences on Spatial Cognition

What affects the speed of acquiring information about the environment, the accuracy of this information, the way individuals organize the information, and differences in ability to recall and use spatial information? The influences may be divided into two main categories: individual differences (e.g., spatial ability, visual impairment, age, gender, and familiarity with the setting), and influences in the physical environment (e.g., a grid arrangement versus a meandering "organic" arrangement).[151] The nature of the connections between influences and spatial cognition may not always be of the "A causes B" nature. Culture is a one example: spatial cognition may be a constitutive part of culture, rather than something "caused by" culture.[152]

PERSONAL. As noted earlier, even shared environments are not cognized in the same way by all their inhabitants. Individual differences must underlie this variability in spatial cognition.[153] The crucial questions are: *Which* individual differences affect our thinking about our everyday settings, and *how* do they affect it? Five of these factors will be discussed in some detail because they have received the most research attention: stage of life, spatial ability, familiarity with the place, gender, and cognitive biases.

However, spatial cognition is also related to many other factors that have received some, but not much attention, including the kind of directions given to the wayfinder,[154] personality,[155] intelligence,[156] self-efficacy,[157] culture,[158,159] education,[160] emotion,[161,162] and time pressure, risk, and interest.[163] Among the more surprising influences on spatial cognition are testosterone level,[164] the level of economic development of countries that one is asked to recall,[165] which direction one is facing when one thinks about place locations,[166] and a strong tendency when wayfinding to select routes heading south![167]

Naturally, features of the environment also affect spatial cognition. However, let's begin with developmental changes.

STAGE OF LIFE. As a toddler, you were not allowed out of the house alone. A few years later, your yard or the block was the limit. Then maybe you were given a bicycle or a skateboard, and the whole neighborhood was yours. As a teen, your horizon may have been the whole community. These expansions in a person's permissible range are accompanied by changes in general cognitive development.[168]

These changes may be described in terms of Jean Piaget's influential theory of cognitive development. Spatial cognition is viewed in this theory as one aspect of the child's more general cognitive unfolding. Early on, children are **egocentric**: they believe they are the center of the world. They perceive environments in terms of how close something in it is to them, whether they can touch it, and whether it is part of them or not. Infants must learn, for example, that those five small pink objects flying around near them are their own toes rather than a tasty five-headed being of independent means.

About at the time of entering school, children enter a stage that allows them to adopt perspectives from viewpoints other than their own; this is the **projective** stage. Children at this stage are able—theoretically—to orient themselves using prominent landmarks. For example, most are able to find their way home from school. Indeed, children aged about 7 use landmarks more than older children or adults do.[169]

Later, at around 11 years of age, most children are able to think in more **abstract** terms. The reflection of this change in spatial cognition is an ability to use abstract concepts such as Euclidean coordinates (grid systems such as latitude and longitude) or directions such as north, south, east, and west.[170] At age 12, children are fooled less often than at age 8 by altered landmarks.[171]

Research generally supports this Piagetan model of children's spatial cognition.[172] However, some believe that researchers who have limited their studies to the laboratory have underestimated the spatial-cognitive abilities of children.[173] For example, some children as young as 12 months old are able to use landmarks.[174] Relatively young children can use aerial maps effectively. Some 6-year-olds can make spatial judgments that appear to require perspective-taking or Euclidean abilities.[175] Children can draw a map of the route from home to school that contains

FIGURE 2–6 Children gradually learn to orient themselves in their homes, neighborhoods, and communities.

much more detail than they can report when asked to tell someone about the same route.[176] In familiar settings, even children as young as 3 have demonstrated that they can use Euclidean knowledge or maps,[177,178] an accomplishment that Piagetans would not expect for almost another decade of life!

The spatial cognitive abilities of children sometimes have been underestimated because their spatial abilities outstrip their verbal abilities. For example, they are able to use a map or to find their way home, but they are not yet able to explain very well how they accomplished the feat.[179] Attention must therefore be paid to the most appropriate method of assessing the spatial cognitive abilities of children (see Figure 2-6).

What about the other end of the developmental spectrum? Older people say they have more difficulty finding their way around unfamiliar places.[180] Most research indicates that spatial ability declines with advancing age,[181-185] although some studies report no decline in performance with age,[186-188] particularly when memory demands are less, such as when directions are given while the person is holding a map.[189] Because quite a bit of research has been conducted on this topic, we know a fair amount about it, and the reality is—as usual—somewhat complex. However, two likely general conclusions are that (1) with advancing age, some spatial abilities decline, others do not, and some may even improve, and (2) older individuals think about space *differently* than younger individuals. For example, elderly individuals may perform better in settings that are familiar and meaningful to them,[190] although even this does not always hold.[191] Older people learn *new* spatial information more slowly than younger people;[192] they may have greater difficulty in learning new routes, finding new routes, and remembering the layout of places.[193] Another problem is that elderly people may *believe* their performance is better when it is actually declining,[194] although they also sometimes report wayfinding to be more difficult than younger people do![195]

These age changes may be caused by both behavioral and physiological changes, such as reduced mobility and sensory ability. For example, no age-related performance decline was found for a task that required no movement through a real setting—that is, participants were asked to recall the spatial location of typed words on cards.[196] In contrast, another study found that after older and younger travelers drove a 211-mile/340-kilometer route along the coast in Australia, the older travelers more frequently mislabeled landmarks.[197] However, older people in this study remembered *more* districts and reported *more* details than did younger travelers. Apparently, older people rely more for their memory of the environment on features that are (1) more meaningful to them, such as buildings that are used more often or more easily, (2) are historical,[198,199] (3) are unique in architectural style,[200] or (4) include landscape elements that make them feel good.[201] Researchers are now investigating which teaching methods will best help older people to learn new environments.[202]

SPATIAL ABILITY. You might think it is obvious that individuals with greater spatial ability perform better on spatial cognition tasks such as wayfinding, and they do,[203,204] but even this is not that simple. Standard psychological tests that measure one's ability to mentally rotate objects or find objects embedded in a complex background do predict how well people learn or remember new settings, but only modestly.[205-207] This is probably because other factors come into play, such as the ability of older children to use abilities that younger children do not yet possess.[208]

Thus, natural talent in spatial cognition does not neatly translate into better real-world spatial-cognitive performance. However, this does not mean spatial ability has no impact on one's life. For example, being able to learn and remember the location and orientation of objects in space without any contextual or background information is a better predictor of whether older adults will use the goods and services in their neighborhoods than how long they have lived in the neighborhood or how mobile they are.[209]

EXPERIENCE. Clearly, as we spend more time in a place our spatial cognitions about it will change. The most obvious change is that our knowledge about it will grow, which means we are usually able to find our way around in it better.[210-212] Sketch maps of the campus made six months apart by new students at a university, for example, showed significant increases not only in the amount of information on the maps, but also in the differentiation and the integration of that information.[213] Students with at least one year's experience at another campus depicted their university with greater configurational accuracy than students with less experience.[214] Wayfinding is more difficult in more complex settings, but experience helps.[215] Experienced taxi drivers perform better than inexperienced drivers; they also know how to use different strategies in different parts of the city.[216] Experience in one place helps in new places:

taxi drivers from one city learned the routes around a new town better than a control group did.[217]

Several other experience-related factors are also related to spatial cognition. For example, drivers may acquire different and perhaps better *organized* environmental information than their passengers even though they do not necessarily acquire *more* information.[218,219] Children who walk to school have better cognitive maps than children who are driven to school.[220] Social class, urban versus rural residence, and husbands versus wives vary in the form and content of spatial knowledge.[221,222] These factors probably indicate that individuals move through cities differently depending on social factors (for example, wealthy urban husbands probably move about more than poor rural wives).[223]

However, more experience in a place does not necessarily mean that people have a more *accurate* mental map of it. In a study of distance judgments in a very large building, the more experienced people were, the more *incorrect* their maps were.[224] The researchers suggest that as we become more familiar with a setting, we change our image of it in ways that help us wayfind better. However, this may require that we develop an inaccurate image of it, in cartographic terms.

When we are aware that it is important to learn the spatial layout of a place, we can do so very quickly,[225] more quickly than when we are not instructed to pay attention to the environment.[226] If we learn only the parts of a building that we need, our knowledge of the whole building may be weak. People who knew nothing about a certain building were asked to memorize floor plans of it. They were then able to find their way around the building significantly better than people who had worked in the building for two years.[227]

Gender. Many studies report differences between males and females in the acquisition, accuracy, organization, and use of spatial information. When there is a difference, it is likely to favor males,[228-234] and women more often say they have difficulty or uncertainty when wayfinding in new settings.[235-238] However, these differences do not always hold. For example, in one study, men were more accurate than women only in locating those places that were difficult to locate.[239] In a Swedish study, men and women either walked or were driven through an unfamiliar residential neighborhood.[240] When they were driven, men learned about the setting slightly faster than women, but when they walked through the setting, men and women learned equally quickly. This suggests that the male advantage is caused by more extensive driving experience. However, other evidence suggests that the difference is present before the driving age.[241] For example, some theorists believe that the difference is based on longstanding evolutionary trends for males to roam further afield than females.[242]

Despite this plausible hypothesis, other evidence suggests that the sexes are *not* different in ability, although men may make spatial decisions faster[243] or express their judgments with more confidence.[244,245] Women may have more anxiety about spatial cognition, as opposed to less actual ability.[246] This suggests again that the gender differences may reflect the different experiences that males and females are likely to have, rather than basic differences in cognitive abilities or tendencies.[247,248] Some direct evidence for this has been reported.[249] For example, boys have more experience because they are typically allowed to roam further than girls; they have larger **home ranges** than girls.[250,251]

Apart from differences in ability, men and women seem to have different ways of thinking about the environment.[252] Men's sketch maps often include more territory[253] and are more gridlike; women's maps tend to be more home-centered.[254] When asked to give directions, men give more distance estimates ("it's about 6 kilometers") and cardinal directions ("west of here") than women.[255] Women seem to base their spatial cognition more on landmarks[256-258] or their experience traveling along paths, whereas men may rely more on map-like mental representations of the city,[259] a pattern that also holds inside buildings.[260]

SPATIAL–COGNITIVE BIASES. Cognitive maps do not match cartographic maps for a variety of reasons, as we have already seen. Beyond these, however, we may err in three predictable ways, which we may call the Euclidean, superordinate-scale, and segmentation biases.

In the **Euclidean bias**, we think of the world as more Euclidean or gridlike than it actually is. On sketch maps, many individuals draw streets that actually converge as if they were parallel, intersections that do not form right angles as if they did, and streets with gentle curves as straight lines.[261-263] When asked to point toward targets that are not visible, people make more mistakes if they are at an intersection that is not a right angle.[264] This makes cities with grid-like street patterns more legible and easier

to navigate than cities with curving, radial, or nonparallel streets.

To illustrate the **superordinate-scale bias**, answer the following three questions for yourself: Which is farther north, Toronto or Minneapolis? Which is farther west, Athens or Warsaw? Which is farther east, Reno or San Diego? In thinking about locations that we are not sure about, we tend to rely on superordinate groupings—that is, larger categories of which the place in question is a member.[265] Toronto is in Canada; Canada is north of the United States; Minneapolis is in the United States; therefore, Toronto must be north of Minneapolis. Athens is in Greece, which has been part of the Western geopolitical alliance, and Warsaw, in Poland, was part of the Eastern bloc for a long time: therefore, Athens must be west of Warsaw. Reno, a city in Nevada, which is a state east of California, where San Diego is located, must be east of San Diego. Each of these lines of reasoning is, of course, incorrect. Using larger categories to reason about the location of places within them sometimes leads to errors in spatial cognition. On the other hand, using the superordinate scale very often results in the correct conclusion; this is why we use it.

The **segmentation bias** pertains to distance judgments. Mentally breaking a route into separate segments seems to alter our distance estimates.[266] Estimates over the whole route, or from segment to segment, increase with objective distance (as they should), but distance estimates *within* segments do not increase with objective distance. Apparently, we do not make reliable distance differentiations for places that are within the same segment of the route.

PHYSICAL INFLUENCES. Which features of the environment affect environmental cognition? Long ago, Kevin Lynch hypothesized that regular, clear paths and highly visible landmarks would improve residents' spatial cognition of cities.[267] Research supports this contention,[268,269] and extended it. For example, distance judgments are more accurate in cities with more regular traffic patterns.[270] In addition, the presence of strongly organizing features in cities, such as rivers, roads, and railroads, improve spatial cognition. Including landmarks when guiding people around a city improves their wayfinding performance.[271]

One might also expect that highly salient (prominent, conspicuous) features of a cityscape would further enhance one's processing of information about it. A study

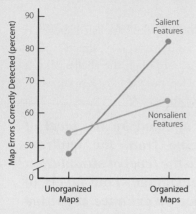

FIGURE 2–7 Accurate map reading depends on how well the map is organized and how salient, visible, or obvious features of the place are rendered on the map.

tested this idea by comparing the speed of processing and the number of errors in the reading of maps that varied both in their degree of organization and in the degree of salience of certain features.[272] As Lynch would have predicted, greater organization improved speed and reduced errors. However, salience *without* organization significantly *harmed* spatial cognition (see Figure 2-7). Apparently, salient features can enhance the spatial cognition of settings that are clearly organized, but can confuse us when their salience is not accompanied by clear organization.

Apart from wayfinding, what might make buildings cognitively stand out or be remembered better? Donald Appleyard pioneered this line of research in Ciudad Guyana, a Venezuelan city that was planned from the ground up. He assessed a variety of relatively objective characteristics of buildings in Ciudad Guyana and compared them with the frequency they were recalled by residents.[273] The better-recalled buildings were tall, freestanding, distinctive in shape, easily visible, frequently used, and had much human movement around them. Each of these characteristics also enhanced resident recall of buildings in Orange, California.[274] However, a few characteristics were found to enhance recall only in Ciudad Guyana (such as the singularity of the building's use) or only in Orange (such as building quality). This suggests, pending further research, that certain building characteristics make a stronger impact on individuals regardless of culture, but others make an impact in one culture but not others.

Features of a city that break up the transportation system may interfere with cognitive mapping, too. Fargo, North Dakota, has a large railroad switching yard in its center. When an overpass that linked the two sides of the switching yard was built, women's estimates of distances between places that had been separated by the switching yard became more accurate.[275] This presumably occurred because women tend to rely on travel experience for distance estimates; when they had to travel further around

the switching yards, even the "as-the-crow-flies" distance seemed greater. When the overpass was built, their new travel experience better informed about the straight-line distance.

One controversy about spatial cognition concerns which features of a new environment are learned first. Some hypothesize that we learn landmarks first, before elaborating paths.[276,277] Others have reached the conclusion that paths and districts are learned first, and then we use landmarks for orientation.[278,279] Evidence supports both positions.[280,281] After a careful review, Gary Evans concluded that both may be true, depending on the physical character of the setting in question.[282] For example, in one study that supported the idea that paths are learned before landmarks, the authors noted that participants were virtually forced to learn the paths first because the distance between landmarks was so great. In other places, where many salient landmarks are available, they may be learned first.

So far we have focused on some features of cities that affect urban spatial cognition. Which features of building interiors influence spatial cognition or wayfinding in them? In general, four factors play a role in this:

GARY EVANS is a major researcher in the areas of environmental cognition and stress.

TOMMY GARLING is a leading Swedish environmental psychologist who has extensively studied environmental perception and cognition, as well as transportation and pro-environmental behavior.

- Signs and numbering systems
- Visibility of the destination and views to outdoors
- Differentiation (the distinctiveness of different parts of the building)
- Configuration (the overall layout of the building)[283]

Thus, in general, one would expect wayfinding to be easier in buildings with clear signs and numbering systems, good visibility, greater differentiation, and simpler configuration.[284] Some research supports this. Wayfinding is easier in buildings that have simpler floor plans.[285] Signs significantly increase the rate of travel through complex buildings and reduce the number of wrong turns and backtracking.[286] However, signs do not fully overcome building complexity; finding one's way around buildings simpler floor plans is easier.

When individuals are learning the layout of a building on their own, they consistently move toward the parts of the building that allow the best surveillance of the building as a whole.[287] Presumably, buildings that have no place from which the rest of the building can be scanned are more difficult to comprehend. Full understanding of a building's layout requires the development of an overall cognitive map; wayfinding that must rely merely on moving from sign to sign or landmark to landmark is limited. In fact, when parts of the building are visually misaligned, wayfinding problems result.[288]

SPACE SYNTAX is a method of analyzing buildings and other places in terms of how the space's physical features affect movement through the space.[289,290] It was devised as an objective way of describing buildings and places, but research shows that sketch maps, which represent the subjective or cognitive view of a place, strongly mirror space syntax analyses of places.[291] In getting to know a new place, we seem to use immediate features that are within our field of view, but later, once we know the place better, our wayfinding attempts are better understood in terms of the space syntax features of the place.[292]

For many reasons, buildings cannot always be constructed for optimal wayfinding. What can be done when a building already exists and is like a maze? We might improve the signage and numbering, but its architectural aspects (i.e., visibility, differentiation, and configuration) are not easy to change. One way to deal with the situation is to teach people how to wayfind in complex buildings. Some have proposed that the fastest way to enhance the spatial cognition of a building is to show people sequences of slides or photos and building models.[293] The models should be simplified—showing the main elements of the building, but not any distracting elements that would not help with wayfinding.

In contrast, sometimes people actually *want* wayfinding to be awful, and are even willing to pay to get lost. In Japan and England, life-scale mazes have become a national pastime.[294] The British Tourist Authority once declared a "Year of the Maze," and in Japan, at least 100 commercial mazes have been constructed. Mazes have been created for enjoyment since ancient Crete. A good maze is one that deliberately violates all four of the principles listed above (a) no signs or numbers, (b) no visibility, (c) no distinctive parts, and (d) very high complexity. Although the challenge of a maze may be fun once or twice, no one likes a maze when rushing to an appointment or to a class.

IN SUM *Cognition is affected by the level of stimulation we receive from the environment in comparison to the level of stimulation to which we are accustomed. Low levels of stimulation can reduce or enhance cognitive abilities. Spatial cognition—the complex way we acquire, process, store, and recall information about everyday settings—is affected by one's stage of life, familiarity or experience with the setting, spatial and perceptual ability, gender, cognitive biases, and features of the city or building. The spatial cognition of children generally follows a sequence moving from egocentric to projective to abstract, although they may move through these stages faster than laboratory studies suggest. The spatial cognition of older people differs from that of younger adults: where their experience is limited by reduced mobility or sensory abilities, they may perform less well. Their memories of the environment are more personalized and are, in some respects, better than those of young adults. Gender differences in spatial cognition exist, but may largely reflect the different travel experiences of men and women. Experience in a setting gives one a fuller and better organized cognitive image of it. Three common cognitive biases are to envision places as more gridlike than they actually are, to wrongly employ larger geographical entities in placing smaller ones, and to be affected by the number of segments or barriers along a path. Spatial cognition is also affected by characteristics of the place about which one is cognizing. For example, spatial cognition of urban forms is improved by clear paths and visible landmarks. Where one of these elements is more common or salient than the other, examples of it will be learned* *first. Some evidence suggests that visibility without organization may detract from effective spatial cognition. At the architectural level, buildings that are tall, free-standing, distinctively shaped, and used often are better recalled than others.*

Theories of Spatial Cognition

How can all this knowledge about how we comprehend everyday settings be integrated? Clearly, information flows from the physical environment to a cognitive apparatus that must ultimately be represented in the brain. Appropriately, the theoretical approaches to the puzzle of spatial cognition to be discussed next complement one another by originating with physical, cognitive, and physiological structures. Even better, although we have a long way to go, some preliminary signposts indicate the direction toward unification of these approaches.

LEGIBILITY: A PHYSICAL PERSPECTIVE. The seminal work of Kevin Lynch[295,296] and Donald Appleyard[297] have been influential in urban planning and environmental psychology. The concept of legibility and its relation to paths, landmarks, edges, nodes, and districts have provided the basic infrastructure for hundreds of studies. The role of information processing in the head is not ignored in this approach (as we shall see later in this section), but it does begin with, and emphasize, the physical arrangement of space.

The principal elements of this physical perspective have already been described. The thrust of the theory is to predict that more legible places are easier to comprehend and use. Lynch's ideas have been studied and applied at scales ranging from buildings to entire cities (see Figure 2-8). For example, to create more legible cities, the theory suggests that urban planners should gradually shape their communities in five ways as the city grows and redevelops:[298]

1. Place landmarks at major decision points in the road system.

2. Keep these landmarks distinctive by maximizing their visibility; this can be accomplished by making them tall, separate from neighboring buildings, unique in architectural style, and into enclosures for activities that result in much public use of the building.

FIGURE 2-8 The Empress Hotel, one of the most legible buildings in Victoria, British Columbia.

3. Primary roads should coincide with the functional boundaries of districts to reinforce edges.

4. Preserve buildings that might serve as good landmarks when a district undergoes extensive redevelopment.

5. Construct landmarks in overly homogeneous districts.

Lynch's ideas also have been applied to you-are-here maps, color-coded buildings, and transit map designs. The latter will be described here; you-are-here maps and color-coding will be described later. Legibility principles have been used to design bus and subway maps that improve comprehension of transit routes. The best of these maps do not represent transit routes cartographically, but in a simplified schematic manner that matches transit riders' experience as they move from point to point in a journey.[299] Maps that use color-coding to enhance legibility of routes give transit riders greater accuracy and confidence, but those that try too hard to be helpful by providing off-route street details result in less accuracy and more frustration.[300]

Maps have not completely solved the problem of environmental orientation. Even experienced subway riders, when asked to take a trip from A to B, chose non-optimal routes more than half the time.[301] The riders had difficulty with subway maps and signs; they often responded by selecting a *familiar* route rather than the *optimal* route to reach their destinations.

In a hospital outpatient department, researchers gave some women hand-held maps to use in locating numerous destinations in the building and other women no map.[302] Those who used the hand-held maps actually took longer to locate the destinations, but they did retrace their steps less often, and they *believed* the map was useful in planning their trip.

INTELLECTUAL GROWTH AND PLANNING: TWO COGNITIVE PERSPECTIVES. The intellectual growth and planning approach emphasizes the role of cognition more than the role of the physical environment. However, the two approaches now are converging. The intellectual growth perspective examines the way individuals develop the capacity to comprehend space. It is concerned with the ways children develop the ability to use spatial information, such as in wayfinding, giving directions, and remembering where places are. Mainly derived from Piagetian theory, it includes the egocentric, place-oriented, and abstract coordinates stages that children are presumed to follow.

Gary Moore offered an extension of these ideas that serves to increase the role of the environment within this approach.[303] He proposed that in each stage children not only know different things about the environment, but they *organize* that knowledge differently. Moore also has suggested that there are conceptual parallels between the childhood progression from stage to stage and the short-term progression that adults move through as they learn a new setting. As a **transactional-constructivist**, Moore asserts that spatial cognition cannot be understood until the transactions that occur between individuals and their settings are understood.[304] He also believes we actively construct the world from data we have gleaned about it (as opposed to those who believe the world reveals itself to us as it is or, as James Gibson asserted, as already constructed.

One relatively simple demonstration of constructivism in children is provided by studies in which children start at a certain home base (*X*) and are taught how to get from *X* to three other places, *A*, *B*, and *C*.[305] The children are not taught how to get from *A* to *B*, from *B* to *C*, or from *A* to *C*, yet they are able to explain the spatial relations between these places. Because the children had no direct experience with them, they must have constructed these spatial relations.

Other researchers have begun to develop formal models that simulate the process by which we make our way through, for example, a new neighborhood.[306] Computer programs have been developed to model the way people gradually learn the spatial features of places.[307] Most such models assume that we create regionalized, hierarchical mental maps.[308] **Regionalization** means that we tend to create groups of locations (e.g., rooms within a large building, buildings within a large city, towns within a geographic region). **Hierarchical organization** means that we create categories within categories, such as cities within countries. Each region may be identified with one or more landmarks, and some theories of spatial cognition focus on the ways that we use landmarks to organize space.[309] Because there is some dispute about the precise definition of a landmark,[310] it may be more accurate to say that regions tend to have cognitive **anchor points**.[311] In everyday spatial behavior, these regionalized and hierarchical mental maps are used whenever we need to plan how to get from *A* to *B*.

Another theory asserts that we base our wayfinding either on visually recognizing key elements of the environment ("Turn right at the library"), or by mentally representing the environment as a map ("Head south for 10 blocks, then turn east").[312] Of course, not all our wayfinding requires conscious planning; many trips are so familiar we traverse them with no planning.[313]

THE THEORY IN PRACTICE. What does all this mean in practice? Many important consequences for spatial cognition of both children and adults are implied by all this research. For example, residents' regionalizations of their neighborhoods do not necessarily correspond to the way that neighborhoods are organized in the political system.[314] If the boundaries drawn by lawmakers for voting districts are quite different from the residents' own images of the neighborhood's boundaries, confusion and conflict may ensue.

Another practical application concerns getting lost (or found). In the case of a lost 3-year-old boy, researchers showed, by reconstructing the paths he took, that his wanderings were not random.[315] Depending on age, experience and the setting, the likely paths taken by lost persons may be predicted with some accuracy. The standard procedures used by rescue officials sometimes involve search strategies, such as following a strict grid pattern, that do not take these most-likely paths into account. Knowledge of a child's developmental stage and the terrain may lead to more efficient search strategies. For example, lost children under age 6 are more often found in open spaces, but lost children in the 6- to 12-year-old range often seek enclosures or refuges when they get lost. Spatial cognition principles have been used to help people with severe mental illnesses to find their way around their communities.[316]

The hierarchical manner in which we organize spatial knowledge means that we construct maps at different levels (like the different magnifications on a microscope), and we are able (under the appropriate conditions) to use whichever "magnification" best suits our needs. For example, if we give people a task in which they are to minimize the total distance they travel to do a series of errands, they are able to recognize and select segments of their trip that are not the shortest they might have chosen in order to accomplish the overall goal of the traveling the shortest *total* distance.[317]

Personal constructions of spatial relations mean that we do not always act according to cartographic reality. For example, cognitive distances are strongly related to where consumers decide to shop—more related than to other factors such as objective distance to the store, socioeconomic factors, or demographic information about the shopper.[318] We shop according to how we *think* the world is organized more than according to how it is actually organized.

Our construction of space also seems to involve some oddly inefficient strategies. **Road climbing** is the tendency to select long, straight routes from our starting point—even when that route is 50 percent longer than other possible routes.[319] However, usually people do employ useful strategies, such as map imagery (remembering a map they have seen, or mentally constructing one for the purpose at hand), or imagining traveling along the route.[320]

The second—but very much related—cognitive perspective involves the role of **plans and goals** in spatial cognition.[321-323] This perspective is concerned with the use of spatial knowledge to plan a series of errands or other spatial tasks to be done in a certain order. The world we cognitively construct depends on the goals and plans we carry with us as we move through the world. For example, individuals who enter a room with the intention to hide something in it or to redecorate it end up with quite different mental maps of the room than individuals who enter it merely to wait.[324]

Like the transactional-constructivists, these theorists assert that we are active agents in our transactions with settings. We develop **action plans** to guide our behavior. Travel plans, which are one kind of action plan, partly determine what sort of spatial information is acquired, how it is organized, and what inferences (or constructions) about settings are drawn by a person (see Figure 2-9). The development of spatial knowledge (and here is one connection to the intellectual growth perspective) is influenced by the nature of the activity we are engaged in.[325]

Much spatial activity is guided by meaningful plans and goals. In laboratory studies, the researcher's goals often replace any goals the study participants might have had. Therefore, to learn more about the role of goals and planning in spatial cognition, we should study people in their own habitats. For example, even short local trips of 20 minutes require as many as 50 wayfinding decisions: Travel planning and execution are considerable cognitive tasks.[326] When individuals have (or are given) specific goals, plans, or tasks that involve spatial relations (such as going to the store for your parents when you were a child or hunting for mushrooms in the woods), their spatial development may proceed more quickly than laboratory-based studies might predict. Wayfinders who have developed expectancies about upcoming path choices are more likely to know when they are on the correct route.[327]

Both criminals and their victims have cognitive maps, like everyone else. Law enforcement is enhanced when it uses cognitive mapping techniques. For example, they can be used to identify "fear zones" in cities and the cognitive maps of criminals.[328] Cognitive maps of crime do not necessarily match official crime statistics. For example, suburbanites may incorrectly locate high levels of crime in the downtown area of cities.[329] On the other side of the law, researchers have helped to construct cognitive map profiles of suspects based on their apparent plans and the actual patterns of crime sites. Serial rapists, for example,

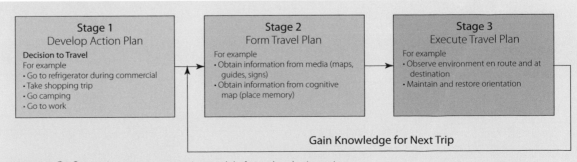

FIGURE 2–9 An information–processing model of travel and orientation.

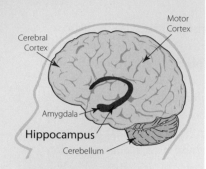

FIGURE 2–10 The hippocampus is the neurological site where much of our spatial cognition occurs.

exhibit non-random spatial patterns in their crimes, making it easier to predict where they are most likely to strike next.[330]

THE HIPPOCAMPUS: A PHYSIOLOGICAL PERSPECTIVE. Too rarely have connections between environmental psychology and the neurosciences been made, although presumably all behavior (including environmentally relevant behavior) is represented one way or another in brain physiology. The most ambitious attempt to link spatial cognition and the brain has been that of John O'Keefe and Lynn Nadel. Working originally from studies on rats, they proposed that the hippocampus, a seahorse-shaped part of the limbic system in the central core of the brain, is the home of the cognitive map[331,332] (see Figure 2-10).

The idea that animal behavior is guided by cognitive maps was introduced to psychology long ago, but not in such specific physiological detail.[333,334] O'Keefe and Nadel's basic idea is that (1) some neurons in the hippocampus are specifically coded for place; (2) networks of such neurons form a framework that represents, in a three-dimensional Euclidean framework, the settings known to the individual; and (3) in humans, the portion of the hippocampus in the left hemisphere houses a semantic or word-based map and the portion in the right hemisphere houses a spatial or pictorial map. O'Keefe and Nadel's theory also postulates the existence of two systems of spatial cognition: the taxon system and the locale system. The **taxon system** guides the routes one takes, using guidance hypotheses and orientation hypotheses. *Guidance hypotheses* specify objects or cues in the setting that should be approached or kept at a certain distance. *Orientation hypotheses* specify how this is to be accomplished behaviorally, such as "Turn right 90 degrees." The **locale system**, as its name suggests, refers to places. *Place hypotheses* are constructions by the brain that organize space knowledge important to the individual. Typical place hypotheses might be: "This is a dangerous place" or "That place usually supplies water

O'Keefe and Nadel originally worked with freely moving rats whose brains were monitored as they explore their settings. However, they have gathered evidence from human neuropsychology that appears to support their ideas. The potential applications of their theory to humans are interesting. They speculate, for example, that language developed primarily as a way for humans to express our place knowledge to others. In humans, *place learning* (learning the names of places) appears to promote the learning of other types of spatial information, such as the sequence or arrangement of landmarks, better than *orientation learning* (learning where to turn left or right).[335] Researchers see connections between the hippocampal model of the cognitive map and the problems experienced by victims of Alzheimer's disease, which affects the hippocampus as well as other regions of the brain, who have difficulty using maps (among their other problems).[336]

The hippocampus is not the only brain location related to cognitive mapping. For example, individuals with damage to the parietal region of the cortex lose the ability to draw maps of familiar places and seem to lose their knowledge of how places they know are arranged in geographic space.[337] Apparently, different parts of the brain are associated with different kinds of spatial cognition.[338] One summary of the research concludes there are five categories of spatial cognition and these are represented in various parts of the brain.[339] This idea is presented in Table 2-1.

One notable theoretical problem should be mentioned. The issue is whether spatial knowledge in humans is stored as **propositions** or as **analogies**. Simply put, the propositional approach hypothesizes that our knowledge of everyday space is stored in the brain as words. The analogical approach hypothesizes that the knowledge is stored as pictorial images. The propositional approach assumes that information is stored in

TABLE 2–1 Locations of Various Spatial-Cognition Functions in the Brain

Spatial Cognition Type	Sample Function	Brain Region
Spatial perception	Object localization	Occipital and parietal lobes
Spatial memory	Short-term memory for space	Hippocampus, thalamus
Spatial attention	Attention to space	Parietal lobe
Spatial operations	Mental rotation	Right parietal lobe
Spatial construction	Assembling parts into a whole	Parietal lobe

abstract networks of meaning, or schemata.[340] The analogical approach assumes it is stored as a model or image of the real world.[341] As often happens in psychology, the resolution of the issue may be that both forms of information storage occur.[342]

A final brain-based theory of spatial cognition is the **world graph**, a representation of relations among situations encountered by the individual.[343] Each situation is said to be encoded in a neural node, but each place may be encoded in several neural nodes. The world graph model appears to explain certain classic findings in animal exploration research and, if extended to humans, would presumably assist in the understanding of cognitive maps.

IN SUM *Five theories of spatial cognition concentrate on the physical environment, cognitive, or its physiological aspects. The legibility approach focuses on how settings, from buildings to cities, should be arranged to promote easy comprehension of them by individuals who need to find their way. Two cognitive theories, the intellectual growth and planning approaches, focus on the ways that children learn to comprehend the settings around them as their cognitive abilities increase and the ways in which our travel plans affect both typical and optimal wayfinding. Two physiological theories, the hippocampal and world graph approaches, examine the basis of wayfinding in the brain. The five theories complement one another because a full understanding of spatial cognition will require knowledge of the physical environment, how we think about those spaces, and the neural basis of it all.*

Spatial Cognition and Design

YOU-ARE-HERE MAPS. How can environmental cognition principles be made useful? One important application is

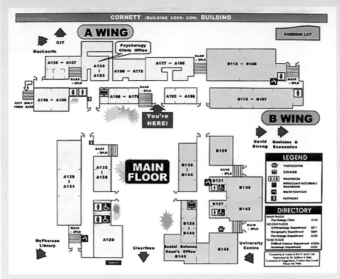

FIGURE 2–11 Based on the text, which you-are-here map is better?

you-are-here maps. Many places, such as large buildings, campuses, and shopping centers, are difficult for people to find their way in or around. Some of them place maps on pedestals or walls near the entrance, showing the layout of the building, complete with a little arrow saying, "You are here." These maps are an attempt to make the building more legible. (In a way, they are admissions that the building is insufficiently legible on its own!) You-are-here maps vary in quality; some succeed in improving the building's legibility; others may be worse with the map than without it (see Figure 2-11). Certain general principles should be followed to make you-are-here maps effective.[344]

Structure-matching means the map should usefully reflect the layout and appearance of the setting it represents. In particular, structure-matching is improved when:

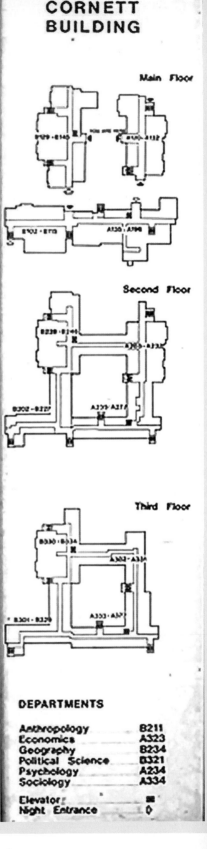

- The map uses labels that resemble actual labels (such as company logos) in the setting.

- The map is placed asymmetrically along the path in which it is placed, so that its viewers can easily see the relative location of the map within the setting.

- The you-are-here symbol on the map points to a little image of the map itself.

- The symbol consists of an arrow pointing to exactly where the viewer is in relation to the map.

Orientation is improved when:

- The map is aligned the same as the setting (e.g., east is east and west is west).

- The map has *forward-up equivalence* (the top of the map represents straight ahead in the actual setting).

In laboratory and field tests, these principles have been shown to significantly improve wayfinding in buildings.[345-347] However, even good you-are-here maps require more cognitive effort than good signs on walls; wayfinders who used signs found their destinations faster than those who used you-are-here maps.[348] Thus, good signs may be better than good you-are-here maps.

Improving Wayfinding with Color-Coding. Buildings may also be made more legible through the use of color-coded paths and carefully researched numbering systems. Painting the floors of a campus building different colors reduced wayfinding errors and improved comprehension of the building by undergraduates.[349] In a hospital, researchers showed that a minor detail such as how the floors below ground are numbered can seriously affect how many patients and visitors get lost on their way to an appointment.[350]

Design to Help People with Alzheimer's Disease. People afflicted with advanced Alzheimer's disease experience problems in wayfinding. Based on interviews and observations, researchers devised a set of design criteria that make spatial navigation for them less difficult.[351] Buildings should vary in form (sameness confuses), minimize building height (elevators cause major anxiety), avoid patterns, dark lines, and dark surfaces in floor coverings (these cause anxiety and disorientation), and use many signs (with large letters).

SUMMARY

In environmental psychology, perception research emphasizes understanding how individuals respond to complex everyday scenes, rather than simplified stimulus presentations. Sometimes scenes must be simulated, as when the goal is to understand reactions to a building that has not yet been built. A person's level of awareness, degree of adaptation, and selectivity in attending to cues, given the massive complexity of real scenes, have major effects on what is perceived. Sometimes this means that we miss important elements of a scene, with negative consequences for health or safety. Environmental perception is not the same for everyone: various personal and cultural differences are associated with seeing the same scene differently. Brunswik's probabilistic functionalism, Gibson's theory of affordances, Berlyne's collative properties, and the phenomenologist's first-person approach all represent valuable ways to understand how we "read" the world.

Environmental cognition other than the comprehension of space focuses on the effect that different levels of stimulation have on how well we think and perform everyday tasks. Spatial cognition has mainly been studied as a form of information processing that strongly differs from the way a machine would process information or how maps depict it, including several known biases that cause errors, but nevertheless it is generally effective. The elements of cognitive maps are studied using sketch maps, model manipulations, distance estimation, and natural observation. Cognitive maps develop along with other cognitive processes in a Piagetian manner, but experience with the environment can speed or slow this development. Legible cities and buildings are easier to comprehend.

Theories of spatial cognition begin from different points of departure: the setting itself, cognitive development, and brain physiology. These theories ultimately may be integrated into a complete model of spatial cognition that considers the same phenomenon at different levels of analysis.

Suggested Supplementary Readings

Carpman, J. R., & Grant, M. A. (2002). Wayfinding: A broad view. In R. B. Bechtel, & A. Churchman (Eds.), *Handbook of environmental psychology* (pp. 427-442). Hoboken, NJ: Wiley.

Devlin, A. (2012). Environmental perception: Wayfinding and spatial cognition. In S. Clayton (Ed.). *The Oxford handbook of environmental and conservation psychology* (pp. 41-64). New York: Oxford

Downs, R. M., & Stea, D. (1977). *Maps in minds: Reflections on cognitive mapping.* San Francisco: Harper & Row.

Garling, T., & Evans, G. W. (1991). *Environment, cognition, and action: An integrative multidisciplinary approach.* New York: Oxford.

Golledge, R. G. (1987). Environmental cognition. In I. Altman, & D. Stokols, (Eds.), *Handbook of environmental psychology.* New York: Wiley.

Kitchin, R. M. (1994). Cognitive maps: What they are and why study them? *Journal of Environmental Psychology, 14,* 1-19.

Lynch, K. (1960). *The image of the city.* Cambridge, MA: MIT Press.

References

1 Ross, H. E. (1974). *Behavior and perception in strange environments.* London: George Allen and Unwin.

2 Ittelson, W. H. (1978). Environmental perception and urban experience. *Environment and Behavior, 10,* 193-213.

3 Gifford, R., & Ng, C. F. (1982). The relative contribution of visual and auditory cues to environmental perception. *Journal of Environmental Psychology, 2,* 275-284.

4 Ittelson, W. H. (1970). Perception of the large-scale environment. *Transactions of the New York Academy of Sciences, 32,* 807-815.

5 Ittelson, W. H. (1973)(Ed.)., *Environment and cognition.* New York: Seminar Press.

6 Ittelson, W. H. (1978). Environmental perception and urban experience. *Environment and Behavior, 10,* 193-213.

7 Sommer, R. (1972). *Design awareness.* New York: Holt, Rinehart and Winston.

8 Gifford, R. (1976). Environmental numbness in the classroom. *Journal of Experimental Education, 44*(3), 47.

9 Huestegge, L., Skottke, M., Andres, S., Muesseler, J., & Debus, G. (2010). The development of hazard perception: Dissociation of visual orientation and hazard processing. *Transportation research. Part E, Logistics and transportation review, 13,* 1-8.

10 Leff, H. (1978). *Experience, environment, and human potential.* New York: Oxford University Press.

11 Gifford, R. (1980). Judgments of the built environment as functions of individual differences and context. *Journal of Man-Environment Relations, 1,* 22-31.

12 Marans, R. W., & Stokols, D. (1993). *Environmental simulation: Research and policy issues.* New York: Plenum.

13 Hetherington, J., Daniel, T. C., & Brown, T. C. (1993). Is motion more important than it sounds? The medium of presentation in environment perception research. *Journal of Environmental Psychology, 13,* 283-291.

14 Appleyard, D., & Craik, K. H. (1978). The Berkeley environmental laboratory and its research program. *International Review of Applied Psychology, 27,* 53-55.

15 McKechnie, G. E. (1977). Simulation techniques in environmental psychology. In D. Stokols (Ed.), *Perspectives on environment and behavior: Conceptual and empirical trends.* New York: Plenum Press.

16 Coeterier, J. F. (1983). A photo validity test. *Journal of Environmental Psychology, 3,* 315323.

17 Sirikasem, P., & Shebilske, W. L. (1991). The perception and metaperception of architectural designs communicated by video-computer imaging. *Psychological Research/Psychologische Forschung, 53,* 113-126.

18 Wood, W. (1972). *An analysis of simulation media.* Unpublished Graduation Project, School of Architecture, University of British Columbia, Vancouver.

19 Stamps, A. E. (1993). Postconstruction validation of photomontage simulations. *Perceptual and Motor Skills, 76*(3, Part 2), 1335-1338.

20 Bateson, J. E., & Hui, M. K. (1992). The ecological validity of photographic slides and videotapes in simulating the service setting. *Journal of Consumer Education, 19,* 271-281.

21 Ishikawa, T., Okabe, A., Sadahiro, Y., & Kakumoto, S. (1998). An experimental analysis of the area of an open space using 3-D stereo dynamic graphics. *Environment and Behavior, 30,* 216-234.

22 Lowenthal, D. (1972). Research on environmental perception and behavior: Perspectives on current problems. *Environment and Behavior, 4,* 333-342.

23 Brunswik, E. (1944). Distal focusing of perception. *Psychological Monographs, 56,* 148.

24 Lynch, K., & Rivkin, M. (1959). A walk around the block. *Landscape, 8,* 24-34.

25 Feimer, N. R. (1984). Environmental perception: The effects of media, evaluative context, and observer sample. *Journal of Environmental Psychology, 4,* 61-80.

26 Wagner, M., Baird, J. C., & Barbaresi, W. (1981). The locus of environmental attention. *Journal of Environmental Psychology, 1,* 195-206.

27 Stevens, S. S. (1975). *Psychophysics: Introduction to its perceptual, neural, and social prospects.* New York: Wiley.

28 Reed, C. F., Lehberger, P. F., & Haase, R. F. (1980). Application of psychophysical scaling to measurement of complexity of houses. *Perceptual and Motor Skills, 50,* 655-660.

29 Coren, S., Porac, C., & Ward, L. M. (1984). *Sensation and perception.* Toronto: Academic Press.

30 Falk, J. H., & Balling, J. D. (2010). Evolutionary influence on human landscape preference. *Environment and Behavior, 42,* 479-493.

31 Kim, T., Jeong, G., Baek, H., Kim, G., Sundaram, T., Kang, H., et al. (2010). Human brain activation in response to visual stimulation with rural and urban scenery pictures: A functional magnetic resonance imaging study. *Science of the Total Environment, 408,* 2600-2607.

32 Hartmann, P., & Apaolaza-Ibáñez, V. (2010). Beyond savanna: An evolutionary and environmental psychology approach to behavioral effects of nature scenery in green advertising. *Journal of Environmental Psychology, 30,* 119-128.

33 Sommer, R. (1997). Further cross-national studies of tree form preference. *Ecological Psychology, 9,* 153-160.

34 Clinton, A., & Devlin, A. S. (2011). 'Is this really a police station?': Police department exteriors and judgments of authority, professionalism, and approachability. *Journal of Environmental Psychology, 31,* 393-406.

35 Nasar, J. L., Valencia, H., Abidin, O., Chueh, S., & Hwang, J. (1985). Out of sight further from mind: Destination visibility and distance perception. *Environment and Behavior, 17,* 627639.

36 Kearney, A. R., & Bradley, G. A. (2011). The effects of viewer attributes on preference for forest scenes: Contributions of attitudes, knowledge, demographic factors, and stakeholder group membership. *Environment and Behavior, 43,* 147-181.

37 Hershberger, R. G. (1968). A study of meaning and architecture. *Man and His Environment, 1*(6), 67.

38 Kaplan, R. (1973). Predictors of environmental preference: Designers and clients. In W. F.

E. Preiser (Ed.), *Environmental design research.* Stroudsberg, PA: Dowden, Hutchinson and Ross.

39 Valadez, J. J. (1984). Diverging meanings of development among architects and three other professional groups. *Journal of Environmental Psychology, 4,* 223-228.

40 Payne, I. (1969). Pupillary responses to architectural stimuli. *ManEnvironmental Systems, 1,* S11.

41 Dantzker, H. C., & Chandrasekaran, D. (2010). Exploring cancer risk perceptions of turf and lawn pesticide professionals in New York State. *Environment and Behavior, 42,* 740-764.

42 Edney, J. J. (1972). Place and space: The effects of experience with a physical locale. *Journal of Experimental Social Psychology, 8,* 124-135.

43 Nasar, J. L., Valencia, H., Abidin, O., Chueh, S., & Hwang, J. (1985). Out of sight further from mind: Destination visibility and distance perception. *Environment and Behavior, 17,* 627-639.

44 Smith, C. D. (1984). The relationship between the pleasingness of landmarks and the judgement of distance in cognitive maps. *Journal of Environmental Psychology, 4,* 229-234.

45 Turnbull, C. (1961). Some observations regarding the experiences and behavior of the Bambuti pygmies. *American Journal of Psychology, 74,* 304308.

46 Coren, S., Porac, C., & Ward, L. M. (1984). *Sensation and perception.* Toronto: Academic Press.

47 Bourg, G., & Castel, P. (2011). The relevance of psychosocial maps in the study of urban districts. *Journal of Environmental Psychology, 31,* 245-256.

48 Wohlwill, J. F. (1973). The environment is not in the head! In W. F. E. Preiser (Ed.), *Environmental design research,* Vol. 2. Stroudsburg, PA: Dowden Hutchinson and Ross.

49 Hendrick, C., Martyniuk, O., Spencer, T. J., & Flynn, J. E. (1977). Procedures for investigating the effect of light on impression: Simulation of a real space by slides. *Environment and Behavior, 9,* 491-510.

50 Kaye, S. M., & Murray, M. A. (1982). Evaluations of an architectural space as a function of variations in furniture arrangement, furniture density, and windows. *Human Factors, 24,* 609-618.

51 Stamps, A. E. (2011). Effects of area, height, elongation, and color on perceived spaciousness. *Environment and Behavior, 43,* 252-273.

52 Thiel, P. (1970). Notes on the description, scaling, notation, and scoring of some perceptual and cognitive attributes of the physical attributes. In H. Proshansky, W., Ittelson, & L. Rivlin (Eds.), *Environmental psychology: Man and his physical setting.* New York: Holt, Rinehart, & Winston.

53 Pederson, D. M., & Topham, T. L. (1990). Perception of enclosure effects of architectural surfaces in a large scale interior space. *Perceptual and Motor Skills, 70,* 299-304.

54 Stamps, A. E. (2005). Enclosure and safety in urbanscapes. *Environment and Behavior, 37,* 102-133.

55 Stamps, A. E. (2010). Effects of permeability on perceived enclosure and spaciousness. *Environment and Behavior, 42,* 864-886.

56 Stamps, A. E., & Smith, S. (2002). Environmental enclosure in urban settings. *Environment and Behavior, 34,* 781-794.

57 Thiel, P., Harrison, E.D., & Alden, R.S. (1986). The perception of spatial enclosure as a function of the position of architectural surfaces. *Environment and Behavior, 18,* 227-245.

58 Dainoff, M. J., Sherman, R. C., Miskie, D., & Grovesnor, J. (1981). Perceived enclosedness of schematic architectural space. *Journal of Experimental Psychology, 7,* 1349-1356.

59 Ross, H. E. (1974). *Behavior and perception in strange environments.* London: George Allen and Unwin.

60 Arthur E. (2012). Atmospheric Permeability and Perceived Enclosure Stamps. *Environment and Behavior, 44,* 427-446.

61 Okabe, A., Aoki, K., & Hamamoto, W. (1986). Distance and direction judgement in a large-scale natural environment: Effects of a slope and winding trail. *Environment and Behavior, 18,* 755-772.

62 Sadalla, E. K., & Magel, S. G. (1980). The perception of traversed distance. *Environment and Behavior, 12,* 65-79.

63 Jansen-Osmann, P., & Wiedenbauer, G. (2004). The influence of turns on distance cognition: New experimental evidence to clarify the route-angularity effect. *Environment and Behavior, 36,* 790-813.

64 Sadalla, E. K., & Staplin, L. J. (1980). The perception of traversed distance: Intersections. *Environment and Behavior, 12,* 167-182.

65 Sadalla, E. K., & Oxley, D. (1984). The perception of room size: The rectangularity illusion. *Environment and Behavior, 16,* 394-405.

66 Cadwallader, M. (1979). Problems in cognitive distance: Implications for cognitive mapping. *Environment and Behavior, 11,* 559-576.

67 Sadalla, E. K., Burroughs, W. J., & Staplin, L. J. (1980). Reference points in spatial cognition. *Journal of Experimental Psychology: Human Learning and Memory, 5,* 516-528.

68 Hirtle, S. C., & Jonides, J. (1985). Evidence of hierarchies in cognitive maps. *Memory and Cognition, 13,* 208-217.

69 Sadalla, E. K., & Oxley, D. (1984). The perception of room size: The rectangularity illusion. *Environment and Behavior, 16,* 394-405.

70 Korte, C., & Grant, R. (1980). Traffic noise, environmental awareness, and pedestrian behavior. *Environment and Behavior, 12,* 408-420.

71 Brunswik, E. (1956). *Perception and the representative design of psychological experiments.* Berkeley: University of California Press.

72 Brunswik, E. (1957). Scope and aspects of the cognitive problem. In H. Gruber, K. R. Hammond, & R. Jessor (Eds.), *Contemporary approaches to cognition: A symposium held at the University of Colorado.* Cambridge, MA: Harvard University Press, p. 5.

73 Craik, K. H., & Appleyard, D. (1980). The streets of San Francisco: Brunswik's lens model applied to urban inference and assessment. *Journal of Social Issues, 36* (3), 72-85.

74 Gibson, J. J. (1966). *The senses considered as perceptual systems.* Boston: Houghton Mifflin.

75 Gibson, J. J. (1979). *The ecological approach to visual perception.* Boston: Houghton Mifflin.

76 Gibson, J. J. (1976). *The theory of affordances and the design of the environment.* Paper presented at the annual meetings of the American Society for Aesthetics, Toronto.

77 Kaplan, S., & Kaplan, R. (1982). *Cognition and environment: Functioning in an uncertain world.* New York: Praeger.

78 Gibson, J. J. (1976). *The theory of affordances and the design of the environment.* Paper presented at the annual meetings of the American Society for Aesthetics, Toronto.

79 Clark, C., & Uzzell, D. L. (2002). The affordances of the home, neighbourhood, school and town centre for adolescents. *Journal of Environmental Psychology, 22,* 95-108.

80 Berlyne, D. E. (1971). *Aesthetics and psychobiology.* New York: AppletonCenturyCrofts.

81 Berlyne, D. E. (1974). (Ed.). *Studies in the new experimental aesthetics: Steps toward an objective psychology of aesthetic appreciation.* New York: Halsted Press.

82 Rapoport, Am., & Kantor, R. E. (1967). Complexity and ambiguity in environmental design. *Journal of the American Institute of Planners, 33,* 210-221.

83 Venturi, R. (1966). *Complexity and contradiction in architecture.* New York: Museum of Modern Art.

84 Wohlwill, J. F. (1976). Environmental aesthetics: The environment as a source of affect. In I. Altman and J. F. Wohlwill (Ed.), *Human behavior and environment,* Vol. 1. New York: Plenum.

85 Wohlwill, J. F. (1976). Environmental aesthetics: The environment as a source of affect. In I. Altman and J. F. Wohlwill (Ed.), *Human behavior and environment,* Vol. 1. New York: Plenum.

86 Wohlwill, J. F. (1976). Environmental aesthetics: The environment as a source of affect. In I. Altman and J. F. Wohlwill (Ed.), *Human behavior and environment,* Vol. 1. New York: Plenum.

87 Heidegger, M. (1971). *Poetry, language, and thought.* New York: Harper and Row.

88 Seamon, D. (1982). The phenomenological contribution to environmental psychology. *Journal of Environmental Psychology, 2,* 119-140.

89 Graumann, C. F. (2002). The phenomenological approach to peopleenvironment studies. In R. B. Bechtel, & A. Churchman (Eds.), *Handbook of environmental psychology* (pp. 95-113). Hoboken, NJ: Wiley.

90 Korosec-Serfaty, P. (1984). The home from attic to cellar. *Journal of Environmental Psychology, 4,* 303-321.

91 Jacobs, J. (1961). *The death and life of great American cities.* New York: Random House.

92 Seamon, D., & Nordin, C. (1980). Marketplace as place ballet: A Swedish example. *Landscape, 24,* 35-41.

93 Tuan, Y. F. (1974). *Topophilia.* Englewood Cliffs, NJ: PrenticeHall.

94 Relph, E. (1976). *Place and placelessness.* London: Pion.

95 Livingstone, D. H., & Harrison, R. T. (1983). Reflections on a phenomenological approach. *Journal of Environmental Psychology, 3,* 295-296.

96 Sixsmith, J. (1983). Comment on "The phenomenological contribution to environmental psychology" by D. Seamon. *Journal of Environmental Psychology, 3,* 109-111.

97 Seamon, D. (1983). Response to Sixsmith's comments on the phenomenological contribution. *Journal of Environmental Psychology, 3,* 199-200.

98 Low, S. M. & Ryan, W. P. (1985). A methodology for the integration of architectural and local perceptions in Oley, Pennsylvania. *Journal of Architectural Planning and Research, 2,* 3-22.

99 Kitchin, R. M. (1994). Cognitive maps: What are they and why study them? *Journal of Environmental Psychology, 14,* 1-19.

100 Downs, R. M., & Stea, D. (1977). *Maps in minds: Reflections on cognitive mapping.* San Francisco: Harper & Row.

101 Mauser, C. (1996). A kaleidoscope model: Defining natural environments. *Journal of Environmental Psychology, 16,* 335-348.

102 Gladwin, T. N., Newburry, W. E., & Reiskin, E. D. (1997). Why is the northern elite mind biased against community, the environment, and a sustainable future? In M. H. Bazerman, & D. M. Messick (Eds.), *Environment, ethics and behavior: The psychology of environmental valuation and degradation.* San Francisco: The New Lexington Press/Jossey-Bass.

103 Bostrom, A., Fischhoff,B., & Morgan, M. (1992). Characterizing mental models of hazardous processes: A methodology and application to radon. *Journal of Social Issues, 48*(4), 85-100.

104 Taylor, J. G, Stewart, T. R., & Downton, M. (1988). Perceptions of drought in the Ogallala Aquifer region. *Environment and Behavior, 20,* 150-175.

105 Brown, R. S., Williams, C. W., & Lees-Haley, P. R. (1994). The effects of hindsight bias and causal attribution on human response to environmental events. *Journal of Applied Social Psychology, 24,* 661-674.

106 Cherulnik, P. D. (1991). Reading restaurant facades: Environmental inference in finding the right place to eat. *Environment and Behavior, 23,* 150-170.

107 Leff, H. L., & Gordon, L. R. (1979). Environmental cognitive sets: A longitudinal study. *Environment and Behavior, 11,* 291-327.

108 Bazerman, M. H., & Moore, D. A. & Gillespie, J. J. (1999). The human mind as a barrier to wiser environmental agreements. *American Behavioral Scientist, 42,* 1277-1300.

109 Chawla, L. (1986). The ecology of environmental memory. *Children's Environments Quarterly, 3,* 34-42.

110 Pinheiro, J. Q. (1998). Determinants of cognitive maps of the world as expressed in sketch maps. *Journal of Environmental Psychology, 18,* 321-339.

111 Peron, E. M., Baroni, M. R., Job, R., & Salmaso, P. (1990). Effects of familiarity in recalling interiors and external places. *Journal of Environmental Psychology, 10,* 255-271.

112 Schiavo, R. S., & McWalter, S. (1990, August). *Building renovation and memorableness.* Paper presented at annual meetings of the American Psychological Association, Boston.

113 Hammitt, W. E. (1987). Visual recognition capacity during outdoor recreation experiences. *Environment and Behavior, 19,* 651-672.

114 Tversky, B. (2000). Remembering spaces. In E. Tulving, F. I. M. Craik et al. (Eds.), *The Oxford Handbook of Memory* (pp. 363-378). New York: Oxford University Press.

115 Wohlwill, J. F. (1966). The physical environment: A problem for a psychology of stimulation. *Journal of Social Issues, 22*(4), 2938.

116 Helson, H. (1964). *Adaptationlevel theory.* New York: Harper and Row.

117 Suedfeld, P., Landon, P. B., & Ballard, E. J. (1983). Effects of reduced stimulation on divergent and convergent thinking. *Environment and Behavior, 15,* 727-738.

118 Kalish, N., Landon, P. B., Rank, D. S., & Suedfeld, P. (1983). Stimulus tasks and environmental characteristics as factors in the cognitive processing of English sentences. *Bulletin of the Psychonomic Society, 21,* 13.

119 Lynch, K. (1960). *The image of the city.* Cambridge, MA: MIT Press.

120 Aragones, J. I., & Arredondo, J. M. (1985). Structure of urban cognitive maps. *Journal of Environmental Psychology, 5,* 197-212.

121 Magana, J. R. (1978). *An empirical and interdisciplinary test of a theory of urban perception.* Doctoral dissertation, University of California, Irvine.

122 Abu-Ghazzeh, T. M. (1996). Movement and wayfinding in the King Saud University built environment: A look at freshman orientation and environmental information. *Journal of Environmental Psychology, 16,* 303-318.

123 Ramadier, T., & Moser, G. (1998). Social legibility, the cognitive map and urban behavior. *Journal of Environmental Psychology, 18,* 307-319.

124 Downs, R. M. (1981). Maps and metaphors. *Professional Geographer, 33,* 287-293.

125 Kaplan, S., & Kaplan, R. (1982). *Cognition and environment: Functioning in an uncertain world.* New York: Praeger.

126 Chase, W. G., & Chi, M. T. H. (1981). Cognitive skill: Implications for spatial skills in largescale environments. In J. H. Harvey (Ed.), *Cognition, social behavior, and the environment.* Hillsdale, NJ: Erlbaum.

127 Golledge, R. G. (1976). Methods and methodological issues in environmental cognition research. In G. T. Moore, & R. G. Golledge (Eds.), *Environmental knowing: Theories, research, and methods.* Stroudsberg, PA: Dowden, Hutchinson & Ross.

128 Kearney, A. R., & Kaplan, S. (1997). Toward a methodology for the measurement of knowledge structures of ordinary people: The Conceptual Content Cognitive Map (3CM). *Environment and Behavior, 29,* 579-617.

129 Tlauka, M., & Wilson, P. N. (1996). Orientation-free representations from navigation through a computer-simulated environment. *Environment and Behavior, 28,* 647-664.

130 Wilson, P. N. (1999). Active exploration of a virtual environment does not promote orientation or memory for objects. *Environment and Behavior, 31,* 752-763.

131 Cutmore, T. R. H., Hine, T. J., Maberly, K. J., Langford, N. M., & Hawgood, G. (2000). Cognitive and gender factors influencing navigation in a virtual environment. *International Journal of Human Computer Studies, 53,* 223-249.

132 Rossano, M. J., West, S. O., Robertson, T. J., Wayne, M. C., & Chase, R. B. (1999). The acquisition of route and survey knowledge from computer models. *Journal of Environmental Psychology, 19,* 101-115.

133 Aadland, J., Beatty, W. W., & Maki, R. H. (1985). Spatial memory for children and adults assessed in the radial maze. *Developmental Psychobiology, 18,* 163-172.

134 Hart, R. (1979). *Children's experience of place.* New York: Irvington.

135 Evans, G. W. (1980). Environmental cognition. *Psychological Bulletin, 88,* 259-267.

136 Baskaya, A., Wilson, C., & Ozcan, Y. Z. (2004). Wayfinding in an unfamiliar environment. Different spatial settings of two polyclinics. *Environment and Behavior, 36,* 839-867.

137 Blades, M. (1990). The reliability of data collected from sketch maps. *Journal of Environmental Psychology, 10,* 327-339.

138 Magana, J. R., Evans, G. W., & Romney, A. K. (1981). Scaling techniques in the analysis of environmental cognition data. *Professional Geographer, 33,* 294-301.

139 Sonnenfeld, J. (1985). Tests of spatial skill: A validation problem. *Man-Environment Systems, 15,* 107- 120.

140 Holahan, C. J., & Dobrowolny, M. B. (1978). Cognitive and behavioral correlates of the spatial environment: An interactional analysis. *Environment and Behavior, 10,* 317-333.

141 O'Neill, M. (1991). A biologically based model of spatial cognition and wayfinding. *Journal of Environmental Psychology, 11,* 299-320.

142 Tlauka, M., & Wilson, P. N. (1996). Orientation-free representations from navigation through a computer-simulated environment. *Environment and Behavior, 28,* 647-664.

143 Baskaya, A., Wilson, C., & Ozcan, Y. Z. (2004). Wayfinding in an unfamiliar environment. Different spatial settings of two polyclinics. *Environment and Behavior, 36,* 839-867.

144 Jansen-Osmann, P. (2002). Using desktop virtual environments to investigate the role of landmarks. *Computers in Human Behavior, 18,* 427-436.

145 Sherman, R. C., Croxton, J., & Giovanatto, J. (1979). Investigating cognitive representations of spatial relations. *Environment and Behavior, 11,* 209-226.

146 Cadwallader, M. (1979). Problems in cognitive distance: Implications for cognitive mapping. *Environment and Behavior, 11,* 559-576.

147 Wiener, J. M., Büchner, S. J. & Hölscher, C. (2009). Taxonomy of Human Wayfinding Tasks: A Knowledge-Based Approach. *Spatial Cognition & Computation: An Interdisciplinary Journal, 9,* 152-165.

148 Waller, G. (1986). The development of route knowledge: Multiple dimensions? *Journal of Environmental Psychology, 6,* 109-119.

149 Kitchin, R. M. (1997). Exploring spatial thought. *Environment and Behavior, 29,* 123-156.

150 Downs, R. M., & Siegel, A. W. (1981). On mapping researchers mapping children mapping space. In L. S. Liben, A. H. Patterson, & N. Newcombe (Eds.), *Spatial representation and behavior across the life span.* New York: Academic Press.

151 Moore, G. T. (1979). Knowing about environmental knowing: The current state of theory and research on environmental cognition. *Environment and Behavior, 11,* 33-70.

152 Heft, H. (2013). Environment, cognition, and culture: Reconsidering the cognitive map. *Journal of Environmental Psychology, 33,* 14-25.

153 Bryant, K. J. (1984). Methodological convergence as an issue within environmental cognition

research. *Journal of Environmental Psychology, 4,* 43-60.

154 Padgitt, A. J., Hund, A. M. (2012). How good are these directions? Determining direction quality and wayfinding efficiency. *Journal of Environmental Psychology, 32*(2), 164-172.

155 Bryant, K. J. (1991). Geographical/spatial orientation ability within real-world and simulated large-scale environments. *Multivariate Behavioral Research, 26,* 109-136.

156 Webley, P. (1981). Sex differences in home range and cognitive maps in eightyear old children. *Journal of Environmental Psychology, 1,* 293-302.

157 Rovine, M. J., & Weisman, G. D. (1989). Sketch-map variables as predictors of way-finding performance. *Journal of Environmental Psychology, 9,* 217-232.

158 Nasar, J. L. (1984). Visual preferences in urban street scenes: A crosscultural comparison between Japan and the United States. *Journal of CrossCultural Psychology, 15,* 79-93.

159 Hund, A. M., Schmettow, M., & Noordzij, M. L. (2012). The impact of culture and recipient perspective on direction giving in the service of wayfinding. *Journal of Environmental Psychology, 32*(4), 327-336.

160 Karan, P. P., Bladen, W. A., & Singh, G. (1980). Slum dwellers' and squatters' images of the city. *Environment and Behavior, 12,* 81-100.

161 Herman, J. F., Miller, B. S., & Shiraki, J. H. (1987). The influence of affective associations on the development of cognitive maps of large environments. *Journal of Environmental Psychology, 7,* 89-98.

162 Anooshian, L. J. & Seibert, P. S. (1997). Effects of emotional mood states in recognizing places: Disentangling conscious and unconscious retrieval. *Environment and Behavior, 29,* 699-733.

163 Coshall, J. T., & Potter, R. B. (1987). Social psychology variations in the distance cognitions of urban consumers in Britain. *Journal of Social Psychology, 127,* 611-618.

164 Janowsky, J. S., Oviatt, S. K., & Orwoll, E. S. (1994). Testosterone influences spatial cognition in older men. *Behavioral Neuroscience, 108,* 325-332.

165 Chokor, B. A. (2003). Pattern of representation of countries in cognitive maps of the world with special reference to Africa. *Journal of Environmental Psychology, 23,* 427-437.

166 Sako, T., Ando, T., & Fukui, I. (1990). Effects of orientation on direction judgment of places. *Proceedings of the 54th Annual Convention of the Japanese Psychological Association, 54,* 533.

167 Brunyé, T. T., Andonova, E., Meneghetti, C., Noordzij, M. L., Pazzaglia, F., Wienemann, R., Mahoney, C. R., & Taylor, H. A. (2012). Planning routes around the world: International evidence for southern route preferences, *Journal of Environmental Psychology, 32*(4), 297-304.

168 Hart, R. A., & Moore, G. T. (1973). The development of spatial cognition: A review. In R. M. Downs, & D. Stea (Eds.), *Image and environment: Cognitive mapping and spatial behavior.* Chicago: Aldine.

169 Jansen-Osmann, P. (2004). The representation of landmarks and routes in children and adults: A study in a virtual environment. *Journal of Environmental Psychology, 24,* 347-357.

170 Hart, R. A., & Moore, G. T. (1973). The development of spatial cognition: A review. In R. M. Downs, & D. Stea (Eds.), *Image and environment: Cognitive mapping and spatial behavior.* Chicago: Aldine.

171 Heth, C. D., & Cornell, E. H. (1998). Characteristics of travel by persons lost in Albertan wilderness areas. *Journal of Environmental Psychology, 18,* 223-235.

172 Evans, G. W. (1980). Environmental cognition. *Psychological Bulletin, 88,* 259267.

173 Spencer, C., & Darvizeh, Z. (1981). The case for developing a cognitive environmental psychology that does not underestimate the abilities of young children. *Journal of Environmental Psychology, 1,* 21-31.

174 Acredolo, L. P. (1988). From signal to "symbol": The development of landmark knowledge from 9 to 13 months. *British Journal of Developmental Psychology, 6,* 369- 372.

175 Biel, A. (1982). Children's spatial representation of their neighborhood: A step towards a general spatial competence. *Journal of Environmental Psychology, 2,* 193-200.

176 Matthews, M. H. (1985). Young children's representations of the environment: A comparison of techniques. *Journal of Environmental Psychology, 5,* 261-278.

177 Conning, A. M., & Byrne, R. W. (1984). Pointing to preschool children's spatial competence: A study in natural settings. *Journal of Environmental Psychology, 4,* 165-175.

178 Stea, D., Kerkman, D. D., Piñon, M. F., Middlebrook, N. N., & Rice, J. L. (2004). Preschoolers use maps to find a hidden object outdoors. *Journal of Environmental Psychology, 24,* 341-345.

179 Neisser, U. (1976). *Cognition and reality.* San Francisco: Freeman.

180 Bryant, K. J. (1991). Geographical/spatial orientation ability within real-world and simulated large-scale environments. *Multivariate Behavioral Research, 26,* 109-136.

181 Ohta, R. J., & Kirasic, K. C. (1983). The investigation of environmental learning in the elderly. In G. D. Rowles & R. J. Ohta (Eds.), *Aging and milieu.* New York: Academic Press.

182 Pearce, P. L. (1981). Route maps: A study of traveller's perceptions of a section of countryside. *Journal of Environmental Psychology, 1,* 141-155.

183 Aubrey, J. B., & Dobbs, A. R. (1989). Age differences in extrapersonal orientation as measured by performance on the Locomotor Maze. *Canadian Journal on Aging, 8,* 333-342.

184 Kirasic, K. C., Allen, G. L., & Haggerty, D. (1992). Age-related differences in adults' macrospatial cognitive processes. *Experimental Aging Research, 18,* 33-39.

185 Aubrey, J. B., & Dobbs, A. R. (1990). Age and sex differences in the mental realignment of maps. *Experimental Aging Research, 16,* 133-139.

186 McCormack, P. (1982). Coding of spatial by young and elderly adults. *Journal of Gerontology, 37,* 80-86.

187 Kirasic, K. C. (1991). Spatial cognition and behavior in young and elderly adults: Implications for learning new environments. *Psychology and Aging, 6,* 10-18.

188 Burns, P. C. (1998). Wayfinding errors while driving. *Journal of Environmental Psychology, 18,* 209-217.

189 Brown, L. N., Lahar, C. J., & Mosley, J. L. (1998). Age and gender-related differences in strategy use for route information: A "map-present" direction-giving paradigm. *Environment and Behavior, 30,* 123-143.

190 Georgemiller, R., & Hassan, F. (1986). Spatial competence: Assessment of route-finding and route-learning, and topographical memory in normal aging. *Clinical Gerontologists, 5,* 19-38.

191 Burns, P. C. (1998). Wayfinding errors while driving. *Journal of Environmental Psychology, 18,* 209-217.

192 Burns, P. C. (1998). Wayfinding errors while driving. *Journal of Environmental Psychology, 18,* 209-217.

193 Ohta, R. J., & Kirasic, K. C. (1983). The investigation of environmental learning in the elderly. In G. D. Rowles & R. J. Ohta (Eds.), *Aging and milieu.* New York: Academic Press.

194 Pearce, P. L. (1981). Route maps: A study of travellers' perceptions of a section of countryside. *Journal of Environmental Psychology, 1,* 141-155.

195 Aubrey, J. B., & Dobbs, A. R. (1989). Age differences in extrapersonal orientation as measured by performance on the Locomotor Maze. *Canadian Journal on Aging, 8,* 333-342.

196 McCormack, P. (1982). Coding of spatial by young and elderly adults. *Journal of Gerontology, 37,* 80-86.

197 Bryant, K. J. (1991). Geographical/spatial orientation ability within real-world and simulated large-scale environments. *Multivariate Behavioral Research, 26,* 109-136.

198 Evans, G. W., Smith, C., & Pezdek, K. (1982). Cognitive maps and urban form. *Journal of the American Planning Association, 48,* 232-244.

199 Porteous, J. D. (1977). *Environment and behavior: Planning and everyday life.* Don Mills, ON: AddisonWesley.

200 Evans, G. W., Brennan, P. L., Skorpanich, M. A., & Held, D. (1984). Cognitive mapping and elderly adults: Verbal and location memory for urban landmarks. *Journal of Gerontology, 39,* 452-457.

201 Bryant, K. J. (1991). Geographical/spatial orientation ability within real-world and simulated large-scale environments. *Multivariate Behavioral Research, 26,* 109-136.

202 Kirasic, K. C., & Mathes, E. A. (1990). Effects of different means for conveying environmental information on elderly adults' spatial cognition and behavior. *Environment and Behavior, 22,* 591-607.

203 Blajenkova, O., & Motes, M. A. (2005). Individual differences in the representations of novel environments. *Journal of Environmental Psychology, 25,* 2005, 97-109.

204 Hund, A. M., & Padgitt, A. J. (2010) Direction giving and following in the service of wayfinding in a complex indoor environment. *Journal of Environmental Psychology, 30,* 553-564.

205 Pearson, J. L., & Ialongo, N. S. (1986). The relationship between spatial ability and environmental knowledge. *Journal of Environmental Psychology, 6,* 299- 304.

206 Pearson, J. L., & Ferguson, L. R. (1989). Gender differences in patterns of spatial ability,

environmental cognition, and math and English achievement in later adolescence. *Adolescence, 24,* 421-431.

207 Cutmore, T. R. H., Hine, T. J., Maberly, K. J., Langford, N. M., & Hawgood, G. (2000). Cognitive and gender factors influencing navigation in a virtual environment. *International Journal of Human Computer Studies, 53,* 223-249.

208 Fenner, J., Heathcote, D., & Jerrans-Smith, J. (2000). The development of wayfinding competency: Asymmetrical effects of visuo-spatial and verbal ability. *Journal of Environmental Psychology, 20,* 165-175.

209 Simon, S. L., Walsh, D. A., Regnier, V. A., & Krauss, I. K. (1992). Spatial cognition and neighborhood use: The relationship in older adults. *Psychology and Aging, 7,* 389-934.

210 Bryant, K. J. (1991). Geographical/spatial orientation ability within real-world and simulated large-scale environments. *Multivariate Behavioral Research, 26,* 109-136.

211 Weisman, J. (1981). Evaluating architectural legibility: Way-finding in the built environment. *Environment and Behavior, 13,* 189-204.

212 Garling, T., Lindberg, E., & Mantyla, T. (1983). Orientation in buildings: Effects of familiarity, visual access, and orientation aids. *Journal of Applied Psychology, 68,* 177-186.

213 Schouela, D. A., Steinberg, L. M., Levelton, L. B., & Wapner, S. (1980). Development of the cognitive organization of an environment. *Canadian Journal of Behaviourial Science, 12,* 116.

214 Kirisic, K. C., Allen, G. L., & Siegel, A. W. (1984). Expression of configurational knowledge of large-scale environments: Students' performance of cognitive tasks. *Environment and Behavior, 16,* 687-712.

215 Aadland, J., Beatty, W. W., & Maki, R. H. (1985). Spatial memory for children and adults assessed in the radial maze. *Developmental Psychobiology, 18,* 163-172.

216 Giraudo, M., & Peruch, P. (1988). Spatio-temporal aspects of the mental representation of urban space. *Journal of Environmental Psychology, 8,* 9-17.

217 Woollett, K., & Maguire, E. A. (2010). The effect of navigational expertise on wayfinding in new environments. *Journal of Environmental Psychology, 30*(4), 565-573.

218 Carr, S., & Schissler, D. (1969). The city as a trip: Perceptual selection and memory in the view from the road. *Environment and Behavior, 1,* 736.

219 Ohta, R. J., & Kirasic, K. C. (1983). The investigation of environmental learning in the elderly. In G. D. Rowles & R. J. Ohta (Eds.), *Aging and milieu.* New York: Academic Press.

220 Rissotto, A., & Tonucci, F. (2002). Freedom of movement and environmental knowledge in elementary school children. *Journal of Environmental Psychology, 22,* 64-77.

221 Orleans, P. (1973). Differential cognition of urban residents: Effects of social scale on mapping. In R. M. Downs, & D. Stea (Eds.), *Image and environment: Cognitive mapping and spatial behavior.* Chicago: Aldine.

222 Windley, P. G., & Vandeventer, W. H. (1982). Environmental cognition of small rural towns: The case for older residents. *Journal of Environmental Psychology, 2,* 285-294.

223 Karan, P. P., Bladen, W. A., & Singh, G. (1980). Slum dwellers' and squatters' images of the city. *Environment and Behavior, 12,* 81-100.

224 Foley, J. E., & Cohen, A. J. (1984). Mental mapping of a megastructure. *Canadian Journal of Psychology, 38,* 440-453.

225 Garling, T., Book, A., Lindberg, E., & Nilsson, T. (1981). Memory for the spatial layout of the everyday physical environment: Factors affecting rate of acquisition. *Journal of Environmental Psychology, 1,* 263-277.

226 Cohen, R., Weatherford, D. L., Lomenick, T., & Koeller, K. (1979). Development of spatial representations: Role of task demands and familiarity with the environment. *Child Development, 50,* 1257-1260.

227 Moeser, S. D. (1988). Cognitive mapping in a complex building. *Environment and Behavior, 20,* 21-49.

228 Ward, S. L., Newcombe, N., & Overton, W. F. (1986). Turn left at the church, or three miles north: A study of direction giving and sex differences. *Environment and Behavior, 18,* 192-213.

229 Acredolo, L. P. (1988). From signal to "symbol": The development of landmark knowledge from 9 to 13 months. *British Journal of Developmental Psychology, 6,* 369- 372.

230 Webley, P., & Whalley, A. (1987). Sex differences in children's environmental cognition. *Journal of Social Psychology, 127,* 223-225.

231 Brown, L. N., Lahar, C. J., & Mosley, J. L. (1998). Age and gender-related differences in strategy use for route information: A "map-present" direction-giving paradigm. *Environment and Behavior, 30,* 123-143.

232 Cutmore, T. R. H., Hine, T. J., Maberly, K. J., Langford, N. M., & Hawgood, G. (2000). Cognitive and gender factors influencing navigation in a virtual environment. *International Journal of Human Computer Studies, 53,* 223-249.

233 Lehnung, M, Leplow, B., Haaland, V. O., Mehdorn, M., & Ferstl, R. (2003). Pointing accuracy is dependent on age, sex, and experience. *Journal of Environmental Psychology, 23,* 419-425.

234 Stone, J. P., & McBeath, M. K. (2010). Gender differences in distance estimates when exposed to multiple routes. *Environment and Behavior, 42,* 469-478.

235 Bryant, K. J. (1991). Geographical/spatial orientation ability within real-world and simulated large-scale environments. *Multivariate Behavioral Research, 26,* 109-136.

236 Lawton, C. A., Charleston, S. I., & Zieles, A. S. (1996). Individual and gender related differences in indoor wayfinding. *Environment and Behavior, 28,* 204-29.

237 Devlin, A. S., & Bernstein, J. (1997). Interactive way-finding: Map style and effectiveness. *Journal of Environmental Psychology, 17,* 99-110.

238 Picucci, L., & Bosco, A. (2011). Besides navigation accuracy: Gender differences in strategy selection and level of spatial confidence. *Journal of Environmental Psychology, 31,* 430-438.

239 Kirisic, K. C., Allen, G. L., & Siegel, A. W. (1984). Expression of configurational knowledge of large-scale environments: Students' performance of cognitive tasks. *Environment and Behavior, 16,* 687-712.

240 Garling, T., Book, A., Lindberg, E., & Nilsson, T. (1981). Memory for the spatial layout of the everyday physical environment: Factors affecting rate of acquisition. *Journal of Environmental Psychology, 1,* 263-277.

241 Beatty, W. W. (2002). Sex differences in geographic knowledge: Driving experience is not essential. *Journal of the International Neuropsychological Society, 8,* 804-810.

242 Jones, C. M., Braithwaite, V. A., & Healy, S. D. (2003). The evolution of sex differences in spatial ability. *Behavioral Neuroscience, 117,* 403-411.

243 Lin, C-T., Huang, T-Y., Lin, W-J., Chang, S-Y., Lin, Y-H., Ko, L-W., Hung, D. L., & Chang, E. C. (2012). Gender differences in wayfinding in virtual environments with global or local landmarks. *Journal of Environmental Psychology, 32*(2), 89-96.

244 Foley, J. E., & Cohen, A. J. (1984). Mental mapping of a megastructure. *Canadian Journal of Psychology, 38,* 440-453.

245 Schmitz, S. (1997). Gender-related strategies in environmental development: Effects of anxiety on wayfinding in and representation of a three-dimensional maze. *Journal of Environmental Psychology, 17,* 215-228.

246 Burns, P. C. (1998). Wayfinding errors while driving. *Journal of Environmental Psychology, 18,* 209-217.

247 Evans, G. W. (1980). Environmental cognition. *Psychological Bulletin, 88,* 259-267.

248 Pearson, J. L., & Ferguson, L. R. (1989). Gender differences in patterns of spatial ability, environmental cognition, and math and English achievement in later adolescence. *Adolescence, 24,* 421-431.

249 Webley, P. (1981). Sex differences in home range and cognitive maps in eightyear old children. *Journal of Environmental Psychology, 1,* 293-302.

250 Matthews, M. H. (1986). Gender, graphicacy and geography. *Educational Review, 38,* 259-271.

251 Matthews, M. H. (1986). The influence of gender on the environmental cognition of young boys and girls. *Journal of Genetic Psychology, 147,* 295-302.

252 Lin, C-T., Huang, T-Y., Lin, W-J., Chang, S-Y., Lin, Y-H., Ko, L-W., Hung, D. L., & Chang, E. C. (2012). Gender differences in wayfinding in virtual environments with global or local landmarks. *Journal of Environmental Psychology, 32*(2), 89-96.

253 Windley, P. G., & Vandeventer, W. H. (1982). Environmental cognition of small rural towns: The case for older residents. *Journal of Environmental Psychology, 2,* 285-294.

254 Orleans, P., & Schmidt, S. (1972). Mapping the city: Environmental cognition of urban residents. In W. J. Mitchell (Ed.), *Environmental design: Research and practice.* Los Angeles: University of California.

255 Ward, S. L., Newcombe, N., & Overton, W. F. (1986). Turn left at the church, or three miles north: A study of direction giving and sex differences. *Environment and Behavior, 18,* 192-213.

256 Picucci, L., & Bosco, A. (2011). Besides navigation accuracy: Gender differences in strategy selection and level of spatial confidence. *Journal of Environmental Psychology, 31,* 430-438.

257 Jansen-Osmann, P. (2004). The representation of landmarks and routes in children and adults: A study in a virtual environment. *Journal of Environmental Psychology, 24,* 347-357.

258 Beatty, W. W. (2002). Sex differences in geographic knowledge: Driving experience is not essential. *Journal of the International Neuropsychological Society, 8,* 804-810.

259 Antes, J. R., McBride, R. B., & Collins, J. D. (1988). The effect of a new city traffic route on the cognitive maps of its residents. *Environment and Behavior, 20,* 75-91.

260 Lawton, C. A. (1996). Strategies for indoor wayfinding: The role of orientation. *Journal of Environmental Psychology, 16,* 137-145.

261 Byrne, R. (1979). Memory for urban geography. *Quarterly Journal of Experimental Psychology, 15,* 157-163.

262 Evans, G. W. (1980). Environmental cognition. *Psychological Bulletin, 88,* 259267.

263 Sadalla, E. K., & Montello, D. R. (1989). Remembering changes in direction. *Environment and Behavior, 21,* 346-363.

264 Montello, D. R. (1991). Spatial orientation and the angularity of urban routes: A field study. *Environment and Behavior, 23,* 47-69.

265 Stevens, A., & Coupe, P. (1978). Distortions in judged spatial relations. *Cognitive Psychology, 10,* 422-437.

266 Allen, G. L., & Kirasic, K. C. (1985). Effects of the cognitive organization of route knowledge on judgments of macrospatial distance. *Memory and Cognition, 13,* 218-227.

267 Ross, H. E. (1974). *Behavior and perception in strange environments.* London: George Allen and Unwin.

268 Appleyard, D. (1976). *Planning a pluralistic city.* Cambridge, MA: MIT Press.

269 Tzamir, Y. (1975). *The impact of spatial regularity and irregularity on cognitive mapping* (Technical Report). Haifa, Israel: TechnionIsrael Institute of Technology, Center for Urban and Regional Studies.

270 Canter, D., & Tagg, S. K. (1975). Distance estimation in cities. *Environment and Behavior, 7,* 59-80.

271 Roger, M., Bonnardel, N., & Le Bigot, L. (2011). Landmarks' use in speech map navigation tasks. *Journal of Environmental Psychology, 31,* 192-199.

272 Holahan, C. J., & Sorenson, P. F. (1985). The role of figural organization in city imageability: An information processing analysis. *Journal of Environmental Psychology, 5,* 279-286.

273 Appleyard, D. (1976). *Planning a pluralistic city.* Cambridge, MA: MIT Press.

274 Evans, G. W., Smith, C., & Pezdek, K. (1982). Cognitive maps and urban form. *Journal of the American Planning Association, 48,* 232-244.

275 Antes, J. R., McBride, R. B., & Collins, J. D. (1988). The effect of a new city traffic route on the cognitive maps of its residents. *Environment and Behavior, 20,* 75-91.

276 Hart, R. A., & Moore, G. T. (1973). The development of spatial cognition: A review. In R. M. Downs & D. Stea (Eds.), *Image and environment: Cognitive mapping and spatial behavior.* Chicago: Aldine.

277 Siegel, A. W., & White, S. H. (1975). The development of spatial representations of largescale environments. In H. W. Reese (Ed.), *Advances in child development and behavior,* Vol. 10. New York: Academic Press.

278 Appleyard, D. (1976). *Planning a pluralistic city.* Cambridge, MA: MIT Press.

279 Lynch, K. (1960). *The image of the city.* Cambridge, MA: MIT Press.

280 Evans, G. W., Marrero, D. G., & Butler, P. A. (1981). Environmental learning and cognitive mapping. *Environment and Behavior, 13,* 83-104.

281 Garling, T., Book, A., Lindberg, E., & Nilsson, T. (1981). Memory for the spatial layout of the everyday physical environment: Factors affecting rate of acquisition. *Journal of Environmental Psychology, 1,* 263-277.

282 Evans, G. W. (1980). Environmental cognition. *Psychological Bulletin, 88,* 259-267.

283 Weisman, G. D. (1979). *Wayfinding in the built environment: A study in architectural legibility.* Doctoral dissertation, University of Michigan, Ann Arbor, MI.

284 Garling, T., Book, A., & Lindberg, E. (1986). Spatial orientation and wayfinding in the designed environment: A conceptual analysis and some suggestions for postoccupancy evaluation. *Journal of Architectural Planning and Research, 3,* 55-64.

285 Weisman, J. (1981). Evaluating architectural legibility: Way-finding in the built environment. *Environment and Behavior, 13,* 189-204.

286 O'Neill, M. J. (1991). Effects of signage and floor plan configuration on wayfinding accuracy. *Environment and Behavior, 23,* 553-574.

287 Peponis, J., Zimring, C., & Choi, Y. K. (1990). Finding the building in wayfinding. *Environment and Behavior, 22,* 555-590.

288 Werner, S., Schindler, L. E. (2004). The role of spatial reference frames in architecture: Misalignment impairs way-finding performance. *Environment and Behavior, 36,* 461-482.

289 Hillier, B. (1999). *Space is the machine: A configurational theory of architecture.* Cambridge University Press.

290 Peponis, J., & Wineman, J. (2002). Spatial structure of environment and behavior. In R. B. Bechtel, & A. Churchman (Eds.), *Handbook of environmental psychology,* 271-291. Hoboken, NJ: Wiley.

291 Kim, Y. O., & Penn, A. (2004). Linking the spatial syntax of cognitive maps to the spatial syntax of the environment. *Environment and Behavior, 36,* 483-504.

292 Haq, S., & Zimring, C. (2003). Just down the road a piece: The development of topological knowledge of building layouts. *Environment and Behavior, 35,* 132-160.

293 Hunt, M. E. (1985). Enhancing a building's imageability. *Journal of Architectural Planning and Research, 2,* 151-168.

294 Wolkomir, R. (1987, December). It is easy to get bushed when you're threading a maze. *Smithsonian, 18,* 109-118.

295 Lynch, K., & Rivkin, M. (1959). A walk around the block. *Landscape, 8,* 2434.

296 Lynch, K. (1960). *The image of the city.* Cambridge, MA: MIT Press.

297 Appleyard, D. (1976). *Planning a pluralistic city.* Cambridge, MA: MIT Press.

298 Evans, G. W., Smith, C., & Pezdek, K. (1982). Cognitive maps and urban form. *Journal of the American Planning Association, 48,* 232-244.

299 Bartram, D. J. (1980). Comprehending spatial information: The relative efficiency of different methods of presenting information about bus routes. *Journal of Applied Psychology, 65,* 103-110.

300 Garland, H. C., Haynes, J. J., & Grubb, G. C. (1979). Transit map color coding and street detail: Effects on trip planning performance. *Environment and Behavior, 11,* 162-184.

301 Bronzaft, A. L., Dobrow, S. B., & O'Hanlon, T. J. (1976). Spatial orientation in a subway. *Environment and Behavior, 8,* 575-594.

302 Wright, P., Hull, A. J., & Lickorish, A. (1993). Navigation in a hospital outpatients' department: The merits of maps and wall signs. *Journal of Architectural and Planning Research, 10,* 76-89.

303 Moore, G. T. (1979). Knowing about environmental knowing: The current state of theory and research on environmental cognition. *Environment and Behavior, 11,* 33-70.

304 Pick, H. L. (1976). Transactionalconstructivist approach to environmental knowing: A commentary. In G. T. Moore & R. G. Golledge (Eds.), *Environmental knowing: Theories, research, and methods.* Stroudsburg, PA: Dowden Hutchinson and Ross.

305 Pick, H. L. (1976). Transactionalconstructivist approach to environmental knowing: A commentary. In G. T. Moore & R. G. Golledge (Eds.), *Environmental knowing: Theories, research, and methods.* Stroudsburg, PA: Dowden Hutchinson and Ross.

306 Golledge, R. G., Smith, T. R., Pellegrino, J. W., Doherty, S., & Marshall, S. P. (1985). A conceptual model and empirical analysis of children's acquisition of spatial knowledge. *Journal of Environmental Psychology, 5,* 125-152.

307 Leiser, D., & Zilbershatz, A. (1989). The traveller: A computational model of spatial network learning. *Environment and Behavior, 21,* 435-463.

308 Couclelis, H., Golledge, R. G., Gale, N., & Tobler, W. (1987). Exploring the anchor-point hypothesis of spatial cognition. *Journal of Environmental Psychology, 7,* 99-122.

309 Sadalla, E. K. (1988). Landmarks in memory. Conference on Landmarks in Spatial Cognition and Spatial Development. *British Journal Of Developmental Psychology, 6,* 386-388.

310 Presson, C. C., & Montello, D. R. (1988). Points of reference in spatial cognition: Stalking the elusive landmark. *British Journal of Developmental Psychology, 6,* 378-381.

311 Couclelis, H., Golledge, R. G., Gale, N., & Tobler, W. (1987). Exploring the anchor-point hypothesis of spatial cognition. *Journal of Environmental Psychology, 7,* 99-122.

312 Aginsky, V., Harris, C., Rensink, R., & Beusmans, J. (1997). Two strategies for learning a route in a driving simulator. *Journal of Environmental Psychology, 17,* 317-331.

313 Gotts, N. M. (1989). Unplanned wayfinding in path- networks: A theoretical study of human problem solving. *Dissertation Abstracts International, 50*(4-B), 1670.

314 Mutter, L. R., & Westphal, J. M. (1986). Perspectives on neighborhoods as park-planning units. *Journal of Architectural and Planning Research, 3,* 149-160.

315 Cornell, E. H., & Heth, C. D. (1984). Report of a missing child. In S. H. White (Chair), *Human development in the real world.* Symposium at the

annual meetings of the American Psychological Association, Toronto.

316 Taylor, B., & Taylor, A. (1993). Wayfinding training for the severely mentally ill. *Families in Society, 74*, 434-440.

317 Saisa, J., & Garling, T. (1987). Sequential spatial choices in the large-scale environment. *Environment and Behavior, 19*, 614-635.

318 Halperin, W. C. (1986). Spatial cognition and consumer behavior: A panel data approach. *Dissertation Abstracts International, 46*(11-A), 34-58.

319 Bailenson, J. N., Shum, M. S., & Uttal, D. H. (1998). Road climbing: Principles governing symmetric route choices in maps. *Journal of Environmental Psychology, 18*, 251-264.

320 Kitchin, R. M. (1997). Exploring spatial thought. *Environment and Behavior, 29*, 123-156.

321 Garling, T., Book, A., & Lindberg, E. (1984). Cognitive mapping of largescale environments: The interrelationship of action plans, acquisition, and orientation. *Environment and Behavior, 16*, 334.

322 Russell, J. A., & Ward, L. M. (1982). Environmental psychology. *Annual Review of Psychology, 33*, 651-688.

323 Gauvain, M. (1993). The development of spatial thinking in everyday activity. *Developmental Review, 13*, 92-121.

324 Ward, L. M., Snodgrass, J., Chew, B.,& Russell, J. A. (1988). The role of plans in cognitive and affective responses to places. *Journal of Environmental Psychology, 8*, 1-8.

325 Gauvain, M. (1993). The development of spatial thinking in everyday activity. *Developmental Review, 13*, 92-121.

326 Passini, R. (1984). Spatial representations: A wayfinding perspective. *Journal of Environmental Psychology, 4*, 153-164.

327 Cornell, E. H., Heth, C. D., & Skoczylas, M. J. (1999). The nature and use of route expectancies following incidental learning. *Journal of Environmental Psychology, 19*, 209-229.

328 Brantingham P. L., & Brantingham, P. J. (1993). Nodes, paths and edges: Considerations on the complexity of crime and the physical environment. *Journal of Environmental Psychology, 13*, 3-28.

329 Pyle, G. F. (1980). Systematic sociospatial variation in perceptions of crime location and severity. In D. E. GeorgesAbeyie & K. D. Harries (Eds.), *Crime: A spatial perspective*. New York: Columbia University Press.

330 Canter, D., & Larkin, P. (1993). The environmental range of serial rapists. *Journal of Environmental Psychology, 13*, 63-70.

331 O'Keefe, J., & Nadel, L. (1974). Maps in the brain. *New Scientist*, 749-751.

332 O'Keefe, J., & Nadel, L. (1978). *The hippocampus as a cognitive map*. Oxford: Clarendon Press.

333 Tolman, E. C. (1932). *Purposive behavior in animals and men*. New York: Century.

334 Tolman, E. C. (1948). Cognitive maps in rats and men. *Psychological Review, 55*, 189-208.

335 Anooshian, L. J. (1996). Diversity within spatial cognition: Strategies underlying spatial knowledge. *Environment and Behavior, 28*, 471-493.

336 Beatty, W. W., & Bernstein, N. (1989). Geographical knowledge in patients with Alzheimer's disease. *Journal of Geriatric Psychiatry and Neurology, 2*, 76-82.

337 De Renzi, E. (1982). Memory disorders following focal neocortical damage. *Philosophical Transactions of the Royal Society of London, 298*, 73-83.

338 Committeri, G., Galati, G., Paradis, A-L., Pizzamiglio, L., Berthoz, A., & LeBihan, D. (2004). Reference frames for spatial cognition: Different brain areas are involved in viewer-, object-, and landmark-centered judgments about object location. *Journal of Cognitive Neuroscience, 16*, 1517-1535.

339 Kritchevshy, M. (1988). The elementary spatial functions of the brain. In J. Stiles-Davis, M. Kritchevsky, & U. Bellugi (Eds.), *Spatial cognition: Brain bases and development*. Hillsdale, NJ: Erlbaum.

340 Neisser, U. (1976). *Cognition and reality*. San Francisco: Freeman.

341 Kosslyn, S. M. (1975). Information representation in visual images. *Cognitive Psychology, 7*, 341-370.

342 Evans, G. W. (1980). Environmental cognition. *Psychological Bulletin, 88*, 259-267.

343 Lieblich, I., & Arbib, M. A. (1982). Multiple representations of space underlying behavior. *The Behavioral and Brain Sciences, 5*, 627-659.

344 Levine, M. (1982). You-are-here maps: Psychological considerations. *Environment and Behavior, 14*, 221-237.

345 Levine, M., Marchon, I., & Hanley, G. (1984). The placement and misplacement of you-are-here maps. *Environment and Behavior, 16*, 139-157.

346 Warren, D. H., Rossano, M. J., & Wear, T. D. (1990). Perception of map-environment correspondence: The roles of features and alignment. *Ecological Psychology, 2*, 131-150.

347 Warren, D. H. & Scott, T. E. (1993). Map alignment in travelling multisegment routes. *Environment and Behavior, 25*, 643-666.

348 Butler, D. L., Acquino, A. L., Hissong, A. A., & Scott, P. A. (1993). Wayfinding by newcomers in a complex building. *Human Factors, 35*, 159-173.

349 Evans, G. W., Fellows, J., Zorn, M., & Doty, K. (1980). Cognitive mapping and architecture. *Journal of Applied Psychology, 65*, 474-478.

350 Carpman, J. R., Grant, M. A., & Simmons, D. A. (198384). Wayfinding in the hospital environment: The impact of various floor numbering alternatives. *Journal of Environmental Systems, 13*, 353-364.

351 Passini, R., Pigot, H., Rainville, C., & Tetreault, M. H. (2000). Wayfinding in a nursing home for advanced dementia of the Alzheimer's type. *Environment and Behavior, 32*, 684-710.

CHAPTER 3:

Environmental Appraisals, Assessments, and Concern

[Beauty] exists merely in the mind which contemplates [things]; and each mind perceives a different beauty. One person may even perceive deformity, where another is sensible of beauty; and every individual ought to acquiesce in his own sentiment, without pretending to regulate those of others.

—DAVID HUME (1757)[1]

TOM AND JANE WERE SITTING IN THE COFFEE SHOP *talking to friends about their camping trip. Someone asked what the park was like.*

"It's incredible," Jane quickly answered. Then she realized that statement was not very informative, so she tried to describe the steep valleys, the granite mountains, and the alpine meadow with its tiny shimmering lakes. Tom broke in to relate how beautiful the deep forest was to him, but Jane looked at him with a puzzled expression.

"That place was creepy," she said, "I felt awful—almost trapped—and there was no sunlight." Now it was Tom's turn to look puzzled. They did not know each other all that well yet.

"I grew up near heavy timber like that," he said, "and we used to spend hours playing in it. It is like being enclosed, but not like being trapped—unless you feel trapped in your own natural world," he joked.

A friend asked if they knew about the new mine planned for the park. "Whaaat?" Tom and Jane exclaimed in unison. "Don't you read the papers?" the friend asked. "Gouge Mines figures there's enough zinc in there to make a pit profitable, as long as they don't have to do too much reclamation of the land. They've offered to build a smelter near there, too, and the locals are already looking forward to jobs."

Tom and Jane looked at each other. "That's unbelievable," they said in unison. "The government has commissioned some kind of study, though," continued the friend. "Something about assessing the impact of the mine and smelter on the scenic quality of the region. They do it by assembling a panel of observers who look at the park before development and simulations of what it would look like afterward."

"Where do I sign up?" asked Tom.

CONSIDER ANY PLACE YOU KNOW—PERHAPS YOUR FAVORITE VACATION SPOT, your bedroom, the building this class is in, or your friend's mountain cottage. Do you care about it? How would you go about describing it? Is it beautiful? Good quality? How does it make you feel? What, if anything, does it mean to you? Is it safe? To what extent, do you think, are your own thoughts and feelings about this place similar to those of your friends, a panel of experts or strangers who visit it? Do different individuals who enter a place experience "different" places?

This chapter continues the discussion, begun in Chapter Two, of the process by which we come to know and understand the everyday physical environment. The initial gathering of information from settings—environmental perception—is often followed by much cognitive and emotional interpretation of that information. The focus in this chapter is on two judgment processes, environmental appraisal and assessment, and on environmental attitudes, which include any attitude toward nature or architecture, although usually the focus is on ecological concern. However, concern for the built environment also deserves some attention. Many people are upset when heritage buildings are destroyed, others are unhappy with condominium towers, or worried about whether a building can withstand an earthquake.

The terms "environmental appraisal" and "environmental assessment" have been used differently by different authors,[2] but in this book the following definitions will be employed. **Environmental appraisals** are an individual's personal impressions of a setting. **Environmental assessments** are based on the pooled impressions of a place by several observers (usually experts or setting users). In studying environmental appraisals, the emphasis is on understanding the person; in studying environmental appraisals, the emphasis is on understanding the place. Many different kinds of appraisals have been studied; six are discussed in this chapter. Four approaches to environmental assessment will be discussed after that.

ENVIRONMENTAL APPRAISALS: PERSONAL IMPRESSIONS OF PLACES

HOW WOULD YOU DESCRIBE THE PLACE WHERE YOU ARE READING THIS? Do you like some places and dislike others? We develop feelings about places. Certain buildings have meaning for us. Some areas seem dangerous. In general, environmental appraisal refers to six kinds of personal impressions: descriptions, evaluations, judgments of beauty, emotional reactions, meanings, and risk.

The six kinds of impressions overlap to a certain extent. For example, if you consider a certain city to be beautiful, you are also likely to report that it gives you good feelings to be there and that it is a good and personally meaningful city. On the other hand, the different kinds of impressions do not *always* follow from one another. For example, a place may be significant to a person, but this meaning may derive from horrible experiences rather than pleasant ones.

TABLE 3–1: A Process Model for the Comprehension of Environmental Displays

Which Observer?	Which Environmental Display Method?	Which Appraisal?	Which Format?
User Groups:	*In Person:*	Description	Free (blank piece of paper)
e.g., Residents	e.g., Walking Through	Evaluation	Checklist
Employees	Driving By	Aesthetic	Scale
Students	Aerial View	Emotional	Viewing Time
Customers	Slides or Photos	Meaning	Beliefs about Human Consequences
	Video or Film	Risk	
Experts:	Models		
e.g., Facility Managers	Sketches or Drawings		
Architects	Audios (soundscapes)		
Real Estate Appraisers	No Presentation		
Special Groups:			
e.g., Elderly			
Introverts			
Poor			
Disabled			
Everyone			
i.e., All Observers			

Thus, different kinds of appraisals may overlap from time to time, but conceptually they are quite distinct.

A useful organizing framework for understanding environmental appraisals and assessments was provided by the pioneer environmental psychologist Kenneth Craik.[3] A slightly adapted version of it is presented in Table 3-1.

The complexity of the process is evident in the many possibilities implied by the Craik's framework. Different kinds of **observers** experience different **environmental displays** in different **presentation formats** and are asked to report their impressions in different **judgment formats**, the accuracy of which may be tested by different **validational criteria**.

Most studies select one or two items from each column of Craik's framework, although a few investigators have systematically compared items from each of several columns within a single study to understand how they interrelate to affect perception.[4] Both environmental appraisals and assessments can be studied within this framework, depending on which elements of it are selected for study and how the resulting data are analyzed. Broad or narrow judgments of either specific settings or the environment (as a global entity) may be studied.

A variety of personal and environmental characteristics—and interactions of them—combine to influence appraisals. Personal characteristics include an individual's stage of life, culture, personality, mood, and experience. The person's plans, goals, and intentions toward the setting are particularly important.[5,6] Environmental characteristics include complexity, naturalness, architectural style, contents, state of repair, and many other relatively objective features.

Descriptions: What Is There?

Environmental description has been left, for most of history, to poets and novelists. The centuries of practice have been fruitful. The most accurate and memorable descriptions of houses, mountains, trees, the sea, farms, towns, and prisons have come from the pens of the best novelists and poets. If the purpose is to produce a penetrating, unforgettable portrait of a place, commission a talented writer to do the job.

If, however, the purpose is to understand how everyday persons think about the settings in their daily lives, or planned settings, or settings new to them, a different strategy may be necessary. In Craik's framework, one suggested method of obtaining descriptions of the environment is to ask individuals to write free descriptions of them—simply give them blank pieces of paper and pens. This strategy can lead to some valuable insights (e.g., which features of the setting are written about first or at all; which themes naturally emerge from the writer's narrative). But there are difficulties, too. Some people are intimidated by a blank piece of paper; some features of the setting that are important to the writer may be inadvertently overlooked; descriptions obtained from different writers may be difficult to compare—if comparison is a goal of the study.

For these reasons, environmental psychologists have tried to develop comprehensive, standardized sets of environmental descriptors. The free-description technique allows the researcher to discover which dimensions observers select to describe a setting. However, when

KENNETH CRAIK provided an essential foundation for the study of environmental personality and environmental assessment.

the purpose of the study is to discover what people think about a setting, or to compare how they think about multiple settings, a standard set of descriptor used as a checklist offers comprehensiveness and, for many people, an easier way to express themselves.

How Many Dimensions? How many distinct dimensions, themes, or factors are needed to describe environments efficiently, but without omitting anything important? The answer, in part, is that different dimensions will emerge depending on which buildings or observers are studied and which individual items are included. Psychologists who study meaning in other areas of psychology[7] were successful in showing that only three dimensions (potency, activity, and evaluation) seemed to fully encompass meaning for many concepts and things, so some early environmental psychologists aimed to discover the fundamental dimensions of architectural meaning.[8-12] This work produced quite a variety of dimensions, some of which arose frequently and others that rarely arose. However, all agreed that simple three-factor systems like the potency, activity, and evaluation system are inadequate to characterize physical environments.

No widely accepted set of dimensions for describing all physical environments has emerged. However, a useful set of central and peripheral dimensions for describing building interiors was proposed by one research team[13] (see Table 3-2).

These dimensions include some that are rather broad in the sense that many features of the building interior contribute to them (e.g., beauty) and others are narrow in that they primarily reflect fewer features (e.g., temperature).

The Description of Cities. Other environmental psychologists have developed similar descriptor sets for cities. Beginning with open-ended questions to a representative sample of town residents, researchers gradually evolved a short but comprehensive list of qualities or dimensions that make up the image of an urban setting.[14] These dimensions are:

- Economic potential (space for commercial or industrial growth)
- Diversity of land use (a combination of recreational, public-service, industrial, commercial, and residential lands)
- Historic significance (historic landmarks, events, boundaries, etc.)
- Fond memories (positive personal memories for residents)
- Appearance of the built environment (age, style, and type of buildings)
- Natural features (water, hills, trees, etc.)
- Movement and location (traffic, walkways, centrality of arrangements, etc.)
- Importance as an activity center (dynamism of public involvement in ceremonies, shopping, sports, public events, etc.).

These dimensions may, of course, vary or be present or absent in any given town. They may vary in different parts of a city. Different dimensions may be more important to residents as a whole or to particular subsets of residents. In general, however, the framework serves as a way to describe urban settings in a relatively compact and efficient manner. These descriptions might be used to chart how the image of a given town changes over time, or to compare cities.

Evaluations and Preferences: Is It Good? Is it Better?

When asked for their impressions of a place, individuals very frequently include comments as to whether they like it or not. Evaluation includes appraisals such as liking, goodness, quality, preference, and monetary value. What influences these evaluative appraisals?

Personal Influences. Whether a personal evaluation is positive or negative depends in part on the person's background. The very same everyday buildings are judged differently based on social class, gender, age, mood, and educational level.[15,16] In one pioneering study, adults were asked to express their preferences among slides depicting scenes of Alaska and Delaware.[17] The observers' preferences were predictable from such influences as their age, gender, and culture. For example, females preferred more richly vegetated and warmer scenes and younger adults preferred the more exotic scenes. Indoors, research suggests that women are more sensitive than men to sensory aspects of the environment, such as lighting, brightness, sounds, and smells. [18,19] Other research shows that older children (16-year olds) prefer more exotic or riskier landscapes than younger children (11-year-olds).[20] Thus, in general, wilder landscapes appear to be preferred more by young adults than by children or older adults. The natives of Delaware and Alaska both preferred scenes of their native land.

Other studies support the idea that familiar landscapes are preferred,[21,22] but this familiarity effect does not always hold. Scots and Australians shown housing scenes from Scotland and Australia preferred scenes from the other country,[23] Japanese and American students preferred street scenes from the other country over street scenes from their own country,[24,25] and Koreans preferred Western landscapes to their own, whereas Westerners preferred Korean landscapes.[26]

Culture and training also matter. For example, Japanese rated certain images of the sea, the mountain, and the river as less pleasant than did Germans, Swedes, and residents of the United States.[27] When various possible nursing home designs were evaluated, nursing home administrators and designers favored designs that promoted social interaction (apparently because they believe that social interaction is desired or needed by nursing home residents). However, the residents themselves consistently favored designs that enhanced their privacy.[28] Preferences among

10 possible housing designs expressed by a special neighborhood design review board showed little correlation with the preferences of the same designs expressed by residents of the neighborhood.[29] Preferences for having controversial facilities such as prisons and landfills differ between planners and everyday residents.[30]

Research shows that architects prefer more unusual house forms while non-architects prefer more typical house forms.[31] Despite (or, perhaps, *because of*) their training, architects have different preferences than non-architects. During their education, architects are socialized by their school and their profession to prefer certain architectural styles.[32] Perhaps as a consequence, architects also do not seem to understand what the public likes. I and others have found that even when they are specifically asked to predict what non-architects will find desirable, architects often are unable to do so.[33,34] This may occur because architects and non-architects apply different interpretational schemes to the judgment of buildings, and architects think more in terms of design issues than "like—dislike" when considering a building.[35]

Preference ratings can differ merely because people happen to make their ratings while thinking about their role in the building (such as judging a house plan as a wife versus judging it without one's wife role in mind).[36] One's personality,[37] stage of development,[38] occupational status,[39] environmental sensitivity,[40] and mental health[41] also influence environmental preferences. Mechanically oriented and older observers like well-lit buildings, and pro-development observers prefer big, new urban buildings.[42,43] In general, individual differences very much influence setting preferences, although some research indicates that the main influences on preference, as you might assume, are physical features of the setting, such as architectural style or elements of the scene.[44-46]

Physical Influences. Features of the setting itself also affect our liking of and preference for places, of course. Among

TABLE 3–2: Semantic Scales to Measure the Meaning of Designed Environments

Factors or Concepts	Primary Scale	and	Alternate Scale
1. General Evaluative	good-bad		pleasing-annoying
2. Utility Evaluative	useful-useless		friendly-hostile
3. Aesthetic Evaluative	unique-common		interesting-boring
4. Activity	active-passive		complex-simple
5. Space	cozy-roomy		private-public
6. Potency	rugged-delicate		rough-smooth
7. Tidiness	clean-dirty		tidy-messy
8. Organization	ordered-chaotic		formal-casual
9. Temperature	warm-cool		hot-cold
10. Lighting	light-dark		bright-dull

Note: Secondary Scales might include old–new, expensive–inexpensive, large–small, exciting–calming, clear–ambiguous, colorful–subdued, safe–dangerous, quiet–noisy, stuffy–drafty.

outdoor settings, would anyone prefer a scene showing an outlet pipe discharging reddish-orange chemicals into a river already full of discarded tires and dubious floating objects over a scene depicting a sunny meadow with wild flowers? But among less dramatically attractive or unattractive scenes, the physical elements associated with visual preference are not obvious; research is necessary to identify cues that lead viewers to prefer one scene over another.[47] For example, my own laboratory has recently concentrated on understanding *why* architects' preferences differ from those of others, by learning which specific features of buildings influence the preferences of the two groups.[48,49]

This approach has also been used to study the preferences of non-architects. For example, on average, rooms with windows are more appealing than rooms without windows,[50] square rooms are preferred over rectangular ones,[51] higher-than-usual ceilings are preferred,[52] and warmer colors are more attractive than others.[53] However, preference is not as simple as a list of features; the context must also be taken into account. For example, window preferences are affected by the size of the room they are in; specifically, we seem to prefer proportionally larger windows in smaller rooms.[54]

Studies of building facades suggest that people generally prefer exteriors that express a sense of the past, have detailed, curved, decorated, grooved, or three-dimensional surfaces that seem to provide shelter and invite touching and exploration.[55] Houses with vegetation on them were significantly more preferred and beautiful, especially those with ivy-covered facades and meadow roofs.[56] When pictures of natural landscapes with cartoon characters were added to a pediatric hospital ward, the children's parents judged it as significantly improved.[57]

Older buildings are generally preferred, as long as they have been well-maintained,[58] and more traditional rural settings are preferred over modern ones.[59] Certain architectural styles are preferred over others,[60] although such stylistic preferences probably will change over time as fashions change. Most people prefer ornate, clean, open, and single-purpose (e.g., residential-use only) buildings.[61]

Preferred city districts tend to have some or all of five features: naturalness, good upkeep, an ordered appearance, openness, and historical significance.[62] The most preferred shopping centers are well-maintained, have attractive window displays, more street activities, and more greenery.[63] A related study disagreed in one respect—it found that more *enclosed* urban spaces were more pleasant, but confirmed the value of other features and added two more: preferred urban scenes have fewer cars and more noise (from human sources, not mechanical noise).[64] People dislike streets with obtrusive signs.[65] As you might expect, streets with more trees and other vegetation are preferred.[66] Similar features are preferred in urban shoreline scenes.[67] Other environmental features that are related to evaluations are more abstract. One early system proposed the following elements (among others), which clearly are more conceptual than those just mentioned: pleasantness, complexity, unity, potency, enclosedness, and originality.[68]

In a classic study, the physical quality of environments was even shown to affect appraisals of other people.[69] Perceivers were placed in messy, closet-like rooms (but the room's qualities were not pointed out to them) and asked to rate the well-being of people in photos. Those placed in messy rooms perceived the people in the photos to be lower in well-being than those who perceived the same photos in tidy rooms. A later study found that this effect depends on the perceiver's expectations of the room's aesthetic qualities. If the perceiver *expects* the room to be beautiful or ugly, the results found in the original study can even be reversed.[70] So, once more, the environment affects appraisals, but personal factors such as the perceiver's expectations can also play a crucial role.

You will recall that Berlyne's collative properties, which were introduced in Chapter 2, are based on physical features of scenes. Among the collative properties are congruity and contrast. In one study, observers were shown simulated landscapes into which various built structures had been placed through the wonders of model-building and photography.[71] Landscape scenes containing buildings judged (by previous observers) to be strongly incongruous with, and in contrast to, the landscape were strongly disliked. This may not be surprising. But do observers like buildings that are very much in context and very low on contrast, or would they prefer buildings with a moderate degree of these qualities? Some preferred the latter over the dullness of buildings that blend in almost too well; other groups showed no preference. Thus, individual differences among observers seem to play a role in the preference of scenes that are low-to-medium in contrast and congruity, but few people prefer strongly contrasting, incongruous developments in landscapes (see Figure 3-1).

Three other collative properties are complexity (i.e., much detail and many design elements), coherence (the degree to which a scene appears ordered or "hangs together"), and novelty (the unusualness of a place's appearance). A study of urban signs found that the most pleasant streets had signs of moderate complexity and high coherence.[72] More complex high-rises are preferred over plainer ones.[73] Residences with more complex facades

FIGURE 3-1 Does the newer building in this scene fit into the landscape or does it make the scene less coherent?

are preferred.[74] Architecturally designed houses tend to be more novel and coherent than non-architect-designed houses, and both architects and non-architects seem to prefer novel but coherent designs.[75, 76] In a different study, only architects preferred novel or atypical houses; non-architects preferred more typical designs.[77] Ferry passengers in British Columbia preferred natural shorelines with small built structures on them over undeveloped shorelines.[78] In general, these results seem to support the notion that moderate complexity, development, or contrast is preferred to very low levels of these qualities. Most people prefer woodlawn (forests with underbrush removed or treed grassy areas) over fields with taller, browner weedy-looking plants, cultivated fields, or scrub land.[79] In general, we seem to prefer tranquil nature scenes.[80,81]

Jack Nasar, who has spent a career in this area, proposes three kinds of important environmental design qualities: formal, symbolic, and schemas.[82] **Formal** qualities include the design's complexity and order. **Symbolic** quality is expressed in the style (e.g., colonial or postmodern). **Schemas** refer to the typicality of the design—is it usual or unusual? Different kinds of evaluation, Nasar has hypothesized, will be based on different qualities. For example, a *pleasant* building (to most eyes) will show orderliness, moderate complexity, and elements of familiar styles. An *exciting* building will be atypical, complex, and low in orderliness. The **typicality** of a scene refers to the degree to which it resembles our mental image of a place of that type. More typicality appears to generate greater preference, at least for desirable places, like pastoral scenes.[83] For undesirable places, such as alleys, greater typicality (the more it looks like a typical alley), generates *less* preference.[84]

Another environment-based approach to scene preference is **prospect-refuge theory**.[85] It proposes, based on evolutionary ideas, that people prefer environments at the edges between open areas (e.g., fields, savannah) and closed areas (e.g., forest or jungle). The open areas provide prospect, the opportunity to see game or danger at some distance, and the closed area provides refuge, the opportunity to hide. Compared to other species, humans are not the strongest or fastest, but we need to eat and to survive. Thus, prospect-refuge theory proposes that we like edge settings so we can "hit and run." In a study that asked recreationists to rate scenes varying in prospect and refuge, the most preferred scenes were those that suggested the viewer was close to a clearly defined refuge but had easy access to an open grassy meadow, thus supporting the theory.[86] Walkways with higher levels of prospect and refuge are more preferred than walks with lower levels of prospect-refuge.[87]

However, the main point of this section is that preference may be explained either in terms of concrete measures such as the number of windows or trees, or in more abstract terms such as coherence, congruity, prospect, and refuge. Clearly, however, preferences are best explained by knowing something about the observer *and* something about the setting.[88] Thus, to fully understand preference, we need to investigate both **consensus** (when virtually everyone agrees on preference) and **contrast** (when some people prefer an environment but others do not).[89] Sometimes, both consensus and contrast occur: this might happen when most people agree about which landscapes are *beautiful*, but cultural differences may cause the same people to vary in their *preferences* for those landscapes.[90]

Finally, natural landscapes may be preferred because they contain **fractals**, that is, elements that, although not of perfect geometric form, are repeated in similar shapes but in different sizes in a scene.[91] Built and natural environments often have fractal characteristics that may include clouds, mountain ranges, and city skylines.

Perceiver-Environment Approaches to Preference. Another perspective on environmental preference essentially fuses person and environment by employing concepts that imply both. In their approach, which draws on cognitive and evolutionary ideas, Stephen and Rachel Kaplan have developed an integrative conceptualization of environmental preference.[92,93] They and others[94] believe that human preference for settings originates in our evolutionary past and in the adaptive value offered by particular settings. For example, children seem to prefer savannah to other landscape types.[95] Because humans originated in the African savannah, the authors suggest that the children's preference for this landscape may indicate an evolutionary basis for landscape preference. However, a simpler explanation may be that people are more familiar with local savannah-like landscapes, and prefer what is familiar.[96]

Because of the vast experience of humans (as a species) with natural landscapes, the Kaplans believe we are able to form preferences after very brief exposure to a new scene. They extend Gibson's idea that environments provide affordances—direct knowledge about the possibilities for orientation, safety, locomotion, and new information. Their idea is that we prefer sites that allow us to accomplish

JACK NASAR is a leading researcher in environmental aesthetics.

STEPHEN KAPLAN has contributed much to the understanding of environmental cognition, particularly of nature scenes, and the understanding of nature as a restorative agent.

central human goals such as being safe and finding food or shelter. Other environmental psychologists agree that we tend to base our preferences on what is important to us or the consequences of our choices.[97,98,99] The Kaplans call the functional qualities of environments that help us meet important goals **cognitive affordances**.

In addition to these basic needs, the Kaplans postulate that humans have a strong desire to make sense of the environment and to be involved with it. One outcome of the need to make sense of places is our construction and use of cognitive maps, as discussed in the last chapter. In general, the Kaplans believe that people prefer landscapes and interior settings that "offer promise of being involving and making sense."[100] Environments may offer this promise either immediately or for the future. When involvement and making sense are combined with immediate or future promise, a 2 x 2 matrix results, yielding four elements of preference. (See Table 3-3).

In the Kaplans' preference framework, **coherence** (making sense immediately) refers to the ease with which a scene can be cognitively organized. **Complexity** (being involved immediately) refers to the scene's capacity to keep an individual busy (occupied without becoming bored or overstimulated). **Legibility** (the promise of making sense in the future) means that the environment appears to be one that could be explored without getting lost; it is arranged in a clear manner. **Mystery** (the promise of future involvement) means that the environment suggests one could learn more, interact more, or be further occupied—if one entered it. These elements are the essence of the manner in which the Kaplans have integrated person and environment considerations in

conceptualizing preference. Consider coherence. Cognitive organization is a human activity, yet some scenes are easier to organize than others. Coherence, therefore, is not *in* our heads or *in* the environment; it is in the way we appraise environments.

For the Kaplans, preference should be predictable from coherence, legibility, complexity, and mystery, but not necessarily in simple ways. Generally, preference should increase as each of these qualities increases, but there are limits. Too much legibility in a setting might necessarily reduce mystery; the setting would be clear but it would lack interest and ultimately be boring. The Kaplans also stress the role of familiarity in preference. When a place is new, strange, or possibly dangerous to us, we prefer more familiar places. For example, studies of woodlands scenes show that more familiar scenes are preferred over less familiar scenes.[101] However, familiarity and making-sense can work in opposite directions. Once we know a place so well that it is very familiar, there may be little new making-sense to be done, and preference for the place may decline. We like to make sense of places, as long as the task is not overwhelming, dangerous, or complete.

Evidence on how cognitive affordances relate to preference has been mounting quickly. For example, scenes with more mystery are often preferred more.[102-112] However, this seems more true for nature scenes (and perhaps individual buildings) than for others (e.g., urban street scenes). Perhaps mysterious scenes are preferable as long as they are not thought to be dangerous, as urban street scenes often are. More complexity also seems to be associated with greater preference, at least in zoos,[113] urban scenes,[114] and rural scenes.[115] More coherence also is generally associated with greater preference.[116-119] The four main cognitive affordances may not be entirely independent of each other; coherent scenes are often perceived as legible scenes, for example. Researchers have begun to try to disentangle these seemingly similar concepts.[120]

One way to obtain a broadly based answer to questions like this is to conduct a **meta-analysis**, a method of statistically combining the results of many studies on one research question in order to reach a more general conclusion. One meta-analysis considered 28 published articles that included a total of 6288 participants and 1820 scenes; it concluded that the relations between the four key cognitive affordances and preferences were far from consistent.[121] Based on the research conducted so far, a likely conclusion is that mystery, complexity, coherence, and legibility are

TABLE 3-3: The Kaplans' Preference Framework.

Availability of Information	Needs	
	Making Sense	Involvement
Present or Immediate	Coherence	Complexity
Future or Promised	Legibility	Mystery

Note: Preference for a scene is believed to be a function of the need to make sense of the scene and the need to be involved in the scene. Information may be immediately available to the observer or promised "around the corner." *Coherent* scenes allow the observer to immediately structure or organize the scene's elements. *Complex* scenes offer much information to keep the observer occupied. *Legible* scenes give the impression to observers that they will not get lost or disoriented. *Mysterious* scenes suggest to observers that they will learn more if they venture into the scene.

differently related to preference in different kinds of environments, rather than having the same relation to preference in all environments. As usual in environmental psychology, the truth is not simple.

Aesthetics: Is It Beautiful?

The third kind of appraisal is of beauty. The working assumption here is that beauty is in the eye of the beholder. For example, not surprisingly, how well maintained a house is affects aesthetic judgments of it.[122] However, if beauty were entirely a property of the environment, then everyone would agree on the beauty or ugliness of every scene. But, obviously, some people think deserts are beautiful, and others do not; some think rocky peaks, chaotic markets, undersea vistas, or skyscrapers are beautiful, but others do not. An Australian study found, for example, that although beauty, averaged across observers, was greatest for natural, green, open grasslands with some water and pathways, each individual observer favored scenes with different combinations of these qualities.[123] A study of rural scenes found that beauty was positively related to scenic complexity, coherence, mystery, and biodiversity, but viewer perceptions of those characteristics themselves were very variable.[124]

Culture and experience are obvious person-based factors related to differences in appraisals of beauty. For example, when the appraisals by tourists and local Balinese of the beauty of Balinese villages, the two groups did agree in most ways, but differences were also found, which the researchers attributed to the tourists' misunderstanding of the meaning of certain landscape features.[125] Another study suggests that the beauty of water scenes changes with the growth of a person's environmental experience. The more one realizes that aquatic plant growth is an outcome of water pollution, rather than a natural phenomenon, the uglier the water scene appears.[126]

Therefore, many appraisals of scenic beauty will vary with culture, and experience, and perhaps evolutionary factors.[127] To a certain extent, beauty clearly is in the eye of the beholder. The real question is to what *degree* this

is true, because those who favor the idea that beauty is mostly determined by features of the scene have strong evidence to present, too. Some scenes are appraised as beautiful by virtually everyone. Although many examples would support this thesis, one less-obvious scene quality is visual penetration—the visual depth of a scene. In a study of the natural beauty of Texas pine and oak forests, greater visual penetration was the best predictor of scenic beauty.[128] Therefore, both viewer and scene must be considered if we are to construct a complete account of environmental aesthetics.

Emotions: How Does It Make You Feel?

BEYOND DESCRIPTION, EVALUATION, AND BEAUTY, a fourth kind of appraisal is how a place makes you feel, that is, affective appraisal.

Is Affect the Same as Evaluation and Aesthetics? Presumably, environments that we appraise as good, preferable, and beautiful will also make us feel pleasant. To some extent then, appraisals of quality, beauty, and pleasant feelings overlap. However, there are valid reasons *not* to conclude that these kinds of appraisal are redundant. First, pleasantness is only one emotion we experience; other emotions may not neatly correspond to evaluation or beauty judgments. Second, emotion (affect) is conceptually distinct from evaluation and beauty. The physiological, behavioral, and cognitive aspects of emotion are quite different from those involved in coldly judging goodness or beauty. Emotion has been described as "a complex state of the human organism, involving not only feelings such as sadness, awe, fear, rage, surprise, joy, but also bodily changes of various kinds, as well as impulses towards all forms of behavior."[129] Third, emotions imply time and ethics.[130] For example, fear is prospective; it ordinarily refers to the future, whereas sadness is retrospective; it usually refers to the past. In

FIGURE 3-2: Two major dimensions of emotion and their hybrids form a circumplex, or circular ordering. Consider your emotions evoked by the setting you are in right now. Where would they fit on the circumplex?

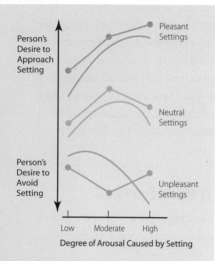

FIGURE 3-3: The pleasure–arousal hypothesis. The desire to approach a setting varies with the setting's pleasure and arousal–eliciting qualities. According to the hypothesis, people prefer to be in places that are very pleasurable and moderately arousing.

terms of ethics, anger is caused by perceived wrong-doing, usually by someone else, and guilt is caused by perceived wrong-doing by oneself. In sum, emotional appraisals are not redundant with evaluative or aesthetic appraisals.

A Model of Emotional Response to Settings.
Before we directly discuss emotional appraisals, the work of two leading investigators of emotion in environmental psychology—James Russell and Albert Mehrabian—should be introduced. They view emotion as a mediator between the environment and personality (as pre-existing influences), and behavior (as the outcome).[131,132] Originally, their research identified three primary emotional responses: pleasure, arousal, and dominance. Later, Russell's research led him to conclude that dominance is a poor third as a primary emotion, and he has concentrated on a model that includes only pleasure and arousal as primary emotions.[133]

The remaining emotions, pleasure and arousal, are viewed as being independent from one other; that is, we may experience any combination of them. The model is a **circumplex**—a circular pattern of emotions which forms an infinite number of combinations of pleasure and arousal based on its two main dimensions (see Figure 3-2). Any combination of these emotions may be elicited by a setting. In this framework, both environmental variables (e.g., light, temperature, or the incoming speed of information) and

personality variables (e.g., sociability or arousal-seeking tendency) are believed to influence the level of emotion experienced in a given setting. These emotions, in turn, influence such key behaviors as the desire to approach or avoid a setting, an employee's work performance, or interpersonal interaction in the setting.

The framework was tested in a series of studies in which verbal descriptions of settings were presented to research participants whose personality tendencies were known and who were asked to report how they would act in the setting.[134] The results can be complex, but one relatively simple example is representative. The curves in Figure 3-3 show Mehrabian and Russell's **pleasure-arousal hypothesis:** That individuals want to approach physical settings which are, apart from their other characteristics, *moderately* arousing and *maximally* pleasurable. Note also that as the pleasantness of a setting increases, the maximum desire to approach it is predicted to occur at higher levels of arousal. The solid lines in Figure 3-3 depict the actual experimental findings.

As predicted, more pleasant settings were viewed as more approachable settings. For settings that were not particularly pleasant or unpleasant, the pleasure-arousal hypothesis was supported. Moderately arousing settings were more desirable than were low or high-arousal settings. However, for pleasant settings, approachability did not decline for highly arousing settings, as the researchers predicted; instead, it increased. For unpleasant settings, moderately arousing settings were the *least* desirable to approach, rather than the most desirable. City skylines seen at night are perceived as more pleasurable and exciting than the same skylines seen during the day.[135] The results of this and other studies show that the emotional impact of the physical environment is indeed systematically related to behavior in them.

Mehrabian and Russell's research program often uses verbal descriptions of all the variables—personality, environment, emotions, and behaviors. This reliance on the self-report method stimulated some critics to charge that the theory merely captures semantic associations among the variables, rather than the emotional impact of real behavior in real settings.[136] However, Russell and his coworkers have defended their finding of a general structure for emotional qualities of settings by showing that the same dimensions emerge from a variety of rating methods,[137] and other research supports the pleasure-arousal hypothesis.[138] In forest scenes, more pleasure and less arousal are experienced when the scene depicts greater accessibility (e.g., an open path).[139] Curvilinear designs for interiors evoke more pleasurable and less arousing (that is, more relaxed and peaceful) reactions than rectilinear interiors, and people expressed greater desire to approach the curvilinear interiors.[140]

In an intriguing study conducted in France, young women in a shopping mall responded more often to an attractive man's request for their phone number when they were in a pleasant-smelling area of the mall.[141] This suggests that even implicit or background pleasantness produces approach behavior.

Meaning: What Is Its Significance?

A FIFTH KIND OF APPRAISAL concerns an environment's meaning. Sometimes the word *meaning* is loosely used to characterize research on environmental perception, description, evaluation, or emotion, but in this chapter the word will refer to four quite distinct processes:

1. *Place attachment*: the profound experience of bonding with a place,

2. *Ideological communication*: the way a building signifies some philosophical, architectural, political concept to those who view it,

3. *Personal communication*: what a building or room "says" to observers about its occupants , and

4. *Purpose*: appraisals of the place's function in relation to its form or appearance.

Place Attachment. Places can acquire great personal meaning. Most appraisals occur after brief exposure to a place, but place attachment usually occurs after long experience. It refers to the richness of meaning that develops with great familiarity.[142,143] Place attachment is important enough that a later chapter will be devoted to it.

Ideological Communication. The second meaning of meaning refers to the abstract concepts that a setting signifies or, despite its designer's intentions, fails to signify.[144] For example, buildings constructed by Hitler's government still communicate the Nazi image intended by their architects.[145] Buildings can reflect the ideals and aspirations of those who construct them, and indeed this is often a goal of the architect. For example, **International Modernism** was an important architectural movement whose proponents believed in purity of form. Modernists were weary of

the excessive ornamentation and detail that characterized older styles; to them, *modern* meant clean lines. Skyscrapers with absolutely regular lines and symmetric strips of windows are typical modernist structures. They thought the rest of us would also appreciate the simple, clear, rectangular lines of their building facades. They were wrong about that.

Charles Jencks, who was influential in developing a reformist architectural movement, thought he had a solution.[146] This movement, **postmodernism**, is based in part on the notion that two codes or sensibilities exist, one used by professional architects and one used by the rest of us. A *code*, in this sense of the word, is an understanding or implicit agreement that certain stylistic elements signify or imply (i.e., mean) certain philosophies or values. Jencks believed that modernist buildings were designed by and to a professional code that was accepted and appreciated among architects. To architects, modernist buildings meant *modern* (new, clean, clear). But the public interpreted the same buildings according to a different code; the same buildings meant *alienation* (cold, hard, forbidding) to them (see Figure 3-4). Postmodernism attempts to incorporate both the architect's code and the public's code, so that they have positive connotations in both codes. Postmodern buildings do not all look the same or mean the same, but some common stylistic threads among postmodern buildings include hints of traditional architectural forms, more curves, and building elements that appear almost out of place or jumbled.

FIGURE 3–4: These are examples of International Modern (*top*) and Postmodern buildings (*bottom*).

Postmodernist architects hope their buildings mean something positive in both the professional code (e.g., witty juxtaposition of historical styles and wise comments on aesthetic principles through the building's design) and in the public code (e.g., "Gee, that reminds me of my grandparents' farm house"). Because these intended meanings are positive, this should lead to greater popular as well as professional liking of postmodern buildings. These ideas were tested by showing examples of modern, transitional, and postmodern buildings to architects and non-architects.[147] The results supported Jencks' dual-coding notion—the idea that architects and non-architects employ different processes to pick up the meaning of buildings. Most architects are now aware of the existence of separate codes for themselves and non-architects, but often they have been unable to use that sensitivity to successfully convey their intended meanings to non-architects through their postmodern buildings.

Personal Communication. Like it or not, the buildings we live in or work in "say" something to others about us. Obvious conclusions are drawn about the wealth of persons who live in shacks versus those who live in mansions, for example. However, observers draw more subtle conclusions, too. For example, residents of higher-status neighborhoods are not only seen as wealthier, but they are also viewed as having more favorable traits.[148,149]

Architectural style also influences inferences about residents. In a study of people who lived in six house styles (Tudor, Farm, Saltbox, Colonial, Mediterranean, and Spanish), researchers found that residents of Farm-style houses as most friendly and Colonial-style houses as least friendly.[150] Those who live in Tudor and Colonial houses were seen as being leaders; residents of Saltbox and Mediterranean styles were not. The identical building, given different labels, will elicit different meanings. For example, an apartment that is said to be public housing provokes less favorable reactions than the same apartment that is said to be a private condominium.[151] Building materials also influence inferences about the occupants. In one study, observers were shown houses made of brick, concrete block, weathered wood, stucco, flagstone, and wooden shingles.[152] Residents of concrete block houses were seen as cold and non-artistic, and residents of wooden shingle houses were seen as warm and creative.

Purpose. The fourth kind of meaning involves the way building or landscape form and function are understood by everyday people. Much modern architecture is ambiguous; if passersby are not given clues (like a sign over the entrance), they may not be able to comprehend what the

purpose or function of the building is. One of the primary concerns of non-architects when looking at buildings is to discover the *purpose* of buildings they take the time to look at.[153] The reason for this concern, presumably, is that a crucial aspect of a building's meaning is bound up with the appropriateness of its form for its function. A famous dictum is that form should follow function, that is, the physical looks of the building should reflect its purpose. Unfortunately, this is often *not* the case.[154] We might like the looks of a certain restaurant, as a restaurant, but we would not like to *live* in the building. For example, a study in the Netherlands found that observers judged a building differently if it was said to be, for example, a city hall, a train station, or was presented with no functional label.[155]

Behavior that people believe occurs in a place is an important influence on the place's meaning. Researchers showed 20 places to observers and asked them:

- Why might one go here?
- What might be done here?
- What activities probably occur here? [156]

The results suggest that place meaning is intricately connected to one's planned activities. Some places are quite behavior-specific; only a few activities are feasible in them (such as a skate park). Others are much less behavior-specific; many activities might occur in them (such as a beach). Places that are less behavior-specific probably have broader meaning. Thus, if your plans are vague or include many possible variations, a behavior-specific place may have little value at the moment. But if you want to go skateboarding, even a beach with its many possible pleasant associations, might not be appreciated.

Turning this around, the purpose of a place can depend on what one wants from it. As one obvious example of this, one can see a forest as a timber supply, or as a place that offers wilderness recreation.[157]

Risk: Is It Safe?

SIXTH AND LAST—BUT CERTAINLY NOT LEAST—many people appraise the likelihood of danger in the places where they live, work, or visit every day. Perhaps some are fortunate enough to proceed through their days without giving much thought to their own safety (or that of their children or loved ones). Unfortunately, many others often feel compelled to judge how safe an environment is when they consider entering it. Risk appraisals include perceived danger from crime, from accidents, and from natural or technological hazards. As usual, risk appraisals vary with the person, environment, and person-environment combinations.

Person-based Influences. Risk perception may be a general disposition; research shows that some people perceive more risk than others across a range of potential threats. A measurement tool, the **Environmental Appraisal Inventory**, has been developed to assess this disposition.[158,159] Risk appraisals vary with several individual differences. For example, the risk from nuclear waste and nuclear energy is appraised as greater by life scientists than by physicists, chemists, and engineers.[160] Among residents, risk appraisal differs with ethnic background,[161,162] gender and educational level (women generally perceive more risk),[163-166] perceived control,[167] dispositional anxiety,[168,169] the distance one lives from the hazardous site,[170,171] and degree of environmental activism or concern.[172-174] Among nuclear power plant employees, those who know less appraise the risks as greater,[175] and experts' risk appraisals depend on the kind of institution in which they work.[176] People who think about nature in different ways (for example, nature as a benign force versus nature as capricious or perverse) evaluate risks differently.[177] Another very important person-based difference is that between experts and laypersons.[178] Many sociopolitical clashes occur because appraisals of safety and security differ for experts and non-experts.

Risk appraisals are multidimensional. One might consider as many as seven dimensions of them: the likelihood of the risk, how acceptable the risk is, how likely it is that exposure will lead to negative outcomes, the severity of the negative outcomes, how personally relevant the causes and consequences of the substance in question are, how much control one has over exposure to it, and how vividly the risk is presented.[179] This multidimensionality guarantees that relations among risk concepts will be complex.

Resident or non-expert opinions are often dismissed by experts. According to one viewpoint, resident reasoning comes in three flavors: ignorance or irrationality, selfishness, and prudence.[180] Put more positively, non-experts think in more social and personal terms about the threat of hazardous facilities. After all they, rather than the experts, are much more likely to live near the threat. Resident appraisals may be "amplified" through social networks, although studies show that these appraisals are often quite rational.[181] Expert views, in contrast, are formed through strong reliance on an objectivist, number-heavy, physical-characteristics approach to safety appraisal.[182] Experts and laypersons have different needs, goals, and methods of gathering information.[183] Laypersons' trust of public officials is low.[184]

Why lay and expert safety appraisals clash is not difficult to see. Now that these disagreements are well-established through many public clashes, each side has begun to anticipate the others' position—LULU (Locally Unwanted Land Use) syndrome is the experts' fear that residents will protest a development, and residents' dread of development is expressed by the well-known Not in My Backyard (NIMBY) syndrome.[185] Government agencies often claim they are committed to communicate information about risks to the public, but often do not live up to this commitment in practice.[186]

In order to get beyond these problems, we need more knowledge about how experts and non-experts think about these issues. The goal is to create a decision-making framework that somehow integrates the experts' obsession with technical detail and the layperson's emphasis on personal and social concerns. Experts must cease dismissing laypersons' appraisals as irrational and begin understanding what is behind their fears.[187] One research team has tackled this problem by comparing lay and expert views on the use of nuclear power in space, although their findings might apply to more down-to-earth problems.[188] An expert-like decision-making model was explicitly compared to a layperson's decision model in terms of the types of background knowledge and beliefs espoused, general beliefs, beliefs that are peripheral to the main issue, incorrect beliefs, and beliefs that are not part of the other side's model.

One intriguing proposal that follows from these ideas is that of a **science court**, a democratic institution before which both sides would debate an issue.[189] The final decision would be made by educated citizens who were informed by expert opinion. However, an alternate approach is to build more trust between experts and residents.[190] Trust may be increased by imposing strict government standards and by giving control over the operation of a facility to local residents.[191] Accurate information that is framed to take into account the personal and social concerns of residents probably helps. When citizens are involved in the risk planning process, they are more likely to accept risks.[192]

Physical Influences. Different environments will be appraised as risky or not by almost everyone: a dark alley at night versus a country lane during the day; a raging, flooded river versus a quiet brook. Among less-obvious comparisons, the average person believes that nuclear power is riskier than pesticides, and that climbing mountains is riskier than skiing.[193]

A study of Scottish children examined which cues children use to appraise the risk of crossing roads.[194] These appraisals are obviously crucial for the safety of children: An incorrect appraisal can be fatal. The study found that younger children (5 to 7 years old) tend to use the presence or absence of cars *in their view* as their criterion for road-crossing safety. That is, they often do not consider oncoming cars that might be obscured from their view by parked cars or shrubs. By age 11 or so, most children factor the possibility of hidden cars into their appraisals of road-crossing safety (see Figure 3-5).

Which environmental factors influence appraisals of safety in parking lots, such as those at shopping centers?[195] The appraised attractiveness and security of parking lots in Georgia increased as the amount of vegetation increased, but their appraised security was high only when the vegetation was well-maintained and appeared to be part of a landscape design. Uncontrolled vegetation seems to suggest an uncared-for jungle-like zone that might harbor violent people. Prospect-refuge theory, discussed earlier as a basis for environmental preference, sometimes can predict which settings people appraise as safe. When they were shown slides that varied in prospect and refuge, college students in one study appraised those higher in prospect and refuge as safer; they also judged scenes with more light

as safer.[196] Walkways with higher levels of prospect and refuge were appraised in another study as less dangerous than walkways with lower levels of prospect-refuge, but perhaps surprisingly, they were not seen as safer from social (human) dangers.[197] Thus, one reason we prefer scenes with prospect and refuge is that we often feel safer in them. Light helps us discern whether a place has prospect and refuge qualities.

Person-Environment Combinations. Risk perception also varies for particular *combinations* of individuals and environments. For example, citizens with greater attachment to a certain city or country tend to see local polluted sites as less polluted (and, therefore, less risky) than other residents who are less attached to their city or country.[198]

IN SUM *Environments may be appraised in six important ways. First, they may simply be described in a free manner; a good poet or novelist probably is best able to select and employ the best dimensions for describing any particular setting. Researchers, nevertheless, have tried to develop standard sets of descriptors to obtain the average person's description of places. One outcome of the many efforts to find such a set has been the finding that certain dimensions emerge repeatedly. Second, evaluative appraisals may take the form of stated preferences, ratings of quality, or rankings of goodness. Early research showed that such personal factors as age, gender, and familiarity with the place and objective features such as room design, congruity, contrast, and complexity play a role in evaluations. Newer approaches integrate person and place factors using concepts that involve person and environment. Preference is a complex outcome of these influences. Third, appraisals of beauty depend on how one weights the different visual elements in a scene, cultural meaning assigned to elements of the scene, the amount of one's environmental knowledge, and person-scene constructs such as visual penetration. Fourth, emotional appraisals are a complex mix of behavioral, cognitive, and physiological responses. Settings evoke combinations*

FIGURE 3-5: When 5-year-olds cross the street, they sometimes pay attention to cues that fail to protect them from oncoming traffic.

of pleasure, arousal, and perhaps feelings of dominance in us. These emotions are linked to behavior in the pleasure-arousal hypothesis, which states that we approach or like places that are more arousing when they are also pleasant. Fifth, environmental meaning includes four aspects: personal attachment or belonging, the building's communication of some architectural or philosophical concept, what a setting says about its occupants, and the communication of its purpose or function. Place attachment is an important process that involves some of the closest personenvironment bonds we ever experience. Part of the art of architecture lies in finding a nonverbal, stylistic way to get a message from the creator of a building to its users. One recent solution, postmodernism, works only for some buildings. Buildings also communicate images about the people who live or work in them. Finally, meaning, in the sense of a building's perceived working function, has strong effects on its appreciation. We do not like buildings that have vague or inappropriate functional meanings. Sixth, appraisals of risk may be made in relation to crime, accidents, and environmental hazards about residences, neighborhoods, dump sites, power plants, or even the world as a whole. As with other appraisals, they vary from person to person and in relation to such physical variables as distance to the problem site and features of the site itself. An important difference is that between experts and everyday people; experts rely more on quantitative criteria in their appraisals of danger, whereas laypersons rely more on personal and social criteria. Efforts are underway to build bridges between these two groups.

PLACES CREATE DIFFERENT IMPRESSIONS in different people, but often, many observers develop similar impressions of a place. In this portion of the chapter, the differences between appraisal and assessments and the varieties of assessments will be described. Several human-based paradigms for assessing environmental quality (as opposed to mechanical means of doing so) will be discussed. The purposes and paradigms of Observer-based environmental assessments will be described. Finally, several typical investigations will be described, to give some flavor of current efforts to assess the quality of natural and built environments.

Distinctions and Definitions

Assessments versus Appraisals. These constructs differ in four ways:

1. Appraisals are *person*-centered; they focus on the way individuals think and feel about the places around them. Assessments are *place*-centered; they focus on the quality of a setting from a broader human perspective. To understand how individuals appraise environments, their judgments of several places from their own world of experience usually are studied. To understand a place, judgments by several observers about one place usually are obtained.

2. Appraisals more often embody psychological constructs (i.e., emotion, meaning, concern, preference). Assessments more often are attempts to measure properties of the setting (e.g., environmental quality), using human perceptual skills. Even similar-sounding appraisals and assessments are conceptually different. For example, a judgment of preference (an appraisal) and a judgment of quality (an assessment) are distinct. Observers may assess the architecture of one city as being of high quality, but nevertheless *prefer* the architecture of another city.[199]

3. Assessments are more likely than appraisals to be undertaken in order to influence public policy. For example, the motive for much landscape assessment research is to help decide which vistas in national parks should be preserved versus exploited for their timber or minerals.

4. Because assessments are place-centered, observers with specific functional relationships to the place usually are selected. These assessors often are experts either in the sense that they have professional training relevant to the setting (e.g., landscape architects assessing the quality of a university's botanical gardens) or in that they have a special interest in the setting (e.g., residents assessing the quality of a proposed housing development in their neighborhood, or hikers who often use a trail).

The Varieties of Place Assessment. Early in the history of environmental psychology, Kenneth Craik described how social scientists were beginning to use psychological assessment techniques, long used primarily to assess persons, to assess places.[200] The personality, intelligence, and other characteristics of individuals can be measured by careful human observation, and the same general set of skills may be applied to the assessment of physical settings. Craik described five kinds of place assessment that might be undertaken.

1. The physical and spatial properties of a setting may be measured. The slope of a valley, the height of a ceiling, the number of days of sunshine, and the number of rooms in a house are a few of the huge number of possible physical or spatial properties that might be assessed.

2. The number and variety of artifacts in a place may be assessed. What kind of furniture is in a living room? Which facilities are present in a campground?

3. The traits of places may be assessed. Is that landscape *inviting*? Is that office *lush*? Is that home *majestic*? Environmental trait assessment must be distinguished from environmental appraisals, which represent the viewpoint of one individual. When a group of carefully selected and trained assessors agree that a certain trait applies to a certain place, we can be more confident that the trait is truly characteristic of the place, rather than a reflection of the needs and experiences of any one individual making an appraisal. The term *personality* is used to describe the overall pattern of a person's traits, so I have proposed the term **environmentality** to describe the overall pattern of an environment's traits. What sort of environmentality does your place have?

4. The behaviors that typically occur in a place may be assessed. As noted earlier, some places support many different human activities (e.g., a park), whereas others support relatively few (e.g., a field of wheat). Two similar places may enclose quite different sets of behaviors (your living room compared to your neighbor's living room).

5. The institutional attributes or social climate of places may be assessed.[201] Is a particular school organized or chaotic, supportive or not? Is a particular hospital of good quality?[202]

IN THE YEARS SINCE CRAIK OFFERED THIS TYPOLOGY, research has been unequally divided among the five kinds of assessments. The urgency of problems such as air pollution and the steady destruction of parklands and wilderness areas has led to legislation aimed at protection of the natural environment. The first step in environmental protection is to determine the location, extent, and severity of the present or potential damage.[203] Consequently, most environmental assessment efforts have focused on one place trait (quality) and on one type of setting (the natural environment). Concern over the deterioration of ecosystems all over the globe has probably explains why this topic has received so much attention at the expense of assessment research on other topics. The dramatic tone taken by some who express these concerns is exemplified by the words of a representative of an environmental defense organization, who was speaking about only one aspect of environmental degradation, visible air pollution: "When we lose visibility... an important part of our vision as a people will be lost."[204]

We should not forget, however, that many other kinds of environmental assessment—such as those involving the great *indoors*, where we spend the vast majority of our time—are also important, and some indoor assessment work is done.[205]

Technical Environmental Assessments versus Observer-based Assessments. As noted earlier, most environmental assessments are done on environmental quality. In general, these assessments may be made by technical or Observer-based means. **Technical environmental assessments (TEAs)** employ mechanical monitoring equipment or other physical means to produce a reading of environment quality. **Observer-based environmental assessments (OBEAs)** employ the perceptual abilities of humans to judge the quality (or other characteristics) of settings. The OBEA is a measure of the quality of the environment as it is *experienced*.[206]

Both TEAs and OBEAs are useful, depending on the goal of the assessment. TEAs are valuable, for example, for assessing levels of hazardous materials in air, water, and soil that humans cannot perceive. OBEAs are more useful when the goal of the study involves assessing quality in terms of the social, aesthetic, preferential, and satisfaction aspects of environmental change. For some purposes, such as measuring the visual impact of air pollution or the aural impact of noise, TEAs and OBEAs can play complementary roles. For example, TEA measures (e.g., the presence or absence of a view or the size of a living room or noise from airplanes) may significantly predict an OBEA measure (e.g., satisfaction with a nursing home or assessments of a wilderness).[207,208]

One might be tempted to think of TEAs as objective measures and OBEAs as subjective measures, but this is inappropriate.[209] TEAs can be subjective in that assessors choose the times and places to sample the environment, and sometimes they interpret the data according to their training and experience. More importantly, choosing which dimension of the environment to examine is subjective. OBEAs may be considered subjective because human observers are assumed to produce widely differing assessments; that is, they are not reliable. This *may* happen, but not necessarily. In many OBEAs, the level of agreement among observers is strikingly high.[210]

Nevertheless, no standardized OBEA yet exists. The very variety in the names given them by different research groups (Perceived Environmental Quality Indices, Visual Impact Assessment, Multiphasic Environmental Assessment Procedure, etc.) is evidence that they are still in the developmental stage. This lack of standardization does not mean today's OBEAs are valueless. They may in fact be both impossible and undesirable to standardize, owing to the vast variety in both settings and assessment purposes. The optimal strategy probably is to develop the best possible OBEA for each type of setting, just as TEAs employ many different specialized machines. Rudolf Moos

and his associates, for example, spent years developing a standard instrument for the assessment of sheltered-care environments,[211] and Kenneth Craik spent years developing procedures for assessing landscapes.[212]

The Uses of Observer-Based Environmental Assessments

ENVIRONMENTAL APPRAISALS ARE PRIMARILY OF INTEREST to those who wish to understand how individuals think and feel about environments. Environmental assessments have a different set of uses.[213] Several of these uses originate with public policy issues because concern for the deteriorating quality of the environment has culminated in laws requiring that environments be monitored. Both TEAs and OBEAs have been undertaken as part of the public push to learn how economic development affects parklands, air, water, and urban areas. However, you might be thinking: What good are these human-based assessments? Aren't machines more objective and accurate? OBEAs have at least five purposes or uses:

1. OBEAs allow comparisons between human and mechanical measures of environmental quality. Large gaps between TEAs and OBEAs might indicate credibility problems for TEAs. Depending on whether the TEA or the OBEA is eventually found to be more accurate, more public education or improved TEA technology might be warranted. However, TEAs and OBEAs do not always differ; they may complement and confirm the other.

2. OBEAs assist in the development of TEAs. Through an OBEA, sites that are high or low in environmental quality can be identified. Subsequently, physical characteristics that differentiate high from low environmental quality sites can be identified so that eventually the environmental quality of sites can be assessed directly from their physical characteristics using TEAs. For example, consider a park manager who has many potential campsites to choose from, but must select only a few for development. A panel of campers could be taken on a tour of potential sites and asked to rank the quality of each as a campsite. Then the physical elements common to sites assessed as high quality may be determined. Future campsite selection then could be based on knowledge of those key physical

elements; future panels of campers would not have to be organized.

3. OBEAs provide knowledge of trends in environmental impact from the human point of view. OBEAs performed at regular intervals during the course of development in urban or park settings can inform policy-makers of the seriousness of the impact at any given stage in a project. Similarly, the progress of environmental protection or enhancement programs can be monitored through OBEAs. For example, in England the Thames River has been subjected to an intensive cleanup program. TEAs that indicate declines in pollution levels are valuable, but OBEAs can demonstrate that London's residents and visitors notice changes in the river's color, smell, and ability to produce fish. Indeed, such a study was conducted on a river in France: Technical indicators of water pollution were compared with the perceptions of riverside campers.[214]

4. OBEAs are useful for assessments of environmental quality that particularly relate to human interaction with the environment. For example, many physical characteristics of sound can be measured mechanically, but sound is not the same as noise. Sound only becomes noise under certain conditions, which include the preferences, goals, and activities of the listeners in the setting. One person's jazz festival is another person's intolerable screeching!

5. OBEAs educate staff in the setting.[215] Park managers, nursing home operators, and planners often feel certain they know all the important issues in their facilities, but they do not. I once attended a meeting of a library board that had constructed a new branch library. It had been open for only a few months. The person who had spent over a year shepherding the project from start to finish questioned the need for an assessment of the library. "We have the best of everything there," he said. The chief librarian turned to him and said, "Bill, I hate to say this, but lighting has already been identified as a problem." Bill confused the goal of getting the library constructed in time and on budget with the goal of ensuring that the building suited the needs of its users. Very often, "on time" and "within budget" are not good enough.

OBEAs may also be used to evaluate buildings, as illustrated in the library story. Environmental assessment is essential for architecture that is well-tailored to the needs of building users. No one person knows all the strengths and weaknesses of a large setting like a library or wilderness area. OBEAs utilize the observations of many individuals to educate those who manage settings. Because this architectural use of OBEAs is a large topic, it will be discussed in detail in the book's final chapter as part of the architectural design process, where the term for essentially the same activity is **post-occupancy evaluation (POE).**

Paradigms and Methodological Considerations

Observer-based environmental assessment may be approached from four different paradigms.[216,217]

The Expert Paradigm. The expert paradigm involves the evaluation of environmental quality by trained observers. The training may be in any of several relevant fields, such as forestry, real estate, landscape architecture, resource management, construction, or engineering. The experts usually rate a setting using principles from their own field, which may include artistic concepts like form, balance, and contrast, or forestry concepts like timber age, density, and health. The expert OBEA, then, is an assessment of a specific dimension of environmental quality made by persons who are skilled in a particular field.

The Psychophysical Paradigm. The psychophysical paradigm uses classic psychological measurement procedures, including categorical ratings, the paired-comparison method, and rank-ordering by observers to produce precise and reliable indexes called **scenic beauty estimations (SBEs).**[218] The SBE method assumes that most of the power to predict judgments of environments resides in the scene rather than in the observer. Thus, in a logical extension of this belief, the psychophysical paradigm has been used to identify properties of settings that reliably lead to judgments of environmental quality. The psychophysical paradigm, then, is Observer-based only in its initial stages, when human observers are used to discover which properties of scenes do result in assessments of beauty or quality. Later, if the paradigm is successful, environmental assessment does not require observers, because each observer is presumed to respond to a given scene in more or less the same way. Knowing that a setting has certain characteristics (and does *not* have others) should allow for the computation of its level of quality or beauty from a prediction equation.

Most research within the psychophysical paradigm concerns the aesthetics of landscapes, especially natural landscapes. Most people find the typical natural landscape more beautiful than the typical urban or suburban scene,[219] and that landscapes seem to produce more positive physiological effects than scenes of built environments.[220] The practical goal of this work has been to discover objective ways of deciding which vistas are beautiful to users of national parks. Is a wilderness scene more beautiful when it includes water? Is a forest view more beautiful when clearings are visible, or when dense tall trees fill the scene?

Research that systematically varies landscape elements in the scene—such as the amount, type, and location (center versus periphery, and near versus far) of vegetation, water, and sky—supports the psychophysical approach by showing that physical elements can explain much of the variability in judgments of aesthetics, with little consideration of individual differences among observers.[221] The power of physical cues to predict judgments of beauty varies from study to study depending on the selection of scenes and observers, but they clearly are a dominant force. In other words, this research suggests that most people will agree on the beauty of any given natural landscape. The challenge is to discover exactly which elements of the landscape are the most influential in defining beauty (see Figure 3-6).

Two recent studies explore this challenge. One studied judged beauty as a function of the distance to a feature in a scene.[222] Six similar scenes were studied; each scene showed a grassy field in the foreground, a small ridge in the middle ground, and a large ridge in the background. Photographs were taken at various distances from the large back ridge in each scene. Scenic beauty varied with the distance to the back ridge but not in a straight-line fashion. The scene was judged more beautiful when the back ridge was either relatively near or relatively far, and less beautiful at intermediate distances. In another study, the placement of vegetation in the scene was a significant predictor of beauty.[223] Scenes in which vegetation was seen in the center middle ground and in the center background were judged more beautiful.

The Cognitive Paradigm. The cognitive paradigm emphasizes human processing of information received from the environment. Observers are presumed to combine many features of the setting into broad assessments such as satisfaction or preference, as in the Brunswick lens model. The psychophysical and cognitive paradigms may be joined into a single entity called the **behavioral paradigm**.[224] In a typical study of this type, people (not surprisingly!) find any sort of mechanical sounds, for example from cars or planes, worsens assessments of natural landscapes, particularly more visually beautiful landscapes.[225]

The Humanistic Paradigm. The humanistic or experiential paradigm focuses on the assessment of an active, sensitive observer who often adopts a phenomenological approach. The social and aesthetic concerns of an involved, sympathetic observer are reflected in humanistic OBEAs.

IN SUM *Environmental assessments, in contrast to environmental appraisals, are place-centered (instead of person-centered), aim to measure physical properties (instead of psychological properties), are more often policy-oriented, rather than oriented to the understanding of individuals, and more often employ observers who have an expert or frequent-user relationship with the place being assessed. Place assessments may take the*

FIGURE 3-6 The scenic beauty estimate (SBE) method can offer a reliable quantitative estimate of this scene's beauty. Based on the method, this is a very beautiful scene.

form of determining a setting's physical and spatial properties, artifacts and objects, traits, behavioral occurrences, or social climate, but researchers have so far concentrated on one trait (environmental quality) in one kind of setting (wilderness). Place assessments may use technical or human means of observations. Each has its place; neither is necessarily more reliable or valid; each employs a variety of instruments (different machines for technical assessments, different questionnaires or rating forms for human observers). OBEAs have at least five purposes. They can allow for comparisons between TEAs and OBEAs, assist in the development of physical measures of environmental quality, provide data on environmental quality trends from the human perspective, provide assessments of quality along dimensions with particular human relevance, and educate the staff of the assessed setting as to its strengths and weaknesses. Four OBEA paradigms may be identified: expert, psychophysical, cognitive, and humanistic. Each has its own values and purposes, which result in different kinds of assessments.

What Is an Environmental Attitude?

ALTHOUGH THEY MIGHT REFER to many aspects of the environment, an **environmental attitude** is broadly defined here as an individual's *concern* for the physical environment as something that is worthy of protection, understanding, or enhancement. How concerned are you about the welfare of your own room, your residence, your neighborhood or city, a nearby wilderness area, or planet Earth? How concerned are others?

Why study environmental attitudes? Although attitudes do not always translate into environmentally friendly behavior, they often do. They also can be very useful for environmental managers such as policy-makers, park superintendents, fish and game officers, forestry officials, building managers, or recycling coordinators.[226] First, knowledge of a group's environmental attitudes can inform managers about the level of support for specific programs or the environment in general. Second, environmental attitudes can help in the setting of environmental goals (e.g., 90 percent of newspaper to be recycled within two years). Third, they can indicate what people are doing about the environment now, or at least what they *intend* to do.

The Components of Environmental Attitudes. Attitudes, in general, are usually said to have three components: cognitive, affective, and conative. For our purposes, the **cognitive component** includes what an individual knows or thinks about an environment. The **affective component** includes one's emotions and feelings about an environment. The **conative component** refers to one's behavioral intentions toward an environment.

Environmental attitudes divide into a **preservation factor** and a **utilization factor**.[227-229] Preservationist attitudes are connected to pro-environmental behavior, that is, saving the environment, and utilizationist attitudes are connected to economic liberalism, which relies on the idea that resources exist to be used and developed.

Theories of Environmental Attitudes and Behavior. Several approaches to understanding environmental concern and its relation to pro-environmental behavior have

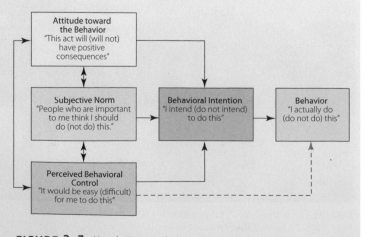

FIGURE 3–7: Ajzen's Theory of Planned Behavior

been developed. Probably the most frequently used is the **theory of planned behavior (TPB)** (see Figure 3-7).[230] It maintains that if a person is to act in an environmentally friendly manner, several factors must precede it. The person first must have had the *intention* to act in that way. However, this intention must be preceded by three conditions: a positive attitude toward the act, the belief that this is the normal or usual way to act, and the belief that one has sufficient control over the situation to be able to engage in pro-environmental action. A positive attitude depends on the person believing that the act will have positive consequences. That the behavior is "normal" is based on social pressure applied by significant others whom the person is motivated to please. Finally, perceived control depends on the belief that one possesses the resources and opportunities to actually engage in the pro-environmental behavior.

The more that all these factors are pointing in the right direction, the more likely that the person will act in a pro-environmental fashion. The theory was supported in a study that Yuko Heath and I conducted to predict who will use public transportation,[231] and other studies that predict who will conserve energy, car pool, and recycle,[232] or which employees intend to engage in pro-environmental actions at work.[233] However, the basic theory has been shown to be more powerful when certain factors are added to the model, such as a person's habits[234] and descriptive norms,[235] that is, what people think is the "usual thing to do," and developing an identity as an environmental person.[236-238]

Norms can be descriptive, as above, or injunctive, that is, a prescription from someone or a group about how one *should* act. Descriptive and injunctive norms may agree, that is, be "aligned," or not. If they are not aligned (e.g., you look around and see what most people are doing, and that is not what someone says people ought to be doing), intentions to engage in environmental behavior—quite understandably—are lower than when the two types of norm are aligned.[239]

A second approach is called the **values-belief-norm (VBN) model** (see Figure 3-8).[240] As its name suggests, it asserts

that the chain leading to pro-environmental behavior begins with a person's values. The more *biospheric*, the more *altruistic*, and the less *egoistic* are one's general values, the more he or she should believe the main tenets of the *New Ecological Paradigm* (NEP), a worldview that envisions the planet as a delicate, threatened, and interconnected system.[241] In turn, believing in the NEP is thought to lead to the belief that certain acts (those that harm the environment) have *adverse consequences*. Still, according to VBN, people will not act in a pro-environmental way if they do not also believe that they are able *to reduce those consequences*. If all these values and beliefs are in place, a person should then have a sense of obligation and develop the *norm* to engage in pro-environmental actions, a concept borrowed from **norm activation theory (NAM)**.

VBN specifies four kinds of actions that a person might take: environmental activism, public non-activist behaviors (e.g., writing letters or attending meetings), private behaviors (e.g., recycling or choosing public transport), and actions within an organization (e.g., trying to get one's workplace or school to reduce its energy use). VBN theory has also received empirical support; it does a good job of accounting for non-activist environmental behaviors.[242-244]

Another approach, the **stage model**, focuses on the changes that a person goes through on the way to more-frequent pro-environmental behavior.[245] It asserts that behavioral change follows a sequence of four stages: pre-decisional, pre-actional, actional, and post-actional. The model further proposes that three separate kinds of intentions (to form a goal to change, to engage in a particular behavior, and to actually implement the behavior) mark the transitions from stage to stage.

Finally, others advocate **self-determination theory (SDT)**[246] as a useful explanation of why people adopt or do not adopt pro-environmental behavior. The basic idea is that intrinsic motivation (doing something for its own

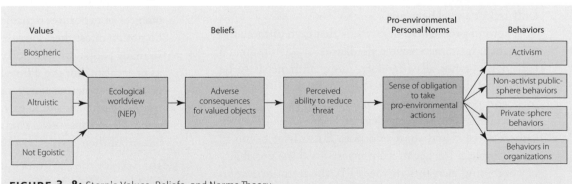

FIGURE 3–8: Stern's Values, Beliefs, and Norms Theory

sake) is a better predictor of the willingness and stability of behavior than extrinsic motivation (doing something for outside rewards). Thus, feeling autonomous and competent is expected to favor the adoption of pro-environmental behavior. One study supports the idea that SDT predicts one pro-environmental behavior (household energy-saving) better than the TPB,[247] and another reports that egoistic, biospheric, and altruistic values predict environmental intentions better than SDT, although these three values are correlated with the SDT constructs.[248]

A different use of these theories than predicting behavior is to use them as a way to discover distinct groups of individuals. For example, five clear groups of transportation users, based on their TPB values, beliefs, and attitudes, were identified in a German study.[249] This segmentation strategy was better able to predict certain travel choices than the traditional way of segmenting populations into cluster groups based on demographic or geographic variables.

Challenges for Theories. One problem, not so much with these theories themselves, but with how they have been studied, at least in this field, is that so far researchers rarely measure the last element in the theories, the actual behavior of individuals. Many studies go only as far as measuring the *intention* to behave. Others use self-reported behavior, indirect measures of behavior, or group measures (e.g., a household's energy use) rather than directly measuring individuals' actual behavior. The most common measure, self-reports, are subject to a variety of influences, such as memory errors or the desire to look good, that reduce their validity as measures of what people really do. In a meta-analysis of studies that measured both self-reported and objective measures of behavior, Christine Kormos and I found a correlation of .46 between them.[250] Is that good, or bad? Let's say it is "not too bad," but far from allowing researchers and policymakers to assume that self-reports truly reflect actual behavior.

A second problem, in my view, is that each of these theories includes *some* valuable predictors of environmental behavior, but not all. Therefore, more effort needs to be devoted to integrating them to find the most useful predictors (and perhaps drop the less-useful predictors), rather than to be single-mindedly devoted to any one of them.[251] Others agree[252] and some efforts to do so have begun.[253] For example, a European team investigated the possibility of combining elements of the TPB, the norm activation model, habit theory, and the ipsative theory of behavior[254] (an approach that takes into account a person's objective and subjective situational constraints).[255] In their attempt to account for peoples' choices of ways to travel, the authors found that their **comprehensive action determination model** accounted for these choices better than any of the separate parts of the model. Another effort combined elements of the NAM and the TPB and learned that the combination worked well than the separate elements.[256]

Measurement Instruments. In order to measure environmental attitudes such as concern or values, reliable and valid measurement instruments are needed. Many instruments have been developed, some for very specific purposes such as ecological concern about consumer products[257] or the transportation of nuclear waste,[258] and others are more general measures. Here is a selection of them, generally arranged by when they were published, that is, from the historical (and perhaps a bit dated) to the current (and thus benefiting from experience):

1. The Maloney-Ward Ecology Inventory contains 45 items arranged in four subscales: affect, knowledge, verbal commitment, and actual commitment.[259,260] Affect relates to the affective component of attitudes; Knowledge to the cognitive component. The latter two represent the conative component: Verbal Commitment measures what respondents *say* they will do for conservation; and Actual Commitment asks them to report what they have actually *done*.

2. The Weigel Environmental Concern Scale[261] is a shorter 16-item scale without separate subscales.

3. A German scale also measures environmental concern, knowledge, and reported behavior.[262]

4. The Environmental Worry Scale was developed to assess workers' anxiety about the effects of their exposure to organic solvents.[263] The health consequences of exposure to many technological hazards do not manifest themselves for many years (if at all), so many people worry. Worry may sound the same as pessimism, but the difference is that pessimism is fatalistic, whereas worry may be the proper and necessary prerequisite to galvanize exposed (and worried) persons into taking action against the hazard or their own exposure to it.

5. The Test for the Environmental Attitudes of Children (TEACH)[264] examines children's level of

agreement with five themes: the interrelationship of all life forms, ownership versus stewardship of the environment, the necessity of action to solve environmental problems, commitment to quality environments, and a sense of awe and wonder toward nature. Another recent scale was also developed for use with children.[265]

6. Some traditional psychological measurement instruments have been revised to include environmental values. One, the Rokeach Value Survey, traditionally assessed the importance to individuals of 20 values, such as equality, a world of peace, family security, and health. It has now been modified to include a 21st value, a clean environment.[266]

7. Another approach is to classify people in terms of *why* they support the environment.[267] Some people (ecocentrics) want to protect nature for its own sake, whereas others (anthropocentrics) support environmental issues because they see nature as the fountain of human comfort, health, and quality of life.[268-270] Individuals who are more ecocentric express greater concern about environmental issues; people who are more anthropocentric express less concern; the Earth, for them, is a source of resources to be used.

8. The Environmentalism Scale[271] measures three forms of environmental attitude: Internal environmentalism refers to person's beliefs about the relations between humanity and nature, and personal relevance to environmental issues. External environmentalism includes attitudes to issues outside the self, such as consumer goods, legislation, and economic aspects of environmental issues. Substantive environmentalism assesses a person's attitudes about the severity of environmental problems, pollution, deforestation, and biological extinction.

9. A scale developed in Germany assesses the degree of hopelessness about the environment that individuals feel.[272] The idea is to measure the degree to which individuals believe it is already too late and to explore the negative consequences when people give up hope that environmental problems can be solved. An international survey revealed that undergraduates from the former socialist countries of Eastern Europe were more pessimistic about the environment than those from Western Europe.[273] This environmental pessimism may have increased, but it isn't exactly new; I knew an extremely bright student in the 1960s who chose not to go to graduate school because he thought the ecology was going to collapse too soon to make going to graduate school worthwhile.

10. Another tool measures environmental values,[274] although the nature and meaning of environmental values are unclear and need some theoretical attention, according to some environmental psychologists.[275]

11. A scale to measure motivation toward proenvironmental behavior and concern has been developed, translated into several languages,[276,277] and validated.[278]

12. A different approach is to measure ecological behaviors as manifestations of concern.[279]

13. A survey of environmental attitudes was developed to measure the attitudes of college students.[280]

14. The New Ecological Paradigm (NEP) scale is a 15-item measure of agreement with a general "planet Earth" perspective.[281] The NEP probably contains some subscales[282] or factors.[283]

15. The Environmental Attitudes Inventory's (EAI) twelve scales purport to capture the main facets measured by all or most of the previous measures.[284]

16. The first of a triad of nature-oriented measures assesses one's Commitment to Nature.[285]

17. The second, with commitment usually comes concern, and the Love and Care for Nature scale, as its name says, focuses on individuals' personal and emotional relationship with nature (or the lack of it, obviously).[286]

18. Third, another scale measures empathy for nature as a personality trait. Dispositional Empathy with Nature is the tendency to understand and share the emotional experience of the natural world.[287]

The reliability and validity of scales like these usually is demonstrated by showing that they have excellent internal consistency reliability and by showing that individuals known to have pro-ecology attitudes (e.g., dedicated members of environmental organizations) have significantly higher scores on them than do individuals who are not members of activist organizations. Thus, when the scales are given to individuals whose environmental attitudes are not yet known, we can be reasonably certain that their scores do, in fact, reflect their pro-environment attitudes. With these instruments, we can begin to answer important questions about environmental attitudes and values, such as the one that follows.

Just How Concerned Are People?

Level of Concern. Isn't *everyone* concerned about the environment these days? Judging from the media, polls, and the general population, one might think so (see Figure 3-9). Certainly it is no longer fashionable to be anti-environment. But privately, some people are not *that* concerned; they may be more concerned with jobs, health, or other considerations than with the environment. A legitimate question is this: Just *how* concerned are people about the environment? How much has this concern changed over the years? Do environmental disasters affect the level of concern?

Projects and websites change, but a team at Yale University has been working on US climate change opinions, for example, and its work is here: *http://environment.yale.edu/climate-communication*. The Pew organization also tracks climate change opinions: *http://www.pewresearch.org*.

Clearly, opinions change, and environmental concern can actually decline over time,[288,289] as well as increase,[290] or both decline and increase.[291] In general, concern for the environment is strong, but perhaps superficial for many

people.[292] Enthusiasm often declines if people believe that the adjustments they would have to make would cramp their lifestyles. Could it be that support for the environment is "strong" but not very committed?

This question can be approached by asking how important the environment is compared to other concerns. One study found that of the Rokeach Value Survey's 21 values, a clean environment was tied for fifth, behind freedom, family security, health, a world at peace, and tied with self-respect.[293] Another disturbing trend is that sometimes greater environmental concern is associated with *lower* levels of objective environmental knowledge.[294]

The Generality and Stability of Environmental Concern. A related issue is the *generality* of environmental concern, in two senses of the term. First, are people equally concerned about all sorts of environments? Some researchers have investigated how concern varies for different parts of the environment; to think that concern does not differ for different places or for different life domains would be simplistic.[295-297] As an example, people seem to have separate (and different) environmental concerns related to transportation, purchasing choices, pollution cleanup, and the public advocacy of their concerns. However, persons who hold pro-environment attitudes in more than one domain do exist, of course, and they may be said to have a **generalized environmental ethic.**[298]

Second, are people equally concerned across time? When something goes wrong, concern rises. For example, after the 1979 Three Mile Island nuclear incident in the United States, concerns about nuclear energy rose until they were about equal to such central life concerns as finances, health, and social well-being.[299] A Dutch study found that concern about nuclear power went from negative, before the 1986 Chernobyl nuclear incident, to very negative one month after the incident, and then back to the original level of negativity a year and a half later.[300] Another Dutch survey found that stability of environmental concern appeared more at the group or average level than at the individual level, where more variability over time occurred.[301] Also, supporters of nuclear energy wavered in their views more than opponents of nuclear energy did. Thus, disaster increases concern, but for some people, it sinks back to pre-disaster levels with time.

FIGURE 3-9: Recycling has become a major way for many people to express their environmental concern in concrete action.

Is Everyone Concerned?

NOT EVERYONE IS EQUALLY CONCERNED about the environment, as we have just seen. Many studies have reported differences in concern, and some of those variations will be presented next, to give the flavor of these differences. You will see that the findings vary; the results depend, in part, on how the question is asked.[302] If you also think of environmental concern as something that varies with age, gender, culture, education, social class, favorite activities, different time periods, and concern for different aspects of the environment, you will be on the right track and prepared for what follows.

Age and Childhood Experiences. Most (but not all[303]) research shows that younger people are more environmentally concerned than older people, at least about the general environment.[304-307] This finding even holds *within* the younger age range; a German study found that 12-year-olds were more concerned than 15- and 18-year-olds.[308] However, environmental concern is quite variable in adults, so it would be a mistake to think that all older people are unconcerned,[309] or that all younger people are concerned.[310]

Three possible interpretations of this (or any) age-related trend are possible. First, it may be that as people age, they become less concerned about the environment; this is a true **age effect**. However, a second possibility is that something important happened to a particular generation (e.g., Baby Boomers) that did not happen to an older generation (for example, children of the Great Depression). Such a **cohort effect** is not caused by aging, but by events that had more of an impact on one age group than another. A third possibility is that the times are changing; that the overall political-social climate is growing more liberal or more conservative, so that *everyone* is more concerned or less concerned about the environment than they used to be. This is called an **era effect**. In a clever study that compared concern across different ages, generations, and eras to answer this question, it appears that the decline in environmental concern with age primarily is an era effect, although true age effects do appear strong for the young-adult age group.[311]

Environmental concern should be distinguished from **ecocentrism**, the belief that nature deserves protection without regard for human costs and benefits. Younger people apparently are *less* eco-centric than older people, on average.[312]

Childhood experiences may account in part for environmental concern; usually children learn these values from their parents.[313] When children spend more time in nature, and they believe that their family values nature, they tend to be more environmentally concerned.[314] Among environmental educators, the strongest predictor of environmental concern is the amount of outdoor experience they had as children.[315] Children who talk about the environment at home, watch nature films, and read about the environment are more concerned.[316] Where in the hierarchy of moral wrongs do children place actions that harm the environment? Apparently, they view such actions as worse than social transgressions, but not as bad as actions that harm people.[317]

Gender. Women (on average![318-321] but not always[322]) report more concern for the environment. However, a different and disturbing gender difference is that women (on average!) are more likely to say they are more upset by anti-environmental events, to say they will do more about the problems, but to report actually doing less and knowing less about environmental problems, than men.[323-325] This pattern—that women express more concern, but men are more knowledgeable—has been confirmed in other studies.[326-329] Perhaps this is one result of social and school systems that discourage girls from early interests in science and the environment. This would strongly suggest that educators should pay more attention to the environmental education of girls and women. Another explanation is that concerns such as health and safety are more important to women, especially women with children at home.[330,331]

Education. Education and knowledge differences are also apparent, although differences can be complex.[332] However, among the differences, business[333] and technology[334] majors are less concerned than others, on average.[335] Students enrolled in a university environmental education (EE) program have significantly greater environmental knowledge, verbal commitment, and actual commitment than similar students who are not enrolled in EE,[336] although it may be that students in EE programs had more environmental concern *before* they entered the EE program,[337,338] so the programs may not *increase* environmental attitudes very much.[339] Performing ecological restoration work is associated with more positive environmental attitudes,[340] as is engaging in more nature-related activities in general.[341] Private school students are more knowledgeable about the environment than public school students.[342] Individuals with more education in general are more concerned about the environment,[343-346] and, for example, tend to recycle more and buy more hybrid vehicles,[347] although one study in Norway found less concern with more education.[348] In Britain, the best discriminator between environmentally concerned and indifferent teens was the amount of environmental knowledge about specific issues they claimed to have, although concerned teens also had more scientific knowledge than unconcerned teens.[349]

Activities. Environmental concern is associated with choice of activities. On average (as always), people who engage in outdoor recreation tend to be concerned about the environment, but this varies with the activity.[350] Those who prefer consumptive outdoor activities (e.g., hunting or fishing) tend to be less concerned than people who engage in non-consumptive activities (e.g., hiking, photography).[351] Members of bicycling organizations are more concerned than members of off-road vehicle organizations.[352] People who spend more time reading newspapers are more concerned, and those who watch more TV are less concerned[353] and less willing to make sacrifices for the environment.[354] However, adolescents who watch more science shows[355] and people who watch more news and nature documentaries are more concerned.[356] Women who engage in more personal health care activities are more concerned.[357]

Identity and Personality. Who are you? Do you think of yourself as part of your community, or separate from it? Would you describe yourself as an environmentalist or green person? Are you agreeable? Conscientious?

Social identity and environmental identity are related to pro-environmental concern and behavior. In general, people with a stronger sense of identity with their society (that is, have a stronger social identity) are more likely to report engaging in pro-environmental behavior.[358] Of course, one might identify with one's community without identifying as a "green" person, or vice versa, so the two forms of identity must be distinguished. However, they lead to the same place: not surprisingly, having an environmental identity is also associated with more environmental concern and action.[359-361]

Environmental identity may be different in that it seems to be a necessary bridge between one's values and one's environmental intentions and reported behaviors.[362] That is, biospheric values may not directly predict intentions and behaviors; they seem to predict environmental identity, which in turn predicts intentions and reported behaviors.

People who are more agreeable, more conscientious, more open to experience[363] and give greater consideration to the future consequences of their current actions[364] all tend to have greater pro-environmental intentions and actions. Emotions also affect environmental intentions: feeling guilty makes people lean toward intending to repair damage, feeling anger makes people want to punish those who damage the environment, and pride in our group's environmental record makes us want to do even more.[365]

Values, Moral Principles, Felt Responsibility, and Worldviews. Values (and related concepts that are relatively stable within a person) are strongly related to environmental attitudes.[366] Despite their definition as "stable," Yuko Howes and I found that values do sometimes vary with the situation, and of course one's values sometimes conflict with each other (e.g., "I am in favor of the environment, but for pleasure I am going to take a nice long shower.") When two values conflict, the degree of difference in the preexisting level of endorsement of the two values is a better predictor of one's attitudes than the endorsement level of either single value.[367]

However, in general and not surprisingly, persons who hold more altruistic and biospheric values and are less egoistic report being more environmentally concerned.[368,369] Individuals who simply have stronger value orientations, are more people-oriented, less authoritarian,[370] more ethics-oriented,[371] and have higher levels of moral development[372] are more environmentally concerned. Those who believe their actions will make a difference[373] and those who are more tolerant and understanding report more environmental concern.[374] Energy-saving in the home is strongly related to holding achievement-related values such as feeling capable and intelligent.[375]

At least in Australia, committed environmentalists have more secular and **post-materialist** values than other people.[376] These values typically are held by more affluent citizens who have less reason to worry about the basic needs of life; they are able to be concerned with "higher-level" goals and actions such as self-improvement, personal freedom, and providing direct input to government. As in personal relationships, commitment to the environment partly is a matter of satisfaction with the other and the investments one has made in the other. In the environmental realm, satisfaction and investments leads to commitment, and commitment leads to reported pro-environmental behavior and willingness to sacrifice for the environment.[377]

Among students, moral principles are better predictors of environmental actions, whereas among community residents, tangible outcomes (such as material economic rewards) are better predictors of environmental actions.[378] Materialists and post-materialists may be concerned about different environmental issues; for example, in Turkey materialists tend to be more concerned about local environmental issues, whereas post-materialists tend to be more interested in global environmental issues.[379] However, post-materialist values sometimes are less important than other factors, such as whether an actual environmental hazard is nearby.[380] Those who believe in free-market principles, that technology will solve our problems, and that economics is the best measure of progress tend to have less environmental concern.[381,382]

As you might expect, feeling responsible is an important part of environmental concern.[383] This feeling of responsibility apparently stems largely from a sense of guilt.[384] In a nationwide sample of Dutch teenagers, environmental concern was strongly connected to willingness to make sacrifices, such as financial sacrifices, for the environment.[385]

One's worldviews are related to one's environmental concern. Among these worldviews, four views about nature have been distinguished.[386] First, those who think of nature as *capricious* believe that she is capable of anything; nature is unpredictable (see Figure 3-10). Second, those who think of nature as *benign* believe that she is very capable of adapting; nature can manage to find its equilibrium again even when she is disturbed. Third, those who think of nature as *ephemeral* believe that she is delicate and fragile; even small disturbances will have drastic consequences. Fourth, those who think of nature as *tolerant/perverse* believe she is able to absorb some disturbance, but beyond a certain limit, she will suddenly collapse.

So, which group do you think is the most concerned about the environment? Those who believe the nature-ephemeral myth are most concerned; those who believe the nature-benign myth are least concerned.[387] A different set of views about nature is that it is sacred in itself, it is sacred because a deity created it, or that it is not sacred.[388] In a large-scale US survey, those who believe it is sacred in itself were more likely to say they had signed an environmental petition or participated in an environmental group. The two groups who believe nature is sacred were more likely to report donating money to environmental groups.

Some people hold egalitarian worldviews while others hold individualistic worldviews. In general, people believe that threats to the environment are weaker in their local area than in distant places,[389] but egalitarians believe this more strongly and individualists believe it less strongly.[390]

Are you an optimist or a pessimist about the environmental future? This worldview matters. In a study of 18 nations, we found a very general tendency for people everywhere to be pessimistic about the future of the environment.[391] However, individuals who are optimistic about the future of the world or our ability to adapt tend to have fewer pro-environmental intentions[392] and to discount the possibility of negative future environmental consequences.[393] At the same time, people in may nations tend to be optimistic about the environmental condition of their own region.[394] So, why worry or change your behavior if the future is far away and, anyway, all will turn out fine around here? Personal optimism may be a good thing, optimism about the environmental future may reduce motivation to act now.

Politics, Religion, and Social Class. Less environmental concern is reported by individuals with conservative political views[395,396] and with fundamentalist Christian beliefs,[397-400] although one study did not find this.[401] The basis for this may be that these political and religious views are closely tied to a mastery-over-nature philosophical perspective, which naturally leads to favorable attitudes toward resource extraction and use, which can lead to environmental degradation.[402,403]

FIGURE 3–10: Some people believe that nature is capricious; that it can do anything and in fact might do so at any time.

At the nation level, some research shows that richer countries have greater environmental concern.[404,405] Other studies suggest that environmentalists tend to be middle-class or upper-middle-class.[406,407] However, a study that compared industrialized and developing nations found that environmental issues were mentioned more frequently than expected in developing countries, and that respondents from developing countries actually expressed higher levels of concern about environmental problems than did respondents from industrialized nations.[408] However, in a study in which occupations were counted at environmentalist group meetings, there were no more occupations from one economic class than another,[409] and one large survey found low-income earners were more concerned than higher-income earners.[410]

This apparent discrepancy may be resolved by noticing that the first studies described compared concern to national wealth, and the second study compared it to individual opinions, a different level of analysis. This idea is supported by a more recent study which found that economic factors predicted environmental concern at the national level, but not at the individual level.[411] Complicating this picture, *within* one African country, wealthier persons better recognized environmental issues than poorer persons.[412] However, this may be the result of educational differences resulting from wealth differences.

Differences in environmental concern by wealth may also depend on global versus local concerns. Citizens of poorer countries are far more concerned about local environmental problems than citizens of wealthy countries; no difference was found in concerns about global problems.[413] This is probably because wealthy people have fewer environmental problems in their communities than poor people do. Furthermore, even if environmental actions save money in the long run, wealthier people can more easily afford the initial costs. (One psychologist decided to turn this into an advantage for the environmental movement by urging his fellow psychologists to invest in companies that produce energy-saving technologies.[414])

Urban-Rural Differences. People who live in rural areas experience the environment in very different ways from their urban counterparts. Does that result in greater or lesser environmental concern? Norwegian farmers are less ecocentric and more anthropocentric than others,[415] and rural Trinidadians also are more anthropocentric than more urbanized societies, as befits their use of natural re-

sources for human ends.[416] In Nevada, however, rural people appear to have more environmental concern than urban people, in that their beliefs in the need to protect water environments is greater.[417] Of course, this may stem from anthropomorphic views. City-dwellers in Rome—at least those who hold more anthropomorphic and egoist views—are more "ambivalent" toward green spaces in their city.[418] Urban students in Germany tend to report greater verbal commitment to environmental issues,[419] and both rural and urban dwellers in British Columbia report relatively high levels of environmental concern .[420]

Cultural and Ethnic Variations. Many variations in environmental concern among ethno-racial and national groups have been reported. Within the US, early research suggesting lower concern among African-Americans has recently been supplanted by studies showing that blacks have similar[421] or greater[422,423] concern than Euro-Americans. The earlier findings may have stemmed from measurement of environmental activities that were less relevant to African-Americans.[424] Immigration to the US by some groups is associated with environmental concern. In one study, more-acculturated Latin-Americans were less concerned than less-acculturated Latin-Americans.[425] Another study found that immigrants in general had similar environmental attitudes as non-immigrants, but that newer immigrants express greater concern than native-born Americans.[426] In general, people in developing countries seem to have as much, or more, environmental concern as people in developed countries.[427]

What do we know about environmental concern around the world? In Spain, survey results suggest that environmentalism has become a "central element" of the Spanish belief system.[428] Chinese teens rate environmental pollution and overpopulation as their greatest concerns, even more important than the death of a parent, fear of nuclear war, or getting a good job.[429] In Kolkata (formerly spelled Calcutta), more than 80 percent of the respondents in a large-scale survey believed that local air pollution was, or was soon to be, a major problem.[430] Brazilian children who live in the rain forest, Portuguese children, and children of the same age in the United States are about equally concerned about the environment.[431,432] However, Thai students—although moderately concerned about the environment—are more concerned about economic, social, political, and educational issues.[433] Thus, in general, environmental concern is near the top of our concerns, even if it is not always the number one priority.

Beyond differences in *levels* of environmental concern, the *structure* of concern varies across different societies.[434,435] For example, in the U.S., people tend to see the issue as humans versus nature, but in Mexico and Brazil, people are more likely to believe that there is no necessary conflict between development and nature.[436,437] Different environmental values (i.e., valuing its preservation versus valuing its utilization) are associated with environmental behavior in different cultures, such as those in Europe, Asia, and South America.[438] Although some observers have portrayed traditional societies as managing their resources well, and as models for modern industrialized societies to emulate, one study concluded that the low-impact practices of traditional societies result less from their reverence for the environment than from low population density, inefficient harvest technologies, and a lack of profitable markets for the resources.[439]

Proximity to, and Threat from, Problem Sites. Finally, although other factors also play a role, people who live further from a problem site such as a landfill or waste disposal site tend to be less concerned, at least about that environmental problem.[440-442] In a southern California study, residents who felt their well-being was more threatened by environmental problems were more likely to engage in recycling, water conservation, less driving, and purchasing environmentally safer products.[443] Not surprisingly, residents are in favor of reducing greenhouse gas emissions if they believe this will not threaten their own jobs.[444]

How to Increase Environmental Concern

Given that environmental concern is widespread, but perhaps not as deep, committed, or universal as might be desirable, how can it be increased?

Environmental Education. One broad answer is education, but just how best to educate people is not fully understood. Environmental education (EE) encompasses a variety of attempts to change attitudes or behavior through many different methods, all of which broadly have a teacher—learner approach. The main methods have been traditional classroom lectures and field trips. Some newer approaches involve use of the media.[445]

Most research on its effectiveness has compared traditional lectures with innovative EE course materials. In a typical study, Australian fifth- and sixth-graders were placed in an EE program called Sunship Earth, and the changes in their environmental knowledge and attitudes before and afterward were compared.[446] The program managed to increase ecological knowledge, but it did not result in more positive environmental attitudes.

One might think the EE is, by its very nature, effective. However, some EE programs have not worked,[447] and others have even backfired; one managed to *reduce* students' empowerment to work on environmental issues.[448] A review of 34 published studies of EE programs found that only 14 reported positive effects.[449] Given that scientific journals often reject studies that find null effects, the true failure rate probably is even higher. Another review showed, surprisingly, that *classroom* programs actually were more effective than *outdoor* EE programs.[450]

Nevertheless, one popular EE approach to increasing environmental concern advocates getting people out into nature. After some Canadian high-school students went into the wilderness for a six-day experience, their environmental knowledge did increase significantly.[451] When the impact of an outdoor education program at summer camp on 9- to 14-year-olds was examined, researchers found that longer programs resulted in greater changes in environmental concern. Greater changes also occurred in first-time campers than in those who had camped before.[452] Involving university students in projects that help restore damaged environments increased their ecological behavior.[453] Some games that combine EE with fun may be useful with children.[454]

More success has been reported with an approach called Issue Investigation and Action Training (IIAT).[455,456] In IIAT, students analyze and investigate specific environmental issues and consider ways to resolve the issue. For example, compared to other 12-year-olds who received standard science instruction, students in the IIAT program increased their environmental knowledge, skills, and beliefs. Another test of IIAT involved teen-aged students in a six-day residential workshop. The outcomes for those who received instruction meant to raise their environmental awareness (only) was compared with outcomes for those who received awareness instruction *and* action strategies.[457] Those who received action strategy training learned more about environmental action and reported engaging in more environment-related behaviors.

Environmental education is now widespread at the college level. One study compared students in standard science courses with those in EE courses.[458] The two groups did not differ in environmental concern, but the EE students were significantly better able to defend their views with facts.

Thus, EE can increase environmental concern, but not every EE program works for every participant. One review of numerous programs produced a list of four guidelines for EE programs that should increase their power to effect change:

- Gear the program to the audience's current level of knowledge, attitude, and moral development.

- Explain both sides of the issue.

- Encourage more direct contact with nature.

- Stimulate a sense of responsibility and personal control.[459]

Based on a review of research, other writers have added nine further guidelines:

- Know the action strategies.

- Employ action skills.

- Enhance environmental attitudes.

- Maintain a sense of control.

- Provide a feeling of personal responsibility.

- Know the issues.

- Encourage social norms in favor of the environment.

- Enhance environmental sensitivity.[460]

- Involve the emotions.[461]

One reason that some EE programs fail, according to the same writers, is an over-reliance on knowledge at the expense of the other guidelines. A key step that is not in the above list is that people with ingrained anti-environmental practices need to *unlearn* those practices, which sometimes they are afraid to do, or are confused about the transition.[462] More recent research suggests that norms may only increase environmental behavior when a threat to one's mortality is salient.[463]

Simulations. Another approach to increasing concern is to simulate environmental situations and outcomes. One professor designed and used a simulation of local energy use and conservation.[464] Compared to other students who received a standard lecture on the same material, those who took part in the simulation showed a greater improvement in energy conservation attitudes and greater likelihood of taking action.

Environmental Stories. Stories (as opposed to straight textbook material!) may be valuable, at least for preteens. Students find stories that depict young people engaging in pro-environmental activities more interesting, and the stories manage to promote increased environmental knowledge and concern at the same time.[465] Environmental stories can be powerful mechanisms for increasing students' sense of hopefulness and power to change the world. And so it happened that, once upon a time, a curious student just like you decided to take a course in environmental psychology…

Guided Group Discussions. Guided group discussion is a way to persuade people in small group to adopt more pro-environmental choices. Neighborhood coffee meetings are the origin of curbside recycling "blue box" programs in Canada. Carol Werner and her colleagues used the technique to reduce the use of toxic products.[466] They believed that a small-group discussion which includes useful information helps to create the sense of a norm favoring pro-environmental behavior, and that promotes the persuasive impact of the information shared in the group.

The Power of Images. Activist organizations such as Greenpeace have long realized the power of the media to affect environmental concern, and they distribute videos of their activities and environmental problems to media outlets. For example, a Greenpeace film showing Russian ships dumping nuclear waste into the sea near Japan had an immediate effect: Russia announced it would stop the dumping. Nevertheless, empirical studies of how such images affect viewers' environmental concern have been strangely lacking. However, a study that I conducted with Donald Hine examined the effect of graphic scenes such as needles washing up on a beach on viewers' environmental attitudes. Compared to a control group that watched architectural images, the graphic scenes produced significantly more verbal commitment and actual financial donations to a local pollution group.[467]

Organized Public Events. Finally, are public events such as Earth Day useful in changing attitudes, or are they just flashy circuses? One researcher seized the opportunity of administering an environmental concern survey six months before and six months after an Earth Day.[468] Although concern was evident before Earth Day, afterwards students showed increased acceptance that environmental problems exist, recycled more, and were more concerned about world population. Events such as Earth Day do seem to have a positive influence.

The Issue Champion. In organizations, responding to environmental issues can be problematic; employees may have individual concerns, but the organization may not act if the employee is not in a secure position. My daughter once tried to get her restaurant to compost the food left on diners' plates, but as a mere hostess her efforts were ignored. A study of two organizations over a year's time showed that, in order to get an organization moving, two conditions must *both* be met:[469] First, the issue needs a champion, someone who will push the issue with management, and second, the issue must mesh with the organization's strategic plans. I would add that the champion must either have some power in the organization or be willing to (potentially) lose her job.

Does Concern Translate to Action?

A CRUCIAL ISSUE IN ENVIRONMENTAL PSYCHOLOGY is whether, or to what extent, individuals follow up their attitudes with action. How many times in your own life have you heard people say they were in favor of something, or intended to do something, but never actually followed through?

Some evidence indicates that links between environmental concern and actual behavior are quite weak,[470,471] although strong connections have also been reported.[472-475] One reason for this discrepancy lies in methodological problems that obscure the true relation between concern and action. One problem concerns the distinction between self-reported behavior and actual, observed behavior. Some studies that claim to find significant links between attitudes and "behavior" actually correlated attitudes with *self-reported* behavior.[476,477] Unfortunately, self-reported behavior does not always match up well with *actual* behavior.[478] Reported (or intended) behaviors and actual behaviors do not even necessarily have the same predictors.[479,480]

A second problem lies in how attitudes are measured: sometimes general attitudes of environmental concern are used to predict specific environmental behaviors, which does not work very well. A better approach is to measure environmental attitudes specific to the behavior in question if one wishes to predict specific environmental behaviors.[481] For example, measuring attitudes toward recycling is likely to yield a better prediction of actual recycling behavior than measuring general environmental attitudes.

A third problem can occur when only one environmental behavior is predicted, and the link between concern and behavior appears weak. When a wider variety of environmental behaviors are examined, the link between attitudes and behavior usually is stronger. One study demonstrated this by investigating the relation between environmental attitudes and numerous individual behaviors, such as circulating a petition, recycling, and recruiting a friend to help in an environmental action project.[482] Correlations with each of these behaviors (alone) were low, suggesting support for the weak-link position. But the correlation with an index composed of all the pro-environment behaviors was much higher, supporting the idea that pro-environment attitudes actually do predict pro-environmental behavior in general.[483] Persons who care about the environment may not engage in this or that *particular* pro-environment activity, but they do take part in *more* activities across the full spectrum of pro-environment activities. Partly to overcome this problem, efforts have been made to construct a standard measure of general ecological behavior that includes multiple behaviors,[484,485] and its value has been demonstrated in several countries.[486,487]

In sum, the connection between environmental attitudes can appear either weak or strong, depending on how the question is studied. However, daily experience and some evidence[488] suggest that however *predictable* individuals' concern may be, that their *level* of concern is much more developed than their actual pro-environmental behavior. This idea is consistent with the **low-cost hypothesis**, which states that environmental attitudes predict whether people will engage in simpler, easier pro-environment acts (e.g., recycling), but do not predict whether they will engage in high-cost behaviors (e.g., giving up their car in favor of public transit).[489] For high-cost behaviors, people start to find reasons why they cannot match their environmental attitudes and intentions with behavior worthy of them. When people experience inconsistency about eco-friendly behavior; ambivalence means that they are less likely to adopt it.[490]

Researchers have begun to explore the ways that people justify the gaps between their environmental attitudes and their actual behaviors.[491, 492] Just what are these justifications?

The Dragons of Inaction. Over the years, I have gathered together a collection of the reasons that we give for not translating our concern into action. At this time, the list includes about 30 "dragons of inaction."[493] These 30 "species" fall into seven "genera." Here, briefly, are examples of each dragon genus. First, we are disposed by our ancient brain to think in terms of the here and now, and therefore we tend to discount the future, when the consequences of our current anti-environmental actions will have a negative impact (**Limited Cognition**). Second, some broad worldviews that themselves are not environmental in nature (for example, that engineers will fix all the problems) tend to reduce motivation for the rest of us to take action (**Ideologies**). Third, like it or not, we are influenced by our significant others, and if they discourage environmental action, for us to take action is an uphill battle (**Other People**). Fourth, we are invested in our current lifestyle and find it hard to divest ourselves of it. "I own this car…you want me to just leave it in the driveway?" (**Sunk Costs**). Fifth, some people basically do not trust experts or scientists (**Discredence**). Sixth, all change (including change toward more pro-environmental behavior) involves risks of various kinds (**Perceived Risks**). Finally, sometimes we do a little and think it is enough, when more and stronger action is needed (**Limited Behavior**).

Key Predictors of Pro-environmental Behavior. Given these issue with the measurement of attitude, and the barriers to action that hold people back, we might well ask which attitudes best predict that people *will* engage in environmentally responsible behavior. A meta-analysis of 315 studies that have examined this question found that the best predictors of responsible environmental behavior are:

- Knowledge of environmental issues.
- Knowledge of action strategies.
- Internal locus of control.
- Verbal commitment.[494]
- Environmental concern.
- A sense of personal responsibility.[495]

Another meta-analysis investigated the relative value of various factors or interventions for promoting pro-environmental behavior;[496] it concluded that the most effective approaches were:

- ➤ Employing cognitive dissonance.
- ➤ Goal setting.
- ➤ Social modeling.
- ➤ Prompts (targeted messages).

A more recent meta-analysis based on 87 publications that included 253 experimental strategies to change observed environmental behaviors concluded that cognitive dissonance-based strategies (e.g., the foot-in-the-door technique) that try to convince people to match their previously stated beliefs with behavior, goal setting, social modeling, and prompts had the strongest effects on behavior.[497] Even a fairly simple but carefully worded and placed prompt (sign) can actually change behavior. For example, Reuven Sussman and I used them to encourage people to turn off the lights in unused rooms, and significant reductions were achieved.[498]

Other kinds of attitudes have recently been shown to be associated with environmental behavior: A willingness to exercise restraint, that is, to be frugal or austere,[499-501] and feelings of responsibility or guilt.[502,503] Also, personal and social norms predict environmental behavior, often better than attitudes.[504-506] Individuals' values, such as openness to change and universalism, also predict it.[507,508] Two strong predictors, not surprisingly, membership in an environmental organization[509] and a commitment to action[510] or to nature.[511] Reading classic books in the environmental literature has a positive effect.[512] An interesting distinction was recently made between "harmonious" passion and "obsessive" passion.[513] Both predict support for typical pro-environmental actions, but it takes obsessive passion to support more radical environmental action. A variety of demographic variables distinguish those who engage in more pro-environmental actions from those who engage in fewer actions. Among these, political liberalism, community involvement, and cosmopolitanism are associated with more environment-friendly behavior.[514]

Finally, individuals probably will not act in an environmentally responsible way if they lack the motivation to do so.[515] Self-determined motivation predicts who will engage in environmental activism[516] and in everyday ecological behaviors.[517] For example, when a researcher was clearly perceived as supporting participants' autonomy, they developed more internalized motivation, which led to more frequent pro-environmental behavior, which in turn predicted intentions to continue striving after the study was over.[518] In a different study, this sequencing of causal factors was taken a step further. A sense of self-efficacy ("I am capable of doing this") led to intrinsic motivation ("I am doing this for myself, not because of some external push"), which in turn seems to cause in-home recycling.[519] When a government is perceived to be supporting its citizens' autonomy in their environmental behavior (as opposed to being perceived as a controlling force), the citizens experience more autonomous motivation, and that, in turn, increases the frequency of their reported pro-environmental behavior.[520] When teens are exposed to more environmental messages from the friends, family, and the media, they develop more biospheric values, which leads to more pro-environmental attitudes, which leads to more environmental intentions, which leads to more reported environmental behaviors.[521]

These studies that examine the possible sequencing of causal factors lead to my next topic.

Mediators, Moderators, and Models. A long list of factors that predict some outcome ultimately is unsatisfying. Environmental psychologists need to organize lists of predictors into a form that is coherent, elegant, and sensible. This quest begins with mediators and moderators, that is, factors that help explain pro-environmental behavior in a more sophisticated way, and are the basis for models. A **moderator** is a variable that represents a group or condition for which a relationship is stronger or weaker. For example, one study examined the link between soil-conservation attitudes in farmers and their actual soil-conservation behavior.[522] The correlation was not very strong in general. However, the farmer's income moderated the relation: The attitude-behavior link was stronger for farmers with higher incomes than for those with lower incomes. Presumably, wealthier farmers are better able to afford to turn their attitudes into reality. In a different study, a certain attitude-behavior relationship was weaker for upper-income individuals, for those with conservative political beliefs, and for those with less education.[523] Other conditions or situations that can moderate (change) the relation between environmental attitudes or values and environmental actions or beliefs include the amount of effort required for the action,[524] whether a person is in an early or late stage of behavior change,[525] whether the environmental nature of the behavior is recognized by the person,[526] whether a decision-maker works for a public- or private-sector orga-

nization,[527] and whether the behavior in question occurs in public or in private.[528]

A **mediator** is a variable that, in a causal sequence, fits *between* the attitude and the behavior. The attitude changes a certain variable (the mediator), which in turn changes the actual behavior. For example, a study of the link between environmental concern and a specific behavior (voting for a bottle-deposit law) discovered that this link was mediated by several variables, including a change in norms.[529] Thus, the conclusion is that attitudes change norms, and then the norms change behavior; if one's norms are *not* altered by one's attitude, the behavior will not change. As another example, a study's goal was to predict who would become involved in a struggle to preserve wetlands.[530] Activism was hypothesized to be a function of a person's personality (urbanism) and knowledge about wetlands, but not directly. The researchers proposed that personality and knowledge would influence two mediators—assessment of the problem and arousal over the problem—and that these two mediators would, in turn, predict activism. The results of the study supported this model.

A Swedish study nicely demonstrates another apparently causal sequence involving mediators.[531] The researchers reasoned that the path to pro-environmental behavior begins with one's general (non-environmental) values (whether a person is a self-enhancer or a self-transcender) and proceeds to environmental values (self-enhancers view the environment as a fountain of resources to enrich their life; self-transcenders view the environment as important in itself, beyond their own self-interest). From there, if pro-environmental behavior is to occur, the person must also be aware that a problem exists (if none is perceived, why act?). The researchers believe that the person further must possess the personal norm to engage in pro-environmental behavior: if it is not "what I usually do," then it will not get done. Their survey of 1,400 Swedes showed that this sequence of general values, environmental values, problem awareness, and personal norms does appear to describe who will, and who will not, engage in pro-environmental behavior.

A meta-analysis generally supported the existence and importance of the variables identified in the meta-analysis described earlier, but also showed that (a) the intention to engage in pro-environmental behavior mediates the impact of personal and social influences on reported actual behavior, (b) personal moral norms influence behavioral intention, and (c) problem awareness is a significant indirect influence on pro-environmental intention; its impact appears to be mediated by moral and social norms, guilt, and attribution processes.[532]

Once a number of mediators and moderators are identified in studies like these, the bases for creating a coherent model are available. Such a model would, on logical and empirical grounds, constitute an organized and efficient set of factors that can strongly predict pro-environmental behavior. The job of the environmental psychologist is not as easy as that may sound (assuming that it does sound easy!). Each species of environmental behavior—for example, energy conservation, anti-nuclear activism, recycling, buying environmentally friendly products, or engaging in environmental protection campaigns—seems to have a different set of significant predictors.[533-537]

Pathways to Action. How can all the information above be used to really change behavior? One broad template suggested by Linda Steg and Charles Vlek includes four steps in this process.[538] Those who hope to increase pro-environmental behavior should (a) choose a specific behavior to be changed, (b) examine the main factors that drive this behavior, (c) design and apply interventions to change it, and (d) evaluate the effectiveness of the interventions. One study of littering serves as an example; the authors observed thousands of people in over 100 locations who littered, or not.[539] About two-thirds of smokers littered their cigarette butts. Younger people littered less. Where litter was already present, people littered more. When a litter receptacle was available, people littered less. However, when it was farther away, they littered more. Thus, the authors followed step one by observing a specific act, step two by demonstrating some of the factors that seem to drive littering (age, norms, availability, and distance to a litter box), and that permits clear inferences about some ways to reduce littering. Step four would follow next, in a new study, once the interventions have been in place for some time.

An approach that sounds similar in broad terms, but differs in some important ways, is applied behavioral analysis, which maintains that positive or negative consequences for behavior are what count. Rather than focusing on attitudes, values, and norms, behavior analysts believe that behavioral change is more likely to occur when social environments are restructured to provide consequences.[540] For example, they would forego trying to change people's minds in favor of simply tripling the deposit on cans and bottles, or instituting a charge for driving downtown, as has been done in London. In adapting applied behavioral analysis ideas to environmental problems, Scott Geller advocates a way to change environmental behavior that may be summed up in the acronym DO-RITE, which stands for the following sequence:[541]

1. **D**efine the target behavior to be changed.
2. **O**bserve the target behavior.
3. **R**ecord the rate of occurrence of the behavior.
4. **I**ntervene with a program that changes the consequences of engaging in that behavior.
5. **T**est the impact of the program by comparing the frequency of the behavior before and after the program.
6. **E**valuate the program. Was it cost-effective? Were the consequences appropriate and strong enough?

Applied behavior analysts believe that environmental messages and lectures have limited value as behavior-change agents. They believe that modeling, hands-on involvement, how-to demonstrations, goal setting, and written commitments are more effective. One review of many behavior-intervention studies concluded that the best ways to change environment-related behavior are to obtain commitments from people, to model or demonstrate desired activities, and to persuade people to set goals.[542] In addition, people must actively care.[543] Another study concludes, however, that the problem of inducing *durable* behavior change is more complex.[544] Often, when applied behavior analytic methods stop, so does the desired behavior.

IN SUM *Environmental concern is an attitude for which behavioral connections are of particular importance. More than a dozen measures of it are available. Early research suggested that the links between environmental concern and action are not very strong, but later work shows that when pro-environmental behavior is more broadly conceived, the links are stronger. Many personal and social factors are correlated with environmental concern and behavior. Concern for the environment often is in the top 5 concerns that individuals have in their whole life, but the amount and stability of concern varies with place and time; concern is not necessarily in-creasing everywhere. Environmental educa-tion does not automatically increase concern or pro-environmental behavior. Programs must be carefully developed. Applied behavior analysis provides another route for increasing the frequency of pro-environmental behav-iors with a more direct, consequence-based approach.*

This chapter is about how we think about the environment. Much recent research has, with justification, dealt with concern for the welfare of the environment, and how that does or does not translate into real action on the part of individuals. However, it opened by describing two other major ways of thinking about the environment, our per-sonal appraisals of buildings and landscapes, and attempts to reach a consensus about environments through human-based environmental assessments. I will conclude with two examples of such assessments.

TWO CASE STUDIES:
AN OBSERVER-BASED
ENVIRONMENTAL ASSESSMENT
AND IMPROVING AN
ENVIRONMENTAL BEHAVIOR

The Scenic Quality of a Valley

Over the last two decades, much theoretical and method-ological progress has been made on OBEAs. OBEAs *are* needed, they can be useful, but they are not always *seen* to be useful by the policy-makers who are in a position to fund them.[545] Yet, because OBEAs have great potential val-ue and because they are needed, researchers have worked hard to develop them.

The natural landscapes of many countries are be-ing eroded quickly. Unspoiled landscape is an important non-renewable resource.[546] Economic development has its benefits, but one of its primary costs is destruction of the land as a setting suitable for native animals and plants and as a place of beauty and quiet recreation for people. Recognizing that economic development will not cease,

policy-makers have enacted legislation that attempts to identify the best landscapes for preservation.

In a series of studies, Erwin Zube and his colleagues examined common assumptions about what constitutes scenic quality.[547] Many observers were shown slides of countryside in the northeast United States; others were taken into the field to see the vistas in person. Observers assessed the scenes using various rating methods. Some of the specific issues in question were (1) which features of the landscape lead observers to assess it as scenic, (2) whether assessors from different walks of life agree what is scenic, and (3) whether slide-simulated scenes produce the same judgments of scenic quality as field viewing of scenes.

On the first issue, Zube and his associates concluded that natural landscapes are more scenic than built ones. Humans "have yet to build a landscape equal in quality to the best in nature."[548] As for specific landscape charac-teristics, the authors report that scenic quality generally increases with ruggedness (e.g., when much variation in vertical elevation appears in the scene), with the amount of shoreline visible in the scene, and with steepness, among other features. The image that comes to mind, then, is the classic postcard photograph of a sparkling lake set in tall mountains.

The second issue is agreement among different kinds of assessors. One cannot expect perfect agreement, but Zube and his associates found quite strong tendencies for diverse groups to agree on the scenic quality of any given scene. The average correlation among groups ranging from secretaries and students to professional environmental de-signers was .77, which is very strong. This does not mean that assessors with different roles may not have somewhat different views or should not be asked to participate in OBEAs.[549] In fact, despite strong agreement among asses-sor groups, there are also significant differences, such as age and cultural variations.[550,551] In the scenic valley study, these differences did not appear because only one culture was studied and because the age groups that appear to have different standards for scenic quality (children and the elderly) did not participate.

The third issue is whether simulations are effective in yielding the same assessments of scenic quality produced by field visits. Of course the outcome depends on the qual-ity of simulation employed. Zube and his associates used color photographs and found very high correlations be-tween assessments made after viewing the photos and after seeing the actual scenes.

Thus, this OBEA provided local authorities with a list of scenes in their district that have high scenic quality, tentatively concluded that scenic quality is highest for unspoiled, rugged terrain with shorelines visible, discovered that scenic quality is quite similar for young to middle-aged adults of different backgrounds but from the same culture, and showed that color photographs effectively simulate field-observed scenic quality.

Encouraging Food Composting

The weight of our environmental choices is increasing, and what we throw out is a large part of this problem. Much of what we toss out ends in landfills, which are not only ugly and replace natural spaces, but emit potent greenhouse gases like carbon dioxide and methane. A fair amount of this waste is organic but it does not decompose because some landfills are designed to prevent that so as to avoid the leeching of toxic chemicals into the soil.

However, most waste could be handled better. One big source of it is all that food that people do not finish, at home or in public. Food composting can reduce waste while creating a valuable soil supplement that is better in some important ways than chemical fertilizers. In sum, food composting helps in three ways: to mitigate climate change, to reduce the pressure on existing landfills, and to improve agricultural soil quality.

Can diners in public places be encouraged to compost their food and associated items? A study led by Reuven Sussman, with colleagues Leila Scannell, Matt Greeno, and me, investigated whether or not visual prompts (signs) and human models could influence food composting in a university cafeteria.[552] Composting information signs and human models were used. The models watched when diners began to approach the garbage and compost bins, and pretended to be diners themselves who just happened to be a bit ahead in their disposal of items. They rather clearly engaged in the appropriate composting bins for food and other items. The choices of over 1,000 real diners who followed the models to the bins were monitored by other researchers who pretending to be dining.

Ideal composting significantly increased relative to the baseline (the rate of appropriate composting *before* the signs and models were introduced) from 12.5% to 20.5%. Ideal composting increased to 42% when two researchers modeled the behavior. Most importantly, the increased composting continued even after the models were removed; it seems that the cafeteria's population of diners had learned to compost more appropriately, and new social norms were created.

SUMMARY

Individuals appraise settings. In doing so, they may describe settings, make personal judgments of the setting's value, aesthetics, emotional impact, meaning, and security. Selected groups of observers can reliably assess places. Although many kinds of place assessments are possible, most so far have focused on the scenic quality of natural settings. Observer-based assessments (OBEAs) are more place- and policy-oriented than are environmental appraisals. They complement technical assessments (TEAs) and are particularly valuable for assessing dimensions of quality that are especially relevant to humans and can serve as educational tools. OBEAs that use expert, psychophysical, cognitive, and humanistic paradigms have been developed. Environmental concern is important for the survival of many plants, animals, and perhaps ourselves. Although it appears strong, commitment may be not as strong as we think. Certainly its strength varies, and pro-environmental behavior does not always follow from environmental concern. The value of OBEAs is demonstrated in an assessment of a scenic river valley, and that of prompts and human modeling for increasing food composting.

Suggested Supplementary Readings

Craik, K. H., & Zube, E. H. (1976)(Eds.). *Perceiving environmental quality*. New York: Plenum.

Geller, E. S. (2002). The challenge of increasing pro-environmental behavior. In R. B. Bechtel, & A. Churchman (Eds.), *Handbook of environmental psychology* (pp. 525-540). Hoboken, NJ: Wiley.

Gifford, R, & McCunn, L. J. (2012). Appraisals of built environments and approaches to their design that promote well-being and behaviour. In Steg, L., van den Berg, A. E., & de Groot, J. I. M. (Eds.)(pp. 87-95). *Environmental psychology: An introduction*. New York: Wiley-Blackwell.

Gifford, R., & Nilsson, A. (2014). Personal and social factors in environmental concern and behavior. *International Journal of Psychology, 49*, 141-157.

Gifford, R., & Sussman, R. (2012). Environmental attitudes. In S. Clayton (Ed.) (2012). *Handbook of environmental and conservation psychology* (pp. 65-80). New York: Cambridge University Press.

Schultz, P. W., & Kaiser, F. G. (2012). Promoting pro-environmental behavior. In S. Clayton, (Ed.)(2012). *Handbook of environmental and conservation psychology* (pp. 556-580). New York: Cambridge University Press.

Steg, L., & Vlek, C. (2009). Encouraging pro-environmental behaviour: An integrative review and research agenda. *Journal of Environmental Psychology, 29*, 309-317.

References

1 Hume, D. (1757). Of the standard of taste (An essay). *Four Dissertations*. Modern reference: Miller, E. F. (Ed). (1987). Of the standard of taste. *Essays: Moral, political and literary* (p. 230). Indianapolis: Literary Classics.

2 Craik, K. H., & Zube, E. H. (1976)(Eds.). *Perceiving environmental quality*. New York: Plenum.

3 Craik, K. H. (1968). The comprehension of the everyday physical environment. *Journal of the American Institute of Planners, 34*, 29-37.

4 Feimer, N. R. (1984). Environmental perception: The effects of media, evaluative context, and observer sample. *Journal of Environmental Psychology, 4*, 61-80.

5 Canter, D. (1985). Intention, meaning and structure: Social action in its physical context. In G. P. Ginsburg, M. Brenner, & M. von Cranach (Eds.). *Discovery strategies in the psychology of action*. Orlando, FL: Academic Press.

6 Ward, L. M. (1977). Multidimensional scaling of the molar physical environment. *Multivariate Behavioral Research, 12*, 2342.

7 Osgood, C., Suci, G., & Tannenbaum, P. (1957). *The measurement of meaning*. Urbana: University of Illinois Press.

8 Canter, D. (1968). *The measurement of meaning in architecture*. Unpublished manuscript, Building Performance Research Unit, Glasgow.

9 Canter, D. (1969). An intergroup comparison of connotative dimensions in architecture. *Environment and Behavior, 1*, 3748.

10 Cass, R. C., & Hershberger, R. G. (1973). *Further toward a set of semantic scales to measure the meaning of designed environments*. Paper presented at the annual meeting of the Environmental Design Research Association, Blacksburg, VA.

11 Collins, J. B. (1969). *Perceptual dimensions of architectural space validated against behavioral criteria*. Unpublished doctoral dissertation, University of Utah, Salt Lake City.

12 Hershberger, R. G. (1972). *Toward a set of semantic scales to measure the meaning of architectural environments*. Paper presented at the annual meeting of the Environmental Design Research Association, Los Angeles.

13 Cass, R. C., & Hershberger, R. G. (1973). *Further toward a set of semantic scales to measure the meaning of designed environments*. Paper presented at the annual meeting of the Environmental Design Research Association, Blacksburg, VA.

14 Sancar, F. H., & Matari, H. (1988). *A situational research approach for discovering the meaning of city image*. Paper presented at the 19th annual meetings of the Environmental Design Research Association, Pomona, CA.

15 Verderber, S., & Moore, G. T. (1977). Building imagery: A comparative study of environmental cognition. *Man-Environment Systems, 7*, 332-341.

16 Gifford, R. (1980). Judgments of the built environment as a function of individual differences and context. *Journal of Man-Environment Relations, 1*, 22-31.

17 Sonnenfeld, J. (1966). Variable values in space and landscape: An inquiry into the nature of environmental necessity. *Journal of Social Issues, 22*, 71-82.

18 Hidayetoglu, M. L., Yildirim, K., & Akalin, A. (2012). The effects of color and light on indoor wayfinding and the evaluation of the perceived environment. *Journal of Environmental Psychology, 32* (1), 50-58.

19 Mourshed, M., & Zhao, Y. (2012). Healthcare providers' perception of design factors related to physical environments in hospitals. *Journal of Environmental Psychology, 32*, 362-370.

20 Bernaldez, F. G., Gallardo, D., & Abello, R. P. (1987). Children's landscape preferences: From rejection to attraction. *Journal of Environmental Psychology, 7*, 169-176.

21 Lyons, E. (1983). Demographic correlates of landscape preference. *Environment and Behavior, 15*, 487511.

22 Pedersen, D. M. (1986). Preferred city size by ruralists and urbanites. *Perceptual and Motor Skills, 63*, 441-442.

23 Canter, D., & Thorne, R. (1972). Attitudes to housing: A cross cultural comparison. *Environment and Behavior, 4*, 332.

24 Nasar, J. L. (1984). Visual preferences in urban street scenes: A crosscultural comparison between Japan and the United States. *Journal of CrossCultural Psychology, 15*, 79-93.

25 Nasar, J. L. (1984). *Cognition in relation to downtown streetscenes: A comparison between Japan and the United States*. Paper presented at the annual conference of the Environmental Design Research Association, JuneJuly.

26 Yang, B., & Brown, T. J. (1992). A cross-cultural comparison of preferences for landscape styles and landscape elements. *Environment and Behavior, 24*, 471-507.

27 Eisler, A. D., Eisler, H., Yoshida, M. (2003). Perception of human ecology: Crosscultural and gender comparisons. *Journal of Environmental Psychology, 23*, 89-101.

28 Duffy, M., Bailey, S., Beck, B., & Barker, D. G. (1986). Preferences in nursing home design: A comparison of residents, administrators, and designers. *Environment and Behavior, 18*, 246-257.

29 Stamps, A. E. (1991). Comparing preferences of neighbors and a neighborhood design review board. *Environment and Behavior, 23*, 618-629.

30 Takahashi, L. M., & Gaber, S. L. (1998). Controversial facility siting in the urban environment. *Environment and Behavior, 30*, 184-215.

31 Nasar, J. L., & Purcell, T. (July, 1990). Beauty and the beast extended: Knowledge structure and evaluations of houses by Australian architects and non-architects. In H. Pamir, V. Imamoglu, & N. Teymur (Eds.), *Culture, space,*

history. Ankara, Turkey: Sevki Vanh Foundation for Architecture.

32   Wilson, M. A. (1996). The socialization of architectural preference. *Journal of Environmental Psychology, 16*, 33-44.

33   Nasar, J. L. (1988). *Architectural symbolism: A study of house-style meanings.* Paper presented at the 19th annual meeting of the Environmental Design Research Association, Pomona, CA.

34   Brown, G. & Gifford, R. (2001). Architects predict lay evaluations of large contemporary buildings: Whose conceptual properties? *Journal of Environmental Psychology, 21*, 93-99.

35   Devlin, K. (1990). An examination of architectural interpretation: Architects versus non-architects. *Journal of Architectural and Planning Research, 7*, 235-244.

36   James, K. (1989). Family-role salience and environmental cognition. *Journal of Environmental Psychology, 9*, 45-55.

37   Kaplan, R. (1977). Patterns of environmental preference. *Environment and Behavior, 9*, 195215.

38   Malinowsky, J. C., & Thurber, C. A. (1996). Developmental shifts in the place of preferences of boys aged 8-16 years. *Journal of Environmental Psychology, 16*, 45-54.

39   Priestley, T., & Evans, G. W. (1996). Resident perceptions of a nearby electric transmission line. *Journal of Environmental Psychology, 16* , 65-74.

40   Iwata, O. (1990). The relationship of social evaluation and subjective sensitivity to environmental evaluation. *Psychologia: An International Journal of Psychology in the Orient, 35*, 69-75.

41   Srinivasan, T. (1987). A study of mental health of the adolescents in relation to geographical environments. *Child Psychiatry Quarterly, 20*, 55-60.

42   Gifford, R. (1980). Environmental dispositions and the evaluation of architectural interiors. *Journal of Research in Personality, 14*, 386-399.

43   Gifford, R. (1980). Environmental dispositions and the evaluation of architectural interiors. *Journal of Research in Personality, 14*, 386399.

44   Stamps III, A. E., & Nasar, J. L. (1997). Design review and public preferences: Effects of geographical location , public consensus, sensation seeking, and architectural styles. *Journal of Environmental Psychology, 17*, 11-32.

45   Stamps, A. E. (1996). People and places: Variance components of environmental preferences. *Perceptual and Motor Skills, 82*, 323-334.

46   Peron, E., Purcell, A. T., Staats, H., Falchero, S., & Lamb, R. J. (1998). Models of preference for outdoor scenes: Some experimental evidence. *Environment and Behavior, 30*, 282-305

47   Im, S. (1984). Visual preferences in enclosed urban spaces: An exploration of a scientific approach to environmental design. *Environment and Behavior, 16*, 235-262.

48   Gifford, R., Hine, D. W., Muller-Clemm, W., Reynolds, Jr., D. J., & Shaw, K. T. (2000). Decoding modern architecture: A lens model approach for understanding the aesthetic differences of architects and laypersons. *Environment and Behavior, 32*, 163-187.

49   Gifford, R., Hine, D. W., Muller-Clemm, W., & Shaw, K. T. (2001). Why architects and laypersons judge buildings differently:

Cognitive properties and physical bases. *Journal of Architectural and Planning Research, 18*, 131-149.

50   Kaye, S. M., & Murray, M. A. (1982). Evaluations of an architectural space as a function of variations in furniture arrangement, furniture density, and windows. *Human Factors, 24*, 609-618.

51   Nasar, J. L. (1981). Responses to different spatial configurations. *Human Factors, 23*, 439-446.

52   Baird, J. C., Cassidy, B., & Kurr, J. (1978). Room preference as a function of architectural features and user activities. *Journal of Applied Psychology, 63*, 719-727.

53   Hidayetoglu, M. L., Yildirim, K., & Akalin, A. (2012). The effects of color and light on indoor wayfinding and the evaluation of the perceived environment. *Journal of Environmental Psychology, 32* (1), 50-58.

54   Butler, D. L., & Steuerwald, B. L. (1991). Effects of view and room size on window size preferences made in models. *Environment and Behavior, 23*, 334-358.

55   Frewald, D. B. (1990). Preferences for older buildings: A psychological approach to architectural design. *Dissertation Abstracts International, 51*, 414-415.

56   White, E. V., & Gatersleben, B. (2011). Greenery on residential buildings: Does it affect preferences and perceptions of beauty? *Journal of Environmental Psychology, 31*, 89-98.

57   Monti, F., Agostini, F., Dellabartola, S., Neri, E., Bozicevic, L., & Pocecco, M. (2012). Pictorial intervention in a pediatric hospital environment: Effects on parental affective perception of the unit. *Journal of Environmental Psychology, 32*, 216-224.

58   Herzog, T. R., & Gale, T. A. (1996). Preference for urban buildings as a function of age and nature context. *Environment and Behavior, 28*, 44-72

59   Strumse, E. (1996). Demographic differences in the visual preferences for agrarian landscapes in western Norway. *Journal of Environmental Psychology, 16*, 17-31

60   Pedersen, D. M. (1986). Perception of interior designs. *Perceptual and Motor Skills, 63*, 671-676.

61   Nasar, J. L. (1983). Adult viewers' preferences in residential scenes: A study of the relationship of environmental attributes to preference. *Environment and Behavior, 15*, 589-614.

62   Nasar, J. L. (1990). The evaluative image of the city. *Journal of the American Planning Association, 56*, 41-53.

63   Oppewal, H., & Timmermans, H. (1999). Modeling consumer perception of public space in shopping centers. *Environment and Behavior, 31*, 45-65.

64   Nasar, J. L. (1987). Environmental correlates of evaluative appraisals of central business district scenes. *Landscape and Urban Planning, 14*, 117-130.

65   Nasar, J., L., & Hong, X. (1999). Visual preferences in urban signscapes. *Environment and Behavior, 31*, 671-691.

66   Wong, K. K. (1990). Scenic quality and cognitive structures of urban environments: The role of scene attributes and

respondent characteristics. *Dissertation Abstracts International, 51*, 22-69.

67   Nasar, J. L. (1987). Physical correlates of perceived quality in lakeshore development. *Leisure Sciences, 9*, 259-279.

68   Kuller, R. (1980). Architecture and emotion. In B. Mikellides (Ed.). *Architecture for people.* London: Studio Vista.

69   Maslow, A. H., & Mintz, N. C. (1956). Effects of aesthetic surrounding: I. Initial effects of three aesthetic conditions upon perceiving "energy" and "well-being" in faces. *Journal of Psychology, 41*, 247-254.

70   Wilmot, D. (1990). Maslow and Mintz revisited. *Journal of Environmental Psychology, 10*, 293-312.

71   Wohlwill, J. F. (1982). The visual impact of development in coastal zone areas. *Coastal Zone Management Journal, 9*, 225-248.

72   Nasar, J. L. (1987). The effect of sign complexity and coherence on the perceived quality of retail scenes. *Journal of the American Planning Association, 53*, 499-509.

73   Stamps, A. E. (1991). Public preferences for high rise buildings: Stylistic and demographic effects. *Perceptual and Motor Skills, 72*, 839-844.

74   Stamps, A. E. (1999). Physical determinants of preference for residential facades. *Environment and Behavior, 31*, 723-751.

75   Devlin, K., & Nasar, J. L. (1989). The beauty and the beast: Some preliminary comparisons of "high" versus "popular" residential architecture and public versus architect judgments of same. *Journal of Environmental Psychology, 9*, 333-334.

76   Stamps, A. E. (1993). Public preferences for residences: Precode, code minimum, and avantgarde architectural styles. *Perceptual and Motor Skills, 77*, 99-103.

77   Purcell, T., & Nasar, J. L. (August, 1990). *Australian architect and non-architect students experiences of American houses.* Paper presented at the Conference of the International Association of Empirical Aesthetics, Budapest, Hungary.

78   Miller, P. A. (1984). *Visual preference and implications for coastal management: A perceptual study of the British Columbia shoreline.* Unpublished doctoral dissertation, University of Michigan, Ann Arbor, MI.

79   Kaplan, R., Kaplan, S., & Brown, T. (1989). Environmental preference: A comparison of four domains of predictors. *Environment and Behavior, 21*, 509-530.

80   Herzog, T. R., & Bosley, P. J. (1992). Tranquility and preference as affective qualities of natural environments. *Journal of Environmental Psychology, 12*, 115-127.

81   Herzog, T. R., & Barnes, G. J. (1999). Tranquility and preference revisited. *Journal of Environmental Psychology, 19*, 171-181.

82   Nasar, J. L. (1994). Urban design aesthetics: The evaluative qualities of building exteriors. *Environment and Behavior, 26*, 377-401.

83   Hagerhall, C. M. (2001). Consensus in landscape preference judgements. *Journal of Environmental Psychology, 21*, 83-92.

84   Herzog, T. R., & Stark, J. L. (2004). Typicality and preference for positively and negatively valued environmental settings. *Journal of Environmental Psychology, 24*, 85-92.

85 Appleton, J. (1975). *The experience of landscape.* New York: Wiley.

86 Ruddell, E. J., & Hammitt, W. E. (1987). Prospect refuge theory: A psychological orientation for edge effect in recreation environments. *Journal of Leisure Research, 19,* 249-260.

87 Andrews, M., & Gatersleben, B. (2010). Variations in perceptions of danger, fear and preference in a simulated natural environment. *Journal of Environmental Psychology, 30,* 473-481.

88 Peterson, G. L., & Neumann, E. S. (1969). Modeling and predicting human response to the visual recreation environment. *Journal of Leisure Research, 1,* 219-237.

89 Abello, R. P., Bernaldez, F. G., & Galiano, E. F. (1986). Consensus and contrast components in landscape preference. *Environment and Behavior, 18,* 155-178.

90 Yi, Y. K. (1993). Affect and cognition interface in aesthetic experiences of landscapes. *Dissertation Abstracts, 53,* 3015-3016.

91 Hagerhall, C. M., Purcell, T., & Taylor, R. (2004). Fractal dimension of landscape silhouette outlines as a predictor of landscape preference. *Journal of Environmental Psychology, 24,* 247-255.

92 Kaplan, S., & Kaplan, R. (1982). *Cognition and environment: Functioning in an uncertain world.* New York: Praeger.

93 Kaplan, S. (1987). Aesthetics, affect, and cognition: Environmental preference from an evolutionary perspective. *Environment and Behavior, 19,* 3-32.

94 Ulrich, R. S. (1983). Aesthetic and affective response to natural environment. *Human behavior and environment: Advances in theory and research, 6,* 85-125.

95 Balling, J. D., & Falk, J. H. (1982). Development of visual preference for natural environments. *Environment and Behavior, 14,* 528.

96 Lyons, E. (1983). Demographic correlates of landscape preference. *Environment and Behavior, 15,* 487-511.

97 Butler, D. L., & Biner, P. M. (1989). Effects of setting on window preferences and factors associated with those preferences. *Environment and Behavior, 21,* 17-31.

98 Lindberg, E., Garling, T., Montgomery, H., & Waara, R. (1986). Preferences for housing aspects: A study of underlying beliefs and values. *Umea Psychological Reports,* No. 184.

99 Carmichael, B. A. (1991). *Tourist image and ski resort choice: An analysis of the Victoria, B. C. skier market.* Unpublished doctoral dissertation, University of Victoria, Victoria, British Columbia.

100 Kaplan, S., & Kaplan, R. (1982). *Cognition and environment: Functioning in an uncertain world.* New York: Praeger, p. 80.

101 Herzog, T. R. (1984). A cognitive analysis of preference for field-and-forest environments. *Landscape Research, 9,* 10-16.

102 Herzog, T. R. (1984). A cognitive analysis of preference for field-and-forest environments. *Landscape Research, 9,* 10-16.

103 Herzog, T. R. (1985). A cognitive analysis of preference for waterscapes. *Journal of Environmental Psychology, 5,* 225-241.

104 Herzog, T. R. (1989). A cognitive analysis of preference for urban nature. *Journal of Environmental Psychology, 9,* 27-43.

105 Herzog, T. R., & Smith, G. A. (1988). Danger, mystery, and environmental preference. *Environment and Behavior, 20,* 320-344.

106 Scott, S. B. (1990). Preference, mystery and visual attributes of interiors: A study of relationships. *Dissertation Abstracts International, 50,* 33-86.

107 Kaplan, R., Kaplan, S., & Brown, T. (1989). Environmental preference: A comparison of four domains of predictors. *Environment and Behavior, 21,* 509-530.

108 Friedman, C., Balling, J. D., & Valadez, J. J. (1985). *Visual preference for office buildings: A comparison of architects and non-architects.* Paper presented at the Annual Meeting of the Environmental Design Research Association, New York City, NY.

109 Gimblett, H. R. (1990). Environmental cognition: The prediction of preference in rural Indiana. *Journal of Architectural Planning and Research, 7,* 222-234.

110 Herzog, T. R., & Miller, E. J. (1998). The role of mystery in perceived danger and environmental preference. *Environment and Behavior, 30,* 429-449.

111 Ikemi, M. (2005). The effects of mystery on preference for residential façades. *Journal of Environmental Psychology, 25,* 167-173.

112 Nasar, J. L., & Cubukcu, E. (2011). Evaluative appraisals of environmental mystery and surprise. *Environment and Behavior, 43,* 387-414.

113 Finlay, T. W. (1990). The prediction of preference evaluations of zoo exhibits: A comparison of the informational and psychophysical theories of environmental preference. *Dissertation Abstracts International, 51,* 427.

114 Herzog, T. R. (1992). A cognitive analysis of preference for urban spaces. *Journal of Environmental Psychology, 12,* 237-248.

115 Gimblett, H. R. (1990). Environmental cognition: The prediction of preference in rural Indiana. *Journal of Architectural Planning and Research, 7,* 222-234.

116 Herzog, T. R. (1984). A cognitive analysis of preference for field-and-forest environments. *Landscape Research, 9,* 10-16.

117 Herzog, T. R. (1985). A cognitive analysis of preference for waterscapes. *Journal of Environmental Psychology, 5,* 225-241.

118 Herzog, T. R. (1989). A cognitive analysis of preference for urban nature. *Journal of Environmental Psychology, 9,* 27-43.

119 Herzog, T. R. (1992). A cognitive analysis of preference for urban spaces. *Journal of Environmental Psychology, 12,* 237-248.

120 Herzog, T. R., & Leverich, O. L. (2003). Searching for legibility. *Environment and Behavior, 35,* ,2003,459477.

121 Stamps, A. E. III (2004). Mystery, complexity, legibility and coherence: A metaanalysis. *Journal of Environmental Psychology, 24,* 116.

122 da Luz Reis, A. T., & Dias Lay, M. C. (2010). Internal and external aesthetics of housing estates. *Environment and Behavior, 42,* 271-294.

123 Fenton, D. M. (1985). Dimensions of meaning in the perception of natural settings and their relationship to Aesthetic response. *Australian Journal of Psychology, 37,* 325-339.

124 van den Berg, A. E., Vlek, C. A., & Coeterier, J. F. (1998). Group differences in the aesthetic evaluation of nature development plans: A multilevel approach. *Journal of Environmental Psychology, 18,* 141-157.

125 Hull, R. B., & Revell, G. R. (1989). Cross-cultural comparison of landscape scenic beauty evaluations: A case study in Bali. *Journal of Environmental Psychology, 9,* 177-191.

126 Thornton, J. A., McMillan, P. H., & Romanovsky, P. (1989). Perceptions of water pollution in South Africa: Case studies from two water bodies (Hartbeesport Dam and Zandvlei). *South African Journal of Psychology, 19,* 199-204.

127 Bourassa, S. C. (1990). A paradigm for landscape aesthetics. *Environment and Behavior, 22,* 787-812.

128 Ruddell, E. J., Gramann, J. H., Rudis, V. A., & Westphal, J. M. (1989). The psychological utility of visual penetration in near-view forest scenic-beauty models. *Environment and Behavior, 21,* 393-410.

129 Kuller, R. (1980). Architecture and emotions. In B. Mikellides (Ed.), *Architecture for people.* Studio Vista, London.

130 Böhm, G. (2003). Emotional reactions to environmental risks: Consequentialist versus ethical evaluation. *Journal of Environmental Psychology, 23,* 199-212.

131 Mehrabian, A., & Russell, J. A. (1974). *An approach to environmental psychology.* Cambridge, Mass: MIT Press.

132 Mehrabian, A., & Russell, J. A. (1975). Environmental effects on affiliation among strangers. *Humanitas, 11,* 219-230.

133 Russell, J. A., Ward, L. M., & Pratt, G. (1981). Affective quality attributed to environments: A factor analytic study. *Environment and Behavior, 13,* 259-288.

134 Mehrabian, A., & Russell, J. A. (1974). *An approach to environmental psychology.* Cambridge, Mass: MIT Press.

135 Nasar, J. L., &Terzano, K. (2010). The desirability of views of city skylines after dark. *Journal of Environmental Psychology, 30,* 215-225.

136 Daniel, T. C., & Ittelson, W. H. (1981). Conditions for environmental perception research: Comment on The psychological representation of molar physical environments by Ward and Russell. *Journal of Experimental Psychology: General, 110,* 153-157.

137 Russell, J. A., & Ward, L. M. (1981). On the psychological reality of environmental meaning: Reply to Daniel and Ittelson. *Journal of Experimental Psychology, 110,* 163-168.

138 Foxall, G. & Greenly, G. (1998). The affective structure of consumer situations. *Environment and Behavior, 30,* 781-798.

139 Staats, H., Gatersleben B., & Hartig, T. (1997). Change in mood as s function of environmental design: Arousal and pleasure on a simulated forest hike. *Journal of Environmental Psychology, 17,* 283-300.

140 Dazkir, S. S., & Read, M. A. (2012). Furniture Forms and Their Influence on Our Emotional Responses Toward Interior Environments. *Environment and Behavior, 44,* 722-732.

141 Guéguen, N. (2012). The sweet smell of… courtship: Effects of pleasant ambient fragrance on women's receptivity to a man's courtship request. *Journal of Environmental Psychology, 32,* 123-125.

142 Gold, J. R., & Burgess, J. (1982). (Eds.), *Valued environments.* London: George Allen & Unwin.

143 Manzo, L. C., & Devine-Wright, P. (Eds.) (2014). *Place attachment: Advances in theory, methods and applications.* New York: Routledge.

144 Hershberger, R. G. (1970). Architecture and meaning. *Journal of Aesthetic Education, 4,* 37-55.

145 Espe, H. (1981). Differences in the perception of National Socialist and Classicist architecture. *Journal of Environmental Psychology, 1,* 33-42.

146 Jencks, C. (1978). Postmodern history. *Architectural Design, 1,* 1358.

147 Groat, L. (1982). Meaning in postmodern architecture: An examination using the multiple sorting task. *Journal of Environmental Psychology, 2,* 322.

148 Cherulnik, P. D., & Souders, S. B. (1984). The social contents of place schemata: People are judged by the places where they live and work. *Population and Environment: Behavioral and Social Issues, 7,* 211-233.

149 Cherulnik, P. D., & Bayless, J. K. (1986). Person perception in environmental context: The influence of residential settings on impressions of their occupants. *Journal of Social Psychology, 126,* 667-673.

150 Nasar, J. L. (1988). *Architectural symbolism: A study of house-style meanings.* Paper presented at the 19th annual meeting of the Environmental Design Research Association, Pomona, CA.

151 Nasar, J. L., & Julian, D. (1985). Effects of labelled meaning on the affective quality of housing scenes. *Journal of Environmental Psychology, 5,* 335-344.

152 Sadalla, E. K., & Sheets, V. L. (1993). Symbolism in building materials: Self-presentational and cognitive components. *Environment and Behavior, 25,* 155-180.

153 Groat, L., & Canter, D. (1979). Does postmodernism communicate? *Progressive Architecture, 12,* 84-87.

154 Nasar, J. L., Stamps, A. E. III, & Hanyu, K.(2005). Form and function in public buildings. *Journal of Environmental Psychology, 25,* 159-165.

155 Prak, N. L., & van Wegen, H. B. R. *The influence of cognitive factors on the perception of buildings.* Paper presented at the annual meeting of the Environmental Design Research Association, Lawrence, Kansas, 1975.

156 Genereux, R. L., Ward, L. M., & Russell, J. A. (1983). The behavioral component of the meaning of places. *Journal of Environmental Psychology, 3,* 43-55.

157 Anderson, N. M., Williams, K. J. H., & Ford, R. M. (2013). Community perceptions of plantation forestry: The association between place meanings and social representations of a contentious rural land use. *Journal of Environmental Psychology, 34,* 121-136.

158 Schmidt, F. N., & Gifford, R. (1989). A dispositional approach to hazard perception: Preliminary development of the Environmental Appraisal Inventory. *Journal of Environmental Psychology, 9,* 57-67.

159 Walsh-Daneshmandi, A., & MacLachlan, M. (2000). Environmental risk to the self: Factor analysis and development of subscales for the Environmental Appraisal Inventory (EAI) with an Irish sample. *Journal of Environmental Psychology, 20,* 141-149.

160 Barke, R. P., &Jenkins-Smith, H. C. (1993). Politics and scientific expertise: Scientists, risk perception, and nuclear waste policy. *Risk Analysis, 13,* 425-439.

161 Vaughn, E., & Nordenstam, B. (1991). The perceptions of environmental risks among ethnically diverse groups. *Journal of Cross-Cultural Psychology, 22,* 29-60.

162 Vaughn, E. (1993). Individual and cultural differences in adaptation to environmental risks. *American Psychologist, 48,* 673-680.

163 Pilisuk, M., Parks, S. H., & Hawkes, G. (1987). Public perception of technological risk. *Social Science Journal, 24,* 403-413.

164 Barke, R. P., Jenkins-Smith, H., & Slovic, P. (1997). Risk perceptions of men and women scientists. *Social Sciences Quarterly, 78,* 167-176.

165 Bord, R. J., & O'Conner, R. E. (1997). The gender gap in environmental attitudes: The case of perceived vulnerability to risk. *Social Science Quarterly, 78,* 830-840.

166 Wilson, M., Daly, M., Grodin, S, & Pratt, A. (1996). Sex differences in valuations of the environment? *Population and Environment: A Journal of Interdisciplinary Studies, 18,* 143-159.

167 Prince-Embury, S., & Rooney, J. F. (1987). Perception of control and faith in experts among residents in the vicinity of Three Mile Island. *Journal of Applied Social Psychology, 17,* 953-968.

168 Larrain Navarro, P., Simpson-Housley, P., & de-Man, A. F. (1987). Anxiety, locus of control and appraisal of air pollution. *Perceptual and Motor Skills, 64,* 811-814.

169 Mehta, M. D., & Simpson-Housley, P. (1994). Trait anxiety and perception of potential nuclear power plant disaster. *Psychological Reports, 74,* 291-295.

170 Pedigo, S. K. (1986). The risks of radiation: A study of the attitudes of a select sample of residents of southeast Tennessee. *Dissertation Abstracts International, 47*(3-B), 1016.

171 Williams, B. L., Brown, S., Greenberg, M., & Kahn, M. A. (1999). Risk perception in context: The Savannah River site stakeholder study. *Risk Analysis, 19,* 1019-1935.

172 Maharik, M., & Fischhoff, B. (1993). Contrasting perceptions of the risks of using nuclear energy sources in space. *Journal of Environmental Psychology, 13,* 243-250.

173 Kuhn, K. M. (2000). Message format and audience values: Interactive effects of uncertainty information and environmental attitudes on perceived risk. *Journal of Environmental Psychology, 20,* 41-51.

174 Der Karabetian, A., Stephenson, K., & Poggi, T. (1996). Environmental risk perception, activism and world-mindedness among samples of British and U. S. college students. *Perceptual and Motor Skills, 83,* 451-462.

175 Sjoberg, L, & Drottz-Sjoberg, B.-M. (1991). Knowledge and risk perception among nuclear power plant employees. *Risk Analysis, 11,* 607-618.

176 Barke, R. P., &Jenkins-Smith, H. C. (1993). Politics and scientific expertise: Scientists, risk perception, and nuclear waste policy. *Risk Analysis, 13,* 425-439.

177 Steg, L., & Sievers, I. (2000). Cultural theory and individual perceptions of environmental risks. *Environment and Behavior, 32,* 250-269.

178 Flynn, J., Slovic, P., & Mertz, C. K. (1993). Decidedly different: Expert and public views of risks from a radioactive waste repository. *Risk Analysis, 13,* 643-648.

179 Vaughan, E. (1986). Some factors influencing the nonexpert's perception and evaluation of environmental risks. *Dissertation Abstracts International, 47,* 1332.

180 Freudenburg, W. R., & Pastor, S. K. (1992). NIMBYs and LULUs: Stalking the syndromes. *Journal of Social Issues, 48,* 39-61.

181 Renn, O., Burns, W. J., Kasperson, J. X., Kasperson, R. E., et al. (1992). The social amplification of risk: Theoretical foundations and empirical applications. *Journal of Social Issues, 48,* 137-160.

182 Cvetkovich, G., & Earle, T. C. (1992). Environmental hazards and the public. *Journal of Social Issues, 48,* 1-20.

183 Brown, P. (1992). Popular epidemiology and toxic waste contamination: Lay and professional ways of knowing. *Journal of Health and Social Behavior, 33,* 267-281.

184 MacGregor, D., Slovic, P., Mason, R. G., Detweiler, J. et al. (1994). Perceived risks of radioactive waste transport though Oregon: Results of a statewide survey. *Risk Analysis, 14,* 5-14.

185 Park, J. J., & Selman, P. (2011). Attitudes toward rural landscape change in England. *Environment and Behavior, 43,* 182-206.

186 Chess, C., & Salomone, K. L. (1992). Rhetoric and reality: Risk communication in government agencies. *Journal of Environmental Education, 23,* 28-33.

187 Wandersman, A. H., & Hallman, W. K. (1993). Are people acting irrationally? Understanding public concerns about environmental threats. *American Psychologist, 48,* 681-686.

188 Maharik, M. & Fischhoff, B. (1992). The risks of using nuclear energy sources in space: Some lay activists' perception. *Risk Analysis, 12,* 383-392.

189 Winder, A. E. (1992-93). Risk assessmentBrisk perception: Who shall decide? *International Quarterly of Community Health Education, 13,* 405-410.

190 Bord, R. J., & O'Connor, R. E. (1992). Determinants of risk perceptions of a hazardous waste site. *Risk Analysis, 12,* 411-416.

191 Kunreuther, H., Easterling, D., Desvouges, W., & Slovic, P. (1990). Public attitudes toward siting a high-level nuclear waste repository in Nevada. *Risk Analysis, 10,* 469-484.

192 Summers, C., & Hine, D. W. (1997). Nuclear waste goes on the road: Risk perceptions and compensatory tradeoffs in single-industry communities. *Canadian Journal of Behavioural Science, 29,* 211-223.

193 Slovic, P., Fischoff, B., & Lichtenstein, S. (1979). Rating the risks. *Environment, 21,* 14-20, 36-39.

194 Ampofo-Boateng, K. (1989). Children's perception of safety and danger on the road. *Dissertation Abstracts International, 49,* 4567-4568.

195 Shaffer, G. S., & Anderson, L. M. (1985). Perceptions of the security and attractiveness of urban parking lots. *Journal of Environmental Psychology, 5,* 311-323.

196 Loewen, L .J., Steel, G. D., & Suedfeld, P. (1993). Perceived safety from crime in the urban environment. *Journal of Environmental Psychology, 13,* 323-331.

197 Andrews, M., & Gatersleben, B. (2010). Variations in perceptions of danger, fear and preference in a simulated natural environment. *Journal of Environmental Psychology, 30,* 473-481.

198 Bonaiuto, M., Breakwell, G. M., & Cano, I. (1996). Identity processes and the environmental threat: The effects of nationalism and local identity upon perception of beach pollution. *Journal of Community and Applied Social Psychology, 6,* 157-175.

199 Craik, K. H. (1971). The assessment of places. In P. McReynolds (Ed.) *Advances in psychological assessment, Vol. 2.* Palo Alto, CA: Science and Behavior Books.

200 Craik, K. H. (1971). The assessment of places. In P. McReynolds (Ed.) *Advances in psychological assessment, Vol. 2.* Palo Alto, CA: Science and Behavior Books.

201 Moos, R. H. (1973). Conceptualizations of human environments. *American Psychologist, 28,* 652-655.

202 Andrade, C., Lima, M. L., & Fornara, F. (2012). Marino Bonaiuto, Users' views of hospital environmental quality: Validation of the Perceived Hospital Environment Quality Indicators (PHEQIs). *Journal of Environmental Psychology, 32,* 97-111.

203 Rowe, R. D., & Chestnut, L. G. (1983). Introduction. In R. D. Rowe & L. G. Chestnut (Eds.), *Managing air quality and scenic resources at national parks and wilderness areas.* Boulder, CO: Westview Press.

204 Yuhnke, R. E. (1983). The importance of visibility protection in the national parks and wilderness. In R. D. Rowe & L. G. Chestnut (Eds.), *Managing air quality and scenic resources at national parks and wilderness parks.* Boulder, CO: Westview Press.

205 Christensen, D. L., & Carp, F. M. (1987). PEQI-based environmental predictors of the residential satisfaction of older women. *Journal of Environmental Psychology, 7,* 45-64.

206 Craik, K. H., & Zube, E. H. (1976)(Eds.). *Perceiving environmental quality.* New York: Plenum.

207 Christensen, D. L., & Carp, F. M. (1987). PEQI-based environmental predictors of the residential satisfaction of older women. *Journal of Environmental Psychology, 7,* 45-64.

208 Benfield, J. A., Bell, P. A., Troup, L. J., & Soderstrom, N. C. (2010). Aesthetic and affective effects of vocal and traffic noise on natural landscape assessment. Journal of Environmental Psychology, 30, 103-111.

209 Zube, E. H. (1980). *Environmental evaluation: Perception and public policy.* Monterey, CA: Brooks/Cole.

210 Anderson, T. W., Zube, E. H., & MacConnell, W. P. (1976). *Predicting scenic resource values: Studies in landscape perception* (Technical report). Amherst: Institute for Man and Environment, University of Massachusetts.

211 Moos, R. H., & Lemke, S. (1984). *Multiphasic environmental assessment procedure.* Unpublished manuscript, Stanford University, Social Ecology Laboratory, Palo Alto, CA.

212 Craik, K. H. (1983). A psychology of large scale environment. In N. R. Feimer & E. S. Geller (Eds.) *Environmental psychology: Directions and perspectives.* New York: Praeger.

213 Craik, K. H., & Zube, E. H. (1976)(Eds.). *Perceiving environmental quality.* New York: Plenum.

214 Moser, G. (1984). Water quality perception, a dynamic perspective. *Journal of Environmental Psychology, 4,* 201-210.

215 Moos, R. H., & Lemke, S. (1984). *Multiphasic environmental assessment procedure.* Unpublished manuscript, Stanford University, Social Ecology Laboratory, Palo Alto, CA.

216 Zube, E. H. (1984). Themes in landscape assessment theory. *Landscape Journal, 3,* 104-110.

217 Zube, E. H., Sell, J. L., & Taylor, J. G. (1982). Landscape perception: Research, application and theory. *Landscape Planning, 9,* 133.

218 Daniel, T. C. (1990). Measuring the quality of the natural environment: A psychophysical approach. *American Psychologist, 45,* 633-637.

219 Kaplan, S., Kaplan, R., & Wendt, J. S. (1972). Rated preference and complexity for natural and urban visual material. *Perception and Psychophysics, 12,* 354-356.

220 Ulrich, R. S. (1981). Natural versus urban scenes: Some psychophysical effects. *Environment and Behavior, 13,* 523-556.

221 Hull, R. B., & Buhyoff, G. J. (1983). Distance and scenic beauty: A nonmontonic relationship. *Environment and Behavior, 15,* 77-91.

222 Hull, R. B., & Buhyoff, G. J. (1983). Distance and scenic beauty: A nonmontonic relationship. *Environment and Behavior, 15,* 77-91.

223 Patsfall, M. R., Feimer, N. R. Buhyoff, G. J., & Wellman, J. D. (1984). The prediction of scenic beauty from landscape content and composition. *Journal of Environmental Psychology, 4,* 726.

224 Zube, E. H. (1984). Themes in landscape assessment theory. *Landscape Journal, 3,* 104-110.

225 Benfield, J. A., Bell, P. A., Troup, L. J., & Soderstrom, N. C. (2010). Aesthetic and affective effects of vocal and traffic noise on natural landscape assessment. *Journal of Environmental Psychology, 30,* 103-111.

226 Heberlein, T. A. (1989). Attitudes and environmental management. *Journal of Social Issues, 45,* 37-57.

227 Milfont, T. L., & Duckitt, J. (2004). The structure of environmental attitudes: A first and sec ondorder confirmatory factor analysis. *Journal of Environmental Psychology, 24,* 289-303.

228 Bogner, F. X., & Wiseman, M. (2002). Environmental perception of French and some Western European secondary school students.

European Journal of Psychology of Education, 17, 318.

229 Munoz, F., Bogner, F., Clement, P., & Carvalho, G. S. (2009). Teachers' conceptions of nature and environment in 16 countries. *Journal of Environmental Psychology, 29,* 407-413.

230 Ajzen, I. (1991). The theory of planned behavior. *Organizational Behavior and Human Decision Processes, 50,* 179-211.

231 Heath, Y., & Gifford, R. (2002). Extending the theory of planned behavior: Predicting the use of public transportation. *Journal of Applied Social Psychology, 32,* 2154-2185.

232 Laudenslager, M. S., & Holt, D. T. (2004). Understanding air force members' intentions to participate in pro-environmental behaviors: An application of the theory of planned behavior. *Perceptual and Motor Skills, 98*(3,Pt2), 1162-1170.

233 Greaves, M., Zibarras, L. D., & Stride, C. (2013). Using the theory of planned behavior to explore environmental behavioral intentions in the workplace. *Journal of Environmental Psychology, 34,* 109-120.

234 Bamberg, S., & Schmidt, P. (2003). Incentives, morality, or habit? Predicting students' car use for university routes with the models of Ajzen, Schwartz and Triandis. *Environment and Behavior, 35,* 264-285.

235 Heath, Y., & Gifford, R. (2002). Extending the theory of planned behavior: Predicting the use of public transportation. *Journal of Applied Social Psychology, 32,* 2154-2185.

236 White, K. M., & Hyde, M. K. (2012). The role of self-perceptions in the prediction of household recycling behavior in Australia. *Environment and Behavior, 44,* 785-799.

237 Fielding, K., McDonald, R., & Louis, W. (2008). Theory of planned behaviour, identity and intentions to engage in environmental activism. *Journal of Environmental Psychology, 28,* 318-326.

238 Whitmarsh, L., & O'Neill, S. (2010). Green identity, green living? the role of pro-environmental self-identity in determining consistency across diverse pro-environmental behaviours. *Journal of Environmental Psychology, 30,* 305-314.

239 Smith, J. R., Louis, W. R., Terry, D. J., Greenaway, K. H., Clarke, M. R., & Cheng, X. (2012). Congruent or conflicted? The impact of injunctive and descriptive norms on environmental intentions. *Journal of Environmental Psychology, 32,* 353-361.

240 Stern, P. (2000). Toward a coherent theory of environmentally significant behavior. *Journal of Social Issues, 56,* 407-424.

241 Dunlap, R. E., van Liere, K. D., Mertig, A. G., & Emmet Jones, R. (2000). Measuring endorsement of the new ecological paradigm: A revised NEP scale. *Journal of Social Issues, 56,* 425-442.

242 Stern, P. (2000). Toward a coherent theory of environmentally significant behavior. *Journal of Social Issues, 56,* 407-424.

243 Steg, L., Dreijerink, L., & Abrahamse, W. (2005). Factors influencing the acceptability of energy policies: A test of VBN theory. *Journal of Environmental Psychology, 25,* 415-425.

244 García Mira, R., Deus, E. R., Rodriguez, M. D., & Martinez, J. R.. (2003). Predicting

environmental attitudes and behavior. In G. Moser, E. Pol, Y. Bernard, M. Bonnes, & J. Corraliza (Eds.), *People, places, and sustainability* (pp. 302-311). Ashland, OH: Hogrefe & Huber.

245 Bamberg, S. (2013). Changing environmentally harmful behaviors: A stage model of self-regulated behavioral change. *Journal of Environmental Psychology, 34,* 151-159.

246 Deci, E. L., & Ryan, R. M. (1985). *Intrinsic motivation and self-determinaton in human behaviour.* New York: Plenum.

247 Webb, D., Soutar, G. N., Mazzarol, T., & Saldaris, P. (2013). Self-determination theory and consumer behavioural change: Evidence from a household energy-saving behaviour study. *Journal of Environmental Psychology, 35,* 59-66.

248 de Groot, J. I. M., Steg, L. (2010). Relationships between value orientations, self-determined motivational types and pro-environmental behavioural intentions. *Journal of Environmental Psychology, 30,* 368-378.

249 Hunecke, M., Haustein, S., Böhler, S., & Grischkat, S. (2010). Attitude-based target groups to reduce the ecological impact of daily mobility behavior. *Environment and Behavior, 42,* 3-43.

250 Kormos, C. & Gifford, R. (in press). The validity of self-report measures of pro-environmental behavior: A meta-analytic review. *Journal of Environmental Psychology.*

251 Gifford, R. (2014). Environmental psychology matters. *Annual Review of Psychology, 65.*

252 Liebe, U., Preisendorfer, P., & Meyerhoff, J. (2011). To pay or not to pay: Competing theories to explain individuals' willingness to pay for public environmental goods. *Environment and Behavior, 43,* 106-130.

253 Cordano, M., Welcomer, S., Scherer, R. F., Pradenas, L., & Parada, V. (2011). A cross-cultural assessment of three theories of pro-environmental behavior: A comparison between business students of Chile and the United States. *Environment and Behavior, 43,* 634-657.

254 Tanner, C. (1999). Constraints on environmental behaviour. *Journal of Environmental Psychology, 19,* 145–157.

255 Klöckner, C. A., & Blöbaum, A. (2010). A comprehensive action determination model: Toward a broader understanding of ecological behaviour using the example of travel mode choice. *Journal of Environmental Psychology, 30,* 574-586.

256 Wall, R., Devine-Wright, P., & Mill, G. (2007). Comparing and combining theories to explain pro-environmental intentions: The case of commuting-mode choice. *Environment and Behavior, 39,* 731-753.

257 Kinnear, T. C., & Taylor, J. R. (1973). The effect of ecological concern on brand perceptions. *Journal of Marketing Research, 10,* 191-197.

258 Larsen, K. S. (1994). Attitudes toward the transportation of nuclear waste: The development of a Likert-type scale. *Journal of Social Psychology, 134,* 27-34.

259 Maloney, M. P., & Ward, M. O. (1973). Ecology: Let's hear from the people. *American Psychologist, 28,* 583586.

260 Maloney, M. P., Ward, M. P., & Braucht, G. N. (1975). A revised scale for the measurement of ecological attitudes and knowledge. *American Psychologist, 30,* 787-790.

261 Weigel, R., & Wiegel, J. (1978). Environmental concern: The development of a measure. *Environment and Behavior, 10,* 315.

262 Schahn, J., & Holzer, E. (1990). Konstruktion, Validerung und Anwendung von Skalen zur Erfassung des individuellen Umweltbewu. (Construction, validation, and application of scales for the measurement of individual environmental concern). *Zeitschrift fur Differentielle und Diagnostische Psychologie, 11,* 185-204.

263 Bowler, R. M., & Schwarzer, R. (1991). Environmental anxiety: Assessing emotional distress and concerns after toxin exposure. *Anxiety Research, 4,* 167-180.

264 Brown-Allen, B. P. (1992). The development of the Test for the Environmental Attitudes of Children. *Dissertation Abstracts International, 52,* 4200-4201.

265 Larson, L. R., Green, G. T., & Castleberry, S. B. (2011). Construction and validation of an instrument to measure environmental orientations in a diverse group of children. *Environment and Behavior, 43,* 72-89.

266 Simmons, D. D., Binney, S. E., & Dodd, B. (1992). Valuing "a clean environment": Factor location, norms, and relation to risks. *Journal of Social Behavior and Personality, 7,* 649-658.

267 Eckersley, R. (1992). *Environmentalism and political theory.* Albany, NY: State University Press.

268 Thompson, S. C. G., & Barton, M. A. (1994). Ecocentric and anthropocentric attitudes toward the environment. *Journal of Environmental Psychology, 14,* 149-157.

269 Grendstad, G., & Wollebaek, D. (1998). Greener still? An empirical examination of Eckersley's ecocentric approach. *Environment and Behavior, 50,* 653-675.

270 Hernandez, B., Ernesto, S., Martinez-Torvisco, J., & Hess, S. (2000). The study of environmental beliefs by facet analysis: Research in the Canary Islands, Spain. *Environment and Behavior, 32,* 612-636.

271 Banerjee, B., & McKeage, K. (1994). How green is my value: Exploring the relationship between environmentalism and materialism. *Advances in Consumer Research, 21,* 147-152.

272 Sohr, S. (1994). Ist es schon "funf nach zwolf"?B Entwicklung einer Skala zu "Okologischer Hoffnungslosigkeit." (Is it "five past twelve" already? Development of a new instrument to measure "ecological hopelessness.") *Praxis der Kinderpsychologie und Kinderpsychiatrie, 43,* 203-208.

273 Larsen, K. S., Groberg, D. H., Simmons, D. D., & Ommundsen, R. (1993). Authoritarianism, perspectives on the environment, and work values among social science students in former socialist and Western societies. *Social Behavior & Personality, 21,* 251-263.

274 Zimmerman, L. K. (1996). The development of an environmental values short form. *Journal of Environmental Education, 28,* 32-37.

275 Reser, J. P., & Bentrupperbäumer, J. M. (2005). What and where are environmental values? Assessing the impacts of current diversity of use of 'environmental' and 'world heritage' values. *Journal of Environmental Psychology, 25,* 125-146.

276 Pelletier, L. G., Tuson, K. M., Green-Demers, I., Noels, K., & Beaton, A. M. (1998). Why are you doing things for the environment? The motivation toward the environment scale. *Journal of Applied Social Psychology, 28,* 437-468.

277 Corraliza, J., & Berenguer, J. (1998). Structure of environmental attitudes: General orientation or attitudinal. *Revista de Psicologia Social, 13,* 339-406.

278 Villacorta, M., Koestner, R.,& Lekes, N. (2003). Further validation of the Motivation Toward the Environment Scale. *Environment and Behavior, 35,* 486-505.

279 Kaiser, F. G. (1998). A general measure of ecological behavior. *Journal of Applied Social Psychology, 28,* 395 - 422.

280 Schindler, F. H. (1999). Development of the survey of environmental issue attitudes. *Journal of Environmental Education, 31,* 12-16.

281 Dunlap, R. E., van Liere, K. D., Mertig, A. G., & Emmet Jones, R. (2000). Measuring endorsement of the new ecological paradigm: A revised NEP scale. *Journal of Social Issues, 56,* 425-442.

282 Noe, F. P., & Snow, R. (1990). The New Environmental Paradigm and further scale analysis. *Journal of Environmental Education, 21,* 20-26.

283 Bechtel, R. B., Verdugo, V. C., & Pinheiro, J. D. Q. (1999). Environmental belief systems: United States, Brazil, and Mexico. *Journal of Cross-Cultural Psychology, 30,* 122-128.

284 Milfont, T. L., & Duckitt, J. (2010). The Environmental Attitudes Inventory: A valid and reliable measure to assess the structure of environmental attitudes. *Journal of Environmental Psychology, 30,* 80-94.

285 Green, J. D., & Reed, A. (2009). Interdependence with the environment: Commitment, interconnectedness, and environmental behavior. *Journal of Environmental Psychology, 29,* 173-180.

286 Perkins, H. E. (2010). Measuring love and care for nature. *Journal of Environmental Psychology, 30,* 455-463.

287 Tam, K.-P. (2013). Dispositional empathy with nature. *Journal of Environmental Psychology, 35,* 92-104.

288 Thompson, J. C., & Gasteiger, E. L. (1985). Environmental attitude survey of university students: 1971 vs. 1981. *Journal of Environmental Education, 17,* 13-22.

289 Gigliotti, L. M. (1992). Environmental attitudes: 20 years of change. *Journal of Environmental Education, 24,* 15-26.

290 Arcury, T. A., & Christianson, E. H. (1990). Environmental worldview in response to environmental problems: Kentucky 1984 and 1988 compared. *Environment and Behavior, 22,* 387-407.

291 Wray-Lake, L., Flanagan, C. A., & Osgood, D. W. (2010). Examining trends in adolescent environmental attitudes, beliefs, and behaviors across three decades. *Environment and Behavior, 42,* 61-85.

292 Krause, D. (1993). Environmental consciousness: An empirical study. *Environment and Behavior, 25,* 126-142.

293 Simmons, D. D., Binney, S. E., & Dodd, B. (1992). Valuing "a clean environment": Factor location, norms, and relation to risks. *Journal of Social Behavior and Personality, 7,* 649-658.

294 Bang, H. K., Ellinger, A. E., Hadjimarcou, J., & Traichal, P. A. (2000). Consumer concern, knowledge, belief, and attitude toward renewable energy: An application of the reasoned action theory. *Psychology and Marketing, 17,* 449-468.

295 Smythe, P. C., & Brook, R. C. (1980). Environmental concerns and actions: A social-psychological investigation. *Canadian Journal of Behavioral Science, 12,* 175-186.

296 Van Liere, K. V., & Dunlap, R. E. (1981). Environmental concern: Does it make a difference how it's measured? *Environment and Behavior, 13,* 651-676.

297 Gigliotti, L. M. (1992). Environmental attitudes: 20 years of change. *Journal of Environmental Education, 24,* 15-26.

298 Painter, J., Semenik, R, & Belk, R. (1983). Is there a generalized energy conservation ethic? A comparison of the determinants of gasoline and home heating energy conservation. *Journal of Economic Psychology, 3,* 317-331.

299 MacGregor, D. (1991). Worry over technological activities and life concerns. *Risk Analysis, 11,* 315-324.

300 Verplanken, B. (1989). Beliefs, attitudes, and intentions toward nuclear energy before and after Chernobyl in a longitudinal within-subjects design. *Environment and Behavior, 21,* 371-392.

301 Midden, C. J., & Verplanken, B. (1990). The stability of nuclear attitudes after Chernobyl. Special Issue: Psychological fallout from the Chernobyl nuclear accident. *Journal of Environmental Psychology, 10,* 111-119.

302 Dietz, T., Stern P. C., & Guagnano, A. (1998). Social structural and social psychological bases of environmental concern. *Environment and Behavior, 30,* 450-471.

303 Grønhøj, A., & Thøgersen, J. (2009). Like father, like son? Intergenerational transmission of values, attitudes, and behaviours in the environmental domain. *Journal of Environmental Psychology, 29,* 414-421.

304 Honnold, J. A. (1984-85). Age and environmental concern: Some specification of effects. *Journal of Environmental Education, 16,* 4-9.

305 Zhang, J. (1993). Environmental hazards in the Chinese public's eyes. *Risk Analysis, 13,* 509-513.

306 Arcury, T. A., & Christianson, E. H. (1993). Rural-urban differences in environmental knowledge and actions. *Journal of Environmental Education, 25,* 19-25.

307 Klineberg, S. L., McKeever, M., & Rothenbach, B. (1998). Demographic predictors of environmental concern: It does make a difference how it's measured. *Social Science Quarterly, 79,* 734-753.

308 Szagun, G., & Mesenholl, E. (1993). Environmental ethics: An empirical study of West German adolescents. *Journal of Environmental Education, 25,* 37-44.

309 Wright, S. D., Caserta, M., & Lund, D. A (2003). Older adults' attitudes, concerns, and support for environmental issues in the 'new

west'. *International Journal of Aging & Human Development, 57,* 151-179.

310 Wray-Lake, L., Flanagan, C. A., & Osgood, D. W. (2010). Examining trends in adolescent environmental attitudes, beliefs, and behaviors across three decades. *Environment and Behavior, 42,* 61-85.

311 Honnold, J. A. (1984-85). Age and environmental concern: some specification of effects. *Journal of Environmental Education, 16,* 4-9.

312 Grendstad, G., & Wollebaek, D. (1998). Greener still? An empirical examination of Eckersley's ecocentric approach. *Environment and Behavior, 50,* 653-675.

313 Grønhøj, A., & Thøgersen, J. (2009). Like father, like son? Intergenerational transmission of values, attitudes, and behaviours in the environmental domain. *Journal of Environmental Psychology, 29,* 414-421.

314 Cheng, J. C.-H., & Monroe, M. C. (2012). Connection to nature: Children's affective attitude toward nature. *Environment and Behavior, 44,* 31-49.

315 Palmer, J. A. (1993). Development of concern for the environment and formative experiences of educators. *Journal of Environmental Education, 24,* 26-30.

316 Eagles, P. F., & Demare, R. (1999). Factors influencing children's environmental attitudes. *Journal of Environmental Education, 30,* 33-37.

317 Hussar, K. M., & Horvath, J. C. (2011). Do children play fair with mother nature? Understanding children's judgments of environmentally harmful actions. *Journal of Environmental Psychology, 31,* 309-313.

318 Gutteling, J. M., & Wiegman, O. (1993). Gender-specific reactions to environmental hazards in the Netherlands. *Sex Roles, 28,* 433-447.

319 Zhang, J. (1993). Environmental hazards in the Chinese public's eyes. *Risk Analysis, 13,* 509-513.

320 Blocker, T. J., & Eckberg, D. L. (1997). Gender and environmentalism: Results from the 1993 General Social Survey. *Social Science Quarterly, 78,* 841-858.

321 Tikka, P. M., Kuitnen, M. T., & Tynys, S. M. (2000). Effects of educational background on students' attitudes, activity levels, and knowledge concerning the environment. *Journal of Environmental Education, 31,* 12-19.

322 Mukherjee, B. N. (1993). Public response to air pollution in Calcutta proper. *Journal of Environmental Psychology, 13,* 207-230.

323 Gifford, R., Hay, R., & Boros, K. (198283). Individual differences in environmental attitudes. *Journal of Environmental Education, 14,* 1923.

324 Arcury, T. A., & Christianson, E. H. (1993). Rural-urban differences in environmental knowledge and actions. *Journal of Environmental Education, 25,* 19-25.

325 Gambro, J. S., & Switzky, H. N. (1999). Variables associated with American high school students knowledge of environmental issues relates to energy and pollution. *Journal of Environmental Education, 30,* 15-22.

326 Stern, P. C., Dietz, T., & Kalof, L. (1993). Value orientations, gender, and environmental concern. *Environment and Behavior, 25,* 322-348.

327 Schahn, J., & Holzer, E. (1990). Studies of individual environmental concern: The role of knowledge, gender, and background variables. *Environment and Behavior, 22,* 767-786.

328 Grieve, K. W., & Van Staden, F. J. (1985). Environmental concern in South Africa: An attitudinal study. *South African Journal of Psychology, 15,* 135-136.

329 Arcury, T. A., Scollay, S. J., & Johnson, T. P. (1987). Sex differences in environmental concern and knowledge: The case of acid rain. *Sex Roles, 16,* 463-472.

330 Davidson D. J., & Freudenburg, W. R. (1996). Gender and environmental risk concerns: A review and analysis of available research. *Environment and Behavior, 28,* 302-339.

331 Dietz, T., Kalof, L., & Stern, P. C. (2002). Gender, values, and environmentalism. *Social Science Quarterly, 83,* 353-364.

332 Bonnes, M., Uzzell, D., Carrus, G., & Kelay, T. (2007). Inhabitants' and Experts' Assessments of Environmental Quality for Urban Sustainability. *Journal of Social Issues, 63,* 59-78.

333 Synodinos, N. E. (1990). Environmental attitudes and knowledge: A comparison of marketing and business students with other groups. *Journal of Business Research, 20,* 161-170.

334 McKnight, M. D. (1991). Socialization into environmentalism: Development of attitudes toward the environment and technology. *Dissertation Abstracts International, 52,* 301.

335 Tikka, P. M., Kuitnen, M. T., & Tynys, S. M. (2000). Effects of educational background on students attitudes, activity levels, and knowledge concerning the environment. *Journal of Environmental Education, 31,* 12-19.

336 Gifford, R., Hay, R., & Boros, K. (198283). Individual differences in environmental attitudes. *Journal of Environmental Education, 14,* 1923.

337 Bogner, F. X. (1998). The influence of short-term outdoor ecology on long-term variables of environmental perspective. *Journal of Environmental Education, 29,* 17-29.

338 Reid, I., & Sa'di, I. (1997). Jordanian and British primary schoolchildren's attitudes towards the environment. *Educational Studies, 23,* 473-480.

339 Bowler, P. A., Kaiser, F. G., & Hartig, T. (1999). A role for ecological restoration work in university environmental education. *Journal of Environmental Education, 30,* 19-26.

340 Tikka, P. M., Kuitnen, M. T., & Tynys, S. M. (2000). Effects of educational background on students' attitudes, activity levels, and knowledge concerning the environment. *Journal of Environmental Education, 31,* 12-19.

341 Hausbeck, K. W., Milbrath, L. W., & Enright, S. M. (1992). Environmental knowledge, awareness and concern among 11th-grade students: New York State. *Journal of Environmental Education, 24,* 27-34.

342 Ostman, R. E., & Parker, J. L. (1987). Impact of education, age, newspapers, and television on environmental knowledge, concerns and behaviors. *Journal of Environmental Education, 19,* 3-9.

343 Arcury, T. A., & Christianson, E. H. (1993). Rural-urban differences in environmental

knowledge and actions. *Journal of Environmental Education, 25,* 19-25.

344 Hsu, S. J., & Rothe, R. E. (1996). An assessment of environmental knowledge and attitudes held by community leaders in the Hualien area of Taiwan. *Journal of Environmental Education, 28,* 24-31.

345 Klineberg, S. L., McKeever, M., & Rothenbach, B. (1998). Demographic predictors of environmental concern: It does make a difference how it's measured. *Social Science Quarterly, 79,* 734-753.

346 Chanda, R. (1999). Correlates and dimensions of environmental quality concern among residents of an African subtropical city: Gaborone, Botswana. *Journal of Environmental Education, 30,* 31-39.

347 Laidley, T. M. (2013). The Influence of Social Class and Cultural Variables on Environmental Behaviors: Municipal-Level Evidence From Massachusetts. *Environment and Behavior, 45,* 170-197.

348 Grendstad, G., & Wollebaek, D. (1998). Greener still? An empirical examination of Eckersley's ecocentric approach. *Environment and Behavior, 50,* 653-675.

349 Lyons, E., & Breakwell, G. M. (1994). Factors predicting environmental concern and indifference in 13- to 16-year-olds. *Environment and Behavior, 26,* 223-238.

350 Teisl, M. F., & O'Brien, K.. (2003). Who cares and who acts? Outdoor recreationists exhibit different levels of environmental concern and behavior. *Environment and Behavior, 35,* 506-522.

351 di Nenna, P. M., Paolillo, V., & Giuliani, M. M. (1987). Le convinzioni ambientaliste dei cacciatori italiani: Indagine conoscitiva per mezzo dell' "I.C.A. test." (Environmental values of Italian hunters: A cognitive study based on the ICA test). *Movimento, 3,* 104-110.

352 Schuett, M. A., & Ostergren, D. (2003). Environmental concern and involvement of individuals in selected voluntary associations. *Journal of Environmental Education, 34,* 30-38.

353 Ostman, R. E., & Parker, J. L. (1987). Impact of education, age, newspapers, and television on environmental knowledge, concerns and behaviors. *Journal of Environmental Education, 19,* 3-9.

354 Shanahan, J., Morgan, M., & Stenbjerre, M. (1997). Green or brown? Television and the cultivation of environmental concern. *Journal of Broadcasting and Electronic Media, 41,* 305-323.

355 Eagles, P. F., & Demare, R. (1999). Factors influencing children's environmental attitudes. *Journal of Environmental Education, 30,* 33-37.

356 Holbert, R. L., Kwak, N., & Shah, D. V. (2003). Environmental concern, patterns of television viewing, and pro-environmental behaviors: Integrating models of media consumption and effects. *Journal of Broadcasting & Electronic Media, 47,* 177-196.

357 Greenwald, J. M.(1993). Environmental attitudes: A structural developmental model. *Dissertation Abstracts International, 53*(12-B), 6550.

358 Dono, J., & Richardson, B. (2010). The relationship between environmental activism, pro-environmental behaviour and social

identity. *Journal of Environmental Psychology, 30,* 178-186.

359 Botetzagias, I., van Schuur, W. (2012). Active Greens: An Analysis of the Determinants of Green Party Members' Activism in Environmental Movements. *Environment and Behavior. 44,* 509-544.

360 Fielding, K., McDonals, R., & Louis, W. (2008). Theory of planned behaviour, identity and intentions to engage in environmental activism. *Journal of Environmental Psychology, 28,* 318-326.

361 Whitmarsh, L., & O'Neill, S. (2010). Green identity, green living? the role of pro-environmental self-identity in determining consistency across diverse pro-environmental behaviours. *Journal of Environmental Psychology, 30,* 305-314.

362 van der Werff, E., Steg, L., Keizer, K. (2013). The value of environmental self-identity: The relationship between biospheric values, environmental self-identity and environmental preferences, intentions and behaviour. *Journal of Environmental Psychology, 34,* 55-63.

363 Milfont, T. L., & Sibley, C. G. (2012). The big five personality traits and environmental engagement: Associations at the individual and societal level. *Journal of Environmental Psychology, 32,* 187-195.

364 Khachatryan, H., Joireman, J., & Casavant, K. (2013). Relating values and consideration of future and immediate consequences to consumer preference for biofuels: A three-dimensional social dilemma analysis. *Journal of Environmental Psychology, 34,* 97-108.

365 Harth, N. S., Leach, C. W., & Kessler, T. (2013). Guilt, anger, and pride about in-group environmental behaviour: Different emotions predict distinct intentions. *Journal of Environmental Psychology, 34,* 18-26.

366 Schultz, P. W., & Zelezny, L. (1999). Values as predictors of environmental attitudes: Evidence for consistency across 14 countries. *Journal of Environmental Psychology, 19,* 255-265.

367 Howes, Y., & Gifford, R. (2009). Stable or dynamic value importance? The interaction between value endorsement level and situational differences on decision-making in environmental issues. *Environment and Behavior, 41,* 549-582.

368 Milfont, T. L., & Gouveia, V. V. (2006). Time perspective and values: An exploratory study of their relations to environmental attitudes. *Journal of Environmental Psychology, 26,* 72-82.

369 Khachatryan, H., Joireman, J., & Casavant, K. (2013). Relating values and consideration of future and immediate consequences to consumer preference for biofuels: A three-dimensional social dilemma analysis. *Journal of Environmental Psychology, 34,* 97-108.

370 Schultz, P. W., & Stone, W. F. (1994). Authoritarianism and attitudes toward the environment. *Environment and Behavior, 26,* 25-37.

371 Borden, R. J., & Francis, J. L. (1978). Who cares about ecology? Personality and sex differences in environmental concern. *Journal of Personality, 46,* 190-203.

372 Swearingen, T. C. (1990). Moral development and environmental ethics. *Dissertation Abstracts International, 50*(12-B, Part 1), 5905.

373 Axelrod, L. J., & Lehman, D. R. (1993). Responding to environmental concerns: What factors guide individual action? *Journal of Environmental Psychology, 13,* 149-159.

374 Kinnear, T. C., Taylor, J. R., & Ahmed, S. A. (1974). Ecologically concerned consumers: Who are they? *Journal of Marketing, 38,* 20-24.

375 Mirosa, M., Lawson, R., & Gnoth, D. Linking Personal Values to Energy-Efficient Behaviors in the Home. *Environment and Behavior, 45,* 455-475.

376 McAllister, I., & Studlar, D. T. (1999). Green versus brown: Explaining environmental commitment in Australia. *Social Science Quarterly, 80,* 775-792.

377 Davis, J. L., Le, B., & Coy, A. E. (2011). Building a model of commitment to the natural environment to predict ecological behavior and willingness to sacrifice. *Journal of Environmental Psychology, 31,* 257-265.

378 Axelrod, L. J., & Lehman, D. R. (1993). Responding to environmental concerns: What factors guide individual action? *Journal of Environmental Psychology, 13,* 149-159.

379 Göksen, F., Adaman, F., Zenginobuz, E. Ü. (2002). On environmental concern, willingness to pay, and postmaterialist values: Evidence from Istanbul. *Environment and Behavior, 34,* 616633.

380 Drori, I., & YuchtmanYaar, E. (2002). Environmental vulnerability in public perceptions and attitudes: The case of Israel's urban centers. *Social Science Quarterly, 83,* 53-63.

381 Kilbourne, W. E., Beckmann, S. C., & Thelen, E. The role of the dominant social paradigm in environmental attitudes: A multinational examination. *Journal of Business Research, 55,* 193-204.

382 Heath, Y., & Gifford, R. (2006). Free-market ideology and environmental degradation. *Environment and Behavior, 38,* 48-71.

383 Kaiser, F. G., Ranney, M., Hartig T., & Bowler, P. A. (1999). Ecological behavior, environmental attitude, and feelings of responsibility for the environment *European Psychologist, 4,* 59-74.

384 Kaiser, F. G., & Shimoda, T. A. (1999). Responsibility as a predictor of ecological behavior. *Journal of Environmental Psychology, 19,* 243-253.

385 Kuhlemeier, H., van den Bergh, H., & Lagerweij, N. (1999). Environmental knowledge, attitudes, and behavior in Dutch secondary education. *Journal of Environmental Education, 30,* 4-14.

386 Adams, J. (1995). *Risk.* London: Routledge, Taylor, & Francis.

387 Poortinga, W., Steg, L., & Vlek, C. (2003). Myths of nature and environmental management strategies. A field study on energy reductions in traffic and transport. In G. Moser, E. Pol, Y. Bernard, M. Bonnes, & J. Corraliza (Eds.), *People, places, and sustainability* (pp. 280290). Ashland, OH: Hogrefe & Huber.

388 Farrell, J. (2013). Environmental Activism and Moral Schemas: Cultural Components of Differential Participation. *Environment and Behavior, 45,* 399-423.

389 Gifford, R., Scannell, L., Kormos, C., Smolova, L., Biel, A., Boncu, S., Corral, V., Hanyu, K, Hine, D. W., Kaiser, F. G., Korpela, K., Lima,

L., Mertig, A. G., Garcia Mira, R., Moser, G., Passafaro, P., Pinheiro, J. Q., Saini, S., Sako, T., Sautkina, E., Savina, Y., Schmuck, P., Schultz, P. W., Sobeck, K., Sundblad, K., & Uzzell, D. (2009). Temporal pessimism and spatial optimism in environmental assessments: An 18-nation study. *Journal of Environmental Psychology, 29*, 1-12.

390 Lima, M. L., & Castro, P. (2005). Cultural theory meets the community: Worldviews and local issues. *Journal of Environmental Psychology, 25*, 23-35.

391 Gifford, R., Scannell, L., Kormos, C., Smolova, L., Biel, A., Boncu, S., Corral, V., Hanyu, K., Hine, D. W., Kaiser, F. G., Korpela, K., Lima, L., Mertig, A. G., Garcia Mira, R., Moser, G., Passafaro, P., Pinheiro, J. Q., Saini, S., Sako, T., Sautkina, E., Savina, Y., Schmuck, P., Schultz, P. W., Sobeck, K., Sundblad, K., & Uzzell, D. (2009). Temporal pessimism and spatial optimism in environmental assessments: An 18-nation study. *Journal of Environmental Psychology, 29*, 1-12.

392 McElwee, R., & Brittain, L. (2009). Optimism for the world's future versus the personal future: Application to environmental attitudes. *Current Psychology, 28*, 133-145.

393 Moser, C., Stauffacher, M., Smieszek, T., Seidl, R., Krütli, P., & Scholz, R W. (2013). Psychological factors in discounting negative impacts of nuclear waste. *Journal of Environmental Psychology, 35*, 121-131.

394 Gifford, R., Scannell, L., Kormos, C., Smolova, L., Biel, A., Boncu, S., Corral, V., Hanyu, K., Hine, D. W., Kaiser, F. G., Korpela, K., Lima, L., Mertig, A. G., Garcia Mira, R., Moser, G., Passafaro, P., Pinheiro, J. Q., Saini, S., Sako, T., Sautkina, E., Savina, Y., Schmuck, P., Schultz, P. W., Sobeck, K., Sundblad, K., & Uzzell, D. (2009). Temporal pessimism and spatial optimism in environmental assessments: An 18-nation study. *Journal of Environmental Psychology, 29*, 1-12.

395 Eiser, J. R., Hannover, B., Mann, L., Morin, M. et al. (1990). Nuclear attitudes after Chernobyl: A cross-national study. *Journal of Environmental Psychology, 10*, 101-110.

396 Schultz, P. W., & Stone, W. F. (1994). Authoritarianism and attitudes toward the environment. *Environment and Behavior, 26*, 25-37.

397 Eckberg, D. L., & Blocker, T. J. (1989). Varieties of religious involvement and environmental concerns: Testing the Lynn White thesis. *Journal for the Scientific Study of Religion, 28*, 509-517.

398 Greeley, A. (1993). Religion and attitudes toward the environment. *Journal for the Scientific Study of Religion, 32*, 19-28.

399 Newhouse, C. H. (1986). An investigation of the relationship between environmental behaviors and personality factors in church members and environmentalists. (Doctoral dissertation, Michigan State University, 1986). *Dissertation Abstracts International, 46*, 3884A.

400 Shultz, P. W., Zeleny, L., & Dalrymple, N. J. (2000). A multinational perspective on the relation between Judeo-Christian religious beliefs and attitudes of environmental concern. *Environment and Behavior, 32*, 576-591.

401 Wolkomir, M., Futreal, M., Woodrum, E., & Hoban, T. (1997). Substantive religious belief and environmentalism. *Social Science Quarterly, 78*, 96-108.

402 Hand, C. M., & Van Liere, K. D. (1984). Religion, mastery-over-nature, and environmental concern. *Social Forces, 63*, 555-570.

403 Eckberg, D. L., & Blocker, T. J. (1996). Christianity, environmentalism, and the theoretical problem of fundamentalism. *Journal for the Scientific Study of Religion, 35*, 343-355.

404 Inglehart, R. (1995). Public support for environmental protection: Objective problems and subjective values in 43 societies. *PS: Political Science and Politics, 28*, 57-72.

405 Franzen, A. (2003). Environmental attitudes in international comparison: An analysis of the ISSP surveys 1993 and 2000. *Social Science Quarterly, 84*, 297-308.

406 Balderjahn, I. (1988). Personality variables and environmental attitudes as predictors of ecologically responsible consumption patterns. Special Issue: Marketing research. *Journal of Business Research, 17*, 51-56.

407 Howard, G. S., Delgado, E., Miller, D., & Gubbins, S. (1993). Transforming values into actions: Ecological preservation though energy conservation. *Counseling Psychologist, 21*, 582-596.

408 Dunlap, R. E., Gallup, G. H., & Gallup, A. M. (1993). Of global concern:Results of the Health and Planet Survey. *Environment, 35*, 7-15, 33-40.

409 Ray, J. J. (1981, March). Are environmental activists middle class? *Tableaus*, pp. 6-7.

410 Uyeki, E. S., & Holland, L. J. (2000). Diffusion of pro-environment attitudes. *American Behavioral Scientist, 43*, 646-662.

411 Kemmelmeier, M., Król, G., & Young, H. K. (2002). Values, economics, and pro-environmental attitudes in 22 societies. *CrossCultural Research: The Journal of Comparative Social Science, 36*, 256-285.

412 Chanda, R. (1999). Correlates and dimensions of environmental quality concern among residents of an African subtropical city: Gaborone, Botswana. *Journal of Environmental Education, 30*, 31-39.

413 Brechin, S. R. (1999). Objective problems, subjective values, and global environmentalism: Evaluating the postmaterialist argument and challenging a new explanation. *Social Science Quarterly, 80*, 793-809.

414 Howard, G. S. (1993). Thoughts on saving our planet: Political, economic, cultural, and bureaucratic impediments to ecological activism. *Counseling Psychologist, 21*, 597-617.

415 Bjerke, T., & Kaltenborn, B. P. (1999). The relationship of ecocentric and anthropocentric motives to attitudes toward large carnivores. *Journal of Environmental Psychology, 19*, 415-421.

416 Rauwald, K. S., & Moore, C. F. (2002). Environmental attitudes as predictors of policy support across three countries. *Environment and Behavior, 34*, 709-739.

417 Kirisioglu, T., Hassenzahl, D. M., & Turan, B. (2013). Urban and rural perceptions of ecological risks to water environments in southern and eastern Nevada. *Journal of Environmental Psychology, 33*, 86-95.

418 Bonnes, M., Passafaro, P., & Carrus, G. (2011). The ambivalence of attitudes toward urban green areas: Between pro-environmental worldviews and daily residential experience. *Environment and Behavior, 43*, 207-232.

419 Bogner, F. X., & Wiseman, M (1997). Environmental perception of rural and urban pupils. *Journal of Environmental Psychology, 17*, 111-122

420 Lutz, A. R., Simpson-Housley, P., & de Man, A. F. (1999). Wilderness: Rural and urban attitudes and perceptions. *Environment and Behavior, 31*, 259-266.

421 Parker, J. D., & McDonough, M H (1999). Environmentalism of African Americans: An analysis of the subculture and barriers theories. *Environment and Behavior, 31*, 155-177.

422 Mohai, P., & Bryant, B. (1998). Is there a "race" effect on concern for environmental quality? *Public Opinion Quarterly, 62*, 475-505.

423 Uyeki, E. S., & Holland, L. J. (2000). Diffusion of pro-environment attitudes. *American Behavioral Scientist, 43*, 646-662.

424 Arp III, W., & Kenny, C. (1996). Black environmentalism in the local community context. *Environment and Behavior, 28*, 267-282.

425 Schultz, P. W., Unipan, J. B., & Gamba, R. J. (2000). Acculturation and ecological worldview among Latino Americans. *Journal of Environmental Education, 31*, 22-27.

426 Hunter, L. M. (2000). A comparison of the environmental attitudes, concern, and behaviors of native-born and foreign-born U. S. residents. *Population and Environment: A Journal of Interdisciplinary Studies, 21*, 565-580.

427 Furman, A. (1998). A note on environmental concern in a developing country: Results from an Istanbul survey. *Environment and Behavior, 30*, 520-534.

428 Herrera, M. (1992). Environmentalism and political participation: Toward a new system of social beliefs and values? *Journal of Applied Social Psychology, 22*, 657-676.

429 Dodds, J., & Lin, C. (1992). Chinese teenagers' concerns about the future: A cross-national comparison. *Adolescence, 27*, 481-486.

430 Dietz, T., Stern P. C., & Guagnano, A. (1998). Social structural and social psychological bases of environmental concern. *Environment and Behavior, 30*, 450-471.

431 Howe, D. C., Kahn, Jr., P. H., &Friedman, B. (1996). Along the Rio Negro: Brazilian children's environmental views and values. *Developmental Psychology, 32*, 979-987.

432 Kahn, P. H. Jr., & Lourenço, O. (2002). Water, air, fire, and earth: A developmental study in Portugal of environmental moral reasoning. *Environment and Behavior, 34*, 405-430.

433 Srichai, N. K. (1989). A study of environmental perceptions and attitudes of selected university students in Thailand. *Dissertation Abstracts International, 50*, 833.

434 Zheng, Y., & Yoshino, R. (2003). Diversity patterns of attitudes toward nature and environment in Japan, USA, and European nations. *Behaviormetrika, 30*, 21-37.

435 Eisler, A. D., Eisler, H., Yoshida, M. (2003). Perception of human ecology: Crosscultural and gender comparisons. *Journal of Environmental Psychology, 23*, 89-101.

436 Corral-Verdugo, V., & Armendariz, L. I. (2000). The "new environmental paradigm" in a Mexican community. *Journal of Environmental Education, 31*, 25-31.

437 Bechtel, R. B., Verdugo, V. C., & Pinheiro, J. D. Q. (1999). Environmental belief systems: United States, Brazil, and Mexico. *Journal of Cross-Cultural Psychology, 30*, 122-128.

438 Boeve-de Pauw, J., & Van Petegem, P. (2013). A Cross-Cultural Study of Environmental Values and Their Effect on the Environmental Behavior of Children. *Environment and Behavior, 45*, 551-583.

439 Low, B. S. (1996). Behavioral ecology of conservation in traditional societies. *Human Nature, 7*, 353-379.

440 Elliott, S. J., Taylor, S. M., Walter, S., Stieb, D., Frank, J., & Eyles, J. (1993). Modelling psychosocial effects of exposure to solid waste facilities. *Social Science and Medicine, 37*, 791-804.

441 Arp III, W., & Kenny, C. (1996). Black environmentalism in the local community context. *Environment and Behavior, 28*, 267-282.

442 Bassett, G. W., Jr., Jenkins-Smith, H. C., & Silva, C. (1996). On-site storage of high level nuclear waste: Attitudes and perceptions of local residents. *Risk Analysis, 16*, 309-319.

443 Baldassare, M., & Katz, C. (1992). The personal threat of environmental problems as predictor of environmental practices. *Environment and Behavior, 24*, 602-616.

444 O'Connor, R. E., Bord, R. J., Yarnal, B., & Wiefek, N. (2002). Who wants to reduce greenhouse gas emissions? *Social Science Quarterly, 83*, 117.

445 Gillilan, S., Werner, C. M., Olson, L., & Adams, D. (1996). Teaching the concept of recycling: A campaign and evaluation. *Journal of Environmental Education, 28*, 11-18.

446 Keen, M. (1991). The effect of the Sunship Earth program on knowledge and attitude development. *Journal of Environmental Education, 22*, 28-32.

447 Eagles, P. F., & Demare, R. (1999). Factors influencing children's environmental attitudes. *Journal of Environmental Education, 30*, 33-37.

448 Bull, J. N. (1993). The effect of participation in an environmental action program on empowerment, interest, and problem-solving skills of inner city students. *Dissertation Abstracts International, 53*, 54-81.

449 Leeming, F. C., Dwyer, W. O., Porter, B. E., & Cobern, M. K. (1993). Outcome research in environmental education: A critical review. *Journal of Environmental Education, 24*, 8-21.

450 Zelezny, L. C. (1999). Educational interventions that improve environmental behaviors: A meta-analysis. *Journal of Environmental Education, 31*, 5-14.

451 Gillett, D. P., Thomas, G. P., Skok, R. L., & McLaughlin, T. F. (1991). The effects of wilderness camping and hiking on the self-concept and the environmental attitudes and knowledge of twelfth graders. *Journal of Environmental Education, 22*, 33-44.

452 Shepard, C. L., & Speelman, L. R. (1985-86). Affecting environmental attitudes through outdoor education. *Journal of Environmental Education, 17*, 20-23.

453 Reid, I., & Sa'di, I. (1997). Jordanian and British primary schoolchildren's attitudes towards the environment. *Educational Studies, 23*, 473-480.

454 Hewitt, P. (1997). Games in instruction leading to environmentally responsible behavior. *Journal of Environmental Education, 28*, 35-37.

455 Ramsey, J. M., & Hungerford, H. (1989). The effects of issue investigation and action training on environmental behavior in seventh grade students. *Journal of Environmental Education, 20*, 29-34.

456 Ramsey, J. M. (1993). The effects of issue investigation and action training on eighth-grade students' environmental behavior. *Journal of Environmental Education, 24*, 31-36.

457 Jordan, J. R., Hungerford, H. R., & Tomera, A. N. (1986). Effects of two residential environmental workshops on high school students. *Journal of Environmental Education, 18*, 15-22.

458 Yount, J. R., & Horton, P. B. (1992). Factors influencing environmental attitude: The relationship between environmental attitude defensibility and cognitive reasoning level. *Journal of Research in Science Teaching, 29*, 1059-1078.

459 Newhouse, N. (1990). Implications of attitude and behavior research for environmental conservation. *Journal of Environmental Education, 22*, 26-32.

460 Boerschig, S., & de Young, R. (1993). Evaluation of selected recycling curricula: Educating the green citizen. *Journal of Environmental Education, 24*, 17-22.

461 Pooley, J. A., & O'Conner, M. (2000). Environmental education and attitudes: Emotions and beliefs are what is needed. *Environment and Behavior, 32*, 711-723.

462 Cegarra-Navarro, J., Eldridge, S., & Martinez-Martinez, A. (2010). Managing environmental knowledge through unlearning in Spanish hospitality companies. *Journal of Environmental Psychology, 30*, 249-257.

463 Fritsche, I., Jonas, E., & Koranyi, N. (2010). Existential threat and compliance with pro-environmental norms. *Journal of Environmental Psychology, 30*, 67-79.

464 Dresner, M. (1989-90). Changing energy end-use patterns as a means of reducing global-warming trends. *Journal of Environmental Education, 21*, 41-46.

465 Monroe, M. C. (1992). The effect of interesting environmental stories on knowledge and action-taking attitudes. *Dissertation Abstracts International, 52*, 38-67.

466 Werner, C. M., & Stanley, C. P. (2011). Guided group discussion and the reported use of toxic products: The persuasiveness of hearing others' views. *Journal of Environmental Psychology, 31*, 289-300.

467 Hine, D. W., & Gifford, R. (1991). Fear appeals, individual differences, and environmental concern. *Journal of Environmental Education, 23*, 36-41.

468 Riesenberg, R. D. (1991, August). *Was Earth Day a moving experience? Pre- and post-environmental attitudes in a midwestern suburban population sample?* Paper presented at the 99th Annual Convention of the American Psychological Association, San Francisco, CA.

469 Bansal, P. (2003). From issues to actions: The importance of individual concerns and organizational values in responding to natural environmental issues. *Organization Science, 14*, 510-527.

470 O'Riordan, T. (1976). Attitudes, behavior, and environmental policy issues. In I. Altman & J. F. Wohlwill (Eds.), *Human behavior and environment: Advances in theory and research* (Vol. 1). New York: Plenum.

471 Scott, D., & Willits, F. K. (1994). Environmental attitudes and behavior: A Pennsylvania survey. *Environment and Behavior, 26*, 239-260.

472 Heberlein, T. A., & Black, J. S. (1981). Cognitive consistency and environmental action. *Environment and Behavior, 13*, 717-734.

473 Vogel, S. (1996). Farmers' environmental attitudes and behavior: A case study for Austria. *Environment and Behavior, 28*, 591-613.

474 Tarrant, M. A., & Cordell, H. K. (1997). The effect of respondent characteristics on general environmental attitude-behavior correspondence. *Environment and Behavior, 29*, 618-637.

475 Iversen, H., & Rundmo, T. (2002). Environmental concern and environmental behaviour among the Norwegian public. *Journal of Risk Research, 5*, 265-279.

476 Dispoto, R. G. (1977). Interrelationships among measures of environmental activity, emotionality, and knowledge. *Education and Psychological Measurement, 37*, 451-459.

477 Borden, R. J., & Schettino, A. P. (1979). Determinants of environmentally responsible behavior. *Journal of Environmental Education, 10*(4), 35-39.

478 Chao, Y., & Lam, S. (2011). Measuring responsible environmental behavior: Self-reported and other-reported measures and their differences in testing a behavioral model. *Environment and Behavior, 43*, 53-71.

479 Syme, G. J., & Nancarrow, B. E. (1992). Predicting public involvement in urban water management and planning. *Environment and Behavior, 24*, 738-758.

480 Manzo, L. C., & Weinstein, N. D. (1987). Behavioral commitment to environmental protection: A study of active and nonactive members of the Sierra Club. *Environment and Behavior, 19*, 673-694.

481 Bamberg, S. (2003). How does environmental concern influence specific environmentally related behaviors? A new answer to an old question. *Journal of Environmental Psychology, 23*, 21-32.

482 Weigel, R. H., & Newman, L. S. (1976). Increasing attitude-behavior correspondence by broadening the scope of behavioral measure. *Journal of Personality and Social Psychology, 33*, 793-802.

483 Kaiser, F. G. (1998). A general measure of ecological behavior. *Journal of Applied Social Psychology, 28*, 395-422.

484 Kaiser, F. G., Woelfing, S., & Fuhrer, U. (1999). Environmental attitude and ecological behavior. *Journal of Environmental Psychology, 19*, 1-19.

485 Kaiser, F. G., Doka, G., Hofstetter, P., & Ranney, M. A. (2003). Ecological behavior and its environmental consequences: A life cycle

assessment of a self-report measure. *Journal of Environmental Psychology, 23,* 11-20.

486 Kaiser, F. G., & Biel, A. (2000). Assessing general ecological behavior: A cross-cultural comparison between Switzerland and Sweden. *European Journal of Psychological Assessment, 16,* 44-52.

487 Kaiser, F. G., & Wilson, M. (2000). Assessing people's general ecological behavior: A cross-cultural measure. *Journal of Applied Social Psychology, 30,* 952-978.

488 Jurin, R., & Fortner, R. W. (2002). Symbolic beliefs as barriers to responsible environmental behavior. *Environmental Education Research, 8,* 373-394.

489 Diekmann, A., & Preisendörfer, P. (2003). Green and greenback: The behavioral effects of environmental attitudes in lowcost and highcost situations. *Rationality and Society, 15,* 441-472.

490 Costarelli, S., & Colloca, P. (2004). The effects of attitudinal ambivalence on pro-environmental behavioral intentions. *Journal of Environmental Psychology, 24,* 279-288.

491 Diekman, A., & Preisendorfer, P. (1992). Personliches umweltverhalten: Diskrepanzen zwischen Anspruch und Wirklichkeit. / Ecology in everyday life: Inconsistencies between environmental attitudes and behavior. *Kolner Zeitschrift fur Soziologie und Sozialpsychologie, 44,* 226-251.

492 Lee, K. (2011). The role of media exposure, social exposure and biospheric value orientation in the environmental attitude-intention-behavior model in adolescents. *Journal of Environmental Psychology, 31,* 301-308.

493 Gifford, R. (2011). The dragons of inaction: Psychological barriers that limit climate change mitigation and adaptation. *American Psychologist, 66,* 290-302.

494 Cottrell, S. (2003). Influence of sociodemographics and environmental attitudes on general responsible environmental behavior among recreational boaters. *Environment and Behavior, 35,* 347-375.

495 Hines, J. M., Hungerford, H. R., & Tomera, A. N. (1986-87). Analysis and synthesis of research on responsible environmental behavior: A meta-analysis. *Journal of Environmental Education, 18,* 1-8.

496 Osbaldiston, R., & Schott, J. P. (2012). Environmental sustainability and behavioral science: Meta-analysis of pro-environmental behavior experiments. *Environment and Behavior, 44,* 257-299.

497 Osbaldiston, R., & Schott, J. P. (2012). Environmental Sustainability and Behavioral Science: Meta-Analysis of Pro-environmental Behavior Experiments. *Environment and Behavior, 44,* 257-299.

498 Sussman, R., & Gifford, R. (2012). Please turn off the lights: The effectiveness of visual prompts. Applied Ergonomics, 43, 596-603.

499 De Young, R. (1996). Some aspects of reduced consumption behavior: The role of intrinsic satisfaction and competence motivation. *Environment and Behavior, 28,* 358-409.

500 Obregon-Salido, F. J., & Corral-Verdugo, V. (1997). Systems of beliefs and environmental conservation behavior in a Mexican community. *Environment and Behavior, 29,* 213-235.

501 Princen, T. (1997). Toward a theory of restraint. *Population and Environment: A Journal of Interdisciplinary Studies, 18,* 233-254.

502 Kaiser, F. G., & Shimoda T. A. (1999). Responsibility as a predictor of ecological behavior. *Journal of Environmental Psychology, 19,* 243-253.

503 .Kaiser, F. G., Ranney, M., Hartig T., & Bowler, P. A. (1999). Ecological behavior, environmental attitude, and feelings of responsibility for the environment. *European Psychologist, 4,* 59-74

504 Widegren, O. (1998). The new environmental paradigm and personal norms. *Environment and Behavior, 30,* 75-100.

505 Harland, P. Staats, H., & Wilke, H. A. M. (1999). Explaining pro-environmental intention and behavior by personal norms and the theory of planned behavior. *Journal of Applied Social Psychology, 29,* 2505-2528.

506 .Steinheider, B., Fay, D., Hilburger, T., Hust, I., Prinz, L., Vogelgesang, F., & Hormuth, S. E. (1999). Soziale normen als praediktoren con umweltbezogenem verhalten./ Social norms as predictors of environmental behavior. *Zeitschrift fur Sozialpsychologie, 30,* 40-56.

507 Schultz, P. W., & Zeleny, L. C. (1998). Values and pro-environmental behavior: A five-country survey. *Journal of Cross Cultural Psychology, 29,* 540-558.

508 Karp, D. G. (1996). Values and their effect on pro-environmental behavior. *Environment and Behavior, 28,* 111-133.

509 McFarlane, B. L., Boxall, P. C. (2003). The role of social psychological and social structural variables in environmental activism: An example of the forest sector. *Journal of Environmental Psychology, 23,* 79-87.

510 Lokhorst, A. M., Werner, C., Staats, H., van Dijk, E., & Gale, J. L. (2013). Commitment and behavior change: A meta-analysis and critical review of commitment-making strategies in environmental research. *Environment and Behavior, 45,* 3-34.

511 Green, J. D., & Reed, A. (2009). Interdependence with the environment: Commitment, interconnectedness, and environmental behavior. *Journal of Environmental Psychology, 29,* 173-180.

512 Mobley, C., Vagias, W., & DeWard, S. (2009). Exploring additional determinants of environmentally responsible behavior: The influence of environmental literature and environmental attitudes. *Environment and Behavior, 42,* 420-447.

513 Gousse-Lessard, A-S., Vallerand, R. J., Carbonneau, N., & Lafrenière, M-A. K. (2013). The role of passion in mainstream and radical behaviors: A look at environmental activism. *Journal of Environmental Psychology, 35,* 18-29.

514 Swenson, M. R., & Wells, W. D. (1997). Useful correlates of pro-environmental behavior. In M. E. Goldberg, M. Fishbein, et al. (Eds.), *Social marketing: Theoretical and practical perspectives. Advertising and consumer psychology* (pp. 91-109). Mahwah, NJ: Erlbaum.

515 Pelletier, L. G., Dion, S., Tuson, K., & Green-Demers, I. (1999). Why do people fail to adopt environmental protective behaviors? Toward a taxonomy of environmental motivation. *Journal of Applied Social Psychology, 29,* 2481-2504.

516 Seguin, C., Pelletier, L. G., & Hunsley, J. (1998). Toward a model of environmental activism. *Environment and Behavior, 30,* 628-652.

517 Green-Demers, I., Pelletier, L. G., & Menard, S. (1997). The impact of behavioral difficulty on the saliency of the association between self-determined motivation and environmental behaviors. *Canadian Journal of Behavioural Science, 29,* 157-166.

518 Osbaldiston, R., & Sheldon, K. M. (2003). Promoting internalized motivation for environmentally responsible behavior: A prospective study of environmental goals. *Journal of Environmental Psychology, 23,* 2003, 349-357.

519 Tabernero, C., & Hernandez, B. (2011). Self-efficacy and intrinsic motivation guiding environmental behavior. *Environment and Behavior, 43,* 658-675.

520 Lavergne, K. J., Sharp, E. C., & Holtby, A. (2010). The role of perceived government style in the facilitation of self-determined and non self-determined motivation for pro-environmental behavior. *Journal of Environmental Psychology, 30,* 169-177.

521 Lee, K. (2011). The role of media exposure, social exposure and biospheric value orientation in the environmental attitude-intention-behavior model in adolescents. *Journal of Environmental Psychology, 31,* 301-308.

522 Lynne, G. D., & Rola, L. R. (1988). Improving attitude-behavior prediction models with economic variables: Farmer actions toward soil conservation. *Journal of Social Psychology, 128,* 19-28.

523 Tarrant, M. A., & Cordell, H. K. (1997). The effect of respondent characteristics on general environmental attitude-behavior correspondence. *Environment and Behavior, 29,* 618-637.

524 Schultz, P. W., & Oskamp, S. (1996). Effort as moderator of the attitude-behavior relationship: General environmental concern and recycling. *Social Science Quarterly, 59,* 375-383.

525 Dahlstrand, U., & Biel, A. (1997). Pro-environmental habits: Propensity levels in behavioral change. *Journal of Applied Psychology, 27,* 588-601.

526 Hormuth, S. E. (1999). Social meaning and social context of environmentally-relevant behavior: Shopping, wrapping, and disposing. *Journal of Environmental Psychology, 19,* 277-286.

527 Nilsson, A., von Borgstede, C., & Biel, A. (2004). Willingness to accept climate change strategies: The effect of values and norms. *Journal of Environmental Psychology, 24,* 267-277.

528 Liu, J. H., & Sibley, C. G. (2004). Attitudes and behavior in social space: Public good interventions based on shared representations and environmental influences. *Journal of Environmental Psychology, 24,* 373-384.

529 Gill, J. D., Crosby, L. A., & Taylor, J. R. (1986). Ecological concern, attitudes, and social norms in voting behavior. *Public Opinion Quarterly, 50,* 537-554.

530 Syme, G. J., Beven, C. E., & Sumner, N. R. (1993). Motivation for reported involvement in local wetland preservation: The roles of knowledge, disposition, problem assessment, and arousal. *Environment and Behavior, 25,* 586-606.

531 Nordlund, A. M., & Garvill, J. (2002). Value structures behind pro-environmental behavior. *Environment and Behavior, 34,* 740-756.

532 Bamberg, S. & Möser, G. (2007). Twenty years after Hines, Hungerford, and Tomera: A new meta-analysis of psycho-social determinants of pro-environmental behaviour. *Journal of Environmental. Psychology, 27,* 14-25.

533 Balderjahn, I. (1988). Personality variables and environmental attitudes as predictors of ecologically responsible consumption patterns. Special Issue: Marketing research. *Journal of Business Research, 17,* 51-56.

534 Sivek, D. J., & Hungerford, H. (1989-90). Predictors of responsible behavior in members of three Wisconsin conservation organizations. *Journal of Environmental Education, 21,* 35-40.

535 Nemiroff, L. S., & McKenzie-Mohr, D. (1992). Determinants and distinguishing variables of pro-disarmament behavior and responsible environmental behavior. *Journal of Social Behavior and Personality, 7,* 1-24.

536 Tanner, C., & Kast, S. (2003). Promoting sustainable consumption: Determinants of green purchases by Swiss consumers. *Psychology & Marketing, 20,* 883-902.

537 Homburg, A., & Stolberg, A. (2006). Explaining pro-environmental behavior with a cognitive theory of stress. *Journal of Environmental Psychology, 26,* 2006, 114.

538 Steg, L., & Vlek, C. (2009). Encouraging pro-environmental behaviour: An integrative review and research agenda. *Journal of Environmental Psychology, 29,* 309-317.

539 Schultz, P. W., Bator, R. J., Large, L. B., Bruni, C. M., & Tabanico, J. J. (2013). Littering in context: Personal and environmental predictors of littering behavior. *Environment and Behavior, 45,* 35-59.

540 Etzioni, A. (1972). Human beings are not very easy to change after all. *Saturday Review,* June 3.

541 Geller, E. S. (1992). Solving environmental problems: A behavior change perspective. In S. Staub & P. Green (Eds.). *Psychology and social responsibility: Facing global challenges.* New York: New York University Press.

542 Dwyer, W. O., Leeming, F. C., Cobern, M. K., Porter, B. E., & Jackson, J. M. (1993). Critical review of behavioral interventions to preserve the environment. *Environment and Behavior, 25,* 275-321.

543 Allen, J. B., & Ferrand, J. (1999). Environmental locus of control, sympathy, and pro-environmental behavior: A test of Geller's actively caring hypothesis. *Environment and Behavior, 31,* 338-353.

544 de Young, R. (1993). Changing behavior and making it stick: The conceptualization and management of conservation behavior. *Environment and Behavior, 25,* 485-505.

545 Hamilton, W. G. (1985). The Okanagan Valley, British Columbia: Visual landscape assessment and planning policy. *Environments, 17,* 46-58.

546 Dearden, P. (1980). Landscape assessment: The last decade. *Canadian Geographer, 24,* 316-325.

547 Zube, E. H., Pitt, D. G., & Anderson, T. W. (1975). Perception and prediction of scenic resource values of the Northeast. In E. H. Zube, R. O. Brush & J. G. Fabos (Eds.), *Landscape assessment: Values, perceptions, and resources.* Stroudsburg, PA: Dowden, Hutchinson and Ross.

548 Zube, E. H., Pitt, D. G., & Anderson, T. W. (1975). Perception and prediction of scenic resource values of the Northeast. In E. H. Zube, R. O. Brush & J. G. Fabos (Eds.), *Landscape assessment: Values, perceptions, and resources.* Stroudsburg, PA: Dowden, Hutchinson and Ross.

549 Craik, K. H. (1983). A role theoretical analysis of scenic quality judgments. In R. D. Rowe & L. G. Chestnut (Eds.), *Managing air quality and scenic resources at national parks and wilderness areas.* Boulder, CO: Westview Press.

550 Zube, E. H., & Pitt, D. G. (1981). Crosscultural perceptions of scenic and heritage landscapes. *Landscape Planning, 8,* 69-87.

551 Zube, E. H., Pitt, D. G., & Evans, G. W. (1983). A life-span developmental study of landscape assessment. *Journal of Environmental Psychology, 3,* 115-128.

552 Sussman, R., Greeno, M., Scannell, L., & Gifford, R. (2013). The effectiveness of models and prompts on waste diversion: A field experiment on composting by cafeteria patrons. *Journal of Applied Social Psychology, 43,* 24–34.

CHAPTER 4:

Personality and Environment

The earliest mark of extraversion in a child is his quick adaptation to the environment, and the extraordinary attention he gives to objects, especially to his effect upon them.

—CARL JUNG[1]

"YOU CAN'T JUST SIGN UP FOR THOSE ENVIRONMENTAL REVIEW PANELS," *said Tom's friend. "Usually only experts or people who visit the place all the time are invited to participate."*

Tom half-heartedly remarked that he went camping in the park several times a year, then he announced that he was off to the carrels to study again. This annoyed Jane slightly.

"Why don't you come with the rest of us to study at Pat's place?" she asked. "Why are you always hiding out alone in that sensory-deprivation chamber?"

Tom reflected. "I guess I've always needed to study in quiet," he said. "Even in high school, when most kids played music in their rooms after being locked in by their parents to do their homework, I liked quiet for studying."

Jane accepted this at face value, but remained skeptical. She had always benefitted from studying in a group of people. She could sweeten the work with conversational breaks, ask questions about difficult concepts, and generally feel less lonely. "Well," she said, trying to change the subject to something less contentious, "what are you going to work on?"

"Becoming enlightened."

"What kind of answer is that?"

"That is one of my major projects, you know," he said. "But I guess you're asking which school project I'm working on. It's an essay on the meaning of place. I'm trying to describe, from my own point of view, why that carrel has become such an important place to me. It's almost like home."

Jane counted to ten, trying not to blow up. "You and that carrel," she finally said. "What kind of person falls in love with a prison cell?"

Tom tried to be conciliatory, but he knew his own longstanding ways. "Sorry," he said, "I guess it takes all kinds."

PERSONALITY MAY SEEM A STRANGE TOPIC in a book about environmental psychology. Often, personality is considered to be something *inside* us, and the environment *outside* us. One might, therefore, wonder what connections exist, if any, between personality and the physical environment. This view is reinforced by a glance at the definitions of *personality* offered by some influential personality theorists. One says that personality is "a person's unique pattern of traits."[2] Another defines it as "the dynamic organization within the individual of those psychophysical systems that determine his [or her] characteristic behavior and thought."[3]

If personality is inside us and the environment is outside us, perhaps they have no connections worthy of study. Some reasons why this conclusion is wrong lead off the next section. After that, the ways that traditional personality variables help us understand person-environment relations are surveyed. Several systems for assessing **environmental personality**, the individual's behavioral tendencies that relate to or have consequences for the physical environment, are discussed. Finally, the chapter closes with a discussion of the uses to which personality may be put in designing environments.

APOLOGIA, BACKGROUND, AND CURRENT SITUATION

Connections Between Personality and the Environment

FIVE REASONS why personality is an integral part of environmental psychology can be discerned:

1. Some personality theorists—from earliest times—have seen personality as intimately related to the physical environment. Even the trait theories, which seem to ignore the environment, intrinsically allow for situational factors when closely examined. For example, the original definition of *extraversion-introversion*, a trait we normally consider to be located inside the person, is based on the person's relationship to the environment. Carl Jung, who devised the concept, said the difference between the extravert and the introvert is based on the person's degree of preference for stimulation from the environment. Of course, merely asserting the existence of a connection between personality and environment does not make it exist. The second reason, however, confirms the first.

2. Knowledge of an individual's traits helps us to understand and predict environmentally relevant behavior. For example, knowledge of whether a person has a sociable and energetic disposition significantly predicts the kind of behavior setting that person is likely to select when given a choice.[4]

3. Apart from traits or dispositions described by traditional personality theorists, such as extraversion or sociability, environmental psychologists have demonstrated that individuals have dispositions that are specifically relevant to person-environment transactions. For example, George McKechnie identified several environmental dispositions, one of which is environmental trust—a measure of the individual's tendency to feel secure in potentially threatening environments.[5]

4. Personal dispositions are central to one of environmental psychology's most important concepts: person-environment compatibility. One of the fundamental goals of designers and architects is to create a good fit between persons and their settings. To accomplish this, one must first be able to accurately assess both persons and environments: if these cannot be accurately assessed, one cannot be sure whether a good match between them has been achieved or not. The assessment of persons yields a pattern of personal dispositions that is an important part of the person half of the person-environment congruence concept.

5. Although the concept has not yet been developed much, we can turn around the notion of personality and apply it to places, instead of people.[6] Plazas, neighborhoods, dwellings, and beaches have enduring characteristics, just like people. The term *environmentality*, introduced in Chapter 3, is appropriate here. Many of the methods and approaches developed over many years by personality psychologists for understanding persons may be used—with minor adaptations—to understand settings too.

Roots of the Connection: Murray and Lewin

Henry Murray's Personology. Actually, the notion that personality and environment influence one another is ancient. Within the modern era, the idea was elaborated most clearly and forcefully by Henry Murray in the 1930s and 1940s, although others have also discussed it.[7] In addition to his psychological interests, Murray was a brilliant all-around scholar who, besides his psychological interests, was a physician who graduated first in his class. He also

HENRY MURRAY invented the concept of press, which included the physical environment.

wrote important literary works, including a classic interpretation of Herman Melville's *Moby Dick*. Not surprisingly, given this breadth of interests, Murray's vision of personality, which he called **personology**, explicitly includes environmental factors.[8]

For Murray, the basic event for personologists to study is the **proceeding**, the initiation and completion of an important behavior sequence. He distinguishes between *internal proceedings*, in which we try to represent, explain, and predict the world to ourselves (e.g., planning, daydreaming, solving problems) and *external proceedings*, in which we interact with other individuals or the physical environment (e.g., conversing, sailing, working). External proceedings have two sides to them: one corresponds to our *experience* of the external proceeding, and the other corresponds to an *objective* account of the behavior sequence. For example, when we sail, we think about and feel the weather, the water, and the boat. Yet our sailing behavior, such as how long and how often we tack, could be measured objectively.

Murray viewed the environment itself as exerting **press**, "the power...to affect the wellbeing of the subject in one way or another"[9] (see Figure 4-1). Press may have a positive or negative influence on us. While sailing, for example, the weather may be warm and sunny with moderate winds, or a sudden squall may capsize us. Press may be social or physical in nature. Most important, press has an experiential side and an objective side, like the external proceeding. **Alpha press** is the environment considered from an objective, third-party point of view. **Beta press** is the environment considered from the individual's own perspective.

Alpha and beta press often closely correspond to one another, but not always. Discrepancies between alpha and beta press may indicate that a person has a problem. Consider a situation in which a room is at 20°C/71°F and someone complains, "It's really cold in here." If we notice this gap between alpha and beta press, we may begin to divine some reason for it. Guessing the person may be coming down with a cold, we might ask, "How are you feeling?" Murray offered several lists of press. These include aspects of both the physical and the social environment. In one list, designed to represent children's press, he included water, weather, and possessions as well as parents, praise, and friendship.[10]

Kurt Lewin's Field Theory. Another theorist whose ideas brought the environment into greater prominence within psychology was Kurt Lewin, who was introduced in Chapter 1. His **field theory** was an attempt to represent the person and the environment in the graphic terms of topology, a branch of mathematics. The *person (P)* is viewed as existing in the *psychological environment (E)*, the person's representation of the physical and social influences in the surroundings. *P* and *E* together comprise the **life space**, the totality of facts inside and outside the person. From these assertions comes Lewin's famous formula, $B=f(P, E)$ (see Figure 4-2).

Outside the life space, the **foreign hull** consists of alien facts—that is, real aspects of the world which have not been incorporated into the life space of a particular individual. For example, there are many corners of the planet that you have never seen or heard of, but they do exist. Of crucial importance, however, is Lewin's contention that the boundary between the life space and the foreign hull is *permeable*. Alien facts may become psychologically important facts, perhaps if you visit one of those corners of the planet. That is why Lewin came to believe that the study of alien

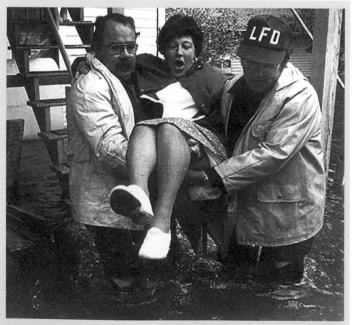

FIGURE 4–1 Floods are one threatening form of environmental press!

facts themselves—an enterprise he termed **psychological ecology**—is worthwhile.[11] One implication of this permeability is that aspects of the physical environment that never before affected an individual in any psychologically important way may begin to do so. Madame Curie was not particularly concerned about the consequences to her health of experimenting with radium. By now, however, we know all too much about the carcinogenic properties of radioactive materials. Concern about them *now* is an important part of living with nuclear power.

A second, and perhaps even more important implication of permeability, is that it is bidirectional. That is, psychological facts also may influence alien facts. This feature of Lewin's theory was early formal recognition of an important current perspective of environmental psychologists: persons should be viewed as active agents of environmental change. Often we are able to choose which setting we wish to use for a given purpose, to alter that setting if need be, and on a larger scale, influence decisions made on environmental issues by governments, business firms, and other organizations. The greenhouse gases we burn contribute to climate change. As we become aware of more elements of the physical environment that affect us, we incorporate more of the foreign hull into our life spaces. This increased awareness does not mean that all of us become environmentally active. Rather, most of us become more active, at least in our own territories, many of us become more active on a larger scale, and nearly all of us could be more active agents of environmental improvement.

A third implication of permeability is that we sometimes affect the foreign hull unintentionally, without realizing either that we have had an effect or the magnitude of that effect. On the societal level, this happened with the widespread use of DDT. For years, we did not realize that DDT was working its way up the food chain and endangering predatory birds by weakening the walls of their eggs. On a personal level, one's decision to reduce, reuse, and recycle affects individuals, organizations, and the physical environment far beyond one's own life space: landfills are one example.

Lewin's theory seems very simple, but it is conceptually powerful and has had enormous impact in psychology. In environmental psychology, it is the basis of several current theories, including ecological psychology and social ecology. The theory has been criticized, however, as being unclear about the difference between the *psychological* environment and the *physical* environment.[12,13] Some critics

maintain that Lewin confused the objective environment and the person's psychological representation of the environment. This confusion has probably made the theory *more* influential rather than less so. Social psychologists have fruitfully taken *E* as the person's cognitive representation of the social and physical world. Some environmental psychologists have fruitfully used *E* as the objective physical world. Both groups have found the theory a useful guiding framework for research. Much applied and theoretical research has been based—sometimes directly, sometimes loosely—on Lewin's ideas. The applied work often employs Lewin's own concept, **action research**,[14] a specific procedure that simultaneously aims to understand and improve social and physical conditions.

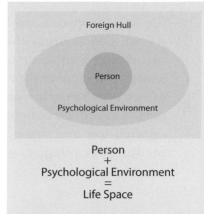

FIGURE 4–2 A simplified depiction of Kurt Lewin's view of persons-in-environments. Each person (P) exists in a psychological environment (E), which, together, comprise the life space (L). Outside L is the foreign hull (F), that part of the objective world that a person has not incorporated into L through perceptions and awareness.

IN SUM *Personality is a part of environmental psychology because traits do not merely refer to persons, but include consideration of how persons interact with their environments, help predict the behavior of individuals in the environment, specifically characterize our environmental tendencies, and form an important part of the person half of person–environment compatibility. The important early formulations of Henry Murray and Kurt Lewin are reviewed because their ideas are still influential. Henry Murray's personology introduced the concepts of alpha and beta press (the actual and perceived power of the environment to affect our welfare), and internal and external proceedings (subjective and objective accounts of the initiation and completion of behavior sequences). Lewin's field theory, which conceptualized persons as actively interacting with their environments in their life spaces, produced the famous formula B = f(P, E). Our representation of the physical environment and some elements of the unrepresented physical environment (the foreign hull) affect our behavior and experience. Lewin's action research concept, in which theory and application are fused, guides many environmental psychologists today.*

TRADITIONAL PERSONALITY DIMENSIONS

WHEN ENVIRONMENTAL PSYCHOLOGY WAS NEW, no one had yet developed measures of personality that were specifically concerned with or designed to assess person-environment transactions. Those who believed that the study of personal dispositions might help us understand behavior in the environment were forced to employ existing measures of personality. Although traditional personality measures were not designed to predict environmentally relevant behaviors, some nevertheless appeared to be useful. Environmental psychologists therefore attempted to use them, in the absence of custom-designed constructs, to help elucidate environment-behavior relations. For example, the frequency of engaging in six outdoor recreation activities was correlated in one study with scores on a general purpose personality test.[15] The results demonstrated that personality is modestly related to one's choice of outdoor activities. These traditional measures were not strong predictors of environmental activities, because they were not designed for that purpose, but they performed fairly well.

This section surveys the outcomes of traditional personality measures in relation to environmental behavior.

The Big Five

PERHAPS THE DOMINANT MODERN CONCEPTUALIZATION of normal personality is the Big Five, which can be remembered easily by its acronym OCEAN: openness (to experience), conscientiousness, extraversion, agreeableness, and neuroticism (also known, in reverse, as emotional stability).

Environmental Concern. The Big Five are related to environmental concern. For example, agreeableness, emotional stability, and conscientiousness are significantly related to biospheric values.[16] Agreeableness, conscientiousness, and openness to experience were strongly related to environmental engagement in another study.[17] In a third study, agreeableness and openness to experience were strongly related to greater environmental concern, and conscientiousness and neuroticism were also related, although less strongly.[18]

Constructs similar to the Big Five's extraversion, such as sociability, outgoing personality, and dispositional warmth, are related to behavior or attitudes in other zones of the environment or in other ways, including social spaces, landscape evaluations, sense of direction, and response to noise.

Social Space. Sociability is predictive of many environmentally relevant behaviors, particularly the use of space. Specifically, this includes preferred interpersonal distance, reactions to high-density situations, and furniture arrangement preferences. Most studies show that outgoing individuals prefer to be physically closer to others than do reserved individuals[19] (see Figure 4-3). For example, extraverted individuals spend more time in lobbies and bars, where more social interaction occurs.[20] Another study showed that more reserved professors arrange their office furniture differently from more outgoing professors.[21] Faculty offices may be characterized as open (when the desk is placed against a far wall, so it does not constitute a barrier between professor and visitor) or closed (when the desk

FIGURE 4–3 Some like to be close.

intervenes between professor and visitor). Outgoing professors more often used the open furniture arrangement.

If sociability were the only influence on social space choices, similar results probably would always be found. However, other factors also affect our preferences.

1. Social factors (such as the number of visitors to the professors' offices in the study just described) might influence their furniture arrangements.[22] Similarly, one might predict that sociable persons would enjoy crowding more than less-sociable persons, and that less-sociable persons would enjoy being alone more than social persons. However, in a study of dormitory residents, outgoing students who lived in high-density dorms reported less stress than reserved students who lived in high-density dorms (as predicted); however, the two groups experienced about the same amount of stress in low-density dorms (where one might expect outgoing students to experience more stress).[23]

2. Demographic factors can moderate relations between personality and environmental behavior. For example, one study found that more-sociable people tend to have more seats per square foot in the entertainment area of their homes than less-sociable people do. They also have more couches and benches (closer seating) than chairs (more isolated seating).[24] However, this seemed to be more true for women than for men.

3. Behavior often is a function of multiple dispositions, not merely one. In a study that examined this idea, I asked participants to draw chairs in a diagram of a room, placing the chairs where they would feel comfortable talking to another person in 18 different social situations.[25] In general, warm individuals placed their chairs closer to the other person than did cold individuals; this is a straightforward relation of the type already discussed. But a more complex pattern was also evident: Those who were colder and *more* ambitious chose significantly larger distances than those who were colder but *less* ambitious. Among warmer individuals, ambitious and non-ambitious individuals did not choose different distances. Thus, if we combine knowledge of at least two dispositions of a person, we can make better predictions about that person's preferred interpersonal distance than if we consider only one disposition.

Landscapes, Sense of Direction, and Noise. Outgoing individuals seem to evaluate landscapes differently than do reserved individuals.[26,27] In one study, individuals who reported needing the support of others found landscapes near San Francisco to be more serene, beautiful, and cultivated than those who reported needing less support from others. In another, outgoing individuals perceived landscapes in the same area as more active and busy than did reserved individuals. These studies demonstrate that personality is connected to environmentally relevant behavior in some less than obvious ways.

Another non-obvious personality-environment relation is the finding that the outgoing-reserved dimension is related to one's sense of direction.[28] More sociable individuals, it seems, are better able to point out correct geographical directions than less sociable individuals. As further evidence that such relations are not obvious, the researcher asked participants how good their sense of direction was, and found no differences between outgoing and reserved individuals. Thus, even those who use their sense of direction more effectively seem to be unaware that they are more skilled than others!

Finally, as predicted by Jung when he first described the concept, extraverts and introverts respond to incoming stimulation, such as noise, differently. In work-like tasks, the performance of neurotic introverts was more adversely affected by noise than was the performance of non-neurotic extraverts.[29] Of course, it is hard to know from this study whether the participants' neuroticism or their extraversion was the more important factor. In another study in which neuroticism was not a factor, extraverts were more annoyed by noise from jet aircraft when the ambient lighting was bright, whereas introverts were more annoyed by it when the lighting was dim.[30]

Locus of Control

SOME PEOPLE BELIEVE they can exert a reasonable amount of control over their own destinies; others believe their lives are strongly influenced by powerful others or by fate. This belief that control is primarily inside or outside oneself (internal versus external locus of control) has been investigated in relation to environmentally relevant behaviors because of its seemingly obvious connection to person-environment relations. In fact, however, most locus of control measures refer to a belief that our lives are controlled by fate, luck, chance, or powerful other *people* rather than by the physical environment. Thus, traditional locus of control measures are not conceptually related to the physical environment. Nevertheless, traditional locus of control has been a significant predictor of environmental attitudes, such as holding more eco-centric values,[31] and behaviors related to the environment. Among the latter are use of social space, response to environmental hazards, pro-environment activities, and preferences for architectural style.

Pro-Environmental Actions. Responsible environmentalism is also affected by locus of control. Generally, those with a more internal locus of control engage in more environmentally responsible behaviors and are more likely to be political activists.[32-35] Regular recyclers were compared with non-recyclers in one study; recyclers were significantly more internal.[36] Internals recycled more even though they also had higher scores on a scale measuring environmental cynicism, that is, they were less optimistic than non-recyclers that their efforts would solve environmental problems.

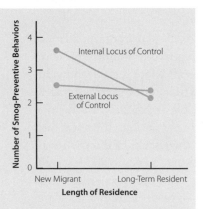

FIGURE 4–4 Whether one copes with air pollution by engaging in behaviors that reduce its impact is a function of both personality and length of residence. Internals who move to Los Angeles initially cope more than newly arrived externals, but as time passes, their coping behavior sags to the level of externals.

Perhaps the internals recycled more because, as measured on another scale, they more strongly believed that environmental problems were their personal responsibility.

Some interactions between locus of control and other factors need more research. For example, in another study of locus of control and anti-pollution behavior, internals were more likely to be engaged in five pro-ecology activities (e.g., joining an environmental group or writing to the government on ecological issues).[37] This is what one would expect. But the researchers also measured the optimism of their participants and found that optimistic internals engaged in more activities than did pessimistic internals. This interaction between locus of control and optimism contrasts with the results in the previous study of recyclers, in which pessimists recycled more. More research is necessary to resolve this discrepancy. However, we may safely conclude that, in general, those who believe they have

some control over their lives do engage in more responsible environmental activities.

When individuals do not believe that they control their lives, both the environment and the self may suffer. Researchers have speculated that a lack of perceived control might lead to frustration, which might manifest itself as vandalism or other environmentally destructive behavior.[38,39] Among the exotic few who have spent the winter in Antarctica, those who feel powerless have the most difficulty adjusting to the harsh environment.[40]

Social Space. Internal versus external locus of control is related to preferences for interpersonal distance and reactions to high population density. Those who believe their lives are controlled by external forces seem to prefer larger interpersonal distances.[41,42] Perhaps those who believe that other people exert considerable influence over them feel more secure if they are literally out of reach. Internals apparently tolerate high densities better than externals.[43,44] In high-density living conditions, a lack of perceived control causes increased psychological distress.[45,46] Possibly internals have learned more and better coping strategies: Those who believe life is reasonably controllable naturally fulfill that belief by developing more and better methods of handling difficult situations, such as high density.

Environmental Hazards. In a study of the manner in which internals and externals respond to some environmental threats, internals believed that luck had less to do with the damage resulting from tornados than externals did.[47] More significantly, internals actually took more of the recommended precautions than externals did. However, as usual, life can be a little more complicated, as researchers who investigated how Los Angeles residents respond to another hazard, air pollution.[48] From the research just described we might expect that internals would cope with smog by engaging in more preventative behaviors than externals would. This was the case for internals who *recently arrived* in Los Angeles; they did take more anti-pollution steps. Unfortunately, however, *long-term* residents who were internals took as few preventative measures as external long-term residents. Sadly, adaptation seemed to dampen the anti-pollution behavior of internals (see Figure 4-4).

Preference for Architectural Styles. Finally, locus of control may be related to preferences for architectural style. Researchers showed slides depicting classical building styles (Renaissance and 1950s International) versus romantic building styles (baroque and 1950s naturalism).[49] Individuals with a tendency toward external locus of control preferred romantic-style buildings, but those with a tendency toward internal locus of control preferred classical-style buildings. To explain this, the researchers speculated that perhaps internality implies the exercise of control, and this preference for control carries over into a preference for more controlled styles and environments. Classical building styles, most architects would agree, include more straight lines and are more severe than the more flowing, rolling lines characteristic of romantic styles.

Other Traditional Dimensions

THE OUTGOING–RESERVED AND INTERNAL–EXTERNAL locus of control dimensions have received the most research attention, but a variety of other personality factors have also been examined. One of these might be called **psychological health**, measured as ego strength, adjustment, self-confidence, or lack of neuroticism. Individuals in good psychological health seem better equipped to withstand the stresses of poor housing,[50] choose more beneficial settings,[51] and even have a better sense of direction.[52]

Conventionality and **traditionalism** have also been examined. Professors with traditional orientations to education reflected this through closed office arrangements, although this was moderated by the number of students the professor advised.[53] As you would expect, more unconventional individuals choose more unconventional places to be,[54] and less conservative individuals recycle more.[55]

Finally, the relevance of a person's **cognitive style** to environmental issues has been examined.[56] One system for describing the way we think holds that a pair of dimensions characterizes much of our cognitive activity.[57] The objective-subjective dimension refers to preferences for "the hard, cold facts" versus preferences for one's own feelings and values. The analytic-holistic dimension refers to a preference for breaking down problems into their parts versus considering the problem as a whole in its context (see Figure 4-5). These dimensions can be combined to form quadrants that represent four cognitive styles. The person who tends to be both analytical and objective is the *analytical scientist*, who focuses on objective facts in a reductionist manner. Perhaps the usual chemist typifies this style. The *systems theorist* prefers an objective approach, but is not so reductionist: the whole interacting system is the focus. Perhaps most biologists adopt this cognitive

style. The *humanist* tends to think in subjective and holistic terms. This person often is the dissident scientist who argues that facts have their place, but in the larger context, feelings and values must be taken into account. The *mystic* prefers a subjective but analytic thinking style: the main concern is to explore the elements of one's own reaction to the external problems the others are working on. The mystic is unlikely to be a scientist, but perhaps a poet or spiritual seeker. Can you imagine how persons with these different cognitive styles might think about nuclear power or pesticide spraying?

A related construct influences how we think about environmental issues. **Cognitive complexity** is the degree to which a person's thoughts about a problem range from simple, concrete, and dichotomous (good-bad, right-wrong) to complex.

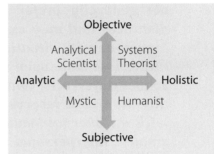

FIGURE 4–5 Two dimensions of cognitive style (analytic–holistic and objective–subjective) describe four general ways of thinking about the environment.

It is also the degree to which one considers self and others, weighs many alternatives, thinks about consequences, and is open to compromise. As one might expect, individuals with greater cognitive complexity think about environmental issues in a more complex way.[58] They see both sides, express more doubts, and are more likely to integrate all the concerns into a compromise proposal.

Personality and Environment

As discussed earlier, personality and the physical setting often act together to influence behavior. To illustrate this in some detail, consider a study of participation in conversations that Timothy Gallagher and I conducted.[59] Neither personality (defensive versus trusting) nor seating arrangement (row versus half-circle) *independently* predicted participation. However, participation was significantly higher for defensive individuals when the chairs were arranged in a row and for trusting individuals when the chairs were arranged in a half-circle. Apparently, when half-circle seating arrangements face participants toward one another, which allows for more visual surveillance than a straight row, the wariness of defensive individuals increases and they "clam up." Trusting individuals, in contrast, apparently feel uncomfortable holding a conversation in a row arrangement and participate less than they would in a half-circle. To predict conversational participation, one needs to know not only an individual's personality, but also the seating arrangement.

IN SUM *Some traditional personality measures assist in the understanding of environment-related behavior even though they were not designed for that purpose. Outgoing individuals generally prefer smaller interpersonal distances and may experience less stress in higher-density situations. They arrange furniture in a more open manner, perceive landscapes differently, and have a better sense of direction than reserved individuals. Persons with an internal locus of control also prefer smaller interpersonal distances and tolerate high density better than those with an external locus of control. Internals often engage in more pro-environment activities, such as recycling, although other factors can alter this. They also may prefer more "controlled" architecture. Psychological health and conventionality have also been linked to environmentally relevant behavior. Spatial behavior is influenced by the joint effects of personality and the physical setting.*

FIGURE 4–6 Thing specialists like to tinker with complex machines.

A BASIC PREMISE OF PERSONALITY THEORY is that researchers should use only dispositions that have been designed for the domain of behavior to be studied. According to this premise, all the foregoing research was ill-advised. But as noted earlier, pioneer environmental psychologists had no purpose-built measures to use in studies of personality and the environment. Such measures have had to be constructed, and this takes time. Because purpose-built measures are newer than the traditional measures, research on the measures designed especially for environmental psychology is less plentiful. Some research is aimed at assessing the reliability and validity of the new measures. Nevertheless, enough research is available to give some flavor of the potential uses of the new measures. A survey of each disposition and some research using it follows.

Person-Thing Orientation

The Disposition. One of the earliest such concepts posits that some individuals are primarily attuned to objects and environments, whereas others are more attuned to people.[60,61] This simple distinction seems appropriate as the first environmental personality dimension. However, person-thing orientation is a trifle more complicated than that. The developer of this concept, Brian Little, proposed that people can be high or low on each of the two orientations, which creates four possible orientations.[62-64] Two of these are obvious: **Person specialists** and **thing specialists** are high on one dimension but low on the other. However, others are **generalists**, who show marked interest in both people *and* things, and **non-specialists**, who are not very interested in either people *or* things. Knowing which of these types best characterizes an individual should enable us to predict some of that person's behavior, including environment-related behavior. Which type would most likely take a computer course? Which would prefer a social psychology course? Which type is best suited to a course in environmental psychology?

The person specialist, according to Little, is likely to have a smaller personal space zone, to use first names in conversations more, and to communicate more. The thing specialist, when not working on a computer or a collection, probably prefers solitary nature walks or gardening, and reads magazines that focus on hobbies, electronics, or other *things* (see Figure 4-6). The generalist cares about both people and things, but may have a problem with information overload. This type of person may be frustrated when attempts to involve an acquaintance who is a computer addict (thing specialist) in a computer club prove futile, and when it is nearly impossible to involve a friend who is majoring in social work (person specialist) to go shopping for a computer.

Individuals in the non-specialist category care most about themselves. Little suggests that a better name for this type might be **self-specialist**. These individuals spend much time attempting to understand and predict their own behavior, and perhaps telling you and everyone else about their progress or lack of progress, which severely limits the amount of time they have to devote to others or the environment.

Little's measures of these dispositions are called the Person-Thing Orientation scales. A different measure of the same basic concept is called **thing-cognitive complexity**, an attempt to assess the complexity of an individual's conceptualization of things.[65] Individuals who are very thing-cognitively complex have many different ways of distinguishing or grouping things or environments. Do you know people who can tell you a million things about different models of computers, and others who hardly know a Mac from a PC?

Research Findings. How might our disposition to specialize in persons or things (or both, or neither) relate to our transactions with the environment? Little reports that person specialists do indeed have more constructs with which to differentiate other individuals; they are more knowledgeable about the myriad types of individuals that exist.[66] Thing specialists use more physicalistic constructs when assessing places, compared to those with low "thing" scores. When Berkeley residents were asked to generate constructs that would distinguish among three local shopping areas, generalists produced the largest number, but person specialists again produced more people-oriented constructs and thing specialists produced more physical constructs.

These results show that the person-thing orientation scale has validity; individuals behave as their score leads us to expect they would. However, one study reported a less obvious finding.[67] When asked to estimate urban distances

(on the order of 6 kilometres, or 4 miles), almost everyone tended to overestimate actual distances, but there were large differences in the amount of error. Generalists only overestimated by 8 percent, followed by thing specialists at 15 percent, person specialists at 33 percent, and non-specialists at 45 percent. Can you explain these results, based on the person-thing orientation model?

Environmental Personality Inventory

The Dispositions. A second early environmental personality typology was constructed by Joseph Sonnenfeld.[68] It includes four traits or dispositions:

1. **Environmental sensitivity.** This is about the amount and complexity of the environment's perceived impact on oneself. When asked whether their home environments have positive, negative, or neutral connotations to them, environmentally sensitive individuals report that many features do have connotations of one sort or another.

2. **Environmental mobility.** By asking individuals to rank how much they would like to visit certain places around the world and how risky and exotic they believe each place to be, one can derive a measure of the individual's mobility. In general, highly mobile individuals are those who would very much like to visit or even migrate to the places they believe are risky and exotic.

3. **Environmental control.** This disposition is related to how much individuals believe the environment controls them, or vice versa, in the case of natural hazards. In the case of flooding, individuals differing on this dimension might prefer to avoid flood plains, work to control flooding, learn to live with floods, or even appreciate the excitement and challenge that floods provide.

4. **Environmental risk-taking.** This disposition describes one's propensity to take risks and to evaluate various activities as being risky or not. Some people climb rock faces, raft down white-water rivers, or race cars, but others would never engage in these activities. This disposition, however, also includes the individual's beliefs about whether these and other more activities are risky or not. Thus, Chris may believe mountain climbing is very risky, yet climb rock cliffs every weekend, whereas Pat climbs

frequently but does not believe climbing is very risky. Lindsay believes climbing is risky and avoids it, and Kim believes that it is not risky but never cares to go. Environmental risk-taking is a combination of whether individuals take risks and whether they are aware that they are taking risks.

Research Findings. People vary on these dispositions, as usual.[69] For example, older people and women are lower on environmental risk-taking, and risky and exotic places are more preferred by younger males. People in business, industrial, and engineering occupations prefer exotic but *not* risky destinations. Those in creative occupations prefer more exotic locales; those in medicine-related fields—perhaps oddly—prefer more risky locations. Individuals who live (or would like to live) in urban areas are highest in environmental sensitivity, but those who were *raised* in large cities are the lowest. Researchers who used a different measure of environmental sensitivity found that it is strongly related to self-reported pro-environmental behavior.[70,71]

The Environmental Response Inventory

The Dispositions. The most ambitious effort to measure environmentally related personality to date is George McKechnie's Environmental Response Inventory (ERI), which contains measures of eight dispositions.[72] McKechnie calls the ERI a broadband assessment instrument,

FIGURE 4–7 Some like them antique.

meaning that for the first time an attempt is made to measure most or all personal dispositions relevant to our everyday interaction with the physical environment. This raises a question: How many such dispositions are there? So far personality researchers who specialize in environmentally relevant behavior have no overall guiding theory to supply an answer to this question,[73] although to develop such a theory would be a very worthy goal. Thus, although the ERI includes more dispositions than any other assessment method to date, it cannot be regarded as comprehensive. Nevertheless, the ERI is the most complete environmental personality assessment system we have. It was developed in a complex, multistage test construction sequence. After much creation, exploration, evaluation, shortening, and testing of the scales, the following eight dispositions were decided upon:

1. **Pastoralism.** The tendency to oppose land development, preserve open space, accept natural forces as influences, and prefer self-sufficiency.

2. **Urbanism.** The tendency to enjoy high-density living and appreciate the varied interpersonal and cultural stimulation found in city life.

3. **Environmental Adaptation.** The tendency to favor the alteration of the environment to suit human needs and desires, oppose development controls, and prefer highly refined settings and objects.

4. **Stimulus Seeking.** The tendency to be interested in travel and exploration, enjoy complex or intense physical sensations, and have very broad interests.

5. **Environmental Trust.** The tendency to be secure in the environment, be competent in finding one's way around, and be unafraid of new places or of being alone.

6. **Antiquarianism.** The tendency to enjoy historical places and things, prefer traditional designs, collect more treasured possessions than most other individuals, and appreciate the products of earlier eras.

7. **Need for Privacy.** The tendency to need isolation, not appreciate neighbors, avoid distraction, and seek solitude.

8. **Mechanical Orientation.** The tendency to enjoy technological and mechanical processes, enjoy working with one's hands, and care about how things work.

We see in these dispositions certain similarities to the earlier systems. For example, stimulus seeking is not unlike Sonnenfeld's environmental mobility. Mechanical orientation is similar to Little's thing-orientation. Nevertheless, McKechnie's system includes some new dispositions and provides a set of concepts that can all be measured at the same time with the same basic instructions and materials. More important, it allows for the beginning of research into the question of how many dimensions of interest to environmental psychologists exist and how they are interrelated. For example, from McKechnie's own work, we know that antiquarianism and pastoralism are strongly correlated (but not so alike that they are redundant), whereas environmental trust and environmental adaptation are completely uncorrelated. Ultimately, one goal is to know all the important dimensions of environmental personality and how they fit together.

An elaboration of one ERI theme develops more differentiated measures of one disposition, antiquarianism[74] (see Figure 4-7). In a study of historic and prehistoric sites in Toronto, four subspecies of the antiquarian personality were uncovered. **Conservation** is the tendency to support (or not) the preservation of historic buildings and archaeological sites. **Heritage** is the tendency to appreciate (or not) the past as a cultural entity that has value in the present as a source of national identity or of lessons that could usefully guide today's decisions. **Experience** is the tendency to desire (or not) direct experience with historic or prehistoric places, such as wanting to visit reconstructed pioneer villages or living in a nice old house. **Interest** is the tendency to think often (or not) about or reflect on past events and places. All four scales are highly correlated with antiquarianism, but the developers of these subspecies offer them as tools for use when the researcher is specifically interested in the different aspects of dispositions toward the past and its artifacts.

Thus far we have focused on the dispositions of environmental personality one at a time. McKechnie's broadband approach opens another possibility: to assess an individual's *pattern* of personal dispositions. For idiographic applications such as designing a home or workspace for one individual, knowing that person's configuration of environmental tendencies could be of considerable value. For example, McKechnie described how the ERI may be used to graphically illustrate the differences between conservation group members, government officials, and members of a fishing and hunting club, or the differences within

a profession, such as student planners versus practicing planners.[75] With eight or more tendencies to consider, this could be a complex decision, but let us consider a relatively simple hypothetical case.

Morgan scores very high on stimulus seeking and antiquarianism, and Leslie scores very high on antiquarianism and very low on stimulus seeking. To keep matters simple, assume both have average scores on the other scales. I see Morgan in an office covered with photos of safaris and mountaintops. On the desk are some pieces of eight found while diving in the Caribbean. A set of genuine armor adorns the corner. An antique map collection fills an entire wall. I see Leslie in an office that also reveals the collector tendency. However, Leslie is into stamps and coins; display cases figure prominently in one corner of the office. In contrast to the electric blue carpet and orange walls of Morgan's office, Leslie has brown carpet and weathered barnboard on one wall. Subdued lighting, Victorian leather furnishings, and bookshelves full of first editions complete the scene in Leslie's office.

The ERI's value has been increased by being adapted for use with children.[76] Many ERI items were adapted to reflect the activities and interests of children as young as age 9, which resulted in the Children's Environmental Response Inventory (CERI). It should allow researchers to discover the tendencies of individual children, understand why they like and dislike certain settings, and assist in planning children's settings.

Research Findings. McKechnie proposed the ERI as a broadband assessment tool useful in any research setting where it is desirable to obtain information about how individuals think about and relate to the everyday physical environment.[77] To this end, I used the ERI to predict how students and residents of towns would judge 10 everyday buildings on a university campus and in the small town surrounding it.[78] Participants were shown color slide sequences of the buildings and asked to rate them on several dimensions. The buildings were divided into several objective categories: newer versus older, larger versus smaller, brightly lit versus dimly lit, and buildings photographed with people versus slides of buildings without people. Pastoralists, antiquarians, and mechanically oriented participants preferred pictures of buildings in which people were not visible over those in which people were present. Recall that these three personality types share strong interests in activities that do not emphasize people. Participants high on the environmental adaptation scale liked larger and newer buildings more than older and smaller ones, but antiquarians, as you might expect, preferred older buildings to newer ones. At a more general level, participants rated the buildings as a whole—that is, an approximation of what they thought of everyday architecture in general. Those high on environmental adaptation liked the buildings; pastoralists and antiquarians disliked them. I concluded that the ERI is indeed a promising tool for understanding which sorts of individuals are likely to prefer which sorts of buildings.

A current problem in medical training is that graduates gravitate more often to urban than to rural areas, resulting in unequal medical services to the population. The ERI was used to identify differences among optometrists who chose to practice in inner city, urban, suburban, and rural locations.[79] Those who located in urban areas scored higher on the urbanism scale. This finding has two implications. First, it shows that the ERI has validity (those who score high on an ERI urbanism scale generally do elect to live in cities). Second, it suggests that the ERI might be used to identify or screen applicants for medical school who are likely to prefer practicing in rural areas, should a medical school be prepared to rectify the imbalance in medical services to rural areas.

Nature Orientation

The Dispositions. How are we psychologically connected to nature (if we are at all)? Quite a number of dispositions have been proposed. Perhaps the first two measures were the nature scale and the romantic escape scale.[80] The **nature** scale taps the tendency to enjoy wilderness, woodlands, campfires, and other outdoor activities in relatively undeveloped places. The **romantic escape** scale also measures one's tendency to get out into natural settings, but with a difference in motivation. The person high on the nature scale wants to head *to* the woods, whereas the romantic escapist wants to flee *from* the urban-suburban life. Since then, researchers have devised measures of the affinity toward nature,[81] the inclusion of nature in self,[82] environmental identity,[83] connectedness to nature,[84] connectivity with nature,[85] commitment to nature,[86] and nature relatedness.[87] Do these sound similar to you? Indeed. A recent study examined the degree to which they overlap and found very strong correlations among them, with a few small differences in how they predicted other variables.[88]

Since then, yet another measure has been developed; it assesses a person's empathy with nature.[89] These are all self-report measures, although two of them ask the person to draw diagrams representing self and nature rather than use agree-disagree statements. But there is another way to assess a person's nature orientation.

Quick, what is the very first word that comes to mind when you read the next word? *Den.* Now, hold on to the word that came to mind for a moment while I explain. So many people are interested in nature these days that some responses to nature questionnaires may represent fashionable or socially desirable answers rather than real interest. For this reason, a measure called the natural environment awareness test (NEAT) was developed.[90] The NEAT uses a word-association approach to overcome the social desirability problem; it assumes that word associations tap a person's true beliefs better than questionnaire items do. Thus, if the first word that came to your mind was *cave, bear,* or *wolf* (or another nature-related word), score one for your nature orientation; if it was *room, study,* or *fireplace* (or other building-related word), then score one for your built-environment orientation. Repeated over 75 words that can have either nature or non-nature associations, the NEAT measures how nature-oriented a person is; the approach is one avenue to investigating nature-relatedness through an **implicit association test.** Another implicit association approach has been developed to overcoming socially desirable responding involves using a game format.[91] One might expect that people have stronger connections to the "nice" aspects of nature than to its "mean" aspect, but apparently we are just as connected to both aspects of nature.[92]

Does nature orientation simultaneously include one's appreciation of nature and the desire to protect it? A large survey in Switzerland suggests that these two aspects of nature orientation are separate.[93] This is not merely hairsplitting: if they are indeed distinct, then policies aimed at enhancing one or the other need to be tailored to that attitude, not aimed at both, which might blunt their impact.

Research Findings. Individuals with different scores on the nature and romantic escape scales do not merely engage in different activities; they do so for different reasons. For example, those who score high on the nature scale engage in their favorite activities in order to gain peace and quiet, to be involved in the process that characterizes the activity, and to be outdoors in natural settings.[94] Studies of the development of an environmental identity in children show that it can be initiated even after short experiences, such as an outdoor lesson about bats.[95] However, like all identity processes, it can only be fully developed after many similar experiences.

Environmental Stimulus Sensitivity

The Dispositions. Are some people more tuned-in to the environment—not only nature, but their surroundings in general? Are some people more able or less able to screen out environmental stimuli than others? Are there individual differences in environmental vulnerability?[96] One family of environmental personality dispositions is geared to such differences. Within this family, three measures, developed separately, deal with how the individual processes incoming stimulation from the environment. One assesses general stimulus sensitivity.[97] Second, the **stimulus screening** disposition, measures an individual's responses ("slow to be aroused" or "quick to adapt") to different kinds of stimuli (sound, texture, odor, and heat) that arrive in different patterns (novel, complex, or sudden).[98] The construct presumes to assess an individual's automatic screening of irrelevant stimuli. Screeners are those who are able to overcome the distraction that irrelevant stimuli cause non-screeners (see Figure 4-8). In general, screeners are believed to be less "arousable" than non-screeners. Third, the **noise sensitivity** scale, developed by Neil Weinstein, focuses on emotional response to noise in the immediate area.[99] Weinstein constructed it under the assumptions that we differ in our initial response to noise and in our abilities to adjust to noise that continues. Noise sensitivity appears to be related to a more general tendency of individuals to be critical or uncritical of their physical surroundings.[100]

Research Findings. These stimulus-sensitivity scales have been shown to predict several environment-related behaviors. Some households are more chaotic than others, but not all parents experience them as chaotic; in one study, only mothers with greater stimulus sensitivity did.[101] We all have our favored and less-favored places, but screeners and non-screeners differ in how they respond to these settings. Non-screeners seem to resist entering disliked settings more than screeners do; once there, they may socialize with others less and work less than screeners do.[102] These findings appear to have important implications for both environmental designers and personnel managers. Anoth-

FIGURE 4–8 Screeners are better able to study in high-stimulus surroundings, like this, than nonscreeners.

er study of screeners' behavior examined the responses of residents to dormitories of different designs.[103] In general, long corridor designs are seen as more crowded and are associated with more behavioral helplessness. However, screeners who lived in long-corridor dormitories adapted to the situation more successfully than did non-screeners.

Research on noise sensitivity shows that the scale can predict responses one would expect it to predict. For example, more noise-sensitive individuals usually perform worse in noisy conditions,[104-106] choose lower levels of noise,[107] listen to music less while working or reading, are more annoyed by noise from nearby roads, report more interference from noise with their daily activities,[108,109] and are more sensitive to other kinds of stimuli.[110] Noise-sensitive college students are more bothered by dormitory noise at the beginning of the school year, and become more disturbed by it by the end of the year.[111] Noise-sensitive students also have a history of lower academic performance, perhaps because of their sensitivity.

These findings are not surprising, but they do demonstrate that individuals who are likely to have negative experiences with noise sources can be identified and should be planned for a long time in advance. Planning for the needs of noise-sensitive individuals is important because they apparently cannot adapt to noise over time.[112,113] Noise sensitivity is not strongly related to objective noise level,[114] because some people are more sensitive to the same level of objectively measured noise than others and because objective noise levels often are unrelated to health or sleep complaints, whereas noise sensitivity in the same space *is* significantly related to health and sleep problems.[115] Thus, planning should not be based simply on objective noise levels; we must determine who in the noisy setting is noise-sensitive and plan for them in particular.

Control-Related Environmental Dispositions

The Dispositions. As noted earlier, the external dimension of traditional locus of control measures does not refer to the physical environment, but to fate, luck, chance, or powerful other people. But control over certain parts of the physical environment is important to people, so environmental psychologists have created special scales to measure perceived control in physical settings. Perceived, actual, and desired[116] control over features of the physical environment are all important. Some of these new control scales are designed for specific environments or purposes. For example, one assesses apartment tenants' degree of perceived control.[117] Faye Schmidt and I developed another control scale, the Environmental Appraisal Inventory (EAI), which concentrates on perceived control over environmental hazards.[118] Across 24 human- and nature-made hazards, some people feel they have more control; others feel more powerless. The EAI also measures how threatening these 24 hazards are to the person, and a recent extension of it assesses how responsible persons feel for each hazard.[119] A concept closely related to control is the belief that things can be improved, or optimism that, *collectively*, people can control the problem even if you cannot personally do so. Such a test, called the Environmental Modifiability Test, was developed for the specific case of air pollution.[120] A third specialized tool, the Environmental Action Internal Control Index, assesses locus of control within the context of pro-environment behavior.[121] It predicts (and initial studies confirm) that internals on the scale will engage in more environmentally responsible actions than externals. A fourth tool for measuring perceived control focuses on control in everyday settings. Stephen Eso and I therefore developed the Survey of Personal Influence in Common Environments (SPICE), which assesses perceived control (and the *importance* of having control) over many elements of three everyday physical settings: home, work or school, and public places (such as streets or retail stores).[122]

Research Findings. Most of the environmental control scales are quite new, and little research has been done with them, although they have many potential purposes. However, one finding is that persons with a greater perceived control over environmental hazards are also more commit-

ted to safeguarding the environment.[123] An important psychological difference is that between *perceived* and *actual* control. In an office work setting, employees who perceived that they had control over the room temperature were more satisfied, but when they were given actual control over the temperature, they were *less* happy.[124] Apparently the employees (and maybe the rest of us) like to feel we have control, but exercising that control takes effort and the cost of this effort cuts into our satisfaction.

IN SUM *Personality dimensions constructed especially for person-environment relations are relatively recent. Five groups or kinds of dimensions have been developed: orientation toward persons or things (or both or neither), concern with perceived or desired control over the physical environment, sensitivity to environmental stimuli, and affinity for nature. Two attempts to assemble a spectrum of environmental personality dimensions are the Environmental Response Inventory and the Environmental Personality Inventory. Personality theory predicts that such measures will be more useful than traditional personality measures for helping us understand person-environment relations because they are tools made specifically for the job.*

THREE USES OF PERSONALITY IN ENVIRONMENTAL DESIGN

I HAVE DESCRIBED IN SOME DETAIL the different approaches to assessing those aspects of personality most relevant to environmental psychology and some of the research linking those instruments to environmentally relevant cognition and behaviors. Perhaps you are still wondering just how such knowledge might be used. Kenneth Craik described three categories of uses to which personality assessments may be put: description, comparison, and prediction.[125]

Description

Description may be accomplished by the judicious use of any or all of the environmental personality measures described above. Whether they are used to describe a single person or the typical member of a certain group, environmental designers cannot take the person into account until the person's qualities are known. Description answers the question, Who is the individual for whom this space will be designed? In addition, the question might be turned around: Who are the architects, the designers, the managers of water resources, the facility managers who allocate and maintain space in organizations? Knowing their personalities helps us understand how they will tend to design and manage the environment.

Comparison

Comparison allows planners, architects, designers, and others to know the *differences* between individuals or groups. For example, knowledge of the differences in personality of typical snowmobilers and cross-country skiers should help park planners to design better new recreation areas and to develop effective policies for existing ones. Many other possible group comparisons might be made as part of the design process. Is the typical student different from the typical professor in terms of environmental tendencies? Are nurses different from physicians? Patients from both nurses and physicians? Every behavior setting includes several user groups. If their typical personalities are different, how so? Clarifying these differences should help designers create settings that better fit the needs of each group.

Prediction

The third use of personality knowledge is prediction. The assessment of individual differences frequently allows a forecast of the satisfaction, productivity, or some relevant behavior of an individual in a given environment. For example, recall that the ERI was used to predict which medical students will migrate. The other uses of prediction from environmental personality measures parallel the chapters of this book. They may be used to understand how individuals think about their surroundings, use the space around them, and manage or squander natural resources.

SUMMARY

This chapter describes the seemingly unlikely connections between personality and the environment. Reasons why environmental psychologists should consider personality are offered. The classic theories of Henry Murray and Kurt Lewin are described. How traditional personality variables (such as outgoing-reserved and internal-external locus of control) help explain behaviors of interest to environmental psychology is discussed. Six systems for assessing environmental personality, and some research using them, are described. The uses of personality assessment in environmental design include description, comparison, and prediction. Knowing the behavioral tendencies of those who are to use or control a setting may help designers produce a more compatible fit between occupant and habitat. Knowing how individuals and groups *differ* on key personality dimensions can help designers become more aware of how settings for different people should reflect their distinct psychological makeups. Knowing the environmental personality of individuals allows better prediction of their satisfaction with and performance in different physical settings.

Suggested Supplementary Readings

Craik, K. H. (1976). The personality research paradigm in environmental psychology. In S. Wapner, S. B. Cohen, & B. Kaplan (Eds.), *Experiencing the environment.* New York: Plenum.

Fridgen, C. (1994). Human disposition toward hazards: Testing the Environmental Appraisal Inventory. *Journal of Environmental Psychology, 14,* 101-111.

Little, B. R. (1987). Personality and environment. In D. Stokols & I. Altman (Eds.). *Handbook of environmental psychology.* New York: Wiley.

McKechnie, G. E. (1977). The environmental response inventory in application. *Environment and Behavior, 9,* 255-276.

References

1 Jung, C. G. (1921/1971). *Psychological types.* Princeton: Princeton University Press.

2 Guilford, J. P. (1959). *Personality.* New York: McGrawHill, p. 5.

3 Allport, G. W. (1961). *Pattern and growth in personality.* New York: Holt, Rinehart and Winston, p. 28.

4 Gormly, J. (1983). Predicting behavior from personality trait scores. *Personality and Social Psychology Bulletin, 9,* 267-270.

5 McKechnie, G. E. (1974). *ERI Manual: Environmental response inventory.* Berkeley, CA: Consulting Psychologists Press.

6 Veness, A. (1987). Place and personality. *Social Science, 72,* 29-33.

7 Campbell, C. M. (1934). *Human personality and the environment.* New York: MacMillan.

8 Murray, H. A. (1938). *Explorations in personality.* New York: Oxford University Press.

9 Murray, H. A. (1938). *Explorations in personality.* New York: Oxford University Press, p. 121.

10 Murray, H. A. (1938). *Explorations in personality.* New York: Oxford University Press.

11 Lewin, K. (1951). *Field theory in social science: Selected theoretical papers.* New York: Harper and Row.

12 Allport, G. W. (1955). *Becoming: Basic considerations for a psychology of personality.*

13 Brunswik, E. (1943). Organismic achievement and environmental probability. *Psychological Review, 50,* 255-272.

14 Sommer, R., & Amick, T. L. (1984). *Action research: Linking research to organizational change.* Davis, CA: Center for Consumer Research, University of California.

15 Driver, B. L., & Knopf, R. C. (1977). Personality, outdoor recreation and expected consequences. *Environment and Behavior, 9,* 169-193.

16 Swami, V., Chamorro-Premuzic, T., Snelgar, R. & Furnham, A. (2009) Egoistic, altruistic, and biospheric environmental concerns: A path analytic investigation of their determinants. *Scandinavian Journal of Psychology, 51,* 139–145.

17 Milfont, T. L., & Sibley, C. G. (2012). The big five personality traits and environmental engagement: Associations at the individual and societal level. *Journal of Environmental Psychology, Volume 32,* 187-195.

18 Hirsh, J. B. (2010). Personality and environmental concern. *Journal of Environmental Psychology, 30,* 245-248.

19 Altman, I. (1975). *The environment and social behavior: Privacy, personal space, territoriality and crowding.* Monterey, CA: Brooks/Cole, p. 73.

20 Eddy, G. L., & Sinnett, R. (1973). Behavior setting utilization by emotionally disturbed college students. *Journal of Consulting and Clinical Psychology, 40,* 210-216.

21 McElroy, J. C., Morrow, P. C., & Ackerman, R. J. (1983). Personality and interior office design: Exploring the accuracy of visitor attributions. *Journal of Applied Psychology, 68,* 541-544.

22 Hensley, W. E. (1982). Professor proxemics: Personality and job demands as factors of faculty office arrangement. *Environment and Behavior, 14,* 581-591.

23 Miller, S., Rossbach, J., & Munson, R. (1981). Social density and affiliative tendency as determinants of dormitory residential outcomes. *Journal of Applied Social Psychology, 11,* 356-365.

24 Osborn, D. R. (1988). Personality traits expressed: Interior design as behavior-setting plan. *Personality and Social Psychology Bulletin, 14,* 368-373.

25 Gifford, R. (1982). Projected interpersonal distance and orientation choices: Personality, sex, and social situation. *Social Psychology Quarterly, 45,* 145-152.

26 Craik, K. H. (1975). Individual variations in landscape description. In E. H. Zube, R. O. Brush, & J. G. Fabos (Eds.), *Landscape assessment: Values, perceptions and resources.* Stroudsberg, PA: Dowden, Hutchinson and Ross.

27 Feimer, N. R. (1981). Personality and sociodemographic variables as sources of variation in environmental perception. In H. M. Proshansky (Chair), *Environmental cognition.* Symposium conducted at the meeting of the American Psychological Association, August. (ERIC Document Reproduction Service No. ED 211-393.)

28 Bryant, K. J. (1982). Personality correlates of sense of direction and geographical orientation. *Journal of Personality and Social Psychology, 43,* 1318-1324.

29 Eysenck, M. W., & Graydon, J. (1989). Susceptibility to distraction as a function of personality. *Personality and Individual Differences, 10,* 681-687.

30 Shigehisa, T., & Gunn, W. J. (1979). Annoyance response to recorded aircraft noise: IV: Effect of intensity of illumination in relation to personality. *Journal of Auditory Research, 19,* 47-58.

31 Boeve-de Pauw, J., Donche, V., & Van Petegem, P. (2011). Adolescents' environmental worldview and personality: An explorative study. *Journal of Environmental Psychology, 31,* 109-117.

32 Sia, A. P., Hungerford, H. R., & Tomera, A. N. (1985-86). Selected predictors of responsible environmental behavior: An analysis. *Journal of Environmental Education, 17,* 31-40.

33 Pettus, A. M., & Giles, M. B. (1987). Personality characteristics and environmental attitudes. *Population & Environment: Behavioral & Social Issues, 9,* 127-137.

34 Huebner, R. B., & Lipsey, M. W. (1981). The relationship of three measures of locus of control to environmental activism. *Basic and Applied Social Psychology, 2,* 45-58.

35 Tucker, Jr.,L. R. (1978). The environmentally concerned citizen: Some correlates. *Environment and Behavior, 10,* 389-418.

36 Arbuthnot, J. (1977). The roles of attitudinal and personality variables in the prediction of environmental behavior and knowledge. *Environment and Behavior, 9,* 217-232.

37 Trigg, L. J., Perlman, D., Perry, R. P., & Janisse, M. P. (1976). Antipollution behavior: A function of perceived outcome and locus of control. *Environment and Behavior, 8,* 307-314.

38 Propst, D. B., & Kurtzz, M. E. (1989). Perceived control-reactance: A framework for understanding leisure behavior in natural settings. *Leisure Studies, 8,* 241-248.

39 Ruback, R. B., & Patniak, R. (1989). Crowding, perceived control, and the destruction of property. *Psychological Studies, 34,* 1-14.

40 Palinkas, L. A. (1985). *Sociocultural influences on psychosocial adjustment in Antarctica.* US Naval Health Research Center Report No. 85-49, 17.

41 Duke, M. P., & Nowicki, S., Jr. (1972). A new measure and social learning model for interpersonal distance. *Journal of Experimental Research in Personality, 6,* 119-132.

42 Heckel, R. V., & Hiers, J. M. (1977). Social distance and locus of control. *Journal of Clinical Psychology, 33,* 469-474.

43 Sundstrom, E. (1978). Crowding as a sequential process: Review of research on the effects of population density on humans. In A. Baum, & Y. M. Epstein (Eds.), *Human response to crowding.* Hillsdale, NJ: Erlbaum.

44 Verbrugge, L. M., & Taylor, R. B. (1980). Consequences of population density and size. *Urban Affairs Quarterly, 16,* 135-160.

45 Ruback, R. B., & Pandey, J. (1991). Crowding, perceived control, and relative power: An analysis of households in India. *Journal of Applied Social Psychology, 21,* 315-344.

46 Lepore, S. J., Evans, G. W., & Schneider, M. L. (1992). Role of control and social support in explaining the stress of hassles and crowding. *Environment and Behavior, 24,* 795-811.

47 Sims, J. H., & Baumann, D. D. (1972). The tornado threat: Coping styles of the North and the South. *Science, 176,* 1386-1391.

48 Evans, G. W., Jacobs, S. V., & Frager, N. B. (1982). Behavioral responses to air pollution. In A. Baum & J. E. Singer (Eds.), *Advances in environmental psychology.* Hillsdale, NJ: Erlbaum.

49 Juhasz, J. B., & Paxson, L. (1978). Personality and preference for architectural style. *Perceptual and Motor Skills, 47,* 241-242.

50 Salling, M., & Harvey, M. E. (1981). Poverty, personality and sensitivity to residential stressors. *Environment and Behavior, 13,* 131-163.

51 Eddy, G. L., & Sinnett, R. (1973). Behavior setting utilization by emotionally disturbed college students. *Journal of Consulting and Clinical Psychology, 40,* 210-216.

52 Bryant, K. J. (1982). Personality correlates of sense of direction and geographical orientation. *Journal of Personality and Social Psychology, 43,* 1318-1324.

53 Hensley, W. E. (1982). Professor proxemics: Personality and job demands as factors of faculty office arrangement. *Environment and Behavior, 14,* 581-591.

54 Eddy, G. L., & Sinnett, R. (1973). Behavior setting utilization by emotionally disturbed college students. *Journal of Consulting and Clinical Psychology, 40,* 210-216.

55 Arbuthnot, J. (1977). The roles of attitudinal and personality variables in the prediction of environmental behavior and knowledge. *Environment and Behavior, 9,* 217-232.

56 Miller, A. (1985). Cognitive styles and environmental problem-solving. *Journal of Environmental Studies, 26,* 21-31.

57 Cotgrove, S. (1982). *Catastrophe or cornucopia.* New York: Wiley.

58 Miller, A. (1982). Environmental problem-solving: Psychosocial factors. *Environmental Management, 6*, 535-541.

59 Gifford, R., & Gallagher, T. M. B. (1985). Sociability: Personality, social context, and physical setting. *Journal of Personality and Social Psychology, 48*, 1015-1023.

60 Cottle, W. C. (1950). A factorial study of the Multiphasic, Strong, Kuder, and Bell inventories using a population of adult males. *Psychometrika, 15*, 25-47.

61 Thurstone, L. L. (1946). Factor analysis and body types. *Psychometrika, 11*, 15-21.

62 Little, B. R. (1968). Factors affecting the use of psychological versus nonpsychological constructs on the Rep Test. *Bulletin of the British Psychological Society, 21*, 113.

63 Little, B. R. (1972). Psychological man as scientist, humanist, and specialist. *Journal of Experimental Research in Personality, 6*, 95-118.

64 Little, B. R. (1976). Specialization and the varieties of human experience: Empirical studies within the personality paradigm. In S. Wapner, S. B. Cohen, & B. Kaplan (Eds.), *Experiencing the environment.* New York: Plenum.

65 Friedman, S. (1974). Relationships among cognitive complexity, interpersonal dimension and spatial preferences and propensities. In S. Friedman, & J. B. Juhasz (Eds.), *Environments: Notes and selections on objects, spaces and behavior.* Belmont, CA: Wadsworth.

66 Little, B. R. (1976). Specialization and the varieties of human experience: Empirical studies within the personality paradigm. In S. Wapner, S. B. Cohen, & B. Kaplan (Eds.), *Experiencing the environment.* New York: Plenum.

67 Little, B. R. (1976). Specialization and the varieties of human experience: Empirical studies within the personality paradigm. In S. Wapner, S. B. Cohen, & B. Kaplan (Eds.), *Experiencing the environment.* New York: Plenum.

68 Sonnenfeld, J. (1969). Personality and behavior in environment. *Proceedings of the Association of American Geographers, 1*, 136-140.

69 Sonnenfeld, J. (1969). Personality and behavior in environment. *Proceedings of the Association of American Geographers, 1*, 136-140.

70 Sivek, D. J., & Hungerford, H. (1989-90). Predictors of responsible behavior in members of three Wisconsin conservation organizations. *Journal of Environmental Education, 21*, 35-40.

71 Sia, A. P., Hungerford, H. R., & Tomera, A. N. (1985-86). Selected predictors of responsible environmental behavior: An analysis. *Journal of Environmental Education, 17*, 31-40.

72 McKechnie, G. E. (1974). *ERI Manual: Environmental response inventory.* Berkeley, CA: Consulting Psychologists Press.

73 Craik, K. H. (1970). Environmental psychology. In T. M. Newcomb (Ed.), *New directions in psychology.* New York: Holt, Rinehart and Winston.

74 Taylor, S. M., & Konrad, V. A. (1980). Scaling dispositions toward the past. *Environment and Behavior, 12*, 283-307.

75 McKechnie, G. E. (1977). The environmental response inventory in application. *Environment and Behavior, 9*, 255-276.

76 Bunting, T. E., & Cousins, L. R. (1985). Environmental dispositions among school-age children: A preliminary investigation. *Environment and Behavior, 17*, 725-768.

77 McKechnie, G. E. (1974). *ERI Manual: Environmental response inventory.* Berkeley, CA: Consulting Psychologists Press.

78 Gifford, R. (1980). Environmental dispositions and the evaluation of architectural interiors. *Journal of Research in Personality, 14*, 386-399.

79 Kegel-Flom, P. (1976). Identifying the potential rural optometrist. *American Journal of Optometry and Physiological Optics, 53*, 479-482.

80 Kaplan, R. (1977). Patterns of environmental preference. *Environment and Behavior, 9*, 195-215.

81 Kals, E., Schumacher, D. & Montada, L. (1999). Emotional affinity toward nature as a motivational basis to protect nature. *Environment & Behavior, 31*, 178-202.

82 Schultz, P. W. (2001). Assessing the structure of environmental concern: Concern for self, other people, and the biosphere. *Journal of Environmental Psychology, 21*, 1-13.

83 Clayton, S. (2003). Environmental identity: A conceptual and an operational definition. In S. Clayton & S. Opotow (Eds.), *Identity and the natural environment: The psychological significance of nature* (pp. 45-65).Cambridge, MA: MIT Press.

84 Mayer, F. S., & Frantz, C. M. (2004). The connectedness to nature scale: A measure of individuals' feeling in community with nature. *Journal of Environmental Psychology, 24*, 503-515.

85 Dutcher, D., Finley, J., Luloff, A., & Johnson, J. (2007). Connectivity with nature as a measure of environmental values. *Environment and Behavior, 39, 474*-493.

86 Davis, J. L., Green, J. D., & Reed, A. (2009). Interdependence with the environment: Commitment, interconnectedness, and environmental behavior. *Journal of Environmental Psychology, 29*, 173-180.

87 Nisbet, E. K. L., Zelenski, J. M., & Murphy, S. A. (2009) The Nature Relatedness Scale: Linking individuals' connection with nature to environmental concern and behavior. *Environment and Behavior, 41*, 715-740.

88 Tam, K.-P. (2013). Concepts and measures related to connection to nature: Similarities and differences. *Journal of Environmental Psychology, 34*, 64-78.

89 Tam, K.-P. (2013). Dispositional empathy with nature. *Journal of Environmental Psychology, 35*, 92-104.

90 Born, T. J., & Wieters, N. E. (1978). Nonreactive measurement of orientation toward the natural environment. *Journal of Environmental Education, 10*, 41-43.

91 Bruni, C. M., & Schultz, P. W. (2010). Implicit beliefs about self and nature: Evidence from an IAT game. *Journal of Environmental Psychology, 30*, 95-102.

92 Bruni, C. M., Chance, R. C., Schultz, P. W., Nolan, J. M. (2012). Natural Connections: Bees Sting and Snakes Bite, But They Are Still Nature. *Environment and Behavior, 44*, 197-215.

93 Kaiser, F. G., Hartig, T., Brugger, A., & Duvier, C. (2013). Environmental Protection and Nature as Distinct Attitudinal Objects: An Application of the Campbell Paradigm. *Environment and Behavior, 45*, 369-398.

94 Kaplan, R. (1977). Patterns of environmental preference. *Environment and Behavior, 9*, 195-215.

95 Kals, E., & Ittner, H. (2003). Children's environmental identity: Indicators and behavioral impacts. In S. Clayton, & S. Opotow, (Eds.), *Identity and the natural environment: The psychological significance of nature.* (pp. 135-157). Cambridge, MA: MIT Press.

96 Iwata, O. (1986). The relationship of personality to environmental vulnerability and pro-environmental orientation. *Progress in Experimental Personality Research, 14*, 165-203.

97 Wachs, T. D. (2013). Relation of maternal personality to perceptions of environmental chaos in the home. *Journal of Environmental Psychology, 34*, 1-9.

98 Mehrabian, A. (1976). *Manual for the questionnaire measure of Stimulus Screening and Arousability.* Unpublished manuscript, University of California at Los Angeles.

99 Weinstein, N. D. (1978). Individual differences in reactions to noise: A longitudinal study in a college dormitory. *Journal of Applied Psychology, 63*, 458-466.

100 Weinstein, N. D. (1980). Individual differences in critical tendencies and noise annoyance. *Journal of Sound and Vibration, 68*, 241-248.

101 Wachs, T. D. (2013). Relation of maternal personality to perceptions of environmental chaos in the home. *Journal of Environmental Psychology, 34*, 1-9.

102 Mehrabian, A. (1978). Characteristic individual reactions to preferred and unpreferred environments. *Journal of Personality, 46*, 717-731.

103 Baum, A., Calesnick, L. E., Davis, G. E., & Gatchel, R. J. (1982). Individual differences in coping with crowding: Stimulus screening and social overload. *Journal of Personality and Social Psychology, 43*, 821-830.

104 Bhatia, P., & Muhar, I. (1988). Noise sensitivity and mental efficiency. *Psychologia: An International Journal of Psychology in the Orient, 31*, 163-169.

105 Jelinkova, Z., Picek, M., & Hyncica, V. (1988). Psychophysiological factors determining responses to noise load. 2nd European International Association for Interdisciplinary Study of Higher Nervous Functions Conference. *Activitas Nervosa Superior, 30*, 146-147.

106 Dornic, S., Laaksonen, T., & Ekehammer, B. (1990). Noise sensitivity: General self-report versus noise effect in laboratory situations. *Reports from the Department of Psychology*, No. 716.

107 Dornic, S., Laaksonen, T., & Ekehammer, B. (1990). Noise sensitivity: General self-report versus noise effect in laboratory situations. *Reports from the Department of Psychology*, No. 716.

108 Matsumura, Y., & Rylander, R. (1991). Noise sensitivity and road traffic annoyance in a population sample. *Journal of Sound and Vibration, 151*, 415-419.

109 Weinstein, N. D. (1980). Individual differences in critical tendencies and noise annoyance. *Journal of Sound and Vibration, 68*, 241-248.

110 Stansfeld, S. A., Clark, C. R., Jenkins, L. M., & Tarnopolsky, A. (1985). Sensitivity to noise in a community sample: I. Measurement of psychiatric disorder and personality. *Psychological Medicine, 15*, 243-254.

[111] Weinstein, N. D. (1978). Individual differences in reactions to noise: A longitudinal study in a college dormitory. *Journal of Applied Psychology, 63,* 458-466.

[112] Bhatia, P., & Muhar, I. (1988). Noise sensitivity and mental efficiency. *Psychologia: An International Journal of Psychology in the Orient, 31,* 163-169.

[113] Weinstein, N. D. (1982). Community noise problems: Evidence against adaptation. *Journal of Environmental Psychology, 2,* 99-108.

[114] Topf, M. (1985). Personal and environmental predictors of patient disturbance due to hospital noise. *Journal of Applied Psychology, 70,* 22-28.

[115] Nivison, M. E., & Endresen, I. M. (1993). An analysis of relationships among environmental noise, annoyance and sensitivity to noise, and the consequences for health and sleep. *Journal of Behavioral Medicine, 16,* 257-276.

[116] Jorgensen, D. O. (1978). Measurement of desire for control of the physical environment. *Psychological Reports, 42,* 603-608.

[117] LeBrasseur, R., Blackford, K., & Whissell, C. (1988). The Leford Test of Tenant Locus of Control: Introducing an effective measure relating locus of control and housing satisfaction. *Environment and Behavior, 20,* 300-319.

[118] Schmidt, F. N., & Gifford, R. (1989). A dispositional approach to hazard perception: Preliminary development of the Environmental Appraisal Inventory. *Journal of Environmental Psychology, 9,* 57-67.

[119] Fridgen, C. (1994). Human disposition toward hazards: Testing the Environmental Appraisal Inventory. *Journal of Environmental Psychology, 14,* 101-111.

[120] Levenson, H. (1973). Perception of environmental modifiability and involvement in antipollution activities. *Journal of Psychology, 84,* 237-239.

[121] Smith-Sebasto, N. J. (1992). Design, development, and validation of an instrument to assess the relationship between locus-of-control of reinforcement and environmentally responsible behavior in university undergraduate students. *Dissertation Abstracts International, 53*(6-A), 17-36.

[122] Eso, S., & Gifford, R. (1994). *Survey of personal influence in common environments.* In preparation, Department of Psychology, University of Victoria.

[123] Fridgen, C. (1994). Human disposition toward hazards: Testing the Environmental Appraisal Inventory. *Journal of Environmental Psychology, 14,* 101-111.

[124] Paciuk, M. T. (1990). The role of personal control of the environment in thermal comfort and satisfaction at the workplace. *Dissertation Abstracts International, 50*(8-A), 22-76.

[125] Craik, K. H. (1976). The personality research paradigm in environmental psychology. In S. Wapner, S. B. Cohen, & B. Kaplan (Eds.), *Experiencing the environment.* New York: Plenum.

Personal Space and Territoriality

The best way to learn the location of invisible boundaries is to keep walking until somebody complains.

—ROBERT SOMMER[1]

Territory...is valued for the way it facilitates making sense, for the opportunity for choice and control it provides, as well as for the many positive associations it comes to have.

—STEPHEN AND RACHEL KAPLAN[2]

A FRIEND INTRODUCED JANE TO AN INTERNATIONAL STUDENT. *He seemed pleasant enough, but for some reason he stood so close to her that she felt overwhelmed and wanted to get away from him. She backed away, but he seemed pushy, and she spent half an hour feeling cornered in a conversation.*

Tom happened to meet Marta, an acquaintance of Jane's, while walking home. She insisted that he come to a postgame celebration. He was not romantically interested in her, but he thought the party might be interesting. As they walked, Marta suddenly took Tom's arm and the two of them were shoulder to shoulder. Tom hoped none of his friends would see him and Marta this way.

Meanwhile, Jane had been thinking of asking for a pay raise. To improve her chances of talking the boss into it, she prepared a mental list of her accomplishments since her last raise, thought about the order in which to present them, and even planned how she would enter the office, where to sit, and how much eye contact to make with the boss.

Precisely at the appointed hour, she knocked on Mrs. Black's door. As she did so, she felt, but then suppressed, the thought that Mrs. Black's office would be very nice to have someday. It had that solid door, that brass nameplate, those leather chairs, and those little conference tables scattered around.

Summoned inside, Jane realized that somehow she had not entered the room with all the panache and presence she had hoped for. Mrs. Black leaned back in her chair. Jane tried to express her reasons for seeking a raise, but somehow the whole idea now seemed rather lifeless. She stammered out her list, confusing her order, and even forgetting some reasons. Finally, although Mrs. Black was pleasant enough, and said she would "think the matter over."

Jane left the office, knowing that her painful recital had not been very convincing. She returned to her own small cubicle, partitioned off in the middle of many other cubicles. She felt comfortable there, at least, with her own pictures and computer, but not at all optimistic about the pay raise.

THE BEST WAY TO EXPLAIN PERSONAL SPACE and territoriality may be to place yourself in these situations faced by Jane and Tom, scenarios in which you are too close to someone, or in "their" space.

Most of the time, when we are comfortable with others, we are not even aware of personal space or territoriality. However, it is always there: just think about giving a hug to the "wrong" person, or entering someone else's room.

This chapter concentrates on one of the most widely studied areas of environmental psychology and one of the least-studied. Over 1,300 studies of personal space have been reported, but far fewer of human territoriality. Everyone possesses and uses personal space every day, and most people have one or more territories, so they are important in our lives. If you have never really thought much about personal space or territoriality before, this chapter may well change the way you think about yourself and others.

WHAT ARE PERSONAL SPACE AND TERRITORIALITY?

Basic Definitions

A SIMPLE DEFINITION OF PERSONAL SPACE was offered by Robert Sommer many years ago: "Personal space refers to an area with invisible boundaries surrounding a person's body into which intruders may not come."[3] This definition can be enlarged by adding that it stretches and shrinks with circumstances and that it operates in conjunction with closely related aspects of social interaction such as angle of orientation (e.g., face-to-face versus side-by-side) and eye contact, and that it is more like a gradient than a clear boundary.[4] Therefore, I define **personal space** as the dynamic spatial component of interpersonal relations. That is, personal space is represented in the changing distance and angle of orientation between individuals as they interact.

The link between personal space and territoriality is that both are space-claiming processes. Personal space is a mobile, "me-centered" territory with no physical aspect other than one's own body. Territories usually are fixed physical spaces, and one's body is not always in the space. Territories are everywhere, once you recognize them. The territory itself usually does not announce itself as a territory, but the *indicators* of territoriality announce it: fences, locks, books spread out on a cafeteria table to save a place, nameplates, no-trespassing signs, gang graffiti. As simple examples, if you look around your classes, you will notice that most of the time, most students sit in the same seats,[5] and if you share meals at home, you will observe that people usually sit in the same seats. Territory extends beyond physical spaces to the world of information and ideas as passwords, copyrights, trademarks, and patents (see Figure 5-1). Despite its pervasiveness, territoriality has not received the amount of study it deserves, partly because it is not as easy to study as some other topics.

An early researcher, Julian Edney, observed that territoriality involves physical space, possession, defense, exclusiveness of use, markers, personalization, and identity.[6] To this list, one could add dominance, control, conflict, security, claim-staking, arousal, and vigilance. In the public mind, territoriality is connected with aggression and violence. However, anti-social behavior actually is a rare manifestation of territoriality, although it receives widespread attention when it occurs. Across all human behavior, territoriality far more often serves two *positive* functions: it reduces conflict and it increases commitment to a setting.[7] Territories are space organizers. Territoriality is not always fair or just, but without it conflict would be much more common; people would be constantly struggling over the ownership and use of every space, object, and idea. Territoriality helps people to fulfil three important needs: for efficacy (to be efficient and competent), for self-identity, and to have a place of one's own.[8]

A simple formal definition of it is not easy to offer, so the following will have to serve as our operating definition:

FIGURE 5-1 Territoriality in the form of steel.

Territoriality is a pattern of behavior and attitudes held by an individual or group related to the perceived, attempted, or actual ownership or control of a definable physical space, object, or idea; it may involve habitual occupation, defense, marking, and personalization of a space, object, or idea. **Marking** means placing an object or substance in a space to indicate one's territorial intentions. Cafeteria diners leave coats or books on a chair or table. Prospectors stake claims. Property owners build fences. Marking serves control needs (that is, it informs others that I "own" this space, such as creating borders or signs that tell others that this space is "mine").[9] **Personalization** means marking in a manner that indicates one's identity. Employees decorate their work spaces with pictures and mementoes. Some car owners purchase vanity license plates with their names or initials on them.

FIGURE 5–2 Observers of birds[11] and animals[12] have long known that certain species maintain characteristic distances between individuals of that species. These distances have biological value; they regulate fundamental processes like food-gathering and mating. Some species at certain times, such as sea lions during breeding, have almost zero personal space; other species, like wolves living in the tundra, have very large ones.

Similarities, Differences, Gradations, and Types

PERSONAL SPACE IS A MOVING TERRITORY; most (not all) territories are fixed. In both cases, entry is by permission, and unauthorized entry is resisted and often is against the law. The borders of territories usually are sharp; those of personal space are more gradual. Both have a communication dimension, but in somewhat different ways. Territories primarily communicate ownership; personal space communicates the nature of the relationship between people.

Edward Hall, a pioneer personal space researcher, observed that interpersonal distance informs both participants and outside observers about the nature of the participants' relationship.[10] For example, you have probably seen couples strolling along, arm in arm. In northern cultures, with some exceptions, the message is that this couple is in a romantic relationship. In Marta's southern culture, as we hope Tom realizes, it often only represents warm friendship.

You probably knew about territories before you read about them here, but did you already know about personal space? Certainly your distancing from others is not random. But were you *aware*, until you read the first part of this chapter, of these behavioral choices you have been making? As an old sage once said, "You don't have to know the laws of physics to shoot a basketball through the hoop." Most of us use personal space every day according to certain rules, yet we have a low level of awareness of these rules and the distancing process. Similarly, we use and honor territories many times each day without much awareness of doing so.

The general tendency to have and defend personal space and territories may be hard-wired in us, but the rules governing their use are acquired. Children gradually learn them; eventually they learn the rules so well that they no longer need to clog their moment-to-moment cognitive processing with them. When these conventions are broken, however, negative consequences follow. First, when someone else is too close or too far away, or enter our territory without warning or permission, we feel uncomfortable. Second, both anecdotal[13] and experimental evidence[14] suggest that when others approach us too closely, we attribute unfavorable traits to them. We conclude that the other person is pushy, rude, cold, or aggressive, whether or not they actually are.

Personal space is divided into gradations and has an objective as well as a subjective dimension to it, and territories are divided into types. Edward Hall described four gradations of personal space, each with a near and far phase (see Figure 5-3).[15] Each provides a different set of sensory information, and each indicates a slightly different relationship between the persons involved.

1. **Intimate distance.** The near phase of intimate distance (0-6"/0-15 cm) is for comforting, protecting, lovemaking, wrestling, and other full-contact activities. People who interact at this distance are on intimate terms, they are behaving within a strict set of rules (e.g., wrestling), or they are expressing strong negative emotions (e.g., an angry player heatedly disputing a referee's decision). The far phase of intimate distance (6-18"/15-45 cm) is used by individuals who are on very close terms. (Note, incidentally, how the English language contains many words that describe the state of human relationships in terms of interpersonal distance, such as *close, in touch,* or *distant*). A typical behavior at this distance is whispering. Generally, the participants in an interaction at this distance are very good friends.

2. **Personal distance.** The near phase (18-30"/45-75 cm) is the zone for those who are familiar with one another and on good terms. Good friends or a happy couple will use this distance to talk. Hall says that if your spouse enters this zone, acquaintances will hardly notice, but if someone else of your spouse's gender comes this close to you, that's "an entirely different story."[16] The far phase of personal distance (2.5-4'/75-120 cm) is used for social interactions between friends and acquaintances. If you observe two classmates who are acquainted but not special friends talking in a hallway, chances are they will be standing in the far phase of personal distance.

3. **Social distance.** Despite the name Hall gave it, this zone is used more for interaction between unacquainted individuals or those transacting business. The near phase (4-7'/1.2-2 m) is the distance someone might select while being introduced to a roommate's mother, or while buying something in a store. The far phase of social distance (7-12'/2-3.5 m) is typical of more formal business transactions. Perhaps Hall should have called it *business distance*.

Here, there is little sense of friendship or even of trying to be friendly. The interaction is best described as the meeting of two organizations' representatives. For example, if the company owned by your roommate's mother is about to buy the store, she and the person's sales boss might interact at this distance.

4. **Public distance.** This zone is used less often by two interacting individuals than by speakers and their audiences. The near phase of public distance (12-25'/3.5-7 m) would be used by a lecturer whose class has grown just large enough that speaking from a seated position no longer feels comfortable. When someone is speaking to a group of 30 or 40, the average distance between speaker and listener is likely to be in this range. The far phase of public distance (over 25'/7 m) is used when ordinary mortals meet important public figures. If you were formally introduced to a head of state, you would probably halt your approach at about this distance. Because it is not easy to hold a normal conversation at this distance, the important public figure must beckon you to come closer if communication between the two of you is to occur.

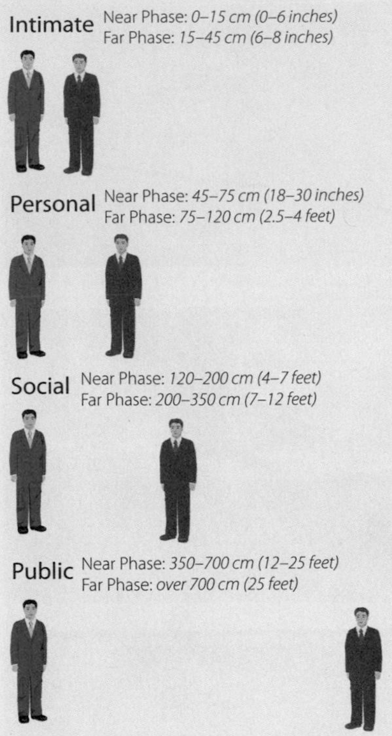

Intimate — Near Phase: 0–15 cm (0–6 inches) / Far Phase: 15–45 cm (6–8 inches)

Personal — Near Phase: 45–75 cm (18–30 inches) / Far Phase: 75–120 cm (2.5–4 feet)

Social — Near Phase: 120–200 cm (4–7 feet) / Far Phase: 200–350 cm (7–12 feet)

Public — Near Phase: 350–700 cm (12–25 feet) / Far Phase: over 700 cm (25 feet)

FIGURE 5–3 Edward Hall first described four major interpersonal distance zones based on the social relation between the two persons.

PERSONAL SPACE HAS ANOTHER, subjective, dimension to it. Notice that all the foregoing descriptions of it refer to objective distances. But when personal space is actually used on a daily basis, we operate on the base of *perceived*, not objective, interpersonal distance. That is, personal space also is a subjective experience. For years, reviews of the personal space literature[17,18] called for research into the cog-

FIGURE 5–4 These are examples of one person's primary, secondary, and public territories.

nitive aspects of personal space. Yet of the hundreds of experiments on personal space, only a few have investigated the experience of personal space. I have suggested that there are two kinds of personal space.[19] **Alpha personal space** is the objective, externally measurable distance and angle between interacting individuals described above. **Beta personal space** is the subjective experience of the distancing process, the individual's *perception* of the distance and angular orientation in a social encounter. One way to investigate beta personal space is to ask individuals at normal interactions to estimate the distance from themselves to the other person.

I found that beta personal space was 24 percent larger than alpha personal space.[20] We seem to believe that we are farther away from the other person than we actually are, or at least say so. At the same time, an **asymmetry effect** in beta personal space seems to exist: while we perceive ourselves to be farther from the other person than we actually are, we generally perceive the other person to be closer to us than he or she actually is.[21] Apparently, we usually think others occupy more of *our* space than we occupy of *their* space. However, the asymmetry seems to operate in reverse (we think we occupy more of *their* space than they do of ours) when few other people are around and we are not particularly self-aware at the moment.[22]

What kinds of territories are there? Some are large, others small, some are nested within others, and some are shared. To understand how territoriality works, it is useful to find a way of classifying territories. Once a good system is discovered, we can study selected territories of a given type and reasonably assume that our findings apply to other territories of the same type. Two main systems with seven distinct types have been proposed.

The Altman system. The key element in Irwin Altman's system is the degree of privacy, affiliation, or accessibility allowed by each type.[23] **Primary territories** are spaces owned by individuals or primary groups, controlled on a relatively permanent basis by them, and central to their daily lives (see Figure 5-4). Examples include one's bedroom or a family's dwelling. The psychological importance of a primary territory to its occupant(s) is always high. **Secondary territories** are less important to us than primary territories, but they do possess moderate significance to their occupants. A person's desk at work, favorite restaurant, locker in the gym, and home playing field are examples. Control of these territories is less essential to the current occupant and is more likely to change, rotate, or be shared with strangers. **Public territories** are areas open to anyone in good standing with the community. Beaches, sidewalks, hotel lobbies, trains, stores, and ski slopes are public territories. Occasionally, because of discrimination or unacceptable behavior, public territories are closed to certain individuals. Bars and taverns, for example, are public territories to anyone of drinking age. However, someone who causes trouble may be banned from the bar. Bouncers are agents of territoriality. In contrast to primary territories, which generally are closed to outsiders, public territories are open to all outsiders who are not specifically excluded.

Objects may not seem like territories, but they do meet some criteria: people mark, personalize, defend, and control their books, coats, bicycles, and computers. A study of drivers found that their relationships with their cars could indeed be matched up with primary, secondary, and public territories as defined above.[24] The notion that cars function as territories is further supported in a study of road rage which found that the number of territory markers on the car (e.g., bumper stickers, decals) and attachment to the vehicle were significant predictors of aggressive driving.[25]

Ideas also may not seem at first to be territories, but in some ways they certainly are. Their creators defend them through patents and copyrights. We have rules against plagiarism. Software authors try to protect ownership of their programs. Our reluctance to consider objects and ideas as territories may stem from our familiarity with the word territoriality as it is used for animals, where it always refers to physical space. Therefore, objects and ideas may be the most human of territories, in the sense that they are based in cognitive processes that are more developed in humans than in other species.[26]

The Lyman and Scott system. This typology proposes two types of territory that are not directly comparable to those in Altman's system.[27] The first of these is **interactional territories**, spaces that are temporarily controlled by a group of interacting individuals. Think of a classroom, a space rented for an event, or a casual game in the park. Little overt marking of these territories may occur, yet entry into them is perceived as interference, rudeness, or "crashing." Second, Lyman and Scott suggest that one's physical self is a **body territory**. This is not the same as personal space, because the boundary is at one's skin rather than at some distance away. Bodies may be entered with permission (as in surgery) or without permission (as in a knife attack), but many people mark and personalize their bodies with makeup, jewelry, tattoos, and clothing, and they certainly defend and try to control access to their bodies.

Types of Infringement

RESEARCH AND EXPERIENCE INDICATE there are several ways that one's personal space or territory may be infringed upon.[28] The most obvious form is **invasion**, in which a person (or group) physically enters the personal space or territory of another without permission, often (in the case of territories) with ownership as the goal. One example might be a parent taking over a child's bedroom for a home office because the child has left for college. The second form of infringement is **violation**, in which the goal is not so much ownership as annoyance or harm. Vandalism, hit-and-run attacks, and burglary fall into this category. The third form of infringement is **contamination**, in which infringers foul someone else's territory by putting something awful in the territory, usually without entering themselves. Examples would be that neighbor who plays loud music, the chemical company that leaves poisonous waste in the ground for later residents to deal with, and a neighbor's pesticide spray drifting into your yard. Even at work, where most people usually try to act in a civil way, infringement over quite a variety of territorial spaces and objects leads to anger and reactions aimed at defending territory.[29] This is especially true in open offices, where boundaries can be vague. Fortunately, some researchers have begun to address the issue by considering physical aspects of offices such as layout and noise, and suggesting conflict management training as a complement to design as a solution to workplace territorial disputes.[30]

Types of Defense

Just as there are a variety of ways to infringe on personal space and territories, there are different ways to defend them. Defenses may be divided into two general types: prevention defenses and reaction defenses.[31,32] Markers such as signs and fences are **prevention defenses** for territories, and perhaps sunglasses, ear buds, or a book held in front of one's face serve to defend one's personal space. Prevention defenses anticipate infringement and act to stop it before it occurs. **Reaction defenses**, in contrast, are responses to an infringement after it actually happens. Examples of reaction defenses range from a "dirty look" to physically striking out at the infringer to legal actions for patent or copyright violations, or simply occupying a place (such as a study carrel or seat in a coffee shop) longer than one otherwise would have.[33] Drivers leaving parking lots found that when another driver was waiting for the spot, drivers took longer to leave than when no one was waiting.[34] (Just what you always thought!) A third type is the **social boundary defense**.[35] Used at the edge of interactional territories, the social boundary defense consists of a ritual engaged in by hosts and visitors (see Figure 5-5). For example, you needed a password to get into the American speakeasies of the 1920s. When Bushmen groups in Africa meet at a border exchange, they exchange certain greetings before they allow outsiders into their

ROBERT SOMMER has pioneered the study of personal space, social design (see Chapter 15), and many other specific behavior settings.

BARBARA BROWN'S work on territoriality and neighborhood life has greatly enhanced our knowledge about how territoriality works in everyday life.

IRWIN ALTMAN'S theory of privacy and related social–environmental processes has been very influential.

FIGURE 5–5 A social boundary type of defense.

territories. The equivalent in the developed world is the customs office at the border. Perhaps the handshake is the social boundary defense for personal space. Social boundary defenses serve to separate unwanted visitors from wanted visitors through social interaction.

IN SUM *Personal space refers to the interpersonal distance and orientation chosen during ongoing social interaction. Territoriality is a pattern of behavior and attitudes held by an individual or group related to the perceived, attempted, or actual ownership or control of a definable physical space, object, or idea. Personal space surrounds each of us all the time, and territories are everywhere, once you start to look. They may originate with our genes, but we learn behavioral conventions in their use as we grow up in each culture. Four gradations of personal space (intimate, personal, social or business, and public) have been identified, and it has both objective and subjective aspects. Seven types of territory (primary, secondary, public, interactional, body, object, and idea) may be distinguished. Personal space and territories may be infringed upon in three general ways: invasion, violation, and contamination. In turn, people utilize preventative, reaction, or social boundary defenses to protect their personal space and territories.*

MEASURING PERSONAL SPACE

THREE GENERAL WAYS TO MEASURE PERSONAL SPACE have been developed, although each has variations, advantages, and disadvantages. Early in the study of personal space, **simulation methods** that involved placing small felt figures on felt boards or making marks on paper were used, but their limitations have caused a great decline in their use. three of these limitations are that research participants (1) are not in real person-to-person interactions when their personal space is being measured and therefore must adjust for scale; (2) must remember distances from previous (actual) encounters; and (3) are quite conscious of the distancing process. To the extent these methods measure the cognitive aspects of personal space, they may be useful measures of beta personal space, but not alpha personal space.

More recently, computer-based methods that use avatars have been developed, and they seem to produce results that mirror studies using live participants.[36] Another approach is to ask people to report their use of space on a questionnaire. The Relational Distance Index measures the reported use of distancing tactics in personal relationships,[37] but it may be subject to some of the same problems as the simulation methods.

Researchers who desire a more realistic measure of alpha personal space have often used the **stop-distance technique**, in which participants usually are studied in a laboratory, but in a real encounter. The participant is asked to stand some distance away and then to walk slowly toward the experimenter and to stop at the point of discomfort. Sometimes the experimenter approaches the participant. The resulting interpersonal distance is taken as a measure of alpha personal space. Occasionally this procedure is repeated for different angles of approach, but most often the two participants face one another during the measurement.

The stop-distance method is very reliable; it tends to yield similar distances each time personal space is measured.[38] What about its validity? Two disadvantages of the simulation methods are overcome in the stop-distance method: the participants themselves take part, rather than felt figures or avatars, so they are not asked to scale down personal space distances, and they need not rely on memory. However, one disadvantage remains: the participant is very aware of the distancing process. Yet whether awareness is a problem is a matter of some debate. Even though measures in which participants are aware of the distancing process correlate poorly with measures in which they are not, the *effects* on both (e.g., gender differences or level of acquaintances) are about the same.[39] However, this may not hold for other variables that affect personal space.[40]

The issue would not matter if stop-distance techniques could be devised that avoid participant awareness. Paul Sacilotto and I did this by simply asking participants who entered a room at a door some distance away (and did not know the study was about personal space) to "come over here and we'll get started."[41] When the participants approached and stopped where they liked, a measurement was made that overcame all three problems with the simulation methods.

I can almost hear you asking, but why not simply study personal space by measuring the unplanned interpersonal distances of individuals in natural settings? This would dispose of all three disadvantages. It would, but there are three other reasons why naturalistic observation is not often used. First, to measure the behavior of people without their prior informed consent is unethical in some circumstances. This can be overcome by asking for consent to use the data afterwards, but two other problems remain.

Another is that measurements made under natural conditions are subject to many uncontrolled variables. For example, if we went to a park and measured personal space between pairs of people there, the pairs probably would include many levels of friendship, topics being discussed, roles, and combinations of personality. Without knowing the status of each person on these variables, explaining why some pairs stood at large interpersonal distances but others stood at small ones would be impossible. One problem with naturalistic measurement of personal space lies in determining the *reasons* for differences in personal space, and that is usually the purpose of the study.

Third, the measurement itself can be tricky. Would you simply estimate the interpersonal distance of each pair from a distance? That would not be very accurate. Would you casually stroll up to them and ask them to freeze so you could stretch a tape between their chests? Even if you are bold enough to do this, your quarries probably would shift their positions by turning to look at you. They may even move back a step or two or run away from this obviously deranged intruder! You could try to photograph the pairs so you could get the distances from the pictures, but there are considerable technical difficulties in translating photographic distances to accurate life-size distances, particularly if the angle of the camera shot is not exactly perpendicular to the conversing couple. These difficulties can and have been overcome, but not often and not easily. For example, in an indoor laboratory, objective distances may be measured with special pressure-sensitive floor mats.[42] That's why stop-distance techniques are used more often than naturalistic methods.

IN SUM *Personal space has been measured using simulation, stop-distance, and naturalistic observation methods. The simulation techniques have flaws, but may be suited to studying beta personal space. The stop-distance technique can, in some variations, overcome these flaws. Naturalistic observation can be technically difficult and often does not allow the investigator to distinguish among different possible reasons for variations in personal space. The researcher must be aware of both the advantages and disadvantages of each method, the theoretical implications of selecting a method, and the pitfalls involved in actually making the measurement.*

MEASURING TERRITORIALITY

TERRITORIALITY, BY ITS VERY NATURE, IS DIFFICULT to study in a laboratory. It often takes time to develop and people need to have a sense of ownership; participants in laboratory studies usually spend an hour or less in the lab. For that reason, the primary methods for studying human territoriality are field experiments, field studies, surveys and interviews, and naturalistic observation. This has an unfortunate consequence: laboratories offer considerable experimental control and without that, conclusions about the causes and effects of territoriality are difficult to draw.

Field *experiments* are attempts to overcome these problems but to also have experimental control and random assignment of participants. Field experiments require unusual creativity and perseverance to design and carry out. A rare example is a study of territoriality and decision making.[43] The purpose of this experiment was to discover whether being in one's own territory gives a person greater influence than a visitor on the outcome of a mutual decision. The researchers also wanted to find out whether dominance (as a personality trait) influenced the process. They asked groups of three students to meet in a room in which one student was resident and the other two were visitors. The group was asked to discuss a budget problem and reach a consensus. Both random assignment and control over the variables were used, so the conclusions could, with some justification, be said to represent causal links (rather than mere associations) between territoriality, trait dominance, and decision making. The random assignment was achieved by selecting on a chance basis which participants participated in their own territory and which were visitors. Control of the trait dominance variable was achieved by assigning one low-, one medium-, and one high-dominance participant to each group of three decision makers. Trait dominance did not affect decision making much. Instead, the final consensus reflected the territory owner's point of view in the debate much more than it reflected the visitors' point of view. The results suggest that if you want decisions to go your way, you should try to get others to discuss the decision at your place. This strategy, it appears, works whether or not you have a dominating personality.

In a typical field *study*, several variables are measured but not controlled by the researcher, and random assignment to the experimental conditions or settings is not used. For example, one field study investigated territoriality on beaches.[44] The researchers observed sunbathers as they marked off territories using towels and umbrellas. The results showed that females claim smaller territories than males, and that mixed-gender groups and larger groups claim less space per person than do same-gender groups and smaller groups. However, because participants were not randomly assigned to the different types of groups, the researchers could not be sure that group size, for example, caused the differences in the size of territories. Some third factor may both cause certain individuals to go to the beach in larger groups and cause these individuals to space themselves rather closely, so that the group as a whole claimed a relatively small space on the beach.

In another field study, the extent to which university students sat in the same seats from day to day was observed.[45] Researchers also use unobtrusive measures, that is, physical indicators of territoriality, such as marking or personalization. In one such study, inner-city Slavic Americans personalized their yards more than their non-Slavic neighbors. The Slavs landscaped their yards more, maintained their houses better, and placed more potted plants in view.[46] One might count books or coats left in cafeterias or coffee shops to "hold my place."

Another way to study territoriality is simply to ask individuals about their behavior and experiences. Self-report methods have the disadvantage that respondents may not be able or willing to report their behavior accurately. However, they have two advantages: the researcher's resources can be stretched to include a much larger number of individuals in the study, and the opinions, beliefs, feelings, and other cognitions of respondents can be studied. A good example is a study of residents of high-rise buildings in Israel.[47] Every member of 45 families, including children over age 5, was asked about their actual territory-relevant behaviors and cognitions. For example, they were asked where in the apartment they chose to engage in specific activities (a behavior question), and who, in their opinion, "owned" various places within the apartment (a cognition question).

IN SUM *Territoriality is nearly always investigated in the field. Researchers occasionally perform true experiments, but more often they examine correlations between territoriality and other behaviors and attitudes, ask for self-reports of territoriality activities, or observe how individuals mark or personalize territories. Because each method has both strengths and weaknesses, researchers should, if possible, employ several methods to answer the research question. If only one method can be used, care must be taken to select the method best suited to the particular research question. For example, if the hypothesis concerns territorial behaviors, naturalistic observation of the behavior is preferable to a questionnaire about the behavior. However, if the question concerns territorial cognitions, a questionnaire or survey is preferable.*

WHAT SIZE IS PERSONAL SPACE? This simple question has been investigated in hundreds of studies since 1959, when the first empirical study of human personal space was published by Robert Sommer. As you might expect, the simple overall conclusion about the size of personal space is this: It depends. What it depends on falls into four broad categories: personal, social, physical, and cultural factors. Bear in mind when reading about these influences that each one assumes "all else is equal," for the sake of reporting them, but in everyday life multiple influences are operating in any given interaction. As always, the findings are average differences, not differences for every person of a given type.

Personal Influences

THE SIZE OF A PERSON'S PERSONAL SPACE is a function, in part, of the characteristics each one of us carries from situation to situation, such as gender, personality, mental health, and age.

Gender. Generally, male-male pairs keep the largest distances,[48-52] followed by female-female pairs and male-female pairs.[53,54] However, results can vary.[55-57] One possible reason is that gender differences in personal space reflect differences in the socialization of males and females rather than biological differences. Depending on their upbringing and other social and cultural influences, men may even interact more closely than women. For example, in a study that focused on gender, race, and age simultaneously, gender influenced personal space only in interaction with race, age, and the other person's gender, not on its own.[58] Girls stay closer to adults when boys and girls play together than when all the children in the play group are girls.[59] Male-female pairs use much more space when the couple are strangers than when they are lovers. Thus, gender is not as powerful a determinant of personal space, on its own, as are some other factors.

Age. Personal space increases with age, at least until early adulthood.[60] Infant personal space is hard to measure because infants have little independent mobility. Developmental psychologists do, however, know that some infants

like to be hugged and others resist contact. Perhaps these young resisters would have larger personal space zones than the huggers if someone could find a way to measure them. By the age of 18 months, however, children already choose different interpersonal distances depending on the person and the situation.[61] By about age 12, children use personal space approximately the way adults do.[62]

Again, other factors play a role, although not to the extent they do with gender. In fact, gender is one such factor. In one study, the personal space of males and females from age 5 to 18 was measured[63] (see Figure 5-6). As usual, older children displayed larger interpersonal distances than younger children. But an age-by-gender interaction was also significant. That is, rather than boys or girls having larger personal space in general, no difference occurs in the size of personal space among younger boys and girls, but older boys chose larger distances than older girls. Culture also can modify the age trend in personal space. For example, children who live in Puerto Rico increase their interpersonal distance at a later age than Puerto Rican children who live in New York.[64]

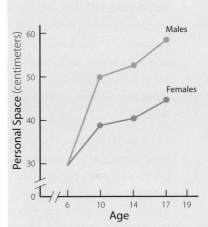

FIGURE 5–6 Personal space increases with age, and males show larger increases than females.

Incidentally, surprisingly little is known about personal space after childhood. As psychologists become more aware of important developmental changes in middle and late adulthood, we realize that personal space may change during these phases of life, too. But so far, no one has investigated this possibility.

Personality. People who are more extraverted, affiliative, or interpersonally warm have smaller personal space zones.[65-67] Those who are field dependent (rely on external cues to make judgments) tend to be warmer and friendly, and they also choose smaller interpersonal distances.[68] I once investigated the whole interpersonal personality domain as it relates to personal space.[69] The strongest correlations involved extraversion and gregariousness (smaller personal space) and coldness and quarrelsomeness (larger personal space). Trait anxiety (as opposed to short-term anxiety) has consistently been linked to larger personal space zones,[70-73] and people who are typically worried about how their views will be received by others also keep larger distances.[74] Type A personalities, persons who are characteristically rushed and competitive, also tend to choose more personal space.[75]

Self-Construal. Do you think of yourself more as a social, interdependent person or more of a personal, independent person? As you might expect, those who think of themselves as social and interdependent (including those who are primed to think that way) choose closer distances than those who think of themselves as personal and independent.[76]

Psychological Disturbance and Violence. Individuals who have some form of emotional problem often have unusual personal space preferences. Because most psychological disturbances involve anxiety and difficulties in communication, interpersonal relationships, and perceptual processes, this is not surprising. The very first empirical study of human personal space examined the interpersonal distances chosen by people with schizophrenia.[77] Compared to hospital employees and non-schizophrenic patients, people with schizophrenia sometimes chose much greater seating distances and sometimes chose much smaller ones.[78] A later study reports that they choose larger distances.[79] Even relatively mild psychological disturbance, for example, in children who had an insecure attachment relationship with their mother and professional caregiver when they were infants, have more permeable personal space, that is, smaller personal space boundaries, and they tolerate greater intrusions into their personal space, compared with children who had two secure attachments in infancy.[80] This pattern seems to hold even in adulthood.[81] However, children who have been physically abused (quite understandably) have larger personal space preferences.[82]

Among prisoners, the interpersonal distance of those with a history of violence is larger than that of nonviolent persons.[83] Those who have clashed with others seem to need to keep a larger "body buffer zone" for security reasons. More recent research indicates that only those violent prisoners who understand nonverbal behavior less and tend toward psychoticism more have larger interpersonal distances,[84] and that when violent persons are allowed to control the distance-choosing process they choose much smaller distances.[85]

One interesting study illustrated the relation between *degree* of disturbance and size of personal space.[86] The personal space of newly admitted patients, who were presumably quite disturbed, was found to be very large. Their personal space was measured every three weeks during their hospital stay. As they improved (by independent judgment), their personal space moved much closer to that of non-patients.

Disabilities. Few studies have examined the interpersonal choices made by people with disabilities. However, one showed that pairs of hearing-impaired children use greater distances than pairs of children with no hearing disability.[87] Another found that children with full-syndrome autism stay closer to adults than children with inactive autism, hyperactivity, or mental retardation.[88]

Social Influences

COLLECTIVELY, THE PERSONAL CHARACTERISTICS just reviewed add up to a generalized personal space tendency that each individual carries from situation to situation. But once individuals enter any social situation, their personal space is influenced by a new set of factors. These social factors may be broadly grouped under the headings of attraction, emotion, cooperation-competition, and status.

Attraction. One of the strongest generalizations in personal space research is that attraction draws us physically closer. In a classic study, drawings of individuals described as good friends were placed closer together than were drawings of strangers.[89] This has been confirmed in naturalistic observations,[90] other cultures,[91] and for children.[92,93]

Among married couples, husbands and wives sit closer than pairs of wives, who sit closer than pairs of husbands, and the greatest distance is between men and women who were not married.[94] Similarity between individuals and pleasantness of manner also operate like attraction. As they increase, personal space decreases.[95-97]

Emotion. Social interaction that includes noticeable emotion affects personal space. Women who see either happiness or sadness in someone's face move relatively close. However, men move closer to happiness than to sadness. Both genders choose a larger distance when they see fear in the other person's face.[98] When two people are engaged in an emotionally intense discussion, others are less likely to walk between them than if no strong emotion is apparent.[99] A few studies have investigated the angry side of interpersonal relations. In one, college men were scolded for being late for the experiment.[100] The experimenter told the participants, none of whom were actually late, "It said on the sign-up sheet to be on time. What's the matter, can't you read?" After a few similar insults, personal space was measured with the stop-distance technique. Not surprisingly, participants who were insulted chose larger personal space zones than did participants who were not insulted. The larger zone was specific to the experimenter who did the insulting; participants did not show larger zones when another person measured their personal space. Criticism and insults lead to dislike, which leads to increased distance.[101]

People choose closer distances when they feel secure and larger distances when they feel unsafe or fearful. For example, when told that a stranger was a non-offender, a non-violent offender, or a violent offender, people chose increasingly larger distances.[102] In another study, participants chose closer distances to an older, well-groomed female than to a scruffy, younger male.[103] Presumably the female inspired less fear than the male, although other factors may have come into play in that study.

Unfortunately, being "different" often leads to greater distancing by others. Participants choose greater distances when the other person is a mental patient, an amputee,[104] a drug user, disabled (wheelchair-bound),[105] a user of a white cane,[106] gay, or fat.[107] The larger distances may, in part, be based on fear of the unfamiliar and in part be based on the difference between the person and society's desirable stereotypes. Stigmatized persons are sensitive to the increase in distance. They realize that although other persons may still be helpful, such as in giving directions when asked,[108] the other's choice of greater interpersonal distance is a telltale sign of their true, unfavorable attitude.

Cooperation-Competition. A third quality of the social situation concerns the competitive or cooperative nature of the interaction. As you might expect, individuals in simulation studies said they would select closer seats when they were cooperating.[109] Moreover, angle of orientation is important. In competitive situations, participants said they would choose more direct orientations (face-to-face), but in more cooperative situations they would choose less direct orientations (side-by-side).

In naturalistic settings, the customs and physical layouts of particular places will alter these tendencies[110] (see

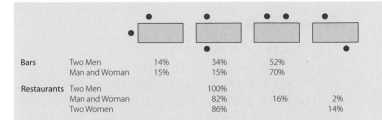

Bars	Two Men	14%	34%	52%
	Man and Woman	15%	15%	70%
Restaurants	Two Men		100%	
	Man and Woman		82%	16%	2%
	Two Women		86%		14%

FIGURE 5–7 These seating choices were observed in three bars and a restaurant. Both the type of setting (bar versus restaurant) and the genders of the pair (MM, FF, MF) affect seating choices.

Figure 5-7). For example, if you went to a fancy, dimly lit restaurant with your dearly beloved—presumably a situation that is more cooperative than competitive—you would probably select seats facing one another. Two men sitting in a singles bar waiting for the right woman to appear—presumably a more competitive than cooperative enterprise—are more likely to sit side by side against a wall. Attorneys who are engaged in cross-examination (an adversarial situation) choose closer distances from the witness than attorneys engaged in direct examination (a cooperative situation with their own witnesses).[111]

The competitive or cooperative quality of a social situation may even affect personal space in *subsequent* situations. In one study, participants played a game with a confederate of the experimenter.[112] The confederates were instructed to use either a very cooperative or very competitive strategy in the game. The interpersonal distance of the participants was observed in another room during a second phase of the experiment. Those who had played with a cooperative confederate selected smaller distances than those who had played with a competitive confederate.

Status. A fourth quality of a social situation pertains to the status, power, or dominance of participants. Generally, others we perceive to be of higher *or* lower status are granted (or banished) to a greater distance. For example, when a high-status person stood near a campus water fountain, fewer passers-by used the fountain than when no one stood near it.[113] Another study found that students sat closer to fellow students and farther from both higher-status others (professors) and lower-status others (a student said to be failing).[114] Thus, personal space is related more to *differences* in status than to the amount of status;[115] the greater the difference in status, the greater the interpersonal distance.[116]

Physical Influences

PERSONAL SPACE IS ALSO INFLUENCED by the physical setting of the interaction. Close distances are more uncomfortable when lighting is dimmer.[117] Smaller distances seem to be preferred in wide or narrow rooms.[118] Individuals use more space in corners of rooms than in the center.[119] Participants who were told to pretend they were theater directors placed actresses farther apart in office waiting rooms than in lobbies or on street corners.[120] Males seem to need more space when the ceiling is lower.[121] People choose larger distances indoors than outdoors.[122] The general conclusion appears to be that we prefer more space between us when the overall supply of physical space is low. However, this may depend on one's purpose. Among bank machine users in Turkey, smaller interpersonal distances were chosen by people waiting in line when density was high, rather than low.[123] Under some circumstances, people use more space outdoors than indoors: Children spread out when they go outside to play compared to their interpersonal distances while playing indoors.[124]

Another physical setting factor is the number of other people around and what they are doing. Individuals in a lab who had been isolated for 90 to 150 minutes selected larger distances than those who were isolated for shorter periods, and larger distances if they thought others would be watching them.[125] Is this true in everyday life? If so, office workers who toil in relative isolation should need more space than those who work with others more. Paul Sacilotto and I compared the personal space of women who spent their working day entering data with that of women in the same building whose jobs offered much more social interaction.[126] The isolates did prefer significantly *more* personal space. Apparently, working in isolation either attracts individuals who already prefer more personal space or, perhaps isolated workers adapt to the isolation and feel less comfortable with other people.

One unusual study examined the effect of weightlessness on interpersonal distance, in an effort to help understand social interaction in space.[127] Weightlessness produces some very odd person-to-person orientations, such as floating prone positions, or head-to-toe arrangements. Generally, the largest interpersonal distances are chosen for the most unusual orientations.

Cultural, Ethnic, Religious, and Legal Variations

NEARLY ALL THE RESEARCH DISCUSSED SO FAR was performed in North America. Yet Edward Hall's original point was that space utilization varies across cultures: Based on his own observations of Arabs, French, South Americans, Japanese, and English, Hall believed that his four zones retained their order but not their size. Let Hall tell his own story:

"I had the good fortune to be visited by a very distinguished and learned man who had been for many years a top-ranking diplomat representing a foreign country...Dr. X was interested in some of the work several of us were doing at the time and asked permission to attend one of my lectures. He came to the front of the class at the end of the lecture to talk over a number of points made in the preceding hour. While talking he became quite involved in the implications of the lecture as well as what he was saying. We started out facing each other and as he talked I became dimly aware that he was standing a little too close and that I was beginning to back up. Fortunately I was able to suppress my first impulse and remain stationary because there was nothing to communicate aggression in his behavior except the conversational distance... Someone who had been so successful in the old school of diplomacy could not possibly let himself communicate something offensive to the other person except outside of his highly trained awareness. By experimenting I was able to observe that as I moved away slightly, there was an associated pattern of interaction. He had more trouble expressing himself. If I shifted to where I felt comfortable (about 21"/53 cm), he looked somewhat puzzled and hurt, almost as though he were saying: "Why is he acting that way? Here I am doing everything I can to talk to him in a friendly manner and he suddenly withdraws. Have I done anything wrong?"[128]

An interaction with a less-sensitive observer than Hall (who eventually rooted himself at the close distance to facilitate the discussion) could have had undesirable repercussions. Remember, people begin to attribute negative characteristics to those who interact with them at inappropriate distances. This can, and indeed *has*, contributed to negative cultural stereotypes.

An early experiment examined cultural differences in some detail.[129] Groups of four male students came to the laboratory and were told they would be observed, but were given no other instructions. Half the groups were composed of Arabs, half of Americans. The average interpersonal distance chosen by Arabs was about the length of an extended arm, but the average interpersonal distance of the Americans was noticeably further. The Arabs touched one another much more often, and their orientation was much more direct. Generally, the Arabs were much more "immediate"[130] than the Americans.

Such findings have led to some overly simplistic generalizations of stereotypes. For example, one researcher asserted that cultures may be described as either *contact* or *non-contact*.[131] Yet two studies[132,133] found that students from alleged "contact cultures" (Latin America, Spain, and Morocco) sit farther apart from one another than do students from a "non-contact culture" (American). Furthermore, not all Latin Americans use the same amount of space.[134] Costa Ricans, for example, choose smaller interpersonal distances than do Panamanians or Colombians. Differences exist among Europeans, too: Dutch pairs use more space than French pairs, who use more space than English pairs.[135] A four-culture study elaborated on this: the largest space was used by Anglo-Saxons (defined as US, UK, and Anglo-Canadians), followed by Asians, Caucasians (defined as Europeans and French-Canadians), and Latinos, who used the least space.[136] Inconsistent subcultural differences have been reported, too. Several studies have shown that African-Americans use more space than whites, but others have shown the reverse or no differences. Like some other black-white differences, the reason may be socioeconomic rather than cultural.[137] Another study supports this conclusion; it showed that black-white differences in personal space decreased as amount of school experience increased.[138]

Despite these cautions about over-generalization, personal space does vary with culture, although not in simple ways. For example, Arab and American males have similar personal space (another contradiction of earlier results!); but Arab and American females do not.[139] Arab females keep larger distances from their female friends too; they place them about as far away as they place male strangers. American students feel more comfortable when a brother and sister sit closer together and two brothers sit farther apart, but Saudi students feel more comfortable the other way around.[140] In general, Japanese use more distance in conversations than Americans, who use more than Venezuelans. However, when Japanese and Venezuelans speak English instead of their native tongue, their conversational distance moves toward that of the Americans.[141] Language, an important part of culture, can modify one's

cultural tendencies to use more or less interpersonal distance (see Figure 5-8). Another important part of culture is religion, and even that is related to personal space choices. In Nigeria, personal space between members of different religions is larger than that between members of the same religion.[142] Pairs of Muslims use smaller interpersonal distances than pairs of Christians.

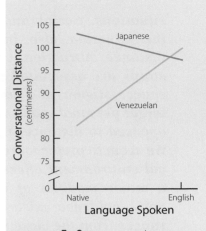

FIGURE 5–8 Interpersonal distancing is affected by the language spoken by conversation partners.

Edward Hall's original goal was to find some reasons for antagonism between cultures; he suggested that the differential use of space was one key factor. A researcher tested this idea by teaching English students how to act more like Arabs in their nonverbal behavior.[143] Arabs who interacted with the trained students liked them more than students who had not received training. Consider the implications for diplomats and for ordinary tourists!

Finally, personal space sometimes is influenced by legal means. For example, spouses sometimes are ordered by courts to keep a certain distance from their partners after they have harassed or abused them. In Boulder, Colorado, the city council passed an ordinance that required pro-life demonstrators to keep a certain fixed distance from women entering an abortion clinic.[144] Pro-life groups challenged this legal enforcement of personal space in court, but based partly on the testimony of Edward Hall and others, the court upheld the ordinance.

IN SUM Personal space may be predicted in part from knowing an individual's characteristics. Males typically use larger distances than females. Young adults typically use more personal space than children. Interpersonally warm and non-anxious individuals choose less personal space than others. Psychological disturbance often leads to more variable or inappropriate personal space. Persons with a history of violence often choose larger interpersonal distances. However, combinations of factors may alter these trends in everyday situations. Social and physical features of the situation also influence interpersonal distance. Attraction, cooperation, and equal status are associated with smaller personal space; stigma and unequal status lead to larger personal space. Angle of orientation, as opposed to distance, is less well understood. We seem to prefer more space when the physical environment offers less room. Culture is a major modifier of interpersonal distance. Some evidence exists for a continuum that ranges from the closeness of Arabs and Latin Americans to the distance of English and Germans. But differences within these groups, occasional results that do not fit this pattern, and other factors such as the language spoken during a particular interaction all may affect personal space. All these factors combine in everyday settings to produce interpersonal distances that are different from what would be expected from consideration of each influence by itself.

INFLUENCES ON TERRITORIALITY

WHO IS TERRITORIAL? Under which conditions does territoriality emerge out of the complexities of human behavior as a distinct pattern? Territoriality is a function of personal, social, physical, and cultural factors.

Personal Influences

Age. Early territoriality has not been studied much, although some sense of it must exist. I recall a dispute with my friend as a 7-year-old over whose Dad owned the sidewalk in front of our house. However, by the time most people are in their mid-teens, they begin to want some territory of their own. Thus, they begin to claim territories in ways outside the conventional legal system, with graffiti,

tagging, and the presence of groups.[145] This leads to occasional conflict when teens occupy a space that older people view as not owned by the teens, such as the area in front of convenience stores. Some store managers have played classical music in front of the store to drive the teens away.

Gender. Territoriality varies with several personal characteristics, but perhaps the most consistent finding is that males claim larger territories than females. This was true in the beach study discussed earlier[146] and in a study of territoriality in dormitories.[147] In the dormitory study, residents were asked to draw on a map of their double-occupancy room which areas the participants considered their own, which parts belonged to their roommate, and which were shared territories. Males drew larger "own" territories than females. Men still hold high-status occupations more often than women, and thereby claim larger spaces at work more often. This suggests that men are more territorial even before they acquire higher status—that is, when both men and women are still in the student phase of their lives.

What of territories in the home? Is a man's home his castle, or does the woman make up for her lack of territory in a work setting by claiming more space at home? A study of Israeli families provides some intriguing answers.[148] First, both parents agreed that the kitchen belongs to the woman. In apparent contradiction, however, over 30 percent of the fathers said the entire home was theirs. On the other hand, more men (48 percent) than women (27 percent) said they had no place of their own at home. Generally, then, women were quite consistent in believing that the home as a whole was a shared territory, but that their own territory was the kitchen. Men delivered a more confused image, more often saying the entire home was theirs, yet granting the kitchen to their wife and also frequently reporting that they actually had no territory at home. Depending on the beliefs in any given home, such a mix of territoriality beliefs could lead to considerable disagreement about who is allowed to do what in which areas of the home.

Other influences. What about such things, as individual differences in personality, or one's background? Territoriality at work seems to vary with employees' need for control.[149] Those who least accepted taking directions from others who were not their supervisors and those who were bothered most by personal space invasions the most also were those who most feared a potential invasion of their workspace. In the investigation of territoriality in shared dormitory rooms described earlier, more intelligent residents of both genders marked off larger areas for themselves, residents of both genders who came from larger homes marked off more space for themselves, and males who were more apprehensive marked off larger territories.[150] Females who were more self-assured but less dominant marked off larger territories. These results suggest that personal history and certain individual differences play an intertwined role in territoriality.

Social Influences

Territorial functioning has been linked to at least five social factors: neighborhood social climate, social class, competition for resources, legal ownership, and task.

Social Climate. The social climate of a neighborhood appears to influence territoriality. In Baltimore districts, congenial social climates were associated with improved territorial functioning.[151] In more congenial neighborhoods, residents were better able to distinguish neighbors from intruders, experienced fewer problems of territorial control, and felt more responsibility for neighborhood space.

Social Class. Territoriality varies with the socioeconomic level of a neighborhood and its residents. At the lowest level are the homeless, who try to create primary territories out of space that is viewed as public territory by most people, such as doorways, lobbies, stations, and parks. Next are young adults, who may officially have some space in their parents' residence but cannot engage in some activities they value at home. They often use cars as primary territories for social interaction, disapproved activities, and sometimes as a means of expressing anger and frustration.[152] In lower-class neighborhoods, a person's house serves a primary territory, but ownership and control often ends at the front door. Just beyond that door unwanted activities may occur, but the resident often feels control over the space outside is impossible and ceases attempts to control it.[153] In middle-class neighborhoods, a sense of territory more often extends to the yard outside and, to some extent, up and down the neighborhood street. In upper-class neighborhoods, territorial functioning sometimes extends to the whole neighborhood. I once took my dog for a walk in a California suburb and was actively watched by residents and even asked as I walked down the street what I was doing there. Although I had no evil intentions, I soon left, and I left feeling as if I were guilty of plotting a burglary. The

FIGURE 5–9 A residential show of territoriality.

most territorial neighborhoods are wealthy enclaves that are literally walled in and have 24-hour security guards (see Figure 5-9). One such gated community in California has over 600 houses.[154]

Competition for Resources. A third social factor is competition for resources. You might expect more territorial behavior when individuals must struggle with others for resources. Everyday experience suggests that when cafeteria chairs, space in the library, or any other resource is in short supply, individuals will begin to mark, personalize, claim, and defend territories to preserve their share of the resource. In contrast, the **cost-benefit theory** of animal territoriality predicts that territoriality is greatest when resources are abundant, because that is when the benefits of territoriality are worth the effort of defending those resources.[155] When resources are scattered and scarce, this theory says, territories must be larger to provide enough food, and the effort of defending such a large space outweighs the meager living the animal can obtain from it. Thus, animals living where resources are difficult to find abandon territoriality in favor of a catch-as-catch-can approach.

Does cost-benefit theory apply to humans? Elizabeth Cashdan's studies of Bushmen help to explain this.[156] In her view, humans control their territories through social boundary defense mechanisms (as noted earlier) in which owner-groups focus on reciprocal access to territories by members of competing owner-groups. The boundary itself is not so important; instead, visitors to a territory must go through various permission rituals to enter an owner's territory. Once they "pay their dues," they are welcome to share in the resources of the territory. Cashdan found that the Bushmen, contrary to cost-benefit theory, are more territorial when resources are scarce than when they are plentiful. That is, Bushmen more often deny outsiders access to the resources they control when resources are limited. If this holds for other human cultures, too, it would confirm that territoriality operates differently in humans and animals.

Legal Ownership. Both renters and homeowners control residential territory, but legal ownership appears to increase the homeowner's territorial behavior.[157] Specifically, homeowners engage in more personalization than renters, although this is not surprising, given the greater commitment of resources made by homeowners. Not all homeowners are equally territorial, but those who are more so make changes to the exteriors of their houses that even naive observers can detect.[158]

Task. One more social situational factor may affect territoriality. When we are in a public territory but engaged in a specific task, we may defend that territory more than if we are not doing anything particular. A study of callers at public telephones (back when these existed!) found that people continued their calls longer when someone was waiting for the phone than when no one was waiting for it[159]—again, just what you always suspected!

Physical Influences

HOW MIGHT THE PHYSICAL SETTING influence someone to be more or less territorial? Most evidence bearing on this question has emerged from the observations and ideas of Jane Jacobs[160] and Oscar Newman[161] that led to **defensible space theory,** which is very similar to **CPTED** (crime prevention through environmental design). The theory deals with residential crime and fear of crime, two phenomena related to territorial invasion. It proposes that certain design features, such as real or symbolic barriers to separate public territory from private territory and opportunities for territory owners to observe suspicious activity in their spaces (surveillance), will increase residents' sense of security and decrease crime in the territory.

Quite a number of field studies have tested defensible space theory, and most provide support for it.[162-164] For example, one would suspect more crime in areas that offer fewer opportunities for surveillance and do not appear be controlled by anyone. A study of the locations of ~~ped-down cars supported those ideas.[165] University ~~ce halls with defensible space features (e.g., ~~as that residents could control and with more

surveillability) suffer less crime than halls on the same campus without such features.[166] A survey of 16 well-conducted studies in which multiple design changes were made in accordance with defensible space theory found reductions in robberies of 30 to 84 percent.[167] Despite these reductions in objective levels of crime, residents' fear of crime is *not* always reduced.[168]

Convenience Stores and Banks. Convenience stores are frequent robbery targets. Those with smaller parking lots and those that do not sell gas, both of which decrease the surveillability of the store's interior, are robbed more, as are stores in more socially disorganized neighborhoods.[169] Several design features are related to increased chances of a holdup.[170] Among these, more robberies occur when the bank has a smaller lobby, a compact, square lobby (as opposed to a wide, rectangular lobby), and larger distances between its teller stations. These features may also be influential because they affect surveillability in the bank lobby. But a key question, of course, is whether criminals themselves respect properties with defensible space features more than those without these features. Here, the theory may require some adjustments. These adjustments concern the underlying reasons for the effectiveness of defensible space features. The features are architectural, and we learned much earlier that it is simplistic to believe that the physical environment determines behavior in a direct way. People often interpret the same environment differently, and some difficulties with defensible space theory occur because criminals do not interpret defensible space features as the theory predicts.

Residences. Julia Macdonald and I examined this question by using the Brunswik lens model. Convicted burglars examined photos of 50 single-family dwellings and rated each one's likelihood of being burglarized.[171] The defensible space features of the houses were then assessed. As the theory predicts, easily surveillable houses were judged to be unlikely burglary targets. However, actual barriers (e.g., fences and visible locks) had no effect on the vulnerability of the houses; the theory predicts that they should. Symbolic barriers, such as extra decorations or fancy gardens, are supposed to communicate to criminals that the residents are especially concerned about their property and are therefore more likely to defend it; symbolic barriers should make burglars shy away. However, the burglars saw houses with symbolic barriers as more vulnerable to burglary (see Figure 5-10).

Why? Interviews after the study revealed that burglars viewed actual barriers as challenges that they could overcome; most fences and locks were not seen as serious barriers to them. The symbolic barriers were interpreted not as signs that the residents were especially vigilant, but as signs that the house probably contained more than the usual amount of valuables: if the residents have the time and money to decorate their house and garden, the burglars reasoned, the residents probably also have a house full of desirable goods. A study of apartment building burglaries confirmed that accessibility (actual barriers) made little difference, but that surveillability reduced burglary.[172] Follow-up studies by my students and me showed that residents and police use different house features to infer that a house is vulnerable to burglary than the burglars themselves do.[173,174] These studies imply that residents and police need to understand the burglar's perspective before they can reduce burglary through residential design.

Interestingly, burglars cannot accurately pick out houses that have already been burglarized from those that have not, but they do use social and physical cues in their guesses.[175] As in our study, they do not see locks and bars as serious impediments, but they worry more about neighbors seeing them and about the residents' territorial concern.

Streets and Disorder. Defensible space theory asserts that both the resident and the criminal are affected by defensible space features. Certain streets in St. Louis have defensible space features, including gateway-like entrances, alterations that restrict traffic flow, and signs that discourage traffic.[176] Residents who live on such streets are more often seen outside their homes, walking and working in their yards. Such behaviors may not be overtly territorial; residents may not think of themselves as guarding the neighborhood, yet they seem to have the effect of discouraging antisocial activity. When streets are "intelligible," that is, understandable and not confusing, more people use them, and this discourages crime.[177] Presumably, intruders are discouraged by this naturally occurring surveillance. Different street forms may facilitate behaviors that are more positive than merely driving burglars away. In comparison to through streets, culs-de-sac seem to promote greater neighborhood attachment among residents.[178] Closer neighborhood ties were reflected in greater concentrations of holiday decorations on culs-de-sac.

Crime in urban neighborhoods is predictable from selected physical cues, including signs of disorder. In a

FIGURE 5–10 Based on the text, which house is most likely to be burglarized? Why?

study of a 48-block area that contains over 500 residences, these physical cues could predict crime better than the estimations of residents who lived in the neighborhood.[179] Interestingly, a study in Australia found that although defensible space features did seem to reduce crime, they did not reduce residents' *fear* of crime.[180]

Cultural Influences

ARE SOME CULTURAL AND ETHNIC GROUPS MORE TERRITORIAL THAN OTHERS? Do different cultures express their territoriality differently? The first question has not yet been clearly answered. A reasonable speculation would be that all human cultures are equally territorial, at least after differences in living conditions are taken into account. A related proposition would be that territoriality is merely expressed differently in different cultures. One investigation of territoriality on French and German beaches[181] was closely patterned on an earlier U.S. study,[182] so that the beach territoriality of Germans, French, and Americans could be compared. The three cultures were similar in *some* respects. For example, in all three cultures larger groups claim smaller per-person spaces, groups composed of males and females claim smaller per-person spaces, and females claim less space than males. Yet in other respects, the cultures differ. The French seem less territorial. They had some difficulty with the very concept of territoriality, often saying that "the beach is for everyone." The Germans engaged in much more marking. They frequently erected sandcastle barriers, signs declaring that "their" area of the beach was "reserved" between two particular dates, and signs indicating that certain areas were reserved for certain groups (families with children here, nudists there, etc.). Finally, the *size* of territories was quite different across the three cultures, although their *shapes* were quite similar. The Germans more often claimed very large territories, but in all three cultures, individuals marked out more elliptical territories and groups marked out more circular territories.

A comparison of U.S. and Turkish college students who shared double-occupancy residence hall rooms reported similar use of space.[183] In both cultures, the men shared less and personalized their space less than women. In both cultures, students who knew their roommates tended to share their belongings and other parts of the room more than students who did not know their roommates previously. This suggests that gender and acquaintance are stronger influences than culture.

How Greek and American groups respond to litter demonstrates again how territoriality is similar yet different across cultures.[184] The experimenters deposited a bag of litter in one of three places: in the front yard, on the sidewalk in front of the house, or on the street curb in front of the house. Bags of litter in the front yards were removed equally quickly in both cultures, but the Americans removed litter placed on the sidewalk or curb faster than Greeks did. Are Americans therefore more territorial than Greeks? The researchers say no; the difference lies in the way the two cultures think of territory around their homes. Americans think of the sidewalk and curb as semi-private so they clean up the litter in "their" territory faster than Greeks, who, the authors suggest, think of the sidewalk and curb as public territory; therefore litter on it is of less concern to them.

Finally, one study reports racial differences in territoriality at drinking fountains.[185] Both blacks and whites were reluctant to intrude on drinkers of the other race, but whites were more reluctant than blacks to intrude. Members of both races tended to drink longer when they were intruded upon than when they were not intruded upon, as if to assert control over their drinking territory. The study of home personalization comparing Slavic-Americans to their non-Slavic neighbors,[186] which found certain differences (discussed earlier), found *no* differences in other comparisons. For example, Slavic and non-Slavic neighbors personalized their front door with their initials at the same rate. Thus, territoriality varies across cultures in some ways but is similar in other ways.

Territoriality is often quite evident in a culture's youth gangs, who must face other gangs on what is nominally public territory. A study that compared British and American gangs found the American gangs to be much more territorial.[187] Does this mean that U.S. youths are more territorial than British youths? Once again, not necessarily. Youths in Britain and in the United States have quite different living conditions. The British gang tends to be a working-class reaction to middle-class values. Because working- and middle-class Britons do not live in the same areas, the gangs need not establish competing territories in their own neighborhoods. They are not fighting one another so much as they are fighting the middle class. American gangs, however, tend to be composed of different racial and ethnic groups who *do* share the same general neighborhood. Territories are carved out and defended because the gangs *are* competing against one another.

IN SUM *Personal, social, physical, and cultural factors can lead to differences in territoriality. Males appear, in general, to manifest more territoriality than females. Territoriality appears to vary with five social factors: ownership, positive social climate, competition for resources, social class, and task. As for physical setting sources of territoriality, defensible space theory argues that physical arrangements increase territoriality feelings and behavior and that this increase leads to a decline in territorial invasions. The*

physical arrangements may be at the block or neighborhood level (altering traffic flow) or at the house level (fences and plantings). Research generally favors the theory, but some defensible space features work in the opposite-from-expected direction. Cultures differ in their expression of territoriality, although the question of whether some cultures are more territorial than others has not been clearly answered.

IN THIS SECTION WE MOVE FROM what causes smaller or larger personal space to what happens after individuals deliberately or innocently choose inappropriate interpersonal distances. The notion of *appropriate* distance is central to personal space. In each situation, only a small range of distances is acceptable. On the too-close side, inappropriate distance will be perceived as invasion of personal space; on the too-far side, it will be perceived as a aloofness or coldness.

Flight and Affect

IF YOU HAVE EVER HAD YOUR PERSONAL SPACE INVADED, you probably felt at least a short burst of emotion.[188] Even when the invasion is excusable, as for example in a crowded elevator, some negative emotion usually surfaces. We might then hypothesize that appropriate distance in a given situation is associated with positive or neutral affect, but too-close and too-far distances lead to negative affect.

Surprisingly few studies have directly tested this idea. However, if avoidance behaviors such as leaving the scene are the result of negative emotions, then there is abundant evidence in favor of this simple hypothesis. The classic evidence comes again from the work of Robert Sommer.[189] He began by simply sitting down quite close (6"/20 cm) to other men who were sitting alone. The men happened to be patients at the mental hospital where Sommer worked,

but as we shall see, the results are similar for other groups of people. After 1 minute, 30 percent of Sommer's participants had moved from their place. After 10 minutes, 55 percent had moved away. Each man whose space was invaded was matched with another seated man whose space was not invaded. After 1 and 10 minutes, 0 percent and 25 percent, respectively, of these controls had moved.

We might infer then, that when someone sits down within your personal space, you are likely to find a reason to leave sooner than you would have otherwise. Later, one of Sommer's female students invaded the personal space of women studying alone in a university library. The closer she sat, the faster they left. Incidentally, less than 2 percent of all the individuals in these studies responded verbally by asking the invader to move or leave. Next, the status of the invader was examined.[190] When the invader was dressed as a faculty member, students fled more quickly than when the invader was dressed as a student. In a shopping mall, women left their seats early when a low-status person sat close to them, but men did not.[191]

A person's gender-role orientation also plays a role. Men with traditional masculine orientations and women with androgynous (balanced masculine-feminine) orientations dislike frontal invasion of their space more than androgynous men and traditional feminine women.[192] Other studies indicate that when friends come very close, positive rather than negative feelings often result,[193] but when the invader is a stranger, particularly a male stranger, negative feelings are aroused.[194]

Attraction

INTUITIVELY, WE MIGHT HYPOTHESIZE that appropriate use of space leads to attraction—or at least does not harm personal relations—whereas inappropriate use of space leads to dislike. Research does support this conclusion, but a problematic word in this simple statement is *appropriate*. The very same distance may be appropriate for one person but not for another. For example, men tolerate invasions by women more than women tolerate invasions by men.[195] In another study, a researcher went to the campus library and looked for a student sitting alone. The researcher then selected a seat next to, one seat away from, or directly across from the student, pretended to read for a short while and then left. Then, a confederate immediately came upon the scene and asked a few questions about the participant's opinion of the researcher. Both male and female students

FIGURE 5–11 Male–female seating reflects mutual attraction.

liked the female researcher who sat very close to them more than they liked the male researcher who sat very close to them.[196] Female students expressed greater attraction for confederates who sat *across* from them, but male students preferred confederates who sat *next* to them. In a study of nurses and patients, male patients liked being touched by female nurses more than female patients did.[197] Ironically, the *nurses* believed that women were more receptive to their touch. Also, the nurses themselves were more comfortable touching their female patients. Thus, appropriateness of distance partly depends on the gender of the person who invades your personal space.

Where do men and women sit in everyday settings? In an observational study, 82 percent of male-female pairs sat across from one another in restaurants, but in bars 70 percent of male-female pairs sat next to one another.[198] This may be influenced both by different seating arrangements in bars and restaurants and the preferences of couples. Either way, it seems that earlier in the evening, at a restaurant, couples usually choose to sit in a pattern which, based on the library study above, facilitates *her* attraction. However, later in the evening at the bar, they choose to sit in a pattern that facilitates *his* attraction (see Figure 5-11).

Neutral or negative feelings in response to personal space invasions also depend on the invader's apparent motives. One important distinction is between intentional invasions and invasions people are forced into, such as in a crowded elevator: Brian O'Connor and I compared the reactions when participants were forced close to another person for a discussion versus when the other person could have stayed further away but moved closer to the participant (12"/30 cm). When the invasion is experienced as intentional, participants evaluated the invader

negatively, but when the invasion was experienced as unavoidable, they did not.[199]

One consequence of attraction is the formation of shared or group personal space. Pairs or larger groups walking along a hallway, for example, seem to form a cohesive whole that becomes an invasion-resistant group space.[200-202]

Arousal

INAPPROPRIATELY CLOSE INTERPERSONAL DISTANCE IS OFTEN VIEWED AS AN INVASION. We feel uncomfortable, and on the physiological level, arousal occurs. This arousal was demonstrated in an unusual and widely discussed study.[203] The researchers hypothesized that arousal caused by spatial invasion would manifest itself in altered patterns of urination. In a lavatory, a hidden camera measured how long it took men to begin urinating and how long they urinated when they were alone, when another man stood one urinal away, and when another man stood at the adjacent urinal. As predicted, urination took longer to begin and lasted less time when someone stood closer. Arousal caused by proximity seems to have literally caused the participants to tense up.

Social Influence

CAN YOU INFLUENCE SOMEONE MERELY BY ADJUSTING YOUR INTERPERSONAL DISTANCE? Research participants were shown films of discussions. Actors who used smaller interpersonal distances and less-direct orientations in the film (more side-by-side than face-to-face) were judged by the film observers to be more persuasive.[204] Notice, however, that this study did not show that individuals who stand close are actually more persuasive, merely that outside observers *perceived* that they were more persuasive. Another study assessed the actual change in listeners' attitudes when a speaker voiced an opinion at close, medium, and far distances.[205] The far speaker had the most influence, contrary to the previous study's conclusion. Possibly, far speakers are more persuasive because listeners are less guarded when the persuader is beyond normal interpersonal distance for persuasion. The two studies illustrate, once again, that perceptions do not always match behavior.

Attribution and Impression Formation

CONSIDER THE FOLLOWING FILM SCENE. You see a man sitting at his desk in an office, sorting through papers. Another man knocks at the door and enters. In one version of the film, the second man begins to speak to the first man from just inside the door. In the second version, he walks over to the desk, produces some papers, and then begins to speak. Observers of this film judge the visiting man to be a subordinate if he stays just inside the door, but more equal in status to the other man if he walks over to the desk.[206] In a later study, participants engaged in a discussion with someone who happened to be a confederate.[207] The confederate sat at four different distances but gave the same answers in response to the participant's questions. When asked to judge the personality of the confederate, participants evaluated the confederate more negatively at larger distances. When a confederate in another study selected a larger-than-normal distance, participants evaluated the confederate as more rejecting and aggressive.[208] A study of police in the Netherlands reports that when suspects engaged in defensive nonverbal behavior in response to a police invasion of their personal space, the police officer interpreted this (often incorrectly) as a sign that the suspect was guilty.[209]

What if the impression comes first—that is, you enter a social situation in which you expect to meet someone with a given set of characteristics? Participants in one study were told they were about to meet someone who was either warm and friendly or unfriendly.[210] The participants chose smaller interpersonal distances for the warm and friendly confederate. Similarly, when observers note that pairs of individuals are physically close together, they will attribute intimacy to the relationship.[211,212]

An important point about these attributions is that they may or may not accurately match individuals' behavior, as we saw earlier in the case of persuasive attempts. The man who stops just inside the office door to talk may simply be a very polite boss rather than a subordinate. Individuals who choose larger interpersonal distances may not have unpleasant personalities, and couples who walk very close to each other may not be lovers. These studies do, however, indicate that observers will form such impressions, accurate or not. What impressions are *your* interpersonal distance choices creating in the minds of others?

Helping Others

INTERPERSONAL DISTANCE SEEMS TO AFFECT THE DESIRE TO HELP OTHERS, but again the relations are not simple. In one study, the personal space of pedestrians was invaded, then the invader dropped something. Even when the dropped object was an important one, moving pedestrians whose space was invaded helped (by picking up the object) less often than did moving pedestrians whose space had not been invaded.[213] Even when the invader is not to blame—when circumstances clearly caused the invasion—helping is still diminished.[214] This makes sense. We would not expect a person who has just been invaded—for whatever reason—to be overly generous. Yet in a subsequent study, requests for help were *more* successful after an invasion.[215] The authors suggest that conflicting results may be the result of different attributions by the invaded individuals in the two studies. In the first study, the invader may have been seen as personally unpleasant, but in the second study the request's importance was salient, and the invasion was not perceived as intentional.

A new study was devised to clear up the confusion by explicitly examining the need of the invader. When the invader pleaded a great need for help *and* stood near, pedestrians offered the most help. When the invader stood near but did not stress a need for help, pedestrians offered the least assistance. At a relatively far distance, this situation was reversed: Invaders who pled low need for assistance received more offers of assistance than those who pled high need.[216] This study is valuable not only for the way it reveals how personal space and helping behavior are linked, but also for once again showing how variables interact to produce results that are not clearly predictable from either variable alone. The earlier studies reached conflicting results because each emphasized only one variable and did not adopt a multivariate approach.

Does increased arousal lead to more or less helping? One study found that those who were invaded did help more;[217] the authors speculated that giving assistance served to reduce the arousal of the person who was invaded. In another, the invader's appearance was discovered to be important: Invaders who looked like punk rockers were given less help than more typical-looking invaders.[218] Interestingly, the two received the same amount of help when they asked for help while standing relatively far away. Invasion by needy or average-looking persons seems to elicit a positive or helpful form of arousal, but invasion by atypical persons seems to cause anxiety (a negative form of arousal) and less empathy for their requests.

Working in Small Groups

IMAGINE WORKING ON A PROJECT with a small group of others. Will the pattern of distances and orientations among you influence productivity or the way the members interact? Research shows that individuals very often say (on questionnaires) that they would select face-to-face arrangements for competition.[219] However, face-to-face seating actually seems to lead to cooperation, not competition.[220] Male participants were asked to play a game in which either a cooperative strategy or a competitive strategy could be used to win. They were asked to sit next to each other or across from each other; in both arrangements they either could see one another or not (a visual barrier was used to accomplish this). Cooperation was greatest in the face-to-face, visual-access condition. So, although such an arrangement is often viewed as competitive, it actually seems to elicit cooperation.

This may happen because the face-to-face arrangement makes the other person very salient. When the other person has so much visual presence, we may be loath to compete, fearing that competition will produce conflict and negative emotions. Perhaps individuals responding to a questionnaire underestimate the emotional power of a face-to-face arrangement, and that is why they report that they would sit face-to-face for competitive activities (the stereotypical arrangement), but actually cooperate more when they are placed in a real face-to-face situation. In another study, groups of four men and women were asked to cooperate with each other or to compete as individuals while at small or large distances.[221] Their task was to solve a complex maze. When the instructions called for participants to compete with each other, performance was better at the larger distance (5'/150 cm) than at the smaller one (2'/60 cm). When the participants were asked to cooperate, however, the smaller distance led to better performance.

In the first study, then, placing a group member in a more visually immediate position, even though it was farther away, led to more cooperation. In this study, bringing individuals closer (without a change in orientation) led to better performance when they were asked to cooperate, but more distant arrangements facilitated performance when the participants were instructed to compete. Cooperation, it seems, occurs more and leads to better performance when group members are made very aware of each other, either because they are face-to-face or because they are very close. Competition occurs more and is associated with higher productivity when the competitors are less-directly oriented or are simply farther apart. These conclusions must be tentative, but the questions they deal with are very important. Millions of employees work in settings where the seating arrangements are based on custom, fashions in office decor, or no rationale at all. These studies suggest that more effective furniture placement could enhance cooperation and productivity.

When employees from different cultures work together in small groups, differences in personal space practices can cause problems.[222] As always with personal space, the problems may not be recognized as being related to this aspect of culturally influenced behavior. Group members may begin to transfer their frustration that is actually based on differences in the use of space to their evaluations of the others' personality or ability. The obvious solution is to recognize the source of the problem and encourage tolerance of differences in the use of space.

IN SUM Personal space is intimately intertwined with numerous facets of human behavior. Changing one's interpersonal distance may allow a person to exert greater social control over another. Moving close in a positive relationship may lead to greater attraction, but doing so when the other person is a stranger may lead to their sudden departure. Impressions are often formed on the basis of interpersonal distances that we observe in others, but these attributions are not always valid. Help may be forthcoming when individuals are physically close and express their need to others. Cooperation occurs more and leads to better performance when individuals are immediate (closer and facing one another). When they are less immediate, performance is better in competitive conditions. Some of these behaviors change if the other person is of the opposite sex, different in status, or creates certain impressions through appearance or apparent motives. Our interpersonal behavior is complex! Let us examine some ideas that offer clarifying principles.

Territoriality functions as a central process in several forms and variations of human behavior.

Personalization and Marking

PERSONALIZATION AND MARKING OCCUR IN A WIDE VARI-ETY OF SETTINGS, INCLUDING SOME YOU MIGHT NOT EX-PECT (see Figure 5-12). For example, one study found that restaurant diners marked their plates by touching them about three times more often when the plate was served by another person than when they served themselves.[223] Because diners probably are not consciously aware that they are marking their places in this manner, some of our marking behavior apparently occurs out of awareness. A similar pattern was found in a video-game arcade.[224] Naturalistic observation of players suggested that players touch the machines to establish territory and touch them longer when others intrude on them. When a confederate of the investigators touched the machines, other players were discouraged from using them.

Of course, personalization and marking are also quite deliberate at times. When property owners erect signs reading "No Hunting," "No Trespassing," "No Agents, Vendors, Solicitors, or Sales Agents", they do so with a clear and conscious purpose. Urban gangs mark their turf boundaries with spray-painted signs on the walls of buildings.[225] We must be careful, however, not to assume that every sign or piece of graffiti is a territorial marker. Graffiti may be mere vandalism, and someone may put a coat on the back of a chair because there is nowhere else to hang it. Personalization and marking serve notice of someone's claim, but if these signs are ignored, the person often does not follow through with stronger defenses of the territory. Personalization seems to be strong enough as a human need that people will find ways to fulfill it even in "non-territorial" offices where it is forbidden.[226] This is especially true when the territory is a public one, such as space at a library table. When an intruder disregards an occupant's territorial markers, the occupant often abandons the space rather than actively defend it.[227]

Personalization can have positive side effects. When residents of a psychiatric ward were allowed to personalize their territories, the social atmosphere of the ward improved.[228] Unfortunately, many organizations discourage personalization. One university, however, encourages it by holding an annual door-painting contest in its dormitories. Personalization of dormitory rooms has also been linked to staying in school (as opposed to dropping out), although of course many other factors influence such a decision.[229]

Aggression and Territorial Defense

In the popular mind, perhaps spurred by stories of violent disputes over territory in some animal species or by media accounts of human territorial conflict, territoriality and aggression are seen as going hand in hand. At the national level, too, the tragedy of war is all too common. Although aggression receives more attention than peaceful coexistence, research in environmental psychology suggests that aggression over individual and small group territories is actually not very common.[230] This, in part, is because humans have developed so many nonviolent ways of settling disputes—language to negotiate with, customs to guide behavior, and a legal system to settle most disputes.

FIGURE 5–12 An example of personalization in a work space.

This is not to say that individuals do not defend their territories. The nonviolent means just listed, and more (e.g., yelling and dirty looks) may be used as territorial defenses. Defense of territory through marking, personalization, and other means is common, however violent defenses are more rare. One such nonviolent defense is vigilance. In an early field study, residents of houses with defense displays (e.g., signs reading "Private Property" or "Keep Out") responded to a knock at the door significantly faster than residents without defense displays.[231] As noted earlier, territory-holders may simply occupy a public space longer,[232] or they may rush to respond to a stranger's entrance more quickly.[233] Unfortunately, aggression does occur under some circumstances. The more a territory is valued, for example, the more likely that territory will be actively defended.[234]

Many societies even condone violence in the defense of a primary territory. For example, homeowners have been acquitted when they shot burglars who invaded their homes. Aggression may also occur when territorial boundaries are vague. When the boundaries between the turf belonging to urban gangs is not clearly agreed upon, more violence occurs than when boundaries are clearly agreed upon.[235]

We may speculate that violence is used as a territoriality defense when all other means have been exhausted, an individual is unaware of alternatives, or an individual is denied other means of defense—such as when some groups, through poverty or discrimination, are denied equal access to the justice system. Sometimes defense is impossible, such as when we are too weak to resist an invasion, when it happens despite our efforts, or when it happens while we are away. Invasion leads to victimization or emotional loss that transcends the material loss. Burglary victims are naturally more upset when the burglary includes some destruction of the house and the loss of personally meaningful items.[236]

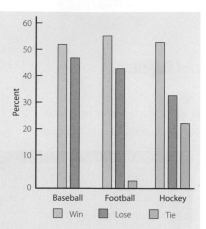

FIGURE 5–13 Outcomes of home games in three professional sports. Differences in winning percentages are not large, but with ties as possible outcomes to their games, hockey teams lose much less often at home than baseball teams.

Dominance and Control

These two terms do not mean quite the same thing.[237] Territoriality has most often been associated with dominance, a social behavior that implies winning. Sometimes dominance or rank in a hierarchy is closely associated with the amount and quality of territory an individual holds, but sometimes it is not. Human territoriality is more closely tied to control, which is a broader concept than dominance. Control refers not only to influence over other individuals, but to influence over space, ideas, and other resources

in the territory. Control may be active, as when control is exercised offensively and is initiated by the territory holder, or passive, as when the territory holder acts defensively, responding to or resisting a challenge by outsiders. We should think more in terms of control, particularly passive control, when considering human territoriality. Individuals rarely engage in direct attempts to assert dominance, but they often may be seen engaging in nonviolent behavior that promotes their control over territories. For example, in a dispute concerning a boundary between two properties, individuals are much more likely to engage in negotiations or a court dispute than in fisticuffs.

In a study of mental hospital patients, the middle and bottom thirds of the dominance hierarchy among both adult and child patients possessed territories on the ward in keeping with their position in the hierarchy: the middle third of the patients had large central territories, and the bottom third had small remote territories.[238,239] The top third of the hierarchy, however, had no particular territory: they wandered freely throughout the setting. In one sense, they had no territory; in another sense, the entire setting was their territory.

In a school for young male offenders, territoriality was correlated with dominance as long as membership in the group remained unchanged.[240] However, when two very dominant individuals left the group, conflict increased and the correlation between dominance and territorial behavior decreased. Later, as group membership grew stable again, the links between territoriality and dominance strengthened among the middle and bottom thirds of the hierarchy. The most dominant individuals, however, were still struggling and had not yet established clear territories. The researchers concluded that, with more time, the group's original strong ties between territorial behavior and dominance might re-emerge. However, there is another possible outcome. The most dominant residents might have established school-wide "territories" that allowed them to move freely throughout the setting. The important point, however, is that the strength of dominance-territoriality relations varies with the situation; shake-ups in the composition of a group as well as other social factors can strengthen or weaken them.

Control and the Home Field Advantage. Does the possession of a territory help humans to dominate activities in it, to win? We have already seen that decisions made on our own turf reflect our own position on the issue more than they reflect others' positions.[241] The courtroom is one place where victories and defeats occur. In an intriguing assessment of a North Carolina courtroom, objectivity and equality between the prosecution and defense were not always reflected in the physical arrangements of the courtroom.[242] After observing the locations of the judge, jury, prosecution, and defense of the courtroom, researchers concluded that the prosecution had a significant advantage over the defense. For example, the prosecution was located nearer the jury, allowing prosecutors to subtly convince jurors that they were literally "on the same side" in the case. Evidence of the value of a primary territory came in a study of favor requests in various territory classifications.[243] The favor was a request to sign a petition that advocated a viewpoint contrary to the beliefs of participants. The participants—particularly men—were more willing to sign such a petition when they were in a "non-territory" than when they were in a primary territory. Apparently, a good way to avoid being talked into something with which you do not agree is to hold the discussion in your personal territory.

Territorial control also appears to affect the outcome of sports events, a phenomenon known as the **home field advantage**. In every league, teams bemoan road trips: they mean travel, which becomes wearisome, and they mean the odds of winning are lower. Or are they? Is the home field advantage myth or reality? Several studies have examined the home and away records of teams in hockey, basketball, baseball, and football.[244,245] In general, home advantage does exist, but it is greater in some sports than others (see Figure 5-13). In a baseball season, home teams won 53 percent of their games. This advantage is small, considering the legends in the game about groundskeepers "doctoring" the playing field to suit the home team or to foil visiting base stealers and bunters. Football teams win about 57 percent of home games, and have about a three-point margin of victory, on average.[246] Professional hockey teams win about 60 percent (wins plus ties are about 70 percent), basketball teams win about 62 percent, and soccer teams win about 67 percent at home. The researchers considered numerous reasons for their findings but concluded that the main reason is fan support, magnified by the form of the physical environment.

Hockey and basketball fans cheer their teams in closed buildings; this intensifies their vocal support for the team when compared to the effect fans can have in baseball and football, where cheers often dissipate into the open sky. Indoor venues also decrease the distance between fans and players, which increases fan input even more. A study of hockey showed that the home advantage grew when the density of the crowd increased.[247] These studies reveal that the home advantage is stronger for indoor sports than for outdoor sports. A study of booing at basketball games revealed that home team performance increased slightly immediately after booing by its fans and that visiting teams committed more fouls and generally performed worse immediately after the booing.[248] A different study found that professional basketball stars (but not non-stars) have fewer fouls called on them during home games.[249] Both studies suggest that referees are influenced by crowds. Yet more evidence that crowd noise helps the home team comes from a study of English football (soccer) referees.[250] In the presence or absence of crowd noise, 40 qualified referees watched various plays on videotape that involved potential fouls. The referees who viewed the plays with background crowd noise were more uncertain in their decision making and awarded significantly fewer fouls against the home team than the referees who watched in silence. Another explanation for the home field advantage is based on player hormone levels.[251] Testosterone levels in male soccer players were found to be significantly higher before a home game than an away game. Rivalry seems to play a role in this. Testosterone levels were higher before playing an "extreme" rival than a "moderate" rival, although self-reported mood was unrelated to testosterone level. This suggests that hormones play a role, but one players are unaware of, if conscious mood levels do not reflect testosterone levels.

The home field advantage can backfire when the pressure to succeed becomes extreme. In baseball's World Series, home teams win over 60 percent of first and second

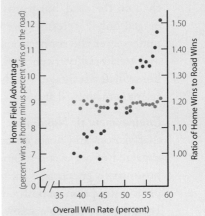

FIGURE 5-14 A puzzle based on the home team effect. Baseball teams with better records win more often at home (see ■ dots). However, this is not simply because they have a better overall win record: Winning teams win a greater percentage of games at home than their overall record would predict, and losing teams win less at home than their overall record would predict (data from James, 1984). Even more striking (see ■ dots on graph), the home field advantage appears to be a constant. Regardless of their overall record, baseball teams win, on average, about 21 percent more home than away games.

games but less than 40 percent of seventh games, when the whole series is decided in one final game.[252] Yet, during the regular season, the home advantage generally is stronger for better teams —those who end up in the World Series. A baseball researcher sorted baseball teams by overall winning percentage and found those that win 55 to 65 percent of their games averaged 12 percent more wins at home than on the road, but teams winning 33 to 43 percent averaged only 7 percent more wins at home.[253] This finding underscores the connections between dominance, control, and territoriality. Even mediocre teams benefit from the home field advantage, but the strength of generally strong teams is magnified at home (see Figure 5-14).

Environmental Numbness. In everyday life, we notice that visitors and hosts enact rituals; the visitor is usually expected to act in a restrained, cautious manner, and the host usually encourages the visitor to feel at home. The implicit assumption on both sides is that the host is in control. The guest's role is to acknowledge this; the host's role is to graciously surrender it. Nevertheless, the visitor's maxim is, "when in Rome, do as the Romans do." Sometimes we are too ready to yield to arrangements in places we do not control. In a study of environmental awareness, I found that students working on a lab assignment for a psychology class went to great lengths not to disturb a furniture arrangement that caused them considerable difficulty in moving around the lab.[254] The students' lack of action was partly caused by their lack of awareness of the physical environment, but some of them later pointed out that "one does not move furniture around except in one's own home." In the lab, there were no explicit prohibitions against moving furniture around, especially if it was interfering with progress in the lab. Yet the students felt that "they" (the lab instructor? the janitor? the university president?) must have wanted the furniture that way. The students felt such a lack of control that they did not even raise the issue of restructuring the furniture arrangements, let alone actively lobby for a change or change things around themselves. I have described this phenomenon as **environmental numbness**. An important consideration in the relation between territory and control, therefore, is whether the territory is primary, secondary, or public. The students in the lab, for example, viewed the lab as a secondary or, more likely, as a public territory.

We should have the most control in our own primary territories. Do individuals at least believe they exert more control in primary territories than in the other kinds? Participants in one study did report feeling more in control when they occupied primary territories (e.g., their bedrooms and bathrooms with closed doors) than they did in secondary territories (e.g., their backyards and the sidewalk in front of their houses), or in public territories (e.g., streets, supermarkets, or recreation areas).[255] One study investigated when pedestrians are more likely to invade the interactional territory formed by two people talking. Pedestrians were more likely to walk between the two conversing people when they were in a secondary territory (their own dormitory corridor) than when they were in a public territory (a classroom building corridor).[256]

IN SUM *We have seen that territoriality is associated with a variety of behaviors: personalization, marking, aggression, dominance, winning, helping, inaction, and control. Personalization and marking are very common (but territoriality is not the basis of every public display). It may occur with or without awareness, may signal ownership but does not always lead to active defense, and it seems to offer psychological benefits to the territory holder beyond merely informing the world of a territorial claim. This does not mean humans never defend territory violently (witness the hundreds of wars and assaults that occur at the national and individual levels), but many more everyday disputes are settled nonviolently. Territoriality does seem to help us control and dominate our territories, but this end is usually accomplished through passive or peaceful means that do not involve direct bullying of others. In the home field advantage in sports, for example, fan support or perhaps "doctoring" the field is used in attempts to control the outcome of the game. We are unlikely to alter furniture or other arrangements in public territories because we do not see them as our own, even when no one else claims the space as a primary territory.*

SO FAR, WE HAVE DEFINED PERSONAL SPACE, described how it may be measured, discussed many influences on it, and surveyed some of its effects on other human behaviors. The time has come to clarify the sources and strands of this complex process. Just how does personal space work?

Learning Personal Space: Social Learning Theory

MOST ENVIRONMENTAL PSYCHOLOGISTS BELIEVE personal space is culturally acquired. However, we should not forget that although many differences exist between cultures and even subcultures,[257] all humans seem to require some amount of personal space. In that sense, personal space is not culturally acquired, but is part of our genetic inheritance as human beings. Not every species is as socially inclined as ours. Therefore, in phylogenetic terms, personal space is genetically acquired, but once we restrict our study to humans, the differences in personal space are the result of the physical setting and personal, social, and cultural influences.

The only theory concerning the *acquisition* of personal space borrows from an approach prominent in other areas of psychology. **Social learning theory** asserts that personal space is a gradually learned behavior resulting from an individual's history of reinforcement.[258] Parents and others often deliver verbal reinforcements to children about the appropriateness of their interpersonal distance: "Don't go near strangers." "Give your Auntie Maud a big kiss, now." "Stay close to your brother on the way to school." Children apparently do learn the rules early. Before they are 2 years [old], children stay closer to Mom in more-stressful and more-structured situations, and roam farther away in free-play situations.[259] By the age of 3, children already stay further from boys than girls, a pattern that generally holds throughout life.[260] Joan Price and I found that by the age of 4, children already follow at least four personal space rules:[261]

1. Boys keep greater distances from boys than girls do from girls.

2. Children stay closer to acquaintances than to strangers.

3. Children stay closer in a formal setting (such as the teacher's office) than in an informal setting (such as their own playroom).

4. If another child is a stranger and the setting is formal, children keep a larger distance than they would from the same stranger in an informal setting. But if the other child is a friend and the setting is formal, they keep a smaller distance than they would even in an informal setting (see Figure 5-15).

We also apparently learn some unfortunate prejudices, such as ageism, by the time we are old enough to go to school. On average, 6-year-olds (but not 4-year-olds) choose larger distances from elderly persons (particularly elderly women) than from younger adults.[262] If we learn this much so young, consider the number of personal space rules we must know by adulthood!

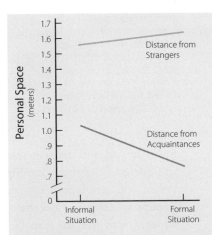

FIGURE 5–15 Even by age 4, children choose different interpersonal distances depending on the situation (formal versus informal) and their relationship with another child (an acquaintance versus a stranger).

Affiliative-Conflict Theory

THE MOST FERTILE THEORY about the function of personal space was originally formulated by Michael Argyle and Janet Dean.[263] The central idea of the affiliative-conflict theory is that it functions to balance our social needs. **Affiliative-conflict theory** maintains that, like cold porcupines, we have conflicting social motives—a desire to draw closer to others and, at the same time, a desire to move away from others. These conflicting tendencies arise because we are simultaneously attracted to others, and we want information from them, but we wish to retain our individuality and freedom, and we do not always want to reveal information about ourselves to them.

Several nonverbal channels (interpersonal amount of eye contact, posture, smiling, and intimacy) and such architectural factors as

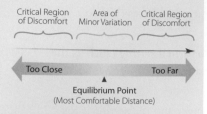

The Interpersonal Distance Continuum

FIGURE 5–16 Interpersonal distance is better viewed as a comfort continuum than as a fixed distance. As distance from an optimal equilibrium point increases or decreases, discomfort grows. Compensatory behaviors (such as averting one's eyes or changing the topic of conversation) can ameliorate mild discomfort from distances that are somewhat too small or large, but not the greater discomfort caused by very large or very small interpersonal distances.

room are involved as individuals seek an equilibrium between their approach and avoidance tendencies.[264] In stable interpersonal relationships, the various channels combine to establish a certain level of intimacy, the equilibrium point. If, for some reason, one person in the relationship alters the equilibrium, then, according to Argyle and Dean's theory, the other will compensate by adjusting one channel or another in an attempt to reestablish the prior level of intimacy.

As an illustration, imagine that you and an acquaintance are strolling along to the cafeteria together, chatting about one of your classes. When you arrive at the cafeteria, you discover that the lineups are long, but because you are hungry both of you squeeze into line anyway. Now you are inappropriately close to your acquaintance; neither of you can avoid it under the circumstances. Affiliative-conflict theory predicts that the resulting disequilibrium in the interpersonal distance channel will be compensated for in other channels. You might reduce eye contact or shift the conversation to less intimate topics. Affiliative-conflict theory has been tested many times; most studies support its basic tenets.[265,266]

The equilibrium varies with circumstances. For example, when interpersonal distance shrinks, eye contact often is reduced too, but the amount of this reduction depends on (1) whether one of the persons actively moves closer (as opposed to already being close), (2) who is speaking and who is listening at the time, (3) whether the pair are friends or strangers, and (4) whether the pair are of the same or opposite genders.[267] Eye contact is likely to be avoided when a same-gender stranger moves closer. The degree to which compensation occurs also depends on personality. Individuals who are more arousable compensate to a lesser degree than those who are less arousable.[268] When people are at the same distance from one another, brighter lighting stimulates more general and intimate

communication.[269] Adjustments of posture, interpersonal distancing, and refrains from establishing eye contact are used to counteract space intrusions.

Affiliative-conflict theory is still evolving.[270] Four recent models represent refinements and extensions of it. These are presented next.

Social Penetration. A major shortcoming of affiliative-conflict theory is its failure to account for certain changes in relationships. When we fall in love, an increase in the nonverbal intimacy of one partner often will be *reciprocated* by the other, rather than compensated for. Instead of moving away when you move close, a romantic partner will maintain the shorter distance or may even move closer to you. In general, when relationships are growing, changing, or dying, affiliative-conflict theory may fail to predict individual responses to disequilibrium.[271] Irwin Altman and his colleagues proposed a form of affiliative-conflict theory that deals with these changes. Their dialectical approach posits that compensatory *and* reciprocal behaviors will occur as individuals gradually adjust to changes in their desired level of interaction with others.[272,273]

Limits of Compensation. Does the basic notion that people will compensate for inappropriate distances work at *any* distance? John Aiello and his colleagues have shown that compensation processes do not work well outside a certain range of distances [274,275] (see Figure 5-16). This is partly caused by growing discomfort as the interpersonal distance becomes more and more inappropriate. In one study, observers were shown videotapes of pairs interacting at different distances. The observers judged the degree of comfort that individuals in the film would feel at the different distances. Maximum comfort was perceived at a moderate distance; at shorter and longer distances the comfort ratings declined.[276] Outside a **critical discomfort region** the usual channels cannot easily be used to restore equilibrium. In several studies Aiello and his colleagues have also found gender differences in the distances at which the critical discomfort region is reached.[277-279] Males show more discomfort as the distance grows inappropriately *close*, but females show more discomfort as the distance grows inappropriately *far*. Women who were too far away from the other person had greater difficulty using any of the other channels to re-establish equilibrium.

Arousal-Cognition. In most versions of affiliative-equilibrium theory, compensation and reciprocation are believed to occur at a very low level of cognitive awareness. However, not all theories discount the role of cognitive processes. If you move too close to someone, you become aroused. This is not surprising; the only mystery might be whether the arousal is negatively toned (annoyance-anger) or positively toned (pleasure-sexual).

Miles Patterson, the chief spokesperson for the arousal approach, believes that changes in arousal have a cognitive component. He asserts that we are aware of changes in our arousal, and we tend to label that change positively or negatively. Patterson predicts that arousal shifts accompanied by positive affect will lead to reciprocation. Only negatively labeled arousal shifts, according to Patterson, lead to the compensatory behaviors described by Argyle and Dean in their affiliative-conflict theory.

Approach-Avoidance. Argyle and Dean's original formulation of affiliative-conflict theory suggested that we use interpersonal distance (and other nonverbal behaviors) to balance conflicting desires to approach and to avoid the other person. Eric Knowles examined this assumption more closely and postulates three clarifications of the approach-avoidance assumption.[280,281] These clarifications also represent a more articulate definition of the comfort concept used by early theorists.

1. Nearly every interpersonal situation involves avoidance tendencies. Even in rewarding relationships, we wish to avoid getting *too* close, involved, or committed.

2. Some interpersonal situations result in approach tendencies; we do want to become involved with some individuals.

3. Discomfort in interpersonal situations results from a discrepancy between approach and avoidance tendencies.

These clarifications are shown in Figure 5-17. In interpersonal situations, individuals who are near one another may be interacting or not (external forces may have put them in proximity, such as in a crowded elevator, bus, or room). The shaded areas in diagrams A and C represent the discrepancy between approach and avoidance tendencies at close and far distances. Diagrams B and D depict the resultant discomfort experienced by a person at these distances.

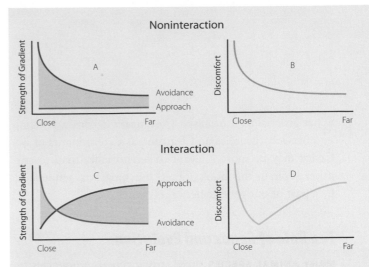

FIGURE 5–17 A more complex view of personal space holds that discomfort depends on whether a person is involved in an interaction with the other person and on the strength of his or her approach and avoidance tendencies toward the other person. When the person is not interacting with the other person (*diagrams* A and B), discomfort does not increase as distance increases. However, when the person is interacting with the other (*diagrams* C and D), discomfort is lowest at an optimal middle distance; the person becomes more uncomfortable when the distance grows too large.

IN SUM Acquisition of the rules concerning interpersonal distance can be characterized by social learning theory. The function of interpersonal distances can be explained by the affiliative equilibrium theory. More encompassing theoretical integrations have begun to appear. The social penetration model emphasizes the role of personal space in the rise and fall of relationships. The limits-of-compensation model highlights the outer limits of interpersonal distance, showing that as discomfort grows, interaction becomes more difficult. The approach–avoidance model hypothesizes differences between the desire to get close to someone and the desire to keep one's distance. Discomfort is seen as the discrepancy between the two desires.

What governs territoriality? The ancient debate in psychology between genetics and learning as determinants of behavior may be more relevant to territoriality than to any other topic in this book. Could our territorial tendencies be a part of our genetic heritage?

The Role of Genes and Evolution

MANY ANIMAL SPECIES show strong genetic tendencies towards territoriality, which has led some theorists to treat human territoriality as a direct extension of animal territoriality. In the forefront of this approach are many European ethologists and some North American writers who have been quick to suggest an instinctual basis for human territoriality.[282] The ethological approach, whether applied to animals or humans, emphasizes the aggression and defense elements of territoriality.

RALPH TAYLOR is a leading researcher of territoriality and urban neighborhoods.

No proof exists that human territoriality is inherited, despite the parallels that can be drawn between some human behaviors and some animal behaviors. Indeed, some writers appear to overlook the fact that not even all animals are territorial; we could, with equal justification, point to our mammalian heritage in support of the position that humans are not instinctually territorial. For example, some of the great apes, our closest relatives, exhibit very little territoriality.

Nevertheless, Ralph Taylor has carefully considered the possible evolutionary and genetic bases for human territoriality, and his view is that territorial functioning is a product of our evolutionary heritage.[283] Our ancient history as bands of hunters roaming the African savannah shaped the general nature of our present territoriality. According to Taylor, because territoriality developed in a small-group context, even today it applies to only individuals and small groups, not to large aggregates such as nations.

Taylor maintains that the behavior processes involved in modern territorial functioning are similar in form to those that evolved long ago, even if they no longer serve quite the same purpose or have the same consequences. Finally, Taylor asserts that the evolutionary basis of territoriality does not mean that it is "hard-wired" into our genes.

An Interaction Organizer

RECALL THAT HUMAN TERRITORIALITY is not often characterized by attempts to dominate visitors.[284] Rather, according to Julian Edney and others, human territoriality serves to organize human behavior so that violence, aggression, and overt domination are unnecessary. When an individual or group controls a setting, many aspects of behavior become ordered, including choice of activities, access to resources, and behavioral customs. Many individuals who have been employed by others dream of owning a business themselves, partly for financial reasons, but also so they can organize and control the policies and physical aspects of their workplace. Children want their own rooms so that their activities and decorations do not have to be negotiated with a sibling. Thus, one motivation for seeking territory is to have the opportunity to obtain these organizing prerogatives.

Territories provide organization and order to communities, small groups, and individuals. Communities benefit mainly because territories geographically fix individuals. Each of us spends considerable time in specific territories. If community members spent time in many different places, we would have a difficult time locating those with whom we want to interact. Thus, territories provide individuals with reliable access to the contacts they need. The community as a whole is better off because time and effort spent in communicating with others is much less than if we had to look everywhere each time we wanted to speak with someone.

Small groups benefit because territorial ownership seems to generate expectations about how visitors and hosts will behave. Clubs and drinking establishments, for example, often have written or unwritten rules of conduct. I once saw a sign erected by the proud owner of a new backyard swimming pool: "We don't swim in your toilet, please don't pee in our pool!" These conventions (particularly those more serious than the pool owner's sign) increase order and security by providing a mutually acceptable set of ground rules on which social behavior can be transacted. As noted earlier, these conventions generally assign control to the host, but the host uses this control to be considerate of the visitor's needs. For example, the host offers the visitor a choice of drinks, serves the visitor first, and suggests where the visitor should sit.

Finally, individuals benefit from the organizing function of territories. Because they control social and resource management aspects of the territory's operation, territory holders are better able to plan and anticipate future events. Familiarity with the territory also gives individuals a sense of competence that would be impossible if they moved randomly from place to place. Individuals gain a sense of identity by simply being spatially separate from others. Also, individuals typically enact long chains of related behaviors. When these occur in a single place, they are better organized and ordered because of the individual's familiarity with the territory. An everyday example is cooking a meal: the process is much easier in our own kitchen than in someone else's kitchen because we know where the ingredients and implements are stored.

IN SUM Theories of territoriality are diverse. Ethology, evolution, organization, and control are quite disparate concepts around which to construct a theory of territoriality. Popular writers have exaggerated the relation between overt aggression and territoriality in humans, perhaps because some are too willing to generalize from animal behavior. However, the most common and positive function of territoriality is to help organize social interaction and organization. If we assume that each of them is partially correct, a future theory that synthesizes them coherently will surely picture human territoriality as an extremely complex process. Despite the diversity in theory, environmental psychologists know enough about territoriality to use their knowledge to improve environmental design. We turn now to that enterprise.

IN THE EARLY DAYS OF PERSONAL SPACE RESEARCH, some researchers dreamt that personal space would be the central part of architectural planning. Robert Sommer subtitled his classic book on personal space *The Behavioral Basis of Design*. Only five years later, however, Sommer realized that personal space would never be *the* cornerstone of architecture.[285] Too many other considerations; local regulations, sites, other social factors, budgets, materials, and aesthetics also influence design. Personal space may not be the essence of environmental design, but it is one important consideration among others. Edward Hall remarked that research on interpersonal distance cannot tell an architect how to design a building, but it certainly can provide the architect with information that can be worked *into* a design. Designers have become more sensitive to the spatial needs of their clients since Sommer's and Hall's books were published.

A number of researchers have specifically examined the role of personal space in the built environment. Most of these studies have concentrated on personal space as reflected in seating arrangements in such public spaces as libraries, airports, schools, offices, and restaurants. Most research has centered on the effect of furniture arrangements on social interaction. Some arrangements seem to foster social interaction and others seem to hinder it. The new digital world of cellphones and the Internet has its own effects on the spatial aspects of interpersonal interaction, these have scarcely been studied so far.[286] Here are three case studies of personal space in architectural design.

Sociopetal and Sociofugal Arrangements

An insightful psychiatrist, Humphrey Osmond, coined the term **sociopetal setting** to describe settings that facilitate social interaction, and **sociofugal setting** to describe settings that discourage social interaction.[287] Osmond himself did not restrict the terms to seating arrangements. He describes, for example, hallways as sociofugal and circular rooms as sociopetal. Most subsequent research, however, has emphasized the sociopetal or sociofugal qualities of seating arrangements. A typical sociopetal arrangement is the dining table in most homes, where family members sit around the table facing one another. A typical sociofugal arrangement is a set of chairs bolted so that chair occupants face outward, away from one another, in different directions. Most seating arrangements fall along a continuum from one extreme to another (see Figure 5-18).

Initially, we may conclude that sociopetal arrangements are good and sociofugal arrangements are bad. After all, we wish to foster social interaction everywhere possible, right? Not necessarily. In some situations minimal social interaction is the goal. For example, in the reading room of a university library, most of us expect others to work quietly. In some community libraries, in contrast, librarians hope to encourage users to discuss issues and ask questions. This, in fact, is the very heart of the matter. Neither sociopetal nor sociofugal designs are inherently good or bad; the questions are: Which behaviors are valued in this particular setting, and which arrangement will encourage these behaviors?

However, designers cannot expect to cause valued behaviors to occur merely by creating one seating arrangement or another. A study I conducted demonstrated that seating arrangements that orient individuals toward one another do not always facilitate conversation.[288] This may be because other factors, like personality, also affect sociability.[289] However, sociopetal and sociofugal seating arrangements do probably encourage or facilitate more or less social interaction in general.

Counseling Settings

A BASIC COMPONENT of many counseling clients' problems is difficulty in communication. People with schizophrenia typically do not communicate well. Those with neuroses may communicate too much but not pleasantly. Even everyday family problems are often based in communication difficulties. Seating arrangements during counseling or therapy may be an important part of success or failure in this delicate situation. Chairs themselves can be psychologically significant.[290] For example, if a person feels ready to crumble emotionally, the therapist could do much better than to offer a folding chair. The chair arrangements recommended by the leaders of four prominent schools of psychotherapy are enlightening.[291]

Freud's approach was very sociofugal; the patient lies on a couch with the analyst sitting at the head of the couch, entirely out of sight. This psychologically distant arrangement was congruent with Freud's belief that such an arrangement facilitates the free expression of repressed ideas.

Harry Stack Sullivan, the father of a more interpersonally oriented school of psychotherapy, recommended an arrangement in which the client and therapist face one another directly, across a desk. Sullivan, who specialized in helping people with schizophrenia, believed this direct orientation promoted communication with the small part of the schizophrenic's personality that still wants to communicate. However, such a direct orientation may overload the therapist; Sullivan ended his own life.

Wilhelm Reich, representing a body-oriented form of psychotherapy, asked his patients to lie on a couch with the therapist sitting beside the couch, facing the patient. This arrangement was rooted in Reich's belief that character defenses in individuals with psychological problems are reflected in rigid muscles and other bodily manifestations. His furniture arrangement was designed to allow the therapist to touch and massage the patient frequently during therapy.

Fritz Perls, the founder of gestalt therapy, believed there should be *no* fixed arrangement of chairs. In fact, he would often direct clients in group therapy to move themselves or the furniture around for different activities, such as role-playing or recounting dreams. Perls sometimes ordered clients to abandon the furniture entirely, in favor of sitting on the floor.

Neighborhoods

WHEN RESIDENTS BELIEVE TOO MUCH TRAFFIC is flowing through their streets, they will often ask cities to restrict the traffic flow in their neighborhoods by blocking off streets. Commuters, however, believe the streets are there to help them get to and from work efficiently. Concerns about children's safety and traffic noise are the neighborhood residents' explicit reasons for the barriers, but the move to territorialize the neighborhood may have less-obvious benefits. Blocking off streets serves to give residents a sense of control and identity. The cars that now move through the streets are neither so numerous nor so foreign; they are owned by neighbors. Because there are fewer cars, residents have a better chance of recognizing strange ones. This may serve to reduce crime, because "different" cars are noticed by residents. Burglars who have several neighborhoods to choose from would be better off selecting a more anonymous neighborhood. Defensible space theory would support neighborhood design changes that increase the residents' sense of ownership, eliminate space about which no one in particular feels vigilant, and increase space that is easily watched by residents.

Changing whole neighborhoods, unfortunately, is politically difficult. Traffic barriers, for example, are opposed not only by commuters who are inconvenienced, but by nearby residents of neighborhoods that will experience increased traffic as a result of the new barriers. Smaller-scale changes, to individual houses, for example, are much easier politically, but may cost the individual homeowner a great deal more. Of course, the problem sometimes can be solved by creating a different street pattern either when a neighborhood is originally designed or by rearranging the street pattern in a block. One study demonstrated that residents of culs-de-sac believe that they have exclusive use of their street, can better distinguish neighbors from strangers, and have safer and better-maintained streets than residents of through streets.[292]

Hospitals

NO ONE LIKES TO BE HOSPITALIZED. Besides the obvious reason (that being in a hospital means illness or injury), another reason we may not enjoy our stay is the way space is managed in hospitals. Unavoidably, we go to a setting where we have no pre-established territory. Immediately, this affects our sense of control and security. Even if we are given a private room or our own bed, we are compelled to perform behaviors (such as sleeping, grooming, and discussing private matters) in a secondary territory that we are used to performing in our own primary territories.[293] If we have no lockable cupboard, for example, our usual sense that we can control our possessions is compromised.

The answer is to allow patients personalization and control wherever possible. Lockable cupboards, viewable bulletin boards, and more table space to display pictures, books, and other meaningful possessions are some suggested design changes. An even simpler rule may be to ask staff to respect the way patients arrange small objects within their reach. Some evidence that the creation of primary territories does have a beneficial effect comes from a study in a nursing home.[294] In double-occupancy rooms, visible markers that divided the room into two separate spaces increased residents' self-esteem and sense of adequacy.

As in most situations, however, there are strong pressures against some of these design changes. Some staff

members complain that tables are cumbersome, cupboards take up valuable space, and bulletin boards are expensive. Some staff object to the inefficiency caused by idiosyncratic arrangements of furniture and personal possessions. The issue is whether institutions primarily exist for the welfare of the patients or the staff.[295] Surprisingly often, judging by the arrangements of hospitals and other institutions, the answer is that staff needs come first.

Staff needs are, of course, legitimate. However, too often, patient needs are underserved because their illness, injury, and temporary status reduce their ability to voice their needs in an effective way. Yet, although each patient is temporary, a permanent stream of similar patients with similar needs flows through the hospital; eventually, many of us will be hospital patients. The best solutions to the staff-versus-patient design dilemma will be reached when designers carefully examine both groups' needs and base architectural changes on the costs and benefits to both groups. More changes favoring patient privacy and territoriality over staff efficiency are needed because, to this point, staff needs usually have prevailed.[296]

FIGURE 5–18 Sociofugal (top) and sociopetal (bottom) seating strongly influences social interaction.

When applied to particular design situations, territoriality should be facilitated in the plans wherever it appears to serve the needs of those who will use the space. That is, based on our list of human behavior patterns that are linked to territoriality, designs for territoriality should attempt to reduce aggression, increase control, and promote a sense of order and security. A rather bold conclusion, supported by some research and refuted by none so far, is this: The more that a building's design can provide primary territories for every person who uses it, the better. Environmental designs that creatively include territoriality can significantly improve quality of life.

SUMMARY

PERSONAL SPACE is the dynamic distance and orientation component of interpersonal relations. It has objective (alpha) and experiential (beta) aspects. Territoriality in humans is a pattern of behavior and experience related to the control (usually by nonviolent means such as occupation, law, custom, and personalization) of physical space, objects and ideas. Seven forms of territory are identified; several infringement and defense strategies are employed in jostling for territory. The best way to measure alpha personal space is the disguised stop-distance technique. Simulation methods may be useful for measuring beta personal space. Field experiments and studies are best for studying territorial behavior, but territorial cognitions are best studied by interviews and questionnaires.

Interpersonal space generally grows with age and with interpersonal coldness. Males have larger personal spaces. Psychologically disturbed individuals have more variable personal space. Personal and situational influences interact, so caution must be exercised in predicting interpersonal distance in everyday social transactions. Attraction and cooperation generally lead to smaller interpersonal distance. Stigma and unequal status lead to larger interpersonal distances. When the physical setting is less spacious, larger interpersonal distances are selected. Cultural differences in interpersonal distance exist, but other factors often operate to alter the simple stereotype of contact versus noncontact cultures. Interpersonal distance may be used to influence others. Inferences about others are often drawn on the basis of the interpersonal distance they choose. Close distances may lead to reciprocation or to flight, depending on the quality of the relationship. They may also evoke helping in others, if a person's need is clearly expressed. Closeness in cooperative circumstances and distance in competitive circumstances lead to better performance.

Males are often more territorial than females. Certain arrangements of dwelling exteriors and street plans may enhance residents' territoriality and reduce crime. Ownership, positive social climate, resource competition, social class, and task are social factors that seem to increase territoriality. Behavior related to territoriality is usually passive, but oriented toward controlling space.

Personalization, marking, and status are used more often than physical aggression.

Integrative models of personal space incorporate its functions as a communication medium that protects us from stress by allowing control of stimulation from others in interpersonal encounters. They emphasize the dynamic nature of relationships, the role of cognitive appraisal, and the management of approach-avoidance conflicts. Theories of territoriality focus on its organizing function and evolution.

Personal space and territoriality are important behavioral bases for the humane design of environments. As the costs of construction rise and more of us are crammed closer and closer together, increasing attention must be paid to the arrangement of space. Personal space transactions are omnipresent and crucial to social interaction, yet they are often unplanned for and go unnoticed. At the very least, we can conclude that designers should offer either a variety of seating arrangements or flexible arrangements, so that individuals can find comfortable spaces for interaction. Designers also should incorporate knowledge about territoriality to build better homes, offices, and institutions. The overall goal is to provide building users with territories that allow them as much control as they are capable of responsibly exercising and as the organizational context allows. When this can be accomplished, territory holders will benefit from a greater sense of self-determination, identity, and perhaps even safety.

Suggested Supplementary Readings

Brown, B. B. (1987). Territoriality. In D. Stokols & I. Altman (Eds.), *Handbook of environmental psychology*. New York: Wiley.

Edney, J. J. (1974). Human territoriality. *Psychological Bulletin, 81*, 959-975.

Hayduk, I. A. (1983). Personal space: Where we now stand. *Psychological Bulletin, 94*, 293-335.

Knowles, E. S. (1989). Spatial behavior of individuals and groups. In P. B. Paulus (Ed.), *Psychology of group influence*. (2nd ed.) Hillsdale, NJ: Erlbaum

Sommer, R. (1969). *Personal space: The behavioral basis of design*. Englewood Cliffs, NJ: Prentice-Hall.

Newman, O. (1972). *Defensible space*. New York: Macmillan.

Taylor, R. B. (2002). *Crime prevention through environmental design (CPTED): Yes, no, maybe, unknowable, and all of the above*. In R. B. Bechtel & A. Churchman (Eds.). *Handbook of environmental psychology* (2ⁿᵈ ed.). New York: Wiley.

References

1 Sommer, R. (1969). *Personal space: The behavioral basis of design* (p. 26). Englewood Cliffs, NJ: Prentice-Hall.

2 2. Kaplan, S., & Kaplan, R. (1978). *Humanscape: Environments for people*. North Scituate, MA: Duxbury Press, p. 264.

3 Sommer, R. (1969). *Personal space: The behavioral basis of design* (p. 26). Englewood Cliffs, NJ: Prentice-Hall.

4 Knowles, E. S. (1980). An affiliative conflict theory of personal and group spacial behavior. In P. B. Paulus (Ed.), *Psychology of group influence*. Hillsdale, NJ: Erlbaum.

5 Costa, M. (2012). Territorial behavior in public settings. *Environment and Behavior, 44*, 713-721.

6 Edney, J. J. (1974). Human territoriality. *Psychological Bulletin, 81*, 959-975.

7 Brown, G., Lawrence, T. B., & Robinson, S. L. (2005). Territoriality in organizations. *Academy of Management Review, 30*, 577-594.

8 Pierce, J. L., Kostova, T., & Dirks, K. T. (2003). The state of psychological ownership: Integrating and extending a century of research. *Review of general research. Review of General Psychology, 7*, 84-107.

9 Brown, G. (2009). Claiming a corner at work: Measuring employee territoriality in their workspaces. *Journal of Environmental Psychology, 29*, 44-52.

10 Hall, E. T. (1959). *The silent language*. Garden City, NY: Doubleday.

11 Howard, E. (1920). *Territory in bird life*. London: John Murray.

12 Hediger, H. (1950). *Wild animals in captivity*. London: Butterworth.

13 Hall, E. T. (1959). *The silent language*. Garden City, NY: Doubleday.

14 Patterson, M. (1968). Spatial factors in social interactions. *Human Relations, 21*, 351-361.

15 Hall, E. T. (1966). *The hidden dimension*. Garden City, NY: Doubleday.

16 Hall, E. T. (1966). *The hidden dimension*. Garden City, NY: Doubleday, p. 113.

17 Evans, G. W., & Howard, R. B. (1973). Personal space. *Psychological Bulletin, 80*, 334-344.

18 Hayduk, L. A. (1978). Personal space: An evaluative and orienting overview. *Psychological Bulletin, 85*, 117-134.

19 Gifford, R., & Price, J. (1979). Personal space in nursery school children. *Canadian Journal of Behavioral Science, 11*, 318-326.

20 Gifford, R. (1983). The experience of personal space: Perception of interpersonal distance. *Journal of Nonverbal Behavior, 7*, 170-178.

21 Codol, J. P., Jarymowicz, M., Kaminska-Feldman, M., & Szuster-Zarojewicz, A. (1989). Asymmetry in the estimation of interpersonal distance and identity affirmation. *European Journal of Social Psychology, 19*, 11-22.

22 Kaminska-Feldman, M. (1991). Self-salience and the autocentric versus allocentric asymmetry effect in interpersonal distance rating. *Cahiers de Psychologie Cognitive, 11*, 669-678.

23 Altman, I. (1975). *The environment and social behavior: Privacy, personal space, territoriality and crowding*. Monterey, CA: Brooks/Cole.

24 Fraine, G., Smith, S. G., Zinkiewicz, L., Chapman, R., & Sheehan, M. (2007). At home on the road? Can drivers' relationships with their cars be associated with territoriality? *Journal of Environmental Psychology, 27*, 204-214.

25 Szlemko, W J. (2008). Territorial Markings as a Predictor of Driver Aggression and Road Rage. *Journal of Applied Social Psychology, 38*, 1664-1688.

26 Altman, I. (1975). *The environment and social behavior: Privacy, personal space, territoriality and crowding*. Monterey, CA: Brooks/Cole.

27 Lyman, S. M., & Scott, M. B. (1967). Territoriality: A neglected sociological dimension. *Social Problems, 15*, 235-249.

28 Lyman, S. M., & Scott, M. B. (1967). Territoriality: A neglected sociological dimension. *Social Problems, 15*, 235-249.

29 Brown, G., & Robinson, S. L. (2011). Reactions to territorial infringement. *Organization Science, 22*, 210-224.

30 Ayoko, O. B., Ashkanasy, N. M., & Jehn, K. A. (2009). Workplace territorial behaviors: A conceptual model of the impact of employees' territorial behaviors on conflict and outcomes in diverse teams. In: 22nd Annual IACM Conference. *22nd Annual International Association of Conflict Management Conference*, Kyoto, Japan, (1-29). 15-19 June, 2009.

31 Knapp, M. L. (1978). *Nonverbal communication in human interaction*. New York: Holt, Rinehart, & Winston.

32 Brown, G. (2009). Claiming a corner at work: Measuring employee territoriality in their workspaces. *Journal of Environmental Psychology, 29*, 44-52.

33 Ruback, R. B., Pape, K. D., & Doriot, P. (1989) Waiting for a phone: Intrusion on callers leads to territorial defense. *Social Psychology Quarterly, 52*, 232-241.

34 Ruback, R. B., & Juieng, D. (1997). Territorial defense in parking lots: Retaliation against waiting drivers. *Journal of Applied Social Psychology, 27*, 821-834.

35 Cashdan, E. (1983). Territoriality among human foragers: Ecological models and an application to four Bushman groups. *Current Anthropology, 24*, 47-66.

36 Bailenson, J. N., Blascovich, J., Beall, A. C., & Loomis, J. M. (2003). Interpersonal distance in immersive virtual environments. *Personality and Social Psychology Bulletin, 29*, 819-833.

37 Hess, J. A. (2003). Measuring distance in personal relationships: The relationship distance index. *Personal Relationships, 10*, 197-215.

38 Hayduk, L. A. (1985). Personal space: The conceptual and measurement implications of structural equation models. *Canadian Journal of Behavioral Science, 17*, 140-149.

39 Knowles, E . S. (1980). An affiliative conflict theory of personal and group spacial behavior. In P.B. Paulus, (Ed.), *Psychology of group influence*. Hillsdale, NJ: Erlbaum.

40 Hayduk, L. A. (1985). Personal space: The conceptual and measurement implications of structural equation models. *Canadian Journal of Behavioral Science, 17*, 140-149.

41 Gifford, R., & Sacilotto, P. (1993). Social isolation and personal space: A field study. *Canadian Journal of Behavioral Science, 25*, 165-174.

42 Barnard, W. A., & Bell, P.A. (1982). An unobtrusive apparatus for measuring interpersonal

distances. *Journal of General Psychology,* 107, 85-90.

43 Taylor, R. B., & Lanni, J. C. (1981). Territorial dominance: The influence of the resident advantage in triadic decision making. *Journal of Personality and Social Psychology, 41,* 909-915.

44 Smith, H. W. (1981) Territorial spacing on a beach revisited: A cross-national exploration. *Social Psychology Quarterly, 44,* 132-137.

45 Costa, M. (2012). Territorial Behavior in Public Settings. *Environment and Behavior, 44,* 713-721.

46 Greenbaum, P. E. & Greenbaum, S. D. (1981). Territorial personalization: Group identity and social interaction in a Slavic-American neighborhood. *Environment and Behavior, 13,* 574-589.

47 Sebba, R., & Churchman, A. (1983). Territories and territoriality in the home. *Environment and Behavior, 15,* 191-210.

48 Bell, P. A., Kline, L. M., & Barnard, W. A. (1988). Friendship and freedom of movement as moderators of sex differences in interpersonal distancing. *Journal of Social Psychology, 128,* 305-310.

49 Gifford, R. (1982). Projected interpersonal distances and orientation choices: Personality, sex, and social situation. *Social Psychology Quarterly, 45,* 145-152.

50 Lott, B. S., & Sommer, R. (1967). Seating arrangements and status. *Journal of Personality and Social Psychology, 7,* 90-95.

51 Pellegrini, R. J., & Empey, J. (1970). Interpersonal spatial orientation in dyads. *Journal of Psychology, 76,* 67-70.

52 Barnard, W. A., & Bell, P. A. (1982). An unobtrusive apparatus for measuring interpersonal distances. *Journal of General Psychology,* 107, 85-90.

53 Kuethe, J. L. (1962). Social schemas. *Journal of Abnormal and Social Psychology, 64,* 31-38.

54 Kuethe, J. L., & Weingartner, H. (1964). Male-female schemata of homosexual and non-homosexual penitentiary inmates. *Journal of Personality, 32,* 23-31.

55 Altman, I. (1975). *The environment and social behavior: Privacy, personal space, territoriality and crowding.* Monterey, CA: Brooks/Cole, p. 75.

56 Balogun, S. K. (1991). The influence of sex and religion on personal space among undergraduate students. *Indian Journal of Behaviour, 15,* 13-20.

57 Atsuko, A. (2003). Gender differences in interpersonal distance: From the view point of oppression hypothesis. *Japanese Journal of Experimental Social Psychology, 42,* 201-218.

58 Severy, L. J., Forsyth, D. R., & Wagner, P. J. (1979). A multimethod assessment of personal space development in female and male, black and white children. *Journal of Nonverbal Behavior, 4,* 68-86.

59 Greeno, C. G. (1990). Gender differences in children's proximity to adults. *Dissertation Abstracts International, 50*(11-B), 5345.

60 Hayduk, L. A. (1985). Personal space: The conceptual and measurement implications of structural equation models. *Canadian Journal of Behavioral Science, 17,* 140-149.

61 Castell, R. (1970). Effect of familiar and unfamiliar environments on proximity behavior of young children. *Journal of Experimental Child Psychology, 9,* 342-347.

62 Evans, G. W., & Howard, R. B. (1973). Personal space. *Psychological Bulletin, 80,* 334-344.

63 Tannis, G. H., & Dabbs, J. M. (1975). Sex, setting and personal space: First grade through college. *Sociometry, 38,* 385-394.

64 Aiello, J. R., & Pagan, G. (1982). Development of personal space among Puerto Ricans. *Journal of Nonverbal Behavior, 7,* 59-80.

65 Cook, M. (1970). Experiments on orientation and proxemics, *Human Relations, 23,* 61-76.

66 Mehrabian, A., & Diamond, S. G. (1971). The effects of furniture arrangement, props, and personality on social interaction. *Journal of Personality and Social Psychology, 20,* 18-30.

67 Patterson, M. L., & Holmes, D. S. (1966). Social interaction correlates of the MMPI extroversion-introversion scale. *American Psychologist, 21,* 18-30.

68 Kline, L. M., Bell, P. A., & Babcock, A. M. (1984). Field dependence and interpersonal distance. *Bulletin of the Psychonomic Society, 2,* 421-422.

69 Gifford, R. (1982). Projected interpersonal distances and orientation choices: Personality, sex, and social situation. *Social Psychology Quarterly, 45,* 145-152.

70 Karabenick, S., & Meisels, M. (1972). Effects of performance evaluation on interpersonal distance. *Journal of Personality, 40,* 275-286.

71 Luft, J. (1966). On nonverbal interaction. *Journal of Psychology, 63,* 261-268.

72 Patterson, M. L. (1973). Stability of nonverbal immediacy behaviors. *Journal of Experimental Social Psychology, 9,* 97-109.

73 Weinstein, L. (1968). The mother-child schema, anxiety, and academic achievement in elementary school boys. *Child Development, 39,* 257-264.

74 Andersen, P. A., & Sull, K. K. (1985). Out of touch, out of reach: Tactile predispositions as predictors of interpersonal distance. *Western Journal of Speech Communication, 49,* 57-72.

75 Strube, M. J., & Werner, C. (1984). Personal space claims as a function of interpersonal threat: The mediating role of need for control. *Journal of Nonverbal Behavior, 8,* 195-209.

76 Holland, R. W., Roeder, U. R., Van Baaren, R. B., Brandt, A. C., & Hannover, B. (2004). Don't stand so close to me: The effects of self-construal on interpersonal closeness. *Psychological Science, 15,* 237-242.

77 Sommer, R. (1959). Studies in personal space. *Sociometry, 22,* 247-260.

78 Horowitz, M. J., Duff, D. F., & Stratton, L. O. (1964). Body-buffer zone: Exploration of personal space. *Archives of General Psychology, 11,* 651-656.

79 Srivastava, P., & Mandal, M. K. (1990). Proximal spacing to facial affect expressions in schizophrenia. *Comprehensive Psychiatry, 31,* 119-124.

80 Bar-Haim, Y., Aviezer, O., Berson, Y., & Sagi, A. (2002). Attachment in infancy and personal space regulation in early adolescence. *Attachment & Human Development, 4,* 68-83.

81 Kaitz, M., Bar-Haim, Y., Lehrer, M., & Grossman, E. (2004). Adult attachment style and interpersonal distance. *Attachment & Human Development, 6,* 285-304.

82 Vranic, A. (2003). Personal space in physically abused children. *Environment and Behavior, 35,* 550-565.

83 Kinzel, A. S. (1970). Body buffer zone in violent prisoners. *American Journal of Psychiatry, 127,* 59-64.

84 Eastwood, L. (1985). Personality, intelligence, and personal space among violent and nonviolent delinquents. *Personality and Individual Differences, 6,* 717-723.

85 Carifio, M. S. (1987). Personal space as a function of violence, race, and control. *Dissertation Abstracts International, 47,* 7-B, 3100.

86 Horowitz, M. J. (1968). Spatial behavior and psychopathology. *Journal of Nervous and Mental Diseases, 146,* 24-35.

87 Jones, E. E. (1985). Interpersonal distancing behavior of hearing-impaired vs. normal-hearing children. *Volta Review, 87,* 223-230.

88 Pedersen, J., Livoir-Petersen, M. F., & Schelde, J. T. (1989). An ethological approach to autism: An analysis of visual behavior and interpersonal contact in a child versus adult interaction. *Acta Psychiatrica Scandinavica, 80,* 346-355.

89 Little, K. B. (1965). Personal space. *Journal of Experimental Social Psychology, 1,* 237-247.

90 Willis, F. N. (1966). Initial speaking distance as a function of the speakers' relationship. *Psychonomic Science, 5,* 221-222.

91 Edwards, D. J. (1972). Approaching the unfamiliar: A study of human interaction distances. *Journal of Behavioral Science, 1,* 249-250.

92 Aiello, J. R., & Cooper, R. E. (1972). The use of personal space as a function of social affect. *Proceedings of the Annual Convention of the American Psychological Association, 7,* 207-208.

93 Strayer, J., & Roberts, W. (1997) ͙ial and verbal measures of children's e͙ ͙ ͙s and empathy. *International Journal ͙ ͙ioral Development, 20,* 385-403.

94 Sinha, S. P., & Mukerjee, N. (͙ adjustment and personal spac͙ *Journal of Social Psychology, 130,* 6͙

95 King, M. G. (1966). Interperso͙ in preschool children and avera͙ distance. *Journal of Genetic Psy͙* 109-116.

96 Rosenfeld, H. M. (1965). Effect of an appro͙ seeking induction on interpersonal proximity. *Psychological Reports, 17,* 120-122.

97 Smith, G. H. (1954). Personality scores and personal distance effect. *Journal of Social Psychology, 39,* 37-62.

98 Mandal, M. K., & Maitra, S. (1985). Perception of facial affect and physical proximity. *Perceptual and Motor Skills, 60,* 782.

99 Rivano-Fischer, M. (1984). Interactional space: Invasion as a function of the type of social interaction. *Psychological Research Bulletin, 24,* 15.

100 O'Neal, E. C., Brunault, M. S., Carifio, M. S., Troutwine, R., & Epstein, J. (1980). Effect

of insult upon personal space preferences. *Journal of Nonverbal Behavior, 5,* 56-62.

101 Guardo, C. J., & Meisels, M. (1971). Child-parent spatial patterns under praise and reproof. *Developmental Psychology, 5,* 365.

102 Skorjanc, A. D. (1991). Differences in interpersonal distance among nonoffenders as a function of perceived violence of offenders. *Perceptual and Motor Skills, 73,* 659-662.

103 Aiken, J. (1991). Come closer-stay back: Interpersonal space preferences. *Dissertation Abstracts International, 51*(9-B), 4639.

104 Kleck, R. E., Buck, P. L., Goller, W. C., London, R. S., Pfeiffer, J. R., & Vukcevic, D. P. (1968). Effect of stigmatizing conditions on the use of personal space. *Psychological Reports, 23,* 111-118.

105 Stephens, K. K., & Clark, D. W. (1987). A pilot study on the effect of visible physical stigma on personal space. *Journal of Applied Rehabilitation Counselling, 18,* 52-54.

106 Conigliaro, L., Cullerton, S., Flynn, K. E., & Roeder, S. (1989). Stigmatizing artifacts and their effect on personal space. *Psychological Reports, 65,* 897-898.

107 Wolfgang, J., & Wolfgang, A. (1971). Explanation of attitudes via physical interpersonal distance toward the obese, drug users, homosexuals, police, and other marginal figures. *Journal of Clinical Psychology, 27,* 510-512.

108 Worthington, M. (1974). Personal space as a function of the stigma effect. *Environmental and Behavior, 6,* 289-295.

109 Sommer, R. (1969). *Personal space: The behavioral basis of design* (p. 26). Englewood Cliffs, NJ: Prentice-Hall.

110 Cook, M. (1970). Experiments on orientation and proxemics, *Human Relations, 23,* 61-76.

111 Brodsky, S. L., Hooper, N. E., Tipper, D. G., & Yates, S. B. (1999). Attorney invasion of witness space. *Law and Psychology Review, 23,* 49-68.

112 Tedesco, J. F., & Fromme, D. K. (1974). Cooperation, competition, and personal space. *Sociometry, 37,* 116-121.

113 Rosenfeld, P., Giacalone, R. A., & Kennedy, J. G. (1987). Of status and suits: Personal space invasions in an administrative setting. *Social Behavior and Personality, 15,* 97-99.

114 Lott, B. S., & Sommer, R. (1967). Seating arrangements and status. *Journal of Personality and Social Psychology, 7,* 90-95.

115 Mehrabian, A. (1969). Significance of posture and position in the communication of attitude and status relationships. *Psychological Bulletin, 71,* 359-373.

116 Gifford, R. (1982). Projected interpersonal distances and orientation choices: Personality, sex, and social situation. *Social Psychology Quarterly, 45,* 145-152.

117 Adams, L., & Zuckerman, D. (1991). The effect of lighting conditions on personal space requirements. *Journal of General Psychology, 118,* 335-340.

118 Daves, W. F., & Swaffer, P. W. (1971). Effect of room size on critical interpersonal distance. *Perceptual and Motor Skills, 33,* 926.

119 Tannis, G. H., & Dabbs, J. M. (1975). Sex, setting and personal space: First grade through college. *Sociometry, 38,* 385-394.

120 Little, K. B. (1965). Personal space. *Journal of Experimental Social Psychology, 1,* 237-247.

121 Savinar, J. (1975). The effect of ceiling height on personal space. Man-Environment Systems, 5, 321-324.

122 Cochran, C. D., Hale, W. D., & Hissam, C. P. (1984). Personal space requirements in indoor versus outdoor locations. *Journal of Psychology, 117,* 121-123.

123 Kaya, N., & Erkip, F. (1999). Invasion of personal space under the condition of short-term crowding: A case study on an automatic teller machine. *Journal of Environmental Psychology, 19,* 183-189.

124 Burgess, J. W., & Fordyce, W. K. (1989). Effects of preschool environments on nonverbal social behavior: Toddlers' interpersonal distances to teachers and classmates change with environmental density, classroom design, and parent-child interactions. *Journal of Child Psychology and Psychiatry and Allied Disciplines, 30,* 261-276.

125 Worchel, S. (1986). The influence of contextual variables on interpersonal spacing. *Journal of Nonverbal Behavior, 10,* 320-254.

126 Gifford, R., & Sacilotto, P. (1993). Social isolation and personal space: A field study. *Canadian Journal of Behavioral Science, 25,* 165-174.

127 Summit, J. E., Westfall, S. C., Sommer, R., & Harrison, A. A. (1992). Weightlessness and interaction distance: A simulation of interpersonal contact in outer space. *Environment and Behavior, 24,* 617-633.

128 Hall, E.T. (1959). *The silent language.* Garden City, NY: Doubleday, p. 161-162.

129 Watson, O. M., & Graves, T. D. (1966). Quantitative research in proxemic behavior. *American Anthropologist, 68,* 971-985.

130 Mehrabian, A. (1966). Immediacy: An indicator of attitudes in linguistic communication. *Journal of Personality, 34,* 26-34.

131 Watson, O. M. (1970). *Proxemic behavior: A cross-cultural study.* The Hague: Mouton.

132 Forston, R. F., & Larson, C. U. (1968). The dynamics of space: An experimental study in proxemic behavior among Latin Americans and North Americans. *Journal of Communication, 18,* 109-116.

133 Mazur, A. (1977). Interpersonal spacing on public benches in "contact" and "noncontact" cultures. *Journal of Social Psychology, 101,* 53-58.

134 Shuter, R. (1976). Proxemics and tactility in Latin America. *Journal of Communication, 26,* 46-52.

135 Remland, M. S., Jones, T. S., & Brinkman, H. (1991). Proxemic and haptic behavior in three European countries. *Journal of Nonverbal Behavior, 15,* 215-232.

136 Beaulieu, C. M. J. (2004). Intercultural study of personal space: A case study. *Journal of Applied Social Psychology, 34,* 794-805.

137 Scherer, S. E. (1974). Proxemic behavior of primary school children as a function of their socioeconomic class and subculture. *Journal of Personality and Social Psychology, 29,* 800-805.

138 Jones, S. E., & Aiello, J. R. (1973). Proxemic behavior of black and white first-, third-, and fifth-grade children. *Journal of Personality and Social Psychology, 25,* 21-27.

139 Sanders, J. L., Hakky, U. M., & Brizzolara, M. M. (1985). Personal space amongst Arabs and Americans. *International Journal of Psychology, 20,* 13-17.

140 Hewitt, J., & Alqahtani, M. A. (2003). Differences between Saudi and U.S. students in reaction to same- and mixed-sex intimacy shown by others. *Journal of Social Psychology, 143,* 233-242.

141 Sussman, N. M., & Rosenfeld, H. M. (1982). Influence of culture, language, and sex on conversational distance. *Journal of Personality and Social Psychology, 42,* 66-74.

142 Balogun, S. K. (1991). Personal space as affected by religions of the approaching and approached people. *Indian Journal of Behaviour, 15,* 45-50.

143 Collett, D. (1971). Training Englishmen in the nonverbal behavior of Arabs. *International Journal of Psychology, 6,* 209-215.

144 Hern, W. (1991). Proxemics: The application of theory to conflict arising from antiabortion demonstrations. *Population and Environment: A Journal of Interdisciplinary Studies, 12,* 379-388.

145 Childress, H. (2004). Teenagers, territory and the appropriation of space. *Childhood: A Global Journal of Child Research, 11,* 195-205.

146 Smith, H. W. (1981) Territorial spacing on a beach revisited: A cross-national exploration. *Social Psychology Quarterly, 44,* 132-137.

147 Mercer, G. W., & Benjamin, M. L. (1980). Spatial behavior of university undergraduates in double occupancy residence rooms: An inventory of effects. *Journal of Applied Social Psychology, 2,* 32-44.

148 Sebba, R., & Churchman, A. (1983). Territories and territoriality in the home. *Environment and Behavior, 15,* 191-210.

149 Wollman, N., Kelly, B. M., & Bordens, K. S. (1994). Environmental and intrapersonal predictors of reactions to potential territorial intrusions in the workplace. *Environment and Behavior, 26,* 179-194.

150 Mercer, G. W., & Benjamin, M. L. (1980). Spatial behavior of university undergraduates in double occupancy residence rooms: An inventory of effects. *Journal of Applied Social Psychology, 2,* 32-44.

151 Taylor, R. B., Gottfredson, S. D., & Brower, S. (1981). Territorial cognitions and social climate in urban neighborhoods. *Basic and Applied Social Psychology, 2,* 289-303.

152 Marsh, P., & Collett, P. (1987) The car as a weapon, *Etc., 44,* 146-151.

153 Taylor, R. B. (1988). *Human territorial functioning: An empirical, evolutionary perspective on individual and small group territorial cognitions, behaviors and consequences.* New York: Cambridge University Press.

154 Taylor, R. B. (1988). *Human territorial functioning: An empirical, evolutionary perspective on individual and small group territorial cognitions, behaviors and consequences.* New York: Cambridge University Press.

155 Cashdan, E. (1983). Territoriality among human foragers: Ecological models and an

application to four Bushman groups. *Current Anthropology, 24,* 47-66.

156 Cashdan, E. (1983). Territoriality among human foragers: Ecological models and an application to four Bushman groups. *Current Anthropology, 24,* 47-66.

157 Greenbaum, P. E. & Greenbaum, S. D. (1981). Territorial personalization: Group identity and social interaction in a Slavic-American neighborhood. *Environment and Behavior, 13,* 574-589.

158 Harris, P. B., & Brown, B. B. (1996). The home and identity display: Interpreting resident territoriality from home exteriors. *Journal of Environmental Psychology, 16,* 187-203.

159 Ruback, R. B., & Juieng, D. (1997). Territorial defense in parking lots: Retaliation against waiting drivers. *Journal of Applied Social Psychology, 27,* 821-834.

160 Jacobs, J. (1961) *The death and life of great American cities.* New York: Vintage.

161 Newman, O. (1972). *Defensible space.* New York: Macmillan.

162 Taylor, R. B. (1988). *Human territorial functioning: An empirical, evolutionary perspective on individual and small group territorial cognitions, behaviors and consequences.* New York: Cambridge University Press..

163 Brown, B. B., & Altman, I. (1983). Territoriality, defensible space, and residential burglary: An environmental analysis. *Journal of Environmental Psychology, 3,* 203-220.

164 Minnery, J. R., Lim, B. (2005). Measuring crime prevention through environmental design. *Journal of Architectural and Planning Research, 22,* 330-341.

165 Ley, D., & Cybriwsky, R. (1974) The spatial ecology of stripped cars. *Environment and Behavior, 6,* 53-68.

166 Sommer, R. (1987). Crime and vandalism in university residence halls: A confirmation of defensible space theory. *Journal of Environmental Psychology, 7,* 1-12.

167 Casteel, C., & Peek-Asa, C. (2000). Effectiveness of crime prevention through environmental design (CPTED) in reducing robberies. *American Journal of Preventive Medicine, 18,* 99-115.

168 Minnery, J. R., Lim, B. (2005). Measuring crime prevention through environmental design. *Journal of Architectural and Planning Research, 22,* 330-341.

169 D'Alessio, S., & Stolzenberg, L. (1990). A crime of convenience: The environment and convenience store robbery. *Environment and Behavior, 22,* 255-271.

170 Wise, J. A., & Wise, B. K. (ca. 1985). *Bank interiors and bank robberies: A design approach to environmental security.* Rolling Meadows, IL: Bank Administration Institute.

171 Macdonald, J. E., & Gifford, R. (1989). Territorial cues and defensible space theory: The burglar's point of view. *Journal of Environmental Psychology, 9,* 193-205.

172 Robinson, M. B., & Robinson, C. E. (1997). Environmental characteristics associated with residential burglaries of student apartment complexes. *Environment and Behavior, 29,* 657-675.

173 Ham-Rowbottom, K. A., Gifford, R., & Shaw, K. T. (1999). Defensible space theory and the police: Assessing the vulnerability of residencies to burglary. *Journal of Environmental Psychology, 19,* 117-129.

174 Shaw, K. T., & Gifford, R. (1994). Residents' and burglars' assessment of burglary risk form defensible space cues. *Journal of Environmental Psychology, 14,* 177-194.

175 Brown, B. B., & Bentley, D. L. (1993). Residential burglars judge risk: The role of territoriality. *Journal of Environmental Psychology, 13,* 51-61.

176 Newman, O. (1980). *Community of interest.* New York: Anchor Press/Doubleday.

177 Chang, D. (2011). Social crime or spatial crime? Exploring the effects of social, economical, and spatial factors on burglary rates. *Environment and Behavior, 43,* 26-52.

178 Brown, B. B., & Werner, C. M. (1985). Social cohesiveness, territoriality, and holiday decorations: The influence of cul-de-sacs. *Environment and Behavior, 17,* 539-565.

179 Perkins, D. D., Wandersman, H. H., Rich, R. C. & Taylor, R. B. (1993). The physical environment of street crime: Defensible space, territoriality, and incivilities. *Journal of Environmental Psychology, 13,* 29-49.

180 Minnery, J. R., & Lim, B. (2005). Measuring crime prevention through environmental design. *Journal of Architectural and Planning Research, 22,* 330-341.

181 Smith, H. W. (1981) Territorial spacing on a beach revisited: A cross-national exploration. *Social Psychology Quarterly, 44,* 132-137.

182 Edney, J. J. , & Jordan-Edney, N. L. (1974) Territorial spacing on a beach. *Sociometry, 37,* 92-104.

183 Kaya, N., Weber, M. J. (2003). Territorial behavior in residence halls: A cross-culture study. *Environment and Behavior, 35,* 400-414.

184 Worchel, S., & Lollis, M. (1982). Reactions to territorial contamination as a function of culture. *Personality and Social Psychology Bulletin, 8,* 370-375.

185 Ruback, R. B., & Snow, J. J. (1993). Territoriality and non-conscious racism at water fountains: Intruders and drinkers (Blacks and Whites) are affected by race. *Environment and Behavior, 25,* 250-267.

186 Greenbaum, P. E. & Greenbaum, S. D. (1981). Territorial personalization: Group identity and social interaction in a Slavic-American neighborhood. *Environment and Behavior, 13,* 574-589.

187 Campbell, A. C., Munce, S., & Galea, J. (1982). American gangs and British subcultures: A comparison. *International Journal of Offender Therapy and Comparative Criminology, 26,* 76-89.

188 Shaw, M. E. (1976). *Group dynamics: The psychology of small group behavior.* New York: McGraw-Hill.

189 Sommer, R. (1969). *Personal space: The behavioral basis of design* (p. 26). Englewood Cliffs, NJ: Prentice-Hall.

190 Barash, D. P. (1973). Human ethology: Personal space reiterated. *Environment and Behavior, 5,* 67-73.

191 Young, A. E., & Guile, M. N. (1987). Departure latency to invasion of personal space: Effects of status and sex. *Perceptual and Motor Skills, 64,* 700-702.

192 Lombardo, J. P. (1986). Interaction of sex and sex role in response to violations of preferred seating arrangements. *Sex Roles, 15,* 173-183.

193 Ashton, N. L., Shaw, M. E., & Worsham, A. P. (1980). Affective reactions to interpersonal distances by friends and strangers. *Bulletin of the Psychonomic Society, 15,* 306-308.

194 Rustemli, A. (1988). The effects of personal space invasion on impressions and decisions. *Journal of Psychology, 122,* 113-118.

195 Hewitt, J., & Henley, R. (1987). Sex differences in reaction to spatial invasion. *Perceptual and Motor Skills, 64,* 809-810.

196 Fisher, J. D., & Byrne, D. (1975). Too close for comfort: Sex differences in response to invasions of personal space. *Journal of Personality and Social Psychology, 32,* 15-21.

197 Lane, P. L. (1989). Nurse-client perceptions: The double standard of touch. *Issues in Mental Health Nursing, 10,* 1-13.

198 Cook, M. (1970). Experiments on orientation and proxemics, *Human Relations, 23,* 61-76.

199 O'Connor, B. P., & Gifford, R. (1988). A test among models of nonverbal immediacy reactions: Arousal labeling, discrepancy-arousal, and social cognition. *Journal of Nonverbal Behavior, 12,* 6-33.

200 Knowles, E. S. (1972). Boundaries around social space: Dyadic responses to an invader. *Environment and Behavior, 4,* 437-445.

201 Knowles, E. S., & Brickner, M. A. (1981). Social cohesion effects on spatial cohesion. *Personality and Social Psychology Bulletin, 7,* 309-313.

202 Rivano-Fischer, M. (1984). Interactional space: Invasion as a function of the type of social interaction. *Psychological Research Bulletin, 24,* 15.

203 Middlemist, R. D., Knowles, E. S., & Matter, C. F. (1976). Personal space invasions in the lavatory: Suggestive evidence for arousal. *Journal of Personality and Social Psychology, 33,* 541-546.

204 Mehrabian, A., & Williams, M. (196?). Nonverbal concomitants of perceived and intended persuasiveness. *Journal of Personality and Social Psychology, 13,* 37-58.

205 Albert, S., & Dabbs, J. M., Jr. (1970). Physical distance and persuasion. *Journal of Personality, 15,* 265-270.

206 Burns, T. (1964, October). Nonverbal communication. *Discovery,* 31-35.

207 Patterson, M. L., & Sechrest, L. B. (1970). Interpersonal distance and impression formation. *Journal of Personality, 38,* 161-166.

208 Aiello, J. R., & Thompson, D. E. (1980). When compensation fails: Mediating effects of sex and locus of control at extended interaction distances. *Basic and Applied Social Psychology, 1,* 65-82.

209 Winkel, F. W., Koppelaar, L., & Vrij, A. (1988). Creating suspects in police-citizen encounters: Two studies on personal space and being suspect. *Social Behavior, 3,* 307-318.

210 Kleck, R. (1969). Physical stigma and task oriented interactions. *Human Relations, 22,* 53-60.

211 Goldring, P. (1967). Role of distance and posture in the evaluation of interactions. *Proceedings of the 75th Annual Convention of the American Psychological Association.*

212 Haase, R. F., & Pepper, D. T., Jr. (1972). Nonverbal components of empathic communication. *Journal of Counseling Psychology, 19,* 417-424.

213 Konecni, V. J., Libuser, L., Morton, H., & Ebbesen, E. B. (1975). Effects of a violation of personal space on escape and helping response. *Journal of Experimental Social Psychology, 11,* 288-299.

214 DeBeer-Kelston, K., Mellon, L., & Solomon, L. Z. (1986). Helping behavior as a function of personal space invasion. *Journal of Social Psychology, 126,* 407-409.

215 Baron, R. A., & Bell, P. A. (1976). Physical distance and helping: Some unexpected benefits of "crowding in" on others. *Journal of Applied Social Psychology, 6,* 95-104.

216 Baron, R. A. (1978). Invasions of personal space and helping: Mediating effects of invader's apparent need. *Journal of Experimental Social Psychology, 14,* 304-312.

217 Buller, D. B. (1987). Communication apprehension and reactions to proxemic violations. *Journal of Nonverbal Behavior, 11,* 13-25.

218 Glick, P., DeMorest, J. A., & Hotze, C. A. (1988). Keeping your distance: Group membership, personal space, and requests for small favors. *Journal of Applied Social Psychology, 18,* 315-330.

219 Sommer, R. (1969). *Personal space: The behavioral basis of design* (p. 26). Englewood Cliffs, NJ: Prentice-Hall.

220 Gardin, H., Kaplan, C. J., Firestone, I. J., & Cowan, G. A. (1973). Proxemic effects on cooperation, attitude, and approach-avoidance in prisoner's dilemma game. *Journal of Personality and Social Psychology, 27,* 13-19.

221 Seta, J. J., Paulus, P. B., & Schkade, J. K. (1976). Effects of group size and proximity under cooperative and competitive conditions. *Journal of Personality and Social Psychology, 34,* 47-53.

222 Ayoko, O. B., & Hartel, C. E. J. (2003). The role of space as both a conflict trigger and a conflict control mechanism in culturally heterogeneous workgroups. *Applied Psychology: An International Review, 52,* 383-412.

223 Truscott, J. C., Parmelee, P., & Werner, C. (1977). Plate touching in restaurants: Preliminary observations of a food-related marking behavior in humans. *Personality and Social Psychology Bulletin, 3,* 425-428.

224 Werner, C., Brown, B., & Damron, G. (1981) Territorial marking in a game arcade. *Journal of Personality and Social Psychology, 41,* 1094-1104.

225 Ley, D., & Cybriwsky, R. (1974). Urban graffiti as territorial markers. *Annals of the Association of American Geographers, 64,* 491-505.

226 Brunia, S. & Gosselink-Hartjes, A. (2009). Personalization in non-territorial offices: a study in human need. *Journal of Corporate Real Estate, 11,* 169-182.

227 Becker, F. D. (1973). Study of spatial markers. *Journal of Personality and Social Psychology, 26,* 439-445.

228 Holahan, C. J. (1976). Environmental change in a psychiatric setting: A social systems analyses. *Human Relations, 29,* 153-166.

229 Vinsel, A., Brown, B. B., Altman, L., & Foss, C. (1980) Privacy regulation, territorial displays and effectiveness of individual functioning. *Journal of Personality and Social Psychology, 39,* 1104-1115.

230 Edney, J. J. (1976). The psychological role of property rights in human behavior. *Environment and Planning: A, 8,* 811-822.

231 Edney, J. J. (1972). Property, possession and permanence: A field study in human territoriality. *Journal of Applied Social Psychology, 2,* 275-282.

232 Ruback, R. B., Pape, K. D., & Doriot, P. (1989) Waiting for a phone: Intrusion on callers leads to territorial defense. *Social Psychology Quarterly, 52,* 232-241.

233 Ruback, B. R., & Kohli, N. (2005). Territoriality at the Magh Mela: The effects of organizational factors and intruder characteristics. *Environment and Behavior, 37,* 178-200.

234 Taylor, R. B., & Brooks, D. K. (1980). Temporary territories: Responses to intrusions in a public setting. *Population and Environment, 3,* 135-145.

235 Ley, D., & Cybriwsky, R. (1974). Urban graffiti as territorial markers. *Annals of the Association of American Geographers, 64,* 491-505.

236 Brown, B. B., & Harris, P. B. (1989). Residential burglary victimization: Reactions to the invasion of a primary territory. *Journal of Environmental Psychology, 9,* 119-132.

237 Edney, J. J. Territoriality and control: A field experiment. *Journal of Personality and Social Psychology, 6,* 1108-1115.

238 Esser A. H. (1968). Dominance hierarchy and clinical course of psychiatrically hospitalized boys. *Child Development, 39,* 147-157.

239 Esser, A. H., Chamberlain, A. S., Chapple, E. D., & Kline, N. S. (1965) Territoriality of patients on a research ward. In J. Wortis (Ed.), *Recent advances in biological psychiatry.* New York: Plenum.

240 Sundstrom, E., & Altman, I. (1974). Field study of territorial behavior and dominance. *Journal of Personality and Social Psychology, 30,* 115-124.

241 Taylor, R. B., & Lanni, J. C. (1981). Territorial dominance: The influence of the resident advantage in triadic decision making. *Journal of Personality and Social Psychology, 41,* 909-915.

242 Austin, W. T. (1982). Portrait of a courtroom: Social and ecological impressions of the adversary process. *Criminal Justice and Behavior, 9,* 286-302.

243 Harris, P. B., & McAndrew, F. T. (1986) Territoriality and compliance: The influence of gender and location on willingness to sign petitions. *Journal of Social Psychology, 126,* 657-662.

244 Schwartz, B., & Barsky, S. F. (1977). The home advantage. *Social Forces, 55,* 641-661.

245 Cornuneya, K. S., & Carron, A. V. (1992). The home advantage in sport competition: A literature review. *Journal of Sport and Exercise Psychology, 14,* 13-27.

246 Acker, J. C. (1997). Location variations in professional football. *Journal of Sport Behavior, 20,* 247-259.

247 Agnew, G. A., & Carron, A. V. (1994). Crowd effects and the home advantage. *International Journal of Sport Psychology, 25,* 53-62.

248 Greer, D. L. (1983). Spectator booing and the home advantage: A study of social influence in the basketball arena. *Social Psychology Quarterly, 46,* 252-261.

249 Lehman, D. R., & Reifman, A. (1987). Spectator influence on basketball officiating. *Journal of Social Psychology 127,* 673-675.

250 Nevill, A. M., Balmer, N. J., & Williams, A. M. (2002). The influence of crowd noise and experience upon refereeing decisions in football. *Psychology of Sport and Exercise, 3,* 261-272.

251 Neave, N., & Wolfson, S. (2003). Testosterone, territoriality, and the 'home advantage'. *Physiology & Behavior, 78,* 269-275.

252 Baumeister, R. F. (1985). The championship choke. *Psychology Today, 19,* 48-52.

253 James, B. (1984). A few words about the home field advantage. In B. James (Ed.), *The Bill James baseball abstract 1984.* New York: Ballantine.

254 Gifford, R. (1976) Environmental numbness in the classroom. *Journal of Experimental Education, 44,* 4-7.

255 Taylor, R. B. & Stough, R. R. (1978). Territorial cognition: Assessing Altman's typology. *Journal of Personality and Social Psychology, 36,* 418-423.

256 Schiavo, R. S., Kobashi, K. C. Quinn, C., Sefcsik, A, & Synn, L. (1990). *Territorial influences on permeability of group spatial boundaries.* Paper presented at the annual meetings of the American Psychological Association, Boston.

257 Baxter, J. C. (1970). Interpersonal spacing in natural settings. *Sociometry, 33,* 444-456.

258 Duke, M. P., & Nowicki, S., Jr. (1972). A new measure and social learning model for interpersonal distance. *Journal of Experimental Research in Personality, 6,* 119-132.

259 Brown, S. R., Pipp, S., Martz, C., Waring. R. (1993). Connection and separation in the mother-infant dyad: Patterns of touch and use of interpersonal space. *Infant Mental Health Journal, 14,* 317-329.

260 Lomranz, J., Shapira, A., Choresh, N., & Gilat, Y. (1975). Children's personal space as a function of age and sex. *Developmental Psychology, 11,* 541-545.

261 Gifford, R., & Price, J. (1979). Personal space in nursery school children. *Canadian Journal of Behavioral Science, 11,* 318-326.

262 Isaacs, L. W., & Bearison, D. J. (1986). The development of children's prejudice against the aged. *International Journal of Aging and Human Development, 23,* 175-194.

263 Argyle, M., & Dean, J. (1965). Eye-contact, distance, and affiliation. *Sociometry, 28,* 289-304.

264 Okken, V., van Rompay, T., & Pruyn, A. (2013). Room to move: On spatial constraints and self-disclosure during intimate conversations. *Environment and Behavior, 45,* 737-760.

265 Patterson, M. L. (1973). Stability of nonverbal immediacy behaviors. *Journal of Experimental Social Psychology, 9,* 97-109.

266 Ajdukovic, D. (1988). A contribution of the methodology of personal space research. *Psychologische Beitrage, 30,* 198-208.

267 Rosenfeld, H. M., Breck, B. E., Smith, S. H., & Kehoe, S. (1984). Intimacy mediators of the proximity-gaze compensation effect: Movement, conversational role, acquaintance, and gender. *Journal of Nonverbal Behavior, 8,* 235-249.

268 Cappella, J. N., & Green, J. O. (1984). The effects of distance and individual differences in arousability on nonverbal involvement: A test of discrepancy-arousal theory. *Journal of Nonverbal Behavior, 8,* 259-286.

269 Gifford, R. (1988). Light, decor, arousal, comfort, and communication. *Journal of Environmental Psychology, 8,* 177-189.

270 Albas, D. C., & Albas, C. A. (1989). Meaning in context: The impact of eye contact and perception of threat on proximity. *Journal of Social Psychology, 129,* 525-531.

271 Hale, J. L., & Burgoon, J. K. (1984). Models of reactions to changes in nonverbal intimacy. *Journal of Nonverbal Behavior, 8,* 287-314.

272 Altman, I., & Taylor, D. A. (1973). *Social penetration: The development of interpersonal relationships.* New York: Holt, Rinehart and Winston.

273 Sundstrom, E., & Altman, I. (1976). Interpersonal relationships and personal space: Research review and theoretical model. *Human Ecology, 4,* 47-67.

274 Aiello, J. R. (1977). A further look at equilibrium theory: Visual interaction as a function of interpersonal distance. *Environmental Psychology and Nonverbal Behavior, 1,* 122-140.

275 Aiello, J. R., Thompson, D. E., & Baum, A. (1981). The symbiotic relationship between social psychology and environmental psychology: Implications from crowding, personal space, and intimacy regulation research. In J. H. Harvey (Ed.), *Cognition, social behavior, and the environment.* Hillsdale, NJ: Erlbaum.

276 Thompson, D. E., Aiello, J. R., & Epstein, Y. (1979). Interpersonal distance preferences. *Journal of Nonverbal Behavior, 4,* 113-118.

277 Aiello, J. R. (1972). A test of equilibrium theory: Visual interaction in relation to orientation, distance and sex of interactants. *Psychonomic Science, 27,* 335-336.

278 Aiello, J. R. (1977). A further look at equilibrium theory: Visual interaction as a function of interpersonal distance. *Environmental Psychology and Nonverbal Behavior, 1,* 122-140.

279 Aiello, J. R., & Thompson, D. E. (1980). When compensation fails: Mediating effects of sex and locus of control at extended interaction distances. *Basic and Applied Social Psychology, 1,* 65-82.

280 Knowles, E. S. (1980). An affiliative conflict theory of personal and group spatial behavior. In P. B. Paulus (Ed.) *Psychology of group influence.* Hillsdale, NJ: Erlbaum.

281 Knowles, E. S. (1989). Spatial behavior of individuals and groups. In P. B. Paulus (Ed.) *Psychology of group influence.* (2nd ed.) Hillsdale, NJ: Erlbaum.

282 Ardrey, R. (1966). *The territorial imperative.* New York: Atheneum.

283 Taylor, R. B. (1988). *Human territorial functioning: An empirical, evolutionary perspective on individual and small group territorial cognitions, behaviors and consequences.* New York: Cambridge University Press.

284 Edney, J. J. (1976). The psychological role of property rights in human behavior. *Environment and Planning: A, 8,* 811-822.

285 Sommer, R. (1974). Looking back at personal space. In J. Lang, C. Burnette, W. Moleski, & D. Vachon (Eds.) *Designing for human behavior: Architecture and behavioral sciences.* Stroudsburg, PA: Dowden, Hutchinson and Ross, p. 205-207.

286 Sommer, R. (2002). Personal space in a digital age. In R. B. Bechtel & A. Churchman (Eds.). *Handbook of environmental psychology.* (pp. 647-660). Hoboken, NJ: Wiley.

287 Osmond, H. (1957). Function as the basis of psychiatric ward design. *Mental Hospitals, 8,* 23-30.

288 Gifford, R. (1981). Sociability: Traits, settings, and interactions. *Journal of Personality and Social Psychology, 41,* 340-347.

289 Gifford, R., & Gallagher, T. M. B. (1985). Sociability: Personality, social context, and physical setting. *Journal of Personality and Social Psychology, 48,* 1015-1023.

290 Winick, C., & Holt, H. (1961). Seating position as nonverbal communication in group analysis. *Psychiatry, 24,* 171-182.

291 Goodman, P. (1964). Seating arrangements: An elementary lecture in functional planning. *Utopian essays and practical proposals.* New York: Random House/Alfred A. Knopf.

292 Je, H. (1987). Urban residential streets: A study of street types and their territorial performances. *Dissertation Abstracts International, 47(7-A),* 23-46.

293 Shumaker, S. A., & Reizenstein, J. E. (1982). Environmental factors affecting inpatient stress in acute care hospitals. In G. W. Evans (Ed.), *Environmental stress.* New York: Cambridge University Press.

294 Nelson, M. N., & Paluck, R. J. (1980) Territorial markings, self-concept, and the mental status of the institutionalized elderly. *Gerontologist 20,* 96-98.

295 Sommer, R. (1969). *Personal space: The behavioral basis of design.* Englewood Cliffs, NJ: Prentice-Hall.

296 Shumaker, S. A., & Reizenstein, J. E. (1982). Environmental factors affecting inpatient stress in acute care hospitals. In G. W. Evans (Ed.), *Environmental stress.* New York: Cambridge University Press.

0 Latane, B. (1981). The psychology of social impact. *American Psychologist, 36,* 343-356.

301 Manning, R. E. (1985). Crowding norms in backcountry settings: A review and synthesis. *Journal of Leisure Research, 17,* 75-89.

302 Barker, R. G. (1968). *Ecological psychology: Concepts and methods for studying the environment of human behavior.* Stanford, CA: Stanford University Press.

303 Wicker, A. W. (1979). *An introduction to ecological psychology.* Monterey, CA: Brooks/Cole.

304 Fischer, C. S. (1976). *The urban experience.* New York: Harcourt Brace Jovanovich.

305 Schmidt, D. E., & Keating, J. P. (1979). Human crowding and personal control: An integration of the research. *Psychological Bulletin, 86,* 680-700.

306 Stokols, D. (1972). On the distinction between density and crowding: Some implications for further research. *Psychological Review, 79,* 275-278.

307 Schopler, J., & Stockdale, J. E. (1977). An interference analysis of crowding. *Environmental Psychology and Nonverbal Behavior, 1,* 81-88.

308 Proshansky, H. M., Ittelson, W. H., & Rivlin, L. G. (1976). Freedom of choice and behavior in a physical setting. In H. M. Proshansky, W. H. Ittelson, & L. G. Rivlin (Eds.), *Environmental psychology: People and their physical settings.* New York: Holt, Rinehart and Winston.

309 Cohen, S. (1978). Environmental load and the allocation of attention. In A. Baum, J. E. Singer, & S. Valins (Eds.), *Advances in environmental psychology* (Vol. 1). Hillsdale, NJ: Erlbaum.

310 Milgram, S. (1970). The experience of living in cities. *Science, 167,* 1461-1468.

311 Wirth, L. (1938). Urbanism as a way of life. *American Journal of Psychology, 44,* 9-14.

312 Simmel, G. (1957). The metropolis and mental life. In P. K. Hatt & A. J. Reiss, Jr. (Eds.), *Cities and societies: The revised reader in urban sociology.* New York: Free Press.

313 Schmidt, D. E., & Keating, J. P. (1979). Human crowding and personal control: An integration of the research. *Psychological Bulletin, 86,* 680-700.

314 Helson, H. (1947). Adaptation level as a frame of reference for prediction of psychophysical data. *American Journal of Psychology, 60,* 1-29.

315 Cox, V. C., Paulus, P. B., & McCain, G. (1984). Prison crowding research: The relevance of prison housing standards and a general approach regarding crowding phenomena. *American Psychologist, 39,* 1148-1160.

316 Bowerman, W. R. (1973). Ambulatory velocity in crowded and uncrowded conditions. *Perceptual and Motor Skills, 36,* 107-111.

317 Baron, R. M., & Rodin, J. (1978). Personal control as a mediator of crowding. In A. Baum, J. E. Singer, & S. Valins (Eds.), *Advances in environmental psychology,* (Vol. 1). Hillsdale, NJ: Erlbaum.

318 Brehm, J. W. (1966). *A theory of psychological reactance.* New York: Academic Press.

319 Milgram, S. (1970). The experience of living in cities. *Science, 167,* 1461-1468.

320 Margulis, S. T. (2003). On the status and contribution of Westin's and Altman's theories of privacy. *Journal of Social Issues, 59,* 411-429.

321 Foddy, W. H., & Finighan, W. R. (1980). The concept of privacy from a symbolic interaction perspective. *Journal for the Theory of Social Behavior, 10,* 1-17.

322 Hammitt, W. E. (2000). The relation between being away and privacy in urban forest recreation environments. *Environment and Behavior, 32,* 521-540.

323 Altman, I. (1975). *The environment and social behavior: Privacy, personal space, territoriality and crowding.* Monterey, CA: Brooks/Cole.

324 Altman, I. (1977). Privacy regulation: Culturally universal or culturally specific? *Journal of Social Issues, 33,* 66-84.

325 Altman, I., Vinsel, A., & Brown, B. B. (1981). Dialectic conceptions in social psychology: An application to social penetration and privacy regulation. *Advances in Experimental Social Psychology, 14,* 107-160.

326 Foddy, W. H. (1984). A critical evaluation of Altman's definition of privacy as a dialectical process. *Journal for the Theory of Social Behavior, 14,* 297-307.

327 Margulis, S. T. (1977). Conceptions of privacy: Current status and next steps. *The Journal of Social Issues, 33,* 5-21.

328 Foddy, W. H. (1984). A critical evaluation of Altman's definition of privacy as a dialectical process. *Journal for the Theory of Social Behavior, 14,* 297-307.

329 Altman, I., Vinsel, A., & Brown, B. B. (1981). Dialectic conceptions in social psychology: An application to social penetration and privacy regulation. *Advances in Experimental Social Psychology, 14,* 107-160.

330 Laufer, R. S., & Wolfe, M. (1977). Privacy as a concept and a social issue: A multidimensional development theory. *Journal of Social Issues, 33,* 22-42.

331 Melton, G. B. (1983). Toward "personhood" for adolescents: Autonomy and privacy as values in public policy. *American Psychologist, 38,* 99-103.

332 Sundstrom, E. (1986). *Workplaces: The psychology of the physical environment in offices and factories.* (pp. 309-311). New York: Cambridge.

333 Archea, J. (1977). The place of architectural factors in behavioral theories of privacy. *Journal of Social Issues, 33,* 116-137.

334 Pastalan, L. A. (1970). Privacy as an expression of human territoriality. In L. A. Pastalan & D. H. Carson (Eds.), *Spatial behavior of older people.* Ann Arbor: University of Michigan Press.

335 Taylor, R. B., & Ferguson, G. (1980). Solitude and intimacy: Linking territoriality and privacy experiences. *Journal of Nonverbal Behavior, 4,* 227-239.

336 Edney, J. J., & Buda, M. A. (1976). Distinguishing territoriality and privacy: Two studies. *Human Ecology, 4,* 283-296.

337 Iwata, O. (1980). Territoriality orientation, privacy orientation and locus of control as determinants of the perception of crowding. *Japanese Psychological Research, 22,* 13-21.

338 Kupritz, V. W. (2000). Privacy management at work: A conceptual model. *Journal of Architectural and Planning Research, 17,* 47-63.

339 Freedman, J. L. (1979). Current status of work on crowding and suggestions for housing design. In J. R. Aiello & A. Baum (Eds.), *Residential crowding and design.* New York: Plenum.

340 Baum, A., & Davis, G. E. (1980). Reducing the stress of high-density living: An architectural intervention. *Journal of Personality and Social Psychology, 38,* 471-481.

341 Evans, G. W. (1979). Design implications of spatial research. In J. R. Aiello & A. Baum, *Residential crowding and design.* New York: Plenum.

342 Schaeffer, M. A., Baum, A., Paulus, P. B., & Gaes, G. G. (1988). Architecturally mediated effects of social density in prison. *Environment and Behavior, 20,* 3-19.

343 Zeisel, J. (1975). *Sociology and architectural design.* New York: Russell Sage Foundation.

344 Vischer, J. C. (1986). The complexity of designing for social mix: An evaluation of site-planning principles. *Journal of Architectural and Planning Research, 3,* 15-31.

345 Wineman, J. D. (1982). The office environment as a source of stress. In G. W. Evans (Ed.), *Environmental stress.* New York: Cambridge University Press.

346 Klitzman, S., & Stellman, J. (1989). The impact of the physical environment on the psychological well-being of office workers. *Social Science and Medicine, 29,* 733-742.

347 Becker, F. D. (1981). *Workspace: Creating environments in organizations.* New York: Praeger.

348 Farrenkopf, T., & Roth, V. (1980). The university faculty office as an environment. *Environment and Behavior, 12,* 467-477.

349 Justa, F. C., & Golan, M. B. (1977). Office design: Is privacy still a problem? *Journal of Architectural Research, 6,* 5-12.

350 Block, L. K., & Stokes, G. S. (1989). Performance and satisfaction in private versus nonprivate working settings. *Environment and Behavior, 21,* 277-297.

351 Kupritz, V. (2003). Accommodating privacy to facilitate new ways of working. *Journal of Architectural and Planning Research, 20,* 122-135.

352 Haans, A., Kaiser, F. G., & de Kort, Y. A. W. (2007). Privacy needs in office environments: Development of two behavior-based scales. *European Psychologist, 12,* 93-102.

353 Cangelosi, V. E., & Lemoine, L. F. (1988). Effects of open versus closed physical environment on employee perception and attitude. *Social Behavior and Personality, 16,* 71-77.

354 Lee, Y. S. (2010). Office layout affecting privacy, interaction, and acoustic quality in LEED-certified buildings. *Building and Environment, 45,* 1594-1600.

355 Tripathi, N. (2002). Seating preference and seat placement as indicators of privacy preference. *Psychological Studies, 47,* 129-138.

356 Ng, C. F., & Gifford, R. (1984). *Speech communication in the office: The effects of background sound level and conversational privacy.* Unpublished manuscript.

CHAPTER 7:

Residential Environmental Psychology

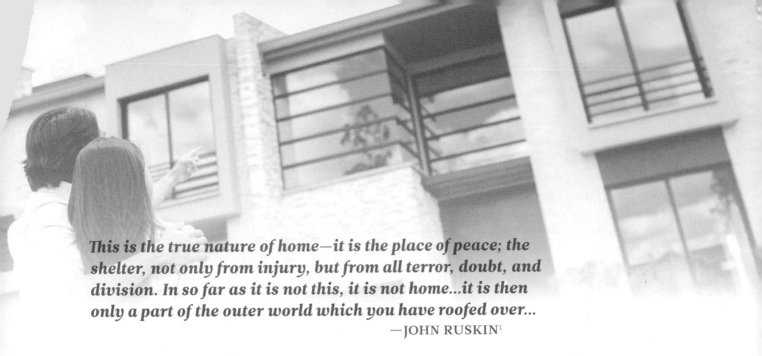

This is the true nature of home—it is the place of peace; the shelter, not only from injury, but from all terror, doubt, and division. In so far as it is not this, it is not home...it is then only a part of the outer world which you have roofed over...

—JOHN RUSKIN[1]

TOM WANDERED AIMLESSLY THROUGH HIS GRANDFATHER'S BIG OLD HOUSE. *He had spent so many childhood hours happily lost in its nooks, playing on the wonderfully smooth worn mahogany stairs and gazing at the titles of the heavy books on the shelves. His grandfather, weakening but still of sound mind, had just announced that, after his death, Tom would inherit the house.*

Tom loved its walls, the rooms, the pictures, the steep roof. Unfortunately, its formerly tranquil semi-rural neighborhood had been overtaken by the city. The house, which properly belonged on a small farm, now was stuck only a block from a busy six-lane road. The ills of the modern city lay just outside the door to the house that belonged to another, more peaceful century. The windows had been broken, and his grandfather had been the victim of three recent break-ins and one mugging.

Tom longed to show the house to Jane, but at the same time he was uncertain whether she would like it. For one thing, the house had been flooded several times in its lifetime; each time, Tom's grandparents had lost heavily. As he was about to abandon his dream of living with Jane in the old place, he remembered a few good points. It was right on a bus line, close to downtown shopping and a great old park, and the property taxes were low.

Finally, he wandered through the spacious rooms, the beautiful woodwork his grandfather had spent years carving, and the high ceilings that made you feel you were in a real house instead of one of those modern cracker boxes. Full of these thoughts, Tom set off to tell Jane of his coming inheritance—his new old home.

HOME IS THE MOST IMPORTANT PLACE IN MOST LIVES. This importance gives it great potential for helping people thrive—or for threatening their very survival. In this chapter, the focus is on the environmental psychology of the residence. The word *home* is used to refer to small spaces, such as one's room, house, apartment or, in the next chapter, to broader areas such as the neighborhood, town, district, or city.

Home usually is the most important refuge from the stresses of work, school, and the street life, and is a major component of life satisfaction.[2] Unfortunately, many people live in residences that do not provide adequate protection and re-juvenation, or have no home at all. When this primary territory does not serve one's basic needs, it can become more hellish than the secondary and public territories we left for the peace of home.

We begin with a definition of home and then explore what makes residences satisfactory or preferable. Next, the way we manage space in the home for work and relaxation is examined, as is the connection between home and self-identity. Then, the positive and negative consequences of living in different residences are considered. Finally, two examples of the application of environmental psychology to the design of homes are offered.

A HOUSE IS NOT A HOME. A house (or apartment, condo, tipi or, in general, any residence) is a physical structure. Home is the rich set of evolving cultural, demographic, and psychological meanings that people attach to that physical structure.[3] Thus, despite real estate advertisements to the contrary, you cannot buy a home. You can buy or rent a residence and, with luck, time, and effort, turn it into a home. Thus, two definitions are needed—one for residence and one for home.

What Is a Residence?

ALTHOUGH THERE ARE MANY FORMS OF RESIDENCES, their common element is that they are physical structures. Instead of trying to list every type of residence (e.g., long-

FIGURE 7–1 Residences take many forms and influence many of our important interactions.

house, farmhouse, penthouse), which would lead to a very long list—particularly if we consider all the variations in housing around the world—a preferable approach is to discover a small number of key dimensions along which every type of residence may be located (see Figure 7-1). Adopting such an approach, Irwin Altman and his colleagues characterized residences along five dimensions: permanent versus temporary, differentiated versus homogeneous, communal versus noncommunal, identity versus communality, and openness versus closedness.[4,5]

1. Residences vary from **permanent** to **temporary**. In industrialized countries, residents usually have permanent dwellings, although apparently this situation is not entirely satisfactory because many householders also maintain temporary residences such as cabins, cottages, and recreational vehicles. In some less-industrialized countries, residents move frequently and often construct temporary homes in new or seasonal places.

2. Residences vary from **differentiated** to **homogeneous**. This refers to the separation, or lack of it, in the functions of rooms. A highly differentiated residence has many rooms, each of which houses a specific activity; in a homogeneous residence nearly any activity may occur in nearly any room. Differentiation, of course, is partly a function of wealth. Poor people rarely have a highly differentiated residence. Little research on the effects of differentiation is available, although presumably it is an important environmental influence on our daily behavior. For example, privacy and territoriality, and perhaps crowding, must be strongly affected by the degree of differentiation in our residences.

3. Residences vary in **communality** and **noncommunality**. This is the degree to which nuclear families live together or in different residences. In many Eastern cultures, several generations of a family live in one household. In some African and Native American cultures, numerous unrelated families live in one residence.

4. Residences vary in **identity** versus **communality**. They often reflect the personal touches of their occupants. *Identity* is the extent to which a residence depicts the unique interests and needs of its residents. *Communality* (the same word as above, but with a different meaning here) is the extent to

which a residence reflects the common stereotype of a home in that culture. A tipi on a suburban lot in North America would be low on communality. The same tipi would be high on communality at a pow-wow on the open plains of the central United States.

5. Residences vary in their **openness** versus **closedness** to outsiders. In some places, houses typically are surrounded by walls or hedges; in others they are not. Residents may be welcoming or cool or even hostile to casual visitors. Thus, dwellings and their occupants signal willingness or unwillingness to interact with neighbors or other visitors. This varies both within and between cultures.

A fascinating panorama of residential variation in these five dimensions may be observed across cultures.[6,7,8] Variation also occurs within any single culture. Yet the psychological effects of these variations are still largely unknown. Environmental psychologists cannot ordinarily conduct field experiments by placing residents randomly in different kinds of homes, so we may never fully understand the effects of different home types. We can and should, however, conduct studies to monitor what happens when individuals move from one type of home to another, such as from the family home to a dormitory or nursing home.

In cultures where the ideal residence probably is permanent, differentiated, and noncommunal, many residents nevertheless reside in homes that are temporary (dormitories, apartments, rented houses), homogeneous (a residence with space for the separation of dining from cooking, or hobbies from entertaining, or laundering from automobile storage, is unaffordable), and communal (roommates are necessary to pay the rent).

Again, What Is Home?

HOME IS A SET OF MEANINGS. Its earliest meaning probably was the village or community of one's origin; not until the sixteenth or seventeenth century did it refer to one's residence.[9] In some barrios in Venezuela, one's dwelling is not distinguished from one's surroundings, even today.[10] Home is so different from the residence that some people may not even live at home, although they always live in their residences. Home, truly, is where the heart is.

Home, like residence, may be described with a set of key dimensions. The six dimensions of home that follow are such that one end is *home* and the other end is *not-a-home* (as opposed to the residence dimensions, both ends of which describe residences, but of different kinds). Certainly not everyone who lives in a residence lives in a home, as the following dimensions of home will make clear. These dimensions of home are haven, order, identity, and connectedness, warmth, and physical suitability.[11-14]

1. Home is a **haven** that surrounds us with privacy, security, refuge, and protection from the slings and arrows of life outside it.

2. Home helps us to know our place in the world. It is a center from which we venture and return; it is one way that we **order** our existence in the world. This ordering is not only spatial, but temporal; home is strongly related to our sense of continuity: childhood experiences, leaving and returning, and the patterning of our daily lives. We learn much about home from trips *away* from home, through contrast.[15] People who commute enough that they need a second residence have a difficult time managing their sense of home.[16]

3. Home is central to our **identity**. As social creatures, home includes for us a sense of family or kinship, ethnic belonging, and socioeconomic status. Home is thus an important part of who we are. Through self-expression and personalization, the home comes to resemble or represent our selves. Home is a symbol of self,[17] "the articulation and confirmation of our very existence."[18] We give the physical structure identity as we transform it from a mere residence into a home, but we also derive our own identity in part *from* that home. Although living rooms, for example, are often portrayed as places for "showing off" to visitors, they are also arranged and decorated to reflect the residents' own identities.[19]

4. Through order and identity, home means **connectedness**,[20] the patterns of spatial and temporal order help us feel connected to certain people, to the place, to the past, and to the future. We feel part of a family or group, and part of a culture.

5. Home is **warmth**. This grows out of the preceding qualities, but goes beyond them. This warmth is like that of the hearth, but is symbolic and interpersonal. That being said, researchers in Hong Kong found that of four building qualities (thermal comfort, air cleanliness, odor, and noise), that thermal comfort was the most important to residents.[21]

6. Home is **physically suitable**. Obviously, this means more than the material physical aspects of the house. It means the physical form and structure of the house matches our psychological needs. Naturally, though, people vary. For example, members of pro-environmental organizations and wildlife students prefer more natural landscapes around their residences, while economics and social science students prefer more neat, well-kept landscapes around theirs.[22]

If we are fortunate to have a place that provides haven, order, identity, connectedness, warmth, and physical suitability, then our residence is very likely to be home. It probably has great personal and social meaning for us, and we likely also experience belongingness, happiness, self-expression, and good relationships within it.[23] To the extent that our residence does *not* have these meanings for us, we are homeless—even if we live in a mansion.

Houselessness and Homelessness

WE USUALLY THINK OF A HOMELESS PERSON as someone without a place to live, a houseless person. However, a person can have a residence and yet be homeless: the place where the person lives has little or no meaning, provides no sense of security, order, identity, connectedness, warmth, or suitability (see Figure 7-2). Some houseless persons have homes but are separated from them. Sometimes this is by choice (e.g., a person prefers the street life or the roaming life for a while); sometimes it is not (e.g., the person was forced away from home, but that residence still has all

FIGURE 7–2 Houselessness and homelessness are major problems in many cities.

the meanings of home). In short, homelessness is not necessarily the same as houselessness. Certainly some of the least fortunate people in the world are those who are both houseless and homeless.

The houseless person who has become homeless probably does so in stages.[24] In the first stage, family support is lost. The person gradually loses the opportunity to rely on family for essential emotional or financial resources. In the second stage, the support of friends from home is lost. Some key elements of home can be provided by friends during or after the loss of family, but once both family and friends are gone, houselessness is much closer to homelessness. In the third stage, the person loses the support of the home community. Some social benefits require an address or roots or connection to others in the community. Without these ties, financial or other supports from the community (even such items as the privilege of owning a library card) may be lost.

Humane solutions to the problem of homelessness must focus on the provision of both housing and support. Merely offering a place to sleep in a large, anonymous shelter is inadequate—so is merely providing hot lunches or emergency clothing allowances. When homeless people in shelters feel a greater loss of control, perhaps from having others both serve them and make the rules, they are more likely to give up looking for a way out of their homelessness.[25] The homeless need an integrated plan aimed at the restoration of both housing and support. One city generously funded a five-step program that offers:

- Basic services such as food, clothing, and showers
- Physical and mental health care
- Shelter
- Employment (including training and transportation)
- Housing that is more permanent than shelters[26]

Probably some people will always be homeless, but perhaps programs like this one can reduce the number almost to those persons who *choose* to be homeless.

This raises the question of choice. Some persons choose houselessness, at least over the shelters that most cities provide. Shelters can be crowded, noisy, lack privacy, and sometimes spread disease; some use them anyway, and some do not. A study of the homeless in Phoenix found that those who "sleep rough" (choose not to use a shelter) are more likely to have experienced court-ordered

psychiatric treatment, consume larger quantities of alcohol more regularly, be Native American, and more frequently work as day laborers than the homeless who use shelters.[27]

Measuring Home

HOW CAN A RESIDENCE OR A HOME BE MEASURED? In the case of a residence, one approach would be to classify it on each of the five physical structure-and-use dimensions used above in the definition of residence (how differentiated versus homogeneous is its interior, how communal are the living arrangements, etc.).

A second approach would be financial: What is the monetary value of the dwelling? Trained real estate assessors can reliably estimate the monetary value of houses.[28]

A third might be a lengthy objective listing of its attributes, such as its age, architectural style, size, number of rooms, etc., such as one finds in a real estate advertisement.

A fourth approach has been to measure the *quality* of a residence for a particular purpose. One such purpose is child development. Several scales have been created to assess the quality of a residence for children.[29-33] These scales typically measure both the physical environment of the residence (e.g., its cleanliness, size, or form) and its social environment (e.g., positiveness of parents' vocal tone; number of stories read). Often their purpose is to measure the residence in order to relate it to mental health[34] or suitability for persons with psychiatric disabilities.[35]

Fifth, some researchers measure what a residence can *do* for a person.[36] For example, David Uzzell and Charlotte Clark did this for adolescents; they found that two important things that a home does for teens is to provide a retreat for themselves and their friends, and a place for seeking security.[37]

Sixth, because home is a set of meanings, another approach to measuring it would assess the meaning of a residence as a home. The best guide probably would be the set of six dimensions outlined above. The more that a residence means to a person on each of the dimensions, the more the residence would be a home. However, no such measure has yet been devised. Maybe *you* should try!

IN SUM *A house is not home. Houses (or, more generally, residences) are physical structures that vary tremendously around the world. They can be described in terms of how open or closed they are, how similar to neighboring*

SUSAN SAEGERT'S research on crowding and on the struggles of poor women to establish liveable residences are landmarks in environmental psychology.

residences they are, how communal or noncommunal they are, whether they are permanent or temporary, how differentiated or homogeneous they are, or on any number of physical features such as number of bedrooms, size and age. Home is a set of meanings such as haven, order, connectedness, warmth, and physical suitability that we bestow on a residence, which in turn becomes part of our own identity. Not everyone has a home; even some people who occupy a house are homeless. Houseless people may have a home—a residence with meaning that, for one reason or another, they are unable to live in. Houselessness is more than lack of a house; many other negative social consequences follow. Individuals who are both houseless and homeless are extremely unfortunate.

An Organizing Framework

IN ORDER TO MAKE SENSE OF RESIDENTIAL environmental psychology, an organizing framework is needed. Several such frameworks have been suggested. According to one, we adapt, adjust, and optimize our residence.[38] That is, to some extent we must **adapt** to parts of our residence that we cannot change. However, we are not passive—where possible, we **adjust** the residence to fit our needs. We **optimize** our space when we develop goals that we think will make the space "fit" us better.

A second framework emphasizes satisfaction with one's housing.[39] María Amérigo and Juan Ignacio Aragonés conceptualize housing satisfaction as an outcome of both objective and subjectively experienced aspects of the residence, as influenced by the resident's personal characteristics. Residential satisfaction, in turn, is postulated as an influence on one's overall life satisfaction and behavioral intentions.

A third framework, developed by Susan Saegert and Gary Evans, focuses on the health implications of housing, particularly for poor people.[40] It urges consideration of factors such as housing markets that constrain residential choice, access to human and social capital, and the role of family dynamics. Saegert and Evans advocate more examination of *cumulative* risks and more sophisticated statistical analyses, including mediator and moderator variables, and the use of multilevel analytical models.

The purpose of these frameworks is to provide an overall picture of the causes and consequences of living in different dwellings. As in previous chapters, four main categories of influence will be considered: personal, social, physical, and cultural factors. The consequences fall into three general categories: attitudes, such as preferences and satisfaction; behavior, such as space management, leisure activities, and arrangement of furniture; and well-being, such as health, stress, fear of crime, and social support.

Figure 7-3 is offered as an organizing framework for housing research. The framework is loosely patterned after Brunswik's lens model (see Chapter 2) and Craik's model of environment comprehension (see Chapter 3). Beginning at the left of the framework, note that each home has thousands of characteristics. Many of these might be unimportant, but others will be very important in the understanding of residential satisfaction, behavior, and well-being.

Next in the framework, researchers must select for study some objective characteristics of the dwelling that they hypothesize have some impact on the resident's satisfaction, behavior, or well-being. Some of these objective characteristics might be the type of housing (single-family dwelling, apartment, condominium), or its age, location, market value, lot size, and architectural style. Some (but obviously not all) of these objective features are perceived by, or salient to, the resident.

How the residence becomes known to an observer or the resident is a factor of its own. A person may experience a dwelling over the span of a few minutes (as a prospective buyer who tours the house) or over many years (in the case of long-term residents). The experiencing of the residence usually is "live," but if the residence happens to be still in its planning stages, it may have to be simulated. The observer's experience with the residence may be thorough, including an inspection of every corner, or cursory, merely viewing the place while driving by.

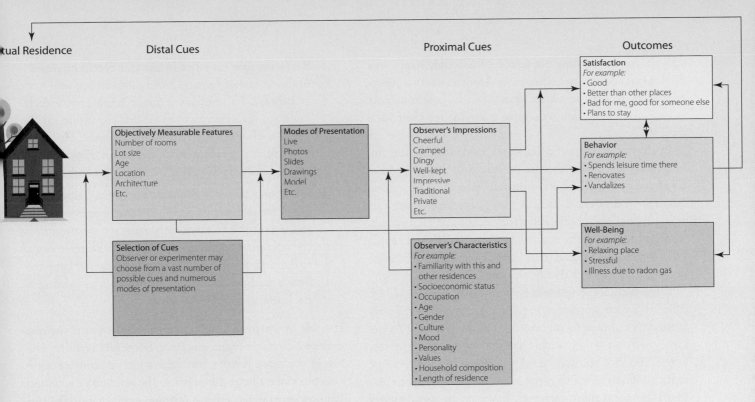

Objectively Measurable Features
Number of rooms
Lot size
Age
Location
Architecture
Etc.

Modes of Presentation
Live
Photos
Slides
Drawings
Model
Etc.

Observer's Impressions
Cheerful
Cramped
Dingy
Well-kept
Impressive
Traditional
Private
Etc.

Satisfaction
For example:
• Good
• Better than other places
• Bad for me, good for someone else
• Plans to stay

Behavior
For example:
• Spends leisure time there
• Renovates
• Vandalizes

Well-Being
For example:
• Relaxing place
• Stressful
• Illness due to radon gas

Selection of Cues
Observer or experimenter may choose from a vast number of possible cues and numerous modes of presentation

Observer's Characteristics
For example:
• Familiarity with this and other residences
• Socioeconomic status
• Occupation
• Age
• Gender
• Culture
• Mood
• Personality
• Values
• Household composition
• Length of residence

FIGURE 7–3 A research model of residential satisfaction, behavior, and well-being.

The next element in the model is the observer. Who is this person (which culture, personality, gender, age, occupation)? How much experience with different residences does this observer have? In evaluating a residence, will the observer compare it to an ideal residence, to past residences, or to standards of residential quality acquired from friends or the media? Is the observer a resident of the dwelling in question, or a passerby, real estate agent, neighbor, or tax assessor?

So far, then, selected distal cues are perceived through two filters: the mode of presentation and the observer's personal characteristics. These interact and, presto, impressions emerge. "Aha," says the observer, "this house is cozy (or grimy, or gloomy, or functional)." The same framework can be used to investigate impressions of the residents themselves.[41] These observer impressions are not, in themselves, conclusions about the ultimate value of the residence. For example, an observer may decide that a house is "traditional," but that does not tell us whether the observer values the house; some people like traditional houses and others do not.

Notice that the model also includes a direct path from the objective characteristics to the outcomes. This is because some effects of the house may occur without the resident's awareness. Remember Lewin's alien hull? For

example, if radon gas leaks into a house and the residents are not aware of it, their health may be seriously affected. Mode of presentation, observer characteristics, and their impressions would be irrelevant.

RESIDENTIAL PREFERENCE, CHOICE, AND SATISFACTION

WHAT SORT OF RESIDENCE WOULD YOU PREFER? Where are you actually living? If you gave different answers to these questions, you know the difference between residential preference and residential choice. If the difference between your preference and your choice is great, you may be unsatisfied with your residence, and it may never develop into a home. Many people prefer what they cannot have and so, for economic or other reasons, they must choose a less-preferred place to live. When we *can* choose what we prefer, we should be most satisfied. However, with trade-offs, a less-preferred dwelling may not be terribly unsatisfying.[42] For example, many individuals would prefer to live in a single-family dwelling but may be reasonably happy in a downtown apartment because it is closer to work, concerts, or friends. Researchers have examined just how much distance some people are willing to trade off for their ideal dwelling.[43]

Both residential preferences and residential choices can be predicted.[44,45] Preferences appear to be more predictable from personal and architectural factors (e.g., a person's values or the physical form of the residence); choices appear to be more predictable from economic factors (e.g., income and cost of the residence). Apparently, even people who live in conventional (that is, not "green") residences are in favor of residences that have more "green" features.[46]

Of course, some residences would make *anyone* dissatisfied. They are so rundown, poorly maintained, or poorly located that almost no one would want to live there. At the same time, some individuals are not satisfied by any residence: they are so fussy, cranky, neurotic, or perfectionist that they find fault with every residence (know anyone like this?). Between these extremes, however, are most homes and most residents. Different residences will satisfy different residents, but a good match between them is most important.[47]

Measuring Residential Satisfaction

TO UNDERSTAND RESIDENTIAL SATISFACTION, IT MUST FIRST BE ADEQUATELY MEASURED. However, measuring it is not as simple as asking, "Do you like your apartment?" For example, a resident's satisfaction can vary depending on whether individuals are asked to compare their residences (e.g., to their previous residence, for example, or to their ideal residence) or not.[48] It can vary for different rooms of the residence, for different qualities of it (e.g., spaciousness, beauty, or lighting), and based on the relation between these qualities and their use by the resident (e.g., lighting for a party versus lighting for washing the dishes).[49]

David Canter described two cognitive processes related to residential satisfaction.[50] The first is that evaluation of a residence's satisfactoriness is necessarily **purposive**. Purposive evaluations have several facets to them: the *level*, *referent*, and *focus* factors.

1. Satisfaction may vary in its specificity or **level**. Residents may be asked to evaluate a single part of the residence (e.g., a bedroom), or a larger portion of it (e.g., the bedrooms as a whole).

2. Residents may be asked to assess different qualities of the residence (e.g., its beauty, lighting, or spaciousness). These qualities are called **referents**; each one suggests a certain purpose that the residence serves well or poorly. The lighting referent, for example, is important when the resident considers lighting tasks such as reading or using a computer.

3. Questions may take **focus** into account. The meaning of focus depends on the referent, but one way to think of it is to ask how broadly we are asking the resident to evaluate something. With reference to lighting, is it the ability of this particular lamp to light a study desk, or is it broader, such as lighting in the home as a whole?

The role of **purpose** emerges when we ask about the resident's relationship *to* the residence. Some feel as if they will live in the place forever, but others intend to move soon. This can make a huge difference in the resident's evaluation. Thus, in general, a resident's purpose in evaluating the residence is itself a crucial factor in satisfaction.

The second cognitive factor, according to Canter, is **comparison**. Whether we explicitly ask observers to compare a specific residence against a series of others or merely ask for a rating of the present one without explicitly pointing out others, they cannot help at least implicitly comparing the residence in question with others in their experience. This means, of course, that different observers will be comparing the present residence against different houses in their experience.

When the observer compares residences, a discrepancy between residences will appear. Some approaches to residential satisfaction focus on this discrepancy between present and past residences, or between present and ideal residences. *Perceived* physical qualities of a residence (such as its appearance and provision for privacy) are important predictors of satisfaction,[51] and so are *preferred* physical qualities. However, the *difference* between perceived and preferred qualities is a separate but important predictor of housing satisfaction.[52]

Enough of these complexities. What is actually known, based on research to date?

Personal Influences

SATISFACTION AND PREFERENCE obviously depend, in part, on the resident. The characteristics of individuals that influence satisfaction include demographic factors, personality, values, expectations, comparisons with other housing, and hopes for the future. These psychological influences on housing satisfaction can be even more important than the type of housing in which one lives.[53] We begin with some examples of demographic indicators of housing satisfaction.

Age and Stage of Life. Differences in preferences for residences are related to one's age or stage in the life cycle. Age-linked differences in satisfaction presumably are caused by changes in a person's needs, purposes, and position in society that usually accompany age.

Over 85 percent of residents of all ages wish to own their dwelling,[54] but families with young children usually prefer the suburbs, whereas many older couples and single residents prefer to live downtown. Not much evidence is available on the residential satisfaction of individuals at the youthful end of the age range. However, one study of children's satisfaction reports that their views are quite similar to those of their parents.[55] One researcher asked 8- to 18-year-olds to draw their ideal homes.[56] Again, as for adults, these residences tended to be single-family dwellings. However, they were larger than their current dwellings and had more leisure-oriented space in them.

In an investigation of preferences for style, younger adults valued more ornate residences, and older adults preferred plainer ones.[57,58] Plainness may not sound attractive, but it does imply simplicity and clarity—attributes that are important to those elderly individuals who find mobility and perception more difficult than they once did. The younger adults liked a residence with mystery, but the older adults did not; they may prefer to find their mystery in a novel, where it will not make their lives more difficult.

The preference of many older people is to stay in their current residence, particularly compared to the alternative of institutional housing. Most people over age 75 prefer to "age in place" and do not spend much time thinking about future residences; they generally want to keep things the same.[59] Older people often prefer adequate, accessible, and personalized homes that will help them fulfil three objectives that are important to them: routines, responsibilities, and reflection.[60]

Another perspective is that the most important elements of residential satisfaction for the elderly are the local area, access to services, relations with neighbors, and the home itself, although the weightings of these four factors vary with the person.[61] The elderly who are satisfied with their home also tend to be less interested in new or different environments, to travel less, and to be happier with their lives than those who are less satisfied with their homes,[62] although sensitive upgrading of the residence makes the elderly[63] (and anyone, I suppose!) feel better. One way to stay at home is to share it with members of another generation. Older homeowners (70+ years) report benefits to their health as well as to their social life from remaining in their home.[64]

Socioeconomic Status. Residential satisfaction is also related to socioeconomic status. In general, of course, wealthier individuals are better able to supply themselves with homes that meet their standards, and are more satisfied. However, wealthier and poorer members of society may be attuned to *different* features of their homes. Wealthier individuals tend to be more sensitive to the aesthetic qualities of their home, and poorer individuals tend to be more sensitive to safety, health, and family needs, as well as aesthetics.[65] Presumably, the wealthier are less sensitive to the other concerns because their safety, health, and family are not in immediate danger, although other explanations are possible. Nevertheless, one implication is that the poor must spend their energy attempting to satisfy a greater number of needs.

Gender and Social Role. Social role influences residential satisfaction. Husbands and wives often disagree on the suitability of a residence. Canadian couples who had recently moved were asked to list the things that made them happy about their new homes and apartments.[66] Among those who moved to a downtown apartment, over 40 percent of the wives mentioned that they were satisfied with the quality of the home, but only 5 percent of the husbands mentioned this. On the other hand, among couples who moved to suburban apartments, over 50 percent of the husbands mentioned quality of the home as a source of their satisfaction, but only 5 percent of the wives did (see Figure 7-4).

As men increasingly enjoy cooking, similarities and differences in men's and women's preferences for kitchen designs become more important.[67] Both men and women prefer kitchens that are open to dining and family room areas over kitchens that are separated from those areas.[68] However, women who work outside the home prefer open kitchens more than those who do not work outside the home.

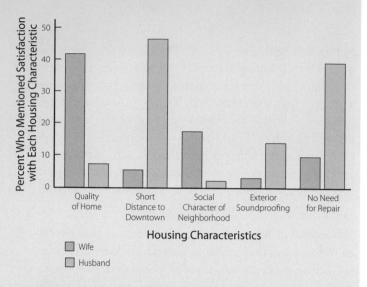

FIGURE 7–4 Husbands and wives who moved to a downtown apartment reported different sources of satisfaction with their new residence.

Despite their agreement on the open-closed aspect of the kitchen, men and women differ in many other kitchen spatial preferences, which can lead to conflict. When men and women are asked to design houses, women design smaller houses with more communal space and more curvature to the walls, and their designs were rated as more original.[69] When men and women designed houses together, the size was larger (like the males' designs) and had even more curvature than the women's designs.

Personality and Values. Personality is correlated with residential satisfaction.[70] For example, in residences with more traffic and disorganization, only mothers who are more stimulus-sensitive tend to see the place as chaotic.[71] Soldiers who are more aggressive are more dissatisfied with their army housing and those with a desire for structure in their lives and those with more nurturing personalities particularly appreciate the physical features of their living environment.[72] Soldiers whose personalities lead them to seek considerable social support more strongly prefer design features that would assist this need, such as more private visiting areas and more telephones.

You would hypothesize that more sociable individuals, given a choice, would select housing that maximizes social interaction. In fact, more affiliative first-year dormitory residents' preferences and actual choices for their second year's housing did tend toward housing that offered potential for more social interaction (e.g., a fraternity versus living alone).[73] This trend even held up for housing choices in

their third year, suggesting that personality is a reasonably long-term predictor of housing preference and choice.

Another key personal predictor of housing preference and choice is one's life values. People tend to favor residences that they believe will help them attain the goals implied by their life values.[74]

Comparisons. If you did not know that your friend lives in a mansion, you might be more satisfied with your hut. We compare residences, such as our previous dwellings with our current one[75] and those of others with our own. Such comparisons can be important sources of satisfaction or dissatisfaction. In a study of Army personnel living in mobile homes and apartments, comparison with other housing accounted for 30 percent of the variance in housing satisfaction—a very significant chunk.[76] However, the grass is not *always* greener on the other side of the fence: when comparing, sometimes the more familiar space is preferred most.[77]

Dreams of the Future. Finally, time is important.[78] Whether one expects improvement in one's housing also affects satisfaction with one's current housing. Thus, several individuals can live in the same place, but some will be happier than the others *if* they expect an improvement.[79] However, those who do not yet live in their dream house are not necessarily dissatisfied with their present dwelling. They seem able to tolerate its limitations as long as their aspirations seem possible. If, for some reason, the dream becomes impossible, however, dissatisfaction naturally grows.

Social Influences

OUR INTERACTIONS WITH OTHER PEOPLE—our ties to them, the norms we share, privacy versus independence, our sense of security—play an important role in residential preference, choice, and satisfaction. In fact, a key part of the definition of home is its social function. The main reasons for satisfaction with dormitories are independence (from parents, presumably), security (compared to off-campus housing), privacy (compared to sharing a house), and socialization (learning the customs of the school). The main reasons for dissatisfaction are visitor restrictions, curfew, and noise.[80] Note that all these reasons are essentially social in one way or another.

Neighbors. Neighbors may be less important than they once were for housing satisfaction, but they still can be important, particularly if they are very good or very bad neighbors. A Spanish study of over 400 housewives found that neighbors and neighborhood attachment were the *most* important factor in residential satisfaction, even more important than objective housing factors.[81] (See Figure 7-5.) Another social factor is the similarity of neighbors; residential satisfaction is greater when residents believe their neighbors are similar to them.[82,83] A related factor is privacy. People prefer housing that provides the balance of separation and togetherness with neighbors that suits them.

Norms. Most of us, when considering a place to live, pay at least some attention to what are the "usual" housing arrangements *for people like ourselves*. Students are often satisfied with a small apartment; university presidents not so much. Social norms for privacy and independence are important factors for elderly people when they select a living arrangement.[84]

Others' Preferences. Another social factor is living-group interaction. In any family or group that decides to live together, considerable negotiation must occur before a particular dwelling is selected for rent or purchase. We all know that such interpersonal politics over housing preferences and choices occur, but research on the topic is scarce. However, if one person's preferences are quite different from another's, but the two are tied together by family or other connections, then the second person will not be very satisfied.

The Shape of Privacy, Security, and Social Interaction. An interesting way to determine individual preferences for residences is to ask people to make a drawing or model. When asked to design a house that would provide privacy, the resulting designs are more differentiated; they contain more rooms, and therefore more corridors and smaller average room size.[85] Houses designed for security are the smallest; smaller houses mean less territory to defend, and they keep occupants closer together, which may aid in the defense of the house. Houses designed for social interaction have greater visibility among their interior spaces and more rounded walls; the latter may reflect natural sociopetal design tendencies.

FIGURE 7–5 Social interaction among neighbors is a key factor in neighborhood success.

Physical Influences

OBVIOUSLY, THE PHYSICAL CHARACTERISTICS of dwellings also significantly affect residents' preferences and satisfaction with them. We will consider five kinds of physical features: housing quality, housing form (e.g., single-family, apartment, etc.), architectural style (e.g., farmhouse, saltbox, colonial), interior (e.g., size, room arrangements, colors, walls, etc.), and outdoor areas (gardens, patios).

Before describing specific research findings, I should emphasize that housing preference research supports two broad conclusions. First, different housing satisfies different people. Therefore, the most important question is *Who* will be happy with *which* housing? Second, some housing is satisfactory to almost no one (even those who live in it, but presumably have no choice)[86] or almost everyone (e.g., very expensive housing).

Given that, which physical characteristics of buildings appeal to *most* people? The residents of one town agreed to a considerable degree in their evaluations of 45 quite variable apartment buildings, even though they came from varying socioeconomic levels and neighborhoods.[87] However, some features swayed them one way or the other. In general, older apartment buildings were preferred over those that looked like multiple-family dwellings, and highly detailed designs were favored over plain and simple designs. This leads to two conclusions that sound contradictory: One is "to each his or her own," and the other is "most people agree which housing is preferable." However contradictory these sound, the truth is that both statements are partly correct, and neither is wholly correct. They are complementary rather than contradictory. With this thought in mind, let's consider the evidence about housing preferences and satisfaction.

Housing Quality. Not surprisingly, people are more satisfied when their housing quality is better. For example, smaller noisy dwellings with fewer rooms generally are less satisfactory.[88] However, sometimes even this simple proposition is less straightforward than one might think. A study of older adults who lived independently in the community found that better housing quality is associated with more positive feelings.[89] But *why?* Further analyses showed that, after controlling for certain other factors, that higher-quality residences seemed to lead to greater place attachment, and that, in turn, seemed to lead to positive feelings. That is, place attachment serves as a *mediator* of the relation between housing quality and positive affect.

Housing Form. William Michelson undertook a large-scale study of Toronto residents who changed residences.[90] Over 50 percent of those who moved to a single-family dwelling said they were "definitely satisfied," but less than 25 percent of those who moved to an apartment said they were "definitely satisfied." This general preference for the single-family dwelling has persisted in North America for many years.[91] Sometimes condominiums or apartments are said to be growing in popularity, but often these reports occur because high cost forces purchasers to rule out single-family dwellings, not because condos or apartments truly are preferred.

Further evidence comes from the negative side of satisfaction. Mobile homes (as an example of a housing form that differs from the "standard" single-family form) are not generally popular, even though one could argue that mobile homes are environmentally preferable—they occupy less land and use less energy, for example. They are particularly dissatisfying to adolescents because schoolmates and others sometimes shun those who live in mobile homes, and this creates a climate of fear and passivity.[92] Of course, mobile homes may be satisfactory for other groups (e.g., the elderly, professionally mobile people, or some military personnel).[93,94]

Architectural Style. How about the style or design of the residence? Preferences for style clearly change in part with changes in fashion. I have lived in my town long enough to recognize which decade a house was built in, because the typical house in a given decade looks much like others built in that decade. Casual observation suggests that when people have the means to convert a preference into an actual choice, they often choose housing that reflects their cultural background.

However, some trends are evident: farmhouse and Tudor-style houses were preferred over saltbox and Mediterranean styles in one study.[95] Apparently, people prefer "moderate"-sized exterior windows.[96] Older people who evaluated assisted-living housing preferred newer and smaller buildings with sheltered entries.[97] I found that seniors who live in congregate care housing are more satisfied when they live in an end unit than in other units.[98] According to "New Urbanists" who build new housing projects that resemble quiet villages of the early 20th century, front porches promote neighborliness and provides other satisfactions such as a place to be alone.[99]

Interior. Housing interiors have not been the subject of as much empirical research as you might think; much effort in interior design is concerned with shifting fashions and artistic statements rather than research as understood in environmental psychology. However, research shows that most individuals prefer higher (than the usual 8-foot/2.4 m) ceilings, flat or sloping ceilings (4:12 slope ratio [vertical-horizontal] but neither larger nor smaller slopes), and walls that meet at 90 degrees or more (not walls that meet at smaller angles).[100]

Everyday experience suggests that the arrangement of rooms (floor plans) can be an important factor in a purchaser's decision. Unfortunately, what little empirical data exists on this question is mixed. American university students preferred floor plans that showed the living room in the upper right-hand corner of the drawing.[101] However, Israeli students express less support the right-hand location.[102] Elderly people (and maybe others?) prefer end-of-corridor units.[103] Much more study is required before any firm conclusions about which individuals prefer which room arrangements can be reached.

Color has been the subject of much research, but most of it has been based on preferences for small patches of color that resemble paint chips, in no particular real-life.[104,105] A study in Japan tried to overcome these limitations by showing slides of living rooms that were painted different colors.[106] The researchers discovered that preference is not merely a matter of hue (that is, red versus blue versus green); it also depends on the hue's saturation (or "denseness") and brightness (from light to dark). Each of these three dimensions of color is related to a different aspect of preference. Hue was *not* strongly related to preference; instead preference was primarily related to perceived warmth (reds are warmer, blues and greens cooler). Saturation (regardless of hue) was most closely related to what we usually call preference: more saturated hues were evaluated as "more elegant," "more comfortable," and "better." Brightness or lightness (regardless of hue) was related to how "active" the room seemed: brighter colors were rated as "fresher," "lighter," and more "cheerful" than darker hues. One important conclusion is that saturation and brightness are at least as important, perhaps more so, than hue, in people's preferences.

Outdoor Areas. The outdoor areas around a residence can make a big difference in satisfaction. The effective use of outdoor open spaces near one's residence is important.[107] Some householders are gardeners and love the space and soil to work in. Gardens can be very important for many householders' physical and mental health, their sense of ownership and identity, as place to socialize, commune with nature, and to grow food.[108] For others, like a former neighbor of mine, gardening is "too much like work."

One need not be a gardener to appreciate nearby green spaces. A study in France found that nearby green space is among the most important determinants of residential satisfaction.[109] (see Figure 7-6). Studies by me and by others report a slightly different outcome: being *near* nature is less important than having a *view* of nature.[110,111]

However, green spaces, in the sense of watered lawns and gardens, are not universally preferred. When the southwest U.S. began to grow rapidly after World War II, the ideal—imported from elsewhere—was a large green lawn. The recent realization that water is not an endless resource has gradually translated into a change of that ideal for many residents of the southwest; they now prefer a residential landscape that complements the dry, almost desert quality of the area to the grassy ideal.[112] As we saw earlier, some prefer more natural, wild yards while others like them neat.[113]

Finally, outdoor areas can also serve as a kind of helpful buffer. Residents of older and newer multi-unit buildings in Israel that differed considerably in status were most satisfied when clear physical boundaries between the buildings were in place.[114]

Cultural Influences

HOUSING VARIES TREMENDOUSLY AROUND THE WORLD. I have seen earthen "beehives" in rural Iran, cedar longhouses in British Columbia, grass huts in India, and floating houses in Kashmir. Even within North America, culture-related variation in housing is large but not so dramatic: the brightly colored exteriors of Portuguese houses, the red-tile roofed villas of Italian suburbanites, the white farmhouses of mid-America, the adobe houses of the southwest U.S. The obvious assumption is that people prefer housing that matches their own cultural background. This is partly because residences that reflect one's culture are designed to complement behavior patterns typical of that culture.

Housing preferences are also based on factors beyond superficial color and form, such as culture. In the Gaza strip, Palestinians who seek new housing base their preferences on issues of gender, politics, religion, kinship, and social relations, with kinship relations and attitudes toward women often crucial criteria.[115] Dwellings also match cultures in another way. An examination of house form across 73 cultures revealed that the extent of partitioning indoor space (differentiation) is related to the degree of sociopolitical complexity in the culture (i.e., how much segmentation, specialization, and hierarchical ordering is typical of the culture).[116] Thus, a worldwide trend is for dwellings to mirror the complexity of their society.

Even in such relatively similar cultures as England and Australia, house forms have significant differences.[117] In many English houses, cleaning the dishes, the clothing, and oneself are closely intertwined, so dishwashing, laundry,

FIGURE 7-6 Gardening is an important source of satisfaction to many residents.

ARZA CHURCHMAN
has long contributed to the environmental psychology of neighborhoods and urban planning, and the role of women in these issues.

and (sometimes) bathing are traditionally done in one room or area. In Australia, these cleaning activities are seen as separate, so the laundry is usually separated from the dishwashing area. In fact, where the laundry *is* placed close to the kitchen in Australian houses, this is a significant source of dissatisfaction. Thus, in general, residential satisfaction seems to be greater when the residence matches the culture.

However, this is not always the case. Scottish and Australian architecture students were shown slides of Scottish and Australian residences.[118] The Scots tended to prefer the traditional bungalow house style typical of Australia, and the Australians tended to prefer the terrace or row housing typical of Scotland. This was true even though a later analysis of the data showed that the two groups comprehended the houses in a similar way.[119] Suddenly, the old adage about the grass being greener on the other side of the fence seems relevant: Individuals do not *always* prefer housing that reflects their own culture.

IN SUM *Residential preferences, choices, and satisfaction reflect what we would like in a residence, what we actually chose, and whether we are happy with it. Measuring these concepts is more complex than it sounds: we need to know just which focus, level, and referents we are interested in, and the answers we get from residents will have comparative and purposive bases to them. Residential evaluations are influenced by such personal characteristics as age, stage in the life cycle, socioeconomic status, personality, values, and hopes for the future. Social factors such as norms, others' preferences, and neighbors also influence these evaluations. Naturally, so do physical and architectural factors like house form, architectural style, floor plan and colors, and outdoor areas. Finally, cultural background strongly affects residential preferences, choices, and satisfaction.*

TO STUDY SATISFACTION *with* a home is much easier to study than behavior *in* the home. Satisfaction may be surveyed in any convenient public or online place where respondents may be found, but many of our beliefs and customs work against allowing researchers to monitor our behavior in the sanctity of our homes. For that reason, less research on this topic is available. Nevertheless, researchers have begun to acquire at least three categories of knowledge about behavior in the home: how different people arrange their home interiors, space management in the home, and home-based leisure. We will consider spatial arrangements first.

How Homes Are Arranged

MANY RESIDENCES LOOK ALMOST IDENTICAL on the outside—think of apartment exteriors or suburban tract houses. However, probably no two house interiors in the whole world are exactly alike. We personalize our living spaces in many wonderful ways. But do all these unique patterns of arrangement have *any* regularities to them? For example, do house arrangements systematically vary by culture or resident personality? When French and Italian living room arrangements were examined, the French living rooms could be described using three dimensions—decoration, functional organization, and structuring of space.[120] For example, at one end of the decoration dimension were living rooms low on ambiguity and complexity; they tended to have velvet antique couches with armrests, copies of period wallpaper, and books for show (not for use) in a wall-unit that also included cupboards and a bar. The Italian living rooms could be described using the same three dimensions, but they tended to be combined differently.

A second study examined only Italian living rooms, and found five major styles arranged in a two-dimensional space characterized by richness versus poorness of the furnishings and symmetry versus asymmetry of their arrangements.[121] Type A living rooms are asymmetric, eccentric, and unconventional; they include mixtures of modern designer furniture and tapestries, silkscreen paintings and antiques. Type B is like Type A except that the objects are less expensive and a little more functional. Type C is the richest; it contains expensive art objects, has wooden floors, and antiques arranged in a ritualistic, ostentatious way. Type D living rooms are cheaper copies of Type Cs: the objects are of the same type and also are arranged ritually, but are reproductions rather than originals and are arranged more symmetrically. The Type E living room contains few valuable articles, and the arrangements are symmetrical. Owners of Types A and B rooms, who tend to be intellectuals and professionals, dislike conspicuous consumption yet prefer artistic decor; the main difference between them is whether they can afford expensive objects. Owners of Types C and D living rooms, who tend to be successful businesspeople, prefer objects that show off their status and refer to the old symbolic order in society. Owners of Type E living rooms tend to be working-class individuals.

Researchers who considered patterns in California single-family dwellings began by describing a wide variety of residences on 38 different dimensions (such as cleanliness, number of books, and need for repair).[122] These were statistically grouped into four factors: disorder-functional complexity (the physical state and maintenance of the home), decorative complexity (material richness), warm-child-oriented (number of child-centered items), and books (number and variety of books). Next, the researchers examined the connection between home type (based on the four factors) and several antecedent factors, such as family type (traditional nuclear family, unmarried parents, communal household, single mother), income, and lifestyle. The goal was to find which of these antecedent factors may have led homeowners to arrange their houses as they did. The homes of unmarried parents had the highest scores on disorder-functional complexity. Their lawns were more overgrown, and their houses were more "funky" than those of traditional-marriage parents. The communal homes had more books than the traditional-marriage homes. Higher-income homes had lower scores on disorder-functional complexity. Surprisingly, as women's income rose, the number and variety of books in the home dropped. Parents with natural-organic lifestyles had homes with higher scores on disorder-functional complexity (see Figure 9-7).

The Spatial Ecology of Home

Women, Men, Children, and Territory. The use of space within the home is not random. People spend more time

FIGURE 9-7 Modern and traditional houses reflect different lifestyles.

in some rooms than others. Recent data are hard to find, but several decades ago, even fully employed women spent more time than fully employed men in the kitchen. (They spent more than twice as much time *alone* in the kitchen).[123] Women reported engaging in more traditional domestic activities, such as baking and laundry and men recalled engaging in more design and building activities.[124] In the living room, bathroom, and bedrooms, women spent more time than men in the company of others—usually with children, and men spent more time than women engaged in passive leisure activities such as reading or watching TV.

M. POWELL LAWTON
extensively studied housing for older people, including ways to enhance the ability of seniors to control their lives through residential technology.

Women who are not employed outside the home spent almost seven times as much time as men on housework and child care. Even when women are fully employed, they spend three times as much time as men on these activities.[125] (Do you think these trends have changed since 1980?)

Privacy in the home becomes more complex when children are around. As they grow up, children are taught which rooms are open to them at which times; later they make privacy demands of their own. Privacy conflicts may occur depending on which activity a person is engaged in, which parent or child desires access, the size of the home, and the accepted child-rearing practices in the home.[126] In a rare study that actually monitored behavior inside homes (as opposed to asking residents to report their activities), cameras were placed in New York homes (with the residents' permission).[127] Although definite territories existed within the homes, the degree to which the boundaries of these territories were respected varied considerably. For example, parents may feel they have the right to enter a teen's bedroom, but do not believe that the teen should enter their bedroom. But both territories are sometimes intruded upon, which creates conflict.

Three strategies for dealing with residential space conflicts have been described.[128] **Time territory strategies** involve rotating a particular space (like the TV area) among family members. **Space territory strategies** attempt to place conflicting activities in different parts of the home. **Cooperation-capitulation arrangements** occur when a dominant family member determines that everyone will engage in one activity, together, at the same time. How is space managed where you live? Who decides?

Consequences of Household Spatial Arrangements. Domestic spatial arrangements affect a variety of behaviors in the home, and they are related to family helpfulness and behavioral choices. For example, the traditional kibbutz in Israel took the radical step of separating parents and children. To discourage "privatism" and individualism in the socialist atmosphere of the traditional kibbutz, children lived in communal houses; parents visited the children's house for a few hours each day.

Recently, as political and social values have changed, some kibbutzim have altered this pattern so that children sleep in their parents' house. The differences between families using the two types of arrangements were compared.[129] Those using family-based sleeping arrangements reported that they helped, supported, and were more committed to one another than families using the communal arrangement. They also said they encouraged family members to act and speak more openly. Those whose children slept communally said they participated in more social and recreational activities and placed more importance on the planning and organization of family activities and responsibilities. These differences are based in part on the differing sleeping arrangements, but also to differences in values between families that have chosen one system or the other.

Child-rearing practices in a fixed amount of space (e.g., two-bedroom apartments) affect parents' behavioral freedom.[130] When parents subscribe to a permissive child-rearing approach, the children's activities usually spill out into the living room and thereby restrict their parents' choices of activities, simply because the limited space available is already covered with the children's toys and possessions. These more permissive parents also complained about noise and lack of privacy. More restrictive parents, of course, are better off in these ways. Their children were required to keep their activities within their own rooms. This may be obvious, but it clearly illustrates how a particular behavior pattern (e.g., child-raising policies) can interact with the physical setting to have important consequences for all residents.

A series of large-scale examinations of mass housing in Russia and Estonia revealed many influences of constructing large numbers of high-rise apartments in cities.[131] This region has, on average, very tall residential buildings. However, most residents must cope with small, poor-quality individual units. One survey question asked how residents would use an extra room if one became available. The answer depended on the current household density. When residents lived in apartments with two fewer rooms than residents, about 80 percent said they would use an extra room as another bedroom or private room. When the number of rooms and people were the same, one-third of the residents said they had no idea what they would do with an extra room, and another one-third said they would use it for a study or work room. When space is short, the kitchen is used for more activities.

Pleasant atmosphere is associated with the interior organization of homes.[132] Based on interviews, pleasantness (or lack of it) seems to be related to five themes: being able to communicate with one another, being accessible to one another, being free to do what one wants, being occupied rather than bored, and being able to relax after working. These themes are related to the organization of the house itself. For example, the lack of order (e.g., a messy table after preparing a meal) interferes for some people with the pleasantness of a meal eaten at the same table. That is, an unpleasant atmosphere results when the "relaxing after work" theme cannot be accomplished (the work in this case is cooking). In another example, more walls were desired by one person because then she could "do more things" with them. Thus, more walls is seen as a way of being occupied rather than bored. In general, a positive or negative home atmosphere depends in part on how the arrangements in the residence support each of the five pleasantness themes for a particular resident.

Admittedly, these few studies offer only hints about the relations between spatial arrangements and behavior in the home. Much more remains to be learned about this important aspect of environmental psychology.

Home Leisure

A PRIMARY PURPOSE OF THE RESIDENCE IS TO PROVIDE A PLACE FOR RELAXATION AND ENTERTAINMENT. Over half of recreational time is spent inside the home,[133] so it is important to understand the role of the physical environment in residential leisure behaviors such as playing games, watching TV, gardening, crafts, reading, and merely lounging. Home-based leisure is strongly affected by the size and differentiation of the home. People who live in bachelor apartments may feel driven away from their small space to find suitable recreation, but denizens of mansions wander from the pool room to the indoor pool to the gift-wrapping room (yes, these exist!) to the bar.

Leisure activities are also driven by one's psychological make-up. For example, residents' environmental identity significantly predicts whether they engage in ecological gardening behavior.[134]

In relatively homogeneous homes, leisure is apt to conflict with other activities; in households where necessity or values favor work, leisure time and quality are likely to suffer. Home-based leisure may seem too commonplace and unimportant for serious attention, but its value in relieving stress and serving as an important vehicle for social bonds within the home seems clear. Consider the results from a study of the home-based leisure activities of adolescents and their families.[135] A strong positive relation was found between the amount of time adolescents spent with their parents in recreational activities at home and their general sense of well-being. Of course, not all leisure activities are equally valuable. Adolescents who watch more television are less oriented to intellectual and cultural activities.

Again, these few studies of home-based leisure suggest that it can have important positive and negative effects, but they remain to be verified, expanded, and refined by future researchers.

IN SUM *The environmental psychology of dwelling interiors is not very developed, partly because studying behavior inside homes meets with understandable resistance. However, we know that residents arrange and decorate their interiors according to certain patterns that reflect such dimensions as simple-complex, conventional-unusual, rich-plain decor, and messy-tidy upkeep. These patterns are related to social class and marital or living arrangement differences. Men, women, and children use the interior dwelling spaces unequally. Children (until the teen years) have restricted territories: parents generally can enter their space, but children generally cannot enter their parents' space. In limited space, residents use time territory strategies, space territory strategies, and cooperation-capitulation arrangements to manage household space. Half our leisure time is spent in the home, but it could be better spent. When teens spend more time sharing leisure with their parents, they report greater well-being. More TV time, however, is associated with less time spent on intellectual and cultural pursuits.*

AS INDICATED IN FIGURE 7-3, our residences can strongly influence well-being. Housing is beneficial when it promotes physical and mental health, and many North Americans are fortunate to have such housing. In the world as a whole, however, experts estimate that a billion people have grossly inadequate housing and 100 million have no housing at all.[136] Many dwellings fail to serve their most basic purpose: to shelter residents from ill-health associated with exposure to the elements or to disease-causing organisms. Particularly in high-density residences that are poorly ventilated, the building serves to increase the rate of communicable diseases such as influenza, tuberculosis, and meningitis,[137] and small children suffer respiratory illnesses caused by burning fuel for heat.[138] Poor quality housing is also associated with poorer mental health.[139,140]

Adapting to a New Residence

ADAPTING TO A NEW RESIDENCE MAY BE RELATIVELY PAIN-LESS, OR VERY DIFFICULT. When the place is inadequate, one's choices are to actively deal with the problem (move, renovate, change activity patterns, or protest) or to be passive (change one's mind instead of the residence or not adapt at all).[141] Distress is a normal response to inadequate housing; well-being is seriously threatened when residents are blocked from changing their residence,[142] cannot move, fail to adapt, or attempt to adapt housing when the residents' efforts are doomed by forces beyond their control (e.g., a nonresponsive landlord or a crumbling house). Residents may then suffer physical or mental stress, live in fear, abuse drugs, have more accidents, or adapt poorly; children may not develop as quickly or as well as they otherwise might. Of course, moving itself can be a source of stress.

One group whose adaptation to new housing has been examined in some detail is the elderly, particularly when they must move to group settings. Besides the loss of privacy and control that results from a move away from one's own home, group settings have a tendency to produce **hyperhabituation**, or the over-adaptation to routines.[143] Relocation of an elderly person even may cause increased susceptibility to illness caused by stress-induced suppression of the immune system.[144] Older people who face such a move may be

helped by giving them a chance to air their feelings, giving them practical information about the new residence,[145] and encouraging **environmental proactivity**—the confidence to make active choices about, help create, and take control of their new housing.[146] The adaptive strategy chosen by older people depends on the kind of problem they face in the home, on their personal style, and on the physical aspects of their residence.[147] A special case of adaptation among older residents is that of the person afflicted with Alzheimer's disease. One study showed that these people adapt better in private rooms than in shared rooms.[148]

Many university students also must adapt to new residences. In one sample of students who left home for college, 31 percent experienced homesickness.[149] Women were more likely to experience it and more likely to suffer some psychological disturbance. Students who did not experience homesickness were more likely to have traveled or lived away from home before going away to college.

High Density at Home

HIGH DENSITY IN THE RESIDENCE was shown in the last chapter to have many adverse effects. Crowding at home, where very important social interaction occurs, has more serious consequences than crowding in public environments.[150] Beginning with mere complaints, a study of Seattle residents showed that residential dissatisfaction was more strongly related to density than to such factors as income, financial value or age of the house, or family size.[151] When household density was 0.4 persons per room or less, residents made 7 percent of possible complaints on a survey; when it exceeded 1 person per room residents made 33 percent of possible complaints.

High-density homes have residents with more psychological distress and psychiatric illness,[152,153] especially for women,[154] and are associated with increased substance abuse,[155] juvenile delinquency, fertility and mortality rates.[156] Furthermore, among preschoolers, cognitive development is significantly slower when children live in residences that were more densely populated and noisy.[157-159] High residential density is linked to school performance.[160-162] The homes of 12-month-old children were surveyed; those with higher indoor densities were found to have poorer physical organization and fewer play materials (even after various statistical controls were applied). Reading performance five years later was lower for children who had fewer play materials at home as 1-year-olds, even after intelligence was controlled for.

High density is even associated with differences in the temperament of toddlers; it predisposes toddlers to lower approachability, less adaptability, higher intensity, and more negative moods.[163] In high-density households, children may receive less attention of a constructive nature,[164] yet may be struck more often by their parents.[165] Thus children from high-density homes may be forced outdoors more often, leading more of them into trouble in the street and in school.[166,167] High-density also affects children's sense of control. Children who lived with many other individuals exercised less control when they *were* given the power to make choices than did children from low-density homes.[168] Children who must live in high density may not learn to persist in tasks or to make active choices when given the chance. Children who live in higher-density homes may be given fewer opportunities to learn about or exercise choice and control than children who live in lower-density homes.

These studies clearly demonstrate that high density in homes has long-term effects on the development of important skills in children and that parent-child relations are disrupted by high indoor density. The negative effects of residential high density may appear smaller than they actually are because families can, with effort, muffle the strain of high-density living by employing various coping strategies. However, this extra effort may cause stress that manifests itself in other ways. High density affects some people more than others. At least in India, crowding is more distressing for women than men.[169] Boys apparently are more sensitive than girls to household population density.[170]

High density may lead residents to believe they have less social support.[171] However, when residents do have social support in a high-density household, it may protect them from these negative outcomes, at least in the short term[172] (see Figure 7-8). Social support is also a factor at the other end of the crowding spectrum: living alone or being lonely. As we saw in the last chapter, at least for women, depression is related to low densities at home as well as high densities.[173] Loneliness is associated with greater residential mobility.[174] Living alone restricts one's social networks not only inside the home, but outside, too. This means that the person who lives alone has fewer social contacts who might provide support when personal adversity strikes.[175]

One might reasonably argue that the true cause of all these woes is poverty rather than high density, which certainly do tend to occur together. Which is the true cause?

FIGURE 7-8 Living in a high-density residence, particularly without much social support, is psychologically risky.

To test this idea, researchers statistically controlled for poverty to determine whether density has an effect *apart* from the effect of poverty.[176] Mental hospital admission rates were predicted reasonably well by density alone, and juvenile delinquency and fertility were also related to density alone, although not as strongly. Although high density is difficult to separate from poverty, it does have a negative effect of its own. Finally, data from 65 countries showed that higher residential densities (persons per room) were correlated with higher murder rates.[177] This introduces our next topic.

Crime, Fear, and Well-being at Home

THREE FURTHER THREATS TO RESIDENTIAL WELL-BEING ARE CRIME, FEAR OF CRIME, AND WELL-BEING. Those fortunate enough to live in safe areas may have difficulty appreciating how stressful it is to experience a burglary or other in-house crime, or to live in fear of intruders.[178] The consequences of having one's primary territory invaded are long-term and cannot always be handled by the resident's own coping efforts.[179] Fear of crime is related to the height of a building, at least for the elderly: more fear was reported in low-rise buildings.[180] Perhaps low-rise buildings seem closer to, and more vulnerable to, crime that invades from the street. Fear has led to the construction of many gated communities. In Brazil, there are so many, even in cities, that they dramatically affect urban form.[181]

Residences are surprisingly dangerous. According to the U.S. National Safety Council, over 8,000 disabling injuries occur each *day* in homes. Almost half of fatal home injuries occur to the elderly. Flooring, stairs, doors, bathtubs, and showers are most dangerous, but elderly people and even designers underestimate the risks of two of these hazards: flooring and doors.[182] Some residences contain toxic substances (e.g., lead paint, off-gassing insulation, mold, etc.). An environmental psychologist created a scale to measure residents' knowledge of indoor hazards.[183] The scale could help identify gaps in residents' knowledge that might be filled, thereby preventing some illnesses caused by these toxic substances.

House Form and Human Dysfunction

OBVIOUSLY, SOME DWELLINGS ARE NOT BEST for some residents, even if they may be suitable for others. One major architectural distinction is between single-family dwellings and multiple-unit dwellings. Many studies paint apartments as poor places for children to grow up and for adults to thrive.[184] Apartment living has been associated with numerous childhood afflictions, including retarded movement skills, more respiratory diseases, more aggression, insomnia, more nervous disorders, reduced social skills, and disrupted play.

If all this is true, we may wonder how any child can survive in an apartment! Although many of the early studies lacked experimental rigor, leading some to question their results, more rigorous studies are now being conducted and they tend to confirm these trends.[185] The physical condition of residences seems to affect children beyond their poor repair or lack of tidiness itself. Cécile Lacombe and I found that as the maintenance of a residence and its immediate neighborhood declines, the frequency of behavior problems in 9-12-year-old children significantly increases.[186] This is not a function of family income; the same relation held even after the results were adjusted for income.

The design of the residence also affects early cognitive development. In a study of 1-year-olds, a key variable was view: Those who had no view outside the home showed slower cognitive development.[187] Residences that provide no "stimulus shelter" for escape, do not encourage exploration, do not offer a variety of play objects over time, and are not physically responsive also produce slower cognitive development.[188]

Although one might think that a stimulus-rich environment would be good for toddlers, one study suggests the opposite. The availability and variety of objects (other than toys) in each toddler's home was measured. The more non-toy objects in the home, the more likely the toddlers were judged by their parents to be moody, intense, and lacking in persistence.[189] Perhaps too many objects frustrate rather than stimulate toddlers; alternately, parents may supply toddlers who already display these qualities with more objects in an attempt to occupy or pacify them.

Even more ways exist in which the child's own household may not be the most advantageous place to develop. A Swedish study of children's play at home found that, in general, play at home often was restricted: parents favored quiet over noisy play, fine motor activities over gross motor activities, and passive rather than active play.[190] Daycare in private homes tends to restrict play in similar ways, whereas purpose-built daycare facilities usually are equipped to support all forms of play. When the intellectual performance of economically disadvantaged children who entered private homes for daycare was compared with that of children who entered purpose-built daycares, the performance of both groups improved initially, but those in the purpose-built daycares maintained their higher levels, whereas the performance of those in private homes actually declined after 18 months.[191]

When families with young children live in high-rises, their parents find it difficult to allow children outside to play. When play is thereby confined largely to the apartment, tension and conflict in the family increases.[192] A Japanese study investigated the rate of development over 1,000 infants who lived in high-rise or low-rise buildings.[193] Those who lived in high-rises were slower to develop independence than those who lived in low-rises. The researchers speculate that this developmental delay occurred because high-rise mothers went outdoors less often and thereby grew over-attached to their children, which slowed the growth of independence in their children.

In sum, housing trends indicate that more of us will be living in apartments. Therefore, even more research is needed on the effects of housing on children, and how their deleterious effects can be overcome.

The architectural form of the residence is also related to the social conditions inside. A study in India, for example, compared the interpersonal climate in single-family dwellings, multi-story apartments, and crowded small houses.[194] Cohesiveness, expressiveness, and active recreation orientation were highest in the single-family dwelling and lowest in the crowded small houses. Residents of the multi-story apartments were loneliest. The residents in the different forms of housing did differ in other ways, such as income and whether members of the extended family lived in the same household, so we cannot be sure that house form caused the differences found in the study. However, the results tentatively challenge the prevailing belief in India that living close together promotes cohesion and decreases conflict.

High-rises may have negative effects, particularly on nuclear families. High-rise and low-rise tenants of the buildings, part of a low-income project in New York, were of similar age, education, and other demographic indicators, but those who lived in high-rises felt more socially overloaded, more anonymous, less safe, less satisfied with their building, and had more difficulty establishing supportive relationships with their neighbors.[195] They also felt more powerless to change building policies and believed they had less privacy.

In reviewing this literature, I concluded that even after adjusting for such moderating factors as income, stage of life, and neighborhood quality, high-rises are less satisfactory than other housing forms for most people: residential life is more impersonal, helping behavior is less frequent, fear of crime is higher, actual crime may be higher, and high-rises may account for a certain percentage of suicides.[196] However, high-rises seem to be better for some people. People over 60 years old have higher morale, on average, in high-rises than in low-rise buildings.[197]

IN SUM *Adapting to a new residence is not always easy for the elderly and some college students. High densities in dwellings are associated with a very wide variety of negative outcomes for adults and children. Some of these are mitigated by social support, if the resident has any. Density and poor residential maintenance appear to have negative effects that go beyond the effects of poverty. Very low densities (living alone) also cause problems for people. High-rises probably are not good for children, and young children may be better off attending a childcare center than if they stay at home.*

PEOPLE MOVE. In any given five-year period, about 45 percent of North Americans, 36 percent of Britons and Japanese, and 48 percent of Australians move.[198] They do so for many reasons, including stress or dissatisfaction associated with their current residence, positive or negative changes in their finances or occupation,[199] and progression through the life cycle, such as going off to college, adding a child to the family, or downsizing after the children leave home.

Some moves have pleasant consequences, and some do not, depending on whether the move was chosen or forced and whether or not it fits the resident's personality, needs, and values. In the earlier part of the century, mobility was associated by some experts with social problems and pathology. Gradually, researchers realized that residential mobility is not always pathological, but often is a normal process caused by life-cycle changes.[200]

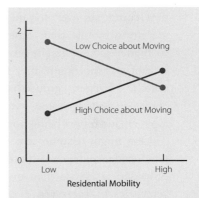

FIGURE 7–9 How moving and illness may be related.

Although not all decisions to move are the result of social problems or dissatisfaction with previous housing, some mobility is associated with adverse outcomes. Mobility is not automatically bad for health, but it can be, depending on a person's residential history, present circumstances, and hopes for the future.[201] For example, among those who move less often, those with less choice about moving report more illness-related symptoms than those who have greater choice about moving[202] (see Figure 7-9). This stress is moderated by personal characteristics: those who are highly mobile and those who are generally less inclined to explore the environment report more illness than those who are more inclined to explore the environment. This suggests that mobility is more damaging to those who move often but do not enjoy seeking out new places.

Mobility may be chosen or forced.[203] The poor and the elderly, whose mobility is often forced, typically experience more crowding after a move. Also, displaced residents often pay more for their new housing than they did for their old housing. More illness is reported among residents who move less often but are unhappy with their present residence and feel they have little choice of residence.[204] Thus, a *lack* of mobility also can be damaging when one's options for moving are restricted.

One group with restricted options is the family headed by a female single parent, which in the United States now comprises over one-quarter of all households. They are more mobile than other households,[205] and, owing to higher rent costs (in relation to income) and relative lack of transportation, they face a more stressful housing search.[206] Even in a group that presumably does have some choice in leaving home—students leaving home for college—many report being homesick.[207]

One might assume that preferences for the potential new residence depends more on the characteristics of the proposed residence than on the resident's personal characteristics.[208] However, a more accurate observation is that the residence's characteristics predict housing preference best *when* they support the resident's values.[209] For example, that the proposed residence is located in a very sociable neighborhood predicts preference for it better if neighborhood socializing is highly valued by the resident.

A change of residence often brings a change in a resident's pattern of activities. Some changes may have been planned and eagerly anticipated; others may not have been foreseen, and come as unpleasant realizations. A study of homeowners who had recently moved from near and far to several Connecticut towns examined the impact of these changes in activity patterns.[210] Positive assessments of the move by residents were related to such changes as increased contact with friends and family, reduced commuting time, increased involvement in religion or community, and improved quality of the residence. Moving may affect children in the sense that parents are less likely to establish social ties in the new neighborhood, which may restrict their childrens' social opportunities.[211]

GIVEN ALL THE PROBLEMS DOCUMENTED by the research literature, environmental psychologists have made many efforts to improve homes. Two examples of environmental psychology applied to the design of homes follow.

Homes for Single-Parent Families

OVER 10 MILLION SINGLE-PARENT FAMILIES live in the United States. Most of these families have female heads and are poor; housing is a big problem for them. Usually single parents must search for housing that was designed in a generic way to suit any group of people living together or housing that was meant for a nuclear family.

However, the single-parent family is neither generic nor nuclear, and it has become a major residential category. Such families need housing that takes its special needs into account. Of course, not even all single-parent families are the same; the number and age of children vary, for example, as does income, whether the single parent works, and the closeness or distance of the absent parent. Nevertheless, how would you design a residence specifically for female-headed single-parent families?

This has been considered by environmental psychologists. Based on an overview of these projects, Kathryn Anthony reports that the most important specific design features of a good project, besides overall quality, are the following: [212]

- On-site or nearby childcare facilities, so parents feel better about working.
- An open kitchen-living room area so parents can cook and watch their children at the same time.
- Separate common areas for children and parents.
- Close proximity to public transportation (single parents often cannot afford cars).
- On-site classroom space (a crucial part of escaping the poverty cycle is education).
- Indoor as well as outdoor play space.

From Building Blocks to a Home

DID YOU EVER BUILD FORTS OR HOUSES as a child? Younger children use building blocks and older children use scrap materials to build play residences. Switzerland had a laboratory where people could build full-scale houses.[213] In the Laboratory for Architectural Experimentation (LEA) at the Federal Institute of Technology at Lausanne, a very large room with high ceilings was the site where residents assemble their dream houses full-scale using lightweight polystyrene blocks and walls. Even two-story simulated houses, complete with doors and windows, could be built and adjusted relatively quickly and easily.

Architects may learn to visualize spaces based on technical drawings, but most people find this difficult. As a researcher at LEA, Roderick Lawrence believed that the third dimension is an essential ingredient for the representation of architectural space to the public. If designers wish to involve residents, and allow them to experience the building much as they would experience the real building, the LEA full-scale approach is valuable.

In one study at LEA, houses that had been simulated were actually constructed later. Researchers then checked whether any changes had been made after the simulation process. The residents had made a few changes, mostly concerning differences in furniture arrangement as envisioned during the simulation versus the way furniture was arranged in the finished house, often because at least some new furniture had been purchased. Architects made a few minor changes involving room sizes and layouts. No design process is perfect, and the LEA experiments revealed a few problems. For example, because the simulation occurred in a lab, some aspects of windows and natural lighting were not well simulated. However, in general, the LEA approach might be tried more widely as designers try to build residences that better suit those who will live in them.

SUMMARY

Home is the most important physical setting for most people. The physical structure (residence, dwelling, house, apartment) is distinct from the meaning structure (home).

Individuals normally called homeless might more properly be called houseless, although if their last residence loses its meaning, they truly are homeless. Residential satisfaction is complex to measure and has many determinants, including stage in the life cycle, socioeconomic status, personality, values, and hopes for the future. Norms, neighbors, and the preferences of others also influence residential satisfaction. Physical features—such as house form, architectural style, floor plan, colors, outdoor areas, and one's cultural background—also affect residential preferences, choices, and satisfaction. People arrange their residential interiors in certain patterns, and these are related to their lifestyle. High indoor density is hard on virtually everyone, but can be tolerable with social support. Adapting to new residences can be stressful. Moving is stressful or not depending on whether a person has some choice in doing so, likes to explore new settings, and likes the present residence.

Suggested Supplementary Readings

Bonaiuto, M. & Alves, S. (2012). Residential places and neighborhoods: Toward healthy life, social integration, and reputable residence. In Clayton, S. D. (Ed.). *The Oxford handbook of environmental and conservation psychology* (pp. 221-247). New York: Oxford.

Evans, G. W., Wells, N. M., & Moch, A. (2003). Housing and mental health: A review of the evidence and a methodological and conceptual critique. *Journal of Social Issues, 59,* 475-500.

Gifford, R. (2007). The consequences of living in high-rise buildings. *Architectural Science Review, 50*(1), 2-17.

Lawrence, R. J. (2002). Healthy residential environments. In R. B. Bechtel & A. Churchman (Eds.), *Handbook of environmental psychology* (pp. 394-412). Hoboken, NJ: Wiley.

Smith, S. G. (1994). The essential qualities of a home. *Journal of Environmental Psychology, 14,* 31-46.

Wells, N. M., & Rollings, K. A. (2012). The natural environment in residential settings: Influences on human health and function. In Clayton, S. D. (Ed.). *The Oxford handbook of environmental and conservation psychology* (pp. 509-523). New York: Oxford.

References

1 Ruskin, J. (1865). *Sesame and lilies*. London: Smith and Elder.

2 Oswald, F., Wahl, H., Mollenkopf, H., & Schilling, O. (2003). Housing and life satisfaction of older adults in two rural regions in Germany. *Research on Aging, 25*, 122-143.

3 Lawrence, R. J. (1987). What makes a house a home? *Environment and Behavior, 19*, 154-168.

4 Altman, I., & Chemers, M. (1980). *Culture and environment*. Monterey, CA: Brooks/Cole.

5 Altman, I., & Gauvain, M. (1981). A cross-cultural and dialectical analysis of homes. In L. Liben, A. Patterson, & N. Newcombe (Eds.), *Spatial representation across the life span*. New York: Academic Press.

6 Rapoport, Am. (1969). *House form and culture*. Englewood Cliffs, NJ: Prentice Hall.

7 Rapoport, Am. (1985). Culture and the urban order. In J. A. Agnew, J. Mercer, & D. E. Sopher (Eds.), *The city in cultural context*. Boston: Allen and Unwin.

8 Altman, I., & Chemers, M. (1980). *Culture and environment*. Monterey, CA: Brooks/Cole.

9 Hayward, D. G. (1975). Home as an environmental and psychological concept. *Landscape, 20*(1), 2-9.

10 Wiesenfeld, E. (1997). Construction of the meaning of a barrio house: The case of a Caracas barrio. *Environment and Behavior, 29*, 34-63.

11 Hayward, D. G. (1975). Home as an environmental and psychological concept. *Landscape, 20*(1), 2-9.

12 Dovey, K. (1985). Home and homelessness. In I. Altman & C. M. Werner (Eds.). *Home environments*. New York: Plenum.

13 Murray, A. (1990). Homelessness: The people. In G. Fallis & A. Murray (Eds.), *Housing and the homeless and poor*. Toronto: University of Toronto Press.

14 Smith, S. G. (1994). The essential qualities of a home. *Journal of Environmental Psychology, 14*, 31-46.

15 Case, D. (1996). Contributions of journeys away to the definition of home: An empirical study of a dialectical process. *Journal of Environmental Psychology, 16*, 1-15.

16 van der Klis, M., & Karsten, L. (2009). Commuting partners, dual residences and the meaning of home. *Journal of Environmental Psychology, 29*, 235-245.

17 Cooper, C. (1976). The house as a symbol of the self. In H. Proshansky, W. H. Ittelson, W., & L. G. Rivlin (Eds.), *Environmental psychology*. New York: Holt, Rinehart and Winston.

18 Stefanovic, I. L. (1992). The experience of place: Housing quality from a phenomenological perspective. *Canadian Journal of Urban Research, 1*, 145-161.

19 Rechavi, T. B. (2009). A room for living: Private and public aspects in the experience of the living room. *Journal of Environmental Psychology, 29*, 133-143.

20 Dovey, K. (1985). Home and homelessness. In I. Altman & C. M. Werner (Eds.). *Home environments*. New York: Plenum.

21 Rechavi, T. B. (2009). A room for living: Private and public aspects in the experience of the living room. *Journal of Environmental Psychology, 29*, 133-143.

22 Zheng, B., Zhang, Y., Chen, J. (2011). Preference to home landscape: wildness or neatness? *Landscape and Urban Planning, 99*, 1-8.

23 Sixsmith, J. (1986). The meaning of home: An exploratory study of environmental experience. *Journal of Environmental Psychology, 6*, 281-298.

24 Baumann, D. J., & Holahan, C. J. (1991). The community psychologist. In R. Gifford (Ed.). *Applied psychology: Variety and opportunity*. Needham Heights, MA: Allyn and Bacon.

25 Burn, S. (1991). Loss of control, attributions, and helplessness in the homeless. *Journal of Applied Social Psychology, 22*, 1161-1174.

26 Baumann, D. J., & Holahan, C. J. (1991). The community psychologist. In R. Gifford (Ed.). *Applied psychology: Variety and opportunity*. Needham Heights, MA: Allyn and Bacon.

27 Larsen, L., Poortinga, E., & Hurdle, D. E. (2004). Sleeping rough: Exploring the differences between shelter-using and non-shelter-using homeless individuals. *Environment and Behavior, 36*, 578-591.

28 Macdonald, J. E., & Gifford, R. (1989). Territorial cues and defensible space theory: The burglar's point of view. *Journal of Environmental Psychology, 9*, 193-205.

29 Caldwell, B. M. (1967). Descriptive evaluations of development and of developmental settings. *Pediatrics, 40*, 46-54.

30 Elardo, E., Bradley, R., & Caldwell, B. M. (1975). The relations of infants' home environment to mental test performance from 6 to 36 months: a longitudinal analysis. *Child Development, 46*, 71-76.

31 Poresky, R. H. (1987). Environmental Assessment Index: Reliability, stability, and validity of the long and short forms. *Educational and Psychological Measurement, 47*, 969-975.

32 Casey, P. H., Bradley, R. H., & Nelson, J. Y. (1988). The clinical assessment of a child's social and physical environment during health visits. *Journal of Developmental and Behavioral Pediatrics, 9*, 333-338.

33 Gifford, R., & Lacombe, C. (2006). Housing quality and children's socioemotional health. *Journal of Housing and the Built Environment, 21*, 177-189.

34 Evans, G. W., Wells, N. M., Chan, H. Y. E., & Saltzman, H. (2000). Housing quality and mental health. *Journal of Consulting and Clinical Psychology, 68*, 526-530.

35 Tsemberis, S., Rogers, E. S., Rodis, E., Dushuttle, P., & Skryha, V. (2003). Housing satisfaction for persons with psychiatric disabilities. *Journal of Community Psychology, 31*, 581-590.

36 Kyttä, M. (2002). Affordances of children's environments in the context of cities, small towns, suburbs and rural villages in Finland and Belarus. *Journal of Environmental Psychology, 22*, 109-123.

37 Clark, C., & Uzzell, D. L. (2002). The affordances of the home, neighbourhood, school and town centre for adolescents. *Journal of Environmental Psychology, 22*, 95-108.

38 .Tognoli J. (1987). Residential environments. In I. Altman & D. Stokols (Eds.), *Handbook of environmental psychology*. New York: Wiley.

39 Amérigo, M., & Aragonés, J. I. (1997). A theoretical and methodological approach to the study of residential satisfaction. *Journal of Environmental Psychology, 17*, 47-57.

40 Saegert, S., & Evans, G. W. (2003). Poverty, housing niches, and health in the United States. *Journal of Social Issues, 59*, 569-589.

41 Gosling, S. D., Ko, S. J., Mannarelli, T., & Morris, M. E. (2002). A room with a cue: Personality judgments based on offices and bedrooms. *Journal of Personality and Social Psychology, 82*, 379-398.

42 Shlay, A. B. (1985). Castles in the sky: Measuring housing and neighborhood ideology. *Environment and Behavior, 17*, 593-626.

43 Chapman, N. J., & Ritzdorf, M. (1986). A trade-off method to assess housing location preferences. *Journal of Environmental Psychology, 6*, 345-358.

44 Lindberg, E., Garling, T., & Montgomery, H. (1986). Beliefs and values as determinants of residential preferences and choices. *Umea Psychological Reports*, Number 194.

45 Lindberg, E., Garling, T., & Montgomery, H. (1989). Preferences for and choices between verbally and numerically described housing alternatives. *Umea Psychological Reports*, Number 189.

46 Noiseux, K., & Hostetler, M. E. (2010). Do homebuyers want green features in their communities? *Environment and Behavior, 42*, 551-580.

47 Moser, G. (2009). Quality of life and sustainability: Toward person–environment congruity. *Journal of Environmental Psychology, 29*, 351-357.

48 Craik, K. H., & Zube, E. H. (1976).(Eds.). *Perceiving environmental quality*. New York: Plenum.

49 Canter, D. (1983). The purposive evaluation of places: A facet approach. *Environment and Behavior, 15*, 659-698.

50 Canter, D. (1983). The purposive evaluation of places: A facet approach. *Environment and Behavior, 15*, 659-698.

51 Weidemann, S., Anderson, J. R., Butterfield, D. I., & O'Donnell, P. M. (1982). Residents' perception of satisfaction and safety: A basis for change in multifamily housing. *Environment and Behavior, 14*, 695-724.

52 Handal, P J., Barling, P. W., & Morrissy, E. (1981). Development of perceived and preferred measures of physical and social characteristics of the residential environment and their relationship and satisfaction. *Journal of Community Psychology, 9*, 118-124.

53 Paulus, P. B., Nagar, D., & Camacho, L. M. (1991). Environmental and psychological factors in reactions to apartments and mobile homes. *Journal of Environmental Psychology, 11*, 143-161.

54 Michelson, W. (1977). *Environmental choice, human behavior and residential satisfaction*. New York: Oxford University Press.

55 Michelson, W. (1977). *Environmental choice, human behavior and residential satisfaction*. New York: Oxford University Press.

56 Schiavo, R. S. (1990). Children's and adolescents' designs of ideal homes. *Children's Environments Quarterly, 7,* 37-46.

57 Nasar, J. L. (1981). Visual preferences of elderly public housing residents: Residential street scenes. *Journal of Environmental Psychology, 1,* 303-313.

58 Nasar, J. L. (1983). Adult viewers' preferences in residential scenes: A study of the relationship of environmental attributes to preference. *Environment and Behavior, 15,* 589-614.

59 Filion, P., Wister, A. V., & Coblentz, E. J. (1992). Subjective dimensions of environmental adaptation among the elderly: A challenge to models of housing policy. *Journal of Housing for the Elderly, 10*(1-2), 3-32.

60 Percival, J. (2002). Domestic spaces: Uses and meanings in the daily lives of older people. *Ageing & Society, 22,* 729-749.

61 Rioux, L., & Werner, C. (2011). Residential satisfaction among aging people living in place. *Journal of Environmental Psychology, 31,* 158-169.

62 Golant, S. M. (1982). Individual differences underlying the dwelling satisfaction of the elderly. *Journal of Social Issues, 38*(3), 121-133.

63 Weenig, M. W. H., & Staats, H. (2010). The impact of a refurbishment of two communal spaces in a care home on residents' subjective well-being. *Journal of Environmental Psychology, 30,* 542-552.

64 Altus, D. E., & Mathews, R. M. (2000). Examining satisfaction of older home owners with intergenerational homesharing. *Journal of Clinical Geropsychology, 6,* 139-147.

65 Salling, M., & Harvey, M. E. (1981). Poverty, personality and sensitivity to residential stressors. *Environment and Behavior, 13,* 131-163.

66 Michelson, W. (1977). *Environmental choice, human behavior and residential satisfaction.* New York: Oxford University Press.

67 Peatross, F. D., & Hasell, M. J. (1992). Changing lives/changing spaces: An investigation of the relationships between gender orientation and behaviors, and spatial preferences in residential kitchens. *Journal of Architectural and Planning Research, 9,* 239-257.

68 Hasell, M. J., Peatross, F. D., & Bono, C. A. (1993). Gender choice and domestic space: Preferences for kitchens in married households. *Journal of Architectural and Planning Research, 10,* 1-22.

69 Keeley, R. M., & Edney, J. J. (1983). Model house designs for privacy, security, and social interaction. *Journal of Social Psychology, 119,* 219-228.

70 Bruin, M. J., & Cook, C. C. (1997). Understanding constraints and residential satisfaction among low-income single-parent families. *Environment and Behavior, 29,* 532-553.

71 Wachs, T. D. (2013). Relation of maternal personality to perceptions of environmental chaos in the home. *Journal of Environmental Psychology, 34,* 1-9.

72 Wiggins, J. S. (1975). *The relationship between personality characteristics and attitudes toward housing and related facilities in six Army posts.* Unpublished manuscript, University of Illinois.

73 Switzer, R., & Taylor, R. B. (1983). Sociability versus privacy of residential choice: Impacts of personality and local social ties. *Basic and Applied Social Psychology, 4,* 123-136.

74 Lindberg, E., Garling, T., & Montgomery, H. (1989). Preferences for and choices between verbally and numerically described housing alternatives. *Umea Psychological Reports,* Number 189.

75 Wiesenfeld, E. (1992). Public housing evaluation in Venezuela: A case study. *Journal of Environmental Psychology, 12,* 213-223.

76 Paulus, P. B., Nagar, D., & Camacho, L. M. (1991). Environmental and psychological factors in reactions to apartments and mobile homes. *Journal of Environmental Psychology, 11,* 143-161.

77 Ritterfeld, U., & Cupchuck, G. C. (1996). Perceptions of interior spaces. *Journal of Environmental Psychology, 16,* 349-360.

78 Michelson, W. (1980). Long and short range criteria for housing choice and environmental behavior. *Journal of Social Issues, 36* (3), 135-149.

79 Paulus, P. B., Nagar, D., & Camacho, L. M. (1991). Environmental and psychological factors in reactions to apartments and mobile homes. *Journal of Environmental Psychology, 11,* 143-161.

80 Popovics, A. J. (1990). Reasons for satisfaction and dissatisfaction with campus housing at an undergraduate school for women. *College Student Journal, 23,* 359-360.

81 Amérigo, M., & Aragonés, J. I. (1990). Residential satisfaction in council housing. *Journal of Environmental Psychology, 10,* 313-325.

82 Amérigo, M., & Aragonés, J. I. (1990). Residential satisfaction in council housing. *Journal of Environmental Psychology, 10,* 313-325.

83 Weidemann, S., & Anderson, J. R. (1985). A conceptual framework for residential satisfaction. In I. Altman & C. M. Werner (Eds.). *Home environments.* New York: Plenum.

84 Wister, A. V. (1985). Living arrangement choices among the elderly. *Canadian Journal on Aging, 4,* 127-144.

85 Keeley, R. M., & Edney, J. J. (1983). Model house designs for privacy, security, and social interaction. *Journal of Social Psychology, 119,* 219-228.

86 Galster, G. C., & Hesser, G. W. (1981). Residential satisfaction: Compositional and contextual correlates. *Environment and Behavior, 13,* 735-758.

87 Widmar, R. (1984). Preferences for multiple-family housing: Some implications for public participation. *Journal of Architectural and Planning Research, 1,* 245-260.

88 Jelinkova, Z., & Picek, M. (1984). *Physical and psychological factors determining population responses to environment.* Presentation at the European C.I.A.N.S Conference, Olomouc, Czechoslovakia.

89 Evans, G. W., Kantrowitz, E., & Eshelman, P. (2002). Housing quality and psychological well-being among the elderly population. *Journals of Gerontology: Series B: Psychological Sciences and Social Sciences, 57B,* P381-P383.

90 Michelson, W. (1977). *Environmental choice, human behavior and residential satisfaction.* New York: Oxford University Press.

91 Marans, R. W. (1976). Perceived quality of residential environments: Some methodological issues. In K. H. Craik & E. H. Zube (Eds.). *Perceiving environmental quality: Research and applications.* New York: Plenum.

92 Miller, S. I., & Evko, B. (1985). An ethnographic study of the influence of a mobile home community on suburban high school students. *Human Relations, 38,* 683-705.

93 Leger, J. M. (1985). The pre-fabricated house: Is it really a home? *Journal of Environmental Psychology, 5,* 345-354.

94 Paulus, P. B., Nagar, D., & Camacho, L. M. (1991). Environmental and psychological factors in reactions to apartments and mobile homes. *Journal of Environmental Psychology, 11,* 143-161.

95 Nasar, J. L.(1989). Symbolic meanings of house styles. *Environment and Behavior, 21,* 235-257.

96 Alkhresheh, M. M. (2012). Preference for void-to-solid ratio in residential facades. *Journal of Environmental Psychology, 32,* 234-245.

97 Marsden, J. P. (1999). Older persons' and family members' perceptions of homeyness in assisted living. *Environment and Behavior, 31,* 84-106.

98 Gifford, R. (1999). *The adjustment of the elderly to congregate care housing.* Report to the Canada Mortgage and Housing Corporation.

99 Brown, B. B., Burton, J. R., & Sweaney, A. L. (1998). Neighbors, households, and front porches: New urbanist community tool or mere nostalgia? *Environment and Behavior, 30,* 579-600.

100 Baird, J. C., Cassidy, B., & Kurr, J. (1978). Room preference as a function of architectural features and user activities. *Journal of Applied Psychology, 63,* 719-727.

101 Cunningham, M. R. (1977). Notes on the psychological basis of environmental design: The right-left dimension in apartment floor plans. *Environment and Behavior, 9,* 125-135.

102 Weisenthal, D. L., & Tubiana, J. H. (1981). Apartment design choices: A study of Israeli and Non-Israeli university students. *Environment and Behavior, 13,* 677-684.

103 Duffy, M., & Willson, V. L. (1984). The role of design factors of the residential environment in the physical and mental health of the elderly. *Journal of Housing for the Elderly, 2,* 37-45.

104 Mahnke, F. H., & Mahnke, R. H. (1987). *Color and light in man-made environments.* New York: Van Nostrand, 1987.

105 Billger, M. (2000). Evaluation of a colour reference box as an aid for identification of colour appearance in rooms. *Colour Research and Application, 25,* 214-225.

106 Kunishima, M., & Yanase, T. (1985). Visual effects of wall colors in living rooms. *Ergonomics, 28,* 869-882.

107 Abu-Ghazzeh, T. M. (1999). Housing layout, social interaction, and the place of contact in Abu-Nuseir, Jordan. *Journal of Environmental Psychology, 19,* 41-73.

108 Freeman, C., Dickinson, K. J. M., Porter, S., & van Heezik, Y. (2012). "My garden is an expression of me": Exploring householders' relationships with their gardens. *Journal of Environmental Psychology, 32,* 135-143.

109 Levy-Leboyer, C., & Ratiu, E. (1993). The need for space and residential satisfaction. *Architecture et Comportement/Architecture and Behavior, 9*, 475-490.

110 Gifford, R. (1999). *The adjustment of the elderly to congregate care housing.* Report to the Canada Mortgage and Housing Corporation.

111 Kearney, A. R. (2006). Residential development patterns and neighborhood satisfaction: Impacts of density and nearby nature. *Environment and Behavior, 38*, 112-139.

112 Saarinen, T. F. (1988). Public perception of the desert in Tucson, Arizona. *Journal of Architectural and Planning Research, 5*, 197-207.

113 Zheng, B., Zhang, Y., Chen, J. (2011). Preference to home landscape: wildness or neatness? *Landscape and Urban Planning, 99*, 1-8.

114 Billig, M., & Churchman, A. (2003). Building walls of brick and breaching walls of separation. *Environment and Behavior, 35*, 227-249.

115 Jabareen, Y. (2005). Culture and housing preferences in a developing city. *Environment and Behavior, 37*, 134-146.

116 Kent, S. (1991). Partitioning space: Cross-cultural factors influencing domestic spatial segmentation. *Environment and Behavior, 23*, 438-473.

117 Lawrence, R. J. (1987). *Housing, dwellings, and homes: Design theory, research, and practice.* New York: Wiley.

118 Canter, D., & Thorne, R. (1972). Attitudes to housing: A cross cultural comparison. *Environment and Behavior, 4*, 3-32.

119 Groves, M., & Thorne, R. (1988). Aspects of housing preference: Revisiting a cross-cultural study with the hindsight of improved data analysis. *Journal of Environmental Psychology, 8*, 45-55.

120 Bonnes, M., Giuliani, M. V., Amoni, F., & Bernard, Y. (1987). Cross-cultural rules for the optimization of the living room. *Environment and Behavior, 19*, 204-227.

121 Amaturo, E., Costagliola, S., & Ragone, G. (1987). Furnishing and status attributes: A sociological study of the living room. *Environment and Behavior, 19*, 228-249.

122 Weisner, T. S., & Weibel, J. C. (1981). Home environments and family lifestyles in California. *Environment and Behavior, 13*, 417-460.

123 Ahrentzen, S., Levine, D. W., & Michelson, W. (1989). Space, time, and activity in the home: A gender analysis. *Journal of Environmental Psychology, 9*, 89-101.

124 Tognoli, J. (1980). Differences in women's and men's responses to domestic space. *Sex Roles, 6*, 833-842.

125 Michelson, W. (1985). *From sun to sun: Daily obligations and community structure in the lives of employed women and their families.* Totowa, NJ: Rowman and Allanheld, pp. 89-101.

126 Parke, R. D., & Sawin, D. B. (1979). Children's privacy in the home: Developmental, ecological, and child-rearing determinants. *Environment and Behavior, 11*, 87-104.

127 Ashcraft, N., & Scheflen, A. (1976). *People space.* Garden City: Anchor.

128 Becker, F. D. (1974). *Design for living: The residents' view of multi-family housing.* Ithaca, NY: Center for Urban Development Research.

129 Raviv, A., & Palgi, Y. (1985). The perception of social-environmental characteristics in kibbutz families with family-based and communal sleeping arrangements. *Journal of Personality and Social Psychology, 49*, 376-385.

130 Blood, R. (1953). A situational approach to the study of permissiveness in child rearing. *American Sociological Review, 18*, 84-87.

131 Kruusvall, J. (1988). Mass housing and psychological research in the Soviet Union. In D. Canter, M. Krampen, & D. Stea (Eds.), *Environmental policy, assessment, and communication.* Aldershot, UK: Avebury.

132 Pennartz, P. J. J. (1986). Atmosphere at home: A qualitative approach. *Journal of Environmental Psychology, 6*, 135-153.

133 Glyptis, S. A., & Chambers, D. A. (1982). No place like home. *Leisure Studies, 1*, 247-262.

134 Kiesling, F. M., & Manning, C. M. (2010). How green is your thumb? Environmental gardening identity and ecological gardening practices. *Journal of Environmental Psychology, 30, 315-327.*

135 McMillan, D. W., & Hiltonsmith, R. W. (1982). Adolescents at home: An exploratory study of the relationship between perception of family social climate, general well-being, and actual behavior in the home setting. *Journal of Youth and Adolescence, 11*, 301-315.

136 Goldstein, G., Novick, R., & Schaefer, M. (1990). Housing, health and well-being: An international perspective. *Journal of Sociology and Social Welfare, 17*, 161-181.

137 Goldstein, G., Novick, R., & Schaefer, M. (1990). Housing, health and well-being: An international perspective. *Journal of Sociology and Social Welfare, 17*, 161-181.

138 Barnes, B. R., Mathee, A., Shafritz, L. B., Krieger, L., & Zimicki, S. (2004). A behavioral intervention to reduce child exposure to indoor air pollution: Identifying possible target behaviors. *Health Education & Behavior, 31*, 306-317.

139 Evans, G. W., Wells N. M., Chan, H. Y. E., & Saltzman, H. (2000). Housing quality and mental health. *Journal of Consulting and Clinical Psychology, 68*, 526-530.

140 Dunn, J. R., & Hayes, M. V. (2000). Social inequality, population health, and housing: A study of two Vancouver neighborhoods. *Social Science & Medicine, 51*, 563-587.

141 Priemus, H. (1986). Housing as a social adaptation process: A conceptual scheme. *Environment and behavior, 18*, 31-52.

142 Kellett, J. (1989). Health and housing. *Journal of Psychosomatic Research, 33*, 255-268.

143 Norris-Baker, C., & Scheidt, R. J. (1989). Habituation theory and environment-aging research: Ennui to joie de vivre? *International Journal of Aging and Human Development, 29*, 241-257.

144 Zaborowski, C. A., Armstrong-Esther, F. M., & Sandilands, M. (1985). Environmental change as a factor in stress in the elderly. *Alberta Psychology, 14*, 10-11, 23-24.

145 Thompson, B. (1989). Preparing elderly people for life in a "home". *British Journal of Occupational Therapy, 52*, 103-104.

146 Lawton, M. P. (1990). Residential environment and self-directedness among older people. *American Psychologist, 45*, 638-640.

147 Slangen de Kort, Y. A. W., Midden, C. J. H., & van Wagenberg, A. F. (1998). Predictors of the adaptive problem-solving of older persons in their homes. *Journal of Environmental Psychology, 18*, 187-197.

148 Morgan D. G., & Stewart, N. J. (1998). Multiple occupancy versus private rooms on dementia care units. *Environment and Behavior, 30*, 487-503.

149 Fisher, S., & Hood, B. (1988). Vulnerability factors in the transition to university: Self-reported mobility history and sex differences as factors in psychological disturbance. *British Journal of Psychology, 79*, 309-320.

150 Stokols, D., Ohlig, W., & Resnick, S. M. (1979). Perceptions of residential crowding, classroom experiences, and student health. In J. R. Aiello & A. Baum (Eds.), *Residential crowding and design.* New York: Plenum.

151 Riemer, S. (1948). Maladjustment to the family home. *American Sociological Review, 10*, 642-648.

152 Kellett, J. (1989). Health and housing. *Journal of Psychosomatic Research, 33*, 255-268.

153 Evans, G. W., Palsane, M. N., Lepore, S. J., & Martin, J. (1989). Residential density and psychological health: The mediating effects of social support. *Journal of Personality and Social Psychology, 57*, 994-999.

154 Regoeczi, W. (2008). Crowding in context: an examination of the differential responses of men and women to high-density living environments. *Journal Of Health And Social Behavior, 49*, 254-268.

155 Tryon, G. S. (1985). An exploratory study of the relationship between residence hall design and student alcohol consumption. *Journal of College Student Personnel, 26*, 372-373.

156 Galle, O. R., & Gove, W. R. (1979). Crowding and behavior in Chicago, 1940-1970. In J. R. Aiello & A. Baum (Eds.), *Residential crowding and design.* New York: Plenum.

157 Wachs, T. D. (1979). Proximal experience and early cognitive-intellectual development: The physical environment. *Merrill-Palmer Quarterly, 25*, 3-41.

158 Heft, H. (1985). High residential density and perceptual-cognitive development: An examination of the effects of crowding and noise in the home. In J. F. Wohlwill & W. van Vliet (Eds.), *Habitats for children: The impacts of density.* Hillsdale, NJ: Erlbaum.

159 Gottfried, A. W., & Gottfried, A. E. (1984). Home environment and cognitive development in young children of middle-socioeconomic-status families. In A. W. Gottfried (Ed.), *Home environment and early cognitive development.* Orlando: Academic Press.

160 Bradley, R. H., & Caldwell, B. M. (1984). The HOME Inventory and family demographics. *Developmental Psychology, 20*, 315-320.

161 Bradley, R. H., & Caldwell, B. M. (1984). The relation of infants' home environments to achievement test performance in first grade: A follow-up study. *Child Development, 55*, 803-809.

162 Saegert, S. (1980). *The effect of residential density on low income children.* Paper presented at the annual meetings of the American Psychological Association, Montreal, September.

163 Wachs, T. D. (1988). Relevance of physical environment influences for toddler temperament. *Infant Behavior and Development, 11*, 431-445.

164 Evans, G., Ricciuti, H., Hope, S., Schoon, I., Bradley, R, Corwyn, R., Hazan, C. (2009). Crowding and cognitive development the mediating role of maternal responsiveness among 36-month-old children. *Environment and Behavior, 2*, 1-14.

165 Booth, A., & Edwards, J. N. (1976). Crowding and family relations. *American Sociological Review, 41*, 308-321.

166 Booth, A., & Johnson, D. R. (1975). The effect of crowding on child health and development. *American Behavioral Scientist, 18*, 736-749.

167 Saegert, S. (1980). *The effect of residential density on low income children.* Paper presented at the annual meetings of the American Psychological Association, Montreal, September.

168 Rodin, J. (1976). Density, perceived choice, and response to controllable and uncontrollable outcomes. *Journal of Experimental Social Psychology, 12*, 564-578.

169 Ruback, R. B., & Pandey, J. (2002). Mental distress and physical symptoms in the slums of New Delhi: The role of individual, household, and neighborhood factors. *Journal of Applied Social Psychology, 32*, 2296-2320.

170 Gottfried, A. W., & Gottfried, A. E. (1984). Home environment and cognitive development in young children of middle-socioeconomic-status families. In A. W. Gottfried (Ed.), *Home environment and early cognitive development.* Orlando: Academic Press.

171 Lakey, B. (1989). Personal and environmental antecedents of perceived social support developed at college. *American Journal of Community Psychology, 17*, 503-519.

172 Evans, G. W., Palsane, M. N., Lepore, S. J., & Martin, J. (1989). Residential density and psychological health: The mediating effects of social support. *Journal of Personality and Social Psychology, 57*, 994-999.

173 Gabe, J., & Williams, P. (2008). Is space bad for your health? The relationship between crowding in the home and emotional distress in women. *Sociology of Health & Illness, 8*, 351-371.

174 Stephan, E., Fath, M., & Lamm, H. (1988). Loneliness as related to various personality and environmental measures: Research with the German adaptation of the UCLA Loneliness Scale. *Social Behavior and Personality, 16*, 169-174.

175 Koller, K, & Gosden, S. (1984). On living alone, social isolation, and psychological disorder. *Australian and New Zealand Journal of Sociology, 20*, 81-92.

176 Galle, O. R., & Gove, W. R. (1979). Crowding and behavior in Chicago, 1940-1970. In J. R. Aiello & A. Baum (Eds.), *Residential crowding and design.* New York: Plenum.

177 Booth, A., & Welch, S. (1973). *The effects of crowding: A cross-national study.* Paper presented at the annual meetings of the American Psychological Association, Montreal, Canada.

178 Korosec-Serfaty, P., & Bolitt, D. (1986). Dwelling and the experience of burglary. *Journal of Environmental Psychology, 6*, 329-344.

179 Brown, B. B., & Harris, P. B. (1989). Residential burglary victimization: Reactions to the invasion of a primary territory. *Journal of Environmental Psychology, 9*, 119-132.

180 Normoyle, J. B., & Foley, J. M. (1988). The defensible space model of fear and elderly public housing residents. *Environment and Behavior, 20*, 50-74.

181 Carvalho, M., George, R. V., & Anthony, K. H. (1997). Residential satisfaction in condominios exclusivos (gate-guarded neighborhoods) in Brazil. *Environment and Behavior, 29*, 734-768.

182 Wells, N. M., & Evans, G. W. (1996). Home injuries of people over age 65: Risk perceptions of the elderly and of those who design for them. *Journal of Environmental Psychology, 16*, 247-257.

183 Rosenthal, S. (2011). Measuring knowledge of indoor environmental hazards. *Journal of Environmental Psychology, 31*, 137-146.

184 van Vliet—, W. (1983). Families in apartment buildings: Sad storeys for children? *Environment and Behavior, 15*, 211-234.

185 Evans, G. W., Lercher, P., & Kofler, W. W. (2002). Crowding and children's mental health: The role of house type. *Journal of Environmental Psychology, 22*, 221-231.

186 Gifford, R., & Lacombe, C. (2006). Housing quality and children's socio-emotional health. *Journal of Housing and the Built Environment, 21*, 177-189.

187 Gottfried, A. W., & Gottfried, A. E. (1984). Home environment and cognitive development in young children of middle-socioeconomic-status families. In A. W. Gottfried (Ed.), *Home environment and early cognitive development.* Orlando: Academic Press.

188 Wachs, T. D. (1979). Proximal experience and early cognitive-intellectual development: The physical environment. *Merrill-Palmer Quarterly, 25*, 3-41.

189 Wachs, T. D. (1988). Relevance of physical environment influences for toddler temperament. *Infant Behavior and Development, 11*, 431-445.

190 Gaunt, L. (1980). Can children play at home? In P. F. Wilkinson (Ed.), *Innovation in play environments.* London: Croom Helm.

191 Golden, M., Rosenblath, L., Grossi, L., Policare, M., Freeman, Jr., H., & Brownlee, E. (1978). *The New York infant day care study.* New York: Medical and Health Research Association of New York City.

192 Becker, F. D. (1974). *Design for living: The residents' view of multi-family housing.* Ithaca, NY: Center for Urban Development Research.

193 Oda, M, Taniguchi, K., Wen, M., & Higurashi, M. (1989). Effects of high-rise living on physical and mental development of children. *Journal of Human Ergology, 18*, 231-235.

194 Dhillon, P. K., & Bhalla, M. (1988). The impact of built-living environment on human behavior: An empirical study. *Journal of the Indian Academy of Applied Psychology, 14*, 16-25.

195 McCarthy, D. P., & Saegert, S. (1978). Residential density, social overload, and social withdrawal. *Human Ecology, 6*, 253-272.

196 Gifford, R. (2007). The consequences of living in high-rise buildings. *Architectural Science Review, 50*, 2-17.

197 Duffy, M., & Willson, V. L. (1984). The role of design factors of the residential environment in the physical and mental health of the elderly. *Journal of Housing for the Elderly, 2*, 37-45.

198 Stokols, D., Shumaker, S. A., & Martinez, J. (1983). Residential mobility and personal well-being. *Journal of Environmental Psychology, 3*, 5-19.

199 Ruback, R. B., Pandey, J., Begum, H. A., Tariq, N., & Kamal, A. (2004). Motivation for and satisfaction with migration: An analysis of migrants to New Delhi, Dhaka and Islamabad. *Environment and Behavior, 36*, 814-838.

200 Rossi, P. H., & Shlay, A. B. (1982). Residential mobility and public policy issues: "Why Families Move" revisited. *Journal of Social Issues, 38*, 21-34.

201 Stokols, D., & Shumaker, S. A. (1982). The psychological context of residential mobility and well-being. *Journal of Social Issues, 38*, 149-171.

202 Stokols, D., Shumaker, S. A., & Martinez, J. (1983). Residential mobility and personal well-being. *Journal of Environmental Psychology, 3*, 5-19.

203 Newman, S. J., & Owen, M. S. (1982). Residential displacement: Extent, nature, and effects. *Journal of Social Issues, 38*(3), 135-148.

204 Stokols, D., Shumaker, S. A., & Martinez, J. (1983). Residential mobility and personal well-being. *Journal of Environmental Psychology, 3*, 5-19.

205 Masnick, G., & Bane, M. J. (1980). *The nation's families: 1960-1990.* Boston: Auburn House.

206 Ahrentzen, S. (1985). Residential fit and mobility among low-income, female-headed family households in the United States. In W. van Vliet, E. Huttman, & Fava (Eds.). *Housing needs and policy approaches: Trends in thirteen countries.* Durham, NC: Duke University Press.

207 Fisher, S., Murray, K., & Frazer, N. A. (1985). Homesickness, health, and efficiency in first year students. *Journal of Environmental Psychology, 5*, 181-195.

208 Clark, W. A. V. (1986). *Human migration.* Beverly Hills, CA: Sage.

209 Lindberg, E., Hartig, T., Garvill, J., & Garling, T. (1992). Residential-location preferences across the life span. *Journal of Environmental Psychology, 12*, 187-198.

210 Walker, P. R. (1992, August). *Residential relocation: Measuring the link between place and identity.* Paper presented at the annual meetings of the American Psychological Association, Washington, DC.

211 Pettit, B., & McLanahan, S. (2003). Residential mobility and children's social capital: Evidence from an experiment. *Social Science Quarterly, 84*, 632-649.

212 Anthony, K. H. (1991). Housing the single-parent family. In W. F. E. Preiser, J. C. Vischer, & E. T. White (Eds.), *Design intervention: Toward a more humane architecture.* New York: Van Nostrand Reinhold.

213 Lawrence, R. J. (1987). *Housing, dwellings, and homes: Design theory, research, and practice.* New York: Wiley.

CHAPTER 8:

Urban Environmental Psychology

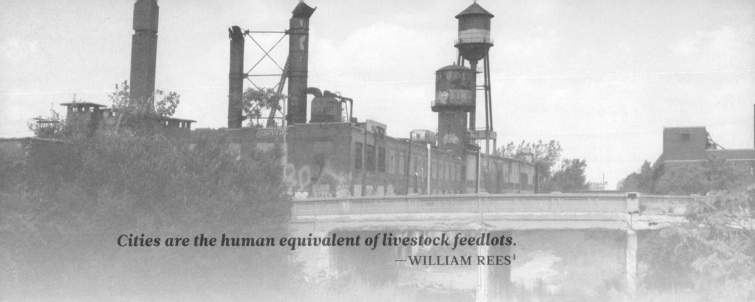

Cities are the human equivalent of livestock feedlots.

—WILLIAM REES[1]

We must restore to the city the maternal life-nurturing functions, the autonomous activities, the symbiotic associations that have long been neglected or suppressed. For the city should be an organ of love.

—LEWIS MUMFORD[2]

"WHAT?" SAID JANE. "I CAN'T HEAR YOU." *Tom laughed and repeated, louder, "What do you think of this awful noise?"*

"You mean the jackhammers or the subway?" asked Jane.

"The whole thing. The whole rotten cacophony," Tom yelled.

"I think it's the price you pay for living in the city," Jane yelled. They were walking home from work, trying to discuss what to do that evening. In order to talk, they entered an espresso bar. It was jammed, they were jostled, but they could hear each other.

"Are you sure you want to live in this neighborhood?" Jane asked. She was debating the wisdom of moving into grandpa's house, which was a block off the main avenue. Tom wanted to. "It's as noisy as a buzz saw at rush hour," he said, "but there's a park close by, we can walk to concerts and the gallery. You can buy almost anything you want without using a car..."

"And get mugged if you don't do these things within a tiny window of time," Jane finished for him. "Or trip over a garbage bag or some wrecked person."

"Like you said, Jane, that's the price you pay. I don't know about you, but I already feel like I'm a part of this neighborhood. I've got genes here, memories of childhood visits. I'm coming home."

"I'm happy for you, Tom. Do you know anyone here?"

"Well, not exactly. But when I go for a walk, I see the same people over and over again. I feel like I know them."

"You feel like you know people that you don't even know? Tom, you have a lot of convincing to do if you want to share this neighborhood with this kid."

THIS CHAPTER EXPLORES PERSON–ENVIRONMENT RELATIONS IN CITIES, public places, the neighborhood, the community, and on the streets. Some of the questions to be addressed are:

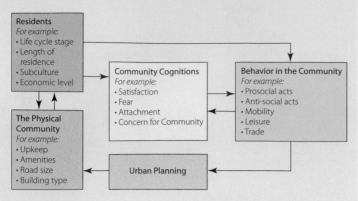

FIGURE 8–1 Model for urban environmental psychology.

- Are cities good for people?

- What constitutes a satisfying neighborhood?

- What are the effects of such community stressors as noise, heat, and air pollution?

- Under which environmental conditions will individuals in public places tend to help or hurt one another?

- What is the nature of social interaction in public places?

- How does the physical environment influence shopping?

A general model for this section is presented in Figure 8-1. The physical aspects of the city (stressors and amenities) and personal factors are presumed to influence the way we think about our cities and neighborhoods (whether we are satisfied or not, fearful or not, attached to them or not, mentally healthy or mentally unhealthy).

In the model, the physical aspects of the city, personal factors, and these cognitions are presumed to affect our actual behavior in urban public places such as streets, parks, and stores. These behaviors may be pro-social, antisocial, or neither; they include everyday behaviors, such as how fast we walk, kids playing in parks, or where we choose to sit in public areas. They also include behavior in retail settings such as our reactions to store music and displays.

The model further proposes that these behaviors, in turn, influence our cognitions (just as cognitions influence behaviors) and the urban planning and design process. The design process, to complete the cycle, influences the physical shape of the city as zoning and other bylaws govern what sort of buildings, streets, and parks get built. The cycle then continues. Environmental psychologists have studied all phases of this model.

A VAST GLOBAL MOVEMENT TO THE CITY IS UNDERWAY. For example, at the beginning of the 20th century, most North Americans lived in rural settings; now most live in cities. From 1970 to 1990, the population of Mexico City increased from 9 million to over 20 million; it is now closer to 30 million. Much of the increase has been caused by migration from the countryside rather than a dramatic increase in the urban birthrate. The rush to the city is a worldwide phenomenon; many other cities also have grown fantastically. What happens once nearly everyone lives so close together?

The Prosecution's Case

CITIES CAN BE VERY STRESSFUL: Noise, traffic, density, and pollution usually are much greater than in rural places. We humans have only lived in such large agglomerations for a tiny fraction of the time we have been a species; it is reasonable to claim that cities are unnatural. Great ancient cities, such as Athens, the cradle of democracy and many of the ideas we hold dear, and Florence, the birthplace of great artists, had only about 25,000 people in their golden ages. Plato claimed that 40,000 was the upper limit to the size of an effective city. Some recent experts claim that 150,000 is the ideal city size.[3] A brain imaging study suggests that we have an inherent preference for viewing natural scenes over urban scenes.[4]

Many people who live in large cities seem to agree that populations of multimillions are too much. Surveys indicate that 60 percent of New Yorkers, 48 percent of Los Angeles' residents, and 43 percent of Bostonians would leave their cities if they could.[5] Out of 192 U.S. cities with populations over 100,000, the average population of the 22 *least* stressful cities was only 116,000.[6] In Canada, city dwellers are 67 percent more likely to be robbed and 44 percent more likely to be beaten up than rural residents.[7]

Ecologically, cities are gluttons. A typical city of 500,000 people who live on about 27,000 acres/11,000 hectares sucks up the natural resources of 6 million acres/2.4 million hectares.[8]

The prosecution rests its case!

The Defense's Case

SOME 5,000 PEDESTRIANS PER HOUR jostle by each other at the corner of 59th Street and Lexington Avenue in New York City. The street is "a collision of senses and sensibilities: shoppers lugging bags, workers toting briefcases, yuppies, beggars, vendors, pickpockets, all against a backdrop of honking horns and the smell of candied nuts..." William Whyte, champion of the city's possibilities, said, "What a carnival!"[9] in an approving manner. He believes that people gravitate *toward* high density and thrive on it. According to Whyte, the vendors, performers, and eccentrics make cities exciting.

Clearly, cities have benefits; besides the interesting street life, these include more cultural, educational, medical, leisure, social, and shopping resources, not to mention greater opportunity for jobs. At least in France, residents of cities report no more stressors such as noise, air pollution, traffic problems, or criminality than residents of rural areas.[10]

The defense rests its case!

WHAT DOES THE EVIDENCE SAY ABOUT THE BENEFITS AND COSTS OF URBAN LIVING? We will consider that after we focus on the basic elements of the topic: neighborhood, city, and urbanite.

WHAT IS A NEIGHBORHOOD?

THE CENTER OF THE MODEL in Figure 8-1 is based on residents' thoughts and feelings about their community, including their beliefs about what their neighborhood *is*, including its spatial extent, their confidence about its future, their safety fears,[11] their attachment to the neighborhood, its meaning to them, their conception of its character,[12] and their overall satisfaction with it.

Are the boundaries of your neighborhood clear to you? Are you sure what your neighborhood means to you? The answers to such questions are not simple. Environmental psychologists have tried to answer them by examining residents' perceptions, cognitions, and definitions of their neighborhoods and communities. Neighborhood is a psychological concept; often legal boundaries (e.g., of a school district or electoral area) are different from those of a neighborhood. This psychological dimension of neighborhoods is illustrated in a Seattle study that asked residents to describe the boundaries of their neighborhood.[13] Not everyone agreed where the boundaries were, yet most respondents did think their neighborhood *had* boundaries.

Within these boundaries, neighborhoods may be urban or suburban; may contain industrial, commercial, or residential development; may have parks; may be old or new, graced with quiet tree-lined streets or split by major roads; and will include varying percentages of high-rise, low-rise, single-family, and other housing forms as residences. The difference between downtown and suburban neighborhoods, in their residents' mental images, is that downtown neighborhoods contain more mixed land uses, more traffic and parking problems, more noise, crowding, stress, danger, pavement, and mess.[14] Despite that, residents who identify with downtown have more positive views of downtown, and those who identify with suburbia have more positive views of suburbia.

Despite this psychological view of neighborhoods, some have tried to define neighborhoods in terms of their physical quality. One outcome of this approach is the Residential Environment Assessment Tool (REAT), which uses an independent observer to assess neighborhoods in an objective checklist manner.[15]

We live in such diverse settings that it may be difficult to imagine how different from one another neighborhoods can be unless you have experienced many of them. However, you can begin to realize the differences by asking yourself three questions: Is there much or little face-to-face interaction in my neighborhood? To what extent do the residents think of themselves as being *of* or *from* this neighborhood? Is there much or little contact between residents of this neighborhood and residents of other neighborhoods?

The answers to these questions may be combined to describe several kinds of neighborhoods.[16] Three will be briefly described. The **integral neighborhood** has much face-to-face interaction, much cohesiveness from neighborhood support of local interest and values, and much participation in organizations outside the neighborhood. The **parochial neighborhood** is like the integral neighborhood except that it has fewer ties to outside organizations; it is inward facing and may even discourage participation in the wider community. The **anomic neighborhood** has little face-to-face contact, little identification, and few ties to the outside world. Do you live in one of these three types?

A different view of them is that neighborhoods consist of three components: social interaction, symbolic interaction, and attachment to people and places.[17] **Social interaction** refers to the ways that neighbors give each other emotional support, supply one another with useful information, and help each other get things done. **Symbolic interaction** refers to mental images of the neighborhood, such as cognitive maps of it and the communication of status through symbols. For example, when people were shown photos of late-19th-century Boston houses and asked which were residences of upper-middle, middle-middle, and lower-middle-class people, the houses still provided usable status cues more than 100 years after they were constructed: the viewers could correctly identify the class of the owners. [18] Agreement about the meaning of neighborhood symbols—in this case the meaning of architectural details—is only one part of the psychological concept of neighborhood, but it is an important part. The third component, **place attachment,** refers to a resident's cognitive-emotional connection to the neighborhood, and will be discussed in another chapter.

WHAT IS A CITY?

YOU MIGHT WELL THINK THAT IS A VERY SILLY QUESTION. "It's a large group of random people and random buildings in one place, that's obvious!" At a superficial level, that is true. But no, as usual, it is not that simple. For example, a study of old and a modern urban developments found that the psychologically meaningful elements in both places were *not* buildings, but such elements as gates, fountains, trees, and gardens.[19] As for the buildings, research shows that they are not merely large random collections of buildings: similar urban forms arose independently in quite different parts of the world, suggesting that there is a reason for the essential form of a city. [20] The study's author believes that the urban form was developed to promote exploration of it, which in turn promotes social interaction. She suggests, in a sort of urban theory of evolution, that early settlements with forms that promoted exploration and social interaction grew into cities, and those that did not died away.

Other scientists have also begun to look at the objective form of cities, in a search for something beyond a random collection of large buildings. They find that some elements that compose the objective face of the city are more informative than others, which makes them more legible and better remembered than others.[21] The grouping of these elements and our categorization of them are what gives meaning to the face of the city.

WHAT IS AN URBANITE?

WHO LIVES IN THE CITY? Urban dwellers are not random either. Ordinarily we think of urbanites in terms of demographics such as income, social class, cultural background, or age. This is reasonable, but a team of Italian environmental psychologists believes that another useful way to think about urbanites is in terms of their behavior patterns, that is, how they *use* the city.[22] Their study in Rome suggests that there are four main types of urbanites. **Neighborhood-confined urbanites** spend most of their time in their residence, rarely go to the city center, but prefer to visit the suburbs when they go out. **Marginal-escape urbanites** stay at home even more, but when they go out in their neighborhood or to the downtown central area (they do not visit the suburbs), it is to "hang out"—just to have a walk, be among people, and enjoy the sights. **Multiplace hyperactive urbanites** go downtown for cultural activities and attend sports and outdoor activities in their own neighborhoods, but also like to go to the suburbs. **Quality-user urbanites** like to go to the downtown central area for specific and cultural activities, such as concerts, to meet friends, to join in political demonstrations, and to buy particular items, but they would not go downtown merely to hang out. They mainly use their own neighborhood only to purchase daily needs; they do not go to the suburbs much. Does one of these types fit you?

ONCE YOU ARE OUTSIDE, ON THE STREETS near your home, are you satisfied with what you see and hear? Does your neighborhood make you feel proud or ashamed? Do you feel as if you would like to escape as soon as possible, or spend your whole life in such a great place? Satisfaction with one's neighborhood obviously is important in its own right, but its importance goes beyond that. Studies show that neighborhood satisfaction is closely related to crucial broader concepts such as a person's satisfaction with the city as a whole,[23] overall psychological well-being,[24] and even satisfaction with life in general.[25]

Measuring Neighborhood Satisfaction. Personal, social, physical, and cultural factors influence one's satisfaction with a community. However, before each of these influences are described, we should consider how to measure community satisfaction. How would you do this? The obvious approach is to simply ask residents, "Are you satisfied with your neighborhood?" However, satisfaction has many dimensions and causes, and it is preferable to measure them with a range of questions, rather than to merely ask the outcome question. Certainly if we hope to improve satisfaction with a particular neighborhood, we must determine which aspects of neighborhood satisfaction are most important and which are within the power of the residents or a government to change.

One way to measure satisfaction is to ask about the extent of positive social relations in the neighborhood, the clarity of the symbolic interactions (clashing meanings lead to confusion and dissension), and strong attachment to the neighborhood.[26] Another view holds that neighborhood satisfaction is composed of residents' satisfaction with the neighborhood's physical condition, political climate, convenience (e.g., access to schools, work, and shopping), and social relations.[27] A third approach consists of a formal checklist of the perceived quality of neighborhoods.[28,29] It includes 19 perceived residential environment quality indicators, each with 3 or 4 items.

In the sections to follow, the factors that influence neighborhood satisfaction will be described. As usual, I group these into personal, social, physical, and cultural sources. My general model (Figure 8-1) suggests that

FIGURE 8–2 Contrasts in neighborhoods: Mixed residential-commercial development (top) is common in cities but is less preferable to most residents than purely residential districts (bottom).

satisfaction may be a direct function of certain personal or physical variables, or it may depend on combinations of person characteristics and physical features. For example, whether a new skateboard park in a neighborhood increases satisfaction probably depends largely on whether you ask a resident who is 14 or 74 years old. People who like trees place more importance on trees when they look for a new place to live.[30]

Personal Influences. Most personal influences on neighborhood satisfaction also depend partly on the neighborhood in question, but some of them may be viewed as mainly personal because they are the cognitions of residents. For example, residents are more satisfied with their neighborhood if it has greater interest for them[31] and when they feel at home in it.[32] When residents believe their current neighborhood is an improvement over their former neighborhood, they will be more satisfied with it.[33] Some residents value their own neighborhood merely *because* they live in it; sometimes even those who live in less-prestigious neighborhoods rate their neighborhood as more prestigious or satisfying than outsiders do.[34, 35]

An attitude of special importance is confidence (or the lack of it) in the neighborhood: when that is strong, residents will stay and improve it. When they are pessimistic about it, they are less likely to stay (if they have any choice), and not likely to renew, renovate, or revitalize it. Indeed, when a government program offered residents incentives to stay and fix up their homes, those who had more confidence in the neighborhood were more likely to stay instead of moving.[36]

Adaptation to the level of stimulation in a neighborhood also affects satisfaction.[37] The large amount of stimulation found in cities may constitute an overload for some people, but be just right for others. You may recall Harry Helson's adaptation-level theory from an earlier chapter; it may help predict who is satisfied with a city or neighborhood and who is not. People who are adapted to quite low levels of stimulation—such as villagers—often find a sudden drastic increase in urban stimulation unpleasant. Similarly, city dwellers who are adapted to lots of action may find villages painfully boring.

Helson suggested that *moderate discrepancies* from one's adaptation level are pleasing.[38] In the case of communities, this might mean that a villager would be pleased by a town but not a city, and that city dwellers would be happier in a small town than in a village. The oft-repeated specter of overload in the city is not true for everyone (remember William Whyte?). After an initial period of actively coping with the higher levels of stimulation found in the city, many new residents find a social and physical niche that protects them from undesirable levels of stimulation. Of course, this protection depends in part on one's resources; for example, one often hears that New York City is a great place to live if you have friends and plenty of money.

Among other personal factors are ownership versus renting (owners are more satisfied) and stage of life (e.g., houses for families and apartments for retired people).[39] Personality-like factors also play a role: some people like cities in general (**urbanophiles**), whereas others do not (**urbanophobes**). Urbanophiles naturally identify with urban life and, perhaps as a psychological defense of their views, tend to underestimate the frequency of incivilities, or bad behavior, in cities; urbanophobes tend to overestimate the their frequency.[40]

Age is another factor. Elderly people often prefer residential areas that are open, well-kept, uniform, organized, and not mysterious.[41] Such places require less cognitive and physical energy to deal with. Which sort of neighborhood is best for children? Suburbia? Maybe not: if a child-friendly neighborhood is defined as one that offers the most opportunities for independent mobility and for accessing environmental affordances (that is, places that facilitate desirable activities), then neighborhoods with moderate urban density may be best.[42] **The key word here is moderate; children who live on busy streets are half as independently mobile as children who do not, and the mobility of girls is doubled when they live on well-connected, low-traffic streets.**[43]

Physical Influences. Satisfaction of course also depends in part on the physical characteristics of the neighborhood itself. However, which physical characteristics matter? Neighborhoods with more natural elements are preferred.[44-48] Neuropsychological studies support this preference for more natural settings.[49] Neighborhoods that appear more open are more satisfying[50,51] and are associated with a stronger sense of community.[52] For most people, a quiet neighborhood is a good neighborhood.[53] Satisfying neighborhoods are free of technological threats, such as power plants and air pollution,[54] and those with more industry are harmful to residents' psychological health.[55] Satisfying neighborhoods are ones that are well-maintained.[56-58] They consist of structures that are more ornate than plain (for younger people anyway), and buildings are single-use (that is, not residential-commercial mixtures).[59] Neighborhoods feel restorative when they have more visual diversity (but not too much height)[60] and are aesthetically pleasant,[61,62] which mainly is a combination of the earlier elements mentioned.

Walkable neighborhoods are satisfying neighborhoods.[63-65] Walkability is the extent to which a neighborhood has pleasant and interesting paths upon which to saunter, meander, promenade, amble, march, ramble, or roam. They have amenities, such as schools, parks, shopping, and recreation facilities, especially ones to which you can stroll, or at least have public transport to reach.[66,67] More amenities also means a stronger sense of community.[68] For the elderly, and probably for others, a more walkable neighborhood includes streets with other people, stairs, marked crossings, trees, front gardens, bus and tram stops, shops, food outlets, and parks, and without litter on the street, high-rise buildings, and high density of dwellings.[69]

The size of a project is an important factor in satisfaction with public housing projects. Since the middle 1970s, the trend in the design of projects has been toward smaller size, and studies show that residents of smaller projects that can fit into other neighborhoods are more satisfied with them.[70] Newness also can help: new residences within older, declining neighborhoods physically revitalize the neighborhood, and those who live in them have greater confidence in the neighborhood than do other residents in the neighborhood.[71]

In sum, most people will be satisfied with a neighborhood with the physical attributes just described: beautiful, green, walkable, relatively small and natural, with good access to needed facilities and services, and this also seems to increase neighborly activities.[72] Other physical qualities, however, may be satisfactory to some residents, but not others.

Which *combinations* of personal qualities and physical features produce neighborhood satisfaction? One example is that older residents prefer outdoor places away from the sun's glare where they can sit and watch people,[73] but not all age groups care about this particular combination of neighborhood features. Children are less annoyed by community noise than adults.[74] In a notable exception to the expected finding, people who live close to a threat (a nuclear plant in England, in this case), *and* have a strong sense of place, perceive *less* risk than those who have a weaker sense of place.[75]

Another example comes from a study of Toronto families who had recently moved. Their satisfaction with physical aspects of the community was strongly influenced by the availability of public transportation and parking facilities, appearance of the neighborhood, and distance to green spaces.[76] However, their satisfaction was moderated by other factors, such as whether the they lived downtown or in the suburbs, and whether they lived in an apartment or a house. For example, the distance to green spaces was a greater source of dissatisfaction for downtown residents than for suburban residents. Lack of public transportation was a bigger source of unhappiness for suburban apartment dwellers than it was for downtown residents.

One surprising source of dissatisfaction involves noise.[77] Because downtowns usually are noisier, you might expect downtown residents to be most upset about noise. However, many more residents of suburban houses in the Toronto study were dissatisfied with noise than were downtown residents. Perhaps downtown residents have adapted to higher noise levels and no longer notice the noise, or maybe suburbanites expect their homes to be even quieter than they are.

Noise is often a problem, yet loud sounds are *not* always annoying (some people like loud concerts or riding motorcycles, for example). Therefore, a reasonable question is: What makes a sound annoying? This depends in part on the listener's perception of the noise-maker's motivation and perceived control over the sound level. Sounds that annoy tend to be—apart from their loudness— less common, apparently avoidable, and occur at night.[78] These factors assist with the prediction of which objective sounds will be experienced as annoying.[79]

DAVID UZZELL
is a leading British environmental psychologist who has investigated many aspects of urban and sustainable behaviors.

The same level of sound is more annoying to people who associate it with other negative events. For example, one intriguing study tested the idea that aircraft noise annoyance is based in part on fears that planes may crash.[80] When annoyance in a community that had recently experienced a plane crash was compared to that in a community with the same level of aircraft noise but no recent crash experience, annoyance indeed was higher in the community that had experienced a crash.

Aircraft noise is source of dissatisfaction in many neighborhoods. Near a busy southern California airport where air traffic alone created an average 65 decibels of sound all day (about as loud as a very busy office), 84 percent of residents said aircraft noise was a problem.[81] However, annoyance was moderated by personal factors: Residents with low perceived control over the noise were more annoyed than residents who believed they could have some control over it, and annoyance was greater among homeowners (as opposed to renters), those with more education, and those who are noise-sensitive.[82] Other studies suggest that annoyance is closely related to one's appraisals of the *trade-offs* between the economic benefits of the noise producer (e.g., airplanes) and its adverse environmental effects.[83]

Can people get used to noise, so that it does not bother them anymore? Strong annoyance can be reduced in the short term, but not in the long term.[84] The same residents were interviewed 4 months and 16 months after a major new highway opened in their community.[85] The new highway raised sound levels 16 to 20 decibels above that in similar neighborhoods with no highway. The residents' annoyance with the increased sound did not decrease in the 12-month interval between surveys, and the residents became more pessimistic about their ability to adapt.

Nevertheless, *some* individuals may be able to adapt to noise better than others. Some of us are more capable than others of screening out unwanted stimulation.[86] Another moderating variable is anxiety level; low-anxiety individuals appear able to adapt to traffic noise, but high-anxiety individuals do not.[87] Other residents seem not to be bothered no matter how much traffic noise surrounds them: in Sweden, the percent of the population that reported being "very annoyed" rose steadily to about 40 percent as the number of heavy vehicles passing by reached about 2,000 per day. However, this percentage did not increase, even when over 9,000 heavy vehicles per day passed by.[88]

Unfortunately, people may adapt to other community problems, such as air pollution. Longtime Los Angeles residents, for example, are equally *capable* of perceiving air pollution as newer residents, but they were significantly less likely to actually report the air on a given day as being polluted.[89] Apparently, at lower pollution levels, they no longer realize that what they see is indeed pollution. Presumably then, long-term residents' satisfaction with their community is not adversely affected by low levels of pollution. This lack of recognition can, of course, be dangerous to one's respiratory health.

Social Influences. What about the social environment of a community? Does satisfaction with a neighborhood depend on the quality of its social life? Surprisingly, social networks may *not* be important sources of satisfaction in many communities. Marc Fried, who coauthored a classic study in favor of the crucial role of social ties for residential satisfaction[90] later claimed that most residential satisfaction is related to the *physical* quality of the neighborhood.[91] When the physical and social features of neighborhoods

were compared, physical features predicted resident satisfaction better.[92] Interviews with 2,500 residents of over 40 municipalities suggested that social ties are an important source of neighborhood satisfaction only to residents who strongly value social ties.

These results suggest that many of us simply no longer value the neighborhood as a source of friends or social support.[93] Instead, we look to work, school, and other non-neighborhood places for our social needs. Of course, the social aspects of the neighborhood are important in that we want our neighbors to be "good" people.[94] However, this does not always mean that we actually want to socialize with these folks! Often, we just hope they are good in the sense that they will not harm us. That leads to the next topic.

Safety fears are a key cause of community satisfaction or dissatisfaction. These fears include parental concerns about possible traffic accidents involving children[95] and widespread fear of crime.[96] Fear of crime discourages older residents from leaving their homes to take the bus,[97] women from using downtown cores[98] and certain areas of college campuses,[99] and generally limits their routine activities.[100] Safety fears have even have adverse effects on the mental health of adults.[101] Feeling good about a community is difficult if every time you go outside, you half expect to get mugged or raped. Places where a potential attacker might hide and dark spots are the worst.[102]

Interestingly, however, fear of crime does not heavily depend on the actual crime rate. It may be inflated by flashy media portrayals or other factors. In a study of Hong Kong and Toronto, Janice Peacock and I found that fear of crime was more closely associated with population density than with actual crime rates.[103] Urban areas that residents *believe* to be dangerous are not always the areas that have the statistically highest rates of crime.[104] Perhaps surprisingly, crime and fear of crime do not always have negative effects on neighborhood satisfaction. For example, a Dutch study found that burglary victims did *not* develop strong negative feelings about their neighborhood.[105] However, an American study reported the more expected outcome that residents who believe their neighborhood to be safer are more satisfied with it.[106]

Defensible space theory, introduced in an earlier chapter, argues that certain arrangements of streets and other public territories create settings in which space is easily surveyed and clearly defined as to ownership.[107] It sometimes is associated with reduced crime rates, and some of its elements can make residents *feel* safer. For example, lighting designed to facilitate surveillance of public areas reduced residents' fear in one study even though crime may not have been reduced.[108] Well-maintained grass and, perhaps surprisingly, more trees make people feel safer.[109] Neighborhood physical decay may, by association, evoke fear of crime, but this may be true only for moderate-income residents, not for all residents.[110]

Despite its complex causes (and non-causes!), fear of crime is an exceedingly important and usually destructive emotion in many communities. It is based, of course, on legitimate concerns, but it unfortunately dampens exploration, activity, and the growth of interpersonal relations in affected neighborhoods.

Cultural Influences. Cities reflect the culture and eras in which they are embedded.[111] Satisfaction with cities that vary with time and culture presumably is a function of congruence between the residents' culture, the era with which they identify,[112] and the physical form of the community.

Diversity that stems from distinct cultural influences may characterize some features of communities, but other features seem to have a near-universal meaning.[113] For example, religious buildings from the cathedral at Chartres to temples in India to basilicas in Milwaukee to sacred buildings in Papua, New Guinea, all use height to express the idea of holiness. Central squares or plazas also show widespread similarity across cultures.

Satisfaction with one's community presumably is a function of whether these near-universal features are present in the built form of our own community. Earlier, I noted that the physical aspects of neighborhoods are more important to many residents than its social features. Some exceptions to this are ethnic or religious groups that explicitly work toward building close physical ties (by buying or renting within one neighborhood) to facilitate close social ties.[114] However, many ethnic group members begin to seek housing outside the traditional ethnic enclave as soon as they have enough money and feel comfortable in the dominant culture.[115] This reinforces the notion that social ties usually or ultimately are less important than the physical qualities of the community for most residents.

Neighborhood Satisfaction as Congruence. Another way to understand whether a person will be satisfied with the neighborhood involves the degree of matching between the person and the neighborhood. What does the person want, and what does the neighborhood have to offer? What might those things be? Congruence is important in six areas: the neighborhood's physical amenities or aesthetics, resource amenities, safety, stimulation versus peacefulness, homogeneity versus heterogeneity, and interaction versus solitude.[116] The more that a resident's needs match what the neighborhood's character in these six areas, the more satisfied the resident is probably will be. Of course, sometimes the same neighborhood is the subject of conflict because it has radically different meaning for different stakeholder groups, as is the case of the proposed redevelopment of an old area of Barcelona.[117]

IN SUM *Neighborhoods are psychological as well as physical. Not everyone who lives in an area would even draw the same boundaries around the neighborhood, and official boundary lines do not always define residents' ideas of their neighborhood. Neighborhoods have different characteristics—some more positive and some more negative—depending on the type of social contact, whether residents feel confident, whether they interact with outsiders ever (or always, by spending most of their time away from the neighborhood), whether they feel attached to or identify with the community, and whether they feel safe. Generally, the neighborhood's physical qualities are more important than its social qualities, unless (on the positive side) residents have special bonds with each other or (on the negative side) residents are at war, or nearly so. A pleasant, green residential-only area is nice, but not everyone's favorite place; more important is whether the neighborhood fills six categories of one's needs and whether one is adapted to its pattern of stimulation.*

THE GROWTH OF COMMUNITIES INTO CITY SCALE automatically means that the ratio of strangers to acquaintances grows. When more people are strangers, treating them as objects or targets is easier. Strength becomes an asset, both for aggressors and for potential victims. No wonder many people find urban outdoor environments threatening, or that urban places are more threatening in the evening and when no one else is around.[118,119] The worse the neighborhood appears to former drug users, the more depressive symptoms they have, regardless of how much social support they have.[120]

A nationwide U.S. study of 207 cities reports that, in general, the largest cities are the worst for children.[121] Not surprisingly, then, a rather broad spectrum of residents now oppose further community growth.[122] Living in a poor urban area seems to make it all worse. Urban residents mistrust others more than suburban residents do, mistrust is deeper in poor neighborhoods than in wealthier ones, poor people mistrust others more than richer people, and mistrust is correlated with perceiving disorder in the neighborhood.[123]

Living in a poor-quality neighborhood not only reduces satisfaction; it increases perceived danger.[124] Cities usually are industrialized, and those who live near industries tend to be poor and to have more mental health problems than other residents.[125] In fact, evidence shows that poor-quality neighborhoods influence depression beyond the effect of poverty itself.[126] Cécile Lacombe and I demonstrated that poor-quality residences are associated with more children's behavior problems, even after the influence of income (and other factors) have been taken into account.[127]

Urbanization itself may have a generally negative impact on mental health. Over the years between 1880 and 1963, a direct regional correlation was found between schizophrenia and urbanization in the United States.[128] In the Netherlands, the incidence of psychosis increases with **urbanicity** (essentially, how close to downtown a person lives), although it is even more common when the person also has a family history of psychosis.[129]

Several explanations for this are possible. One is the **drift hypothesis**, which asserts that people who already have problems migrate (drift) into cities, as opposed to the hypothesis that stressors encountered *in* the city are the cause of their problems. However, contrasting evidence—that physically bad neighborhoods may be the cause of the problem—comes from a rare experimental study in which some families were moved from a bad neighborhood to a good one and some were not.[130] Later, when the mental health of those who moved was compared with that of those who stayed behind, a significant difference was found: the movers improved. However, both the drift hypothesis and the bad-neighborhood hypothesis may be true.

Whatever the cause, cities do have a greater proportion of people with schizophrenia than rural areas, and this concentration itself causes problems. If community stress is also represented by rates of crime, alcoholism, divorce, and suicide, then the drift hypothesis seems to be confirmed by differences in these problems among U.S. cities. The growing cities of the sunbelt in Florida, California, Nevada, Texas, Arizona, and Oklahoma have 22 of the 25 most-stressful cities out of 286 studied.[131,132] Only one city out of the 25 least stressful cities is located in those states. The logical conclusion is that stress is a product of migration. Either troubled people move and bring their troubles with them, or increased population causes disorganization and stress even among the long-term residents of the destination cities, or both.

One model of the connection between the physical design of a community and mental health proposes that the following features may be especially important in causing mental health problems: high density, through streets, poor upkeep of public places, a lack of community meeting places, and high-rise residences.[133] Persistent noise from planes and trains is more than dissatisfying: it can be harmful to health,[134] children's reading skills,[135] and cognitive performance.[136] Children in poor-quality neighborhoods have more emotional and behavioral problems,[137-139] although other influences also play a role. For example, a positive experience in a poor neighborhood reduces the impact of the bad conditions, but exposure to violence makes their effect even worse.[140] Residents of polluted communities report more illness and less satisfaction with community life.[141] Design elements are not equally stressful to everyone (in fact, high-rises may be *less* stressful for some residents), but most of these elements may be stressful to most residents.

FIGURE 8-3 Contrasting views of urban environments. These two summer scenes involve infrastructure and cooling, water-based play: one based around strong infrastructure and healthy community interaction among people of varying backgrounds, the other on infrastructure decay. In many inner cities, community (rather than municipal) control of a fire hydrant occurs when public pools and other facilities close.

Anti-social Behavior in the Urban Environment

DRIVE-BY SHOOTINGS AND CARJACKINGS are two recent and serious manifestations of urban antisocial behavior. Less dramatic but equally disturbing incidents also occur: a subway attendant reminds a patron that smoking is not permitted, and the patron snarls, "OK, come here. I'll butt it out on your forehead!" A pedestrian fed up with cyclists who ride on the sidewalk sticks an umbrella into the spokes of a passing bike. A few blocks later, the courier who was riding the bike hammers his fist into the side of a car that approaches too close.

Environmental psychologists have contributed in many ways to the understanding and reduction of antisocial behavior. One striking example is the accurate postdiction of where serial killers commit their crimes.[142] Another is understanding the mobility of criminals, who sometimes prey on their (usually) relatively poor neighbors, but also engage in "outbound offending" in which they travel to more affluent areas to engage in property theft.[143] Crimes are strongly influenced by "directionality," that is, they do not occur randomly in every direction from the criminal's residence; most occur within one 45-degree cone shape from the criminal's residence.[144] Elements of houses also matter: front porches (surveillance opportunities) and well-kept front lawns and gardens (territoriality indicators) can discourage various kinds of incivilities, which help to create more walkable neighborhoods.[145]

Community Design and Local Conditions

CRIME AND VANDALISM are linked to, or facilitated by, certain aspects of the physical nature of a community. Consider one small, everyday anti-social act; parking in spaces that are reserved for people with disabilities. The usual marking for such spaces is a symbol painted on the pavement. Merely adding an upright sign significantly deters drivers without disabilities from parking in these spaces.[146]

Crime as a function of the environment was discussed earlier, when defensible space theory was described. Areas with defensible space usually have less crime, but defensible space does not always reduce residents' *fear* of crime.[147] When an area seems more residential, with few through streets and little public parking, it usually will experience less crime than houses on the edges of such areas.[148,149] The general principle is to reduce the passage of strangers through the area, which increases bonds among residents and helps them to spot suspicious activity. This notion that more-public areas are more vulnerable is confirmed by reports that more crimes are committed at the edges of central downtown districts.[150]

Among other connections between crime and urban features, blocks with houses that have been burglarized have more street signs.[151] Possibly, streets with more signs indicate a more public area with less control by residents, which may be attractive to criminals. Apartments nearer parking lots and recreation areas are burglarized more, as are stores and residences near corners. Somewhat contrary to this overall picture, streets with heavier traffic may experience less crime—perhaps more cars means more chance of being observed.[152]

Neighborhood design and poverty fit together in an unfortunate pairing. More stores sell alcohol in poorer neighborhoods, which is associated with lower levels of social cohesion.[153] In turn, lower social cohesion is related to more perceived neighborhood problems with youth alcohol and drug use, which is related to neighborhood youth drug and alcohol arrests.

More crime occurs in taller apartments and apartments with more than 5 units per floor or 50 total units.[154] This probably occurs because residents of larger buildings are less likely to know one another, tend to treat each other as strangers, and lose the ability to recognize who lives in the building and who does not. This makes entry by criminals easier. Many gated communities have sprung up, partly out of fears about crime. Residents in one study did feel safer, but actual crime rates were not lower and, surprisingly, the general sense of community was lower than in a non-gated community.[155]

Some design changes do seem to help. A neighborhood in Dayton, Ohio, with a high crime rate incorporated some defensible space changes.[156] Many entrances to the neighborhood were closed, speed bumps were installed to slow down traffic, gates with the neighborhood logo were installed, and the community was divided into five mini-neighborhoods with physical barriers. Two years later, traffic was down 67 percent, violent crime declined by 50 percent, and total crime by 26 percent.

However, some areas with defensible space have serious crime problems anyway. That is partly because *defensible* space (the physical layout) does not necessarily translate into *defended* space (residents actually acting against crime by keeping an eye out or reporting suspicious activity). This can happen, for example, if the neighborhood is not sufficiently cohesive to act together against criminal elements.[157] Defensible space *sets the stage* for crime reduction by making it easier, almost automatic, for residents to fight crime through visual surveillance of outdoor areas, but if residents are unable or unwilling to act on what they see, crime will not be deterred. A second reason that defensible space does not guarantee a crime-free neighborhood is that not all criminals pay attention to the environment. Less-experienced criminals motivated by thrill-seeking, social approval, or under the influence of drugs or alcohol use less

rational criteria for choosing a target and may simply not pay attention to defensible space features of the setting.[158]

When the crime scene is a particular building (such as a convenience store) rather than an entire neighborhood, defensible space design principles may be more successful. One chain of stores incorporated a series of changes such as putting cash registers in front of windows and removing window ads to make the interior more surveillable. Robberies declined 30 percent compared to other stores that were not redesigned.[159] An analysis of bank robberies and sales of stolen property in sting operations showed that bank robbers select locations in the bank that enable them to systematically control seeing and being seen during the crime and that stolen-property salespersons were more tense and left the scene more quickly when the transaction occurred in a setting that limited their surveillability.[160]

Another design factor is physical diversity in a neighborhood. In her influential book, *The Death and Life of Great American Cities*, Jane Jacobs speculated that diversity (defined as short blocks, mixed land use, old and new buildings, and concentrated use of space) increases public social interaction among residents, which thereby helps to discourage crime.[161] A Toronto study of these ideas found support for the idea that more physically diverse districts do have more neighboring and less crime.[162] However, the connection between more neighboring and less crime was not significant. Thus, physical diversity may indeed discourage crime, but for reasons *other* than the creation of more social interaction among residents.

Researchers in the Netherlands developed a checklist for assessing the crime vulnerability of neighborhoods.[163] Six main elements comprise this checklist:

- The potential visibility of public areas (lines of sight).
- The actual presence of residents (to take advantage of these sightlines).
- Social involvement (residents care enough to maintain buildings and act against criminals).
- Access and escape routes (for both criminals and victims).
- Attractiveness (assuming that beauty evokes care in residents and decay informs criminals that the residents have little vigilance).
- The vulnerability of materials (locks, presence of easily vandalized walls, etc.).

The checklist's primary aim is to identify areas that are susceptible to vandalism, but it may be further developed as a tool against other crimes, like burglary and assault.

Vandalism is a widespread destructive behavior. However, not every alteration of public territory is vandalism. Robert Sommer distinguished between vandalism and people's art.[164] Vandals are destructive or egocentric; they break off a young tree or scrawl their own name on a subway wall. Artists' goals include beautifying an ugly environment, and these public artists usually seek anonymity as they creatively enhance a bleak place. Tagging, the highly stylized spray-paint signatures, can be vandalism or people's art.

Some damage in neighborhoods occurs according to the **broken window hypothesis**. This idea, which goes back over 40 years to early environmental psychology research which showed that litter begets more litter,[165, 166] is that when a place is already slightly degraded, people will tend to further degrade it[167,168] and to think of the area as socially disordered.[169] In part, people see litter, vandalism, or even theft as the norm and tend to follow that norm. Of course, this can be remedied by cleaning and repairing a neighborhood, so that a new norm to treat the neighborhood with respect is established.

Trees as crime-prevention agents? Well, yes and no. When they are grown in the public parts of streets, they are associated with lower crime rates.[170] However, small trees on house lots are associated with more crime, perhaps because they reduce surveillability, which aids burglars, but large trees on house lots are associated with less crime.

Weather

CRIME IS RELATED TO WEATHER. Perhaps the most-researched weather variable is temperature. A popular idea is that high temperatures causes riots and other social aggression.[171] Police have subscribed to this notion for a long time,[172] but public awareness of the hypothesis was heightened by a 1968 report from the United States Riot Commission.[173] The Commission's figures indicated that every 1967 riot in the United States (except one) began when the temperature was at least 80°F/27°C. The Commission did not intend this as proof that heat causes aggression. However, as sometimes happens when informal studies confirm an intuitively attractive idea, many readers accepted the data as proof that high temperatures cause riots and crime.

What is the empirical evidence?

Records over a 4-year period *did* show that riots increase with temperature—up to about 83°F/28°C.[174] Some crimes (assault, burglary, collective violence, and rape) increase with temperature up to about 85°F/29°C.[175] (A similar trend occurs in sport. Baseball pitchers hit twice as many batters when temperatures are in the 90s°F/30s°C as when temperatures are cooler.)[176] In Sao Paulo, Brazil, homicides increase with the temperature, but particularly when people are poor and have free time, such as evenings, weekends, and during the summer.[177] However, at even higher temperatures, crime seems to decrease. The curvilinear pattern holds for certain times, such as daylight hours and spring months.[178]

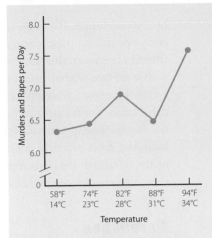

FIGURE 8–4 This shows the number of murders and rapes per day in Houston, Texas, as a function of the maximum temperature on the day of the crime. Violence generally increases across this temperature range rather than peaking at a moderately high temperature.

One group of researchers suggested that, over a certain temperature, heat discomfort may be *too* high to promote riots. This sparked a hot(!) controversy. A different group of researchers reexamined the temperature and riot records and pointed out a **base-rate problem**, that is, the number of riots decreased on very hot days simply because fewer very hot days occur.[179] They suggested that when the base-rate problem was corrected for, antisocial behavior does, after all, rise steadily with temperature. That is, although there are few very hot days, the chances of a riot on those very hot days does continue to increase.

Other field studies also show that, within the normal range of temperatures (up to about 95°F/36°C), the hotter it is, the more aggressive acts occur.[180,181] Yet another study replicated these findings and showed that this is particularly true for violent (as opposed to nonviolent) crimes[182] (see Figure 8-4). Thus, field studies support the linear hypothesis (more heat equals more aggression) rather than the curvilinear hypothesis (aggression peaks at moderately hot temperatures and declines in very hot temperatures).[183]

However, the original researchers' basic contention that antisocial behavior declines at very high temperatures must be true at sufficiently high temperatures. My own experience, when I was a student working in peach orchards in the summer when the temperature was about 113°F/45°C, is that no one wishes even to *move*, let alone run amok in a riot. However, and this is the important and ominous conclusion, the temperature at which aggression begins to decline because potential aggressors are too hot is rather high. For most *practical* purposes, that is, across the range of temperatures that most people experience most of the time, aggression does increase with temperature.

Air Pollution

PURE AIR CAN BE CONTAMINATED WITH CHEMICALS THAT ARE ODORLESS and by those with a foul smell. Bad odors negatively affect mood and attraction to others. For example, students exposed to a bad-smelling pollutant judged peers (shown in photographs) lower on a scale of well-being,[184] and a moderately bad odor facilitated aggression (giving electric shocks).[185]

This led environmental psychologists to search for links between air pollution and social pathology in community settings. Indeed, higher levels of photochemical oxidants in the air have been correlated with more domestic disputes and more instances of psychiatric disturbance.[186,187] Correlation does not imply causation, but the researchers were aware of this and were able to eliminate several alternative explanations for their findings, which suggests that the link *may* be causal.

If these findings are confirmed by subsequent research, the implications are very important, for two reasons. First, it is not terribly surprising to hear that high temperatures and loud noise harm social relations, but we do not usually think of air pollution as an antisocial agent. Air pollution may be a hidden cause of aggression. Second, activists committed to fighting air pollution could reasonably argue that air pollution erodes more than paint, vegetation, and the pH balance of lakes. It may erode human relations.

IN SUM *Personal safety is a very important urban problem. Some danger is caused by poverty and social breakdown, but defensible space principles combined with a take-back-the-streets community attitude can significantly reduce crime. Other physical forces facilitate aggressiveness, though. Higher temperatures, up to about 85°F/29°C, appear to increase the risk of violence. A less obvious aggression-causing problem may be air pollution; in addition to being a health risk, it may also trigger violence in some individuals.*

HELPFULNESS IN THE CITY

ENVIRONMENTAL FACTORS HAVE BEEN LINKED with helpfulness, and the lack of it, as we shall see next.

Weather

A curious researcher asked people to help him with a questionnaire under different climatic conditions.[188] He found that temperature affected how much participants were willing to help, but the effect was not the same in the summer as it was in the winter. In summer, they helped more on cooler days, but in winter they helped more on warmer days. He concluded that we help more when the weather is "nice" (that is, warm winter days and cool summer days). The same researcher also asked restaurant workers to keep track of their tips each day and found that they received more tips on sunny days (in the spring).

Assuming that most of us think of sunshine as pleasant, this supports the following nice-weather hypothesis: We are more willing to help when it is sunny (but not too hot). Other factors can overwhelm weather as an influence. When a person on crutches needed help, over 95 percent of passersby helped whether the temperature was hot, cold, or comfortable.[189] That almost everyone helped certainly is good news.

Noise

Helping is not always facilitated by environmental variables. Loud noise reduces helping. If the noise is very loud, many people try to escape it, rather than help someone in need. Loud noise may reduce helping because in attempting to escape, our attention is narrowed. We walk faster and gaze straight ahead more.[190]

A moderating factor, as in the weather example above, is the seriousness of the other person's predicament. If someone's life is in danger, most of us probably would risk noise loud enough to hurt our ears in order to render assistance. However if the other person's only problem is a dropped book, we may not help. For example, construction noise (92 decibels, as opposed to 72 decibels away from the construction) hindered individuals from giving a small amount of money to a person who asked for some.[191] Panhandlers are advised to avoid noisy street corners.

The seriousness factor was supported in another study in which researchers observed how many passersby helped a person who dropped an armload of books.[192] They arranged for a nearby lawn mower with no muffler to be running during the incident (87 decibels) or not (about 50 decibels). In addition, the person who dropped the books either was wearing a cast or not. Without a cast, the book dropper was helped by 20 percent of passersby in the less-noisy condition and by 10 percent of them in the noisier condition. A much larger difference occurred when a cast was worn. In the less-noisy condition, 80 percent helped, but only 15 percent in the noisier condition.

Apparently, helping in extreme temperatures and in noise is a different matter. Why should this be? One possibility is that we can usually anticipate and dress for cold or hot temperatures, and thereby reduce the adverse effects of temperature. However, when we encounter noise in public places, we cannot easily counter the annoyance, except by leaving. When the noise is localized (as with a lawn mower or jackhammer), we realize that a little fast walking, which incidentally also carries us past the person who needs help, will get us beyond the awful din.

A possible explanation for these findings is that noise seems to affect how we think about others. When individuals were asked to form impressions of others under low- and high-noise conditions, their judgments of others were more *extreme*. Noise, perhaps because it acts as a general arousal agent, influences people to reach stronger conclusions about others than they might make under normal conditions.[193] This could mean more dislike for a stranger who is not in distress, and more sympathy for one who is.

Number of People

THE NUMBER OF BYSTANDERS IS RELATED TO HELPING. This idea was strengthened by the many studies stimulated by a 1964 episode in which a young woman, Kitty Genovese, was killed on a New York street while 38 neighbors watched without helping her.[194] (I must report that although this crime has become a standard in social psychology textbooks, it may simply be untrue that many witnesses saw and did not act.) However, the principle may be true: on the very day I am writing this, the newspaper reported the killing of a teen while many people watched. Subsequent research has found that, under most conditions, the more individuals who witness someone having a problem, the smaller the odds that any one of them will help.

In one field study, the experimenter appeared to lose her contact lens in a mall. Helping behavior was defined as the length of time that the nearby people helped her look for it. When the mall was moderately full, people helped less than when it was moderately empty.[195] In another field study, density in the immediate vicinity of the person needing help was more closely related to helping (high density was associated with less helpfulness) than was density at the community-wide level.[196] At a broader level, as we saw in an earlier chapter, city density is negatively correlated with helpfulness in many cities.[197]

Urbanites do, of course, help those in need under some conditions. Once again, moderating variables—such as being very busy[198] and where one is raised—play an important and sometimes counter-intuitive role. For example, people who were raised in the *city* helped more than those who were raised in the country.[199] Thus, high immediate density may cause unhelpful behavior, but personal characteristics of the potential helper and certain circumstances other than the high density surrounding the event also affect helping behavior.

Behavior in smaller cities may be more helpful in small ways such as holding a department store door open for the next person, although in another study, when big-city shoppers saw someone else being helpful, they were more likely to be helpful, too.[200] Cities sometimes are viewed as unrelenting sources of noise, crime, ugliness, and crowding. The overload approach suggests that urban stimulation is so great that individuals are *forced* to become apathetic and rude.[201] They must select cues and pay attention only to the most important part of their environment, which means ignoring other sights that might seem important to outsiders.

However, Stanley Milgram painted city dwellers as people doing the best they can in a place that tended to "deform" them. This perspective may have improved the

FIGURE 8–5 Most of the time, interaction on the street seems minimal. However, although "nothing" seems to be happening, we usually are monitoring the behavior of others carefully.

image of city dwellers by arguing that they could not help being rude and unhelpful, but city dwellers are not always like that anyway, as we saw earlier. Of course city dwellers are sometimes less friendly to neighbors and strangers than are rural residents, but research shows that they are equally involved with family and relatives.[202,203]

Community Design and the Immediate Surroundings

HELPFULNESS APPEARS TO DEPEND IN PART ON THE COMPLEXITY OF A COMMUNITY SETTING. When people were asked for directions in complex street environments (many signs, more people, more noise, larger buildings) or simple street environments and in pleasant and less pleasant street environments, women helped more in the complex settings, and men helped more in the simple settings.[204] Several explanations for this are possible, but one based on crowding research is that women are more likely than men to be cooperative and helpful when the population density is high. The pleasantness of the setting did not affect helpfulness. However, in another study, pedestrians were more helpful in the same part of town after a shopping mall was constructed than before it was constructed.[205] The mall apparently improved the pleasantness of the district as judged by pedestrians, which in turn increased their helpfulness. These conflicting results on the pro-social effects of street pleasantness require further research.

The immediate environment also affects helpfulness. When an apparently blind person dropped a glove, he was helped significantly more than when the same person appeared to be sighted, but only when the immediate area was free of cigarette smoke.[206] When cigarette smoke was present, help behavior declined, particularly for the blind person, enough so he no longer received more assistance than the sighted person. Older people who live in poor neighborhoods are more often "hostile," according to one study, and that leads them to be less helpful to others in their social network.[207]

Critics of the Internet have speculated that it works against neighborhood cohesion because residents spend much time online, which detracts from time spent with neighbors. However, a study of a suburb back when not everyone was online found, surprisingly, that residents who were online actually knew more neighbors and communicated with them more than those who were not online.[208] Part of the explanation was a local online discussion group, but, nevertheless, the Internet actually seemed to promote neighborhood interaction in this instance.

IN SUM *Acts of kindness sometimes occur more often in nice weather, when little noise is present unless the needy person is very needy, on pleasantly designed streets, and when the presence of others does not make people feel as if their help is unnecessary.*

NOT EVERYTHING WE DO on the streets of the community involves crime, vandalism, or helping. In fact, most of the time in public spaces, we merely watch, walk, sit, talk to others, or quietly enjoy life. Let's consider these simple but important behaviors and their relation to the physical features of outdoor space (see Figure 8-5).

Watching

WE SPEND MUCH OF OUR TIME IN PUBLIC PLACES SIMPLY LOOKING. What are we looking at? People and things. A more interesting question is: How are we looking? Donald Appleyard suggested that when people are in public spaces, they are looking in one of three modes:[209]

1. In **responsive mode**, people look in a receptive, passive manner and see other people and things as a sensory experience, almost as a form of entertainment or recreation. They may see people, gardens, graffiti, and signs, but they are "just looking," much as when they are window shopping.

2. In **operational mode**, people look in a problem-solving way. Imagine that while on a walk in responsive mode you become lost; now you start to pay attention to signs and look for familiar landmarks. When we visually explore our surroundings with a purpose, whether it is finding our way, looking for an address or seeking a particular store, we are in operational mode. We look because we need something.

3. In **inferential mode**, people look at their surroundings as a medium of communication. They are looking for messages, particularly social messages, and instead of objects, they see symbols, markers, or indicators. People do not see the same messages and may even infer contrasting messages from the same object. I see an empty lot, the developer sees a building site. In inferential mode, we see meaning, although we often see different meanings.

Walking and Health

Mental health benefits. Walking is an important behavior, even if it is neglected by many people in this age of automated transport and ubiquitous screens (sometimes I think we are moving toward a time when we rarely look at the real world, but rather move from one fascinating screen to another, 24/7).

One psychologist maintains that walking is one kind of cure:

> One goes for a walk to get the stuck, depressed state of mind...into an organic rhythm...With the soul-calming language of walking, the dartings of the mind begin to form into a direction...We may be driving, literally *driving* ourselves crazy by not attending to the fundamental human need of walking.[210]

Walkability. Unfortunately, many places are not designed for walkers. Such areas lack in *walkability*, as mentioned earlier, that is in physical features that make people *want* to walk. In such places, walking is so unusual that pedestrians feel uncomfortable, concerned that passing motorists will think them odd, or perhaps, too poor to own a car. A colleague who was attending a conference in Los Angeles decided to take a break and went for a walk outside. A motorist stopped and offered her some coins, assuming that if she was walking, she must be poor and homeless.

Standardized ways of measuring the walkability of neighborhoods have been developed,[211-213] and examined as to how well they predict actual walking[214] and other outcomes. For example, low-walkability of an area, less walking, and more driving are significantly related to obesity.[215] Walkability influences people to visit neighborhood parks more.[216] Walkable blocks encourage more use of public transit.[217]

Neighborhoods with new urbanist characteristics encourage more walking, at least among the elderly.[218] They provide more traffic safety, pleasure, and perceived safety than traditional suburban areas, and children too walk more when they live on more walkable routes.[219] A minor downside is that when an entire development is designed for walkability, pedestrians may stick to a few routes, rather than choose all the walkable paths equally.[220]

Of course, other factors, such as the weather, also affect how much people walk. For example, an increase of 5 °C (about 8 °F) is associated with 14% more walkers, and snow decreases walking by over 20%.[221] Where neighborhood design or the weather do not facilitate walking, alternatives sometimes exist. Many elderly people have taken up mall-walking—that is, programmed early-morning walks in indoor shopping centers.[222] Despite their often-negative image, malls do at least provide a place to walk, particularly when the weather is bad. They have grown larger and increasingly connected to other malls and related structures until, in some places, they are like cities within cities. For example, Montreal has a weatherproof network of malls and tunnels over 14 kilometers/8 miles long; one can wander past or into many residential buildings, offices, theaters, over 1,000 stores, 100 restaurants, and subways without ever setting foot on a traditional street.

Walking Speed. Walking is an interesting behavior in itself. For example, average pedestrian velocity is strongly related to community size; the larger the population, the faster people walk.[223,224] This appears to be a culture-free trend; the data were collected in villages, towns, and cities in 8 countries. The trend is so clear that the investigators proposed a precise mathematical formula for walking velocity: $V = .86 \log P + .05$, where V is velocity and P is the population of the community.

When I first read about this research, I was skeptical. So, some students and I tested it in the town where I taught at the time.[225] We were amazed to find that the average walking velocity of individuals in our town was *exactly* that predicted by the formula. Although the grand average of all individual pedestrian velocities conformed to the formula, we found that pedestrian velocities reliably vary from the overall average under certain conditions. For example, groups walk slower than individuals, pedestrians walk faster downhill and faster in the rain, and males walk faster than females. These effects are additive: A lone male walking downhill in the rain walks over 30 percent faster than a group of women walking uphill on a nice day! Other studies report that older people walk faster than younger people[226] and that people walk faster in cooler temperatures.[227]

Walk Where? When people walk, they also make many decisions, most of which are hardly conscious. For example, they decide where and when to cross the street, how to interact with other pedestrians, and which route to take, but not very consciously.[228] A study in which adults and children were observed as they walked through a community and then were interviewed about their route choices found that pedestrians generally choose the shortest route (no surprise there!), but that children select more complex routes than adults, and that women select more complex routes than men.[229] When these pedestrians were asked why they took certain routes, the answer almost always referred to some physical feature of the neighborhood, such as the attractiveness of a route or the location of a certain building along the way.

Walking and Others. For the most part, even though we would feel very strange if we were the only ones on the street, we try to avoid contact with most individuals in public. For example, commuters are less willing to make eye contact with a stranger in the city than they are with the same stranger in the suburbs.[230] Urbanites operate according to a **mini-max principle**: Minimize involvement with others but maximize social order.[231] A good example of this principle is provided by research on pedestrian behavior.[232] Films of urban pedestrians were analyzed, and researchers found they consistently followed certain rules, although not with much awareness. These rules promote noncontact and cooperation. For example, when pedestrians are headed on a collision course with one another, one of them will move aside when the distance between them is about 7 feet/2.1 meters when the sidewalk density is low, and at about 5 feet/1.5 meters when the sidewalk density is high. Other common patterns that pedestrians use as they make their way along a sidewalk full of strangers include the step-and-slide pattern, the head-over-the-shoulder pattern, and the spread effect.

Walk More! Environmental psychologists are allied with health psychologists in trying to encourage more walking: when people walk more, they are healthier and they may drive less. We might encourage walking by getting people to commit to walking a certain amount, or by getting them to make active plans about what to do on the walk. Both strategies work, but people are more satisfied with their walking when they make active plans.[233] Not surprisingly, people choose to walk more when they feel safe, traffic is lighter, and the area is visually pleasant, but the configuration of the streets matters, too.[234] **Integrated street patterns** are those in which one must make many turns from a given stretch of street to reach the other street segments in the neighborhood. These patterns seem to discourage walking.

Hanging Out

YOUNG PEOPLE GATHER WITH FRIENDS in their neighborhoods. Hanging out often occurs in the **fourth environment**, that is anywhere *except* home, playgrounds, and other places meant for kids.[235] Although this may seem an uneventful everyday activity, this neighborhood exploration is important for development and results in the learning of spatial knowledge and competence. The area encompassed by the fourth environment is larger for those who live in the country and for those with more money; in the suburbs, it is larger for boys and for older teens.[236] Teens prefer natural areas if they are available, away from people other than their friends.[237]

Hanging out may have a generally negative reputation, but that stereotype was challenged by a study which showed that teens who were more socially connected—which can occur through hanging out more—had higher levels of civic engagement.[238] Of course, as they get older, teens often gradually lose their social and activity ties to their neighborhood in favor of wider stomping grounds.[239]

Despite the developmental importance of playing or hanging out in the neighborhood, today's urban neighborhood environments are less supportive of children's play, and children use the neighborhood less for play than children in past decades.[240] This may be the result of increased safety concerns and adult-supervised activities. However, the amount of play in modern neighborhoods also is strongly related to greenery; where there are trees and grass, children play about twice as much.[241]

Teens are not the only people who hang out in public areas. Adults, children, and elderly people also gather in parks, malls, and on street corners. Social interaction clearly depends on both the actual and the perceived physical environment; spaciousness is particularly important.[242] Some groups hang out to socialize and others hang out to check out that everything around their place is OK.[243]

Who hangs out the most in malls? If you said teens, you would be wrong: the most frequent category of person to be found sitting around was elderly men.[244] In a city where people over 65 represent about 9 percent of the population, they accounted for up to 50 percent of those sitting in the malls; teens were actually *under*-represented, based on their percent of the population! Obviously, older people like to hang out, too.

Active use of the neighborhood may be important and healthy for the elderly. Yet older people's use of the neighborhood often is limited; this makes them "spatially disadvantaged."[245] The question arises as to what influences the older person's getting out of the house. Answer: their ability to learn and remember locations better predicts their use of the neighborhood than their degree of mobility or the length of time they have lived in the neighborhood.[246]

Homeless and poor people also hang out on the streets. In some cities, they also spend much time sitting in building lobbies. This form of hanging out, loitering, annoys some building owners and middle-class individuals. For example, in 1994, Seattle began enforcing a law that forbade sitting or lying on downtown sidewalks between 7 A.M. and 9 P.M.[247]

MIRILIA BONNES is one of the most important Italian environmental psychologists, and with her team has extensively studied cities and urban satisfaction.

Familiar Strangers

SOMETIMES STRANGERS BECOME FAMILIAR. In an interesting article, Stanley Milgram described how some members of the anonymous mass of people we encounter in our daily lives become known quantities, even though we almost never talk to them.[248] Do you often see the same people at your transit stop, the same jogger or skateboarder, the same person in the purple coat? Even in a large city, certain individuals, both normal and odd, regularly cross our paths, but we do not talk to them.

Milgram called such individuals our **familiar strangers**. He asked his students to photograph groups of commuters waiting for the subway or bus. The photographs were then showed to some of the commuters in the picture, who were asked about the other individuals in the picture. About 90 percent of them recognized at least one person; the average person pointed out four others that they recognized but had never spoken to.

Many commuters said they often think about these familiar strangers, noticing when they get a new coat or trying to figure out what kind of life they lead. One of Milgram's respondents said she once helped a woman who had collapsed on the street. Why? The woman had been

FIGURE 8–6 Some familiar strangers wait for a bus.

SHOPPING IS AN ESSENTIAL HUMAN ACTIVITY. It has always had social and recreational aspects as well as the utilitarian function of obtaining the basic necessities and desirable luxuries of life. Many forces shape our shopping habits; among these are physical setting influences such as location of the store, decor, lighting, weather, sounds, crowding, smells, and displays.

In-store environmental cues, or **atmospherics** (combinations of lighting, music, scent, etc.), affect consumer spending,[249] behavior, and feelings.[250] Retailers have become conscious of environmental psychology.[251]

one of her familiar strangers for years (see Figure 8-6). Sometimes the harshness and anonymity of city streets is overemphasized. Although cities are polluted with crime and fear of crime, these studies show that we do take others into account, sometimes in a very positive way.

IN SUM *We do much on city streets that seems close to nothing, perhaps because we do most of it automatically, without reflecting. However, upon closer examination, this "nothing" turns out to be a fascinating mixture of thoughts and activities. We monitor our progress through the city in responsive, operational, or inferential modes. We walk at a speed that reflects the pulse (or at least the size) of the city. Our walks follow planned patterns even when we are unaware of our plans. We carefully avoid interaction, but maximize social order. Elderly men hang out in malls more than teens do. We know some people that we do not really know—our familiar strangers.*

Consuming Environmentally

RECENT YEARS HAVE SEEN VERY LARGE INCREASES in the sale of organic foods and other environmentally friendly products. Some people are more willing than others to pay a little more for these products; one main segment of these consumers is married women with children at home.[252] If consumers buy one such product, are they more likely to buy other environmentally friendly products, or do they tend to buy just the one? In Denmark, instances of multiple product purchasing (across categories of products) do occur, but not as often as one might think.[253] Apparently, for many people, buying one environment-friendly product actually reduces the frequency of buying others. However, consumers who hold strong environmentalist norms or **universalist values** (that is, a person who seeks social justice and tolerance for all, promotes peace and equality, and believes war should be entered as a last resort to achieve a lasting peace) are an exception: they are more likely to buy environmentally friendly products in multiple categories.

Location, Size, and Attractiveness

AN OLD ADAGE IN THE RETAIL TRADE is that the three most important keys to retail success are (a) location, (b) location, and (c) location. Research tends to substantiate this claim, although of course location is not the entire story. When other factors are equal, most shoppers choose the closest store that stocks what they want to buy. Shoppers

FIGURE 8–7 Cognition and behavior in relation to the physical design of retail settings is an important part of environmental psychology.

also tend to choose the largest store. Size and location, explain much variance in consumer choice of stores.[254] In an analogy to the physical laws of attraction among astronomical bodies, this approach is called the **gravitation model**: if all other factors are equal, consumers gravitate to larger stores and to closer stores.

Another key variable in this gravitation model is the attractiveness of the product. For especially attractive products (usually the more expensive ones), the gravitational effect of size and location is weakened and shoppers will travel farther. The practice of leaving one's own community to buy goods is called **outshopping.** In one small city, 34 percent of furniture and 33 percent of cars were outshopped, but only 4 percent of food and groceries were.[255] Outshopping declines with age. Older people are more likely to confine their shopping to the home neighborhood, a finding that reinforces the gravitation model.[256]

Layout

LARGE STORES MAY DRAW MORE SHOPPERS, but not every shopper is happy with the impersonal environment often characteristic of these retail settings. Robert Sommer and his colleagues compared the social and physical qualities of supermarkets with those of farmer's markets. In farmer's markets, shoppers more often arrive in groups and spend more time interacting with the sellers and with other shoppers.[257] They observed that the spatial layout of supermarkets (block shape, aisle orientation, linear checkout arrangements) is a key factor in their sacrifice of friendliness in favor of traffic efficiency.

The length of aisles also affects buying behavior. When aisles are shorter, shoppers often just look down the aisle rather than walk down it.[258] Long aisles cannot be so easily surveyed, so shoppers walk down them and more often fall victim to impulse buying of attractive items they did not intend to buy before entering the store.

As more people register their dissatisfaction with settings that encourage alienation, shopping environment design and behavior will become more sensitive to the social needs of shoppers. Cooperative stores, with layouts that match the co-op not-for-profit philosophy, may become more popular.[259] You may have noticed that clerks make an effort to be nice at the check-out counter.

One layout does not fit all, as you might expect. For example, shoppers who are task-oriented prefer more spacious stores, and recreational shoppers prefer more stores with arousing colors (red more than blue).[260] That leads to the next retail design consideration.

Emotional Impact

THE EMOTIONAL QUALITY OF A RETAIL ENVIRONMENT is important. Store-induced pleasure and arousal have strong effects on shoppers' intended behaviors.[261] Consistent with Mehrabian and Russell's pleasure-arousal hypothesis, such shopping-related intentions as the time spent browsing, the tendency to spend more money than planned, and the likelihood of returning to the store all increase when pleasant stores were also arousing. When stores are neutral or unpleasant, arousal did not increase these intentions.

One modifier of these findings may be gender: the quality of shopping facilities apparently is more important to women than to men.[262] An extension of the Mehrabian-Russell model has been proposed. It originally stated that environmental features (atmospherics in the case of stores) influence the shopper's emotions (pleasure, arousal, and sometimes dominance), which then influence the shopper's approach or avoidance of the product. The extension proposes that between the emotional response and the approach behavior stages, shoppers must elaborate their imagery of the product and be motivated to shop.[263]

Density

CROWDING IN THE SHOPPING ENVIRONMENT is another physical setting influence on consumer behavior. Objective density affects shoppers' perceptions and cognitions about the store.[264] Feelings of crowding lead to dissatisfaction[265] and adaptive strategies, such as leaving the store earlier than planned. The shopper's attitudes toward the store may then take a negative turn.

An interesting examination of the urban overload hypothesis compared the interactions between customers and staff in post offices and delicatessens that varied in location from urban to rural.[266] As predicted, urban locations were busier and the social interactions in them were briefer than in the rural locations. Even when the number of customers in the urban locations was relatively low, interaction was still less in them. Apparently, the low-interaction habits developed in busy times carry over to times when stimulus overload is not present.

Display and Signage

PURCHASING IS AFFECTED BY HOW GOODS ARE DISPLAYED. Most research has been conducted in grocery stores. Shelf height, end-aisle placement, and location within the store all affect both normal buying and impulse buying.[267] For example, items placed on the end of an aisle will sometimes stimulate sales of that item. However, because shoppers searching for that product no longer need to travel down those long aisles where the item normally is located, overall store sales may suffer (see Figure 8-7).

If the shopper does make the journey down the aisle, the height of an item affects its sales. The sales of the same jars of applesauce increased fivefold when they were moved from waist level to eye level.[268] Basics like dairy products are usually placed at the back of the store so the shopper is drawn past nonessentials that may be purchased impulsively.

Another key layout variable is store cleanliness; clean stores attract more customers.[269] Signs often display an item's name and price, but they may also contain other elements, and this can affect impulse buying. Signs with promotional information (e.g., offering discounts or reduced prices) and atmosphere engagement (e.g., with some style and attractiveness) increased impulse buying.[270]

Music

MUSIC HAS SIGNIFICANT EFFECTS ON BEHAVIOR in retail stores and restaurants, although some of these effects may be indirect.[271] When fast music was played in a supermarket, shoppers walked significantly faster than when slow music was played.[272] More important from the store's perspective, shoppers bought more when the music was slow, presumably because they had more time to look at products. Most interesting, perhaps, was the study's finding that when customers were asked as they left the store if they recalled whether music had been playing while they shopped, there were no significant differences in the three conditions. Apparently, shoppers can be induced to buy more without realizing that the key factor is environmental - the tempo of the music.

Music's volume also may be influential: consumers who shopped when loud music was playing finished shopping more quickly than those who shopped when the music was quieter, but they spent the same amount of money.[273] Thus, the tempo of the music affects both the shopper's pace and the amount purchased, but the volume of music affects only their pace.

The tempo and genre of music also affects eating and drinking. When the tempo was slow, customers stayed 25 percent longer and spent almost 50 percent more on bar purchases.[274] In another restaurant, fast music significantly increased the pace of eating (bites per minute), although total meal time was the same as for slower music.[275] Once again, patrons were unaware of the music's effect on them. Finally, in British restaurants, patrons spent more money when classical music was played.[276, 277] Put on that Mozart, Store Manager!

Lighting

BRIGHT LIGHTING, DIM LIGHTING, SPOT LIGHTING: all have been linked in story and legend to consumer behavior. In reality, few in-store studies have been published, so the facts largely remain to be discovered. However, in a wine store, customers examined and handled merchandise more often under brighter lighting.[278] As usual, it's not that simple. In a hardware store and a clothing store, the effect of supplemental lighting was investigated. Consumers did touch and pick up the hardware tools (but not belts in the clothing store) more under the extra lighting, but they actually spent more time looking at the tools when the extra lighting was *absent*.[279] More research needed!

Scents

SOME PEOPLE HAVE LONG SUSPECTED THAT PLEASANT SCENTS AFFECT SHOPPING BEHAVIOR, and now evidence is beginning to arrive. However, the effects are not as simple as spraying a pleasant odor to produce a sale. For example, the scent must be congruent with the product[280] and with the sort of customer the store attracts.[281] As long as the scent is congruent with the product, consumers' evaluations of it are influenced by it even when they notice the scent and are motivated to "correct" for the effect of the scent "Oh, I see they are trying to get me to buy this thing by spraying patchouli all over it! Hmm, well, I guess I like it anyway."

Two competing theories about *how* and *why* scents are important were compared in Montreal.[282] Mehrabian and Russell's model (that environmental cues influence emotions, which in turn influence approach or avoidance) was compared to a model which proposes that shoppers'

perceptions of the store and product quality mediate (that is, are causal intermediate steps between) the effects of scent on emotions and spending behaviors. This latter model seemed to predict shopper responses better.

IN SUM *The physical environment is not widely studied as a factor in retail behavior, but awareness of, and research on, its influence is growing. Well-known factors include store location and size. At the interior level, the way that shelves, aisles, displays, lighting, and odors affect the emotions and behavior of consumers is gradually becoming clear. We even seem to eat and shop to the beat.*

URBAN ENVIRONMENTAL DESIGN

Defensible Space in Row Housing

OSCAR NEWMAN'S IDEAS ABOUT DEFENSIBLE SPACE have been controversial for years. Many environmental psychologists believe they have some validity, yet the research supporting the concept—as with any field of research—has been problematic. Here we take a closer look at an actual project of Newman's: renovations of a low-income housing project adjacent to the south Bronx, in New York.

Clason Point Gardens consists of row-house clusters housing from 12 to 40 families per cluster. One of the goals of the renovations was to increase defensible space, thereby reducing both fear of crime and actual crime. Following defensible space principles, the renovations (1) assigned as much public space as possible to the control of specific families, using both substantial and symbolic fencing; (2) reduced the number of pedestrian routes through the project and improved lighting along the paths; and (3) improved the project's image and encouraged a sense of personal ownership by resurfacing the dwellings and giving different colors to individual dwellings.

FIGURE 8-8 How many of William Whyte's recommended design elements are evident in this view of a small campus plaza?

Newman reported that residents took new pride in their dwellings, planted grass, added their own new modifications, and even swept the public sidewalks. According to Newman, maintenance costs and crime both were reduced significantly. Serious crimes like burglary, assault, and robbery reportedly dropped by 61.5 percent. The number of residents who said they felt they had the right to question strangers in the project doubled.

The results were not entirely positive,[283] but the renovations do appear to have had a generally beneficial effect on Clason Point Gardens.

Plazas as Social Spaces

WILLIAM WHYTE DOCUMENTED the amount of positive social interaction (as opposed to carefully managed social avoidance) in cities.[284] He emphasized the desirability of design features that promote positive social interaction in public places.[285] In particular, Whyte extensively studied urban plazas, searching for characteristics that distinguish beneficial plazas from useless open spaces.

Over several years, he and his coworkers observed and filmed 18 plazas in New York City. They counted how many individuals used each plaza on pleasant days and began to relate usage rates to various features of the plazas. In general, plazas become more useful as the number of amenities rise. For example, many unused plazas simply have no place for people to sit, and available seating area obviously is crucial.[286] Some other features of successful plazas

include water (fountains and pools), food stands, trees, and activities to watch (jugglers, mimes, and buskers). The siting of plazas is also important. Successful plazas have a sunny orientation in cool cities (or a shady orientation in hot cities), provide shelter from wind, and are located on busy streets at street level rather than hidden away or on a different level than the street (see Figure 8-8).

Years ago, the City of New York offered developers a deal: For each square unit of plaza they included in a new project, their new building could exceed normal zoning restrictions by ten square units. This practice, called **bonus density**, did increase New York's supply of open space downtown. Unfortunately, the new plazas tended to be vast empty spaces devoid of the features just described. So, recognizing this, revised bonus density rules were instituted. New York would only award bonus density if developers offered plazas that included many of the amenities identified by Whyte. These second-generation plazas are markedly improved social spaces that increase the city's pleasantness. Bonus density practices have now spread to practically every city.

Bringing a Neighborhood to Life

MANY NEIGHBORHOODS ARE DEAD. Sure, people live there, but no one speaks to anyone except to complain, few people except troublemakers use the sidewalks or parks, and traffic moves quickly through the streets. Sidney Brower has spent years developing and testing ideas for enlivening neighborhoods in Baltimore. His book, *Design in Familiar Places*, concludes with a list of guidelines for bringing communities to life.[287] Some of the guidelines require more time, capital, and energy than others, but all are attainable with community will. Some require city approval and therefore resident organization, but are worth the effort. An overall plan helps, but it need not be implemented all at once. Here are some of Brower's guidelines:

1. *Keep the street front alive*. Take steps to encourage residents to walk, stroll, and play on the sidewalks. This encourages social interaction and enables natural surveillance over street activities. Find a legitimate use for every public space, so that people routinely visit all areas of the neighborhood and there are no dead spaces. Once some residents are outside, using public space, others will feel safe doing so; security and socializing go

hand in hand. Ensure that every space belongs to, or is managed by, a specific person or group.

2. *Give residents things to do and places to be.* For some, this means benches; for others it might be horseshoes, hopscotch, street vendors, or library vans. Encourage street recreation by blocking off alleys, parking lots, or streets. Some areas, such as sidewalks themselves, must be preserved from fast, rough play for older people to enjoy walking or watching. Think of ways to incorporate recreation into a linked system of spaces between and around dwellings.

3. *Reduce the speed and number of cars.* Can the cars be rerouted at night, slowed with speed bumps, or stopped at certain times with temporary barricades? Speed zones enhanced with speed bumps reduce traffic by up to 30 percent and accidents with injuries by about 25 percent. Residents accept them because they feel safer and the neighborhood is quieter and more suitable for walking.[288,289] However, do not ban cars completely; residents in cars help to maintain a street presence.

4. *Residences should open to the street, not from some central courtyard.* When buildings present their back to the street, the street is ignored and street life shrivels.

5. *Make parks more attractive to adults.* Parks relegated to juvenile use operate at juvenile developmental levels. What might adults like to do in the park? Barbecues? Informal concerts? Mini-dramas? Where possible, incorporate all age groups in all activities, so that competition between the geriatric play-reading and the kids' ball game does not degenerate into intergroup hostility. Can some kids have roles in the play? Can some adults play in, coach, or referee the ball games?

6. *Distinguish between home-based recreation and park activities.* Parks are for noisier, louder activities (even when adults participate, too). Do not put houses immediately beside parks if possible; use a buffer of stores, or recreation centers, or other semi-public structures.

THESE GUIDELINES CAN TAKE MUCH TIME AND EFFORT; residents should form an organization to share the work. They should persuade the city to help with money, advice, and equipment; success is in the interest of all citizens. The best arrangement is an equal partnership between officials and residents, residents should not expect or allow city officials to do it all. Officials need local experience and contacts with local residents to make it work.

SUMMARY

FOR OUR PURPOSES, CITIES AND NEIGHBORHOODS are psychological entities more than geographical entities. They have different personalities depending on how their residents interact with each other and with outsiders, whether residents feel confident, attached, and secure, or not. The neighborhood's physical qualities are more important than its social qualities for most people, but neither suburban nor urban communities are everyone's favorite; the key is whether the community satisfies its residents' needs and whether the resident is adapted to its pattern of stimulation. Urban dwellers face many stressors, and urbanization itself is a major one. Safety is a very important urban concern; city dwellers are so used to following many habits and rules for safety that they often overlook the psychological cost of constant alertness. Defensible space, combined with an actively aware neighborhood, can reduce the threat. However, high temperatures and air pollution increase the risk of violence. People are more helpful in quiet sunny weather and perhaps on pleasantly designed streets, when not too many others are around. On city streets, automatic behavior includes observing one's surroundings in particular modes, walking at a pace that correlates with the city's size, and avoiding interaction with strangers yet becoming quite familiar with some of them. The environmental psychology of shopping includes the influence of store location, size, layout, and display of goods. Basic and important behaviors such as looking, buying, eating, and drinking are influenced by retail lighting, music, density, and scents.

Suggested Supplementary Readings

Bonaiuto, M. & Alves, S. (2012). Residential places and neighborhoods: Toward healthy life, social integration, and reputable residence. In Clayton, S. D. (Ed.). *The Oxford handbook of environmental and conservation psychology* (pp. 221-247). New York: Oxford.

Churchman, A. (2002). Environmental psychology and urban planning: Where can the twain meet? In R. B. Bechtel & A. Churchman (Eds.), *Handbook of environmental psychology* (pp. 191-200). Hoboken, NJ: Wiley.

Daniel, T., & Daniel, K. (2003). *The environmental planning handbook for sustainable communities and regions.* Chicago: APA Planners Press.

Francis, M., & Lorenzo, R. (2006). Children and city design: Proactive process and the 'renewal' of childhood. In C. Spencer & M. Blades (Eds.), *Children and their environments: Learning, using and designing spaces* (pp. 217-237). New York: Cambridge University Press.

Moser, G. (2012). Cities. In Clayton, S. D. (Ed.). *The Oxford handbook of environmental and conservation psychology* (pp. 203-220). New York: Oxford.

Ng, C. F. (2003). Satisfying shoppers' psychological needs: From public market to cyber-mall. *Journal of Environmental Psychology, 23,* 427-237.

Whyte, W. H. (1980). *The social life of small urban spaces.* New York: The Conservation Foundation.

References

1 Honey, K. (1999, January 26). Cities getting too big for the planet, professor says. *The Globe and Mail,* p. A7.

2 2. Mumford, L. (1961). *The city in history: Its origins, its transformations, its prospects.* New York: Harcourt, Brace, and World.

3 Graham, C. (1993, January 14). We may have genetic need to live in smaller cities. Victoria *Times-Colonist,* p. A-4.

4 Kim, T., Jeong, G., Baek, H., Kim, G., Sundaram, T., Kang, H., et al. (2010). Human brain activation in response to visual stimulation with rural and urban scenery pictures: A functional magnetic resonance imaging study. *Science of the Total Environment, 408,* 2600-2607.

5 Graham, C. (1993, January 14). We may have genetic need to live in smaller cities. Victoria *Times-Colonist,* p. A-4.

6 Graham, C. (1993, January 14). We may have genetic need to live in smaller cities. Victoria *Times-Colonist,* p. A-4.

7 Fischer, D. (1994, December 22). Life more peaceful in the country, statistics say. Vancouver *Sun,* p. A-8.

8 Mumford, L. (1961). *The city in history: Its origins, its transformations, its prospects.* New York: Harcourt, Brace, and World.

9 Hall, S. (1989). Standing on those corners, watching all the folks go by. *Smithsonian Magazine, 19,* 119-131.

10 Moser, G., & Robin, M. (2006). Environmental annoyances: An urban-specific threat to quality of life? *European Review of Applied Psychology, 56,* 35-41.

11 Taylor, R. B., Shumaker, S. A., & Gottfredson, S. D. (1985). Neighborhood-level links between physical features and local sentiments: Deterioration, fear of crime, and confidence. *Journal of Architectural and Planning Research, 2,* 261-275.

12 Green, R. (1999). Meaning and form in community perception of town character. *Journal of Environmental Psychology, 19,* 311-329.

13 Guest, A. M., & Lee, B. A. (1984). How urbanites define their neighborhoods. *Population & Environment: Behavioral & Social Issues, 7,* 32-56.

14 Feldman, R. M. (1987). Generic conceptions of place: The public views the city/suburb distinction. *Dissertation Abstracts International, 47*(9-B), 3942.

15 Dunstan, F., Weaver, N., Araya, R., Bell, T., Lannon, S., Lewis, G., Patterson, J., Thomas, H., Jones, P., & Palmer, S. (2005). An observation tool to assist with the assessment of urban residential environments. *Journal of Environmental Psychology, 25,* 293-305.

16 Rivlin, L. G. (1982). Group membership and place meanings in an urban neighborhood. *Journal of Social Issues, 38,* 75-93.

17 Unger, D. G., & Wandersman, A. (1985). The importance of neighbors: The social, cognitive, and affective components of neighboring. *American Journal of Community Psychology, 13,* 139-169.

18 Cherulnik, P. D., & Wilderman, S. K. (1986). Symbols of status in urban neighborhoods: Contemporary perceptions of nineteenth-century Boston. *Environment and Behavior, 18,* 604-622.

19 Wells, J. C., & Baldwin, E. D. (2012). Historic preservation, significance, and age value: A comparative phenomenology of historic Charleston and the nearby new-urbanist community of I'On. *Journal of Environmental Psychology, 32,* 384-400.

20 Betz, V. M. (2003). The city as invention: An environmental psychological approach to the origins of urban life. *Dissertation Abstracts International Section A: Humanities and Social Sciences, 63(11-A),* 3988.

21 Haken, H., & Portugali, J. (2003). The face of the city is its information. *Journal of Environmental Psychology, 23,* 385-408.

22 Bonaiuto, M.., Bonnes, M., & Continisio, M. (2004). Neighborhood evaluation within a multiplace perspective on urban activities. *Environment and Behavior, 36,* 41-69.

23 Demick, J., Hoffman, A., & Wapner, S (1985). Residential context and environmental change as determinants of urban experience. *Children's Environments Quarterly, 2,* 44-54.

24 Carp, F. M., & Christensen, D. L. (1986). Older women living alone: Technical environment assessment of psychological well-being. *Research on Aging, 8,* 407-425.

25 Fried, M. (1982). Residential attachment: Sources of residential and community satisfaction. *Journal of Social Issues, 38*(3), 107-119.

26 Unger, D. G., & Wandersman, A. (1985). The importance of neighbors: The social, cognitive, and affective components of neighboring. *American Journal of Community Psychology, 13,* 139-169.

27 Fried, M. (1984). The structure and significance of community satisfaction. *Population & Environment: Behavioral and Social Issues, 7,* 61-86.

28 Bonaiuto, M., Fornara, F., & Bonnes, M. (2006). Perceived residential environment quality in middle- and low-extension Italian cities. *European Review of Applied Psychology / Revue Européenne de Psychologie Appliquée, 56,* 23-34.

29 Fornara, F., Bonaiuto, M., & Bonnes, M. (2010). Cross-validation of abbreviated Perceived Residential Environment Quality (PREQ) and Neighborhood Attachment (NA) indicators. *Environment and Behavior, 42,* 171-196.

30 Jones, R. E., Davis, K. L., & Bradford, J. (2013). The Value of Trees: Factors Influencing Homeowner Support for Protecting Local Urban Trees. *Environment and Behavior, 45,* 650-676.

31 Jirovec, R. L., Jirovec, M. M., & Bosse, R. (1985). Residential satisfaction as a function of micro and macro environmental conditions

among urban elderly men. *Research on Aging, 7*, 601-616.

32 Lord, D. J., & Rent, G. S. (1987). Residential satisfaction in scattered-site public housing projects. *The Social Science Journal, 24*, 287-302.

33 Lord, D. J., & Rent, G. S. (1987). Residential satisfaction in scattered-site public housing projects. *The Social Science Journal, 24*, 287-302.

34 Cunningham, J. D. (1984). Egotism in prestige ratings of Sydney suburbs: Where I live is better than you think. *Australian Journal of Psychology, 36*, 429-438.

35 Whitley, R., & Prince, M. (2005). Are inner-cities bad for your health? Comparisons of residents' and third parties' perceptions of the urban neighborhood of Gospel Oak, London. *Sociology of Health & Illness, 27*, 44-67.

36 Varady, D. P. (1986). Neighborhood confidence: A critical factor in neighborhood revitalization? *Environment and Behavior, 18*, 480-501.

37 Geller, D. (1980). Responses to urban stimuli: A balanced approach. *Journal of Social Issues, 36*, 86-100.

38 Helson, H. (1964). *Adaptation-level theory*. New York: Harper and Row.

39 Michelson, W. (1977). *Environmental choice, human behavior and residential satisfaction*. New York: Oxford University Press.

40 Félonneau, M. (2004). Love and loathing of the city: Urbanophilia and urbanophobia, topological identity and perceived incivilities. *Journal of Environmental Psychology, 24*, 43-52.

41 Nasar, J. L. (1981). Visual preferences of elderly public housing residents: Residential street scenes. *Journal of Environmental Psychology, 1*, 303-313.

42 Broberg, A., Kyttä, M., & Fagerholm, N. (2013). Child-friendly urban structures: Bullerby revisited. *Journal of Environmental Psychology, 35*, 110-120.

43 Villanueva, K., Giles-Corti, B., Bulsara, M., Timperio, A., McCormack, G., Beesley, B., et al. (2013). Do Children Travel to and What Local Opportunities Are Available? The Relationship Between Neighborhood Destinations and Children's Independent Mobility. *Environment and Behavior, 45*, 679-705.

44 Taylor, R. B. (1982). Neighborhood physical environment and stress. In G. W. Evans (Ed.), *Environmental stress*. New York: Cambridge University Press.

45 Hull, R. B., & Harvey, A. (1989). Explaining the emotion people experience in suburban parks. *Environment and Behavior, 21*, 323-345.

46 Kearney, A. R. (2006). Residential development patterns and neighborhood satisfaction: Impacts of density and nearby nature. *Environment and Behavior, 38*, 112-139.

47 Honold, J., Beyer, R., Lakes, T. & van der Meer, E. (2012). Multiple environmental burdens and neighborhood-related health of city residents. *Journal of Environmental Psychology, 32*, 305-317.

48 Hur, M., Nasar, J, L., & Chun, B. (2010). Neighborhood satisfaction, physical and perceived naturalness and openness. *Journal of Environmental Psychology, 30*, 52-59.

49 Kim, T., Jeong, G., Baek, H., Kim, G., Sundaram, T., Kang, H., et al. (2010). Human brain activation in response to visual stimulation with rural and urban scenery pictures: A functional magnetic resonance imaging study. *Science of the Total Environment, 408*, 2600-2607.

50 Nasar, J. L. (1983). Adult viewers' preferences in residential scenes: A study of the relationship of environmental attributes to preference. *Environment and Behavior, 15*, 589-614.

51 Garcia-Maria, R., Arce, C., & Sabucedo, J. M. (1997). Perceived quality of neighborhoods in a city in the northwest Spain: An individual differences scaling approach. *Journal of Environmental Psychology, 17*, 243-252.

52 Francis, J., Giles-Corti, B., Wood, L., & Knuiman, M. (2012). Creating sense of community: The role of public space. *Journal of Environmental Psychology, 32*, 401-409.

53 Honold, J., Beyer, R., Lakes, T. & van der Meer, E. (2012). Multiple environmental burdens and neighborhood-related health of city residents. *Journal of Environmental Psychology, 32*, 305-317.

54 Honold, J., Beyer, R., Lakes, T. & van der Meer, E. (2012). Multiple environmental burdens and neighborhood-related health of city residents. *Journal of Environmental Psychology, 32*, 305-317.

55 Marques, S., & Lima, M. L. (2011). Living in grey areas: Industrial activity and psychological health. *Journal of Environmental Psychology, 31*, 314-322.

56 Taylor, R. B. (1982). Neighborhood physical environment and stress. In G. W. Evans (Ed.), *Environmental stress*. New York: Cambridge University Press.

57 Nasar, J. L. (1983). Adult viewers' preferences in residential scenes: A study of the relationship of environmental attributes to preference. *Environment and Behavior, 15*, 589-614.

58 Garcia-Maria, R., Arce, C., & Sabucedo, J. M. (1997). Perceived quality of neighborhoods in a city in the northwest Spain: An individual differences scaling approach. *Journal of Environmental Psychology, 17*, 243-252.

59 Nasar, J. L. (1983). Adult viewers' preferences in residential scenes: A study of the relationship of environmental attributes to preference. *Environment and Behavior, 15*, 589-614.

60 Lindal, P. J., & Hartig, T. (2013). Architectural variation, building height, and the restorative quality of urban residential streetscapes. *Journal of Environmental Psychology, 33*, 26-36.

61 Jirovec, R. L., Jirovec, M. M., & Bosse, R. (1985). Residential satisfaction as a function of micro and macro environmental conditions among urban elderly men. *Research on Aging, 7*, 601-616.

62 Widgery, R. N. (1982). Satisfaction with the quality of urban life: A predictive model. *American Journal of Community Psychology, 10*, 37-48.

63 Hull, R. B., & Harvey, A. (1989). Explaining the emotion people experience in suburban parks. *Environment and Behavior, 21*, 323-345.

64 Kearney, A. R. (2006). Residential development patterns and neighborhood satisfaction: Impacts of density and nearby nature. *Environment and Behavior, 38*, 112-139.

65 Honold, J., Beyer, R., Lakes, T. & van der Meer, E. (2012). Multiple environmental burdens and neighborhood-related health of city residents. *Journal of Environmental Psychology, 32*, 305-317.

66 Lord, D. J., & Rent, G. S. (1987). Residential satisfaction in scattered-site public housing projects. *The Social Science Journal, 24*, 287-302.

67 Brown, B. B., & Werner, C. M. (2011). The residents' benefits and concerns before and after a new rail stop: Do residents get what they expect? *Environment and Behavior, 43*, 789-806.

68 Francis, J., Giles-Corti, B., Wood, L., & Knuiman, M. (2012). Creating sense of community: The role of public space. *Journal of Environmental Psychology, 32*, 401-409.

69 Borst, H. C., Miedema, H. M. E., de Vries, S. I., Graham, J. M. A., & van Dongen, J. E. F. (2008). Relationships between street characteristics and perceived attractiveness for walking reported by elderly people. *Journal of Environmental Psychology, 28*, 353-361.

70 Lord, D. J., & Rent, G. S. (1987). Residential satisfaction in scattered-site public housing projects. *The Social Science Journal, 24*, 287-302.

71 Brown, G., Brown, B. B., & Perkins, D. D. (2004). New housing as neighborhood revitalization: Place attachment and confidence among residents. *Environment and Behavior, 36*, 749-775.

72 Wilkerson, A., Carlson, N. E., Yen, I. H., & Michael, Y. L. (2012). Neighborhood physical features and relationships with neighbors: Does positive physical environment increase neighborliness? *Environment and Behavior, 44*, 595-615.

73 Regnier, V. (1985). Using outdoor space more effectively. *Generations, 9*, 22-24.

74 Babisch, W., Schulz, C., Seiwert, M., & Conrad, A. (2012). Noise annoyance as reported by 8- to 14-year-old children. *Environment and Behavior, 44*, 68-86.

75 Venables, D., Pidgeon, N. F., Parkhill, K. A., Henwood, K. L., & Simmons, P. (2012). Living with nuclear power: Sense of place, proximity, and risk perceptions in local host communities. *Journal of Environmental Psychology, 32*, 371-383.

76 Michelson, W. (1977). *Environmental choice, human behavior and residential satisfaction*. New York: Oxford University Press.

77 Llewellyn, L. G. (1981). The social cost of urban transportation. In I. Altman, J. Wohlwill, & P. B. Everett (Eds.), *Transportation and behavior*. New York: Plenum.

78 Levy-Leboyer, C. (1991). Neighborhood noise annoyance. *Journal of Environmental Psychology, 11*, 75-86.

79 Green, D. M., & Fidell, S. (1991). Variability in the criterion for reporting annoyance in community noise surveys. *Journal of the Acoustical Society of America, 89*, 234-243.

80 Moran, S. V., Gunn, W. J., & Loeb, M. (1981). Annoyance by aircraft noise and fear of overflying aircraft in relation to attitudes toward the environment and community. *The Journal of Auditory Research, 21*, 217-225.

81 Jue, G. M., Shumaker, S. A., & Evans, G. W. (1984). Community opinion concerning airport noise-abatement alternatives. *Journal of Environmental Psychology, 4*, 337-345.

[82] Miedema, H. N. E., & Vox, H. (1999). Demographic and attitudinal factors that modify annoyance from transportation noise. *Journal of Acoustical Society of America, 105,* 3336-3344.

[83] Staples, S. L., Cornelius, R. R., & Gibbs, M. S. (1999). Noise disturbance from a developing airport: Perceived risk or general annoyance? *Environment and Behavior, 31,* 692-710.

[84] Fidell, S., & Silvati, L. (1991). An assessment of the effect of residential acoustic insulation on prevalence of annoyance in an airport community. *Journal of the Acoustical Society of America, 89,* 244-247.

[85] Weinstein, N. D. (1982). Community noise problems: Evidence against adaptation. *Journal of Environmental Psychology, 2,* 87-97.

[86] Mehrabian, A. (1977). Individual differences in stimulus screening and arousability. *Journal of Personality, 45,* 237-250.

[87] Jonah, B. A., Bradley, J. S., & Dawson, N. E. (1981). Predicting individual subjective responses and traffic noise. *Journal of Applied Psychology, 66,* 490-501.

[88] Björkman, M. (1991). Community noise annoyance: Importance of noise levels and the number of noise events. *Journal of Sound and Vibration, 151,* 497-503.

[89] Evans, G. W., Jacobs, S. V., & Frager, N. B. (1982). Adaptation to air pollution. *Journal of Environmental Psychology, 2,* 99-108.

[90] Fried, M., & Gleicher, P. (1961). Some sources of satisfaction in an urban slum. *Journal of the American Institute of Planners, 27,* 305-315.

[91] Fried, M. (1982). Residential attachment: Sources of residential and community satisfaction. *Journal of Social Issues, 38*(3), 107-119.

[92] Handal, P., Barling, P., & Morrissy, E. (1981). Development of perceived and preferred measures of physical and social characteristics of the residential environment and their relationship and satisfaction. *Journal of Community Psychology, 9,* 118-124.

[93] Dassopoulos, A. (2011). Do perceptions of social cohesion, social support, and social control mediate the effects of local community participation on neighborhood satisfaction? *Environment and Behavior, 43,* 546-565.

[94] Lord, D. J., & Rent, G. S. (1987). Residential satisfaction in scattered-site public housing projects. *The Social Science Journal, 24,* 287-302.

[95] Garling, T., Svensson-Garling, A., & Valsiner, J. (1984). Parental concern about children's traffic safety in residential neighborhoods. *Journal of Environmental Psychology, 4,* 235-252.

[96] Cook, C. C. (1988). Components of neighborhood satisfaction: Responses from urban and suburban single-parent women. *Environment and Behavior, 20,* 115-149.

[97] Patterson, A. H. (1985). Fear of crime and other barriers to use of public transportation by the elderly. *Journal of Architectural and Planning Research, 2,* 277-288.

[98] Hassinger, J. (1985). Fear of crime in public environments. *Journal of Architectural and Planning Research, 2,* 289-300.

[99] Kirk, N. L. (1988). *Factors affecting perceptions of safety in a campus environment.* Nineteenth Annual Conference of the Environmental Design Research Association, Pomona, California.

[100] Keane, C. (1998). Evaluating the influence of fear of crime as an environmental mobility restrictor on women's routine activities. *Environment and Behavior, 30,* 60-74.

[101] White, M., Kasl, S. V., Zahner, G. E., & Will, J. C. (1987). Perceived crime in the neighborhood and mental health of women and children. *Environment and Behavior, 19,* 588-613.

[102] Nasar, J. L. & Jones, K. M. (1997). Landscape of fear and stress. *Environment and Behavior, 29,* 291-323.

[103] Gifford, R., & Peacock, J. (1979). Crowding: More fearsome than crime-provoking? Comparison of an Asian city and a North American city. *Psychologia, 22,* 79-83.

[104] Kirk, N. L. (1988). *Factors affecting perceptions of safety in a campus environment.* Nineteenth Annual Conference of the Environmental Design Research Association, Pomona, California.

[105] Van der Wurff, A., & Stringer, P. (1989). Postvictimization fear of crime: Differences in the perceptions of people and places. *Journal of Interpersonal Violence, 4,* 469-481.

[106] Baba, Y., & Austin, D. M. (1989). Neighborhood environmental satisfaction, victimization, and social participation as determinants of perceived neighborhood safety. *Environment and Behavior, 21,* 763-780.

[107] Newman, O. (1972). *Defensible space.* New York: MacMillan.

[108] Tien, J., O'Donnell, V. F., Barnett, A., & Mirchandani, P. B. (1979). *Street lighting projects.* Washington, DC: U.S. Department of Justice.

[109] Kuo, F. E., Bacaicoa, M., & Sullivan, W. C. (1998). Transforming inner-city landscapes: Trees, sense of safety and preference. *Environment and Behavior, 30,* 28-59.

[110] Taylor, R. B. (1982). Neighborhood physical environment and stress. In G. W. Evans (Ed.), *Environmental stress.* New York: Cambridge University Press.

[111] Rapoport, Am. (1985). Culture and the urban order. In J. A. Agnew, J. Mercer, & D. E. Sopher (Eds.), *The city in cultural context.* Boston: Allen and Unwin.

[112] Gifford, R. (1984-1985). Age, era and life perspective: Emotional connotations of the 1920s through the 1980s to individuals in their twenties through their eighties. *International Journal of Aging and Human Development, 20,* 33-40.

[113] Rapoport, Am. (1982). *The meaning of the built environment: A nonverbal communication approach.* Beverly Hills, CA: Sage.

[114] Rivlin, L. G. (1982). Group membership and place meanings in an urban neighborhood. *Journal of Social Issues, 38,* 75-93.

[115] Loo, C., & Mar, D. (1982). Desired residential mobility in a low income ethnic community: A case study of Chinatown. *Journal of Social Issues, 38*(3), 95-106.

[116] Kahana, E., Lovegreen, L., Kahana, B., & Kahana, M. (2003). Person, environment, and personenvironment fit as influences on residential satisfaction of elders. *Environment and Behavior, 35,* 434453.

[117] Di Masso, A., Dixon, J., & Pol, E. (2011). On the contested nature of place: 'Figuera's Well', 'The Hole of Shame' and the ideological struggle over public space in Barcelona. *Journal of Environmental Psychology, 31,* 231-244.

[118] Nelson, T. M., & Loewen, L. J. (1993). Factors affecting perception of outdoor public environments. *Perceptual and Motor Skills, 76,* 139-146.

[119] Devlin, A. S. (1999, August). *City behavior and precautionary measures.* Paper presented at the annual meetings of the American Psychological Association.

[120] Latkin, C. A., & Curry, A. D. (2003). Stressful neighborhoods and depression: A prospective study of the impact of neighborhood disorder. *Journal of Health and Social Behavior, 44,* 34-44.

[121] Forum on Environment and Human Behavior. (1995, June). *Zero population growth report.* Washington, DC: ZPG Publications.

[122] Habe, R. (1989). Community growth gaming: A survey method. *Environment and Behavior, 21,* 298-322.

[123] Ross, C. R., Mirowsky, J., & Pribesh, S. (2002). Disadvantage, disorder, and urban mistrust. *City & Community, 1,* 59-82.

[124] Austin, D. M., Furr, L. A., & Spine, M. (2002). The effects of neighborhood conditions on perceptions of safety. *Journal of Criminal Justice, 30,* 417-427.

[125] Downey, L., & Van Willigen, M. (2005). Environmental stressors: The mental health impacts of living near industrial activity. *Journal of Health and Social Behavior, 46,* 289-305.

[126] Cutrona, C. E., Wallace, G., & Wesner, K. A. (2006). Neighborhood characteristics and depression: An examination of stress processes. *Current Directions in Psychological Science, 15,* 188-192.

[127] Gifford, R., & Lacombe, C. (2006). Housing quality and children's socioemotional health. *Journal of Housing and the Built Environment, 21,* 177-189.

[128] Torrey, E. F., & Bowler, A. (1990). Geographical distribution of insanity in America: Evidence for an urban factor. *Schizophrenia Bulletin, 16,* 591-604.

[129] Van Os, J., Hanssen, M., Bak, M., Bijl, R. V., & Vollebergh, W. (2003). Do urbanicity and familial liability coparticipate in causing psychosis? *American Journal of Psychiatry, 160,* 477-482.

[130] Leventhal, T., & Brooks-Gunn, J. (2003). Moving to opportunity: An experimental study of neighborhood effects on mental health. *American Journal of Public Health, 93,* 1576-1582.

[131] Levine, R. V., Miyake, K., & Lee, M. (1989). Places rated revisited: Psycho-social pathology in metropolitan areas. *Environment and Behavior, 21,* 531-553.

[132] Levine, R. (1988). City stress index: 25 best, 25 worst. *Psychology Today, 22*(11), 52-58.

[133] Rohe, W. M. (1985). Urban planning and mental health. In A. Wandersman & R. Hess, *Beyond the individual: Environmental approaches and prevention,* New York: The Haworth Press.

[134] Bronzaft, A. L., Ahern, K. D., McGinn, R., O'Conner, J., & Savino, B. (1998). Aircraft noise: A potential health hazard. *Environment and Behavior, 30,* 101-113.

[135] Evans, G. W., & Maxwell, L. (1997). Chronic noise exposure and reading deficits: The

mediating effects of language acquisition. *Environment and Behavior, 29*, 638-656.

136 Tassi, P., Rohmer, O., Bonnefond, A., Margiocchi, F., Poisson, F., & Schimchowitsch, S. (2013). Long term exposure to nocturnal railway noise produces chronic signs of cognitive deficits and diurnal sleepiness. *Journal of Environmental Psychology, 33*, 45-52.

137 Caspi, A., Taylor, A., Moffitt, T. E., & Plomin, R. (2000). Neighborhood deprivation affects children's mental health: Environmental risks identified in a genetic design. *Psychological Science, 11*, 338-342.

138 Gifford, R., & Lacombe, C. (2006). Housing quality and children's socioemotional health. *Journal of Housing and the Built Environment, 21*, 177-189.

139 Moren-Cross, J. L., Wright, D. R., LaGory, M., & Lanzi, R. G. (2006). Perceived neighborhood characteristics and problem behavior among disadvantaged children. *Child Psychiatry & Human Development, 36*, 273-294.

140 Stiffman, A. R., Halley-Ives, E., Elze, D., Johnson, S., & Dore, P. (1999). Impact of environment on adolescent mental health and behavior: Structural equation modeling. *American Journal of Orthopsychiatry, 69*, 73-86.

141 Adeola, F. O. (2000). Endangered community, enduring people: Toxic contamination, health, and adaptive, responses in a local context. *Environment and Behavior, 32*, 209-249.

142 Canter, D., & Larkin, P. (1993). The environmental range of serial rapists. *Journal of Environmental Psychology, 13*, 63-69.

143 Van Daele, S., & Beken, T. V. (2011). Outbound offending: The journey to crime and crime sprees. *Journal of Environmental Psychology, 31*, 70-78.

144 Frank, R., Andresen, M. A., & Brantingham, P. L. (2012). Criminal directionality and the structure of urban form. *Journal of Environmental Psychology, 2*, 37-42.

145 Foster, S., Giles-Corti, B., & Knuiman, M. (2011). Creating safe walkable streetscapes: Does house design and upkeep discourage incivilities in suburban neighbourhoods? *Journal of Environmental Psychology, 31*, 79-88.

146 Suarez de Balcazar, Y., Fawcett, S. B., & Balcaazar, F. E. (1988). Effects of environmental design and police enforcement on violations of a handicapped parking ordinance. *Journal of Applied Behavior Analysis, 21*, 291-298.

147 Marzbali, M. H., Abdullah, A., Razak, N. A., & Tilaki, M. J. M. (2012). The influence of crime prevention through environmental design on victimisation and fear of crime. *Journal of Environmental Psychology, 32*, 79-88.

148 Krupat, E., & Kubzansky, P. E. (1987). Designing to deter crime. *Psychology Today, 21*, 58-61.

149 Brantingham, P. S., & Brantingham, P. L. (1977). *A theoretical model of crime site selection.* Presentation at the American Society of Criminology Meetings, Atlanta.

150 Rand, G. (1984). Crime and environment: A review of the literature and its implications for urban architecture and planning. *Journal of Architecture and Planning Research, 1*, 3-19.

151 Brown, B. B. (1980). *Territoriality, defensible space, and residential burglary.* Master's thesis, University of Utah.

152 Rand, G. (1984). Crime and environment: A review of the literature and its implications for urban architecture and planning. *Journal of Architecture and Planning Research, 1*, 3-19.

153 Duncan, S. C., Duncan, T. E., & Strycker, L. A. (2002). A multilevel analysis of neighborhood context and youth alcohol and drug problems. *Prevention Science, 3*, 125-133.

154 Rand, G. (1984). Crime and environment: A review of the literature and its implications for urban architecture and planning. *Journal of Architecture and Planning Research, 1*, 3-19.

155 Wilson-Doenges, G. (2000). An exploration of sense of community and fear of crime in gated communities. *Environment and Behavior, 32*, 597-611.

156 Cose, E. (1994, July 11). Drawing up safer cities. *Newsweek*, p. 57.

157 Merry, S. E. (1981). *Urban danger: Life in a neighborhood of strangers.* Philadelphia: Temple University Press.

158 Rand, G. (1984). Crime and environment: A review of the literature and its implications for urban architecture and planning. *Journal of Architecture and Planning Research, 1*, 3-19.

159 Krupat, E., & Kubzansky, P. E. (1987). Designing to deter crime. *Psychology Today, 21*, 58-61.

160 Archea, J. C. (1985). The use of architectural props in the conduct of criminal acts. *Journal of Architectural and Planning Research, 2*, 245-259.

161 Jacobs, J. (1961). *The death and life of great American cities.* New York: Random House.

162 Fowler, E. P. (1987). Street management and city design. *Social Forces, 66*, 365-389.

163 van der Voordt, T. J. M., & van Wegen, H. B. R. (1990). Testing building plans for public safety: Usefulness of the Delft checklist. *Housing and Environmental Research, 5*, 129-154.

164 Sommer, R. (1972). *Design awareness.* New York: Holt, Rinehart and Winston.

165 Heberlein, T. A. Moral norms, threatened sanctions, and littering behavior. (Doctoral dissertation, University of Wisconsin-Madison, 1971). *DissertationAbstracts International, 1972, 32*, 5906A. (University Microfilms No. 7202, 639).

166 Finnie, W. C. Field experiments in litter control. *Environment and Behavior, 1973, 5, 123-144.*

167 Pitner, R. O., Yu, M., & Brown, E. (2012). Making neighborhoods safer: Examining predictors of residents' concerns about neighborhood safety. *Journal of Environmental Psychology, 32*, 43-49.

168 Keize, K., Lindenberg, S., & Steg, L. (2008). The spreading of disorder. *Science, 322*(5908), 1681-1685.

169 Toet, A., & van Schaik, M. G. (2012). Effects of signals of disorder on fear of crime in real and virtual environment. *Journal of Environmental Psychology, 32*, 260-276.

170 Donovan, G. H., & Prestemon, J. P. (2012). The effect of trees on crime in Portland, Oregon. *Environment and Behavior, 44*, 3-30.

171 Harries, K. D., & Stadler, S. J. (1983). Determinism revisited: Assault and heat stress in Dallas, 1980. *Environment and Behavior, 15*, 235-256.

172 Bell, P. A., & Greene, T. C. (1982). Thermal stress: Physiological, comfort, performance and social effects of hot and cold environments. In G. W. Evans (Ed.), *Environmental stress.* New York: Cambridge University Press.

173 United States Riot Commission. (1968). *Report of the National Advisory Commission on Civil Disorders.* Bantam: New York, NY.

174 Baron, R. A., & Ransberger, V. M. (1978). Ambient temperature and the occurrence of collective violence: The long hot summer revisited. *Journal of Personality and Social Psychology, 36*, 351-360.

175 Cohn, E. (1990). Weather and crime. *British Journal of Criminology, 30*, 51-64.

176 Byrne, G. (1988). Putting heat on the ball. *Science, 242*, 518.

177 Ceccato, V. (2005). Homicide in São Paulo, Brazil: Assessing spatial-temporal and weather variations. *Journal of Environmental Psychology, 25*, 307-321.

178 Rotton, J., & Cohn, E. G. (2000). Violence is a curvilinear function of temperature in Dallas: A replication. *Journal of Personality and Social Psychology, 78*, 1074-1081.

179 Carlsmith, J. M., & Anderson, C. A. (1979). Ambient temperature and the occurrence of collective violence: A new analysis. *Journal of Personality and Social Psychology, 37*, 327-334.

180 Anderson, C. A., & Anderson, D. C. (1984). Ambient temperature and violent crime: Tests of the linear and curvilinear hypotheses. *Journal of Personality and Social Psychology, 46*, 91-97.

181 Rotton, J. L. (1982, August). *Temperature, humidity, and violent crime.* Paper presented at the annual meetings of the American Psychological Association, Washington, DC.

182 Anderson, C. A. (1987). Temperature and aggression: effects on quarterly, yearly and city rates of violent and nonviolent crime. *Journal of Personality and Social Psychology, 52*, 1161-1173.

183 Anderson, C. A. (2001). Heat and violence. *Psychological Science, 10*, 33-38.

184 Rotton, J. (1983). Affective and cognitive consequences of malodorous pollution. *Basic and Applied Social Psychology, 4*, 171-191.

185 Rotton, J., Frey, J., Barry, T., Milligan, M., & Fitzpatrick, M. (1979). The air pollution experience and physical aggression. *Journal of Applied Social Psychology, 9*, 397-412.

186 Rotton, J., & Frey, J. (1984). Psychological costs of air pollution: Atmospheric conditions, seasonal trends, and psychiatric emergencies. *Population and Environment, 7*

187 Rotton, J., & Frey, J. (1985). Air pollution, weather, and violent crimes: Concomitant time-series analysis of archival data. *Journal of Personality and Social Psychology, 49*, 1207-1220.

188 Cunningham, M. R. (1979). Weather, mood, and helping behavior: Quasi-experiments with the sunshine samaritan. *Journal of Personality and Social Psychology, 37*, 1947-1956.

189 Schneider, F. W., Lesko, W. A., & Garrett, W. A. (1980). Helping behavior in hot, comfortable and cold temperatures. *Environment and Behavior, 12*, 231-240.

190 Korte, C., & Grant, R. (1980). Traffic noise, environmental awareness, and pedestrian behavior. *Environment and Behavior, 12,* 408-420.

191 Page, R. A. (1977). Noise and helping behavior. *Environment and Behavior, 9,* 311-334.

192 Mathews, K. E. Jr., & Canon, L. K. (1975). Environmental noise level as a determinant of helping behavior. *Journal of Personality and Social Psychology, 32,* 571-577.

193 Siegel, J. M., & Steele, C. M. (1980). Environmental distraction and interpersonal judgments. *British Journal of Social and Clinical Psychology, 19,* 23-32.

194 Latane, B., & Darley, J. M. (1970). *The unresponsive bystander: Why doesn't he help?* New York: Appleton-Century-Crofts.

195 Cohen, S., & Spacapan, S. (1978). The aftereffects of stress: An additional interpretation. *Environmental Psychology and Nonverbal Behavior, 3,* 43-57.

196 Kammann, R., Thomson, R., & Irwin, R. (1979). Unhelpful behavior in the street: City size or immediate pedestrian density? *Environment and Behavior, 11,* 245-250.

197 Levine, R. V., Martinez, T. S., Brase, G., & Sorenson, K. (1994). Helping in 36 U.S. cities. *Journal of Personality and Social Psychology, 67,* 69-82.

198 Cohen, S., & Spacapan, S. (1978). The aftereffects of stress: An additional interpretation. *Environmental Psychology and Nonverbal Behavior, 3,* 43-57.

199 Weiner, F. H. (1976). Altruism, ambience, and action: The effects of rural and urban rearing on helping behavior. *Journal of Personality and Social Psychology, 34,* 112-124.

200 Moser, G., & Corroyer, D. (2001). Politeness in the urban environment: Is city life still synonymous with civility. *Environment and Behavior, 33,* 417-485.

201 Milgram, S. (1970). The experience of living in cities. *Science, 167,* 1461-1468.

202 Franck, K. A. (1980). Friends and strangers: The social experience of living in urban and non-urban settings. *Journal of Social Issues, 36,* 52-71.

203 Korte, C. (1980). Urban-nonurban differences in social behavior and social psychological models of urban impact. *Journal of Social Issues, 36,* 29-51.

204 Amato, P. R. (1981). The effects of environmental complexity and pleasantness on prosocial behaviour: A field study. *Australian Journal of Psychology, 33,* 285-295.

205 Amato, P. R. (1981). The impact of the built environment on prosocial and affiliative behavior: A field study of the Townsville City mall. *Australian Journal of Psychology, 33,* 297-303.

206 Bennett, R., & Casey, D. (1989, August). *Ambient cigarette smoke and environmental load: Effects on prosocial behavior.* Paper presented at the annual meetings of the American Psychological Association, New Orleans.

207 Krause, N. (2011). Neighborhood conditions and helping behavior in late life. *Journal of Environmental Psychology, 31,* 62-69.

208 Hampton, K., & Wellman, B. (2003). Neighboring in netville: How the Internet supports community and social capital in a wired suburb. *City & Community, 2,* 277-311.

209 Appleyard, D. (1976). *Planning a pluralist city.* Cambridge, MA: MIT Press.

210 Hillman, J., Whyte, W. H., & Erickson, A. (1980). *The city as dwelling: Walking, sitting, shaping.* Center for Civic Leadership, University of Dallas, Texas., p. 3.

211 Ewing, R., Handy, S., Brownson, R. C., Clemente, O., & Winston, E. (2006). Identifying and measuring urban design qualities related to walkability. *Journal of Physical Activity & Health, 3,* S223-S240.

212 Day, K., Boarnet, M., Alfonzo, M., & Forsyth, A. (2006). The Irvine Minnesota Inventory to measure built environments: Development. *American Journal of Preventive Medicine, 30,* 144-152.

213 Samarasekara, G. N., Fukahori, K., & Kubota, Y. (2011). Environmental correlates that provide walkability cues for tourists: An analysis based on walking decision narrations. *Environment and Behavior, 43,* 501-524.

214 Boarnet, M. G., Forsyth, A., Day, K., & Oakes, J. M. (2011). The street level built environment and physical activity and walking: Results of a predictive validity study for the Irvine Minnesota Inventory. *Environment and Behavior, 43,* 735-775.

215 Frank, L. D., Andresen, M. A., & Schmid, T. L. (2004). Obesity relationships with community design, physical activity, and time spent in cars. *American Journal of Preventive Medicine, 27,* 87-96.

216 Dills, J. E., Rutt, C. D., & Mumford, K. G. (2012). Objectively measuring route-to-park walkability in Atlanta, Georgia. *Environment and Behavior, 44,* 841-860.

217 Werner, C. M., Brown, B. B., & Gallimore, J. (2010). Light rail use is more likely on "walkable" blocks: Further support for using micro-level environmental audit measures. *Journal of Environmental Psychology, 30,* 206-214.

218 Patterson, P. K., & Chapman, N. J. (2004). Urban form and older residents' service use, walking, driving, quality of life, and neighborhood satisfaction. *American Journal of Health Promotion, 19,* 45-52.

219 Gallimore, J. M., Brown, B. B., & Werner, C. M. (2011). Walking routes to school in new urban and suburban neighborhoods: An environmental walkability analysis of blocks and routes. *Journal of Environmental Psychology, 31,* 184-191.

220 Zook, J. B., Lu, Y., Glanz, K., & Zimring, C. (2012). Design and pedestrianism in a smart growth development. *Environment and Behavior, 44,* 216-234.

221 de Montigny, L., Ling, R., & Zacharias, J. (2012). The effects of weather on walking rates in nine cities. *Environment and Behavior, 44,* 821-840.

222 Fletcher, S., &Macauley, C. (1983). The shopping mall as a therapeutic arena. *Geriatric Nursing 4,* 105-106.

223 Börnstein, M. H., & Börnstein, H. G. (1976). The pace of life. *Nature, 259,* 557-558.

224 Bornstein, M. H. (1979). The pace of life: Revisited. *International Journal of Psychology, 14,* 83-90.

225 Gifford, R., Ward, J., & Dahms, W. (1977). Pedestrian velocities: A multivariate study of social and environmental effects. *Journal of Human Movement Studies, 3,* 66-68.

226 Wirtz, P., & Ried, G. (1992). The pace of life reanalysed: Why does walking speed of pedestrians correlate with city size? *Behaviour, 123,* 77-83.

227 Rotton, J., Shats, M., & Standers, R. (1990). Temperature and pedestrian tempo: Walking without awareness. *Environment and Behavior, 22,* 650-674.

228 Hill, M. R. (1984). Walking, crossing streets, and choosing pedestrian routes: A survey of recent insights from the social/behavioral sciences. *University of Nebraska Studies, new series no. 66.*

229 Hill, M. R. (1984). Walking, crossing streets, and choosing pedestrian routes: A survey of recent insights from the social/behavioral sciences. *University of Nebraska Studies, new series no. 66.*

230 McCauley, D., Coleman, G., & De Fusco, P. (1978). Commuters' eye contact with strangers in city and suburban train stations: Evidence of short-term adaptation to interpersonal overload in the city. *Environmental Psychology and Nonverbal Behavior, 2,* 215-225.

231 Lofland, L. (1973). *A world of strangers.* New York: Basic Books.

232 Wolff, M. (1973). Notes on the behavior of pedestrians. In A. Brienbaum & E. Sagarin (Eds.), *People in places: The sociology of the familiar.* New York: Praeger.

233 Duvall, J. (2013). Using engagement-based strategies to alter perceptions of the walking environment. *Environment and Behavior, 45,* 303-322.

234 Koohsari, M. J., Karakiewicz, J. A., & Kaczynski, A. T. (2013). Public open space and walking: The role of proximity, perceptual qualities of the surrounding built environment, and street configuration. *Environment and Behavior, 45,* 706-736.

235 van Vliet—, W. (1983). Exploring the fourth environment: An examination of the home range of city and suburban teenagers. *Environment and Behavior, 15,* 567-588.

236 van Vliet—, W. (1983). Exploring the fourth environment: An examination of the home range of city and suburban teenagers. *Environment and Behavior, 15,* 567-588.

237 Owens, D. D. (1981). Ridesharing programs: Governmental response to urban transportation problems. *Environment and Behavior, 13,* 311-330.

238 Lenzi, M., Vieno, A., Pastore, M., & Santinello, M. (2013). Neighborhood social connectedness and adolescent civic engagement: An integrative model. *Journal of Environmental Psychology, 34,* 45-54.

239 Schiavo, S. R. (1988). Age differences in assessment and use of a suburban neighborhood among children and adolescents. *Children's Environments Quarterly, 5,* 4-9.

240 Gaster, S. (1991). Urban children's access to their neighborhood: Changes over three generations. *Environment and Behavior, 23,* 70-85.

241 Skjaeveland, O., & Garling, T. (1997). Effects of interactional space on neighbouring. *Journal of Environmental Psychology, 17,* 181-198.

242 Taylor, A. F., Wiley, A., Kuo, F. E., & Sullivan, W. C. (1998). Growing up in the inner city:

Green spaces as places to grow. *Environment and Behavior, 30*, 3-27.

243 Nation, M., Fortney, T., & Wandersman, A. (2010). Race, place, and neighboring: Social ties among neighbors in urban, suburban, and rural contexts. *Environment and Behavior, 42*, 581-596.

244 Brown, D., Sijpkes, P., & MacLean, M. (1986). The community role of public indoor space. *Journal of Architecture and Planning Research, 3*, 161-172.

245 Smith, G. C.(1991). Grocery shopping patterns of the ambulatory urban elderly. *Environment and Behavior, 23*, 86-114.

246 Simon, S. L., Walsh, D. A., Regnier, V. A., & Krauss, I. K. (1992). Spatial cognition and neighborhood use: The relationship in older adults. *Psychology and Aging, 7*, 389-394.

247 Seattle stomps on vagrancy. (1994, May 24). Victoria *Times-Colonist*, p. A5.

248 Milgram, S. (1977). *The individual in a social world: Essays and experiments.* Reading, MA: Addison-Wesley.

249 Turley, L. W., & Milliman, R. E. (2000). Atmospheric effects on shopping behavior: A review of the experimental evidence. *Journal of Business Research, 49*, 193-211.

250 El Sayed, I. M., Farrag, D. A., & Belk, R. W. (2003). The effects of physical surroundings on Egyptian consumers' emotional states and buying intentions. *Journal of International Consumer Marketing, 16*, 5-27.

251 Donovan. R. J., & Rossiter, J. R. (1982). Store atmosphere: An environmental psychology approach. *Journal of Retailing, 58*, 34-57.

252 Laroche, M., Bergeron, J., & Barbaro-Forleo, G. (2001). Targeting consumers who are willing to pay more for environmentally friendly products. *Journal of Consumer Marketing, 21*, 503-520

253 Thögersen, J., & Ölander, F. (2003). Spillover of environment-friendly consumer behaviour. *Journal of Environmental Psychology, 23*, 225-236.

254 Hawkins, D. I., Best, R. J., & Coney, K. A. (1983). *Consumer behavior: Implications for marketing strategy.* Plano, TX: Business Publications.

255 Williams, R. (1981, October-November). Outshopping: Problem or opportunity? *Arizona Business, 27*, 9.

256 Smith, G. C.(1991). Grocery shopping patterns of the ambulatory urban elderly. *Environment and Behavior, 23*, 86-114.

257 Sommer, R., Herrick, J., & Sommer, T. R. (1981). The behavioral ecology of supermarkets and farmers' markets. *Journal of Environmental Psychology, 1*, 13-19.

258 May, F. E. (1969). Buying behavior: Some research findings. In J. U. McNeal (Ed.), *Dimensions of buying behavior.* New York: Appleton-Century-Crofts.

259 Sommer, R. (1998). Shopping at the co-op. *Journal of Environmental Psychology, 18*, 45-53.

260 van Rompay, T. J. L., Tanja-Dijkstra, K., Verhoeven, J. W. M., & van Es, A. F. (2012). On Store Design and Consumer Motivation: Spatial Control and Arousal in the Retail Context. *Environment and Behavior, 44*, 800-820

261 Donovan. R. J., & Rossiter, J. R. (1982). Store atmosphere: An environmental psychology approach. *Journal of Retailing, 58*, 34-57.

262 Jansen-Verbeke, M. (1987). Women, shopping and leisure. *Leisure Studies, 6*, 71-86.

263 Roy, A., & Tai, S. T. C. (2003). Store environment and shopping behavior: The role of imagery elaboration and shopping orientation. *Journal of International Consumer Marketing, 15*, 71-99.

264 Harrell, G., Hutt, M., & Anderson, J. (1980). Path analysis of buyer behavior under conditions of crowding. *Journal of Marketing Research, 17*, 45-51.

265 Machleit, K. A., Eroglu, S. A., & Mantel, S. P. (2000). Perceived retail crowding and shopping satisfaction: What modifies this relationship? *Journal of Consumer Psychology, 9*, 29-42.

266 Segal, M. E., & McCauley, C. R. (1986). The sociability of commercial exchange in rural, suburban, and urban locations: A test of the urban overload hypothesis. *Basic and Applied Social Psychology, 7*, 115-135.

267 Cohen, P. (1981). *Consumer behavior.* New York: Random House.

268 Leed, T. W., & German, G. A. (1973). *Food merchandising: Principles and practices.* New York: Chain Store Age Books.

269 Patricios, N. N. (1979). Human aspects of planning shopping centers. *Environment and Behavior, 11*, 511-538.

270 Zhou, L., & Wong, A. (2003). Consumer impulse buying and in-store stimuli in Chinese supermarkets. *Journal of International Consumer Marketing, 16*, 37-53.

271 Dubé, L., & Morin, S. (2001). Background music pleasure and store evaluation: Intensity effects and psychological mechanisms. *Journal of Business Research, 54*, 107-113.

272 Milliman, R. E. (1982). Using background music to affect the behavior of supermarket shoppers. *Journal of Marketing, 46*, 86-91.

273 Smith, P. C., & Curnow, R. (1966). Arousal hypotheses and the effects of music on purchasing behavior. *Journal of Applied Psychology, 50*, 255-256.

274 Milliman, R. E. (1982). Using background music to affect the behavior of supermarket shoppers. *Journal of Marketing, 46*, 86-91.

275 Roballey, T. C., McGreevy, C., Rongo, R. R., Schwantes, M. L., Steger, P. J., Wininger, M. A., & Gardner, E. B. (1985). The effect of music on eating behavior. *Bulletin of the Psychonomic Society, 23*, 221-222.

276 North, A. C., & Hargreaves, D. J. (1998). The effect of music on atmosphere and purchase intentions in a cafeteria. *Journal of Applied Social Psychology, 28*, 2254-2273.

277 North, A. C., Shilcock, A., & Hargreaves, D. J. (2003). The effect of musical style on restaurant customers' spending. *Environment and Behavior, 35*, 712-718.

278 Areni, C. S., & Kim, D. (1994). The influence of in-store lighting on consumers' examination of merchandise in a wine store. *International Journal of Research in Marketing, 11*, 117-125.

279 Summers, T. A., & Hebert, P. R. (2001). Shedding some light on store atmospherics: Influence of illumination on consumer behavior. *Journal of Business Research, 54*, 145-150.

280 Bosmans, A. (2006). Scents and sensibility: When do (in)congruent ambient scents influence product evaluations? *Journal of Marketing, 70*, 32-43.

281 Douce, L., & Janssens, W. (2013). The presence of a pleasant ambient scent in a fashion store: The moderating role of shopping motivation and affect intensity. *Environment and Behavior, 45*, 215-238.

282 Chebat, J., & Michon, R. (2003). Impact of ambient odors on mall shoppers' emotions, cognition, and spending: A test of competitive causal theories. *Journal of Business Research, 56*, 529-539.

283 Kohn, I. R., Franck, K. A., & Fox, A. S. (1975). *Defensible space modifications in row-house communities.* Report to the National Science Foundation. New York: Institute for Community Design Analysis.

284 Whyte, W. H. (1974). The best street life in the world. *New York Magazine, 15*, 26-33.

285 Whyte, W. H. (1980). *The social life of small urban spaces.* New York: The Conservation Foundation.

286 Nasar, J. L. (1990). Patterns of behavior in urban public spaces. *Journal of Architectural and Planning Research, 7*, 71-85.

287 Brower, S. (1988). *Design in familiar places: What makes home environments look good.* New York: Praeger.

288 Vis, A. A., Dijkstra, A., & Slop, M. (1992). Safety effects of 30 Km/h zones in the Netherlands. *Accident Analysis and Prevention, 24*, 75-86.

289 Zaidel, D., Hakkert, A. S., & Pistiner, A. H. (1992). The use of road humps for moderating speeds on urban streets. *Accident Analysis and Prevention, 24*, 45-56.

The Psychology of Place Attachment

LEILA SCANNELL AND ROBERT GIFFORD

> "Home is not simply a mark upon a map any more than a river's just water. It is the place at the centre of the compass from which every arrow radiates and where the heart is fixed. It is a force that forever draws us back or lures us on. For where the home is, there lies hope. And a future waits. And everything is possible."

—HEIDI THOMAS, *Call the Midwife*
BBC TELEVISION SERIES, SEASON 2, EPISODE 7

"I STILL CAN'T BELIEVE THEY WANT TO TRANSFER YOU TO THE NEW OFFICE," SAID JANE. "Work wouldn't be the same without you. Any thoughts on the move now that you've gotten to know the town a bit better?"

Amber frowned. "It was good that we were able to help set things up in person. But to be honest, I'm still undecided. They want a response by Monday."

The seatbelt sign lit up. "Good afternoon ladies and gentleman. We are nearing our destination. Thank you for flying with us today. Prepare the cabin for landing."

Jane pressed her forehead to the window and looked down. The city appeared miniature.

Amber leaned over to take a look. "I sometimes forget how much I love this place until I'm away from it."

"How long have you lived here?" asked Jane.

"About 15 years now. When I moved here with my parents, it felt familiar — like we instantly fit in to our neighbourhood. It's still so strange that they sold their house and moved downtown. I wish I could see the inside again. Our place was west of City Hall. It's right next to that big pond. See it?"

Jane nodded. "I love that part of town. So much character."

"Growing up, it seemed to be the most perfect neighbourhood in the world. We'd often play down in the ravine when we were kids. These days, I bring the dog there for walks sometimes, and it feels like stepping into the past."

"I know what you mean," said Jane. "There's where I play soccer. Oh—and there's the inner harbor. Tom and I went kayaking on our first date. And then there's Tom's grandfather's house, which he just inherited. If you look north west, you can see a chain of islands. That's where we go camping sometimes. It's like this city helps you to map out your life."

"This is a great city," said Amber. "Leaving for a new job would be really tough."

"I know," said Jane. "I'm pretty sure that I'll never move, if I can help it."

TAKE A FEW MINUTES AND THINK OF A PLACE THAT IS MEANINGFUL FOR YOU—a place that you really feel connected to. This could be any type of place, from any time, for any reason. Perhaps it is a childhood home, a favorite camping spot, a city you long to return to, or the country where you were born. Maybe it is your bedroom, a particular park bench, a place of spiritual significance, or the place where you first met your significant other. Most people can readily conjure up at least one place that is important to them. This cognitive-emotional bond that individuals develop towards places is known as **place attachment.**

After we have long or intense experiences with them, places can acquire great personal meaning. In contrast, most of the appraisals already discussed may be made after brief exposure to a place, although our appraisals of its quality or beauty might change after we have had the benefit of longer experience with it. Place attachment has some serious implications; it can even kill. In a later chapter we shall see that a major reason people often do not abandon locations that are prone to deadly natural hazards such as floods, earthquakes, and hurricanes is their deeply felt connection to a place.

Place is the setting for life's actions. It is where we conduct our day-to-day activities, where we journey to, and where we and our ancestors have traversed. Because of this, place attachment finds a home across disciplines, albeit sometimes by different names or related constructs. Humanistic geographers, for example, have described **topophilia**, meaning love of place, and "sense of place," which is often defined similarly to place attachment.[1,2] Sociologists and community psychologists discuss "community ties" and "sense of community."[3] Indeed, these disciplines generated the bases of research on affective ties to place.

Environmental psychologists were drawn to the topic in the 1980s and 1990s, as part of the overarching inquiry into the interactions between the physical environment and the individual. Earlier work focused more on territoriality and residential satisfaction, but since then, psychological research on place attachment has expanded. For example, a literature search on PsycInfo using the terms "place attachment" and "sense of place" published in psychology journals revealed that place attachment research has nearly quadrupled in the past 20 years. Many of these studies have aimed to define exactly what the nature of person-place bonds seems to be. This has resulted in many types and subtypes of place attachment which, once taken together, give a sense of the variety of attachments that can be developed towards meaningful places.

Defining Place Attachment: Person, Process, Place Framework

RECOGNIZING THE NEED TO TAKE STOCK of the many definitions of place attachment, we organized them into a tripartite framework, consisting of person, place, and process dimensions (Figure 9-1).[4] Thus, given any place attachment, the framework leads us to consider *who* is attached, *what* they are attached to, and *how* (psychologically) they are expressing their attachment.

Who is Attached? The **person dimension** describes the people who are attached, and whether their attachment rests in individually based meanings (e.g., personal experience), collectively based meanings (e.g., cultural or religious significance) or a combination of both. Specifically, the attachment may be at the *individual* level when the place is meaningful for personal reasons, such as the memorable events that occurred there. For example, someone might be attached to Montreal because that is where she lived when she first moved away from her family home to go to university, and thus where she experienced the milestones of young adulthood. The attachment may be at the *collective* level when the place is meaningful as determined by group members; for example, many Jews are attached to Israel because the religion has designated this place as sacred.[5,6]

How Are They Attached? The second dimension is the **psychological process dimension**, which refers to how we express and experience our attachments through affect, cognition, and behavior. Bonds toward a place include an *affective*, or emotional component, and many place attachment researchers define place attachment as having some sort of emotional bond. Most of these emotions toward the important place are positive, such as feeling love, happiness, joy, pride, and contentment when going to (or thinking about) one's place.[7-11] However, individuals can sometimes hold negative or ambivalent feelings toward their important places when they represent painful memories or when the place has disappeared or changed.[12]

Our ties to place are also *cognitive*, because they include the knowledge, memories, and beliefs that make a place meaningful. Cognitively, as one becomes attached to a place, they develop a mental representation of that place, containing a mental map and route knowledge of the place's arrangement,[13] as well as other information such as knowledge about the history of the place, and particular place affordances. Other than mental representations of structural and symbolic aspects of the place, cognitive connections to place involve memories of the place, its people, and the events that have occurred there. [14,15]

Place attachment is also expressed through particular behaviors. When attached to places where they do not live, people often voluntarily visit that place, sometimes at much cost. Some people return to the same vacation spot year after year. Others make religious pilgrimages to sacred places.[16] For example, most Muslims try to make a pilgrimage to Mecca at least once in their lives if they are physically and financially able.

Interestingly, attachment behaviors can emerge as part of design and construction efforts. New places are sometimes built to resemble residents' former homes or communities. In one study of American Mormons living in Mexico, settlements featured wide streets, fields in town, and manicured lawns, rather than traditional Mexican features.[17] Place attachment also plays a role in the decision to restore places to their original states rather than building anew. After facing destruction from a tornado, the community of Xenia, Ohio was rebuilt close to its former state, reflecting the residents' desire to revive Xenia as they knew it, instead of reinventing it anew.[18]

To What Are They Attached? The third dimension of place attachment is the **place dimension**: what is it about the *place* that we are attached to? Attachments can center on a variety of place types of different scales, but researchers tend to emphasize the social and physical qualities of the important place, given that place attachments can be rooted in social ties or can stem from aesthetic or landscape features. These social and physical qualities will be elaborated upon later.

Related Constructs: Place Identity and Place Dependence

WE HAVE SEVERAL KINDS OF PSYCHOLOGICAL TIES TO PLACES. Each taps a slightly different aspect of how we

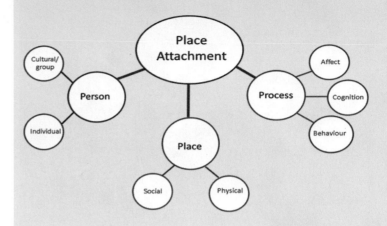

FIGURE 9–1 The person–process–place framework of place attachment.

relate to the important places in our lives. Besides place attachment, two others deserve mention.

Place Identity. Although place identity is related to place attachment,[19,20] it is distinct: place identity is about one's incorporation of a place into the larger concept of self.[21,22] It endows a person with a sense of continuity, self-esteem, self-efficacy (a sense of being able to get things done), and a sense of distinctiveness (from people who live elsewhere).[23] Thus, *who* we are can also include *where* we are. We give ourselves names that reflect our place attachments: Britain has its Fenmen, the United States its New Yorkers, and Canada its Maritimers. University students identify with their schools, and residents of counties, states, districts, provinces, and territories identify with these jurisdictions. At smaller scales, many people identify with their neighborhoods, boroughs, farms, or even houses.

Place Dependence. Sometimes called "functional attachment," place dependence refers to the ability of a place to satisfy needs and goals, or the extent to which the physical characteristics of the place provide the appropriate resources for one's preferred activities.[24,25] That is, we become dependent on places when their features are congruent with our goals. *Generic* place dependence is attachment to a certain *category* of place, based on its function. For example, mountain bikers might be attached to communities that are close to good mountain bike trails (Figure 9-2). *Geographic* place dependence is attachment to a *particular* place, based on its function. For example, some mountain bikers might be attached to the Great Divide Mountain Bike Route, a trail of more than 4,000 km that runs from Banff, Canada, to New Mexico, USA, because it provides them with optimally challenging terrain.

FIGURE 9–2 Places of attachment can support our preferred activities and hobbies.

IN SUM *The various definitions of place attachment have been organized into a tripartite framework, including, person, place, and psychological process dimensions. A variety of related concepts, such as topophilia, sense of place, sense of community, place identity, and place dependence have also been proposed.*

PLACE ATTACHMENT MEASURES AND METHODS

RESEARCHERS WHO STUDY PLACE ATTACHMENT have generally taken one of two approaches: (1) a quantitative approach, where the strength and type of the attachment is translated into numeric terms appropriate for further statistical analyses (e.g., such as investigating correlations among place attachment and other constructs), or (2) a qualitative approach, where the varied meanings and personal experiences of the attachment are articulated by individuals, and then summarized into prominent themes by researchers. Because each method has its limits, a greater diversity of approaches to research methods and measurement will be important for future studies on place attachment.

Self-reported Place Attachment

One method of ascertaining individuals' feelings, thoughts, and motivations is simply to ask them. Not all psychological constructs can be observed, and survey research offers a feasible way to gather information about one's inner processes. This is especially relevant to place attachment because its cognitive-emotional elements are not easily observable.

The majority of place attachment research in environmental psychology measures the strength of the bond between persons and places with self-reports.[26-32] Items on the Sense of Place Scale assess the degree of various aspects of attachment to lakeshore property, including affect (e.g., *"I really miss my lake property when I'm away from it for too long"*) cognition, conceptualized in their scale as place identity (*"My lake property reflects the type of person I am"*), and behavior, conceptualized as place dependence (*"My lake property is the best place for doing the things that I enjoy most"*).[33]

The variety of questions and types of attachments assessed in such self-reports reflects the plethora of place attachment definitions that have been proposed.[34] After measuring place attachment this way, researchers could investigate whether place attachment strength correlates with other variables, such as particular behaviors, or they could explore how the various dimensions of place attachment interrelate.

Unfortunately, some self-report-based place attachment studies are weakened by limited measures. Some lack survey development, standardization, or construct validity. One study assessed place attachment with a single five-point Likert item: *"Do you think the area in which you live is a good place to live?"*[35] This problematic item may better cluster with constructs such as neighborhood satisfaction or quality perception rather than place attachment. Using multi-item reliable measures with established reliability and validity is essential for better place attachment research.

Qualitative Approaches to Place Attachment

SOME RESEARCHERS EMPHASIZE that place attachments involve rich subjective meanings that cannot be captured by self-reports; for this reason, a qualitative approach may be suitable.[36] Similarly, some suggest that qualitative research is the best type of methodology to investigate place meaning because it can better represent the depth and complexity of the bond.[37] Whereas quantitative research identifies and predicts phenomena within a sample that will generalize to a larger population, qualitative research generates a deep understanding of phenomena, such as through case studies or ethnographies. Instead of generalizability, concepts explored through qualitative analyses have transferability; that is, themes that emerge from data can be thought of as abstract concepts with potential relevance to other cases.

Person-place concepts have been explored through semi-structured interviews and other qualitative methodologies. In one study, individuals' descriptions of place memories and meanings were coded into themes and used to develop theories about how place attachment grows.[38] In another, the relation between place attachment and mobility was explored through qualitative interviews with 14 respondents.[39] Qualitative approaches sometimes combine interviews with visual methods such as having participants take photographs, draw, or use maps as points of discussion about their important places.[40-42] Although qualitative methodologies have been of great value in the study of place attachment,[43-45] they are limited in their generalizability to broader populations, and in their ability to explicate the causal aspects of place attachment processes.

Combining qualitative and quantitative approaches does not solve the problem, but it can be used to balance some of their strengths and weaknesses. In a study that used mixed methods, participants marked places on a map with tokens of different psychological importance weights (e.g., 5-50) and place values (e.g., aesthetic value, recreation value, cultural value), and then explained why those places were meaningful to them.[46,47] Such an approach provides numeric data enriched with a description of place meaning.

Other Measures and Methods

Experiments. Because self-reports and qualitative methods pose particular limitations, place attachment researchers will need to expand their measures and methods. We have endeavored to begin this expansion in two experiments.[48] In the first, we manipulated place attachment by having participants either visualize a place to which they were attached or, for the control group, a place with which they were familiar but not attached. Those who visualized a place of attachment reported feeling stronger current levels of self-esteem, meaning, and belonging. Manipulating place attachment (rather than simply measuring it) allows

researchers to move beyond correlational and qualitative findings, into the realm of experiments where causal conclusions are more likely to be valid.

In the second study, we adapted a method that had been used in interpersonal attachment research[49] to investigate whether places of attachment are "sought out" following a stressful situation. Each participant provided a list of names of places to which they were attached, as well as names of places to which they were not attached. Using a reaction-time-based task on the computer, we then measured "seeking out" a place of attachment according to how quickly participants could identify place attachment words that appeared on their computer screens.

Not surprisingly, participants responded more quickly to names of places to which they were attached compared to names of familiar places, unfamiliar places, or nonsense words. Making a mistake during the word recognition task was more stressful; this threat slowed their subsequent performance for every type of word, but interestingly, it *improved* their performance for place attachment words. Making a mistake is a type of threat that led people to seek comfort from their place of attachment. This supports the idea that we cognitively seek out places to which we are attached when presented with a stressor or threat. Perhaps more importantly, the task is a measure of place attachment that taps into automatic processing and therefore offers an alternative to measuring place attachment using self-reports.

Observation. Another way of avoiding some of the biases associated with self-reports and interviews is to observe behaviors that likely represent place attachment. One way to measure behavioral indicators of place attachment is to count proximity-seeking efforts, such as the frequency of homesick students calling home.[50] In general, however, observations of place attachment behaviors are lacking. Field experiments in which place attachment behaviors are observed in varying conditions would add much to the construct and internal validity of place attachment and its processes. A list of observable behaviors that indicate place attachment has not yet been generated, but would be a valuable addition to the literature. Which behaviors do you think would be good indicators of place attachment?

Place attachment research would benefit from measuring it in new ways, and using experiments, observations of people, and other approaches. As a whole, environmental psychology, like some other areas of psychology, relies too much on self-reports; this can introduce **mono-method bias**, in which the apparent overlap or agreement between two measures may be shared because both use the same methodology.[51] To reduce this mono-method bias and methodological stagnation, it is crucial that place attachment researchers adopt new operationalizations and research designs.

IN SUM *Place attachment is usually investigated through quantitative self-reports, or qualitative approaches, such as in-depth interviews. Both methods have their strengths and weaknesses, but one notable weakness shared by both is their limited ability to make causal inferences. Experimental methodologies where participants are randomly assigned to various conditions, and place attachment is manipulated or measured in new ways, would therefore add much to the validity of place attachment research findings, and would help environmental psychology in general escape the trap of the mono-method bias.*

INFLUENCES ON PLACE ATTACHMENT

Personal Factors

PLACE ATTACHMENTS ARE AND HAVE BEEN IMPORTANT TO HUMANS ACROSS CULTURES, PLACES, AND ERAS; however, the type and degree of place attachment can differ depending on various factors, some of which relate to the individual. Time, congruence, mobility, ownership, social status, gender, stage of development, sexuality, and personality differences are some of these personal factors known to influence place attachment.

Time. The most consistent predictor of place attachment is the amount of time that an individual has spent in the place.[52,53] Place attachments do not usually form instantaneously (although this is possible), but tend to strengthen with accumulated positive interactions, and memories that accrue after months and years. Over time, the place becomes a referent for the past, providing an individual with a sense of continuity; this phenomenon is known as **place-referent continuity**.[54]

The degree of the individual's history with the place shapes the nature of the attachment.[55] People with little or no attachment, such as tourists, have a **superficial sense of place**, in which positive feelings rest on aesthetic or entertaining features of the place. Others, such as young children or seasonal visitors, have a developing, yet still weak bond called a **partial sense of place** that includes positive feelings without a commitment to stay. Longer-term residents develop a more stable bond called a **personal sense of place**. These residents typically possess more local knowledge, larger social networks, and greater community involvement. Stronger still is an **ancestral sense of place**, the bond that develops among residents who were raised in the place, and that persists even if the person should have to leave it. Finally, the most intense bond is a **cultural sense of place**, whereby the place is historically connected to one's tribe or cultural group. For example, Maoris in New Zealand may have a cultural sense of place that is deeper than that experienced by non-Maoris. Residential status also has implications for place identity; natives tend to have similar degrees of place attachment and identity, whereas non-natives tend to have lower levels of place identity than attachment.[56]

Congruence. Although time certainly plays a role in place attachment, it is not always required; sometimes place attachments form more quickly, almost like love at first sight. This is more likely to occur when individuals experience congruence; the term **place-congruent continuity** describes the sense that a particular place fits with aspects of the self.[57] A newcomer to a rural lake town in British Columbia once told me about his sense of instant connection to the place: "I drove my car around the bend and saw the lake, and at that moment, I knew I was home and would never move away." Faster-forming place attachments can also occur when a person feels that the place has qualities reminiscent of a previous place of attachment, such as similar climate, or other features.[58] This is called **settlement identity**.[59] For example, a prospective homebuyer may seek out a single family dwelling on a cul-de-sac because her childhood home was in a similar type of neighborhood (Figure 9-3). You might take a moment consider the types of place attachment that you have.

Mobility. If place attachment generally grows with the amount of time spent in a place, then does it decline with increases in **mobility**? Indeed, some evidence does suggest that individuals who are more mobile tend to have weaker place attachment[60] and, conversely, that people who are more attached to a place are less willing to move away.[61,62] However, mobility certainly does not always undermine the experience of place attachment.[63,64] One obvious reason for this is that even when we move, we can maintain connections to place in a variety of ways, such as **place elasticity**, in which a place is "stretched" closer to the distant person through communications and media (e.g., Internet, phone, television), and knowing that (usually) we can return to the place when we feel the need to.[65]

In this increasingly mobile world, many of us become attached to more than one place, forming multiple place bonds.[66] In Sweden, frequent travelers (compared to less frequent travelers) had stronger attachment to places of larger scales, such as countries, yet their attachment to the local communities was as strong as that of the less-frequent travelers.[67] Interestingly, the frequent travelers actually were *more* involved in community and local issues than less-frequent travelers, indicating that their mobility did not detract from their local place attachment. Others have also argued that that "roots" (i.e., place attachment) and "routes" (mobility) are not always at odds.[68] For some people, being away can *strengthen* ties to home through homesickness,[69] or through appreciating the qualities of one's place that may have previously been taken for granted.[70] Thus, mobility is relevant for place attachment, but it does not always dilute place bonds (Figure 9-4).

Ownership. Owning predicts place attachment.[71-73] Those who own their place tend to be more attached, although the direction of this relation is unclear. Does ownership itself increase the strength of the attachment through commitment, time, identity, and other factors, or does feeling an affinity for a place lead people to purchase it? Although ownership is important, it is not essential: people who do not own or control a place can still be attached to it, as is seen, for example, among low-income Americans living in social housing[74] or children who play in green spaces owned by municipalities or landlords.[75] Although a lack of ownership can be disempowering for those in place, it does not obviate the existence of the bond.

Social Status. Through indicators such as income, occupation, and level of education, one's social status is related to

FIGURE 9-3 We can be attached to certain types of places, such houses on culs-de-sac, rather than to specific places.

FIGURE 9-4 Mobility and place attachment are not always at odds.

place attachment. For a long time, place attachment was assumed to be at odds with social status; for example, securing a good job can necessitate moving away from a place to which one is attached. The career path in academia often requires moving to distant universities before attaining a long-term position as a professor. Perhaps because of this, place attachment remains weaker among the highly educated.[76]

More recently, however, this view has been challenged, after considering that the *type* of place attachment makes a difference.[77] People stronger in what has been called "everyday rootedness," in which attachment to place is taken for granted tend to have lower levels of education.[78] However, people with stronger "ideological rootedness," in which

FIGURE 9-5 Children's favorite places can support their development.

individuals select their place of attachment and are more involved in the community, tend to be more highly educated. Therefore, although social status can be linked to higher rates of mobility and weaker local ties, those with high socioeconomic status also tend to be homeowners who are able to select where they live.[79]

Gender. This is another personal factor that can influence the meaning and strength of place attachment, although sometimes it does not matter.[80] Within traditional (patriarchal) gender roles, home may be a haven for men, but a workplace for women.[81] Despite this possible ambivalent experience of home for women, their degree of attachment is not always weaker. In Spain, if not elsewhere, women report stronger place attachment than do men at three spatial levels (i.e., home, neighborhood, and city).[82] The place attachment of women is more often social, whereas men's attachment is more often based on activities.[83] Therefore, the relation between gender and place attachment is complex, and requires further work to disentangle these discrepant findings.

Development. Place attachment is relevant to a person's developmental needs. Certainly it is important for children's development;[84] a child's favorite places can support play, mastery, and exploration[85] (Figure 9-5), as well as problem-solving and emotion-regulation.[86] In addition, the favorite places selected by children are influenced by their range of exploration, their rural or urban residency, their familiarity with and previous exposure to, various environments, and the environmental preferences of their peers.[87,88] This varies with temperament: among boys attending a summer camp, those with more negative emotions were likely to select solitary or novel places, whereas those with more

positive emotions were likely to select social places.[89] Adolescents with higher academic achievement, fewer social ties, and fewer opportunities for local employment showed declining place attachment over a two-year period, but it remained stable among adolescents who had lower academic achievement, stronger identification with their parents, and stronger religiosity.[90]

Place attachments are relevant to developmental processes in young adulthood too, such as providing a suitable location for raising a family and finding work.[91] Deciding to stay in a place after university is more likely among those who prioritize wanting a family, and other goals involving affiliation with others. In contrast, those for whom career goals are more central are more likely to decide to leave. Place preferences therefore interact with one's motivations and life goals.[92] Place attachment (and in particular, a sense of being connected to place through social bonding) is greater among residents with children.[93] Later in life, place ties also assist with social support,[94] as well as with self-reflection and connecting to the past.[95]

Sexuality. The experience of place attachment can also differ depending on one's sexual orientation. For example, lesbian mothers seem more likely to be attached to their residential community when the neighborhood has at least one lesbian-gay-bisexual-transgender (LGBT) organization.[96] Not surprisingly, place attachments develop for places where LGBT individuals feel safe and free from discrimination.[97] In some cases, LGBT individuals have used place to define their community values and ultimately represent their identities beyond that of sexuality; in West Hollywood, for example, residents have created a community that represents not only their sexualities and genders, but also the creative and progressive political aspects of their identities.[98]

Personality differences. Our dispositions probably also play a role in place attachment, although this is an understudied topic. In Italy, residents with insecure interpersonal attachment styles (such as being anxious and preoccupied with, or avoidant towards, close relationships) reported weaker attachment to their community, fewer neighborhood social bonds, and lower levels of satisfaction.[99] Interpersonal attachment styles therefore seem to affect the nature of the bonds with one's current place, and they also appear to influence ties to a former place. Children with an anxious attachment style are much more likely to experience homesickness than their secure counterparts, who are more independent and willing to explore while they are away from home.[100]

The Social Context

THE PPP MODEL INTRODUCED EARLIER specifies that place attachments vary in their degree of emphasis on the social features of a place. Places often include people, who influence the meaning, experiences, and activities inherent in a place. For example, you might be attached to a place where you often hang out with close friends, or to a place where family members live, or a place where you feel you fit in and belong. As a classic study in Boston showed, attachment is not necessarily reduced by the physical decay of a community,[101-103] perhaps because attachment is related to *perceived* neighborhood quality, and that certainly includes the quality of social relations.[104]

Social Interactions. The prevalence and kind of social interactions that occur in a given place are associated with place attachment.[105,106] For example, as you would expect, neighborhood attachment is stronger when one lives near acquaintances, friends,[107, 108] and family[109, 110] (see Figure 9-6). Frequent social interactions are important, even including brief amicable verbal and nonverbal interactions with neighbors (e.g., smiling, saying hello), but of course more involved forms of social support, too.[111]

Social Capital. Sociologists and community psychologists have similarly emphasized community ties.[112-114] Being connected with others in the community can provide individuals with a variety of advantages, ranging from practical support (e.g., sharing childcare, tools and equipment, and carpooling), informational support (e.g., how to perform certain tasks; where to go to access resources), safety (e.g., extra pairs of eyes to mind one's home when they are away), and emotional support (e.g., empathy and caring during times of stress). The advantages that stem from social networks are known as **social capital**. Collectively, a community can come together to secure needed resources,[115] create and maintain good environmental quality,[116] and respond during emergencies.[117] On the flip side, social disorder is destructive to place attachment: Among four types of stressors (physical disorder, social disorder, victimization, and perception of crime), social disorder had the most negative impact on neighborhood attachment.[118]

FIGURE 9–6 Attachment to place can include connections to family.

Homogeneity. How similar or different are you from your neighbors? In general, neighborhood attachment tends to be stronger when individuals perceive that others are **socially homogeneous,** or similar to them.[119] Living near others of similar socioeconomic status, religion, and ethnic or racial background for example, although not necessary for place attachment to develop, certainly contribute to one's sense of belonging. Social homogeneity also builds social capital, given that group advantages emerge from proximity to one's in-group.

On the other hand, diversity can be an attractive feature of places, such as when family residents want their children to be exposed to different ways of life,[120] or when immigrants are beginning to adjust to living in a new country.[121] Indeed, diversity can be a valued and appreciated aspect of place.[122] Taken together, this research suggests that commonality and difference both play a role in the development and experience of place attachment.

The Physical Context

WHICH PHYSICAL FEATURES ARE ASSOCIATED WITH PLACE ATTACHMENT? Some researchers find little connection with the local physical environment,[123] but others do find strong connections. For example, evidence shows that one key factor is interaction with nature, either through the creation and maintenance of a garden[124] (Figure 9-7) or access to a natural area.[125] Although place attachment may explain why many residents of contaminated communities do not move away any more often than residents of un-contaminated communities do,[126] polluted communities, not surprisingly, attract fewer new residents. Which other physical features influence place attachment?

FIGURE 9-7 Studies have found links between gardening and place attachment.

Dwelling. People who live in single-family dwellings are more likely to be "rooted," longer-term residents with plans to stay, than people who live in multi-unit residences.[127] Better housing quality is obviously important,[128] as is smaller building size,[129] possibly because smaller places require less upkeep and can be more easily personalized. Of course, dwellings contain many other physical characteristics, but their impact on place attachment has not yet been thoroughly examined.

Streets and Neighborhoods. At the street level, residents of culs-de-sac develop more attachment to the neighborhood than residents of through streets.[130] The noise level and busyness of the street is also important. Women who live on quieter streets are more likely to have a sense of belonging to the neighborhood.[131] Busy streets discourage belongingness by restricting *space appropriation*, the feeling that outdoor areas exist for the use of residents (as opposed to being the domain of strangers who are merely passing through).

The presence in neighborhoods of distinctive

FIGURE 9-8 Place attachment can be to large-scale places, such as a country, or small-scale places, such as a bedroom.

features such as unique physical terrains or urban designs is related to greater identification with the place.[132] Neighborhoods with main streets that serve as central corridors with access to amenities tend to have a greater sense of community than suburban-style neighborhoods or high-density neighborhoods without prominent main streets.[133] The design of a neighborhood also appears to foster place attachment. **New urbanist communities** are designed with narrow streets, prominent porches, and small lots, with the idea of discouraging the use of cars and encouraging walking. Compared with a nearby traditional suburban community, a new urbanist community had greater place attachment and sense of community, perhaps because residents walked more and therefore met their neighbors more, and because the higher density of residences allowed for more natural areas to be left in the community.[134]

Community Size. Some researchers have wondered whether the population of a community can influence place attachment: do small town residents feel more attached than big city dwellers? The answer to this question is unclear. Sometimes attachment is found to increase as communities are smaller,[135,136] and other times attachment is found to increase as communities are larger.[137] Perhaps community size itself is far less important than other factors, such as the nature of social ties.[138]

Scale. Places of attachment vary in their spatial scale, ranging from very small (e.g., a hammock on the deck or a room in a house; Figure 9-8) to medium (e.g., a house or a park or a neighborhood) to large (e.g., a country or a continent). Despite this variation in place types, place attachment has most commonly been examined at the neighborhood level, in part because the phenomenon was investigated extensively by community psychologists.[139] Unlike community size, spatial level does seem to matter for place attachment, in a U-shaped pattern: place attachment is usually, but not always, stronger for home and city than for neighborhood.[140-143]

Similarity of Physical Features across Places. Physical features can link together place attachments, or create *categories* of places to which people become attached.[144] For example, some of us are city people; others are suburbanites, and yet others are country folk. As noted earlier, settlement identity is attachment to a specific category of place rather than to a particular place. A person who moves from one city to another, for example, may experience a smaller disruption or loss of place attachment than a person who moves from one settlement type to another, such as from suburbia to downtown. This allows for a continuity of place attachment even if one must move. Sometimes the transfer centers on a certain physical feature, rather than an entire place category. For example, when a place contains physical features that resemble childhood places,[145] or places from one's country of origin,[146] or a similar climate, attachment can emerge.

Culture and Ethnic Factors

PLACE ATTACHMENT IS IMPORTANT TO HUMANS ACROSS CULTURES, PLACE TYPES, AND ERAS. However, its type, degree, and expression does vary cross-culturally. Setha Low reviewed the world literature on place attachment and determined that it has six cultural means of transmission: genealogy, loss and destruction, ownership, cosmology, pilgrimage, and narrative.[147,148]

1. **Genealogy** links persons with places through the historical identification of a place with a family. For example, one might feel connected to a church where their grandparents were married and eventually buried (Figure 9-9). In some places such as Spain and Japan, people's names and community names are the same, or houses occupied by generations have the same name as the family.

2. **Loss and destruction** sometimes builds or strengthens place attachment. Those who yearned for Israel before it was established, mourn the loss of redeveloped urban districts, or grieve for towns lost in earthquakes develop fierce attachments to places that might exist, and even to places that never again will exist.

3. **Ownership** is a more familiar mechanism through which place attachment can be created. When we own a place for a long time, it becomes a part of us, and we of it. In one culture, people and their places are said to share blood. Ownership need not be in the legal sense; it can be through symbolic or psychological ownership, as when Detroit residents joined together to plant trees in formerly ugly vacant lots, which both improved the landscape and increased their place attachment.[149]

FIGURE 9-9 Genealogical links to place include churches and cemeteries.

4. **Cosmological** place attachment refers to a culture's religious and mythological views on person-place attachment. Many places are experienced by their natives as the center of the universe. From a cosmopolitan, objective perspective, this may seem absurd (how many places can be the center?), but deep within the cultural meanings of each such place, the center of the town or village or shrine truly is the spiritual center of the world.

5. People can be attached to places they merely visit; when a place is sacred to them and they make a **pilgrimage** there, they experience another kind of place attachment. This sort of attachment usually is religious (Mecca, Jerusalem, Banares, Amritsar), but it can be secular. Serious baseball fans feel an attachment to Cooperstown, New York, where the Hall of Fame stores relics of their heroes; they literally make pilgrimages to the small town.

6. The term **narrative** refers to stories; place attachment can develop through stories that explain the important issues and questions of life in terms of people-place interactions. Stories tell residents how to interact with or respect their land and often include accounts of how the land strikes back if it is not treated properly.

Culturally determined meanings can therefore influence which types of places are deemed worthy of attachment, as well as how the attachment forms and is expressed. Despite these differences, place attachment is prevalent in

FIGURE 9-10 Studies predict that people who are more attached to a place will perceive it to be less polluted.

influence which places one becomes attached to, how this attachment develops, and how it is expressed. Despite variations in it, place attachment is common or even universal across cultures, past and present.

many cultures. An analysis of the relation between religion and place attachment shows that connections to place are found in many religious groups and historical periods.[150] Descriptions of places of worship, sacred structures, burial sites, places in nature, and mythical sites abound in ancient and contemporary texts. Other scholars have detailed the importance of place evident in medieval and contemporary literary works.[151] From such works, place attachment appears important across cultures and historical periods.

Scientific interest in place attachment has grown considerably in the last 10 years. Perhaps this has occurred in response to threats to place attachment, including increased human mobility, placelessness, climate change, or other global forces.[152] Although it takes different forms in different places, environmental psychologists tentatively concluded that it is virtually a universal human experience.

IN SUM *Several personal factors, including the length of time spent in a place, the degree of congruence between a place and one's identity, one's mobility and social status, place ownership, gender and sexuality, developmental goals, and personality attributes, have been identified as relevant to place attachment. Social ties can also contribute to, or stem from, one's place attachment. Place can become meaningful through interactions with others, and the resources, or social capital, we derive from such interactions. Homogeneity and diversity are two other social factors important to place attachment. Some physical and design features have been found to predict place attachment. Cultural factors also*

PSYCHOLOGICAL OUTCOMES OF PLACE ATTACHMENT

PLACE ATTACHMENT IS A PHENOMENON THAT GIVES US INSIGHT INTO THE HUMAN EXPERIENCE. As Edward Relph declared, "to be human is to live in a world that is filled with significant places: to be human is to have and to know your place."[153] Therefore, environmental psychologists recognize that person-environment interactions are sometimes founded on deep emotional ties to places. Place attachment can also help us understand and predict a variety of other outcomes. It has implications for perceptions, behaviors, and emotional outcomes.

Place Perception

THOSE WHO ARE ATTACHED TO A PLACE perceive it differently from those who are not attached. You may come to know every path and corner and hidden staircase of a place to which you are attached; the casual visitor does not. Beyond these detailed mental maps, places of attachment are imbued with personal meanings and layers from the past. Further, because an important place often merges with aspects of one's self-identity,[154,155] place perception can be unconsciously motivated by self-serving biases: the general finding is that place attachment has a positive influence on place perceptions (Figure 9-10). In other words, being attached to a place is like wearing rose-colored glasses, and its flaws and dangers become less apparent. For example, Israelis living in the Gaza strip (i.e., prior to the 2005 disengagement) who were more attached to the area perceived Gaza as less dangerous.[156]

This perceptual bias appears common for many types of places of attachment. Residents who identify with downtown have more positive views of downtown (despite the fact that downtown neighborhoods contain more mixed land uses, traffic and parking problems, noise, crowding, stress, danger, and pavement), and those who identify with suburbia have more positive views of suburbia.[157,158] Residents who are more attached to their neighborhoods perceive fewer problems on their block, such as suspected drug dealings, graffiti, traffic, and noise.[159]

Perceptions of natural environments can similarly be distorted among the attached. Lakeside property owners are more attached and more satisfied with certain attributes of a lake, such as its scenery, water quality, and number of users.[160] Attachment to an area tends to result in higher attractiveness ratings of landscapes in that area.[161] Consistent with these findings, individuals with a strong sense of local and national identity perceived fewer pollutants on local and national public beaches (respectively) than those who identified less strongly with them.[162]

Social identity theory[163] can help explain this tendency of strongly attached and identified residents to inflate the positive qualities of their neighborhoods.[164] Identity gains definition through one's social groups as well as the places to which one belongs,[165,166] and so the attributes of these groups and places have implications for self-esteem. When characteristics of one's group or place are unfavorable, individuals will downplay, ignore, or positively reinterpret them so that self-esteem can be maintained.

So, place attachment seems to alter environmental perceptions, but environments can also influence place attachment. Pleasing physical and social features encourage place attachment by attracting people to an area, and involving them in it.[167] Place attachment tends to vary for neighborhoods of objectively different environmental quality. Although, as noted earlier, people tend to view their neighborhood positively, residents of lower-quality neighborhoods identify less strongly with them than residents of higher-quality neighborhoods, even when the neighborhoods are similar in size and in the sociodemographic characteristics of residents.[168]

In sum, place attachment can alter one's judgments of a place's quality (perhaps as a way to bolster one's self-esteem), and attachments occur more frequently for higher-quality places. Both processes probably operate simultaneously.

FIGURE 9–11 Place attachment can lead us to maintain our place.

Place Preservation and Pro-environmental Behavior

PLACE ATTACHMENT IS NOT MERELY RELATED TO OUR EMOTIONS AND THOUGHTS; it also has implications for behavior. One of its key behavioral outcomes is stewardship; people want to protect their place, provide the necessary upkeep and maintenance, and preserve its special meanings. For example, those who are more attached to their residence are more likely to make repairs,[169] mow the lawn,[170] and remove nearby litter[171] (Figure 9-11). In general, people will act to defend their place from hypothetical and real threats, such as increases in lake pollution from motorboats,[172] a proposed freeway,[173] or other large-scale development projects.[174]

The stewardship behaviors that have attracted the most interest are pro-environmental. People with stronger place attachments tend to perform more pro-environmental behaviors, either as a direct attempt to preserve the place and protect it from damage, or as an indirect result of internalizing the community's values of environmental protection. As one example, youth who had worked on a natural resource project who were more emotionally connected to the place reported engaging in more environmentally responsible behaviors in their day-to-day lives.[175] Sometimes people with stronger place attachment perform fewer pro-environmental behaviors,[176] probably because their place was already fine, and so they did not need to take action.

One way of resolving this discrepancy is to consider the place dimension of place attachment.[177] When individuals are more attached to the *community* aspects of the place, pro-environmental behavior is likely only if that community espouses pro-environmental values. For example, students who attend a university that is renowned for its

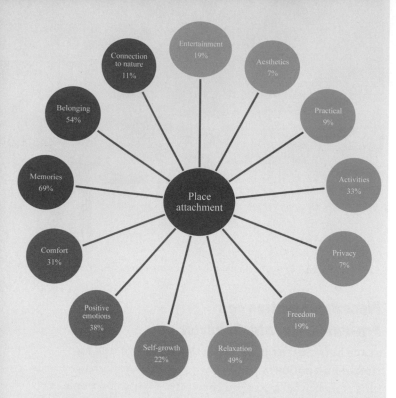

FIGURE 9–12 Thirteen functions of place attachment (Leila Scannell).

sustainability efforts would more likely adopt pro-environmental attitudes and behaviors than students when attend a university with few sustainability efforts. Some communities simply do not prioritize environmental issues, and so pro-environmental behavior will not be influenced by a community-based attachment. Place attachment that is based in the *natural* aspects of a place, however, is a stronger predictor of pro-environmental behavior. Similarly, people who have a strong environmental identity[178] and define themselves as part of nature, are also more likely to report engaging in pro-environmental behavior.

However, being attached to a place does not always lead to pro-environmental actions. Some inflict environmental harm, such as using pesticides to produce a weed-free lawn, burning wood to create a cozy living room atmosphere, or traveling long distances to faraway places to which one is attached.[179-182] Furthermore, people generally want to protect the meaning of the place to which they are attached, but meanings can vary among place users. For example, a proposed hydropower plant development was opposed by residents who were attached to specific parts of a municipality, but it was supported by residents who were attached to the municipality as a whole.[183] Recreationists who reported a strong sense of place identity with the Appalachian Trail were more concerned about problems such as crowding, litter, and noise. However, recreationists who reported a strong sense of place dependence viewed the trail as more important for supporting their recreational activities.[184]

Place Loss

AT SOME POINT, THROUGH MOBILITY, divorce, conviction of a crime, mental disability, natural or technological disaster, forced relocation, or pure exhaustion in old age, many of us lose our cherished places. Sometimes, the value of a place is revealed most clearly to us when the settings we hold most dear are threatened or lost. One poignant form of community attachment occurs in dying towns that have lost most of their population. In the U. S. Midwest, literally thousands of communities died in the 20th century, and many are barely surviving today.[185] Yet attachment to such towns is often intense, perhaps because every factor mentioned above that promotes place attachment is present. That many older residents cling to their dying towns is evidence that economic factors are not the most important aspect of community attachment.[186]

Environmental psychologists are keenly interested in how people experience and adjust to place loss. Marc Fried and his colleagues were among the first to recognize and document the effects of displacement, in their classic investigation of a redevelopment project in the West End of Boston.[187] Although the physical quality of the neighborhood was quite dilapidated, the residents (composed mainly of white ethnic immigrants) expressed strong feelings of attachment to their community. The structural improvements planned for the neighborhood meant that the residents would lose their familiar structures and social settings, and that most of the residents would be forced to move. After the reconstruction, residents expressed mourning and displayed symptoms of grief that Fried argued are comparable to the effects of separation from a loved one.

Place Loss Among Aboriginal Peoples. Place loss among aboriginal peoples supports the idea that displacement can have serious psychological consequences.[188] Place meanings often are more conscious and central among First Nations people than among other North Americans. They include, for example, sacred meanings, connections to ancestors, spirits, nature, food, medicines, customs, and ways of life.[189] These strong connections to place make place loss particularly devastating. Aboriginal peoples worldwide have faced disproportionate dislocation, such as from colonialism, and other actions of those in power. One example is the place loss of the Cheslatta T'En people, whose traditional lands were flooded to create a hydroelectric dam in British Columbia.[190] The dislocation of the residents was forcible and sudden, and farms, communities, and cemeteries were destroyed. Following this, the Cheslatta T'En faced many social and spiritual losses; rates of alcoholism, suicide, health problems, and unemployment increased as a direct result of the loss of their place. Although their well-being has improved in recent years, some scholars have pointed out that few indigenous people fully recover from place disruption.[191]

Place Loss from Migration. The effects of displacement can also arise from voluntary or temporary migration. If you have ever studied away from your childhood home or traveled for an extended period of time, you may have experienced feelings of homesickness. Those who experience place attachment most strongly may have the most personal difficulty with changing or losing places.[192] For example, Chinese students living in Australia who were not well-adjusted had more health problems and lower grades than those who had become somewhat attached to the new environment.[193] The psychological outcomes of moving away from home to a new school or university can sometimes include the loss of sense of belonging, continuity, and self-identity.[194]

What can people do to avoid homesickness and displacement? One effective process is **interchangeability**, which involves seeking out similarities between new and old environments.[195] If a Canadian were living in Taiwan, for example, she might occasionally seek out Western food and other Canadians with whom she can relate. Seeking out areas in the new environment that have home-like qualities is another example of interchangeability. One might feel attached to the beach because her hometown was located near the ocean. Others might bring familiar objects from their homes and be better adjusted. In a psychological sense, a person is not truly displaced when surrounded by referents of home. In general, making links to, and symbolic representations of one's attached place appears to minimize the effects of displacement.

Place attachment also affects how people prepare for *anticipated* place loss, such as from natural disasters. In India, residents who live in areas susceptible to flooding have different degrees of flood preparedness depending

FIGURE 9–13 We can be attached to places that connect us to the past.

on their type of place attachment: those with genealogical (e.g., family ties) and economic (e.g., investment or ownership) place attachment are more prepared than were those with religious place attachment.[196]

Place Attachment and Well-being

PLACE ATTACHMENT HAS IMPORTANT IMPLICATIONS FOR ONE'S WELL-BEING. This notion is supported by studies that document the negative psychological consequences of displacement as well as studies that demonstrate the positive effects of place attachment on well-being. By definition, place attachment is an emotional bond to a place.[197-202] Thus, the experience of place attachment is often characterized by feelings of happiness and comfort.[203] Even in war-torn areas, place attachment is positively associated with life satisfaction.[204]

The Benefits of Place Attachment. What is it about place attachment that benefits us psychologically? A content analysis of Canadians' written descriptions of their places of attachment that I (LS) conducted uncovered 13 benefits: memories, belonging, relaxation, positive emotions, activity support, comfort, self-growth, control, entertainment, connection to nature, practical benefits, privacy, and aesthetics (see Figure 9-12).

The most common benefit was **memories**, mentioned by approximately two-thirds of the sample. Important places can memorialize past events and people, provide a sense of continuity over time[205,206] and serve as a symbolic time-machine into the past (Figure 9-13). The place can also serve as the site of ongoing traditions, such as annual

FIGURE 9–14 Activity support is a common benefit of place attachment.

holiday gatherings or cultural events.[207] Thus, place attachment preserves important memories, and provides the framework for forming new ones.

Belonging was the second-most commonly mentioned benefit of place attachment. It includes feelings of having roots in a place, fitting in, or connecting with others. Indeed, the need to belong appears to be one of the fundamental psychological needs,[208, 209] and ties to a place can help us satisfy it. Places provide belonging when they symbolize one's social group, or offer a venue conducive to meeting up with others.

Places of attachment also frequently offer **relaxation**. For some, this is the immediate stress relief of coming home after a long day of work, or it is leaving for a meaningful vacation place that allows an escape from the everyday routine. Children also seek out their favorite places for relaxation or coping with negative emotions.[210] As you will read in a later chapter, certain places possess restorative properties that include coherence, compatibility, being away, and fascination; places of attachment are especially likely to contain these four properties.[211]

Positive emotions, such as happiness, joy, and love, are also part of place attachment, as is inherent in many definitions and measures of the construct.[212-217] As one person said, "When I'm in [my hometown] I feel at ease, at peace, and happy. The world seems OK again when I'm there."

Activity support was the fifth most-common benefit of place attachment. Places can facilitate one's desired activities and goals. As mentioned earlier, this particular mode of attachment has been termed place dependence,[218,219] in which one becomes dependent on the unique features of a place for enabling a preferred activity. For example, a surfer may be attached to a particular beach or region with reliably big surf (Figure 9-14).

Places of attachment can benefit us by providing **physical and psychological comfort**. Architects, engineers and interior designers calculate physical comfort as it relates to temperature, noise, lighting, air quality, and design.[220,221] People who are attached to larger spaces, such as cities or regions often cite weather as a source of place-attachment related comfort; some have greater attachment to places with climates that resemble those of their childhood places.[222] Comfort is also an important psychological benefit, particularly when a place provides a sense of safety and security.

Places of attachment can also play a role in **self-growth** processes, such as introspection, problem-solving, goal-setting, and making personal changes. This could occur either directly, when the place holds opportunities and resources for self-change, such as new people, activities, or environments, or it could occur indirectly, such as when the environment is conducive to problem-solving and contemplation.

A sense of **control,** autonomy, and freedom can also be helped or hindered by place. People benefit when places of attachment can be altered to suit their needs, offer the freedom to make their own choices, and allow for self-expression. The importance of control over various environmental elements is one theme that recurs in this book, and it certainly is also an important function of place attachment functioning.

Some places of attachment are that because they provide us with **entertainment.** The level of stimulation in these places is experienced as interesting, novel, exciting, fun, or exhilarating. For example, attachment to a particular city, commercial venue, busy park, or vacation destination might provide this benefit. As you may recall from Chapter 2, slight deviations in environmental stimulation (i.e., from the usual) can be enjoyable.[223] Therefore, entertainment and relaxation are both benefits of place attachment where the level of environmental stimulation is relevant.

Connecting to nature is a need that likely evolved from our early ancestral environments[224] and so many people appreciate places of attachment that enable communion with nature (Figure 9-15). This instinctive connection has the ability to restore positive affect, improve cognitive processes[225] and reduce the symptoms of attention deficit disorder.[226]

Place attachment may also support well-being when the place provides **practical benefits** such as access to services and amenities. Life can be easier with proximity to grocery stores, community centers, and medical facilities, or access to particular types of resource centers (e.g., for single-parents), or support groups (e.g., such as Alcoholics Anonymous). Such features have been linked to neighborhood satisfaction and overall quality of life.[227,228]

Privacy is another benefit of place attachment. For example, one person was attached to the Pilbara desert in Australia because it allowed him a chance for solitude. Attachment to an apartment is stronger when the apartment facilitates privacy.[229]

Place attachments are sometimes formed and continued because of their aesthetic value. Benefiting from the **aesthetic** features of environments also has evolutionary roots; we prefer aesthetically pleasing environments because those were the ones likely to contain resources or other features conducive to survival.[230] Among park visitors, aesthetic features are even more important than natural features,[231] supporting the role of beauty in place preferences.

In sum, place attachment contributes to well-being in at least 13 psychologically relevant ways. These benefits even seem to accrue from place attachment at a distance.

The "Shadow Side" of Place Attachment. Although place attachment clearly is good for our well-being, person-place bonds can be associated with ambivalent emotions and experiences.[232] For example, memories of home can be both joyful and painful. The negative components of place attachment, have been called its "shadow side."[233] If you live in social housing as a result of poverty, your attachment may well involve negative aspects caused by the stigma attached to living in social housing.[234] However, despite the stigma, many residents report a strong sense of community and general residential satisfaction.

Place attachment can also interfere with well-being when one is attached to a place, but lacks control, such as when powerful others impose discordant meanings and policies on it, or in extreme cases, destroy it.[235] Another negative outcome of place attachment is "place bondage," when individuals continue to cling to places that inflict harm or fail to meet a variety of other needs.[236] An extreme example would be when residents refuse to leave their homes in the event of a disaster, such as those who refuse to evacuate despite warnings of an impending flood.[237]

Non-attachment. Some people say that they do not have a place of attachment, challenging the assumption that

FIGURE 9–15 Connection to nature is a benefit of place attachment.

attachment is a good or necessary phenomenon. Indeed, some Buddhist philosophers depict any type of attachment as a negative force in which an individual grasps at or clings to the bond.[238] A state of "non-attachment," in contrast, is said to offer a preferable state of flexibility, a lack of fixation on attachment objects, and tolerance to the impermanence of bonds. In this view, developing attachment bonds is not optimal; rather, learning that such bonds are constructed, mutable representations may be more adaptive.

IN SUM *Being attached to a place has a number of psychological outcomes. One is that those who are more attached tend to perceive their place in a more positive light than do those who are less attached. Another implication is that people who are more attached are more likely to take action to protect their place from changes they perceive to be threatening. The negative effects of displacement support the notion that individuals are motivated to maintain attachment to places, and that failure to do so may result in negative psychological outcomes. Aboriginal peoples have historically experienced much place loss, which harm individuals and their entire community. Some processes that appear to aid the transition between old and new environments have been identified. Place attachment usually benefits well-being through at least 13 psychological benefits such as memory support, belongingness, relaxation, positive emotions, activity support, physical and psychological comfort, as well as several others. The shadow side of place attachment means that it can have certain negative impacts, too. Advocates of non-attachment challenge the assumption that attachment of any sort is good for us.*

Developmental Theories of Place Attachment

SOME THEORIES of place attachment postulate how the bonds initially develop. In childhood, the development of place attachment may intermingle with the processes of interpersonal attachment that occur between children and their primary caregivers, such as parents. One proposal is that children begin to associate the close ties they hold toward their parents with surrounding places.[239,240] That is, home comes to represent Mom and Dad (or another primary caregiver), and so emotional bonds to parents generalize to the child's residence. Over time, the scale of the bond expands from the home to the neighborhood to the broader community, all of which are assumed to provide refuge and a sense of security.

According to a different perspective, when caregivers provide a safe haven, this sense of security enables children to venture out and explore nearby places.[241] Emotional ties to place therefore, are rooted in the mastery, freedom, and adventure that children experience through such exploratory ventures. If threats appear, children may return to the safe haven of their guardians once again. Therefore, place attachment in childhood may stem from secure interpersonal attachments to caregivers. However, not all children are afforded secure interpersonal relationships, which raises questions about whether their relationships with place differ, and which processes are involved in their development of place attachment.

In adulthood, the bonds can develop in at least two ways: *place-congruent continuity*, in which attachments form to places that seem to represent or fit with self-attributes, and *place-referent continuity*, in which attachments form to places where links to the past and memories have accumulated.[242]

The developmental theories of place attachment have begun to paint a picture of how attachment can arise in childhood and adulthood. However, these ideas so far are purely theoretical (without empirical validation), or obtained by having adults think retrospectively about their childhood attachments. Observations of infants and children would add much to the understanding of how place attachment forms and changes over time.

Place Attachment: Parallel with Interpersonal Attachment?

ONE WAY TO UNDERSTAND how place attachment, a relatively new topic of study, operates psychologically is to compare it with theories about topics that seem to bear a strong resemblance. One obvious possibility is that affective bonding to places may share some principles with affective bonding to other people. John Bowlby and Mary Salter Ainsworth pioneered the study of interpersonal attachment in the middle 1960s.[243-245] According to Bowlby, interpersonal attachment is an evolved behavior that increases children's chances of survival; those who can remain close to their caregivers are able to receive the care they need and avoid predators and other threats. Specifically, internal or external cues such as threats activate the attachment system, which prompts a host of behaviors (e.g., crying, or seeking out the caregiver) that ultimately allow the child to regain proximity to their caregiver. Once proximity is attained, individuals experience a sense of security. This secure base also enables exploration of the broader environment. Over time, repeated interactions with one's caregiver generate mental models about what to expect in relationship with others.

Many of the processes of interpersonal attachment do appear relevant for place attachment.[246,247] Proximity-seeking is not limited to caregivers; people tend to seek closeness to their important places, sometimes in person, and sometimes cognitively. Making a trip to one's hometown during the holidays, daydreaming about a favorite place, or purchasing a home in a certain city or region[249] are all ways of attaining proximity to place. The desire to remain connected to place is also reflected in the naming and building of new settlements.

Like interpersonal attachment, place attachment also seems to offer a sense of security. For some, home is a "haven" where one can obtain refuge from threats[249-253] and it is the secure base from which the broader world can be explored.[254-256] Finally, as mentioned earlier, separation distress can occur following unwanted place loss, just as distress follows separation from a significant other.[257-259]

Other principles of attachment theory may similarly apply to place attachment. For example, a large proportion of interpersonal attachment research has documented the stable individual differences in relating to other people, called "attachment styles."[260-264] Theorists have considered the existence of comparable styles of relating to place.[265] For example, some people are chronically anxious about losing their place. Others may chronically resist remaining in any one place for long, wanting to move often, and avoid growing roots that are too deep. Others may be "secure" in that they receive comfort from their place of attachment, but are able to leave it, striking a balance between security and exploration. Despite the plausibility of these parallel styles of place attachment, the idea lacks much evidence so far.

Place Processes

PHENOMENOLOGIST DAVID SEAMON, who studies the richness of individual experiences and the nature of existence, asserts that understanding the key processes of place is an important first step to understanding place attachment. He describes six processes that generate (or erode) place.[266] **Place interaction** refers to the usual actions, routines, and activities that occur in a place. Many routines come together to give the place meaning. For example, in a cafeteria, cooks are preparing and serving meals, some patrons are lining up and purchasing their food, and others are eating. Places of attachment can support particular routines and habits that contribute to the connection over time. **Place identity**, already described, refers to the merging of self and the physical environment, and it can arise from frequent place interaction; with time, and habitual interaction, place can become part of who we are. **Place release** is the experience of unexpected, serendipitous happenings in a place. Witnessing a pod of whales in the ocean, running into an old friend in a coffee shop, or happening upon a flash mob downtown are all examples of place release. These pleasurable occurrences punctuate a place as memorable and meaningful.

Place realization refers to the distinctiveness and character of a place. As Seamon says, this would be noticing the "London-ness of London." It is important to place attachment, which tends to be stronger for places of distinct

character.[267] A fifth important place process is **place creation**, which can occur though design, building, personalization, hosting events, or other means. This process can enhance the other processes, and contributes to feelings of attachment. Finally, **place intensification** occurs when the design of the place serves the needs of the human activities that occur there. Through design, place interactions and routines are reinforced and become stable over time. For example, a comfortable atmosphere might enhance patronage of a local pub.

The Meaning-Mediated Model

THE MEANING-MEDIATED MODEL OF PLACE ATTACHMENT aims to explain the role of physical features such as dwelling type or the presence of nature in encouraging neighborhood attachment to form.[268] According to Richard Stedman, we do not become directly attached to tangible objects or sensory experiences offered by various environments, we bond to the meanings that we have projected upon these places. What does that special park, house of worship, street, theatre, or mountain mean to you? In this model, the physical environment itself limits the possible meanings an environment may acquire; it "sets bounds and gives form to [social] constructions."[269] The meanings one may bestow on a park are unlikely to be the same as those one bestows on a street or theater. Certain landscape elements appear particularly important to attachment, such as water quality and level of development, because those elements give rise to certain meanings that are conducive to attachment (or not).

Stages of Place Attachment Disruption

HAVE YOU EVER MOVED AWAY from somewhere that you didn't want to leave? If so, the bond to your place may have been disrupted. Disruptions can occur when physical, legal, or social changes interfere with the appearance, use or meaning of the place.[270]

Two models explain the stages involved in such disruption. In the three-stage model, disruption occurs prior to, during, and after the change.[271] First comes a period of pre-disruption, before the detachment occurs. For example, this might result from securing a job in another city and preparing to move there. Second, the disruption itself occurs when the person must actually depart. In the third stage, a period of post-disruption, attachments are

HAROLD PROSHANSKY
helped found the first graduate program in environmental psychology and produced valuable studies of place identity.

reconciled, by maintaining a connection to the old place, establishing new attachments, or both.

A more elaborate five-stage model emphasizes the role of meaning in place attachment disruption[272] Stage 1 is becoming aware of the proposals for place change, and learning about the types of changes that are slated to occur. Stage 2 involves interpreting the meaning of the change, and considering how it will impact oneself and one's place. Stage 3 is evaluating the outcomes of the change, determining whether these will be predominantly negative or positive. Stage 4 is coping, when individuals consider various coping strategies, such as denial or resistance to the change. Stage 5 is the action phase, when individuals implement the strategy that was previously considered. One key criticism of existing place attachment theories is that they lack dynamism, and are more often descriptive or structural, and less often process-oriented[273]; however, theories of place disruption and development are two that describe the unfolding processes of place attachment.

IN SUM, *much of the place attachment literature is descriptive, but several interesting theories are now being developed. Developmental theories postulate how place attachment can co-occur with certain developmental milestones. Theories of interpersonal attachment can be used to understand how we relate to place, although this line of research is still new. Phenomenological theories detail key place processes that can affect place attachment. The meaning-mediated model suggests that individuals become attached to place meanings, which are constrained by physical characteristics of the place. Theories of place attachment disruption outline the stages that occur when person-place bonds are broken.*

Coffee Shop Design for Place Attachment

FOR SOME PEOPLE, THE NEIGHBORHOOD COFFEE SHOP is an important place of attachment; you may spend long hours studying there, or you may frequent it on your way to work, or perhaps it is where you convene with your friends on a Tuesday night. Beyond their caffeine supply, coffee shops are social gathering places, and so they have the potential to contribute to a sense of community and local attachment. They can also define the character of a neighborhood. People do form affective bonds to coffee shops.[274] Of particular interest to designers and coffee shop managers is which physical features, such as layout and décor, and which social features, such as social support, may promote affective bonding to their venues (Figure 9-16).

To investigate this, three distinct coffee shops in the same town were selected: a converted auto-repair shop, patronized mostly by university students; an artsy-historical space next to a small lake, patronized by local residents; and a large national chain coffee shop with a bookstore attached, patronized by students as well as community members.[275] Observations, interviews, and surveys were used to explore the key social and physical indicators of place attachment to the coffee shops. Using these multiple methods, five physical features were identified:

1. **Cleanliness** is one factor that participants reported would support their repeated patronage, potentially leading to attachment over time. Other than regular maintenance, an impression of cleanliness can be achieved through particular design features, such as finish materials on floors and walls, and particular fabrics on furniture.

2. **Aroma.** The smell of coffee and baked goods was important to participants. Few studies have investigated the role of smell in developing place attachment, but given the ability of certain smells to evoke affective memories, it is not surprising that smell should be relevant to place attachment. Designers could enhance or regulate this feature through ventilation systems.

3. **Lighting**. Coffee shops that engender attachment should provide adequate lighting. Because place attachment often involves the congruence between one's activities and the features of the place, lighting may be designed with typical coffee shop activities in mind, such as reading, socializing, or relaxing.

4. **Comfortable seating**. Some patrons expressed preferences for comfortable furniture, such as couches rather than wooden chairs. Although managers may wish to encourage the development of place attachment, seating that is too comfortable also encourages lingering for a longer period than is desired, inhibiting seating for others. Thus, designers must consider the preferences of the users alongside the business goals of the management.

5. **Views**. Like other types of spaces (e.g., residences, work places), coffee shops are preferred when they incorporate windows with views to the outside.

Of course, place attachment is not derived solely from physical features, as the meaning mediated model asserts, but it also strongly relates to social characteristics of the environment. At least six social features appear relevant to place attachment in coffee shops.

1. **Opportunity to linger**. As we know, place attachment usually takes time to develop, and so allowing people to linger may be one contributing social factor. Coffee shops that allow patrons to linger were also those with the highest rates of observed social interaction.

2. **Control**. Patrons emphasized the importance of having control over some aspects of the coffee shop, whether it was simply having a "usual" chair, or having a say in how the coffee shop should be run. Management can encourage this feature by asking patrons for feedback, and allowing them to alter the space if possible (e.g., ensuring that tables and chairs are movable.)

3. **Trust and belonging**. A public space such as a coffee shop is one in which feeling accepted and welcome are crucial. This generates a sense of belongingness in which feeling socially comfortable in a coffee shop can translate into feeling connected to the broader community. Managers can promote this experience by creating policies against discrimination of patrons,

FIGURE 9–16 Coffee shops can be designed with place attachment in mind.

promoting diversity among employees, and offering the venue to various community groups.

4. **Activity support**. Recall that place dependence emerges when we become attached to places that support our ability to execute our desired activities. Coffee shops can offer such venues, such as for students who are studying, or community members who are holding formal or informal meetings. Thus, designers may investigate local patrons' desired activities and try to incorporate those activities into coffee shop design.

5. **Social presence**. Merely being around others can reduce loneliness and encourage attachment to the community, especially when those others are familiar. Coffee shops with regular customers appear to help meet this need. Remember "familiar strangers" from an earlier chapter?

6. **Social support**. Patrons expressed the importance of the coffee shop as a venue for social support. Using the space to confide in and connect with others serves the individual's needs, and builds social capital in the community.

This list of physical and social features may serve as a starting point for designers. However, because the relations between these features and place attachment were not formally studied, this model remains preliminary, and would benefit from empirical validation.

Place Attachment in Retirement Communities

AN AGING POPULATION means that in some parts of the world, such as Canada, the US, Western Europe, and Japan, the number of people living in retirement communities is increasing. Despite the benefits of such communities, elderly persons' transition to living in a new place can be extremely difficult, especially if they are leaving a long-time residence, are recently widowed, or are experiencing physical and mental health challenges.

Two psychological factors important to adjustment and overall quality of life in the new community are place attachment and social support; the new place is beneficial when it offers a sense of belonging and comfort, as well as staff members and other residents who can provide emotional and tangible support beyond that supplied by the new resident's family.[276] Researchers have begun to identify which design features contribute to place attachment and social support in retirement communities.

A new continuing care retirement facility in the United States surveyed elderly residents who had lived there for 18 months.[277] The researchers also collected a variety of information about the physical environment. Three design features significantly predicted place attachment: (1) a short walking distance between one's unit and the main activity center; (2) a high probability of encountering other residents near one's unit, defined as having neighbors on both sides, and having intersecting pedestrian paths near the front door; and (3) the presence of garden space.

The first two of these factors seem to increase place attachment through involvement in the residential community and increasing social interaction; both were also correlated with perceived social support. Gardening space, however, was not correlated with social support, so it may exert its influence on place attachment through other mechanisms, such as psychological restoration, control, or aesthetics. Of course, many other physical features, such as décor, can also contribute to (or detract from) the degree of attachment to retirement communities. How residential communities can manage to connect residents to their past places is another question that research on place attachment with elderly residents can help us to answer.

AS THESE EXAMPLES SHOW, spaces can be designed with place attachment in mind, by incorporating physical features that are expected to directly increase place attachment, and by designing spaces that facilitate social interaction. Coffee shops and retirement communities are two examples of places that can benefit from place attachment-relevant design. More research is needed to test the causal impact of such design changes on place attachment strength.

SUMMARY

PLACE IS A CENTRAL PART OF THE HUMAN EXPERIENCE, because every life and all of our lives happen in physical settings. Some settings are particularly meaningful and central to our identities. The phenomenon of place attachment is multi-dimensional: they involve many place types, modes of generating meaning, and psychological processes. Certain places possess physical and social attributes that make them more likely candidates for attachment. Once that bond has formed, we often experience improved well-being although, like other relationships, place bonds can also have a shadow side. Research on place attachment has greatly increased in recent years, but the methodological approaches to studying it are still fairly limited; we will know more about the causal mechanisms of place attachment once we begin to study it using experimental designs.

Suggested Supplementary Readings

Altman, I., & Low, S. M. (Eds.) (1992). *Place attachment*. New York: Plenum.

Clayton, S., & Opotow, S. (Eds.). *Identity and the natural environment: The psychological significance of nature*. Cambridge, MA: MIT Press.

Devine-Wright, P., & Howes, Y. (2010). Disruption to place attachment and the protection of restorative environments: A wind energy case study. *Journal of Environmental Psychology, 30*, 271-280.

Fried, M. (1963). Grieving for a lost home. In L. J. Duhl (Ed.), *The urban condition: People and policy in the metropolis* (pp. 124-152). New York: Simon & Schuster.

Giuliani, M. V. (2003). Theory of attachment and place attachment. In M. Bonnes, T. Lee, & M. Bonaiuto (Eds.), *Psychological theories for environmental issues* (pp.137-170).Aldershot: Ashgate.

Lewicka, M. (2011). Place attachment: How far have we come in the last 40 years? *Journal of Environmental Psychology, 31*, 207-230.

Manzo, L. C., & Devine-Wright, P. (Eds.) (2014). *Place attachment: Advances in theory, methods, and applications*. New York, NY: Routledge.

Mazumdar, S., & Mazumdar, S. (2004). Religion and place attachment: A study of sacred places. *Journal of Environmental Psychology, 24*, 385-397.

Morgan, P. (2010). Towards a developmental theory of place attachment. *Journal of Environmental Psychology, 30*, 11-22.

Proshansky, H. M., Fabian, A. K., & Kaminoff, R. (1983). Place-identity: Physical world socialization of the self. *Journal of Environmental Psychology, 3*, 57-83.

Scannell, L., & Gifford, R. (2010). Defining place attachment: A tripartite organizing framework. *Journal of Environmental Psychology, 30*, 1-10.

References

[1] Relph, E. (1976). *Place and placelessness*. London: Pion Limited.

[2] Tuan, Y.-F. (1974). *Topophilia: A study of environmental perception, attitudes, and values*. Englewood Cliffs, N.J.: Prentice-Hall.

[3] Kasarda, J. D., & Janowitz, M. (1974). Community attachment in mass society. *American Sociological Review, 39*, 328–339.

[4] Scannell, L., & Gifford, R. (2010a). Defining place attachment: A tripartite organizing framework. *Journal of Environmental Psychology, 30*, 1-10.

[5] Billig, M. (2006). Is my home my castle? Place attachment, risk perception, and religious faith. *Environment and Behavior, 38*, 248-265.

[6] Mazumdar, S., & Mazumdar, S. (2004). Religion and place attachment: A study of sacred places. *Journal of Environmental Psychology, 24*, 385-397.

[7] Hidalgo, M. C., & Hernández, B. (2001). Place attachment: Conceptual and empirical questions. *Journal of Environmental Psychology, 21*, 273-281.

[8] Giuliani, M. V. (2003). Theory of attachment and place attachment. In M. Bonnes, T. Lee, & M. Bonaiuto (Eds.), *Psychological theories for environmental issues* (pp. 137-170).Aldershot: Ashgate.

[9] Cuba, L., & Hummon, D. M. (1993). A place to call home: Identification with dwelling, community, and region. *Sociological Quarterly, 34*, 111–131.

[10] Mesch, G. S., & Manor, O. (1998). Social ties, environmental perception, and local attachment. *Environment and Behavior, 30*, 227-245.

[11] Riley, R. B. (1992). Attachment to the ordinary landscape. In I. Altman, & S. M. Low (Eds.), *Place attachment* (pp. 13-35). New York: Plenum Press.

[12] Manzo, L. C. (2003). Beyond house and haven: Toward a revisioning of emotional relationships with places. *Journal of Environmental Psychology, 23*, 47-61.

[13] Golledge, R. G., & Stimson, R. J. (1997). *Spatial behavior: A geographic perspective*. New York: Guilford.

[14] Cooper Marcus, C. (1992). Environmental memories. In I. Altman, & S. M. Low (Eds.), *Place attachment* (pp. 87-112). New York: Plenum.

[15] Twigger-Ross, C. L., & Uzzell, D. L. (1996). Place and identity processes. *Journal of Environmental Psychology, 16*, 205-220.

[16] Mazumdar, S., & Mazumdar, S. (2004). Religion and place attachment: A study of sacred places. *Journal of Environmental Psychology, 24*, 385-397.

[17] Smith, J. S., & White, B. N. (2004). Detached from their homeland: The Latter-Day Saints of Chihuahua, Mexico. *Journal of Cultural Geography, 21*, 57-76.

[18] Francaviglia, R. V. (1978). Xenia rebuilds: Effects of pre-disaster conditioning on post-disaster redevelopment. *Journal of the American Institute of Planners, 44*, 13–24.

[19] Altman, I., & Low, S. M. (Eds.) (1992). *Place attachment*. New York: Plenum.

[20] Stedman, R. C. (2002). Toward a social psychology of place. *Environment and Behavior, 34*, 561-581.

[21] Proshansky, H. M. (1978). The city and self-identity. *Environment and Behavior, 10*, 147-169.

[22] Proshansky, H. M., Fabian, A. K., & Kaminoff, R. (1983). Place-identity: Physical world socialization of the self. *Journal of Environmental Psychology, 3*, 5783.

[23] Twigger-Ross, C. L. & Uzzell, D. L. (1996). Place and identity processes. *Journal of Environmental Psychology, 16*, 205-220.

[24] Moore, R. L., & Graefe, A. R. (1994). Attachments to recreation settings. *Leisure Sciences, 16*, 17-31.

[25] Stokols, D., & Shumaker, S. A. (1981). People in places: A transactional view of settings. In J. Harvey (Ed.), *Cognition, social behavior, and the environment* (pp. 441–488). Hillsdale, NJ: Erlbaum.

[26] Billig, M., Kohn, R., & Levav, I. (2006). Anticipatory stress in the population facing forced removal from the Gaza strip. *Journal of Nervous and Mental Disease, 194*, 195-200.

[27] Bonaiuto, M., Fornara, F., & Bonnes, M. (2006). Perceived residential environment quality in middle- and low-extension Italian cities. *European Review of Applied Psychology, 56*, 23-34.

[28] Jorgensen, B. S., & Stedman, R. C. (2001). Sense of place as an attitude: Lakeshore owners' attitudes toward their properties. *Journal of Environmental Psychology, 21*, 233-248.

[29] Scopelliti, M., & Tiberio, L. (2010). Homesickness in university students: The role of multiple place attachment. *Environment and Behavior, 42*, 335-350.

30 Twigger, C. (1992). *Psychological attachment to place: London Docklands—a case study*. Paper presented at the Annual British Psychological Society Conference, Scarborough, U.K, April 5–8.

31 Williams, D. R., & Roggenbuck, J. W. (1989, October). *Measuring place attachment: Some preliminary results*. Paper presented at the NRPA Symposium on Leisure Research, San Antonio, Texas.

32 Giuliani, M. V. (2003). Theory of attachment and place attachment. In M. Bonnes, T. Lee, & M. Bonaiuto (Eds.), *Psychological theories for environmental issues* (pp. 137-170). Aldershot: Ashgate.

33 Jorgensen, B. S., & Stedman, R. C. (2001). Sense of place as an attitude: Lakeshore owners' attitudes toward their properties. *Journal of Environmental Psychology, 21*, 233-248.

34 Scannell, L., & Gifford, R. (2010a). Defining place attachment: A tripartite organizing framework. *Journal of Environmental Psychology, 30*, 1-10.

35 Dallago, L., Perkins, D. D., Santinello, M., Boyce, W., Molcho, M., & Morgan, A. (2009). Adolescent place attachment, social capital, and perceived safety: A comparison of 13 countries. *American Journal of Community Psychology, 44*, 148-160.

36 Fishwick, L., & Vining, J. (1992). Toward a phenomenology of recreation place. *Journal of Environmental Psychology, 12*, 57-63.

37 Mazumdar, S. (2005). Religious place attachment, squatting and "qualitative" research: A commentary. *Journal of Environmental Psychology, 25*, 87-95.

38 Morgan, P. (2010). Towards a developmental theory of place attachment. *Journal of Environmental Psychology, 30*, 11-22.

39 Gustafson, P. (2001). Roots and routes: Exploring the relationship between place attachment and mobility. *Environment and Behavior, 33*, 667-686.

40 Boğaç, C. (2009). Place attachment in a foreign settlement. *Journal of Environmental Psychology, 29*, 267–278.

41 Beckley, T., Stedman, R.C., Wallace, S., & Ambard, M. (2007). Snapshots of what matters most: Using resident employed photography to articulate attachment to place. *Society & Natural Resources, 20*, 913-29.

42 Stedman, R.C., Beckley, T., Wallace, S. & Ambard, M. (2004). A picture and 1000 words: Using resident-employed photography to understand attachment to high amenity places. *Journal of Leisure Research, 36*, 580-606.

43 Ryan, M. M., & Ogilvie, M. (2001). Examining the effects of environmental interchangability with overseas students: A cross cultural comparison. *Journal of Marketing and Logistics, 13*, 63-74.

44 **Steel, G. D. (2000). Polar bonds: Environmental relationships in the polar regions. *Environment and Behavior, 32*, 796-816.**

45 van der Klis, M., & Karsten, L. (2009). Commuting partners, dual residences, and the meaning of home. *Journal of Environmental Psychology, 29*, 235-245.

46 Brown, G. (2005). Mapping spatial attributes in survey research for natural resource management: Methods and applications. *Society and Natural Resources, 18*, 17-39.

47 Brown, G. & Raymond, C. (2007). The relationship between place attachment and landscape values: Toward mapping place attachment. *Applied Geography, 27*, 89–111

48 Scannell, L. (2013). The bases of bonding: Comparing the functions of place and interpersonal attachment. Unpublished Dissertation. University of Victoria

49 Mikulincer, M., Gillath, O., & Shaver, P. R. (2002). Activation of the attachment system in adulthood: Threat-related primes increase the accessibility of mental representations of attachment figures. *Journal of Personality and Social Psychology, 83*, 881-895.

50 Tognoli, J. (2003). Leaving home: Homesickness, place attachment, and transition among residential college students. *Journal of College Student Psychotherapy, 18*, 35-48.

51 Winkel, G., Saegert, S., & Evans, G. W. (2009). An ecological perspective on theory, methods, and analysis in environmental psychology: Advances and challenges. *Journal of Environmental Psychology, 29*, 318-328.

52 Brown, B., Perkins, D. D., & Brown, G. (2003). Place attachment in a revitalizing neighborhood: Individual and block levels of analysis. *Journal of Environmental Psychology, 23*, 259-271.

53 Lewicka, M. (2011). Place attachment: How far have we come in the last 40 years? *Journal of Environmental Psychology, 31*, 207-230.

54 Twigger-Ross, C. L., & Uzzell, D. L. (1996). Place and identity processes. *Journal of Environmental Psychology, 16*, 205-220.

55 Hay, R. (1998). Sense of place in developmental context. *Journal of Environmental Psychology, 18*, 5-29.

56 Hernández, B., Hidalgo, M. C., Salazar-Laplace, M. E., & Hess, S. (2007). Place attachment and place identity in natives and non-natives. *Journal of Environmental Psychology, 27*, 310–319.

57 Twigger-Ross, C. L., & Uzzell, D. L. (1996). Place and identity processes. *Journal of Environmental Psychology, 16*, 205-220.

58 Knez, I. (2005). Attachment and identity as related to a place and its perceived climate. *Journal of Environmental Psychology, 25*, 207-218.

59 Feldman, R. M. (1990). Settlement-identity: Psychological bonds with home places in a mobile society. *Environment and Behavior, 22*, 183-229.

60 Fuhrer, U., Kaiser, F. G., & Hartig, T. (1993). Place attachment and mobility during leisure time. *Journal of Environmental Psychology, 13*, 309–321.

61 Marsh, B. (1987). Continuity and decline in the anthracite towns of Pennsylvania. *Annals of the Association of American Geographers, 77*, 337–352.

62 McHugh, K. E., & Mings, R. C. (1996). The circle of migration: Attachment to place in aging. *Annals of the Association of American Geographers, 86*, 530-550.

63 Cuba, L., & Hummon, D. M. (1993). A place to call home: Identification with dwelling, community, and region. *Sociological Quarterly, 34*, 111–131.

64 Gustafson, P. (2001). Roots and routes: Exploring the relationship between place attachment and mobility. *Environment and Behavior, 33*, 667-686.

65 Barcus, H. R., & Brunn, S. D. (2010). Place elasticity: Exploring a new conceptualization of mobility and place attachment in rural America. *Geografiska Annaler: Series B, Human Geography, 92*, 281-295.

66 Giuliani, M. V., Ferrara, F., & Barabotti, S. (2003). One attachment or more?. In G. Moser, E. Pol, Y. Bernard, M. Bonnes, J. Corraliza, & M.V. Giuliani (Eds.), *People, Places, and Sustainability: 21st Century Metropolis* (pp. 111-122). Göttingen, Germany: Hogrefe & Huber.

67 Gustafson, P. (2009). Mobility and territorial belonging. *Environment and Behavior, 41*, 490-508.

68 Gustafson, P. (2001). Roots and routes: Exploring the relationship between place attachment and mobility. *Environment and Behavior, 33*, 667-686.

69 Tognoli, J. (2003). Leaving home: Homesickness, place attachment, and transition among residential college students. *Journal of College Student Psychotherapy, 18*, 35-48.

70 Case, D. (1996). Contributions of journeys away to the definition of home: An empirical study of a dialectical process. *Journal of Environmental Psychology, 16*, 1-15.

71 Bolan, M. (1997). The mobility experience and neighborhood attachment. *Demography, 34*, 225-237.

72 Brown, B., Perkins, D. D., & Brown, G. (2003). Place attachment in a revitalizing neighborhood: Individual and block levels of analysis. *Journal of Environmental Psychology, 23*, 259-271.

73 Mesch, G. S., & Manor, O. (1998). Social ties, environmental perception, and local attachment. *Environment and Behavior, 30*, 227-245.

74 Manzo, L. C. (2014). Exploring the shadow side: Place attachment in the context of stigma, displacement, and social housing. In L. C. Manzo & P. Devine-Wright (Eds.), *Place attachment: Advances in theory, methods, and applications.* (pp. 165-176). New York, NY: Routledge.

75 Spencer, C. & Woolley, H. (2000). Children and the city: A summary of recent environmental psychology research. *Child: Care, Health and Development, 26*, 181-198.

76 Riger, S., & Lavrakas, P. J. (1981). Community ties: Patterns of attachment and social interaction in urban neighborhoods. *American Journal of Community Psychology, 9*, 55-66.

77 Lewicka, M. (2013). Localism and activity as two dimensions of people-place bonding: The role of cultural capital. *Journal of Environmental Psychology, 36*, 43-53.

78 Hummon, D. M. (1992). Community attachment: Local sentiment and sense of place. In I. Altman & S. Low (Eds), *Place Attachment*, New York: Plenum.

79 Lewicka, M. (2011). Place attachment: How far have we come in the last 40 years? *Journal of Environmental Psychology, 31*, 207-230.

80 Lewicka, M. (2005). Ways to make people active: Role of place attachment, cultural capital and neighborhood ties. *Journal of Environmental Psychology, 4*, 381–395.

81 Ahrentzen, S. B. (1992). Home as a workplace in the lives of women. In I. Altman, & S. M.

Low (Eds.), *Place attachment* (pp. 113-138). New York: Plenum.

82 Hidalgo, M. C., & Hernández, B. (2001). Place attachment: Conceptual and empirical questions. *Journal of Environmental Psychology, 21*, 273-281.

83 Pretty, G. H., Chipuer, H., & Bramston, P. (2003). Sense of place amongst adolescents and adults in two rural Australian towns: the discriminating features of place attachment, sense of community and place dependence in relation to place identity. *Journal of Environmental Psychology, 23*, 273–287.

84 Spencer, C., & Woolley, H. (2000). Children and the city: A summary of recent environmental psychology research. *Child: Care, Health and Development, 26*, 181-198.

85 Morgan, P. (2010). Towards a developmental theory of place attachment. *Journal of Environmental Psychology, 30*, 11-22.

86 Korpela, K. M., Kytta, M., & Hartig, T. (2002). Children's favorite places: Restorative experience, self-regulation and children's place preferences. *Journal of Environmental Psychology, 22*, 387-398.

87 Korpela, K. (2002). Children's environment. In R. B. Bechtel, & A. Churchman (Eds.) *Handbook of environmental psychology.* New York: John Wiley & Sons, 363-373.

88 Malinowski, J. C., & Thurber, C. A. (1996). Developmental shifts in the place preferences of boys aged 8-16 years. *Journal of Environmental Psychology, 16*, 45-54.

89 Thurber, C. A., & Malinowski, J. C. (1999). Environmental correlates of negative emotions in children. *Environment & Behavior, 31*, 487-513.

90 Elder, G. H., King, V., & Conger, R. D. (1996). Attachment to place and migration prospects: A developmental perspective. *Journal of Research on Adolescence, 6*, 397–425.

91 Hay, R. (1998). Sense of place in developmental context. *Journal of Environmental Psychology, 18*, 5-29.

92 Frieze, I. H., Hansen, S. B., & Boneva, B. (2006). The migrant personality and college students' plans for geographic mobility. *Journal of Environmental Psychology, 26*, 170-177.

93 Riger, S., & Lavrakas, P. J. (1981). Community ties: Patterns of attachment and social interaction in urban neighborhoods. *American Journal of Community Psychology, 9*, 55-66.

94 Sugihara, S., & Evans, G. W. (2000). Place attachment and social support at continuing care retirement communities. *Environment & Behavior, 32*, 400-409.

95 Twigger-Ross, C. L., & Uzzell, D. L. (1996). Place and identity processes. *Journal of Environmental Psychology, 16*, 205-220.

96 Oswald, R., & Lazarevic, V. (2011). You live *where*?! Lesbian mothers' attachment to non-metropolitan communities. *Family Relations, 60*, 373-386.

97 Manzo, L. C. (2005). For better or worse: Exploring multiple dimensions of place meaning. *Journal of Environmental Psychology, 25*, 67-86.

98 Forest, B. (1995). West Hollywood as symbol: The significance of place in the construction of a gay identity. *Environment and Planning D: Society and Space, 13*, 133–157.

99 Tartaglia, S. (2006). A preliminary study for a new model of sense of community. *Journal of Community Psychology, 34*, 25-36.

100 Thurber, C. A., & Sigman, M. D. (1998). Preliminary models of risk and protective factors for childhood homesickness: Review and empirical synthesis. *Child Development, 69*, 903-934.

101 Fried, M., & Gleicher, P. (1961). Some sources of residential satisfaction in an urban slum. *Journal of the American Institute of Planners, 27*, 305-315.

102 Taylor, R. B. (1982). Neighborhood physical environment and stress. In G. W. Evans (Ed.), *Environmental stress.* New York: Cambridge University Press.

103 Woldoff, R. A. (2002). The effects of local stressors on neighborhood attachment. *Social Forces, 81*, 87-116.

104 Bonaiuto, M., Aiello, A., Perugini, M., Bonnes, M., & Ercolani, A. P. (1999). Multidimensional perception of residential environment quality and neighborhood attachment in the urban environment. *Journal of Environmental Psychology, 19*, 331-352.

105 Fried, M. (1963). Grieving for a lost home. In L. J. Duhl (Ed.), *The urban condition: People and policy in the metropolis* (pp. 124-152). New York: Simon & Schuster.

106 Hidalgo, M. C., & Hernández, B. (2001). Place attachment: Conceptual and empirical questions. *Journal of Environmental Psychology, 21*, 273-281.

107 Mesch, G. S., & Manor, O. (1998). Social ties, environmental perception, and local attachment. *Environment and Behavior, 30*, 227-245.

108 Chow, K., & Healey, M. (2008). Place attachment and place identity: First-year undergraduates making the transition from home to university, *Journal of Environmental Psychology, 28*, 362-372.

109 Kasarda, J. D., & Janowitz, M. (1974). Community attachment in mass society. *American Sociological Review, 39*, 328–339.

110 Chow, K., & Healey, M. (2008). Place attachment and place identity: First-year undergraduates making the transition from home to university, *Journal of Environmental Psychology, 28*, 362-372.

111 Woldoff, R. A. (2002). The effects of local stressors on neighborhood attachment. *Social Forces, 81*, 87-116.

112 Perkins, D. D. & Long, D. A. (2002). Neighborhood sense of community and social capital: A multi-level analysis. In A. Fisher, C. Sonn, & B. Bishop (Eds.), *Psychological sense of community: Research, applications, and implications* (pp. 291-318). New York: Plenum.

113 Pretty, G. H., Chipuer, H., & Bramston, P. (2003). Sense of place amongst adolescents and adults in two rural Australian towns: the discriminating features of place attachment, sense of community and place dependence in relation to place identity. *Journal of Environmental Psychology, 23*, 273–287.

114 Kasarda, J. D., & Janowitz, M. (1974). Community attachment in mass society. *American Sociological Review, 39*, 328–339.

115 Robison, L., Schmid, A., & Siles, M. (2002). Is social capital really capital? *Review of Social Economy, 60*, 1-21.

116 Pretty, J., & Ward, H. (2001). Social capital and the environment. *World Development, 29*, 209–227.

117 Murphy, B. L. (2007). Locating social capital in resilient community-level emergency management, *Natural Hazards, 41*, 297-315.

118 Woldoff, R. A. (2002). The effects of local stressors on neighborhood attachment. *Social Forces, 81*, 87-116.

119 Twigger, C. (1992). *Psychological attachment to place: London Docklands—a case study.* Paper presented at the Annual British Psychological Society Conference, Scarborough, U.K, April 5–8.

120 Gifford, R., Lacombe, C., Kormos, C., & Scannell, L. (2008). *Families living downtown: Challenges and benefits.* Report for the Canada Mortgage and Housing Corporation.

121 Sonn, C. C. (2002). Immigrant adaptation. In A. T. Fisher, C. C. Sonn & B. J. Bishop (Eds.), *Psychological sense of community: Research, applications, and implications* (pp. 205-222). New York: Kluwer Academic/Plenum Publishers.

122 Manzo, L. C., Kleit, R. G., & Couch, D. (2008). Moving once is like having your house on fire three times: The experience of place and displacement among residents of a public housing site. *Urban Studies, 45*, 1855-1878.

123 Aguilar, M. A. (2002). Identity and daily space in two municipalities in Mexico City. *Environment and Behavior, 34*, 111-121.

124 Sime, J. D., & Kimura, M. (1988). *Home gardens: Attachment to the natural environment and the experience of time from a Western and Japanese perspective.* Nineteenth Annual Conference of the Environmental Design Research Association, Pomona, California.

125 Catrill, J. G. (1998). The environmental self and a sense of place: Communication foundations for regional ecosystem management. *Journal of Applied Communication Research, 26*, 301-318.

126 Hunter, L. M. (1998). The association between environmental risk and internal migration flows. *Population and Environment: A Journal of Interdisciplinary Studies, 19*, 247-277.

127 Riger, S., & Lavrakas, P. J. (1981). Community ties: Patterns of attachment and social interaction in urban neighborhoods. *American Journal of Community Psychology, 9*, 55-66.

128 Fried, M. (1982). Residential attachment: Sources of residential and community satisfaction. *Journal of Social Issues, 38*, 107-120.

129 Lewicka, M. (2010). What makes neighbourhood different from home and city? Effects of place scale on place attachment. *Journal of Environmental Psychology, 30*, 35–51.

130 Brown, B. B., & Werner, C. M. (1985). Social cohesiveness, territoriality, and holiday decorations: The influence of cul-de-sacs. *Environment and Behavior, 17*, 539-565.

131 Pinet, C. (1988). *A "sense of belonging" in the neighborhood: The effect of traffic on space appropriation.* Nineteenth Annual Conference of the Environmental Design Research Association, Pomona, California.

132 Uzzell, D., Pol, E., & Badenas, D. (2002). Place identification, social cohesion, and environmental sustainability. *Environment and Behavior, 34*, 26-53.

133 Pendola, R. & Gen, S. (2008). Does "Main Street" promote sense of community? A comparison of San Francisco neighborhoods. *Environment and Behavior, 40,* 545-574.

134 Kim, J., & Kaplan, R. (2004). Physical and psychological factors in sense of community: New urbanist Kentlands and nearby Orchard Village. *Environment and Behavior, 36,* 313-340.

135 Lewicka, M. (2005). Ways to make people active: Role of place attachment, cultural capital and neighborhood ties. *Journal of Environmental Psychology, 4,* 381–395.

136 Wilson, G., & Baldassare, M. (1996). Overall "Sense of Community" in a suburban region: The effects of localism, privacy, and urbanization. *Environment and Behavior, 28,* 27-43.

137 Theodori, G. L., & Luloff, A. E. (2000). Urbanization and community attachment in rural areas. *Society and Natural Resources, 13,* 399-420.

138 Kasarda, J. D., & Janowitz, M. (1974). Community attachment in mass society. *American Sociological Review, 39,* 328–339.

139 Lewicka, M. (2011). Place attachment: How far have we come in the last 40 years? *Journal of Environmental Psychology, 31,* 207-230.

140 Hidalgo, M. C., & Hernández, B. (2001). Place attachment: Conceptual and empirical questions. *Journal of Environmental Psychology, 21,* 273-281.

141 Hernandez, B., Hidalgo, M. C., Salazar-Laplace, M. E., & Hess, S. (2007). Place attachment and place identity in natives and non-natives. *Journal of Environmental Psychology, 27,* 310–319.

142 Lewicka, M. (2008). Place attachment, place identity and place memory: Restoring the forgotten city past. *Journal of Environmental Psychology, 28,* 209-231.

143 Laczko, L. S. (2005). National and local attachments in a changing world system: Evidence from an international survey. *International Review of Sociology, 15,* 517–528.

144 Feldman, R. M. (1996). Constancy and change in attachments to types of settlements. *Environment and Behavior, 28,* 419-445.

145 Knez, I. (2005). Attachment and identity as related to a place and its perceived climate. *Journal of Environmental Psychology, 25,* 207-218.

146 Ryan, M. M., & Ogilvie, M. (2001). Examining the effects of environmental interchangability with overseas students: A cross cultural comparison. *Journal of Marketing and Logistics, 13,* 63-74.

147 Low, S. M. (1992). Symbolic ties that bind. Place attachment in the plaza. In I. Altman, & S. M. Low (Eds.), *Place attachment* (pp. 165-185). New York and London: Plenum Press.

148 Low, S. M. (1990). Cross-cultural place attachment: A preliminary typology. In Y. Yoshitake, R. B. Bechtel, T. Takahashi, & Asai, M. (Eds.), *Current issues in environment-behavior research.* Tokyo: University of Tokyo.

149 Austin, M. E., & Kaplan, R. (2003). Identity, involvement, and expertise in the inner city: Some benefits of tree-planting projects. In S. Clayton & S. Opotow (Eds.), *Identity and the natural environment: The psychological significance of nature* (pp. 205-225). Cambridge, MA: MIT Press.

150 Mazumdar, S., & Mazumdar, S. (2004). Religion and place attachment: A study of sacred places. *Journal of Environmental Psychology, 24,* 385-397.

151 Lutwack, L. (1984). The role of place in literature. Syracuse, NY: Syracuse University Press.

152 Lewicka, M. (2011). Place attachment: How far have we come in the last 40 years? *Journal of Environmental Psychology, 31,* 207-230.

153 Relph, E. (1976). *Place and placelessness.* London: Pion Limited.

154 Proshansky, H. M. (1978). The city and self-identity. *Environment and Behavior, 10,* 147-169.

155 Proshansky, H. M., Fabian, A. K., & Kaminoff, R. (1983). Place-identity. *Journal of Environmental Psychology, 3,* 57-83.

156 Billig, M. (2006). Is my home my castle? Place attachment, risk perception, and religious faith. *Environment and Behavior, 38,* 248-265.

157 Lalli, M. (1992). Urban-related identity: Theory, measurement and empirical findings. *Journal of Environmental Psychology, 12,* 285-303.

158 Feldman, R. M. (1990). Settlement-identity: Psychological bonds with home places in a mobile society. *Environment and Behavior, 22,* 183-229.

159 Brown, B., Perkins, D. D., & Brown, G. (2003). Place attachment in a revitalizing neighborhood: Individual and block levels of analysis. *Journal of Environmental Psychology, 23,* 259-271.

160 Stedman, R. (2003). Is it really just a social construction? The contribution of the physical environment to sense of place. *Society and Natural Resources, 16,* 671-685.

161 Kaltenborn, B. P., & Bjerke, T. (2002). Associations between landscape preferences and place attachment: A study in Røros, southern Norway. *Landscape Research, 27,* 381-396.

162 Bonaiuto, M., Breakwell, G. M., & Cano, I. (1996). Identity processes and environmental threat: The effects of nationalism and local identity upon perception of beach pollution. *Journal of Community & Applied Social Psychology, 6,* 157-175.

163 Tajfel, H. (1978). *Differentiation between social groups.* Academic Press, London.

164 Bonaiuto, M., Breakwell, G. M., & Cano, I. (1996). Identity processes and environmental threat: The effects of nationalism and local identity upon perception of beach pollution. *Journal of Community & Applied Social Psychology, 6,* 157-175.

165 Proshansky, H. M. (1978). The city and self-identity. *Environment and Behavior, 10,* 147-169.

166 Proshansky, H. M., Fabian, A. K., & Kaminoff, R. (1983). Place-identity. *Journal of Environmental Psychology, 3,* 57-83.

167 Mesch, G. S., & Manor, O. (1998). Social ties, environmental perception, and local attachment. *Environment and Behavior, 30,* 227-245.

168 Uzzell, D., Pol, E., & Badenas, D. (2002). Place identification, social cohesion, and environmental sustainability. *Environment and Behavior, 34,* 26-53.

169 Saegert, S. (1989). Unlikely leaders, extreme circumstances: Older black women building community households. *American Journal of Community Psychology, 17,* 295-316.

170 Brown, B. B., & Perkins, D. D. (1992). Disruptions in place attachment. In I. Altman & S. Low (Eds.), *Place attachment* (pp. 279-304). New York: Plenum.

171 Worchel, S. &, Lollis, M. (1982). Reactions to territorial contamination as a function of culture. *Personality and Social Psychology Bulletin, 8,* 370–375.

172 Stedman, R. (2002). Toward a social psychology of place. *Environment and Behavior 34,* 561-581.

173 Nordenstam, B. J. (1994, March). *When communities say NIMBY to their LULUS: Factors influencing environmental and social impact perception.* Paper presented at the 14th Annual Meeting of the International Association for Impact Assessment, Quebec, Canada.

174 Vorkinn, M., & Riese, H. (2001). Environmental concern in a local context: The significance of place attachment. *Environment & Behavior, 33,* 249-263.

175 Vaske, J. J., & Kobrin, K. C. (2001). Place attachment and environmentally responsible behavior. *Journal of Environmental Education, 32,* 16-21.

176 Uzzell, D., Pol, E., & Badenas, D. (2002). Place identification, social cohesion, and environmental sustainability. *Environment and Behavior, 34,* 26-53.

177 Scannell, L., & Gifford, R. (2010b). The relations between natural and civic place attachment and pro-environmental behavior. *Journal of Environmental Psychology, 30,* 289-297.

178 Clayton, S., & Opotow, S. (2003). Introduction: Identity and the natural environment. In S. Clayton, & S. Opotow (Eds.), *Identity and the natural environment: The psychological significance of nature* (pp. 1-11). Cambridge, MA: MIT Press.

179 Brown, B. B., Altman, I., & Werner, C. M. (2012). Place attachment. In S. J. Smith (Ed.), *The international encyclopedia of housing and home* (pp. 83-188). Oxford, UK: Elsevier.

180 Devine-Wright, P. and Howes, Y. (2010). Disruption to place attachment and the protection of restorative environments: A wind energy case study. *Journal of Environmental Psychology, 30,* 271-280.

181 Edelstein, M. R. (1988). *Contaminated communities: The social and psychological impacts of residential toxic exposure.* Boulder, CO: Westview.

182 Kyle, G. T., Graefe, A., Manning, R. E., & Bacon, J. (2004). Effect of involvement and place attachment on recreationists' perceptions of setting density. *Journal of Leisure Research, 36,* 209-231.

183 Vorkinn, M., & Riese, H. (2001). Environmental concern in a local context: The significance of place attachment. *Environment & Behavior, 33,* 249-263.

184 Kyle, G. T., Graefe, A., Manning, R. E., & Bacon, J. (2004). Effect of involvement and place attachment on recreationists' perceptions of setting density. *Journal of Leisure Research, 36,* 209-231.

185 Norris-Baker, C., & Scheidt, R. J. (1990). Place attachment among older residents of a "ghost town": A transactional approach. *Proceedings of the 21st annual conference of the Environmental Design Research Association, 21,* 333-340.

186 Kaplan, R. (1985). Nature at the doorstep: Residential satisfaction and the

nearby environment. *Journal of Architecture and Planning Research, 2*, 115-127.

187 Fried, M. (1963). Grieving for a lost home. In L. J. Duhl (Ed.), *The urban condition: People and policy in the metropolis* (pp. 124-152). New York: Simon & Schuster.

188 West, R. A. (2003). *Place psychological experience: A Native American perspective.* ProQuest Information & Learning.

189 Windsor, J. E. & McVey, J. A. (2005). Annihilation of both place and sense of place: The experience of the Cheslatta T'En Canadian First Nation within the context of large-scale environmental projects. *Geographical Journal, 171,* 146–65.

190 Windsor, J. E. & McVey, J. A. (2005). Annihilation of both place and sense of place: The experience of the Cheslatta T'En Canadian First Nation within the context of large-scale environmental projects. *Geographical Journal, 171,* 146–65.

191 Fisher, W. F. (1999). Going under: Indigenous peoples and the struggle against large dams. *Cultural Survival Quarterly, 23,* 29-32.

192 McAndrew, F. T. (1998). The measurement of "rootedness" and the prediction of attachment to home-towns in college students. *Journal of Environmental Psychology, 18,* 409-471.

193 Hornsey, M., & Gallois, C. (1998). The impact of interpersonal and intergroup communication accommodation on perceptions of Chinese students in Australia. *Journal of Language and Social Psychology, 17,* 323-347

194 Chow, K., & Healey, M. (2008). Place attachment and place identity: First-year undergraduates making the transition from home to university, *Journal of Environmental Psychology, 28,* 362-372.

195 Ryan, M. M., & Ogilvie, M. (2001). Examining the effects of environmental interchangability with overseas students: A cross cultural comparison. *Journal of Marketing and Logistics, 13,* 63-74.

196 Mishra, S., Mazumdar, S., & Suar D. (2010). Place attachment and flood preparedness. *Journal of Environmental Psychology, 30,* 187-197.

197 Cuba, L., & Hummon, D. M. (1993). A place to call home: Identification with dwelling, community, and region. *Sociological Quarterly, 34,* 111–131.

198 Riley, R. B. (1992). Attachment to the ordinary landscape. In I. Altman, & S. M. Low (Eds.), *Place attachment* (pp. 13-35). New York: Plenum.

199 Fullilove, M. T. (1996). Psychiatric implications of displacement: Contributions from the psychology of place. *American Journal of Psychiatry, 153,* 1516-1523

200 Giuliani, M. V. (2003). Theory of attachment and place attachment. In M. Bonnes, T. Lee, & M. Bonaiuto (Eds.), *Psychological theories for environmental issues* (pp. 137-170). Aldershot: Ashgate.

201 Hidalgo, M. C., & Hernández, B. (2001). Place attachment: Conceptual and empirical questions. *Journal of Environmental Psychology, 21,* 273-281.

202 Mesch, G. S., & Manor, O. (1998). Social ties, environmental perception, and local attachment. *Environment and Behavior, 30,* 227-245.

203 Giuliani, M. V. (2003). Theory of attachment and place attachment. In M. Bonnes, T. Lee, & M.

Bonaiuto (Eds.), *Psychological theories for environmental issues* (pp. 137-170). Aldershot: Ashgate.

204 Billig, M., Kohn, R., & Levav, I. (2006). Anticipatory stress in the population facing forced removal from the Gaza strip. *Journal of Nervous and Mental Disease, 194,* 195-200.

205 Cooper Marcus, C. (1992). Environmental memories. In I. Altman, & S. M. Low (Eds.), *Place attachment* (pp. 87-112). New York: Plenum.

206 Twigger-Ross, C. L., & Uzzell, D. L. (1996). Place and identity processes. *Journal of Environmental Psychology, 16,* 205-220.

207 Low, S. M., & Altman, I. (1992). Place attachment: A conceptual inquiry. In I. Altman, & S. M. Low (Eds.), *Place attachment* (pp. 1-12). New York: Plenum.

208 Baumeiser, R. F., & Leary, M. R. (1995). The need to belong: Desire for interpersonal attachments as a fundamental human motivation. *Psychological Bulletin, 117,* 497- 529.

209 Pittman, T. S., & Zeigler, K. R. (2007). Basic human needs. In A. W. Kruglanski & E. T. Higgins (Eds.), *Social psychology: Handbook of basic principles, 2nd ed.* (pp. 473-489). New York: Guilford.

210 Korpela, K. M., Kytta M., & Hartig, T. (2002). Children's favorite places: Restorative experience, self-regulation and children's place preferences. *Journal of Environmental Psychology, 22,* 387-398.

211 Hartig, T., Kaiser, F. G., & Bowler, P. A. (2001). Psychological restoration in nature as a positive motivation for ecological behavior. *Environment and Behavior, 33,* 590-607.

212 Cuba, L., & Hummon, D. M. (1993). A place to call home: Identification with dwelling, community, and region. *Sociological Quarterly, 34,* 111–131.

213 Fullilove, M. T. (1996). Psychiatric implications of displacement: Contributions from the psychology of place. *American Journal of Psychiatry, 153,* 1516-1523

214 Giuliani, M. V. (2003). Theory of attachment and place attachment. In M. Bonnes, T. Lee, & M. Bonaiuto (Eds.), *Psychological theories for environmental issues* (pp. 137-170). Aldershot: Ashgate.

215 Hidalgo, M. C., & Hernández, B. (2001). Place attachment: Conceptual and empirical questions. *Journal of Environmental Psychology, 21,* 273-281.

216 Mesch, G. S., & Manor, O. (1998). Social ties, environmental perception, and local attachment. *Environment and Behavior, 30,* 227-245.

217 Riley, R. B. (1992). Attachment to the ordinary landscape. In I. Altman, & S. M. Low (Eds.), *Place attachment* (pp. 13-35). New York: Plenum Press.

218 Moore, R. L., & Graefe, A. R. (1994). Attachments to recreation settings. *Leisure Sciences, 16,* 17-31.

219 Stokols, D., & Shumaker, S. A. (1981). People in places: A transactional view of settings. In J. Harvey (Ed.), *Cognition, social behavior, and the environment* (pp. 441–488). Hillsdale, NJ: Erlbaum.

220 Charles, K. E. (2003). Fanger's thermal comfort and draught models (NRC/IRC Client Report B3205.XX). Ottawa, ON: National Research Council of Canada, Institute for Research in Construction.

221 Roulet, C.-A.; Johner, N.; Foradini, F.; Bluyssen, P.; Cox, C.; Fernandes, E.; Muller, B.; Aizlewood, C. 2006. Perceived health and comfort in relation to energy use and building characteristics. *Building Research & Information, 34* (5), 467-474.

222 Knez, I. (2005). Attachment and identity as related to a place and its perceived climate. *Journal of Environmental Psychology, 25,* 207-218.

223 Wohlwill, J. F. (1966). The physical environment: A problem for a psychology of stimulation. *Journal of Social Issues, 22,* 29-38.

224 Ulrich, R. S. (1993). Biophilia, biophobia, and natural landscapes. In S. R. Kellert & E. O. Wilson (Eds.), *The biophilia hypothesis* (pp. 73–137). Washington, D.C.: Island Press.

225 Kaplan, S. (1995). The restorative benefits of nature: Toward an integrative framework. *Journal of Environmental Psychology, 15,* 169-182.

226 Taylor, A. F., Kuo, F. E., & Sullivan, W. C. (2001). Coping with ADD – the surprising connection to green play settings. *Environment and Behavior, 33,* 54-77.

227 Ng, S. H., Kam, P. K., & Pong, R. W. M. (2005). People living in ageing buildings: Their quality of life and sense of belonging. *Journal of Environmental Psychology, 25,* 347–360.

228 Field, A., Witten, K., Robinson, E., Pledger, M. (2004). Who gets to what? Access to community resources in two New Zealand cities. *Urban Policy and Research, 22.* 189- 205.

229 Brown, B. B., & Werner, C. M. (1985). Social cohesiveness, territoriality, and holiday decorations: The influence of cul-de-sacs. *Environment and Behavior, 17,* 539-565.

230 Dutton, D. (2003). Aesthetics and evolutionary psychology. In J. Levison (Ed.), *The Oxford handbook for aesthetics.* New York: Oxford University Press.

231 Hwang, S. N., Lee, C., & Chen, H. J. (2005). The Relationship among tourists' involvement, place attachment and interpretation satisfaction in Taiwan's national parks. *Tourism Management, 26,* 143–156.

232 Manzo, L. C. (2003). Beyond house and haven: Toward a revisioning of emotional relationships with places. *Journal of Environmental Psychology, 23,* 47-61.

233 Chawla, L. (1992). Childhood place attachments. *Human Behavior & Environment: Advances in Theory & Research, 12,* 63-86.

234 Manzo, L. C. (2014). Exploring the shadow side: Place attachment in the context of stigma, displacement, and social housing. In L. C. Manzo & P. Devine-Wright (Eds.), *Place attachment: Advances in theory, methods, and applications.* (pp. 165-176). New York, NY: Routledge.

235 Windsor, J. E. & McVey, J. A. (2005). Annihilation of both place and sense of place: The experience of the Cheslatta T'En Canadian First Nation within the context of large-scale environmental projects. *Geographical Journal, 171,* 146–65.

236 Rubinstein, R. L., & Parmelee, P. A. (1992). Attachment to place and the representation of the life course by the elderly. In I. Altman, & S. M. Low (Eds.), *Place attachment* (pp. 139–163). New York: Plenum.

237 Fried, M. (2000). Continuities and discontinuities of place. *Journal of Environmental Psychology, 20*, 193-205.

238 Sahdra, B., Shaver, P., & Brown, K. (2010). A scale to measure non-attachment: A Buddhist complement to western research on attachment and adaptive functioning. *Journal of Personality Assessment, 92*, 116-127.

239 Hay, R. (1998). Sense of place in developmental context. *Journal of Environmental Psychology, 18*, 5-29.

240 Fried, M. (2000). Continuities and discontinuities of place. *Journal of Environmental Psychology, 20*, 193-205.

241 Morgan, P. (2010). Towards a developmental theory of place attachment. *Journal of Environmental Psychology, 30*, 11-22.

242 Twigger-Ross, C. L., & Uzzell, D. L. (1996). Place and identity processes. *Journal of Environmental Psychology, 16*, 205-220.

243 Bowlby, J. (1969). *Attachment and loss: Vol. 1. Attachment*. New York: Basic Books.

244 Bowlby, J. (1982). *Attachment and loss: Vol. 1. Attachment* (2nd ed.). New York: Basic Books.

245 Ainsworth, M. D. S. (1967). *Infancy in Uganda: Infant care and the growth of love*. Baltimore: Johns Hopkins University Press.

246 Giuliani, M. V. (2003). Theory of attachment and place attachment. In M. Bonnes, T. Lee, & M. Bonaiuto (Eds.), *Psychological theories for environmental issues* (pp. 137-170). Aldershot: Ashgate.

247 Scannell, L., & Gifford, R. (2014). Comparing the theories of interpersonal and place attachment. In L. C. Manzo & P. Devine-Wright (Eds.), *Place attachment: Advances in theory, methods, and applications* (pp. 23-36). New York, NY: Routledge.

248 Kelly, G., & Hosking, K. (2008). Nonpermanent residents, place attachment, and "sea change" communities. *Environment and Behavior, 40*, 575-594.

249 Brown, B.B., & Perkins, D.D. (1992). Disruptions in place attachment. In I. Altman & S. Low (Eds.), *Place attachment* (pp. 279-304). New York: Plenum.

250 Harris, P. B., Brown, B. B., & Werner, C. M. (1996). Privacy regulation and place attachment: Predicting attachments to a student family housing facility. *Journal of Environmental Psychology, 16*, 287–301.

251 Fried, M. (2000). Continuities and discontinuities of place. *Journal of Environmental Psychology, 20*, 193-205.

252 Korpela, K. M., Kytta M., & Hartig, T. (2002). Children's favorite places: Restorative experience, self-regulation and children's place preferences. *Journal of Environmental Psychology, 22*, 387-398.

253 Shumaker, S. A., & Taylor, R. B. (1983). Toward a clarification of people-place relationships: A model of attachment to place. In N. R. Feimer, & E. S. Geller (Eds.), *Environmental psychology: Directions and perspectives* (pp. 219-256). New York: Praeger.

254 Dupuis, A., & Thorns, D. C. (1996). Meanings of home for older homeowners. *Housing Studies, 11*, 485-501.

255 Saunders, P. (1990). *A nation of homeowners*. London: Unwin Hyman.

256 Sixsmith, J. (1986). The meaning of home: An exploratory study of environmental experience. *Journal of Environmental Psychology, 6*, 281-298.

257 Fried, M. (1963). Grieving for a lost home. In L. J. Duhl (Ed.), *The urban condition: People and policy in the metropolis* (pp. 124-152). New York: Simon & Schuster.

258 Fullilove, M. T. (1996). Psychiatric implications of displacement: Contributions from the psychology of place. *American Journal of Psychiatry, 153*, 1516-1523

259 Windsor, J. E. & McVey, J. A. (2005). Annihilation of both place and sense of place: The experience of the Cheslatta T'En Canadian First Nation within the context of large-scale environmental projects. *Geographical Journal, 171*, 146–65.

260 Ainsworth, M. D. S. (1967). *Infancy in Uganda: Infant care and the growth of love*. Baltimore: Johns Hopkins University Press.

261 Ainsworth. M. D. S., Blehar, M., Waters, E., & Wall, S. (1978). *Patterns of attachment: A psychological study of the strange situation*. Hillsdale, NJ: Erlbaum.

262 Bartholomew, K., & Horowitz, L. M. (1991). Attachment styles among young adults: A test of a four-category model. *Journal of Personality and Social Psychology, 61*, 226-244.

263 Main, M., & Solomon, J. (1990). Procedures for identifying infants as disorganized/ disoriented during the Ainsworth Strange Situation. In Greenberg, M. T., Cicchetti, D., & Cummings, M. (Eds.), *Attachment in the preschool years: Theory, research, and intervention* (pp. 121-160). Chicago: The University of Chicago Press.

264 Shaver, P. R., & Mikulincer, M. (2007). Attachment theory and research: Core concepts, basic principles, conceptual bridges. In A. W. Kruglanski, & E. T. Higgins (Eds.), *Social psychology: Handbook of basic principles* (2nd ed.) (pp. 650-677). New York: Guilford.

265 McBain, K. A. (2010). *Adult attachment theory and attachment to place: What makes a house a home?* Unpublished Dissertation. James Cook University.

266 Seamon, D. (2014). Place attachment and phenomenology: The synergistic dynamism of place. In L. Manzo & P. Devine-Wright (Eds). *Place attachment: Advances in theory, methods and research*, (pp. 11-22). New York: Routledge/Francis & Taylor.

267 Twigger-Ross, C. L., & Uzzell, D. L. (1996). Place and identity processes. *Journal of Environmental Psychology, 16*, 205-220.

268 Stedman, R. (2003). Is it really just a social construction? The contribution of the physical environment to sense of place. *Society and Natural Resources, 16*, 671-685.

269 Stedman, R. (2003). Is it really just a social construction? The contribution of the physical environment to sense of place. *Society and Natural Resources, 16*, p. 671.

270 Devine-Wright, P. (2009). Rethinking Nimbyism: the role of place attachment and place identity in explaining place protective action. *Journal of Community and Applied Social Psychology, 19*, 426-441.

271 Brown, B.B., & Perkins, D.D. (1992). Disruptions in place attachment. In I. Altman & S. Low (Eds.), *Place attachment* (pp. 279-304). New York: Plenum.

272 Devine-Wright, P. (2009). Rethinking Nimbyism: the role of place attachment and place identity in explaining place protective action. *Journal of Community and Applied Social Psychology, 19*, 426-441.

273 Devine-Wright, P. (2009). Rethinking Nimbyism: the role of place attachment and place identity in explaining place protective action. *Journal of Community and Applied Social Psychology, 19*, 426-441.

274 Tumanan, M., & Lansangan, J. (2012). More than just a cuppa coffee: A multi-dimensional approach towards analysing the factors that define place attachment. *International Journal of Hospitality Management, 31*, 529-534.

275 Waxman, L., (2006). The coffee shop: Social and physical factors influencing place attachment. *Journal of Interior Design, 31*, 35–53.

276 Sugihara, S., & Evans, G. W. (2000). Place attachment and social support at continuing care retirement communities. *Environment & Behavior, 32*, 400-409.

277 Sugihara, S., & Evans, G. W. (2000). Place attachment and social support at continuing care retirement communities. *Environment & Behavior, 32*, 400-409.

CHAPTER 10:

Educational Environmental Psychology

Nowhere else are large groups of individuals packed so closely together for so many hours, yet expected to perform at peak efficiency on difficult learning tasks and to interact harmoniously.

—CAROL WEINSTEIN[1]

WALKING THROUGH THE WOODS TO THE UNIVERSITY'S FIELD STATION *where they had a lab for their forestry class, Tom and Jane started reminiscing about the schools they had attended. Jane's inner-city school sat in the middle of an expanse of asphalt, surrounded by wire fences. "The windows were tall and narrow, and the globe lamps hung down on long wires. In those ancient rooms with tall ceilings, I felt small and out of place," Jane recalled. "I can still see those big old oak desks with generations of initials carved upon initials."*

"Sounds like doom itself to me," said Tom. He had grown up in a rural district that was being swallowed by suburbia. "My elementary school was certainly different. It was almost new—only one storey and surrounded by grassy fields."

He thought for a minute. "There was something else quite different from yours. It was one of those open-plan schools. You know, with big spaces where the teachers could merge their classes or divide them up by subject instead of by age. I remember some of the teachers just couldn't handle it. They would try to fence the rest of the school out with filing cabinets and bulletin boards."

"Sounds like chaos itself to me," said Jane, gently mocking him.

"You're right, actually. The noise level would steadily rise all day until you could hardly hear the bell at the end of the last period."

"That's strange—your whole school experience must have been so different from mine. Those old rooms were like caverns, huge and quiet. Your voice would sort of disappear into space." Jane actually shuddered as the sounds and smells came back to her. "Maybe the place seemed like that because our high school only had 1,100 students left and the place was built for 2,000."

Tom was surprised. "Really? My schools were always too full. My high school was crowded the day it opened, and by the time I graduated, it had 900 students—and it was built for 600."

Lost in these musings, they suddenly found themselves in front of the field station. "Well, back to forest ecology," said Jane.

LEARNING IS A CENTRAL PART OF EVERYONE'S LIFE. We often associate learning with school, but of course much learning also occurs before we reach school age, outside school hours, and after we have completed school. It often occurs even when we do not think of ourselves as learning, such as

302

when we take a stroll through the woods or when we talk over the events of the day with friends. Learning occurs in places where it is the designated purpose of the setting (for example schools, seminars, practice fields, libraries, conservatories, museums, and training grounds) but also in places in which the learning is incidental to the primary purpose of the setting (for example, playgrounds, street corners, parks, dinner tables, family rooms, offices, and hallways).

This chapter is concerned with the role of the physical environment in learning, including such influences as architecture, noise, light, temperature, crowding, furniture arrangement, and room design. We will also discuss the nature of learning *about* the environment, and the process of developing environmental competence (see Figures 10-1 and 10-2).

From the very large amount of attention paid to *non*-physical factors in learning, such as teaching style or educational philosophy, one might conclude that physical factors are not very important. Yet studies do report dramatic changes in behavior that are associated with the physical aspects of learning environments. For example, when a typical sterile Introductory Psychology classroom was changed into one with softer lighting, plants, posters, cushions, and rugs, exam scores after five weeks were significantly higher than those of students who spent five weeks in a similar room that had not been modified.[2] Physical factors *can* make a significant difference!

Society spends vast sums to educate individuals of all ages. Environmental psychologists believe that educational settings can and should make education both more efficient and more enjoyable. The physical setting may not make or break education on its own—to believe that would be a naive form of architectural determinism—but it can interact with non-environmental factors either to promote or to hinder the learning process.

The general framework for this chapter is presented in Figure 10-3. It proposes that the personal characteristics of students (past school experience, attitudes toward learning, age, gender, personality) interact with physical features of the learning setting (its size, noise level, climate, population density, and design) and the social-organizational climate (rules, curriculum, teaching style, progressive or traditional orientation) to produce learning-related attitudes (satisfaction with school, dissatisfaction with classroom, commitment to learning) and behaviors (class participation, attention to learning materials, questioning,

FIGURE 10-1 People spend years in schools; their physical environments have strong effects on their learning and other behaviors.

FIGURE 10-2 Learning also occurs outdoors and on non-academic topics.

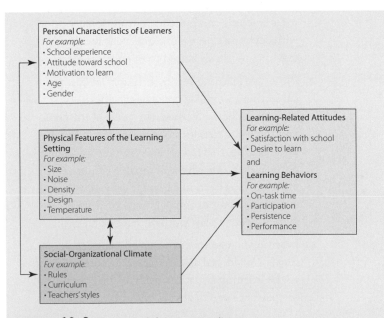

FIGURE 10-3 A framework for conceptualizing person-environment relations in learning settings.

appropriate or inappropriate activity, persistence, creativity, and of course, learning and performance).

Interactions among these factors should be considered where possible. Consider a typical study that included both personal and environmental factors and found important interactions.[3] The researchers sought to discover whether open-plan school designs were equally beneficial to students from urban and suburban neighborhoods. Suburban students achieved about as much in open-plan and traditional schools, but urban students achieved more in traditional schools than in open-plan schools. This shows that one cannot simply conclude open-plan schools are better or worse or all students. The interaction of a personal and an environmental variable suggests the more accurate conclusion that some designs are better for some students.

Carol Weinstein summarized four assumptions made by environmental psychologists who study learning and the physical environment:[4]

1. The physical setting does not teach directly, but it can facilitate or hinder learning, both directly and symbolically. Loud noise, for example, may directly interfere with the transmission of information from teacher to learner. A drab, untidy classroom may symbolize to learners that the school and teacher care little about their progress.

2. The effects of the physical setting on learning are not universal, but are moderated by the social and instructional context. For example, open-plan schools work poorly when educators merely import their teaching methods from traditional schools with separate classrooms, but work better when teaching methods suited to open space are used.

3. No single learning setting is best. The best physical settings are those congruent with the type of material being learned, the goals of the class, and the characteristics of the learners. The very same setting, therefore, may produce wonderful results in one case and terrible results in another. This becomes dramatically obvious if you think, for example, how well children would learn to play football in a hockey rink.

4. Learning is maximized when the physical setting is considered as carefully as are other aspects of the learning situation, such as the curriculum, the teacher's verbal ability, and other teaching aids. Unfortunately, most educational programs still pay little attention to the physical setting.[5]

The task of environmental psychologists who study learning is to identify conditions under which physical and non-physical elements of the setting combine to result in improved learning. But what *is* it? Learning usually is defined as a relatively permanent change in behavior that occurs as result of experience. That may be true, but the learning experience includes more than that. This chapter examines the effects of the physical environment on four dimensions of learning: learning itself, feelings about learning, social behavior related to learning, and health and stress related to learning. Beginning with a look at how settings as a whole affect these dimensions of learning, the chapter examines the effects of more specific physical variables, including noise, light, color, temperature, crowding, and room arrangements.

THE SETTING AS A WHOLE

SCHOOL BUILDINGS AND GROUNDS, as a group, are physically very variable. Some are large, some small; some look like Monopoly hotels, some look like one-storey geometric designs constructed of children's play blocks, some have large grassy fields, some have only asphalt yards. How do such variations in the overall architecture of schools affect learning?

Size

IS THERE A RELATION BETWEEN LEARNING AND THE SIZE OF A SCHOOL? In a classic study, five US high schools ranging in size from 35 to 2,300 students were compared.[5] Size matters! First, the larger schools offered a wider variety of instruction to their students. Variety did not, however, increase as fast as size. Thus, a school that is much larger than another offers its students only slightly greater choice of classes.

Second, participation in activities outside regular class hours was about the same for large and small schools. The important difference is that students in smaller schools participate in more kinds of extracurricular activities, and they much more often participate in central or responsible positions.

Third, students in large schools reported that their satisfactions were more often derived from vicarious experience (such as being *from* the school that won a championship), whereas students in smaller schools reported that their satisfactions came more from direct participation (such as being part of the newspaper staff). Students from small schools more often believed their participation helped them to learn skills, be challenged, engage in important activities, be valued by others, and be involved in an active group.[6] On the other hand, students from large schools more often believed their participation helped them enjoy being part of the organization, learn about school activities, and gain credit for classes.

Fourth, students from small schools reported more achievements in writing, music, drama, and leadership (defined as public recognition of their efforts, such as getting a poem published or winning an election) than did students from large schools.[7]

A key factor underlying most of the school size findings we have discussed is that activities in small schools are chronically understaffed. Students in small schools are almost forced to accept a more active, central, and challenging role because often no one else is available to do the job. Of course, some activities *within* small schools happen to be overstaffed and some *within* large schools are understaffed. The evidence suggests that the outcomes (involvement, challenge, skill development, and being valued) in such situations are like those for small and large schools. That is, the degree of over- or understaffing of a particular activity is the critical variable, rather than the size of the school, although small schools do generally have more understaffed behavior settings than large schools.

Plan and Façade

ANOTHER CHARACTERISTIC OF THE SETTING as a whole that affects learning is the overall plan of the school. A basic architectural distinction may be drawn between schools that are decentralized, with numerous smaller separate buildings, and schools that are centralized, with one or two large buildings. Hundreds of students in three high schools that varied in centralization were interviewed.[8] Students in the decentralized campus needed more time to move from class to class. Time spent in transit restricts between-class student-teacher conversation: Students and teachers interacted 20 percent less in decentralized school classrooms. This suggests that learning itself is adversely affected by decentralized school designs.

The exterior of the school building, its façade, creates an impression. When students in Germany were shown a starkly simple modern façade and another that formed a colorful composite of styles, they preferred the latter.[9] The researcher hypothesized that preferred façades are ones that students care about and will be less likely to vandalize. Think about your secondary school's main façade. How did it make you feel?

School equipment, grounds, and even getting to school influence students. For example, as you would expect, giving young students something to play on, indoors and out, leads to more physical activity on their part.[10] Students who attend schools with larger grounds have lower body mass indexes (BMIs).[11] Some schools have tall fences surrounding entirely paved grounds whereas others have no fences, large areas of grass, and sometimes even trees. In Sweden, more spacious preschool environments with trees, shrubbery, and uneven ground are associated with more physical activity[12] and less inattention[13] than preschools without those features, and in Virginia, more trees and spacious grounds are correlated with more time spent outside by pupils.[14]

Condition, Age, and Neighborhood

DOES THE PHYSICAL CONDITION OF A SCHOOL AFFECT LEARNING? The question is not easy to answer because the quality of a school's physical plant usually is tied to other relevant factors such as neighborhood quality and the socioeconomic status of its students. Nevertheless, a reasonable hypothesis is that a dilapidated learning setting will harm the attitudes of both students and teachers, which will result in less learning. Unfortunately, many schools are in poor condition.[15,16] In dilapidated schools, students are absent more often and score lower on standardized tests.[17]

Trying to learn in a school located in a troubled neighborhood is a challenge for students; difficulties within and without the school itself present many difficulties for disadvantaged students. Environmental stressors, including noise, crowding, and pollution are strongly linked to learned helplessness, which very likely affects learning in an adverse way.[18]

Students do more poorly when schools in bad condition are combined with higher mobility rates for

FIGURE 10-4 Classroom walls naturally affect what students see and learn; they should be carefully arranged.

HOW DO WALLS, CEILINGS, WINDOWS, AND OTHER ELEMENTS OF THE SCHOOL INTERIOR AFFECT LEARNING? You might think this was all worked out years ago, but continuing changes in school design demonstrate that the elusive goal of an ideal classroom has yet to be achieved.

Walls and Ceilings

HOW MIGHT EVEN THE WALLS AND CEILINGS in classrooms matter? In grade-school classrooms, the height of ceilings, the percent of permanent (versus nonpermanent) walls, and the percent of the classroom perimeter that was open (versus having walls) was measured. Teachers and students reported more distractions from in-class noise and from visitors in classrooms with more nonpermanent walls and more open perimeters. Teachers were more satisfied with classrooms that had higher ceilings, and students were also less satisfied with the classroom as a whole when it had more open perimeter space and more nonpermanent walls.[21] In general, this study supports the value of permanent walls that enclose the whole room and higher classroom ceilings. However, ceiling height may even affect behavior, at least for very young students; in a childcare center, more cooperative behavior occurred when ceiling height was more variable.[22]

Classroom walls are often used without much thought. Assignments, posters, and completed work are put up more on the basis of wherever an empty space can be found than on any evidence-based criterion (see Figure 10-4). However, one educator believes that carefully designed classroom walls can have a strong impact on learning.[23] He argues that walls should do one of three jobs, and that each kind of wall should be in a certain location within the classroom.

An **acquisition wall** should include the chalkboard and a bulletin board and be in the front of the room. Only material related to new concepts and concepts that students are struggling with should be placed on this wall; anything else interferes with the acquisition or learning function of this wall. **Maintenance walls** should be along the sides of the room where they may be seen but are less focal than the acquisition wall. These walls are for material that helps

students.[19] Might transferring students to better schools in less-troubled neighborhoods help (even though that would add to their mobility)? As part of a large project in New York City, some students in low-income neighborhoods were transferred and some were not, on a random basis.[20] This did have positive effects on boys aged 11 to 18, whose academic achievement was lower than that of girls in their former school, but which rose to equal the achievement of girls in the better school.

IN SUM *Physical features of the learning setting as a whole affect pupil performance. Many learning experiences are affected by school size, which is often linked to differential staffing of key behavior settings. Students in large schools have an edge in the variety of things they can learn about, yet partly because time at school is limited, students in large schools do not actually participate in more activities than students in small schools. Students in large schools more often learn and enjoy as spectators; students in small schools more often learn and enjoy as participants. In most areas of learning, students in small schools achieve more because they develop competence through direct involvement in activities. However, when activities in large schools are understaffed and activities in small schools are overstaffed, these outcomes may be reversed. Decentralizing school buildings may decrease student-teacher interaction. Not surprisingly, schools in good repair help students learn.*

students review and more fully understand material they already know fairly well. They serve to reassure students. Other material, such as students' work, notices about school activities, etc., should not be on these walls to interfere with the maintenance function. Finally, the **dynamic wall** should be at the back of the room. It is so named because it should be changed often; it contains student work, school notices, holiday decorations, and other material important for organizational or social reasons. The overall rationale of this system is to focus students' attention on learning materials. A small study that compared a typical classroom with one that used the system seemed to show increased learning in the three-wall system.

At the college level, walls can matter too; depending on what is displayed on them, they may influence students' cognitive fatigue. When students were asked to imagine being fatigued, they reported that murals depicting dramatic nature scenes seemed more restorative than even real but plain outdoor scenes seen through windows.[24] The implications for walls in post-secondary institutions are obvious.

Equipment and Attractiveness

EQUIPMENT AND OBJECTS IN THE CLASSROOM are also of obvious importance. Few or old educational materials seem likely to create competition for resources and even aggression in younger students, and apathetic or poor attitudes in older students. Among preschoolers, activities such as type of play are clearly affected by which kinds of equipment are available.[25] This is an obvious but sometimes overlooked facet of the classroom: What happens in the way of learning-related behavior is partly a function of what is available to students.

Having a classroom that seems attractive, comfortable, and has interesting equipment is important; better environments are associated with better student attitudes toward science and better science grades.[26] What happens if students are actually asked what they would like? Five- and 6-year-olds were shown simplified pictures of indoor and outdoor school settings that varied in size, shape, color, complexity, texture, and lighting.[27] Girls preferred settings with more windows, color, texture, shapes, and lighting; boys preferred larger settings than girls did.

Results like these pose a challenge to school designers: how to design a single school that satisfies both genders. This is not a mere matter of taste: children actually learn

better[28] and feel better[29] when their learning environment matches their preferences. When young students can put their preferences into practice by personalizing their classroom environment, their self-esteem increases.[30]

Learning in Familiar Contexts

DECADES AGO, A PSYCHOLOGIST POSTULATED that learning is partially dependent on the background context in which it occurs.[31] If so, this **familiar-context effect** means that students' recall for material learned in a particular place is better in that same place than in a different place. Indeed, several studies support the existence of the effect. For example, college students perform better on exams when they are tested in the room where they learned the material than when they are tested in an unfamiliar room.[32]

In a dramatic field example, when divers were given a list of words to memorize either on dry land or underwater and then asked to recall them either on dry land or underwater, they recalled more words in the same setting in which they learned them, whether that was underwater or on dry land.[33] Apparently, placing the learner in the physical setting where the learning originally occurred (if that is possible) produces the best recall of the learned material. The greater difference between the two places, the greater the decline in performance.[34]

How does the familiar-context effect work? One explanation is that the novel nature of new contexts distracts students. A second explanation is that the learned material is associated with the environmental context through a process like classical conditioning, even though the context had no direct role in the teaching-learning process.[35] An interesting study supports this idea. Participants were asked to recall memorized words in a novel setting and in a familiar setting. When the participants in the novel setting had their associations to the original learning setting strengthened (the experimenter asked them to vividly recall it or showed them slides of it), their performance was about as good as that of participants who learned and recalled words in the same setting. Thus, the familiar-context effect works even when the learner actively remembers the room in which the material was learned, without actually being in the room.[36]

However, not every study supports the familiar-context effect.[37] The studies above examined recall. Distance estimation, a skill we all learn to some extent (although rarely in a formal learning setting) seems to be actually more accurate in novel environments than in familiar ones.[38] It seems to apply more to short-term memory than long-term memory,[39] and for recall memory more than recognition memory.[40,41] (Recall memory is used when a person must remember something without seeing the possible answers; recognition memory is used when a person sees potential answers and must choose the correct one.)

IN SUM *Interior school architecture has a variety of influences on students and teachers. Temporary or low walls increase distractibility. Acquisition, maintenance, and dynamic walls can be strategically used to match students' normal viewing patterns with current versus background educational information. Having a school one finds attractive is associated with better grades, but boys and girls may not find the same decor attractive. When we learn in a given setting, that material is better recalled in the same setting—or when a vivid memory of that setting is evoked.*

NOISE

Some classrooms are noisy, particularly those in urban areas or near trains, busy roads, or airports. Studies in Hong Kong[42] and Greece,[43] as well as many in North America, confirm that noise is prevalent in some schools. By definition, noise is annoying[44] and therefore unacceptable on that basis alone. But does noise hinder learning or other educational processes? Common sense certainly suggests that it does.

Squelching Noise

TEACHERS SPEND MUCH TIME combating noise in the classroom, which suggests that they believe it harms learning. Psychologists with a behaviorist approach have investigated methods of controlling noise, such as installing voice-activated relays. For example, in a home economics class, the teacher allowed students to listen to their favorite radio station as long as the sound level stayed below a certain level. When the sound exceeded this level, the relay automatically turned off the radio.[45] In another class, if a certain noise level was not exceeded for 10 minutes, students were given 2 extra minutes of gym and a 2-minute break from study period.[46] In an elementary school version of this anti-noise strategy, quiet periods in the classroom automatically lit up one light after another on a smiling clown figure, but loud noise extinguished the lights.[47]

These efforts to quell noise are based on the premise that noise harms classroom performance. But what is the scientific evidence? Some authors have argued that under certain conditions noise does not affect performance and that, under others, noise may even enhance performance.[48]

Performance

THE RELATION BETWEEN NOISE AND LEARNING IS COMPLEX BECAUSE ITS EFFECTS DEPEND ON:

- The properties of the noise itself (loudness, pitch, continuity, meaningfulness, reverberation).
- The characteristics of the learner (gender, motivation, personality, intelligence, feelings of control).
- The nature of the task (reading, memorizing, problem solving, listening, motor).
- The situation (lab versus field setting, time of day, whether the noise is expected or unexpected).
- Learning versus performance (whether noise had its effect during the learning of the material or during the performance of material that had been learned).

With these complexities in mind, let us examine the available evidence concerning noise in educational settings. When the psychomotor performance of preschoolers whose daycare was near or far from train noise was assessed, that of children in the nearer preschool was worse.[49] Among 9-year-olds, even those who lived in relatively moderate but chronic noise had memory deficits, compared to similar children who lived in quiet areas.[50]

Other schools are plagued by the noise of aircraft takeoffs and landings. The mathematics and reading achievement of third-graders in an area of Los Angeles that experiences an overflight every 2 minutes of the school day was measured.[51] Their scores were compared with those of students who worked in classrooms that had sound insulation (16 decibels quieter) and with those of children who went to schools out of the air corridor (22 decibels quieter). The reading scores of children in sound-insulated classrooms were significantly higher than those in noisy classrooms. Surprisingly, the scores of children in the sound-insulated classrooms were even higher than those of children in the schools away from the air corridor. The schools away from the air corridor may have been different in some other way (such as poorer quality teaching), or perhaps the children in the sound-insulated classrooms were so glad to come into a relatively quiet classroom from the thunderous outdoors that they were happy to work on their schoolwork!

Taking advantage of a real-life situation that allowed for something close to a true experiment, the performance of children in Germany who lived near an old airport that was closing and a new one that was opening was measured before and after the closure and the opening, at both sites.[52] After the switch, the long-term memory and reading of the children exposed to the noise at the new airport was impaired, and the same processes were improved in the group at the old airport after it closed. Short-term memory also improved in this group after the old airport was closed. At the new airport, the speech perception of the newly noise-exposed group was impaired. The quasi-experimental nature of this study provides very strong evidence that aircraft noise affects learning.

However, speech noise may be more harmful to prose memory than aircraft noise,[53] presumably because both prose and speech involve words, whereas aircraft noise does not.

Arline Bronzaft assessed the impact of noise from trains that passed one side of a New York school frequently. Classrooms on that side of the building were very noisy; those on the other side of the building was relatively quiet. The reading ability of children on both sides was measured, and the reading scores of children on the noisy side of the school were significantly lower.[54] In a classic case of environmental psychology making a difference, the local government was persuaded to install rubber sound-reducing materials on the train tracks. When the children's reading scores were measured again one year later, the differences in scores between the sides of school had disappeared.

However, under some unusual conditions, performance actually improves when noise is louder. In Nigeria, for example, university students were better able to recall words in 100-decibel noise than in 60-decibel noise.[55] The researcher notes that this may be influenced by the Nigerian cultural context, but better performance in higher noise also occurs for certain other groups, as we shall see.

Given such findings, environmental psychologists now try to identify specific conditions in which noise affects performance, and how it does, if it does at all. We now know, for example, that noise affects different kinds of memory. One relatively well-controlled study showed that noise *during* learning reduces later performance more than noise at the time of *recalling* the learned material.[56]

In Sweden, road and aircraft noise during the reading of a text strongly impaired 12-14-year-old children's recall and recognition memory of it,[57] although among 18-20-year-olds, recall memory was impaired but recognition memory was not.[58] Another Swedish study investigated how irrelevant speech and traffic noise affects the episodic and semantic memory of young teens.[59] Episodic memory is about remembering when events occurred, how they changed, and how they are related to each other, and semantic memory is about factual, unchanging knowledge of the world. Only irrelevant speech affected both recognition and recall of both episodic and semantic memory. This probably occurred because speech, which is verbal in nature, interfered with the learning of the text, which of course was verbal in nature.

The effects of noise go beyond memory. In Europe, aircraft noise exposure was significantly associated with increased hyperactivity scores, and road traffic noise was significantly associated with lower scores on a conduct problems measure.[60]

Noise is not merely about the volume of sound. One of its other dimensions is reverberation. Classrooms with more reverberation have adverse effects on speech perception and short-term memory and other tasks, children report the room as noisier, and they say that their relationships with other students and their peers and teachers are worse than do children in classrooms with less reverberation.[61]

We should not forget teachers in all this; they are in classrooms all day too! Their memory is also affected; for example, traffic noise impairs teachers' recall memory.[62] Greater reverberation and noise exposure are also associated with teachers' low job satisfaction, lack of energy after work, interest in leaving the job, lower motivation, and even more sleepiness![63,64]

Personal Influences. The effects of noise clearly vary with characteristics of the learner. One such individual difference is gender. For example, when adults do arithmetic, noise seems to slow women, but not men.[65] First to fifth-grade children worked at visual puzzles in somewhat noisy (70 decibels) or fairly quiet (40 decibels) classrooms. In the noisy conditions, boys solved more puzzles than girls,

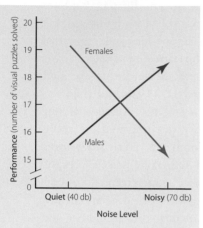

but in the quiet conditions, girls solved more puzzles than boys. [66] These results have an important side note: if the performances of boys and girls in this study had been lumped together (as they are in some noise studies), the data would have (falsely) shown no difference in performance between noisy and quiet conditions. A subsequent study of college students confirmed these results.[67]

FIGURE 10–5 Performance of a moderately difficult task varies with noise and gender. Females, as a group, perform better in quiet; males, as a group, perform better in noise.

This is important because it shows that statistical interactions (in these cases, that girls perform better in quiet and boys perform better in noise) can be overlooked if the results are not broken down by gender (see Figure 10-5). In another example, when students were rated by their teachers on their ability to work independently in a focused way and to follow directions carefully, noise appeared (again) to have no effect until the data for boys and girls were considered separately: then it revealed that noise had a significant negative impact on boys.[68]

A second example of the importance of individual differences is provided by a review of the evidence on noise and learning among exceptional children: it concluded that moderate noise actually helps hyperactive children learn, but not autistic children.[69] Apparently, loud music encourages hyperactive children to be less disruptive and less verbally aggressive, but autistic children often respond to noise by becoming even more passive and repetitive than usual in their actions.

Responses to noise are influenced by personality, too. People with an internal locus of control had better reading comprehension in noisy conditions, and those with an external locus of control were better in quiet conditions.[70]

When introverts were asked to carefully watch certain things, their performance improved over time when the

noise level was lower and worsened over time when noise was louder. This was reversed for extraverts: their performance worsened over time in low noise but improved in louder noise.[71]

Intelligence and originality also appear to affect performance in connection with noise. When the reading scores of 12-year-olds were compared in noisy and quiet conditions, those with higher intelligence test scores performed better in low noise, whereas those with lower test scores actually performed better in louder noise.[72] When university students who were exposed to 60, 80, and 100 decibels were given creativity tasks, highly original (but not other) students were more creative at lower *and* higher noise levels than at the moderate noise level.[73]

Finally, individual differences also matter in terms of **setting congruence** (person-environment matching). For example, children in daycare who were used to noisy conditions performed better in noisy conditions and those who were used to quiet conditions performed better in quiet.[74] Similarly, sixth-graders who preferred a relatively noisy classroom performed better in a noisy room; those who preferred a quiet room performed better in a quiet room.[75]

To integrate some of these results, imagine a class project in which students are asked to read a story looking for details; imagine also that the room is quite noisy. Less intelligent boys with an internal locus of control should do better than more intelligent girls with an external locus of control. Furthermore, if the former also are extraverts, they may do better as time goes on, but if the latter happen to be introverts, may perform worse as time goes on. Those who are used to a noisy classroom should do better than those who are used to a quiet classroom. Of course, this scenario has not been confirmed as a whole in an experiment, but is what we might expect, based on the studies just described.

The Task and the Situation. So far, the role of the material to be learned has not been emphasized. One review of the literature concluded that for difficult tasks, individual differences fade. For example, both ordinary and exceptional children performed difficult tasks less well in noisy conditions than in quiet conditions.[76]

Conditions besides the noise, the learner, and the task can affect learning. For example, student performance can depend on whether the test occurs in the morning or the afternoon and whether the learner expects a recall or recognition test of memory![77] Instructions also matter. When college students were given instructions about solving a spatial puzzle on Rubik's cubes, verbal instructions produced better performance when the room was noisy, but visual instructions produced better performance when the room was quiet.[78]

Type of Noise. Noise, apart from being loud, may be continuous or intermittent, even-pitched or variable, harsh or melodious, meaningful (as in speech or song) or not (as in mechanical noise), and may reverberate much or little. Type of noise affects learning. For example, college students were asked to recall numbers that had been shown to them.[79] They could recall the numbers better when noise in the background was not meaningful than when it was meaningful (speech).

The Aftereffects of Noise. A few investigators have tried to determine whether noise affects learning *after* the noise has ceased. The Los Angeles air corridor study, described earlier, discovered learning decrements even when students were away from the noise they normally experienced. The evidence is mixed, but the majority of studies support the conclusion that the effects of noise outlast the noise itself.[80]

In the best-known examination of this issue, third- to fifth-graders who lived in apartments built over a busy road were tested on their reading ability.[81] All children were tested in quiet conditions, but those who lived in noisier apartments scored lower than those who lived in quieter apartments. In another study, children from homes their parents described as noisy performed more poorly in quiet conditions than children from homes described as quiet.[82]

How does noise harm a learner's performance after it is no longer present? At least four possible reasons have been identified.[83]

1. Noise during the learning process may interfere with moment-to-moment communication between student and teacher. The student may miss key instructions, or the teacher may be forced to repeat instructions often so that less material can be covered in a class period. A cumulative deficiency may then develop over the course of the school year that affects learning even in quiet situations.

2. Noise may interfere with the development of the student's strategies for processing information. Learning is subsequently impaired even in quiet surroundings because the student uses inadequate strategies for thinking about the material to be learned.

3. When noise is beyond the control of students—as it often is—their sense of personal control may be damaged. When they attempt to master a new concept later, even in quiet, that sense of personal control, so important to learning, may not be there.

4. Continued loud noise raises the learner's blood pressure semi-permanently. This chronic increase in physiological arousal may interfere with learning even in quiet periods. We have focused in this section on the effects of noise on performance, but this is evidence that noise also can affect the health of students.

Feelings

BY DEFINITION, NOISE IS UNWANTED SOUND; literally, it is annoying. In classrooms, then, noise is nearly always unwelcome, although we must remember that not all loud sound is noise, at least not for everyone. Nevertheless, perhaps the single most common statement in public schools is "Quiet down, now, class." This may be because teachers report being more noise-sensitive, report more stress from noise, and experience classroom noise as more unpredictable than students.[84]

The bothersomeness (noisiness) of sound varies with certain circumstances and personal qualities. For example, students in general (in both elementary and high school, and in both traditional and open-plan schools) report they are more distracted or annoyed by social conversations[85] or chatter[86] than by schoolwork-related conversations. Even when objective sound levels are the same, sound is more distracting in non-laboratory settings than in laboratory settings and more bothersome when classroom density is higher.

On the personal side, students who report being more noise-sensitive and less able to adapt to noise are, naturally, more annoyed by the same sounds than other students.[87] Teachers are as concerned about *potential* noise as they are about existing noise. Some teachers, especially in open-plan schools, modify their instructional methods to avoid creating noise. However, some effective methods of teaching naturally produce relatively high sound levels. Thus, teachers' fear of noise may sometimes lead them to avoid good teaching methods.[88]

A Solution?

SOMETIMES, FOR EXAMPLE DURING CONSTRUCTION or where road traffic is close and loud, noise is unavoidable. What might be done? One investigator suggests students could put small foam noise-reducers in their ears.[89] His study done in 13 high schools found that these cheap little foamies reduced the loss in performance caused by noise on cognitive and motor tasks. Do you think this is a good idea?

IN SUM *Evidence strongly suggests that noise interferes with learning both while it occurs and, if the learner is subjected to noise for long periods, even after it is gone. Noisy classrooms may impair the performance of girls more than boys, those with an external locus of control, more intelligent students, that of autistic children more than hyperactive children, and that of most children when the task is difficult. Noise may hinder performance by interfering with information processing, lowering the student's perception of control, and increasing blood pressure. Noise is more bothersome in non-laboratory settings, high-density settings, and when it concerns social rather than schoolwork topics. To combat noise, instructors have changed their methods—sometimes sacrificing a good method for a quiet one—and sometimes have successfully employed behavior modification techniques such as sound-activated electrical relays that control reinforcers such as music and extra recess time to reduce sound levels.*

THE HUMAN EYE IS REMARKABLY ABLE TO ADAPT to various levels of light intensity. After a few minutes to adjust, students can read just as fast at 3 foot-candles/32 lux (very dim light) as they can at 53 foot-candles/570 lux (standard classroom lighting).[90] This ability to adjust is fortunate because one study found that the actual light intensity at students' desktops varied from 8 foot-candles/86 lux to 1,000 foot-candles/10,760 lux (the latter results when direct sunlight streams through a window onto a desk).[91] So how does lighting affect performance in an educational setting?

Performance

Type of Light. Are full-spectrum (also known as daylight) fluorescent lamps better than typical cool-white fluorescent lamps? They are more expensive, so their value should be demonstrated before considerable extra funds are spent. First-grade students in four classrooms were filmed during regular school activities.[92] All classrooms were windowless, to control for any effects of sunlight. Two classrooms contained cool-white fluorescent lamps, and two contained daylight lamps. The children in the daylight condition paid more attention to the teacher and were less fidgety. On reading and other tests, one class with the daylight lamps scored better than both classes with cool-white lamps, but the other class with daylight lamps scored worse than both classes with cool-white lamps.

Therefore, on the whole, some learning and learning-related behaviors seem to be affected by the difference in type of light; however, the study's methodology has been criticized.[93] I will list the criticisms because they apply to other studies, not only of lighting but of other environmental variables, and therefore they have broader implications for critically evaluating research reports, something you may have to do in your career.

1. The children apparently were not randomly assigned to classrooms. Thus, the differences in behavior may have preceded the lighting experiment and had nothing to do with light.

2. The total amount of light apparently was not carefully controlled; the classrooms may have had not only different bulbs, but different intensities of light.

3. Teachers may have influenced the results through their teaching methods (they do not seem to have been randomly assigned either) or through their knowledge and expectations of the two kinds of lighting.

4. The experimenters did not explain exactly how they observed and scored the children's behavior. This makes it impossible for subsequent researchers to critique or replicate the study.

5. The observers may have been aware of which lighting condition they were observing (the report did not specify whether the study was double-blind). If they were, their own expectations about the outcome of the study may have influenced the results.

6. The experimenters report no estimate of the observers' inter-rater reliability. We cannot be sure the behaviors were measured similarly across observers or consistently over time for the same observer.

7. The report was not clear whether the observations were done at the same time in the four classrooms. If they were not, differences could be due to natural fluctuations in classroom activity, such as increased restlessness just before lunch and recess breaks.

Most published lighting studies have carefully controlled most of these sources of error. In one of these, college women performed learning-related tasks under cool-white and daylight lamps.[94] The experimenters even controlled for veiling reflection, a source of error not on the list of problems above. (Veiling reflection results when a light source bounces off a work surface into a person's eyes.) The conclusion of this well-controlled study was that basic information processing related to decision-making was better under daylight (full-spectrum) fluorescent lamps than under common cool-white fluorescent lamps.

Another well-controlled study found that some effects of lighting require weeks of exposure before they appear.[95] Several tests and observations of elementary school children's behavior were made over 20 weeks under cool-white and daylight (full-spectrum) bulbs. After 2 weeks, no significant differences were found. However, after 7 to 8 weeks, children exposed to daylight bulbs experienced a significant *decrease* in the strength of their grip and in

the number of gross motor movements, and an *increase* in hand steadiness (see Figure 10-6). These findings are consistent with the hypothesis that cool-white bulbs are more physiologically arousing than daylight bulbs.

Two other relatively well-controlled studies show that cool-white fluorescent lamps increase the hyperactive behavior of children who are already prone to autism and other emotional disturbances.[96,97] In the first of these, autistic children engaged in more repetitive behaviors under fluorescent lamps than under incandescent lamps. The increases ranged from zero to a doubling of repetitive behavior, suggesting again that the effects of lighting vary across individuals.[98] Despite these results, a review of studies conducted between 1941 and 1999 concluded that full-spectrum lighting has no dramatic effects on behavior or health.[99]

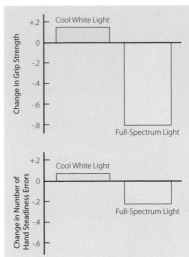

FIGURE 10–6 Lighting and elementary pupil performance are related. In a carefully designed study, children who worked for several weeks at school in full–spectrum lighting made fewer errors on a hand steadiness task than those who worked under fluorescent lighting. However, fluorescent lighting produced greater grip strength than the full–spectrum lighting did.

Amount of Light. As noted earlier, the human eye is very flexible in its light requirements. Although certain tasks require more light because the object is difficult to see, most classrooms do not fall into this category. Although the amount of light in an educational setting may not be crucial, it still can have an important role to play. In one study, students in classrooms with more natural (window) light scored 7 to 26% better or faster in math and reading tests.[100]

However, different students may learn better under different levels of light. One such individual difference, the **dark-interval threshold** (DIT), has been shown to affect children's reading performance.[101] DIT is the shortest dark interval between the presentation of two bright images that a person can detect. Students with short DITs read more accurately in bright light than in dim light, but students with long DITs read more accurately in dim light than bright light. The amount of light students prefer also may affect their performance. Those who prefer bright light perform better in bright light, and those who prefer dim light perform better in dim light.[102]

Hue (Color). Contemporary aesthetic standards seem to favor bright hues for learning settings. Whether this preference merely reflects today's fashions or actually helps to promote learning is subject to debate. One study reported in the popular press[103] claimed that IQ scores measured in bright rooms (blue, orange, yellow) were 26 points higher than those in drab rooms (white, brown, black). A 53 percent increase in friendly behaviors in orange rooms was also reported. Many of the problems with experimental control listed earlier were also present in this study, so these dramatic results must be classified as suggestive rather than conclusive.

A study that carefully controlled the properties of color in a specially constructed learning setting found that, contrary to conventional wisdom, red was no more arousing than blue or yellow. Performance of math, reading, and motor tasks did not significantly vary in red, blue, and yellow rooms.[104] Similar results have been found in other studies.[105] However, in child care centers, variation in wall color (as opposed to uniform color) has been associated with more cooperative behavior.[106]

Feelings and Beliefs

LIGHTING AND COLOR ARE IMPORTANT TO MANY PEOPLE. The media frequently carry stories connecting certain kinds of light with psychological and physiological disturbances. Most of this research has focused on fluorescent lighting. Because it is undeniably more energy efficient and economical than traditional incandescent lighting, fluorescent lighting gradually has become standard in schools and most other public building interiors.

Despite the prevalence of fluorescent lighting, few find it aesthetically pleasing, and many consider it a necessary evil rather than welcome progress.[107] My students and I discovered that a large percentage of people believe that fluorescent lighting is harmful to health.[108] Several improved kinds of fluorescent lamps have been developed in response to these criticisms, such as the full-spectrum or daylight lamp mentioned above. It radiates a spectrum closer to that of natural sunlight, which accounts for its support. However, as noted earlier, it is more expensive, and the evidence for its superiority is unclear.

Health and Stress

LIGHT CAN AFFECT HEALTH when people receive too little natural light, but few people are shielded from sunlight to that extent. Health problems said to be caused by lighting type itself may of course be caused by other factors.

In Sweden, students in windowless classrooms with full-spectrum lamps experienced two-month delays in the annual spring production of morning cortisol, a stress hormone, which is associated with sociability and the ability to concentrate.[109] The authors believe their findings are sufficiently important to recommend that no child be placed in a classroom without windows or full-spectrum lighting.

Fluorescent lighting in good condition has not been shown to cause any negative health effects. However, complaints about them are heard. Do these complaints merely reflect a nostalgic preference for the old familiar forms of light (incandescent bulbs), or are they really a menace to our well-being? Probably not. However, as is true for every aspect of the physical environment, the preferences of individuals who work or live in a building should be respected when possible. In principle, we should not have to demonstrate that something in the environment fries our brains or causes insanity before it is replaced. On the other hand, if one option costs significantly more than another, the space manager (the school board, in this case) may be forced to consider whether the cheaper alternative (fluorescent lighting) actually harms students and teachers or merely displeases them.

What about color? Many believe that greens and blues are calming and that reds and oranges are arousing. Actually, the evidence is not clear, partly because many studies that seem to support this were done by asking people to report how they would feel after looking at small colored cards such as you find in paint stores. However, one study in actual rooms did find that blue was more calming than red or yellow.[110] Another very careful study in real rooms found no differences in physiological measures of arousal between red, yellow, and blue rooms.[111] Is it possible that we merely *think* color affects us, perhaps because we associate colors with hot and cold objects in nature (reddish-orange fires and cold, blue waters)?

IN SUM *Incandescent lighting is preferred by many, but it is more expensive than fluorescent lighting. Full-spectrum lighting has a more natural range of light, but is more* *expensive than typical cool-white lighting, and is not clearly better (or worse) for people; meanwhile, fluorescent lighting has not been shown to have dramatic negative effects on performance or health, although it does seem to affect some basic kinds of cognitive and motor activities. As with noise, the important effects may be on specific subgroups of individuals; when studies of whole classes or schools are done, large effects on a few learners may be obscured by the absence of effects on most learners.*

INDOOR CLIMATE

Performance

INDOOR CLIMATE—TEMPERATURE, HUMIDITY, AND AIR CIRCULATION—CERTAINLY AFFECTS LEARNING, and occasionally health: pollutants from outdoors and from old pools of water in ventilation systems may contribute to the high number of students suffering from asthma.[112] Indoor climate is not an important issue in many schools where temperature and humidity are well-controlled.

However, where indoor climate does vary noticeably, learning is affected in complex, and sometimes unexpected, ways. For example, you might suppose that the most comfortable indoor climate would produce the best performance. This is not true. The best performance by British students on tests occurred when the temperature was slightly *below* the optimal comfort level.[113] Performance was also better when humidity was low and air circulated moderately. Similar findings have been reported in work settings, as we shall see in that chapter.

Some relatively simple relations between indoor climate and performance have been reported. In the gymnasium, rising temperatures are correlated with poorer fitness and performance.[114] In Sweden, the performance of language tasks by elementary school children was worse

in warm than in moderate temperatures.[115] In Portland, Oregon, air-conditioned and non-air-conditioned schools, matched geographically and in the socioeconomic status of the students, were selected for study. Comparisons of performance in subjects ranging from spelling to languages to mathematics were made. In schools with no indoor climate controls, the temperatures were higher and fluctuated more; when the temperature rose in these schools, the performance of students declined.[116] These effects occurred only when the outdoor temperature was relatively warm; in the cool fall of the year, performance was not correlated with temperature.

Children in another study read in controlled temperatures ranging from 68°-86°F/20°-30°C.[117] Their reading performance declined as the temperature rose, but at the highest temperature, they rose again slightly! We might intuitively expect that performance changes steadily in one direction or the other as the temperature increases or decreases, but the relation may not be linear after all. (Recall the temperature and aggression debate in an earlier chapter?)

Feelings

BOTH TEACHERS AND LEARNERS want the classroom atmosphere to be pleasant, of course, but no single set of conditions is pleasant for everyone. Engineers have sought the perfect set of temperature and humidity parameters within which most people feel comfortable for many years. Such standards have been published, but they are thermal comfort envelopes (*ranges* of temperature and humidity levels, rather than precise numbers) within which most individuals prefer indoor climates.

The type of activity engaged in affects climate preferences. Clearly, students who are physically active (e.g., in the gym) will have different preferences than students who are reading at a desk. Another factor is the length of time spent in the classroom. Students change classes or go outside for recesses. Teachers and students may develop preferences for different climates because they have different patterns of physical activity, and students change temperature and humidity levels more often as they move in and out of the classroom.[118]

IN SUM *Few simple, direct relations exist between indoor climate and educational behavior; some combination of person and setting variables may "mediate, transmit, modify, or resist" the variations of climate.*[119] **Research is difficult because indoor climate is composed of many possible patterns of temperature, humidity, and air movement. Perhaps the best-supported conclusion is that performance is best in slightly cool but not humid classrooms.**[120] **Even when care is taken in the control of indoor climates, the levels of temperature and humidity inevitably must be a compromise that considers individual differences in amount of clothing, type of activity, and indoor-outdoor movement.**

SPACE

THE AMOUNT OF SPACE AVAILABLE and how that space is arranged and designed in learning settings has been researched considerably more than indoor climate. Each major outcome (performance, feelings, and social behavior) is considered as a function of spatial density, spatial arrangements, and design.

Performance

Density. Are high-density classrooms a hazard to student achievement? One study of 24 years' worth of school records showed that higher density actually was associated with *higher* achievement scores,[121] although class densities in this study were never very high. In contrast, a meta-analysis of class size (which probably is strongly related to classroom density) that examined 725 comparisons of larger and smaller classes in 77 different studies found that achievement increased as class size decreased.[122] However, this trend was most pronounced for class sizes in the 15 to 20 range, not for larger classes. When special education students worked in low or high social density, their on-task time was greater in low density.[123] Yet other studies find no effect of density. Clearly, high density harms learning under some, but not all, conditions.

Part of the confusion may be caused by teachers' perceptions of larger classes. In a rare experimental study, 62 fourth-grade classes and teachers were randomly assigned to class sizes of 16, 23, 30, or 37 for two school years in a row.[124] Student performance across numerous measures did not vary with class size. (One exception was that mathematics achievement was better in classes of 16 compared to 30 or 37.) However, 81 percent of the teachers *believed* that student performance in small classes was generally better.

Mobility almost certainly is one harmful moderating factor; higher classroom density cuts into performance when the task requires mobility or physical interaction among students.[125] Reading comprehension on a given afternoon is not necessarily affected simply because there are many students in the room. However, performance in a laboratory where students must move about from a supply counter to a work space to instruments might well be damaged by high density. Similarly, one might expect that learning in a pure lecture format would not be affected by increasing density—as long as enough air to breathe and space to write are available. But learning that relies on discussion in groups might be harmed by increases in density.[126]

As we have seen, the effects of classroom density depend on several factors, such as student motivation.[127] Students read a long story in either high or low social density, studied it in lecture, discussion, or independent-study conditions, and were either motivated by possible monetary prizes or not. Achievement on a multiple-choice test was, in general, greater in low density. However, it was also affected by learning format; it was lowest when students worked independently, and surprisingly, it was greater in the low-motivation condition. The researchers explain the latter in terms of too much arousal (e.g., high motivation plus high density plus the stimulation from group discussion) can actually reduce performance. Again, gender can be one of those other factors: performance was hindered by greater spatial densities, but only for girls, and more behavior problems were found, but only for boys.[128] In classrooms, high density must be considered as one arousal agent, but in conjunction with other influences on student performance.

Crowding, as distinct from density, may occur when a learner feels that the available space does not allow for appropriate distance between others, perceives a shortage of resources, such as the lack of needed equipment and materials, or defines a certain combination of density, task, and other individuals present as crowded.[129] In another demonstration that density and crowding are not always the same, only students whose performance in a high-density room was below average found the room crowded.[130]

Sometimes whether behavior is affected by density or by crowding is unclear. In a study of kindergartners, attentiveness to the teacher was measured under two conditions: when the children crowded round to listen to a story versus when they sat in separate, dispersed spaces.[131] Attentiveness was clearly greater when the children were not close together. At least four possible reasons for this may be advanced. In the dispersed condition, (1) each child was able to see and hear better, (2) each child experienced less interference—or attention-diverting camaraderie—from other children, (3) fewer children defined the dispersed condition as crowded, or (4) having a space of one's own clarified activities and reduced conflict between children.

To sort out such explanations, density and other relevant variables must be systematically varied, which is not always easy. When density and the amount of materials available to children were carefully varied, greater density and fewer materials resulted in "behavior inconsistent with learning."[132] The most learning-related behavior occurred when density was high *and* amount of materials was high (see Figure 10-7).

In high-density conditions, learning complex concepts may be more difficult than learning simple concepts.[133] Lurene Haines and I examined student performance of arithmetic concepts that are relatively complex for 10-year-olds as a function of density and territoriality.[134] Four classrooms of the same size that naturally varied in social density (32 students versus 22 students) were selected. In one high and one low-density classroom, territoriality was encouraged; students were assured they would keep the same desk, and they were given name tags to affix to their desks. In the other class, the normal policy of periodic desk-switching was in force, and students were discouraged from personalizing their desks. Pre- and posttest scores on arithmetic tests over a 6-week period were administered. Students in low-density classes scored significantly better than students in high-density classes. In addition, an interaction between density and territoriality was found: in high-density classes, students whose territoriality was encouraged learned more than students whose territoriality was not encouraged, but in low-density classes, students

whose territoriality was encouraged learned less. Thus, low density is better for learning, but if a class is stuck with high density, encouraging students to feel that they have a secure place of their own helps.

Among preschoolers, the chief effect of varying spatial density in the range of 25-75 sq. ft./2.3-7 m² per child is to influence the amount and kind of activities they engage in.[135] When given more space, the children engage in more running, chasing, and vigorous uses of their play equipment. When given less space, more physical contact and more use of equipment for climbing and sliding occurs. Using social density (the number of children per activity center) as the measure, as the ratio increases, off-task time increases.[136]

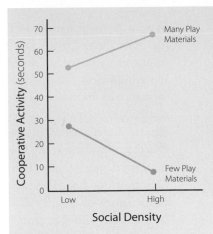

FIGURE 10–7 Cooperation among pre-school children partly depends on so-cial density and resource availability. More cooperation occurs when more play materials are available. As social density increases, the cooperation of those with half as many play materials declines to almost zero.

Teachers, of course, also spend much time in classrooms. How do they respond to higher density? One of two architecturally identical junior high schools experienced a 43 percent decrease in pupils, which we can assume resulted in decreased social density in many classrooms. In this school, teacher absenteeism significantly declined.[137] In denser elementary school classrooms, teachers (but not students) said they experienced more restricted movement and crowding.[138] When we recall that in many classrooms, students sit while teachers circulate, this makes sense.

In classrooms with cluster seating, larger clusters make students feel more distracted and crowded than teachers do, but small clusters make teachers feel more distracted and crowded than students.[139] This contrast in crowding presumably is also caused by the different ways that students and teachers use classroom space. Their different perspectives seem to affect crowding. When students, teachers, and administrators were asked to place figures in a model classroom to the point where one more figure would make the room crowded, students inserted the fewest figures. Teachers inserted more, and administrators inserted the most figures into the model classrooms.[140]

Spatial Arrangements and Classroom Design. Can learning be facilitated by certain furniture arrangements or by improved decor? What are the effects of open classrooms? Do windowless classrooms harm performance? Can performance be improved by selecting certain seat positions in the learning setting? Little evidence is available about the effects of chair arrangements on learning itself, but their effects on learning-related behaviors such as paying attention, participation, use of learning materials, and grades have been studied. For example, most[141-143] but not all[144] comparisons of traditional rows versus the newer cluster-style seating find that rows produce up to twice as much educationally oriented student activity and one-third as much disruptive activity. Single large-circle arrangements produce more on-task learning activity than rows.[145] Table arrangements may produce more interaction among students.[146] Visual barriers, such as walls and partitions, appear to affect the social behavior of 2-year-olds; when they are visually separated from adults, they behave in a more self-centered way and get into more conflicts.[147] Visual access to adults appears to encourage more friendly, cooperative play in this age group.

Does changing the overall design of the learning setting, rather than merely the seating arrangements, affect learning-related activities? A "soft" classroom, mentioned at the beginning of the chapter, resulted in significantly better grades on Introductory Psychology tests. In a comparison of two third-grade classrooms that were similar in most respects, students in one class had longer attention spans, were more involved in their schoolwork, and were less noisy.[148] The comparison was a quasi-experiment rather than a true experiment, but the differences appeared to be caused by these differences:

1. In the better class, the teacher's desk was in a corner. She could not easily direct activities from there and therefore was forced to move throughout the room, which resulted in closer supervision of students. In the other class, the teacher's desk was in the middle of the room; she tended to sit there rather than move through the class to supervise students more personally.

2. Desks in the better class were arranged so that a maximum of two or three students could work together, but in the other class, up to 12 desks were placed in each cluster.

3. Different activities in the better class were separated by barriers (bookcases, etc.). In the other class, incompatible activities (such as ones that produce noise versus others that require concentration) were not very well separated.

IN ANOTHER QUASI–EXPERIMENT, changes to a classroom were made to meet a teacher's specific goals, which were to increase use of certain classroom areas that students were not using much, to make each classroom area more versatile, so that a variety of activities could occur in each one, and to increase the students' use of learning materials that they could manipulate and rearrange themselves.[149] Furniture was rearranged, and tables, shelves, and individual study carrels were added. The children's behavior was carefully measured before the changes were made, and some time was allowed to pass after the changes were made, so that behavioral changes could not be ascribed to the mere novelty of the design alterations. Then the children's behavior was measured again; the design changes did result in improvements in the learning-related behaviors desired by the teacher.

In a daycare center, children had difficulty staying involved in activities. Because one of the main ways that preschoolers (and everyone!) learn is through involvement, the spatial arrangements of the daycare were analyzed, and certain design changes were recommended.[150] Clear boundaries were established between different activity areas, traffic paths were rearranged so that children were not forced to cut through the playhouse to get to the blocks, and learning materials were placed in easy-to-reach, clearly organized arrangements. Again, comparing previous behavior with post-design changes in learning-related behavior showed that children spent more time involved in learning activities and in more constructive play.

In a major Canadian study involving over 1,000 preschoolers in 38 classrooms observed over three years, randomly arranged classrooms were compared with deliberately arranged (that is, five groups of educational activities were placed in specific locations) classrooms.[151] The rest of the program (time schedules, equipment, teacher-student communication) was similar in the random and deliberate classrooms. Children in deliberate classrooms had significantly better scores on creative productivity and creative skills, generalization of number concepts, language use, and utilization of pre-reading materials. Carefully planned locations for different kinds of educational activities appears to be an important factor in preschool development.[152] Finally, when 130 classrooms were surveyed, few had special areas for reading (library corners), but where those were in place, students engaged in more literature activities.[153]

What about the decor of classrooms? The effect of carpeting and thin screens (for visual but not auditory privacy) were investigated in a nursery school.[154] Carpeting increased the amount of time the staff spent in direct, close, educational activities with the children. The screens led teachers to engage in more administrative, noneducational activities. Carpeted rooms with no visual screens produce the highest teacher-student involvement in the nursery school. Carpeting seems to allow more direct interaction because noise is lower, and the absence of screens discourages teachers from leaving to do paperwork, because they are more visible to others.

Some educators believe that classrooms should be decorated with many pictures, posters, illustrations, and other visual images. The educational effects of visual complexity (number of colorful pictures and posters on the wall) were examined.[155] Perhaps surprisingly, 8- and 10-year-old children actually learned best in the plainest learning setting; the more background visual stimulation provided by the room's decor, the less children learned. We must be cautious about generalizing these results to actual classrooms, because this study took place in a trailer, the only persons present were the experimenter and one child at a time, and the time span of the study was short. Nevertheless, the study suggests that plentiful visual stimulation may interfere with learning. Another study of decor investigated the persistence of children in rooms decorated with happy, neutral, and sad pictures.[156] Children in the happy settings persisted longest on their work. Presumably very few teachers would display sad pictures anyway, but the study underscores the idea that learning-related behavior can be affected by room decor.

Do windows in classrooms make any difference? Windowless schools have been built assuming that costs will decline because the school offers fewer glass targets to vandals, because fewer windows means lower heating and cooling costs, and windows supposedly distract students from classwork. Windowless environments have little positive *or* negative impact on the achievement of students.[157] This does not mean, however, that students *like* windowless classrooms, as we shall see later.

Is there a best place to sit in the traditional classroom? The center or middle of the classroom has been called the **action zone**. Attention to this aspect of classrooms began with a very large 1921 study of college students in which seating was more or less random (alphabetical). Grades in the front rows were 3 to 8 percent lower than those in the middle rows, and grades then declined toward the rear, with a sharp drop in the last few rows.[158] A modern study showed a similar pattern when students could choose their own seats.[159] Later research reported that students who sit in the action zone get higher grades[160] and participate more.[161,162] They are more attentive, spend more time in learning-related activities, and are absent less.[163-165] The action zone appears to produce better grades.

So, in that class in which you are having trouble, all you have to do is move into the action zone, right? Not necessarily. Not every study finds the action-zone effect,[166,167] or qualified results. In one, participation was higher in the action zone, but only when students selected their own seats; grades were not higher either when students chose seats or when they did not.[168] In another, higher grades occurred in the action zone when students selected their seats, but no differences in participation occurred.[169]

Perhaps students who sit in the action zone are those who already have considerable interest and talent in that subject; their success may not be caused by their choice of seats, but rather may reflect their liking for that subject, or other factors. We do know, for example, that students who choose action-zone seating are zealous or even overzealous,[170] and have higher self-esteem,[171,172] or at least have higher self-esteem about their school work.[173] Women choose seats in the front more often and receive higher grades, at least in psychology.[174] Students are very aware of the implications of seating location for their social lives, their control over classmates and teachers, and their academic accomplishments.[175]

On the other hand, perhaps the action zone itself does matter, in the sense that students are able see and hear better, become more involved in the course, receive more attention from the teacher, and consequently feel better about themselves and school. In real classrooms, at least the first of these assertions probably is true. Students who like a subject and have a knack for it gravitate to the action zone, and from that vantage point, they see, hear, and may be treated better than students outside the action zone.

But the question remains: Can one really benefit from by moving into the action zone when one otherwise might sit in a back corner? One researcher decided to apply the full experimental approach to the question by randomly assigning some students to the action zone and others outside it, and allowed students in an equivalent class to choose their own seats.[176] Regardless of whether students were assigned seats or given their choice, those who sat in the middle got better grades than those who sat on the sides; they also liked the course more and liked the instructor more. Perhaps the conflicting results may be explained in part by taking differences in students into account. The role of individual differences was examined by randomly assigning students previously known to be vocal or quiet to the action zone and outside it.[177] (see Figure 10-8). Vocal students who were assigned to the action zone participated much more than vocal students who were assigned to sit outside the action zone. However, students known to be quiet did *not* participate more after being assigned to the action zone. One reviewer of this literature concluded that the action zone has little effect on performance but does influence attitudes and participation.[178]

One other major space factor may affect learning. This is the **open-plan classroom**, in which large spaces (usually in grade schools or secondary schools) are shared by more than one class. Many were built over the last several decades, and many studies examined their effectiveness. Open-plan classrooms often have noise problems; open-plan preschools in Scotland sometimes reached 98 decibels, and students received significantly less instruction in educationally valuable activities than did students in more traditional preschools with more separated spaces.[179] However, not every study reaches negative conclusions. When the reading performance of elementary students in open classrooms in which the noise levels were naturally high and low, no differences in accuracy or speed were found either for good or poor readers.[180]

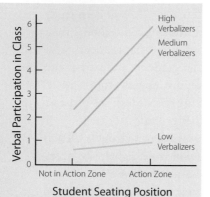

FIGURE 10–8 Participation in class depends on the students' pre–existing tendencies to contribute to discussions and where the students fit in the room. High and medium verbalizers contribute more if they sit in the central "action zone," but quiet students do not.

Probably the biggest single problem with open-plan classrooms is that teachers often are not adequately trained in their use. Many teachers try to apply teaching methods suited to traditional walled classrooms to open classrooms, with unsatisfactory results. When 21 open-space schools were examined, two-thirds did not have educational programs suitable for open space.[181] From a behavior-setting theory perspective, open space without an appropriate program is a violation of **synomorphy**, the Roger Barker principle that physical and social aspects of the setting should fit together well.

Teachers who use traditional methods in open-plan schools often try to create walls with whatever materials are at hand—bookcases, dividers, file cabinets, easels, and so on.[182] They are upset at noise distraction, which probably hinders their effectiveness as teachers. They may avoid useful but relatively loud activities in their own space in order to avoid bothering neighboring classes.[183] Open-plan schools, then, have decidedly negative implications for learning when the educational program is geared to the traditional walled classroom.

When open-plan classrooms are matched with open-plan teaching methods, which include team-teaching and less frequent but more intimate contact with students, some positive changes result.[184] For example, students seem to develop more initiative and autonomy. Because more activities occur simultaneously, students may learn to cope with distraction better than those in quieter, more focused traditional classrooms. If so, children educated in open-plan classrooms should be able to concentrate better, which should allow them to work more persistently. This idea was tested by giving puzzles to students from open-plan and traditional classrooms; the open-plan students worked more persistently on the puzzles.[185] On the negative side, students in open-plan classrooms (even with appropriate programs) may spend more time in transition between activities and on off-task activities[186] and spend less time than those in traditional classrooms actually engaged in educational activity.[187]

Overall, neither open-plan nor traditional classrooms produce clearly superior student achievement in general,[188] but the advocates of open-plan education never claimed it would produce higher achievement levels. Instead, open-plan schools are promoted as a more suitable arrangement by those who think of learners as active, curious, and responsible.

Therefore, when students are not motivated and responsible, open-plan classrooms may not be appropriate. Children with socioeconomic, intellectual, or developmental problems perform worse in open-space classrooms.[189-191] The average student may score higher on standard achievement tests in a traditional setting,[192,193] and the good student may score higher in open-plan classrooms.[194] The parents of creative children may prefer open classrooms because they have educational goals other than scoring high on achievement tests, such as the development of their child's social or artistic skills.

However, when school administrators believe there are enough problems with open-plan classrooms, they are faced with the problem of reshaping large open spaces to fit traditional teaching styles. Environmental psychologists have been involved in remodeling them. The addition and careful placement of sound-absorbent partitions can turn a poorly functioning classroom into one where more relevant questions are asked of the teacher, traffic flows are separated from work areas, and privacy is increased.[195]

As I stress throughout the book, behavior is a product of the interaction of personal attributes, the sociocultural context, and the physical environment. One study of open-space classrooms should be singled out because it paid particular attention to these interactions. When both the student's degree of motivation and the type of classroom were used to predict achievement and other learning-related behavior, students who were self-directed but not academically inclined had more discipline problems in traditional classes than in open-plan classrooms.[196] However, the same students had higher achievement scores in traditional classrooms than in open-plan classrooms (see Figure 10-9).

Students can also play a role in classroom design and its outcomes. In a study early in my career, when I was teaching a laboratory, I arranged the chairs in the room in such a way that it was difficult (but not impossible) to move around the room.[197] I then watched students as they went about their business, and discovered that very, very few students attempted to ease their mobility and comfort by moving the furniture and chairs (it was not difficult to do so). The students were doing a good job with their lab task, but they were almost entirely unaware of their surroundings, even though the surroundings were causing them to squeeze between desks and chairs many times. I call this phenomenon **environmental numbness**, and have seen similar behavior in many other settings (not to mention numbness in the sense of a lack of awareness that one may be causing to the planet by not engaging in pro-environmental behavior). Recently, a study in Brazil took up this theme, advocating that students become more aware of the possibilities to increase their physical comfort in classrooms.[198] Students (and many others in life) seem to think that some unknown "they" want furniture a certain way, yet "they" often do not care or even exist. Unless a clear rule against doing so exists, move that furniture around until it suits you!

The design of the physical setting must not be considered separately from what Roger Barker, Paul Gump, and other ecological psychologists call the *program*.[199] In the case of the learning setting, the program is the social environment, including the curriculum and the teaching style. A particular physical setting might be very beneficial for one educational program, but not for another. This means that much research that examines the value of particular physical arrangements for particular educational programs remains to be done.

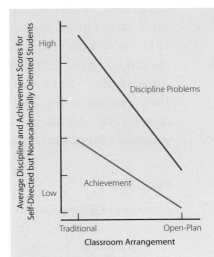

FIGURE 10-9 Classroom arrangements affect student outcomes. Self-directed but non-academically inclined students, for example, seem to have fewer discipline problems in open-plan arrangements compared to those in traditional arrangements, but they also demonstrate lower achievement in open-plan arrangements.

IN SUM *The amount, arrangement, and design of space in educational settings is very important for classroom performance and related behaviors. High density may affect learning when the activity involves physical movement around the classroom, when learning depends on some classroom resource that is less plentiful than the number of learners, when a particular situation seems crowded to a learner, and when the concept to be learned is complex. Among preschoolers, high density alters the child's choice of activities. Numerous classroom arrangement features have been linked to educational performance. Benefits appear to accrue in classrooms that have the teacher's desk in a corner, have different kinds of activities carefully arranged and separated, possess library corners, and are carpeted. Action-zone seating benefits some students. Open-space classrooms have positive outcomes when teachers use techniques suited to open-plan classrooms and students have fewer behavioral or other problems. They can be noisy, but also can foster student autonomy. All these findings depend in part on grade level and teaching style.*

Feelings

OUR SURVEY TO THIS POINT has mainly focused on classroom *behavior*. How do the physical features of learning settings affect the *feelings* of students and teachers?

Density. Increasing the number of individuals per unit of space (density) does not necessarily lead to increased discomfort (crowding). Nevertheless, high density in classrooms often does, in fact, lead to crowding. When over 30 classes that met in the same college classroom were examined, as the number of students in the class rose from 5 to 22, the number of complaints about room size and ventilation approximately doubled.[200] High density usually increases discomfort, but performance may not be affected if the task does not last very long. If all of one's classes are over-populated, however, crowding discomfort may well lead to performance decrements.

Spatial Arrangements and Classroom Design. Many secondary students' feelings about the layout of schools may be represented by one who said in an interview:

> I'd like comfortable chairs...ones that have cushions so your back doesn't hurt and your bottom either. I'd like us sitting around...looking at each other, not in a line...I'd like a sink, where you could get water to drink, and you wouldn't have to ask the teacher to go down the hall...We could have our books in a bookcase, and we wouldn't have to sit in the same place all the time...most of all [a skylight, so I could] just look up and see the sky and the clouds and the sun...and you'd like it better, being in school.[201]

Other students are asking for some of the same design elements, but for some new ones, too. In 1990, British Columbia students were asked to write essays on "My School."[202] Besides skylights, they suggested that classrooms should have lofts, playhouses, refrigerators, and computers that allow them to access resources outside the school, such as libraries and museums (at least the computer part has often come true). Classrooms should have emergency supplies, they said, such as blankets in the case of earthquakes. They suggested that merely having windows is not enough—there are too many awful or sterile views out too many windows. Playgrounds should include gardens, some suggested.

Many educators have wondered why we persist in making classrooms hard and linear when many students would prefer softer, rounded ones. Several possible reasons may be advanced:

- The burden of advocating and executing changes usually falls on an overworked teacher who often ends up accepting the traditional classroom rather than pursuing change in addition to normal duties.

- Custodians often complain that such changes upset their work routines.

- Administrators resist offering financial support.

- Some educators, parents, and even students believe the hard, linear classroom is best for learning.

- Whether or not any of these beliefs are valid, they usually triumph. Most classrooms remain relatively hard and linear. Some researchers have explored the roots of these preferences for the traditional classroom. Some teachers' support for it appears to be related, in part, to their need for control. When teachers were asked to choose among a variety of classroom layouts, those with a high need for control selected traditional formations in which the teacher was in a clear position of control, but those with a low need for control preferred formations in which the teacher was not so obviously in a controlling position.[203]

Satisfaction with the classroom is also, in part, a function of its physical characteristics. When a room has fewer solid walls, teachers believe there are more visual and aural distractions.[204] When a room has lower ceilings, they report more visual and movement distractions. As noted above, satisfaction is also a function of synomorphy, the congruence between program and setting. Teachers who use open-plan teaching methods and operate in open-plan environments are more satisfied than teachers in traditional classrooms.[205]

Satisfaction also depends, of course, on individual and other differences. For example, students also differ in their spatial preferences. Troubled adolescents prefer larger interpersonal distances than others, and students prefer larger interpersonal distances in the morning than in the afternoon.[206] Open-plan classrooms seem to cause greater anxiety about schoolwork among students than traditional classrooms do.[207]

Once again, these results suggest that no single classroom design is likely to satisfy everyone. Is it possible, then, to build a school that makes most of its users happy? Probably not, but one solution is to create **pluralistic schools**—designs that accommodate differences in preference by providing several kinds of space within a single school.[208] When schools are built or remodeled, uniform designs might be avoided in favor of a variety of classroom plans that satisfy the needs of different users. Class size and density in a pluralistic school might be arranged so that problem students are given a little more room and schedules arranged so that students engage in more individual work in the morning and more interactive work, such as discussions and labs, in the afternoon.

Many students express a desire for more time alone, away from the harried life in the classroom. Open-plan classrooms, in particular, can be noisy and overstimulating.[209,210] Most of us need to get away from it all at least briefly during the day, but public school children are given few opportunities to be alone. Of course, schools have the responsibility to preserve the health and welfare of their students, but must that require constant surveillance?

Windows have little impact on actual academic performance, but studies of student feelings about windows have reached mixed conclusions. One early investigation found generally positive feelings about windowless classrooms,[211] but later surveys report ambivalence or dislike of them.[212] Perhaps the reason for the mixed results is time: preference for windowless classrooms at one new school turned into dislike after one year.[213] The belief that students in windowless classrooms are deprived of something important received support in an intriguing study that asked children in both kinds of classrooms to draw pictures of schools.[214] Students in the windowless school included significantly more windows in their drawings than did

FIGURE 10–10 High–density classrooms may harm academic performance and create dissatisfaction.

students in schools with windows. One might conclude that when students are deprived of windows, they psychologically compensate by creating mental images of a school that includes what their actual school lacks.

So far, the feelings or perceptions of those who are neither students nor teachers have not been considered: principals, office staff and visiting parents. When such outsiders were shown slides of vacant classrooms that were either open-plan or traditional, and were either neat or messy, they inferred that teachers in neat classrooms were significantly more organized, responsive, and creative than teachers in messy classrooms.[215] They also felt that open-plan teachers probably were more responsive and creative than teachers in traditional classrooms, and that students in neat classrooms probably were happier and better behaved than students in messy classrooms. Classroom arrangements send messages to outside observers; the messages may or may not be valid, but they are certainly sent—and received.

Social Behavior

Density. What are the effects of high or low densities on social behavior in the classroom? In some places, fiscal restraint has meant higher classroom densities than in the recent past (see Figure 10-10). Most research has focused on the negative side of social behavior, such as aggression (or the lack of it). Originally, research produced mixed results, but perhaps because social density (number of people in the same space changes) and spatial density (amount of space for the same number of people changes) were not distinguished. Gradually, environmental psychologists realized that increases in social density seem to be associated with increases in aggression, but increases in spatial density are not.[216] Why might this be?

Changes in density may or may not be accompanied by changes in the amount of resources (access to the teacher, toys, lab equipment) available to each student. When more students are added to the same room (an increase in social density), the result may be greater competition for resources that have *not* increased. However, when a class of children is moved from a larger classroom to a smaller one (an increase in spatial density), the students probably have access to the same amount of resources, and there is still one teacher for the same number of students. Indeed, children in high-density situations with more resources are less aggressive than children in high-density situations with fewer resources.[217] However, as we would predict from the social—spatial density distinction, when spatial density is increased not by shifting to a smaller classroom, but by slicing an existing classroom in half, aggression does increase.[218] That was because many resources also were divided when the room was halved.

The effects of density are modified by the classroom's program. For example, high-density situations discourage students from selecting activities that require much concentration.[219] Teachers who are faced with large classes may modify their lesson plans to avoid confrontations among students.[220]

Architectural features such as ceiling height and perimeter space also may modify the effects of density.[221] Imagine the difference in perceived crowding between a windowless basement room with one tiny door and a low ceiling and another one with the same floor size except that it is a second-floor room with a panoramic view, high ceilings, and double sliding-glass doors. When perceived spaciousness is increased by these architectural features, aggression and other antisocial behaviors may decrease. Obviously, then, the number of persons present is only a starting point for considering the effects of density.[222] The type of density, the availability of key resources, the program, and architectural features other than floor size are also important. Confusion in the findings of early studies on density and aggression is largely resolved when these physical-setting factors are considered.

Classroom aggression may depend on the physical or mental ability of students. In classes of disabled children, more aggression occurred when social density was greater. When social density was first increased and then decreased, aggression increased and then decreased.[223] When the immediate workspace of some second-graders was decreased, aggression increased 100 percent for boys and 130 percent for girls.[224] Yet when the density in a college classroom was doubled, no aggression was reported, even though students reported being less comfortable, satisfied, and happy.[225] The obvious conclusion is that as students gain cognitive skills and are socialized against overt aggression, they feel worse, but do not (usually!) strike out against their fellow students.

Aggression is not the only social behavior affected by classroom density. Students tend to withdraw and behave randomly, deviantly, or as spectators (rather than as participants) in high-density classrooms.[226] Withdrawal from social interaction occurs at both very high and very low densities.[227] This implies that classroom involvement is greatest at moderate density; based on these studies, this would be about 30-40 sq. ft./2.8-3.7 m^2 per student.

Unfortunately, very little research on the relation between classroom density and positive social behaviors has been reported. However, installing partitions in classrooms to separate various activities seems to increase cooperation.[228]

Spatial Arrangements. Classroom layout affects the social interaction of both teachers and students, and students are known to be aware of the spatial features of their environments and to choose their spaces according to possibilities and their preferred activities.[229] Researchers examined the effects of special **privacy booths** for elementary school students.[230] These miniature rooms, where students could be alone during regular school hours were very popular—for a while. For the first 10 days that the booths were installed, about 70 percent of the students visited the booths each day. Over the next two weeks, however, usage averaged about 15 percent, and after 25 days less than 5 percent of the students used the booths each day.

The privacy booth experiment appears to have been a surprising failure; the students seemed not to value the booths except as a novelty. However, the children in this study happened to be those who had abundant opportunities for privacy at home. Children without so much privacy at home might use privacy booths more. At the more personal level, some children consistently used the booth more than others: Boys who were rated by their teachers as more distractible, more aggressive, and less sociable used the booths more and girls who sought more privacy at home used the classroom booths more. Thus, privacy booths benefit some children.

Unexpected findings also emerged from another study of student privacy.[231] Students in elementary school classrooms that allowed for privacy (they had separate rather than shared desks and secluded study areas within the classroom) reported that they had less privacy than did students in classrooms *without* amenities for privacy. This may have occurred because students were not allowed free access to the secluded study areas. When one can see but not enter a desirable place, one may feel less privacy than if the desirable option was not available at all. The design lesson may be this: If expectations are raised by providing something desirable, but use of that new facility is restricted, discontent may be greater than if the desirable feature had never been built.

Social interaction is different in open-plan and traditional classrooms. Because classes in open-plan spaces are often combined, teachers interact with one another more, students meet with teachers more, and students move around more than in traditional classrooms.[232] This increased interaction may, of course, create more noise and disruption than in traditional classrooms.[233] Open classroom space may be associated with more aggression, at least at the preschool stage.[234,235] Despite this image of barely controlled chaos, more students report being able to find an adequate place to study by themselves in open-plan classrooms than in traditional classrooms.[236]

In this section, several major environmental influences on the learning process have been reviewed. As elsewhere in environmental psychology, multiple influences on different sorts of people have a variety of outcomes. Is there a way to integrate this knowledge? If we had an overall integrative framework, it might aid understanding and also provide a clear set of guidelines for the design of learning settings.

One proposed framework is the **optimal stimulation** approach.[237,238] Its proponents suggest that all the influences we have discussed—noise, light, space, resources, and climate—may be characterized as presenting the learner with too little, too much, or optimal stimulation. Regardless of which modality the stimulation arrives in, the assumption is that teachers and learners perform better, feel better, and interact better when the total amount of stimulation is "optimal." But how much stimulation is optimal? The optimal level is the amount required to produce an arousal level in the individual that produces the best work, the best feelings, and the best social interaction of which the individual is capable. Still the question remains: How much stimulation is needed to produce the ideal amount of arousal? The exact numbers are not known, but we can often make some tentative statements about this.[239]

1. *Individual differences.* Hyperactive children need more stimulation than typical children who, in turn, need more stimulation than autistic children.

2. *Type of activity.* We all perform or feel better during certain activities when little physical stimulation comes our way (e.g., studying for an examination), but we also perform or feel better during activities when much stimulation is present (e.g., dancing).

3. *Length of time.* From the time a situation is new to us until it begins to fatigue or bore us, the optimal level of stimulation changes. Normally, the longer we are in the same setting, the more we adapt to the stimulation it offers, so that the optimal level of it rises with time.

Eventually, researchers might be able to identify the quantity of stimulation that is optimal for each individual's personal qualities, current activity, in what social company, and length of exposure to the activity.

IN SUM *The amount and arrangement of space in educational settings is very important for classroom performance and behavior, yet much remains to be learned. High density may harm learning when the activity involves physical movement around the classroom, when learning depends on some classroom resource that is less plentiful than the number of learners, when a particular situation feels crowded to a particular learner, and when the concept to be learned is complex. Space in classrooms also affects student and teacher feelings. Most students and teachers prefer lower-density classrooms, because lower densities usually feel less crowded. Providing satisfying physical arrangements within schools is best accomplished by creating a variety of layouts. Softer, more homelike classrooms will not become common until attitudes change. School authorities must be willing to spend a bit more, janitors must be willing to deal with rooms that are probably harder to clean, and parents must be willing to believe that a good education is possible in a non-traditional classroom. Students probably would not have to change their attitudes very much at all. Increased social density leads to increased aggression and withdrawal when other resources, architectural features, and teaching style do not counteract it. Attempts to provide more privacy for most students in the classroom have so far not been very successful, but some students appear to benefit. Open-plan classrooms increase social interaction. Classroom arrangements should provide "optimal" stimulation, although the appropriate amount in any given situation cannot yet be specified. However, each student's need for stimulation, the type of activity, with whom, and the length of time spent engaged in the activity will have to be considered to discover these amounts.*

ENVIRONMENTAL COMPETENCE

AS NOTED AT THE OUTSET OF THIS CHAPTER, not all learning occurs in classrooms. In this section, we focus on learning *about* the environment. According to Fritz Steele, who has written extensively about the topic, **environmental competence** is "people's ability to deal with their immediate surroundings in an effective and stimulating manner."[240] It includes many aspects of interaction with the environment, such as wayfinding, sense of direction, knowledge of the best and worst parts of a city, knowledge of and appreciation for different architectural styles, knowing the power structure of an organization so that design modifications might be lobbied for instead of merely commented upon, skill in navigation or wilderness hiking, outdoor skills,

and the ability to personalize a setting quickly (see Figure 10-11).

People begin to develop environmental competence at birth, and many seek to increase it throughout their lives by traveling or paying special attention to local settings. Yet, little formal attention is given to the development of environmental competence after early childhood. In youth and adulthood, people are often left to develop environmental competence on their own. In parallel with this neglect, environmental competence has not been studied very much. Nevertheless, enough work has been completed—and the topic is important enough—to devote this space to it. After discussing the nature of environmental competence, we will turn to methods for developing it further.

The Varieties of Environmental Competence

STEELE PROPOSED THREE KINDS OF ENVIRONMENTAL COMPETENCE,[241] and later studies confirm most of these types.[242] The first kind includes one's **personal style, attitudes, and awareness**. Thus, part of environmental competence is awareness of one's own environmentally relevant skills, abilities, needs, and values. Do you know where you stand on environmental issues? Have you ever actively assessed your own needs for space? Do you believe you could find your way out of a forest if you lost your way?

Skill in perceiving the environment without too much distortion or too many blind spots is another aspect of this personal dimension of environmental competence. Do you know anyone who consistently misjudges physical distances? Anyone who seems to be completely out of touch with their physical surroundings? Curiosity about the environment—the desire to explore new settings and learn more about familiar ones—is also very important. Someone who is not curious about the environment is unlikely to develop much competence in it.

The second kind of environmental competence concerns the individual's **knowledge about the surroundings**. This includes scientific knowledge relevant to environmental issues, knowing how to get around in a particular building or city or wilderness area, and knowing how to find out how to get around. Some students have acquired knowledge about how to get around that labyrinthine campus building; however, others get lost in it even after months of trying and are too embarrassed to inquire.

Environmental psychologists have studied this problem with a view to better understanding how individuals get lost and which strategies they employ as they struggle to find their way back. For example, the behavior of hunters lost in the mountains has been investigated, as has which medium (slides, videotapes, or walking) helps young children learn a route best.[243] (Answer: walking.)

Steele says that technical knowledge of one's surroundings—for example, knowing the difference between fluorescent and incandescent lighting—is an important component of environmental competence because it provides a person with design possibilities to draw upon if we design, or help design a home, office, or other place. These design possibilities may then be offered to those charged with the maintenance and modification of the building. Not everyone cares enough to bother offering, pushing, petitioning, or politicking over design changes, but without some knowledge of design possibilities, they probably would never bother.

Knowledge about people in relation to settings is another aspect of knowledge about one's surroundings. From those who know little or nothing about any part of the environment to those who take their PhDs in a specialized area, the range of environmental knowledge across individuals is immense. For example, when my students and I explored individual differences in knowledge about environmental issues, we found that natural science majors know more than social science or non-science majors and that environmental studies students know more about them than students who are not in environmental studies.[244]

Knowledge about how the social and political system deals with the physical setting is the final aspect of environmental knowledge. For example, what are the rules of the game governing getting a rare species declared as endangered? Who knows how many of the species are left, or who finally decides that the species is endangered? Who decides whether to move, or who gets which office? When are the meetings about this held? The environmentally competent person will discover at least some of the answers to the questions above, and perhaps try to exert some influence. The environmentally incompetent individual is likely to shrug and give up the quest almost before it begins.

The third kind of environmental competence described by Steele involves **practical skills** related to the environment. These practical skills include being able to scout a setting, match oneself with appropriate settings for different activities, personalize a setting and creative custodianship.

Scouting is the ability to get the feel of a place and to systematically canvass it through focused searching. As an example, I once hosted an eminent, much-traveled environmental psychologist. Lunch time arrived and I could not think of a restaurant suited to the occasion. We began scouting, and within minutes, under the direction of my guest, who had no experience in my city but has great scouting ability, we found a very suitable restaurant.

Matching is the ability to find the right place for the right activity at the right time. Have you *actively* considered, for example, just where you work best? The difference between successful and unsuccessful students often is that successful students discover the physical and temporal conditions in which they work well. Socially, some individuals seem to have a knack for selecting places for getting together that make the event worthwhile; others rarely think of the place to meet, focusing exclusively on the social aspects of the meeting.

The ability to *personalize* a setting well and

FIGURE 10–11 Learning often occurs outside the classroom, too. The physical environment, including you-are-here signs, influences this learning.

quickly is another useful practical aspect of environmental competence. College students, for example, move relatively often. Some seem to be able to transform a barren room into a glowing reflection of themselves, whereas others manifest no interest or ability in personalizing, sometimes preferring to complain about the plainness of the building. At the public school level, one enlightened architect developed a service to provide inexpensive materials for teachers and students to personalize their classrooms.[245] Amazingly, some organizations actually prohibit employees from personalizing their work spaces, thereby actively blocking the

FIGURE 10–12 In this environmental education class, students played representatives of a mining company and an environmental activist group to experience some of the dialog that occurs between developers and conservationists.

development of environmental competence in their employees. They seem to believe that environmental competence may lead to agitation for more democratic decision-making on design questions.[246] They are probably correct!

Finally, *creative custodianship* is Steele's term for the practical skill involved in using a setting without unduly upsetting the place's essential character in the process. For example, some campers go to great lengths to leave no trace of their temporary habitation. A few vandals, on the other hand, go to great lengths to ensure their presence *does* leave an ugly and preferably permanent mark on the environment. No one's environmental competence is perfect; many of us need to improve it in some or many areas. We turn now to ways of increasing environmental competence.

Developing Environmental Competence

Formal Education. Of course, many forms of formal, recognized environmental competence are taught in post-secondary schools, including architecture, landscape architecture, town planning, environmental studies, and geography, as well as environmental psychology; perhaps the most extensive training in environmental competence occurs in the military.[247] However, Steele asserts that high schools and colleges ought to teach courses in environmental competence in the broad sense of creating a citizenry interested in and knowledgeable about local everyday physical settings. This teaching would create ordinary citizens who are capable of responsible criticism of those settings, when criticism is needed.

One form of environmental competence (or the lack of it) is that of teachers in the classroom. This sense of it refers to how the classroom as a physical setting can be used to enhance learning. Researchers have interviewed teachers and observed them as they gave their lessons to learn more about how the arrangement of furniture, learning centers, and other elements of the physical classroom influence their students' learning.[248]

With the growth of environmental awareness, many traditional classes in biology and geography have been transformed into environmental education classes. The emphasis shifted from mere description of nature to stressing the fragility and limitedness of planet Earth. New curricula were quickly developed, such as a series of "environmental encounters" that were proposed for the whole public school age range, from kindergarten to the end of high school[249] (see Figure 10-12). Evidence of its continuing vitality is the continuing stream of environmental education curriculum guides and manuals.[250,251] For example, a Swiss team developed a program called "Nature on the Way to School" that teaches children to recognize species and biodiversity as they walk to school.[252] Children from 8 to 16 who went through the program learned to notice a significantly greater number of species. Another approach is to use the school grounds themselves as a setting for increasing the environmental awareness of children.[253]

Proposing environmental education is one thing; whether it is effective is another. The evidence is mixed. Some classes increase students' knowledge, as you would expect.[254] But the field trip, that hallowed and beloved institution, has not always fared so well. Summer students aged 10 to 13 years old were taught two principles of plant ecology in their home schoolyard and in a natural setting (on a field trip).[255] Learning was significantly better in the home schoolyard than on the field trip. The novelty of a day out of school is pleasant, but it may interfere with the learning of concepts. On the other hand, students on a field trip may learn something different or more important than the intended environmental concepts. Educators must decide just what they hope to gain from a field trip.

How effective are different methods of teaching environmental competence? Teachers often believe that active-involvement instructional methods (e.g., debates, simulation games, field trips) are the most effective, but most teachers actually use passive-involvement methods (e.g., lectures and readings).[256] Apparently, the effective teaching of environmental competence within the formal school system is hindered by a reluctance to relinquish the traditional forms of knowledge transmission—ones developed to teach classical disciplines such as philosophy and history.

Teachers' beliefs about the value of active involvement have been substantiated.[257] High-school students who participated in a 6-day program received either instruction in environmental issues or instruction plus information on environmental action strategies.[258] As you might expect, those who received only instruction did not increase their environmental activities over the next two months, but those who were taught action strategies did.

Active-involvement alternatives do exist within formal educational settings. Many university-based science programs that provide symbiotic links with the National Park Service in the United States have been established.[259] Environmental competence is not limited to concern about nature; it involves the built environment too. Some students are being taught how to design settings, including their own classrooms. Children as young as age 8 have been taught enough architecture in hour-long, once-a-week sessions to produce good-quality designs for classrooms and other settings.[260]

Another alternative to the plain lecture is the simulation exercise. Instructors teach about such issues as resource depletion through games that show what happens when resources are used too quickly.[261] One such simulation exercise that concerned energy conservation was directly compared to the traditional lecture as a way of changing attitudes and behavior.[262] Students who took part in the simulation showed an increase in positive attitudes toward attitude change and a greater likelihood of taking action.

We must not forget that environmental problems can be frightening, particularly to younger students. We need more concern, but an unintended effect of some curricula is to unduly scare students—something that adds to the problems rather than ameliorating them. Environmental education programs should stress that problems exist, but that with new skills we can overcome them.[263]

Informal Programs. A wide variety of programs promote environmental awareness in community settings. Some resemble school programs, but are aimed at community adults. For example, a Texas program focused on water quality problems.[264] Five months after 51 adults had completed the program, they still reported greater awareness of the problems and felt confident about discussing them in public.

Robert Sommer described many awareness-enhancing programs that focus on the built environment in his book *Design Awareness*.[265] One school gave 4-year-olds the task of designing their own classroom. Another taught children about personal space and crowding by drawing circles on the floor and asking the students to squeeze into the circumferences of the circles.

Environmental psychologists have conducted workshops in schools and hospitals that serve to sensitize staff to the environment as it is experienced by their clients. Many physicians, for example, have never rolled down a hospital corridor on a gurney. When teachers are asked to sit in a student's desk for an hour without leaving it, they better understand why some children are fidgety and restless. The environmental competence developed in these workshops can help to create settings that reflect new respect for the needs of those who usually have little input into design decisions: students, patients, clients.

Outdoor environmental competence, such as that gained through outdoor challenge programs and interpretation trails, also have received attention. One of the earliest examined the effects of taking part in an outdoor challenge program. Adolescent boys spent 2 weeks in a large primitive forest, working on survival skills.[266] By their own account, the boys felt that the experience significantly improved a variety of skills, including their knowledge of the woods, map-reading, compass use, food-finding, and ecological knowledge.

The interpretation trail is an increasingly common feature of our parks. Guides take individuals or small groups on short hikes, pointing out forest delights that might otherwise be overlooked. In one study, the merits of interpretations that emphasize a sensory approach (including many opportunities and exhortations to listen, touch, smell, and even taste the forest) were compared to a nonsensory approach in which the emphasis was more on verbal information.[267] The sensory approach led to more expressions of enjoyment from the hikers, but the nonsensory approach led hikers to ask more questions and to engage in more social interaction. Investigations like this will help to fine-tune the process of developing environmental competence.

IN SUM *Environmental competence involves learning about the environment. Three kinds include (1) personal style, attitudes and awareness of physical setting; (2) knowledge*

FIGURE 10-13 The soft classroom at the University of California, Davis.

of physical settings, including technical knowledge, how to unearth new information, knowledge about how social systems control space, and knowledge of person-environment relations; and (3) practical environmental skills such as scouting, matching, personalization, and creative custodianship. Programs in and out of school teach many different facets of environmental competence, from basic environmental ethics to campfire starting to architectural design. Although many subareas of environmental competence have received considerable attention, the concept as a whole so far has not received much attention.

LEARNING AND ENVIRONMENTAL DESIGN

ENVIRONMENTAL PSYCHOLOGISTS HAVE BEEN INVOLVED IN THE DESIGN OF MANY EDUCATIONAL SETTINGS. In this section, two examples of educational design research by environmental psychologists are presented: efforts toward better kindergarten classrooms and college classrooms.

Kindergarten Classrooms

YOU MAY RECALL from research described earlier that few elementary school classrooms have library corners, but where they exist, students use them frequently. That study was correlational; the use of library corners may have been caused by other factors—such as teachers who stressed reading—as much as it was caused by the library corners themselves.

To test the idea that having a library corner directly leads to increased literature activities when students have a choice of activities, Lesley Mandel Morrow and Carol Weinstein conducted a more experimental study of 13 kindergarten classrooms.[268] None of the classrooms already possessed special library corners or much preexisting literature activity. Each classroom was randomly assigned to one of four conditions: control (no changes), new library corner, library program, or both new library corner and program.

After allowing some time for the novelty of the changes to wear off, the researchers measured how often children accessed the literature during their free-play periods. The number of children who used library materials during free play rose about *twentyfold* in the new library corner condition. Introducing a new library program also raised the number of users almost fivefold. The combination of library corner plus program also produced more reading, but not more than a new library corner alone or a new library program alone. In the control classrooms, usage remained significantly lower than in all three experimental conditions. Gender differences were found: girls used literature more than boys in all three experimental conditions.

Thus, the mere existence of a library corner in a kindergarten classroom increases children's use of literature. The challenge for future research in this area would be to design a library corner that will attract boys!

A College Classroom

ALL OF US HAVE SAT THROUGH CLASSES IN PLAIN, BORING, HARD ROOMS. We can cope with such rooms; they probably do not cause brain damage or cocaine addiction. Nevertheless, they are not pleasant. If they could be made at least slightly more tolerable, would they help in any measurable way?

Robert Sommer and Helge Olsen redesigned a plain 30-seat college classroom at the University of California.[269] With a very small budget, they changed it into a soft classroom with semicircular, cushion-covered bench seating, adjustable lighting, a small carpet, and some other decoration (see Figure 10-13).

Compared to participation in traditional classrooms of similar size, student participation increased markedly in the soft classroom. The number of statements per student tripled, and the percentage of students who spoke in class approximately doubled. The soft classroom, contrary to the expectations of some, was not damaged or vandalized even though some of its components were vulnerable to vandals. Besides the dramatic increase in participation, students using the room wrote many glowing comments about it in a logbook placed in the soft classroom.

Seventeen years after it was built, the soft classroom still elicited more discussion from students.[270] This research, together with Wollin and Montagne's work, described at the start of the chapter, which showed that soft classrooms for Introductory Psychology improved exam performance, suggests a tentative conclusion: college classrooms need not be plain and hard. In fact, the early evidence suggests that inexpensive changes to make them more pleasant have very tangible benefits.

SUMMARY

EDUCATIONAL ACTIVITIES—including learning, participation, classroom social interaction, and feelings about school settings—are affected in important ways by the physical school setting, in conjunction with other factors such as teaching style and age of the learner. The size, plan, and condition of the setting as a whole is one set of influences. Noise has a larger effect than light and climate, but this may occur because in many schools the latter two are usually provided at reasonably acceptable levels, whereas noise often varies widely from classroom to classroom. Budget crunches have created space crunches. The resulting larger class sizes (increased social density) have been linked to numerous difficulties in learning. Open-plan classrooms can work well when (and only when) teachers are appropriately trained and students are able to handle the flexibility they

provide. Aggression and withdrawal accompany greatly increased social density. Environmental competence refers to learning about environments, including buildings and the great outdoors. It involves a personal dimension (one's orientation toward learning more about the environment), technical and social knowledge of specific settings, and practical skills. All forms of environmental competence may be developed through programs in and out of schools, although these programs must be carefully designed or they may not be effective. Examples include lessons in resource conservation, field trips, and workshops for adults. Two design research interventions are described in which the use of library materials was increased in kindergarten and participation (and even grades) in college classes was increased through design changes.

Suggested Supplementary Readings

Bronzaft, A. L. (1981). The effect of a noise abatement program on reading ability. *Journal of Environmental Psychology, 1*, 215222.

Pederson, D. M. (1999). Dimensions of environmental competence. *Journal of Environmental Psychology, 19*, 303-308.

Rivlin, L. G., & Weinstein, C. S. (1984). Educational issues, school settings, and environmental psychology. *Journal of Environmental Psychology, 4*, 347-364.

Sanoff, H., & Walden, R. (2012). School environments. In Clayton, S. D. (Ed.). *The Oxford handbook of environmental and conservation psychology* (pp. 276-294). New York: Oxford.

Steele, F. (1980). Defining and developing environmental competence. In C. P. Alderfer & C. L. Cooper (Eds.), *Advances in Experimental Social Processes, 2*, 225-244.

References

1   Weinstein, C. (1979). The physical environment of the school: A review of the research. *Review of Educational Research, 49*, 577-610.

2   Wollin, D. D., & Montagne, M. (1981). College classroom environment: Effects of sterility versus amiability on student and teacher performance. *Environment and Behavior, 13*, 707-716.

3   Traub, R. E., & Weiss, J. (1974). Studying openness in education: An Ontario example. *Journal of Research and Development in Education, 8*, 4759.

4   Weinstein, C. S. (1981). Classroom design as an external condition for learning. *Educational Technology, 21*, 12-19.

5   Gump, P. V., & Friesen, W. V. (1964). Participation in nonclass settings. In R. G. Barker & P. V. Gump (Eds.), *Big school, small school: High school size and student behavior*. Stanford, CA: Stanford University Press.

6   Gump, P. V., & Friesen, W. V. (1964). Satisfactions derived from nonclass settings. In R. G. Barker & P. V. Gump (Eds.), *Big school, small school: High school size and student behavior*. Stanford, CA: Stanford University Press.

7   Baird, L. L. (1969). Big school, small school: A critical examination of the hypothesis. *Journal of Educational Psychology, 60*, 286-303.

8   Myrick, R., & Marx, B. S. (1968) cited in R. H. Moos (1976). *The human context: Environmental determinants of behavior*. New York: Wiley.

9   Rittelmeyer, C. (1987). Meaning fields of the architecture of school buildings: An empirical study toward perception and evaluation of different school facades by students. *Psychologie in Erziehung und Unterricht, 34*, 171-177.

10 Sugiyama, T., Okely, A. D., Masters, J. M., & Moore, G. T. (2012). Attributes of Child Care Centers and Outdoor Play Areas Associated With Preschoolers' Physical Activity and Sedentary Behavior. *Environment and Behavior, 44*, 334-349.

11 Ozdemir, A., & Yilmaz, O. (2008). Assessment of outdoor school environments and physical activity in ankara's primary schools. *Journal of Environmental Psychology, 28*, 287-300.

12 Boldemann, C., Blennow, M., Dal, H., Mårtensson, F., Raustorp, A., Yuen, K., & Wester, U. (2006). Impact of preschool environment upon children's physical activity and sun exposure. *Preventive Medicine: An International Journal Devoted to Practice and Theory, 42*, 301-308.

13 Mårtensson, F., Boldemann, C., Söderström, M., Blennow, M., Englund, J., & Grahn, P. (2009). Outdoor environmental assessment of attention promoting settings for preschool children. *Health & Place, 15*, 1149-1157.

14 Arbogast, K. L., Kane, B. C. P., Kirwan, J. L., & Hertel, B. R. (2009). Vegetation and outdoor recess time at elementary schools: What are the connections? *Journal of Environmental Psychology, 29*, 450-456.

15 Piccigallo, P. R. (1989). Renovating urban schools is fundamental to improving them. *Phi Delta Kappan*, 402-406.

16 Decrepit schools linked to learning woes. (1993, October 6), Victoria *Times-Colonist*, p. A9.

17 Durán-Narucki, V. (2008). School building condition, school attendance, and academic achievement in new york city public schools: A mediation model. *Journal of Environmental Psychology, 28*, 278-286.

18 Evans, G. W., & Stecker, R. (2004). Motivational consequences of environmental stress. *Journal of Environmental Psychology, 24*, 143-165.

19 Evans, G. W., Yoo, M. J., & Sipple, J. (2010). The ecological context of student achievement: School building quality effects are exacerbated by high levels of student mobility. *Journal of Environmental Psychology, 30*, 239-244.

20 Leventhal, T., & Brooks-Gunn, J. (2004). A randomized study of neighborhood effects on low-income children's educational outcomes. *Developmental Psychology, 40*, 488-507.

21 Ahrentzen, S. (1981). The environmental and social context of distraction in the classroom. In A. E. Osterberg, C. P. Tiernan, & R. A. Findlay (Eds.), *Design research interactions*. Ames, IA: Environmental Design Research Association, pp. 241-250.

22 Read, M. A., Sugawara, A. I., & Brandt, J. A. (1999). Impact of space and color in the physical environment on preschool children's cooperative behavior. *Environment and Behavior, 31*, 413-428.

23 Creekmore, W. N. (1987). Effective use of classroom walls. *Academic Therapy, 22*, 341-348.

24 Felsten, G. (2009). Where to take a study break on the college campus: An attention restoration theory perspective. *Journal of Environmental Psychology, 29*, 160-167.

25 Pellegrini, A. D. (1985). Social-cognitive aspects of children's play: The effects of age, gender, and activity centers. *Journal of Applied Developmental Psychology, 6*, 129-140.

26 Talton, E. L., & Simpson, R. D. (1987). Relationships of attitude toward classroom environment with attitude toward and achievement in science among tenth grade biology students. *Journal of Research in Science Teaching, 24*, 507-525.

27 Cohen, S., & Trostle, S. L. (1990). Young children's preferences for school-related physical-environmental setting characteristics. *Environment and Behavior, 22*, 753-766.

28 Dunn, R. (1987). Research on instructional environments: Implications for student achievement and attitudes. *Professional School Psychology, 2*, 43-52.

29 Bilewicz, M., & Klebaniuk, J. (2013). Psychological consequences of religious symbols in public space: Crucifix display at a public university. *Journal of Environmental Psychology, 35*, 10-17.

30 Maxwell, L. E., & Chmielewski, E. J. (2008). Environmental personalization and elementary school children's self-esteem. *Journal of Environmental Psychology, 28*, 143-153.

31 McGeoch, J. A. (1942). *The psychology of human learning*. New York: Longmans, Green, p. 501.

32 Abernathy, E. M. (1940). The effect of changed environmental conditions upon the result of college examinations. *Journal of Psychology, 10*, 293-301.

33 Godden, D. R., & Baddeley, A. D. (1975). Context-dependent memory in two natural environments: On land and underwater. *British Journal of Psychology, 66*, 325-331.

34 Weir, W., & May, R. B. (1988). Environmental context and student performance. *Canadian Journal of Education, 13*, 505-510.

35 Nixon, S. J., & Kanak N. J. (1985). A theoretical account of the effects of environmental context upon cognitive processes. *Bulletin of the Psychomonic Society, 23*, 139-142.

36 Smith, S. M. (1979). Remembering in and out of context. *Journal of Experimental Psychology, 5*, 460-471.

37 Farnsworth, P. R. (1934). Examinations in familiar and unfamiliar surroundings. *Journal of Social Psychology, 4*, 128-129.

38 Cohen, R., Weatherford, D. L., Lomenick, T., & Koeller, K. (1979). Development of spatial representations: Role of task demands and familiarity with the environment. *Child Development, 50*, 1257-1260.

39 Smith S. M. (1986). Environmental context-dependent recognition memory using a short-term memory task for input. *Memory and Cognition, 14*, 347-354.

40 Eich, E. (1985). Context, memory, and integrated item/context imagery. *Journal of Experimental Psychology: Learning, Memory, and Cognition, 11*, 764-770.

41 Canas, J. J., & Nelson, D. L. (1986). Recognition and environmental context: The effect of testing by phone. *Bulletin of the Psychonomic Society, 24*, 407-409.

42 Choi, C. Y., & McPherson, B. (2005). Noise levels in Hong Kong primary schools: Implications for classroom listening. *International Journal of Disability, Development and Education, 52*, 345-360.

43 Skarlatos, D., & Manatakis, M. (2003). Effects of classroom noise on students and teachers in Greece. *Perceptual and Motor Skills, 96*, 539-544.

44 Clark, C., Head, J., & Stansfeld, S. A. (2013). Longitudinal effects of aircraft noise exposure on children's health and cognition: A six-year follow-up of the UK RANCH cohort. *Journal of Environmental Psychology, 35*, 1-9.

45 Wilson, C. W., & Hopkins, B. L. (1973). The effects of contingent music on the intensity of noise in junior home economics classes. *Journal of Applied Behavior Analysis, 6*, 269-275.

46 Schmidt, G. W., & Ulrich, R. E. (1969). Effects of group contingent events upon classroom noise. *Journal of Applied Behavior Analysis, 2*, 171-179.

47 Strang, H. R., & George, J. R. (1975). Clowning around to stop clowning around: A brief report on an automated approach to monitor, record, and control classroom noise. *Journal of Applied Behavior Analysis, 8*, 471-474.

48 Hockey, G. R. J., & Hamilton, P. (1970). Arousal and information selection in short-term memory. *Nature, 226*, 866-867.

49 Hambrick-Dixon, P. J. (1988). The effect of elevated subway train noise over time on Black children's visual vigilance performance. *Journal of Environmental Psychology, 8*, 299-314.

50 Lercher, P., Evans, G. W., & Meis, M. (2003). Ambient noise and cognitive processes among primary schoolchildren. *Environment and Behavior, 35*, 725-735.

51 Cohen, S., Evans, G. W., Krantz, D. S., Stokols, D., & Kelly, S. (1981). Aircraft noise and children: Longitudinal and cross-sectional evidence on adaptation to noise and the effectiveness of noise abatement. *Journal of Personality and Social Psychology, 40*, 331-345.

52 Hygge, S., Evans, G. W., & Bullinger, M. (2002). A prospective study of some effects of aircraft noise on cognitive performance in schoolchildren. *Psychological Science, 13*, 469-474.

53 Sörqvist, P. (2010). Effects of aircraft noise and speech on prose memory: What role for working memory capacity? *Journal of Environmental Psychology, 30*, 112-118.

54 Bronzaft, A. L. (1981). The effect of a noise abatement program on reading ability. *Journal of Environmental Psychology, 1*, 215-222.

55 Madu, S. N. (1990). Effect of noise on memory and recall among Nigerian students. *Journal of African Psychology, 1*, 15-23.

56 Bell, P. A., Hess, S., Hill, E., Kukas, S., Richards, R. W., and Sargent, D. (1984). Noise and context-dependent memory. *Bulletin of the Psychonomic Society, 22*, 99100.

57 Hygge, S. (2003). Classroom experiments on the effects of different noise sources and sound levels on long-term recall and recognition in children. *Applied Cognitive Psychology, 17*, 895-914.

58 Hygge, S., Boman, E., & Enmarker, I. (2003). The effects of road traffic noise and meaningful irrelevant speech on different memory systems. *Scandinavian Journal of Psychology, 44*, 13-21.

59 Boman, E. (2004). The effects of noise and gender on children's episodic and semantic memory. *Scandinavian Journal of Psychology, 45*, 407-416.

60 Stansfeld, S. A., Clark, C., Cameron, R. M., Alfred, T., Head, J., Haines, M. M., et al. (2009). Aircraft and road traffic noise exposure and children's mental health. *Journal of Environmental Psychology, 29*, 203-207.

61 Klatte, M., Hellbrück, J., Seidel, J., & Leistner, P. (2010). Effects of classroom acoustics on performance and well-being in elementary school children: A field study. *Environment and Behavior, 42*, 659-692.

62 Enmarker, I. (2004). The effects of meaningful irrelevant speech and road traffic noise on teachers' attention, episodic and semantic memory. *Scandinavian Journal of Psychology, 45*, 393-405.

63 Kristiansen, J., Persson, R., Lund, S. P., Shibuya, H., & Nielsen, P. (2013). Moberg Effects of Classroom Acoustics and Self-Reported Noise Exposure on Teachers' Well-Being. *Environment and Behavior, 45*, 283-300.

64 Kristiansen, J., Lund, S. P., Nielsen, P. M., Persson, R., & Shibuya, H. (2011). Determinants of noise annoyance in teachers from schools with different classroom reverberation times. *Journal of Environmental Psychology, 31*, 383-392.

65 Gulian, E., & Thomas, J. R. (1986). The effects of noise, cognitive set and gender on mental arithmetic performance. *British Journal of Psychology, 77*, 503-511.

66 Christie, D. J., & Glickman, C. D. (1980). The effects of classroom noise on children: Evidence for sex differences. *Psychology in the Schools, 17*, 405408.

67 Hykin, S. (1984). *The effects of classroom noise on adults: Evidence for sex differences.* Unpublished master's thesis, University of Victoria, Victoria, British Columbia.

68 Belojevic, G., Evans, G. W., Paunovic, K., & Jakovljevic, B. (2012). Traffic noise and executive functioning in urban primary school children: The moderating role of gender. *Journal of Environmental Psychology, 32*, 337-341.

69 Zentall, S. S. (1983). Learning environments: A review of physical and temporal factors. *EEQ: Exceptional Education Quarterly, 4*, 90-115.

70 Collins-Eiland, K., Dansereau, D. F., Brooks, L. W., & Holley, C. D. (1986). Effect of conversational noise, locus of control, and field dependence/independence on the performance of academic tasks. *Contemporary Educational Psychology, 11*, 139-149.

71 Geen, R. G., McCown, E. J., & Broyles, J. W. (1985). Effects of noise on sensitivity of introverts and extraverts to signals in a vigilance task. *Personality and Individual Differences, 6*, 237-241.

72 Edmonds, E. M., & Smith. L. R. (1985). Students' performance as a function of sex, noise, and intelligence. *Psychological Reports, 56*, 727-730.

73 Toplyn, G., & Maguire, W. (1991). The differential effect of noise on creative task performance. *Creativity Research Journal, 4*, 337-347.

74 Hambrick-Dixon, P. J. (1988). The effect of elevated subway train noise over time on Black children's visual vigilance performance. *Journal of Environmental Psychology, 8*, 299-314.

75 Pizzo, J., Dunn, R., & Dunn, K. J. (1990). A sound approach to improving reading: Responding to students' learning styles. *Journal of Reading, Writing, and Learning Disabilities International, 6*, 249-260.

76 Zentall, S. S. (1983). Learning environments: A review of physical and temporal factors. *EEQ: Exceptional Education Quarterly, 4*, 90-115.

77 Breen-Lewis, K., & Wilding, J. (1984). Noise, time of day and test expectations in recall and recognition. *British Journal of Psychology, 75*, 51-63.

78 Hartley, L. R., Boultwood, B., & Dunne, M. P. (1987). Noise and verbal or spatial solutions of Rubik's cube. *Ergonomics, 30*, 503-509.

79 Salame, P., & Baddeley, A. (1987). Noise, unattended speech and short-term memory. *Ergonomics, 30*, 1185-1194.

80 Cohen, S., & Weinstein, N. (1982). Nonauditory effects of noise on behavior and health. In G. W. Evans (Ed.), *Environmental stress.* New York: Cambridge University Press.

81 Cohen, S., Glass, D. C., & Singer, J. E. (1973). Apartment noise, auditory discrimination and reading ability in children. *Journal of Experimental Social Psychology, 9*, 407-422.

82 Heft, H. (1979). Background and focal environmental conditions of the home and attention in young children. *Journal of Applied Social Psychology, 9*, 47-69.

83 Cohen, S., & Weinstein, N. (1982). Nonauditory effects of noise on behavior and health. In G. W. Evans (Ed.), *Environmental stress.* New York: Cambridge University Press.

84 Enmarker, I, & Boman, E. (2004). Noise annoyance responses of middle school pupils and teachers. *Journal of Environmental Psychology, 24*, 527-536.

85 Brunetti, F. (1972). Noise, distraction and privacy in conventional and open school environments. In W. J. Mitchell (Ed.), *Environmental design: Research and practice.* Los Angeles: University of California.

86 Enmarker, I, & Boman, E. (2004). Noise annoyance responses of middle school pupils and teachers. *Journal of Environmental Psychology, 24*, 527-536.

87 Boman, E., & Enmarker, I. (2004). Factors affecting pupils' noise annoyance in school: The building and testing of models. *Environment and Behavior, 36*, 207-228.

88 Ahrentzen, S., Jue, G. M., Skorpanich, M. A., & Evans, G. W. (1982). School environments and stress. In G. W. Evans (Ed.), *Environmental stress.* New York: Cambridge University Press. (pp. 224-255).

89 Miller, G. M. (1988). Effects of a hearing protection device on cognitive and motor performance of students in noisy environments. *Dissertation Abstracts International, 47.*

90 Stein, C. (1975). School lighting reevaluated. *American School and University, 48*, 70-78.

91 Stein, C. (1975). School lighting reevaluated. *American School and University, 48*, 70-78.

92 Mayron, L. W., Ott, J. N., Nations, R., & Mayron, E. L. (1974). Light, radiation, and academic behavior. *Academic Therapy, 10*, 441-448.

93 Fletcher, D. (1983). Effects of classroom lighting on the behavior of exceptional children. *EEQ: Exceptional Education Quarterly, 4*, 75-89.

94 Dalezman, Jones, Bevlig, Polf & Keeny, cited in Mayron, L. W., Ott, J. N., Nations, R., & Mayron, E. L. (1974).

95 Munson, P., & Ferguson, R. (1985). *The extravisual effects of fluorescent illumination on the behavior of school children.* Manuscript unpublished, University of Victoria.

96 Colman, R., Frankel, F., Ritvo, E., & Freeman, B. (1976). The effects of fluorescent and incandescent illumination upon repetitive behavior in autistic children. *Journal of Autism and Childhood Schizophrenia, 6*, 157-162.

97 Painter, M. (197677). Fluorescent lights and hyperactivity in children: An experiment. *Academic Therapy, 12*, 181-184.

98 Fletcher, D. (1983). Effects of classroom lighting on the behavior of exceptional children. *EEQ: Exceptional Education Quarterly, 4*, 75-89.

99 McColl, S. L., & Veitch, J. A. (2001). Full-spectrum fluorescent lighting: A review of its effects on physiology and health. *Psychological Medicine, 31*, 949-964.

100 Hedge, A. (2000). Where are we in understanding the effects of where we are? *Ergonomics, 43*, 1019-1029.

101 Riding, R. J., & Pugh, J. C. (1987). Dark-interval-threshold, illumination level and children's reading performance. *Journal of Research in Reading, 10,* 21-28.

102 Dunn, R. S., Krimsky, J. S., Murray, J. B., & Quinn, P. J. (1985). Light up their lives: A review of research on the effects of lighting on children's achievement and behavior. *Reading Teacher, 38,* 863-869.

103 Blue is beautiful. (1973, September 17). *Time,* (Canadian edition), p. 66.

104 Fehrman, K. R. (1987). The effects of interior pigment color on school task performance mediated by arousal. *Dissertation Abstracts International,* 48(4-A), 819.

105 Rosenstein, L. D. (1985). Effect of color of the environment on task performance and mood of males and females with high or low scores on the Scholastic Aptitude Test. *Perceptual and Motor Skills, 60,* 550.

106 Pellegrini, A. D. (1985). Social-cognitive aspects of children's play: The effects of age, gender, and activity centers. *Journal of Applied Developmental Psychology, 6,* 129-140.

107 Taylor, L. (1980, May 24). Improved lighting may make brighter work. *The Financial Post,* p. 25.

108 Veitch, J. A., Hine, D. W., & Gifford, R. (1993). End users' knowledge, beliefs, and preferences for lighting. *Journal of Interior Design, 19,* 15-26.

109 Kuller, R., & Lindsten, C. (1992). Health and behavior of children in classrooms with and without windows. *Journal of Environmental Psychology, 12,* 305-317.

110 Blue is beautiful. (1973, September 17). *Time* (Canadian edition), p. 66.

111 Rosenstein, L. D. (1985). Effect of color of the environment on task performance and mood of males and females with high or low scores on the Scholastic Aptitude Test. *Perceptual and Motor Skills, 60,* 550.

112 Czubaj, C. A. (2002). School indoor air quality. *Journal of Instructional Psychology, 29,* 317-321.

113 Auliciems, A. (1969). Effects of weather on indoor thermal comfort. *International Journal of Biometerology, 13,* 147-162.

114 Flatt, D. L. (1975). The effects of high temperature upon performance of certain physical tasks by high school students. *Dissertation Abstracts International, 35,* 7678A.

115 Ryd, H., & Wyon, D. P. Methods of evaluating human stress due to climate. *National Swedish Institute for Building Research,* 1970, Document 6.

116 Pepler, R. D. (1971). Variations in students' test performances and in classroom temperatures in climate controlled and nonclimate controlled schools. *ASHRAE Transactions, 77,* 35-42.

117 Wyon, D. P. (1970). Studies of children under imposed noise and heat stress. *Ergonomics, 13,* 598-612.

118 Moos, R., & Sommers, P. (1976). The architectural environment: Physical space and building design. In R. Moos, *The human context: Environmental determinants of behavior.* New York: Wiley.

119 Moos, R., & Sommers, P. (1976). The architectural environment: Physical space and building design. In R. Moos, *The human context:*

Environmental determinants of behavior. New York: Wiley.

120 Ahrentzen, S., Jue, G. M., Skorpanich, M. A., & Evans, G. W. (1982). School environments and stress. In G. W. Evans (Ed.), *Environmental stress.* New York: Cambridge University Press. (pp. 224-255).

121 Weldon, D. E., Loewy, J. H., Winer, J. I., & Elkin, D. J. (1981). Crowding and classroom learning. *Journal of Experimental Education, 49,* 160-176.

122 Glass, G. V., & Smith, M. L. (1978). *Meta-analysis of research on the relationship of class size and achievement.* San Francisco: The Far West Laboratory for Educational Research and Development.

123 Thomas, K. G. (1987). The effects of high and low social density on on-task behavior and correctness of work sheet completion of special education students. *Dissertation Abstracts International, 48,* 630-631.

124 Shapson, S. M. (1980). An experimental study of the effects of class size. *American Educational Research Journal, 17,* 141-152.

125 Heller, J. F., Groff, B. D., & Solomon, S. (1977). A. Toward an understanding of crowding: The role of physical interaction. *Journal of Personality and Social Psychology, 35,* 183-190.

126 Weinstein, C. (1979). The physical environment of the school: A review of the research. *Review of Educational Research, 49,* 577-610.

127 Weldon, D. E., Loewy, J. H., Winer, J. I., & Elkin, D. J. (1981). Crowding and classroom learning. *Journal of Experimental Education, 49,* 160-176.

128 Maxwell, L. E. (2003). Home and school density effects on elementary school children: The role of spatial density. *Environment and Behavior, 35,* 566-578.

129 Epstein, Y. M., & Karlin, R. A. (1975). Effects of acute experimental crowding. *Journal of Applied Social Psychology, 5,* 34-53.

130 Gochman, I. R., & Keating, J. P. (1976). *Perceived crowding as a function of unsuccessful goal attainment.* Paper presented at the annual meeting of the Western Psychological Association, Los Angeles.

131 Krantz, P. J., & Risley, T. R. (1977). Behavioral ecology in the classroom. In K. D. O'Leary & S. G. O'Leary (Eds.), *Classroom management: The successful use of behavior modification,* New York: Permagon Press.

132 Rohe, W., & Patterson, A. H. (1974). The effects of varied levels of resources and density on behavior in a day care center. In D. Carson (Ed.), *Manenvironment interactions: Evaluations and applications.* Stroudsberg, PA: Dowden, Hutchinson and Ross.

133 Evans, G. W. (1978). Human spatial behavior: The arousal model. In A. Baum & Y. Epstein (Eds.), *Human response to crowding.* Hillsdale, NJ: Erlbaum.

134 Haines, L. L. (1985). *Density and territoriality: The effects on classroom performance.* Unpublished Honors thesis, University of Victoria, Victoria, British Columbia.

135 Smith, P., & Connolly, K. (1977). Social and aggressive behavior in preschool children as a function of crowding. *Social Science Information, 16,* 601-620.

136 Kantrowitz, E. J., & Evans, G. W. (2004). The relation between the ratio of children per activity area and off-task behavior and type of play in day care centers. *Environment and Behavior, 36,* 541-557.

137 McCain, G., Cox, V. C., Paulus, P. B., Luke, A., & Abadzi, H. (1985). Some effects of reduction of extra-classroom crowding in a school environment. *Journal of Applied Social Psychology, 15,* 503-515.

138 Ahrentzen, S. (1980). *Environmentbehavior relations in the classroom setting: A multimodal research perspective.* Unpublished Master's thesis, University of California, Irvine.

139 Ahrentzen, S. (1981). The environmental and social context of distraction in the classroom. In A. E. Osterberg, C. P. Tiernan, & R. A. Findlay (Eds.), *Design research interactions.* Ames, IA: Environmental Design Research Association, pp. 241-250.

140 Weldon, D. E., Loewy, J. H., Winer, J. I., & Elkin, D. J. (1981). Crowding and classroom learning. *Journal of Experimental Education, 49,* 160-176.

141 Axelrod, S., Hall, R. V., & Tams, A. (1979). Comparison of two common classroom seating arrangements. *Academic Therapy, 15,* 29-36.

142 Wheldall, K., Morriss, M. Vaughan, P., & Ng, Y. Y. (1981). Rows vs. tables: An example of the use of behavioral ecology in two classes of elevenyearold children. *Educational Psychology, 1,* 171-184.

143 Wheldall, K., & Lam, Y. Y. (1987). Rows versus tables: II: The effects of two classroom seating arrangements on classroom disruption rate, on-task behavior and teacher behavior in three special school classes. *Educational Psychology, 7,* 303-312.

144 Rosenfield, P., Lambert, N. M., & Black, A. (1985). Desk arrangement effects on pupil classroom behavior. *Journal of Educational Psychology, 77,* 101-108.

145 Rosenfield, P., Lambert, N. M., & Black, A. (1985). Desk arrangement effects on pupil classroom behavior. *Journal of Educational Psychology, 77,* 101-108.

146 Gill, W. M. (1977). A look at the change to open-plan schools in New Zealand. *New Zealand Journal of Educational Studies, 12,* 3-16.

147 Legendre, A., & Fontaine, A. M. (1991). The effects of visual boundaries in two-year-olds' playrooms. *Children's Environments Quarterly, 8,* 2-16.

148 Zifferblatt, S. M. (1972). Architecture and human behavior: Toward increased understanding of a functional relationship. *Educational Technology, 12,* 54-57.

149 Weinstein, C. S. (1977). Modifying student behavior in an open classroom through changes in the physical design. *American Education Research Journal, 14,* 249-262.

150 Perkins, cited in Weinstein, 1981.

151 Nash, B. C. (1981). The effects of classroom spatial organization on four and fiveyear-old children's learning. *British Journal of Educational Psychology, 51,* 144-155.

152 Trawick-Smith, J. (1992). A descriptive study of spatial arrangement in a family day care home. *Child and Youth Care Forum, 21,* 263-276.

153 Morrow, L. M. (1982). Relationships between literature programs, library corner designs, and children's use of literature. *Journal of Educational Research, 75*, 339-344.

154 Neill, S. R. St. J. (1982). Experimental alterations in playroom layout and their effect on staff and child behavior. *Educational Psychology, 2*, 103-119.

155 Porteous, C. W. (1972). *Learning as a function of molar environmental complexity.* Unpublished master's thesis, University of Victoria, Victoria, British Columbia.

156 Santrock, J. W. (1976). Affect and facilitative self control: Influence of ecological setting, cognition, and social agent. *Journal of Educational Psychology, 68*, 529-535.

157 Ahrentzen, S., Jue, G. M., Skorpanich, M. A., & Evans, G. W. (1982). School environments and stress. In G. W. Evans (Ed.), *Environmental stress.* New York: Cambridge University Press. (pp. 224-255).

158 Griffith, C. R. (1921). A comment upon the psychology of the audience. *Psychological Monographs, 30*(136), 36-47.

159 Brooks, C. I., & Rebeta, J. L. (1991). College classroom ecology: The relation of sex of student to classroom performance and seating preference. *Environment and Behavior, 23*, 305-313.

160 Becker, F. D., Sommer, R., Bee, J., & Oxley, B. (1973). College classroom ecology. *Sociometry, 36*, 514-525.

161 Sommer (1967). Classroom ecology. *Journal of Applied Behavioral Science, 3*, 489-503.

162 Hillmann, R. B., Brooks, C. I., & O'Brien, J. P. (1991). Differences in self-esteem of college freshmen as a function of classroom seating-row preference. *Psychological Record, 41*, 315-320.

163 Hillmann, R. B., Brooks, C. I., & O'Brien, J. P. (1991). Differences in self-esteem of college freshmen as a function of classroom seating-row preference. *Psychological Record, 41*, 315-320.

164 Schwebel, A. I., & Cherlin, D. L. (1972). Physical and social distancing in teacherpupil relationships. *Journal of Educational Psychology, 63*, 543-550.

165 Hillmann, R. B., Brooks, C. I., & O'Brien, J. P. (1991). Differences in self-esteem of college freshmen as a function of classroom seating-row preference. *Psychological Record, 41*, 315-320.

166 Buckalew, L. W., Daly, J. D., & Coffield, K. E. (1986). Relationship of initial class attendance and seating location to academic performance in psychology classes. *Bulletin of the Psychonomic Society, 24*, 63-64.

167 Millard, R. J., & Stimpson, D. V. (1980). Enjoyment and productivity as a function of classroom seating location. *Perceptual and Motor Skills, 50*, 439-44.

168 Wulf, K. M. (1977). Relationship of assigned classroom seating area to achievement variables. *Educational Research Quarterly, 21*, 56-62.

169 Levine, D. W., O'Neal, E. C., Garwood, S. G. and McDonald, P. J. (1980). Classroom ecology: The effects of seating position on grades and participation. *Personality and Social Psychology Bulletin, 6*, 409-412.

170 Walberg, H. (1969). Physical and psychological distance in the classroom. *School Review, 77*, 6470.

171 Dykman, B. M., & Reis, H. T. (1979). Personality correlates of classroom seating position. *Journal of Educational Psychology, 71*, 346-354.

172 Hillmann, R. B., Brooks, C. I., & O'Brien, J. P. (1991). Differences in self-esteem of college freshmen as a function of classroom seating-row preference. *Psychological Record, 41*, 315-320.

173 Morrison, T. L., & Thomas, M. D. (1975). Selfesteem and classroom participation. *Journal of Educational Research, 68*, 374-377.

174 Brooks, C. I., & Rebeta, J. L. (1991). College classroom ecology: The relation of sex of student to classroom performance and seating preference. *Environment and Behavior, 23*, 305-313.

175 MacPherson, J. C. (1984). Environments and interaction in row and column classrooms. *Environment and Behavior, 16*, 481-502.

176 Stires, L. (1980). Classroom seating location, student grades, and attitudes: Environment or selfselection? *Environment and Behavior, 12*, 241-254.

177 Koneya, M. (1976). Location and interaction in row and column seating arrangements. *Environment and Behavior, 8*, 265-282.

178 Montello, D. R. (1988). Classroom seating location and its effect on course achievement, participation, and attitudes. *Journal of Environmental Psychology, 8*, 149-157.

179 Neill, S. R. St. J., & Denham, E. J. M. (1982). The effects of preschool building design. *Educational Research, 24*, 107-111.

180 Weinstein, C. S., & Weinstein, N. D. (1979). Noise and reading performance in an open space school. *Journal of Educational Research, 72*, 210-213.

181 Gump, P. V., & Ross, R. (1977). The fit of milieu and program in school environments. In H. McGurk (Ed.), *Ecological factors in human development.* New York: Elsevier NorthHolland.

182 Ross, R. P. (1980). Modification of space in open plan schools: An examination of the press toward synomorphy. In R. R. Stough & A. Wandersman (Eds.), *Optimizing environments: Research, practice, and policy.* Washington, DC: Environmental Design Research Association.

183 Gump, P. V. (1978). School environments. In I. Altman & J. F. Wohlwill (Eds.), *Children and the environment.* New York: Plenum.

184 Gump, P. V. (1978). School environments. In I. Altman & J. F. Wohlwill (Eds.), *Children and the environment.* New York: Plenum.

185 Reiss, S., & Dyhaldo, N. (1975). Persistence, achievement and openspace environments. *Journal of Educational Psychology, 67*, 506-513.

186 Cotterell, J. L. (1984). Effects of school architectural design on student and teacher anxiety. *Environment and Behavior, 16*, 455-479.

187 Gump, P. V. (1978). School environments. In I. Altman & J. F. Wohlwill (Eds.), *Children and the environment.* New York: Plenum.

188 Ahrentzen, S., Jue, G. M., Skorpanich, M. A., & Evans, G. W. (1982). School environments and stress. In G. W. Evans (Ed.), *Environmental stress.* New York: Cambridge University Press. (pp. 224-255).

189 Bell, A. E., Switzer, F., & Zipursky, M. (1974). Open area education: An advantage or disadvantage for beginners? *Perceptual and Motor Skills, 39*, 407-416.

190 Grapko, M. F., cited in Weinstein, 1979.

191 Traub, R. E., & Weiss, J. (1974). Studying openness in education: An Ontario example. *Journal of Research and Development in Education, 8*, 47-59.

192 Bell, A. E., Switzer, F., & Zipursky, M. (1974). Open area education: An advantage or disadvantage for beginners? *Perceptual and Motor Skills, 39*, 407-416.

193 Wright, R. J. (1975). The affective and cognitive consequences of an open education elementary school. *American Educational Research Journal, 12*, 449-468.

194 Gran, B., & Engquist, O. (1979). In King, J. & Marans, R. W. *The physical environment and the learning process: A survey of recent research.* Ann Arbor, MI: University of Michigan, Architectural Research Laboratory.

195 Evans, G. W., & Lovell, B. (1979). Design modification in an open plan school. *Journal of Educational Psychology, 71*, 41-49.

196 Solomon, D., & Kendall, A. J. (1976). Individual characteristics and children's performance in "open" and "traditional" classroom settings. *Journal of Educational Psychology, 68*, 613-625.

197 Gifford, R. (1976). Environmental numbness in the classroom. *Journal of Experimental Education, 44*, 47.

198 Bernardi, N., & Kowaltowski, D. C. C. K. (2006). Environmental comfort in school buildings: A case study of awareness and participation of users. *Environment and Behavior, 38*, 155-172.

199 Gump, P. V. (1978). School environments. In I. Altman & J. F. Wohlwill (Eds.), *Children and the environment.* New York: Plenum.

200 Sommer, R., & Becker, F. D. (1971). Room density and user satisfaction. *Environment and Behavior, 3*, 412417.

201 Coles, R. (1969). Those places they call schools. *Harvard Educational Review: Architecture and Education, 39*, 46-57.

202 Hathaway, W. E. (1990). Planning schools for the 21st century. *The Canadian School Executive, 10*, 3-10.

203 Feitler, F. C., Weiner, W., & Blumberg, A. (1970). *The relationship between interpersonal relations orientations and preferred classroom physical settings.* Paper presented at the annual meeting of the American Educational Research Association, Minneapolis.

204 Ahrentzen, S., & Evans, G. W. (1984). Distraction, privacy, and classroom design. *Environment and Behavior, 16*, 437-454.

205 Traub, R., Weiss, J., & Fisher, C. (1977). *Openness in schools: An evaluation study.* Ottawa: Ontario Institute for Studies in Education.

206 Krovetz, M. L. (1977). Who needs what when: Design of pluralistic learning environments. In D. Stokols (Ed.), *Perspectives on environment and behavior: Theory, research and applications.* New York: Plenum Press.

207 Cotterell, J. L. (1984). Effects of school architectural design on student and teacher anxiety. *Environment and Behavior, 16,* 455-479.

208 Krovetz, M. L. (1977). Who needs what when: Design of pluralistic learning environments. In D. Stokols (Ed.), *Perspectives on environment and behavior: Theory, research and applications.* New York: Plenum Press.

209 Walberg, H. (1969). Physical and psychological distance in the classroom. *School Review, 77,* 64-70.

210 Rothenberg, M., cited in Krovetz, 1977.

211 Chambers, J. A. (196364). A study of attitudes and feelings toward windowless classrooms. *Dissertations Abstracts International, 24,* 4498.

212 Weinstein, C. (1979). The physical environment of the school: A review of the research. *Review of Educational Research, 49,* 577-610.

213 Collins, B. L. (1965). Windows and people: Alternative survey. Psychological reactions to environments with and without windows. *National Bureau of Standards Building Science Series,* No. 70. Washington, DC: Institute for Applied Technology.

214 Karmel, L. J. (1965). Effects of windowless classroom environment on high school students. *Perceptual and Motor Skills, 20,* 277-278.

215 Weinstein, C. S., & Woolfolk, A. E. (1981). The classroom setting as a source of expectations about teachers and pupils. *Journal of Environmental Psychology, 1,* 117-129.

216 Weinstein, C. (1979). The physical environment of the school: A review of the research. *Review of Educational Research, 49,* 577-610.

217 Rohe, W., & Patterson, A. H. (1974). The effects of varied levels of resources and density on behavior in a day care center. In D. Carson (Ed.), *Man-environment interactions: Evaluations and applications.* Stroudsberg, PA: Dowden, Hutchinson and Ross.

218 Rohe, W. M., & Nuffer, E. L. (1977). *The effects of density and partitioning on children's behavior.* Paper presented at the annual meetings of the American Psychological Association, San Francisco, CA.

219 Rohe, W. M., & Nuffer, E. L. (1977). *The effects of density and partitioning on children's behavior.* Paper presented at the annual meetings of the American Psychological Association, San Francisco, CA.

220 Fagot, B. I. (1977). Variations in density: Effect on task and social behaviors of preschool children. *Developmental Psychology, 13,* 166-167.

221 Ahrentzen, S., Jue, G. M., Skorpanich, M. A., & Evans, G. W. (1982). School environments and stress. In G. W. Evans (Ed.), *Environmental stress.* New York: Cambridge University Press. (pp. 224-255).

222 Gump, P. V. (1978). School environments. In I. Altman & J. F. Wohlwill (Eds.), *Children and the environment.* New York: Plenum.

223 McAfee, J. K. (1987). Classroom density and the aggressive behavior of handicapped children. *Education and Treatment of Children, 10,* 134-145.

224 Sherrill, A. A. (1986). Elementary classroom crowding and student aggressive behaviors. *Dissertation Abstracts International, 47,* 1146.

225 Banzinger, G. (1982). Teaching about crowding: students as an independent variable. *Teaching of Psychology, 9,* 241-242.

226 Weinstein, C. (1979). The physical environment of the school: A review of the research. *Review of Educational Research, 49,* 577-610.

227 Shapiro, S. (1975). Preschool ecology: A study of three environmental variables. *Reading Improvement, 12,* 236-241.

228 Rohe, W. M., & Nuffer, E. L. (1977). *The effects of density and partitioning on children's behavior.* Paper presented at the annual meetings of the American Psychological Association, San Francisco, CA.

229 Kasal, A., & Do an, F. (2010). Fifth-, sixth-, and seventh- grade students' use of non-classroom spaces during recess: The case of three private schools in Izmir, Turkey. *Journal of Environmental Psychology, 30,* 518-532.

230 Weinstein, C. S. (1982). Privacy-seeking behavior in an elementary classroom. *Journal of Environmental Psychology, 2,* 23-35.

231 Ahrentzen, S., & Evans, G. W. (1984). Distraction, privacy, and classroom design. *Environment and Behavior, 16,* 437-454.

232 Weinstein, C. (1979). The physical environment of the school: A review of the research. *Review of Educational Research, 49,* 577-610.

233 Stebbins, R. A. (1973). Physical context influences on behavior: The case of classroom disorderliness. *Environment and Behavior, 5,* 291-314.

234 Neill, S. R. St. J. (1982). Preschool design and child behavior. *Journal of Child Psychology and Psychiatry, 23,* 309-318.

235 Neill, S. R. St. J., & Denham, E. J. M. (1982). The effects of preschool building design. *Educational Research, 24,* 107-111.

236 Brunetti, F. (1972). Noise, distraction and privacy in conventional and open school environments. In W. J. Mitchell (Ed.), *Environmental design: Research and practice.* Los Angeles: University of California. 29-38.

237 Wohlwill, J. F. (1966). The physical environment: A problem for a psychology of stimulation. *Journal of Social Issues, 22,* 29-30.

238 Zentall, S. S. (1983). Learning environments: A review of physical and temporal factors. *EEQ: Exceptional Education Quarterly, 4,* 90-115.

239 Zentall, S. S. (1983). Learning environments: A review of physical and temporal factors. *EEQ: Exceptional Education Quarterly, 4,* 90-115.

240 Steele, F. (1980). Defining and developing environmental competence. In C. P. Alderfer & C. L. Cooper (Eds.), *Advances in experiential social processes, 2,* 225-244, p. 225.

241 Steele, F. (1980). Defining and developing environmental competence. In C. P. Alderfer & C. L. Cooper (Eds.), *Advances in experiential social processes, 2,* 225-244, p. 225.

242 Pederson, D. M. (1999). Dimensions of environmental competence. *Journal of Environmental Psychology, 19,* 303-308.

243 Cornell, E. H., & Hay, D. H. (1984). Children's acquisition of a route via different media. *Environment and Behavior, 16,* 627-641.

244 Gifford, R., Hay, R., & Boros, K. (1982-83). Individual differences in environmental attitudes. *Journal of Environmental Education, 14,* 19-23.

245 Sommer, R. (1972). *Design awareness.* New York: Holt, Rinehart and Winston.

246 Steele, F. (1980). Defining and developing environmental competence. In C. P. Alderfer & C. L. Cooper (Eds.), *Advances in experiential social processes, 2,* 225-244, p. 225.

247 Steele, F. (1980). Defining and developing environmental competence. In C. P. Alderfer & C. L. Cooper (Eds.), *Advances in experiential social processes, 2,* 225-244, p. 225.

248 Martin, S. H. (2002). The classroom environment and its effects on the practice of teachers. *Journal of Environmental Psychology, 22,* 139-156.

249 Stapp, W. B. (1971). An environmental education program (K12) based on environmental encounters. *Environment and Behavior, 3,* 263-283.

250 Robinson, B., & Wolfson, E. (1982). *Environmental education: A manual for elementary educators.* New York: Teachers College Press.

251 Brody, M. (2005). Learning in nature. *Environmental Education Research, 11,* 603-621.

252 Lindemann-Matthies, P. (2002). The influence of an educational program on children's perception of biodiversity. *Journal of Environmental Education, 33,* 22-31.

253 Malone, K., & Tranter, P. J. (2003). School grounds as sites for learning: Making the most of environmental opportunities. *Environmental Education Research, 9,* 283-303.

254 Bradley, J. C., Waliczek, T. M., Zajicek, J. M. (1999). Relationship between environmental knowledge and environmental attitude of high school students. *Journal of Environmental Education, 30,* 17-21.

255 Martin, W. W., Falk, J. H., & Balling, J. D. (1981). Environmental effects on learning: The outdoor field trip. *Science Education, 65,* 301-309.

256 Schwab, K. E. (198283). Instructional methods: Their use and effectiveness in environmental education. *Journal of Environmental Education, 14,* 8-12.

257 Ramsey, J. M. & Hungerford, H. (1989). The effects of issue investigation and action training on environmental behavior in seventh grade students. *Journal of Environmental Education, 20,* 29-34.

258 Jordan, J. R., Hungerford, H. R., & Tomera, A. N. (1986). Effects of two residential environmental workshops on high school students. *Journal of Environmental Education, 18,* 15-22.

259 Agee, J. K., Field, D. R., & Starkey, E. E. (198283). Cooperative parks studies unit: University-based science programs in the national park service. *Journal of Environmental Education, 14,* 24-28.

260 van Wagenberg, D., Krasner, M., & Krasner, L. C. (1981). Children planning an ideal classroom: Environmental design in an elementary school. *Environment and Behavior, 13,* 349359.

261 Powers, R. B. (1985-86). The Commons Game: Teaching students about social dilemmas. *Journal of Environmental Education, 17,* 4-10.

262 Dresner, M. (1989-90). Changing energy end-use patterns as a means of reducing global-warming trends. *Journal of Environmental Education, 21*(2), 41-46.

263 Carlander, M. (1988). Atomalderns barn: Att arbeta for fred, miljo och globalt medansvar med barn pa lag-och mellanstadiet. / Nuclear-age children: Working for peace, the environment and global responsibility with children in grades 1-6. *American Psychology Association, 39,* 110.

264 Westphal, J. M., & Halverson, W. F. (1985-86). Assessing the long-term effects of an environmental education program: A pragmatic approach. *Journal of Environmental Education, 17*(2), 26-30.

265 Sommer, R. (1972). *Design awareness.* New York: Holt, Rinehart and Winston.

266 Kaplan, R. (1974). Some psychological benefits of an outdoor challenge program. *Environment and Behavior, 6,* 101-116.

267 Brockmeyer, F. M., Bowman, M., & Mullins, G. W. (198283). Sensory versus non-sensory interpretation: A study of senior citizen's preferences. *Journal of Environmental Education, 14,* 37.

268 Morrow, L. M., & Weinstein, C. S. (1982). Increasing children's use of literature through program and physical design changes. *Elementary School Journal, 83,* 131-137.

269 Sommer, R., & Olsen, H. (1980). The soft classroom. *Environment and Behavior, 12,* 316.

270 Wong, C. Y., Sommer, R., Cook, R. (1992). The soft classroom 17 years later. *Journal of Environmental Psychology, 12,* 337-343.

Workplace Environmental Psychology

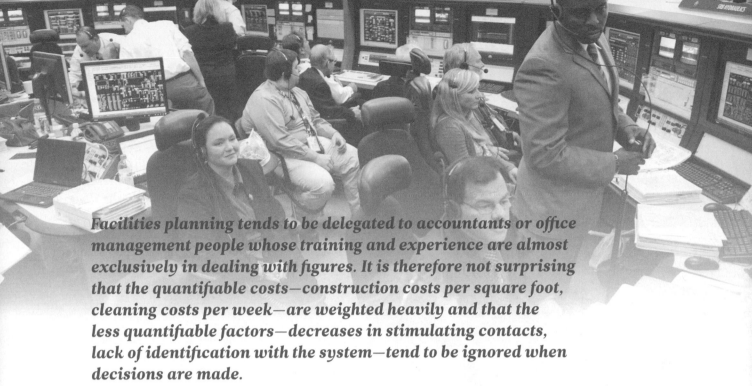

Facilities planning tends to be delegated to accountants or office management people whose training and experience are almost exclusively in dealing with figures. It is therefore not surprising that the quantifiable costs—construction costs per square foot, cleaning costs per week—are weighted heavily and that the less quantifiable factors—decreases in stimulating contacts, lack of identification with the system—tend to be ignored when decisions are made.

—FRED STEELE[1]

TOM STRUGGLED INTO CONSCIOUSNESS AS THE RADIO DRIBBLED OUT THE DREARY 7 A.M. *news. After dragging himself through the bathroom and kitchen, he went outside—only to discover that his car had a flat tire. "What do I do now?" he moaned to himself.*

If he wanted to make it to work on time, the only choice was to take the bus. The bus schedule was in a drawer somewhere, but of course he could not find it. Tom stood in drizzling rain for 20 minutes before the bus pulled up. The driver tossed out a cheery, "Morning, there! Wet today, isn't it!" All this for a part-time job, Tom thought.

After the bus dropped him off, Tom passed a machine shop as he waded his way to his office. Even if he were in a good mood, he muttered to himself, he wouldn't understand how those people could stand all that noise of machinery and yelling. He sat down at his desk, wishing he could just quietly let his clothes dry and his emotional health improve. Unfortunately, the open plan of his office made him the center of attention, and he felt compelled to pretend the whole situation was humorous. This did not improve his mood at all.

Throughout the day, he waited for a minute when his coworkers were all away from their desks so he could call Jane for a little sympathy, but there was not one moment when he was left alone. However, most of them didn't seem to mind calling to place bets, arrange parties, or talk to their friends.

Between his own desire for a moment's solitude and the steady stream of distracting conversations that he couldn't help overhearing, Tom was a wreck by the end of the day. He was determined to ride off into the sunset, even if it was on a bus. Then he remembered that his place was east of the office.

Without a doubt, he thought, we're going somewhere calm, sunny—and cheap—as soon as we can both get some time off.

WORKING CAN PROVIDE SOME OF THE BEST AND SOME OF THE WORST EXPERIENCES IN LIFE. For Sigmund Freud, it was one of the two major paths to fulfillment (the other is love, of course). Many fac-

FIGURE 11–1 Adults spend much of their lives in factories and offices. The effects of these settings deserve close study.

tors determine a person's productivity, stress, and satisfaction at work, but for decades, psychologists have realized that the physical environment is an important influence on employee productivity and satisfaction (see Figure 11-1). In this chapter, we consider the relations between the physical environment and (a) getting *to* work, (b) performance, feelings, social behavior, health, and stress *at* work, and (c) trying to enjoy life *after* work (by getting away). Throughout, we must resist the tempting but simplistic notion that changes in the physical setting will directly determine employee behavior. We will begin with a famous example.

EARLY RESEARCHERS HYPOTHESIZED that environment-behavior relations operated according to simple environmental determinism. The famous Hawthorne studies included a dozen years of work on the effects of the physical environment on the productivity and satisfaction of assembly-line workers at the Hawthorne plant of the Western Electric Company, near Chicago.[2] Many separate studies were completed, and the meaning of the voluminous results is still debated, nine decades later. Nevertheless, certain basic conclusions from the Hawthorne studies are widely accepted.

For example, early on, researchers hypothesized that changing the level of lighting on an assembly line would affect productivity. This is a straightforward hypothesis that anyone new to environmental psychology might reasonably propose: If workers can see better, they probably will be able to assemble more items, and production will rise. However, in several separate studies, production did *not* reliably vary with lighting level. At one stage, the amount of light was even reduced by 70 percent without a loss of productivity. The researchers became convinced that something very odd was happening when they replaced a set of lights with bulbs *of the same wattage* and found that the employees expressed satisfaction with the "increased illumination."

Some observers took these results as evidence that the physical environment at work is not important. Because the Hawthorne studies were one of the first large-scale investigations of environment and behavior, this conclusion probably set back the development of environmental psychology by three decades. Unfortunately, the conclusion is wrong. A more accurate view is that employee-environment relations are complex. Three important findings of the Hawthorne studies were overlooked by those who concluded the environment was unimportant.[3]

1. The findings refute an assumption that is itself faulty. The simplistic notion that lighting directly affects work output is a form of naive environmental determinism. Environmental psychologists believe that physical setting influences are mediated by employee perceptions, beliefs, preferences, experience,

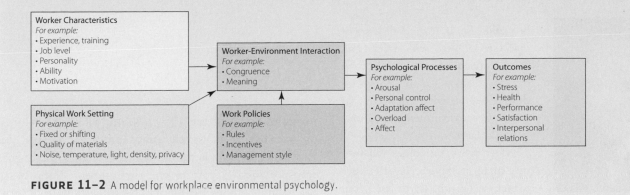

FIGURE 11–2 A model for workplace environmental psychology.

and personality. For example, the behavior of employees in the Hawthorne studies was clearly affected by their *perceptions* of the work environment. In the bulb-changing study, for example, employees probably assumed that if management went to the trouble and expense to replace a bulb, it must have been deficient; a new bulb must be an improvement.

2. The conclusion focuses on one environmental variable when a *different* environmental variable, more subtle but perhaps more important for that very reason, was operative.[4] Employees in some of the Hawthorne studies were moved to a different room, away from most employees. This room made the employees feel special, and *its* physical features may have affected performance more than the environmental factors chosen for examination by the researchers.

3. The layout of the room facilitated social contact among employees. This probably encouraged the employees to form and maintain informal norms about how much to produce in a given day.

In general, the Hawthorne studies disconfirm naive determinism, but they do confirm that physical settings have important influences on work behavior. However, these influences are more complex than the researchers thought. They involve broader, more subtle aspects of the setting, which in turn are influenced by employee characteristics (see Figure 11-2).

The work environment can be considered not only as a collection of physical stimuli (noise, light, temperature, etc.), but also as a physical structure (size, furniture, hallways, etc.), a place of beauty (or not), as a symbolic artifact (the meaning or image of the work setting), a place with which an employee identifies (or not),[5] and a place that "works" (that is, facilitates the tasks to be accomplished)

or not.[6,7] Each employee is experienced or not, noise-sensitive or not, senior or junior, motivated to work or not, etc. Fundamental psychological processes such as arousal, overload, affect, adaptation, and personal control are integral to employee-environment interactions. These employee-environment interactions lead to outcomes which, in general, may be categorized as performance, health or stress, satisfaction, and interpersonal relations.

One example of the modern approach to environmental psychology on the job examined how an employee's private self-consciousness moderates the effects of an unpleasant physical workplace.[8] **Private self-consciousness** (PSC) is the tendency to compare one's desired condition with one's actual condition; some people monitor this difference between their ideal and reality frequently, and some do not. When the work environment is objectively worse (more dangerous, high or low temperature, air pollution, noise), high-PSC employees experience more distress than low-PSC employees do. (If you have worked so far in your life, would you say that you are high- or low-PSC?)

More generally, the physical environment at work affects some employees more, or differently, than others. In another illustration, overloaded employees report fewer adverse reactions to heat and high density than employees who are not overloaded.[9] Apparently, overworked employees cannot or will not allow environmental problems to intrude into their consciousness. Whether this is wise or healthy is another matter, of course.

The physical environment at work is crucial to employees' performance, satisfaction, social relations, and health, but also to the organizations for which they work. Over the 40-year life cycle of an office building, only about 2 to 3 percent of all expenditures are on the initial costs of the physical environment; in contrast, about 90 percent is spent on salaries and benefits.[10] If the 2 to 3 percent is well-spent, very large savings on the 90 percent might

FRANK BECKER'S studies of quality work environments have been influential.

be achieved. If it is poorly spent, many employees will suffer (and, as a consequence, so will their organizations). Good workplace design begins with knowledge of employee-environment relations in workplaces.

Most work outcomes fall into one of four major categories: performance (productivity itself, but also such indicators as resignation rate, time spent in the office, and attendance), feelings (satisfaction, evaluations, attitudes, emotions, and perceptions), health and stress (morale, positive or negative changes in body or mind), and social behavior (spatial behavior, interpersonal interaction, privacy, status).

What affects these four kinds of work activity? Five major aspects of the physical setting that affect them include: sound (noise, music), the indoor climate (heat, cold, humidity), air (pollution, freshness), light and color (sunlight, incandescent, fluorescent, windows, views), and space (amount of it, arrangement of work stations). A general concern that applies to all these physical aspects of the workplace is a sense of control. Perceived control over the physical workspace (e.g., being able to adjust it to suit one's needs and preferences) increases not only job satisfaction, but also a feeling of stronger cohesiveness among colleagues.[11] Organizations can help increase this sense not only by providing adjustable furniture and ways to customize lighting and other aspects of the environment at each workstation, but also through training programs.[12]

We will soon stroll through the known relations between the four major categories of work activities and the five major environmental aspects of workspaces. First, however, we should "get to work," which of course is an important a part of the environmental psychology of work.

PERHAPS BECAUSE WE ARE THINKING OF OTHER THINGS, OR BECAUSE IT IS OFTEN UNPLEASANT, or because the experience literally is *transit*ory, we can easily forget that transportation is part of the environment. Cars, buses, roads, and rail lines are important settings both to the traveler and to residents of the neighborhoods through which they pass. Transportation, of course, plays a very large role in our lives. In economic terms, many of the largest corporations either manufacture vehicles or produce goods for vehicles. The cultural and social life of some developed nations is interwoven with the myths and realities of cars.

Environmental psychologists investigate many transportation-related behaviors, attitudes, impacts, and choices,[13] including such issues as: How do commuters choose their mode of transport, and how can those choices be changed? What is the impact of each transportation mode on the commuter? What is the impact of the traffic created by commuters on neighborhood residents? How do commuters view the places they pass through on the way to work? What role can transportation choices play in energy conservation? Can we design urban transit systems that meet the needs of both commuters and the residents of neighborhoods through which they move?

Driving Around in My Automobile

Fun, Fun, Fun? Cars are fun and convenient; they can bring status, privacy, and a sense of control to our lives. In many North American cities, more than 90 percent of employees drive a car to work (although in New York, Boston, and Washington DC, over 50 percent use public transit).

Cars are convenient, but they are also a threat to ourselves, the environment, and the rest of the living world. The current transportation system has been declared unsustainable by the Organization of Economic Cooperation and Development (OECD), an international council with 100 nations as members or associates. Over 30,000 people have been killed by or in cars *every year* in the United States, although the annual toll has been declining from the all-time high of over 54,589 in 1972, and nearly proportional numbers are killed in many industrialized countries. This does not include the much larger number of people who are seriously injured by cars.

Beyond that, huge numbers of animals are killed by cars, and many natural areas are split and despoiled by roads and highways. Despite improvements in their engines, cars remain an important contributor of greenhouse gases to climate change. In being habituated or even addicted to cars, people tend to ignore these facts. Many of these problems have been described, and some solutions have been offered.[14]

Commuting to and from work is a major part of the driving that people do. Thus, many or even most people in the developed world use the most expensive form of travel, which translates to ease for self, but damage to the ecosystem. For these reasons, many see the automobile as dysfunctional and unsustainable. It requires enormous expenditures by individuals, and by governments, which are responsible for providing and maintaining the road system, and of course, the government is us, too (through taxes).

Because most people continue to choose cars over urban transit, even when they know cars are very expensive, Joseph Reser raised this question: Are we actually *addicted* to automobiles?[15] Reser acknowledges that cars do serve several important perceived needs besides mere transportation, including a sense of freedom, a way to express oneself, privacy and security, status, convenience, and an opportunity to exert control over a powerful machine. He concludes that for many people, the use of cars is an adaptive response to a stressful macro-environment.

Who Uses Cars, and Why? Who uses which form of transit? People who have cars and higher incomes use public transit less.[16] Those who believe public transit is easy to use, reliable, safe, and uncrowded use urban transit more.[17] Those who have bad memories of transit, hate to be tied to fixed schedules, and believe that only the poor use public transit tend to use urban transit less.[18]

Environmental psychologists have investigated the transportation choices of commuters by trying to discover what information commuters themselves use in deciding how to get to work. For example, Levin and Louviere describe how concepts from psychology and economics may be blended to produce a behavioral choice model of the commuter's choice process.[19] The blend includes objective facts, such as the cost of urban transit, and subjective impressions, such as the commuter's attitudes toward urban transit. Even when a commuter's subjective impressions are incorrect, they play a major role in transit choices. For example, Levin and Louviere found that commuters who choose to drive cars markedly underestimate the overall cost of operating their cars.

The Consequences of Commuting

WHETHER WE TAKE A CAR OR USE PUBLIC TRANSIT, we commute to work when we choose, or are forced by circumstance, to live too far from work to walk or cycle. What are the behavioral and emotional consequences of driving to work? One important consequence is stress. All forms of commuting have their sources of stress. When we drive, we must deal with people who impede our progress. In one survey of automobile drivers, 12 percent of the men and 18 percent of the women said that at times they could gladly kill another driver![20] Not surprisingly, then, one behavioral effect of driving is an increase in adverse physiological reactions, such as chest pain and other forms of stress.[21]

What exactly makes commuting stressful? One factor is the predictability of the trip. If a person has made the journey many times in a highly predictable mode, commuting may be relatively painless, but as the journey becomes more unpredictable ("Will the bus be late? Will the traffic keep me from arriving on time?"), commuting becomes more stressful.[22] Adverse reactions to commuting are linked to personal characteristics and to the number of hindrances commuters face on the journey (measured as the time and distance from home to work). Commuters who drive longer distances have higher blood pressure. The more interchanges commuters must negotiate on their way to work, the more days they are ill enough to be hospitalized.[23]

Commuting also includes risks from others who drive dangerously. One danger in this situation is the aggressive driver. Who are these people, anyway? Apparently, they usually have hostile, sensation-seeking, competitive personalities, are driving without passengers, and are late.[24]

Can Commuters Be Pried from Their Cars? Several suggestions have been made. Joseph Reser's is to alter the negative aspects of the environment that cars help people to overcome (e.g., crowding on buses). Other environmental psychologists scrutinize both transportation alternatives (for example, suggesting how to make public transit more desirable) and commuters. For example, Israeli bus riders' perceptions of their transit system were sought, with the

FIGURE 11-3 Car-sharing is a small but growing solution for those who wish to reduce their car use.

goal of altering the bus service to fit their preferences.[25] The notion of evaluating transport services from the user's point of view seems obvious, but has not been done often enough.

Levin and Louviere's behavioral choice modeling approach proposes two general solutions to the problem. First, we could provide more objective information, such as presenting the true costs and benefits of alternative forms of transit. Often, but not always, this information suggests that we should build better urban transit systems, and use them. Second, we could find ways to change commuters' choices; this usually means finding ways to encourage commuters who drive to work alone to use public transit or to create and use ride-sharing opportunities.

In one attempt to do this, bus fares were reduced to zero in non-rush hours.[26] Ridership increased, but because such a large proportion of people drive cars, even free fares did not significantly reduce auto traffic in the city, and this approach may cost more than a transit authority can afford. Other solutions must be considered. One low-cost solution might be to ask drivers to commit themselves to a certain amount of bus riding. Getting commuters who normally drove to work to commit themselves to taking the bus twice a week was just as effective as giving away free tickets in increasing bus use.[27]

Christine Kormos and I asked drivers to reduce their vehicle use by 25 percent and informed them that others had switched to sustainable forms of transportation. Those in a high-social-norm condition decreased their commuting-related private vehicle use by approximately five times, compared to baseline.[28]

Environmental psychologists also attempt to understand why some programs are more effective than others.

For example, one might interview commuters who stay in a ride-sharing program and those who drop out, seeking variables that distinguish between the groups. Once such variables are identified, programs might be retooled so they respond better to the needs of commuters. Four factors distinguish successful groups from unsuccessful groups: whether the group can find a mutually acceptable pickup and drop-off route, the quality of agreements made in the group, the degree of similarity among the group members, and perceived equity (that is, the fairness of costs and benefits).[29]

Another option is car-sharing, which also has environmental and personal advantages (see Figure 11-3). Several programs were tried in England.[30] Each began with publicity ranging from an article in the company paper to posters, newspaper stories, and television ads. Only a small percentage (less than 2 percent) of the target populations joined the programs and survived the critical first few days of trying them out. About 10 percent of the participants who joined dropped out every 6 months, so that 4 years later about half the arrangements had disappeared. In the end, these programs did not change the transit patterns of about 98 percent of the individuals they were aimed at. Joseph Reser might say that addictions are hard to break.

On the other hand, car-sharing did change the lives of those who joined by saving them money and by enriching their social lives. It may be done informally with friends or colleagues, through one's employer, or as part of a commercial program. Portland, Oregon, had the first commercial car-sharing organization in the United States. Members joined because they occasionally needed a vehicle and wanted to save money. The advantage to the environment is that even though members did not drive less, they used fewer vehicles: 26 percent sold their personal vehicles, and 53 percent were able to avoid an intended purchase. Beyond that, most members reported that they walked, cycled, and took public transit more.[31] Addictions *can* be beaten!

Those who will not or truly cannot give up their cars have partially solved the stress problem another way: rather than give up their cars, commuters have turned their cars into pleasurable cocoons that are nearly as comfortable as home, with good sound systems, heated seats and steering wheels, and cup holders. I am told that some commuters in Bangkok cook their meals on portable stoves placed on the passenger seat because congestion makes their trip to work last hours.

Speaking of congestion, that is another important stressor for many commuters. Different ways of reducing it have been suggested (besides the old solution of simply building more roads with more lanes). London uses the toll system: drivers must pay every day to enter central London…or take public transit, which suddenly becomes much more attractive. About 30 percent fewer cars entered the congestion zone of central London after the toll system was implemented.

Might other methods work? Drivers who frequently experienced congestion were asked about two road pricing policies, one aimed at decreasing congestion (by instituting tolls) and one aimed at solving environmental problems (by charging more for bigger cars).[32] Both were acceptable *when* drivers expected that the policy would work if implemented.

For those who wish to try a different way to get to work, alternatives do exist. Public transit and cycling are the most obvious. Live too far away from work of school for those options? No local transit, or it is unattractive? Another partial solution, one that reduces driving a little and helps with health too, is to drive to within a certain distance of work or school (your choice; as far away as you can manage) and then walk the rest of the way. That's been my own choice for years. Another benefit (which happens to be the case for me, too): commuters who have some physical activity in their commute also spend more time exercising and otherwise being physically active.[33]

IN SUM *Most research on getting to work has been broadly concerned with encouraging people to choose less energy-intensive means of commuting as part of the general drive towards sustainability. Environmental psychologists have created demographic profiles of car and urban transit riders, devised models of commuter preference, provided positive information about urban transit, evaluated existing transit systems, offered reduced fares, and promoted car sharing. Commuting often is stressful, but the majority still drive, suggesting that the description of it as an addiction is not completely wrong. However, the more promising approaches are being sorted out from the less promising ones, and progress must be made, because the worldwide growth in cars and driving is not sustainable.*

SOUND, NOISE, AND MUSIC

ON THE JOB, SOUND may come from jackhammers, office machines, background music, co-workers talking, and many other sources. Some of these sounds may be expected, natural, or even desirable—silence is not always pleasant—but others may be unwanted and annoying. Fancy formulae exist for specifying the conditions under which sound is likely to be labeled noise,[34] but the most straightforward way to define it is this: **Noise** is unwanted sound. (In case you were wondering, desirable and beautiful sound, in contrast, is called **euphony.**)

Noise bothers a huge number of employees, and not only in industrial settings. One study found that 99 percent of office employees report that noise (mainly telephones ringing and people talking in the background) impairs their concentration.[35]

Whether a particular sound is heard as noise or euphony depends on the individual and the situation. One person's euphony may be another person's noise: A whisper at 2 yd./m (30 decibels) may be euphonic, and a rocket lifting off at 300 yards/m (200 decibels) may be noise. However, to the workers who labored long and hard to enable that rocket to lift off, the 200 decibels may be euphonious. To give you a sense of "normal," noise levels in typical offices average about 45 decibels and range from about 40 to 60 decibels.[36]

Noise and Performance

EARLY NOISE RESEARCH FOCUSED ON HEARING DAMAGE from loud industrial sounds. Even today, many industrial workers are exposed to sound levels that can cause either temporary or permanent hearing damage. More workers today use hearing protection devices, but a recent study found that manufacturers' ratings of the degree to which

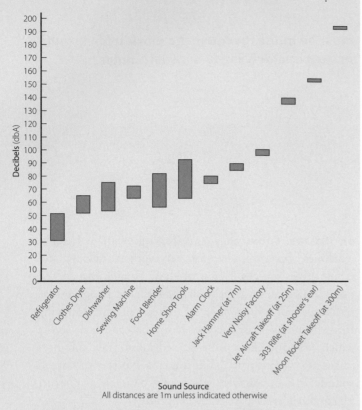

FIGURE 11–4 The loudness of some familiar sound sources. The dBA is a measure that weights objective sound pressure to approximate the human perception of loudness.

these devices reduce sound are substantially overestimated; they may not provide as much protection as they claim.[37]

Usually, individuals who lose their hearing do not lose it suddenly; instead, the lowest level of sound that they can detect at a given frequency gradually rises—that is, a shift in the hearing threshold develops. A **temporary threshold shift (TTS)** is one that reverses itself within 16 hours (about the length of time between leaving the noise source at work and returning to it the next day.) If a threshold shift repeatedly is allowed to last into the next workday, it may become a **permanent threshold shift (PTS)**. This process may easily go unnoticed, and the victim may gradually lose considerable hearing ability. A TTS can occur after only 10 minutes of 100 decibel sound,[38] a sound level that may be found in very noisy factories and in many concerts and nightclubs. TTS can also occur after 90 minutes of 90 decibels, a sound level found in many factories; it is about the loudness of noisier kitchen waste disposers and electric lawn mowers at a distance of 3 ft./1 m.[39] (See Figure 11-4). For these reasons, occupational health and safety standards are set in terms of length of exposure to a given level of sound. For example, in one jurisdiction,

workers may be exposed to 105 decibels, but for no more than 15 minutes, whereas they may be exposed to 99 decibels for an hour, or to 90 decibels for 8 hours.[40]

Sound levels in offices rarely reach levels that endanger hearing, but that does not mean sound is unimportant in offices. Other factors (such as the source, meaning, controllability, and predictability of the sound) may be more important than the loudness of the sound. As the sound's *source* becomes more relevant to an employee, as its *meaning* grows, and as its *controllability* and *predictability* decrease, a sound is more likely to be perceived as noise and to negatively affect work behavior. Whether noise affects actual productivity at realistic sound levels in actual offices is not yet clear,[41] but it can.[42]

Many employees and researchers *believe* that noise interferes with performance, but the evidence itself is contradictory. In fact, noise occasionally has even been shown to improve work performance.[43,44] Noise-performance relations remain unclear partly because of inadequate research funding, which has been less than one-twentieth of the amount spent on noise-induced hearing loss.[45] This is unfortunate because sound itself and research on sound effects on behavior are both extremely complex.[46]

In a good example of the complex relations between noise and productivity, people were asked to proofread in a room that either was quiet or received intermittent bursts of sound at 70 decibels.[47] They were able to detect as many spelling errors and they could recall the passages they had proofread as well in the noisy condition as they could in the quiet condition. Conclusion one: Performance is *not* affected by noise. However, the people could not detect as many grammatical errors when it was noisy. Conclusion two: Performance (of another kind) *is* affected by noise. When the room was noisy, they started working more slowly and they worked less steadily. Conclusion three: Performance (of yet other kinds) *is* affected by noise. Yet, in the noisy room, participants actually worked *more accurately*. Conclusion four: Performance is *improved* by noise!

Varying results like these illustrate six conclusions that a sophisticated consumer of the noise literature will learn. First, the *task* matters. Work may be grouped into four broad types of tasks: cognitive (reading, writing, reasoning, creative), vigilance (monitoring people, a machine, or a production line), motor (manual manipulation of tools), and social (meetings, evaluations of employees). For a particular employee, a given task may be familiar and well-learned or not. Tasks may be relatively simple or complex.

We may be asked to engage in one task at a time or several. The task may be an expected part of one's routine or the boss' idea of a new direction.

Based on this, one broad conclusion is that employee performance will not be affected by continuous loud noise when an employee (1) performs a routine task, (2) merely needs to react to signals at certain definite times, (3) is informed when to be ready, and (4) is given clear visual signals.[48] Examples of work fitting this description include servicing a machine one knows well or writing a routine letter. Tasks that are often affected by noise include those that ask the employee to pay attention to multiple sources of information or to perform more than one task at a time.[49] If an employee must monitor several other employees or machines, or think carefully while performing, performance is more likely to be affected.

The effects of noise differ for simple versus complex tasks. A typical finding is that noise hinders the performance of complex tasks more than it hinders the performance of simple tasks.[50] In fact, noise sometimes *improves* the performance of simple tasks.[51] For example, if a person works in a skateboard factory and has assembled the same skateboard model a thousand times, some noise (that is not too irritating) might physiologically arouse the employee enough to speed up work on this very well-learned task. This is an extension of the **Yerkes-Dodson hypothesis**, which states that performance is better at moderate levels of arousal than at either low or high levels of arousal. A little arousal "pushes" performance of a simple task up toward the peak of this inverted-U-shaped function, but a further dose of arousal (too much noise) may push performance over the peak and down (see Figure 11-5).

When one of several tasks is more important, noise tends to increase the effort expended on less-important tasks.[52] Consider, for example, the difference between finding spelling errors and finding grammatical errors. For some people, spelling errors almost leap off the page; performance on this almost automatic task may not be affected for them. On the other hand, the detection of grammatical errors requires more thought, and performance is more likely to suffer as one's effort shifts to searching for spelling errors. Finally, manual tasks are not as easily affected by noise. The performance of manual labor is not affected much by noise, but employees tend to *believe* they are working harder. In fact, they may indeed be working harder at the cognitive level in order to maintain the expected level of performance at the objective level.[53,54]

Second, *employee characteristics*, such as gender, age, and personality matter. For example, under noisy conditions, women slowed their work *pace* but men did not (*accuracy* was the same for both).[55] Performance can be affected by age: noise slows reaction time and harms the memory of older people more than younger people.[56,57] However, older people may perform some tasks better: in noisy conditions, older men responded more accurately than young and middle-aged men to non-obvious events that occurred during a task.[58]

Personality also modifies work performance in noise. As you would expect, the performance of noise-sensitive workers is adversely affected by noise.[59] Some are able to screen out unwanted stimuli better than others.[60] Possibly, screeners can tune out noise because they have developed coping strategies that nonscreeners do not have.

Extraverts prefer more stimulation in general, and sound in particular, than introverts;[61] noise harms the reading comprehension of introverts more than that of extraverts.[62] The performance of introverts is more affected than that of extraverts by distractions that are similar to others that are important to the task.[63] Introverts seem to perform tasks under noisy conditions better in the evening; extraverts perform the same tasks better at midday.[64]

In low-noise conditions, people with an external locus of control comprehend reading material better than those with an internal locus of control.[65] The performance of creative employees appears to follow the Yerkes-Dodson hypothesis (better performance at moderate levels of noise or arousal), but the performance of less-creative employees does not.[66]

Third, *characteristics of the sound itself* are important. As you know, sound may be loud or soft, high or low, continuous or intermittent, familiar or novel, meaningful or not, musical, mechanical, masked by other sounds, natural, or human. One of the clearest findings is that *novel* sounds reduce performance.[67] Because novelty wears off, the same sound may not affect performance shortly after its introduction. Loud and uncontrollable noise causes people to

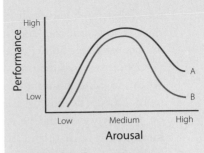

FIGURE 11–5 According to the Yerkes-Dodson hypothesis, performance is better for easier tasks (naturally), but this difference is greater when a worker is more physiologically aroused

remember more negatively toned trait words and worsens their moods, but this does not happen as much either in loud controllable noise or quieter uncontrollable noise.[68]

Cognitive tasks may not be affected much by a steady "white" noise, but mixtures of sounds that are heard in many offices (keyboards, background speech, and music) do interfere with the performance of cognitive tasks.[69] Intermittent noise often causes temporary setbacks in performance during the noise.

Some employees are able to compensate for losses during noisy periods with increased efficiency during quiet periods, so that their overall performance is similar to that under uniformly quiet conditions.[70,71] When noise is unpredictable, coping strategies are more difficult to implement, so performance may suffer more than when the noise is intermittent but somewhat predictable. When noise is masked (not reduced in volume, but "covered" with white noise so that its distinctive elements are reduced), performance of some tasks improves.[72]

Fourth, certain *employee-noise combinations* affect performance. For example, employees may perform better when the ambient sound level matches their preferred sound level.[73] Those who have had more time to adapt to noise may learn new material faster.[74] Employees who have control over sound probably are less affected by it than are employees who do not have control over the sound or whether it is on or off.[75] Employees who can turn on a sound (such as some music) when they believe it will not affect their present task and turn it off when it bothers them will probably accomplish more than employees who have no choice in the matter.

Fifth, aspects of *the environment* affect the relation between noise and performance, but not always in expected ways. For example, one might guess that when noise and vibration are present, performance of a cognitive task such as doing arithmetic in your head would worsen, but actually performance was no worse when the noise and vibration were present in subjectively equal amounts. However, performance *did* decline when either noise or vibration was subjectively lower than the other.[76]

Sixth, as we saw in an earlier chapter, noise can affect performance *after it ends*.[77-80] However, performance is not always worse:[81] it can actually be better when moderate noise is followed by an easy task *or* loud noise is followed by a difficult task.[82] Furthermore, what an employee experiences after the noise ends can also play a role. After spending a few hours doing office work, with its

usual noises, people either watched a nature film about a river, with river sounds, or merely heard the river's sounds. Those who both saw and heard the river felt more energetic than those who merely heard the river sounds.[83]

Music and Performance

DOES MUSIC AFFECT PERFORMANCE? Sometimes music can speed people up or slow them down, as we saw in earlier chapters. However, the effects of music are not that simple. They depend on the kind of music, the type of work, and the characteristics of the individual employee.

Some studies do support the idea that music improves productivity,[84] but three problems cloud this research. First, some of this music research omitted key elements, such as control groups. Second, if the music on the job was a novelty, its positive effects might have been caused by that, rather than the music itself. Third, some studies examined only simple, repetitive tasks, which leaves open the question of its effects on cognitively demanding work.

Nevertheless, light music can increase productivity even in modern workplaces, with their greater cognitive demands, although sometimes it does harm performance.[85] When you consider the vast variety of tasks that employees undertake at work, and the vast variety of musical styles, tempos, and volumes, you will agree that no simple conclusion can be drawn at present. Music *may* increase (or decrease) productivity, but the conditions that do so have yet to be clearly identified; future research is needed.

Feelings about Noise

AS DEFINED EARLIER, NOISE IS UNWANTED SOUND. If you ask industrial or office workers their opinion about noise, they quite naturally will tell you they do not like it and wish it would go away, and that noise adversely affects their own productivity. Not all noise is equally aversive: for example, noise that an employee experiences as relevant is less annoying than irrelevant noise,[86] it is worse in open-plan than closed offices,[87] people with neurotic tendencies seem to experience the same noise as more annoying,[88] and women report being more annoyed.[89]

Overall, noise is rated as an important problem by employees. In a typical survey, over 1,000 office workers rated the "opportunity to concentrate without noise and other distractions" as the *single most desirable* office characteristic (out of 17 choices). In rating their own workspace, all but

2 of the 17 office characteristics were rated *more* satisfactory than "the opportunity to concentrate without noise."[90] In another survey of employees at 58 sites, job satisfaction declined as noise from people talking and telephones ringing increased.[91] In short, office employees believe that noise is a serious problem.

However, a clear gap exists between the results of the productivity studies and the attitude studies. Actual performance often is unchanged by noise (although sometimes it is),[92,93] yet many employees clearly believe that noise detracts from their work. Who is correct? One answer may be that researchers have not yet examined sufficiently sensitive measures of productivity. That is, perhaps productivity truly declines in noisy conditions, but the measures of productivity used have been insufficiently sensitive to detect the decline. Also, sometimes only short exposures to noise are examined, but at work some employees are subjected to years of it. The effects of noise on productivity may be gradual and cumulative.

Second, perhaps employees do not really know themselves. Employees do not usually keep objective counts of their own productivity, so their opinions about noise and productivity may be formed in good faith, but are simply inaccurate. For example, participants in one study *believed* that noise hurt their performance when it did not.[94]

A third possibility is that both viewpoints are correct. Because employees whose work slows in noisy periods are often able to work faster and better during quiet periods, their overall performance could appear unaffected. However, to struggle during noisy periods and to compensate during quiet periods in order to achieve the same overall level of performance requires greater effort and more-effective coping strategies than does performance during uniformly quiet work sessions. This gives the appearance of "no" decrement in performance, with stress being experienced by employees.

As I have often noted, environmental influences—in this case, noise—do not act alone. In Israel, a study of absenteeism among 802 employees showed that noise was a significant predictor of absenteeism, but that it interacted with gender and job complexity: absenteeism was greatest for women with more complex jobs who labored in noisier conditions.[95] Noise—or the lack of it, quiet—also can have indirect effects. Stress on the job reduces job satisfaction and organizational commitment, but if employees are provided with a quiet environment, the effect of stress on satisfaction and commitment is much reduced.[96]

Of course, the objectively loudest work settings are in industry, but industrial work tends to include those types of tasks, described earlier, that are least affected by loud sounds (see Figure 11-6). However, even in industrial settings, workers feel better when the sound levels are reduced. When company morale was examined after employees moved to a new site with strongly reduced noise levels, job satisfaction, environmental satisfaction, stress, ease of communication, attitude toward the company, and company attachment all improved.[97]

FIGURE 11–6 One very noisy job.

Feelings about Music

EMPLOYEE ATTITUDES TOWARD MUSIC ARE CLEARER. Most like it and *believe* that it improves their productivity. However, up to 10 percent of employees definitely do *not* like music at work. Sometimes this is a function of the type of music played and sometimes employees find that it interferes with their work. Music should be introduced to the workplace very carefully. As discussed earlier, it may raise or lower productivity. However, because 90 percent or more of employees prefer music, removing it once it is installed is likely to cause bad feelings among the vast majority of employees.

Health and Stress

PHYSIOLOGICAL CHANGES CAUSED BY SOUND in workplaces are limited, for the most part, to hearing loss. Long-term noise exposure may even change the brain. Among workers who had five or more years of chronic noise exposure on the job, the strength and the hemispheric organization of their speech-sound discrimination changed, and the speed of their other sound processing decreased.[98] Prolonged loud sound may have effects that go beyond hearing and sound processing. A review of 40 studies concluded that

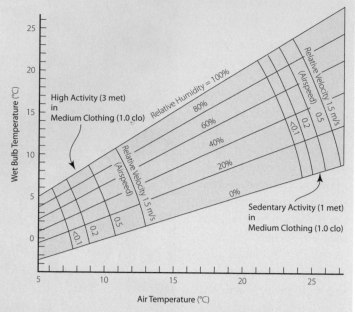

FIGURE 11–7 Comfort zones that simultaneously take into account temperature, humidity, air speed, activity level, and amount of clothing have been developed.

employees who are exposed to unpredictable noise for at least three years and whose work involves mental concentration have at least a 60 percent higher chance of cardiovascular disease than other employees.[99] Unfortunately, many of the studies were unable to separate noise effects from other aversive factors that were present at the same time. Nevertheless, the conclusion is consistent with the idea that employees who must expend extra effort coping with loud noise suffer long-term consequences.

Noisy factories seem to have another side-effect, perhaps less critical, but certainly undesirable: more laryngitis and sore throats! All that yelling required to make oneself heard on a noisy factory floor seems to increase the frequency of throat problems.[100] Low-level noise, such as that found in offices, may produce stress-caused reactions such as reduced motivation to solve problems or fewer attempts to improve one's work conditions, yet does not seem to result in an increase in *perceived* stress.[101] This suggests that even in less-loud noise, stress may occur even though employees do not report any.

Stress can pile up, not only from noise, but from other workplace sources, as we shall see later. The build-up is the result of complex, multiple stressors. A model of cumulative risk has been developed and tested, and it successfully predicts employee well-being.[102] Once stressed, employees understandably have a need to recover. This level of need for recovery can now be assessed with a recently developed scale.[103]

Social Behavior

A KEY SOCIAL EFFECT OF NOISE IS TO IMPAIR EMPLOYEE PRIVACY. The ideal workplace should be sufficiently quiet to permit concentration and communication without too much difficulty. Open-plan offices should be suffused with enough masking sound to allow for conversational privacy.[104] Existing open-plan offices very often are deficient in acoustical privacy, with up to 90 percent of employees unhappy about the lack of opportunity to converse confidentially.[105,106] Even among office employees who are generally satisfied with the physical aspects of their office, mechanical noise (such as telephone, heating and ventilation equipment) and human noise (overheard conversations) are associated with increased tension, depression, anger, and fatigue.[107]

Office privacy is also importantly influenced by spatial arrangements. Generally, walls and partitions provide a greater sense of privacy,[108-110] but open-plan offices are often deficient in sound insulation. In addition to depriving employees of privacy, noise may make them less helpful. Participants exposed to 85 decibels were less likely to help another person who had just dropped something than were participants exposed to 65 decibels or less.[111] The implications for jobs in which the primary function of employees is to help clients, customers, or coworkers are obvious.

Noise even seems to influence employees' judgments about their coworkers. Students playing the role of managers were given the resumés of five newly hired applicants.[112] These student-managers were asked to consider the qualifications of the five new employees and then to recommend a starting salary for each one. They made their recommendations after reading the new employees' resumés either in a room where the sound level was about 53 decibels (normal office sound level) or a room where the sound level was about 75 decibels (loud but realistic office sound level). The student-managers in the noisier room recommended starting salaries for the same five new employees that were significantly less than those made by student-managers in the quieter room. This result, which was later replicated, has enormous implications not only for pay recommendations, but for other kinds of recommendations made at work, and for interpersonal attitudes among coworkers.

IN SUM *Noise has many effects on work activities and feelings. In industrial settings, it can* *cause serious hearing loss. Loud noise is particularly dangerous when employees do not realize that deafness comes slowly and almost imperceptibly. Despite the common supposition that noise affects performance, research in natural settings shows (a) how complex the issue is and (b) that performance decrements depend on the task, the person, and the type of noise. Noise harms performance when certain combinations of employee, task, and type of noise co-occur, but not under some other circumstances. For certain routine tasks, noise may even arouse an employee enough to improve performance. Music may improve performance, but research on the topic is suspect. Once again, no universal effect is to be expected: performance effects, if any, are a function of person, task, and music. Noise is disliked by definition but, for the most part, employees like music on the job. They generally think noise hinders and music helps their performance. Noise is a serious problem in modern open-plan offices. Employees find sound a problem both coming and going: sound entering their workspace is annoying, and when their own words escape over partitions too easily their privacy is compromised. Office noise may even affect important interpersonal behavior, from mere impressions of others to important judgments regarding them. Some research suggests that long-term exposure to loud sound has serious physiological effects that extend beyond hearing loss.*

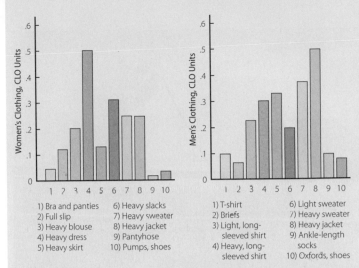

FIGURE 11–8 The CLO is a measure of the capacity of each clothing article to insulate a person.

INDOOR CLIMATE

HEAT AND COLD CAN AFFECT MOST WORK BEHAVIOR BUT, AS USUAL, THEIR EFFECTS ARE COMPLEX. Temperature itself is multifaceted. The temperature of the air alone does not help us understand its influences on work behavior very well. A hot dry atmosphere is quite different from a hot humid one, and the degree of air movement further affects the character of the atmosphere. **Effective temperature**—an index composed of air temperature, humidity, and air movement measures—has replaced that of simple temperature as a better indicator of indoor climate (see Figure 11-7).

The effects of temperature depend on the type of work being done, the amount of clothing worn, and the length of time spent in high or low effective temperature. My sister, who lives in the country, tells me that firewood warms her twice—once when she cuts and splits it, and again when she burns it. As I sit writing this, and as you sit reading it, very little heat is generated; a higher effective temperature obviously is necessary for comfort when we are writing or reading than for my sister when she is chopping wood. The effect of temperature on work depends in part on how much clothing we wear. Researchers have even invented a scale (the unit is called the **clo**) to measure exactly how much each piece of clothing helps to keep us warm[113] (see Figure 11-8).

Another complexity in temperature research is that **core body temperature** is sometimes more important than effective temperature. Core body temperature takes some time to change, so short-term exposure to a wide variety of effective temperatures may not affect work behavior. Most of the time, most employees are not seriously affected by cold or heat. When the ambient temperature is low or high, they often can adjust it or at least adjust their clothing. Even though they may not be perfectly comfortable, they do not feel the same level of distress as they would to

FIGURE 11–9 Some jobs, such as that of these welders who are working outside, must be done in very cold conditions, and the low temperatures can affect performance.

other uncontrolled variables in their environment, such as noise. Nevertheless, some consequences of heat and cold may be found for most types of work.

Performance

EVERY POSSIBLE OUTCOME HAS BEEN REPORTED FOR HEAT AND COLD—performance declines when it is hot and when it is cold; performance increases when it is hot and when it is cold; performance is unchanged when it is hot and when it is cold. Increases *and* decreases in performance at the same time have even been reported.[114] For example, people whose body temperature was high were asked to detect certain signals. Compared to those whose body temperature was lower, they detected more signals correctly (better performance) but they also made more false detections (worse performance).

Nevertheless, certain general patterns in the research findings do exist. For example, as temperatures rise into the very hot range, productivity definitely drops, especially for heavy manual labor,[115] but sometimes even for complex cognitive work.[116] Another relatively consistent result is that cold temperatures negatively affect the performance of work that requires fine movements and sensitive touch from an employee's hands.[117,118] Interestingly, the performance of such tasks does not gradually slip as the temperature drops, but seems to hold up well until hand-skin temperature reaches a certain point (about 57° F/14°C), then drops off quickly.

As in classrooms, cool (not cold) offices, may *improve* the performance of cognitive tasks and reduce post-work fatigue, even though employees prefer warmer temperatures.[119] In general, the more complex the task, the more that performance will worsen with heat or cold. Tasks that require vigilance and dual tasks appear to be performed best in moderately warm temperatures (80°-88°F/27°-31°C), but tracking tasks and learning tasks are performed best at slightly lower temperatures.[120]

The length of time an employee is exposed to heat or cold can change whether or not temperature affects performance. Cognitive performance is essentially unaffected up to 100° F/38°C, if the employee must only work 30 minutes. However, if the employee must work three hours, the maximum temperature before cognitive performance is affected is about 87° F/30.5°C.[121]

Outcomes that do not conform to these basic trends are caused by factors besides temperature itself. Examples include which task is being performed and whether the employee is acclimatized, believes the temperature is controllable, has coping strategies, and is motivated. One obvious coping strategy, for example, is to adjust the amount of clothing one wears. When office work was performed in cool (65° F/18°C) or warm (78° F/25.5°C) temperatures with the same degree of humidity, lightly dressed men performed best in the warm conditions and worst in the cool conditions, but heavily dressed men performed best in cool and worst in warm conditions.[122]

Workers often are able to think of other, more complex ways of overcoming inappropriate temperatures. The point is that where coping strategies exist and are used, questions about how temperature affects performance become irrelevant. The more useful questions are about how and why employees cope with, or fail to cope with, unusual temperatures.

Feelings

FEELINGS ABOUT TEMPERATURE ARE USUALLY STATED IN TERMS OF COMFORT. Much engineering research has been devoted to finding the ideal effective temperature. Obviously, no single temperature is best, but the modern approach has been to identify **comfort zones.** For example, an office employee working at a desk while wearing light clothing in a room with 45 percent humidity will be comfortable when the temperature is between 75° and 80° F (24° and 26.5°C). A field study showed that the limits of comfort under typical humidity and clothing conditions are 70° to 80° F (21° and 26.5°C)[123] (see Figure 11-9).

Feelings about temperature are affected not only by the actual temperature, but by what the individual *thinks* the temperature is, and even by room decor. Individuals report feeling warmer, at equal temperatures, when the heating devices in a room are pointed out to them, the decor is more luxurious, and thermometers are fixed to report higher than actual temperatures.[124] For example, college students were asked how comfortable they were when an actual increase of 5° F (2°C) occurred and when they were led to believe that such an increase had occurred.[125] The students reported similar changes in comfort for the real and the fake temperature increases. The fake heating strategy may be unethical as an energy conservation tactic, but it illustrates the Hawthorne principle: One's *perception* of a situation is often more important than the objective characteristics of the situation.

Perceived control affects satisfaction with temperature. When employees believe they have some control over the room temperature, their satisfaction with the actual temperature is greater.[126] Interestingly, however, *having* that control also has its drawbacks; the effort implied by being responsible for the temperature seems to cause some dissatisfaction. Thus, employees sometimes want control but not to have the responsibility that comes with control.

One might think environments that are ideal in terms of comfort would be ideal in terms of performance—that a comfortable employee is a productive employee. Again, this common-sense hypothesis is not true. Performance of office-like work was significantly better in temperatures about 18°F/9°C below the comfort envelope standard.[127] Despite saying they were too cool, workers in the cool conditions also reported feeling more energetic at the end of an hour's work than at the beginning of the session! (In warm conditions, their reported energy *declined* during the hour.)

Health and Stress

TEMPERATURE STRESS DEPENDS on effective temperature, duration of exposure, and the amount and type of protective clothing. Lasting physiological changes from high or low temperatures take a long time to develop, unless the temperatures are extreme (e.g., if a person touches a flame or falls through the ice into a freezing lake). Apart from these extremes, the human body is wonderfully able to adapt to a wide range of environmental conditions. The Inuit (formerly known as Eskimo) have adapted well to very cold conditions. Inuit adults work and their children play outdoors in temperatures that would make those of us who live farther south scurry for warmth.

On the hot side of the temperature spectrum, while visiting India I saw hod-carriers who ran all day in the summer heat with heavy loads of bricks on their backs. Clearly, individuals can adapt to severe conditions, but physiological changes, or **temperature stress,** will occur as they acclimatize, and may occur even after they are acclimatized. For example, fishermen who work the cold northern Atlantic waters actually undergo semi-permanent physiological changes in their hands that allow them to avoid discomfort and frostbite longer than non-acclimatized individuals.[128] Individuals differ in acclimatization—some seem to adapt better than others—but this is less important in determining temperature stress than one's length of exposure.[129] Although most individuals who have the time to adapt to large temperature changes can do so, some never acclimatize. Among people in very cold conditions, those who are older, more depressed, and have no previous cold-caused injury are less likely to engage in preventative actions than others.[130] Both heat and cold have acute effects on cardiovascular disease when people are exposed to them over long periods of time.[131]

Social Behavior

HOW DOES TEMPERATURE AFFECT INTERPERSONAL RELATIONS? We must recall that many work settings have well-controlled temperatures, so heat or cold sufficiently extreme to affect social behavior is uncommon. The simple assumption might be that when moderately hot temperatures occur, employees will be more aggressive toward their co-workers. However, the relation between heat and aggression varies with other factors, too, such as the length of exposure, whether a person has access to fluids, and even whether those fluids are alcohol-based drinks or not.[132] We must be cautious in our conclusions about how heat affects aggression at work.

IN SUM *Indoor climate is best measured by effective temperature, which includes humidity and air movement as well as temperature.*

Relatively extreme effective temperatures do not affect many work behaviors unless core body temperature is altered. The effects of temperature are also usually muffled by access to appropriate clothing. The amazing variety of temperature effects reported partly are the result of these measurement and clothing factors, as well as one's degree of acclimatization, knowledge of coping strategies, motivation, and the type of work. Engineers have outlined well-described comfort envelopes, but environmental psychologists have discovered that comfort depends on perception as well as actual effective temperature and that optimal performance may be found outside the comfort envelope. Temperature stress occurs when individuals are initially subjected to temperatures far outside the comfort zone, but many people can adapt to these more extreme temperatures after longer-term exposure to them.

AIR

THE INGREDIENTS IN WORKPLACE AIR can play an important role in work behavior and health. Considerable concern has been expressed over the effects of air pollutants in offices, particularly in newer buildings that are tightly sealed for energy conservation, with recirculated air replacing openable windows. Sometimes the ventilation equipment malfunctions, filters are not maintained properly, or intakes suck in tainted air and distribute it. In one infamous case, air from a government health building's lab was circulated to offices. The air contained viruses that had been sent to the lab for testing. Ironically, many employees got sick in a building devoted to the promotion of health!

Performance

DOES AIR QUALITY AFFECT ACTUAL PERFORMANCE AT WORK? We do know that commuters trying to *reach* work occasionally have problems, such as when carbon monoxide levels on roads are high enough to affect driving ability.[133] Employees engaged in normal amounts of manual labor apparently are unaffected by moderate doses of carbon monoxide,[134] although some of these results are based on short-term exposure of healthy young males. Carbon monoxide and other pollutants may yet be found to affect performance in more sensitive groups or over longer time periods.[135]

Other kinds of work are affected by carbon monoxide and other air pollutants that restrict the oxygen-carrying capacity of the blood. For example, when a job calls for prolonged alertness but generally involves low stimulation, performance may be affected by moderate levels of carbon monoxide.[136] Such concentrations may be found in buildings close to major roadways.

Carbon monoxide is poisonous but odorless. Bad-smelling air seems to have its own effects; it impaired performance of a relatively complex task (proofreading) but not of a relatively simple one (simple arithmetic).[137] When the air smelled bad *and* participants believed they could not avoid the smell, their persistence at working on puzzles declined significantly.[138]

Another aspect of air that has been suspected of affecting performance is the level of **air ionization**. Clean rural air contains about 1,200 positive and 1,000 negative ions per cubic centimeter of air, but modern urban air-conditioned offices contain only about 150 positive and 50 negative ions (the beneficial ones, in this case), per cubic centimeter.[139] On the assumption that modern industrial cities and workplaces are deficient in negative ions, some individuals have become convinced that negative ion generators are valuable (I know of two reputable environmental psychologists who had the machines in their offices).

The popular press and manufacturers of ion generators have made so many exaggerated claims about the alleged benefits of negative air ions that many other environmental psychologists scoff at any mention of air ions (except, of course, my two acquaintances!). The United States Food and Drug Administration even prohibited the sale of ion generators back in the mid-1950s. However, very high ion concentrations may affect performance. When individuals who did not know that ions were being tested, but were exposed to negative ion concentrations over 4,000 per cubic centimeter, their reaction times were significantly faster and they had better motor coordination.[140] Very high levels of negative ions also significantly improved basic perceptual motor tasks,[141] but some studies report no effects of negative or positive ions.[142-144]

As is often the case, individual differences matter. Some people may be more ion-sensitive than others.[145] Air ions may affect men but not women.[146] (see Figure 11-10). Type A personalities (irritable, consistent sense of urgency, strong reactions to stress) exhibited more aggression (delivered more heat to others in a lab experiment) when high levels of negative ions were present than when low levels of negative ions were present. The latter results are puzzling because negative ions are generally thought to provide beneficial outcomes. One suggestion is that negative ions act as arousal agents, magnifying natural tendencies; for Type A individuals, this may cause an increase in aggressiveness. This magnification effect of negative ions was replicated: higher levels of them produced more arousal and seemed to intensify either positive or negative feelings about other people, and caused people to make more errors on a simple cognitive task, as if they were too aroused to be accurate.[147] Perhaps the conclusion here is that ions have complex effects that vary with different individuals, and that others are not affected at all. The possible benefits of fragrances on work performance have been investigated. They do improve performance on certain tasks, such as monitoring simple displays on a computer screen and completing word puzzles.[148,149] Despite claims to the contrary, probably no particular fragrance has special power; rather, any fragrance that a person finds pleasant will work. However, the effects of fragrances appear to decline over the course of an hour or so, and they now are banned in many workplaces because some people have adverse health reactions to them.

Feelings

THE QUALITY OF AIR AT WORK is a growing concern as speculation and knowledge about potentially harmful fumes from office machines and building materials increases. Among office workers, air quality is one of the most important factors in the environment.[150] Apparently, many more office workers feel like complaining about air quality than actually do so.[151] How much air-related dissatisfaction exists? Over a thousand employees in nine buildings were surveyed; 75 percent reported that too little air circulated "sometimes" or "often," 77 percent said the temperature was too cold, and 72 percent said it was too hot "sometimes" or "often."[152]

These problems have led to the development of a formula to predict how many employees will complain about drafts.[153] For example, at 72°F/22°C and air movement of 8 inches/0.2 meters/second, around 20 percent of employees will complain of drafts, but at the same temperature and air movement of 12 inches/0.3 meters/second, around 40 percent will complain.

A true story about air in a factory illustrates how important employee *perceptions* of environmental conditions can be.[154] Many complaints about the stuffiness and lack of movement of the air in the factory were

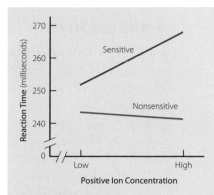

FIGURE 11–10 A simple behavior (reaction time) that is important in many tasks such as driving and operating equipment is harmed by high concentrations of positive air ions for those who are ion–sensitive (i.e., have low automatic lability) but not for those who are not ion–sensitive.

received, but when the ventilation system was thoroughly checked, no problems were discovered. Many of this factory's employees had worked outdoors most of their lives, and they felt that buildings *must* be stuffy and breezeless. Then someone devised the idea of attaching streamers to the ventilation outlets near the ceiling. When the employees could see the streamers flying, their complaints about air movement stopped.

Those negative ions are at it again, this time with feelings. In the offices of a large insurance company in Britain, employees working in greater concentrations of negative ions felt warmer and more alert; they also judged the environment as fresher.[155] Others reported feeling more relaxed and stimulated and less irritable and depressed after six hours of negative ion exposure.[156]

Finally, what about fragrances and feelings? In short, they are risky; as noted above, some people have medical sensitivities, but of course others may be impressed by a fine fragrance. In an interesting mock job interview study, applicants either wore scents or did not.[157] Female interviewers gave more positive evaluations to applicants who wore fragrances than to those who did not, but male interviewers gave more positive evaluations to applicants who wore no scent than they gave to those who did wear some. Conclusion: know who will interview you! Altering the local airspace may be perceived as air *pollution* or air *enhancement*.

Health and Stress

AIR QUALITY CAN HAVE DRASTIC EFFECTS ON HEALTH, as the relatives of many Legionnaires who attended the fateful convention in 1976 that killed 29 people, made 182 others ill, and gave birth to a new phrase (Legionnaire's Disease) will testify. Modern ventilation systems are capable of moving air very efficiently, but if an airborne disease agent gets into the system, the same efficiency becomes a severe liability. Besides disease-causing microorganisms, air can carry other agents that make people ill, including ozone (emitted by some office machines), tiny airborne particles from asbestos (found in many office buildings of a certain age), cigarette smoke in some places, and organic solvents such as benzene (found in copy machine toner). Most of these agents have been linked to serious diseases, such as cancer, and to a wide variety of troublesome minor problems including eye irritation, respiratory tract problems, allergies, thyroid disturbance, gastrointestinal cramps, and others.[158] Both white- and blue-collar workers are exposed to bad air. One survey found that more than 50 percent of factory workers say they are exposed to hazardous air pollution in their work.[159]

Sick buildings are structures that contain airborne health-threatening substances. **Sick building syndrome** refers to the collection of health problems linked to these substances. Two syndromes have been distinguished: **building-related illness** (a cluster of symptoms found in all office buildings to differing degrees), and **building-specific illness** (a cluster of symptoms that occurs only in air-conditioned buildings).[160]

Sick building syndrome is very common. At one point, the Environmental Protection Agency estimated that 20 to 30 percent of all U.S. office buildings cause health problems—including at the EPA itself![161] Precisely what causes sick building syndrome is unclear, perhaps because there are multiple causes and multiple symptoms in employees. Modern chemicals, tight sealing, poor ventilation, noxious fungi, poor duct design, a history of smoking, physiological susceptibility, mass psychogenic illness (workers

frightening one another into illness), and "complaining personality" have all been offered as possible causes.[162,163] Conflict and poor communication about the issue itself may lead to the persistence of the symptoms.[164]

The sick building phenomenon became so widely known that one advertisement for an office building to rent sported this headline: "Enjoy Fresh Air! You can open our office windows." Of course, how fresh that outdoor air is depends on where you live; in some places the filtered indoor air may be cleaner than outdoor air. Also, two virtues clash when windows open: the fresh air is usually nice, but heated (or cooled) air simultaneously leaves, which is not very good for energy conservation.

Whether any particular employee is affected by air quality depends on the concentration of the hazardous agent, the coping strategies of the employee, the employee's basic physiological sensitivity, and whether the employee has control of temperature and ventilation. In general, sick building syndrome is partly explained by environmental factors and partly by personal factors.[165] Relatively low levels of oxygen in a tightly sealed building, for example, may affect only those workers who do not get outside for a break or those who require larger amounts of oxygen (such as employees engaged in heavy labor).

However, when oxygen levels sink very low, nearly everyone will be affected. Some years ago, the trading floor of the Toronto Stock Exchange had to be cleared when many employees and traders began to faint, speak incoherently, and complain of numbness in their chests. Apparently, all the doors and windows had been closed, and the busy traders simply used up all the available oxygen! Air conditioning alone (without any airborne pathogens) can cause eye, nose, and throat irritation.[166]

Interestingly, merely having control over air quality or not is related to employee health. Employees who could not control the air conditioning in their workspace were three times as likely to report building illness symptoms such as headaches, fatigue, and respiratory irritation as employees who could control the air conditioning in their space.[167] Finally, air ions have been implicated in health as well as performance and feelings. The frequency of headaches was compared when negative ion generators were on and off (without the knowledge of the employees); when they were on, headache reports dropped by about 40 percent.[168]

Social Behavior

AIR IN A WORKPLACE CAN EVEN AFFECT SOCIAL RELA-TIONS. Most relevant studies have focused on cigarette smoke and bad odors. Smoking indoors has drastically declined, but still exists in some places. The general trend is that people like others whose smoking preferences match their own.[169,170] Bad odors are also not very common in most workplaces, but they too do occur sometimes. Attraction to others in odoriferous settings depends on attitude similarity; if people think alike, bad smells actually seem to *increase* attraction.[171] Sharing an odor disaster with someone similar to ourselves apparently causes people to draw together. As for others…not so much: moderately bad odors in the presence of unfamiliar others actually led people in an experiment to shock an unfamiliar other person more.[172] Motivation to work matters. When people were highly motivated to work, their annoyance with cigarette smoke was relatively small, but when they were not very motivated to work, they were much more annoyed by cigarette smoke.[173]

IN SUM *Several components of air—including carbon monoxide, air ions, and bad odors—may affect performance, but the effects are not striking under normal conditions. Extremely high concentrations of negative ions may facilitate some basic cognitive processes, but for many people who are not ion-sensitive, these effects are not strong. However, long-term exposure, differential physiological sensitivity, and psychological moderators such as perceived control and motivation to work help to explain why the performance of some individuals is affected but that of others is not. When it carries chemical impurities or disease-causing organisms, air can seriously impair health. Air quality is a growing concern of employees. Lack of control over noticeably bad air may affect persistence at work and, in some circumstances, foster negative feelings among employees.*

LIGHT AND COLOR

LIGHT IS, OF COURSE, ESSENTIAL TO WORK. Without it, few jobs can be performed at all. Fortunately, natural or artificial light is nearly always available. Research on light primarily involves comparisons of different light:

- Sources (e.g., sunlight, incandescent, fluorescent, sodium vapor),
- Fixtures (e.g., ceiling, desk, floor lamp, etc.),
- Amounts (illuminance), and
- Arrangements (angle at which it strikes the work surface, uniform versus non-uniform).

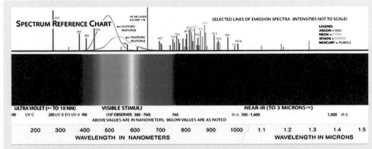

FIGURE 11–11 The full spectrum of light, including both the visible and invisible portions of it. UV is ultraviolet light, and IR is infrared light.

Light sources vary in which parts of the visible spectrum are emphasized, which means they have different color tones (see Figure 11-11). Color is less essential than light in the workplace, but it is nevertheless important for safety coding and wayfinding. Until recently, lighting primarily was studied from an engineering standpoint, using specialized equipment and terminology.

However, in the search for optimal lighting from a purely technical point of view, the human dimension sometimes gets lost. For example, one of the main reasons for the widespread installation of fluorescent tubes is their energy efficiency. An incandescent bulb transforms about 10 percent of the electricity it uses into light; the other 90 percent is transformed into heat. The ratio for a typical fluorescent bulb is about 20 percent light to 80 percent heat. The newer LED lamps are even more efficient. However, many people simply do not like the color or intensity of their light. Therefore, attention now focuses more on the concept of **lighting quality**, which takes into account individual well-being as well as architectural and economic factors.[174,175]

How does light affect performance, feelings, social behavior, health, and safety? We first consider performance.

Performance

A META-ANALYSIS THAT DONALD HINE, JENNIFER VEITCH, AND I CONDUCTED demonstrated that within the normal range of lighting, from slightly dim to quite bright, performance of office tasks improves with more light.[176,177] However, this statement requires several qualifications.

1. Optimal light level depends on the task. Proofreading fine print obviously requires much more light than a roundtable discussion.

2. The work surface is important. If the surface is shiny, higher light levels—especially from undiffused sources such as a bare bulb—will cause glare, which can hinder the performance of many tasks.

3. The angle of the light is important. For some tasks, performance is enhanced when light is very diffused. Surgery and assembly-line work are examples. For other tasks, the definition of surfaces provided by shadows means that carefully angled lighting is best. Examples of such tasks include searching for flaws in fabrics or other manufactured objects that should have uniform surfaces.

For these reasons, one conclusion on which engineers and environmental psychologists agree is that lighting should be tailored, if possible, to each task and individual. If implemented, this policy would probably result in much greater use of immediate or local lighting and decreased use of lighting intended to serve everyone working in a large area. One positive effect of more localized lighting would be energy savings realized from the reduced use of light in work areas that do not require their current, probably excessive, levels of light.[178] Energy-efficient lighting does not seem to harm work performance,[179] and even when workers are able to choose their level of lighting, most choose levels that are within energy conservation guidelines.[180]

The full-spectrum lamp has received much attention, primarily for its alleged effect on seasonal affective disorder (see Figure 11-11). Such reports have led some observers to assume that full-spectrum lighting must have a broad range of benefits, such as improved performance for typical (non-depressed) office employees. Paul Boray,

Lorne Rosenblood, and I compared full-spectrum lamps with regular cool white and warm white lamps.[181] Over a broad range of cognitive tasks, we found no performance increment for full-spectrum bulbs, and a later review of the research literature came to the same conclusion.[182] In a follow-up study, Jennifer Veitch, Donald Hine, and I investigated the possibility that *belief* in the full-spectrum lamp produced performance increases.[183] As before, no performance-enhancing qualities of full-spectrum lamps were found, but when people were *told* that full-spectrum lamps had benefits, their reading performance increased. Oddly, however, reading performance also improved when they were told that claims about the benefits of the lamps were highly exaggerated!

Increased light appears to increase arousal level. A clear demonstration of this came in an investigation of the alertness of shift workers.[184] After working one night under quite dim light, employees worked the next night under dim, moderate, or bright illumination. Those who worked in the brightest condition were the most alert, and their cognitive performance was significantly enhanced. Alertness is a problem with shift work, so attempts have been made to adjust employees' biological clocks to cause them to be more alert at night and less alert during the day.[185] A light was used as a "pacemaker" to gradually adapt the employees to brightness at night and darkness during the day; this seemed to be effective.

Four methods of lighting graveyard shifts (midnight to morning) were compared.[186] Special skylights were used that could keep illumination high, low, increase it across the shift, or decrease it across the shift. High but decreasing light levels improved performance on complex cognitive tasks, compared to the other conditions. Brighter light seems to physiologically arouse employees; decreasing levels appear to be effective because high levels of light at the start of a shift counteract the normal sleepiness at that time of day. Apparently, once aroused at the start of a shift, employees do not need continuing stimulation from light.

Light levels may influence the amount of time that employees spend in the office. Employees are more likely to leave a darker office when given the choice, such as eating lunch away from the office versus eating at their desks.[187]

As always, outcomes depend on the task. Creativity is an important type of performance in many occupations. Should the light be bright to stimulate it? Actually, no: people appear to be more creative in the dark![188] Darkness seems to create a sense of freedom from constraints, which opens the door to thinking in a more risky, exploratory way. Need an idea? Turn out the lights!

In general, giving employees control over their work environment and other aspects of their jobs is a good idea, and often produces better performance. Is the same true for lighting? In a simulated office, Jennifer Veitch and I gave some people control over the type of lighting they could use while others were denied control. Those who were given control performed *less* well on creativity tasks than those denied control.[189] This was unexpected, but it is consistent with the idea (introduced earlier) that although control often is desirable, it carries with it the cost of being responsible and having to make decisions. Perhaps this "cost of being in control" affects creative work.

As noted earlier, little quality research on color has been conducted that directly relates to workplaces. Color may have unexpected effects. Would you guess that office workers type faster in offices with red or blue walls? They typed in red or blue office settings, and then typed again either in the same-colored setting or the other-colored setting. They made no more errors in one color setting or the other, but they made more errors when they were moved to the different-colored setting.[190]

Feelings

SOME SURVEYS INDICATE THAT MOST EMPLOYEES are generally satisfied with lighting,[191] but others report that complaints are frequent.[192] The resolution of this contradiction probably rests with the type of work an employee does. Those who perform visually demanding work often believe lighting is inadequate, but those whose work is not visually demanding believe their light is adequate. The importance of lighting varies with office type: employees in enclosed offices say that lighting is more important than do employees in open-plan offices.[193] In general, darker offices and factories may be less satisfying.[194,195]

Some types of lighting produce dissatisfaction because they render colors strangely. Many people have had the experience of buying clothing that appears apricot in the store, but looks more like diseased carrot at home. At work, poor lighting can do the same to skin color. When people were asked to judge the acceptability of a familiar face (their own) under several different light sources, incandescent and warm-white incandescent lamps were the most acceptable, followed by cool white and "improved" mercury lamps.[196] At the bottom were two kinds of high-pressure sodium lamps. The importance of semi-permanent off-color appearance at work has not yet been demonstrated, but it would not seem to be conducive to good interpersonal relations on the job. Individuals find a variety of light sources and types more interesting than single-source lighting or repetitive use of one kind of fixture.[197]

Employee feelings about another source of light are clear: Light from outdoors is very desirable.[198] Although sunlight has high potential for glare, employees like to be located near a window. Those who are located farther from a window are more often unhappy about lighting. Greater sunlight penetration is associated with greater job satisfaction.[199] Too much sunlight penetration, however, is not relaxing.[200] Windows, of course, also offer views, which contribute to satisfaction,[201] and buffer the effects of job stress.[202] Windows offer the opportunity to stay in touch with conditions in the outside world—weather, time of day, and the action on the street. Windows probably do not improve work performance,[203,204] but they do reduce boredom and increase overall job satisfaction.[205]

Given the usual complexity of person-environment relations, one study adopted a broad approach to predicting outcomes from daylighting; it included personal influences (e.g., gender), building influences (e.g., quality of the view to outdoors), and perceptions of the environment (e.g., impressions of the office) as predictors of physical and psychological discomfort, sleep quality, and environmental utility.[206] Attractive window views reduced discomfort (which improved sleep quality at home!), but close proximity to a window and perceiving the lighting to be of lower quality was associated with thermal and glare problems.

"Here's an idea: let's use very high-resolution display screens to replace actual windows! Employees can see nature on the screen, and then we don't need to have windows in our offices!" Well, no; at least in terms of recovery from the kind of mild stress one finds at work, this does not work.[207] Actual windows reduce stress, but fancy screens are no better at doing that than a blank wall.

Employees in windowless offices try to compensate anyway; they put two[208] or three[209] times as much visual material—especially on nature themes—on their walls as occupants of windowed offices, and are five times more likely to bring plants into their offices.[210] Workers even desire interior windows (from room to room), especially if the room seen through the interior window has a window to the outdoors.[211] Given that employees definitely prefer windows, researchers now examine more specific questions. Apparently people prefer proportionately larger windows in smaller rooms, for example, and smaller windows for a computer work room than for an office.[212]

So far we have concentrated on feelings *about* lighting. What sort of feelings are created *by* lighting? Lighting designers certainly believe that different arrangements of light create different moods, but evidence concerning this belief is not abundant. Fortunately, a model developed by Jennifer Veitch, Guy Newsham, Peter Boyce, and others provides a framework for pursuing these questions. For example, they find that employees' appraisals of lighting influence their aesthetic judgments and mood, and this in turn influences their work engagement.[213] The *amount* of light affects mood; when people rated literary passages under bright, typical, or dim light, they gave the passages more extreme emotional ratings under bright *or* dim light than under normal light.[214] This suggests that emotion is heightened by lighting that strongly differs (in amount) from the level that one is used to.

Gender may matter. In the same typical office light, women rate the lighting as more glaring and intense than men,[215] and women experienced more bluish light as "warmer." This may be because they find themselves in a better mood in the more bluish light.[216]

Health, Aging, Stress, and Safety

LIGHT IS IMPORTANT FOR HEALTH. Ultraviolet light, rare indoors, assists in the formation of vitamin D and in the body's processing of calcium. The advent of artificial lighting has changed the biological rhythms of most industrialized peoples. Glare causes eyestrain, and it is found in a surprising variety of places in the typical office, from shiny pages in a book or magazine (indirect glare) to sunlight streaming into our eyes from behind someone a person is talking to (direct glare).

As we age, the ability of our eyes to gather light diminishes; a person needs more light to experience the same level of environmental illumination. People 60 years old, on average, need about three times as much illumination as people 20 years old.[217] Thus, workplace lighting should take into account the age of employees, but merely increasing the level of light is not always the best strategy: the possible associated increase in glare must also be considered.[218] In addition, high illumination levels from fluorescent lamps, especially full-spectrum lamps, make offices less desirable in social terms, increases visual discomfort, and physiologically arouses people.[219]

Control over lighting at work may affect our health beyond eye strain alone. Employees in one large-scale survey who personally could change their lighting conditions were three times less likely to report building illness symptoms.[220]

Employee safety, particularly in industrial settings, is obviously threatened by inadequate lighting. Considerable research has been devoted to, for example, the reduction of glare from dangerous areas such as the surface of the saw bed in the vicinity of power saw blades. Proper illumination in transit areas of a building also prevents accidents. In European factory studies, increases in illumination levels from 14 to 93 footcandles/150 to 1,000 lux have resulted in accident rate reductions of 50 percent.[221]

Social Behavior

DOES LIGHT AFFECT SOCIAL BEHAVIOR ON THE JOB? Lighting occasionally prompts discussions about how bad or good it is or whether it makes employees appear look attractive or not to others. Apart from the study that examined the acceptability of one's own face under different light sources, only one study has examined whether others look more or less attractive, and in it my colleagues and I found no evidence that full-spectrum or regular fluorescent lamps make any difference.[222]

However, different *amounts* of light may affect appraisals of other employees' work.[223] When lighting level was quite low (14 footcandles/150 lux), performance appraisals were more positive and people were more willing to donate volunteer time than when the lighting level was quite high (139 footcandles/1,500 lux). This is somewhat surprising because, according to the arousal model, increased illumination should produce more activity in general and more communication in particular. One study supports this counter-intuitive result, but another supports the arousal model. The first found that brighter light produced *less* "conversational energy" than soft light, contrary to theory.[224] In the second, I found that when participants wrote letters to one another, they wrote more intimate things and wrote for a longer time in brighter light, which is consistent with the arousal view.[225]

Different spectral qualities of light (slightly different color tones) may affect certain other judgments at work.

Warm-white fluorescent lamps, which look slightly more orange-red, may produce a greater desire to resolve conflicts through collaboration and to donate more time; cool-white lamps may produce a desire to resolve conflicts through avoidance.[226]

IN SUM *Light affects work behavior primarily when it is insufficient (leading to low productivity and accidents) or improperly placed (leading to glare and eyestrain). Office lighting often is excessive. Many employees dislike fluorescent and other newer forms of lighting, some of which distort color. Carefully placed local lighting could resolve some of these problems. Access to natural light and views is psychologically important.*

SPACE: DENSITY AND ARRANGEMENTS

HOW DOES SPACE—THE AMOUNT OF IT AND HOW IT IS ARRANGED—AFFECT EMPLOYEES? This chapter emphasizes research in traditional office and shop settings, which comprise most contemporary work settings. However, the growth of computers and related telecommunications systems is now increasing the feasibility of working away from the traditional workplace. This totally different use of space for work will be briefly discussed first.

Working Away From Work

WORKING AWAY FROM THE CENTRAL OFFICE is called **telecommuting**.[227] In the popular media, articles about telecommuting depict a smiling employee sitting in a home office, working at a computer in front of a large picture window looking over an idyllic scene. Some suggest that soon most of us will be working at home. However, a more thoughtful analysis shows that telecommuting is not for everyone. It may promise an end to commuting, reductions in the burning of carbon for driving, and a reduction in the cost of working for the employee (such as clothing costs), but it has more potential for employees whose work is based on information than for those in manufacturing, it can conflict with home life, it may create social isolation,

and it can pose supervisory problems. Even some employees whose job *could* largely be accomplished at home prefer the office as a place that is specifically set aside for work, keeps them in touch with co-workers, and sustains their motivation.[228] Nevertheless, telecommuting may be right for some employees. Female insurance claims processors, for example, were very satisfied with it, and the practice resulted in a 69 percent drop in absenteeism and a 10 percent increase in productivity.[229]

Traditional research on workspaces emphasizes the study of **human factors**, also called **ergonomics**. Volumes of information have been produced on how machines ought to be designed to suit human needs at the immediate workstation—for example, how best to lay out the controls in airplane cockpits or how chairs for secretaries ought to be designed.[230] Environmental psychologists are more interested in how best to arrange the office or industrial floor as a whole. Some workers toil in very cramped spaces, such as submarines; others work in spaces that are too wide open for them (there is a basis for all those lonesome cowboy songs!). In some offices and industrial settings, space may be almost entirely open, such as in an airplane manufacturer's hangar or the office bullpen, or it may be so private that employees must pass several guardian secretaries to gain the ear of the big boss. What *is* known about the effects of spatial arrangements?

Performance

FEW STUDIES HAVE COMPARED ACTUAL JOB PERFORMANCE IN DIFFERENT WORKSPACE ARRANGEMENTS. One difficulty is in measuring performance accurately, particularly in white-collar jobs, although some useful beginnings have been made.[231] Somewhat indirect measures of performance such as withdrawal (leaving the workplace when the employee has a choice) and turnover (the rate of resignations) have been used. For example, when an office has fewer barriers (walls or partitions), withdrawal rates are higher.[232] If we can generalize from laboratory studies, offices with high employee densities (i.e., little space for each person) jeopardize performance, especially if the work involves physical mobility and interaction.[233]

The amount and arrangement of space have joint effects. When less space is available so that employees are closer together *and* fewer barriers or enclosures are present, higher turnover and withdrawal rates occur.[234] Performance ratings decline when employees work in offices with a combination of higher density and closer interpersonal distances, and when they have difficulty screening out unwanted stimulation.[235] In plain language, when employees are squeezed together and have few physical barriers to ease the high density, they leave.

Open-plan arrangements are said to facilitate communication, which sounds as if they would increase productivity. Unfortunately, this does not always follow, mainly because the increased communication often is not work-oriented; often, it is more social or irrelevant in nature than productive.[236] Are interviews conducted in offices affected by privacy or sound level? Cheuk Fan Ng and I found that low privacy plus high sound levels understandably produces dissatisfaction, but interviewees did not speak *less* with the interviewer.[237] When irrelevant speech abounds, employees believe that their workload is higher, and it affects their performance.[238] In a sense, their workload *is* higher, because they spend extra effort to tune out the irrelevant speech.

Attitudes about spatial arrangements may not correspond to performance-related behaviors in those arrangements. Professors usually can choose to spend parts of their work days in their office, at the library, or at home. The actual number of occupied and unoccupied faculty offices in colleges that had open-plan or private offices were counted. Even though faculty in the open-plan arrangements expressed dissatisfaction with working there, they were present in their offices just as often as were faculty in private offices.[239] Motivated employees strive to do their work even in environments they do not like. They may often be successful in doing so, but the cost of coping with an inhospitable setting over the long term may be high.

Many people keep plants in their offices. Some employees believe they clean the air and improve comfort, creativity, health, and productivity.[240] However, plants may not be universally beneficial: employees' moods improved with the number of plants, but their performance actually *declined* as the number of plants increased.[241] The role of plants needs more research, because for others, the presence of plants improved performance immediately after a demanding cognitive task, but not shortly afterward.[242] In my own office, I have several plants; I just like them.

Not every feature of offices affects performance. When people could choose their own locations in a room, they tended to choose seating near windows for sunlight and outdoor views, but they did not necessarily perform better there. They also tended to believe that visual glare caused by sunlight would hinder their performance, but it did not, at least as much as they thought it would.[243]

Feelings

AS IN EVERY SETTING, HIGH POPULATION DENSITY often leads to feelings of being crowded, which leads to other negative outcomes. In a medical clinic, employees with less space per person felt more crowded, were late for work more often, more often wanted a transfer, and reported lower job satisfaction.[244] However, this was not universally the case: employees who were very busy or whose jobs required them to move around did not show this pattern.

When spatial arrangements are inadequate, employees sometimes are quite willing to say so, and sometimes they try to escape that location or are more often tardy or absent. Too often, however, employees adapt to bad situations, or do not realize that the surroundings could be better. As mentioned in earlier chapters, I call this unfortunate form of passive adaptation to a dysfunctional setting environmental numbness.[245] In such cases, employees do not spontaneously report their feelings about the workplace. Overloaded employees may be even more environmentally numb than others; overworked clerical employees actually complain *less* than others about temperature and density problems.[246]

On the other hand, if employees are directly asked their opinions and feelings about their workplace, they will respond quickly and fully. Where I teach, for example, we sent out a long survey on the office environment to campus employees. In only a few days, with no reminders, over 80 percent of the surveys were returned—an exceptionally high return rate for mass-distributed surveys.

The biggest issue in workplace arrangements at present is whether or not open-plan offices are beneficial. The majority of employee reactions to open-plan offices are negative.[247] Furthermore, the negative opinions often do not change with time.[248] Not surprisingly, employees who are not stimulus-screeners have a hard time in open-plan offices.[249] A few positive responses come from employees who recently moved from dingy, cramped former offices into bright new ones (a novelty effect), or from employees who enjoy the social aspects of work more than they enjoy the work itself.

Open-plan offices have been defended (against high-walled cubicles and private offices) as spaces in which employees can more easily "read" cues from others.[250]

When some researchers were moved to an open-plan space, they generally liked the new arrangements, but the new arrangements did not produce the expected increase in collaboration.[251]

Supervisory or professional employees and those whose work requires confidentiality, are especially unhappy with open-space designs.[252] That different groups of employees are affected differently also emerged when professional, managerial, and clerical employees moved from traditional enclosed offices to open-plan offices. Professionals were affected least; clerical and managerial employees the most.[253] Clerical staff actually experienced an increase in privacy and the adequacy of their work area; managers reported that their privacy and work area worsened.

Despite the bulk of negative evidence, the percentage of all offices that are arranged in open plans continues to increase. Why do open-plan arrangements continue to grow in popularity? One reason is that employee resentment has taken a long time to be documented, collated, and fed back to organization heads. Second, some organizations appear to believe that territoriality is bad, and deliberately create office space to minimize it. However, as we learned in an earlier chapter, territoriality usually does not mean conflict; instead it usually provides order and the chance for a person to establish an identity. Thus, when one organization decided to eliminate territories and personalization through design, the result was that employees felt that their work identity was threatened, and they began to use various tactics to regain their lost sense of identity.[254] Third, organization heads are still being sold very effectively on the alleged advantages of open-plan offices, including cost savings by putting more employees in less overall space, and better tax breaks on furniture. For example, a marketing manager for open-plan systems will argue that carpeting costs can be cut by 20-30 percent because installers do not have to cut around walls and partitions.[255]

What are the long-term consequences of choosing tax breaks and an immediate 20-30 percent saving on carpet costs over the considerable dissatisfaction of employees? Employees are not merely dissatisfied with open-plan offices, they also begin to feel their jobs are less significant.[256] They begin to believe their tasks are less significant and they spend less discretionary time (during coffee breaks and lunch) in the office.[257] A few organizations have begun to respond to these problems. One computer company, for example, has implemented a "neighborhood" concept—small groups of employees in an open area, but with walls

FIGURE 11–12 Office appearance creates impressions. What sort of impression would you develop about this office's occupant?

between the neighborhoods. Whether the open-plan office can be adapted to fit human needs remains to be demonstrated; its research record to date is generally poor, except for a "honeymoon" effect at first, when all is shiny and new.

Is the problem with open-plan offices caused by a lack of privacy or by the sheer number of others one can see? Is it a matter of working with a large or small *number* of coworkers or one of spatial density or arrangements?[258] This perspective, based on Roger Barker's behavior setting and staffing theories, hypothesizes that when too many or too few staff members operate behavior settings, performance and feelings are affected.[259,260] In 22 bank branches that varied in size, employees in small branches did report greater **setting claim**—that is, the sense that they are needed, perform important jobs, and work hard. In turn, greater setting claim was significantly related to greater job satisfaction, greater identification with the bank, and less tardiness. Thus, space in the sense of staffing level is another important component of feelings about work.

Environmental psychologists have begun to examine combined environmental influences at work. For example, employees are more dissatisfied when they work in offices with higher densities, closer interpersonal distances, *and* they have difficulty screening out unwanted stimulation.[261] When offices have few enclosures, place employees close together, are relatively dark, and are occupied by larger numbers of employees, dissatisfaction is, not surprisingly, higher.[262]

Another dimension of feelings in offices is the reactions of visitors. Have you ever entered someone's office and quickly developed an impression of the person who works there? Desk placement, display of status symbols, and tidiness are related to visitors' feelings and on their perceptions of the office occupant[263] (see Figure 11-12).

Some findings were obvious. For example, a tidy office creates the impression that the occupant is organized, a display of status symbols (such as diplomas and awards) makes visitors believe the occupant is higher in rank, and a messy desk makes them think the occupant is busy and rushed. Other findings are less obvious. An office with neat stacks of papers—as opposed to an office that is messy or extremely tidy—makes visitors feel comfortable and welcome. Visitors also seem to think that occupants of such offices are high achievers.

Desk placement may be open (that is, placed against a wall so that the office occupant has no barriers between self and a visitor), or closed (that is, placed between self and visitor). Open arrangements make visitors feel welcome and suggest to them that the office occupant is extraverted and has confidence in dealing with others. Informal seating positions (kitty-corner or side-by-side) elicit more positive evaluations of the office occupant's concern for visitors than do more formal seating positions (e.g., directly opposite).[264] When office occupants choose to sit at a small conference table in the office rather than at a desk, they are seen as more friendly, caring, helpful, and open-minded, but less authoritative. Thus, the mere arrangement of one's office can create important differences in the impressions of visitors.

The visitor's personality makes a difference, too. For example, not everyone prefers tidy offices; sensation-seekers seem to prefer messier offices than nonsensation-seekers.[265] Whether the office's occupant is present also seems to matter: A messy office *without* an occupant produces favorable ratings of the occupant, but these impressions were lessened or even reversed when the occupant is present in the midst of a messy office.[266]

The impression of the organization as a whole depends in part on visitor impressions of reception or lobby areas. Most organizations are aware of this and make some effort to create a positive impression with their reception areas. But what *is* a positive impression, exactly? One view is that such areas vary in two important ways: the amount of *control* and the amount of *consideration* implied by the decor of the lobby or reception area.[267] The message that control (order, stability, rigidity) is important to an organization is conveyed by the display of flags, official seals, logos, and emblems. The message that consideration (warmth, comfort, ease, and goodness of communication) is important is conveyed by plants, art, magazines, and furniture arranged in a sociopetal manner.

However, these control and consideration dimensions are not salient to everyone. Students who saw reception areas differentiated them only on the basis of high versus low consideration, whereas executives differentiated them on the basis of both dimensions.[268] Thus, in general, visitors' perceptions of organizations are based in part on the design and decor of reception areas, but visitors are variably sensitive to the variations.

Health and Stress

MIGHT THE VERY ARRANGEMENT AND AMOUNT OF SPACE IN AN OFFICE AFFECT EMPLOYEE HEALTH? That health might be affected by poor air quality, extreme temperatures, or even noise seems likely, but space and the building design itself? Apparently so. Office employees who worked with fewer enclosures surrounding them and with more other employees reported more fatigue and psychosomatic complaints, particularly if they were nonscreeners.[269] When 1,200 employees who worked in enclosed versus open-plan offices were surveyed, about 40 percent of employees in the open-plan offices said they "frequently" suffered from headaches, whereas only 20 percent of employees in enclosed offices said they "frequently" had headaches.[270] That employee health may be compromised by open-plan arrangements is serious and warrants further investigation: satisfaction, productivity, and interpersonal relations all must suffer if employees are often tired or feeling sick at work.

On the positive side, some building features have the potential to improve employee health. As concern about unhealthy body weight increases, researchers are looking for ways to encourage more physical activity during the course of working. One such tactic is to encourage the use of stairs. For example, placing motivational signs throughout a building and playing various types of music in the stairwell both significantly increased stair use.[271] Another approach to increasing stair use is to "squeeze" people a bit by reducing the number of operating elevators.[272] Those who need elevators for physical reasons still have them, but those who are capable of using stairs are "nudged" in that direction.

Social Behavior

OPEN-PLAN OFFICES ARE SUPPOSED TO FACILITATE COMMUNICATION. Most, but not all, research supports this view. The mixed results occur because different kinds of communication may increase or decrease in open offices. As explained earlier, necessary and desirable communication may decrease, but unwanted and interfering communication also increases.[273] In open-plan offices, compared with enclosed offices, supervisory feedback and communication with other departments is greater, but confidential communication is less.[274]

In two high-tech firms, the presence of more enclosures actually was associated with *increased* communication—having a door or walls or higher partitions was correlated with increased time spent working with others.[275] Thus, open-plan offices may increase communication, but this is not always desirable; in fact, enclosed office arrangements may encourage more *useful* forms of communication.

One form of useful communication is collaboration. Which characteristics of their workplace leads employees to believe that their space supports collaboration? These are distances, from one's workstation (a) to a meeting space, (b) to shared service areas, (c) to kitchen or coffee area, and the percentage of floor space designated for shared services and amenities.[276]

Another dimension of social behavior—status—is related to office arrangements. Supervisory employees typically have different kinds of space than nonsupervisory employees. They usually have more space, more freedom to personalize, more expensive furniture, and more means of regulating the access of others to their space, such as walls and doors.[277] Space and furnishings are very important to employees; the best way to show just how important they are is to suggest that either might be taken away from them. This threat of environmental deprivation even makes normally soft-spoken executives turn red and turn up the volume.[278]

The pursuit of status often is considered hollow and vain, but status symbols can help to create and develop the impression among employees that a sense of order guides the organization's allocation of resources (such as space). The larger, more private, or better-furnished office is also one way to recognize and reward achievement.[279] Status-seeking does become an end in itself for some people, but when workspace arrangements are carefully managed, larger and better workspaces may be one reasonable way to concretely inform employees that the organization values their work.

Privacy is another aspect of office social life. How do employees try to achieve it? They use verbal means (e.g., "I'm busy, please come back later"), nonverbal means (e.g.,

a sign on the door), and environmental means (e.g., closing the door) for regulating interaction. However, we do not always want to turn others away too obviously. For example, school administrators avoided using privacy mechanisms that required direct rejection of others (e.g., asking them to call back or to schedule an appointment with a secretary). Instead, they tended to use indirect forms of rejection (e.g., avoiding others by coming in early or staying late) and favored combinations of mechanisms that all sent the same message, especially when this could be justified by a heavy workload or confidential meeting.[280]

Anyone who has ever worked anywhere knows that territoriality is a workplace process. Sometimes territories are worked out harmoniously, and sometimes the process produces clear winners and losers. Graham Brown discovered four main dimensions of workplace territoriality.[281] First, **identity-oriented marking**, that is, labeling something as one's own. Second, **control-oriented marking** includes actions like creating a border around one's workspace (e.g., with filing cabinets, in an open office area). Third, **anticipatory defending behaviors** include actions such as locking physical spaces or creating passwords that others do not know; the goal is to prevent entry before it is attempted. Fourth, **reactionary defending behaviors** occur in response to perceived attempts to infringe on one's space. For example, if someone enters another's space but is not welcome, the territory holder may give the infringer a mean look.

A behavior on the border between personal and social is the personalization of one's space. Some organizations forbid any posters, pictures, or other employee contributions to the decor, fearing that an expensive overall interior design scheme will be compromised. Therefore, not surprisingly, organizational policies predict the degree of personalization more strongly than employee personality does.[282] However, anti-personalization edicts may backfire. When employees are heavily restricted, they lose a feeling of personal control over their work, and that can increase stress, decrease satisfaction, and, perhaps, decrease productivity.[283] Facility managers are faced with a choice. Are the aesthetic values of a uniform design scheme more important than the dissatisfaction of their employees?

As the world's workplace becomes increasingly fluid and international, the potential for difficulties in social relations based on cultural differences grows.[284] Culturally heterogeneous workgroups are, as the name implies, groups of employees from different backgrounds whose

FIGURE 11–13 One classic destination: a Greek island.

arrangements. Many open-plan arrangements reduce desirable communication and increase undesirable communication. Office arrangements lead visitors to form impressions of the office-holder's character and status. Some organizations restrict the degree to which employees may arrange or personalize their offices and fail to adequately consult employees when offices are planned. These policies may backfire in the sense that unhappy employees are less productive and tend to leave when they can.

jobs involve working together. One very visible group that has experienced occasional problems are the international crews aboard the International Space Station.[285] Problems can arise from different ideas about how to use the available space, barriers to being able to retreat from others when some privacy is needed, and differences in territoriality as understood within different cultures can be problematic. For example, Cécile Lacombe and I found numerous cultural differences in preferences for the interior design of the International Space Station.[286]

At present, the vast majority of workplaces are designed *for* employees, rather than *with* them. Recently, movement in this direction has resulted in tentative or even token efforts to involve employees, but they are not yet sufficient in most cases. Designers undoubtedly have good intentions, but without fully involving those who know themselves and their work best—the employees—their designs usually will suffer, often in important ways. Employee performance, feelings, and social behavior are importantly affected by spatial arrangements. Employee participation in design will be covered in detail in a later chapter, but the important point at present is simply that much more needs to be done to involve employees in the shaping of the spaces in which they will spend many hours of their lives.

IN SUM *Naturally occurring spatial arrangements have few documented effects on performance, but employees are very sensitive to space, and unhappy with many existing*

TRAVEL: GETTING AWAY TO A NEW ENVIRONMENT

FOR MOST EMPLOYEES, THE TIME FOR A VACATION OR HOLIDAY EVENTUALLY ARRIVES. Over the last century, the amount of time the average person spends at work has been shrinking; employees have more and more time for leisure. Workers can choose to leave their everyday surroundings for any of a vast array of destinations (see Figure 11-13). Leisure-related behavior has been under increasing scrutiny by a variety of social scientists, including environmental psychologists.[287] This section examines the environmental psychology of travel, which includes the study of tourist behavior, cognitive images of exotic destinations, choice of travel mode, and related phenomena.[288,289] Touring has a life cycle all of its own; its five temporal stages are:

● Anticipation
● Travel to the destination
● On-site behavior
● Return travel
● Recollection[290]

A similar model (see Figure 11-14) provides a framework for research on travel behavior that is congruent with this book's general approach to environmental psychology. In this model, persons who differ in motives, personality, age, gender, and other individual ways consider traveling. In the *choice phase*, they may choose *not* to travel because of some barrier (more on travel barriers soon). If they do choose to travel, they select an activity and a destination, which may be nearly automatic (e.g., "We always go to the mountains in the spring.") or be the subject of much discussion and study.

Once a place and activity are selected and the trip begins, the traveler enters the *experience phase*. This includes all the events and occurrences from departure to return, such as the travel itself, the weather, the interactions with people, and the on-site activities that were the reason for the trip. These events lead to *outcomes*, such as whether or not the motives for going were fulfilled, general satisfaction or dissatisfaction, and safety or harm. The *return phase* includes the trip home and subsequent trip-related thoughts and actions. Is the traveler rested, relaxed, a better person, broke? Do travelers tell others positive or negative things about their trips? Do they force their pictures on unsuspecting friends? Do they plan to repeat the trip?

Travel is part of environmental psychology for two main reasons. First, by traveling to environments away from their usual haunts, individuals alter themselves, sometimes radically. But not everyone travels. Who travels, and who does not? Why travel, and why not? What do travelers *do* in their temporary environments? What are the effects of destination environments on travelers? Second, travel has a significant impact on destination environments. In which ways are destinations harmed by tourism? Are they enhanced in any way?

We begin with the traveler; later the focus will be on the destination.

Who Goes (and Who Does Not)?

SOME PEOPLE GO ON VACATION EVERY CHANCE THEY GET; OTHERS WORK YEARS WITHOUT TAKING A VACATION. Personal experience suggests that one reason for traveling or not is whether a person's job satisfaction and involvement are high or low. Some people's jobs are everything to them; others cannot wait to get away. Sometimes a job that once was almost everything is now almost nothing. Apart from this, researchers speak of barriers to leisure or travel, such as lack of time, lack of money, lack of desirable places to go, and crowding.[291] A **barrier** is any factor that precludes or limits an individual's travel.[292] In general, barriers may be personal (fear of travel, no interest in exploring, love of home), environmental (poor sites or destinations), inter-

personal (poor social relations either at the destination or during the process of deciding where to go or whether to go, no one to go with), or resource problems (not enough money or time).

But, of course, many employees *do* get away. These decisions result in the interesting concept of **travel careers.**[293] When you think about it, each of us has a travel history: we have traveled much or little, to many or few places that are exotic or conventional. As we shall see later, one's past travel career influences the outcome of one's next trip.

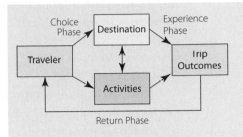

FIGURE 11–14 A basic model for the environmental psychology of tourism.

The mix of travel motives, travel careers, and demographic variables such as age, gender, and children (or not) results in certain identifiable groupings of travelers.

These are called **segments** by marketers, who study them in order to promote travel to particular destinations. Numerous segments have been described, but one set of five segments that was developed to understand the main groupings of travelers to outdoor recreation destinations will serve as an example.[294] The five segments are the excitement-seeking competitives (one likely destination: white-water rafting), the get-away actives (sightseeing), the fitness-driven (walking for pleasure), the health-conscious sociables (picnicking), and the unstressed and unmotivated (driving for pleasure). Many segments, like this one, are based on the reasons or motives for travel. We turn now to that topic.

Why Go?

INDIVIDUALS WHO HAVE UNFULFILLING JOBS MAY FIND THIS QUESTION RIDICULOUS; obviously, you go away to escape from a workplace that offers little except a means of supporting the parts of your life that are more pleasant than work. Individuals lucky enough to love their work must ask the question seriously. Many individuals, however, even in cultures that are well-known for devotion to work, currently believe there is more to life than job satisfaction. Among Germans, who have a reputation as diligent workers, about half preferred their leisure time to their work time by the 1980s, whereas 20 years earlier only one-third preferred leisure to work.[295]

The motives for leisure and travel have been extensively examined; from 4 to 48 different motives have been reported. A typical survey of the reasons for taking vacations yielded the following responses: rest and relaxation (63 percent), to escape routine (52 percent), to visit friends and relatives (45 percent), and to explore new places (35 percent).[296]

To some extent, of course, motives on the longer lists overlap with each other. Seven relatively distinct motives that I find in most studies, however, are:

- *Social.* To interact with family and friends away from one's usual setting.

- *Escape.* To get away, find peace and quiet, avoid routine and others' expectations.

- *Play.* To have fun, be entertained, seek pleasure.

- *Nature.* To enjoy the unbuilt environment.

- *Growth.* To improve oneself, learn, explore.

- *Challenge.* To test oneself, become fit, hone skills, be competitive or alert.

- *Recognition.* To be known for taking this trip, to increase one's status.

Obviously, different motives fuel different trips to different places by different persons. As just one example, how might the leisure motives of men and women differ? Biological sex was not related to motives, but sex-role orientation was.[297] Feminine individuals were more likely to seek an escape from reality and masculine individuals were more likely to seek challenge or competitiveness. Even those heading to a single destination may be driven by different motives; more-specialized hikers, for example, seek autonomy, exercise, achievement, and nature more than less-specialized hikers.[298]

Travel may result from an attempt to optimize a trade-off between contrasting motives: to leave the familiar parts of their lives behind (e.g., to achieve growth or to escape) and the desire to retain certain rewarding aspects of their lives at home, such as their safety and health. [299] When we leave home, we gain novelty and, we hope, pleasant experiences in the sun, among ruins, in museums, with distant friends or relatives, on the water, or in the wilderness. However, we then leave behind some or all family and friends, our sure knowledge of our surroundings, and

a tried and tested pattern of living. We take a chance on airplanes, roads, unfamiliar places, unknown systems of medicine, law, economics, and daily customs.

Some people find this trade-off decision very easy to make; others experience difficulty deciding what to do. Most of us eventually are willing and eager to fly away. Each person must solve the tension between the need for novelty and the need for familiarity in order to achieve optimal experiences. If the decision is to go, then we must decide *where* to go. As for us, for now, we just take the very short journey to the next line in this book.

Go Where?

MOST RECREATIONAL TRAVEL DESTINATIONS ARE:

- The homes of family or friends
- Resorts (often in sunny places)
- Rural or wilderness locations
- Cities worth touring
- Planned leisure developments (e.g., theme parks)
- Religious shrines

Some destinations, of course, offer more than one attribute. For example, Athens is a sunny place that also has great touristic value, and a religious shrine may be located in a pleasant rural setting. In the choice phase, we weigh our images of the places we are considering as one factor in the selection of a destination. Our images of places are based on a mix of personal experience (if we have been there before), word of mouth, advertisements, and stories about the place in the media. One outcome of a visit is that our image of the destination often changes.

Because it would take centuries to study every travel destination, researchers have tried to classify destinations into types. The assumption is that if we can discover something important about one kind of destination, it might well apply to other destinations of the same kind, which would save having to study every destination individually. One such distinction is between authentic and staged destinations.[300] **Authentic destinations** offer experiences that travelers believe are genuine. Such places usually are natural (like wilderness) or, in the case of built-up areas, places that have not been specifically altered to attract travelers. **Staged destinations** are those that, although they may be pleasurable, do not provide a sense of genuineness. They typically include elements designed for travelers, the epitome of which are theme parks, which do not even have residents—only employees trained to enact fantasy roles.

Authentic destinations generally are preferred, but not by everyone.[301] Travelers with more extensive travel careers especially like authentic destinations, and those with less extensive travel careers considered the staged destinations more satisfying. Destinations must balance tourism value with other considerations. For example, some wilderness areas derive income from timber and from tourism. These two sources of income clash; many tourists do not want to visit forest areas with even small clear-cuts, but they are especially negative about visiting areas with large clear-cuts.[302]

Do What?

TRAVELERS ENGAGE IN MANY FORMS OF BEHAVIOR, OF COURSE. One important activity is seeking and developing knowledge about one's new surroundings. In one example of knowledge-development research, first-time visitors to Oxford, England, were asked to draw cognitive maps of Oxford to determine how much they had learned about it.[303] As expected, those who had been in the city longer drew maps that included more landmarks, streets, and districts, and were more accurate. Tourists whose accommodations were on the periphery of the city also seemed to understand the city better, presumably because they traveled more widely during their stay.

Another common tourist behavior is asking for help. In 120 bus terminals from Portland, Oregon, to New Orleans, Louisiana, Australian and American travelers asked fellow passengers and total strangers for information. They more often received a helping response from fellow passengers than from total strangers, and the longer the others had been fellow passengers, the more likely they were to offer help. Female travelers were helped more than male travelers, and male Australian travelers received more help than male American travelers.[304] Australian males probably were perceived as foreign tourists, legitimizing their requests for help; the American male tourist was not seen as foreign, and therefore his requests were viewed as less legitimate, and perhaps having other motives.

Managers of national parks and commercial theme parks are concerned about the flow of tourists through their settings. Commercial operators wish to design their settings to maximize flow and minimize traffic pathways and customer discomfort; in national parks, the rationing

FIGURE 11–15 Appreciative versus consummatory recreation. The person in the top picture is appreciating nature (just looking at it); the one in the bottom picture is consuming nature (trying to shoot it).

of entry in the busy summer season encourages research into tourist activities like length of stay and rate of travel through the park.[305] Most research is motivated by marketing and promotion goals and therefore is aimed at getting travelers to choose a certain destination. Surprisingly little research has been done on just what travelers do once they reach their destinations.

Just as with travelers and motives, many different travel activities exist. One distinction among activities (again, the purpose is to investigate *classes* of activities because studying every form of travel activity is impossible) is that between appreciative and consumptive travel activities (see Figure 11-15). As the terms imply, **appreciative activities** are those in which the goal is to see or experience something without taking or destroying the object of admiration (e.g., photography, sightseeing, bird watching).

Consumptive activities involve the removal, or consumption, of at least some of that which one goes to see (e.g., hunting, fishing). Those who prefer these two kinds of activity differ; for example, those who choose appreciative activities tend to have stronger pro-environmental attitudes than those who choose consumptive activities.[306]

With What Outcomes?

The Impact of Destination Environments on Travelers. Traveling, of course, usually has multiple effects on the traveler. One's knowledge and experience may be enriched, one's circle of friends may enlarge, and one hopes to feel refreshed and ready to return home to a familiar life. Of course, travelers often experience anxiety, discomfort, illness, theft, exhaustion, loss, and stress. Travel usually has both positive and negative outcomes that depend partly on the experience and partly on the traveler.

Let's begin on the positive side. One writer claims that 44 psychological benefits may be derived from outdoor leisure activities alone.[307] Among these are improvements in physical and mental health, life satisfaction, and personal growth. Some environments are more likely to produce positive outcomes than others. Wilderness backpacking, for example, restores travelers more, on average, than non-wilderness vacations.[308] Extended time in the wilderness results in greater self-actualization.[309] After a wilderness experience, life seems less cluttered, travelers are more mindful of those close to them, and more focused on activities that are important to them.[310]

However, characteristics of travelers make a difference, too. One is experience, which tends to make one's preferences more specific, which usually means more difficult to satisfy.[311] On one's first trip to Paris, just *being* in the fabled Left Bank is exciting. One's tenth trip to Paris may not be satisfying unless more particular events occur, such as meeting a certain kind of person in a certain kind of Left Bank bistro. A tour of a national wildlife refuge that featured wild birds was more satisfying to visitors who knew less about birds.[312] More knowledgeable bird watchers need to see more exotic birds in order to be as satisfied as those who know little about wild birds.

Travelers' satisfaction is related to their preferences and expectations. Do you prefer to see others engaged in what you are doing, or to be doing it alone? Some inner-tube floaters prefer floating when many other floaters are nearby while others dream of being the only floater on the

river.[313] Specialization and experience help to explain why satisfaction varies when the density of inner-tube floaters on a river is identical.[314] Preferences and expectations can conflict. If they match (for example, you prefer sunny weather for your beach trip and you also expect it based on the season or a weather forecast), all is good. However, what if you prefer to visit museums when you travel, but happen to visit a place that you expect (maybe because it is a sleepy little town?) has no museums? Will you be more satisfied if the sleepy little town turns out to have a museum after all (thus matching your preference) or turns out not to have one (thus matching your expectation)? At least among campers, their' *preferences* for various features of a campsite were more related to their satisfaction than their *expectations* about those features.[315]

Pilgrimages are an ancient travel practice that continues today. The traditional pilgrimage involves a journey to a religious site to fulfill a spiritual goal or for healing, although secular pilgrimages occur (must see the Barcelona football stadium? The Rock and Roll Hall of Fame? The original Starbucks in Seattle?). One famous pilgrimage destination is Lourdes, the French site that over 3 million Christians visit every year. Many hope for physical health benefits, but emotional benefits have been examined, too. The anxiety and depression of pilgrims was measured one month before their trip, one month after their trip, and 10 months later. Anxiety and depression significantly declined following the pilgrimage and stayed significantly lower for the 10 months after the pilgrimage.[316] (Of course, whether Lourdes itself or some other aspect of the journey caused the emotional improvement is not certain, but presumably the pilgrims do not care; for them, the trip had a positive effect.)

As usual, travel outcomes depend to some extent on the match between the traveler and the destination.[317] For example, people with higher scores on the Urbanism scale of the Environmental Response Inventory experienced a smaller reduction in occupational strain after a nature holiday than vacationers who scored lower on the scale. Campsites vary; some have features that appeal to some campers and others that appeal to other campers.[318] This, of course, can be generalized to all types of travelers and destinations.

Unfortunately, traveling can also result in negative experiences. Some tourists react to their new situation, with its lack of familiarity and routine, by going into **environment shock**. The moods of visitors to a resort on a tropical island noticeably worsened on the second and third days of their stay. Minor health complaints also peaked in this period, lending credence to the environment shock notion.[319] Getting away from it all can have even worse complications. Hawaiian authorities recognize the "coconuts and bananas syndrome," which refers to the myth believed by some stray wanderers that life is so easy in the tropics that one can simply pick food off the trees.[320] "Coconuts and bananas" tourists tend to be young, unmarried, and unemployed, and sometimes even have psychiatric breakdowns when they discover that life is not that easy, even in Hawaii. Tourists who hold unrealistic expectations (such as believing they will see grass huts on Waikiki Beach) have about ten times the psychiatric admission rate of other tourists. The broader message, of course, is that tourist destinations can be stressful if a traveler expects that a destination will solve most of life's problems.

Finally, visiting a destination almost always changes the traveler's image of that destination. The ideal images that travelers had about the wet northern tropics in Australia were compared to the actual images they developed as a result of visiting the area.[321] Both *positive divergences* (that is, ways in which the area was better than expected, such as roads being less crowded than expected, and seeing more wildlife than expected) and *negative divergences* (e.g., the climate and road conditions were worse than expected) were found. Similarly, the images of British Columbia changed for Japanese exchange students as a result of a study visit.[322] The climate was better than they expected, and the pace of travel was less hectic than they expected. However, reaching natural surroundings was more difficult than the students anticipated.

The Impact of Travelers on Destination Environments.

So, sometimes travelers have personal growth experiences, and sometimes they go bananas. What happens to the environments they visit? Although tourists bring revenue, they sometimes also may bring unpleasant attitudes and behaviors. The environmental impact of travelers is now recognized: beer cans on mountain peaks, the use of scarce ground water in dry resort areas, land development pressures, and locally inappropriate behavior (see Figure 11-16). Even simple, innocent, natural behaviors can cause problems. The famous prehistoric paintings in the caves at Lascaux, France, were so damaged by the mere breathing of tourists that the French government had to close them. Crime rates are also affected by tourists. Tourist centers

FIGURE 11-16 The impact of travelers on one destination: Resident anger.

have significantly more of certain types of crimes than non-tourist areas.[323]

The negative impact of tourists can be reduced.[324] The design of two English stately houses that are open to the public will serve as an example. In one, trees and gardens are arranged so that numerous tourists do not detract from the aesthetic experience of visiting the home. It has always had a public life and, in fact, would look odd deserted. The other's garden was designed for the contemplation of nature in solitude; when many tourists are present, the whole effect is ruined.

In general, we may have to discourage **romantic tourism**, in which the ideal vacation consists of a lone individual or pair of lovers in an uninhabited tourist destination—whether that's a famous garden, unspoiled wilderness, or tropical beach. Given the finite number of undeveloped wild beaches and wilderness areas, romantic tourism will eventually lead to disappointment and unmet expectations on the part of travelers. It fosters the relentless development of ever-more-remote beaches and wilderness areas to satisfy romantic tourists. Instead, much better use of existing tourist areas could be made. For example, the provision of more extensive signs and maps could educate travelers about appealing places off the beaten track in established tourist areas.

The environmental psychology of travel is young; the research described here represents the early efforts in an area that will grow. Too many studies rely solely on surveys and are primarily conducted for marketing and

FIGURE 12-17 A loosely coupled setting: Telecommuting offices in a suburban mall save employees most of their commuting.

advertising purposes.[325] Understanding travelers' actual behaviors is important and interesting in its own right. The topic may seem frivolous, but travel has important impacts on the traveler, the destination, and the economy. Gaining more knowledge of traveler-destination transactions will be invaluable for designing highly adapted destinations (e.g., amusement parks and resorts) and planning for the survival of more vulnerable destinations (e.g., wildernesses, heritage buildings, and archeological sites).

IN SUM *The environmental psychology of travel is a new but growing area. Travelers affect destinations and are affected by them. Anticipation, travel, and recollection of travel involve environmental perception and cognition. Recreational travel is an environmental trade-off, but as society is able to provide citizens with more disposable income and time, it is a trade-off many are pursuing. Destination selection, acquisition of knowledge about destination, and tourist behavior along the road are a few areas of developing research. Some destinations bring relief from anxiety; others throw travelers into environment shock. Travelers ruin some physical settings and enhance almost none; romantic tourism is an undesirable luxury. More careful planning of destination sites might spread the impact of visitors, offer more authentic experiences, and educate travelers while offering them solace from the working world.*

ENVIRONMENTAL PSYCHOLOGISTS have been involved in the design of many work settings, from basic noise and light consultations, to complete building design and renovation. Better workplace design is not only a basic right of employees, but can save money for organizations. Improved layout and enclosure in offices, for example, leads to productivity increases of 15 percent for managers and professional-technical employees, and 17.5 percent for clerical workers,[326] and up to 50 percent increases with better workplace designs.[327]

In this section, two settings are selected as examples of applied research that illustrate major themes in this chapter.

Loosely Coupled Work Settings

COMPUTER-ASSISTED WORK DECENTRALIZATION (CAWD) or **loose coupling** is a concept which assumes that things are less interdependent than we normally think. One architectural implication is that placing all the units of an organization under one roof is not always necessary or desirable. An early loose-coupling solution was to encourage or even require employees to work at home, but that only works for a few employees. Yet CAWD does allow for working outside the office, and good reasons exist for decentralizing work if possible. One is to help solve the problem of too many cars by essentially replacing many commuting vehicles with communications cables.

One approach has been tested in Sweden: employees work neither at home nor at the office, but in a **neighborhood work center** (**NWC**).[328] The experimental NWC was opened in a small town 30 miles from Stockholm. It occupied space in a shopping center. Employees from a variety of organizations worked in the same place and shared equipment. Their reasons for agreeing to trying out the NWC concept included being closer to their families, avoiding crowding at their main office, cutting commuting costs, and the availability of some equipment at the NWC that was unavailable in their main office (see Figure 12-17).

As in many experiments, the NWC experienced both successes and challenges. Some employees could work who simply would not be able to work otherwise, because of the difficulty of commuting. Others benefit from the special equipment, and some from being able to work with a spouse. On the other hand, the NWC was unsatisfactory for some employees because confidential documents were not entirely secure, it was too isolated, or they simply lacked commitment to the NWC concept.

The neighborhood work center is an interesting idea, and further experience will yield a profile of the kind of employee and organization for which it is best-suited. The question is not whether work settings should be loosely coupled or not; it is *which* work settings and employees are most beneficial when they are loosely coupled.

Acoustic Privacy in Open-Plan Offices

AS WE SAW EARLIER, OPEN-PLAN OFFICES are increasingly common. However, a big problem with them is acoustic privacy. Employees are concerned about their conversations leaking to others *and* about unwanted speech floating into their work area. However, if open-plan offices are carefully designed, acoustic privacy can be acceptable. How can we design for acoustic privacy?

A procedure has been created that allows designers to assess the level of acoustic privacy between any two desks in an office.[329] This "ready reckoner" allows designers to create offices that maximize acoustic privacy without wasting space. (One *could* create excellent acoustic privacy by simply placing desks very far apart, but space is expensive.) The procedure involves measuring five things: (a) the distance between workstations, (b) the prevailing background machine noise, (c) the level of conversational sound, (d) whether there are any partitions between the speaker and the listener, and (e) speaker-listener orientation (e.g., back-to-back or face-to-face). The combination of these factors determines the **articulation index**, the percentage of spoken words understood by a listener. Acoustic privacy is worse when the articulation index is high.

In general, acoustic privacy will be worse when employees are closer together, background noise is low, the speaker and listener face each other, and the situation calls for louder speech (e.g., in conferences as opposed to two-person conversations). Here are two examples using the "ready reckoner." When the employees are 9 ft./3 m apart from chair to chair, with no partitions between them, with the background noise level at 45 decibels and the speech level is normal (60 decibels), and the speaker faces 180 degrees from the listener (they are back-to-back), the articulation index is .14 (that is, about 1 word out of 7 can be understood), which the procedure's creator says is "acceptable" speech privacy. In contrast, when the employees are 15 ft./5 m apart, with no partitions, 45 decibels of background noise, a 60-decibel speech level, but the speaker and listener face *toward* each other, the articulation index is .57, which translates to "nil" speech privacy.

SUMMARY

COMMUTING TO WORK, WORKING, AND GETTING AWAY from work are all fertile fields of study for the environmental psychologist. Commuting is not good for the commuter or the environment, so environmental psychologists have been searching for ways to reduce car commuting. Noise—unwanted sound, by definition—has complex effects on work performance. Some conditions under which it is likely to improve or harm performance have now been tentatively identified. In industrial settings, noise often impairs hearing without the victim's awareness; it has also been linked to health problems. Noise in offices, where work often involves considerable cognitive processing and sensitive social interaction, is an important problem. Few performance effects have been documented, but privacy complaints are widespread in typical open-plan offices.

Most employees can control temperature through clothing or other protective devices, enough that it has no strong effects on performance. In experimental situations in which temperature is varied strongly, the same pattern of complex effects observed for noise are reported. Temperature swings can be annoying in buildings with inadequate heating and cooling systems. Performance may be optimal at temperatures below typical comfort zones, which may create conflict between the goals of creating pleasant work settings and creating efficient ones. Long-term extreme temperatures are stressful, but humans have considerable adaptive capacity for temperature.

Airborne disease agents can cause health problems, but air ions and malodors have weak effects on most individuals. Certain employees, however, have ion sensitivities that make them more susceptible than most people. Lighting is a problem primarily when it is too bright or placed inappropriately for a task. Lower levels of more localized light, and more sunlight where possible, would increase employee satisfaction. Spatial arrangements should reflect the employee's need for interaction with others, which varies with the task and the employee. As with noise, the problem is essentially one of privacy.

Recreational travel involves most areas of environmental psychology; the difference is that the setting is typically unfamiliar but desirable. Little research about the traveler's perceptions, thought processes, social interactions, and learning have yet appeared, but what we do know offers tantalizing glimpses of an interesting new area of research.

Suggested Supplementary Readings

Becker, F. D. (1981). *Workspace: Creating environments in organizations.* New York: Praeger.

Garling, T., & Steg, L. (2007). *Threats from car traffic to the quality of life: Problems, causes, and solutions.* Amsterdam: Elsevier.

McCoy, J. M. (2002). Work environments. In R. B. Bechtel & A. Churchman (Eds), *Handbook of environmental psychology* (pp. 443-460). Hoboken, NJ: Wiley.

Oborne, D. J., & Gruneberg, M. M. (Eds.)(1983). *The physical environment at work.* New York: Wiley.

Sundstrom, E. (1986). *Work places.* New York: Cambridge University Press.

Veitch, J. (2012). Work environments. In Clayton, S. D. (Ed.). *The Oxford handbook of environmental and conservation psychology* (pp. 248-275). New York: Oxford.

Vischer, J. (2005). *Space meets status: Designing workplace performance.* London: Routledge Spon Press.

References

1   Steele, F. I. (1973). *Physical settings and organization development*. Don Mills, ON: Addison-Wesley.

2   Roethlisberger, F. J., & Dickson, W. J. (1939). *Management and the worker*. Cambridge, MA: Harvard University Press.

3   Steele, F. I. (1973). *Physical settings and organization development*. Don Mills, ON: Addison-Wesley.

4   Steele, F. I. (1973). *Physical settings and organization development*. Don Mills, ON: Addison-Wesley.

5   Rooney, D., Paulsen, N., Callan, V., Brabant, M., Callois, C., & Jones, E. (2010). A new role of place identity in managing organizational change. *Management Communication Quarterly, 24*, 44-75.

6   Davis, T. R. (1984). The influence of the physical environment in offices. *Academy of Management Review, 9*, 271-283.

7   Vilnai-Yavetz, I., Rafaeli, A., & Yaacov, C. S. (2005). Instrumentality, aesthetics, and symbolism of design. *Environment and Behavior, 37*, 533-551.

8   Frone, M. R. (1989). Chronic occupational stressors, self-focused attention, and well-being: Testing a cybernetic model of stress. *Journal of Applied Psychology, 74*, 876-883.

9   Sutton, R. I., & Rafaeli, A. (1987). Characteristics of work stations as potential occupational stressors. *Academy of Management Journal, 30*, 260-276.

10 Wineman, J. D. (Ed.)(1986). *Behavioral issues in office design*. New York: Van Nostrand Reinhold.

11 Lee, S. Y., & Brand, J. L. (2005). Effects of control over office workspace on perceptions of the work environment and work outcomes. *Journal of Environmental Psychology, 25*, 323-333.

12 Huang, Y., Robertson, M. M., & Chang, K. (2004). The role of environmental control on environmental satisfaction, communication, and psychological stress: Effects of office ergonomics training. *Environment and Behavior, 36*, 617-637.

13 Altman, I., Wohlwill, J. F., & Everett, P. B. (Eds.), *Transportation and behavior*. New York: Plenum.

14 Garling, T., & Steg, L. (2007). *Threats from car traffic to the quality of life: Problems, causes, and solutions*. Amsterdam: Elsevier.

15 Reser, J. (1980). Automobile addiction: Real or imagined? *Man-environment Systems, 10*, 279-287.

16 Hartgen, D. T. (1974). Attitudinal and situational variables influencing urban mode choice: Some empirical findings. *Transportation, 3*, 377-392.

17 Tischer, M. L., & Phillips, R. V. (1979). The relationship between transportation perceptions and behaviors over time. *Transportation, 8*, 21-33.

18 Gilbert, G., & Foerster, J. F. (1977). The importance of attitudes in the decision to use mass transit. *Transportation, 6*, 321-332.

19 Levin, I., & Louviere, J. (1981). Psychological contributions to travel demand modelling. In I. Altman, J. F. Wohlwill, & P. B. Everett (Eds.), *Transportation and behavior*. New York: Plenum.

20 Turner, C. W., Layton, J. F., & Simons, L. S. (1975). Naturalistic studies of aggressive behavior: Aggressive stimuli, victim visibility, and horn honking. *Journal of Personality and Social Psychology, 31*, 1098-1107.

21 Aronow, W. S., Harris, C. N., Isbell, M. W., Rokaw, M. D., & Imparto, B. (1972). Effect of freeway travel on angina pectoris. *Annals of Internal Medicine, 77*, 669-676.

22 Evans, G. W., Wener, R. E., & Phillips, D. (2002). The morning rush hour: Predictability and commuter stress. *Environment and Behavior, 34*, 521-530.

23 Stokols, D., & Novaco, R. W. (1981). Transportation and well-being: An ecological perspective. In I. Altman, J. F. Wohlwill, & P. B. Everett (Eds.), *Transportation and behavior*. New York: Plenum.

24 Harris, P. B., & Houston, J. M. (2010). Recklessness in context: Individual and situational correlates to aggressive driving. *Environment and Behavior, 42*, 44-60.

25 Stern, E. (1982). Bus services in rural areas. *Environment and Behavior, 14*, 94-112.

26 Studenmund, A. H., & Connor, D. (1982). The free-fare transit experiments. *Transportation Research, 16*, 261-269.

27 Bachman, W., & Katzev, R. (1982). The effects of non-contingent free bus tickets and personal commitment on urban bus ridership. *Transportation Research, 16A*, 103-108.

28 Kormos, C., Gifford, R., & Brown, E. (2014). The influence of descriptive social norm information on sustainable transportation behavior: A field experiment. *Environment and Behavior*.

29 Owens, D. D. (1981). Ridesharing programs: Governmental response to urban transportation problems. *Environment and Behavior, 13*, 311-330.

30 Bonsall, P., Spencer, A., & Tang, W. (1983). Ridesharing in Great Britain: Performance and impact of the Yorkshire schemes. *Transportation Research, 17*, 169-181.

31 Katzev, R. (2003). Car sharing: A new approach to urban transportation problems. *Analyses of Social Issues and Public Policy (ASAP), 3*, 65-86.

32 Schuitema, G., Steg, L., & Rothengatter, J. A. (2010). The acceptability, personal outcome expectations, and expected effects of transport pricing policies. *Journal of Environmental Psychology, 30*, 587-593.

33 Terzano, K., & Morckel, V. C. (2011). Walk or bike to a healthier life: Commuting behavior and recreational physical activity. *Environment and Behavior, 43*, 488-500.

34 Dunn, B. E. (1979). The noise environment of man. In H. W. Jones (Ed.), *Noise in the human environment*, (Vol. 2). Edmonton, Alberta: Environmental Council of Alberta.

35 Banbury, S. P., Berry, D. C. (2005). Office noise and employee concentration: Identifying causes of disruption and potential improvements. *Ergonomics, 48*, 25-37.

36 Moreland, J. B. (1988). Ambient noise measurements in open-plan offices. *Journal of the Acoustical Society of America, 83*, 1683-1685.

37 Park, M.-Y., & Casali, J. G. (1991). A controlled investigation of in-field attenuation performance of selected insert, earmuff, and canal cap hearing protectors. *Human Factors, 33*, 693-714.

38 Dunn, B. E. (1979). The noise environment of man. In H. W. Jones (Ed.), *Noise in the human environment*, (Vol. 2). Edmonton, Alberta: Environmental Council of Alberta.

39 Reif, Z. F., & Vermeulen, P. J. (1979). Noise from domestic appliances, construction, and industry. In H. W. Jones (Ed.), *Noise in the human environment*, (Vol. 2), Edmonton, Alberta: Environmental Council of Alberta.

40 Workers' Compensation Board of British Columbia. (1979). *Industrial Health Safety Regulations*. Richmond, B. C.: Workers Compensation Board of British Columbia.

41 Broadbent, D. E. (1979). Human performance and noise. In C. M. Harris (Ed.), *Handbook of noise control*, New York: McGraw Hill.

42 Jahncke, H., Hygge, S., Halin, N., Green, A. M., & Dimberg, K. (2011). Open-plan office noise: Cognitive performance and restoration. *Journal of Environmental Psychology, 31*, 373-382.

43 Miller, J. D. (1974). Effects of noise on people. *Journal of the Acoustical Society of America, 56*, 729-764.

44 Harrison, D. W., & Kelly, P. L. (1989). Age differences in cardiovascular and cognitive performance under noise conditions. *Perceptual & Motor Skills, 69*, 547-554.

45 Goldstein, J., & Dejoy, D. M. (1980). Behavioral and performance effects of noise: Perspectives for research. In J. V. Tobias, G. Jansen, & W. D. Ward (Eds.), *Proceedings of the third international congress on noise as a public health problem*. Rockville, MD: American Speech-Language-Hearing Association.

46 Baker, M. A., & Holding, D. H. (1993). The effects of noise and speech on cognitive task performance. *Journal of General Psychology, 120*, 339-355.

47 Weinstein, N. D. (1974). Effect of noise on intellectual performance. *Journal of Applied Psychology, 59*, 548-554.

48 Broadbent, D. E. (1979). Human performance and noise. In C. M. Harris (Ed.), *Handbook of noise control*, New York: McGraw-Hill.

49 Cohen, S., & Weinstein, N. (1982). Nonauditory effects of noise on behavior and health. In G. W. Evans (Ed.), *Environmental stress*. New York: Cambridge University Press.

50 Nagar, D., & Pandey, J. (1987). Affect and performance on cognitive task as a function of crowding and noise. *Journal of Applied Social Psychology, 17*, 147-157.

51 Reid, D. B., & Paulhus, D. L. (1987). *After-effects of noise on cognitive performance*. Poster presented at the annual meetings of the Canadian Psychological Association.

52 Broadbent, D. E. (1979). Human performance and noise. In C. M. Harris (Ed.), *Handbook of noise control*, New York: McGraw-Hill.

53 Albery, W. B. (1989). The effect of sustained acceleration and noise on workload in human operators. *Aviation, Space, & Environmental Medicine, 60*, 943-948.

54 Levy-Leboyer, C. (1989). Noise effects on two industrial tasks. *Work and Stress, 3*, 315-322.

55 Gulian, E., & Thomas, J. R. (1986). The effects of noise, cognitive set and gender on mental arithmetic performance. *British Journal of Psychology, 77*, 503-511.

56 Lahtela, K., Niemi, P., Kuusela, V., & Hypen, K. (1986). Noise and visual choice-reaction time:

A large-scale population survey. *Scandinavian Journal of Psychology, 27,* 52-57.

57 Jennings, J. R., Nebes, R., & Brock, K. (1988). Memory retrieval in noise and psychophysiological response in the young and old. *Psychophysiology, 25,* 633-644.

58 Jennings, J. R., Brock, K., & Nebes, R. (1989). Aging but not arousal influences the effect of environmental noise on the span of attention. *Experimental Aging Research, 15,* 61-71.

59 Bhatia, P., Shipira, & Muhar, I. S. (1991). Effect of low and high intensity noise on work efficiency. *Psychologia: An International Journal of Psychology in the Orient, 34,* 259- 265.

60 Mehrabian, A. (1977). Individual differences in stimulus screening and arousability. *Journal of Personality, 45,* 237-250.

61 Ng, C. F. (1989). Office worker performance and satisfaction: The effects of office noise and individual characteristics. *Dissertation Abstracts International, 50*(5-B), 2190-2191.

62 Standing, L., Lynn, D., & Moxness, K. (1990). Effects of noise upon introverts and extroverts. *Bulletin of the Psychonomic Society, 28,* 138-140.

63 Eysenck, M. W., & Graydon, J. (1989). Susceptibility to distraction as a function of personality. *Personality and Individual Differences, 10,* 681-686.

64 Matthews, G. (1985). The effects of extraversion and arousal on intelligence test performance. *British Journal of Psychology, 76,* 479-493.

65 Veitch, J. (1990). Office noise and illumination effects on reading comprehension. *Journal of Environmental Psychology, 10,* 209-217.

66 Toplyn, G. A. (1988). The differential effect of noise on creative task performance. *Dissertation Abstracts International, 48,* 3718.

67 Broadbent, D. E. (1979). Human performance and noise. In C. M. Harris (Ed.)., *Handbook of noise control,* New York: McGraw-Hill.

68 Willner, P., & Neiva, J. (1986). Brief exposure to uncontrollable but not to controllable noise biases the retrieval of information from memory. *British Journal of Clinical Psychology, 25,* 93-100.

69 Smith, A. P. (1985). The effects of different types of noise on semantic processing and syntactic reasoning. *Acta Psychologica, 58,* 263-273.

70 Broadbent, D. E. (1979). Human performance and noise. In C. M. Harris (Ed.)., *Handbook of noise control,* New York: McGraw-Hill.

71 Tafalla, R. J. (1990). Noise, physiology and human performance: The potential role of effort. *Dissertation Abstracts International, 51*(3-B), 1551.

72 Loewen, L. J., & Suedfeld, P. (1992). Cognitive and arousal effects of masking office noise. *Environment and Behavior, 24,* 381-395.

73 Ng, C. F. (1989). Office worker performance and satisfaction: The effects of office noise and individual characteristics. *Dissertation Abstracts International, 50*(5-B), 2190-2191.

74 Srivastava, R. (1988). Adaptation with noise and its psychological consequences. *Perspectives in Psychological Researches, 11,* 1-27.

75 Willner, P., & Neiva, J. (1986). Brief exposure to uncontrollable but not to controllable noise biases the retrieval of information from memory. *British Journal of Clinical Psychology, 25,* 93-100.

76 Champion, D. F. (1987). Some effects of combination of noise and vibration on the performance of a cognitive task. *Dissertation Abstracts International, 47*(10-B), 4296.

77 Glass, D. C., & Singer, J. E. (1972). *Urban stress: Experiments on noise and social stressors.* New York: Academic Press.

78 Agrawal, K. (1988). Dependence proneness as related to post- stress frustration-tolerance and performance. *Indian Journal of Current Psychological Research, 3,* 55-59.

79 Davidson, L. M., Hagmann, J., & Baum, A. (1990). An exploration of a possible physiological explanation for stressor aftereffects. *Journal of Applied Social Psychology, 20,* 869-880.

80 Evans, G. W., Allen, K. M., Tafalla, R. , & O'Meara, T. (1996). Multiple stressors: Performance, psychophysiological and affective responses. *Journal of Environmental Psychology, 16,* 147-154.

81 Reid, D. B., & Paulhus, D. L. (1987). *After-effects of noise on cognitive performance.* Poster presented at the annual meetings of the Canadian Psychological Association.

82 Klein, K., & Beith, B. (1985). Re-examination of residual arousal as an explanation of aftereffects: Frustration tolerance versus response speed. *Journal of Applied Psychology, 70,* 642-650.

83 Jahncke, H., Hygge, S., Halin, N., Green, A. M., & Dimberg, K. (2011). Open-plan office noise: Cognitive performance and restoration. *Journal of Environmental Psychology, 31,* 373-382.

84 Fox, J. G. (1983). Industrial music. In D. J. Oborne & M. M. Gruneberg (Eds.) *The physical environment at work.* New York: Wiley.

85 Fox, J. G. (1983). Industrial music. In D. J. Oborne & M. M. Gruneberg (Eds.) *The physical environment at work.* New York: Wiley.

86 Harcum, E. R. (1987). Disturbance ratings for relevant and irrelevant noise during performance of a cognitive task. *Perceptual and Motor Skills, 65,* 333-334.

87 Harris, L., & Associates. (1978). *The Steelcase national study of office environments: Do they work?* Grand Rapids, MI: Steelcase Inc.

88 de Barbenza, C. M., de Uhrlandt, M. S., & de Vila, N. C. (1985). Noise in the work environment. *Revista de Psicologia General Aplicada, 40,* 945-952.

89 Kjellberg, A., Landstrom, U., Tesarz, M., Söderberg, L., & Åkerlund, E. (1996). The effects of nonphysical noise characteristics, ongoing task and noise sensitivity on annoyance and distraction due to noise at work. *Journal of Environmental Psychology, 16,* 123-136

90 Harris, L., & Associates. (1978). *The Steelcase national study of office environments: Do they work?* Grand Rapids, MI: Steelcase Inc.

91 Sundstrom, E., Burt, R., & Kamp, D. (1980). Privacy at work: Architectural correlates of job satisfaction and job performance. *Academy of Management Journal, 23,* 101-117.

92 Sundstrom, E., Town, J. P., Osborn, D. P., Rice, R. W., Konar, E., Mandel, D., & Brill, M. (1994). Office noise, satisfaction, and performance. *Environment and Behavior, 26,* 195-222.

93 Champion, D. F. (1987). Some effects of combination of noise and vibration on the performance of a cognitive task. *Dissertation Abstracts International, 47*(10-B), 4296.

94 Weinstein, N. D. (1977). Noise and intellectual performance: A confirmation and extension. *Journal of Applied Psychology, 62,* 104-126.

95 Fried, Y., Melamed, S., & Ben-David, H. A. (2002). The joint effects of noise, job complexity, and gender on employee sickness absence: An exploratory study across 21 organizations: The CORDIS study. *Journal of Occupational and Organizational Psychology, 75,* 131-144.

96 Leather, P., Beale, D., & Sullivan, L. (2003). Noise, psychosocial stress and their interaction in the workplace. *Journal of Environmental Psychology, 23,* 213-222.

97 Raffaello, M., & Maass, A. (2002). Chronic exposure to noise in industry: The effects on satisfaction, stress symptoms, and company attachment. *Environment and Behavior, 34,* 651-671.

98 Brattico, E., Kujala, T., Tervaniemi, M., Alku, P., Ambrosi, L. S., & Monitillo, V., S. (2005). Long-term exposure to occupational noise alters the cortical organization of sound processing. *Clinical Neurophysiology, 116,* 190-203.

99 Welch, B. L. *Extra-auditory health effects of industrial noise: Survey of foreign literature.* Aerospace Medical Research Laboratory, Aerospace Medical Division, Airforce Systems Command, Wright-Patterson AFB, June 1979.

100 Cohen, A. (1969). Effects of noise on psychological state. *Noise as a public health hazard.* Washington, DC: American Speech and Hearing Association.

101 Evans, G. W., & Johnson, D. (2000). Stress and open-office noise. *Journal of Applied Psychology, 85,* 779-783.

102 Evans, G. W., Becker, F. D., Zahn, A., Bilotta, E., & Keesee, A. M. (2012). Capturing the ecology of workplace stress with cumulative risk assessment. *Environment and Behavior, 44,* 136-154.

103 Smolders, K. C. H. J., de Kort, Y. A. W., Tenner, A. D., & Kaiser, F. G. (2012). Need for recovery in offices: Behavior-based assessment. *Journal of Environmental Psychology, 32,* 126-134.

104 Lewis, P., & O'Sullivan, P. (1974). Acoustic privacy in office design. *Journal of Architectural Research, 3,* 48-51.

105 Goodrich, R. (1982). Seven office evaluations: A review. *Environment and Behavior, 8,* 175-190.

106 Hedge, A. (1982). The open-plan office: A systematic investigation of employee reactions to their work environment. *Environment and Behavior, 14,* 519-542.

107 McDowell, K., & Carlson, K. (1984). *The effects of attributes of office environments on employee mood.* Paper presented at the annual meetings of the Canadian Psychological Association meeting, Ottawa, June.

108 Sundstrom, E., Burt, R., & Kamp, D. (1980). Privacy at work: Architectural correlates of job satisfaction and job performance. *Academy of Management Journal, 23;* 101-117.

109 Sundstrom, E., Herbert, R. K., & Brown, D. W. (1982). Privacy and communication in an open-plan office: A case study. *Environment and Behavior, 14,* 379-392.

110 Sundstrom, E., Town, J. P., Brown, D. W., Forman, A., & McGee, C. (1982). Physical enclosure, type of job, and privacy in the office. *Environment and Behavior, 14,* 543-559.

111 Mathews, K. E. Jr., & Canon, L. K.(1975) Environmental noise level as a determinant of

helping behavior. *Journal of Personality and Social Psychology, 32*, 571-577.

112 Sauser, W. I., Jr., Arauz, C. G., & Chambers, R. M. (1978). Exploring the relationship between level of office noise and salary recommendations: A preliminary research note. *Journal of Management, 4*, 57-63.

113 Rohles, F. H., Jr., Konz, S., & Munson, D. (1980). Estimating occupant satisfaction from effective temperature. *Proceedings of the Human Factors Society, 24*, 223-227.

114 Bell, P. A., & Greene, T. C. (1982). Thermal stress: Physiological, comfort, performance and social effects of hot and cold environments. In G. W. Evans (Ed.) *Environmental stress*. New York: Cambridge University Press.

115 McCormick, E. J. (1976). *Human factors in engineering and design*. New York: McGraw-Hill.

116 Gaoua, N., Grantham, J., Racinais, S., & El Massioui, F. (2012). Sensory displeasure reduces complex cognitive performance in the heat. *Journal of Environmental Psychology, 32*, 158-163.

117 Fox, W. F. (1967). Human performance in the cold. *Human Factors, 9*, 203-220.

118 Enander, A. (1987). Effects of moderate cold on performance of psychomotor and cognitive tasks. *Ergonomics, 30*, 1431- 1445.

119 Nelson, T. M., Nilsson, T. H., & Hopkins, G. W. (1987). Thermal comfort: Advantages and deviations. *Ashrae Transactions, 93*.

120 Enander, A. E., & Hygge, S. (1990). Thermal stress and human performance. *Scandinavian Journal of Work, Environment, and Health, 16*, 44-50.

121 McCormick, E. J. (1976). *Human factors in engineering and design*. New York: McGraw-Hill.

122 Vickroy, S. C., Shaw, J. B., & Fisher, C. D. (1982). Effects of temperature, clothing, and task complexity on task performance and satisfaction. *Journal of Applied Psychology, 67*, 97-102.

123 Markee White, N. L. (1987). Quantifications of factors influencing thermal comfort in an office environment: Implications for energy conservation. *Dissertation Abstracts International, 47*(12-B), 4843.

124 Rice, B. (1980). Cooling by deception. *Psychology Today, 14*, 20.

125 Stramler, C. S., Kleiss, J. A., & Howell, W. C. (1983). Thermal sensation shifts induced by physical and psychological means. *Journal of Applied Psychology, 68*, 187-193.

126 Paciuk, M. (1990). The role of personal control of the environment in thermal comfort and satisfaction at the workplace. *Dissertation Abstracts International, 50*(8-A), 2276.

127 Nelson, T. M., Nilsson, T. H., & Johnson, M. (1984). Interaction of temperature, illuminance and apparent time on sedentary work fatigue. *Ergonomics, 27*, 89-101.

128 LeBlanc, J. (1975). *Man in the cold*. Springfield, IL: Thomas.

129 Bell, P. A., & Greene, T. C. (1982). Thermal stress: Physiological, comfort, performance and social effects of hot and cold environments. In G. W. Evans (Ed.) *Environmental stress*. New York: Cambridge University Press.

130 Vickers, R. R., & Hervig, L. K. (1984). *Predictors of cold weather health behaviors*. San Diego, CA:

US Naval Health Research Center, Health Psychology Dept.

131 Kristensen, T. S. (1989). Cardiovascular diseases and the work environment: A critical review of the epidemiologic literature on nonchemical factors. *Scandinavian Journal of Work, Environment and Health, 15*, 165-179.

132

Bell, P. A., & Greene, T. C. (1982). Thermal stress: Physiological, comfort, performance and social effects of hot and cold environments. In G. W. Evans (Ed.) *Environmental stress*. New York: Cambridge University Press.

133 Moos, R. H. (1976). *The human context. Environmental determinants of behavior*. New York: Wiley.

134 National Academy of Sciences. (1977). *Medical and biological effects of environmental pollutants*. Washington, DC: National Academy of Sciences.

135 Evans, G. W., & Jacobs, S. V. (1982). Air pollution and human behavior. In G. W. Evans (Ed.), *Environmental stress*. New York: Cambridge University Press.

136 Evans, G. W., & Jacobs, S. V. (1982). Air pollution and human behavior. In G. W. Evans (Ed.), *Environmental stress*. New York: Cambridge University Press.

137 Rotton, J. (1983). Affective and cognitive consequences of malodorous pollution. *Basic and Applied Social Psychology, 4*, 171-191.

138 Rotton, J., cited in Evans & Jacobs, 1982.

139 Hawkins, L. H. (1981). The influence of air ions, temperature, and humidity on subjective wellbeing and comfort. *Journal of Environmental Psychology, 1*, 279-292.

140 Hawkins, L. H., & Barker, T. (1978). Air ions and human performance. *Ergonomics, 21*, 273-278.

141 Tom, G., Poole, M. F., Galla, J., & Berrier, J. (1981). The influence of negative air ions on human performance and mood. *Human Factors, 23*, 633-636.

142 Farmer, E. W., & Bendix, A. (1982). Geophysical variables and behavior: V. Human performance in ionized air. *Perceptual and Motor Skills, 54*, 403-412.

143 Kozena, L., Frantik, E., & Lajcikova, A. (1988). Artificial air ionization does not compensate for deleterious effects of monotony in healthy young subjects. *Activitas Nervosa Superior, 30*, 255-258.

144 Charry, J. M., & Hawkinshire, F. B. W. (1981). Effects of atmospheric electricity on some substrates of disordered social behavior. *Journal of Personal and Social Psychology, 41*, 185-197.

145 Charry, J. M., & Hawkinshire, F. B. W. (1981). Effects of atmospheric electricity on some substrates of disordered social behavior. *Journal of Personal and Social Psychology, 41*, 185-197.

146 Baron, R. A. (1987). Effects of negative ions on cognitive performance. *Journal of Applied Psychology, 72*, 131-137.

147 Baron, R. A. (1987). Effects of negative ions on interpersonal attraction: Evidence for intensification. *Journal of Personality and Social Psychology, 52*, 547-553.

148 Warm, J. S., Dember, W. N., & Parasuraman, R. (1991). Effects of olfactory stimulation on performance and stress in a visual sustained attention task. *Journal of the Society of Cosmetic Chemists, 42*, 330-351.

149 Baron, R. A. (1994). The physical environment of work settings: Effects on task performance, interpersonal relations, and job satisfaction. *Research in Organizational Behavior, 16*, 1-46.

150 Harris, L., & Associates. (1978). *The Steelcase national study of office environments: Do they work?* Grand Rapids, MI: Steelcase Inc.

151 Rankin, R. E. (1969). Air pollution control and public apathy. *Journal of Air Pollution Control Association, 19*, 565-569.

152 Sterling, E. M. (1986). Indoor air quality- total environment performance: Comfort and productivity issues in modern office buildings. *Resource- The Canadian Journal of Real Estate*, 21-24.

153 Fanger, P. O., & Christensen, N. K. (1987). Prediction of draft. *ASHRAE Journal, 29*, 30-31.

154 Schultz, D. P. (1982). *Psychology and industry today*. New York: MacMillan.

155 Hawkins, L. H. (1981). The influence of air ions, temperature, and humidity on subjective wellbeing and comfort. *Journal of Environmental Psychology, 1*, 279-292.

156 Buckalew, L. W., & Rizzuto, A. (1982). Subjective response to negative air ion exposure. *Aviation, Space, and Environmental Medicine, 53*, 822-823.

157 Baron, R. A. (1983). Sweet smell of success? The impact of pleasant artificial scents on evaluations of job applicants. *Journal of Applied Psychology, 68*, 709-713.

158 Evans, G. W., & Jacobs, S. V. (1982). Air pollution and human behavior. In G. W. Evans (Ed.), *Environmental stress*. New York: Cambridge University Press.

159 Baron, R. A. (1994). The physical environment of work settings: Effects on task performance, interpersonal relations, and job satisfaction. *Research in Organizational Behavior, 16*, 1-46.

160 Hedge, A., Sterling, E. M., & Sterling, T. D. (1986). Building illness indices based on questionnaire responses. *Proceeding IAQ/86 Managing Indoor Air for Health and Energy conservation*, 31-43.

161 Adler, T. (1992). Chemicals just one part of indoor-air problems. *American Psychological Association Monitor, 23*, 35, 71.

162 Ryan, C. M., & Morrow, L. A. (1992). Dysfunctional buildings or dysfunctional people: An examination of the sick building syndrome and allied disorders. *Journal of Clinical and Consulting Psychology, 60*, 220-224.

163 Bauer, R. M., Greve, K. W., Besch, E. L., Schramke, C. J. et al. (1992). The role of psychological factors in the report of building-related symptoms in sick building syndrome. *Journal of Consulting and Clinical Psychology, 60*, 213-219.

164 Thoern, A. (2000). Emergence and preservation of a chronically sick building. *Journal of Epidemiology and Community Health, 54*, 552-556.

165 Norback, D., Michel, I., & Widstrom, J. (1990). Indoor air quality and personal factors related to the sick building syndrome. *Scandinavian Journal of Work, Environment and Health, 16*, 121-128.

166 Turiel, I., Hollowell, C. D., Miksch, R. R., Rudy, J. V., & Young, R. A. (1983). The effects of reduced ventilation on indoor air quality in an office building. *Atmospheric Environment, 17*,

167 Sterling, E. M. (1986). Indoor air quality- total environment performance: Comfort and productivity issues in modern office buildings. *Resource-The Canadian Journal of Real Estate*, 21-24.

168 Hawkins, L. H. (1982). Air ions and office health. *Occupational Health*, 116-124.

169 Bleda, P. R., & Sandman, P. H. (1977). In smoke's way: Socioemotional reactions to another's smoking. *Journal of Applied Psychology, 62*, 452-458.

170 Jones, J. W., & Bogat, A. G. (1978). Air pollution and human aggression. *Psychological Reports, 43*, 721-722.

171 Rotton, J., Barry, T., Frey, J., & Soler, E. (1978). Air pollution and interpersonal attraction. *Journal of Applied Social Psychology, 8*, 57-71.

172 Rotton, J., Frey, J., Barry, T., Milligan, M., & Fitzpatrick, M. (1979). The air pollution experience and interpersonal aggression. *Journal of Applied Social Psychology, 9*, 397-412.

173 Stone, J., Breidenbach, S., & Heimstra, N. (1979). Annoyance response of non-smokers to cigarette smoke. *Perceptual and Motor Skills, 49*, 907-916.

174 Veitch, J. A. (2000, July). *Lighting guidelines from lighting quality research.* Paper presented at the CIBSE/ILE Lighting Conference, York, UK.

175 Veitch, J. A. (2000). *Psychological processes influencing lighting quality.* National Research Council of Canada, Ottawa, ON.

176 Barnaby, J. F. (1980). Lighting for productivity gains. *Lighting Design and Application*, 20-28.

177 Gifford, R., Hine, D. W., & Veitch, J. A. (1997). Meta-analysis for environment-behavior research, illuminated with a study of lighting level effects on office task performance. In G. T. Moore & R. W. Marans (Eds.), *Advances in environment, behavior, and design. Vol. 4: The integration of theory, research, and utilization.* New York: Plenum.

178 Boyce, P. R. (1981). *Human factors in lighting.* London: Applied Science Publishers.

179 Katzev, R. (1992). The impact of energy-efficient office lighting strategies on employee satisfaction and productivity. *Environment and Behavior, 24*, 759-778.

180 Veitch, J. A., & Newsham, G. R. (1999). *Exercised control, lighting choices, and energy use: An office simulation experiment.* National Research Council of Canada, Ottawa, ON.

181 Boray, P. F., Gifford, R., & Rosenblood, L. (1989). Effects of warm white, cool white and full-spectrum fluorescent lighting on simple cognitive performance, mood and ratings of others. *Journal of Environmental Psychology, 9*, 297-307.

182 McColl, S. L., & Veitch, J. A. (2001). Full-spectrum fluorescent lighting: A review of its effects on physiology and health. *Psychological Medicine, 31*, 949-964.

183 Veitch, J A., Gifford, R., & Hine, D. W. (1991). Demand characteristics and full spectrum lighting effects on performance and mood. *Journal of Environmental Psychology, 11*, 87-95.

184 Campbell, S. S., & Dawson, D. (1990). Enhancement of nighttime alertness and performance with bright ambient light. *Physiology & Behavior, 48*, 317-320.

185 Czeisler, C. A., Johnson, M. P., Duffy, J. F., Brown, E. N. et al. (1990). Exposure to bright light and darkness to treat physiologic maladaptation to night work. *New England Journal of Medicine, 322*, 1253-1259.

186 Boyce, P. R., Beckstead, J. W., Eklund, N. H., Stobel, R. W., & Rea, M. S. (1993). Lighting the graveyard shift: The influence of a daylight-simulating skylight on the task performance and mood of night-shift worker. *Bilaga*, 35-38.

187 Oldham, G. R., & Fried, Y. (1987). Employee reactions to workplace characteristics. *Journal of Applied Psychology, 72*, 75-80.

188 Steidle, A., & Werth, L. (2013). Freedom from constraints: Darkness and dim illumination promote creativity. *Journal of Environmental Psychology, 35*, 67-80.

189 Veitch, J. A., & Gifford, R. (1996). Choice, perceived control, and performance decrements in physical environment. *Journal of Environmental Psychology, 16*, 269-276.

190 Kwallek, N., Lewis, C. M., & Robbins, A. S. (1988). Effects of office interior color on workers' mood and productivity. *Perceptual and Motor Skills, 66*, 123-128.

191 Wineman, J. D. (1982). The office environment as a source of stress. In G. W. Evans (Ed.), *Environmental stress.* New York: Cambridge University Press.

192 Megaw, E. D., & Bellamy, L. J. (1983). Illumination at work. In D. J. Oborne & M. M. Gruneberg (Eds.), *The physical environment at work.* New York: Wiley.

193 Marans, R. W., & Yan, X. (1989). Lighting quality and environmental satisfaction in open and enclosed offices. *Journal of Architectural Planning and Research, 6*, 118-131.

194 Oldham, G. R., & Fried, Y. (1987). Employee reactions to workplace characteristics. *Journal of Applied Psychology, 72*, 75-80.

195 Bhattacharya, S. K., Tripathi, S. R., & Kashyap, S. K. (1989). Evaluation of lighting conditions in relation to visual comfort in workplaces of weavers in a textile mill. *Journal of Human Ergology, 18*, 213-221.

196 Chao, A., & Bennett, C. A. (1981). Lamps for lighting people. *Proceedings of the Human Factors Society, 25*, 485-487.

197 Flynn, J. E., Hendrick, C., Spencer, T., & Martyniuk, D. (1979). The effects of light source color on user impression and satisfaction. *Journal of the Illuminating Engineering Society, 6*, 167-179.

198 Wineman, J. D. (1982). The office environment as a source of stress. In G. W. Evans (Ed.), *Environmental stress.* New York: Cambridge University Press.

199 Leather, P., Pygras, M., Beale, D., & Lawrence, C. (1998). Windows in the workplace: Sunlight, view, and occupational stress. *Environment and Behavior, 30*, 739-762.

200 Boubekri, M., Hull, R. B., & Boyer, L. L. (1991). Impact of window size and sunlight penetration on office workers' mood and satisfaction: A novel way of assessing sunlight. *Environment and Behavior, 23*, 474-493.

201 Farrenkopf, T., & Roth, V. (1980). The university faculty office as an environment. *Environment and Behavior, 12*, 467-477.

202 Leather, P., Pygras, M., Beale, D., & Lawrence, C. (1998). Windows in the workplace: Sunlight, view, and occupational stress. *Environment and Behavior, 30*, 739-762

203 Stone, N. J., & Irvine, J. M. (1994). Direct or indirect window access, task type, and performance. *Journal of Environmental Psychology, 14*, 57-63.

204 Stone, N. J, & English, A. J. (1998). Task type, posters, and workspace color on mood, satisfaction, and performance. *Journal of Environmental Psychology, 18*, 175-185.

205 Finnegan, M. C., & Solomon, L. Z. (1981). Work attitudes in windowed vs. windowless environments. *Journal of Social Psychology, 115*, 291-292.

206 Aries, M. B. C., Veitch, J. A., & Newsham, G. R. (2010). Windows, view, and office characteristics predict physical and psychological discomfort. *Journal of Environmental Psychology, 30*, 533-541.

207 Kahn, P H. (2008). A plasma display window?—The shifting baseline problem in a technologically mediated natural world. *Journal of Environmental Psychology, 28*, 192-199.

208 Heerwagen, J. H., & Orians, G. H. (1986). Adaptations to windowlessness: A study of the use of visual decor in windowed and windowless offices. *Environment and Behavior, 18*, 623-639.

209 Bringslimark, T., Hartig, T., & Patil, G. G. (2011). Adaptation to windowlessness: Do office workers compensate for a lack of visual access to the outdoors? *Environment and Behavior, 43*, 469-487.

210 Bringslimark, T., Hartig, T., & Patil, G. G. (2011). Adaptation to windowlessness: Do office workers compensate for a lack of visual access to the outdoors? *Environment and Behavior, 43*, 469-487.

211 Biner, P. M., Butler, D. L., & Winsted, D. E. (1991). Inside windows: An alternative to conventional windows in offices and other settings. *Environment and Behavior, 23*, 359-382.

212 Butler, D. L., & Steuerwald, B. L. (1991). Effects of view and room size on window size preferences made in models. *Environment and Behavior, 23*, 334-358.

213 Veitch, J. A., Stokkermans, M. G. M., Newsham, G. R. (2013). Linking Lighting Appraisals to Work Behaviors. *Environment and Behavior, 45*, 198-214.

214 Kaye, S. & Larson, S. (1992). *Illumination levels and the perceived emotionality of literary passages.* Unpublished manuscript.

215 Veitch, J. A. (2000). *Psychological processes influencing lighting quality.* National Research Council of Canada, Ottawa, ON.

216 Knez, I., & Enmarker, I. (1998). Effects of office lighting on mood and cognitive performance and a gender effect in work-related judgment. *Environment and Behavior, 30*, 553-567.

217 Weale, R. A. (1961). Retinal illumination and age. *Transactions of the Illumination Engineering Society, 26*, 95-100.

218 Briggs, R. P. (1986). Visual changes among older workers: Implications for workstation design. *Proceedings of the Human Factors Society*, 801-803.

219 Kuller, R., & Wetterberg, L. (1993). Melatonin, cortisol, EEG, ECG and subjective comfort in healthy humans: Impact of two fluorescent lamp types at two light intensities. *Lighting Research and Technology, 25*, 71-81.

220 Sterling, E. M. (1986). Indoor air quality- total environment performance: Comfort and productivity issues in modern office buildings. *Resource-The Canadian Journal of Real Estate*, 21-24.

221 Bennett, C. A. (1974). Let's shed a little light. In D. H. Carson (Ed.), *Man-environment*

interactions: Evaluations and applications, Part 2. Stroudsberg, PA: Dowden, Hutchinson, & Ross.

222 Boray, P. F., Gifford, R., & Rosenblood, L. (1989). Effects of warm white, cool white and full-spectrum fluorescent lighting on simple cognitive performance, mood and ratings of others. *Journal of Environmental Psychology, 9*, 297-307.

223 Baron, R. A., Rea, M. S., & Daniels, S. G. (1992). Effects of indoor lighting (illuminance and spectral distribution) on the performance of cognitive tasks and interpersonal behaviors: The potential mediation role of positive affect. *Motivation and Emotion, 16*, 1-33.

224 Veitch, J. A., & Kaye, S. M. (1988). Illumination effects on conversational sound levels and job candidate evaluation. *Journal of Environmental Psychology, 8*, 223-233.

225 Gifford, R. (1988). Light, decor, arousal, comfort and communication. *Journal of Environmental Psychology, 8*, 177-189.

226 Baron, R. A., Rea, M. S., & Daniels, S. G. (1992). Effects of indoor lighting (illuminance and spectral distribution) on the performance of cognitive tasks and interpersonal behaviors: The potential mediation role of positive affect. *Motivation and Emotion, 16*, 1-33.

227 Becker, F. D. (1984). Loosely-coupled settings: A strategy for computer-aided work decentralization. In B. Staw & L. L. Cumming (Eds.), *Research in organizational behavior.* Greenwich, CT: JAI Press.

228 Becker, F. D. (1984). Loosely-coupled settings: A strategy for computer-aided work decentralization. In B. Staw & L. L. Cumming (Eds.), *Research in organizational behavior.* Greenwich, CT: JAI Press.

229 Swartz, J. (1986). Computer commuters busier and happier. *American Psychological Association Monitor, 17*, 8.

230 McCormick, E. J. (1976). *Human factors in engineering and design.* New York: McGraw-Hill.

231 Simon, S. E. (1987). Productivity, efficiency and effectiveness: simple indicators of agency performance. *Journal of Rehabilitative Administration, 11*, 4-10.

232 Oldham, G. R., & Fried, Y. (1987). Employee reactions to workplace characteristics. *Journal of Applied Psychology, 72*, 75-80.

233 Heller, J. F., Groff, B. D., & Solomon, S. (1977).A. Toward an understanding of crowding: The role of physical interaction. *Journal of Personality and Social Psychology, 35*, 183-190.

234 Oldham, G. R., & Fried, Y. (1987). Employee reactions to workplace characteristics. *Journal of Applied Psychology, 72*, 75-80.

235 Oldham, G. R., Kulik, C. T., & Stepina, L. P. (1991). Physical environments and employee reactions: Effects of stimulus-screening skills and job complexity. *Academy of Management Journal, 34*, 929-938.

236 Wineman, J. D. (1982). The office environment as a source of stress. In G. W. Evans (Ed.), *Environmental stress.* New York: Cambridge University Press.

237 Ng, C. F., & Gifford, R. (1984). *Speech communication in the office: The effects of background sound level and conversational privacy.* Unpublished manuscripts, University of Victoria.

238 Smith-Jackson, T. L., & Klein, K. W. (2009). Open-plan offices: Task performance and mental workload. *Journal of Environmental Psychology, 29*, 279-289.

239 Becker, F., Gield, B., Gaylin, K., & Sayer, S. (1983). Office design in a community college: Effect on work and communication patterns. *Environment and Behavior, 15*, 699-726.

240 Smith, A. & Pitt, M. (2009). Sustainable workplace: improving staff health and well-being using plants. *Journal of Corporate Real Estate, 11*, 52-63.

241 Larsen, L. Adams, J., Deal, B., Kweon, B. S., & Tyler, E. (1998). Plants in the workplace: The effects of plant density on productivity, attitudes, and perceptions. *Environment and Behavior, 30*, 261-281.

242 Raanaas, R. K., Evensen, K. H., Rich, D., Sjostrom, G., & Patil, G. (2011). Benefits of indoor plants on attention capacity in an office setting. *Journal of Environmental Psychology, 31*, 99-105.

243 Wang, N., & Boubekri, M. (2010). Investigation of declared seating preference and measured cognitive performance in a sunlit room. *Journal of Environmental Psychology, 30*, 226-238.

244 May, D. R., Oldham, G. R., & Rathert, C. (2005). Employee affective and behavioral reactions to the spatial density of physical work environments. *Human Resource Management, 44*, 21-33.

245 Gifford, R. (1976). Environmental numbness in the classroom. *Journal of Experimental Education, 44*, 4-7.

246 Sutton, R. I., & Rafaeli, A. (1987). Characteristics of work stations as potential occupational stressors. *Academy of Management Journal, 30*, 260-276.

247 Ng, C. F., & Gifford, R. (1984). *Speech communication in the office: The effects of background sound level and conversational privacy.* Unpublished manuscripts, University of Victoria.

248 Brennan, A., Chugh, J. S., & Kline, T. (2002). Traditional versus open office design: A longitudinal study. *Environment and Behavior, 34*, 279-299.

249 Maher, A., & Von Hippel, C. (2005). Individual differences in employee reactions to open-plan offices. *Journal of Environmental Psychology, 25*, 219-229.

250 Murray, B. (2002). There's nothing good about working in a cubicle, study finds. *Monitor on Psychology, 33*, 11.

251 Lansdale, M., Parkin, J., Austin, S., & Baguley, T. (2011). Designing for interaction in research environments: A case study. *Journal of Environmental Psychology, 31*, 407-420.

252 Posehn, K. (1984). *An environmental evaluation of open plan offices.* Paper presented at the Canadian Psychological Association annual meetings, Ottawa.

253 Zalesny, M. D., & Farace, R. V. (1987). Traditional versus open offices: A comparison of sociotechnical, social relations, and symbolic meaning perspectives. *Academy of Management Journal, 30*, 240-259.

254 Elsbach, K. D. (2003). Relating physical environment to self-categorizations: Identity threat and affirmation in a non-territorial office space. *Administrative Science Quarterly, 48*, 622-654.

255 Tausz, A. (1979, October 20th). Landscape of the future. *The Financial Post*, p. S10.

256 Oldham, G. R., & Brass, D. J. (1979). Employee reactions to an open-plan office: A naturally occurring quasi-experiment. *Administrative Science Quarterly, 24*, 267-284.

257 Oldham, G. R., & Rotchford, N. L. (1983). Relationships between office characteristics and employee reactions: A study of physical environment. *Administrative Science Quarterly, 28*, 542-556.

258 Oxley, D., & Barrera, M, Jr. (1984). Undermanning theory and the workplace: Implications of setting size for job satisfaction and social support. *Environment and Behavior, 16*, 211-234.

259 Barker, R. G. (1968). *Ecological psychology: Concepts and methods for studying the environment of human behavior.* Stanford, CA: Stanford University Press.

260 Wicker, A. W. (1979). *An introduction to ecological psychology.* Monterey, CA: Brooks/Cole.

261 Oldham, G. R., Kulik, C. T., & Stepina, L. P. (1991). Physical environments and employee reactions: Effects of stimulus-screening skills and job complexity. *Academy of Management Journal, 34*, 929-938.

262 Oldham, G. R., & Fried, Y. (1987). Employee reactions to workplace characteristics. *Journal of Applied Psychology, 72*, 75-80.

263 Morrow, P. C., & McElroy, J. C. (1981). Interior office design and visitor response: A constructive replication. *Journal of Applied Psychology, 66*, 646-650.

264 Becker, F. D., Gield, B., & Froggat, C. C. (1983). Seating positions and impression formation in an office setting. *Journal of Environmental Psychology, 3*, 253-261.

265 Samuelson, D. J., & Lindauer, M. S. (1976). Perception, evaluation, and performance in a neat and messy room by high and low sensation seekers. *Environment and Behavior, 8*, 291-306.

266 Sitton, S. (1984). The messy desk effect: How tidiness affects the perception of others. *The Journal of Psychology, 117*, 263-267.

267 Ornstein, S. (1992). First impressions of the symbolic meanings connoted by reception area design. *Environment and Behavior, 24*, 85-110.

268 Ornstein, S. (1992). First impressions of the symbolic meanings connoted by reception area design. *Environment and Behavior, 24*, 85-110.

269 Fried, Y. (1990). Workspace characteristics, behavioral interferences, and screening ability as joint predictors of employee reactions: An examination of the intensification approach. *Journal of Organizational Behavior, 11*, 267-280.

270 Hedge, A. (1984). Evidence of a relationship between office design and self-reports of ill health among office workers in the United Kingdom. *Journal of Architectural and Planning Research, 1*, 163-174.

271 Angelique, N., Yore, M. M., Ham, S. A., & Dietz, W. H. (2004). Increasing stair use in a worksite through environmental changes. *American Journal of Health Promotion, 18*, 312-315.

272 Olander, E. K., & Eves, F. F. (2011). Elevator availability and its impact on stair use in a workplace. *Journal of Environmental Psychology, 31*, 200-206.

273 Wineman, J. D. (1982). The office environment as a source of stress. In G. W. Evans (Ed.), *Environmental stress.* New York: Cambridge University Press.

274 Sundstom, E., Herbert, R. K., & Brown, D. W. (1982). Privacy and communication in an open-plan office: A case study. *Environment and Behavior, 14,* 379-392.

275 Hatch, M. J. (1987). Physical barriers, task characteristics, and interaction activity in research and development firms. *Administrative Science Quarterly, 32,* 387-399.

276 Hua, Y., Loftness, V., Heerwagen, J. H., & Powell, K. M. (2011). Relationship between workplace spatial settings and occupant-perceived support for collaboration. *Environment and Behavior, 43,* 807-826.

277 Konar, E., Sundstrom, E., Brady, C., Mandel, D., & Rice, R. W. (1982). Status demarcation in the office. *Environment and Behavior, 4,* 561-580.

278 Mazumdar, S. (1992). "Sir, please do not take away my cubicle." The phenomenon of environmental deprivation. *Environment and Behavior, 24,* 691-722.

279 Becker, F. D. (1981). *Workspace: Creating environments in organizations.* New York: Praeger.

280 Werner, C. M., & Haggard, L. M. (1992). Avoiding intrusions at the office: Privacy regulation on typical and high solitude days. *Basic and Applied Social Psychology, 13,* 181-193.

281 Brown, G. (2009). Claiming a corner at work: Measuring employee territoriality in their workspaces. *Journal of Environmental Psychology, 29,* 44-52.

282 Wells, M., & Thelen, L. (2002). What does your workspace say about you? The influence of personality, status, and workspace on personalization. *Environment and Behavior, 34,* 300-321.

283 Karasek, R. A. (1979). Jr. Job demands, job decision latitude and mental strain Implications for job redesign. *Administrative Science Quarterly, 24,* 285-308.

284 Ayoko, O. B., & Härtel, C. E., J. (2003). The role of space as both a conflict trigger and a conflict control mechanism in culturally heterogeneous workgroups. *Applied Psychology: An International Review, 52,* 383-412.

285 Kanas, N. (1998). Psychosocial issues affecting crews during long-duration international space missions. *Acta Astronautica, 42,* 1-8.

286 Gifford, R., & Lacombe, C. (2006). *The habitability of spacecraft: Assessments of a virtual reality simulation of the ISS across cultural, personality, and individual differences.* Report to the Canadian Space Agency.

287 Mercer, D. C. (1976). Motivational and social aspects of recreational behavior. In I. Altman & J. F. Wohlwill (Eds.), *Human behavior and environment* (Vol. 1). New York: Plenum.

288 Pearce, P. L. (1982). *The social psychology of tourist behavior.* Oxford: Pergamon.

289 Stringer, P. (1984). Studies in the socio-environmental psychology of tourism. *Annals of Tourism Research, 11,* 147-166.

290 Fridgen, J. D. (1984). Environmental psychology and tourism. *Annals of Tourism Research, 11,* 19-39.

291 Schreyer, R. *Motivation for participation in outdoor recreation and barriers to that participation- A commentary on salient issues.* Salt Lake City, UT: The President's Commission on Americans Outdoors.

292 Ellis, G. D., & Rademacher, C. (1986). *Barriers to recreation participation.* Salt Lake City, UT: The President's Commission on Americans Outdoors.

293 Pearce, P. L., & Moscardo, G. M. (1985). The relationship between travellers' career levels and the concept of authenticity. *Australian Journal of Psychology, 37,* 157-174.

294 President's Commission on Americans Outdoors (1986). *Participation in outdoor recreation among American adults and the motivations which drive participation.* Market Opinion Research.

295 Germans now putting leisure ahead of jobs. (1984, January 8). Victoria *Times-Colonist,* p. C7.

296 Rubenstein, C. (1980). Survey report: How Americans view vacations. *Psychology Today, 13,* 62-66, 71-76.

297 Hirschman, E. C. (1984). Leisure motives and sex roles. *Journal of Leisure Research, 16,* 209-223.

298 Virden, R. J. (1986). The effects of recreation specialization and motivations on the environmental setting preferences of backcountry hikers. *Dissertation Abstracts International, 47*(6-A), 2314.

299 Iso-Ahola, S. E. (1983). Towards a social psychology of recreational travel. *Leisure Studies, 2,* 45-56.

300 Pearce, P. L., & Moscardo, G. M. (1985). The relationship between travellers' career levels and the concept of authenticity. *Australian Journal of Psychology, 37,* 157-174.

301 Pearce, P. L., & Moscardo, G. M. (1985). The relationship between travellers' career levels and the concept of authenticity. *Australian Journal of Psychology, 37,* 157-174.

302 Yuan, S. M. (1993). The relationship between tourism and timber harvesting: A social-psychological approach. *Dissertation Abstracts International, 53*(7-B), 3841.

303 Pearce, P. L. (1977). Mental souvenirs: A study of tourists and their city maps. *Australian Journal of Psychology, 29,* 203-210.

304 Pearce, P. L. (1980). Strangers, travellers, and greyhound terminals: A study of small-scale helping behaviors. *Journal of Personality and Social Psychology, 38,* 935-940.

305 Gustke, L. D., & Hodgson, R. W. (1980). The rate of travel along an interpretive trail: The effect of an environmental discontinuity. *Environment and Behavior, 12,* 53-63.

306 Jackson, E. L. (1986). Outdoor recreation participation and attitudes to the environment. *Leisure Studies, 5,* 1-23.

307 Tinsley, H. E. A. (1986). *Motivations to participate in recreation: Their identification and measurement.* Carbondale, IL: The President's Commission on Americans Outdoors.

308 Hartig, T., Mang, M., & Evans, G. W. (1991). Restorative effects of natural environment experiences. *Environment and Behavior, 23,* 3-26.

309 Young, R. A., & Crandall, R. (1985, July). *Self- actualization and wilderness use: A panel story.* Paper presented at the National Wilderness Research Conference, Fort Collins, CO.

310 Talbot, J. F., & Kaplan, S. (1986). Perspectives on wilderness: Re-examining the value of extended wilderness experiences. *Journal of Environmental Psychology, 6,* 177-188.

311 Schreyer, R., & Beaulieu, J. T. (1986). Attribute preferences for wildland recreation settings. *Journal of Leisure Research, 18,* 231-247.

312 Applegate, J. E., & Clark, K. E. (1987). Satisfaction levels of birdwatchers: An observation on the consumptive-nonconsumptive continuum. *Leisure Sciences, 9,* 129-134.

313 Ditton, R. B., Fedler, A. J., & Graefe, A. R. (1983). Factors contributing to perceptions of recreational crowding. *Leisure Sciences, 5,* 273-288.

314 Hammitt, W. E., McDonald, C. D., & Noe, F. P. (1984). Use level and encounters: Important variables of perceived crowding among nonspecialized recreationists. *Journal of Leisure Research, 16,* 1-8.

315 Dorfman, P. W. (1979). Measurement and meaning of recreation satisfaction. *Environment and Behavior, 11,* 483-510.

316 Morris, P. A. (1982). The effect of pilgrimage on anxiety, depression, and religious attitude. *Psychological Medicine, 12,* 291-294.

317 Macdonald, J. E. (1994). *The restorative effects of a vacation from work: The role of novelty, positive affect, and nature.* Unpublished doctoral dissertation, University of Victoria.

318 Dorfman, P. W. (1979). Measurement and meaning of recreation satisfaction. *Environment and Behavior, 11,* 483-510.

319 Pearce, P. L. (1981). Environment shock: A study of tourists' reactions to two tropical islands. *Journal of Applied Social Psychology, 11,* 268-280.

320 Streltzer, J. (1979). Psychiatric emergencies in travellers to Hawaii. *Comprehensive Psychiatry, 20,* 463-468.

321 Ross, G. F. (1991). Tourist destination images of the wet tropical rainforests of North Queensland. *Australian Psychologist, 26,* 153-157.

322 Andressen, B. (1987). *Travel and geographic learning: A study of perception and attitude change in a Japanese tourist segment.* Unpublished doctoral dissertation, The University of Victoria, Victoria, B.C.

323 Walmsley, D. J., Boskovic, R. M., & Pigram, J. J. (1983). Tourism and crime: An Australian perspective. *Journal of Leisure Research, 15,* 136-155.

324 Walter, J. A. (1982). Social limits to tourism. *Leisure Studies, 1,* 295-304.

325 Pearce, P. L., & Moscardo, G. (1985). Tourist theme parks: Research practices and possibilities. *Australian Psychologist, 20,* 303-312.

326 Brill, M., Margulis, S. T., & Konar, E. (1984). *Using office design to increase productivity.* Buffalo, NY: Buffalo Organization for Social and Technological Innovation.

327 Gifford, R. (1992). *Performance and related outcomes of inadequate offices: An annotated bibliography.* Report to the British Columbia Buildings Corporation.

328 Becker, F. D. (1984). Loosely-coupled settings: A strategy for computer-aided work decentralization. In B. Staw & L. L. Cumming (Eds.), *Research in organizational behavior.* Greenwich, CT: JAI Press.

329 Hegvold, L. W. (1971). *Acoustical design of open-planned offices.* Ottawa, ON: National Research Council of Canada, Division of Building Research.

Natural Environmental Psychology

Nature's peace will flow into you as sunshine flows into trees. The winds blow their own freshness into you and the storms their energy, while cares drop off like autumn leaves.

— JOHN MUIR[1]

Poor naked wretches, wheresoe'er you are,
That bide the pelting of this pitiless storm,
How shall your houseless heads and unfed sides,
Your looped and window'd raggedness, defend you
From seasons such as these?

— SHAKESPEARE, *King Lear*

JANE LIFTED HER HEAD AND PEEKED OUT THE TENT FLAP. *Dawn had not yet arrived, but she could see light anyway. Even though the night was crystalline cold, she crawled out of her sleeping bag to see more. Once outside, she saw Venus huge and low in the sky. It seemed almost as big and bright as a full moon. Entranced, she silently stared, wonderstruck, for several minutes.*

"Tom," she finally said, "You have to see this."

Mumble.

"Tom, wake up. Come see." Tom dragged himself into consciousness. He had been in the middle of a bad dream. The new old house he had inherited from his grandfather had been swept away in a flood. He and Jane had just moved in, but already the house had become a part of them; to see it floating away, tilted at a crazy angle, was terrifying.

"Jeez, I'm glad you woke me up," he said. "You wouldn't believe what happened to the house in my dream."

"Look," said Jane, distracted. "Isn't it amazing? Do you think Venus really affects love down here?"

"I don't know. But I remember once when we were sitting outside in the dark last July, it made a great conversation piece. I've never seen it this big though."

Tom made breakfast, and as the sun rose, they sat next to the fire, talking and soaking up its heat like the ancients. Jane remarked how she felt like a new person after a few days in the woods. Tom noticed that this was in marked contrast to her initial comments, which were more along the lines of how she was going to get behind at work.

"It's hard to get me to go outdoors, but now it's going to be hard to drag me back to work," she said.

THIS CHAPTER IS ABOUT THE GREAT OUTDOORS. It covers a lot of territory—from cosmic rays to local weather patterns, from wilderness to floods. This chapter is about nature— as a huge force on our behavior, thoughts, and feelings, as a victim of our unsympathetic actions, as a wondrous restorative agent for our stressed-out souls (see Figure 12-1), and as an awesome source of power to disrupt our lives.

The first part of the chapter, on extraterrestrial and atmospheric environmental psychology, examines influences from far away (deep space) to near at hand (weather and climate)—influences over which we have little control. The second part of the chapter considers the hypothesis that nature provides an enhancing, restorative tonic for the mind and body. But we are not always nice, and neither is nature. Part three considers the immense "hit" that nature can deliver with a mere shrug of her shoulders—natural disasters. We also threaten each other with technological hazards.

FIGURE 12-1 Many people bring as much nature indoors as possible.

EXTRATERRESTRIAL AND ATMOSPHERIC FORCES

IS OUR BEHAVIOR OR FUNDAMENTAL NATURE AFFECTED BY FORCES BEYOND EARTH? This may seem unlikely to skeptics, but the answer is yes—in some ways. First, current views of cosmology argue that the whole planet Earth is spun-off star matter. Not only the Earth itself, but all upon it is highly developed star dust. You are star dust. Second, all that happens on the Earth is powered by the sun, either directly through solar power or indirectly through the use of stored solar power. Coal, gas, and oil are simply plant-stored solar power; hydro-electric power is based on the sun lifting water into the atmosphere so it can return to Earth as rain, and most of our food is produced through photosynthesis.

"Sure, sure," you say—"but what about our everyday actions, tendencies, hopes, and beliefs?" In some very basic ways, the sun influences those too. Prolonged sunny weather induces us to go to the beach, play summer sports, to garden; the lack of it creates good conditions for staying indoors or engaging in winter sports. "Yes," you say, "we don't need research to prove that." Perhaps you are asking—"Are there any more mysterious, less-obvious, exotic deep-space influences on us?" Well, maybe.

Deep Space and Heavenly Bodies

WE BEGIN WITH the furthest-out potential influences, and move earthward.

Cosmic Rays. Possible connections between outer space phenomena and earthly actions have been investigated. For example, variations in cosmic ray activity was associated with psychiatric hospital admissions and behavioral disturbances in people afflicted with schizophrenia.[2] Although the effect was very small, hospital admissions increased with cosmic ray activity; behavioral disturbances increased for some persons with schizophrenia, but decreased for others. Possibly, although much more research is necessary, the flow of neutrons from cosmic rays somehow affects people with schizophrenia.

Planets: Is Astrology Valid? Are the positions of planets at birth and later personality related? Do astrology's claims have any validity? Among eminent French scientists, a significantly high proportion of introverts were born when Saturn had just risen or just passed overhead, and extraverts were more likely to be born when Mars or Jupiter had just risen or passed overhead.[3] However, a major problem is that no causal mechanism for these findings is available. *How* might planetary position possibly affect the personality of a child who is being born?

The Moon: Is Lunacy Real? The belief that the moon influences strange behavior goes back at least to 400 B.C. and has had prominent supporters through the centuries.[4] Half of undergraduates in one survey agreed with the statement that, "Some people behave strangely when the moon is full."[5] Even higher percentages of police officers believe the full moon affects people.[6] What does the evidence say? Published studies do report significant connections between phases of the moon and such behaviors as calls to counseling centers, psychiatric hospital admissions, and homicides.[7] However, critics say these results probably are due to type I errors and the file-drawer problem.

A **type I error** occurs when a researcher accepts a significant result as true when actually it is untrue. They can occur when an investigator computes many statistical tests in a set of data and finds a few significant results. For example, if 20 statistical tests are computed at the .05 level of significance, one test can be expected to appear significant purely by chance. If the researcher is able to publish that one result, that published article will help create the false impression that a genuine effect has been found. The **file-drawer problem** refers to the 19 null results, which tend to get filed away, so that the scientific world is unaware that 20 tests were conducted, not the one that was published. This way, type I errors may appear in scientific journals. The innocent inquirer who then searches the published scientific literature finds the one significant results, which creates the impression that the phenomenon is real.

The lunacy hypothesis—the moon causes bad and crazy behavior—has been declared dead,[8] but it still lives for some who believe it has not been fairly evaluated.[9] However, as with the planetary-position study described earlier, a major problem is the lack of a plausible causal mechanism. One theory that seems reasonable at first glance suggests that the moon's gravitational influence on bodily fluids causes tides like those caused by the moon in oceans, and somehow these "biological tides" result in lunacy behaviors.[10] Unfortunately, the moon's gravitational force on a person is over 5,000 times weaker than that of the Earth; even a large building tugs on your bodily fluids harder when you walk by it than the moon does.[11] The moon's gravitational effect is far too weak to affect our bodily fluids. A subsequent analysis examined eight other

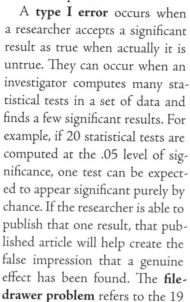

JAMES ROTTON'S work on the effects of air pollution and lunar influences showed that the former may be more important than we thought and the latter may be less important than we thought.

possible causal mechanisms and concluded that none were credible.[12]

Nevertheless, James Rotton and I. W. Kelly took the trouble to assemble every lunacy study they could find (117 data sets in 37 studies) and performed a meta-analysis on them.[13] In a **meta-analysis,** the results of all known relevant studies are quantitatively combined to estimate the magnitude of an effect. **Effect sizes** computed in meta-analyses are usually expressed, like correlation coefficients, as a value that ranges from 0 to 1, where 0 indicates no relationship and 1 indicates a complete explanation of an outcome by the hypothesized influence. Rotton and Kelly's meta-analysis yielded an effect size of 0.01; lunar influences therefore explain about one hundredth of 1 percent of the variation in behaviors usually associated with lunacy.

Earthly Forces

LET US MOVE A LITTLE CLOSER TO HOME—THE ATMOSPHERE. What effects do climate, the weather, and the seasons have on people?

Weather, Climate, and Seasons. Influences from specific meteorological components (e.g., sunshine, rain, wind, temperature, and humidity in different seasons and climates) cannot be examined in field experiments because these components of weather cannot be separated from one another or controlled in everyday life. Investigators cannot special-order different combinations of outdoor weather variables. One way to get around this problem is to use special statistical procedures to control for the influence of some variables (e.g., wind or humidity) in order to isolate the effects of others (e.g., temperature). If such procedures are not employed in field studies, conclusions can be flawed.

Special climate chambers are able to vary different climate elements in a systematic way, which helps in terms of a purely scientific experiment, but of course a certain element of realism is lost when a study is done in a sealed chamber. Also, participants in climate chamber experiments may perceive the experimenter's purpose and respond to conditions as they think the experimenter wants them to,[14] or respond differently merely because they are so aware of the artificial climate.

Apart from these research problems, everyday experience suggests that weather does influence many people. One street survey, for example, found that 71 percent of people said that their mood was affected by that day's weather, including 39 percent who said that it affected their mood "strongly" or "very strongly."[15] So, millions of people *believe* their mood is influenced by the weather. What about their behavior?

Consider the effects of one weather variable, temperature. As we learned in an earlier chapter, temperature clearly influences human behavior; as the temperature moves from comfortable to hot, collective violence such as riots, domestic violence, assaults, and rape increase,[16, 17] up to the point where most people are too hot to bother striking out. Cooler-than-normal July temperatures may be depressing,[18] perhaps because hopes and expectations for warmer weather are dashed.

If high temperatures do cause aggression, do even higher temperatures cause even more aggression? The answer is that aggression increases with temperature to a certain point and then decreases when the temperature becomes too hot for people to function.[19,20] The only issue is the exact temperature at which aggression reaches its maximum. Some "cool" studies have tested these ideas in real-world settings. In Phoenix, Arizona, researchers in cars were deliberately slow to move after a stoplight turned green.[21] They counted the rate of horn-honking in cars stuck behind them. Especially among drivers who appeared not to have air-conditioned cars, horn-honking increased directly with temperature. Horn-honking increased right up to 118°F/47°C. However, this is an "easy" way to aggress; more physically demanding forms of aggression probably diminish at a lower temperature.

Sunny weather may have a dark side. In Tokyo, higher rates of murder, manslaughter, and bodily injury resulting in death occur on sunny days than on non-sunny days.[22] Might even *global* warming cause crime, in addition to all its other well-publicized effects? Serious crimes such as assault, rape, burglary and robbery (but not murders) were positively correlated with average annual temperatures in the U.S. across the five decades from 1950 to 1999.[23]

But *why* does heat cause aggression? We must ask the same question we did of the more cosmic would-be causes of human behavior: Is there a plausible causal mechanism? Do high temperatures have a direct effect, or do they trigger some other process or interact with social or cultural factors, or both?[24] Five models of the heat-aggression relation have been proposed.[25, 26]

1. The **negative affect escape model** proposes that increasing discomfort from heat causes aggression up to a point, but in very hot temperatures the motive to escape the heat becomes stronger than the motive to aggress. This model is the basis of the idea that the heat-aggression relation is curvilinear (that aggression rises with temperature to a point, and then falls).

2. The **excitation transfer-misattribution model** proposes that when the temperature rises, people experience a general increase in physiological arousal. They look for a reason for this increased arousal; if they do not realize that it is caused by the temperature, they look for other causes. If this search happens to focus on another person who seems annoying, they are more likely to decide that their arousal actually must be anger at this person, and they become aggressive.

3. The **cognitive neoassociation model** asserts that over time people learn to associate uncomfortable conditions (such as extreme temperatures) with aggressive thoughts and emotions. Aggression may occur even when no one who seems particularly annoying is around.

4. The **general affective model** predicts that emotions worsen as the temperature rises, so aggression rises linearly with temperature.[27]

5. **Routine activity theory** maintains that patterns of behavior is the real key: More aggression occurs in warm periods, because people go out more when it is warm than when it is cold.[28,29]

Quite possibly, all these models contribute to a full explanation, although further research may support one more than the others.

So far the emphasis has been on heat; less research has examined the effects of cold temperatures. Cold also may lead to aggressiveness, but of a different sort; whereas high temperatures increase aggression slowly and produce aggressive acts that are not particularly specific to ambient events (such as insults), cold temperatures tend to produce aggressive acts that are swift and more specifically directed toward ambient events.[30] Cold temperatures are not strongly related to crime patterns except robbery;[31] cold-weather robbing may reflect a survival strategy for people who desperately need food or shelter.[32]

Temperature is also associated with behaviors such as emergency room visits and calls to suicide prevention lines, but probably in an indirect manner.[33] Warm weather brings people outside to work and play, and they injure themselves more often than in cold weather. People stay indoors more when it is cold, which induces "cabin fever" and depression, which in turn leads to more calls to help lines.

Sunshine obviously is related to temperature, but not always (e.g., cold, sunny days do occur), and it seems to elicit a somewhat different set of behaviors. People were asked to help with a questionnaire and told that they could answer as many questions as they wished and, separately, the amount of tips received by servers in restaurants was counted.[34] On sunny days, people volunteered to answer more questionnaire items and they gave more tips. Probably not incidentally, the servers' moods also were better on sunny days! Other studies show that tipping increases when customers *think* the weather is sunny, even when it is not.[35]

Sunshine can improve the spirits *too* much for some people: The incidence of mania rises in the long days of summer.[36] At the other end of the spectrum, lack of sunlight is associated with **seasonal affective disorder** (SAD), a form of clinical depression that varies with season. SAD affects up to 9 percent of the population of the U.S., with more of these people living in more northern latitudes; up to 20 percent of Swedish people reportedly suffer from it. Larger numbers of people suffer from subsyndromal (that is, nonclinical) SAD.[37] The lack of sunshine and higher latitudes are significantly correlated with suicide rates in Japan.[38]

Another meteorological component, ozone level, is worth mentioning because it is less obvious, yet may be an important factor in human behavior; higher levels of ozone in the atmosphere were associated with more family disturbances severe enough to result in calls to the police.[39] The same study illustrates the valuable point that weather *combinations* may be more important than levels of individual weather variables. Assaults and family disturbances tended to occur just after days that were warmer and dryer, with lower winds.

We think of some weather combinations as "bad" weather, which usually means cold, wet, and windy weather with fluctuating barometric pressure; "good" weather is warm, dry, and calm with stable barometric pressure. Preschoolers' play may be affected by these weather patterns. Good weather and weather changing from good to bad is associated with more playing with objects than other children; bad weather and weather changing from bad to good is associated with more playing with other children than objects.[40]

In 49 U.S. cities, "bad" weather has been associated with a *lower* suicide rate.[41] People born in the first quarter of the year (January through March) when more "bad" weather occurs have greater-than-expected number of psychiatric problems.[42,43] This may be especially true for females, for whom the risk is 28 percent higher in February than in July.[44] Bad weather may—indirectly—cause schizophrenia. Bad weather increases the chances of getting the flu, and the anti-bodies produced by the mother to combat influenza during a crucial stage of pregnancy may also harm the developing child's brain.

Consideration of long-term weather combinations, or climate, led to some rather grand theories of climate in the first decades of the 20th century. The most notable of these was Huntington's **cyclonic theory**, which argued that people born in the northern temperate zones (northern Europe, North America) attained the highest level of technology and civilization because of the moderate but very changeable weather in those latitudes. The idea was that people in these zones learned to work hard during good weather because the weather might turn bad at any time. This theory has fallen into disfavor because of its questionable assumptions about whose civilization is "highest" and its determinist tone.

Nevertheless, some cross-cultural climate research is still undertaken. Apparently, cooler countries experienced greater economic prosperity over the last three decades of the 20th century.[45] Across 71 countries including both especially hot and cool countries, wealth predicts happiness: wealthy countries are, as nations, happier than poorer nations.[46] The authors explained this as a result, in part, of wealthier nations having more resources to deal with extreme heat or cold. However, even *among* wealthier nations, hotter and colder countries are happier than more temperate ones, suggesting that climate itself is important. Similarly, *among* poorer nations, the temperate countries are happier than the hotter or poorer ones; once gain, the cause may be climate-related.

Climate is also related to national levels of altruism: it is highest in cold, wealthier nations (higher than in hot wealthy nations, so again, wealth is not the main factor), and lowest in cold, poorer nations (lower than in hot, poorer nations, so again climate, not poverty, seems to be what matters).

Geo- and Electromagnetic Forces. The Earth's geomagnetic field varies, and strong variations are called **geomagnetic storms**. In Britain, over a 10-year period, admissions to psychiatric hospital of depressive-phase manic-depressive individuals rose by 36 percent in the second week following geomagnetic storms.[47] Some evidence even suggests that 20th century wars were related to changes in geomagnetic activity.[48]

On the subject of magnetic forces, do electric power lines and other sources of electromagnetic power affect human behavior or well-being? Over 2 million miles of power lines crisscross the U.S. One review concludes that they have no important effects,[49] but another reports that several independent studies show an association between electrical power distribution and childhood leukemia, with possible health effects to adults.[50]

Of more immediate psychological importance may be differing *perceptions* of power lines' potential effects. Technical experts are baffled by the public's continuing concerns in the absence of any hard evidence that power lines cause physiological or psychological damage. Some members of the public are equally baffled why the experts dismiss their concerns.[51] Clearly, as we saw in Chapter 3, one useful approach is to understand the bases of experts' and laypersons' beliefs; the two groups literally may be thinking about different things as they arrive at their views.

IN SUM *A few studies suggest that extraterrestrial forces from cosmic rays, planets, and the moon may be associated with human behavior, but these results probably are Type I errors. In any case, no one has suggested a reasonable mechanism by which such forces would wield their influence. Weather influences human behavior in many obvious ways and some less-obvious ways. Aggressiveness rises with temperature to a point and then declines. Ozone levels may influence violence. Electromagnetic radiation may affect public fears more than it affects health.*

NATURE AS A RESTORATIVE AGENT

PEOPLE HAVE BELIEVED FOR A LONG TIME THAT NATURE IS GOOD FOR THEM. Even back when the world's largest cities were small by today's standards, the hanging gardens of Babylon and walled gardens in Mesopotamia were nurtured so that those early urbanites could maintain some contact with nature. Ancient Romans brought trees into the city and prized mansions that overlooked open fields. The most famous early American landscape architect, Frederick Law Olmsted, created Central Park in New York City and other urban parks explicitly because he (and those who commissioned his work) believed that nature is beneficial to the emotional and physiological health of people.[52]

As reported in earlier chapters, people much prefer to look at nature scenes than urban scenes,[53] a preference that some theorists assert is innate.[54] To restore themselves of attentional fatigue, people say they prefer a walk in the forest twice as strongly as a walk through an urban center.[55] In British Columbia, over half of the adult population considers outdoor recreation to be "very important" to them, and 84 percent report that it is of at least "some" importance to them.[56] Even though about three-quarters of Canadians live in cities, 70 percent participate in wildlife-related activities, and 22 percent take special trips to watch, study, feed, or photograph wildlife in a given year.[57]

Even when nature is potentially dangerous, many people want to experience it; in one survey, 42 percent of those who visited the outdoors responded positively to the idea of hiking in an area which was posted with a sign warning of bears in the area. Over 85 percent said they would like to see a grizzly bear in the wild from a safe distance.[58]

Some observers believe that nature is even more important to people today than it was in ancient days. As people are increasingly cocooned in an industrial, urbanized environment, they are increasingly alienated from nature.[59] That may be why we strongly dislike the sounds of the developed world, such as aircraft noise, in natural settings.[60] Most modern academic authors[61-63] assert that nature is good for people in a variety of ways. But what exactly does this mean?

What Needs Restoring?

ENVIRONMENTAL PSYCHOLOGISTS HAVE TRIED to identify, in more precise terms than everyday phrases such as "to recharge my batteries," why people seek out nature. Until the presumed outcomes of experiencing nature are clearly spelled out, testing the hypothesis that nature is "good for us" is impossible. Researchers have hypothesized that exposure to nature improves our health, speeds our recovery of attentional capacity, or from physical illness, or identified experiences and needs that they believe nature provides but that we cannot easily obtain in urban environments.

Many authors have attempted to list all the reasons, experiences, motives, or benefits that people associate with nature or outdoor recreation. These lists have included up to 40 or 50 items, with considerable repetition within lists and from list to list. To simplify things, I examined many of these lists in order to create a complete but relatively short, non-overlapping set of benefits associated with nature.[64] Here are they are:

- Cognitive freedom
- Escape
- Experience nature
- Growth
- Challenge
- Guidance
- Social
- Health
- Self-control
- Ecosystem connectedness

The first is **cognitive freedom**.[65] Being in nature provides a feeling that we have the freedom to pay attention to whatever we wish, *when* we choose to do so. This is said to restore attentional capacity. Nature also allows for a sense of **escape**—the chance to be relatively free from the rules and constraints of society. Of course, one is not truly free in nature and rules still exist, but for many people the rules and constraints are sufficiently different and less demanding in a natural setting that they experience considerable cognitive freedom and escape.

However, we go to nature for reasons other than to escape everyday life. We may need to be in nature for its own sake, that is, to **experience nature**. Once there, people have a fourth reason for being in nature: to seek **growth**,

the chance to develop themselves and learn what the natural environment has to teach them. This growth can be in their skills, knowledge of the woods, self-knowledge, self-actualization, or in one's spiritual domain.

Fifth, some people go to nature for the **challenge**, or what has been called the adrenalin experience[66]—the excitement that emerges in potentially dangerous situations such as white-water rafting, encountering a bear, or rock climbing. Of course, one can have an adrenalin experience crossing a busy street in any big city, but the difference is that in nature one often *chooses* such an experience.

Sixth, when the challenge involves responsibility for others (such as being a youth group leader), a person may seek a **guidance** experience. The chance to lead a group may be particularly important to someone whose city job involves little opportunity for leadership. Most of the experiences already described involve a seventh, **social** dimension that is different from social life in the city. One spends time with different people in different activities; even being in nature with your family or friends is a different social experience than in the city. Thus, we can be socially restored by nature.

The eighth reason for being in nature is that it is often said to improve our **health**, both mental and physical, through the fresh air and exercise it offers. Ninth, nature can provide a therapeutic experience by giving its visitors a chance to exert **self-control**,[67] a kind of self-confidence in which one feels able to accept whatever comes and adapt to it. The tenth, but certainly not least, reason for being in nature goes beyond the immediate experience of trees and streams; it is to sense **ecosystem connectedness**, the awareness that we are part of the immensity of nature and the cosmos.[68,69]

Does Nature Restore Us?

CASUAL EXPERIENCE SUGGESTS that these experiences and benefits occur, at least for some people sometimes. People *say* they are more restored by nature than by other environments.[70] They claim that their favorite outdoor places are more restorative than their favorite urban places.[71] However, casual experience and stated preferences do not scientifically prove that nature has benefits for people. What does the research say? Research on the benefits of nature has asked two basic questions: Does being *in* nature benefit us? Can nature benefit people who merely have a *view* of nature?

Being in Nature. One would think that being in nature would be beneficial. However, we should remember that nature is not always benign. A cougar attacked and nearly killed a boy on the island where I live, although the attack was rare. On the day that I am writing this, a massive landslide killed up to 18 people in Washington State. Superstorms and earthquakes are nature, too. Clearly, being in nature can be far from restorative.

However, are safe nature outings on pleasant days restorative? They seem to improve directed-attention performance[72,73] and to increase one's sense of vitality.[74] Even being in simulated nature seems to offer most of the stress-reduction benefits of actual nature, although being in actual nature leads to stronger feelings of altered states of consciousness and energy.[75]

In a direct comparison of settings, when backpackers who took a wilderness vacation, a non-wilderness vacation, or no vacation were compared, they felt better and performed better on a proofreading task after they returned.[76] (Interestingly, the backpackers actually felt *worse* immediately after returning, but better some time later. Possibly they were a bit depressed at first about the return to society!) These findings were confirmed in later studies; the difference was that stressed people took a walk in a park versus a walk in a built-up area or staying indoors.[77] Workers who took a vacation in nature returned to work more restored (less personal strain) than those who took an urban vacation, particularly employees with less-urban orientations.[78] When physiological stress measures were taken four times a day, people randomly assigned to forests were significantly less stressed than those assigned to urban settings.[79] Restoration from being in nature does not seem to be strongly affected by having to share the trails with other people.[80]

Longer and frequent visits of green spaces in urban areas are viewed by city dwellers as beneficial, especially during very hot periods,[81] and longer outdoor experiences are more restorative,[82] although bringing the children along is less restorative.[83] When children with ADHD took guided walks in a city park versus two other urban settings, they concentrated better after the walk in the park.[84]

Wilderness experiences may foster **self-actualization,** the fulfillment of one's potential for personal growth and psychological health. Individuals who spent time in wilderness areas were more self-actualized than those who did not,[85] and campers who appreciated wilderness more were slightly more self-actualized.[86] These correlational data

do not *prove* that going into the wilderness increases self-actualization, but they are consistent with that hypothesis.

Some varieties of nature may be restorative than others: coastal areas, forests, moors, and mountains appear to be more restorative than urban parks and playing fields.[87] Perceived restorativeness, as opposed to restorativeness assessed by some an objective measure, can vary with the very same place depending on temporary factors such as the air or water quality on a particular day.[88]

Finally, is living *near* nature beneficial? Within urban areas, more green space is associated with fewer health problems: people with more green space in a 3 km/2 mile radius around them were less affected by stressful life events than those without such a "buffer zone."[89] Among children who live in rural areas, the life stress of those who live near natural areas is lower than that of children who do not live

RACHEL KAPLAN was among the first to investigate the psychological benefits of nature.

near natural areas.[90] On the other hand, bringing nature (plants) indoors, although an ancient practice that many would claim is beneficial for emotional states, pain perception and management, creativity, task-performance, and autonomic arousal, does not have uniform support in research conducted so far.[91]

Views of Nature. Merely looking at nature seems to help restore people. In a classic study conducted by Roger Ulrich, surgery patients who had a view of nature out their hospital room windows (as opposed to a view of a brick building) recovered faster: they had shorter hospital stays, fewer problems noted by nurses, and fewer post-operative medical problems.[92] Prisoners with nature views are less likely than those with non-nature views to make sick calls[93] or to report stress-related minor illnesses such as headaches and upset stomachs.[94] Looking at nature improves one's mood, and to some extent it improves concentration.[95] Students rate dramatic nature murals, especially those with water, as more restorative than views of real but less-exciting nature that include buildings, and they rate views with no nature as least restorative. [96]

More generally, viewing natural landscapes is associated with positive health effects, including short-term recovery from stress or mental fatigue, faster physical recovery from illness, and long-term overall improvement on health and well-being.[97] Girls (but not boys—here begins the "not always" part!) who have more natural views from their residence show more self-discipline (concentration, impulse inhibition, and delay of gratification), which may be important skills for avoiding problems that preteens can experience.[98]

In a laboratory study, people were shown a stress-inducing film about workplace accidents and then shown one of 6 short films that depicted either natural or urban scenes.[99] Those who were shown nature scenes recovered from the stressful experience faster, according to both self-report and physiological measures (see Figure 12-2). Individuals who watched a video of nature-dominated drives experienced less stress, recovered more quickly from stress, and were less likely to experience stress later.[100] Other studies have demonstrated a reduction in heart rate, signaling stress reduction,[101] and that vegetation on the side of the road in a video-simulated driving study resulted in greater tolerance of frustration, which might mitigate road rage.[102]

However, not every study confirms the idea that nature views are beneficial. For example, nursing-home patients that my colleagues and I studied who had a nature view suffered a significant *decline* in mental status one month after admission to the home.[103] Others report that scenes with water in them, whether in nature *or* in built-up areas are perceived as restorative.[104] This opens the door to the question: is nature the only restorative agent, and if not, what else has that effect?

Is Nature the Only Restorative Agent?

SOME HAVE PROPOSED that restoration does not derive from nature itself, or solely from nature, but from aspects of nature that may be found in other settings. What about calm, beautiful, well-designed buildings? Some houses of worship can also be restorative,[105] and people rate buildings with more "entropy" (that is, summed architectural variation) as being more restorative.[106] In Italy, different aspects of restoration are possible in different places (including buildings) for people at different stages of life.[107]

More broadly, the **affective-arousal approach** asserts that nature's benefits derive from the positive emotions it elicits in us, and that any calm, peaceful setting will have similar benefits.[108] A similar idea is that we get overloaded by stimuli in the built environment, and nature usually provides a reduction in stimulus level, which is restorative; the implication is that any environment that reduces the bombardment is restorative.[109]

Another proposal asserts that culture is the driving factor; that some people learn through their culture to love nature and to dislike cities; therefore, the apparent benefits of nature derive more from being in a loved place than from nature itself.[110]

How Does Nature Restore Us?

IF IT IS NATURE THAT RESTORES US, two major theories propose why it does so. One, originated by Stephan Kaplan, is **attention restoration theory**.[111] Nature, according to this view, is inherently fascinating; it compels our involuntary attention, which requires little or no effort; we simply take in the scene without effort. This is restorative because ordinarily, in our workaday world, we are required to actively focus our attention most or all the time. Focused attention is taxing; we get mentally tired. Nature provides a setting for non-taxing involuntary attention, and we are gradually refreshed by being in it. This approach is based on the recharging of our capacity for attention—a *cognitive* approach.

The other major theory is the evolutionary approach taken by Roger Ulrich and his colleagues.[112,113] This theory takes a firmer position that nature is necessary for restoration. Nature may be one of the few settings that is fascinating, but there are others—beautiful art, one's child or lover, for example. However, the basic thesis of this **biophilia approach** is that humans evolved for two million years in natural environments, and we have only lived in cities for a tiny fraction of that time. Thus, genetically, we are much more adapted to natural than to built settings. Being in nature is like going home, genetically. We are where we belong, where we fit in, and this is very restorative. This

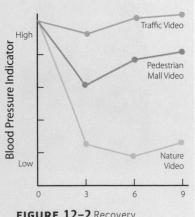

FIGURE 12–2 Recovery (in minutes) from stress after seeing videos of nature versus videos of malls.

approach assumes that nature makes us feel good—an *affective* approach.

Of course, both theories may be true; they are not necessarily opposed to each other. When researchers tried to distinguish between them, affective but not cognitive changes were found, but the authors suggest that perhaps the cognitive changes take longer to unfold (than the time the participants were in the experiment), and the participants saw nature photos, rather than being in nature.[114] Clearly, more research is needed on this important question.

A different approach suggests that nature restores people by drawing them to it, which in turn promotes healthy activities. Thus, for example, when neighborhoods have trees and green spaces, people tend to use those spaces more than other spaces that lack trees and plants for their play and social activities, which facilitates exercise and helps to knit neighborhoods together as vital places to live.[115] Similarly, when people walk in nature, they are cognitively engaged, and reap more psychological benefits.[116]

Identity, Connectedness, and Nature

ENVIRONMENTAL PSYCHOLOGISTS EXPLORE THE RELATION OF SELF TO NATURE, or **environmental identity**, and measures of this have been developed.[117-119] How deeply do people identify with nature? What are the consequences of doing so, or not? Certainly not everyone develops an identity with nature or the environment, and people whose values are more self-oriented are more easily distracted from any connection to nature that they may have.[120]

When people spend more time in nature, they tend to develop an identity with it.[121] Environmental psychologists have speculated that if people identify with nature, they will be motivated to act to protect nature, just as they would act to protect themselves.[122] Unconscious identification with nature is associated with more explicit concern for the environment,[123] and greater inclusion of nature in the self is associated with greater self-reported pro-environmental behavior.[124]

Robert Sommer has underlined this connection by pointing out how trees, one of the most important aspects of nature, have been incorporated into our individual and collective identities through such practices as naming many of the streets we *live* on (not so much the downtown *business* streets) after trees, thinking of ourselves as being part of a family tree, etc.[125]

However, evidence about whether the typical person is more identified with nature or the built world is mixed,[126] and environmental identity may vary with the seasons.[127] Other evidence suggests that *emotional* connections to nature may be stronger influences on a person's intention to visit nature than one's *identification* with nature.[128] Nevertheless, an entire book was devoted to the idea that we are split from nature and need to heal this split.[129] Ironically, making nature part of ourselves may be "loving it to death" as more and more people visit wilderness areas, bringing noise and air pollution, not to mention motorized vehicles, into the heart of natural areas.[130]

IN SUM *People have always believed that nature is restorative, even though it can be destructive, too. Different ways in which nature can benefit us include facilitating cognitive freedom, ecosystem connectedness, escape, challenge, experiencing nature, growth, guidance, a renewed social life, self control, and health. Being in nature, even merely viewing nature, or living near nature can have restorative effects, although some researchers maintain that the same effects might be gained by certain features of civilization. The two main mechanisms by which nature restores us are through refreshing our attentional capacity and improving our moods by being "home."*

NATURAL AND TECHNOLOGICAL HAZARDS

Big Trouble

A PRIMARY HUMAN GOAL, and certainly one pursued by environmental psychologists, is to forestall the possibility of violent death and destruction from fire, storm, flood, tsunami, explosion, meltdown, avalanche, earthquake, pollution, or other major hazards. Despite these efforts, the

FIGURE 12–3 December 26, 2004: Thailand faces the Indian Ocean tsunami.

annual death toll from such hazards is large: each year on average about 250,000 people are killed by extreme events of nature,[131] and in some years more than that are killed in a single event. The great 2004 tsunami in the Indian Ocean killed over 230,000 people in 14 countries (see Figure 12-3). In 2012, Hurricane Sandy killed 285 people in the New York area and caused more than $68 billion in damage. Its category-3 fury was exceeded by Hurricane Katrina in 2005, which killed at least 1,836 people and devastated many southern coastal U.S. towns, most notably New Orleans. Less well-known today is the 1928 Okeechobee Hurricane, which killed over 4,000 people in Florida and the Caribbean.

Yet even these hurricanes cause much less damage than earthquakes and volcanoes do. Mount Vesuvius buried the entire town of Pompeii 19 centuries ago. A great earthquake and tsunami in 1755 killed 60,000 to 100,000 residents of Lisbon. The 1883 Krakatoa volcano killed about 36,000 people. In 1976, a huge earthquake in Tangshan, China, killed between 250,000 (the official estimate) and 800,000 (an unofficial estimate) people. By some estimates, the number of catastrophes seems to be increasing.[132] Other important disasters inflict less obvious but nevertheless important damage. For example, air pollution kills many people (for example, about 1,700 each year in Toronto and Montreal).[133]

Disasters do not strike humanity equally. Apart from Hurricanes Sandy and Katrina, fate appears kind to North America, which received fewer great natural blows than other continents. However, within North America, some groups face greater risks than others. For example, the elderly make up about 12 percent of the U.S. population, but comprise 29 percent of annual deaths by fire.[134] African-Americans are more likely than Euro-Americans to live near hazardous waste sites.[135]

The scientific study of environmental hazards harks back to 1917, when a Red Cross supply ship collided with another ship loaded with 3,000 tons of TNT and other explosive materials in the harbor at Halifax, Nova Scotia. The resulting explosion was the largest ever recorded until the first atomic bombs were dropped. It killed about 2,000 people, injured about 8,000, and flattened many homes in Halifax and the neighboring town of Dartmouth. One can still see pieces of the ships embedded in the walls of surviving buildings. The social-psychological responses of the victims were studied, and recommendations were made for methods to avoid future disasters and to improve community relief efforts if they did recur.[136] However, we have more to learn more about human response to the threat and the reality of environmental hazards. This section covers human preparation and response to these environmental disasters. Unfortunately, it also must cover human failure to prepare for and respond to them.

Definitions and Distinctions

ENVIRONMENTAL HAZARDS may be easier to characterize by listing common types than by attempting a formal definition, but the following definition is reasonably accurate and comprehensive (see Figure 12-4). **Environmental hazards** are events of unusually large magnitude, often unpredictable and allowing little or no preparation, that cause death or injury to many people, destroy much property, and disrupt many social and economic activities. Sometimes they are *nonevents*—hazards that have no single low point, no particular "crunch" time, such as drought and air pollution. As a preliminary step to organizing knowledge about hazards, some have tried to classify them.[137]

Nearly everyone's home is threatened by one or more possible disasters. Some of these are **natural hazards**: flood, fire, storm, earthquake, heat or cold wave, volcano, drought, tsunami, avalanche, and so on. **Technological hazards**, in contrast, result from human works: nuclear plant accidents, radioactive or chemical spills and seepages, nuclear bombs, landmines, falling space debris, large explosions, floods caused by broken dams, and so on. Of course, combinations are possible—heavy rains can cause a dam to break, or an earthquake might cause a chemical spill.

Apart from their natural or human origins, these two kinds of environmental hazards differ in other ways, although these differences are not always clear.[138] According to one view, technological catastrophes are more likely than natural ones to have direct long-term effects, to have effects far beyond the original place of impact, and to threaten people differently than natural hazards do.[139] For example, the 1979 nuclear accident at Three Mile Island likely had physical and psychological effects that spread farther and last longer than those from a tropical storm.

Both technological and natural hazards may have important *indirect* long-term effects, not all of which are bad. For example, the eruption of the volcano Santorini ruined the Minoan civilization, but that calamity also stimulated the rise of Greek culture, a major basis of our own civilization. Most large disasters spark legislation, which governs building codes and zoning for many subsequent years, and that presumably ameliorates future hazards.[140]

Natural hazards usually occur rather suddenly (drought is one exception), but technological hazards often act slowly (explosions are an exception). Climate change is a special case of technological hazard, in the sense that it is largely caused by people using technology to burn carbon. Another "slow" problem in the poorer parts of many urban areas is lead contamination. Lead occurs in some paints, in soil and air near smelters, printing factories, foundries and other industrial plants, and in traffic fumes. It has been associated with mental retardation, hyperactivity, a variety of illnesses,[141] and even to crime rates, again particularly in poorer areas.[142] Lead is not the only hazard: many environmental chemicals pose hazards for brain development and health, which of course can lead to a variety of behavioral problems later in life.[143]

Preparation for, and response to, environmental hazards may be divided into three phases. *Before* the calamity, individuals who differ in age, education, and attachment to the community have (a) more or less knowledge about hazards and differing perceptions of the risk from a given hazard, (b) more or less experience with previous hazards, and (c) more or less education about hazards. *During* a calamity, individuals obviously experience a great deal of stress. They may be killed, injured, extremely frightened, stressed, lose friends or relatives, and see their property destroyed. *After* the calamity, victims must somehow cope with the experience. They seek a variety of solutions to future occurrences as well as compensation for their losses. Let us begin at the beginning—before calamity strikes.

Before the Calamity

Awareness: Knowing What Is Possible. Before disaster strikes, most of us are engaged in our normal routines. We may be aware that disaster is possible, our disaster plans may be in place (but probably not), and unless someone refreshes our memory, we pay little attention to the possibility. After all, environmental disasters are relatively rare in each person's life, most of us have never experienced one, and many other causes kill people more frequently. However, just one volcanic eruption, tornado, meltdown, hurricane, bomb, quake, flood, or fire easily can end your life. Which of these disasters is most likely to strike *your* community? Are you ready?

Attitudes: Thoughts and Feelings about Hazards. Given that individuals are aware of potential hazards, what do they think and feel about them? Attitudes about environmental hazards are important to understand because they are related to the degree of preparation that people engage in, and preparation often is the key to survival.

Attitudes toward hazards include the following:

- Knowledge about the possibility of a disaster.
- Risk perceptions about hazards, including the discounting of information
- Opinions for or against hazardous technological developments.
- Trust or the lack of it in authorities in charge of hazards.
- Beliefs about the costs and benefits of technological developments.
- Feelings about potential hazards, such as fear or anxiety.
- Behavioral intentions or tendencies, such as planning to prepare, or coping style.

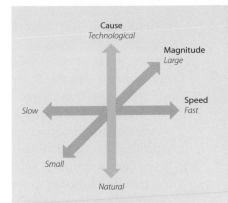

FIGURE 12–4 A way to classify environmental hazards: natural versus technological in origin, slow versus fast in speed, and large versus small in impact.

Attitudes are related clusters of thoughts and feelings. For example, higher levels of concern, less trust in officials, greater perceived risk, increased fear and anxiety, greater opposition to hazardous technology, and environmentalism tend to be found together.[144-150] Part of the reason for favoring or opposing hazardous technology sites is related to one's perceived outcomes from such sites. For example, individuals opposed to an arsenic-emitting smelter believed they were more vulnerable to its effects and had less choice about being exposed to the emissions.[151] When people believe that society is able to adapt to future challenges, they tend to discount negative future consequences more, but when they are more emotionally involved with the future, they discount them less.[152]

Perhaps the most important attitude toward technological hazards is general favorability (or not) toward technologies that might produce disasters or hazards. Those who favor such technologies tend to be less worried about them and less willing to prepare for disaster; those who oppose these technologies tend to be more fearful, concerned, and willing to prepare for disaster. Furthermore, those who favor technological developments such as nuclear power or hazardous waste disposal plants assign more credibility or weight to the project's benefits than to its costs. Nuclear plants provide power and jobs; waste disposal sites provide jobs. These are immediate and tangible benefits. The risks to health, the landscape, property values, and the social fabric of the community usually are less tangible, would occur later, and are more difficult to prove.

Attitudes: The Hazard Itself and Proximity to It. Some hazards are feared more than others; for example, nuclear power plants generally are more fearsome than oil developments.[153] Little is known about which hazards are more or less objectively dangerous than others, but some evidence about the likelihood of various hazards will be presented later in this chapter.

Naturally, proximity to an environmental hazard influences concern. Three kinds of "close" may be identified: physical proximity to the actual site, place attachment or length of residence in the community where the site is located, and experiential closeness (that is, having experienced the hazard before). First, consider living physically close to a hazardous site. One would expect that living close would lead to greater concern and opposition to an environmental hazard, and less trust of official warnings; indeed, this is often the case.[154-157] In accordance with this

idea, social scientists have created **risk perception shadows**—maps that show the degree of perceived risk as a function of distance from a hazard.[158]

However, concern does not always rise directly with closeness. For example, residents who lived near solid waste disposal facilities in Florida did not think of them as more dangerous than residents who lived farther away.[159] In fact, the reverse sometimes occurs. Northeastern U.S. residents whose community had *more* radon gas—that is, they were literally closer to it—tended to *underestimate* its health risks, whereas those whose community had *less* radon tended to *overestimate* its risks.[160]

As these results imply, sometimes—particularly if a hazard is difficult to control—residents deny or downplay the danger, even when it is inside their own homes. Students who lived in a dormitory with very poor seismic safety ratings were more likely to deny the seriousness of the situation than students who lived in dorms with good seismic ratings.[161] Teens who lived 3 mi./5 km from a nuclear power plant were less fearful of it than were teens who lived 64 mi./105 km away.[162] Agricultural workers who believe that finding an alternative occupation would be difficult also believe their risk from pesticides is less.[163] Residents who live near a large waste incinerator[164] and a new oil refinery[165] habituated to it after some time, yet another example of environmental numbness.[166] Living close to a hazard sometimes is viewed as an amenity as well as a risk.[167]

The second form of closeness is place attachment or length of residence in the community. Permanent community residents tend to favor proposed nuclear power plants, coal liquefaction plants, and arsenic-emitting smelters more than short-term residents,[168,169] perhaps because they have a strong sense of place, even though a hazard looms nearby.[170] For technological hazards, at least, familiar risks—assuming familiarity grows with length of residence—appear to be more tolerable than unfamiliar risks. However, for natural hazards, residents who have lived in an area longer believe the probability of a future earthquake is higher.[171]

The third form of close is experience or familiarity with hazards. Experience with hazards obviously affects attitudes toward them; for example, people who had experienced a disastrous earthquake were more concerned about future quakes than those with no experience.[172,173] Immigrant Mexican farm workers believe the risk to themselves from pesticide exposure is greater if they have experienced harm from pesticides previously and believe exposure to pesticide is unavoidable.[174]

In contrast, residents of a community that already had a nuclear power plant were *more* favorable to a new plant than residents of other communities in the area.[175] Presumably, as the benefits of the plant accrued and no costs were salient, acceptance grows. An examination of the fears of Washington State residents 5 months before and 1 month after the Chernobyl accident revealed that people thought about and discussed a nearby nuclear plant more after Chernobyl, and their expectation that they would develop cancer or suffer genetic changes actually declined.[176]

Attitudes and Personality: Who Is Concerned? Attitudes toward environmental hazards are partly rooted in individual differences (e.g., gender, age, education, personality, and social influences). For example, women fear or oppose such hazardous technical developments more than men;[177-180] they also have greater concerns about such natural hazards as tornadoes[181] and earthquakes.[182] Married people and those with children at home are more concerned than non-parents.[183,184] Younger people usually report being more concerned or fearful,[185,186] but sometimes older people are more concerned.[187] These clusters of thoughts and feelings appear to be similar across cultures.[188] More educated people tend to have fewer fears and concerns about hazards.[189-192] This is consistent with research which shows that more "sophisticated" individuals are less vulnerable to threats of other kinds.[193] This does not mean that more educated people think hazards are less likely—in fact they even may believe hazards are *more* likely[194]—but simply that they are less fearful about them.

As a student and I discovered in creating an instrument to measure individuals' assessments of the risk to themselves, to the environment, and of their ability to deflect a risk if it arose, risk perception tendencies may constitute a personality disposition.[195] Consistent with this idea, people who are fearful or concerned about one hazard tend to be concerned about other hazards.[196] As you would expect, persons who are dispositionally more anxious or less trusting are more likely to be concerned about hazards[197] and to expect greater risks of death and damage from them.[198,199] Specific risks cause dispositionally anxious persons more anxiety.[200] A further problem for people with their higher level of anxiety is that they are more likely to deny the importance of an actual disaster warning when it arrives.[201]

Individuals with an internal locus of control are more likely to be aware that a hazard exists[202] and, perhaps because they are accustomed to thinking that they can change things, they experience more stress when an environmental threat that is very difficult to change is near their home.[203] Similarly, people who tend to cope with stressors in a problem-solving manner (as opposed to those who fight stress by working on their own emotions) experience more stress when the threat is a hazardous waste dump that is already in place, and therefore very difficult to change.[204]

Personality consists of an interrelated set of dispositions. When statements about hazards made by residents who live near a large chemical-industrial complex in the Netherlands were examined, they fell into four major patterns,[205] which might be called **hazard response personalities**. The patterns show an ordered increase in anxiety and concern. The least anxious pattern is the Secure personality, whose attitude is, "What hazard? Is there a hazard around here?" The second is the Accepting personality, who tends to say, "Well, it's not good, but life is a trade-off—if we want modern goods, we have to accept some risks." Then comes the Defensive personality, who claims "It isn't all that bad, you know; people exaggerate these risks." Fourth and most anxious is the Vigilant personality, who believes "They don't tell you everything; reality is probably worse than they or anyone knows." Which of these is closest to your own hazard response personality?

Attitudes toward hazardous technology also depend on the importance that individuals place on previous problems with the technology. For example, people who downplayed the importance of the Three Mile Island nuclear plant problems were more accepting of a local nuclear power plant.[206] Apparently, denial can mutate into positive attitudes.[207]

Attitudes: The Role of Information. What we think, feel, and do depends in part on what we hear and from whom we hear it. For example, social interaction can make attitudes stronger or push them in the opposite direction. When people in an affected area discuss natural or technological hazards, risk may be **socially amplified**,[208] that is, one's risk estimates can be increased, decreased, or otherwise shaped by the social, cultural, psychological, and institutional context in which risk is discussed. Simply put, people can alarm *or* assure one another. Perhaps in part because we tend to discuss hazards with others who share our views, we have a tendency toward **false consensus**, the belief that more others have the same beliefs as ourselves than actually is the case.[209]

Having heard emergency information before a traumatic disaster like a fire seems to reduce the emotional distress people feel when they actually experience a fire.[210] In China, people who had recently been through a magnitude 8.0 earthquake that killed 70,000 people, wounded 370,000, and caused $85 billion in damage heard either positive or negative information and whether it came from someone familiar (word-of-mouth) or from a public source.[211] The credibility of, and the risk perceptions about, what they heard was most strongly influenced by negative information they heard word-of-mouth.

However, attitudes toward environmental hazards are also influenced by media coverage.[212] The **heuristic** (inferential rule) used by individuals to estimate their probability of being harmed can be unduly influenced by the availability of fallible indicators, such as the high degree of memorability and imaginability of the event caused by extensive media coverage.[213]

Documentaries can significantly shift attitudes about nuclear power,[214] although not every study agrees that they can really change a person's perception of risk.[215] The primary purpose of documentaries usually is to inform people, rather than to warn them, but other media presentations, such as public service messages, are designed to warn. Four public service ads, designed to warn about earthquakes, contained either a picture of earthquake damage or not, and contained estimates of the likelihood a future quake or not.[216] Those with images were more likely to motivate people to prepare for an earthquake than those without pictures; the estimates of quake likelihood had no effect.

Public officials must be careful with their warnings; the prediction of a quake that did not happen produced mild but widespread stress disorders in children.[217] Another reason that warnings must be carefully planned is that people respond differently depending on which medium carries the warning to them,[218] warnings carried by newspapers and TV, for example, vary in memorability, vividness, and imaginability.

Attitudes: Experts versus Laypersons. An important difference in attitudes about hazards is that between experts (who presumably have technical education on the topic) and laypersons (who presumably do not).[219] Compare, in Table 13-1, the risk rankings (out of 30 risks presented) of

some technological hazards by League of Women Voters members, college students, and experts.[220] Such disagreements reflect the serious policy, planning, and expenditure conflicts between environmental activists, middle-class citizens, and experts. They also create an ominous potential for chaos in the event of large-scale disaster because the biggest difference is between experts and laypersons. Five possible reasons for these disagreements have been advanced.[221]

1. Experts and the rest of us speak different languages when it comes to hazard risks. To experts, for example, the very word *risk* tends to mean "average casualties per year." To nonexperts, however, *risk* often means that plus other factors, such as the risk to oneself.

2. Experts and non-experts may be trying to solve different problems. When faced with a particular risk, the two groups may perceive different sets of possible solutions and different sets of potential consequences of the risk. They may think they are struggling with the same threat, but their differing conceptions of that threat mean that they often are not actually on the same track.

3. Experts and laypersons often disagree about which solutions are feasible. In considering what should be done about a risk, experts often are aware of a greater variety of possible technological solutions, but they also feel constrained to limit their actions to a certain policy mandate or budget. Concerned citizens, on the other hand, tend to see political action as a solution—that is, changing the policy or budget rather than being constrained by it.

4. Experts and laypersons may actually see the facts differently. This may arise because experts withhold some key information, because non-experts fail to do their homework, because the mass media sometimes distorts facts, or because the two groups gained their facts from different sources.

5. Experts try to consider risks and benefits separately, but most laypersons do not separate the two. For example, if you give people more information about the *benefits* of pesticides, they begin to associate fewer *risks* with pesticides, even though nothing was said about the risks.[222]

TABLE 13–1 Rankings of Technological Risks by Three Societal Groups

	League of Women Voters	College Students	Experts
Nuclear power	1	1	20
Pesticides	9	4	8
Motor vehicles	2	5	1
Hunting	13	18	23
Skiing	21	25	30
Mountain climbing	15	12	29
Electric power	18	19	9

Note: Ratings of the risk from selected environmental hazards by college students, League of Women Voters members, and experts. Raters judged the risk of 30 hazards (low ranking signifies high risk).

Experts often describe lay estimates of risk as unreasonable or even irrational because they differ from their estimates which are based on technical and quantitative analyses. However, unreasonable or irrational risk perceptions would make no sense; in reality, the risk perceptions of laypersons make considerable sense when the context of their perceptions is understood.[223] That is, laypersons view risks in quite understandable ways that reflect their own personal, cultural, political, and economic situation.[224,225] Put another way, experts employ a **technical model** for estimating risk that places more value on rationality, efficiency, and expertise while laypersons base their risk estimates on a **democratic model** that places more emphasis on personal, experiential, and social values.[226] In England, for example, many people were opposed to a new nuclear plant who were not anti-nuclear in principle (e.g., they were not worried about health or safety), but because they believed it posed a threat to the landscape.[227]

So, who is correct in these disagreements—experts or laypersons? You might assume that the experts are correct. However, for at least some technologies, the experts themselves disagree with one another, so they cannot always be correct. Furthermore, experts are not always confident about their assessments of how environmental hazards will affect people.[228] In fact, sometimes no "correct" answer exists—at least until much later, when time and experience show who was correct.

However, laypersons also often misperceive risks, too, and their tendency to think unclearly about the hazard has even been given a name: **bounded rationality**.[229] People often incorrectly estimate the odds that a particular environmental hazard will affect them. For example, when individuals were asked the odds of a lightning strike in comparison to another hazard, botulism, a potentially fatal form of food poisoning, their average response was that botulism was 3.33 times more likely; actually, lightning is 52 times more likely![230] Another famous example of risk misperception was provided by the falling of *Skylab* in July, 1979.[231] On the day before the expected crash, Israelis were asked what their chances of being injured by falling debris were, on a scale of 0 percent to 100 percent. Over half the respondents gave an answers over 1 percent, which itself is a very large overestimate. One expert calculated that the odds of *Skylab* striking any specific person were about 1 in 200 billion.[232] The misperceptions were related to several personal characteristics: Younger individuals, women, less-educated individuals, and more-anxious individuals overestimated their chances of being struck by *Skylab*.

Can anything be done about the differences between lay and expert risk perception? Certainly. Many procedures have been identified that should help bring experts and laypersons closer together in a joint effort to combat hazards. Seven of these follow.

1. The mental models used by laypersons and experts should be identified and compared. This has been done for some hazards: lay versus expert opinion about the use of nuclear power in space was literally mapped out models of how each group thinks about it.[233]

2. Concepts and terminology must be agreed upon. People cannot have a fruitful discussion unless their definitions of key concepts are the same. For example, does the word *risk* refer solely to the odds of being injured, or can it include other forms of harm?

3. Gaps in technical knowledge should be eliminated. Lay people must recognize the need to learn factual material, even though the discussions probably need to go beyond facts.

4. Alternative solutions and possible consequences must be clarified. The feasibility of technical and political strategies for nullifying hazards must be discussed.

5. All pertinent facts, including the sources of those facts, must be disclosed and recognized.

6. The similarities and differences of the mental models (exactly what is believed to cause what) should be made clear to everyone.

7. Ideas and issues that have no place in the discussion should be recognized and kept out of the discussion.

Preparedness. When environmental psychologists assume their role as problem solvers, one goal is to convince people threatened by an environmental hazard to engage in preparation strategies. Obviously, knowing who is likely to be prepared and what sort of influences can be used to increase preparedness among individuals who are not prepared is important.[234] For example, people's estimates of how *likely* a disaster often are not correlated with their preparedness, but their *worry* about a potential disaster is; put in psychological terms, cognitive factors matter less than emotional factors.[235]

Preparedness comes in several varieties. A person might go online for flood preparedness information, call local authorities for a pamphlet on how to upgrade the house to withstand a hurricane, stock the cellar with food and first-aid supplies and radio batteries in case of a tornado, wear protective clothing when using pesticides, or organize a meeting to oppose a proposed local hazardous waste dump. More generally, we can say that preparation can take four forms: information-seeking, household readiness, self-protective behavior, and political involvement.

In an example of the first form, residents of one community were threatened by water contamination.[236] Those who sought information about how to reduce their risk from contaminated water tended to be those who perceived their personal risk to be greater and those who trusted the experts' ability to solve the problem less. As expected, the information-seekers knew more about how to combat the water problem, and thus were more prepared.

The second form of preparedness is household readiness. The goal is to convince all residents who might be struck by an environmental hazard to prepare their residences as much as possible and to learn what to do if disaster strikes. To achieve this goal, emergency planners

should know who is likely to have already prepared; this ensures that efforts to improve preparedness can be targeted more efficiently. We know, for example, that men and women tend to prepare differently[237] and that those who have more choice about, and commitment to, preparing for disaster probably will do more preparation.[238]

Typically, attempts to predict who will and who will not ready their households are based on such person- and situation-based factors as gender, age, proximity to the danger, expectations, and environmental concern. For example, a residents in a flood-threatened area who had taken out flood insurance tended to be employed and better-educated than those who had not.[239] In India, flood preparedness was related to three kinds of place attachment (economic, genealogical, and religious). Those with genealogical and economic place attachment prepared for floods, but those with religious place attachment did not.[240] What others *expect* a person to believe (such as that nothing can be done about flooding, or that something *can* be done) and the person's belief that a given behavior *will* have consequences (such as that fastening bookshelves to walls will—or will not—prevent injury during an earthquake) also predict preparedness.[241,242]

Bounded rationality can affect whether people prepare for disaster or no; some residents tend to perceive and adopt a narrower than necessary range of **adjustments** (preparations) to the possibility of a disaster.[243] Often, of course, *no* adjustments are made—people simply wait for disaster to strike. Even when people do make adjustments, such as taking out insurance or stocking emergency food, they tend to make fewer adjustments than available knowledge would call for. People also tend to be aware of fewer adjustments than are actually available. We also seem to prefer the **crisis response**—that is, to wait until disaster strikes before preparing for the *next* one.

When we misperceive risks, we do so in a variety of creative ways.[244] Some of us believe that hazards occur in cycles and "it isn't time yet." Others place too much faith in such protective devices as dams. Some deny that the hazard exists at all. One flood victim, when asked why he had not prepared, answered that he didn't prepare because floods do not happen in his town—only "high water."

The third form of preparedness is self-protective behavior. Self-protective behavior is most likely to occur in persons who know about the risk, believe they have some control over their own health and job, and believe that precautions really work.[245] Women, at least in one study, took more steps to avoid exposure than men.[246] Perhaps counter-intuitively, those who already suffer from an ailment related to a hazard—such as lung-diseased people who live in an area with serious air pollution—may take *fewer* precautions.[247] Perhaps they believe the damage has already been done and it will not worsen, or perhaps whatever influenced them to endanger themselves in the first place continues to influence them even after their health has been damaged.

The fourth, and probably most effective, form of preparation for potential disaster is political involvement. Residents can indirectly prepare by putting pressure on lax policymakers and enforcement officers. About 70 percent of the damage by hurricanes in Texas and North Carolina was the result of poor building code enforcement.[248] In areas where building codes were strictly enforced, only 3 percent of affected dwellings suffered major structural damage. In the case of Hurricane Andrew, the building codes were excellent, but enforcement was lax, and experts say that 4 to 6 billion dollars could have been saved by stronger enforcement of the building codes.

When hazardous waste facilities are proposed in one's community, some people donate time or money and organize or attend meetings. Who *are* these people? In a rural community near Phoenix, Arizona, those who became involved were more likely to use **problem-focused coping**, that is, trying to solve problems by changing the source of their stress rather than **emotion-focused coping**, that is, trying to solve problems by changing their own emotional reactions to the source of their stress.[249] In Australia, residents facing a proposal to site a hazardous waste facility who became slightly involved politically (e.g., signing a petition or attending a meeting) tended to be those who have lived longer in the neighborhood or have children; those who became more seriously involved tended to be those with a greater financial stake (e.g., greater property value).[250]

Unfortunately, many residents never become politically active. The town with the "number one toxic waste dump" in the United States has a "conspicuous absence of...sustained and forceful protest" about the dump.[251] The town's residents, in general, have a high level of trust in government, which apparently reduces their perceived need to protest. The minority of residents who became involved tended to be those who believed they can make a difference, were more educated, and were married. In another town in which exceptionally high levels of dioxin were found,

the community response was very low. Interviews with residents revealed that three factors contributed to this.[252] First, widespread knowledge that the town had an ugly industrial history dampened the shock value of the news. Second, that a government agency discovered the problem and "managed" impressions about it tended to defuse public controversy. Third, local elected officials who might have led protests tended to support the government's decisions rather than criticize them. In general, protest can be dampened by the control and management of information by prominent persons, and apathy can be increased by assertions that the problem is not new or surprising.

Experimental (as opposed to correlational) approaches to learning *how* individuals become politically involved is in its infancy. However, Donald Hine and I showed people images depicting serious water pollution—such as images of police officers collecting medical refuse on a beach and poisoned fish washed up on a shore *or* a set of control images that did not depict water pollution.[253] When they were later asked for help by an environmental group, those who were shown the pollution images offered significantly more verbal commitment to a local water pollution activist group, and they backed up their verbal commitment with more donations than the latter group. This was not surprising, but it was did help initiate a causal approach to the problem, as opposed to the usual correlational approach, which does not allow for drawing causal conclusions.

How can more people be convinced to prepare? One influence that *ought* to be facilitating our preparations for environmental hazards, but is *not* working very well, is education. Educational programs about disaster are often fragmented and, consequently, so is individual knowledge of local potential disasters.[254] Publicity about disaster plans can be surprisingly poor at raising community awareness.[255] Experts warn of a pervasive myth called the **knowledge deficit model** that may be expressed as follows: If we educate, that will change attitudes, which in turn will change behavior.[256]

This sequence simply does not occur in most environmental hazard situations; education must be followed by further measures. For example, a program developed to reduce residents' use and waste of toxic household products, the usual persuasive and education-oriented messages, were supplemented by a carefully designed group discussion.[257] After the discussion, 33 percent had begun proper disposal and 36 percent had begun sharing leftover products with their neighbors rather than disposing of them.

FIGURE 12–5 Hazard warnings are not always heeded.

Where disasters are frequent, preparations are more often incorporated into daily living. Thus, education in the absence of any recent disaster may be ineffective, but frequent or recent experience is a great teacher. For example, those who live in Bangladesh's delta area suffer from frequent storms and floods. They are very poor, yet they still invest much effort in small levees, elevated platforms for themselves and their livestock, and special anchoring devices. Experience is effective even when the disaster is rare. Some 22 years after a tornado ripped through Flint, Michigan, residents who lived near the path of the tornado were interviewed.[258] Residents who were aware of the tornado were more likely to make preparations, such as taking shelter upon hearing a tornado warning and having tornado insurance than residents who had actually experienced the tornado. However, where disasters have not occurred, at least in residents' memory, preparations are rare. This means that the most dangerous environmental hazards are the rare but large ones. Most of us are aware that cataclysmic events may occur *somewhere*, but this does not often lead to action unless they happened locally.[259]

What about warning threatened residents (see Figure 12-5)? If you received a letter describing a possible earthquake or hurricane in your community, would you actually take steps to increase your household readiness? That depends in part on what the letter says. Altogether, 16 different forms of a warning letter were sent to people in Los Angeles.[260] Each letter included material that emphasized one side or the other of four themes: the quake is highly likely (or not), the severity of the quake was likely to be great (or not), being prepared is likely to reduce damage (or not), and getting prepared is easy (or not). Merely receiving this letter (regardless of which version) made little difference in the residents' preparedness, but certain forms of it were effective. In particular, letters asserting that the probability of a quake was high and that preparation does help to reduce the damage caused by the quake significantly increased preparedness.

For effective action on the part of potential victims, vague warnings will not suffice. Where warnings are possible, they should:

- Be clear, containing specific directions.
- Come from a credible source.
- Be reinforced socially at the local level.
- Use an appropriate medium of communication.

These findings are encouraging in that they suggest better preparedness need not result only from bitter experience; if people can be made aware of specific hazard possibilities, they may be better prepared for disaster. Simulations and field exercises also clearly improve preparedness.[261]

During the Calamity

UNTIL THIS POINT, THE DISASTER HAS NOT HAPPENED. The next section deals with what happens when the potential hazard becomes actual. What do we know about behavior, thoughts, and feelings as the disaster unfolds?

The First Moments: Stand Up and Protect. When the disaster strikes, do people panic? Actually, most individuals do *not* panic during disaster: many cases of victims acting as calmly, rationally, and effectively as possible under the circumstances have been documented.[262,263] So, just what *are* they doing? Japanese people who underwent a 1982 earthquake that measured 7.1 on the Richter scale were asked exactly what they did during the 30-second quake.[264] The average person engaged in five separate actions and moved 27 feet/9 meters. About half turned off gas valves or gas flames (good idea), over one-third grabbed freestanding cabinets to keep them and their contents from falling (bad idea), about a quarter went outside (often a bad idea), and about 20 percent helped others (usually a good idea).

The Japanese study was followed up among people who lived near the center of the 1989 Loma Prieta earthquake in California. This quake was the same strength as the earlier Japanese one, but its main shock was shorter (10 to 12 seconds). Virtually everyone responded first by standing up (if they were not already standing) and walking (bad idea). About 93 percent were in position to be hit by flying debris. However, by the end of the shock, about half had assumed a more protected position (good idea). The average person moved about 14 feet/4.2 meters and engaged in four distinct actions. Half sought a protected place for shelter. A fifth did nothing; they just stood or sat in place waiting for the quake to cease. Another fifth helped someone else. Only 7 percent went outside, but of course there was less time to get outside during the Loma Prieta quake than during the Japanese quake.

Not everyone responds the same. The Loma Prieta residents were mostly middle-class Anglos, and about half were retired. Hispanic agricultural workers were also interviewed; they generally were younger, poorer, and had more children at home. They had the same initial reaction (get up!), but they then moved around more, tried to help others (their children, especially) more, and went outside more. Thus, the immediate response to sudden disaster includes some similarities and some differences depending on economic status, stage of the family cycle, and culture (see Figure 12-6).

Some people do react to disaster by collapsing completely or acting in ways that endanger their own and others' lives. Other common soon-after reactions to disaster include confusion, irritability, lethargy, withdrawal, and crying.[265] How these stress reactions might be ameliorated will be discussed later, but panic behavior is important because it is dangerous. Therefore, one research goal is to discover who is likely to panic, under which specific circumstances, and to find ways to reduce panic in future disasters. For example, among flood victims, the calmer individuals were those who knew more about the flood hazard in their area.[266] Presumably, knowledge about a hazard helps a person feel more control or certainty even when the water is rising.

A special case is the person at the operational center of a disaster, such as someone who works at a nuclear plant when things start to go wrong. These employees may experience even more stress than others because they have the same fears as everyone else, but also feel responsible for causing the problem, solving it, or both. During the Three Mile Island nuclear incident, employees naturally felt significantly more tension than employees at other nearby nuclear plants.[267] In particular, they felt overloaded, and they experienced considerable conflict about what to do because of the uncertainty at the plant and how this might affect their own families.

FIGURE 12–6 A rare photo of what individuals do *during* earthquakes.

The Immediate Aftermath

IMMEDIATELY AFTER DISASTERS STRIKE, many survivors leave the building or the community. Building evacuation is a crucial process because it can be done very successfully (no injuries) or very unsuccessfully (many deaths). Evacuation from the community is a big decision that can have both benefits (safety from further exposure to the hazard) and costs (possible looting of one's home, the expense of traveling, traffic jams). Evacuation from a building depends in part on the design of the building, such as whether it has enough doors, stairs, and exit signs, and in the right locations. When a fire alarm sounds, for example, more people are likely to leave safely if exit instructions are clear and more exits are available.[268]

Terrible disasters such as the New York attacks on the World Trade Center in which many trapped people died have helped refine building design rules into most building codes; safety legislation is in place and safety equipment is available.[269] However, the immediate human response to danger is still not fully understood, and evacuations may be unsuccessful even when the building's design follows the building code.

In England, researchers examined what shoppers and staff did as they became aware of a large fire that killed 50 people in a store.[270] Designers of escape routes often follow the **physical science and complementary panic model**, which assumes that when people realize they are in danger, they will head for emergency exits, assuming they are nearby and visible. The **affiliative model**, in contrast, predicts that people will move toward their companions first. What happened? Interviews revealed that shoppers mainly

FIGURE 12–7 New Orleans, August 29, 2005, in the aftermath of Hurricane Katrina.

conformed to the affiliative model, but staff mainly conformed to the physical science model. Of course, shoppers were much more likely than staff to be accompanied by friends or family. Thus, it appears that the affiliative model holds when loved ones are near, and is the model of choice when people could follow either model, but the physical science model holds when loved ones are not nearby.

Proactive approaches to evacuation do not assume that good signs and exits will be enough to get everyone out safely. For example, a Japanese study compared the **Follow Directions method**, in which leaders *tell* people where to go with loud voices and vigorous gestures, with the **Follow Me method**, in which leaders actually *take* a few people where they should go.[271] The results showed that the Follow Me method worked best when each leader had a few (four or so) people to guide, but the Follow Directions

model worked better when each leader had to guide many more people.

Evacuations also occur at the community level. Typically, authorities call for everyone to leave, but not everyone does. One famous case was a man who had lived on Mount St. Helens for a long time; he was told that an eruption was imminent and asked to leave, but did not, and was never seen again. Who evacuated, who did not, and why, after a nuclear incident is instructive.[272] Nearby residents received conflicting information and had to decide for themselves what was best. About one-third of the residents within 20 miles/32 kilometers of the plant decided to leave. About two-thirds later said they left after hearing the governor's call for evacuation. About half returned after a week, and almost everyone returned within two weeks. About 60 percent said they left out of fear for their children or their health. Evacuation rates varied depending on one's situation: residents were more likely to leave if they lived closer to the plant, were younger, if the household was larger (usually when small children were involved, and had neighbors who also left). However, about 40 percent said they left because of the uncertainty caused by conflicting reports and unclear leadership.

Many residents left out of uncertainty; that should not be the reason for leaving. Residents should hear clear, uniform calls to stay or to leave, and obviously the calls should be correct—no false positives (go when it is not necessary) or false negatives (stay when you should have evacuated). Evacuation rates should not differ by demographic category. In the cases of hurricanes Hugo and Andrew, residents who had evacuated in a previous hurricane were three times more likely to evacuate this time; women were twice as likely as men to evacuate; and that African-Americans were half as likely as whites and Latinos to evacuate.[273] Clearly, calls to evacuate should pay particular attention to groups that are less likely to heed the call to leave.

One surprisingly frequent and positive immediate post-disaster phenomenon is the **therapeutic community**, when even unrelated people work hard together during the disaster or very soon afterward. Therapeutic communities often develop in response to fast-acting natural disasters, but not for slow-moving technological disasters. During two technological hazard events—aerial pesticide spraying and the disposal of asbestos—therapeutic communities did not develop.[274] This may be because the hazard's effects unfold slowly, because of confusion about who is or is not a victim, and because of community conflict about whether a hazard truly exists at all.

After the Calamity

WHAT HAPPENS SHORTLY AFTER THE DISASTER? In the case of natural disasters, this refers to what happens after the immediate worst, sometimes called the **low point**. In the case of technological hazards, this refers to what happens soon after people realize that a serious threat exists. What do people typically think, what do they do, and what are the effects on their mental health?

The most compelling reason for learning more about what happens after a disaster is that the post-disaster phase also happens to be the period preceding the next disaster.[275] This includes learning about what happens soon after a disaster and learning how society and individuals go about mitigating future disasters (see Figure 12-7).

Soon After: Cognition. Worry soars after incidents like the Fukushima nuclear disaster, or even the Three Mile Island nuclear plant accident, which caused almost no immediate injury or death. Trust in nuclear power declines, even far from the site of the problem.[276] Daily concern rises to the point where worries about nuclear energy equal worries over money, health, and friendship.[277]

The severity of damage to one's home can affect victims' memory long after the event. In one case, those who suffered least *and* most recalled less than those who suffered moderately.[278] Czech children who lived in a heavily polluted area could not remember things as well as a matched group who lived in an unpolluted area.[279]

Women, on average, worry more than men and experience more stress[280,281] in such situations, and this may cause them to cope more actively than men. This may occur because men, on average, show more trust in technology.[282] Some people deny the reality of a threat that is real but has not yet had a clear impact on them. Fishers in a Puerto Rican estuary that was contaminated by mercury were aware of the threat, but denied that it was important or believed that the "real" contamination was elsewhere in the estuary.[283] These thoughts enabled them to keep eating the fish they caught in the estuary.

Who is to blame? Who should pay? Victims of disasters typically want *someone* to pay. In natural disasters, victims expect the government to help; in technological disasters, they expect both the government and any company

involved to pay. The issue of who should pay how much in technological disasters is complex and depends on whether the company or organization was following safety guidelines and using the best available technology when the accident happened.[284] For example, in a hypothetical flood scenario, the more severe the flood, the more that women blamed an official in charge of levee maintenance. Men, in contrast, were more likely to check whether the official had been doing the job properly, and based their blame on that criterion rather than on the severity of the flood.[285]

Unfortunately for victims, people who are unaffected by the disaster sometimes see the *victims* as guilty,[286] a tendency known as **blaming the victim**. "Well, they shouldn't have been living in that area, anyway. They knew floods can happen there." The **just-world belief** is that people generally get what they deserve and deserve what they get. This may not be fair or true, but it helps people cope when they are faced with much stress, such as from a big earthquake. After a big Chinese earthquake, this was confirmed, especially for those who suffered the greatest losses.[287]

Before a disaster happens, many individuals believe they will be able to control dangerous events—the **illusion of control**. When fate spares such a person, especially if neighbors are struck, this illusion is strengthened.[288] Thus, if a disaster injures or kills only a fraction of the people in a community, many other residents will tend to believe even more than before that they can handle future disasters. This can be a big mistake.

Will the disaster happen again? Will there be serious aftershocks, new flooding, another emission of radioactivity? Beliefs about the future vary with other beliefs. In the case of technological hazards, those who supported a technology before it caused a problem tend to think it will not happen again, whereas those who opposed the technology think that it will.[289] In the case of natural hazards, those who feared the disaster more than others before it happened are more likely to fear that it will happen again.[290]

Will others help? After a flood, the disaster made survivors believe the social support available to them was reduced.[291] This makes sense when we recall that some sources of support may themselves be incapacitated or have their own problems.

Soon After: Behavior. Besides these cognitions, how do victims and others behave? Do residents move out of the area? Do they protest or organize against the causes of the disaster? What happens in their close relationships and to their community?

Unless a disaster is extreme, most residents do not move. Ties to jobs, family, friends, and the physical setting result in place attachment, which tends to keep people in a place even after a disaster. After one frightening but non-explosive nuclear incident, for example, only about 2 percent of residents who lived within five miles/eight kilometers had

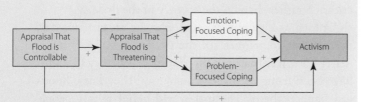

FIGURE 13–8 This model predicts who will engage in activism and who will not.

moved away a year later.[292] As might be expected, those who leave fear the threat more and those who stay have more faith that experts can ease the threat.[293] However, the rate of moving (2 percent) was the same *before* the incident, and even though movers *said* they moved because of the incident, their attitudes toward the incident were no different from those who did not move.[294] However, people who moved *into* the neighborhood tended to have favorable attitudes toward the nuclear plant.

If most people do not leave unless the disaster is extreme, do they remain passive or do they become active in fighting the source of the disaster? Among people who lived in a flood-stricken area, some became activists and some did not (see Figure 13-8).[295] Who chooses which path will be described in some detail because the same pattern may apply to activism in the face of other environmental threats and disasters. First, residents must perceive the flood (or whatever the disaster happens to be) as controllable. One might think that floods cannot be controlled, but levees and dams usually have been constructed to prevent flooding, and so many people will believe the flood could have been controlled by a *better* system of engineering. (Such disasters again show how the distinction between natural and technological hazards is not always clear.) Second, residents who believed floods are *not* controllable tended to deal with the disaster through emotion-focused coping—going inside themselves to cope, whereas those who believed that floods *are* controllable tended to see floods as a future threat. Third, seeing the floods as a future threat

was associated more strongly with problem-focused coping—the tendency to deal with a stressor by attacking it. Finally, problem-focused coping was strongly associated with activism.

Unfortunately, disasters may split communities when activists committed to different perceptions of, and solutions to, the problem argue with each other, try to recruit other residents, and sometimes clash with residents who believe there is no real problem. In Centralia, Pennsylvania, an underground coal fire has burned for at least 50 years; as many as seven groups once existed to fight the problem, and yet some residents believed the whole thing was a hoax. However, the mine fire is real, and of Centralia's 1,400 residents in 1960, seven remain in late 2013. Experts say the underground coal will burn for a thousand years.

Other post-disaster behavioral changes that have been documented include the rate of marriage among disaster survivors. In six large-scale U.S. disasters, marriage and divorce were not much affected.[296] However, the huge 1976 Tangshan earthquake in China had an important effect. Remarriage after the death of a spouse is traditionally discouraged in China, but 2,000 of 3,000 widowed people in Tangshan remarried within a few years, primarily to provide economic security and to ease their personal suffering.[297] After the Mount Saint Helens eruption in 1980, alcohol abuse, family stress, illness, and violence increased.[298] One positive ray of light emerged: a 90-percent decrease in child abuse. Unfortunately, other forms of domestic violence rose by almost 50 percent.

As many as 100,000 sites in the United States alone are threatened by toxic waste dump sites. (Can you imagine how many toxic sites we humans have created around the whole globe?) When members of a community become aware of this problem, ties to the community are weakened by learning that the community is contaminated and during struggles over the best solution or form of activism.[299] After the Exxon oil spill in Alaska, traditional social relations in the area declined, people engaged in less fishing and hunting, residents believed their health declined, and drug use, alcohol use, and domestic violence increased.[300] Sadly, survivors receive less help than they expected they would receive before the disaster.[301] Disagreements in the wake of the disaster about what to do next lead to a reduced sense of community.[302] After a big Australian bush fire, families experienced more conflict, withdrawal, irritability, and mothers tended to overprotect their children.[303] Sadly, survivors receive less help than they expected they would receive before the disaster.[304] Politics matter. Liberals are likely to favor aid even to survivors who had not acted responsibly, but conservatives are not.[305]

After some disasters, mental health professionals band together to provide relief for the survivors' typical feelings of grief, guilt, isolation, anger, depression, and anxiety.[306] Special response teams have been organized in the United States,[307,308] Mexico,[309] Australia,[310,311] and other countries after major disasters. The concept of mental health rescue teams to complement traditional rescue workers has grown; after the big Kobe earthquake in early 1995, I received an email note from Japan pleading for U.S. mental health rescue teams to come over and help survivors, and the same happened after Hurricane Katrina.

Soon After: Mental Health. Next we consider another major outcome of disasters, stress and other mental health problems. Surviving victims, of course, suffer considerable stress from the losses they suffer and from the shock of experiencing an overwhelming event (see Table 13-2a and b). Clearly, when the disaster is greater, worry will be greater and, as will we see later, may cause mental health problems. After the 911 attack in New York, about 60 percent of the residents of the nearby Chinatown had 4 or more emotional symptoms, and among those who lost a loved one, the figure rose to 90 percent.[312] Immediately, many victims show signs of **post-traumatic stress disorder** (**PTSD**), but depression, phobias,[313] and medically unexplained symptoms such as abdominal pain, vomiting, nausea, fainting, amnesia, and even paralysis[314] are also seen. After the 1989 Loma Prieta earthquake near San Francisco, college students had many more nightmares than students in another (unaffected) town.[315]

After major natural and technological disasters, when the impact is strong and swift, the outcome for many persons is moderate to severe cases of post-traumatic stress disorder. Residents who lived near a nuclear reactor incident reported feeling less control over their lives and performed more poorly on tasks measuring persistence; those who reported more loss of their sense of control also had more symptoms of stress.[316] Nearby residents, particularly men, showed elevated levels of biochemicals associated with stress for at least 17 months after the accident.[317] After a tornado, rescue team members found people mowing lawns that were not there anymore, and others trying to glue together chairs in the midst of completely destroyed homes.[318]

Victims sometimes avoid the overwhelming reality facing them. For example, residents of Armero, Colombia, who survived a 1985 volcano and mudslide that killed about 22,000 people often did not want to know the full

TABLE 13–2a Harold Foster's System for Assessing the Impact of Environmental Hazards and Some Stress Scores for Selected Large Events

Infrastructural Stress Values			
Magnitude	Designation	Characteristics	Stress Value
I	Very minor	Noticed only by instruments	0
II	Minor	Noticed only by sensitive people	2
III	Significant	Noticed by most people including those indoors	5
IV	Moderate	Everyone fully aware of event. Some inconvenience experienced, including transportation delays	10
V	Rather pronounced	Widespread sorrow. Everyone greatly inconvenienced; normal routines disrupted. Minor damage to fittings and unstable objects. Some crop damage.	17
VI	Pronounced	Many people disrupted and some frightened. Minor damage to old or poorly constructed buildings. Transportation halted completely. Extensive crop damage.	25
VII	Very pronounced	Everyone disturbed; many frightened. Event remembered for many years. Considerable damage to poorly built structures. Crops destroyed. High livestock losses. Most people suffer financial losses.	65
VIII	Destructive	Many injured. Some panic. Numerous normal buildings severely damaged. Heavy loss of livestock.	80
IX	Very destructive	Widespread initial disorganization. Area evacuated or left by refugees. Fatalities common. Routeways blocked. Agriculture severely affected for many years.	100
X	Disastrous	Many fatalities. Masonry and frame structures collapse. Hazard-proofed buildings suffer considerable damage. Massive rebuilding necessary.	145
XI	Very disastrous	Major international media coverage. Worldwide appeals for aid. Majority of population killed or injured. Wide range of buildings destroyed. Agriculture may never be reestablished.	180
XII	Catastrophic	Future textbook example. All facilities completely destroyed; often little sign of wreckage. Surface elevation may be altered. Site often abandoned. Rare survivors become life-long curiosities.	200

extent of the tragedy and resorted to primitive ("magical") thinking styles.[319] More broadly, suicides increase by 63 percent in the first year after an earthquake, by 31 percent after a hurricane, and by 14 percent in the first four years after a flood.[320]

Obviously such people need psychological first aid. A meta-analysis of 52 studies showed that, compared to normal conditions, a 17-percent increase in the rate of psychopathology occurs in the wake of disaster.[321] This is an average; in the Armero disaster mentioned earlier, major depression and post-traumatic stress disorder affected about 50 percent of the survivors.[322] Interestingly, even the form of temporary housing people are placed in after a disaster can influence their psychological health. After an earthquake in Italy, some were placed in converted shipping containers while others were placed in dachas (like a cabin or cottage); the dacha residents experienced significantly less emotional stress.[323]

Foster developed a formula to estimate total community stress (Magnitude, above) from the number of casualties, damage to the infrastructure (Stress Value, Table 13-2a), total population affected, and whether the disaster occurred in a developing or developed nation.

Reactions to disasters vary with individual differences. In some cases, individual differences predict mental health outcomes better than the severity of the disaster.[324-326] For example, women appear more strongly affected by disaster. Adolescent girls report more nightmares and fear of being alone than adolescent boys.[327] Among tornado victims, younger people experienced more physical stress, anxiety, and disruption to their social life than older people, possibly because older people have learned more coping mechanisms,[328,329] although sometimes older people suffer more than younger people.[330] Distress is also greater when victims mistrust authorities.[331] Surprisingly, among people struck by Hurricane Hugo, those who had taken part in disaster education and other preparedness activities manifested *more* physiological and psychological stress than those who had not![332]

The amount of stress caused by a disaster partly depends on one's circumstances before it strikes. Not surprisingly, people who show signs of distress before the disaster tend to experience more stress afterward.[333] In the case of Hurricane Hugo, for example, victims who had higher levels of stress because of financial, family, and physical problems before the hurricane exhibited more psychological stress afterward than other victims.[334] Child

victims of Hurricane Andrew reported more stress when they had parents who were in conflict; this was particularly true of Hispanic children.[335] Children whose academic achievement had been higher experienced less stress from the same hurricane.[336]

A formula has been created to estimate the amount of distress after disasters:[337]

$$\text{Distress} = \frac{\text{Exposure to Stressors} + \text{Vulnerability}}{\text{Psychological Resources} + \text{Social Resources}}$$

Which is more stressful, natural or technological disasters? Although some technological disasters cause more stress and mental health problems than natural hazards,[338-340] a meta-analysis found that in general, natural hazards cause more mental health problems. Apart from any difference in the *magnitude* of a disaster, which obviously can account for differences in stress levels, the primary psychological difference between natural and technological disasters is the potential for blame: blaming someone for a nuclear plant meltdown is easier than blaming someone for an earthquake. Evidence from non-disaster clinical situations suggests that stress tends to be lower when the victim has someone else to blame, so this may be why stress is greater after natural rather than technological disasters.[341]

However, if the blame is assigned to *oneself* (or a group to which you belong), the stress might be greater, not less.[342] This can happen, for example, if community residents blame themselves for allowing a hazardous waste dump site or other environmental threat in their community, or failing to adequately prepare for the disaster. Nevertheless, technological disasters may cause more total stress because their effects, or the effects that people worry about, usually persist much longer than for most natural disasters and have no particular worst moment or low point that passes.[343] A tornado may rip a person's roof off, but the repairs are done relatively soon; the threat to the person's health from the toxins in a nearby hazardous waste dump, on the other hand, continues for years.

How can disaster stress be relieved? Survivors must cope somehow. Some do so by using problem-focused coping and some use emotion-focused coping. Still others use denial to reduce the reality of disaster stress. Each style may help, depending on the nature of the disaster. When the problem is very difficult to change, a problem-focused approach may actually increase one's distress, because one is trying to solve an insoluble problem. The Three Mile Island nuclear incident apparently was handled better by people who used an emotion-focused coping style,[344,345] although younger residents in the area who used a more problem-focused approach to the restart of the nuclear plant seemed to experience less stress.[346]

Fortunately, many mental health problems decline with time after the disaster.[347] However, this does not occur always or very rapidly. Two years after an Australian earthquake, substantial mental health problems persisted.[348] Among victims of the large Armero mudslide, the rate of emotional distress over a four-year period declined from 65 percent to 31 percent.[349] One could say that stress declined by 50 percent, but one could also say that, after four years, almost a third of the population was still suffering. Psychological testing more than a dozen years after the great Tanshan earthquake showed that survivors were still affected.[350]

Unfortunately, some disasters do *not* subside. For example, natural disasters (such as drought) and technological hazards (such as pollution) can continue for a long time. People stuck in these circumstances truly are stuck: their home, which once had all the positive qualities of a home, now becomes a semi-permanent "place of danger and defilement."[351] Furthermore, when a disaster becomes widely known, few others want to live there either, and the residence's value plummets. Not only do residents lose their home in the psychological sense that their identity, security, and place attachment are damaged, but they also lose financially.[352] This is very stressful and can last a long time if moving is unaffordable.

Some victims are helped by friends or family; social support is a key element in recovery from disaster stress.[353] However, it may help more in some ethnic groups than others.[354] Social support helps more when the victim experiences lower rather than higher levels of stress, and it helps when it comes from one's supervisor (as opposed to one's peers).

However, social support sometimes may not help, or may even *worsen* stress.[355] After one incident, women were not helped by social support.[356] Having the support of family members sometimes does *not* reduce stress, but having the support of (non-family) others does.[357,358] Stress actually increased when, after a nuclear incident, supervisors were offered support from other supervisors and non-supervisors were offered help from other non-supervisors. In general, social support helps disaster victims, but it does not help everyone.

Apart from coping style and social support, survivors appear to follow a three-part **social stage model** of coping with their stress.[359] First, they openly talk and think about it for about two weeks after the disaster. Second, for about six weeks they inhibit talking about it, but continue to think about it. During this stage, distress can increase, perhaps because victims are thinking but not talking. Third, an indefinitely long adaptation stage arrives, during which

TABLE 13–2b Examples of Event Magnitude

Event	Location	Date	Magnitude
Plague (Black Death)	Europe-Asia	14th century	10.9
Spanish Armada	British coastal waters	July 21–29, 1588	7.2
Black Hole of Calcutta	Bengal, India	1756	5.0
Eruption of Mt. Pele	Martinique	May 8, 1902	7.3
Landslide	Frank, Alberta, Canada	April 29, 1903	5.1
Titanic sunk by iceberg	North Atlantic ocean	April 14–15, 1912	6.1
World War I	Europe	1914–1918	10.5
Munitions ship explosion	Halifax, Nova Scotia	1917	7.1
Train derailment in tunnel	Mondane, France	Dec. 12, 1917	5.2
Great Purge	USSR	1936–1938	10.2
World War II	Global	1939–1945	11.1
Atomic bomb	Hiroshima, Japan	Aug. 6, 1945	8.2
Tsunami	Hawaiian Islands	April 1, 1946	5.8
USS *Thresher* lost	Off Cape Cod, Mass.	April 10, 1963	4.7
Glacier avalanche	Yungay, Peru	May 31, 1970	8.1
Mass poisoning from fungicide-treated grain	Iraq	1971	7.4
Flood	Rapid City, S.D.	June, 1972	6.6
Earthquake	Managua, Nicaragua	Dec. 23, 1972	7.9
Tornado	Xenia, Ohio	April 3, 1974	6.4
Indian Ocean tsunami		December, 2004	8.5
Hurricane Katrina	New Orleans	August, 2005	8.2

Note: Foster developed a formula to estimate total community stress (Magnitude, above) from the number of casualties, damage to the infrastructure (Stress Value, Table 13-2a), total population affected, and whether the disaster occurred in a developing or developed nation.

FIGURE 12–9 The aftermath of the 1980 Mount Saint Helens explosion for one local residence.

victims neither talk nor think about the disaster. This does not mean that the disaster's effects are gone; symptoms may remain under the surface for years, or forever.[360]

Later: Mitigating Future Hazards. Over the years, a large and well-coordinated international effort toward improving society's response to disasters has evolved. These efforts have sought to:

- Assess the extent of human occupancy of hazard zones.

- Identify the full range of possible human adjustment to the hazard.

- Study how individuals perceive and estimate the occurrence of the hazard.

- Describe how damage-reducing strategies are adopted.

- Estimate the optimal set of adjustments, taking social and cultural consequences into account.[361]

A considerable body of knowledge and many organizations have developed since the Halifax explosion of 1917 to implement these goals. These include (1) research on how best to warn people faced with a disaster, (2) attempts to model behavior during disasters in order to better anticipate how officials and ordinary individuals will respond when the "big one" happens, and (3) contributions to public policy concerning natural and technological disasters.

First, psychologists investigate what and how to communicate risks and warnings.[362] In some disasters, residents have received conflicting information and false comforting words. On the other hand, information should not alarm residents to the point that they cannot act in a manner that helps themselves and others. Clearly, the information should be expert and credible,[363] and should use plain language and reflect goals shared by authorities and residents.[364]

Second, psychologists have tried to model the ways that authorities and victims will behave during a disaster. Just as one might study how a new jet design might react by using a wind tunnel, social scientists work at predicting behavior during disasters. In one such study, 60 families participated in a simulation of the personal and family decisions they would make if faced with a volcanic disaster like Mount Saint Helens.[365] In another, the goal was to understand international negotiation over ozone-depletion issues among scientists and diplomats.[366] Although findings from such simulations need to be checked against the reality of behavior in real disasters, the knowledge gained in them is still very useful as a way of approximating what people will do, without having to wait for a disaster (see Figure 13-9).

Third, psychologists have assisted in formulating government policy on environmental hazards. Elected and appointed officials must make many decisions that influence whether and how people prepare for or respond to disaster. However, psychologists are better qualified to investigate the stressfulness of living near a toxic waste dump or who in a community is likely to test their home for radon gas.[367] Research, for example, on which ethnic groups are more likely to adopt safety measures when dealing with pesticides can have a significant positive impact on government policies concerning pesticide exposure.[368] In general, government policy does alter human behavior, and psychologists who study natural and technological hazards can help develop policy that will reduce both the risk and the magnitude of a disaster's impact when it comes.

We return now to the actions of everyday people after the disaster. Faced with possible loss of life, property losses, and greatly increased stress, what can individuals do? Actions may be divided into **adjustments** (short-term responses) to hazards, and **adaptations** (long-term responses) to them. Adaptations include fundamental changes throughout the social fabric or even the biology of the species, and are perhaps best studied by anthropologists or biologists. Adjustments include purchasing insurance, devising warning systems, constructing dams and levees (for floods), designing shock-resistant buildings (for earthquakes, storms, and bombs), or simply bearing the cost of the disaster. Adjustments may be grouped into three categories: reducing one's vulnerability to the hazard, accepting losses by bearing them (alone or by sharing), and leaving a hazardous location.

The latter adjustment, moving away, may seem the most logical, but it is rare, as we saw earlier. (The exodus from New Orleans following Hurricane Katrina is an exception.) Why do individuals, especially those who are repeatedly subjected to hazards, not simply move away? In Los Angeles, where earthquakes are always possible, neither the objective earthquake hazard (e.g., living near a fault) nor perceived hazards (e.g., fear of quakes) predicted residents' intentions to move away.[369] Instead, moving was related to place attachment. Older individuals, those with children, those who owned a home, and those who were satisfied with their community did *not* intend to move, but those were less attached to the community *did* intend to move. In an area of Hamilton, Ontario, that is subject to multiple hazards, residents do not move primarily because of place attachment and the relatively low housing costs there.[370]

If residents will not move, what should be done? Disaster victims in developed countries generally favor technological and engineering solutions to environmental hazards.[371] Flood plain residents in Australia are very aware of the flood hazard, yet most make few adjustments, favoring the construction of dams, levees, and other public works to solve the problem.[372] The attitude is, "I don't want to move; fix the environment."

In general, individuals' adjustments to environmental hazards are not very impressive. Despite occasional heroics during a calamity, the larger scenario is one in which many people fail to prepare for disaster, deny or underestimate the probability of being victimized (except when the hazard is highly publicized, in which case they often overestimate their chances of being a victim), fail to move away from hazardous locations, yet expect to be protected from the hazard by engineers paid for largely by other taxpayers, and hope to be compensated by the government when disaster strikes! (Incidentally, the latter is not a good bet; in major disasters, government aid rarely covers more than one-third of actual losses).

I will close with a challenge: Can you construct a defense against this unflattering portrait? That is, can you think of any justifiable reasons for the lack of self-protective behavior? By the way, what preparations have you made for the hazards that might strike *your* area?

IN SUM *A person's attitudes about environmental risk—including awareness of a hazard's existence, assessments of a disaster's likelihood, evaluation of hazardous technologies as desirable or not, and trust or distrust of authorities—are related to numerous personal and environmental factors, including gender, education, proximity, disaster experience, and media exposure. However, once formed, these attitudes toward hazards are in turn related to the level and type of each person's preparedness for disaster. People may be aware of a threat; they may have complex attitudes toward it, experts, and authorities; they often perceive risk differently from the experts; they may be breathing toxins, but have no symptoms yet; they may or may not have prepared themselves and their residences; they may be apathetic or politically active. Still, the fears have not been realized. Most homes are subject to one or more serious environmental hazards, some natural and others technological. Before the calamity occurs, governments attempt to reduce risk through engineering and education, but when neither of these are effective, many lives can be lost. Specific warnings and awareness-raising simulations can help, but effective personal action is often blunted by the tendency to bounded rationality, under-preparation, crisis response, and risk misperception. During a disaster, losses may be high, but individuals generally act in relatively rational ways. The outcome of disaster is stress in many forms. Some forms of coping reduce stress better than others. Place attachment and economic factors often prevent residents from vacating high-risk areas; they would rather see governments engage in massive public works to protect their homes.*

Hospital Design for Psychological Health

THE VERY WORD *hospital* conjures up images of institutional green walls, sterile trays, gleaming instruments, and cold, inward-looking interiors. Health-care workers do their best to help, but the building usually offers all the reassurance, warmth, and natural feel of an oil tanker. Hospitals do not have to be that way. They need to be clean and functional for medical procedures, but not all areas need to be sterile, either figuratively or literally. What *should* they be like?

For one thing, hospitals should be psychologically supportive.[373] To the extent that architecture can facilitate healing, it should. According to Roger Ulrich, architecture can be supportive and foster health by reducing stress, which is an impediment to recovery.[374] In general, this can be accomplished in two ways. First, the building should not cause patients (or visitors and staff) any *further* stress than they already must face. It should not be crowded, noisy, difficult to find one's way around in, spread noxious air, or have bad lighting. Second, it should provide exposure to physical features of the environment that reduce stress. The designed environment can reduce stress by (a) enhancing social support, (b) providing a sense of control, and (c) offering access to positive distractions in the physical surroundings. Social support can be enhanced by increasing the potential for social interaction through flexible, sociopetal seating arrangements in patient rooms and lounges. Sense of control can be improved by giving patients more or easier control over temperature, drapes, television, their beds, and privacy. Based on the research described earlier about the health-related consequences of viewing nature, Ulrich also advocates giving patients and staff more pleasant, natural views or art in their hospital spaces. These might be views of trees, water, animals, fish in an aquarium, or at least, some sky.

Housing Disaster Victims

EMERGENCY HOUSING IS NEEDED AT MANY SITES AROUND THE WORLD EACH YEAR. The art and science of providing shelter for disaster survivors is relatively new and is still developing. Probably no donations of emergency shelter by outside countries occurred before World War II, yet within 10 days of a large 1976 quake in Turkey, over 6,500 tents were delivered.[375]

Many technologically advanced solutions to post-disaster housing have been devised, including parachutes that turn into freestanding tents ready for immediate occupancy on landing, polyurethane igloos, and instant floating marina-like shelters for flood victims. The UN and other agencies have sponsored competitions for emergency housing designs that are low in cost, lightweight, collapsible, easy to erect, and sturdy.

However, these well-intentioned temporary shelter solutions may not be what disaster victims actually need. Ian Davis, who has extensive experience with international agencies that provide disaster shelter, listed seven unsupported beliefs about emergency housing:[376]

1. "After disasters there is a need for many new shelters." Actually, most families only go to official shelters when all else has failed.

2. "Survivors show no clear patterns of housing preference after a disaster." Actually, a clear order of preferences usually emerges: Go to (a) the homes of friends and family, (b) locally improvised shelters, (c) converted buildings such as school gymnasiums, and only finally (d) officially provided shelter.

3. "Compulsory evacuation is an effective policy." In fact, place attachment is so strong that no such evacuation in the last forty years has been very successful.

4. "Tents make an effective shelter." Actually, despite stockpiles of up to 10,000 tents in various places around the world, tents tend to be late in arriving and underused once they arrive.

5. "Emergency shelter is a matter of life and death." Actually, it usually is not; local coping mechanisms take care of most serious threats.

6. "In disastrous circumstances people will be prepared to live in unusual housing." In fact, novel housing is often rejected as culturally alien (remember, the need for *any* official housing is lower than often thought).

7. "In a disaster, people are willing to live communally." In fact, people usually become more inward, clutching to their family unit where possible.

FOUR FURTHER MYTHS pertain to the reconstruction phase:

1. "Temporary housing is needed prior to re-construction." Actually reconstruction of regular dwellings starts—at least in developing countries—immediately, and survivors usually ignore temporary housing.

2. "An important priority is clearing rubble." In fact, except for clearing access roads, the rubble is often best left in place, to be recycled into new homes, at least in less-developed countries.

3. "Crash programs by agencies and governments are an effective way of solving post-disaster housing needs." In fact, local people usually respond faster and better in rebuilding.

4. "Community relocation is ideal." So far, most attempts to relocate entire communities have been unsatisfactory.

Given all this negativity, what does Davis suggest? A prime goal of those who would like to help in some way should be to train local people how to rebuild their own houses with safer materials and, if possible, in a safer site nearby. The safer design should, of course, respect local cultural traditions.[377] These efforts should be at the grassroots level, rather than persuading governments to institute new building codes that often have no practical influence on house construction. Meetings in villages and comic-book depictions of safe construction techniques are more likely to change the house construction techniques that are passed down the generations.

SUMMARY

A few studies report that extra-terrestrial forces from cosmic rays, planets, or the moon affect human behavior, but these results probably are false-positive errors. No one has suggested a plausible mechanism by which such forces would influence people. Aggressiveness rises with temperature to a point and then declines. Ozone levels may influence violence. Electromagnetic radiation may affect public fears more than it affects health. Most people believe that nature restores them, and "nice" nature does, but obviously it can be very destructive too. Nature restores by facilitating cognitive freedom, ecosystem connectedness, escape, challenge, growth, experiencing nature, guidance, a renewed social life, enhancing self control, and health. Being in nature, even merely seeing nature, apparently is restorative. The two main mechanisms by which nature restores are by refreshing attentional capacity and improving moods. These mechanisms are not limited to nature; other settings can restore us, too. Attitudes about environmental risk—including awareness of a hazard's existence, assessments of a disaster's likelihood, evaluation of hazardous technologies as desirable or not, and trust or distrust of authorities—are related to gender, education, proximity, disaster experience, and media exposure. Once formed, those attitudes toward hazards are in turn related to the quality of preparedness for disaster. Laypersons perceive risk differently than experts do; efforts toward mutual understanding are necessary. In the precalamity phase, governments attempt to reduce risk through engineering and education, but when neither of these are effective, many lives are lost. Specific warnings and awarenessraising simulations can help, but effective personal action is often blunted by bounded rationality, underpreparation, crisis response, and risk misperception. During a disaster, losses may be high, but individuals generally act in relatively rational ways. The outcome of disaster for survivors is stress in many forms. Some forms of coping reduce stress better than others. Place attachment and economic factors often prevent residents from vacating high-risk areas; they would rather see governments engage in massive public works to protect their homes.

Suggested Supplementary Readings

Altman, I., & Wohlwill, J. F. (1983) (Eds.). *Behavior and the natural environment.* New York: Plenum.

Lindell, M. K.. (2012). Response to environmental disasters. In Clayton, S. D. (Ed.). *The Oxford handbook of environmental and conservation psychology* (pp. 391-413). New York: Oxford.

Peek, L. A., & Mileti, D. S. (2012). The history and future of disaster research. In R. B. Bechtel & A. Churchman (Eds.), *Handbook of environmental psychology* (pp. 511-524). Hoboken, NJ: Wiley.

Schultz, P. W. (2002). Inclusion with nature: The psychology of human-nature relations. In P. Schmuck & P. W. Schultz (Eds.), *Psychology of sustainable development* (pp. 61-78). Dordrecht, Netherlands: Kluwer Academic.

Staats, H. (2012). Restorative environments. In Clayton, S. D. (Ed.). *The Oxford handbook of environmental and conservation psychology* (pp. 445-458). New York: Oxford.

Ulrich, R. S. (1993). Biophilia, biophobia, and natural landscapes. In S. R. Kellert & E. O. Wilson (Eds.) *The biophilia hypothesis.* Washington, DC: Island Press/Shearwater Books.

Winter, D. (2003). *Ecological psychology: Healing the split between planet and self.* Mahwah, NJ: Erlbaum.

References

[1] Quoted from p. 3 of Hartig T., Mang, M., & Evans, G. W. (1991). Restorative effects of natural environment experiences. *Environment and Behavior, 23,* 3-26.

[2] Friedman, H., Becker, R. O., & Bachman, C. H. (1965). Psychiatric ward behavior and geophysical parameters. *Nature, 205,* 1050-1052.

[3] Gauquelin, M., Gauquelin, F., & Eysenck, S. B. G. (1979). Personality and position of the planets at birth: An empirical study. *British Journal of Social and Clinical Psychology, 18,* 71-75.

[4] Cooke, D. J., & Coles, E. M. (1978). The concept of lunacy: A review. *Psychological Reports, 42,* 891-897.

[5] Rotton, J., & Kelly, I. W. (1985). A scale for assessing belief in lunar effects: Reliability and concurrent validity. *Psychological Reports, 57,* 239-245.

[6] Rotton, J., Kelly, I. W., & Elortegui, P. (1986). Assessing belief in lunar effects: Known-groups validation. *Psychological Reports, 59,* 171-174.

[7] Garzino, S. J. (1982). Lunar effects on mental behavior: A defense of the empirical research. *Environment and Behavior, 14,* 395-417.

[8] Campbell, D. E., & Beets, J. L. (1978). Lunacy and the moon. *Psychological Bulletin, 85,* 1123-1129.

[9] Garzino, S. J. (1982). Lunar effects on mental behavior: A defense of the empirical research. *Environment and Behavior, 14,* 395-417.

[10] Abel, E. L. (1976). *Moon madness:* Greenwich, CT: Fawcett.

[11] Campbell, D. E. (1982). Lunar-lunacy research: When enough is enough. *Environment and Behavior, 14,* 418-424.

[12] Culver, R., Rotton, J., & Kelly, I. W. (1988). Geophysical variables and behavior: XLIX. Moon mechanisms and myths: A critical appraisal of explanations of purported lunar effects on human behavior. *Psychological Reports, 62,* 683-710.

[13] Rotton, J., & Kelly, I. W. (1985). Much ado about the full moon: A meta-analysis of lunar-lunacy research. *Psychological Bulletin, 97,* 286-306.

[14] Dubitsky, S., Weber, R., & Rotton, J. (1993). Heat, hostility and immune function: The moderating effects of gender and demand characteristics. *Psychonomic Society, 31,* 534-536.

[15] Schneider, F. W., & Whalley, A. M. (1980). Unpublished data University of Windsor.

[16] Cohn, E. G. (1990). Weather and crime. *British Journal of Criminology, 30,* 51-64.

[17] Anderson, C. A. (1989). Temperature and aggression: Ubiquitous effects of heat on occurrence of human violence. *Psychological Bulletin, 106,* 74-96.

[18] Hartig, T., Catalano, R., & Ong, M. (2007). Cold summer weather, constrained restoration, and the use of antidepressants in Sweden. *Journal of Environmental Psychology, 27,* 107-116.

[19] Rotton, J., & Cohn, E. G. (2000). Violence is a curvilinear function of temperature in Dallas: A replication. *Journal of Personality and Social Psychology, 78,* 1074-1081.

[20] Cohn, E. G., & Rotton, J. (1997). Assault as a function of time and temperature: A moderator-variable time-series analysis. *Journal of Personality and Social Psychology, 72,* 1322-1334.

[21] Kenrick, D. T., & MacFarlane, S. W. (1986). Ambient temperature and horn honking: A field study of the heat-aggression relationship. *Environment and Behavior, 18,* 179-191.

[22] Ikegaya, H., & Suganami, H. (2008). Correlation between Climate and Crime in Eastern Tokyo. *Canadian Journal Of Criminology & Criminal Justice, 50,* 225-238.

[23] Rotton, J., & Cohn, E. G. (2003). Global warming and U.S. crime rates: An application of routine activity theory. *Environment and Behavior, 35,* 802-825.

[24] Rotton, J. (1986). Determinism redux: Climate and cultural correlates of violence. *Environment and Behavior, 18,* 346-368.

[25] Anderson, C. A. (1989). Temperature and aggression: Ubiquitous effects of heat on occurrence of human violence. *Psychological Bulletin, 106,* 74-96.

[26] Bell, P. A. (1992). In defense of the negative affect escape model of heat and aggression. *Psychological Bulletin, 111,* 342-346.

[27] Anderson, C.A., & Anderson, K. B. (1998). Temperature and aggression: Paradox, controversy and a (fairly) clear picture. In R. Geen & E. Donnerstein (Eds.) *Human aggression: Theories, research, and implications for social policy.* San Diego: Academic Press.

[28] Anderson, C. A., & Anderson, K. B. (1998). Temperature and aggression: Paradox, controversy, and a (fairly) clear picture. In R. Geen & E. Donnerstein (Eds.), *Human aggression: Theories, research, and implications for social policy.* San Diego: Academic Press (pp. 240-298).

[29] Ceccato, V. (2005). Homicide in São Paulo, Brazil: Assessing spatial-temporal and weather variations. *Journal of Environmental Psychology, 25,* 307-321.

[30] Boyanowski, E., cited in Cohn, E. G. (1990). Weather and crime. *British Journal of Criminology, 30,* 51-64.

[31] Cohn, E. G. (1990). Weather and crime. *British Journal of Criminology, 30,* 51-64.

[32] Cohn, E. G. (1990). Weather and crime. *British Journal of Criminology, 30,* 51-64.

[33] Sandilands, M. L., & Christman, G. (1987). *The effects of weather variables and month on frequency of call to a crisis line and visits to an emergency ward.* Unpublished paper presented at the annual convention of the Canadian Psychological Association, Vancouver.

[34] Cunningham, M. R. (1979). Weather, mood, and helping behavior: Quasi experiments with

the sunshine Samaritan. *Journal of Personality and Social Psychology, 37,* 1947-1956.

35 Rind, B. (1996). Effect of beliefs about weather conditions on tipping. *Journal of Applied Psychology, 26,* 137-147

36 Carney, P. A., Fitzgerald, C. T., & Monaghan, C. E. (1988). Influence of climate on the prevalence of mania. *British Journal of Psychiatry, 152,* 820-823.

37 Low, K. G. (1998). Seasonal affective disorder in college students: Prevalence and latitude. *Journal of American College Health, 47,* 135-137.

38 Terao, T., Soeda, S., Yoshimura, R., & Iwata, N. (2002). Effect of latitude on suicide rates in Japan. *The Lancet, 360,* 1892.

39 Rotton, J., & Frey, J. (1985). Air pollution, weather, and violent crimes: Concomitant time-series analysis of archival data. *Journal of Personality and Social Psychology, 49,* 1207-1220.

40 Essa, E. L., Hilton, J. M., & Murray, C. I. (1990). The relationship between weather and preschoolers' behavior. *Children's Environments Quarterly, 7,* 32-36.

41 Lester, D. (1996). A hazardous environment and city suicides. *Perceptual and Motor Skills, 82,* 1330.

42 Campbell, D. E. & Beets, J. L. (1977). Meteorological variables and behavior: An annotated bibliography. *Catalog of Selected Documents in Psychology, 7,* 1.

43 Kinney, D. K., Jacobsen, B., Jansson, L., Faber, B., Tramer, S. J., & Suozzo, M. (2000). Winter birth and biological family history in adopted schizophrenics. *Schizophrenia Research, 44,* 95-103.

44 Takei, N., Sham, P., O'Callaghan, E., Murray, G. K., Glove, G., & Murray, R. M. (1994). Prenatal exposure to influenza and the development of schizophrenia: Is the effect confined to females? *American Journal of Psychiatry, 151,* 117-119.

45 de Vliert, E. V., Kluwer, E. S., & Lynn, R. (2000). Citizens of warmer countries are more competitive and poorer: Culture or chance? *Journal of Economic Psychology, 21,* 143-165

46 Van de Vliert, E., Huang, X., & Parker, P. M. (2004). Do colder and hotter climates make richer societies more, but poorer societies less, happy and altruistic? *Journal of Environmental Psychology, 24,* 17-30.

47 Kay, R. W. (1994). Geomagnetic storms: Association with incidence of depression as measured by hospital admission. *British Journal of Psychiatry, 164,* 403-409.

48 Persinger, M. A. (1999). Wars and increased solar-geomagnetic activity: Aggression or change in intraspecies dominance? *Perceptual and Motor Skills, 88,* 1351-1355.

49 Gamberale, F. (1990). Physiological and psychological effects of exposure to extremely low frequency electric and magnetic fields on humans. *Scandinavian Journal of Work, Environment and Health, 16,* 51-54.

50 O'Connor, M. E. (1993). Psychological studies in nonionizing electromagnetic energy research. *Journal of General Psychology, 120,* 33-47.

51 Furby, L., Slovic, P., Fischhoff, B., & Gregory, R. (1988). Public perceptions of electric power transmission lines. *Journal of Environmental Psychology, 8,* 19-43.

52 Ulrich, R. S., & Parsons, R. (1992). Influences of passive experiences with plants on individual well-being and health. In D. Relf (Ed.), *The role of horticulture in human well-being and social development.* Forest Grove, OR: Timber Press.

53 van den Berg, A. E., Koole, S. L., & van der Wulp, N. Y. (2003). Environmental preference and restoration: (How) are they related? *Journal of Environmental Psychology, 23,* 135-146.

54 Falk, J. H., & Balling, J. D. (2010). Evolutionary influence on human landscape preference. *Environment and Behavior, 42,* 479-493.

55 Staats, H., Kieviet, A., & Hartig, T. (2003). Where to recover from attentional fatigue: An expectancy-value analysis of environmental preference. *Journal of Environmental Psychology, 23,* 147-157.

56 Outdoor Recreation Council of British Columbia. (1990). Surveys finds outdoor recreation very important to British Columbians. *The Outdoor Report, 4,* 2.

57 Environment Canada. (1989). *The importance of wildlife to Canadians in 1987: Highlights of a national survey.* Environment Canada, Canadian Wildlife Service.

58 Sandilands, M., & Cairns, J. (1988). *Hikers' attitudes towards bears and Zuckerman's thrill and adventure seeking scale.* Paper presented at the Canadian Psychological Association annual meetings.

59 Ryzhikov, A. I. (1992). Nature and man: Psychological problems of alienation. *Journal of Russian & East European Psychology, 30,* 37-44.

60 Mace, B. L., Corser, G. C., Zitting, L., & Denison, J. (2013). Effects of overflights on the national park experience. *Journal of Environmental Psychology, 35,* 30-39.

61 Kellert, S. R. (1997). *Kinship to mastery: Biophilia in human evolution and development.* Washington, DC: Island Press.

62 Kaplan, S. (1995). The restorative benefits of nature: Towards an integrative framework. *Journal of Environmental Psychology, 15,* 169-182.

63 Ulrich, R. S. (1993). Biophilia, biopho[...] and natural landscapes. In S. R. K[...] E. O. Wilson (Eds.) *The bio[...]* Washington, DC: Isla[...] Books.

64 Gifford, [...] Report [...]

65 Hammitt, [...] sions of w[...] *Behavior, 14[...]*

66 Fiedeldey, A[...] ture on hikin[...] *Dissertation Ab[...]* 6698-6699.

67 Scherl, L. M. [...] Understanding th[...] individual-wildern[...] self-control. *Leisure S[...]*

68 Fiedeldey, A. C. (1[...] ture on hiking trails:[...] *Dissertation Abstracts I[...]* 6698-6699.

69 Snyder, J. S. (1989). Th[...] ally feeling connected to [...] *Abstracts International, 49(9-B[...]*

70 Herzog, T. R., Black, A. M., Fountaine, K. A., & Knotts, D. J. (1997). Reflection and attentional recovery as distinctive benefits of restorative environments. *Journal of Environmental Psychology, 17,* 165-170.

71 Korpela, K. I., Ylen, M., Tyrvainen, L., & Silvennoinen, H. (2010). Favorite green, waterside and urban environments, restorative experiences and perceived health in Finland. *Health Promotion International, 25,* 200-209.

72 Berman, M., Jonides, J., & Kaplan, S. (2008). The cognitive benefits of interacting with nature. *Psychological Science, 19,* 1207-1212.

73 Mayer, F., Frantz, C., Bruehlman-Senecal, E., & Dolliver, K. (2009). Why is nature beneficial? The role of connectedness to nature. *Environment and Behavior, 41,* 607-643.

74 Ryan, R. M., Weinstein, N., Bernstein, J., Brown, K. W., Mistretta, L., & Gagné, M. (2010). Vitalizing effects of being outdoors and in nature. *Journal of Environmental Psychology, 30,* 159-168.

75 Kjellgren, A., & Buhrkall, H. (2010). A comparison of the restorative effect of a natural environment with that of a simulated natural environment. *Journal of Environmental Psychology, 30,* 464-472.

76 Quoted from p. 3 of Hartig T., Mang, M., & Evans, G. W. (1991). Restorative effects of natural environment experiences. *Environment and Behavior, 23,* 3-26.

77 Hartig, T., Evans, G. W., Jamner, L. D., Davis, D. S., & Gärling, T. (2003). Tracking restoration in natural and urban field settings. *Journal of Environmental Psychology, 23,* 109-123.

78 Macdonald, J. E. (1994). The restorative effects of a vacation from work: The role of [...]elty, positive affect, and nature. Un[...] doctoral dissertation, Universi[...]

79 Lee, J., Park, B., Tsune[...] Miyazaki, Y. (20[...] ing real for[...] with [...]

98

99 Ev[...] Env[...]

100 Parsons, R.[...] Fiorito,[...] urban envir[...] Stress rec[...] Psychology, 11[...]

101 Hebl, M. R.[...] (1998). The view f[...] for stress recovery a[...] *of Environmental Psycho[...]*

Laumann, K.[...] Gärling, T[...] (2003). Selective attention and[...] sponses to natural and urb[...] *Journal of Environmental Psych[...]*

102 Cackowski, J. M., & Nasar, J. [...] restorative effects of a roadside [...] Implications for automobile dr[...] and frustration. *Environment and Be[...]*

103 O'Connor, B. P., Davidson, H., & Gif[...] (1991). Window view, social exposure [...] nursing home adaptation. *Canadian Journal o[...] Aging, 10,* 216-223.

736-751.

[86] Shin, W. S. (1993). Self-actualization and wilderness attitudes: A replication. *Journal of Social Behavior and Personality, 8,* 241-256.

[87] White, M. P., Pahl, S., Ashbullby, K., Herbert, S., & Depledge, M. H. (2013). Feelings of restoration from recent nature visits. *Journal of Environmental Psychology, 35,* 40-51.

[88] Hipp, J. A., & Ogunseitan, O. A. (2011). Effect of environmental conditions on perceived psychological restorativeness of coastal parks. *Journal of Environmental Psychology, 31,* 421-429.

[89] van den Berg, A. E., Maas, J., Verheij, R. A., & Groenewegen, P. P. (2010). Green space as a buffer between stressful life events and health. *Social Science & Medicine, 70,* 1203-1210.

[90] Wells, N. M., & Evans, G. W. (2003). Nearby nature: A buffer of life stress among rural children. *Environment and Behavior, 35,* 311-330.

[91] Bringslimark, T., Hartig, T., & Patil, G. G. (2009). The psychological benefits of indoor plants: A critical review of the experimental literature. *Journal of Environmental Psychology, 29,* 422-433.

[92] Ulrich, R. S. (1984). View through a window may influence recovery from surgery. *Science, 224,* 420-421.

[93] Moore, E. O. (1982). A prison environment's effect on health care service demands. *Journal of Environmental Systems, 11,* 17-34.

[94] West, M. J. (1985). University of Washington Masters thesis cited in Ulrich (1993).

[95] Van den Berg, A. E., Koole, S. L., & Van der Wulp, N. Y. (2003). Environment preference and restoration: (How) are they related? *Journal of Environmental Psychology, 23,* 135-146.

[96] Felsten, G. (2009). Where to take a study break on the college campus: An attention restoration theory perspective. *Journal of Environmental Psychology, 29,* 160-167.

[97] Velardea, M. D., Fryb, G., & Tveit, M. (2007). Health effects of viewing landscapes: Landscape types in environmental psychology. *Urban Forestry & Urban Greening, 6,* 199-212.

[Taylor], A. F., Kuo, F. E., & Sullivan, W. C. (2002). Views of nature and self-discipline: [evi]dence from inner city children. *Journal of [Envir]onmental Psychology, 22,* 49-63.

[R]. S., Simons, R. F., Losito, B. D., [E.], Miles, M. A., & Zelson, M. (1991). [reco]very during exposure to natural and [urban envir]onments. *Journal of Environmental [Psychol.],* 201-230.

[ssinary], L. G, Ulrich, R. S., [Grossman-Alexander], M. [from] the road: Implications [and] immunization. *Journal [of...ology, 18,* 113-140.

[, & Stormark], K. M. [and] heart rate re[...an] environments. [...ogy, 23,* 125-134.

[, (2003). The [...vegetation: [...er] anger [...avior, 35,*

[..d], R. [...nd]

[104] White, M., Smith, A., Humphryes, K., Pahl, S., Snelling, D., & Depledge, M. (2010). Blue space: The importance of water for preference, affect, and restorativeness ratings of natural and built scenes. *Journal of Environmental Psychology, 30,* 482-493.

[105] Herzog, T. R., Ouellette, P., Rolens, J. R., & Koenigs, A. M. (2010). Houses of worship as restorative environments. *Environment and Behavior, 42,* 395-419.

[106] Lindal, P. J., & Hartig, T. (2013). Architectural variation, building height, and the restorative quality of urban residential streetscapes. *Journal of Environmental Psychology, 33,* 26-36.

[107] Scopelliti, M., & Giuliani, M. V. (2004). Choosing restorative environments across the lifespan: A matter of place experience. *Journal of Environmental Psychology, 24,* 423-437.

[108] Mehrabian, A., & Russell, J. A. (1974). *An approach to environmental psychology.* Cambridge, MA: MIT Press.

[109] Cohen, S. (1978). Environmental load and all the allocation of attention. In A. Baum, J. E. Singer, & S. Valins (Eds.), *Advances in environmental psychology*, Vol. 1. Hillsdale, NJ: Erlbaum.

[110] Tuan, Y. F. (1974). *Topophilia: A study of environmental protection, attitudes, and values.* Englewood Cliffs, NJ: Prentice Hall.

[111] Kaplan, S. (1995). The restorative benefits of nature: Towards an integrative framework. *Journal of Environmental Psychology, 15,* 169-182.

[112] Ulrich, R. S., Simons, R. F., Losito, B. D., Fiorito, E., Miles, M. A., & Zelson, M. (1991). Stress recovery during exposure to natural and urban environments. *Journal of Environmental Psychology, 11,* 201-230.

[113] Ulrich, R. S. (1993). Biophilia, biophobia, and natural landscapes. In S. R. Kellert & E. O. Wilson (Eds.) *The biophilia hypothesis.* Washington, DC: Island Press/Shearwater Books.

[114] Hartig, T., Book, A., Garvill, J., Olsson, T., & Garling, T. (2008). Environmental influences on psychological restoration. *Scandinavian Journal of Psychology, 37,* 378-393.

[115] Scopelliti, M., & Giuliani, M. V. (2004). Choosing restorative environments across the lifespan: A matter of place experience. *Journal of Environmental Psychology, 24,* 423-437.

[116] Duvall, J. (2011). Enhancing the benefits of outdoor walking with cognitive engagement strategies. *Journal of Environmental Psychology, 31,* 27-35.

[117] Clayton, S. (2003). Environmental identity: A conceptual and an operational definition. In S. Clayton & S. Opotow (Eds.), *Identity and the natural environment: The psychological significance of nature* (pp. 45-65).Cambridge, MA: MIT Press.

[118] Clayton, S. (2003). Environmental identity: A conceptual and an operational definition. In S. Clayton & S. Opotow (Eds), *Identity and the natural environment: The psychological significance of nature* (pp. 45-65).Cambridge, MA: MIT Press.

[119] Mayer, F. S., & Frantz, C. M. (2004). The connectedness to nature scale: A measure of individuals' feeling in community with nature. *Journal of Environmental Psychology, 24,* 503-515.

[120] Frantz, C., Mayer, F. S., & Rock, M. (2005). The influence of selfawareness on connectedness to nature. *Journal of Environmental Psychology, 25,* 427436.

[121] Mayer, F., Frantz, C., Bruehlman-Senecal, E., & Dolliver, K. (2009). Why is nature beneficial? The role of connectedness to nature. *Environment and Behavior, 41,* 607-643.

[122] Clayton, S., & Opotow, S. (Eds). (2003). *Identity and the natural environment: The psychological significance of nature.* Cambridge, MA: MIT Press.

[123] Schultz, P. W., Shriver, C., Tabanico, J. J., & Khazian, A. M. (2004). Implicit connections with nature. *Journal of Environmental Psychology, 24,* 31-42.

[124] Davis, J. L., Green, J. D., & Reed, A. (2009). Interdependence with the environment: Commitment, interconnectedness, and environmental behavior. *Journal of Environmental Psychology, 29,* 173-180.

[125] Sommer, R. (2003). Trees and human identity. In S. Clayton & S. Opotow, S. (Eds.), *Identity and the natural environment: The psychological significance of nature* (pp. 179-204). Cambridge, MA: MIT Press.

[126] Verges, M., & Duffy, S. (2010). Connected to birds but not bees: Valence moderates implicit associations with nature. *Environment and Behavior, 42,* 625-642.

[127] Duffy, S., & Verges, M. (2010). Forces of nature affect implicit connections with nature. *Environment and Behavior, 42,* 723-739.

[128] Hinds, J., & Sparks, P. (2008). Engaging with the natural environment: The role of affective connection and identity. *Journal of Environmental Psychology, 28,* 109-120.

[129] Winter, D. (2003). *Ecological psychology: Healing the split between planet and self.* Mahwah, NJ: Erlbaum.

[130] Mace, B. L., Bell, P. A., & Loomis, R. J. (2004). Visibility and natural quiet in national parks and wilderness areas: Psychological considerations. *Environment and Behavior, 36,* 5-31.

[131] Burton, I., Kates, R. W., & White, G. F. (1978). *The environment as hazard.* New York: Oxford.

[132] Baum, A., & Fleming, I. (1993). Implications of psychological research on stress and technological accidents. *American Psychologist, 48,* 665-672.

[133] Study shows heat and smog are killers. CBC online story, June 6, 2005.

[134] Gulaid, J. A., Sacks, J. J., & Sattin, R. W. (1988). Deaths from residential fires among older people, United States, 1984. *Journal of the American Geriatrics Society, 37,* 331-334.

[135] Adeola, F. O. (1994). Environmental hazards, health, and racial inequity in hazardous waste distribution. *Environment and Behavior, 26,* 99-126.

[136] O'Riordan, T. (1984). Attitudes, behavior, and environmental policy issues. In I. Altman & J. F. Wohlwill (Eds.), *Human behavior and environment: Advances in theory and research* (Vol. 1). New York: Plenum.

[137] Cvetkovich, G., & Earle, T. C. (1985). Classifying hazardous events. *Journal of Environmental Psychology, 5,* 5-53.

138 Cvetkovich, G., & Earle, T. C. (1985). Classifying hazardous events. *Journal of Environmental Psychology*, 5, 5-53.

139 Baum, A., Fleming, R., & Davidson, L. M. (1983). Natural disaster and technological catastrophe. *Environment and Behavior*, 15, 333-354.

140 Foster, H. D. (1980). *Disaster planning: The preservation of life and property*. New York: Springer-Verlag.

141 Spreen, O., Tupper, D., Risser, A., Tuokko, H., & Edgell, D. (1984). *Human developmental neuropsychology*. New York: Oxford University Press.

142 Stretesky, P. B., & Lynch, M. J. (2004). The relationship between lead and crime. *Journal of Health and Social Behavior*, 45, 214-229.

143 Koger, S. M., Schettler, T., & Weiss, B. (2005). Environmental toxicants and developmental disabilities: A challenge for psychologists. *American Psychologist*, 60, 243-255.

144 Bord, R. J., & O'Connor, R. E. (1992). Determinants of risk perceptions of a hazardous waste site. *Risk Analysis*, 12, 411-416.

145 Levi, D. J., & Holder, E. E. (1988). Psychological factors in the nuclear power controversy. *Political Psychology*, 9, 445-457.

146 Sjoberg, L., & Drottz-Sjoberg, B. (1991). Knowledge and risk perception among nuclear power plant employees. *Risk Analysis*, 11, 607-618.

147 Pilisuk, M., & Acredolo, C. (1988). Fear of technological hazards: One concern or many? *Social Behavior*, 3, 17-24.

148 van der Pligt, J. (1985). Public attitudes to nuclear energy: Salience and anxiety. *Journal of Environmental Psychology*, 5, 87-97.

149 Levi, D. J., & Holder, E. E. (1986). Nuclear power: The dynamics of acceptability. *Environment and Behavior*, 18, 385-395.

150 Binney, S. E., Mason, R., Martsolf, S. W., & Detweiler, J. H. (1996). Credibility, public trust, and the transport of radioactive waste through local communities. *Environment and Behaviour*, 28, 283-301.

151 Baird, B. N. R. (1986). Tolerance for environmental health risks: The influence of knowledge, benefits, voluntariness, and environmental attitudes. *Risk Analysis*, 6, 425-435.

152 Moser, C., Stauffacher, M., Smieszek, T., Seidl, R., Krütli, P., & Scholz, R. W. (2013). Psychological factors in discounting negative impacts of nuclear waste. *Journal of Environmental Psychology*, 35, 121-131.

153 Eiser, J. R., Spears, R., Webley, P., & van der Pligt, J. (1988). Local residents' attitudes to oil and nuclear developments. *Social Behavior*, 3, 237-253.

154 Van der Pligt, J., Eiser, J. R., & Spears, R. (1986). Construction of a nuclear power station in one's locality: Attitudes and salience. *Basic & Applied Social Psychology*, 7, 1-15.

155 Wiegman, O., Boer, H., Gutteling, J. M., & Komilis, E. et al. (1992). The development of reactions of the public to warning and emergency situations in France, Greece, and the Netherlands. *Journal of Social Psychology*, 132, 101-116.

156 Eraenen, L. (1997). Finnish reactions facing the threat of nuclear accidents in Russian nuclear power plants. *Patient Education and Counseling*, 30, 83-94.

157 Lima, M. L. (2004). On the influence of risk perception on mental health: Living near an incinerator. *Journal of Environmental Psychology*, 24, 2004, 7184.

158 Stoffle, R. W., Traugott, M. W., Stone, J. V., McIntyre, P. D. et al. (1991). Risk perception mapping: Using ethnography to define the locally affected population for a low-level radioactive waste storage facility in Michigan. *American Anthropologist*, 93, 611-635.

159 Johnson, R. J., & Scicchitano, M. J. (2012). Don't Call Me NIMBY: Public attitudes toward solid waste facilities. *Environment and Behavior*, 44, 410-426.

160 Hostetler, A. J. (1987). Radon's origin alters perception of its risks. *American Psychological Association Monitor*, 18, 21.

161 Lehman, D. R., & Taylor, S. E. (1987). Date with an earthquake: Coping with a probable, unpredictable disaster. *Personality and Social Psychology Bulletin*, 13, 546-555.

162 Spielberg, W. E. (1987). Living with Indian Point: A study investigating the relationship between stress, time distortion, ideology, coping style and expressed vulnerability of high school students in close residence to a nuclear power plant. *Dissertation Abstracts International*, 47(9-B), 3971-3972.

163 Vaughan, E., & Nordenstam, B. (1989, August). *Farmworkers and pesticide exposure: Perceived risk, psychological distress, and health*. Paper presented at the 97th annual convention of American Psychological Association, New Orleans, LA.

164 Lima, M. L. (2004). On the influence of risk perception on mental health: Living near an incinerator. *Journal of Environmental Psychology*, 24, 2004, 7184.

165 Luginaah, I. N., Taylor, S. M., Elliot, S. J., & Eyles, J. D. (2002). Community reappraisal of the perceived health effects of a petroleum refinery. *Social Science & Medicine*, 55, 47-61.

166 Gifford, R. (1976). Environmental numbness in the classroom. *Journal of Experimental Education*, 44(3), 4-7.

167 Zhang, Y., Hwang, S. N., & Lindell, M. K. (2010). Hazard proximity or risk perception? Evaluating effects of natural and technological hazards on housing values. *Environment and Behavior*, 42, 597-624.

168 Stout-Wiegand, N., & Trent, R. B. (1984-85). Comparison of students' and non-student residents' attitudes toward local energy developments: Environmentalism versus economic interest. *Environmental Education*, 16, 29-35.

169 Baird, B. N. R. (1986). Tolerance for environmental health risks: The influence of knowledge, benefits, voluntariness, and environmental attitudes. *Risk Analysis*, 6, 425-435.

170 Venables, D., Pidgeon, N. F., Parkhill, K. A., Henwood, K. L. & Simmons, P. (2012). Living with nuclear power: Sense of place, proximity, and risk perceptions in local host communities. *Journal of Environmental Psychology*, 32, 371-383.

171 de Man, A., & Simpson-Housley, P. (1988). Correlates of responses to two potential hazards. *Journal of Social Psychology*, 128, 385-391.

172 Dooley, D., Catalano, R., Mishra, S., & Serxner, S. (1992). Earthquake preparedness: Predictors in a community survey. *Journal of Applied Social Psychology*, 22, 451-470.

173 Moore, D. P., & Moore, J. W. (1996). Post-hurricane burnout: An island township's experience. *Environment and Behaviour*, 28, 134-155.

174 Vaughan, E. (1993). Chronic exposure to an environmental hazard: Risk perceptions and self-protective behavior. *Health Psychology*, 12, 74-85.

175 Van der Pligt, J., Eiser, J. R., & Spears, R. (1986). Construction of a nuclear power station in one's locality: Attitudes and salience. *Basic & Applied Social Psychology*, 7, 1-15.

176 Lindell, M. K., & Perry, R. W. (1990). Effects of the Chernobyl accident on public perceptions of nuclear plant accident risks. *Risk Analysis*, 10, 393-399.

177 Pilisuk, M., & Acredolo, C. (1988). Fear of technological hazards: One concern or many? *Social Behavior*, 3, 17-24.

178 Kraus, N., Malmfors, T., & Slovic, P. (1992). Intuitive toxicology: Expert and lay judgements of chemical risks. *Risk Analysis*, 12, 215-232.

179 Brody, C. J. (1984). Differences by sex in support for nuclear power. *Social Forces*, 63, 209-228.

180 Lai, J. C., & Tao, J. (2003). Perception of environmental hazards in Hong Kong Chinese. *Risk Analysis*, 23, 669-684.

181 deMan, A., & Simpson-Housley, P. (1987). Factors in perception of tornado hazard: An exploratory study. *Social Behavior and Personality*, 15, 13-19.

182 Dooley, D., Catalano, R., Mishra, S., & Serxner, S. (1992). Earthquake preparedness: Predictors in a community survey. *Journal of Applied Social Psychology*, 22, 451-470.

183 Dooley, D., Catalano, R., Mishra, S., & Serxner, S. (1992). Earthquake preparedness: Predictors in a community survey. *Journal of Applied Social Psychology*, 22, 451-470.

184 McClelland G. H., Schulze, W. D., & Hurd, B. (1990). The effects of risk beliefs on property values: A case study of a hazardous waste site. *Risk Analysis*, 10, 485-497.

185 Dooley, D., Catalano, R., Mishra, S., & Serxner, S. (1992). Earthquake preparedness: Predictors in a community survey. *Journal of Applied Social Psychology*, 22, 451-470.

186 McClelland G. H., Schulze, W. D., & Hurd, B. (1990). The effects of risk beliefs on property values: A case study of a hazardous waste site. *Risk Analysis*, 10, 485-497.

187 Lai, J. C., & Tao, J. (2003). Perception of environmental hazards in Hong Kong Chinese. *Risk Analysis*, 23, 669-684.

188 Vari, A., Kemp, R., & Mumpower, J. L. (1991). Public concerns about LLRW facility siting: A comparative study. *Journal of Cross-Cultural Psychology*, 22, 83-102.

189 Pilisuk, M., & Acredolo, C. (1988). Fear of technological hazards: One concern or many? *Social Behavior*, 3, 17-24.

190 de Man, A. F., & Simpson-Housley, P. (1987). Factors in perception of earthquake hazard. *Perceptual and Motor Skills*, 64, 815-820.

191 Pilisuk, M., Parks, S. H., & Hawkes, G. (1987). Public perception of technological risk. *Social Science Journal*, *24*, 403-413.

192 Lai, J. C., & Tao, J. (2003). Perception of environmental hazards in Hong Kong Chinese. *Risk Analysis*, *23*, 669-684.

193 Lazarus, R. S. (1966). *Psychological stress and the coping process*. New York: McGraw-Hill.

194 de Man, A. F., & Simpson-Housley, P. (1987). Factors in perception of earthquake hazard. *Perceptual and Motor Skills*, *64*, 815-820.

195 Schmidt, F. N., & Gifford, R. (1989). A dispositional approach to hazard perception: Preliminary development of the Environmental Appraisal Inventory. *Journal of Environmental Psychology*, *9*, 57-67.

196 Schmidt, F. N., & Gifford, R. (1989). A dispositional approach to hazard perception: Preliminary development of the Environmental Appraisal Inventory. *Journal of Environmental Psychology*, *9*, 57-67.

197 Larrain Navarro, P., Simpson-Housley, P., & de Man, A. F. (1987). Anxiety, locus of control and appraisal of air pollution. *Perceptual and Motor Skills*, *64*, 811-814.

198 Krugman, M., & Yoder, C. Y. (1992, August). *Trust and anxiety influence the perception of environmental risks*. Poster presented at the American Psychological Association annual convention, Washington, DC.

199 Simpson-Housley, P., de Man, A. F., & Yachnin, R. (1986). Trait-anxiety and appraisal of flood hazard, a brief comment. *Psychological Reports*, *58*, 509-510.

200 de Man, A. F., & Simpson-Housley, P. (1987). Factors in perception of earthquake hazard. *Perceptual and Motor Skills*, *64*, 815-820.

201 de Man, A. F., Simpson-Housley, P., Curtis, F., & Smith, D. (1984). Trait anxiety and response to potential flood disaster. *Psychological Reports*, *54*, 507-512.

202 Larrain Navarro, P., Simpson-Housley, P., & de Man, A. F. (1987). Anxiety, locus of control and appraisal of air pollution. *Perceptual and Motor Skills*, *64*, 811-814.

203 Spielberg, W. E. (1987). Living with Indian Point: A study investigating the relationship between stress, time distortion, ideology, coping style and expressed vulnerability of high school students in close residence to a nuclear power plant. *Dissertation Abstracts International*, *47*(9-B), 3971-3972.

204 Hallman, W. K. (1990). Coping with an environmental stressor: Perception of risk, attribution of responsibility and psychological distress in a community living near a hazardous waste facility. *Dissertation Abstracts International*, *51*(1-B), 474-475.

205 Stallen, P. J. M., & Tomas, A. (1988). Public concern about industrial hazards. *Risk Analysis*, *8*, 237-245.

206 Hughey, J. B., & Sundstrom, E. (1988). Perceptions of Three Mile Island and acceptance of a nuclear power plant in a distant community. *Journal of Applied Social Psychology*, *18*, 880-890.

207 Baldwin, T. K. (1993). Response to an earthquake prediction in southeast Missouri: A study in pluralistic ignorance. *Dissertation Abstracts International*, *53*(9-A), 3025-3026.

208 Renn, O., Burns, W. J., Kasperson, J. X., Kasperson, R. E., et al. (1992). The social amplification of risk: Theoretical foundations and empirical applications. *Journal of Social Issues*, *48*(4), 137-160.

209 van der Pligt, J., van der Linden, J., & Ester, P. (1982). Attitudes to nuclear energy: Beliefs, values and false consensus. *Journal of Environmental Psychology*, *2*, 221-231.

210 Knuth, D., Kehl, D., Hulse, L., & Schmidt, S. (2013). Perievent distress during fires – The impact of perceived emergency knowledge. *Journal of Environmental Psychology, 34*, 10-17.

211 Zhu, D., Xie, X., & Gan, Y. (2011). Information source and valence: How information credibility influences earthquake risk perception. *Journal of Environmental Psychology, 31*, 129-136.

212 McClelland G. H., Schulze, W. D., & Hurd, B. (1990). The effects of risk beliefs on property values: A case study of a hazardous waste site. *Risk Analysis*, *10*, 485-497.

213 Slovic, P., Fischhoff, B., & Lichtenstein, S. (1979). Rating the risks. *Environment*, *21*, 14-20, 36-39.

214 van der Pligt, J., Eiser, J. R., & Spears, R. (1987). Nuclear waste: Facts, fears, and attitudes. *Journal of Applied Social Psychology*, *17*, 453-470.

215 Wober, M., & Gunter, B. (1985). Patterns of television viewing and of perceptions of hazards to life. *Journal of Environmental Psychology*, *5*, 99-108.

216 Bochniak, S., & Lammers, H. B. (1991). Effect of numbers vs pictures on perceived effectiveness of a public safety awareness advertisement. *Perceptual and Motor Skills*, *73*, 77-78.

217 Kiser, L., Heston, J., Hickerson, S., & Millsap, P. (1993). Anticipatory stress in children and adolescents. *American Journal of Psychiatry*, *150*, 87-92.

218 Spencer, J. W., Seydlitz, R., Laska, S., & Triche, E., (1992). The different influences of newspaper and television news reports of a natural hazard on response behavior. *Communication Research*, *19*, 299-325.

219 van der Pligt, J. (1985). Public attitudes to nuclear energy: Salience and anxiety. *Journal of Environmental Psychology*, *5*, 87-97.

220 Slovic, P., Fischhoff, B., & Lichtenstein, S. (1979). Rating the risks. *Environment*, *21*, 14-20, 36-39.

221 Slovic, P. ,Fischhoff, B., & Lichtenstrin, S. (1986). Regulation of risk: A psychological perspective. In R. Noll (Ed.), *Social science and regulatory policy*. Berkeley, CA: University of California Press.

222 Alhakami, A. S. (1992). A psychological study of the inverse relationship between perceived risk and perceived benefit of technological hazards. *Dissertation Abstracts International*, *52*(9-B), 5004.

223 Wandersman, A. H., & Hallman, W. K. (1993). Are people acting irrationally? Understanding public concerns about environmental threats. *American Psychologist*, *48*, 681-686.

224 Vaughan, E. (1993). Individual and cultural differences in adaptation to environmental risks. *American Psychologist*, *48*, 673-680.

225 Douglas, M., & Wildavsky, A. (1982). *Risk and culture*. Los Angeles: University of California Press.

226 Fiorino, D. J. (1989). Technical and democratic values in risk analysis. *Risk Analysis*, *9*, 293-299.

227 Eiser, J. R., Spears, R., & Webley, P. (1988). Predicting attitudes to oil and to nuclear energy. *Journal of Environmental Psychology*, *8*, 141-147.

228 Kraus, N., Malmfors, T., & Slovic, P. (1992). Intuitive toxicology: Expert and lay judgements of chemical risks. *Risk Analysis*, *12*, 215-232.

229 Slovic, P., Kunreuther, H., & White, G. F. (1974). Decision processes, rationality, and adjustment to natural hazards. In G. F. White (Ed.), *Natural hazards: Local, national, global*. New York: Oxford University Press.

230 Slovic, P. (1978). The psychology of protective behavior. *Journal of Safety Research*, *10*, 58-68.

231 Kushnir, T. (1982). Skylab effects: Psychological reactions to a human-made environmental hazard. *Environment and Behavior*, *14*, 84-93.

232 Logsdon, T. (1983). The orbiting junkyard. *Technology Illustrated*, *3*, 30-34.

233 Maharik, M., & Fischhoff, B. (1992). The risks of using nuclear energy sources in space: Some lay activists' perceptions. *Risk Analysis*, *12*, 383-392.

234 Lindell, M. K., & Perry, R. W. (2000). Household adjustment to earthquake hazard: A review of research. *Environment and Behavior*, *32*, 461-501.

235 Miceli, R., Sotgiu, I., & Settanni, M. (2008). Disaster preparedness and perception of flood risk: A study in an alpine valley in Italy. *Journal of Environmental Psychology, 28*, 164-173.

236 Cvetkovich, G., & Earle, T. C. (1988). Judgement and hazard adaptation: A longitudinal study of responses to risks of water contamination. 11th conference on: Subjective probability, utility and decision making (1987, Cambridge, England). *Acta Psychologica*, *68*, 343-353.

237 Mulilis, J. P., & Bovalino, K. (1998). *Masculine and feminine dimensions of tornado preparedness*. Presented at the Annual Convention of the American Psychological Association, San Francisco.

238 Mulilis, J. P. , Duvall, T. S., & Rombach, D. (1999). *Effects of commitment and choice on responsibility on tornado preparedness*. Presented at the annual meeting of the American Psychological Association, Boston.

239 Lave, T. R., & Lave, L. B. (1991). Public perception of the risks of floods: Implications for communication. *Risk Analysis*, *11*, 255-267.

240 Mishra, S., Mazumdar, S., & Suar, D. (2010). Place attachment and flood preparedness. *Journal of Environmental Psychology, 30*, 187-197.

241 Bertness, J. E. (1987). Hazard perception research: A critique and proposal. *Dissertation Abstracts International*, *47*(9-A), 3528.

242 Vaughan, E. (1993). Individual and cultural differences in adaptation to environmental risks. *American Psychologist*, *48*, 673-680.

243 Slovic, P., Kunreuther, H., & White, G. F. (1974). Decision processes, rationality, and

adjustment to natural hazards. In G. F. White (Ed.), *Natural hazards: Local, national, global.* New York: Oxford University Press.

244 Jackson, E. L. (1981). Response to earthquake hazard: The west coast of North America. *Environment and Behavior, 13,* 387-416.

245 Sims, J. H., & Baumann, D. D. (1983). The tornado threat: Coping styles of the North and South. *Science, 176,* 1386-1391.

246 Skov, T., Cordtz, T., Jensen, L. K., Saugman, P., et al., (1991). Modifications of health behaviour in response to air pollution notifications in Copenhagen. *Social Science & Medicine, 33,* 621-626.

247 Skov, T., Cordtz, T., Jensen, L. K., Saugman, P., et al., (1991). Modifications of health behaviour in response to air pollution notifications in Copenhagen. *Social Science & Medicine, 33,* 621-626.

248 Mulady, J. J. (1994). Building codes: They're not just hot air. *Natural hazards Observer, 18*(3), 4-5.

249 Bachrach, K. M., & Zautra, A. J. (1985). Coping with a community stressor: The threat of a hazardous waste facility. *Journal of Health and Social Behavior, 26,* 127-141.

250 Cook, J. R. (1983). Citizen response in a neighborhood under threat. *American Journal of Community Psychology, 11,* 459- 471.

251 Kaminstein, D. S. (1991). Toxic passivity: A study of the lack of protest in an environmentally threatened community. *Dissertation Abstracts International, 52*(3-B), 1778-1779.

252 Zavestoski, S., Mignano, F., Agnello, K., Darroch, F., & Abrams, K. (2002). Toxicity and complicity: Explaining consensual community response to a chronic technological disaster. *Sociological Quarterly, 43,* 385-406.

253 Hine, D. W., & Gifford, R. (1991). Fear appeals, individual differences, and environmental concern. *Journal of Environmental Education, 23*(1), 36-41.

254 Sorenson, J. H. (1983). Knowing how to behave under the threat of disaster: Can it be explained? *Environment and Behavior, 15,* 438-457.

255 Nasar, J. L., & Greenberg, M. L. (1984). The preparedness and reactions of citizens to warnings and crisis relocation for nuclear attack. *Journal of Applied Social Psychology, 14,* 487-500.

256 Sims, J. H., & Baumann, D. D. (1983). The tornado threat: Coping styles of the North and South. *Science, 176,* 1386-1391.

257 Werner, C. M. (2003). Changing homeowners' use of toxic household products: A transactional approach. *Journal of Environmental Psychology, 23,* 33-45.

258 Hanson, S., Vitek, J. D., & Hanson, P. O. (1979). Natural disaster: Long-range impact on human responses to future disaster threats. *Environment and Behavior, 11,* 268-284.

259 Sims, J. H., & Baumann, D. D. (1983). The tornado threat: Coping styles of the North and South. *Science, 176,* 1386-1391.

260 Mulilis, J., & Lippa, R. (1990). Behavioral change in earthquake preparedness due to negative threat appeals: A test of protection motivation theory. *Journal of Applied Social Psychology, 20,* 619-638.

261 Foster, H. D. (1980). *Disaster planning: The preservation of life and property.* New York: Springer-Verlag.

262 Quarantelli, E. L. (1976). *Human response in stress situations.* Laurel, MD: John Hopkins University Press.

263 Laska, S. B. (1990). Homeowner adaptation to flooding: An application of the general hazards coping theory. *Environment and Behavior, 22,* 320-357.

264 Archea, J. (1990). Two earthquakes: Three human conditions. In Y. Yoshitake, R. B. Bechtel, T. Takahashi, & M. Asai (Eds.), *Current issues in environment-behavior research.* University of Tokyo.

265 Weinrich, S., Hardin, S. B., & Johnson, M. (1990). Nurses respond to hurricane Hugo victims' disaster stress. *Archives of Psychiatric Nursing, 4,* 195-205.

266 Hansson, R. O., Noules, D., & Bellovich, S, J. (1982). Knowledge warning and stress: A study of comparative roles in an urban floodplain. *Environment and Behavior, 14,* 171-185.

267 Chisholm, R. F., Kasl, S. V., & Eskenazi, B. (1983). The nature and predictors of job related tension in a crisis situation: Reactions of nuclear workers to the three mile island accident. *Academy of Management Journal, 26,* 385-405.

268 Johnson, N. R., & Feinberg, W. E. (1997). The impact of exit instruction and number of exits in fire emergencies: A computer simulation investigation. *Journal of Environmental Psychology, 17,* 123-133.

269 Sugiman, T., & Misumi, J. (1988). Development of a new evacuation method for emergencies: Control of collective behavior by emergent small groups. *Journal of Applied Psychology, 73,* 3-10.

270 Sime, J. D. (1985). Movement toward the familiar: Person and place affiliation in a fire entrapment setting. *Environment and Behavior, 17,* 697-724.

271 Sugiman, T., & Misumi, J. (1988). Development of a new evacuation method for emergencies: Control of collective behavior by emergent small groups. *Journal of Applied Psychology, 73,* 3-10.

272 Cutter, S., & Barnes, K. (1982). Evacuation behavior and Three Mile Island. *Disasters, 6,* 116-124.

273 Riad, J. K., Norris, F. H., & Ruback, R. B. (1995). *Predicting evacuation in two major disasters.* Presented at the annual meeting of the American Psychological Association, New York.

274 Cuthbertson, B. H., & Nigg, J. M. (1987). Technological disaster and the nontherapeutic community: A question of true victimization. *Environment and Behavior, 19,* 462-483.

275 Hallman, W. K. (1990). Coping with an environmental stressor: Perception of risk, attribution of responsibility and psychological distress in a community living near a hazardous waste facility. *Dissertation Abstracts International, 51*(1-B), 474-475.

276 Prati, G., & Zani, B. (2013). The Effect of the Fukushima Nuclear Accident on Risk Perception, Antinuclear Behavioral Intentions, Attitude, Trust, Environmental Beliefs, and Values. *Environment and Behavior, 45,* 782-798.

277 MacGregor, D. (1991). Worry over technological activities and life concerns. *Risk Analysis, 11,* 315-324.

278 Parker, J. F., Bahrick, L., & Fivush, R. (2000). *Young mothers' memory for a natural disaster: The effects of stress.* Presented at the SARMAC Conference, Miami Beach.

279 Arochova, O., Kontrova, J., Lipkova, V., & Liska, J. (1988). Effect of toxic atmosphere emissions on cognitive performance by children. *Studia Psychologica, 30,* 101-114.

280 Van-Haaften, E. H., Van-de-Vijver, F. J. R. (1999). Dealing with extreme environmental degradation: Stress and marginalization of Sahel dwellers. *Psychological Psychiatry and Psychiatric Epidemiology, 34,* 376-382.

281 Ferraro, F. R., Morton, M., Zink, J., & Jacobson, B. (1999). Impact of the 1997 flood on cognitive performance in the elderly. *Clinical Gerontologist, 20,* 79-82.

282 Mardberg, B., Carlstedt, L., Stalberg-Carlstedt, B., & Shalit, B. (1987). Sex differences in perception of threat from the Chernobyl accident. *Perceptual & Motor Skills, 65,* 228.

283 Burger, J., & Gochfeld, M. (1991). Fishing a Superfund site: Dissonance and risk perception of environmental hazards by fishermen in Puerto Rico. *Risk Analysis, 11,* 269-277.

284 Baron, J., Gowda, R., & Kunreuther, H. (1993). Attitudes toward managing hazardous waste: What should be cleaned up and who should pay for it? *Risk Analysis, 13,* 183-192.

285 deMan, A., Simpson-Housley, P., & Curtis, F. (1985). Assignment of responsibility and flood hazard in Catahoula County, Louisiana. *Environment and Behavior, 17,* 371-386.

286 Yates, S. (1992). Lay attributions about distress after a natural disaster. *Personality & Social Psychology Bulletin, 18,* 217-222.

287 Xie, X., Liu, H., & Gan, Y. (2011). Belief in a just world when encountering the 5/12 Wenchuan Earthquake. *Environment and Behavior, 43,* 566-586.

288 Parker, S. D., Brewer, M. B., & Spencer, J. R. (1980). Natural disaster, perceived control and attributions to fate. *Personality & Social Psychology Bulletin, 6,* 454-459.

289 Plous, S. (1991). Biases in the assimilation of technological breakdowns: Do accidents make us safer? *Journal of Applied Social Psychology, 21,* 1058-1082.

290 Shippee, G. E., Bradford, R., & Gregory, W. L. (1982). Community perceptions of natural disasters and post-disaster mental health services. *Journal of Community Psychology, 10,* 23-28.

291 Kaniasty, K., & Norris, F. H. (1993). A test of the social support deterioration model in the context of natural disaster. *Journal of Personality and Social Psychology, 64,* 395-408.

292 Goldhaber, M. K., Houts, P. S., & DiSabella, R. (1983). Moving after the crisis: A prospective study of Three Mile Island area population mobility. *Environment and Behavior, 15,* 93-120.

293 Prince-Embury, S., & Rooney, J. F. (1989). A comparison of residents who moved versus those who remained prior to restart of Three Mile Island. *Journal of Applied Social Psychology, 19,* 959-975.

294 Goldhaber, M. K., Houts, P. S., & DiSabella, R. (1983). Moving after the crisis: A prospective study of Three Mile Island area population mobility. *Environment and Behavior, 15,* 93-120.

295 Rochford, E. B. Jr., & Blocker, T. J. (1991). Coping with "natural" hazards as stressors: The predictors of activism in a flood disaster. *Environment and Behavior, 23,* 171-194.

296 Aguirre, B. E. (1982). The long term effects of major natural disasters on marriage and divorce: An ecological study. *Victimology: An International Journal, 5,* 298-307.

297 Chen, X., Dai, K., & Parnell, A. (1992). Disaster tradition and change: Remarriage and family reconstruction in a post-earthquake community in the People's Republic of China. *Journal of Comparative Family Studies, 23,* 115-132.

298 Adams, P. R., & Adams, G. R. (1984). Mount St. Helen's ashfall: Evidence for a disaster stress reaction. *American Psychologist, 39,* 252-260.

299 Edelstein, M. R., & Wandersman, A. (1987). Community dynamics in coping with toxic contaminants. In I. Altman & A. Wandersman (Eds.), *Neighborhood and community environments.* New York: Plenum.

300 Palinkas, L. A., Downs, M. A., Petterson, J. S., & Russell, J. (1993). Social, cultural, and psychological impacts of the Exxon Valdez oil spill. *Human Organization, 52,* 1-13.

301 Kaniasty, K. Z., Norris, F. H., & Murrell, S. A. (1990). Received and perceived social support following natural disaster. *Journal of Applied Social Psychology, 20,* 85-114.

302 Unger, D. G., Wandersman, A., & Hallman, W. (1992). Living near a hazardous waste facility: Coping with individual and family distress. *American Journal of Orthopsychiatry, 62,* 55-70.

303 McFarlane, A. C. (1987). Family functioning and overprotection following a natural disaster: The longitudinal effects of post-traumatic morbidity. *Australian & New Zealand Journal of Psychiatry, 21,* 210-218.

304 Kaniasty, K. Z., Norris, F. H., & Murrell, S. A. (1990). Received and perceived social support following natural disaster. *Journal of Applied Social Psychology, 20,* 85-114.

305 Skitka, L. J. (1999). Ideological and attributional boundaries on public compassion: Reactions to individuals and communities affected by a natural disaster. *Personality and Social Psychology Bulletin, 25,* 793-808.

306 McLeod, B. (1984). In the wake of disaster. *Psychology Today, 18,* 54-58.

307 Thaggard, S. L. (1991). The Huntsville tornado of 1989: A psychiatrist's perspective. *Psychiatric Annals, 21,* 553-555.

308 Ponton L. E., & Bryant, E. C. (1991). After the earthquake: Organizing to respond to children and adolescents. *Psychiatric Annals, 21,* 539-546.

309 Berman, R., & Roel, G. (1993). Encounter with death and destruction: The 1985 Mexico City earthquake. Special section: In times of national crisis. *Group Analysis, 26,* 81-89.

310 McFarlane, A. C. (1989). The prevention and management of the psychiatric morbidity of natural disasters: An Australian experience. *Stress Medicine, 5,* 29-36.

311 Raphael, B., & Meldrum, L. (1993). The evolution of mental health responses and research in Australian disasters. *Journal of Traumatic Stress, 6,* 65-89.

312 Chen, H. C., Chung, H., Chen, T., Fang, L., & Chen, J-P. (2003). The emotional distress in a community after the terrorists attack on the World Trade Center. *Community Mental Health Journal, 39,* 157-165.

313 Horowitz, M. J., Stinson, C., & Field, N. (1991). Natural disasters and stress response syndromes. *Psychiatric Annals, 21,* 556-562.

314 Escobar, J. I., Canino, G., Rubio-Stipec, M., & Bravo, M. (1992). Somatic symptoms after a natural disaster: A prospective study. *American Journal of Psychiatry, 149,* 965-967.

315 Wood, J. M., Bootzin, R. R., Rosenhan, D., Nolen-Hoeksema, S., et al. (1992). Effects of the 1989 San Francisco earthquake on frequency and content of nightmares. *Journal of Abnormal Psychology, 101,* 219-224.

316 Davidson, L. M., Baum, A., & Collins, D. L. (1982). Stress and control-related problems at Three Mile Island. *Journal of Applied Social Psychology, 12,* 349-359.

317 Schaeffer, M. A., & Baum, A. (1984). Adrenal cortical response to stress at Three Mile Island. *Psychosomatic Medicine, 46,* 227-237.

318 DeAngelis, T. (1991). Psychologists bring disaster victims help. *APA Monitor, 22,* 24.

319 Cohen, R. E. (1987). The Armero tragedy: Lessons for mental health professionals. *Hospital & Community Psychiatry, 38,* 1316-1321.

320 Krug, E. G., Kreesnow, M. J., Peddicord, J. P., Dahlberg, L. L., Powell, K. E., Crosby, A. E., & Annest, J. L. (1998). Suicide after natural disasters. *New England Journal of Medicine, 338,* 373-378.

321 Rubonis, A. V., & Bickman, L. (1991). Psychological impairment in the wake of disaster: The disaster- psychopathology relationship. *Psychological Bulletin, 109,* 384-399.

322 Lima, B. R., & Pai, S. (1992-93). Responses to the psychological consequences of disasters in Latin America. *International Journal of Mental Health, 21,* 59- ?1.

323 Caia, G., & Maass, A. (2010). Container vs. dacha: The psychological effects of temporary housing characteristics on earthquake survivors. *Journal of Environmental Psychology, 30,* 60-66.

324 Carr, V. J., Lewin, T. J., Kenardy, J. A, Webster, R. A., & et al. (1997). Psychosocial sequelae of the 1989 Newcastle earthquake: III. Role of Vulnerability factors in post-disaster morbidity. *Psychological Medicine, 27,* 179-190.

325 Matthies, E., Hoeger, R., & Guski, R. (2000). Living on polluted soil: Determinants of stress symptoms. *Environment and Behaviour, 32,* 270-286.

326 Benight, C., Swift, E., Sanger, J., Smith, A., & Zeppelin, D. (1999). Coping self-efficacy as a mediator of distress following a natural disaster. *Journal of Applied Social Psychology, 29,* 2443-2464.

327 Seroka, C. M., Knapp, C., Knight, S., Siemon, C. R., & Starbuck, S. (1986). A comprehensive program for postdisaster counseling. *The Journal of Contemporary Social Work,* 37-44.

328 Bell, B. D. (1978). Disaster impact and response: Overcoming the thousand natural shocks. *The Gerontologist, 18,* 531-540.

329 Kato, H., Asukai, N., Miyaki, Y., Minakawa, K., & et al. (1996). Post-traumatic symptoms among younger and elderly evacuees in the early staged following the 1995 Hanshin-Awaji earthquake in Japan. *Acata Psychiatrica Scandinavica, 93,* 477-481.

330 Lewin, T. J., Carr, V. J., & Webster, R. A. (1998). Recovery from post-earthquake psychological morbidity: Who suffers and who recovers? *Australian and New Zealand Journal of Psychiatry, 32,* 15-20.

331 Goldsteen, R., Schorr, J. K., & Goldsteen, K. S. (1989). Longitudinal study of appraisal at Three Mile Island: Implications for life event research. *Social Science and Medicine, 28,* 389-398.

332 Faupel, C. E., & Styles, S. P. (1993). Disaster education, household preparedness, and stress responses following Hurricane Hugo. *Environment and Behavior, 25,* 228-249.

333 Nolen-Hoeksema, S., & Morrow, J. (1991). A prospective study of depression and posttraumatic stress symptoms after a natural disaster: The 1989 Loma Prieta earthquake. *Journal of Personality & Social Psychology, 61,* 115-121.

334 Norris, F. N., & Uhl, G. A. (1993). Chronic stress as a mediator of acute stress: The case of Hurricane Hugo. *Journal of Applied Social Psychology, 23,* 1263-1284.

335 Wasserstein, S. B., La Greca, A. M., & Silverman, W. K. (1994). *Hurricane Andrew: Parent conflict as a moderator of children's adjustment.* Presentation at the annual meetings of the American Psychological Association, Los Angeles.

336 Vincent, N. R., La Greca, A. M., & Silverman, W. K., Wasserstein, S. B., & Prinstein, M. J. (1994). *Predicting children's responses to natural disasters: Role of academic achievement.* Presentation at the annual meetings of the American Psychological Association, Los Angeles.

337 Vitaliano, P. P., Maiuro, R. D., Bolton, P. A., & Armsden, G. C. (1987). A psychoepidemiologic approach to the study of disaster. *Journal of Community Psychology, 15,* 99-122.

338 Baum, A. (1988). Disasters, natural and otherwise. *Psychology Today, 22,* 57-60.

339 Baum, A., Fleming, R., & Davidson, L. M. (1983). Natural disaster and technological catastrophe. *Environment and Behavior, 15,* 333-354.

340 Baum, A., Fleming, I., Israel, A., & O'Keeffe, M. K. (1992). Symptoms of chronic stress following a natural disaster and discovery of a human-made hazard. *Environment and Behavior, 24,* 347-365.

341 Rubonis, A. V., & Bickman, L. (1991). Psychological impairment in the wake of disaster: The disaster-psychopathology relationship. *Psychological Bulletin, 109,* 384-399.

342 Hallman, W. K. (1990). Coping with an environmental stressor: Perception of risk, attribution of responsibility and psychological distress in a community living near a

hazardous waste facility. *Dissertation Abstracts International*, *51*(1-B), 474-475.

343 Baum, A., Fleming, R., & Davidson, L. M. (1983). Natural disaster and technological catastrophe. *Environment and Behavior*, *15*, 333-354.

344 Baum, A., Fleming, R., & Singer, J. E. (1983). Coping with victimization by technological disaster. *Journal of Social Issues*, *39*(2), 117-138.

345 Collins, D. L., Baum, A., & Singer, J. E. (1983). Coping with chronic stress at Three Mile Island: Psychological and biochemical evidence. *Health Psychology*, *2*, 149-166.

346 Prince-Embury, S., & Rooney, J. F. (1990). Life stage differences in resident coping with restart of the Three Mile Island nuclear generating facility. *Journal of Social Psychology*, *130*, 771-779.

347 Rubonis, A. V., & Bickman, L. (1991). Psychological impairment in the wake of disaster: The disaster-psychopathology relationship. *Psychological Bulletin*, *109*, 384-399.

348 Carr, V. J., Lewin, T. J., Kenardy, J. A., Webster, R. A., et al. (1997). Psychological sequelae of the 1989 Newcastle earthquake: II. Exposure and morbidity profile during the first 2 years post-disaster. *Psychological Medicine*, *27*, 167-178.

349 Lima, B. R., Pai, S., Toledo, V., Caris, L. et al. (1993). Emotional distress in disaster victims: A follow-up study. *Journal of Nervous & Mental Disease*, *181*, 388-393.

350 Zhang, H.-C., & Zhang, Y.-Z. (1991). Psychological consequences of earthquake disaster survivors. *International Journal of Psychology*, *26*, 613-621.

351 Edelstein, M. R. (1986). Toxic exposure and the inversion of the home. *Journal of Architectural & Planning Research*, *3*, 237-251.

352 Preston, V., Taylor, S. M., & Hodge, D. C. (1983). Adjustment to natural and technological hazards: A study of an urban residential community. *Environment and Behavior*, *15*, 143-164.

353 Fleming, R., Baum, A., Gisriel, M. M., & Gatchel, R. J. (1982). Mediating influences of social support on stress at Three Mile Island. *Journal of Human Stress*, 8, 14-22.

354 Palinkas, L. A., Russell, J., Downs, M. A., & Petterson, J. S. (1992). Ethnic differences in stress, coping, and depressive symptoms after the Exxon Valdez oil spill. *Journal of Nervous & Mental Disease*, *180*, 287-295.

355 Chisholm, R. F., Kasl, S. V., & Mueller, L. (1986). The effects of social support on nuclear workers response to the Three Mile Island accident. *Journal of Occupational Behaviour*, *7*, 179-193.

356 Solomon, Z. (1985). Stress, social support and affective disorders in mothers of pre-school children: A test of the stress-buffering effect of social support. *Social Psychiatry*, *20*, 100-105.

357 Solomon, S. D., Bravo, M., Rubio-Stipec, M., & Canino, G. J. (1993). Effect of family role on response to disaster. *Journal of Traumatic Stress*, *6*, 255-269.

358 Jeney-Gammon, P., Daugherty, T. K., Finch, A. J., Belter, R. W., et al. (1993). Children's coping styles and report of depressive symptoms following a natural disaster. *Journal of Genetic Psychology*, *154*, 259-267.

359 Pennebaker, J. W., & Harber, K. D. (1993). A social stage model of collective coping: The Loma Prieta earthquake and the Persian gulf. *Journal of Social Issues*, *49*(4), 125-145.

360 Murphy, S. A. (1986). Perceptions of stress, coping, and recovery one and three years after a natural disaster. *Issues in Mental Health Nursing*, *8*, 63-77.

361 Burton, I., Kates R. W., & White, G. F. (1978). *The environment as hazard*. New York: Oxford.

362 Weinstein, N. D., Sandman, P. M., & Roberts, N. E. (1990). Determinants of self-protective behavior. Home radon testing. *Journal of Applied Social Psychology*, *20*, 783-801.

363 McCallum, D. B., Hammond, S. L., & Covello, V. T. (1991). Communicating about environmental risks: How the public uses and perceives information sources. *Health Education Quarterly*, *18*, 349-361.

364 deMarchi, B. (1991). The Seveso Directive: An Italian pilot study in enabling communication. *Risk Analysis*, *11*, 207-215.

365 Ekker, K., Gifford, G., Leik, S. A., & Leik, R. K. (1988). Using microcomputer game-simulation experiments to study family response to the Mt. St. Helens eruptions. *Social Science Computer Review*, *6*, 90-105.

366 Druckman, D. (1993). The situational levers of negotiating flexibility. *Journal of Conflict Resolution*, *37*, 236-276.

367 Fischhoff, B. (1990). Psychology and public policy: Tool or toolmaker? *American Psychologist*, *45*, 647-653.

368 Vaughan, E. (1993). Individual and cultural differences in adaptation to environmental risks. *American Psychologist*, *48*, 673-680.

369 Kiecolt, K. J., & Nigg, J. M. (1982). Mobility and perceptions of a hazardous waste environment. *Environment and Behavior*, *14*, 131-154.

370 Preston, V., Taylor, S. M., & Hodge, D. C. (1983). Adjustment to natural and technological hazards: A study of an urban residential community. *Environment and Behavior*, *15*, 143- 164.

371 Ives, S. M., & Furuseth, D. J. (1983). Immediate response to headwater flooding in Charlotte, North Carolina. *Environment and Behavior*, *15*, 512-525.

372 Payne, R. J., & Pigram, J. J. (1981). Changing evaluations of flood plain hazard: The Hunter River Valley, Australia. *Environment and Behavior*, *13*, 461-480.

373 Ruga, W. (1989). Designing for the six senses. *Journal of Health Care Interior Design*, *1*, 29-34.

374 Ulrich, R. S. (1991). Effects of interior design on wellness: Theory and recent scientific research. *Journal of Health Care Interior Design*, *3*, 97-109.

375 Davis, I. (1978). *Shelter after disaster*. Oxford: Oxford Polytechnic Press.

376 Davis, I. (1978). *Shelter after disaster*. Oxford: Oxford Polytechnic Press.

377 Rapoport, A. (1969). *House form and culture*. Englewood Cliffs, NJ: Prentice Hall.

CHAPTER 13:

The Psychology of Climate Change

REUVEN SUSSMAN AND ROBERT GIFFORD

To anyone who continues to deny the reality that is climate change, I dare you to get off your ivory tower and away from the comfort of your armchair. I dare you to go to the islands of the Pacific, the islands of the Caribbean and the islands of the Indian Ocean and see the impacts of rising sea levels; to the mountainous regions of the Himalayas and the Andes to see communities confronting glacial floods, to the Arctic where communities grapple with the fast-dwindling polar ice caps... to the vast savannas of Africa where climate change has likewise become a matter of life and death as food and water become scarce...

— NADEREV (YEB) SAÑO
LEAD NEGOTIATOR FOR THE PHILIPPINES
AT A UN CLIMATE SUMMIT MEETING IN WARSAW, NOVEMBER 11, 2013

TOM AND JANE WERE SITTING IN THE SUN AT A PATIO RESTAURANT OVERLOOKING THE HARBOR, HAVING A TALL COOL ONE. *It was one of those perfect afternoons, with no wind, a bright blue sky, and just the right temperature.*

"Wouldn't it be nice if every day were like this?" Jane mused.

"I guess so," said Tom, "but I wonder if that would get boring. Anyway, with the climate changing, I guess we can be sure that every day won't be like this one."

"My uncle is sure that's all a hoax," Jane laughed. "He says he doesn't see any changes he hasn't seen before."

"Well," said Tom, "I guess he doesn't pay much attention to the news or to people who study climate change professionally. I heard that our brains haven't evolved much since we humans lived on the savannah 30,000 years ago. And what did we care about then? Nothing that we couldn't see, and nothing that was beyond our nomadic range. The here and now. So even though we are now able to measure and think about global events, I'm not surprised that some people stick to what they can personally see and hear."

"Yes," Jane agreed, "plus, he's very comfortable in his lifestyle, and I think he feels threatened by people who say we need to change."

"Wow! What's that?" Tom suddenly exclaimed. "That...that's a brown pelican out there! I've never seen one up here before. The last one I saw was when we were down in Mazatlán!"

"And I guess she wouldn't be up here if she didn't have some of her Mexican diet swimming around in our harbor, too, would she?" Jane added with a knowing smile.

FIGURE 13–1 The consumption of coal, oil, natural gas, and other fossil fuels is a major driver of global climate change.

the commission stated that "most of the observed warming of the past 50 years is attributable to human activities." In its fourth report (2007),[2] the IPCC stated that "most of the observed increase in global average temperatures since the mid-20th century is very likely due to the observed increase in anthropogenic [human-caused] greenhouse gas concentrations." The fifth report, published in 2014, stated that every person on Earth will be affected by climate change.

THE HUMAN CAUSES OF CLIMATE CHANGE

CLIMATE CHANGE IS EXACTLY WHAT IT SOUNDS LIKE— LONG-TERM VARIATION IN THE EARTH'S TEMPERATURE, wind patterns, atmosphere, hydrosphere (water), cryosphere (snow, ice, and permafrost) and biosphere (plants and animals). Climate change is not the same as daily changes in the weather. Essentially, climate change is defined by its effects on all of the earth's systems (including us!). Although the earth's climate also changes naturally, substantial scientific evidence now demonstrates that systematic climate change is occurring at a global scale because of increases in the earth's temperature, and these changes are most likely driven by human behavior.[1]

Beginning in 1990, the United Nations recognized the importance of climate change by commissioning a group of international scientists to publish a report every few years on the state of climate change research. This is called the Intergovernmental Panel on Climate Change (IPCC). In 1995, the IPCC stated that "humans are having a discernible influence on the earth's climate." In 2001,

How Human Activities Cause Climate Change

ALTHOUGH AWARENESS AND CONCERN about climate change have increased since the 1990s, many people are still unclear about the basic causes and consequences of the phenomenon.[3-5] Therefore, a primer on climate change and human behavior follows.

Global warming occurs because certain gases in the atmosphere (collectively called greenhouse gases) warm the earth by helping to trap heat from the sun instead of allowing it to radiate back into outer space. The concentration of greenhouse gases in the atmosphere has naturally fluctuated over the earth's 4.5 billion year history from volcanic eruptions and other natural processes, but since the industrial revolution 150 years ago, greenhouse gas levels have increased very quickly and natural processes do not sufficiently explain the change.[6] This has led to a predictable rise in the earth's average temperature.[7]

Human activities are the *primary* causes of current global climate change because they directly or indirectly lead to the release of greenhouse gas emissions.[8] Carbon dioxide is produced as a by-product of burning gas, oil, coal, natural gas, or any other fossil fuel (Figure 13-1). Thus, every time we drive a car or fly on a plane we are causing the release of greenhouse gases into the atmosphere. We also warm the earth by using electricity at home, school, and work, if that electricity is generated by burning fossil fuels.[9,10] Less obviously, our purchase decisions affect greenhouse gas emissions. All goods require energy to be produced and distributed, so the more goods we buy and the further away they come from, the more greenhouse gases get emitted.

Methane is another important gas, and it is 25 times more potent as a greenhouse gas than carbon dioxide on an equal-weight basis. Farm animals produce much methane (Figure 13-2), and some comes from rotting food and the breakdown of other organic material in landfills. This is also a human-caused source of greenhouse gas in the sense that people raise animals in unprecedented numbers for consumption of milk and meat.[11]

FIGURE 13–2 Farm animals produce methane.

Another way that people are indirectly causing climate change is by altering the biosphere. The earth's natural ability to sequester carbon is embodied by plants[12] and the oceans. Large forests, such as the Amazon rainforest and northern boreal forests are responsible for a significant amount of carbon capture. However, these are being cut down or burned at increasing rates to make space for agriculture, heating, and construction.[13] Although many forests are replanted after being cut down, older trees sequester more carbon than younger trees and the rate of cut is faster than the rate of replenishment.[14]

In sum, we produce the carbon dioxide and methane that heat the globe directly when we burn fossil fuels, and indirectly through our purchases and our diets. We need to eat and we need other necessities, but we can also make *consumption behavior* choices that use less energy: driving less, eating differently, purchasing items made from recycled material, and buying carbon offset credits are a few examples. Ultimately, the goal is to live *sustainably*,[15] which means, in one sense, emitting only as many greenhouse gases as can be naturally absorbed by the earth.

Currently, people in developed countries emit much more greenhouse gas per person than people in developing countries.[16] The amount of carbon emitted by an average North American, for example, is 16 times greater than that of an average African.[17] Even though birth rates in developing countries are higher than in developed countries, the per-person emissions are lower and in many cases, the overall level of emissions is lower.

However, as developing countries steadily become richer, their citizens purchase more goods, travel longer distances and generally increase their consumption. The ability of the earth to absorb current levels of greenhouse gases is already falling behind our consumption levels. If developing countries also maintain or increase their levels of consumption, temperatures will continue to increase. Therefore, both consumption behavior and population growth play vital roles in climate change.

Environmental psychologists are uniquely positioned to study the causes of consumption choices, attitudes about and perceptions of climate change, and methods for encouraging people to engage in *climate action* (actions to mitigate climate change such as reducing consumption). They also investigate why some people support government or industrial initiatives to mitigate climate change (while others do not) and they examine how cultural beliefs and social norms affect perceptions of climate change

FIGURE 13–3 Pine beetle infestation. The orange and burgundy trees are dead.

and climate action. All of these psychological processes are vital if we are to reduce greenhouse gas emissions and slow global warming.

The Physical and Social Consequences of Climate Change

MOST METEOROLOGISTS HAVE SHIFTED from using the term "global warming" to using the term "climate change" because it better describes the complexity of the phenomenon. Surface temperatures are rising around the world, but this results in a variety of effects in different regions (beyond the warming itself). For example, western Canada has recently experienced longer, warmer summers with better growing conditions for agriculture, but in sub-Saharan Africa and Australia increased temperatures are resulting in droughts and desertification.[18] In an unfair twist of fate, developing

countries (typically located in warmer southern climates) are expected to experience the harshest effects of climate change even though their citizens contribute fewer greenhouse gas emissions per capita.[19] Therefore, climate change has social impacts as well as physical impacts: the divide between "have" and "have-not" countries is likely to increase.

However, the negative effects of climate change are not restricted to developing countries or those that already experience typically warmer temperatures. Warmer temperatures in western Canada have also (among other impacts) facilitated the mountain pine beetle's destruction of huge swathes of forest (Figure 13-3). Colder winter temperatures once killed these insects, but today the winters are not cold or long enough to do so.[20] In the same way, mosquitoes and other insects that carry diseases (in other parts of the world) also benefit from warmer weather, and this leads to increased rates of disease and mortality.[21] In general, the negative effects of global climate change are likely to far outweigh the shorter-term positive effects experienced by some regions.

The IPCC has described a number of potential large-scale consequences of climate change.[22] Higher maximum and minimum global temperatures may well lead to increased heat-related health problems and deaths and to create more droughts and negative outcomes for agriculture. Events like the heat wave of 2003 in France that resulted in 14,947 deaths (60% more than usual) in just one month may become more likely.[23] Climate change may result in more illness because disease-carrying insects and animals can now move into new, warmer territories. Other animals and plants will disappear because they cannot live in warmer temperatures or their food sources have become scarce. Warmer temperatures also lead to sea-level rise because warmer oceans will expand, and large-scale ice melting in northern regions will add to their total volume. Sea-level rise could spell disaster for many major cities that are located on ocean coasts.

Droughts and desertification will occur with global temperature increases, and other regions will experience increased intense precipitation and other extreme weather events, such as tornadoes and cyclones. This is likely to mean more floods, soil erosion, mudslides, damage to coastal infrastructure and ecosystems, and infectious disease epidemics (see Figure 13-4).

These and many other complex physical effects of climate change are already occurring. For environmental and other psychologists, the important outcomes of these physical effects are the psychological and social effects on people who are experiencing them. Psychologists play an important role in understanding the impacts of climate change on mental health, for aiding people to *adapt* to and *cope* with these stressful changes, and to learn why people and communities choose to *prepare* (or not) for climate change. The remainder of this chapter will describe research that focuses on the psychological processes associated with climate change.

Have you ever wondered why some people deny that the current climate changes are anthropogenic (human-driven)? What are the best ways to communicate information about climate change? How can climate-positive action be encouraged? Are you concerned about how people might be psychologically affected by climate change or how they could adapt to it or cope with it? This chapter will touch on each of these topics by focusing on three main areas of climate change psychology research: perceptions of climate change, the impact of climate change, and the psychology of encouraging climate action.

FIGURE 13–4 A Spring 1995 landslide (and debris flow, at bottom) in La Conchita, California.

HOW IS CLIMATE CHANGE PSYCHOLOGY STUDIED?

ENVIRONMENTAL PSYCHOLOGISTS INVESTIGATE the human aspects of climate change in one or more of four basic ways: through surveys, qualitative methods, experiments, or observations of behavior. All are meant to learn about people's knowledge, concern, awareness, values, feelings, beliefs, intentions, and actual behavior related to climate change.

Surveys and Polls

AMONG SURVEYS, SOME LARGE-SCALE OPINION POLLS ask just one question, such as "You may have heard about the idea that the world's temperatures may have been going up slowly over the past 100 years. What is your personal opinion on this—do you think this has probably been happening, or do you think it probably hasn't been happening?" [24] Other surveys ask multiple questions, trying to understand the finer nuances of community thinking. [25] Still others use

validated measures, based on a particular theory. [26] Polls provide important "snapshot" information about climate change opinions and attitudes, while surveys that include validated psychological scales provide more theory-driven, comprehensive information and therefore produce higher quality information. Several such instruments have been created or adapted to measure perceptions of climate change, [27,28] motivation for climate action, [29] and coping with climate change. [30]

Qualitative Methods

QUALITATIVE STUDIES INVOLVE INTERVIEWS of individuals or analyses of the texts of government debates, news, or statements on social media. The value of the qualitative approach is to let people's own perspectives "drive" the study, rather than asking them predetermined, closed-ended questions. Such questions may limit the findings to what the investigator asks, and therefore miss some of what is going on in the mind of the respondent.

By looking for patterns across multiple interviews, researchers can understand public *narratives* about climate change and, in doing so, make inferences about how the public may think about the topic. In one such project, 235 individuals from public, private, and non-profit sectors affected by (or contributing to) climate change were interviewed to ascertain their understandings of how climate change works and the types of behaviors that may contribute to it.[31] Most qualitative interview studies involve far fewer participants (the example above was exceptional) and, therefore, may be less representative of the general population. However, they also tend to provide more detailed information about the thoughts of each respondent.

Content analysis of news reports, political rhetoric transcripts, or other public documents is another form of qualitative research for climate change psychology. For example, newspaper stories have had their content analyzed for changes in wordings, perspectives, and themes over several decades, so that we can learn how public perceptions of global warming have changed over time.[32-35] The public statements and documents of various industries have been analyzed to understand how their climate change strategies and self-presentations have changed.[36,37] Content analysis has been used to understand how climate change topics are integrated into classroom education.[38] This strategy requires careful· reading and categorizing of many texts in order to discern patterns within them. Occasionally, advanced computer-aided techniques can aid in the process.[39]

Qualitative and survey methods have different advantages: the former usually is deeper, and the latter usually is broader. Qualitative research is useful for discovering nuances within attitudes and motivations, whereas survey approaches are better for learning whether different constructs (e.g., knowledge about climate change and concern about climate change) are correlated or not, and often are more representative of a population's views.

Experimental Methods

A PROBLEM WITH BOTH QUALITATIVE AND SURVEY methods is that although they *describe* what people say about climate change, they cannot determine what *caused* those statements. For that purpose, experimental research is the best tool. Experimental methods, which use random as-

signment of participants to conditions and experimenter control of what participants hear or experience, allow for the inference of causality.[40] For example, researchers can test the effectiveness of different messages using experimental methods

Observing Behavior

FINALLY, ENVIRONMENTAL PSYCHOLOGISTS OBSERVE ACTUAL BEHAVIOR. This is very important, although it can be difficult to do; watching whether a large sample of people actually drive much or little, turn down their thermostats or not, or take long or short showers is not easy. However, as I (RG) have written: "…to be blunt, not concern for the environment, not felt responsibility, not subjective norms, not attitude towards the behavior, not goals, and not even behavioral intentions solve environmental problems. Only actual behavior will bring a resolution."[41]

PERCEPTIONS OF CLIMATE CHANGE

Awareness, Belief, Knowledge, and Concern About Climate Change

"GLOBAL WARMING IS HAPPENING BECAUSE HUMAN ACTIVITIES ARE CREATING A HOLE IN THE EARTH'S OZONE LAYER." False. In fact, ozone depletion is caused by the release of chlorofluorocarbons (CFCs) often found in appliances such as old refrigerators or air conditioning units, whereas global warming is created by the release of greenhouse gases (usually) through burning fossil fuels. However, if you have confused the ozone issue with climate change, you are not alone. The misconception that ozone depletion is related to climate change is common among children and adults alike.[42- 45]

Since the late 1980s, public awareness of climate change, belief in its existence, and knowledge of its causes and consequences have generally increased. In a review of hundreds of questions from 70 American polls conducted between the 1986 and 2007, several interesting patterns

FIGURE 13–5 Retreating glaciers have become an iconic symbol of climate change. In many parts of the world, glaciers are an important source of fresh water in summer months, and their retreat and disappearance reduces reliable sources of water for drinking and agriculture. This glacier, in central British Columbia, has rapidly retreated since the 1940s. Before that time, any pictures from this location would have been taken from beneath the glacier. The entire mile-wide lake at the bottom of this photo has been formed by melt. In 1967, the glacier melted away from the valley wall enough to un-dam the lake it had formed. The glacier continues to diminish.

emerged.[46] One of the clearest is that the level of *awareness of the issue* increased from only 39% in 1986 to 80-90% in the early 1990s when the percentage seemed to plateau.

People's *belief that climate change is real* depends slightly on how the question is phrased. When asked, "Do you believe the theory that increased carbon dioxide and other gases released into the atmosphere will, unchecked, lead to global warming and an increase in average temperatures, or not?" 67-77% agreed that "yes, it will result in an increase." When asked, "How convinced are you that global warming or the greenhouse effect is actually happening—would you say that you are completely convinced, mostly convinced, not so convinced, or not convinced at all?" 56-69% agreed that they were "completely convinced" or "mostly convinced".

As another example of how the wording of the question matters, when polls ask, "What is the most important problem facing this country today?" few respondents answer "climate change" or environmental problems. However, many more give environmental answers if the question is, "What is the most serious problem that will face the world in the future if nothing is done to stop it?" [47]

The belief that a *scientific consensus* about climate change exists is more consistent across polls, and it has steadily increased from 28% in 1994 to 65% in 2006. The belief that it is an *immediate threat* has increased from about 50% to about 60%.

The polling data on *knowledge of climate change* shows that, although most Americans have a better understanding of the causes and consequences of climate change now than when the issue first appeared in the public eye,[48] many still have misconceptions and incorrect notions. Apart from conflation of the ozone issue with climate change, many people are also not clear about how climate change is caused. The belief that human activity may cause climate change is growing in acceptance, but the link between fossil-fuel burning and climate change is still not well understood by many people.[49] One American poll

FIGURE 13-6 Storm damage has traditionally been seen as a low-probability, high-consequence risk.

it ranged from about 30% to 40%.[58] Concern about climate change seems to wane when issues such as the economy or terrorism gain public interest.[59] Thus, many people apparently care about climate change as long as they think that nothing else "more important" is happening.

In other countries, answers can be different. For example, in Europe when respondents were given nine possible issues and asked, "Which are most serious?" 51% percent mentioned climate change as one of the world's most serious problems and 20% stated it was the most serious problem.[60] In a 39-nation survey, the United States was among the six countries least likely to rate global climate change as a major threat,[61] although around 40% of Americans *are* concerned.

Naturally, concern varies across individuals. Females usually report more concern than males,[62-64] although this is not always the case.[65] Individuals who trust scientists tend to be more concerned than others,[66] although some are less concerned because they think that scientists will invent a solution to the problem.[67] Others believe that climate change is a "classed issue"; that is, less important to people who face economic hardship and more important to those who are economically comfortable.[68] However, one study suggests that wealthier citizens are *less* concerned about climate change.[69]

Concern, knowledge, perceived efficacy, guilt, and behavior. Feeling concerned is important because, as you would expect, it is ordinarily correlated with more reported pro-climate behavior or greater willingness to act.[70,71] But just how does concern translate to willingness to act? A key may be *perceived self-efficacy*, the belief that one's actions can make a difference. For example, concern *mediates* the effect of knowledge on self-efficacy.[72] That is, people who are knowledgeable but *not* concerned do not experience self-efficacy and therefore are less likely to take action;

from 2000 found that less than 65% of respondents properly identified burning coal as a cause of climate change,[50] and in 2009 another survey found a similar result.[51] In the UK, carbon is often seen as pollution, without a complete understanding of how it contributes to climate change.[52] In general, awareness of, belief in, and knowledge about climate change have increased, but all these need to be further increased.

Awareness versus Knowledge versus Concern. Climate change *knowledge* is not synonymous with climate change *concern*. Knowing that a problem exists is not necessarily enough to generate *concern* about it. In some cases, knowledge is associated with more worry about the problem[53] and sometimes more knowledge is actually associated with *less* concern.[54,55] This may be because people have two kinds of thoughts about climate change: actual knowledge and "meta-knowledge" (i.e., confidence in one's knowledge).[56] Sometimes people who have incorrect knowledge but high confidence in that knowledge (i.e., they are confident about their false beliefs) are less likely be concerned.

Awareness of climate change problems does not necessarily lead to concern or intentions to change behavior.[57] In a series of polls between 1997 and 2007, perceptions of climate change as "personally important" reached a peak of 52% ("very" or "extremely" important) in 2007, and the percentage of Americans who worried "a great deal" about people who are knowledgeable *and* concerned do feel as if they can make a difference. *Collective guilt* also affects some people's willingness to act.[73] They are more willing to take action if they feel regret or guilty that their fellow citizens produce too many greenhouse gas emissions. People who are knowledgeable about climate change but do not experience this sense of collective guilt are less willing to take action.

Many citizens say they care about the issue, but few take any civic action or even pay attention to what the government is doing about climate change.[74] Before the public becomes more "carbon capable" (capable of taking action to mitigate climate change), social and structural changes that support climate action may need to be implemented.

Experts versus laypersons. Climate change experts such as employees of the US Environmental Protection Agency, geographers, meteorologists, and full-time researchers base their understandings of the problem on different information than most members of the general public. Most laypeople get their information from television or Internet sources,[75,76] but experts spend more time thinking about the problem and base their knowledge on data they have personally gathered or interpreted. Therefore, as you would expect, climate change researchers have more knowledge and confidence in that knowledge than journalists or politicians, who in turn, have more than members of the general public.[77]

Beyond that, experts and the rest of us have different concerns. Laypersons tend to be more concerned about low-probability, high-consequence risks, whereas professionals are more concerned about long-term, ecosystem-level risks (see Figure 13-6).[78] At least back in 2000, experts perceived risks to ecosystems as having slightly *lower* impacts, yet also being less avoidable, more acceptable, and less understandable than laypersons did.[79]

The reputation of climate scientists and trust in the scientific community has been called into question by people who claim that research on the idea of anthropogenic climate change is a lucrative business. In essence, they claim that climate scientists are "in it for the money" and that is why they report that anthropogenic climate change is happening. However, the data do not support this claim. In a survey of US climate change researchers, opinions on the subject were not predicted by a variety of other "fame and fortune"-related factors.[80]

Politics. In developed countries around the world, and especially in the US, political ideologies are among the strongest predictors of climate change perceptions. People with conservative political views and Americans who tend to vote Republican are generally more skeptical of anthropogenic climate change and believe it poses less of a risk than do liberals or Americans who vote Democrat.[81] This is probably because political views affect general environmental attitudes which, in turn, affect belief in anthropogenic climate change.[82] Words matter. Democrats usually believe that climate change is occurring, regardless of what it is called, but Republicans are more likely to believe that the phenomenon is occurring when it is called climate change than when it is called global warming.[83]

Between 2001 and 2010, the division of opinion between Democrats and Republicans in the United States on the climate change issue increased.[84] At the beginning of the millennium, scientific research on climate change was generally accepted by members of all political parties (even if the solutions were controversial), but today belief (or not) in the *science* of climate change is part of Americans' political identities; rejecting the science behind climate change is a part of conservative Republican ideology. Even those who have personal experience with climate change, extreme weather, and physical changes to the planet are less likely to believe in climate change if they identify as Republican.[85] Some evidence suggests that knowledge of climate change will only lead to concern about climate change when Americans trust scientists or are *not* Republican.[86]

The Perception of Risk

HUMANS ARE EVOLVED TO RESPOND TO IMMEDIATE, CLEAR, AND PRESENT DANGER. We are good at assessing risks and taking action for hazards that are certain and nearby. When a person threatens another person with a knife, for example, that person knows almost instinctively how to respond. Climate change is a different kind of hazard. Some psychologists argue that humans fail to understand and respond to climate change because it poses a type of risk that we are not "wired" to deal with — one that is uncertain, distant and devoid of emotional connection.[87,88]

Therefore, people tend to believe that climate change consequences will occur in distant places and future times.[89,90] This belief that climate change is *psychologically distant* leads to a lack of concern and preparedness to act.[91]

It also contributes to psychologically *discounting* the risk of climate change and reducing motivation to take immediate action. Indeed, taking action often requires a degree of self-sacrifice that could put one at a disadvantage compared to others, and the benefits of those actions are likely to be experienced only by future generations. By this reasoning, then, any person taking immediate climate action is acting irrationally.[92] In contrast, most people perceived the ozone depletion problem to be immediate, concrete, and relevant to everyday behaviors, and therefore that issue gained better traction with marked reductions in the ozone hole over the past few decades.[93] Those who experience climate change as an immediate threat will be more likely to take action to stop it.

The role of emotion in understanding risk is vital. Perceptions of risk are not typically arrived at analytically or rationally. Instead, our emotional processes are responsible for risk perception.[94] Risk perception is often driven less by thinking than by a *feeling* such as fear, anxiety, or dread.[95] When the brain's analytical system and emotional system disagree, as in the case with phobias, the emotional system usually wins;[96] we know how we should act, but we cannot bring ourselves to do it. Therefore, climate change, which is understood almost exclusively at an analytical level through statistics and second-hand information, is devoid of an emotional connection and evokes a reduced perception of risk. In the end, many of us are not as concerned as we know that we should be.[97]

Although climate change certainly may be understood through analytical reasoning, this type of thinking often is ineffective unless guided by emotion.[98] If climate change is presented in a way that evokes an emotional reaction rather than as an abstract, statistical, time-delayed problem, concern and action would increase.[99,100]

Personal experience. Experience with the immediate environment can influence one's current thoughts about climate change. For example, when people completed climate change surveys on hot days (or days that were perceived as warmer than usual), they reported being more concerned about climate change and were more likely to donate money to a climate change-related charity.[101,102] In France, even completing a climate change questionnaire in a room with several dead plants led to increased belief in climate change.[103]

Direct experience with climate change-related events outside the lab is also associated with perceptions of climate change risk. The beliefs of Americans about climate change are primarily driven by personal observations, weather, and physical changes on the planet.[104] The presence of heat waves and droughts, for example, increases belief in climate change and support for environmental regulation.[105, 106] Private forest owners in Europe who experience the effects of climate change are more likely to believe that climate change is happening and are more likely to take steps to adapt to the problem.[107] People who experience air pollution are more likely to develop pro-environmental values than those who do not and are more likely to cite pollution as a source of climate change.[108] Those who live on a coastline or in low-lying areas are likely to perceive the risk of sea-level rise.[109]

However, experience with climate change does not always lead to increased belief in the phenomenon; attitudes and values may override experience in some cases.[110] Flood victims are no more likely than non-victims to implicate climate change as a cause of floods.[111] Experts, environmentalists, and people who keep up with the news are less influenced by the immediate environment than the information they get from other sources,[112, 113] probably because these more informed people have opinions that are more strongly held, and therefore are less likely to be swayed by peripheral cues such as the state of the immediate environment.[114]

Many who are *vulnerable* but have not yet experienced the effects of climate change are unlikely to believe that it is occurring. Nevada farmers, despite being quite vulnerable to the risk of drought (see Figure 13-7), are less likely to perceive an increased risk of climate change unless they (a) are able to associate droughts with climate change, (b) already believe that humans cause climate change, and (c) are *not* Republican.[115] Other vulnerable communities do see climate change as a looming threat. Dutch homeowners who live along a river delta are willing to pay more than necessary for flood insurance based on their climate change concerns,[116] and some citizens of small islands in the South Pacific have begun purchasing land in Australia out of concern that their homes will soon be drowned by rising sea levels.[117]

In order for people in vulnerable areas to perceive the risk of climate change, the risk often must be salient or overt.[118] People who live where the risk is less salient are less likely to perceive one, even if their area is actually *more* prone to climate change-related disasters such as severe floods.[119]

Communicating Climate Change

Media portrayals. Media portrayals of climate change both reflect and dictate the public's perceptions of the topic. By analyzing the content of news stories and other public discourses over time, we can understand how the public climate change narrative has evolved and how media portrayals could be modified to increase concern about climate change.

In content analyses of UK and American newspaper coverage of climate change between 1980 and 2003, three distinct "circuits" were found.[120,121] The first circuit emphasized scientific consensus and the serious risk of climate change. During the second circuit, discussion of climate change moved from the basic science to controversy about policy. During this time, media eventually latched on to the term "sustainable development" (i.e., growing businesses and the economy using practices that do not emit more carbon or pollution than the earth can naturally process) as one that describes a policy solution that most people could accept. During the third circuit, American news sources focused primarily on the economics of climate change policy, and UK newspapers portrayed the issue as more urgent and as the cause of many "extreme weather events," such as the hottest temperatures in European history.

Since the publication of the US and UK reports in 1999 and 2003, respectively, climate change has been featured in even more print media coverage. A Canadian report suggests that unprecedented numbers of climate change-related news stories were published in later years (2007/2008), but with thematically narrower foci than previously.[122] Although climate change is being discussed more frequently, it has now become part of the status quo and is only mentioned superficially. In-depth treatments of ecological, economic, or health issues related to climate change are rarely presented now, perhaps because media writers assume that the general public already knows this information and is no longer interested in hearing it.

In many ways, media coverage of climate change is rather similar around the world, but some small differences do exist. For example, American media tend to resist using the *precautionary principle* (that is, if a policy is suspected of causing harm, those who advocate the policy must prove its safety before it can be implemented) for dealing with climate change, because it is seen as a threat to American economic interests.[123] In Canada, the coverage of climate

FIGURE 13-7 Droughts and desertification will occur with global temperature increases.

change in print media is highly influenced by American politics and, although controversy is frequently worked into the stories, debates are less often staged in Canadian media between climate change scientists and skeptics in order to present "two sides" of a climate change story.[124] Thus, American media may be slightly more negative, skeptical, and apprehensive about climate change issues than other Western countries.

However, despite increasing certainty about climate change in the scientific community, debate continues in the public and political spheres. Not surprisingly then, people who get their information from science news sources believe that climate change poses a larger risk than people who get their information from political news sources.[125]

Films. Humans are naturally inclined to understand and remember stories. Hence, media portrayals and cultural perspectives on climate change are sometimes referred to as *narratives*. Different narratives have the ability to evoke different emotions and promote or inhibit behaviors. When it comes to promoting narratives, movies can be powerful tools because they provide rich, in-depth, multi-sensory information that can make issues appear less psychologically distant.[126]

Studies of people who watched the popular climate-change movies *An Inconvenient Truth* (documentary) or *The Day After Tomorrow* (science fiction) reveal that immediately after the watching the films, viewers reported being more concerned about climate change and more motivated to engage in climate action.[127,128] In the case of *An Inconvenient Truth*, viewers also became more knowledgeable after watching the movie and, in the case of *The Day After Tomorrow*, viewers developed emotional reactions such as anxiety about climate change that strongly motivated climate action.

However, concern waned with time; neither film was particularly successful at motivating *actual* climate action. Viewers of *The Day After Tomorrow*, having recognized the film as a work of fiction, also became slightly skeptical of the likelihood of the types of extreme climate change events portrayed in the film. Nevertheless, in the final analysis of these two films, researchers concluded that any film that increases positive awareness of climate change in the general public on a large scale is beneficial. Watching films that promote climate change skepticism has the opposite effect (that is, decreasing concern about climate change), perhaps because the concern of viewers was already high, and could only decline.[129]

Films may not motivate actual behavior on their own, but as part of an educational program, they can be useful. For example, people who watched a film about someone affected by climate change and then were instructed to take that person's perspective, were subsequently more likely to take a brochure about climate change, spend longer reading the brochure, and report stronger intentions to engage in substantial climate action than participants in two other control groups.[130] Thus, the power of films lies in making climate change more immediate and salient, but moving viewers to action seems to require further engagement with them.

Crafting a climate change message. Which kinds of messages will motivate people to engage in climate action? Messages can take many forms. Sometimes those that, in-

tuitively, you would expect to be effective are not the most effective. Most energy experts, for example, believed that a financial message for energy conservation (save money by conserving energy) would be most effective, and that a normative message (conserve energy because your neighbors are doing it) would be least effective.[131] In reality, the normative message was more than three times as effective as the financial message.[132] Fortunately, telling the experts this changed their minds.[133] This was an important demonstration of how technical experts and environmental psychologists can and should work together.

Research on climate change messaging has examined three broad aspects of the communication process: the *message*, the *source* and the *audience*. The climate change message itself has probably received the most attention. Because climate change is psychologically distant, uncertain, and devoid of immediate emotion, most messaging efforts seek methods for making it more salient, certain, and emotional for the audience.

The message: reducing uncertainty. Certainty about a problem can affect how people respond to it. In commons dilemma simulations, when people are uncertain about how much of a shared resource remains in the pool, they are more likely to over-exploit the resource.[134] If even one person in a group holds a dissenting opinion, others are less likely to be convinced.[135] When people read a (fabricated) news story about ice thinning in the Arctic that included an additional paragraph about two scientists who disagreed about the cause of the thinning ice, they were significantly less convinced of the certainty of climate change than people who were not exposed to the paragraph.[136] Therefore, when news media outlets present a *debate* about the existence of climate change (when none really exists) or make statements such as "The IPCC now reports that scientists are 95% certain that climate change is happening due to human causes" followed by "skeptics point out that climate warming plateaued for a 15-year period despite rising greenhouse gas emissions," they severely damage the effectiveness of messages encouraging climate action.

Unfortunately, the nature of science is that conclusions are never absolutely certain. Some laypersons, therefore, see this lack of absolute certainty as a questionable lack of surety. For example, the 2007 IPCC report, which was carefully written by scientists, was perceived by readers as less certain than its authors intended.[137] Climate-change awareness campaigns with ambivalence risk being unsuccessful. This was the case in a Swedish campaign where, despite good intentions on the part of the government, the campaign was unable to present a coherent "story" to describe the problem and solutions, which led to a disappointing result.[138] This challenge should not be underestimated; the nature and complexity inherent in climate change can be difficult to explain simply and clearly.

Climate change certainty may be increased by presenting clear information. Deniers of global warming have argued that earth's temperatures stopped rising in 1998. This conclusion is disputed by climate scientists who point out that when temperatures from the last 120 years are taken into account, the recent plateau does not significantly change their conclusions that temperatures continue to rise. When ordinary pedestrians in Australia were shown the trend in global temperatures in a graph they, like the experts, came to the same conclusion – that temperatures would continue to rise.[139] Furthermore, when the same data was presented as "share prices" for a fictitious company, participants made the same estimation about increasing prices in the future (these predictions were free of any preconceived notions the people may have had about global warming). In some cases then, simply presenting climate change data to people can lead them to clear conclusions and increased certainty that anthropogenic climate change is occurring.

The message: emotion and salience. Does seeing a negative, fear-inducing image of hurricane damage *help* or *hurt* the climate change cause? The answer is...both. Creating an emotional connection in a climate change message is important for gaining the audience's attention, but fear-inducing images have the unfortunate effect of making message recipients feel helpless, overwhelmed and ultimately *de*-motivated to engage in climate action.[140] This may be caused by one's *belief in a just world*. Many people justify their current lifestyles and attitudes by believing that the world is a just and fair place, which leads to the belief that everyone gets what they deserve: poor people are poor because they don't work hard enough, sick people are sick because they don't take care of themselves, etc. Global warming contradicts these beliefs because its effects are severe and arbitrary. Therefore, people with a strong belief in a just world tend to respond to dire messages about climate change by discounting its importance or denying it outright.[141] This leads to a reduced motivation to act.

However, if persuasive arguments accompany messages that induce negative emotions, attitudes toward climate-related action become *more* favorable.[142] According to the *elaboration likelihood model*, people are more likely to process information if it pertains to a topic with which they are highly involved.[143] Stirring up negative emotions increases people's involvement in climate change and, consequently, motivates them to pay attention to strong arguments about it.[144]

Using messages and images that induce positive emotions may be more effective than negative emotions for encouraging climate action. Images such as wind turbines, solar panels on top of buildings, or people cycling link concerns about climate change to solutions and help motivate climate action rather than overwhelm message recipients.[145] A newly developed computer program called *carbon.to* builds on positive emotions research by presenting climate change statistics in a way that is fun and playful.[146] Although the program could benefit from further testing and research, initial users find it to be effective and useful.

Given the psychologically distant nature of climate change, sometimes simply making the problem more salient can increase concern or motivation to act. For example, showing people potential future landscapes of areas affected by climate change is a powerful way to increase concern and willingness to act.[147]

The message: promotion versus prevention. Messages that emphasize climate change *prevention* instruct recipients to act now in order to *avoid* future problems; those that emphasize *promotion* instruct people to take action in order to achieve a desirable future. The slight, but important, difference can change the way people think about taking action. Louise Comeau and I (RG) conducted a telephone survey in which the first statements emphasized positive, group-oriented motivation (e.g., "We help solve climate change when we take transit, compost, or buy green energy.") or statements that emphasized sacrifices (e.g., "I am going to have to get used to driving less, turning off the lights, and turning down the heat."). People could agree or disagree with these statements. However, merely presenting the positive-phrased statements led people to stronger intentions to engage in climate action.[148]

If recipients of the message are not very concerned about climate change, a *prevention*-focused message may be more effective. When people with less concern were shown advertisements that included the prevention-focused heading "Prevent an unhealthy natural environment," rather than the promotion-focused "Enjoy a healthier natural environment," their intention to live more sustainably and buy more environmentally friendly products increased.[149] People with greater concern responded more positively to the promotion-focused headline. This demonstrates the importance of considering one's audience when crafting a climate change communication.

The source of the message. When evaluating climate change messages, recipients look to the source of the message as an important piece of information, especially if they are not highly involved with the topic. If the source is credible, attractive, and trustworthy, the communication is given more value. When readers get climate change information from textbooks or official government documents, for instance, they find the information more trustworthy than if it comes from a newspaper or industry.[150] Companies, however, can appear more trustworthy if they appear to be arguing *against* their best interests (and have an honest reputation to begin with).[151] Some have suggested that elderly people could be good campaigners for climate action because they appear wise and concerned about future generations, and because they would achieve a sense of self-fulfillment and pride in leaving behind a positive legacy.[152]

The credibility of the source can be augmented if the source appears to represent multiple perspectives. When people read information about carbon-capture-and-storage technology, for example, the same information is judged as higher in quality if it purportedly comes from an environmental organization *in collaboration* with an oil company, than if it comes from only one of the stakeholders.[153]

Paying attention to sources matters. Individuals who read about climate change from multiple sources were more likely to understand the material if they also remembered the sources.[154] Therefore, encouraging people to attend to the material's sources may improve their ability to learn about climate change.

The message's audience. The same message will be received differently by different people. Therefore, in designing a message, many audience characteristics must be considered. For example, does a particular audience already accept the idea of climate change, or not? People who already have strong views one way or another will be more difficult to change and are unlikely to be affected by controversy in a climate change newspaper story,[155] or be affected by

the state of their immediate surroundings.[156,157] People who know relatively little about climate change are poorer consumers of information about it, and therefore are more likely to trust sources that are objectively less trustworthy; they also have difficulty separating relevant from irrelevant information.[158] As noted earlier, individuals with less concern about climate change are more persuaded by prevention-focused messages than promotion-focused messages.[159] Among those Internet users who perceive media reports on climate change to be generally exaggerated, more Internet use is associated with *decreased* knowledge, awareness, and intentions related to climate change.[160]

In the US, Republicans and people with conservative ideologies are also less likely to be susceptible to climate action messages. When people were asked to read stories about how climate change could affect the health of people, Republicans identified less with victims and were consequently less likely to support climate change policy.[161]

Trust in science and scientists are also audience factors that play a role in how climate change communications are received. When scientists make a plea for climate action, recipients of that plea are, not surprisingly, more willing to act if they trust the scientists than if they do not. Additionally, scientists are more persuasive if they tell their audience what it expects to hear: if recipients expect the scientist to merely inform them, an informational approach is more convincing; if they expect the scientist to attempt to persuade them, then a persuasive approach is more effective.[162]

Audience expectations and motivations are important factors for their comprehension of climate change. People who expect the issue to be simple do not get as much out of reading multiple texts as people who expect the issue to be complex and multi-faceted, and those who believe that one's opinions on climate change should be based on rules of inquiry and weighing multiple sources of information also comprehend the issues better after reading multiple sources.[163]

Climate change education. Teaching about climate change in school has become common practice around the world (see Figure 13-8). Resolving ambiguities and confusion about the issue at young ages may facilitate knowledge and concern later. In children, these confusions are more common than in adults. Greek, Turkish, and American children have some knowledge of climate change, but they still conflate the issue with ozone depletion,[164] and are rather unfamiliar with the potential causes of and solutions to the problem.[165-167]

Integration of climate change education into classes on non-environmental topics may be an effective way of normalizing the subject and making it part of everyday life (and perhaps influencing everyday behavior). Given that the topic is related to a wide variety of subjects, teachers have proposed integrating it into quite varying classes, such as business,[168] management,[169] and mathematics.[170] In some environment-focused university classes, the curriculum could also be improved—by adding climate change *psychology* components.[171]

Methods for teaching students about climate change range in effectiveness. As for most subjects, students learn best about climate change when they are engaged with the material. This can be achieved cognitively, by asking students to engage in discussions, consult experts, summarize climate change texts (or construct arguments based on those texts), or engage in reflective writing.[172,173] Students who are taught to think critically are more likely to believe that anthropogenic climate change is plausible than students who are taught about climate change without a critical-thinking component.[174] Engagement can also be facilitated by role-playing a mock environmental summit,[175] pitting students in multi-school negotiations,[176] or using computer-simulated climate change experiments.[177] Including cartoons in climate-change classes also has the effect of relieving boredom and getting students excited about the material.[178] In general, hands-on activities, visual aids, and experience in natural field settings provide the best environment for learning about climate change.[179-181]

Out-of-school programs can be useful for increasing students' awareness and knowledge of climate change, as well as perceived self-efficacy for potential climate action. Although some instructors suggest that environmental organizations are better off doing in-class presentations,[182] extra-curricular programs can be quite effective as well.[183-185] For example, one program in rural Uganda (an area strongly affected by climate change) successfully increased knowledge, leadership, social awareness, self-efficacy, connection to nature, political awareness, and commitment to civic action among its 16- to 24-year-old participants by using a two- to three-day field workshop in national forest settings.[186]

FIGURE 13-8 Students at Maryvale Preparatory School near Baltimore use a NASA visualization program in the classroom to better understand the galaxy and our own planet. NASA's application content reflects a strong focus on Earth science.

Denial

WHEN WE ACCEPT THAT HUMANS CAUSE CLIMATE CHANGE, we must accept that *we* are part of the problem. The idea that we may be living in a way that will lead to the demise of the world as we know it can be a tough pill to swallow, especially for those who believe in a just world, make their living by contributing to climate change, or believe that acquiring material objects makes them happy. According to cognitive dissonance theory, a person whose beliefs and behavior conflict is motivated to change one of those so that the conflict is reduced.[187] For some people, knowing that climate change is happening because of human behavior motivates them to change their behavior. For others, it motivates attitude change: they prefer to change their thoughts about climate change (toward disbelief) than to change their anti-environmental behavior.

Denial versus skepticism. Climate change deniers are not skeptics, although some use that term. True skeptics critique both sides of an argument and admit uncertainties on both sides.[188] Scientists, who deal in probabilities and degrees of uncertainty, are closer to being true skeptics than climate change "skeptics" who hold their negative beliefs in the face of overwhelming evidence to the contrary.

In general, belief in anthropogenic climate change is widespread. Belief in scientific consensus about the issue has increased, and more people seem to think that climate change is an immediate threat than earlier. However, some recent polls suggest that in recent years concern about climate has decreased[189] Between 2002 and 2008, alarmist images (e.g., that climate change will be a catastrophe) increased, but only slightly; and the use of these images declined in 2010. Americans were asked to "provide the first word, thought, image, or phrase that comes to mind when thinking about global warming" every year from 2002 to 2010.[190] "Naysayer affective images" (e.g., "hoax") increased from less than 10% in 2002 to 23% in 2010. The most common type of naysayer images were conspiracy theories ("scam," "hoax," etc.), or flat denial ("it's not happening"). One of the most common images in 2002, ice melting, was half as common in 2010 as it was 2002 (20% vs 10%).[191]

Types of Denial. Not all deniers hold the same beliefs. One researcher, who did use the term skeptics, suggested three types: Trend skeptics, attribution skeptics and impact skeptics. [192] All three deny climate change, but in slightly different ways. *Trend skeptics* deny the trend of increasing earth temperatures. *Attribution skeptics* accept the trend but attribute it to natural causes. *Impact skeptics* accept that humans cause climate change but believe the impacts will be neutral or even beneficial. Australian deniers tend to be attribution skeptics.[193] Scottish cattle farmers, who are responsible for large amounts of methane, tend much more toward impact skepticism.[194]

More recently a new form of denial may be emerging. The "non-denier denier" or "greenhouse-lite" denier[195,196] does not deny global warming outright, but denies the necessity to act. The non-denier denier is a construction of various special interest groups (such as oil and automotive companies) to discourage support for climate action.[197] These groups generally accept the science of climate change, but suggest that it is too late to change (mitigate, slow down, stop) the problem, so we should accept it

and adapt. For example, one prominent purveyor of this viewpoint[198] argues that, although anthropogenic climate change is occurring, we should assign higher priority (and funding) to other issues such as poverty, HIV, or malaria that can be solved with enough financial investment. This argument ignores that problems such as malaria and poverty are linked to climate change, that climate change may have more widespread and devastating effects than other problems, and that addressing these problems can be done while addressing climate change at the same time.

Five Strategies for Denial. Climate-change deniers use five main strategies to maintain their beliefs: *Conspiracy theories, fake experts, cherry-picking, impossible expectations*, and *logical fallacies*.[199]

Conspiracy theories about climate change tend to center on climate scientists and their motivations. If scientists have ulterior motives such as career advancement, fame, or fortune, then their scientific findings can be called into question or dismissed outright. When climate scientists' personal email communications were leaked to the public in November, 2009 (dubbed "climategate" by the media), this was exactly the sort of evidence deniers needed to confirm their theories. However, deniers took the email quotes out of context to support their theories without question. Several international committees later investigated the emails and the research, finding that they were not guilty of any wrongdoing, that their research was rigorous, and that the scientists' honesty was not in question,[200,201] but deniers continue to point to the emails as evidence of a climate change conspiracy.

Fake experts are cited by climate-change deniers to show that no scientific consensus about climate change exists. These "experts" are not actually experts at all, but individuals with opinions about climate change that have written books or published articles on the subject without a background in climate science, meteorology, or geography (often with a conspicuous lack of evidence for their cases, or supported by articles written by other fake experts). Fake experts are created by interest groups (e.g., conservative organizations, media, Republican politicians, and contrarian scientists) in order to affect public perception of debate.[202- 203 204] One commonly cited petition supposedly shows that 31,000 scientists reject the science behind the theory of anthropogenic climate change.[205] However, a closer look reveals that this petition contains signatures by anyone with a bachelor of science degree (computer science, mechanical engineering, zoology, etc.) and only 0.1% of the signatories are actual climate scientists.

Cherry-picking refers to deniers' tendency to accept only the small number of studies (or parts of studies) that cast doubt on climate science while ignoring the massive collection of studies that support it. For example, one published study suggested that the famous "hockey stick" graph showing that global warming has increased dramatically in the past 100 years compared to the previous 900 years was calculated using flawed statistics.[206,207] Deniers point to this single study as proof that anthropogenic global warming is not occurring despite the appearance of several later peer-reviewed climate studies that have found similar temperature trends.[208] Other commonly cited pieces of "denial evidence" have also been disconfirmed by peer-reviewed research. These include "global warming stopped in 1998," "the sun is responsible for global warming," and that "global warming is good."[209] The scientific method requires working with probabilities rather than certainty and involves some critique and disagreement among researchers in order to move forward. Thus, some research will appear that disagrees with or changes parts of the greater premise, but evaluating the overall weight of evidence, rather than cherry-picking, is the only way to obtain an understanding that is closest to the truth.

Impossible expectations of what research can deliver enable climate change deniers to avoid taking action. For example, deniers hold the idea that climate models are unreliable—"How can meteorologists predict what will happen in 20 years when they can't predict the weather next week?" This is a conflation of the terms *weather* and *climate*. Specific weather patterns are difficult to predict, but climate (average temperatures over long periods) is more easily and accurately predicted. Climate models from 20 years ago do not map on to current observed climate patterns *perfectly*, but they do correspond closely enough to be considered more than coincidental.[210]

Logical fallacies are raised by deniers to explain why anthropogenic climate change is not occurring. The most common is that climate has changed in the past because of natural processes; it must therefore be occurring again for the same reasons.[211] Climate scientists do not deny that natural processes contribute to climate change, but after these natural processes are accounted for, a great deal of climate change is still best explained by human causes.

Correlates of, and Reasons for, Denial. The denial of anthropogenic climate change is correlated with various demographic factors, values, and beliefs.[212] The Scottish cattle farmers mentioned earlier are motivated to deny climate change because they contribute methane to the atmosphere and might prefer to maintain their beliefs rather than change their behaviors. However, some do *not* deny the problem: those who have experience, values, or education that convinced them otherwise.[213] Similarly, Australians' climate change denial is associated with low levels of pro-environmental behavior, conservative political orientation, external locus of responsibility ("I didn't cause the problem"), negative cognitive evaluations of responding to climate change (e.g., "Responding to climate change will cost a lot of money"), and lack of perceived moral duty to act.[214]

Personal values and beliefs are key predictors of climate change denial. In addition to having a lower felt obligation to act, weaker general environmental values, and stronger economic values,[215,216] climate change deniers are more likely to believe in free-market ideology, have more environmental apathy, weaker beliefs that their behavior can make a difference, and less ecocentrism (i.e., nature-centered systems of values).[217] People who are generally contrarian and believe in such conspiracy theories as a faked NASA moon landing or that HIV does not cause AIDS are also more likely to deny climate change.[218]

But why do people go to such great lengths to deny climate change? One theory about the root causes of climate change denial is system justification.[219] According to this idea, people are motivated to defend and justify the status quo because it helps them to maintain a sense of certainty and stability, provides a feeling of safety, and allows them to relate to others within the same social system. People who benefit from the status quo are especially likely to engage in system justification because they want to feel that they deserve what they have. When the status quo is challenged, as climate change does, people are more likely to deny that information; it is easier to deny climate change than to admit that they might need to change their lifestyle and values. System justification may be the reason why males, conservatives, and people with strong national patriotism are more likely to deny climate change.[220-222]

Communicating with Deniers. Deniers pay attention to and are influenced by media that reinforce their beliefs, as do many other people. Unfortunately, the media deniers attend to generally are not credible sources interested in disseminating the truth about climate change. Denial of climate change in the public sphere has increased in recent years as a direct result of concerted efforts by stakeholders and lobby groups who have a vested interest in preventing action to deal with climate change.[223-225]

Changing the opinions of entrenched climate change deniers is more difficult than convincing someone who is merely uninformed or apathetic about the issue. However, some have tried to solve this problem. The most promising avenue, perhaps surprisingly, involves system justification. If climate action can be framed in a way that *supports* the status quo rather than rejects it,[226] that argument has a better chance of being accepted by deniers. For example, framing an appeal for climate action as "patriotic" may be an effective way of using *system justification* to promote climate-positive attitudes.[227]

Climate change denial is less likely to occur when people feel good about themselves. When people think about the kind deeds they have done for others, they are less likely to deny climate change.[228] They also tend to take more personal responsibility for climate change and put less responsibility exclusively on big business or stakeholders. Therefore, messages that remind deniers of their better social moments may be effective.

If changing *behavior* of deniers, rather than their attitudes, is the goal of a communication, then suggesting non-climate-related reasons for behavior may be the most effective approach. In a large online survey of Dutch citizens, researchers found that people who denied climate change were unlikely to support the idea of eating less meat if it were presented as a "climate protective" action.[229] The researchers propose that perhaps some climate actions should be presented as beneficial for non-environmental reasons (e.g., health or cost).

IN SUM *Climate change psychology is the study of how humans understand climate change, as well as motivation for human behavior that contributes to climate change, prevents climate change or adapts to climate change. It is studied using qualitative, survey, and experimental methods. Although knowledge, awareness, and belief in climate change have increased over recent years, this has not always translated into increases in climate-positive action. Individual differences affect*

perceptions of climate change. For example, experts perceive climate change differently (and support different climate action policies) than most others, and conservatives are least likely to believe that anthropogenic climate change is happening. One reason that climate change risk perception is lower than it should be is that the risk is psychologically distant. When climate change is experienced directly or through films, perceptions of risk increase. Changing climate change attitudes and behaviors can be accomplished through communication and education. Effective climate change communication considers the message itself, source of the message, and the different audiences for the message.

DEALING WITH THE IMPACTS OF CLIMATE CHANGE

CLIMATE CHANGE HAS FAR-REACHING PHYSICAL EFFECTS that create psychological and community impacts. For example, one direct effect will be to make some plant and animal species extinct. Climate change also results in more extreme weather events, and therefore communities and individuals will have to deal with the social and psychological outcomes of those hazards (as in Figure 13-9, for example). Droughts and floods may lead to increased competition and consequent racism and intergroup violence. If climate change causes the destruction of homes or communities, forcing people to relocate, then the experience of losing the place to which they are attached will be stressful. This section presents research that addresses the psychological and social impacts of climate change.

Psychological and Social Impacts

THE EFFECTS OF CLIMATE CHANGE ARE MORE THAN PHYSICAL. Environmental psychologists have identified three types of climate change impacts: direct (acute or traumatic), indirect (uncertainty and threats of future problems), and psychosocial (community and post-disaster adjustment).[230] As an example at the interpersonal level, when people are asked to think about the consequences of climate change, they tend to become more conservative in their thinking, and this affects their perception of others.[231] They engage in more system justification, develop more authoritarian attitudes, and are more likely to derogate criminals.

At the community level, people who are well-off and well-prepared *before* climate-related events occur experience smaller impacts, and they cope and adapt better.[232] Unfortunately, this means that climate change causes the disparity between "haves" and "have-nots" to increase. For example, across 158 countries, poor countries were hit harder than rich ones by climate change, and rich people in poor countries were still able to live long lives.[233] Therefore, an important goal for environmental psychologists and policy-makers is to promote resiliency and empowerment, especially among poorer citizens, to provide treatment for acute issues and to introduce policies to deal with the effects of climate change.[234]

Crime and unrest. Environmental psychologists have documented an association between heat and aggressive behavior, as we saw in an earlier chapter. An increase in temperature caused by climate change may be an important additional cause of aggression: some estimate that assaults and murders in the United States might increase by at least 24,000 per year following an increase of only a few degrees in the average temperature.[235]

The physical effects of climate change seem to make people more likely to break the law because it causes both increased strain on individuals and more opportunities to commit crimes.[236] It also leads to reduced social control, reduced social support, and increased social conflict because community members become more desperate for scarce resources. Climate change even seems to foster more favorable attitudes toward crime and increase individuals' criminal traits.[237] Indeed, US intelligence services have publicly discussed the impending security threats that climate change may bring.[238]

Mental health. The stress induced by climate change can be a factor in depression, anxiety, and even suicide.[239,240] Suicide rates in Australia and Italy are mildly correlated with hot temperatures, particularly for males.[241,242] Older Australian farmers and indigenous peoples, who already must cope with significant daily stress, suffer more mental

FIGURE 13−9 Landslide damage in Honduras, in the aftermath of Hurricane Mitch. The hurricane caused more than 9,000 deaths, and 9,000 were left missing, making it one of the most deadly hurricanes in history.

health problems related to climate change.[243-245] Like Inuit communities in Canada,[246] these groups experience a significant sense of loss when their local landscape changes, leading to inability to survive using traditional methods.

The effects of flooding, extreme weather, infectious diseases, droughts and famine are the likely causes of most mental health problems,[247,248] but they may be minimized by effective policies and social preparedness. The excessive number of deaths in France's unprecedented 2003 heat wave, for example, were largely a result of socioeconomic vulnerability.[249] Not surprisingly then, mental health professionals suggest educating people about the potential consequences of climate change.[250]

Positive impacts. Not all the impacts are negative. In the face of climate change, a few psychological benefits can emerge. One is that climate change can be viewed as a shared problem that groups must work together to solve.[251] Bringing up a local catastrophe caused by climate change among Arab Israelis reduced support for war and increased support for peaceful reconciliation. Feelings of shared humanity and possible mortality can trump thoughts of war and conflict.[252] Working together to prevent climate change also has the positive effect of facilitating collective engagement and the positive emotions that go along with it,[253,254] including increasing self-efficacy beliefs, social competence, and a sense of civic responsibility.[255]

followed by appraisals of the stressor and pre-response interpretations and motivations. Two types of appraisals occur: *threat appraisal*, in which people try to determine how serious or harmful the stressor or problem is, and *coping appraisal*, in which people try to figure out what they can do about the problem. At the same time (before responding), people experience several "pre-response" interpretations and motivations: *affect* (emotions such as worry, fear or anxiety), *attribution* ("Did I cause the problem and am I responsible for fixing it?"), and *motivation* (such as wanting to reduce uncertainty about the problem). This is followed by *intra-individual responses* (such as emotion regulation or denial), and *behavioral responses* (such as seeking information, talking to people, or taking action). All of these can be either constructive or destructive, and together they result in positive or negative impacts on the individual and community, which then feed back to inform the individual's reappraisals of the problem.

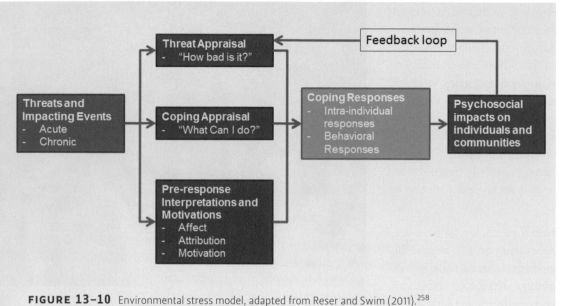

FIGURE 13–10 Environmental stress model, adapted from Reser and Swim (2011).[258]

Coping and Adapting to Climate Change

WHETHER OR NOT PEOPLE BELIEVE that climate change is occurring, many are already dealing with its effects. How people respond to these effects can affect their psychological well-being. Two important reactions are *coping* and *adapting*. Coping is how one responds to an impact over a fairly short time period, and adaptation is dealing with change that one has experienced, or is expecting to experience, over a longer duration.[256]

Climate change is a stressor—it causes events and circumstances that, if not alleviated, can evoke stress reactions that are harmful to physical and mental health. Stress and coping have traditionally been examined in relation to health, but environmental psychologists have created a stress and coping model as they relate to climate change[257] (see Figure 13-10).

Climate change-caused stressors such as acute events (e.g., a hurricane) or chronic events (e.g., a drought) are

At each step in the model, certain factors can influence how people will respond. Among these are characteristics of individuals (their resilience, sensitivity, or optimism), characteristics of the stressor or physical environment (how harmful it actually is), and characteristics of the community (e.g., the social capital of the community). For example, when considering rising sea levels, people who live in coastal communities probably think and act differently than others who live inland.

The physical environment plays an obvious role in *threat appraisal* depending on the magnitude of the event. However, if individuals believe they can take actions that will mitigate the problem (i.e., they have stronger self-efficacy beliefs), then their *coping appraisal* may compensate for the perception of the problem as a dangerous threat. Furthermore, if the community itself is supportive of its members, then the threat may evoke more positive pre-response interpretations and motivations (e.g., less anxiety and more motivation to take action). The sum of these (sometimes contrasting) appraisals, interpretations ,and motivations will determine each individual's response to the threat and, thus, their overall ability to cope with and adapt to climate-related events.[259]

Types of Coping. Eight types of psychological coping strategies for dealing with the *idea* of climate change have been identified.[260] These are:

- Expression of emotions (coping by expressing emotions such as mourning or anger),

- Problem solving (cognitions and actions that focus on the problem to be solved, including acquiring knowledge or social support),

- The denial of guilt (coping by refusing to acknowledge responsibility),

- Relativization (coping by minimizing the problem),

- Self-protection (changing behavior to focus on personal health),

- Pleasure (coping by concentrating on the pleasure-producing value of the endangered environment),

- Wishful thinking (coping by thinking of alternative solutions, based on hope and anticipation of a positive outcome), and

- Resignation (coping by accepting the situation as it is, and believing that conditions cannot be changed).

These strategies fall into two overarching styles. Emotional expression, problem solving, and self-protection are considered *problem-focused* coping strategies because they are proactive and take action to deal with the psychological impacts of thinking about climate change. Denial, relativization, and pleasure are considered *de-problematization-focused* coping strategies because they involve downplaying or avoiding of the problem.

In a similar taxonomy, three climate change coping strategies were proposed: *meaning-focused coping* (also known as emotion-focused coping, in which individuals reappraise the problem to deal with the stress constructively), *problem-focused coping* (in which individuals search for information about what they can do and act on it), and *de-emphasizing the seriousness* of climate change (in which they ignore the problem).[261] People tend to use them differently at different stages of life: children tend to use

problem-focused coping less, and de-emphasizing more for dealing with the worry generated by climate change than young adults, and they develop hope from trusting in experts and technological development more than young adults do.[262]

Although problem-focused coping often can be a healthy way of dealing with stress, the young people who used problem-focused coping were more likely to worry and those who used meaning-focused coping were happier, more optimistic, and more satisfied with life,[263] probably because problem-focused coping is not very effective for dealing with uncontrollable stressors. Interestingly, those who engaged in meaning-focused coping were more likely to take climate action than those who de-emphasized the threat. According to these studies, therefore, coping with climate change may be different than coping with other stressors.

Adaptation to climate change is improved through preparedness and, unfortunately, some of the worst-affected and most vulnerable areas in the world are the least prepared and poorest equipped to deal with the problem. Along the River Meghna in Bangladesh, for instance, residents with the greatest risk of flooding from climate change are also those with the lowest incomes and poorest access to community assets. Thus, they are least prepared at the individual and community levels, and least likely to successfully adapt or cope with eventual flooding.[264]

IN SUM *Climate change impacts may be direct, indirect, or psychosocial. Its influence in raising temperatures even a few degrees may lead to more crime and more mental health problems. However, working together to mitigate climate change can also have some positive psychological benefits. Coping and adapting to climate change occurs after threat appraisals, coping appraisals and pre-response interpretations and motivations. Numerous types of coping have been identified, some of which are healthier than others. The negative consequences of climate change to humans may be mitigated by effective preparation, policies and adaptation, but the poorest and least-prepared populations are, unfortunately, also the most likely to bear the brunt of the problem.*

IF CLIMATE CHANGE IS POTENTIALLY THE GREATEST THREAT TO HUMANITY, why aren't people doing everything they can to stop it? Why do people continue to consume instead of conserving energy and resources? How can we apply psychological research to get people to change their behavior and live more sustainably? These questions will be addressed in the final section of this chapter.

Psychological Barriers to Climate Action

BARRIERS TO BEHAVIOR CHANGE can be structural or psychological. Structural barriers are generally outside of a person's immediate control. For example, a structural barrier could be the physical environment ("I can't take public transport because it doesn't exist where I live."), or a person's financial situation ("I can't install solar panels because the up-front costs are too high."). Nevertheless, most people who are not severely restricted by structural barriers could be doing more to reduce their carbon footprint. Behavior change by these people is inhibited by *psychological barriers*.

Psychological barriers to climate action, which I (RG) call the *dragons of inaction*, can be divided into seven basic genera: Limited cognition, ideologies, other people, sunk costs, discredence, perceived risk, and limited behavior.[265]

Limited cognition. Many people lack a full understanding of climate change and, rather than leading them to use caution, this unfortunately results in continuing in some destructive behaviors. This genus of dragon includes *ignorance* (not knowing about the problem), *uncertainty* (being unsure about the problem and its consequences), *environmental numbness* (being unaware of or bored with hearing about what is happening with the climate), and *judgmental discounting* (seeing the problem as less important because it is psychologically distant). These may all be related to another dragon within this genus: that we have an *ancient brain* (which evolved to pay attention to immediate and present events). Limited cognition also includes weak *self-efficacy* and *optimism bias* (a tendency to think that everything will work out fine, even if we do not change our behavior).

Ideologies. These dragons include overarching beliefs about the world as a whole that influence climate change beliefs as a part of a whole worldview. They include beliefs about social and economic systems such as the belief that free-market capitalism is the best economic system, *system justification* (the belief that the status quo is best, as explained earlier), that outside powers can save humanity (such as *religious powers* or Mother Nature), and *technosalvation* (engineers will invent technological solutions to the problem).

Other people. As social animals, humans are strongly influenced by others we like or admire. If those others are not acting sustainably, then we are less likely act sustainably. This happens through the processes of *social comparison* (observing others to learn the proper course of action) and *perceived inequity* ("it's unfair if I'm the only one who changes"). Other people also influence us through *social norms and networks* (if people in our social network behave unsustainably, then we are more likely to do the same).

Sunk costs. People who have some investment in unsustainable behavior find changing this behavior difficult. This dragon genus includes *financial investments*, such as owning oil stock or a car, which makes driving more likely. This is related to another sunk cost, *behavioral momentum* (habit). Habitual behaviors make life easier because they require relatively little brain power to carry out, and this is precisely what makes them difficult to change. Habitual behaviors that produce excessive greenhouse gas emissions are difficult dragons to slay. Another dragon, *conflicting values, goals and aspirations*, can prevent behavior change when pro-environmental ideas take a back seat to other goals (e.g., "I want to drive less…but I want to save time."). Finally, when people do not feel *place attachment* to where they live, they may be less likely to engage in pro-environmental behavior to save or enhance it.

Discredence. The fourth dragon genus involves viewing experts or authorities in an excessively negative light. This can take the form of *mistrust* (e.g., not believing that scientists or policy-makers are dependable sources of accurate information) and *denial* (e.g., refusing to accept evidence supporting climate change). Discredence can also include negative responses to opportunities for action such as *perceived program inadequacy* (e.g., not wanting to participate in climate action programs because they are perceived as ineffective), or *reactance* (doing the opposite of what's asked as a response to perceived infringement on one's freedom).

Perceived risk. Any behavior change involves some degree of risk, and climate-positive behaviors are no different. If the perceived risks of some pro-climate action outweigh its perceived benefits, then people are less likely to change. Six types of risks associated with adopting a new behavior have been identified: *functional* (e.g., "Will an electric vehicle strand me on my way to work because the battery runs out?"), *physical* (e.g., "I feel less safe biking than driving."), *financial* (e.g., the initial costs of new solar panels are known, but the long-term savings are unknown), *social* (e.g., driving a sports car is cooler than taking the bus), *psychological* (e.g., lower self-esteem or self-confidence as a consequence of taking the bus), and *temporal* (e.g., time lost to investigating the feasibility of some change if it might not work out).

Limited behavior. The final genus of climate action dragon does not involve complete inaction, but rather not enough action. The two species of dragon in this genus are *tokenism* (engaging a small action and then believing that no further action is necessary because "I've done enough."), and the *rebound effect* ("Honey, I bought a hybrid, let's drive to Alaska."). The rebound effect is rewarding yourself in a net climate-negative way for having made a small climate-positive decision.

Encouraging Individual Climate Action

PEOPLE CAN ENGAGE IN MANY DIFFERENT PRO–ENVIRONMENTAL BEHAVIORS. Some conserve natural resources (e.g., recycling), others prevent water pollution (e.g., buying biodegradable soap), or minimize environmental toxins (e.g., buying organic food). Behaviors that specifically count as *climate action* behaviors include driving less, purchasing locally produced products, installing solar panels, taking shorter showers, changing eating habits, turning off unused appliances, and many others. The list is so long that,

FIGURE 13–11 Damage to New Jersey coastal communities in the aftermath of Hurricane Sandy, 2012.

for many environmental psychologists, climate action *is* pro-environmental behavior. Therefore, this section will describe theories of general pro-environmental behavior, because they apply to most climate actions, and interventions that target specific climate actions. These fall into two main categories: individualistic theories and altruistic theories.[266]

Individualistic and altruistic theories. Individualistic approaches emphasize pro-environmental behavior as a result of self-relevant motives, that is, because they think they have something to gain. One example is the operant conditioning approach, which suggests that people increase behaviors that are rewarded and decrease behaviors that are punished.[267] If laws reward pro-environmental behavior and punish anti-environmental behavior, then people should learn to behave pro-environmentally. For example, financial incentives (rewards) and disincentives (punishments) can change household energy consumption behaviors and therefore reduce greenhouse gas emissions.[268,269] In Switzerland, perceived costs and benefits are the strongest predictors of willingness to take climate action and to support climate policy measures.[270]

A second example of individualistic theory is the theory of planned behavior,[271] which was introduced in an earlier chapter. According to this theory, intentions are the best predictors of behavior, and they are, in turn, predicted by attitudes about the behavior (thoughts and feelings), subjective norms (perceptions of others' support for, and engagement in, the behavior), and perceived behavioral control over the behavior (difficulty of engaging in the behavior).

The theory of planned behavior has been used to explain general pro-environmental behavior and specific climate actions. For example, *intentions* to recycle, carpool, and conserve energy are predictable from one's attitudes, subjective norms, and perceived behavioral control.[272] In one experiment, changing attitudes by inducing fear of future climate change consequences or changing perceived behavioral control by inducing perceptions of group efficacy increased climate action intentions.[273]

In particular, attitudes toward climate action have been studied extensively as predictors of intentions to act. For example, attitudes about the power of different climate actions to have an impact affect intentions. If people believe their actions will have a strong impact on climate change, they are more likely to intend to engage in them.[274,275]

Pro-environmental actions are often taken even if the action has no direct benefit for the person. For example, to save old-growth forests, many people sign petitions or participate in protests without any benefit to themselves, and some have even gone to jail for their efforts. Such behaviors are not well-explained by individualistic theories; these might be called altruistic theories.

Altruistic theories propose that pro-environmental behavior is motivated by values that transcend individuals' concerns with their own interests. For example, behavior may be a product of environmental consciousness,[276,277] prosocial moral norms,[278] self-transcendent values,[279] or a positive social value orientation.[280] People who think that climate change is an important issue are more willing to sacrifice to protect the environment.[281]

The line between altruistic and individualistic theories, however, is often blurred. In one theory of pro-environmental behavior, taking climate action is similar to helping a stranger in need; altruistic motivations interact with individualistic motivations. An individual must (1) notice the problem, (2) interpret it as an emergency, (3) take responsibility, (4) overcome barriers to action (such as the dragons described earlier), and (5) weigh the costs of action against the benefits.[282] In another theory, having a "green identity" predicts engaging in climate action. People with green identities see the environment as part of their self-concept and therefore take action to protect it.[283-284]

[285] Whether these people engage in climate action for altruistic or individualistic reasons is debatable.

Interestingly, some of the most impactful climate actions, such as reduced car use, are not motivated by environmental values. People may ride their bikes, for example, not because they are trying to mitigate climate change by driving less, but because they are trying to stay healthy or save money.[286] Other climate-friendly behaviors, such as eating less meat or purchasing an electric vehicle, are often motivated by financial or health concerns rather than pro-environmental values.[287,288] Of course, that is fine: the actions are still helping the environment, even if the motivation is not environmental. Thus, when encouraging pro-environmental behavior, environmental psychologists consider people's already-held values and tailor an intervention to match those values. For example, your conservative friend who thinks that climate change is a big hoax might be interested in saving money. You would be wise to tell your friend how much money will be saved by getting a bike, without mentioning the environment once.

Interventions to encourage climate action. Given that individuals are motivated by a variety of pro-environmental and non-environmental values, and that their social, economic, and geographic situations may differ greatly, no single intervention can be considered the "gold standard" or best intervention available. Climate action interventions should be designed for certain individuals in specific situations doing particular behaviors, and they should be tested before being implemented.[289] Some of the major approaches employ information, feedback, financial incentives, and social influence.

The most common approach for encouraging climate action is to inform people about the problem. This approach works best when targeting individuals who might not know about climate change (e.g., they are held back by the *limited cognition* dragon). Information campaigns have been used to reduce household energy use[290] and change travel mode choices,[291] among others.

However, information alone is typically not enough for most people to encourage climate action. Information is useful for increasing climate change knowledge, belief, and concern, but this is often not accompanied by action. Action is more likely if people are actively engaged in the material. For example, using a guided group discussion, in which group members are encouraged to actively discuss the value of climate action rather than simply listening to a lecture, can encourage them to turn off unused lights in public buildings.[292] Similarly, merely watching a climate change film is not as effective for encouraging climate action as asking viewers to watch the film and then take the perspective of climate change victims within the film.[293] For people who are already "on-board" with climate change, information delivered as a sign in an appropriate location (e.g., "please turn off the lights" above a light switch) may be enough to trigger climate action.[294]

A second strategy involves feeding information back to people about the impact of their choices. When people are uncertain about their impact, they tend to believe that they are acting appropriately, even when they are not. Accurate feedback reduces uncertainty and shows individuals their true impact. Often this is enough to trigger climate-friendly action; when feedback about energy use was provided to households, they reduced their energy use by 5% to 12%.[295]

If feedback is to be effective, it should be presented immediately after the behavior so that the person clearly sees the link between behavior and energy use, and is more likely to change behavior. Therefore, monthly utility bills are not particularly effective forms of feedback, and so this intervention strategy requires some technological advances and investment (e.g., small displays in the kitchen or elsewhere that residents spend much time, so they will see their energy usage). Real-time feedback devices available to retail consumers already exist and, in some regions, residential dwellings are also now equipped with "smart meters" that allow customers to see their daily electricity use online.[296,297] These advances make the feedback strategy more feasible than it once was.

A third approach, based on operant conditioning, involves awarding financial incentives for climate-positive choices that make the behavior more likely to recur. Financial incentives may include rewards for decreasing energy use, reducing electricity prices at peak times, and providing rebates for investment in household energy efficiency.[298, 299]

Financial incentives can be very effective but they have disadvantages: (a) their costs may be high, possibly so high that the intervention is not worth the benefits it brings, (b) among people who are motivated only by financial rewards, climate-positive behavior will cease when the reward is removed, and (c) money is sometimes spent rewarding people who were already willing to engage in the action for altruistic reasons. Nevertheless, combining financial incentives with other interventions can improve effectiveness and increase climate action.[300,301]

Fourth, some interventions involve social motives and interactions. We are social animals. Public sector employees with strong pro-environmental values, for example, often will only accept climate change policies if there is also a social norm of acceptance.[302] Social interventions involve setting norms or making people aware of existing norms. Significant others become the focus and are particularly useful for overcoming the "other people" dragon of inaction. These interventions are appealing because they have the potential to be self-perpetuating, less expensive, and more enduring.

Social interventions can include techniques such as interviewing members of a community and tailoring a pro-environmental campaign to that community,[303] involving real-life social networks,[304] or involving virtual social networks.[305] The presence of others often can make people feel more accountable and therefore increase the likelihood of reducing energy use. In a related approach, getting people to make a public commitment to reduce energy can result in increased conservation.[306–308]

When admired others, or even just peers, model energy conservation, for example, onlookers are influenced to join in and engage in those behaviors, too.[309,310] Seeing people engage in pro-environmental behavior has the effect of making that behavior seem acceptable (like a norm) and it has the bonus effect of showing people *how* to do the behavior; both of which increase the likelihood of action. Leading by example and *being the change you want to see* can make an important difference.

IN SUM *Climate action may be inhibited by seven categories of psychological barriers, or encouraged by individualistic or altruistic motivations. Several theories explain why people choose to engage in positive climate action. Information, feedback, financial incentives and social interventions have all been used to engage people in climate action. Each of these interventions has benefits and drawbacks. Policy changes will be most effective if they consider the psychological drivers of climate-related behavior discussed in this chapter.*

SUMMARY

CURRENT GLOBAL WARMING is largely caused by human consumption choices such as the way we eat, the choice of products we buy and the ways we choose to travel. The greenhouse gases produced by the processes associated with these choices already affect the planet and the people living on it. Climate change psychology is the study of how we perceive climate change, cope with or adapt to it, or encourage action to mitigate it. Each of these facets can be studied using surveys, polls, qualitative methods, experiments, or behavioral observations. Climate change awareness, belief, knowledge and concern are not always related. One can be knowledgeable or aware without being concerned, and belief, knowledge or concern may not always translate into action. Perceptions of risks from climate change may be related to experiencing the problem directly or becoming emotional about it. Therefore, successful climate change communications facilitate an emotional response and make the problem seem immediate and certain. The small percentage of people who deny climate change use a variety of techniques to maintain their denial in the face of strong supporting evidence. Couching climate action in terms of values that are important to the denier (or using non-environmental justifications entirely) may be the best method to encourage deniers to take action. The physical effects of climate change (droughts, extreme weather, etc.) bring with them a host of psychological and social impacts. Those who are better prepared for these effects will suffer reduced impacts. However, the best prepared are usually the wealthiest, and climate change is likely to have the harshest effects on the poorest areas of the world. People may fail to take climate action because at least seven categories of psychological barriers prevent them from doing so. Encouraging climate action requires addressing the barriers that are present in a particular situation. Some popular and effective interventions include social, incentive, feedback, and information interventions. The theories underlying these interventions may be individualistic, altruistic, or a combination of both. Climate change is a large, daunting and potentially devastating problem to deal with, but if we understand why it is a problem and how to encourage individual action to solve it, we *can* make a difference. Denying the problem won't make it go away, but changing our behavior will help to minimize its human and biospheric damage.

Suggested Supplementary Readings

Berners-Lee, M. (2011). *How bad are bananas? The carbon footprint of everything.* Berkeley, CA: Greystone.

CRED (2009). *The psychology of climate change communication: A guide for scientists, journalists, educators, political aides, and the interested public.* New York, NY: Center for Research on Environmental Decisions.

Gifford, R., Kormos, C., & McIntyre, A. (2011). *Behavioral dimensions of climate change: Drivers, responses, barriers, and interventions.* WIREs Climate Change. Doi 10.1002/wcc.143

Swim, J. (Ed.). (2011). Special issue: Psychology and global climate change. *American Psychologist, 66,* 241–328.

Washington, H. (2011). *Climate change denial: Heads in the sand.* New York, NY: Taylor & Francis.

References

1 IPCC. (2007). *Climate Change 2007* (Assessment No. 4). Cambridge, UK and New York, USA: Cambridge University Press.

2 IPCC. (2007). *Climate Change 2007* (Assessment No. 4). Cambridge, UK and New York, USA: Cambridge University Press.

3 Nisbet, M. C., & Myers, T. (2007). The polls—trends: Twenty years of public opinion about global warming. *Public Opinion Quarterly, 71,* 444-470.

4 Kilinç, A., Boyes, E., & Stanisstreet, M. (2011). Turkish school students and global warming: Beliefs and willingness to act. *Eurasia Journal of Mathematics, Science & Technology Education, 7,* 121-134.

5 Santos, M. A. O. D. (2012). Investigating consumer knowledge of global warming based on Rogers' knowledge stage of the innovation decision process. *International Journal of Consumer Studies, 36,* 385-393.

6 Mann, M. E., Zhang, Z., Hughes, M. K., Bradley, R. S., Miller, S. K., Rutherford, S., & Ni, F. (2008). Proxy-based reconstructions of hemispheric and global surface temperature variations over the past two millennia. *Proceedings of the National Academy of Sciences, 105,* 13252-13257.

7 Mann, M. E., Zhang, Z., Hughes, M. K., Bradley, R. S., Miller, S. K., Rutherford, S., & Ni, F. (2008). Proxy-based reconstructions of hemispheric and global surface temperature variations over the past two millennia. *Proceedings of the National Academy of Sciences, 105,* 13252-13257.

8 IPCC. (2007). *Climate Change 2007* (Assessment No. 4). Cambridge, UK and New York, USA: Cambridge University Press.

9 IEA. (2011). *International Energy Agency: Climate and electricity annual data and analyses.* France: International Energy Agency.

10 IEA. (2013). *International Energy Agency: Key world energy statistics 2013.* France: International Energy Agency.

11 Steinfeld, H., Gerber, P., Wassenaar, T., Castel, V., Rosales, M., & de Haan, C. (2006). *Livestock's long shadow: Environmental Issues and Options.* Rome, Italy: Food and agriculture organization of the United Nations.

12 Lewis, S. L., Lopez-Gonzalez, G., Sonké, B., Affum-Baffoe, K., Baker, T. R., Ojo, L. O., Phillips, O. L., Reitsma, J. M., White, L., & Comiskey, J. A. (2009). Increasing carbon storage in intact African tropical forests. *Nature, 457,* 1003-1006.

13 FAO. (2012). *State of the World's Forests 2012.* Rome, Italy: Food and Agriculture Organization of the UN.

14 UN. (1992). *Rio declaration on environment and development.* Retrieved 11/28, 2013, from http://www.un.org/documents/ga/conf151/aconf15126-1annex1.htm

15 UN. (1992). *Rio declaration on environment and development.* Retrieved 11/28, 2013, from http://www.un.org/documents/ga/conf151/aconf15126-1annex1.htm

16 IEA. (2013). *International Energy Agency: Key world energy statistics 2013.* France: International Energy Agency.

17 Boden, T. A., Marland, G., & Andres, R. J. (2008). *U.S. Department of Energy: Global, Regional, and National Fossil-Fuel CO2 Emissions.* Oak Ridge, Tennessee: Carbon Dioxide Information Analysis Center.

18 Dai, A. (2011). Drought under global warming: A review. *Wiley Interdisciplinary Reviews: Climate Change, 2,* 45-65.

19 Easterbrook, G. (2007). Global warming: Who loses—and who wins? *Atlantic Monthly, 199,* 52-64.

20 Carroll, A. L., Taylor, S. W., Régnière, J., & Safranyik, L. (2003). Effect of climate change on range expansion by the mountain pine beetle in British Columbia. *Pages 223-232 in TL Shore Et Al.(Eds) Mountain Pine Beetle Symposium: Challenges and Solutions, Oct. 30-31, 2003. Kelowna BC. Natural Resources Canada, Infromation Report BC-X-399, Victoria, Canada.*

21 IPCC. (2007). *Climate Change 2007* (Assessment No. 4). Cambridge, UK and New York, USA: Cambridge University Press.

22 IPCC. (2007). *Climate Change 2007* (Assessment No. 4). Cambridge, UK and New York, USA: Cambridge University Press.

23 Poumadère, M., Mays, C., Le Mer, S., & Blong, R. (2005). The 2003 heat wave in France: Dangerous climate change here and now. *Risk Analysis, 25,* 1483-1494.

24 Nisbet, M. C., & Myers, T. (2007). The polls—trends: Twenty years of public opinion about global warming. *Public Opinion Quarterly, 71,* 444-470.

25 Gifford, R., & Comeau, L. A. (2011). Message framing influences perceived climate change competence, engagement, and behavioral intentions. *Global Environmental Change, 21,* 1301-1307.

26 Islam, M. M., Barnes, A., & Toma, L. (2013). An investigation into climate change skepticism among farmers. *Journal of Environmental Psychology, 34,* 137-150.

27 Dijkstra, E. M., & Goedhart, M. J. (2012). Development and validation of the ACSI: Measuring students' science attitudes, pro-environmental behaviour, climate change attitudes and knowledge. *Environmental Education Research, 18,* 733-749.

28 Lazo, J. K., Kinnell, J., & Fisher, A. (2000). Expert and layperson perceptions of ecosystem risk. *Risk Analysis, 20,* 179-193.

29 Clark, C. F., Kotchen, M. J., & Moore, M. R. (2003). Internal and external influences on pro-environmental behavior: Participation in a green electricity program. *Journal of Environmental Psychology, 23,* 237-246.

30 Homburg, A., Stolberg, A., & Wagner, U. (2007). Coping with global environmental problems: Development and first validation of scales. *Environment and Behavior, 39,* 754-778.

31 Norton, T., Sias, P., & Brown, S. (2011). Experiencing and managing uncertainty about climate change. *Journal of Applied Communication Research, 39,* 290-309.

32 Kirilenko, A., Stepchenkova, S., Romsdahl, R., & Mattis, K. (2012). Computer-assisted analysis of public discourse: A case study of the precautionary principle in the US and UK press. *Quality & Quantity: International Journal of Methodology, 46,* 501-522.

33 Smith, J. (2…
sion makin…
Analysis, 25, …

34 Carvalho, A…
cuits of clim…
papers, 1985…

35 McComas, …
stories abou…
the impact…
Communica…

36 Domenec, F.…
letters publi…
tween 2003 …
Management, 16, 296-311.

37 Daub, S. J. (2010). Negotiating sustainability: Climate change framing in the communications, energy and paperworkers union. *Symbolic Interaction, 33,* 115-140.

38 Dalelo, A. (2012). Loss of biodiversity and climate change as presented in biology curricula for Ethiopian schools: Implications for action-oriented environmental education. *International Journal of Environmental and Science Education, 7,* 619-638.

39 Kirilenko, A., Stepchenkova, S., Romsdahl, R., & Mattis, K. (2012). Computer-assisted analysis of public discourse: A case study of the precautionary principle in the US and UK press. *Quality & Quantity: International Journal of Methodology, 46,* 501-522.

40 Joireman, J., Truelove, H. B., & Duell, B. (2010). Effect of outdoor temperature, heat primes and anchoring on belief in global warming. *Journal of Environmental Psychology, 30,* 358-367.

41 Gifford, R. (2014). Environmental psychology matters. *Annual Review of Psychology, 65,* 541-580, p. 552.

42 Nisbet, M. C., & Myers, T. (2007). The polls—trends: Twenty years of public opinion about global warming. *Public Opinion Quarterly, 71,* 444-470.

43 Liarakou, G., Athanasiadis, I., & Gavrilakis, C. (2011). What Greek secondary school students believe about climate change. *International Journal of Environmental and Science Education, 6,* 79-98.

44 Chowdhury, P. D., Haque, C. E., & Driedger, S. M. (2012). Public versus expert knowledge and perception of climate change-induced heat wave risk: A modified mental model approach. *Journal of Risk Research, 15,* 149-168. doi:10.1080/1366 9877.2011.601319

45 Reynolds, T. W., Bostrom, A., Read, D., & Morgan, M. G. (2010). Now what do people know about global climate change? Survey studies of educated laypeople. *Risk Analysis, 30,* 1520-1538.

46 Nisbet, M. C., & Myers, T. (2007). The polls—trends: Twenty years of public opinion about global warming. *Public Opinion Quarterly, 71,* 444-470.

47 Yeager, D. S., Larson, S. B., Krosnick, J. A., & Tompson, T. (2011). Measuring Americans' issue priorities: A new version of the Most Important Problem question reveals more concern about global warming and the environment. *Public Opinion Quarterly, 75,* 125-138.

48 Reynolds, T. W., Bostrom, A., Read, D., & Morgan, M. G. (2010). Now what do people know about global climate change? Survey

49 studies of edu…
1520-1538. …

Santos, …
sumer…
Ro…

...ated laypeople. *Risk Analysis, 30,*

...M. A. O. D. (2012). Investigating con-...knowledge of global warming based on ...gers' knowledge stage of the innovation deci-...ion process. *International Journal of Consumer Studies, 36,* 385-393.

50 Nisbet, M. C., & Myers, T. (2007). The polls—trends: Twenty years of public opinion about global warming. *Public Opinion Quarterly, 71,* 444-470.

51 Reynolds, T. W., Bostrom, A., Read, D., & Morgan, M. G. (2010). Now what do people know about global climate change? Survey studies of educated laypeople. *Risk Analysis, 30,* 1520-1538.

52 Whitmarsh, L., Seyfang, G., & O'Neill, S. (2011). Public engagement with carbon and climate change: To what extent is the public 'carbon capable'? *Global Environmental Change, 21,* 56-65.

53 Sundblad, E., Biel, A., & Gärling, T. (2007). Cognitive and affective risk judgements related to climate change. *Journal of Environmental Psychology, 27,* 97-106.

54 Ungar, S. (2000). Knowledge, ignorance and the popular culture: climate change versus the ozone hole. *Public Understanding of Science, 9,* 297-312.

55 Kellstedt, P. M., Zahran, S., & Vedlitz, A. (2008). Personal efficacy, the information environment, and attitudes toward global warming and climate change in the United States. *Risk Analysis, 28,* 113-126.

56 Scannell, L., & Grouzet, F. M. E. (2010). The metacognitions of climate change. *New Ideas in Psychology, 28,* 94-103.

57 Schuetz, S., Bhattarai, J., Mealy, B., Schuetz, S., Swopes, N., Harvey, D., Berletic, L., Knapp, B., & Ohlms, K. (2011). What? The earth is sick? Undergraduate students awareness of environmental problems: A qualitative study. *Ecopsychology, 3,* 269-276.

58 Nisbet, M. C., & Myers, T. (2007). The polls—trends: Twenty years of public opinion about global warming. *Public Opinion Quarterly, 71,* 444-470.

59 Nisbet, M. C., & Myers, T. (2007). The polls—trends: Twenty years of public opinion about global warming. *Public Opinion Quarterly, 71,* 444-470.

60 European Commission. (2011). *Special Eurobarometer 372.* Retrieved 09/21, 2013, from http://ec.europa.eu/public_opinion/archives/ebs/ebs_372_en.pdf

61 Pew Research Center (2013). Climate change and financial instability seen as top threats. *Pew Research Global Attitudes Project.* Retrieved 04/15, 2014, from http://www.pewglobal.org/files/2013/06/Pew-Research-Center-Global-Attitudes-Project-Global-Threats-Report-FINAL-June-24-20131.pdf

62 Sundblad, E., Biel, A., & Gärling, T. (2007). Cognitive and affective risk judgments related to climate change. *Journal of Environmental Psychology, 27,* 97-106.

63 Davidson, D. J., & Haan, M. (2012). Gender, political ideology, and climate change beliefs in an extractive industry community. *Population and Environment: A Journal of Interdisciplinary Studies, 34,* 217-234.

64 Safi, A. S., Smith, W. J. J., & Liu, Z. (2012). Rural Nevada and climate change: Vulnerability, beliefs, and risk perception. *Risk Analysis, 32,* 1041-1059.

65 Kellstedt, P. M., Zahran, S., & Vedlitz, A. (2008). Personal efficacy, the information environment, and attitudes toward global warming and climate change in the United States. *Risk Analysis, 28,* 113-126.

66 Malka, A., Krosnick, J. A., & Langer, G. (2009). The association of knowledge with concern about global warming: Trusted information sources shape public thinking. *Risk Analysis, 29,* 633-647.

67 Kellstedt, P. M., Zahran, S., & Vedlitz, A. (2008). Personal efficacy, the information environment, and attitudes toward global warming and climate change in the United States. *Risk Analysis, 28,* 113-126.

68 Laidley, T. (2013). Climate, class and culture: Political issues as cultural signifiers in the US. *The Sociological Review, 61,* 153-171.

69 Slimak, M. W., & Dietz, T. (2006). Personal values, beliefs, and ecological risk perception. *Risk Analysis, 26,* 1689-1705.

70 Semenza, J. C., Hall, D. E., Wilson, D. J., Bontempo, B. D., Sailor, D. J., & George, L. A. (2008). Public perception of climate change: Voluntary mitigation and barriers to behavior change. *American Journal of Preventive Medicine, 35,* 479-487.

71 Milfont, T. L. (2012). The interplay between knowledge, perceived efficacy, and concern about global warming and climate change: A one-year longitudinal study. *Risk Analysis, 32,* 1003-1020.

72 Milfont, T. L. (2012). The interplay between knowledge, perceived efficacy, and concern about global warming and climate change: A one-year longitudinal study. *Risk Analysis, 32,* 1003-1020.

73 Ferguson, M. A., & Branscombe, N. R. (2010). Collective guilt mediates the effect of beliefs about global warming on willingness to engage in mitigation behavior. *Journal of Environmental Psychology, 30,* 135-142.

74 Whitmarsh, L., Seyfang, G., & O'Neill, S. (2011). Public engagement with carbon and climate change: To what extent is the public 'carbon capable'? *Global Environmental Change, 21,* 56-65.

75 Liarakou, G., Athanasiadis, I., & Gavrilakis, C. (2011). What Greek secondary school students believe about climate change. *International Journal of Environmental and Science Education, 6,* 79-98.

76 Taddicken, M. (2013). Climate change from the user's perspective: The impact of mass media and internet use and individual and moderating variables on knowledge and attitudes. *Journal of Media Psychology: Theories, Methods, and Applications, 25,* 39-52.

77 Sundblad, E., Biel, A., & Gärling, T. (2009). Knowledge and confidence in knowledge about climate change among experts, journalists, politicians, and laypersons. *Environment and Behavior, 41,* 281-302.

78 Slimak, M. W., & Dietz, T. (2006). Personal values, beliefs, and ecological risk perception. *Risk Analysis, 26,* 1689-1705.

79 Lazo, J. K., Kinnell, J., & Fisher, A. (2000). Expert and layperson perceptions of ecosystem risk. *Risk Analysis, 20,* 179-193.

80 Farnsworth, S. J., & Lichter, S. R. (2012). The structure of scientific opinion on climate change. *International Journal of Public Opinion Research, 24,* 93-103.

81 Etkin, D., & Ho, E. (2007). Climate change: Perceptions and discourse of risk. *Journal of Risk Research, 10,* 623-641.

82 Slimak, M. W., & Dietz, T. (2006). Personal Values, Beliefs, and Ecological Risk Perception. *Risk Analysis, 26,* 1689-1705.

83 Schuldt, J. P., Konrath, S. H., & Schwarz, N. (2011). "Global warming" or "climate change"? Whether the planet is warming depends on question wording. *Public Opinion Quarterly, 75,* 115-124.

84 McCright, A. M., & Dunlap, R. E. (2011). The politicization of climate change and polarization in the American public's views of global warming, 2001–2010. *The Sociological Quarterly, 52,* 155-194.

85 Borick, C. P., & Rabe, B. G. (2010). A reason to believe: Examining the factors that determine individual views on global warming. *Social Science Quarterly, 91,* 777-800.

86 Malka, A., Krosnick, J. A., & Langer, G. (2009). The association of knowledge with concern about global warming: Trusted information sources shape public thinking. *Risk Analysis, 29,* 633-647.

87 Gardner, G. T., & Stern, P. C. (1996). *Environmental problems and human behavior.* Allyn & Bacon.

88 Gifford, R. (2011). The dragons of inaction: Psychological barriers that limit climate change mitigation and adaptation. *American Psychologist, 66,* 290-302.

89 Gifford, R., Scannell, L., Kormos, C., Smolova, L., Biel, A., Boncu, S., Corral, V., Güntherf, H., Hanyu, K., & Hine, D. (2009). Temporal pessimism and spatial optimism in environmental assessments: An 18-nation study. *Journal of Environmental Psychology, 29,* 1-12.

90 Leiserowitz, A. A. (2005). American Risk Perceptions: Is Climate Change Dangerous? *Risk Analysis, 25,* 1433-1442.

91 Spence, A., Poortinga, W., & Pidgeon, N. (2012). The psychological distance of climate change. *Risk Analysis, 32,* 957-972.

92 Etkin, D., & Ho, E. (2007). Climate change: Perceptions and discourse of risk. *Journal of Risk Research, 10,* 623-641.

93 Ungar, S. (2000). Knowledge, ignorance and the popular culture: climate change versus the ozone hole. *Public Understanding of Science, 9,* 297-312.

94 Epstein, S. (1994). Integration of the cognitive and the psychodynamic unconscious. *American Psychologist, 49,* 709.

95 Loewenstein, G. F., Weber, E. U., Hsee, C. K., & Welch, N. (2001). Risk as feelings. *Psychological Bulletin, 127,* 267.

96 Loewenstein, G. F., Weber, E. U., Hsee, C. K., & Welch, N. (2001). Risk as feelings. *Psychological Bulletin, 127,* 267.

97 Weber, E. U. (2006). Experience-based and description-based perceptions of long-term risk: Why global warming does not scare us (yet). *Climatic Change, 77,* 103-120.

98 Damasio, A. (2005). *Descartes' error: Emotion, reason, and the human brain* Penguin. com.

99 Weber, E. U. (2006). Experience-based and description-based perceptions of long-term risk:

Why global warming does not scare us (yet). *Climatic Change, 77*, 103-120.

100 Roeser, S. (2012). Risk communication, public engagement, and climate change: A role for emotions. *Risk Analysis, 32*, 1033-1040.

101 Li, Y., Johnson, E. J., & Zaval, L. (2011). Local warming: Daily temperature change influences belief in global warming. *Psychological Science, 22*, 454-459.

102 Joireman, J., Truelove, H. B., & Duell, B. (2010). Effect of outdoor temperature, heat primes and anchoring on belief in global warming. *Journal of Environmental Psychology, 30*, 358-367.

103 Guéguen, N. (2012). Dead indoor plants strengthen belief in global warming. *Journal of Environmental Psychology, 32*, 173-177.

104 Borick, C. P., & Rabe, B. G. (2010). A reason to believe: Examining the factors that determine individual views on global warming. *Social Science Quarterly, 91*, 777-800.

105 Chowdhury, P. D., Haque, C. E., & Driedger, S. M. (2012). Public versus expert knowledge and perception of climate change-induced heat wave risk: A modified mental model approach. *Journal of Risk Research, 15*, 149-168.

106 Owen, A. L., Conover, E., Videras, J., & Wu, S. (2012). Heat waves, droughts, and preferences for environmental policy. *Journal of Policy Analysis and Management, 31*, 556-577.

107 Blennow, K., Persson, J., Tomé, M., & Hanewinke, M. (2012). Climate change: Believing and seeing implies adapting. *PLoS ONE, 7*

108 Whitmarsh, L. (2008). Are flood victims more concerned about climate change than other people? The role of direct experience in risk perception and behavioural response. *Journal of Risk Research, 11*, 351-374.

109 Brody, S. D., Zahran, S., Vedlitz, A., & Grover, H. (2008). Examining the relationship between physical vulnerability and public perceptions of global climate change in the United States. *Environment and Behavior, 40*, 72-95.

110 Brody, S. D., Zahran, S., Vedlitz, A., & Grover, H. (2008). Examining the relationship between physical vulnerability and public perceptions of global climate change in the United States. *Environment and Behavior, 40*, 72-95.

111 Whitmarsh, L. (2008). Are flood victims more concerned about climate change than other people? The role of direct experience in risk perception and behavioural response. *Journal of Risk Research, 11*, 351-374.

112 Chowdhury, P. D., Haque, C. E., & Driedger, S. M. (2012). Public versus expert knowledge and perception of climate change-induced heat wave risk: A modified mental model approach. *Journal of Risk Research, 15*, 149-168. doi:10.1080/1366 9877.2011.601319

113 Owen, A. L., Conover, E., Videras, J., & Wu, S. (2012). Heat waves, droughts, and preferences for environmental policy. *Journal of Policy Analysis and Management, 31*, 556-577.

114 Petty, R. E., Haugtvedt, C. P., & Smith, S. M. (1995). Elaboration as a determinant of attitude strength: Creating attitudes that are persistent, resistant, and predictive of behavior. In J. A. Krosnick (Ed.), *Attitude strength: Antecedents and consequences.* (pp. 93-130). Hillsdale, NJ England: Lawrence Erlbaum Associates, Inc.

115 Safi, A. S., Smith, W. J. J., & Liu, Z. (2012). Rural Nevada and climate change: Vulnerability, beliefs, and risk perception. *Risk Analysis, 32*, 1041-1059.

116 Botzen, W. J. W., & van, d. B. (2012). Risk attitudes to low-probability climate change risks: WTP for flood insurance. *Journal of Economic Behavior & Organization, 82*, 151-166.

117 Mortreux, C., & Barnett, J. (2009). Climate change, migration and adaptation in Funafuti, Tuvalu. *Global Environmental Change, 19*, 105-112.

118 Brody, S. D., Zahran, S., Vedlitz, A., & Grover, H. (2008). Examining the relationship between physical vulnerability and public perceptions of global climate change in the United States. *Environment and Behavior, 40*, 72-95.

119 Brody, S. D., Zahran, S., Vedlitz, A., & Grover, H. (2008). Examining the relationship between physical vulnerability and public perceptions of global climate change in the United States. *Environment and Behavior, 40*, 72-95.

120 Carvalho, A., & Burgess, J. (2005). Cultural circuits of climate Change in U.K. broadsheet newspapers, 1985-2003. *Risk Analysis, 25*, 1457-1469.

121 McComas, K., & Shanahan, J. (1999). Telling stories about global climate change: Measuring the impact of narratives on issue cycles. *Communication Research, 26*, 30-57.

122 Young, N., & Dugas, E. (2011). Representations of climate change in Canadian national print media: The banalization of global warming. *Canadian Review of Sociology, 48*, 1-22.

123 Kirilenko, A., Stepchenkova, S., Romsdahl, R., & Mattis, K. (2012). Computer-assisted analysis of public discourse: A case study of the precautionary principle in the US and UK press. *Quality & Quantity: International Journal of Methodology, 46*, 501-522.

124 Young, N., & Dugas, E. (2011). Representations of climate change in Canadian national print media: The banalization of global warming. *Canadian Review of Sociology, 48*, 1-22.

125 Zhao, X., Leiserowitz, A. A., Maibach, E. W., & Roser-Renouf, C. (2011). Attention to science/environment news positively predicts and attention to political news negatively predicts global warming risk perceptions and policy support. *Journal of Communication, 61*, 713-731.

126 Pahl, S., & Bauer, J. (2013). Overcoming the distance: Perspective taking with future humans improves environmental engagement. *Environment and Behavior, 45*, 155-169.

127 Nolan, J. M. (2010). "An inconvenient truth" increases knowledge, concern, and willingness to reduce greenhouse gases. *Environment and Behavior, 42*, 643-658.

128 Lowe, T., Brown, K., Dessai, S., de França Doria, M., Haynes, K., & Vincent, K. (2006). Does tomorrow ever come? Disaster narrative and public perceptions of climate change. *Public Understanding of Science, 15*, 435-457.

129 Greitemeyer, T. (2013). Beware of climate change skeptic films. *Journal of Environmental Psychology, 35*, 105-109.

130 Pahl, S., & Bauer, J. (2013). Overcoming the distance: Perspective taking with future humans improves environmental engagement. *Environment and Behavior, 45*, 155-169.

131 Nolan, J. M., Kenefick, J., & Schultz, P. W. (2011). Normative messages promoting energy conservation will be underestimated by experts... unless you show them the data. *Social Influence, 6*, 169-180.

132 Nolan, J. M., Schultz, W. P., Cialdini, R. B., Goldstein, N. J., & Griskevicius, V. (2008). Normative social influence is underdetected. *Personality and Social Psychology Bulletin, 34*, 913-923.

133 Nolan, J. M., Kenefick, J., & Schultz, P. W. (2011). Normative messages promoting energy conservation will be underestimated by experts... unless you show them the data. *Social Influence, 6*, 169-180.

134 Hine, D. W., & Gifford, R. (1996). Individual restraint and group efficiency in commons dilemmas: The effects of two types of environmental uncertainty. *Journal of Applied Social Psychology, 26*, 993-1009.

135 Asch, S. E. (1956). Studies of independence and conformity: A minority of one against a unanimous majority. *Psychological Monographs, 70*, 1-70.

136 Corbett, J. B., & Durfee, J. L. (2004). Testing public (un) certainty of science media representations of global warming. *Science Communication, 26*, 129-151.

137 Budescu, D. V., Broomell, S., & Por, H. (2009). Improving communication of uncertainty in the reports of the intergovernmental panel on climate change. *Psychological Science, 20*, 299-308.

138 Uggla, Y. (2008). Strategies to create risk awareness and legitimacy: The Swedish climate campaign. *Journal of Risk Research, 11*, 719-734.

139 Lewandowsky, S. (2011). Popular consensus: Climate change is set to continue. *Psychological Science, 22*, 460-463. doi:10.1177/0956797611402515

140 O'Neill, S., & Nicholson-Cole, S. (2009). "Fear won't do it" Promoting positive engagement with climate change through visual and iconic representations. *Science Communication, 30*, 355-379.

141 Feinberg, M., & Willer, R. (2011). Apocalypse soon? Dire messages reduce belief in global warming by contradicting just-world beliefs. *Psychological Science, 22*, 34-38.

142 Meijnders, A. L., Midden, C. J. H., & Wilke, H. A. M. (2001). Role of negative emotion in communication about CO_2 risks. *Risk Analysis, 21*, 955-966.

143 Petty, R. E., Haugtvedt, C. P., & Smith, S. M. (1995). Elaboration as a determinant of attitude strength: Creating attitudes that are persistent, resistant, and predictive of behavior. In J. A. Krosnick (Ed.), *Attitude strength: Antecedents and consequences.* (pp. 93-130). Hillsdale, NJ England: Lawrence Erlbaum Associates, Inc.

144 Meijnders, A. L., Midden, C. J. H., & Wilke, H. A. M. (2001). Role of negative emotion in communication about CO_2 risks. *Risk Analysis, 21*, 955-966.

145 O'Neill, S., & Nicholson-Cole, S. (2009). "Fear won't do it" Promoting positive engagement with climate change through visual and iconic representations. *Science Communication, 30*, 355-379.

146 Zapico, J. L., Guath, M., & Turpeinen, M. (2011). Kilograms or cups of tea: Comparing footprints for better CO_2 understanding. *PsychNology Journal, 9*, 43-54.

147 Sheppard, S. R. (2005). Landscape visualisation and climate change: the potential for influencing

perceptions and behaviour. *Environmental Science & Policy, 8*, 637-654.

148 Gifford, R., & Comeau, L. A. (2011). Message framing influences perceived climate change competence, engagement, and behavioral intentions. *Global Environmental Change, 21*, 1301-1307.

149 Newman, C. L., Howlett, E., Burton, S., Kozup, J. C., & Tangari, A. H. (2012). The influence of consumer concern about global climate change on framing effects for environmental sustainability messages. *International Journal of Advertising: The Quarterly Review of Marketing Communications, 31*, 511-527.

150 Bråten, I., Strømsø, H. I., & Salmerón, L. (2011). Trust and mistrust when students read multiple information sources about climate change. *Learning and Instruction, 21*, 180-192.

151 Terwel, B. W., Harinck, F., Ellemers, N., & Daamen, D. D. L. (2009). How organizational motives and communications affect public trust in organizations: The case of carbon dioxide capture and storage, *Journal of Environmental Psychology, 29*, 290-299.

152 Frumkin, H., Fried, L., & Moody, R. (2012). Aging, climate change, and legacy thinking. *American Journal of Public Health, 102*, 1434-1438.

153 Ter Mors, E., Weenig, M. W. H., Ellemers, N., & Daamen, D. D. L. (2010). Effective communication about complex environmental issues: Perceived quality of information about carbon dioxide capture and storage (CCS) depends on stakeholder collaboration. *Journal of Environmental Psychology, 30*, 347-357.

154 Strømsø, H. I., Bråten, I., & Britt, M. A. (2010). Reading multiple texts about climate change: The relationship between memory for sources and text comprehension. *Learning and Instruction, 20*, 192-204.

155 Corbett, J. B., & Durfee, J. L. (2004). Testing public (un) certainty of science media representations of global warming. *Science Communication, 26*, 129-151.

156 Chowdhury, P. D., Haque, C. E., & Driedger, S. M. (2012). Public versus expert knowledge and perception of climate change-induced heat wave risk: A modified mental model approach. *Journal of Risk Research, 15*, 149-168.

157 Owen, A. L., Conover, E., Videras, J., & Wu, S. (2012). Heat waves, droughts, and preferences for environmental policy. *Journal of Policy Analysis and Management, 31*, 556-577.

158 Bråten, I., Strømsø, H. I., & Salmerón, L. (2011). Trust and mistrust when students read multiple information sources about climate change. *Learning and Instruction, 21*, 180-192.

159 Newman, C. L., Howlett, E., Burton, S., Kozup, J. C., & Tangari, A. H. (2012). The influence of consumer concern about global climate change on framing effects for environmental sustainability messages. *International Journal of Advertising: The Quarterly Review of Marketing Communications, 31*, 511-527.

160 Taddicken, M. (2013). Climate change from the user's perspective: The impact of mass media and internet use and individual and moderating variables on knowledge and attitudes. *Journal of Media Psychology: Theories, Methods, and Applications, 25*, 39-52.

161 Hart, P. S., & Nisbet, E. C. (2012). Boomerang effects in science communication: How motivated reasoning and identity cues amplify opinion polarization about climate mitigation policies. *Communication Research, 39*, 701-723.

162 Rabinovich, A., Morton, T. A., & Birney, M. E. (2012). Communicating climate science: The role of perceived communicator's motives. *Journal of Environmental Psychology, 32*, 11-18.

163 Bråten, I., & Strømsø, H. I. (2010). When law students read multiple documents about global warming: Examining the role of topic-specific beliefs about the nature of knowledge and knowing. *Instructional Science, 38*, 635-657.

164 Liarakou, G., Athanasiadis, I., & Gavrilakis, C. (2011). What Greek secondary school students believe about climate change. *International Journal of Environmental and Science Education, 6*, 79-98.

165 Kilinç, A., Boyes, E., & Stanisstreet, M. (2011). Turkish school students and global warming: Beliefs and willingness to act. *Eurasia Journal of Mathematics, Science & Technology Education, 7*, 121-134.

166 Liarakou, G., Athanasiadis, I., & Gavrilakis, C. (2011). What Greek secondary school students believe about climate change. *International Journal of Environmental and Science Education, 6*, 79-98.

167 Shepardson, D. P., Niyogi, D., Choi, S., & Charusombat, U. (2009). Seventh grade students' conceptions of global warming and climate change. *Environmental Education Research, 15*, 549-570.

168 Takacs, C. H. (2013). Teaching about climate change in the business curriculum: An introductory module and resource list. *Journal of Education for Business, 88*, 176-183.

169 Paschall, M., & Wüstenhagen, R. (2012). More than a game: Learning about climate change through role-play. *Journal of Management Education, 36*, 510-543.

170 Renert, M., & Davis, B. (2012). Ecological sustainability and mathematics education: Integrally connected. *Journal of Integral Theory and Practice, 7*, 94-104.

171 Jacobson, S. K., Carlton, J. S., & Devitt, S. E. C. (2012). Infusing the psychology of climate change into environmental curricula. *Ecopsychology, 4*, 94-101.

172 Johnson, L. R., Johnson-Pynn, J., Lugumya, D. L., Kityo, R., & Drescher, C. F. (2013). Cultivating youth's capacity to address climate change in Uganda. *International Perspectives in Psychology: Research, Practice, Consultation, 2*, 29-44.

173 Bråten, I., & Strømsø, H. I. (2010). Effects of task instruction and personal epistemology on the understanding of multiple texts about climate change. *Discourse Processes, 47*, 1-31.

174 Lombardi, D., Sinatra, G. M., & Nussbaum, E. M. (2013). Plausibility reappraisals and shifts in middle school students' climate change conceptions. *Learning and Instruction, 27*, 50-62.

175 Rebich, S., & Gautier, C. (2005). Concept mapping to reveal prior knowledge and conceptual change in a mock summit course on global climate change. *Journal of Geoscience Education, 53*, 355.

176 Paschall, M., & Wüstenhagen, R. (2012). More than a game: Learning about climate change

through role-play. *Journal of Management Education, 36*, 510-543.

177 Varma, K., & Linn, M. C. (2012). Using interactive technology to support students' understanding of the greenhouse effect and global warming. *Journal of Science Education and Technology, 21*, 453-464.

178 Oluk, S., & Özalp, I. (2007). The teaching of global environmental problems according to the constructivist approach: As a focal point of the problem and the availability of concept cartoons. *Kuram Ve Uygulamada Egitim Bilimleri, 7*, 881-896.

179 Johnson, L. R., Johnson-Pynn, J., Lugumya, D. L., Kityo, R., & Drescher, C. F. (2013). Cultivating youth's capacity to address climate change in Uganda. *International Perspectives in Psychology: Research, Practice, Consultation, 2*, 29-44.

180 Taber, F., & Taylor, N. (2009). Climate of concern — A search for effective strategies for teaching children about global warming. *International Journal of Environmental and Science Education, 4*, 97-116.

181 Bozdogan, A. E. (2011). A collection of studies conducted in education about 'global warming' problem. *Kuram Ve Uygulamada Egitim Bilimleri, 11*, 1618-1624.

182 Porter, D., Weaver, A. J., & Raptis, H. (2012). Assessing students' learning about fundamental concepts of climate change under two different conditions. *Environmental Education Research, 18*, 665-686.

183 Liarakou, G., Athanasiadis, I., & Gavrilakis, C. (2011). What Greek secondary school students believe about climate change. *International Journal of Environmental and Science Education, 6*, 79-98.

184 Johnson, L. R., Johnson-Pynn, J., Lugumya, D. L., Kityo, R., & Drescher, C. F. (2013). Cultivating youth's capacity to address climate change in Uganda. *International Perspectives in Psychology: Research, Practice, Consultation, 2*, 29-44.

185 Devine-Wright, P., Devine-Wright, H., & Fleming, P. (2004). Situational influences upon children's beliefs about global warming and energy. *Environmental Education Research, 10*, 493-506.

186 Johnson, L. R., Johnson-Pynn, J., Lugumya, D. L., Kityo, R., & Drescher, C. F. (2013). Cultivating youth's capacity to address climate change in Uganda. *International Perspectives in Psychology: Research, Practice, Consultation, 2*, 29-44.

187 Festinger, L. (1957). *A theory of cognitive dissonance* Stanford University Press.

188 Pittock, A. (2009). *Climate change: the science, impacts and solutions.* CSIRO PUBLISHING.

189 ABC. (2009). *Australian Broadcast Corporation: Climate change falling off policy radar.* Retrieved 11/29, 2013, from http://www.abc.net.au/news/2009-10-13/climate-change-falling-off-policy-radar/1101842

190 Smith, N., & Leiserowitz, A. (2012). The rise of global warming skepticism: Exploring affective image associations in the United States over time. *Risk Analysis, 32*, 1021-1032.

191 Smith, N., & Leiserowitz, A. (2012). The rise of global warming skepticism: Exploring affective image associations in the United States over time. *Risk Analysis, 32*, 1021-1032.

192 Rahmstorf, S. (2003). *Weather catastrophes and climate change: The climate sceptics*. Munich, Germany: Munich Re.

193 Leviston, Z., & Walker, I. (2012). Beliefs and denials about climate change: An Australian perspective. *Ecopsychology, 4*, 277-285.

194 Islam, M. M., Barnes, A., & Toma, L. (2013). An investigation into climate change skepticism among farmers. *Journal of Environmental Psychology, 34*, 137-150.

195 Enting, I. G. (2007). *Twisted: the distorted mathematics of greenhouse denial* Ian Enting.

196 Hoggan, J. (2009). *Climate cover-up: The crusade to deny global warming* Greystone Books Ltd.

197 Washington, H. (2011). *Climate change denial: Heads in the sand*. New York, NY: Taylor & Francis.

198 Lomborg, B. (2001). *The skeptical environmentalist: measuring the real state of the world* Cambridge University Press.

199 Diethelm, P., & McKee, M. (2009). Denialism: what is it and how should scientists respond? *The European Journal of Public Health, 19*, 2-4.

200 Boulton, G., Clarke, P., Eyton, D. & Norton, J. (2010). *The Independent Climate Change E-mails Review*. Retrieved 11/28, 2013, from http://citeseerx.ist.psu.edu/viewdoc/download?doi=10.1.1.179.2074&rep=rep1&type=pdf

201 Willis, P., Blackman-Woods, R., Boswell, T., Cawsey, I., Dorries, N., Harris, E., Iddon, B., Marsden, G., Naysmith, D., Spink, B., Stewart, I., Stringer, G., Turner, D., & Wilson, R. (2010). *The Disclosure of Climate Data from the Climatic Research Unit at the University of East Anglia: Eighth Report of Session 2009-10*. Washington, D.C.: The Stationery Office.

202 Hoggan, J. (2009). *Climate cover-up: The crusade to deny global warming* Greystone Books Ltd.

203 Washington, H. (2011). *Climate change denial: Heads in the sand*. New York, NY: Taylor & Francis.

204 Nagel, J. (2011). Climate change, public opinion, and the military security complex. *The Sociological Quarterly, 52*, 203-210.

205 OISM. (2008). *Petition Project, Oregon Institute of Science and Medicine*. Retrieved 11/29, 2013, from www.petitionproject.org

206 Bradley, R. S., Mann, M., & Hughes, M. K. (1999). Northern hemisphere temperatures during the past millennium: inferences, uncertainties, and limitations. *Geophysical Research Letters, 26*, 759-762.

207 McIntyre, S., & McKitrick, R. (2005). Hockey sticks, principal components, and spurious significance. *Geophysical Research Letters, 32*, L03710.

208 Mann, M. E., Zhang, Z., Hughes, M. K., Bradley, R. S., Miller, S. K., Rutherford, S., & Ni, F. (2008). Proxy-based reconstructions of hemispheric and global surface temperature variations over the past two millennia. *Proceedings of the National Academy of Sciences, 105*, 13252-13257.

209 Washington, H. (2011). *Climate change denial: Heads in the sand*. New York, NY: Taylor & Francis.

210 Washington, H. (2011). *Climate change denial: Heads in the sand*. New York, NY: Taylor & Francis.

211 Plimer, I. R. (2009). *Heaven and earth* Taylor Trade.

212 McCright, A. M. (2011). Cool dudes: The denial of climate change among conservative white males in the United States. *Global Environmental Change, 21*, 1163-1172.

213 Islam, M. M., Barnes, A., & Toma, L. (2013). An investigation into climate change skepticism among farmers. *Journal of Environmental Psychology, 34*, 137-150.

214 Leviston, Z., & Walker, I. (2012). Beliefs and denials about climate change: An Australian perspective. *Ecopsychology, 4*, 277-285.

215 Islam, M. M., Barnes, A., & Toma, L. (2013). An investigation into climate change skepticism among farmers. *Journal of Environmental Psychology, 34*, 137-150.

216 Leviston, Z., & Walker, I. (2012). Beliefs and denials about climate change: An Australian perspective. *Ecopsychology, 4*, 277-285.

217 Heath, Y., & Gifford, R. (2006). Free-Market Ideology and Environmental Degradation: The Case of Belief in Global Climate Change. *Environment and Behavior, 38*, 48-71.

218 Lewandowsky, S., Oberauer, K., & Gignac, G. E. (2013). NASA faked the moon landing—therefore, (climate) science is a hoax: An anatomy of the motivated rejection of science. *Psychological Science, 24*, 622-633.

219 Jost, J. T., Banaji, M. R., & Nosek, B. A. (2004). A decade of system justification theory: Accumulated evidence of conscious and unconscious bolstering of the status quo. *Political Psychology, 25*, 881-919.

220 Feinberg, M., & Willer, R. (2011). Apocalypse soon? Dire messages reduce belief in global warming by contradicting just-world beliefs. *Psychological Science, 22*, 34-38.

221 Feinberg, M., & Willer, R. (2011). Apocalypse soon? Dire messages reduce belief in global warming by contradicting just-world beliefs. *Psychological Science, 22*, 34-38.

222 Feygina, I., Goldsmith, R. E., & Jost, J. T. (2010). System justification and the disruption of environmental goal-setting: A self-regulatory perspective. In Y. Trope (Ed.), *Self control in society, mind, and brain*. (pp. 490-505). New York, NY US: Oxford University Press.

223 Hoggan, J. (2009). *Climate cover-up: The crusade to deny global warming* Greystone Books Ltd.

224 Washington, H. (2011). *Climate change denial: Heads in the sand*. New York, NY: Taylor & Francis.

225 Nagel, J. (2011). Climate change, public opinion, and the military security complex. *The Sociological Quarterly, 52*, 203-210.

226 Feygina, I., Jost, J. T., & Goldsmith, R. E. (2010). System justification, the denial of global warming, and the possibility of "system-sanctioned change". *Personality and Social Psychology Bulletin, 36*, 326-338.

227 Feygina, I., Jost, J. T., & Goldsmith, R. E. (2010). System justification, the denial of global warming, and the possibility of "system-sanctioned change". *Personality and Social Psychology Bulletin, 36*, 326-338.

228 Sparks, P., Jessop, D. C., Chapman, J., & Holmes, K. (2010). Pro-environmental actions, climate change, and defensiveness: Do self-affirmations make a difference to people's motives and beliefs about making a difference? *British Journal of Social Psychology, 49*, 553-568.

229 de Boer, J., Schösler, H., & Boersema, J. J. (2013). Climate change and meat eating: An inconvenient couple? *Journal of Environmental Psychology, 33*, 1-8.

230 Doherty, T. J., & Clayton, S. (2011). The psychological impacts of global climate change. *American Psychologist, 66*, 265-276. doi:10.1037/a0023141

231 Fritsche, I., Cohrs, J. C., Kessler, T., & Bauer, J. (2012). Global warming is breeding social conflict: The subtle impact of climate change threat on authoritarian tendencies. *Journal of Environmental Psychology, 32*, 1-10.

232 Poumadère, M., Mays, C., Le Mer, S., & Blong, R. (2005). The 2003 Heat Wave in France: Dangerous Climate Change Here and Now. *Risk Analysis, 25*, 1483-1494.

233 Tang, K. K., Petrie, D., & Rao, D. S. P. (2009). The income-climate trap of health development: A comparative analysis of African and Non-African countries. *Social Science & Medicine, 69*, 1099-1106.

234 Doherty, T. J., & Clayton, S. (2011). The psychological impacts of global climate change. *American Psychologist, 66*, 265-276.

235 Anderson, C. A., Anderson, K. B., Dorr, N., DeNeve, K. M., & Flanagan, M. (2000). Temperature and aggression. *Advances in Experimental Social Psychology, 32*, 63-133.

236 Agnew, R. (2012). Dire forecast: A theoretical model of the impact of climate change on crime. *Theoretical Criminology, 16*, 21-42.

237 Agnew, R. (2012). Dire forecast: A theoretical model of the impact of climate change on crime. *Theoretical Criminology, 16*, 21-42.

238 Yeoman, B. (2009). Tomorrow's wars. *On Earth, 31*, 18-19.

239 Blashki, G. A., Burke, S., Fritze, J. G., & Wiseman, J. (2008). Hope, despair and transformation: Climate change and the promotion of mental health and wellbeing. *International Journal of Mental Health Systems, 2*

240 Page, L. A., & Howard, L. M. (2010). The impact of climate change on mental health (but will mental health be discussed at Copenhagen?). *Psychological Medicine, 40*, 177-180.

241 Hanigan, I. C., Butler, C. D., Kokic, P. N., & Hutchinson, M. F. (2012). Suicide and drought in New South Wales, Australia, 1970–2007. *PNAS Proceedings of the National Academy of Sciences of the United States of America, 109*, 13950-13955.

242 Preti, A., Lentini, G., & Maugeri, M. (2007). Global warming possibly linked to an enhanced risk of suicide: Data from Italy, 1974-2003. *Journal of Affective Disorders, 102*, 19-25.

243 Polain, J. D., Berry, H. L., & Hoskin, J. O. (2011). Rapid change, climate adversity and the next 'big dry': Older farmers' mental health. *The Australian Journal of Rural Health, 19*, 239-243.

244 Hunter, E. (2009). 'Radical hope' and rain: Climate change and the mental health of Indigenous residents of northern Australia. *Australasian Psychiatry, 17*, 445-452.

245 Berry, H. L., Hogan, A., Owen, J., Rickwood, D., & Fragar, L. (2011). Climate change and farmers' mental health: Risks and responses. *Asia-Pacific Journal of Public Health, 23*, 119S-132S.

246 Cunsolo Willox, A., Harper, S. L., Ford, J. D., Landman, K., Houle, K., & Edge, V. L. (2012).

"From this place and of this place:" Climate change, sense of place, and health in Nunatsiavut, Canada. *Social Science & Medicine, 75*, 538-547.

247 Crabtree, A. (2012). Climate change and mental health following flood disasters in developing countries, a review of the epidemiological literature: What do we know, what is being recommended? *Australasian Journal of Disaster and Trauma Studies, 2012*, 21-29.

248 McMichael, A. J., Woodruff, R. E., & Hales, S. (2006). Climate change and human health: Present and future risks. *The Lancet, 367*, 859-869.

249 Poumadère, M., Mays, C., Le Mer, S., & Blong, R. (2005). The 2003 Heat Wave in France: Dangerous Climate Change Here and Now. *Risk Analysis, 25*, 1483-1494.

250 Cornforth, S. C. (2008). Life's span, global warming and ethics: Do counsellors have a part to play in averting a potential catastrophe? *International Journal for the Advancement of Counselling, 30*, 145-154. d

251 Pyszczynski, T., Motyl, M., Vail, K. E. I.,II, Hirschberger, G., Arndt, J., & Kesebir, P. (2012). Drawing attention to global climate change decreases support for war. *Peace and Conflict: Journal of Peace Psychology, 18*, 354-368.

252 Pyszczynski, T., Motyl, M., Vail, K. E. I.,II, Hirschberger, G., Arndt, J., & Kesebir, P. (2012). Drawing attention to global climate change decreases support for war. *Peace and Conflict: Journal of Peace Psychology, 18*, 354-368.

253 Maiteny, P. T. (2002). Mind in the gap: Summary of research exploring 'inner' influences on pro-sustainability learning and behaviour. *Environmental Education Research, 8*, 299-306.

254 Langford, I. H. (2002). An existential approach to risk perception. *Risk Analysis, 22*, 101-120.

255 Johnson, L. R., Johnson-Pynn, J. S., & Pynn, T. M. (2007). Youth civic engagement in China: Results from a program promoting environmental activism. *Journal of Adolescent Research, 22*, 355-386.

256 IRIN. (2012). *Climate Change: Coping Versus Adapting.* Retrieved 12/02, 2013, from http://www.irinnews.org/report/95224/climate-change-coping-versus-adapting

257 Reser, J. P., & Swim, J. K. (2011). Adapting to and coping with the threat and impacts of climate change. *American Psychologist, 66*, 277-289.

258 Reser, J. P., & Swim, J. K. (2011). Adapting to and coping with the threat and impacts of climate change. *American Psychologist, 66*, 277-289.

259 Reser, J. P., & Swim, J. K. (2011). Adapting to and coping with the threat and impacts of climate change. *American Psychologist, 66*, 277-289.

260 Homburg, A., Stolberg, A., & Wagner, U. (2007). Coping with global environmental problems: Development and first validation of scales. *Environment and Behavior, 39*, 754-778.

261 Ojala, M. (2012). How do children cope with global climate change? Coping strategies, engagement, and well-being. *Journal of Environmental Psychology, 32*, 225-233.

262 Ojala, M. (2013). Regulating worry, promoting hope: How do children, adolescents, and young adults cope with climate change? *International Journal of Environmental and Science Education, 8*, 537-561.

263 Ojala, M. (2012). How do children cope with global climate change? Coping strategies, engagement, and well-being. *Journal of Environmental Psychology, 32*, 225-233.

264 Brouwer, R., Akter, S., Brander, L., & Haque, E. (2007). Socioeconomic vulnerability and adaptation to environmental risk: A case study of climate change and flooding in Bangladesh. *Risk Analysis, 27*, 313-326.

265 Gifford, R. (2011). The dragons of inaction: Psychological barriers that limit climate change mitigation and adaptation. *American Psychologist, 66*, 290-302.

266 Stern, P. C. (2011). Contributions of psychology to limiting climate change. *American Psychologist, 66*, 303-314.

267 Skinner, B. F. (1938). The behavior of organisms: An experimental analysis.

268 Geller, E. S., Winett, R. A., & Everett, P. B. (1982). *Preserving the Environment: New Strategies for Behavior Change.* New York: Pergamon Press.

269 Lehman, P. K., & Geller, E. S. (2005). Behavior analysis and environmental protection: Accomplishments and potential for more. *Behavior and Social Issues, 13*, 13-32.

270 Tobler, C., Visschers, V. H. M., & Siegrist, M. (2012). Addressing climate change: Determinants of consumers' willingness to act and to support policy measures. *Journal of Environmental Psychology, 32*, 197-207.

271 Ajzen, I. (1991). The theory of planned behavior. *Organizational Behavior and Human Decision Processes, 50*, 179-211.

272 Laudenslager, M. S., Holt, D. T., & Lofgren, S. T. (2004). Understanding air force members' intentions to participate in pro-environmental behaviors: An application of the theory of planned behavior. *Perceptual and Motor Skills, 98*, 1162-1170.

273 van Zomeren, M., Spears, R., & Leach, C. W. (2010). Experimental evidence for a dual pathway model analysis of coping with the climate crisis. *Journal of Environmental Psychology, 30*, 339-346.

274 Kilinç, A., Boyes, E., & Stanisstreet, M. (2011). Turkish school students and global warming: Beliefs and willingness to act. *Eurasia Journal of Mathematics, Science & Technology Education, 7*, 121-134.

275 Truelove, H. B., & Parks, C. (2012). Perceptions of behaviors that cause and mitigate global warming and intentions to perform these behaviors. *Journal of Environmental Psychology, 32*, 246-259.

276 Dunlap, R. E., & Van Liere, K. D. (1978). The "new environmental paradigm": A proposed measuring instrument and preliminary results. *Journal of Environmental Education, 9*, 10-19.

277 Dunlap, R. E., Van Liere, K. D., Mertig, A. G., & Emmet Jones, R. (2000). Measuring endorsement of the new ecological paradigm: A revised NEP scale. *Journal of Social Issues, 56*, 425-442.

278 Schwartz, S. H. (1992). Universals in the content and structure of values: Theoretical advances and empirical tests in 20 countries. *Advances in Experimental Social Psychology, 25*, 1-65.

279 Stern, P. C., Dietz, T., Abel, T., Guagnano, G. A., & Kalof, L. (1999). A value-belief-norm theory of support for social movements: The case of environmentalism. *Human Ecology Review, 6*, 81-98.

280 Van Lange, P. A., & Joireman, J. A. (2008). How we can promote behavior that serves all of us in the future. *Social Issues and Policy Review, 2*, 127-157.

281 Liu, J. H., & Sibley, C. G. (2012). Hope for the future? Understanding self-sacrifice among young citizens of the world in the face of global warming. *Analyses of Social Issues and Public Policy (ASAP), 12*, 190-203.

282 Frantz, C. M., & Mayer, F. S. (2009). The emergency of climate change: Why are we failing to take action. *Analyses of Social Issues and Public Policy (ASAP), 9*, 205-222.

283 Clark, C. F., Kotchen, M. J., & Moore, M. R. (2003). Internal and external influences on pro-environmental behavior: Participation in a green electricity program. *Journal of Environmental Psychology, 23*, 237-246.

284 Ferguson, M. A., & Branscombe, N. R. (2010). Collective guilt mediates the effect of beliefs about global warming on willingness to engage in mitigation behavior. *Journal of Environmental Psychology, 30*, 135-142.

285 Swim, J. K., & Becker, J. C. (2012). Country contexts and individuals' climate change mitigating behaviors: A comparison of U.S. versus German individuals' efforts to reduce energy use. *Journal of Social Issues, 68*, 571-591.

286 Whitmarsh, L. (2009). Behavioural responses to climate change: Asymmetry of intentions and impacts. *Journal of Environmental Psychology, 29*, 13-23.

287 de Boer, J., Schösler, H., & Boersema, J. J. (2013). Climate change and meat eating: An inconvenient couple? *Journal of Environmental Psychology, 33*, 1-8.

288 Caperello, N. D., & Kurani, K. S. (2012). Households' stories of their encounters with a plug-in hybrid electric vehicle. *Environment and Behavior, 44*, 493-508.

289 Steg, L., & Vlek, C. (2009). Encouraging pro-environmental behaviour: An integrative review and research agenda. *Journal of Environmental Psychology, 29*, 309-317.

290 Abrahamse, W., Steg, L., Vlek, C., & Rothengatter, T. (2005). A review of intervention studies aimed at household energy conservation. *Journal of Environmental Psychology, 25*, 273-291.

291 Bamberg, S., & Möser, G. (2007). Twenty years after Hines, Hungerford, and Tomera: A new meta-analysis of psycho-social determinants of pro-environmental behaviour. *Journal of Environmental Psychology, 27*, 14-25.

292 Werner, C. M., Cook, S., Colby, J., & Lim, H. (2012). 'Lights out' in university classrooms: Brief group discussion can change behavior. *Journal of Environmental Psychology, 32*, 418-426.

293 Pahl, S., & Bauer, J. (2013). Overcoming the distance: Perspective taking with future humans improves environmental engagement. *Environment and Behavior, 45*, 155-169.

294 Sussman, R., & Gifford, R. (2012). Please turn off the lights: The effectiveness of visual prompts. *Applied Ergonomics, 43*, 455-638.

295 Fischer, P., Greitemeyer, T., & Frey, D. (2008). Self-regulation and selective exposure: the impact of depleted self-regulation resources on confirmatory information processing. *Journal of Personality and Social Psychology, 94*, 382.

296 Bartusch, C., & Porathe, T. (2011). Climate-smart information design: Visualizing residential electricity use over the Internet. *Information Design Journal, 19*, 3-17.

297 Hyvönen, K., Saastamoinen, M., Hongisto, M., Kallio, A., & Södergård, C. (2012). A monitoring and feedback service as a way to reduce the greenhouse gas emissions of consumption. *International Journal of Consumer Studies, 36*, 221-227.

298 Abrahamse, W., Steg, L., Vlek, C., & Rothengatter, T. (2005). A review of intervention studies aimed at household energy conservation. *Journal of Environmental Psychology, 25*, 273-291.

299 Staats, H., Harland, P., & Wilke, H. A. (2004). Effecting durable change a team approach to improve environmental behavior in the household. *Environment and Behavior, 36*, 341-367.

300 Stern, P. C. (1986). Blind spots in policy analysis: What economics doesn't say about energy use. *Journal of Policy Analysis and Management, 5*, 200-227.

301 Hirst, E. (1987). Individual and institutional behavior related to energy efficiency in buildings. *Journal of Environmental Systems, 16*, 57-74.

302 Nilsson, A., von Borgstede, C., & Biel, A. (2004). Willingness to accept climate change strategies: The effect of values and norms, *Journal of Environmental Psychology, 24*, 267-277.

303 McKenzie-Mohr, D., & Smith, W. A. (1999). *Fostering sustainable behavior: An introduction to community-based social marketing.* Gabriola Island, B.C: New Society Pub.

304 Darley, J. M. (1978). Energy conservation techniques as innovations, and their diffusion. *Energy and Buildings, 1*, 339-343.

305 Robelia, B. A., Greenhow, C., & Burton, L. (2011). Environmental learning in online social networks: Adopting environmentally responsible behaviors. *Environmental Education Research, 17*, 553-575.

306 Katzev, R. D., & Johnson, T. R. (1983). A social-psychological analysis of residential electricity consumption: the impact of minimal justification techniques. *Journal of Economic Psychology, 3*, 267-284.

307 Katzev, R.D., Johnson, T.R. (1984). Comparing the effects of monetary incentives and foot-in-the-door strategies in promoting residential electricity conservation. *Journal of Applied Social Psychology, 14*, 12–27.

308 Pallak, M.S., Cummings, N. (1976). Commitment and voluntary energy conservation. *Personality and Social Psychology Bulletin, 2*, 27–31.

309 Winett, R. A. (1982). The effects of videotape modeling and daily feedback on residential electricity conservation, home temperature and humidity, perceived comfort, and clothing worn: Winter and summer. *Journal of Applied Behavior Analysis, 15*, 381-402.

310 Aronson, E., & O'Leary, M. (1982-83). The Relative Effectiveness of Models and Prompts on Energy Conservation: A Field Experiment in a Shower Room. *Journal of Environmental Systems, 12*, 219-224.

CHAPTER 14:

Sustainability: Managing Limited Resources

Freedom in a commons brings ruin to all.

—GARRETT HARDIN[1]

MOVING DAY ARRIVED. *Tom and Jane at last were able to move into the house his grandfather had given him. The excitement of having so much space and being together in it was almost too much. They sat among the cardboard boxes in the kitchen with friends who had helped them move, sipping tea.*

"Well," asked one friend, "What are you going to do with this place after you're settled in? Build a swimming pool?"

"You're kidding, I hope," Jane replied. "Not only do we have barely enough money to heat the place. And now—you heard the mayor's speech, didn't you?"

The town's reserves of water were virtually depleted in the drought, and the mayor had appealed to residents not to use any water except for drinking, cooking, personal hygiene, and one weekly bath. "We couldn't very well justify a private pool now," she said.

"One thing we will have to do," Tom broke in, "is put some insulation in the walls. I looked inside one wall and there was absolutely none there! I don't know how Gramps lived through the winter."

"Someday I'd like to investigate solar heating," said Jane. "We have a good southern exposure in the back."

"I guess you two will just have to keep each other warm until you save up a little!" a friend replied.

After a moment's reflection, one of their friends brightened up. "I saw enough bottles in the basement that if you took them all to the recycling place, you'd probably have enough to pay for solar heating," he laughed.

AFTER YEARS OF PUBLIC DEBATE, ENVIRONMENTAL RESOURCE ISSUES ARE FAMILIAR TO ALL OF US. We are quite aware that, on one hand, some vital natural resources are being depleted quickly, while on the other hand, there is an oversupply of undesirable by-products from our use of those same natural resources (e.g., carbon dioxide and chemical pollution). The world struggles toward the goal of **sustainability**, which is defined as development that "meets the needs of the present without compromising the ability of future generations to meet their own needs."[2]

This chapter considers the psychological processes involved in sustainability, which can also be defined as the effective management of environmental resources. Although policy-makers

FIGURE 14–1 Recycling has become a widespread practice, but it is an easy sustainability behavior. The more challenging behaviors, such as driving less, are more difficult to achieve.

often look to economics, political science, or engineering for the solutions to sustainability, environmental psychology has a crucial role to play.[3,4]

What are these "environmental resources" we use sustainably or not? This may seem either obvious or mysterious. Those who think it's obvious might say, "Well, fish, trees, water!" However, those who think it's mysterious might say, "Well, what about the energy used to make a car or a glass of beer, take shower, or the environmental cost of growing cotton for jeans or to fly home for the holidays, or the impact of food as a waste product?" Indeed, environmental resources are part of virtually everything we do, all day long. We cannot use *no* resources, but we certainly can use them more carefully.

So, once more, what *are* environmental resources? Rather than list each of the thousands of them, we can think of them as falling into five main categories. These categories overlap in important ways (everything is connected!), but we can look at "environmental resources" through these five lenses. First, we use **energy** for many of our endeavors. Second, the **food** (and drink) we consume is grown, transported, and disposed of. Third, we buy **material goods**, from computers to clothing to cars. Fourth, we **waste** portions of everything we acquire. Fifth, **transportation** moves us (and our food, material goods, and waste!) all around the town and the planet.

The ways that environmental psychologists examine these five categories of environmental resources include our *values* (broad preferences about how things should be), *attitudes* (thoughts, intentions, goals) toward using them, our *behaviors* (actual adopting, using, disposing) with them, and *interventions* to change unsustainable uses of them.

I used the word *management* earlier. Here the term refers to the *rate* and *quality* of each individual's use of these resources. The rate of this process is often quantifiable, although the quality of the process is often debatable (see Figure 14-1). Much environmental management is done at the macro level by governments, corporations, and other organizations. Environmental psychologists usually are more interested in the resource management behavior of individuals and small groups—resource management at the micro level, although some are involved with larger entities. Both levels are important, but the crucial aspect of micro-level resource management is that it sums up to the macro level in mysterious, irrational, yet all-important ways. We are 7 billion resource managers. We range from subsistence farmers in very poor countries to binners sorting out recyclables from garbage in our cities to middle-class people trying to decide whether to buy an SUV, a hybrid, or a bicycle, to the CEOs of the companies making those cars.

After some key concepts are defined, we will examine the main research strategies used by environmental psychologists to understand resource management. Next, the factors that promote sustainability will be surveyed, and key theories about resource management will be described. The latter part of the chapter is devoted to four important cases of resource management: air pollution, water conservation, energy conservation, and recycling. The basic question underlying this chapter is this: Can we achieve sustainability, or better yet, can we achieve what has been called sustainable happiness, that is, happiness that does not exploit other people, the environment, or future generations?[5]

SUSTAINABILITY AS A COMMONS DILEMMA

MY OWN VISION OF THE PROBLEM IS BEST DESCRIBED BY THE NOTION OF THE COMMONS DILEMMA, and much of the chapter is framed by this notion. What is this "commons"? Originally, a commons was a central open space in the heart of a settlement. It was owned by all the citizens of the settlement and therefore by no citizen in particular. Today, we would probably call such spaces urban parks. Any citizen is welcome to use the park for picnics, sports, or just strolling, or the open ocean for fishing. In the old days when economies were more agriculturally based, people also grazed their animals on the commons. As long as there was room and grass enough on the commons for everyone, it was a tranquil place.

In most commons, however, the day eventually arrived when someone added a new cow to the commons and was perceived as using the commons for grazing more than he or she should. In the ensuing discussions, the management of commons space often will be a hot topic. The owner of the offending cow may have countered with the opinion that "it's a free country, isn't it?" The issue becomes freedom in the commons.[6] (See Figure 14-2)

I chose the commons as a metaphor for discussing the problem of sustainability because it seems vivid and appropriate. Now there is evidence that its basic storyline is more memorable than other environmental messages.[7] Other North American and European social scientists also advocate thinking of environmental problems in this way.[8,9]

Commons are established on the assumption that the supply of the resource can meet the demands of the community. Eighteenth-century economists such as Adam Smith did not much consider the boundaries or limits that are inherent in commons. Each individual was therefore free to exploit resources as much as possible, because in exploiting the resource for his or her own benefit, the individual was believed to be guided by an "invisible hand" to benefit the whole community. If a farmer could grow enough wheat to make himself rich, he would also employ people to assist him, buy more goods from others, and donate more to charity. Given the world population and state of technology at the time, this was not an unreasonable viewpoint in the 18th century.

However, an early 19th-century economist, William Lloyd, was one of the first to see a problem with this. He wrote:

> If a person puts more cattle into his own field, the amount of the subsistence which they consume is all deducted from that which was at the command of his original stock [of cattle]; and if, before, there was no more than a [bare] sufficiency of pasture, he reaps no benefit from the additional cattle, what is gained in one way being lost in another. But if he puts more cattle on a common, the food which they consume forms a deduction which is shared between all the cattle...that of others as [well as] his own... and only a small part of it from his own cattle...[10]

FIGURE 14–2 This is what happens when "harvesters" have the mechanical power to take resources faster than the resource can regenerate itself.

The essential difference between the ideas of Smith and Lloyd is that Lloyd recognized that many resources are limited. By the 1960s, the problem became clear and acute. In a desirable but limited commons, individuals tend to act in self-interest. In a famous article, Garrett Hardin asserted that a process called the "tragedy of the commons" begins. "Each man [or woman] is locked into a system that compels him [or her] to increase his [or her] herd without limit—in a world that is limited. Ruin is the destination toward which all men [and women] rush, each pursuing his [or her] own best interest."[11]

Many social scientists and philosophers now recognize that grazing land, as in the metaphor of the commons, is merely one of many resources that are limited and held in common. The same basic ideas apply to overpopulation, air pollution, oil, whales, buffalo, energy brownouts, water shortages, congested radio bands, food supplies, and many other resources.

Thus, a **commons** is any desirable environmental resource held jointly by a group of individuals. It could be one pond owned by three families, it could be a national forest owned by the citizens of a nation, or it could be the global supply of oxygen, which presumably is owned indirectly by all people. Some resources renew themselves very quickly (solar and wind), some relatively quickly (such as grass for grazing or river water for electric power), others not so quickly (such as trees in a forest), and some very slowly or not at all (oil or endangered species). Once people have the means to harvest the resource more quickly than it regenerates, the resource is in danger.

Despite the knowledge that natural resources are being depleted rapidly, people do not seem to be able to stop. In fact, we are depleting them *faster* since we became aware of ecological shortages back in the 1970s. This is explicitly contrary to the definition of sustainable development. Hardin believed that reversing our tragic path toward ruin is difficult or impossible. He did not believe that technical expertise would solve the problem. The only thing that can save us, according to Hardin, is a "fundamental extension of morality." By this assertion, Hardin means that we must abolish the freedom of the commons and institute "mutual coercion, mutually agreed-upon." That is, society must agree, through laws and regulations, to severely limit individual freedom to exploit the commons.

Of course, through regulations, we already do impose some restraints, such as catch limits for fish or limits to forest cuts, but Hardin was not optimistic that society can accomplish this limitation, mainly because the individual freedom to exploit resources is so deeply valued by many members of society.

ROBYN DAWES'
thinking and research forms much of the basis for research in commons dilemmas and resource management.

Hardin's provocative pessimism has spurred much debate and research. I must add that not every thinker agrees with Hardin's premise. For example, the economist Julian Simon[12] and the statistician Bjorn Lomborg[13] have strenuously argued that resource shortages are overrated and that people will always find ways to deal with the short-term resource problems that they do admit occur.

Self-Interest and the Public Interest

EARLIER, I USED THE PHRASE COMMONS DILEMMA. What is the *dilemma* part? This is the difficult choice whether to act in self-interest or in the public interest. To paraphrase Hamlet: To get ahead or to cooperate, that is the question! In times of plenty when the resource is virtually inexhaustible, we might be able to take as much as we can, but when the resource is finite, we must choose between self-interest and sharing: that's the dilemma.

One can act in self-interest in two basic ways: by *taking* (having a nice long shower during a drought) or by *giving* (throwing recyclables in the garbage). Either way, the self-interest choice is easier or more rewarding, at least in the short run. The public-spirited act is often more expensive,

difficult, or time-consuming and less immediately rewarding than the self-serving act. This observation has led some observers to conclude that self-serving behavior is natural. If by "natural" these observers mean "unchangeable part of human nature," then most environmental psychologists would disagree. They assume that certain influences promote self-serving behavior and others promote public-interest behavior.

Environmental psychologists do not accept Hardin's argument that we will *always* act in self-interest; we consider the issue of how individuals will behave in a limited commons to be an empirical question and that, ultimately, solutions can be found. We know that sometimes individuals *do* act in the public interest rather than in self-interest. Many individuals will walk out of their way to deposit litter in a garbage can, voluntarily limit the number of children they have, or turn down their thermostats. On the other hand, we can all recall occasions when we or others acted in self interest. Thus, the key questions are: *Under which conditions* do individuals act in self interest? How can we *change* that?

Before surveying the research on which conditions lead to self-serving or public-interest behavior, a brief discussion of the several types of dilemmas is warranted.

Commons Dilemmas, Social Traps, and Social Dilemmas

THE TERM COMMONS DILEMMA (also sometimes called resource dilemma) was inspired by the thought of Lloyd and Hardin, but was first used by Robyn Dawes.[14] He saw it as part of a family of similar problems that share certain characteristics that he called **social dilemmas**.[15] Commons dilemmas (the focus of this chapter) refer to choices we make about the use of natural resources. Social traps are about the temporal dilemma created when individuals (or society) succumb to short-term rewards that have some built-in and gradual cost that eventually becomes very large.[16] Classic social traps include overeating, smoking, and the use of some pesticides. Public goods problems refer to one's choice to contribute (or not) to something that would benefit the community as a whole (such as donating blood or giving to a fund to purchase parkland). The ethical dilemma in a public goods problem is this: if you never donate blood, should you ask for it later if you need a blood transfusion? Should you use that park that you did not help purchase?

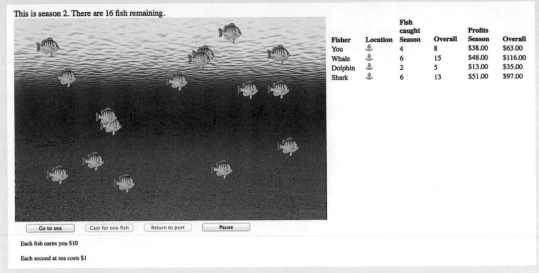

This is season 2. There are 16 fish remaining.

Fisher	Location	Fish caught Season	Overall	Profits Season	Overall
You	⚓	4	8	$38.00	$63.00
Whale	⚓	6	15	$48.00	$116.00
Dolphin	⚓	2	5	$13.00	$35.00
Shark	⚓	6	13	$51.00	$97.00

Go to sea　　Cast for one fish　　Return to port　　Pause

Each fish earns you $10

Each second at sea costs $1

FIGURE 14–3 FISH 4.0 is a microworld developed by Robert Gifford and his colleagues for studying the choices people make when harvesting limited natural resources.

In formal terms, the defining characteristics of a social dilemma are that (1) each participant receives more (or is penalized less) for a self-interest choice than for a public-interest choice, and (2) the participants as a group benefit more if they all choose to act in the public interest, than if they all choose to act in self-interest.[17]

Research Strategies

COMMONS DILEMMAS MAY BE STUDIED FROM SEVERAL PERSPECTIVES.[18] First, choices in a commons dilemma may be characterized as cooperative (oriented toward mutual gains), individualistic (oriented toward self gain), or competitive (oriented toward self's gain *relative* to others' gain).[19] Second, they may also be viewed as a form of group problem-solving.[20] Third, some researchers have focused on the formation of coalitions and the use of power in managing the commons.[21] Finally, applied behavior analysts see commons dilemmas as a set of behaviors governed by reinforcements and learning processes.

Field Experiments and Studies. Commons dilemmas certainly are complex situations that include each of these dimensions. How can they be studied? Field *experiments* require that the experimenter have control of the resource and the situation, which of course can be very difficult for a researcher to obtain. Field *studies* do not include the same degree of control over the resource and the situation, but the consequence is that a variety of explanations for the results must be entertained, because the lack of control allows many variables to potentially influence behavior in the commons.

Microworlds. You are in front of computer and a virtual ocean is on the screen. A dozen fish are swimming around. You can catch as many as you want. You know that at the end of each season, the number of fish that remain in the ocean will spawn so that the number doubles for the next season. However, two other people are also fishing from this same ocean.

How many fish will you take in this season?

This is the commons dilemma in a microcosm. Environmental psychologists study commons dilemmas by using these kinds of simulated commons, or microworlds.[22-28] Just as everyday commons dilemmas differ from situation to situation, so can microworlds. The rules and values of the resources in both real and simulated dilemmas vary considerably. The number of participants, the amount of the resource, and many other factors are systematically changed to determine each factor's importance.

Self-interest is the most attractive choice, but each participant is best-off if no one else **defects** (that is, takes more than a sustainable amount of the resource), next best-off if everyone cooperates (everyone takes a sustainable amount), and worst-off if everyone defects.[29]

From an early simple simulated commons dilemma that offered people the chance to take walnuts from a bowl (and trade them for money),[30] the idea has been technologically upgraded several times, and perhaps the most sophisticated microworld now is FISH 4.0, an online program that includes many research parameters and several ways of measuring fishers' choices in the commons.[31]

Microworlds evoke the obvious suspicion that behavior in them will not match behavior in everyday, real commons. For example, if the exercise is to be a valid indicator of behavior in a real-world commons, the symbolic resources should have enough value that harvesters take the simulation seriously. Most studies conducted so far have offered limited payoffs. Observations of research participants suggest, however, that even small payoffs can produce behavior which *seems* quite similar to that which could be expected in a real, valuable commons.

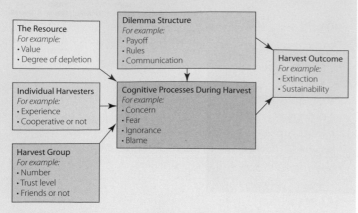

FIGURE 14–4 An overview of the natural resource management process.

For example, in a study in which participants could win no more than $10.50, participants were so caught up in the dilemma that defectors were sworn at, unrequited cooperators cried, stormed out of the room, and told defectors they "would have to live with their decisions for the rest of their lives."[32] Some participants have threatened ("jokingly") to beat up defectors, to destroy their reputations, and even to kill them![33] In my own lab, participants have said such things as "You greedy pig!" and "You die!" and "I could have smashed some heads."[34] Thus, despite the lack of field investigations, research using microworlds may have reasonable ecological validity.

Grounded Theory Analysis. Almost all studies in this area apply a set of conditions to the participants, then measure differences in harvesting behavior. Such a "black box" strategy ignores the thinking process engaged in by group members as they grapple with the dilemma. Donald Hine and I claimed that examining the "online thinking" of group members as they grapple with the dilemma is important. One way to do this is through **grounded theory analysis**, a method of scientifically examining subjective experience.[35] Indeed, by using this approach, we found that harvesters consider a number of factors as they make their decisions that researchers had not yet thought about.[36]

IN SUM *Each of us manages a steady supply of natural resources that have been converted into products we use every day. Some of these resources come from limited sources called commons. A commons is a pool of desirable materials that may be harvested by a number of individuals or organizations that all have access to it. Commons dilemmas occur when* harvesters can extract natural resources faster than the resource can regenerate; individuals then must decide whether to maximize their own gain or the gain of the group, including themselves. Social traps are similar, but emphasize the time dimension; we are trapped as a result of the eventual outcome of repeatedly yielding to short-term rewards while ignoring long-term costs. Social dilemma is the general term for these conflicts. Field experiments on social dilemmas are nearly impossible, and field studies are uncommon. Many laboratory studies of commons dilemmas have been conducted instead. The dynamics of commons dilemmas are very complex; some microworlds can take into account a large number of the many dimensions of everyday commons dilemmas. Judging from participants' reactions, microworlds may be more representative of everyday behavior than one might think.*

The Role of Environmental Psychology

SUSTAINABILITY IS ABOUT HUMAN BEHAVIOR. Therefore, it is yet another problem that environmental psychology can help solve, and the field is ready and able to do so.[37,38] Those who make decisions about resource management, whether as private individuals, or even as chief executive officers of large corporations, are nevertheless individuals, and that is the province of psychology.

WHAT INFLUENCES SUSTAINABILITY– RELATED BEHAVIOR?

IN MOST STUDIES OF SUSTAINABILITY, THE FUNDAMENTAL QUESTION IS THIS: UNDER WHICH CONDITIONS WILL PEOPLE COOPERATE—THAT IS, ACT SUSTAINABLY—OR NOT? What influences individuals to harvest much or little from a valuable, shared, limited, slowly regenerating resource?

The influences may be placed into four categories for now (see Figure 14-4). Later a more complete model will be introduced that will supersede this simple framework.

1. *The resource*: Is it important to the participants, is it nearly depleted or relatively plentiful?

2. *The participants as individuals*: Are they old or young? Experienced or not? Do they hold cooperative values or not?

3. *The participants as group members*: How many are there? Do they trust or know each other? Are they friends or strangers?

4. *Structure of the dilemma*: What are the rules and regulations surrounding one's decisions? What are the payoffs for cooperation and penalties for defection?

All of these matter, often in combination. In the following paragraphs, each is emphasized in turn for the sake of discussion, but sometimes multiple factors must be mentioned to accurately characterize an investigation.

The Resource

THREE CHARACTERISTICS OF THE RESOURCE (value, abundance, and certainty) all affect rates of cooperation among harvesters. First, as the value of the resource increases, the rate of cooperation decreases.[39] Second, the abundance of the resource also is important: if plenty exists, a dilemma does not. If the resource is almost extinguished, will people cooperate more than when it was relatively plentiful, or will they scramble to get what they can before the resource is totally exhausted? Early studies compared behavior in commons that were pure or half-ruined. The experimental situation was analogous to decisions to pollute (that is, where "giving" is the self-interest choice, rather than decisions to harvest, where taking is the self-interest choice). Participants cooperated significantly more in the half-ruined situation[40,41] (see Figure 14-5). In one way, these results are grounds for optimism; when we inherit partly ruined surroundings, we seem to (finally) cooperate. Unfortunately, from another perspective, when people inherit pure surroundings, apparently they will act selfishly *until* things are half-ruined.

However, a different study examined a harvest situation (as opposed to the pollution situation) in which students worked for course credits.[42] When fewer course credits were available in the commons, fewer cooperative responses occurred than when many course credits were available. This finding conflicts with those in the study

above. Perhaps the difference lies in whether the dilemma is framed as a "give-some" dilemma or a "take-some" dilemma. People may cooperate more in half-*polluted* commons, but act in self-interest more in half-*harvested* commons.

Resources may decline at different rates. Does it matter how quickly the water, trees, or fish are disappearing? That may depend on whether the harvesters are trusting individuals or not.[43] When the resource depletes slowly, harvesters seem to increase their take as time goes on. Less-trusting people harvested at about the same rate regardless of how fast the resource disappeared, but more-trusting people harvested more when the resource was depleting slowly and less when the resource was rapidly disappearing. Thus, trusting harvesters seem to be sensitive to the speed of resource depletion, but distrusting harvesters seem not to be.

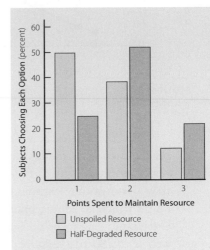

FIGURE 14–5 As the environment is degraded, it is treated with more respect. Swedish teenagers in this simulation spent more money to maintain the resource if they were given a half-ruined resource than if they were given an unspoiled resource.

Resources can disappear for different reasons, and this affects cooperation, too. What is the difference in cooperation if the resource is being depleted by *human* overharvesting versus some *natural* cause, such as disease or a climate shift? Apparently, if people think other *people* are depleting the resource, they want to get some too, but if *nature* is depleting the resource, they are more willing to restrain their harvests.[44]

Finally, the certainty of the resource matters. We can't always be sure exactly how much of a resource is available for harvest. No one knows exactly how many whales or salmon are in the sea, or how much oil remains in the earth. Most early simulations of commons dilemmas presented exact amounts to harvesters, but recently researchers have examined resource uncertainty as a factor in cooperation. Low levels of uncertainty may not affect cooperation,[45] but higher levels do: when uncertainty is at least moderate, harvesters increase their take.[46,47]

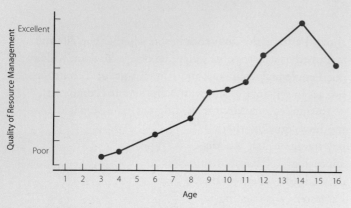

FIGURE 14–6 Quality of resource management in a simulated resource management task by groups of children from ages 3 to 16.

Given that the exact amount of many resources is not precisely known, this is a disturbing finding. When harvesters are faced with a range of possible harvest amounts, they optimistically assume the larger numbers are accurate,[48] which of course suits a self-interested perspective. Uncertainty can focus on resource replenishment *rates* as well as their actual amounts. We cannot be sure how fast whales will reproduce, or how long trees will take to reach maturity, or how many fish will spawn; we have only estimates. Once again, as uncertainty about replenishment rate grows, people seem to believe the more optimistic estimates and harvest more.[49] This also suits their self-interest.

The Harvesters

PERSONAL QUALITIES THAT HARVESTERS BRING TO THE DILEMMA (e.g., their age, gender, personality, and social values) affect cooperation. Often, however, the effects of these factors depend on some others aspect of the dilemma. For example, men and women as a whole cooperate about equally, but men cooperate more (and women do not) when group members trust and can communicate with each other.[50]

Age, education, and income. The ability to work together toward sound management of the commons generally increases with age, at least up to the late teens. Nursery school children are primarily "own-gain oriented."[51] I used a commons dilemma simulation to study groups of children from age 3 to 16.[52] As age increased, cooperation increased. By age 14, groups were harvesting up to 85 percent of the maximum possible points while maintaining the health of the commons. At age 16, however, a drop in cooperativeness was observed. I remarked, half-seriously, that maybe we should turn over the management of natural resources to 14-year-olds (see Figure 14-6).

Up to age 5 or so, most children are unable to grasp the idea that one may have to give up an immediate gain for a long-term gain. However, from about age 5 to 14, children are increasingly able to understand the value of cooperation. After age 14 or so, cooperative behavior probably depends largely on "life" factors other than cognitive development. Perhaps in our late teens idealism declines as working and other experience "teach" young people that the world is a competitive place where each person must get whatever he or she can. Another study also showed that 18- to 20-year-olds employ quite *low* levels of cooperation.[53] A slight increase in cooperation may occur across the 18-to-40 age range.[54] Older people have not been studied in microworlds, but perhaps studies showing that older people litter less than younger people give a hint.[55,56]

At least in the case of adopting solar thermal energy, but probably for other cooperative choices, more education and higher incomes are associated with more cooperation.[57]

Gender. Do males or females cooperate more in commons dilemmas? Females probably receive more socialization to cooperate than do males. In reasonably similar commons dilemma simulations, one study found that females consistently cooperated more than males,[58] but another found no differences between males and females.[59] The only study to examine gender differences as its central concern found no differences in actual cooperation, although women gave more moral reasons for their actions than men[60] and sometimes women show more emotional concern.[61] Gender, like age after the mid-teens, is probably less influential than other factors.

Personality. Early researchers proposed three basic personality types: the person who consistently tries to cooperate, even when that strategy results in losses, the person who quickly settles into an uncooperative stance and refuses to budge even when others try to cooperate, and a third person who falls in between these extremes.[62]

An early researcher postulated the existence of a **1/*n*th personality**, the tendency to cooperate or adopt public interest strategies,[63] and found that 1/*n*th personalities did indeed act in the public interest more often than non-1/*n*th personalities. No overall gender differences were found, but the combination of gender and personality affected harvesting. Males who were high on the 1/*n*th personality dimension cooperated no more or less than men who were low on it. However, high 1/*n*th females cooperated much more than did low 1/*n*th females. Thus, gender and personality seem to *interact* to predict who will act in the public interest.

A nearly opposite sort of person is the **narcissist**, who thinks of self first. These folks, not surprisingly, harvest selfishly.[64] A similar personality type, the **egocentric**, also tends to over-harvest in resource dilemmas[65] and be less supportive of biofuels.[66]

Values. Social values also influence behavior in the commons. Three types of common **social value orientation** are cooperativeness (the belief that I should maximize my profit *and* your profit), competitiveness (I maximize my profit *relative* to yours), and individualism (I maximize my profit with no particular concern for your profit).[67] Less common orientations are *altruism* (I maximize your profit *over* my own) and the *murder-suicide* type (I minimize both my profit *and* your profit).

Generally, as would be expected, persons who hold cooperative values do restrain their harvests in commons dilemmas.[68,69] However, other factors can modify this. For example, cooperative harvesters who hear a message promoting cooperation cooperate more than those who do not hear it, but this further depends on the other harvesters' cooperativeness.[70] What if a harvester is known by other harvesters to be cooperative or greedy? As you might expect, group members who are known to be cooperative elicit more cooperation from others.[71]

Another sort of value, **biospheric**, reflects a strong and stable concern for life on the planet. Those with stronger biospheric values tend to support the use of biofuels.[72] Finally, some evidence suggests that environmental cooperativeness only follows from biospheric values if a person also has a strong environmental identity.[73]

Motivation. Are you passionate? How so? **Harmonious passion** means striving toward a chosen goal, but in a way that allows choice among one's other goals; **obsessive passion** involves a kind of tunnel vision in which one goal is so strong that others are lost. Both forms are associated with mainstream environmental cooperation, but only obsessive motivation is associated with support for radical environmentalism.

Another view of motivation puts **autonomy** at the center, suggesting that when we do something, it is based on a continuum of autonomy that ranges from *external* (controlled) to *introjected* (to avoid guilt or shame) to *identified* (personally endorsed) to *integrated* (congruent with values, goals and needs that are part of self). This range of motivation predicts reported household energy-saving behavior well; in fact, better than such other influences such as intentions, subjective norms, perceived behavioral control, and past behavior.[74] As an example, in China, when *transformational leadership* (that is, when the leader connects the followers' sense of identity and self to the project, inspires and challenges them, etc.) in environmental matters was strong, it was positively related to reported environmental behavior, but when transformational leadership was weak, external motivation was negatively related to reported environmental behavior.[75]

Attitudes. Environmental cooperativeness is related to a one's **consideration of future consequences**. Those who report considering future consequences more tend to favor using public transportation,[76] the use of biofuels,[77] and have positive attitudes toward green sources of electricity.[78]

Experience, Education, and Knowledge. Harvesters' prior experience and knowledge affect environmental cooperation. For example, **social uncertainty**—a person's lack of confidence about how others will act—-may be important.[79] People new to understanding the commons and the dilemma involved may have only a vague idea how their actions affect the commons as a whole. If so, giving them prior experience or knowledge about it (such as you are getting right now!) might improve their performance in a later commons dilemma. Evidence supports this hypothesis; better understanding of the commons dilemma is associated with more cooperation.[80] Experience as a one-person manager of a commons (perhaps your first time paying the utility bills as an adult?) was better than prior group experience (say as part of your family) in subsequent commons management situations.[81] Presumably, in the simpler context of one-person management, we learn more about how our actions affect the commons.

Experience in the sense of simply having more knowledge about environmental issues is also associated with more responsible environmental behavior.[82,83] For example, useful information about the environmental impact of food purchase choices strengthens shoppers' intention to buy locally produced, seasonal, and environmentally certified products and increased the actual buying of certified and fair trade products.[84]

However, as we saw in an earlier chapter, environmental education programs are not always effective.[85] More needs to be learned about how best to develop and deliver these programs, so they are more consistently effective. For example, the false consensus effect (believing that others think the same as you even when they may not) can play a role in whether an EE program changes behavior. Participants in one program who believed that most (51%-54%) of the others in their program would contribute money and volunteer work for environmental causes contributed; those who believed that fewer (28%-35%) of their classmates would contribute, did not.[86]

The Harvesters as Group Members

ONCE INDIVIDUAL HARVESTERS ARE PART OF A GROUP, a complex mix of interactions that influence environmental harvesting begins to occur among the members. These include the size of the group, conformity, trust, friendship, sense of community, and perceived equity.

Number of Harvesters. Group size affects harvesting. Nearly every study of group size has found that behavior in resource management tends increasingly toward self-interest as group size increases.[87] Cooperation declines both as the number of harvesters rises and as the number of groups *within* a commons with a constant total membership rises.[88] This is very bad news for a planet with 7 billion people.

Why does this happen?

1. As group size increases, the harm from any one person or group's defection is spread thin among the general population.

2. Defection often is less visible to others in larger groups.

3. The effect of the harm done is less visible to the defector;[89] it is easier to inflict pain if you do not have to watch others experience their loss.

4. Negative feedback to the defector is more difficult to sustain in larger groups.

The upper population limit for a well-functioning (cooperative) commons may be as low as 150 members.[90] Trust in others—a key component of cooperation—helps cooperation in groups of three but not even in groups of seven harvesters, suggesting that trust helps most in very small groups.[91] This suggests that in larger commons (such as towns, cities, and the Earth as a whole), Garrett Hardin's pessimism may be well justified unless other, more positive, factors can improve management of the commons.

Conformity, Modeling, and Comparison. The commons can be confusing, particularly to new harvesters. One way to deal with this problem is to check out what others are doing—play it safe and simply do what others do.[92,93] This conformist tendency influenced harvesting even when verbal warnings were issued, the probability of punishment was present, and even when conformist harvesting was against the harvester's own best interests![94] Inexperience in a complicated situation seems to produce strong tendencies to conformity as harvesters desperately try to figure out the best course of action.

Fortunately, conformity can be a positive influence if harvesters copy others who are acting sustainably. Reuven Sussman and I examined whether conformity to others could encourage the use of public food compost bins in a shopping center food court and a fast-food restaurant.[95] Confederates watched for diners who had finished eating and were headed toward the garbage and compost bins. The confederates inserted themselves just ahead of the diner, and conscientiously disposed of food and garbage in the recommended way. Diners who had a confederate ahead of them were far more likely to do the right thing than diners who did not have a confederate ahead of them. Interestingly, in the same study signs were places on tabletops to encourage composting. They were ineffective; humans as models were effective. Similarly, but within a commons dilemma, when one harvester sacrificed self-interest, other harvesters subsequently conserved more.[96,97]

When harvesters were told that others were *under*-using the commons, they increased their own use of it; this sounds like nonconformity.[98] However, when they were told that most others were under-using the resource, but a few others were over-harvesting, they over-harvested; this is conformity to a selfish model. When told that the commons was being *over*used by others, participants increased their own harvests (conformity again) when they had little trust in other harvesters, but decreased their own harvests (nonconformity) when they trusted the others. In sum, the rule-of-thumb appears to be this: conform if it suits your self-interest and you do not trust others, but act sustainably if the resource is endangered and you do trust the others.

What happens when harvesters see no single pattern of harvesting, so they can't conform to any one pattern? As above, when some other harvesters take more, and some less, many harvesters choose to take more.[99,100] "Oh, if you can take *that* many, I guess it's OK for me to do so, too."

Another kind of comparison occurs when people think about the past, present, and future. For example, when shown images of a woman in the future who was negatively impacted by environmental events and taking her perspective, people engaged in more environment-positive actions.[101] Yet in another study, after comparing their peers to people in the past few decades, people said they were *more* willing to make sustainable choices, but after comparing their peers to people in the future, they said they were *less* willing to make sustainable choices.[102] Why do you think that happens?

Friendship. The quality of relations among harvesters is important. As you might assume, as friendship grows, cooperation grows.[103] Friends know one another's needs; they may draw upon past experience that probably includes some give and take; they have a stake in continuing their good relations, which favors cooperation over self-interested harvesting. Happily, harvesters do not seem to require pre-existing friendship before they cooperate; when they know strangers have attitudes identical to their own, they cooperate more.[104] Of course, when group members are not friends, or even worse, when are enemies…well, you can imagine that outcome.

Trust. Another important positive factor is trust. One would expect that, like friendship, trust is associated with cooperation in commons dilemmas. However, when Donald Hine and I tested this idea in a meta-analysis, we were surprised to find that across the existing research literature, trust has little effect on cooperation.[105] The reason appears to be that the effect of trust depends quite heavily on certain other factors, so that its effect *in general* is weak, although it is associated with cooperation in some circumstances.

For example, as noted earlier, trusting participants cooperate more only in smaller groups[106] and only when they know how much others are cooperating, not when others' harvest behavior is not known to the group as a whole.[107] Again as noted earlier, cooperation increases for men but not women when group members trust one another and can communicate with each other.[108] The effect of trust also depends on how quickly the resource is being depleted. Those who do not trust others much harvest about the same amount regardless of how fast the resource is being harvested, but those who do trust others harvest more when the resource pool is full, and less when it is almost

FIGURE 14–7 Commons already are governed in various ways. Do you think this sign will effectively protect this resource?

empty.[109] Thus, the influence of interpersonal trust is positive, but its influence is easily modified by other factors.

Sense of Community. When harvesters think of themselves more as individuals than as group members, they over-harvest more.[110] Having a sense of community or group identity, is important[111] and it can provide a positive glow in the dilemma. A very hopeful sign is that not much seems to be required to create enough group identity to improve cooperation. The only difference between "high-identity" and "low-identity" harvesters in one study was that the high-identity harvesters came to the lab as a group and received their instructions together. That's all it took for them to cooperate more.[112] Possible lesson for everyday sustainability: create a sense of community, and perhaps that is not as difficult as it sounds.

The Structure of the Dilemma

THE RULES, CUSTOMS, NORMS, AND CIRCUMSTANCES OF COMMONS DILEMMAS VARY. Whatever the state of the resource itself, or the qualities of the harvesters, these formal and informal structural elements of the dilemma itself will themselves play an important role in determining the quality of resource management. These structural elements include the nature of the rewards and punishments for harvesting, whether or not harvesters are educated about commons dilemmas, whether they may communicate with each other, whether the resource is partitioned into territories, rules about who may harvest how much in which order, and the different ways of governing dilemma situations (see Figure 14-7).

Payoffs, Rewards, and Punishments. What is the effect of delivering rewards or punishments to harvesters, instead of merely asking them to cooperate? Naturally, paying for cooperation tends to increase it and punishing defection tend to reduce it, although neither has an absolute or universal impact on harvesters. However, if the reward for cooperation is high enough, or the penalty for defection is strong enough, the commons dilemma is virtually not a dilemma anymore.[113] However, within a payoff structure that retains the essence of the dilemma, smaller rewards do lead to less harvesting and higher rewards do lead to more harvesting,[114] and penalties will reduce defection.[115]

So, we should just reward people for acting sustainably, and punish them for defecting, right? Unfortunately, managers of everyday commons often do not have enough money or policing power at their disposal to transform them into non-dilemmas. For example, horns from endangered rhinos bring thousands of dollars to poachers, but governments cannot afford to pay every potential poacher the same amount *not* to poach or to hire enough park rangers to be certain that no poaching occurs.

An important question with a less obvious answer is whether rewards *or* punishments are more effective in producing cooperation. Positive incentives evoked more cooperation than negative incentives in one study,[116] but in another, rewards and punishments were equally effective,[117] and in a third, overconsumption decreased as the probability of punishment rose.[118] Incidentally, the rewards do not have to be monetary. Verbal reinforcements such as "Good choice!" after a cooperative harvest was sufficient to improve cooperation in two studies.[119,120] Because of its important implications for how to manage real-world resources, this question needs more research.

The absolute size of a reward is not always what is most important; sometimes the key is the *relative* size of the reward (for example, some sports stars sulk when they are paid "only" $3 million per year, because another player is paid $5 million). When the size of the harvester's own gain (high or low) and the size of the gain for all harvesters (high or low) were separately varied, the harvester's own gain affected cooperation much more.[121] However, in two other studies, when harvesters were told that the group's total winnings would be divided equally among them, they cooperated more than when individuals each could take home their own profits.[122,123]

Such discrepancies may be caused by the complexity of the dilemma's rules.[124] Harvesters may act selfishly not because they do not care about others, but because they comprehend just enough of the rules to understand what *might* happen to *themselves* as the dilemma progresses. When the rules are too complex, in the real world as well as in a microworld, harvesters may give up trying to discover how to serve the public interest and simply look after themselves as best they can. When the rules are simpler, cooperation does increase when others' welfare is at stake.

The rewards and punishments discussed so far are administered by an external authority (the researcher, essentially taking the role of government). Paul Bell and colleagues asked what happens when rewards and punishments are administered by the harvesters themselves. In one such scenario, the harvesters were given the opportunity to punish those who acted in self-interest.[125] After every set of five choices, they could vote to penalize others; if two of the five group members voted to sanction a third participant, the latter lost 5 points; if three voted to sanction a fourth, the loss was 10 points; if four participants all voted to punish a fifth, the fifth participant lost 15 points. Perhaps not surprisingly, cooperation was higher when this sort of punishment by "armed cooperators" was part of the dilemma's structure. However, sanctioning systems are not free in the real world. Harvesters themselves may well be willing to fine others who are greedy, but a policing system requires money and the will to establish and operate it, and vigilantism is usually frowned upon. As if to support this point, when harvesters were able to sanction others, but they were charged for policing services (which would be analogous to local taxes in the everyday world), the sanctioning system did not improve the overall functioning of the dilemma.[126]

Enlightenment. Before people enter a commons dilemma, one might attempt to persuade harvesters to "do the right thing." One might try to *induce* morality by delivering a short "sermon" to harvesters, mentioning the benefits of cooperation, public-interest ethics, resource exploitation, the sad case of blue whales, and so on. When this was done, compared to a group that received no sermon, the harvest-

PAUL BELL has investigated many factors that affect cooperation in commons dilemmas.

ers did cooperate more.[127] Advocating either the Golden Rule or altruism also produces greater cooperation than if no moral guidelines were advocated.[128] Pro-sustainable morality can be induced, at least temporarily, by appeals to high moral standards.

Communication. When harvesters talk to each other, it helps; communication is crucial for sustainability in a commons. In everyday life, communication may not occur because the harvesters choose not to talk to one another, or because communication is forbidden by superiors or governments, or because harvesters rarely encounter one another. The choice not to communicate may result from self-interest combined with good fortune, as when the old prospector finally discovers a gold mine or when a whaler sights a rare blue whale. In ocean fish wars, an increasingly common occurrence, governments may forbid fishermen from divulging the size of their catches to avoid international diplomatic trouble. Those who poach orangutans in Borneo may not communicate because they rarely meet one another during their poaching forays.

On the positive side, when communication occurs, management of the commons improves.[129,130,131,132,133] Communication among group members serves a number of beneficial functions. It can help to

- Clarify payoffs
- Reach agreements on harvesting (such as taking turns).
- Reduce distrust.
- Enhance group identity.
- Encourage public commitment to cooperation[134] (in a public discussion, harvesters are not likely to advocate defection).
- Devise penalties for not following agreements.
- Elicit promises to cooperate.[135]

The development of these **group-regarding motives** may be a necessary and nearly sufficient condition for good management of the commons and group harvesting success.[136] When group members think they will be meeting and communicating in the future, cooperation is better.[137]

Communication may also overcome the negative influence of "bad apples." When a confederate joined a commons dilemma and was instructed to act in self-interest while other harvesters were allowed to communicate, the selfish confederate's presence did not reduce cooperation.

However, when communication was not permitted, the selfish confederate's presence did result in significantly more self-interested choices on the part of others.[138]

However, communication is not always beneficial. For example, it may lead to cooperation only among better-adjusted individuals.[139] It may facilitate the performance of trusting males but not trusting females.[140] In the real world, communication is not free—someone must invest time, effort, or cash to establish and maintain communication. When communication is not free, its benefits are reduced (but not eliminated).[141]

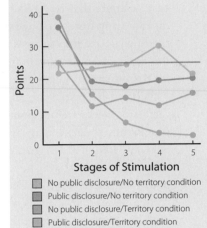

FIGURE 14-8 The effects of resource visibility and territories on harvesting. As harvesting rate deviates from the optimal rate, the outlook for the resource worsens. Across several stages of this simulation, the most favorable harvesting rates occurred when the resource was visible and territories existed.

Public Disclosure. Transparency is also crucial. Are the harvests by those with access to the commons made public or kept private? When harvesters could see how each of the others was acting, two out of three measures of cooperation rose significantly[142] (see Figure 14-8). The evidence on this is clear: public disclosure increases the number of public-interest choices.[143-146] As noted earlier, trust is a positive influence, but it is very dependent on other factors. Without knowing what others are taking, trust may diminish. The positive effect of trust on cooperation in one study occurred only when harvesters knew others' harvest totals and, more importantly, when harvesters *knew that others knew* what they were taking.[147]

Harvest Rules. What is the effect of varying some of the rules? For example, the effect of putting a limit on the maximum harvest each season was that harvesters cooperated earlier in the sequence, but less later.[148] What if harvesters are allowed to donate resources back to the pool? This would be analogous to a wealthy lumber baron personally financing a tree-planting project, or a poor but generous woodcutter volunteering time to plant trees. When donations are possible, the resource is depleted less quickly.[149] Although some harvesters are greedy, others are not; to permit donations is to allow generous harvesters to "give something back."

A few harvesters do not even wait for someone to tell them they can donate. One of the most touching moments in my own research career occurred when a 4-year-old girl in one of my early studies saw that the resources (in this case, walnuts that could be traded later for cookies) were disappearing from the bowl that held them. She looked at the bowl, looked at her own stash, looked at me, and then put some of her own walnuts back so more were available for the other girls in her group.

What if harvesters are allowed to steal from other harvesters? Thieves are not popular, and thieves are not given permission to steal in the everyday world, but…what if, anyway? Perhaps if harvesters take resources from each other, they at least will not be taking from the common pool of resources, which should help to preserve the resource. Indeed, in a study that punished over-harvesting, but allowed theft, theft *did* increase, and the resource was better preserved.[150] However, when theft *was* punished, over-harvesting occurred, and the resource was more rapidly depleted. Given that neither stealing nor over-harvesting are desirable, which policy would you implement if you were in charge of a commons dilemma?

Resource Partitioning. If the commons is divided into portions, each of which is managed by a separate harvester, will management of the entire commons be better than if no subdivisions are made? One of the few field studies examined two lobster fishing arrangements in Maine.[151] In one, the commons is open; all fishers who operate out of a given harbor have equal access to the lobsters in the vicinity of the harbor. In the other, fishers are organized into groups. Each group holds a clearly defined territory from which other groups are barred. In the subdivided commons, lobster management is better. More and larger lobsters result, and each fisher makes more money.

Of course, because this study was done in the field, one cannot be sure that lobster stocks were equal for the subdivided and undivided commons *before* the researcher began collecting data, and many other aspects of the two arrangements may be different. However, laboratory studies also support the value of subdividing the commons.[152] When subdividing versus no subdividing and reinforcements versus no reinforcements were compared, subdivision improved management of the commons, but reinforcements did not bring *further* improvement.[153] Harvesters in these studies use the resource in a manner that simultaneously earns them more and leaves more of the resource in the commons. This is the very definition of good resource management.

These results might be applied to the management of energy sources in everyday life. If the total pool of electricity, natural gas, or gasoline could be divided into small pools controlled by neighborhoods or apartment blocks, fewer brownouts and gasoline shortages might occur. This has been called decentralized generation or **district energy**. Subdividing the commons may make external reinforcements, such as rewards and punishments, less necessary.

Equity. In the real world, some harvesters enter commons dilemmas with more resources than others (e.g., a lobster fisher may inherit a prime territory from a parent, or a rich person may decide to enter the poaching business and starts out by buying the best equipment money can buy). Some harvesters reap more than others through greater effort, skill, greed, or persistence. These differences are of two types: inequality is a difference in the *actual* amount of resources, and inequity is a difference in the *perceived fairness* of the amount of resources. If Chris fishes 12 hours every day and Kim fishes 8 hours a day, Chris is likely to catch more fish (harvests unequal), but many people would say their harvests were *equitable* because Chris works longer than Kim.

So, what happens when harvesters are told that at the end of the dilemma, no matter what happens to the resource, all harvests will be split equally? In one study, cooperation was better in the sense that all harvests were larger.[154] However, when inequality or inequity in the harvest or distribution of resources was present, decreased cooperation resulted.[155,156] Equal outcomes may produce the greatest cooperation in a commons dilemma, but not all harvesters are happy with the practice. Some harvesters in both simulated resource management dilemmas[157] and in real-world energy conservation[158] do not feel that forced equality is fair. These, of course, tend to be individuals who prefer the individual-gain orientation to the justice-for-all orientation. Cohesive (that is, friendly) groups seem to use equality as the basis of distributing the resources they harvest, whereas non-cohesive groups seem to use equity as the basis.[159]

Governance. Which structural solutions, that is, forms of government, do harvesters prefer? The obvious reason for this is so that we eventually can recommend how commons dilemmas ought to be run.

Wanting to vote for a leader is particularly popular when the resource is overused,[160] when harvesters are allowed to freely take more of the resource (as opposed to being limited in their harvests), and when the amount of others' harvests varies more.[161,162] Harvesters are more likely to vote for a leader to run the commons when they believe the cause of non-cooperation is that the task is difficult rather than that other harvesters are greedy.[163] Finally, cooperative harvesters are more likely than non-cooperators to vote for an elected leader when the commons is overused; non-cooperators are against having elected leaders regardless of the state of the resource.[164] These self-interested persons presumably do not want any leaders slowing up their harvesting and presumably do not care about the resource itself. Voting for a leader is more popular than forced-equal outcomes.[165]

Once leaders are elected in the commons, how can they maintain support among the harvesters? One thing is clear: leaders' support will vanish if harvesters see leaders allocate relatively more of the harvested resource to themselves and other harvesters.[166] Interestingly, leadership does not always produce more cooperation; voluntary leaders did not produce more cooperation than leaderless groups did.[167] Generally, one would expect leadership—at least high-quality leadership—to improve management of the commons. Perhaps that is true in larger groups, and small groups do not need a leader.

What to Do?

IN EVERYDAY LIFE, SOME COMMONS DILEMMAS ARE MANAGED WELL. In some places hunted wildlife such as ducks and deer are managed relatively well by systems of permits, seasons, and hunting rules. Some local fisheries are well-managed through local customs;[168] however, the list of commons that are poorly managed is long, and these problems have stimulated the mass of research just sampled. The important question is whether commons that are now managed poorly can be managed better. What, if anything, can be done?

As noted earlier, in his classic article, Garrett Hardin was pessimistic.[169] Early on, environmental psychologists suggested there is more hope for solutions than Hardin thought, but others were more skeptical.[170,171] The many studies conducted in the last three decades place experts in a better position to resolve this dispute. Each real-world commons needs its own analysis, but from the results of the studies above, a tentative set of general recommendations that might lead to more socially responsible management of the commons might be constructed. (Skip down to the IN SUM section if you want to see the list now.)

In general, what might be done? Some have suggested that a dictator should be appointed, with the hope that the dictator would use power in a wise and benevolent way.[172,173] Others might advocate a sort of environmental Walden Two (a fictional utopia invented by B. F. Skinner) where public-interest behavior in the commons is positively reinforced. Third, the existing governmental framework might be used to lobby for legislative enactment of rules that enforce cooperation in the commons. Finally, some would advocate that friendship, trust, and communication be encouraged, perhaps in a more decentralized and territorialized system than now exists.[174]

Central to the issue is an ancient problem: How to allocate resources in the first place?[175] This is, in the broadest and deepest sense of politics, a political question. If we think of society as, in part, a system for distributing resources, how should society be run? Thoughtful marketing professors suggest that the main barriers to increased cooperation are (1) the desire to maintain one's own freedom, (2) the desire to avoid being a sucker (cooperating when no one else does), (3) self-interest, and (4) mistrust of others.[176] They described some ways that cooperation might be sold to "me-firsters" using marketing strategies originally developed for conventional retail products such as soap. Can we use marketing techniques to convince selfish people to be cooperative?

Another approach to understanding commons dilemmas (which, of course, is a beginning toward overcoming them) is in the arena of theory. If people can view them from the vantage point of a coherent framework, perhaps other solutions will become apparent. After this summary, those theories will be discussed.

IN SUM *The quality of resource management depends on the resource itself, the characteristics of participants, and the rules of the game. Cooperation seems to decline as the importance of the resource increases and to improve as the resource is depleted—two ominous signs. As children develop, their ability to manage commons dilemmas increases. One might advocate that, when a commons dilemma exists, part of the resource should be allocated to each participant to manage, that friendship and trust should be encouraged among the participants, and that the total number of participants be kept small. In addition, one might advocate that participants should communicate, make public choices, and be subject to punishment for selfish decisions, although positive incentives for cooperation are even more effective. Further, individuals should be given experience operating the commons, and the benefits of altruism in the commons should be pointed out. Last, but certainly not least, payoffs for cooperation should be increased, if possible.*

THEORIES OF COMMONS DILEMMAS

THE MAJOR INFLUENCES ON INDIVIDUAL CHOICE IN COMMONS DILEMMAS have been discussed, but the larger perspectives that attempt to integrate knowledge about social and commons dilemmas still need to be examined. This section briefly reviews six theories: biosocial theory, tragic-choice theory, social-trap and behaviorist theory, limited processing theory, structural/goal expectation theory, and my attempt at a general theory. Each theory offers a different perspective, some broader and some narrower. Of course, each theory probably holds part of the truth. In addition, Donald Hine and I have proposed that over the course of a commons dilemma, different influences are strongest at different times.[177]

Biosocial Theories

THE FIRST APPROACH INCLUDES SEVERAL THEORIES WHICH SHARE THE BROAD VIEW that behavior in the commons is largely a function of the genetic or biological makeup of humans.[178] They agree that competitiveness or selfishness dominate human action, but vary in the degree to which these tendencies are expressed in aggression. One competition-based but less aggressive view holds that animals manage commons by establishing territories, perhaps with some initial violence, but that these territories are subsequently maintained with little serious violence.[179] The territories serve several functions, but in terms of commons management, resources are preserved by spreading the animals out in space and limiting new population, both of which reduce consumption of food resources in any particular territory.

An extension of this theory argues that, in humans, the competitiveness for territory reaches more aggressive levels, emerging as violence, fraud, and deceit.[180] No one would deny that these behaviors occur in humans; the controversial tenet of this theory is that a competitive urge for territory, rooted in our genes, is the *cause* of it. This theory asserts that territories are the basis of the social hierarchy in society, which in turn controls the distribution of resources, which is where the management of the commons comes in. Inequality is seen as the natural basis of society, and the most resources go to people highest in the hierarchy.

Both forms of the theory believe that altruism exists, although perhaps only for competitive reasons. At best, wealthy persons give money (e.g., a scholarship) to poorer persons (students) so the wealthy person can later employ the better-trained person to help the wealthy person become even richer. At worst, wealthy persons give money to the poor merely so the poor will survive to comprise a group of people to which the wealthy person can feel superior!

A third biosocial approach differs in that adherents believe altruism directed at society in general simply does not exist.[181] The **selfish gene theory** proposes that aid and assistance *only* occur where a gene might ensure its own survival. Thus, one shares resources with one's children, but not with those who do not carry one's genes.

Tragic-Choice Theory

MOST OF US WOULD PREFER A WORLD WITHOUT COMMONS DILEMMAS. The dream of sufficient food, land, and energy for everyone is very attractive. Yet, when we look around, we see that whether or not the world has enough resources for everyone—and some experts believe it does—existing resources clearly are not equally allocated. Tragic-choice theory is largely phrased in terms we have called *macro* or societal-level decision making.[182] However, many of the concepts in it may be extended to the *micro* or individual level.

The theory begins with the fundamental assumption that this inequality, and the resulting scarcity and suffering, are natural and therefore nearly impossible to change. In this way it is similar to the biosocial theories. Tragic-choice theory goes on to offer an explanation of commons dilemmas that is controversial and not pleasant to hear. In fact, the theory itself predicts that people will not be receptive to it because, its proponents argue, some widely held ideals are simply incompatible.

Two such ideals are freedom and equality. Tragic-choice theory maintains that these two goals are fundamentally incompatible. Freedom means the opportunity to get ahead—that is, to be "more equal" than others.[183] The theory also claims that democracy does *not* lead to equal allocation.[184] Tragic-choice theory maintains that equal, or more nearly equal, allocation of resources is possible, but that it could only be accomplished by a much more powerful central authority than most citizens would tolerate. That is, without freedom for most citizens.

The theory further posits that scarcity originates in a **first-order determination**—that is, a conscious decision *not* to produce as much as could be produced.[185] One of the clearest examples of a first-order determination is the sometimes profitable decision not to produce as much food (e.g., as dairy products, grains) as *could* be produced. Such decisions are defended as ways to stabilize commodity prices, but in fact, the theory says, they serve to assist or enrich producers at the expense of other members of the commons. These decisions to create scarcity are followed by **second-order determinations**—decisions about how to distribute the now-insufficient supply of goods. In contrast to the cry, "All persons are created equal," tragic-choice theory claims it is unfortunate but true that our allocation policies clearly show that we do not value every person equally (see Figure 14-9).

To disguise the conflict between the *ideal* of equality and the *fact* of inequality, various devices exist to support second-order determinations.[186] One is to offer much-publicized resources to a few of the needy, but not to offer adequate resources to the most of the needy most of the time. (Examples of this are when a wealthy philanthropist selects one worthy charity to benefit while ignoring other equally worthy causes, or when the homeless are given turkey on Christmas but on no other day of the year.) The allocation problem is also avoided through political

FIGURE 14-9 Second-order determinations lead to the familiar spectacle of poor persons against rich backdrops.

devices (citizens hand decision-making power—and their guilt about inequality—to someone else); the free market victim-blaming rationalization ("if those people really wanted a slice of the pie, they would work harder"); and custom ("we've always done it this way").

At the individual level, tragic-choice theory predicts that people will engage in self-interest behaviors because they accept one or more of these devices as justifications for getting ahead by overusing the commons. The only way out, according to the theory, is to be more honest and aware of our relation to the suffering of others. No specific technological or legislative solution is offered. Perhaps a bit more perspective-taking (seeing the world from the disadvantaged person's point of view) would help.[187]

Social-Trap and Reinforcement Theories

JOHN PLATT'S SOCIAL-TRAP THEORY is based on reinforcement.[188] The problem in a social trap, from Platt's point of view, is that too many people reward themselves too immediately. For example, if a person is holding an empty fast-food package and does not see a trash can nearby, the immediately rewarding act is to litter (the person's hands are free of a burden), but of course when this person and others repeatedly litter, the whole area will eventually be visually ruined by litter.

The social-trap theory solution is to examine the reinforcement structure of the commons dilemma and to rearrange the timing and the value of reinforcements to reverse the pending disaster. In some commons, this is not only a workable solution, it is a solution that is already working. Most fish and game laws work reasonably well, for example.

In general, in a social-trap or applied behavior analysis approach, the antecedent conditions (events that lead up to the harvest choice, including education, prompting, goal setting, and commitment) and consequence procedures (post-choice events such as reinforcement and punish-

FIGURE 14–10 Commons managers sometimes draw attention to fragile elements of the ecosystem, hoping that their message will be heeded by recreational tourists.

ment) must be carefully considered if more cooperation is to be elicited in larger-scale, longer-term, everyday commons dilemmas[189] (see Figure 14-10). A primary reason that commons are mismanaged, according to social-trap theory, is that reinforcements for public-interest acts are not only smaller than those for self-interest acts, but they are not often *contingent* on the public-interest behavior; that is, they are offered long after the occurrence of the public-spirited act. Our only material reward for not littering, for example, is a tiny reduction in taxes (because fewer trash collectors and landfill sites are needed) at some distant future time.

However, many commons dilemmas are harder to resolve than littering, because the *values* of citizens differ.[190] Even those who litter will admit that it is not a good idea. But when not everyone agrees on values, delivering those immediate reinforcements can produce sparks. In a large public aquarium, five Orca whales died some years ago. When it applied to capture more, the community was split on the value of displaying captured whales. The ensuing debate made it clear that there was no general agreement on whether capturing and displaying whales (presumably of some educational value) or leaving them in their open-ocean habitat (the natural thing to do) was the public-interest choice. (Postscript: the aquarium eventually closed completely.)

One solution is to place control of the resource in government hands, but two obvious problems arise with this solution. First, if individuals hand absolute control to a government, who controls the controllers?[191] Second, if individuals democratically elect a government and the government begins to force public interest behavior (by restricting the harvesting of fish or trees), it may well be voted out of office in favor of a government that promises the "freedom to harvest." Once again, if the commons is limited, defection will occur and disaster may ensue.

In agreeing with Hardin, Platt believes that the root problem is too many people, rather than too few resources. However, some proposals for reducing the population are ominous (witness the Holocaust and other genocides). Even relatively benign approaches to population control are sometimes seen as morally unacceptable, or as attempts by the First World to control the Third World.

However, if the world population cannot be reduced, then Platt and Hardin believed that we must dispense either with the ideal of equality (in resources) or the ideal of freedom (to "get ahead"). Influenced as he is by B. F. Skinner (the author of a book appropriately titled *Beyond Freedom and Dignity*), Platt suggests that we should sacrifice freedom. Beyond freedom (to a benevolent but authoritarian dictator) lies the possibility of justice and equality.

Limited Processing Theory

ROBYN DAWES, WHO PROPOSED LIMITED PROCESSING THEORY, believed that in many situations individuals do not behave in a rational manner.[192] By this, he does not mean that people act irrationally in the sense of derangement. Rather, they often coolly and calmly act non-rationally.

Two basic modes of non-rationality may be distinguished. First, people sometimes simply do not pay much attention to what they are doing. For example, people may litter, catch a fish, or leave a light on after they leave a room without any thought about the sustainability consequences of their act. Habits control many behaviors that affect the environment; consider that habit of driving each day or leaving lights on or turning them off. Some habits are "acting habits" in which the habit is to do something; others are "non-acting habits," in which the habit is to not do something.[193] Either way, defection without a conscious choice to defect may occur.

Second, people may act non-rationally even when they have a basic understanding of commons dilemmas and an awareness that they are making a choice. This can happen when the structure of the commons dilemma is too complex to understand or when no one has explained that a particular behavior happens to be a defection. Consider the African villager who poaches a rare rhinoceros in order to sell the horn for its alleged medicinal properties. This is defection, from our point of view, but the villager may not understand or agree with our assessment that taking the rhinoceros constitutes defection; rather it is seen as a way to feed a family.

Dawes suggested that much defection can be explained in terms of limited processing theory, and the way to overcome it is obvious, although not easy to accomplish. We must increase the awareness in offenders that certain behaviors constitute defection and that alternative behaviors will result in positive long-term outcomes. However, one problem with this solution is that defection sometimes harms one commons but helps another. The African villager who poaches rhino contributes to the demise of an endangered species, but the money gained probably enriches the villager's family and community, allowing a child to go to school or the villager to purchase a farm machine so more food can be produced for that family. This complication leads to moral and political dilemmas, rather than to purely strictly economic or psychological ones, like the commons dilemma.

Structural/Goal Expectation Theory

STRUCTURAL/GOAL EXPECTATION THEORY ASSERTS that a small but clear set of conditions is required for cooperation to occur.[194] First, the harvesters must agree that mutual cooperation is desirable. This will occur when harvesters realize they are interdependent and that defection cannot continue for long. Second, the harvesters must realize that harvest cooperation based on individual, voluntary decisions does not work. Third, they must agree that a "structural" change (i.e., an elected leader who controls behavior in the commons) is necessary and will be effective (e.g., the leader would make or receive the harvest and then allocate it to each harvester).[195]

For cooperation to occur, structural/goal expectation theory says that harvesters must change their belief that free access to the commons is desirable to the belief that a leader-controlled system will work. Obviously, this does not always happen, which is why—according to this theory—cooperation does not always happen. For example, if harvesters believe the cause of bad management is a personal quality of other harvesters (e.g., greediness), they may be less likely to accept the third condition above (that leadership would be effective) than if they believe the problem is that the management of the commons is very complex (but which a talented leader could handle).

Although evidence reviewed earlier shows that depleted commons generally lead to acceptance of the leader idea, this may not be enough, harvesters must also believe the problem is one that a leader *could* solve.[196] The theory is not clear on whether cooperation might be achieved in any other way, but it implies there *are* no other viable ways. So far, the theory focuses on predicting which conditions are necessary for cooperation, but says little about how to get harvesters to alter their beliefs.

Toward a General Theory

SOME ENVIRONMENTAL PSYCHOLOGISTS have begun to attempt the creation of integrated and unified theories that include most or all the main influences on whether individuals cooperate in commons dilemmas, and therefore believe and act in pro-environmental ways. One such model uses a computer simulation that integrates social and ecological information.[197] By entering the results of numerous completed studies into the simulation program, and then varying some of the parameters, their program very rapidly displays what would happen over the course of time. Another, three-motive theory, postulates that sustainability-related decisions are based on three motives: self-interest (greed, or the desire to get ahead), the desire to act responsibly (not to deplete the resource too much), and conformity (to make decisions not very different from what others are doing).[198]

My own general theory grew out of reviewing the literature over several decades. Rather than continuing to simply list influences on resource management, I began to organize them into a single inclusive framework (see Figure

14-11). This framework proposes that choices made in a social or commons dilemma are a function of five major kinds of influences. First, the decisions made by a person who is faced with a resource management choice (which is, most of us, much of the time!) are partly governed by *ambient geophysical conditions* (for example, fishers cannot fish during big storms, many forests are closed during dry periods for fear of fire, and householders turn up the heat when the temperature outside goes down).

Second, our decisions obviously are influenced in part by *rules and pricing* (laws, regulations, fees, taxes, and fines). Not everyone follows the rules and regulations all the time, but they do influence many or most of our decisions once they are in place. Third, *person factors* (dispositions, values, experiences, wealth, knowledge, etc.) clearly affect our choices. Fourth, *salient others* in our social world, including friends, family, admired other decision-makers, those who might be monitoring our choices, and the number of other harvesters all influence our decisions. Fifth, the level of *technology* used obviously influences the amount that we

are able to take, and not all of us possesses the same level of technology: for example, compare the fishing catch of an angler with that of a factory ship.

Even with all these influences, some people are simply unaware that they are managing a resource, whereas others (you and I!) are very aware of it: this awareness or lack of it clearly affects resource management decisions. The decisions themselves, whether to take much or a little, to cooperate or defect, are the heart of the matter. Although a function of all the foregoing influences, these decisions can follow a variety of different strategies (or sometimes even no clear strategy).

These strategies result in various sorts of financial, emotional, and social outcomes for us, over the long term: wealth, poverty, satisfaction, frustration, admiration, or reprobation. When aggregated across billions of decision-makers, the environment (water, air, trees, fish, animals, birds) is profoundly affected by these decisions. Finally, in turn, these changes in the environment come back to affect us (drought, scarcity of fish, polluted air, global warming).

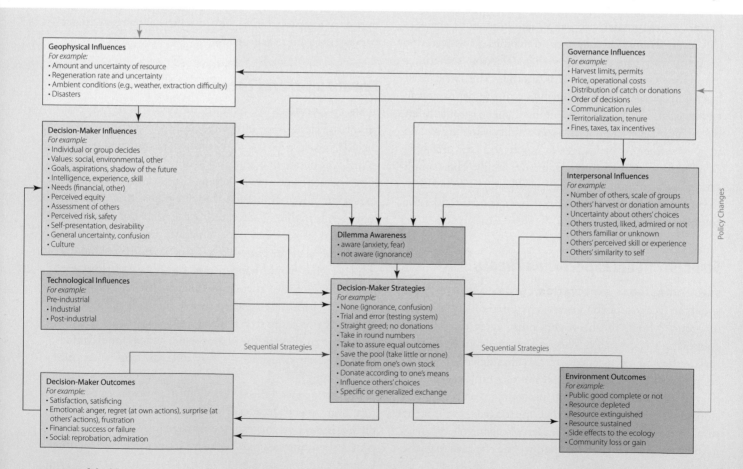

FIGURE 14–11 My general model for social dilemmas, including commons dilemmas and resource dilemmas. Compare with the simpler overview in Figure 14-4.

Fortunately, these environmental outcomes do cause changes in the regulations (e.g., a climate accord or new regulations limiting hunting or logging), although loosening of regulations also occurs, which foster defection. The whole cycle goes round and round in a dynamic dance, and we do not know with certainty how it will end.

IN SUM *Six theories of commons dilemmas have been described. Biosocial theory claims that self-interest is genetic; two forms of it differ about how much aggressiveness accompanies this self-interest. Tragic-choice theory maintains that self interest cannot be overcome except by the creation of a very strong central authority; this is unpleasant but necessary for the survival of the commons. Without such a central authority, the production and distribution of resources will be organized so as to benefit the wealthy at the expense of both the poor and the commons. Social-trap theory applies a reinforcement perspective to commons dilemmas. It suggests that better management of the commons would follow from a restructuring of reinforcement timing. Like tragic-choice theory, a centralized authority appears necessary. Limited processing theory postulates that most individuals act selfishly, not because they are evil, but because the dangers of defection simply do not occur to them. Its solution is clear: Make more individuals aware of the consequences of overusing resources that are in limited supply. Structural/goal expectancy theory again asserts the need for a central authority. This leader should be elected, and the harvesters must believe that mutual cooperation is necessary. Finally, I have tried to "put it all together" in a complex model that includes all the major categories of influence on choices we make in the commons.*

DEFECTION: SELF-INTERESTED BEHAVIOR

THE FOCUS NOW TURNS TO FOUR CRUCIAL EXAMPLES OF HUMAN BEHAVIOR that affect sustainability and are everyday commons dilemmas: air pollution, water conservation, energy conservation, and recycling. In the terminology of this chapter, the act of polluting or the choice to use an unsustainable amount of water or energy resources are defecting behaviors. Many people think of pollution as something produced by large anonymous organizations rather than themselves, and much pollution is, indeed, produced from large plants and factories. However, a surprising amount of pollution and overuse of resources can be traced to the decisions and acts of individuals. That is why pollution and conservation may be described as behavioral problems, why including them in a discussion of individual resource management strategies is reasonable, and why so much research directed at pollution control involves attempts to change the behavior of individuals.

One important form of pollution is automobile exhaust. However, environmental psychologists have also studied wood smoke pollution, noise pollution, visual pollution (the imposition of ugliness on the landscape), and litter. The ecological consequences of some behavior choices are ambiguous. For example, whether using paper diapers (which are disposable) or cloth diapers (which use hot water and detergent to clean) is environmentally preferable has been debated. Fortunately, environmental psychologists are investigating this very issue by examining the life cycles of competing products.[199]

The Problem

ALTHOUGH ABOUT 70 PERCENT OF THE PLANET'S SUR-
FACE IS COVERED WITH WATER, MUCH LESS IS SUITABLE
FOR HUMAN CONSUMPTION AND USE. About 3 percent of
the world's water is fresh water; the rest is salt water. Two-
thirds of the fresh water is tied up in glaciers (so far!), and
much of the rest is tied up in the soil or deep aquifers. Thus,
roughly .01 percent of all the water on Earth is accessible
to humans; this arrives via precipitation.

Furthermore, the distribution of available fresh water
is very uneven. People in some countries walk great distances each day solely to obtain water and bring it home.
For now, water is not difficult to find in most industrialized countries, but it could be in the not-too-distant future. A United Nations report estimates that 20 percent
of the world's population already do not have enough to
drink, and that by 2023 the amount available per person
will drop by one-third.[200]

Water management occurs on all levels. In the household, we use it for bathing, gardening, cooking, and sewage.
Very large quantities are also used for farming, industrial,
and recreation. Therefore, in the terminology of this chapter, harvesters include individuals, farmers, governments,
private companies, and industry. But even the larger entities are composed of individuals who make decisions on
behalf of those large entities. Thus, psychological factors
are important at all levels of analysis. An important problem is that people seem to fall victim to several biases in
thinking about water use.[201]

Who Conserves and What Helps?

RESEARCH ON WATER CONSERVATION BEHAVIOR IS STILL
IN ITS INFANCY. However, early research on the topic indicates that water consumption by households can be
predicted from their level of environmental awareness,
personal involvement (thinking about water as a finite
resource), water-use habits, and income, but among these
factors, personal involvement and habits appear to be the
most important factors.[202]

As in other areas of environmental research, attitudes
toward water use are not very strongly related to actual
water consumption. When several potential influences on
water use in household appliances such as washing machines were examined, informative labels attached to the
appliances resulted in a 23 percent reduction in water use,
but leaflets and feedback were not very effective.[203] Some
writers have argued that communities can foster restraint
in the use of water among residents who feel attached to
their community.[204] Water use is greater when residents
feel less attached to their community and pay a fixed rate
for it (as opposed to paying in proportion to how much
water they use).[205] Women report more affective concern
about the possibility of water shortages.[206]

The Consequences

THE ARID AND SEMI-ARID AREAS OF THE GLOBE have about
20 percent of the world population, but receive only about
2 percent of global water runoff. Events in these areas
demonstrate the life-and-death nature of resource management. The shrinking supply of water (per capita) implies strong potential for conflict, partly because, of major
river basins in the world, about 261 extend over at least
two international boundaries. About 145 nations depend
on river systems shared with other nations for portions of
their freshwater supply.

Conflict over water is not new, and certainly it can occur in modern times. As the dry areas of the planet reach
for water that is not there, conflict will ensue. For example, according to some authors, the Mideast Six-Day War
in 1967 was actually triggered by squabbling over water
rights to tributaries of the Jordan River. Boutros Boutros-
Ghali, the former Secretary-General of the UN, said, "The
next war in our region will be over the waters of the Nile,
not politics." Without improvements in water conservation, this could be true in other areas of the world. The
population of the world doubled between 1950 and 1990,
but global water use tripled in the same period. Because of
population growth, available freshwater supplies per capita
in the world decreased by one-third in just 22 years, from
1970 to 1992, and this situation has worsened since then.
Global water use is not sustainable.

TWO RESEARCHERS WERE WALKING THROUGH A CAMPUS HOUSING COMPLEX ONE DAY. They were studying energy conservation practices and had decided to have a look around the real world. Although it was a cold day, they noticed the distinctive sound of an air conditioner coming from one apartment. Upon knocking and asking a few questions, they discovered that the resident did not like the high temperatures in the apartment produced by the furnace, which was running full blast. To adjust the temperature, he had turned on the air conditioner![207]

Because most energy we use comes from natural resources, energy conservation is a commons dilemma and a central component of sustainability.[208] In commons dilemma terms, many energy resources (e.g., oil, coal, natural gas, and wood) renew themselves so slowly (how much new natural gas will be created by nature during our lifetimes?) that they are usually referred to as *non*renewable energy sources. Although hydroelectric power on a given river renews itself whenever rain falls, no new rivers are being created.

Energy conservation was an important public issue in the 1970s when oil price hikes caused shortages. Then a gradual relaxation of prices made many people complacent about the issue. However, the recent resurgence of general environmental interest and high fuel prices have caused renewed interest in energy conservation.[209] The price of energy certainly is not the only important motive for energy conservation.[210] Nevertheless, we still use energy much faster than it is being created, and not everyone uses it equitably. The amount of energy used in the United States for air conditioning *alone* was nearly equal to the *total* amount of energy used until recently in China; the per capita use of energy in developing countries is only about 1 per cent of per capita use in Canada.[211]

Government and industry are the biggest energy users,[212] but residential users also have control over the disposition of many resources. Where I live, for example, industry uses about one-third of the electricity, commercial organizations use about one-third; behavior in the home can significantly affect energy conservation.[213] Experts have estimated that energy use in typical existing houses and apartments could be reduced by up to 50 percent.[214]

The savings could, of course, be used for many purposes: to reduce the cost of energy to the consumer, to finance deserving social programs (how about more student loans at lower interest rates?), and to ease national dependence on distant, tenuous sources of energy. These savings may be accomplished partly by technological advances, partly by changing the behavior patterns of residents, and best by integrated programs that include both.[215] Changing residential energy conservation by changing behavior has been largely overlooked and holds great promise.[216]

PAUL STERN has investigated the important psychological and technical factors that influence energy conservation.

This is not to imply that changing behavior is easy. I have identified over 30 psychological barriers to change.[217] People may have too little knowledge about ways to reduce their household energy use, may not think these savings are important, may think achieving them is too expensive.[218] They may largely operate from habit. For example, perhaps the most important variable under the immediate control of people at home is thermostat setting. For high-frequency resource management behaviors such as turning down the thermostat each evening, the best predictor of future behavior is past behavior: Those who *have* been doing it will continue to do it.[219] One challenge for environmental psychologists, then, is to get homeowners *started* in conservation so that they will continue to help conserve. High energy use is tied to self-esteem for some people; to cut back implies giving up on their vision of a better life.[220]

Another challenge is posed by the recognition that home energy conservation is affected not only by simple daily choices such as whether to turn the thermostat down, but by larger choices such as where to live and other demographic characteristics. Energy use is well-predicted by climate, house characteristics (fireplace, fuel source, single-family versus multiple-family), resident characteristics (bigger, wealthier families with more members use the most energy), and attitudes (beliefs that energy conservation is important).[221]

Further challenges occur when behavior-change programs are viewed by residents as infringements on their freedom. The programs do not always fit easily into

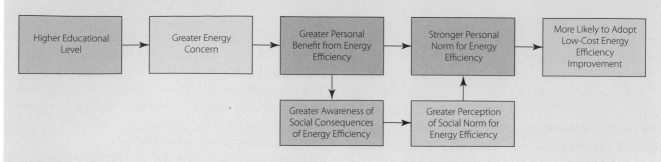

FIGURE 14-12 The more important causal influences on who will (and who will not) acquire low-cost energy efficiency devices.

residents' lifestyles, and they can be quite labor-intensive and costly. Despite these problems, residential energy conservation holds great potential for easing pressure on diminishing supplies of nonrenewable resources. The environmental psychologist's challenge is to discover ways to improve energy consumption patterns in homes inexpensively and help preserve the home as a haven from excessive outside pressures.

Technological solutions to the energy problem receive more attention than psychological approaches. In many instances, however, all the technology in the world will not save one kilowatt-hour if consumer behavior does not change. Some of the methods used to promote energy conservation include appeals from authorities, educational campaigns, providing feedback about rates of energy use, and reinforcing conservation practices with money or rebates. However, before we try to change behavior, we need to know who already conserves energy, and when. Then we know where to aim energy conservation programs.

Who Conserves, Under Which Conditions?

ALTHOUGH EVERYONE HAS BECOME AWARE OF ENERGY SHORTAGES, not everyone adopts energy conservation measures. Environmental psychologists have begun to construct models to predict who will engage in energy-saving behavior and who will not.[222] A basic distinction is that between antecedent influences (factors present before the conservation behavior occurs or not), and consequence influences (factors that occur after the conservation behavior occurs or does not). For example, attitudes and goal-setting are antecedent influences, and rewards and feedback are consequence influences. Another broad distinction is that between internal factors, such as a person's values, and external factors, such as the price of energy. This section examines some of these factors (see Figure 14-12).

Attitudes, Knowledge, Values, Motives, and Norms. Several attitudes are strongly related to energy use: whether or not a person thinks energy use is important for comfort and health, whether or not the energy savings seem to be worth the effort of conserving, whether or not one's efforts as an individual can make any difference, and whether or not energy problems are viewed as real.[223] These four attitudes predict over half of the variance in actual electricity usage by households.[224]

Among other beliefs, people who participated in a green electricity program tend to have some motives (biocentric) that are stronger than other motives (altruistic or egoistic).[225] People with different views of nature favor different policy approaches to energy conservation.[226] Those who believe in nature as benign (that it can absorb damage we inflict on it and always find some balance) tend to favor market-oriented solutions most and government regulation least; they prefer technological solutions over behavioral solutions to environmental problems. Those who see nature as tolerant (that it can absorb some damage, but beyond a certain amount of damage it will collapse) tend to favor government regulation most and market-oriented solutions least. Those who think of nature as ephemeral (that it is fragile and even small disturbances will have important consequences) tend to favor behavior-based solutions over technological solutions.

Favorable attitudes toward conservation do not necessarily lead to actually turning down the thermostat, changing furnace filters, or caulking,[227] or even having a commitment to do such things.[228] Even concerned citizens tend to adopt only conservation behaviors that are familiar and easy to engage in.[229] Sometimes energy conservation practices are adopted for a brief period, then abandoned.[230] People often exaggerate the conservation actions they have taken.[231]

Worse yet, attitudes often are based on overconfidence about what a person knows. A survey of California residents found that *claimed* knowledge about particular energy-saving programs was much greater than *actual* knowledge of them.[232] For example, when asked to rank the energy requirements of various household appliances, people tend to believe that larger machines use more energy than smaller ones, even though this is not always the case.[233] How can citizens save energy if they think they know more than they actually do? Consider a simple process such as how a thermostat works. Interviews with householders show that a quarter to a half of people think thermostats work like valves (you turn the knob up to produce more heat or turn it down to produce less heat) instead of as feedback devices (you set a temperature; the thermostat then senses the current temperature and turns the furnace on or off to maintain that temperature).[234]

Furthermore, many people who *say* they have undertaken some action to save energy really have not done so.[235] Even individuals who attended an intensive energy conservation workshop and generally emerged with increased concern about conservation and optimism that they could make a substantial difference in overall savings usually did not actually change their behavior or their homes.[236] In a subsequent home check, only 11 percent of the workshop attendees had installed a water flow restrictor and only 1 of 70 had lowered the water heater thermostat as a result of the workshop. Unfortunately, people often confuse what they *believe* with what they *think* they know and what they *think* they have done with what they have *actually* done. And, of course, actions are what conserve energy, not intentions or beliefs. Therefore, we must be particularly skeptical of research that is based only on attitudes or unconfirmed verbal reports of energy conservation behavior.

Not all the attitude research is negative. Although energy-related attitudes are not great predictors of actual behavior, they do help. For example, in a study that tried to predict thermostat-setting behavior, knowing a person's attitudes helped to predict who turned thermostats down and who did not even *after* such as variables as the dwelling's physical characteristics, the person's demographic characteristics, and economic data were used as predictors.[237]

Furthermore, if a longer sequence of factors is considered, the results may be more encouraging. For example, willingness to conserve by reducing one's driving was predicted well when the following model was used: the person's values and awareness of the problem influenced the person's own norms, and that in turn influenced the person's willingness to reduce driving.[238] Furthermore, knowledge of attitudes can be used to guide energy policy. For example, individuals whose attitudes include accepting personal responsibility for energy conservation are more likely to be in favor of individual-level solutions (e.g., thermostat setbacks and a reduction of travel), whereas those who assign the cause of energy problems to causes outside themselves (e.g., oil companies and government) are more likely to favor outside solutions.[239] Pro-environmentalists tend to favor "soft" solutions such as solar power and reduction in energy use, whereas non-environmentalists tend to favor "hard" solutions such as nuclear power or new dams.[240]

Pro-conservation attitudes are best promoted by a strategy that emphasizes the desirable consequences of conservation rather than one that focuses on negative issues such as whether environmental problems really exist or not.[241] Attitudes do not predict conservation behavior very well, but they are an important first step. Finally, believing that one is competent or able to make the necessary changes to one's dwelling is important.[242]

Income and Status. Relatively high- and very low-income earners conserve more. Consumers with relatively high incomes are better educated and better able to afford the initial startup costs of some alternatives.[243] Solar energy, for example, is relatively expensive to begin with, and its costs take several years to repay through energy savings; it is not very feasible for low-income or mobile consumers.[244] In surveys, higher-status persons *report* (for what it is worth!) that they adopt conservation practices more.[245]

Very low-income groups in North America and in developing countries already conserve more, partly because they have much less money to spend on the more-important energy costs (heating, cooling), let alone energy-gobbling gadgets. Thus, one prime target of conservation programs is higher-income individuals who have not yet changed their lifestyles. These individuals are especially ripe because they use more energy at present, but also usually believe that conservation is desirable.

Ownership and Building Type. Homeowners take more actions than renters to make their dwellings energy-efficient, but they do not reduce energy-using activities any more than renters.[246] Residents who live in multiple-unit dwellings with a single electrical meter tend to conserve less. In many such buildings constructed before energy prices rose dramatically, only one gas or electric meter was installed for the whole building; energy was not expensive, but installing separate meters in every unit was. Many landlords are thereby forced to include the cost of utilities in the rent, because they cannot easily compute how much each resident uses. When someone else pays for your utilities, the temptation to defect is strong. If the air-conditioner controls are closer than the furnace controls, why not just cool off your overheated place with the air conditioner? In the case of residential energy, the cost is largely passed on to one's neighbors in a manner that is directly analogous to William Lloyd's parable of the villagers and their cattle.

Lifestyle, Age, and Experience. As might be expected, people who tend toward lifestyles characterized by "voluntary simplicity," engage in more conservation than do those whose lifestyle is not characterized this way.[247] Those whose lives have been directly touched by energy shortages, or believe their health and comfort are threatened by shortages, are more likely to take action.[248] Understandably, people who are home during the day use more energy, and those with small children use more heat at night.[249] The elderly use more heat at night[250] and during the day,[251] partly because they are more worried about their health. Older people are slower to adopt other conservation techniques, too.[252] This may be because conservation programs have not yet been designed for the needs of older people.

Provoking Energy Conservation

NOW THAT WE HAVE A SENSE OF WHO TENDS TO CONSERVE UNDER WHICH CONDITIONS, we can survey the different suggestions for how to increase energy conservation in the future.

Appeals from Authorities. In the scenario that opens this chapter, the mayor of a town facing a water shortage appeals for citizens to use less water. How well do such appeals work? In the United States, the best-known appeal was one made on national TV by President Carter in 1977. Two studies seized this opportunity to evaluate the effectiveness of this appeal. One surveyed over 400 residents and found that 27 percent of the households had reduced their thermostats to the recommended 65°F/18°C.[253] Unfortunately, some who had not even heard the appeal also lowered their thermostats, so the appeal itself may not have been the reason for the lowered thermostats.

In another study, an energy conservation program was already underway when Carter's appeal came.[254] An appeal from the governor came at about the same time. The investigator was thus able to compare the existing program, which was behaviorally oriented, and Carter's appeal. President Carter's appeal was much more effective than the behavioral program. The behavioral program was then refined to include group meetings and more incentives. The refined program was more effective than the gubernatorial appeal.

Appeals and other strategies to induce behavior changes in consumers must be evaluated against the change caused by price increases; energy conservation behavior certainly is spurred in part by simple economic factors.[255] A comparative review concluded that appeals from authorities are useful over and above economic considerations, but not universally so.[256] The response varies with climate and type of energy used in the home. Presumably, the appeal's effectiveness also will vary with the attractiveness of the leader.

Educational Campaigns. The most widely used strategy to promote energy conservation is to distribute pamphlets, letters, flyers, stickers, and booklets describing how one might conserve energy around the home. This approach is relatively inexpensive and seems rational: If consumers are told how they can save money, surely they will take advantage of the information. Unfortunately, as noted earlier, most studies show that the distribution of energy conservation literature alone does *not* have a significant impact on behavior,[257-259] although some studies do report significant changes.[260,261] Even when educational aids are not immediately effective, they do serve to *prime* consumers, so that later intervention strategies will work better.

Perhaps we need to start earlier, when consumers of energy are still in school. The U.S. government placed about 140 Energy-Environment Simulators in schools.[262] They compress 100 years into 1 minute; students try to maintain viable sources of energy under a variety of conditions such as a cutoff of Mideast oil, the development of new technology for producing energy, or an increase in population. These simulators and other realistic exercises should help raise awareness of the problems involved in energy conservation and may foster increased conservation behavior.[263]

Another educational approach is to use the power of the media, which some see as the best method of achieving significant energy savings.[264] Based on social psychological principles, a media campaign should (a) come from a believable source, such as an admired person, (b) contain a specific message, (c) be presented in a vivid manner, and (d) let people know what they are losing by not conserving.[265] An Australian study measured the effectiveness of a 30-second commercial that advocated conservation of gasoline.[266] It found that after 4 weeks of intensive airplay, the commercial had a small but significant effect on self-reported conservation of gasoline.

The most effective approach might be to tailor messages to processes that underlie behavior change, that is, awareness of the problem, deciding to change, and actually initiating and implementing change.[267] If so, the messages should target peoples' intrinsic goals, such as health and well-being, less than their extrinsic goals, such as saving money.

Commitment. Individuals who have in some way made a public commitment to energy conservation usually save more than those who have not.[268,269, 270] Obviously, if I have announced to my neighbors that I am careful to turn off lights in rooms I am not using, I feel pressure not to have them pass by and notice that every room in my house is lighted.

The logical extension of this idea was tested. If public commitment leads to conservation, will stronger public commitment lead to even more energy conservation? Small businesses were invited to participate in a conservation program.[271] All were told that the program included a community relations component. They might be assigned, randomly, to a mild commitment condition (their business listed in a newspaper advertisement thanking firms in the small town where the study occurred for their participation), a strong commitment condition (nearly the same ad, except that newspaper readers could tell exactly how much each business had conserved), or a control condition (no ad exposure). The control condition produced the least conservation, as expected. However, the strong commitment condition produced *less* conservation than did the mild commitment condition. Perhaps this happened because the strong-commitment firms were placed under too much pressure and they felt trapped.

However, commitment *usually* is effective; a meta-analysis confirmed this.[272] As the authors note, to understand when commitment will be effective and when it will not be, environmental psychologists will need to take a closer look at the psychological mechanisms underlying commitment. One investigation that did this found that people who tend to distrust others tend to favor public commitment when they expect that others will also contribute, whereas people who tend to trust others favor public commitment when they expect that others will *not* also contribute.[273]

Feedback. Assuming that a consumer is inclined toward saving energy, a basic principle is that providing feedback about the rate of energy use will facilitate behavior change. Of course, consumers already receive feedback every month or two in the form of a bill. However, this information is often ineffective as a behavior change agent because it arrives long after the behavior in question and it is too diffuse. Consumers are usually unaware just which appliance or heater was used, on which days they used energy extravagantly, or whether an increased bill reflects increased usage or increased utility prices.

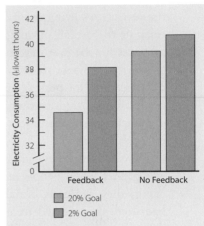

FIGURE 14–13 Daily average electricity consumption (adjusted for pre–study consumption rates) of townhouse residents in four conditions. Giving residents moderately difficult goals and feedback produces the most savings.

Environmental psychologists who have investigated the effectiveness of feedback have offered energy-use information to the consumer much more frequently—sometimes even an immediate, continuous read-out of how much energy is being used. For example, householders were told four times per week how much electricity they had used in comparison to an amount predicted for them on the basis of outdoor temperature and other factors.[274] Compared to a no-feedback control group, the informed residents used 10.6 percent less electricity. Other feedback studies report savings in the range of 5-15 percent [275,276] (see Figure 14-13). These savings do not sound very dramatic until they are multiplied by the number of residential units in a whole country; then the potential value of frequent feedback is clear.

A review of 38 studies of feedback concluded that it is effective, particularly if it is given frequently.[277] The effectiveness of feedback may increase when it is even more immediate. In pilot programs, this approach has evolved from one that hand-delivers a written record of use to feedback delivered to home computers; computer-delivered feedback is very conservation-effective.[278] Feedback can also be delivered via a digital readout on the wall of the consumer's living room. Because consumers may lose track of the overall meaning of a continuous display, usage rates for the past day and week are also displayed. In California, although continuous displays combined with different rates for peak versus off-peak electricity use did not manage to reduce overall energy consumption, they did at least cause consumers to shift their electricity use to off-peak periods.[279]

Here's another key: in the Netherlands, conservation was greater when people were not only told how much energy they had used, but also how much another group had used; this seemed to arouse competitive motives.[280] When strategies are combined, savings are even better: daily feedback plus a commitment to save resulted in significant natural gas conservation.[281] When a combination of tailored information, goal setting, and tailored feedback was employed to reduce energy use in the Netherlands, a 5% reduction in direct energy use was achieved.[282]

Goal Setting. Energy savings are easier to achieve when individuals are also asked to meet relatively difficult, but voluntarily chosen, goals—such as a 20 percent saving.[283] Interestingly, some people respond to goal, they set themselves, but others need to have goals set for them. Both self-set and assigned goals can be effective, but for different social orientations: pro-self individuals saved more energy when they set their own goals; pro-social individuals saved more energy when the goal was set for them.[284]

According to feedback intervention theory,[285] goals also should match in terms of level. For example, a person whose goal is "to act in a pro-environmental way," that is, a general goal, may not respond to information about a specific environmental action (e.g., turning off the light when leaving a room) as well as another person with a more specific goal, such as turning off those lights.[286]

Modeling and Prompts. People learn from watching others. This principle has been shown to increase energy and water conservation behavior. In university gym showers, despite signs urging people to soap up while the water was turned off and to take short showers, only 6 percent did. A larger sign increased compliance to 19 percent, but the sign was a target for aggressive remarks and minor vandalism. However, when a confederate of the experimenter modeled the desirable behaviors, half of the others soaped up with the water off and took shorter showers. When two students modeled, 67 percent of others complied.[287]

Signs alone can save energy, and are very cost-effective. In public buildings, people often leave the lights on when they leave washrooms. However, in less-busy times, lights are illuminating empty spaces. Carefully designed signs (polite, giving a reason) induced washrooms users to turn off lights in university washrooms, and the improved behavior persisted during an 11-week follow-up period.[288]

Monetary Rewards. For many people, the most effective behavior change agent is money. An obvious strategy is to offer grants, loans, or rebates for saving energy. The early studies of this strategy were full of promise: individuals responded extremely well. However, if a conservation program based on financial reward is to have wide-ranging potential, it must be cost-effective, at least in the long run. Fortunately, careful planning of rebates, grants, and loans can make monetary payoffs cost-effective.[289-291]

Home Audit Programs. Energy utility companies and governments also have tried to provoke conservation through programs in which a company representative visits the house and examines its energy-wasting capacity. Typically, the auditor points out problems, suggests that repairs be done, offers an attractive grant or loan for major refits, and suggests reputable contractors. The success of such programs is variable; a national average might be about 15 percent of householders who go on to make the necessary changes to weatherproof their houses.

Psychologists have improved that success rate by training auditors in how to communicate with householders.[292] For example, auditors were told to use vivid examples, such as saying, "If you were to add up all the cracks under these doors, the effect is the same as if you had a hole the size of a basketball in your wall." The auditors were told to focus on loss rather than gain, such as saying, "If you don't fix cracks, it's your hard-earned cash going right out the window." The auditors were also trained to induce investment or commitment in the audit process by getting householders to follow them around the house, help take measurements, and actually look at the cracks. Together, these changes to the auditor's style produced a cooperation rate of about 60 percent, roughly four times the usual rate.

Designing For Energy Conservation

ENERGY-USE PATTERNS ARE RELATIVELY RESISTANT TO CHANGE. Major Western countries reduced their demand for oil by only 2 percent even during the energy-conscious 1970s.[293] High rates of usage are part of the lifestyle of many consumers. They may not wish to change; if they do, they may find it difficult to maintain interest in an energy conservation program. This leaves a great deal of potential for increased conservation.

Weather remains the single largest predictor of what consumers will do with their heating and cooling machines. Feedback and tailored rebates to individual consumers may help increase conservation by small percentages that add up to large national savings. Research into newer aspects of energy conservation—such as field studies of adjustment to non-optimal temperatures, modeling and peak-load management—may help.[294] The promised savings of "up to 50 percent" may not be realized until (1) behavioral and cognitive approaches, (2) hardware improvements, and (3) economic considerations are integrated.[295,296]

Structural changes perhaps are the best solutions, where they can be implemented, because they involve a single event (buy and install), rather than having to train people to make daily decisions in favor of conservation. Some structural changes (solar panels, insulation) are expensive, but not all are (low-flow showerheads, weather-stripping). Giving residents a small canister designed to improve combustion and help wood fires burn more efficiently was shown to be effective on its own.[297]

When structural changes can be built in from the beginning, they are cheaper than retrofitting them. One small community can serve as an example. Developers in Davis, California, went far beyond merely adding solar panels to the houses in their project.[298] Davis can be very hot in the summer; their designs take advantage of natural ventilation patterns to reduce the need for air conditioning. Excess heat in some developments comes from broad expanses of pavement; in this development the pavement area was reduced by narrowing streets and clustering homes.[299] The development also has water conservation features, and parts of a preexisting orchard were retained. The developers lived in the development, so that assistance with technical problems is close at hand. Energy conservation is not merely turning the thermostat down. It is part of a pattern of living that includes voluntary lifestyle simplicity[300] and environmental designs that make it easy to conserve.

IN SUM *Energy use is a commons dilemma when it is easier to waste energy, particularly from nonrenewable sources in the service of short-term goals, than it is to conserve it for the future. Savings of up to 50 percent could be achieved in ideal conditions, which would include an integration of psychological, economic, and structural contributions. Conservers include those with enough money to purchase energy-saving devices so they can save over the long haul; those who must conserve because they cannot afford much gasoline, air conditioning, or fuel oil; those who have adopted a voluntary simple lifestyle and feel a personal responsibility for energy problems; those who are willing to make moderate public commitments toward energy conservation; and those whose energy is not monitored with a shared meter. Conservation may be enhanced in the short term by appeals from authorities. Educational campaigns seem to change attitudes, priming individuals for changing behavior, but energy-use habits are relatively difficult to change. Feedback and goal setting have achieved 20-percent savings. Monetary approaches have a cost-benefit problem: they sometimes cost more than they save. The case of a housing development that integrated several design innovations with a group of ecologically oriented residents was described as an important step toward the upper limit of 50-percent energy savings.*

AIR POLLUTION: A COMMONS DILEMMA

THE BY-PRODUCTS OF CIVILIZATION that are released into the air constitute a "give-some" type of commons dilemma (see Figure 14-14). Greenhouse gas emissions may be the

FIGURE 14-14 A "give-some" form of bad resource management, as opposed to the "take-some" form exemplified by overfishing or clear-cutting practices in the lumber industry..

most important problem facing the planet today, but even they are only part of the air pollution problem. For example, small particulates from burning wood and fossil fuels cause many problems of their own. In all its manifestations, air pollution is a huge problem for the health of people and other living things, as well as for the atmosphere that surrounds everything on earth.

Myths About Air Pollution

MANY PEOPLE have erroneous ideas about air pollution:

1. *Air pollution is a big-city problem.* When air pollution residues were measured in the blood of blood donors who live in rural and urban settings, overexposure to carbon monoxide was found to be common even in rural areas.[301] For example, the worst air pollution in Canada occurs in a fairly small town in the far north.[302] The cause: extensive wood-burning for heat, combined with a valley location and climatic tendency toward inversions. Of course air pollution is a big-city problem too, but it is not limited to cities.

2. *Air pollution is a relatively new problem.* Although it is worsening in some places, air pollution is considerably less now than it was 100 years ago in some industrial cities, such as London. This is partly because coal and wood are no longer as commonly used in cities for home heating and cooking. Although air pollution is not new, recently smoke pollution has resurfaced as a problem in some parts of North America. In areas with a reasonable supply of firewood, many residents burn wood to heat their homes and some neighborhoods have a serious problem.

3. *Air pollution is an outdoor phenomenon.* Outdoor air is drawn into homes and many workplaces. People normally do not notice air pollution indoors because it is not dense enough to see, and some is odorless.

4. *Air pollution may affect health, but not behavior.* Obviously, air pollution can have drastic health effects. In one especially bad month (December, 1952) the deaths of about 3,500 individuals in London were attributed to air pollution. An extensive catalog of health problems that may be caused by air pollution has been assembled.[303] Very careful studies have demonstrated that residents of places with more airborne particulates have shorter lives.[304] Globally, about two million people die each year from causes related to air pollution. However, studies also have shown that air pollution has distinctly *behavioral* effects in addition to the much-publicized effects on health, and some are cited in this chapter.

5. *Air pollution is caused by factories, not people.* Over 80 million tons of carbon monoxide alone are released into the atmosphere each year in North America from transportation sources, and most transportation still involves one or two individuals driving a car.[305] Incidentally these pollution figures, mind-boggling as they are, do not include other common air pollutants such as sulfur dioxide, nitrogen dioxide, and particulates (tiny particles produced during combustion).

6. *Incineration destroys toxins.* When wastes are burned, the particulates go into the air. However, in many incinerators, ash or finer particles still contain dangerous compounds. Even state-of-the-art incinerators with the latest "scrubbers" do not entirely destroy toxins: many are left in the ash inside the incinerator after the waste in burned and must be put *somewhere* afterward.

If those are the myths, what are the facts?

Air Pollution and Behavior

EXPERIMENTAL STUDIES OF AIR POLLUTION are relatively rare. Often, the studies have ethical problems, and not surprisingly, participants who are willing to inhale carbon monoxide to advance scientific knowledge are difficult to find. The existing evidence indicates that common air pollutants affect the range of our behavior, basic psychological processes, and perhaps, attraction, aggression, and schizophrenia.

Restriction of Activities. When I was thirteen, I attended school in such a polluted area that students were sometimes required to wear gas masks whenever they went outside. Try playing your favorite sport in a gas mask! Clearly, the first behavioral effect of air pollution is that one's behavior sometimes is *constrained* to a narrower range than is desirable.

Cognitive Performance. The second behavioral effect of air pollution is that excessive levels of carbon monoxide negatively affect such basic cognitive activities as reaction time and arithmetic ability,[306] the ability to judge time,[307] and the ability to detect changes in light intensity.[308] These alterations of basic behavior may not sound exciting to anyone except experimental psychologists with specialized interests in them. However, these basic behaviors are the building blocks of such important behaviors as driving and problem-solving. People do not *feel* any different when they are exposed to levels of carbon monoxide high enough to affect their performance. Because of this lack of awareness, people often fail to avoid either the carbon monoxide or the behavior it may be affecting.

The evidence concerning driving accidents is not clearcut; some studies report no relation, but others show small but significant correlations between accident rates and levels of carbon monoxide on the road or at the place of work just left by the driver.[309] The lack of clarity in this applied research should not be taken as proof that air pollution does *not* affect complex behaviors; the problems of conducting research on this complicated but everyday phenomenon may obscure its subtle effects on key everyday behaviors.

Social Behavior. Air pollution may affect social and interpersonal processes, including domestic violence, as discussed earlier. People exposed to cigarette smoke are more aggressive than those who were not.[310] Air pollution is correlated both with the total number of psychiatric emergency room visits and to the number of schizophrenia-related visits.[311] Correlational data do not *prove* that air pollution drives people crazy, but the data do suggest that individuals who are having difficulties even in clean air may find that the slight performance decrements caused by air pollution are enough to throw them off balance.

Adapting to Air Pollution. Given its unpleasant aesthetic qualities and its effects on health and behavior, environmental psychologists have wondered why public outcries against air pollution have not been louder. For example, in preparation for the 1984 Olympics, Los Angeles tried to implement strict controls in an attempt to improve its Smog City image, and Beijing did the same for the 2008 Olympics. But why did it take an event like the Olympics for these cities to implement the controls?

Two general answers may be offered: adaptation and perceived costs. In most instances, air pollution increases gradually. This allows time for a population to get used to the decrease in visual quality, the increase in eye irritation, and the small decrements in cognitive performance. The **Weber-Fechner law** of psychophysics says that noticeable differences in the level of a stimulus change with the overall intensity of the stimulus. That is, when little pollution is present, a small increase will be noticed, but when more is present, the same size increase will no longer be noticed.[312,313] The same principle may apply to all resource management situations. When the pool of resources is large, a few defections will go unnoticed, but when the pool is nearly depleted, a defection is very obvious. One piece of litter in a spotless hallway stands out, but one piece of litter added to many others will not be noticed.

A second reason for inaction is the perceived cost of action. If someone's job depends on air pollution, that person will be reluctant to struggle against it. What if one of the costs of installing expensive "scrubbers" in the smokestacks includes your own layoff?[314] If the cost of cleaning up the atmosphere to a commuter is bicycling to work through all kinds of weather, is the effort worthwhile? Public interest choices are desirable, but how many comfort losses will individuals absorb?

To both the adaptation and perceived cost problems, the concerned environmental psychologist has an answer. Implied in both equity and limited processing theories, the answers are to increase awareness of the long-term costs of defection and to find ways to increase equity. Changing behavior may require Herculean efforts on the part of concerned citizens.

IN SUM *Air pollution is a "give-some" form of commons dilemma. Many individuals and organizations cleanse their own hands but dirty the commons. Air pollution is an old problem caused by individuals as well as industry that occurs in both rural and urban areas, indoors and outdoors, and affects behavior as well as health. Its behavioral effects are subtle but probably include constraining the kinds of activities people engage in, mildly impairing cognitive processing, and increasing interpersonal and psychiatric problems. Efforts directed against air pollution have been blunted by the tendency to adapt to it and by the high perceived cost of correcting it.*

RECYCLING: A COMMONS DILEMMA

NATIONAL GEOGRAPHIC MAGAZINE ONCE FEATURED A STORY FULL OF GARBAGE. Instead of the usual exotic and beautiful scenes for which the magazine is famous, its pages were filled with pictures of human beings scuttling over mountains of trash. In many countries, whole classes of people are engaged full-time in processing garbage. They sort out the valuable materials, fight over rights to the garbage of the wealthy, and often live at the disposal site. This is hardly an attractive scene. Yet the only difference between these people and other people is that they work near the end of

a disposal process and the rest of us work at the beginning (see Figure 14-15).

Each of us is curator of a steady stream of natural resources that have been transformed into usable goods. Of course, most people do not realize this; they simply think they are recycling or throwing out the garbage. Yet it remains true that many times daily each of us decides how to manage the flow of paper, glass, metal, food, water, and oil that comes to us so routinely. In some places, most of these products are discarded into unsorted general garbage, to be collected, transported, crushed, burned, and bulldozed at a cost of billions each year.[315] We certainly do not want to appear wasteful, but in some societies, we are.[316]

Some recycling is easy (low-cost to us, such as paper into a nearby receptacle designed for that purpose), and some is more difficult (high cost to us, such as finding where to properly recycle paint or chemicals); these have different psychological drivers, and therefore require different strategies to increase their rates of recycling.[317]

In the language of this chapter, the public-interest choice is to find ways not to use, or at least to *reuse*, resources, not to toss them into messy unsorted piles. The key to managing resources in the public interest is to change this common practice of having a single bag or can for throwing away anything no longer wanted. Two forms of resource recovery may be distinguished: **recycling** occurs when waste material is processed to recreate the original product, and **reclaiming** occurs when the waste material is processed to create a different product.[318] *Recycled* paper may go from being a sheet of paper to being a shopping bag. *Reclaimed* tires have been used as an ingredient in paving mixes for airport runways and for streets. Apparently, bits of tire help prevent cracking in the pavement during cold weather.

Technical Problem or Human Problem?

RESOURCE RECOVERY MAY BE VIEWED as a technical problem, as a behavioral problem, or both. The purely technical approaches tend to allow consumers to send in mixed garbage in the traditional manner; the separation and recovery of materials is done at a central plant. Such high-technology solutions tend to maximize both consumer convenience and expense.[319] However, the expense (and high-technology plants can be very expensive) is—unfortunately—remote in time for most people, and it forms an indeterminate part of the consumer's tax bill. Thus, in the short run, the technical solution is often more attractive.

The alternative, to consider resource recovery as a behavioral problem, focuses on persuading consumers to reduce their original use of materials, to separate, to prepare, and sometimes to deliver their discarded items at the beginning of the waste disposal process. This can be bothersome. Yet because the high-tech solution is often more expensive (sometimes more so than the old bulldozing-for-landfill approach it is supposed to replace), the public interest choice is probably the low-tech, consumer-based form of resource recovery.

Recycling is a commons dilemma and a key part of sustainability. One community of about 200,000 people, with a recycling rate of about 68 percent, saves 70,000 trees in one year.[320] However, even this level of recycling diverts only about 4 percent of the material from that community's traditional garbage stream.

Who Recycles, and Who Does Not?

IN GENERAL, PEOPLE WHO (a) are motivated to recycle, (b) have positive attitudes about recycling, and (c) have strategies for accomplishing the task recycle more.[321] Not surprisingly, individuals with greater environmental knowledge, awareness, or commitment tend to recycle more [322-325] and homeowners recycle more.[326,327] Recyclers also tend to have higher incomes and more education.[328] People who find ways to make it more interesting and manageable also recycle more.[329]

Ethnic differences in recycling exist in the U.S. (Caucasians most, African-Americans and Asians next, Hispanics least), but there and in other countries,[330] these differences may be more a matter of differences in access to recycling facilities than to ethnicity itself.[331,332] In support of this, residents with access to a structured recycling program and ample room to store their materials before recycling are much more likely to recycle.[333] Access to programs and lack of access probably are stronger influences *against* recycling than environmental attitudes are as *pro*-recycling forces.

Most people *say* they recycle; even decades ago, 81 percent of college students and 58 percent of community householders said they recycle.[334,335] However, not everyone recycles yet, and as usual, self-reports may not be entirely valid.[336] When people were asked if they recycled and then their recycling was checked, higher-income

FIGURE 14–15 "Dumpster divers" or "binners" may be found even in well-off places. They search for food, and they help recycle cans and other materials that others find too much trouble to recycle.

households claimed they recycled more than did lower-income households, but actually they did not.[337]

If possible, researchers try to have an integrated theory about what they are investigating, rather than a mere list of influences. In Scotland, theory of planned behavior was used to predict the intention to recycle.[338] It proposes that a chain of factors must be in place. The intention to recycle must be preceded by the person's belief that it is the normal thing to do, and the person must have a positive attitude toward recycling. In turn, the person must believe recycling is normal if it is the normal behavior of significant others, and the person is motivated to please these significant others. The positive attitude depends on the person believing that the act will have positive consequences. Finally, potential recyclers must believe that they have sufficient control over the situation to be able to recycle. In this study, all these factors were in place, except that in order to have the intention to recycle, people did not necessarily have to believe that recycling is the normal thing to do. In Italy and Australia, when people have adopted an identity that includes "being a recycler," predictions of who intends to recycle are improved over the use of the theory of planned behavior alone,[339,340] suggesting that the theory needs to be expanded.

How To Encourage Recycling

MANY PEOPLE NOW RECYCLE, BUT MILLIONS STILL DO NOT. How can these holdouts be encouraged to responsibly manage the valuable resources passing through their households?

The Recycling Program. Programs work better if the target group is involved in designing the program.[341] Specific elements of a recycling program can influence rates of recycling. For example, programs that accept **commingled** materials (all recyclables are placed in one container, as opposed to separate materials in separate containers) achieve very high participation rates, although the method was not directly compared with separated-materials programs.[342, 343] Recycling containers is another program element, and the more different kinds of containers, the less recycling is done.[344] Programs should remind people, with signs or other messages, that they are in favor of recycling; it happens with greater frequency when beliefs about it are top-of-mind.[345]

STUART OSKAMP has been at the forefront of research on pro-environmental behavior for many years.

Educate, Prompt, Reward. Some answers to the question of how to increase recycling are, by now, familiar: educate, prompt, and reward it. Increasing awareness through speeches, personal communication, television, and pamphlets works,[346-350] although the effects of the media may be greater for those with more education.[351] Some see the problem as a marketing issue: The same arsenal of techniques should be used to sell recycling as to sell commercial products.[352] Reminding people to recycle with signs and labeled receptacles works,[353,354] and using positive reinforcement works.[355]

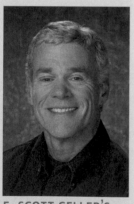

E. SCOTT GELLER'S work provides a blueprint for improving the state of the environment.

Less obvious is that positive appeals have the strongest effect on recycling *attitudes*, but negative messages (such as describing the social and environmental risks of *not* recycling) have the strongest effect on recycling *behavior*.[356]

Different strategies may work with *recycling* of materials as opposed to their *re-use*, at least for children: parental modeling of the behavior and sanctions worked best for recycling, whereas communication about the problem worked best for re-use of materials.[357]

In other cultures, some of the factors so far mentioned also influence recycling, but other factors that fit the culture may also be important. For example, in collectivist China, concern for the community is the strongest predictor of recycling.[358]

In a Virginia university, recycling was prompted by the delivery of a flyer once a week to every resident of two dormitories. Less than 3 percent of the residents responded, but even this small number of recyclers produced about 45 pounds of paper per week.[359] Two reward systems were also tried. In one, a competition between dorms offered a monetary prize to the dorm that recycled the most paper. This strategy produced about 544 pounds of paper per week, over ten times as much as the flyer-only strategy, participation rates doubled. The other reward system offered raffle coupons for prizes for each pound of recyclable paper brought in. This yielded about 820 pounds per week, and participation was four times greater than in the flyer-only condition.

This study illustrates both the advantages and disadvantages of the behavioral approach to recycling. The rewards increased recycling over the flyer-only baseline, but when they were discontinued, recycling fell back to baseline levels. Thus, reward strategies must be continued in order to promote recycling in the long run.[360] Also, rewards cost money and the labor to run contests and competitions is not free; one danger is that the costs of these strategies may exceed the benefits from increased recycling. Interestingly, in the prompt (flyer) condition, recycling actually was higher in the weeks after prompting ended than during the prompting phase. Prompts may not be as immediately effective as monetary rewards, but their effect may last longer, and they may cost less. Signs are another form of prompting, of course, but their placement is very important. Placing them very close to the containers can dramatically increase the rate of recycling.[361]

Block Leaders. A different strategy is to locate individuals on each block (or equivalent) who might encourage their neighbors to recycle.[362] When these block leaders each approached several of their neighbors, recycling increased significantly; it even increased compared to recycling by other neighbors who received the same plea in written form instead of in person.[363] In a similar approach, recycling also will increase when "significant others" are depicted recycling.[364]

Commitment and Feedback. Asking people to make a commitment to recycle also works.[365,366] In a retirement home, when residents were asked to make a commitment as part of a group, their recycling increased by 47 percent.[367] However, among college students, those who made a personal commitment kept recycling at a higher level longer than students who made a commitment as a group. Incidentally, the effect of the personal commitment also lasted longer than the effect of a token reward for recycling. This is encouraging, given the disadvantages of paying people to recycle noted above.

Incidentally, which do you think works better—an educational approach or feedback? Over 5 months, Michigan university students in dormitories were educated about the need for recycling or given posted feedback once per month about the actual amount they had recycled; the feedback group recycled significantly more.[368] Feedback that suggests recycling is the usual (normative) thing to do increases it.[369]

Regulations. Some people believe that morality cannot be legislated. Generally, this is not the case for recycling. Although some people react against recycling regulations, most people accept bottle refund laws, for example.[370] Laws are effective in cleaning up the streets. Before and after a bottle bill was enacted, the number of cans and bottles observed each day dropped from 4 per block to 2 per block![371] The law had a tremendous effect, but notice that laws are not a panacea: some litter remained. In Japan, a "demanding" rule to recycle was successful even though the social benefits of recycling could have been emphasized more and the government could have discussed the rule with the populace more.[372]

Integrated Approaches. Combine the strategies for maximum effectiveness. One such approach is the information-motivation-behavior skills model.[373] Its basic premise is that if people have all three of these, the frequency of the behavior in question should increase, but a deficiency in any of the three should lead to decreased frequency. The model began with health behaviors, but appears to work with curbside recycling, too.[374]

The most effective approaches will be an integrated program combining as many of these strategies and factors as possible. The following factors all can play important roles in recycling:

- How much awareness and information people have about recycling.
- Who the potential recycler is, in demographic terms
- Convenience: make it easy
- The economic payoff
- Attitudes toward recycling
- Local norms about recycling
- Policies or regulations[375,376]

In different places and for different materials to be recycled, some of these factors will be more important than others. That's why other researchers stress that recycling programs should offer potential recyclers a variety of reasons to recycle; the idea is that everyone will find one or more of the reasons persuasive.[377]

SUMMARY

MANY NATURAL RESOURCES ARE COMMONS, that is, desirable commodities that many individuals or organizations are capable of over-using, either raw or after being transformed into a multitude of products. When the rate of harvesting can exceed the rate at which the resource replenishes itself, a commons dilemma exists. Harvesters must decide whether to get rich or comfortable quickly or, through restraint, to benefit all harvesters more moderately with the crucial consequence that the commons is preserved for the future. Through field studies and laboratory simulations, environmental psychologists have identified which characteristics of the resource and its harvesters and which rules promote cooperation rather than defection. Theories of commons dilemmas offer political solutions, systematically consider the many dimensions of commons dilemmas, propose reinforcement strategies, and note that most individuals are basically unaware of commons dilemmas. The theories, therefore, raise important questions as they provide a way of understanding behavior in the commons. For example, *should* individuals cooperate—choosing in broadest terms justice over freedom? If forced to choose, many choose freedom: the freedom to burn fossil fuels, to "harvest" forests, to turn up the heat or air conditioning if they wish, to throw food and unwanted goods into landfills. The chapter has reviewed the case for justice. Simulation research and real-world experience clearly shows that freedom—that beautiful word—easily can lead to ruination. Some theorists believe we are already too far along the defection trail to reverse the tragic course; most environmental psychologists believe it is not too late. Educational campaigns are the start, but they do not work by themselves. Changed attitudes do not lead to changed behavior often enough. Water use, pollution, energy conservation, and recycling are everyday instances of commons dilemmas. Strategies for behavior change are evolving: appeals from respected leaders, moral arguments for justice, prompts, feedback, goal-setting, obtaining public commitments from consumers, changing payoffs to favor conservation instead of exploitation, public disclosure of defections, increased communication among commons members, careful arrangement and design of the physical setting, provision of smaller resource territories for which individuals feel more responsible, and last (but most important), the fostering of trust and friendship. Friendship is the most important because it may allow us a little of that almost unaffordable luxury, freedom. Julian Edney observed that friendship, with its "sympathetic and mutual awareness of each others' condition, needs, and feelings," may be the vehicle by which we eventually achieve both justice *and* freedom.[378]

Suggested Supplementary Readings

Abrahamse, W., Steg, L., Vlek, C., & Rothengatter, T. (2005). A review of intervention studies aimed at household energy conservation. *Journal of Environmental Psychology, 25,* 273-291.

Bonnes, M., & Bonaiuto, M. (2002). Environmental psychology: From spatial-physical environment to sustainable development. In R. B. Bechtel & A. Churchman (Eds.), *Handbook of environmental psychology* (pp. 28-54). Hoboken, NJ: Wiley.

Dawes, R. M., & Messick, D. M. (2000). Social dilemmas. *International Journal of Psychology, 35,* 111-116.

Edney, J. J. (1984). Rationality and social justice. *Human Relations, 37,* 163-180.

Geller, E. S., Winett, R. A., & Everett, P. B. (1982). *Preserving the environment.* New York: Pergamon.

Kurz, T. (2002). The psychology of environmentally sustainable behavior: Fitting together pieces of the puzzle. *Analyses of Social Issues and Public Policy (ASAP), 2,* 257-27

Hardin, G. (1968) The tragedy of the commons. *Science, 162,* 1243-1248.

Ostrom, E., Dietz, T., Dolsak, N., Stern, P. C., Stonich, S. (Eds.)(2002). *The drama of the commons.* Washington, DC: National Academy Press.

Schmuck, P., & Schultz, P. W. (Eds.)(2002). *Psychology of sustainable development.* Dordrecht, Netherlands: Kluwer Academic.

Schultz, P. W., & Kaiser, F. G. (2012). Promoting pro-environmental behavior. In Clayton, S. D. (Ed.). *The Oxford handbook of environmental and conservation psychology* (pp. 556-580). New York: Oxford.

Stern, P. C. (1992). What psychology knows about energy conservation. *American Psychologist, 47,* 1224-1232.

References

1 Hardin, G. (1968). The tragedy of the commons. *Science, 162*, 1243-1248.

2 World Commission on Environment and Development (1987). *Our common future.* New York: Oxford. (p. 8).

3 Hardin, G. (1968). The tragedy of the commons. *Science, 162*, 1243-1248.

4 Koger, S. M. & Scott, B. A. (2007). Psychology and environmental sustainability: A call for integration. *Teaching of Psychology, 34*, 10-18.

5 O'Brien, C. (2008). Sustainable happiness: How happiness studies can contribute to a more sustainable future. *Canadian Psychology/Psychologie canadienne, 49*, 289-295

6 Hardin, G. (1968). The tragedy of the commons. *Science, 162*, 1243-1248.

7 Mio, J. S., Thompson, S. C., & Givens, G. H. (1993). The commons dilemma as metaphor: Memory, influence, and implications for environmental conservation. *Metaphor and Symbolic Activity, 8*, 23-42.

8 Joireman, J. (2005). Environmental problems as social dilemmas: The temporal dimension. In A. Strathman & J. Joireman (Eds.), *Understanding behavior in the context of time: Theory, research, and application* (pp. 289-304). Mahwah, NJ: Erlbaum.

9 Vlek, C. A. J. (2003). Globalisation, commons dilemmas and sustainable quality of life: What do we need, what can we do, what may we achieve? In R. Mira, C. J. M. Sabucedo, & M. J. Romay (Eds.), *Culture, environmental action and sustainability* (pp. 42-60). Ashland, OH: Hogrefe & Huber.

10 Lloyd, W. F. *Lectures on population, value, poor laws and rent.* New York: August M. Kelley, 1837/1968.

11 Hardin, G. (1968). The tragedy of the commons. *Science, 162*, 12431248, p. 1244.

12 Simon, J. (1981). *The ultimate resource.* Princeton, NJ: Princeton University Press.

13 Lomborg, B. (Ed.)(2004). *Global crises, global solutions.* Cambridge, UK: Cambridge University Press.

14 Dawes, R. M. (1973). The commons dilemma game: An *N*-person mixed motive game with a dominating strategy for defection. *ORI Research Bulletin, 13*,1-12.

15 Dawes, R. M. (1980). Social dilemmas. *Annual Review of Psychology, 31*, 169193.

16 Platt, J. (1973). Social traps. *American Psychologist, 28*, 641-651.

17 Dawes, R. M. (1980). Social dilemmas. *Annual Review of Psychology, 31*, 169-193.

18 Edney, J. J., & Harper, C. S. (1978). The commons dilemma: A review of contributions from psychology. *Environmental Management, 2*, 491-507.

19 McClintock, C. G., Moskowitz, J. M., & McClintock, E. (1977). Variations in preferences for individualistic, competitive, and cooperative outcomes as a function of age, game class, and task in nursery school children. *Child Development, 48*, 1080-1085.

20 Mintz, A. (1951). Nonadaptive group behavior. *Journal of Abnormal Social Psychology, 46*, 150-159.

21 Rapoport, An., & Kahan, J. P. (1976). When three is not always two against one: Coalitions in experimental three person cooperative games. *Journal of Experimental Social Psychology, 12*, 253-273.

22 Chapman, J., Hu, L., & Mullen, B. (1986). GROUP1 and GROUP2: BASIC programs for laboratory research on the commons dilemma and group persuasion. *Behavior Research Methods, Instruments, and Computers, 18*, 466-467.

23 Powers, R. B. (1987). Bringing the commons into a large university classroom. *Simulation and Games, 18*, 443-457.

24 Kirts, C. A., Tumeo, M. A., & Sinz, J. M. (1991). The COMMONS GAME: Its instructional value when used in a natural resources management context. *Simulation and Gaming, 22*, 5-18.

25 Fusco, M. E., Bell, P. A., Jorgenson, M. D., & Smith, J. M. (1991). Using a computer to study the commons dilemma. *Simulation and Gaming, 22*, 67-74.

26 Summers, C. (1993). *Natural resource management decisions: An interactive, animated simulation model.* Proceedings of the Society for Computer Simulation, San Diego.

27 Akimov, V., & Soutchanski, M. (1994). Automata simulation of *N*-person social dilemma games. *Journal of Conflict Resolution, 38*, 138-148.

28 Tsai, Y. M. (1993). Social conflict and social cooperation: Simulating "the tragedy of the commons." *Simulation and Gaming, 24*, 356-362.

29 Dawes, R. M. (1980). Social dilemmas. *Annual Review of Psychology, 31*, 169-193.

30 Edney, J. J. (1979). The nuts game: A concise commons dilemma analog. *Environmental Psychology and Nonverbal Behavior, 3*, 252-254.

31 Gifford, R. FISH 4.0. See http://web.uvic.ca/~rgifford/fish/

32 Dawes, R. M., McTavish, J., & Shaklee, H. (1977). Behavior communication and assumptions about other people's behavior in a common dilemma situation. *Journal of Personality and Social Psychology, 35*, 111.

33 34. Bonacich, P. (1976). Secrecy and solidarity. *Sociometry, 39*, 200-208.

34 Tindall, D. B., & O'Connor, B. (1987, June). *Attitudes, social identity, social values, and behavior in a commons dilemma.* Paper presented at the Canadian Psychological Association Conference, Vancouver, B.C.

35 Strauss, A., & Corbin, J. (1990). *Basics of qualitative research: Grounded theory procedures and techniques.* Newbury Park; CA: Sage.

36 Hine, D. W., & Gifford, R. (1997). What harvesters really think about in commons dilemma simulations: A grounded theory analysis. *Canadian Journal of Behavioural Sciences, 29*, 180-194.

37 Oskamp, S., & Schultz, P. W. (2006). Using psychological science to achieve ecological sustainability. In S. I. Donaldson, D. E. Berger, & K. Pezdek (Eds.), *Applied psychology: New frontiers and rewarding careers* (pp. 81-106). Mahwah, NJ: Erlbaum.

38 Schmuck, P., & Vlek, C. (2003). Psychologists can do much to support sustainable development. *European Psychologist, 8*, 66-76.

39 Kelley, H. H., Condry, J. C., Jr., Dahlke, A. E., & Hill, A. H. (1965). Collective behavior in a simulated panic situation. *Journal of Experimental Social Psychology, 1*, 20-54.

40 Watzke, G. E., Dana, J. M., Doktor, R. H., & Rubenstein, F. D. (1972). An experimental study of individual vs. group interest. *Acta Sociologica, 15*, 366-370.

41 Rubenstein, F. D., Watzke, G., Doktor, R. H., & Dana, J. (1975). The effect of two incentive schemes upon the conservation of shared resource by fiveperson groups. *Organizational Behavior and Human Performance, 13*, 330-338.

42 Brechner, K. C. (1977). An experimental analysis of social traps. *Journal of Experimental Social Psychology, 13*, 552-564.

43 Brann, P., & Foddy, M. (1987). Trust and the consumption of a deteriorating common resource. *Journal of Conflict Resolution, 31*, 615-630.

44 Rutte, C. G., Wilke, H. A., & Messick, D. M. (1987). Scarcity or abundance caused by people or the environment as determinants of behavior in the resource dilemma. *Journal of Experimental Social Psychology, 23*, 208-216.

45 Samuelson, C. D., & Hannula, K. A. *Group identity and environmental uncertainty in a sequential resource dilemma.* Unpublished manuscript, Texas A & M University, Department of Psychology, College Station.

46 Budescu, D. V., Rapoport, A., & Suleiman, R. (1990). Resource dilemmas with environmental uncertainty and asymmetric players. *European Journal of Social Psychology, 20*, 475-487.

47 Hine, D. W., & Gifford, R. (1996). Individual restraint and group efficiency in commons dilemmas: The effects of toe types of environmental uncertainty in pool size and regeneration rate. *Journal of Applied Social Psychology, 26*, 993-1009.

48 Gustafsson, M. (1999). *Explanations of effects of resource uncertainty in social dilemmas.* Sweden: Göteborg University, Department of Psychology.

49 Hine, D. W., & Gifford, R.(1996). Individual restraint and group efficiency in commons dilemmas: The effects of toe types of environmental uncertainty in pool size and regeneration rate. *Journal of Applied Social Psychology, 26,* 993-1009.

50 Moore, S. F., Shaffer, L. S., Pollak, E. L., & Taylor-Lemeke, P. (1987). The effects of interpersonal trust and prior commons problem experience on commons management. *Journal of Social Psychology, 127*, 19-29.

51 McClintock, C. G., Moskowitz, J. M., & McClintock, E. (1977). Variations in preferences for individualistic, competitive, and cooperative outcomes as a function of age, game class, and task in nursery school children. *Child Development, 48*, 1080-1085.

52 Gifford, R. (1982). Children and the commons dilemma. *Journal of Applied Social Psychology, 12*, 269-280.

53 Edney, J. J. (1979). The nuts game: A concise commons dilemma analog. *Environmental Psychology and Nonverbal Behavior, 3*, 252-254.

54 Bixenstine, V. E., & Douglas, J. (1967). Effects of psychopathology on group consensus and cooperative choice in a sixperson game. *Journal of Personality and Social Psychology, 5*, 32-37.

55 Bator, R. J., Bryan, A. D., & Schultz, P. W. (2011). Who gives a hoot? Intercept surveys of litterers and disposers. *Environment and Behavior, 43*, 295-315.

56 Schultz, P. W., Bator, R. J., Large, L. B., Bruni, C. M., & Tabanico, J. J. (2013). Littering in context:

Personal and environmental predictors of littering behavior. *Environment and Behavior, 45*, 35-59.

57 Schelly, C. (2010). Testing residential solar thermal adoption. *Environment and Behavior, 42*, 151-170.

58 Vinacke, W. E., Mogy, R., Powers, W., Langan, C., & Beck, R. (1974). Accomodative strategy and communication in a three-person matrix game. *Journal of Personality and Social Psychology, 29*, 509-525.

59 Caldwell, M. D. (1976). Communication and sex effects in a fiveperson prisoner dilemma game. *Journal of Personality and Social Psychology, 33*, 273-280.

60 Javine, D. L. (1986). *A gender comparison: cooperation for the public good*. Unpublished doctoral dissertation, University of Nevada, Reno.

61 Larson, K. L., Ibes, D. C., & White, D. D. (2011). Gendered perspectives about water risks and policy strategies: A tripartite conceptual approach. *Environment and Behavior, 43*, 415-438.

62 Rapoport, An., Chammah, A., Dwyer, J., and Gyr, J. (1962). Threeperson nonzerosum nonnegotiable games. *Behavioral Science, 7*, 38-58.

63 Meux, E. P. (1973). Concern for the common good in an Nperson game. *Journal of Personality and Social Psychology, 28*, 414-418.

64 Campbell, W. K., Bush, C. P., Brunell, A. B., & Shelton, J. (2005). Understanding the social costs of narcissism: The case of the tragedy of the commons. *Personality and Social Psychology Bulletin, 31*, 1358-1368.

65 Biel, A., & Garling, T. (1995). The role of uncertainty on resource dilemmas. *Journal of Environmental Psychology, 15*, 221-233.

66 Khachatryan, H., Joireman, J., & Casavant, K. (2013). Relating values and consideration of future and immediate consequences to consumer preference for biofuels: A three-dimensional social dilemma analysis. *Journal of Environmental Psychology, 34*, 97-108.

67 Liebrand, W. B. G., Jansen, R. W., Rijken, V. M., & Suhre, C. J.(1986). Might over morality: Social values and the perception of other players in experimental games. *Journal of Experimental Social Psychology, 22*, 203-215.

68 Hine, D. W., & Gifford, R. (1993, June). *The commons dilemma: A quantitative review*. Paper presented at the annual convention of the Canadian Psychological Association, Calgary.

69 Hine, D. W., & Gifford, R. (1996). Attributions about self and others in commons dilemmas. *European Journal of Social Psychology, 26*, 429-445.

70 Sattler, D. N., & Kerr, N. L. (1991). Might versus morality explored: Motivational and cognitive bases for social motives. *Journal of Personality and Social Psychology, 60*, 756-765.

71 Wedekind, C. & Milinski, M. (2000 May). Cooperation through image scoring in humans. *Science, 288*, 850-852.

72 Khachatryan, H., Joireman, J., & Casavant, K. (2013). Relating values and consideration of future and immediate consequences to consumer preference for biofuels: A three-dimensional social dilemma analysis. *Journal of Environmental Psychology, 34*, 97-108.

73 van der Werff, E., Steg, L., & Keizer, K. (2013). The value of environmental self-identity: The relationship between biospheric values, environmental self-identity and environmental

preferences, intentions and behaviour. *Journal of Environmental Psychology, 34*, 55-63.

74 Webb, D., Soutar, G. N., Mazzarol, T., & Saldaris, P. (2013). Self-determination theory and consumer behavioural change: Evidence from a household energy-saving behaviour study. *Journal of Environmental Psychology, 35*, 59-66.

75 Graves, L. M., Sarkis, J., & Zhu, Q. (2013). How transformational leadership and employee motivation combine to predict employee pro-environmental behaviors in China. *Journal of Environmental Psychology, 35*, 81-91.

76 Joireman, J. (2005). Environmental problems as social dilemmas: The temporal dimension. In A. Strathman, & J. Joireman (Eds.), *Understanding behavior in the context of time: Theory, research, and application* (pp. 289-304). Mahwah, NJ: Erlbaum.

77 Khachatryan, H., Joireman, J., & Casavant, K. (2013). Relating values and consideration of future and immediate consequences to consumer preference for biofuels: A three-dimensional social dilemma analysis. *Journal of Environmental Psychology, 34*, 97-108.

78 Hansla, A., Gamble, A., Juliusson, A., & Gärling, T. (2008). Psychological determinants of attitude towards and willingness to pay for green electricity. *Energy Policy, 36*, 768-774.

79 Wade-Benzoni, K. A., Tenbrunsel, A. E., & Bazerman, M. H. (1996). Egocentric interpretations of fairness in asymmetric, environmental social dilemmas: Explaining harvesting behavior and the role of communication. *Organizational Behavior and Human Decision Processes, 67*, 111-126.

80 Tindall, D. B., & O'Connor, B. (1987, June). *Attitudes, social identity, social values, and behavior in a commons dilemma*. Paper presented at the Canadian Psychological Association Conference, Vancouver, B.C.

81 Allison, S. T., & Messick, D. M. (1985). Effects of experience on performance in a replenishable resource trap. *Journal of Personality and Social Psychology, 49*, 943-948.

82 Hines, J. M., Hungerford, H. R., & Tomera, A. N. (1986-87). Analysis and synthesis of research on responsible environmental behavior: A meta-analysis. *Journal of Environmental Education, 18*(2), 1-8.

83 Werner, C. M., Cook, S., Colby, J., & Lim, H.-J. (2012). "Lights out" in university classrooms: Brief group discussion can change behavior. *Journal of Environmental Psychology, 32*, 418-426.

84 Hanss, D., & Böhm, G. (2013). Promoting purchases of sustainable groceries: An intervention study. *Journal of Environmental Psychology, 33*, 53-67.

85 Collado, S., Staats, H., & Corraliza, J. A. (2013). Experiencing nature in children's summer camps: Affective, cognitive and behavioural consequences. *Journal of Environmental Psychology, 33*, 37-44.

86 Hovardas, T., & Korfiatis, K. (2012). Effects of an environmental education course on consensus estimates for proenvironmental intentions. *Environment and Behavior, 44*, 760-784.

87 Dawes, R. M. (1980). Social dilemmas. *Annual Review of Psychology, 31*, 169-193.

88 Komorita, S. S., & Lapworth, C. W. (1982). Cooperative choice among individuals versus groups in an Nperson dilemma situation. *Journal of Personality and Social Psychology, 42*, 487496.

89 Edney, J. J. (1981). Paradoxes on the commons: Scarcity and the problem of equality. *Journal of Community Psychology, 9*, 334.

90 Edney, J. J. (1981). Paradoxes on the commons: Scarcity and the problem of equality. *Journal of Community Psychology, 9*, 334.

91 Sato, K. (1989). Trust and feedback in a social dilemma. *Japanese Journal of Experimental Social Psychology, 29*, 123-128.

92 Messick, D. M., Wilke, H., Brewer, M. B., Kramer, R. M., Zemke, P. E., & Lui, L. (1983). Individual adaptations and structural change as solutions to social dilemmas. *Journal of Personality and Social Psychology, 44*, 294-309.

93 Fleishman, J. A. (1988). The effects of decision framing and others' behavior on cooperation in a social dilemma. *Journal of Conflict Resolution, 32*, 162-180.

94 Smith, J. M., Bell, P. A., & Fusco, M. E. (1988). The influence of attraction on a simulated commons dilemma. *Journal of General Psychology, 115*, 277-283.

95 Sussman, R., & Gifford, R. (2013). Be the change you want to see: Modeling food composting in public places. *Environment and Behavior, 45*, 323-343.

96 Nonami, H. (1996). The self-sacrificing minority and saving victims of environmental problems as a social conflict situation. *Psychologia: An International Journal of Psychology in the Orient, 39*, 33-41.

97 Nonami, H. (1997). The effects of a self-sacrificing minority on pro-environmental norms and behavior: An investigation using a sea pollution game. *Japanese Psychological Research, 39*, 65-74.

98 Hine, D. W., & Gifford, R. (1997). What harvester really think about in commons dilemma simulations: A grounded theory analysis. *Canadian Journal of Behavioural Sciences, 29*, 180-194.

99 Messick, D. M. (1984). Solving social dilemmas: Individual and collective approaches. *Representative Research in Social Psychology, 14*, 72-87.

100 Smith, J. M. (1989). The effects of others' behavior, punishment, and warning in behavior in a simulated commons dilemma. *Dissertation Abstracts International, 50 (3-B)*, 1140-1141.

101 Pahl, S., & Bauer, J. (2013). Overcoming the distance: Perspective taking with future humans improves environmental engagement. *Environment and Behavior, 45*, 155-169.

102 Ferguson, M. A., Branscombe, N. R., & Reynolds, K. J. (2011). The effect of intergroup comparison on willingness to perform sustainable behavior. *Journal of Environmental Psychology, 31*, 275-281.

103 Grzelak, J., & Tyska, T. (1974). Some preliminary experiments on cooperation in nperson games. *Polish Psychological Bulletin, 5*, 8091.

104 Smith, J. M., Bell, P. A., & Fusco, M. E. (1988). The influence of attraction on a simulated commons dilemma. *Journal of General Psychology, 115*, 277-283.

105 Hine, D. W., & Gifford, R. (1993, June). *The commons dilemma: A quantitative review*. Paper presented at the annual convention of the Canadian Psychological Association, Calgary.

106 Sato, K. (1989). Trust and feedback in a social dilemma. *Japanese Journal of Experimental Social Psychology, 29*, 123-128.

107 Sato, K. (1989). Trust and feedback in a social dilemma. *Japanese Journal of Experimental Social Psychology, 29*, 123-128.

108 Moore, S. F., Shaffer, L. S., Pollak, E. L., & Taylor-Lemeke, P. (1987). The effects of interpersonal trust and prior commons problem experience on commons management. *Journal of Social Psychology, 127*, 19-29.

109 Brann, P., & Foddy, M. (1987). Trust and the consumption of a deteriorating common resource. *Journal of Conflict Resolution, 31*, 615-630.

110 Tindall, D. B., & O'Connor, B. (1987, June). *Attitudes, social identity, social values, and behavior in a commons dilemma.* Paper presented at the Canadian Psychological Association Conference, Vancouver, B.C.

111 Dawes, R. M., & Messick, D. M. (2000). Social dilemmas. *International Journal of Psychology, 35*, 111-116.

112 Samuelson, C. D., & Hannula, K. A. *Group identity and environmental uncertainty in a sequential resource dilemma.* Unpublished manuscript, Texas A & M University, Department of Psychology, College Station.

113 Dawes, R. M. (1980). Social dilemmas. *Annual Review of Psychology, 31*, 169-193.

114 Allison, S. T., & Messick, D. M. (1990). Social decision heuristics in the use of shared resources. *Journal of Behavioral Decision Making, 3*, 195-204.

115 Harvey, M. L., Bell, P. A., & Birjulin, A. A. (1993). Punishment and type of feedback in a simulated commons dilemma. *Psychological Reports, 73*, 447-450.

116 Komorita, S. S., & Barth, J. M. (1985). Components of reward in social dilemmas. *Journal of Personality and Social Psychology, 48*, 364-373.

117 Wit, A., & Wilke, H. A. (1990). The presentation of rewards and punishments in a simulated social dilemma. *Social Behavior, 5*, 231-245.

118 Bell, P. A., Petersen, T. R., & Hautaluoma, J. E. (1989). The effect of punishment probability on overconsumption and stealing in a simulated commons. *Journal of Applied Social Psychology, 19*, 1483-1495.

119 Birjulin, A. A., Smith, J. M., & Bell P. A. (1993). Monetary reward, verbal reinforcement and harvest strategy of others in a simulated commons dilemma. *Journal of Social Psychology, 133*, 207-214.

120 Martichuski, D. K., & Bell, P. A. (1991). Reward, punishment, privatization, and moral suasion in a commons dilemma. *Journal of Applied Social Psychology, 21*, 1356-1369.

121 Kelley, H. H., & Grzelak, J. (1972). Conflict between individual and common interest in an *n*person relationship. *Journal of Personality and Social Psychology, 21*, 19097.

122 Edney, J. J., & Bell, P. A. (1983). The commons dilemma: Comparing altruism, the golden rule, perfect equality of outcomes, and territoriality. *Social Science Journal, 20*, 23-33.

123 Edney, J. J., & Bell, P. A. (1984). Sharing scarce resources: Groupoutcome orientation, external disaster, and stealing in a simulated commons. *Small Group Behavior, 15*, 87-108.

124 Edney, J. J., & Harper, C. S. (1978). The commons dilemma: A review of contributions from psychology. *Environmental Management, 2*, 491-507.

125 Caldwell, M. D. (1976). Communication and sex effects in a fiveperson prisoner dilemma game.

126 Ostrom, E., Walker, J., & Gardner, R. (1990, August-September). *Sanctioning by participants in collective action problems.* Paper presented at the 1990 Annual Meetings of the American Political Science Association, San Francisco, CA.

127 Dawes, R. M. (1980). Social dilemmas. *Annual Review of Psychology, 31*, 169-193.

128 Edney, J. J., & Bell, P. A. (1983). The commons dilemma: Comparing altruism, the golden rule, perfect equality of outcomes, and territoriality. *Social Science Journal, 20*, 23-33.

129 Brechner, K. C. (1976). An experimental analysis of social traps. *Journal of Experimental Social Psychology, 13*, 552-564.

130 Caldwell, M. D. (1976). Communication and sex effects in a fiveperson prisoner dilemma game. *Journal of Personality and Social Psychology, 33*, 273-280.

131 Dawes, R. M., McTavish, J., & Shaklee, H. (1977). Behavior communication and assumptions about other people's behavior in a common dilemma situation. *Journal of Personality and Social Psychology, 35*, 111.

132 Edney, J. J., & Harper, C. S. (1978). The commons dilemma: A review of contributions from psychology. *Environmental Management, 2*, 491-507.

133 Moore, S. F., Shaffer, L. S., Pollak, E. L., & Taylor-Lemeke, P. (1987). The effects of interpersonal trust and prior commons problem experience on commons management. *Journal of Social Psychology, 127*, 19-29.

134 Kerr, N. L., & Kaufman-Gilliland, C. M. (1994). Communication, commitment, and cooperation in social dilemma. *Journal of Personality and Social Psychology, 66*, 513-529.

135 Orbell, J. M., Van de Kragt, A. J., & Dawes, R. M. (1988). Explaining discussion-induced cooperation. *Journal of Personality and Social Psychology, 54*, 811-819.

136 Dawes, R. M., Orbell, J. M., & van de Kragt, A. J. C. (1985). *Doing well and doing good as ways of resolving social dilemma.* Unpublished manuscript.

137 Levine, B. L. (1987). Community psychology of managing the commons: A simulation study comparing the effect of alternative social arrangements on groups' performance, perceptions, and values with special reference to sense of community. *Dissertation Abstracts International, 47*(11-B), 4701.

138 Jerdee, T. H., & Rosen, B. (1974). Effects of opportunity to communicate and visibility of individual decisions on behavior in the common interest. *Journal of Applied Psychology, 59*, 712-716.

139 Bixenstine, V. E., & Douglas, J. (1967). Effects of psychopathology on group consensus and cooperative choice in a sixperson game. *Journal of Personality and Social Psychology, 5*, 32-37.

140 Moore, S. F., Shaffer, L. S., Pollak, E. L., & Taylor-Lemeke, P. (1987). The effects of interpersonal trust and prior commons problem experience on commons management. *Journal of Social Psychology, 127*, 19-29.

141 Ostrom, E., & Walker, J. M. (1989, August-September). *Communication in a commons: cooperation without external enforcement.* Paper presented at the American Political Science Association meetings, Atlanta, GA.

142 Cass, R. C., & Edney, J. J. (1978). The commons dilemma: A simulation testing the effects of resource visibility and territorial division. *Human Ecology, 6*, 371-386.

143 Bixenstine, V. E., Levitt, C. A., & Wilson, K. R. (1966). Collaboration among six persons in a prisoner's dilemma game. *Journal of Conflict Resolution, 10*, 488-496.

144 Jerdee, T. H., & Rosen, B. (1974). Effects of opportunity to communicate and visibility of individual decisions on behavior in the common interest. *Journal of Applied Psychology, 59*, 712-716.

145 Fox, J., & Guyer, M. (1978). Public choice and cooperation in an *n*person prisoner's dilemma. *Journal of Conflict Resolution, 22*, 468-481.

146 Batson, C. D., Ahmad, N., Yin, J., Bedell, S. J., Johnson, J. W., Templin, C. M., & Whiteside, A. (1999). Two threats to the common good: Self interests egoism and empathy-induced altruism. *Personality and Social Psychology Bulletin, 25*, 3-16.

147 Sato, K. (1989). Trust and feedback in a social dilemma. *Japanese Journal of Experimental Social Psychology, 29*, 123-128.

148 Rapoport, A. (1988). Provision of step-level public goods: effects of inequality in resources. *Journal of Personality and Social Psychology, 54*, 432-440.

149 Naseth, G. J. (1990). The effects of warning of impending resource depletion, resource control and environmental attitudes on behavior in a social dilemma. *Dissertation Abstracts International, 51*(3-B), 1549.

150 Bell, P. A., Petersen, T. R., & Hautaluoma, J. E. (1989). The effect of punishment probability on overconsumption and stealing in a simulated commons. *Journal of Applied Social Psychology, 19*, 1483-1495.

151 Acheson, J. M. (1975). The lobster fiefs: Economic and ecological effects of territoriality in the Maine lobster industry. *Human Ecology, 3*, 183-207.

152 Cass, R. C., & Edney, J. J. (1978). The commons dilemma: A simulation testing the effects of resource visibility and territorial division. *Human Ecology, 6*, 371-386.

153 Martichuski, D. K., & Bell, P. A. (1991). Reward, punishment, privatization, and moral suasion in a commons dilemma. *Journal of Applied Social Psychology, 21*, 1356-1369.

154 Edney, J. J., & Bell, P. A. (1987). Freedom and equality in a simulated commons. *Political Psychology, 8*, 229-243.

155 Aquino, K., Steisel, V., & Kay, A. (1992). The effects of resource distribution, voice, and decision framing on the provision of public goods. *Journal of Conflict Resolution, 36*, 665-687.

156 Messick, D. M. (1984). Solving social dilemmas: Individual and collective approaches. *Representative Research in Social Psychology, 14*, 72-87.

157 Edney, J. J., & Bell, P. A. (1983). The commons dilemma: Comparing altruism, the golden rule, perfect equality of outcomes, and territoriality. *Social Science Journal, 20*, 23-33.

158 Bennett, P. D., & Moore, N. K. (1981). Consumers' preferences for alternative energy conservation policies: A tradeoff analysis. *Journal of Consumer Research, 8*, 313-321.

159 Sattler, D. N. (1991). Effects of group cohesion, beliefs of own deserving, and beliefs of

other's deserving on cooperation in social dilemmas. *Dissertation Abstracts International*, 52(1-B), 575.

160 Samuelson, C. D., Messick, D. M., Rutte, C. G., & Wilke, H. (1984). Individual and structural solutions to resource dilemmas in two cultures. *Journal of Personality and Social Psychology*, 47, 94-104.

161 Samuelson, C. D., & Messick, D. M. (1986). Inequities in access to and use of shared resources in social dilemmas. *Journal of Personality and Social Psychology*, 51, 960-967.

162 Samuelson, C. D., & Messick, D. M. (1986). Alternative structural solutions to resource dilemmas. *Organizational Behavior & Human Decision Processes*, 37, 139-155.

163 Samuelson, C. D. (1991). Perceived task difficulty, causal attributions, and preferences for structural change in resource dilemmas. *Personality and Social Psychology Bulletin*, 17, 181-187.

164 Samuelson, C. D. (1993). *Evaluation of allocation systems in resource dilemmas: Effects of social values, perceived resource use, and outcome inequity.* Unpublished manuscript.

165 Samuelson, C. D., & Messick, D. M. (1986). Alternative structural solutions to resource dilemmas. *Organizational Behavior & Human Decision Processes*, 37, 139-155.

166 Wit, A., & Wilke, H. (1988). Subordinates' endorsement of an allocating leader in a commons dilemma: An equity theoretical approach. *Journal of Economic Psychology*, 9, 151-168.

167 Edney, J. J., & Harper, C. S. (1978). Heroism in a resource crisis: A simulation study. *Environmental Management*, 2, 523-527.

168 Leal, D. R. (1998). Community-run fisheries: Avoiding the "tragedy of the commons." *Pollution and Environment: A Journal of Interdisciplinary Studies*, 19, 225-245.

169 Hardin, G. (1968). The tragedy of the commons. *Science*, 162, 1243-1248.

170 Edney, J. J. (1980). The commons problem: Alternative perspectives. *American Psychologist*, 35, 131-150.

171 Shippee, G. (1981). Energy policymaking and Edney's dilemma. *American Psychologist*, 36, 216-217.

172 Hardin, G. (1968). The tragedy of the commons. *Science*, 162, 1243-1248.

173 Ophuls, W. (1973). Leviathan or oblivion? In H. E. Daly (Ed.), *Toward a steady-state economy*. San Francisco: Freeman.

174 Fox, J. R. (1985). Psychology, ideology, utopia and the commons. *American Psychologist*, 40, 48-58.

175 Edney, J. J. (1981). Paradoxes on the commons: Scarcity and the problem of equality. *Journal of Community Psychology*, 9, 334.

176 Wiener, J. L., & Doescher, T. A. (1991). A framework for promoting cooperation. *Journal of Marketing*, 55, 38-47.

177 Gifford, R., & Hine, D. W. (1997).Toward cooperation in commons dilemmas. *Canadian Journal of Behavioural Sciences*, 29, 167-179.

178 Edney, J. J. (1980). The commons problem: Alternative perspectives. *American Psychologist*, 35, 131-150.

179 Wynne-Edwards, V. C. (1965). Self-regulating systems in populations of animals. *Science*, 147, 1543-1548.

180 Ardrey, R. (1970). *The social contract*. New York: Dell.

181 Dawkins, R. (1976). *The selfish gene*. New York: Oxford.

182 Calabresi, G., & Bobbitt, P.(1978). *Tragic choices*. New York: Norton.

183 Edney, J. J. (1981). Paradoxes on the commons: Scarcity and the problem of equality. *Journal of Community Psychology*, 9, 334.

184 Hardin, G. (1968). The tragedy of the commons. *Science*, 162, 12431248.

185 Calabresi, G., & Bobbitt, P.(1978). *Tragic choices*. New York: Norton.

186 Edney, J. J. (1981). Paradoxes on the commons: Scarcity and the problem of equality. *Journal of Community Psychology*, 9, 334.

187 Pahl, S., & Bauer, J. (2013). Overcoming the distance: Perspective taking with future humans improves environmental engagement. *Environment and Behavior*, 45, 155-169.

188 Platt, J. (1973). Social traps. *American Psychologist*, 28, 641-651.

189 Geller, E. S. (1989). Applied behavior analysis and social marketing: an integration for environmental preservation. *Journal of Social Issues*, 45(1), 17-36.

190 Edney, J. J. (1981). Paradoxes on the commons: Scarcity and the problem of equality. *Journal of Community Psychology*, 9, 334.

191 Hardin, G. (1968). The tragedy of the commons. *Science*, 162, 1243-1248.

192 Dawes, R. M. (1980). Social dilemmas. *Annual Review of Psychology*, 31, 169-193.

193 de Vries, P., Aarts, H., & Midden, C. J. H. (2011). Changing simple energy-related consumer behaviors: How the enactment of intentions is thwarted by acting and non-acting habits. *Environment and Behavior*, 43, 612-633.

194 Yamagishi, T. (1986). The structural/goal expectation theory of cooperation in social dilemmas. In E. J. Lawler & B. Markovsky (Eds.), *Advances in group processes* (Vol. 3), Greenwich, CT: JAI Press.

195 Samuelson, C. D. (1991). Perceived task difficulty, causal attributions, and preferences for structural change in resource dilemmas. *Personality and Social Psychology Bulletin*, 17, 181-187.

196 Samuelson, C. D. (1991). Perceived task difficulty, causal attributions, and preferences for structural change in resource dilemmas. *Personality and Social Psychology Bulletin*, 17, 181-187.

197 Mosler, H., & Brucks, W. M. (2003). Integrating commons dilemma findings in a general dynamic model of cooperative behavior in resource crisis. *European Journal of Social Psychology*, 33, 119-133.

198 Messick, D. M., Wilke, H., Brewer, M. B., Kramer, R. M., Zemke, P. E., & Lui, L. (1983). Individual adaptations and structural change as solutions to social dilemmas. *Journal of Personality and Social Psychology*, 44, 294309.

199 Kaiser, F. G., Doka, G., Hofstetter, P., & Ranney, M. A. (2003). Ecological behavior and its environmental consequences: A life cycle assessment of a self-report measure. *Journal of Environmental Psychology*, 23, 11-20.

200 Gregory, G. D., & Di Leo, M. (2003). Repeated behavior and environmental psychology: The role of personal involvement and habit formation in explaining water consumption. *Journal of Applied Social Psychology*, 33, 1261-1296.

201 Gregory, G. D., & Di Leo, M. (2003). Repeated behavior and environmental psychology: The role of personal involvement and habit formation in explaining water consumption. *Journal of Applied Social Psychology*, 33, 1261-1296.

202 Gregory, G. D., & Di Leo, M. (2003). Repeated behavior and environmental psychology: The role of personal involvement and habit formation in explaining water consumption. *Journal of Applied Social Psychology*, 33, 1261-1296.

203 Kurz, T., Donaghue, N., & Walker, I. (2005). Utilizing a social-ecological framework to promote water and energy conservation: A field experiment. *Journal of Applied Social Psychology*, 35, 1281-1300.

204 Van Vugt, M. (2002). Central, individual, or collective control? Social dilemma strategies for natural resource management. *American Behavioral Scientist*, 45, 783-800.

205 Gregory, G. D., & Di Leo, M. (2003). Repeated behavior and environmental psychology: The role of personal involvement and habit formation in explaining water consumption. *Journal of Applied Social Psychology*, 33, 1261-1296.

206 Larson, K. L., Ibes, D. C., & White, D. D. (2011). Gendered perspectives about water risks and policy strategies: A tripartite conceptual approach. *Environment and Behavior*, 43, 415-438.

207 Cone, J. D., & Hayes, S.C. (1980). *Environmental problems: Behavioral Solutions*. Monterey, CA: Brooks/Cole.

208 Samuelson, C. D. (1990). Energy conservation: A social dilemma approach. *Social Behavior*, 5, 207-230.

209 Kempton, W., Darley, J. M., & Stern, P. C. (1992). Psychological research for the new energy problems: Strategies and opportunities. *American Psychologist*, 47, 1213-1223.

210 Stern, P. C. (1992). What psychology knows about energy conservation. *American Psychologist*, 47, 1224-1232.

211 Energy facts. (1993, March 18). Victoria *Times-Colonist*, D-1.

212 Stern, P. C., & Gardner, G. T. (1981). The place of behavior change in the management of environmental problems. *Journal Environmental Policy*, 2, 213-240.

213 Geller, E. S. (1983). The energy crisis and behavioral science: A conceptual framework for largescale intervention. In A. W. Childs & G. B. Melton (Eds.), *Rural psychology*. New York: Plenum.

214 Socolow, R. H. (1978). *Saving energy in the home*. Cambridge, MA: Ballinger.

215 Geller, E. S., Winett, R. A., & Everett, P. B. (1982). *Preserving the environment*. New York: Pergamon.

216 Stern, P. C., & Aronson, E. (1984). (Eds.), *Energy use: The human dimension*. New York: Freeman.

217 Gifford, R. (2011). The dragons of inaction: Psychological barriers that limit climate change mitigation and adaptation. *American Psychologist*, 66, 290-302.

218 Steg, L. (2008). Promoting household energy conservation. *Energy Policy*, 36, 4449-4453.

219 Macey, S. M., & Brown, M. A. (1983). Residential energy conservation: The role of past experience in repetitive household behavior. *Environment and Behavior, 15*, 123-141.

220 Schulz, D. A. (1985). Self esteem and energy use: Toward the internalization of a conservation ethic. *Marriage and Family Review, 9*, 67-80.

221 Ritchie, J. R. B., McDougall, G., & Claxton, J. D. (1981). Complexities of household energy consumption and conservation. *Journal of Consumer Research, 8*, 233-242.

222 Black, J. S., Stern, P. C., & Elworth, J. T. (1985). Personal and contextual influences on household energy adaptations. *Journal of Applied Psychology, 70*, 3-21.

223 Samuelson, C. D., & Biek, M. (1991). Attitudes toward energy conservation: A confirmatory factor analysis. *Journal of Applied Social Psychology, 21*, 549-568.

224 Becker, L. J., Seligman, C., Fazio, R. H., & Darley, J. M. (1981). Relating attitudes to residential energy use. *Environment and Behavior, 13*, 560-609.

225 Clark, C. F., Kotchen, M. J., & Moore, M. R. (2003). Internal and external influences on pro-environmental behavior: Participation in a green electricity program. *Journal of Environmental Psychology, 23*, 237-246.

226 Poortinga, W., Steg, L., & Vlek, C. (2003). Myths of nature and environmental management strategies. A field study on energy reductions in traffic and transport. In G. Moser, E. Pol, Y. Bernard, M. Bonnes, & J. A. Corraliza (Eds.), *People, places, and sustainability* (pp. 280-290). Ashland, OH: Hogrefe & Huber.

227 Olsen, M. E. (1981). Consumers' attitudes toward energy conservation. *Journal of Social Issues, 37*(2), 108131.

228 Neuman, K. (1986). Personal values and commitment to energy conservation. *Environment and Behavior, 18*, 53-74.

229 Simmons, D. A., Talbot, J. F., & Kaplan, R. (198485). Energy in daily activities: Muddling toward conservation. *Journal of Environmental Systems, 14*, 147-155.

230 Kantola, S. J., Syme, G. J., & Campbell, N. A. (1984). Cognitive dissonance and energy conservation. *Journal of Applied Psychology, 69*, 416421.

231 Hirst, E., & Goeltz, R. (1985). Accuracy of self-reports: Energy conservation surveys. *Social Science Journal, 22*, 19-30.

232 Costanzo, M., Archer, D., Aronson, E., & Pettigrew, T. (1986). Energy conservation behavior: The difficult path from information to action. *American Psychologist, 41*, 521-528

233 Baird, J. C., & Brier, J. M. (1981). Perceptual awareness of energy requirements of familiar objects. *Journal of Applied Psychology, 66*, 90-96.

234 Kempton, W. (1986). Two theories of home heat control. *Cognitive Science, 10*, 75-90.

235 Kantola, S. J., Syme, G. J., & Campbell, N. A. (1984). Cognitive dissonance and energy conservation. *Journal of Applied Psychology, 69*, 416-421.

236 Geller, E. S. (1981). Evaluating energy conservation programs: Is verbal report enough? *Journal of Consumer Research, 8*, 331-335.

237 Peters, J. S. (1990). Integrating psychological and economic perspectives on energy consumption: The determinants of thermostat setting behavior. *Dissertation Abstracts International, 51*(4-B), 2116-2117.

238 Nordlund, A. M., & Garvill, J. (2003). Effects of values, problem awareness, and personal norm on willingness to reduce personal car use. *Journal of Environmental Psychology, 23*, 339-347.

239 Belk, R., Painter, J., & Semenik, R. (1981). Preferred solutions to the energy crisis as a function of causal attributions. *Journal of Consumer Research, 8*, 306-312.

240 Jackson, E. L. (1985). Environmental attitudes and preferences for energy resource options. *Journal of Environmental Education, 17*(1), 23-30.

241 Taschian, R. O., & Slama, M. E. (1985). Survey data on attitudes and behaviors relevant to energy: Implications for policy. *Marriage & Family Review, 9*, 29-51.

242 Wentworth, W. R. (1989). Energy conservation attitudes, intentions, and behaviors of homeowners in Staten Island, New York. *Dissertation Abstracts International, 49*(8-B), 3505.

243 Marshall, M. J. (1987). Social-psychological correlates of household energy conservation activities. *Dissertation Abstracts International, 48*(1-B), 301-302.

244 Labay, D. G., & Kinnear, T. C. (1981). Exploring the consumer decision process in the adoption of solar energy systems. *Journal of Consumer Research, 8*, 271-278.

245 Griffin, R. J., Glynn, C. J., & McLeod, J. M. (1986). Energy and communication: Social status in a tale of two cities. *Man-Environment Systems, 16*, 34-44.

246 Marshall, M. J. (1987). Social-psychological correlates of household energy conservation activities. *Dissertation Abstracts International, 48*(1-B), 301-302.

247 LeonardBarton, D. (1981). Voluntary simplicity lifestyles and energy conservation. *Journal of Consumer Research, 8*, 243-252.

248 Olsen, M. E. (1981). Consumers' attitudes toward energy conservation. *Journal of Social Issues, 37*(2), 108-131.

249 Peters, J. S. (1990). Integrating psychological and economic perspectives on energy consumption: The determinants of thermostat setting behavior. *Dissertation Abstracts International, 51*(4-B), 2116-2117.

250 Macey, S. M. (1989). Hypothermia and energy conservation: A tradeoff for elderly persons? *International Journal of Aging and Human Development, 29*, 151-161.

251 Peters, J. S. (1990). Integrating psychological and economic perspectives on energy consumption: The determinants of thermostat setting behavior. *Dissertation Abstracts International, 51*(4-B), 2116-2117.

252 Griffin, R. J. (1989). Communication and the adoption of energy conservation measures by the elderly. *Journal of Environmental Education, 20*(4), 19-28.

253 Luyben, P. D. (1982). Prompting thermostat setting behavior: Public response to a presidential appeal for conservation. *Environment and Behavior, 14*, 113-128.

254 Wodarski, J. B. (1982). National and state appeals for energy conservation: A behavioral analysis of effects. *Behavioral Engineering, 7*, 119-130.

255 Winkler, R. C., & Winett, R. A. (1982). Behavioral interventions in resource management: A systems approach based on behavioral economics. *American Psychologist, 37*, 421-435.

256 Walker, J. M. (1980). Voluntary response to energy conservation appeals. *Journal of Consumer Research, 7*, 8892.

257 Cone, J. D., & Hayes, S.C. (1980). *Environmental problems: Behavioral solutions.* Monterey, CA: Brooks/Cole.

258 Geller, E. S., Winett, R. A., & Everett, P. B. (1982). *Preserving the environment.* New York: Pergamon.

259 Kurz, T., Donaghue, N., & Walker, I. (2005). Utilizing a social-ecological framework to promote water and energy conservation: A field experiment. *Journal of Applied Social Psychology, 35*, 1281-1300.

260 Staats, H., van Leeuwen, E., & Wit, A. (2000). A longitudinal study of informational interventions to save energy in an office building. *Journal of Applied Behavior Analysis, 33*, 101-104.

261 Hine, D. W., Bhullar, N., Marks, A. D. G., Kelly, P., & Scott, J. G. (2011). Comparing the effectiveness of education and technology in reducing wood smoke pollution: A field experiment. *Journal of Environmental Psychology, 31*, 282-288.

262 Zielinski, E. J., & Bethel, L. J. (1983). Winning the energy game. *The Science Teacher, 50*, 55-56.

263 Dresner, M. (1989-90). Changing energy end-use patterns as a means of reducing global-warming trends. *Journal of Environmental Education, 21*(2), 41-46,

264 Parthasarathy, R. (1989). Psychological or attitudinal factors which influence the introduction of energy conservation technologies. *Abhigyan*, Fall, 36-47.

265 Seligman, C. (1985). Information and energy conservation. *Marriage and Family Review, 9*, 135-149.

266 Syme, G. J., Seligman, C., Kantola, S. J., & MacPherson, D. K. (1987). Evaluating a television campaign to promote petrol conservation. *Environment and Behavior, 19*, 444-461.

267 Pelletier, L., & Sharp, E. (2008). Persuasive communication and proenvironmental behaviours: How message tailoring and message framing can improve the integration of behaviours through self-determined motivation. *Canadian Psychology/Psychologie canadienne, 49*, 210-217.

268 Pallak, M. S., & Cummings, W. (1976). Commitment and voluntary energy conservation. *Personality and Social Psychology Bulletin, 2*, 27-30.

269 Katzev, R., & Wang, T. (1994). Can commitment change behavior? A case study of environmental actions. *Journal of Social Behavior and Personality, 9*, 13-26.

270 Lokhorst, A. M., Werner, C., Staats, H., van Dijk, E., & Gale, J. L. (2013). Commitment and behavior change: A meta-analysis and critical review of commitment-making strategies in environmental research. *Environment and Behavior, 45*, 3-34.

271 Shippee, G., & Gregory, W. L. (1982). Public commitment and energy conservation. *American Journal of Community Psychology, 10*, 81-93.

272 Lokhorst, A. M., Werner, C., Staats, H., van Dijk, E., & Gale, J. L. (2013). Commitment and behavior change: A meta-analysis and critical review of commitment-making strategies in environmental research. *Environment and Behavior, 45*, 3-34.

273 Lokhorst, A. M., van Dijk, E., & Staats, H. (2009). Public commitment making as a structural solution in social dilemmas. *Journal of Environmental Psychology, 29*, 400-406.

274 Seligman, C., & Darley, J. M. (1977). Feedback as a means of decreasing residential energy consumption. *Journal of Applied Psychology, 62,* 363-368.

275 Geller, E. S., Winett, R. A., & Everett, P. B. (1982). *Preserving the environment.* New York: Pergamon.

276 Siero, S., Boon, M., Kok, G., & Siero F. (1989). Modification of driving behavior in a large transport organization: A field experiment. *Journal of Applied Psychology, 74,* 417-423.

277 Abrahamse, W., Steg, L., Vlek, C., & Rothengatter, T. (2005). A review of intervention studies aimed at household energy conservation. *Journal of Environmental Psychology, 25,* 273-291.

278 Brandon, G., & Lewis, A. (1999). Reducing household energy consumption: A qualitative and quantitative field study. *Journal of Environmental Psychology, 19,* 75-85.

279 Sexton, R. J., Johnson, N. B., & Konakayama, A. (1987). Consumer response to continuous-display electricity-use monitors in a time-of-use pricing experiment. *Journal of Consumer Research, 14,* 55-62.

280 Siero, F. W., Bakker, A. B., Dekker, G. B., van den Burg, M. T. C. (1996). Changing organizational energy consumption behaviour through comparative feedback. *Journal of Environmental Psychology, 16,* 235-246.

281 Van Houwelingen, J. H., & Van Raaij, W. F. (1989). The effect of goal-setting and daily electronic feedback on in-home energy use. *Journal of Consumer Research, 16,* 98-105.

282 Abrahamse, W., Steg, L., Vlek, C., & Rothengatter, T. (2007). The effect of tailored information, goal setting, and tailored feedback on household energy use, energy-related behaviors, and behavioral antecedents. *Journal of Environmental Psychology, 27,* 265-276.

283 Becker, L. J. (1978). Joint effect of feedback and goal setting on performance: A field study of residential energy conservation. *Journal of Applied Psychology, 63,* 428-433.

284 McCalley, L. T., & Midden, C. J. H. (2002). Energy conservation through product-integrated feedback: The roles of goal-setting and social orientation. *Journal of Economic Psychology, 23,* 589-603.

285 Kluger, A. N., & DeNisi, A. (1996). The effects of feedback interventions on performance: A historical review, a meta-analysis, and a preliminary feedback intervention theory. *Psychological Bulletin, 119,* 254-284.

286 McCalley, L. T., de Vries, P. W., & Midden, C. J. H. (2011). Consumer response to product-integrated energy feedback: Behavior, goal level shifts, and energy conservation. *Environment and Behavior, 43,* 525-545.

287 Aronson, E., & O'Leary, M. (1977). The relative effectiveness of models and prompts on energy conservation: A field experiment in a shower room. *Journal of Environmental Systems, 12,* 219-224.

288 Sussman, R, & Gifford, R. (2012). Please turn off the lights: The effectiveness of visual prompts. *Applied Ergonomics, 43,* 596-603.

289 Winett, R. A., Neale, M. S., & Grier, H. C. (1979). Effects of selfmonitoring and feedback on residential electricity consumption. *Journal of Applied Behavior Analysis, 12,* 173-184.

290 Winett, R. A., Neale, M. S., Williams, K. R., Yokley, J., & Kauder, H. (1979). The effects of individual and group feedback on residential electricity consumption: Three replications. *Journal of Environmental Systems, 8,* 217-233.

291 Hollenbeck, B. G. (1986). Reducing residential energy consumption: The effects of government subsidies on energy conservation. *Dissertation Abstracts International, 47*(1-B), 376.

292 Gonzales, M. H., Aronson, E., & Costanzo, M. A. (1988). Using social cognition and persuasion to promote energy conservation: A quasi-experiment. *Journal of Applied Social Psychology, 18,* 1049-1066.

293 McDougall, G. H. G., Claxton, J. D., Ritchie, J. R. B., & Anderson, C. D. (1981). Consumer energy research: A review. *Journal of Consumer Research, 8,* 343-354.

294 Geller, E. S., Winett, R. A., & Everett, P. B. (1982). *Preserving the environment.* New York: Pergamon.

295 Stern, P. C. (1984). (Ed.), *Improving energy demand analysis.* Washington: National Academy Press.

296 Winkler, R. C., & Winett, R. A. (1982). Behavioral interventions in resource management: A systems approach based on behavioral economics. *American Psychologist, 37,* 421-435.

297 Hine, D. W., Bhullar, N., Marks, A. D. G., Kelly, P., & Scott, J. G. (2011). Comparing the effectiveness of education and technology in reducing wood smoke pollution: A field experiment. *Journal of Environmental Psychology, 31,* 282-288.

298 Corbett, M. N. (1981). *A better place to live: New designs for tomorrow's communities.* Emmaus, PA: Rodale.

299 Sommer, R. (1983). *Social design: Creating buildings with people in mind.* Englewood Cliffs, NJ: PrenticeHall.

300 LeonardBarton, D. (1981). Voluntary simplicity lifestyles and energy conservation. *Journal of Consumer Research, 8,* 243-252.

301 Stewart, R., Baretta, E., Platte, L., Stewart, M. T., Kalbfleisch, J., Van Yserloo, B., and Rimm, A. (1974). Carboxyhemoglobin levels in American blood donors. *Journal of the American Medical Association, 229,* 1187-1195.

302 Wilson, G. (1987). Where there's smoke... *Conserver Society Notes, 14,* 53-55.

303 Sommers, P., Van Dort, B., & Moos, R. (1976). Noise and air pollution. In R. Moos (Ed.), *The human context: Environmental determinants of behavior.* New York: Wiley.

304 Jerrett, M., Buzzelli, M., Burnett, R. T., & DeLuca, P. F. (2005). Particulate air pollution, social confounders, and mortality in small areas of an industrial city. *Social Science & Medicine, 60,* 2845-2863.

305 Rose, E. F., & Rose, M. (1971). Carbon monoxide: A challenge to the physician. *Clinical Medicine, 78,* 12-19.

306 Schulte, J. H. (1963). Effects of mild carbon monoxide intoxication. *Archives of Environmental Health, 7,* 524-530.

307 Beard, R. R., & Wertheim, G. A. (1967). Behavioral impairment associated with small doses of carbon monoxide. *American Journal of Public Health, 57,* 2012-2022.

308 Horvath, S. M., Dahms, T. E., & O'Hanlon, J. F. (1971). Carbon monoxide and human vigilance: A deleterious effect of present urban concentrations. *Archives of Environmental Health, 23,* 343-347.

309 Sommers, P., Van Dort, B., & Moos, R. (1976). Noise and air pollution. In R. Moos (Ed.), *The human context: Environmental determinants of behavior.* New York: Wiley.

310 Jones, J. W., & Bogat, A. G. (1978). Air pollution and human aggression. *Psychological Reports, 43,* 721-722.

311 Briere, J., Downes, A., & Spensley, J. (1983). Summer in the city: Weather conditions and psychiatric emergencyroom visits. *Journal of Abnormal Psychology, 92,* 77-80.

312 Sommer, R. (1972). *Design awareness.* New York: Holt, Rinehart and Winston.

313 Evans, G. W., Jacobs, S. V., & Frager, N. B. (1982). Behavioral responses to air pollution. In A. Baum & J. E. Singer (Eds.), *Advances in environmental psychology.* Hillsdale, NJ: Erlbaum.

314 Wall, G. (1973). Public response to air pollution in South Yorkshire, England. *Environment and Behavior, 5,* 219-248.

315 Purcell, A. H. (1981, February). The world's trashiest people: Will they clean up their act or throw away their future? *The Futurist,* 51-59.

316 Arkes, H. R., & Hutzel, L. (1997). Waste heuristics: The desire not to waste versus the desire for new things. In M. H. Bazerman, D. M. Messick, et al (Eds.), *Environment, ethics, and behavior: The psychology of environmental valuation and degradation.* San Francisco, CA: The New Lexington Press/Jossey-Bass Inc.

317 Andersson, M., & von Borgstede, C. (2010). Differentiation of determinants of low-cost and high-cost recycling. *Journal of Environmental Psychology, 30,* 402-408.

318 Geller, E. S., Winett, R. A., & Everett, P. B. (1982). *Preserving the environment.* New York: Pergamon.

319 Geller, E. S., Winett, R. A., & Everett, P. B. (1982). *Preserving the environment.* New York: Pergamon.

320 Blue boxes' trees tallied. Victoria *Times-Colonist,* March, 1990.

321 Scott, D. (1999). Equal opportunity, unequal results: Determinants of household recycling intensity. *Environment and Behavior, 31,* 267-290.

322 Vining, J., & Ebreo, A. (1992). Predicting recycling behavior from global and specific environmental attitudes and changes in recycling opportunities. *Journal of Applied Social Psychology, 22,* 1580-1607.

323 Simmons, D., & Widmar, R. (1990). Motivations and barriers to recycling: Toward a strategy for public education. *Journal of Environmental Education, 22*(1), 13-18.

324 Lansana, F. M. (1992). Distinguishing potential recyclers from nonrecyclers: A basis for developing recycling strategies. *Journal of Environmental Education, 23*(2), 16-23.

325 Kallgren, C. A., & Wood, W. (1986). Access to attitude-relevant information in memory as a determinant of attitude-behavior consistency. *Journal of Experimental Social Psychology, 22,* 328-338.

326 Lansana, F. M. (1992). Distinguishing potential recyclers from nonrecyclers: A basis for developing recycling strategies. *Journal of Environmental Education, 23*(2), 16-23.

327 Oskamp, S., Harrington, M. J., Edwards, T. C., Sherwood D. L., et al. (1991). Factors influencing household recycling behavior. *Environment and Behavior, 23,* 494-519.

328 Katzev, R., Blake, G., & Messer, B. (1993). Determinants of participation in multi-family recycling programs. *Journal of Applied Social Psychology, 23*, 374-385.

329 Werner, C. M., Rhodes, M. U., & Partain, K. K. (1998). Designing effective instructional signs with schema theory: Case studies of polystyrene recycling. *Environment and Behavior, 30*, 709-735.

330 Chen, M., & Tung, P. (2010). The moderating effect of perceived lack of facilities on consumers' recycling intentions. *Environment and Behavior, 42*, 824-844.

331 Howenstine, E. (1993). Market segmentation for recycling. *Environment and Behavior, 25*, 86-102.

332 Berger, I. E. (1997). The demographics of recycling and the structure of environmental behavior. *Environment and Behavior, 29*, 515-531.

333 Derksen, L., & Gartrell, J. (1993). The social context of recycling. *American Sociological Review, 58*, 434-442.

334 Williams, E. (1991). College students and recycling: Their attitudes and behaviors. *Journal of College Student Development, 32*, 86-88.

335 Oskamp, S., Harrington, M. J., Edwards, T. C., Sherwood D. L., et al. (1991). Factors influencing household recycling behavior. *Environment and Behavior, 23*, 494-519.

336 Corral-Verdugo, V. (1997). Dual "realities" of conservation behavior: Self-reports vs. observations of re-use and recycling behavior. *Journal of Environmental Psychology, 17*, 135-145.

337 McGuire, R. H. (1984). Recycling: Great expectations and garbage outcomes. Special Issue: household refuse analysis-theory, method, and applications in social science. *American Behavioral Scientist, 28*, 93-114.

338 Knussen, C., Yule, F., MacKenzie, J., & Wells, M. (2004). An analysis of intentions to recycle household waste: The roles of past behavior, perceived habit, and perceived lack of facilities. *Journal of Environmental Psychology, 24*, 237-246.

339 Mannetti, L., Pierro, A., & Livi, S. (2004). Recycling: Planned and self-expressive behavior. *Journal of Environmental Psychology, 24*, 227-236.

340 White, K. M., & Hyde, M. K. (2012). The role of self-perceptions in the prediction of household recycling behavior in Australia. *Environment and Behavior, 44*, 785-799.

341 Matthies, E., & Kroemker, D. (2000). Participatory planning: A heuristic for adjusting to the context. *Journal of Environmental Psychology, 20*, 65-74.

342 Gamba, R. J., & Oskamp, S. (1994). Factors influencing community residents' participation in commingled curbside recycling programs. *Environment and Behavior, 26*, 587-612.

343 Oskamp, S., Zelezny, L., Schultz, P. W., Hurin, S., & Burkhardt, R. (1996). Commingled versus separated curbside recycling: Does sorting matter? *Environment and Behavior, 28*, 73-91.

344 Katzev, R., Blake, G., & Messer, B. (1993). Determinants of participation in multi-family recycling programs. *Journal of Applied Social Psychology, 23*, 374-385.

345 Kallgren, C. A., & Wood, W. (1986). Access to attitude-relevant information in memory as a determinant of attitude-behavior consistency. *Journal of Experimental Social Psychology, 22*, 328-338.

346 Hopper, J. R., & Nielsen, J. M. (1991). Recycling as altruistic behavior: Normative and behavioral strategies to expand participation in a community recycling program. *Environment and Behavior, 23*, 195-220.

347 Burn, S. M., & Oskamp, S. (1986). Increasing community recycling with persuasive communication and public commitment. *Journal of Applied Social Psychology, 16*, 29-41.

348 de Young, R., Duncan, A., Frank, J., Gill, N., et al. (1993). Promoting source reduction behavior: The role of motivational information. *Environment and Behavior, 25*, 70-85.

349 Margai, F. L. (1997). Analyzing changes in waste reduction behavior in a low-income urban community following a public outreach program. *Environment and Behavior, 29*, 769-792.

350 Nyamwange, M. (1996). Public perception of strategies for increasing participation in recycling programs. *Journal of Environmental Education, 27*(4), 9-22.

351 Martinez, M. D., & Scicchitano. M. J. (1998). Who listens to trash talk?: Education and public media effects on recycling behavior. *Social Science Quarterly, 79*, 287-300.

352 Shrum, L. J., Lowrey, T. M., & McCarty, J. A. (1994). Recycling as a marketing problem: A framework for strategy development. *Psychology and Marketing, 11*, 393-416.

353 Katzev, R., & Mishima, H. R. (1992). The use of posted feedback to promote recycling. *Psychological Reports, 71*, 259-264.

354 Werner, C. M., & Maleka, E. (1998). Motivations and behaviors that support recycling. *Journal of Environmental Psychology, 18*, 373-386.

355 Diamond, W. D., & Loewy, B. Z. (1991). Effects of probabilistic rewards on recycling attitudes and behavior. *Journal of Applied Social Psychology, 21*, 1590-1607.

356 Lord, K. R. (1994). Motivating recycling behavior: A quasi-experimental investigation of message and source strategies. *Psychology and Marketing, 11*, 341-358.

357 Matthies, E., Selge, S., & Klöckner, C. A. (2012). The role of parental behaviour for the development of behaviour specific environmental norms – The example of recycling and re-use behaviour. *Journal of Environmental Psychology, 32*, 277-284.

358 Tang, Z., Chen, X., & Luo, J. (2011). Determining socio-psychological drivers for rural household recycling behavior in developing countries: A case study from Wugan, Hunan, China. *Environment and Behavior, 43*, 848-877.

359 Witmer, J. F., & Geller, E. S. (1976). Facilitating paper recycling: Effects of prompts, raffles, and contests. *Journal of Applied Behavior Analysis, 9*, 315322.

360 Porter, B. E., Leeming, F. C., & Dwyer, W. O. (1995). Solid waste recovery: A review of behavioral programs to increase recycling. *Environment and Behavior, 27*, 122-152.

361 Austin, J., Hatfield, D. B., Grindle, A. C., & Bailey, J. S. (1993). Increasing recycling in office environments: The effects of specific, informative cues. *Journal of Applied Behavior Analysis, 26*, 247-253.

362 Hopper, J. R., & Nielsen, J. M. (1991). Recycling as altruistic behavior: Normative and behavioral strategies to expand participation in a community recycling program. *Environment and Behavior, 23*, 195-220.

363 Burn, S. M. (1991). Social psychology and the stimulation of recycling behaviors: The block leader approach. *Journal of Applied Social Psychology, 21*, 611-629.

364 Kahle, L. R., & Beatty, S. E. (1987). Cognitive consequences of legislating postpurchase behavior: Growing up with the bottle bill. *Journal of Applied Social Psychology, 17*, 828-843.

365 de Young, R., Duncan, A., Frank, J., Gill, N., et al. (1993). Promoting source reduction behavior: The role of motivational information. *Environment and Behavior, 25*, 70-85.

366 Werner, C. M., Turner, J., Shipman, K., Twitchell, F. S., Dickson, B. R., Bruschke, G. V., & von Bismark, W. B. (1995). Commitment, behavior, and attitude change: An analysis of voluntary recycling. *Journal of Environmental Psychology, 15*, 197-208.

367 Wang, T. H., & Katzev, R. D. (1990). Group commitment and resource conservation: Two field experiments on promoting recycling. *Journal of Applied Social Psychology, 20*, 265-272.

368 Goldenhar, L. M. (1991). Understanding, predicting, and influencing recycling behavior: The future generation. *Dissertation Abstracts International, 52*(3-B), 1379.

369 Schultz, P. W. (1999). Changing behavior with normative feedback interventions: A field experiment on curbside recycling. *Basic and Applied Social Psychology, 21*, 35-36.

370 Crosby, L. A., & Taylor, J. R. (1982). Consumer satisfaction with Michigan's container deposit law - an ecological perspective. *Journal of Marketing, 46*, 47-60.

371 Trinkhaus, J. (1984). A bottle law: an informal look. *Perceptual and Motor Skills, 59*, 806.

372 Ohnuma, S., Hirose, Y., Karasawa, K., Yorifuji, K., & Sugiura, J. (2005). Why do residents accept a demanding rule? Fairness and social benefit as determinants of approval of a recycling system. *Japanese Psychological Research, 47*, 1-11.

373 Fisher, J. D., & Fisher, W. A. (2002). The information–motivation–behavioral skills model. In R.J. DiClemente, R.A. Crosby, C. Kegler (Eds.), *Emerging theories in health promotion practice and research*. San Francisco: Jossey-Bass.

374 Seacat, J. D., & Northrup, D. (2010). An information–motivation–behavioral skills assessment of curbside recycling behavior. *Journal of Environmental Psychology, 30*, 393-401.

375 Wright, R. E. (1992). An investigation of the relative importance of factors influencing recycling behavior. *Dissertation Abstracts International, 52*(11-A), 4008-4009.

376 Lansana, F. (1992). Modeling household participation rates in recycling programs: An analysis of spatio-temporal variations. *Dissertation Abstracts International, 52*(7-A), 2673.

377 Simmons, D., & Widmar, R. (1990). Motivations and barriers to recycling: Toward a strategy for public education. *Journal of Environmental Education, 22*(1), 13-18.

378 Edney, J. J. (1984). Rationality and social justice. *Human Relations, 37*, 163-180.

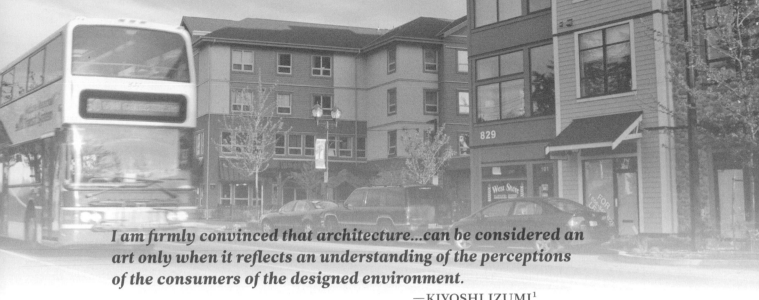

I am firmly convinced that architecture...can be considered an art only when it reflects an understanding of the perceptions of the consumers of the designed environment.

—KIYOSHI IZUMI[1]

TOM AND JANE WERE SPENDING A LEISURELY SATURDAY AFTERNOON AT THEIR LOCAL LIBRARY, WHICH HAD OPENED A FEW WEEKS EARLIER. *Tom had checked out a book on renovating old houses. They were reading the paper, trading small talk on current issues and the bizarre story of the day ("10-year-old girl, discovered by primitive tribes, lives with pack of panthers and goes about on all fours, fighting with the panthers for food and trying to leap into trees").*

A young woman approached them. "Excuse me," said she, "I am conducting a study of this library, and I wonder if you would mind telling me your opinions of it?" Tom and Jane agreed, but groaned silently. They had responded to more than their share of questionnaires that year at school. "Now they're even invading public territories," Tom thought to himself.

The questionnaire covered various aspects of the library, such as spatial layout, lighting, windows, and noise. It asked their reasons for coming to the branch library and for any special complaints or compliments they wished to offer about it.

The woman returned in a few minutes for their completed questionnaires. She explained that similar questionnaires had been distributed in the old library, for comparison purposes.

"I have to tell you, too," she said somewhat hesitantly, "that I have been watching you two for the last half hour." Tom and Jane looked at each other quickly, then back at the researcher. "In our evaluation we want to learn how people actually use the library as well as how they feel about it. You see, our study of the old library showed that people were afraid to talk aloud to each other and that it took a long time for people to find the books they were looking for."

"This new design is supposed to make you feel more like talking because we've separated the study area from the light-reading area. All those maps and signs, together with carefully planned arrangement of the card catalog and stacks are supposed to help you find things faster. Do you realize that it took you 38 seconds to find the book you're holding?"

This long speech took Tom and Jane a bit by surprise. They stared for a minute, then Jane stammered, "I guess your project seems like a good idea..."

The woman leaned closer. "I have to ask," she said, "what were you reading in the paper that was so hilarious?"

IN MANY OF THE FOREGOING CHAPTERS, WE SURVEYED RESEARCH AND THEORY in those areas of environmental psychology that relate to person-setting relations. For some readers, this may be enough; to understand something of how and why individuals interact with the physical environment satisfies one's curiosity. For these readers, I have tried to present some *principles* of environmental psychology. Other readers may be hoping for something more. Examples of design applications were offered in earlier chapters, but we have not yet directly examined the process of designing environments or the role of social science in the design process.

This chapter is especially for readers who have been patiently waiting for a fuller treatment of the *practice* of environmental psychology in environmental design—about putting environment-behavior knowledge to work to improve buildings and other physical settings. The chapter begins with a description of social design, a process that can improve the habitability of buildings. Next, the goals, problems, and advantages of including social science in architecture are considered. Then the social design process is described, and I focus on its two most important phases: programming and post-occupancy evaluation. The chapter closes with descriptions of several examples of programming and post-occupancy evaluations.

SOCIAL DESIGN

MANY, MANY BUILDINGS HAVE BEEN CONSTRUCTED THAT DID NOT ADEQUATELY CONSIDER the needs of the people who would use them. Some buildings might even be called inhumane. However, more-humane buildings can be designed. This process, developed over the last several decades under a variety of names, might best be called **social design.**[2,3] Most generally, it involves studying how settings can best serve human desires and requirements. It must be distinguished from technical design research (for example, on the performance of building materials).

A Definition

ROBERT SOMMER, A PIONEER DEVELOPER OF THESE IDEAS, characterizes social design as follows:

Social design is working with people rather than for them; involving people in the planning and management of the spaces around them; educating them to use the environment wisely and creatively to achieve a harmonious balance between the social, physical, and natural environment; to develop an awareness of beauty, a sense of responsibility, to the Earth's environment and to other living creatures; to generate, compile, and make available information about the effects of human activities on the biotic and physical environment, including the effects of the built environment on human beings. Social designers cannot achieve these objectives working by themselves. The goals can be realized only within the structures of larger organizations, which include the people for whom a project is planned.[4]

Social design may be distinguished from formal design (the traditional approach).[5] **Formal design** favors an approach that may be described as large-scale, corporate, high-cost, exclusive, authoritarian, tending to high-tech solutions, and primarily concerned with style, the paying client, and a national or international focus. In contrast, social design favors an approach that may be described as small-scale, human-oriented, low-cost, inclusive, democratic, tending to appropriate technology, and concerned with meaning and context, undertaken with those will use the building as well as the paying client, and a local focus.

Although these distinctions provide the flavor of social design, they may not all apply in every design project. For example, social design may cost a little more, at least initially, but it may save much more over the life of the building. Social design techniques may be applied to large-scale projects as well as small-scale projects. The difference between social design and formal design is that in a large-scale project, the social designer often pays more attention to specific behavior settings *within* the large project. In a large office complex, for example, the individual needs and activities of employees are more likely to be researched and incorporated into the building design. Others have more recently elaborated on ideas similar to social design.[6]

The Need

Architecture as a Limited Discipline. Certainly portions of the built environment need improvement. One well-publicized example is a large St. Louis apartment complex that was completed in 1954 called Pruitt-Igoe. It was de-

FIGURE 15–1 The Pruitt–Igoe housing project in St. Louis.

signed with the admirable intention of replacing deteriorating inner-city housing. The complex, which contained 33 11-story buildings for about 12,000 people, was praised in an architectural journal for having no wasted space, vandal-resistant features, and individualistic design.[7] The Pruitt-Igoe design saved space in part by having elevators stop only at every third floor, so most residents would walk up or down one flight of stairs to their apartments. Altogether, Pruitt-Igoe cost about $1,000 less per unit to build than comparable buildings of the time.

The design changes were considered so admirable that the architect even applied for a patent on the design. However, problems appeared soon after it opened. The failure to carefully examine its design in relation to human behavior contributed to high rates of fear, vandalism, vacancy, and serious crime. A particular problem was crime in the stairwells that residents were forced to use because of the innovative elevator savings plan. The situation was so bad that, after only 18 years, the city demolished the entire complex. Whether the architect received his patent is unknown, but he did go on to design the World Trade Towers in New York!

Pruitt-Igoe is the most dramatic example of building design failure—part of the demolition was shown on national television—but many other buildings also pose problems for their users (see Figure 15-1).

What causes these problems? For three reasons, we must assume that architects do their best: They have personal standards of excellence and ethics, they are legally responsible for the design of their buildings, and they want to enhance their reputations and win recognition. The last reason can be problematic: one key to success for architects is to win prizes. Virtually all prizes are awarded by committees of architects. Thus, a prize-winning architect is one who impresses...*other architects*.

A central problem is that architects often view their designs differently from those who will occupy their creations. Buildings can be evaluated similarly even by different groups of laypersons, such as students and professors,[8] but buildings often quite literally *mean* different things to architects than they do to others.[9]

In one design competition for an actual building, rankings by architectural experts of the five entries were compared with rankings by 65 non-architects; both groups were given the same criteria to use.[10] The experts' first choice was ranked fourth out of the five entries by the non-architects. In another competition, evaluations of new housing projects were made by a design competition jury, a trained but independent observer, and residents of the projects.[11] The observer's ranking of the projects was exactly the reverse of the design jury's. One reason in this instance was the use of different criteria: The design jury relied heavily on attractiveness or aesthetics, and judged mainly from drawings and photos, while the observer and the residents used two further criteria—the quality of construction and livability. Graham Brown and I took another approach: we asked architects to predict how everyday persons would respond to a collection of 42 modern office buildings. They failed miserably as a group, although a few did moderately well.[12]

My lab has tried to understand the underlying reasons for these differences.[13] We showed 42 large contemporary buildings to practicing architects and to laypersons, and asked for their aesthetic evaluations of them. The usual group differences were found. Then we used Brunswik's lens model to discover just *which* distal cues (59 objective features of each building) and *which* proximal cues (complexity, clarity, friendliness, originality, meaningfulness, and ruggedness) each group was using to reach their aesthetic conclusions. The lens model analyses revealed how the two groups processed the distal cues into proximal cues and then into aesthetic conclusions. In this way, we can learn how a building's physical features are interpreted differently by the two groups, which leads them to experience different proximal properties, which in turn leads to different aesthetic conclusions.

The differences in the meaning of buildings lead to differences in design preferences. When architects and nursing home residents were shown a series of alternative designs for nursing homes, many differences were found.[14] Generally, architects preferred designs that promoted social interaction, thinking that was what residents wanted or needed, but the residents preferred designs that promoted privacy. This illustrates a key point: Architects act in good faith but often misjudge client needs.

By learning how a building's features are comprehended and interpreted by architects and community members, the way toward better mutual understanding is open. Indeed, the ideal building, in terms of aesthetics, is possible. In another study, we found buildings in four possible categories: ones that both architects and laypersons thought were ugly, one that architects liked but laypersons did not, ones that laypersons liked but architects did not… and some that *both* groups found beautiful.[15]

Recently, researchers have begun to examine how and why architects develop their design preferences. For example, during the course of architecture school, the immersion of students in architectural style builds into them an increasingly complex cognitive structure about styles[16]—as

it should. Researchers have tried to describe the cognitive processes involved in design process, to get "inside the architect's head."[17,18] Unfortunately, architecture schools sometimes promote the ideas that good architects are creative geniuses or stars who will or should operate in a patriarchal, hierarchical, power-oriented, and competitive manner.[19] Fortunately, this is changing. A growing number of professional designers see themselves as negotiators, communicators, or researchers.[20]

Obviously, designers must learn to see the built world through the eyes of their clients so they can appreciate their needs and perceptions. (You may wish to glance again at the quotation that opens this chapter.) This does not mean, however, that architects should throw out all their training and expertise, and design buildings exactly as a group of unsophisticated users want them to. Instead, designers must more often become **enabling practitioners**— that is, experts who actively listen to, and collaborate with, building users.[21] But because architects often have more than enough trouble dealing with many technical aspects of a design, and because most architects have little training in social science, they usually cannot perform an adequate social design of a building. They need the assistance of a professional social designer.

Architecture as Art

DESIGN EDUCATION AND DESIGN COMPETITIONS often encourage designers to emphasize the aesthetic dimension of architecture at the expense of the setting's functional value. Environments should, of course, be both beautiful *and* functional for their occupants. Unfortunately, attempts to create fashionable works of art dominated architecture for a long time—and still do. Architectural magazines still use expensive photography and glossy paper to show off buildings, but often no people are visible in the scenes. One is tempted to conclude that these unpeopled buildingscapes accurately reflect many designers' interests.

One of the most influential architects in the world, Philip Johnson, once said: "The job of the architect is to create beautiful buildings. That's all."[22] In an advertisement placed in my local newspaper by the company he founded, a tribute to a retiring architect states that he "is certainly not discarding his brush or his palette. His keen interest in Architecture as a Fine Art remains intense." These architectural formalists think of buildings more as paintings or sculpture than as habitats.[23] Commenting on the way

FIGURE 15–2 An example of vernacular architecture: a Kwakwaka'wakw (*Kwakiutl*) longhouse on Vancouver Island.

children's spaces are designed, for example, one observer noted that designers think more about such visual qualities as the geometry of the space, perspective, and vista than about children's preferences or developmental needs.[24]

Growing Collaboration. Fortunately, the times have been changing since environmental psychology began in the 1960s. Many—but certainly not all—architects now recognize the importance of designing for the human use of buildings, as well as aesthetics. For example, in the early 1970s the American Institute of Architects sponsored a conference that served as an early "summit meeting" between social scientists and designers.[25] Participants at this early conference outlined several key roles that social scientist consultants might play, including evaluating building habitability, defining the psychological needs of occupants, and training occupants in the optimal use of buildings.

While architects were mesmerized by the aesthetic properties of geometric space, psychologists sometimes neglected the physical context of behavior. In the growing collaboration, real people were imagined in designed spaces, a concept that might be called **place-making**.[26,27] To make a place, architects and social designers work together to create a space with a human face, or an "envelope for behavior." The social-versus-formal design approaches need not be adversarial. If formal designers try to make beautiful buildings for the multi-sensory pleasure of the building's *users*, then aesthetic pursuits serve at least one of the social designer's goals.[28] Beautiful buildings can actually improve our perceptions of each other, facilitate social interaction, and assist occupants in some less-direct ways, such as enhancing tourism or a city's reputation.

Actually, consultation with building users was not new in the early 1970s, although perhaps it had been forgotten by many designers. Way back in 1914, one office design team "spent several months in consultation, asking advice, and studying the needs of every department and of every individual,"[29] although these consultations primarily concerned one aspect of design—the physical distance between employees.

Nevertheless, by the late 1960s, entire organizations, such as the Environmental Design Research Association (EDRA) and the International Association for the Study of People and their Physical Surroundings (IAPS) were devoted to the cooperation of designers, and social designers sprang up and remain active. Social design researchers make their living from their contributions to the design process; most operate as one- or two-person offices, much like clinical psychologists or physicians. Some individual collaborations between psychologists and architects have lasted 15 years or more.[30] The user-centered approach is still being elaborated,[31] and it is even applied to the building of environments for humans in outer space.[32] For example, my own company was asked to evaluate the international space station as a basis for future long-duration space travel.[33]

When and How Social Design Helps. Social design is not *always* needed in the design process. It may not be required, for example, in times and places where buildings are constructed by small communities in which everyone works together in accordance with a time-tested architectural tradition. These traditions, called **preindustrial vernacular**,[34] evolved over a long period, so that the architecture already fits community and cultural norms, individual interests, local climate, geography, and materials quite well. When community members are both the builders and the occupants, the design process does not need separate financiers, architects, boards of directors, construction firms, or even social designers (see Figure 15-2).

However, in the developed nations of the world, the division of labor has produced considerable role specialization. As work is split more narrowly and each person's entire career is reduced to one phase of the fundamental processes in society—such as the creation of buildings—communication among the principal players in the design process tends to diminish. The **principal players** in building include the client (who puts up the money), the designer (architect, planner), the engineer (on larger projects), various construction specialists such as electricians and plumbers, and most important, the everyday building user, occupant, or visitor. Why "most important"? Because after all the other principal players leave for their next project, the everyday users of the building will have to live with it for the life of the building...a very long time.

IN SUM *Some buildings are human disasters; others are "merely" persistent nuisances to those who use them. Social design is a way of creating buildings that fit occupants and users better, by involving them in the planning process. Social design is needed in societies that have splintered the building-creation process into many specialist roles. It is a remedy for the malady in which architects saw themselves primarily as artists, ignoring the basic needs and activities of occupants. This malady is now widely recognized, yet many buildings are still constructed without significant user involvement.*

SOCIAL RESEARCH IN THE DESIGN PROCESS

BEFORE DELVING INTO A STAGE-BY-STAGE EXAMINATION OF OUR PRIMARY CONCERN—the design process—let's take a step back to consider the goals, advantages, and problems of the social science contribution to environmental design.

The Goals

SOCIAL DESIGN RESEARCHERS and practitioners pursue six general goals, some broader than others, some overlapping with others.

1. Create physical settings that **match** the needs and activities of their occupants. This goal, probably the most important of all, is variously called *habitability, congruence,* or *goodness of fit.*

2. **Satisfy** building users. Occupant satisfaction is important because they must spend significant parts of their lives working, residing, or relaxing in the setting.

3. **Change behavior.** Such changes might include increasing office-worker productivity, enhancing social ties among institutionalized elderly people, reducing aggression in a prison, or increasing communication among employees in an office. This goal can be both difficult to attain and controversial, as we shall see later.

4. Enhance the occupant's **personal control.**[35] The more building users are able to alter the setting to make it suit their needs, the less stressful that setting will be.

5. Facilitate **social support.**[36] Designs that encourage cooperation, assistance, and support are desirable primarily for building occupants who are disadvantaged in one way or another, but also for active and successful individuals.

6. Employ **imageability.** This refers to the ability of the building to help occupants and especially visitors and newcomers to find their way around without getting lost or confused.

Let us examine each of these goals more closely.

Matching. Matching refers to how well the occupant's activities and needs are met by the setting. Ideally, of course, buildings should perfectly match their occupants' needs and behavior. Whether the degree of match is high or low sometimes depends in part on whose viewpoint is considered.[37] You may recall the difference between alpha and beta press, a distinction made by the personality theorist Henry Murray between actual and perceived influences on human behavior. Similarly, alpha and beta forms of matching may be distinguished. The alpha form of matching, **congruence,** refers to how well the setting fits the person from an objective point of view. The beta form, **habitability**, is "environmental quality as perceived by occupants of buildings or facilities."[38]

All the principal players in the design process hope, of course, that both perceived and actual matches are good. The possibility remains, however, that a team of design experts could *declare* that congruence had been achieved when the occupants believe that it has not. Unfortunately, significant disagreements between experts and users have indeed been demonstrated in several studies of residential environments. For example, professional planners believed that a certain high-quality neighborhood was related to how open, interesting, and pleasant it was, but neighborhood residents believed high quality was related solely to how pleasant it was.[39]

Such clashes mean that efforts must be made not only to improve the fit between users and their environments, but also to reduce differences between designers' and occupants' definitions of good design. Because users' actual activities are sometimes easier to document than their needs, clashes may be resolved if data on activities are collected. When alpha and beta press are the same—such as when a building user has a clear-cut need that everyone perceives—the design implications are clear, but the design still does not always meet this need. For example, persons with physical disabilities often have obvious clear-cut needs, such as smooth ramps for those in wheelchairs. Yet too many buildings used by people in wheelchairs still lack ramps. Similarly, aged people whose perceptual and cognitive abilities have markedly declined have specific design needs that are often not provided.[40-42]

Nevertheless, building guidelines for people with specific characteristics are a good idea, and many lists of guidelines have been prepared. For example, one considers the proper design for relatively able-bodied older people.[43] Recommended design features for psychiatric patients were among the first to receive attention from social designers,[44] and continue to be issued.[45-48] Another setting that has been the focus of many recommendations is the daycare center.[49,50] A set of design guidelines has even been

FIGURE 15-3 The habitability of a community library is enhanced by good lighting and considered approaches to the needs of librarians and patrons of all ages.

created to reduce a drastic behavior—suicide—among jail inmates.[51]

Satisfaction. Habitability corresponds to occupant satisfaction; congruence is the expert's opinion that the occupant is satisfied. However, other principal players may or may not be satisfied with the building. Some architects, for example, hope their buildings will work as statements of minimalist or post-modernist aesthetic design principles. The paying client might be primarily satisfied if the project is completed within its budget. Most social design researchers would be satisfied if their work contributed to a habitable structure.

Behavior Change. Many projects implicitly or explicitly embody someone's hope that occupant behavior will change for the better. When all the principal players, including the occupants, agree that a certain pattern of behavior needs encouragement (or discouragement) from the design, the design process may proceed smoothly. In a New York psychiatric hospital, the violent behavior of some severely psychotic patients was one target when renovation designs were considered; the new design significantly reduced this violence.[52] After careful design changes, museum visitors paid more attention to exhibits.[53] By merely adding tabletop partitions between pairs of students with profound developmental disabilities, the amount of on-task behavior of the students by a significant amount was increased.[54] To increase physical activity in the struggle against obesity, environmental psychologists use signs and decorations to encourage building users to choose the stairs over the elevator.[55]

However, principal players sometimes disagree about who should change which behaviors. Clients who pay for new or renovated workplaces, for example, often expect that the new design will increase employee productivity. When faced with this expectation, the social design researcher is in the uncomfortable position of being asked to use the environment to squeeze more productivity out of employees. The very thought of attempting to manipulate employees for the benefit of an organization is unpleasant for many practitioners. Occupant satisfaction is usually the goal of practitioners and other principal players who are particularly sympathetic to the needs of the building user. Some social designers even see the process as part of a worldwide concern for human rights; after all, social design began with attempts to provide the benefits of design to the unfortunate, such as psychiatric patients and the poor.[56] This activist tradition still fuels the efforts of many environmental psychologists.

Regardless of one's point of view, social design is necessarily political in the original sense of discussing and debating policy. Some observers contend that design programs embody the nature of social power in the organization that will occupy the building.[57] Others argue that designers and evaluators of designs *cannot* be objective (even if they think they are) because their work always endorses—implicitly if not explicitly—a set of values about social relationships and social power that would be made concrete in their building plans.[58,59]

Building design almost necessarily implies trade-offs. These usually cannot be decided by purely objective means; values must enter the design process. Different building users naturally will have different values (and, therefore, different design preferences) that the environmental psychologist will encounter without even trying. Social designers must examine their own values, too, as they relate to the project, the clients, and the negotiation process.[60] After deciding who their values allow them to represent, practitioners try to discover and advocate the most advantageous set of trade-offs, based on the best obtainable information.

What happens, then, when work efficiency is promoted as more important than other goals, such as employee

satisfaction? Paying clients who engage a social researcher often expect productivity gains in return for their investment. Robert Sommer agonized over these questions for years. In his book *Social Design*, he offered three primary answers to "the productivity question."[61] First, he believes the research evidence demonstrates that design *can* sometimes raise productivity. However, because design-behavior relations are complex and influenced by many factors, we cannot know in advance whether a new building design will actually boost productivity.

A second response is that social research is, in a modern democracy, a basic right of those who must occupy buildings for large parts of their lives. Social research, from this point of view, is valuable in its own right, and should not have to be justified in productivity terms.

Third, one might question why some paying clients are so productivity-conscious in the first place. "Those who ask the productivity question would like to put dollar signs on positive experiences."[62] Productivity and satisfaction sometimes are conflicting goals, with some principal players stressing one more than the other. Of course, both goals are desirable, but many situations arise where productivity and satisfaction goals are in conflict. When this happens, practitioners are forced to decide what their own political and economic values are.

Personal Control. Social design should provide occupants with real options to control their proximate environment. What does this mean, in specific terms? Consider, for example, my own office. It has a temperature control unit on the wall, but it is closed, with no adjustment lever; I cannot change the temperature. Office workers often cannot control the lighting or open windows. Stress often is related to lack of personal control over physical and social input. Noise, unwanted social contact, congestion, a lack of design coherence or places of refuge are primary sources of stress,[63] yet social design can anticipate and attempt to overcome them or at least buffer building users from them.

Social Support. Many social problems would be eased if more and better social support were available.[64] Common psychological problems such as depression and anxiety have been shown to increase when social support is absent or inadequate.[65] What can social design do for social support?

At the smallest scale, furniture arrangement, studies show that sociopetal arrangements can foster more interaction.[66] At the building level, open-space areas may be arranged to facilitate social interaction.[67] Of course, if the personal control goal as well as the social support goal is to be met, the increased social interaction must be occupant-controllable; building users should be able to find social interaction when and if they want it, but not be faced with unwanted encounters. In office buildings, social support may be fostered through the provision of high-quality lounge space for employees. The mere existence of such space does not guarantee that valuable social support will be available, but with inadequate space for employees to share coffee and conversation, the likelihood of social networks declines.

Finally, social support may result from a design that provides optimal privacy (that is, being able to filter one's interactions). Consider shelters for victims of domestic violence. A study of alternate designs for such shelters found that designs characterized by anonymity and safety were most preferred.[68] Sometimes social support is maximized when a person simultaneously can be near a helper and far from an abuser.

Imageability. Buildings should be imageable, that is, clearly understandable, to their users.[69] When people enter a building, they should immediately be able to find their way around or, in more technical terms, be capable of *purposeful mobility.* In plain language, they should not get lost. I find it astounding how often I enter a building that is unfamiliar to me, even new buildings, and cannot figure out where to go next. Unless you realize that buildings should be imageable, there is a tendency to blame ourselves ("I never did have a good sense of direction"). Sometimes observation reveals that you are not the first to have problems: Perhaps you have seen handmade signs tacked up that someone working in the building has made, either to be helpful or to save answering the same question about where such-and-such is for the hundredth time.

The Problems

The Gap. Designers in our society are almost completely separated from those who will actually use their buildings. You use numerous buildings every day and you will spend the vast majority of your life in one building or another. When was the last time you sat down with an architect to discuss any building that you have ever used? (see Figure 15-4). The paying client (often a board of directors) is the missing link between the designer and the occupant.

Architects communicate extensively with the client or facility managers who work for the client. However, the architect, the paying client, and the facility manager are not very likely to spend much time in the building after the opening-day ceremonies. If paying clients do use the building, they are likely to occupy a special area or floor of the building. In general, a serious gap exists between designer and occupant.

Resistance. Not everyone involved in the design process sees the advantages of social research. In the absence of legal requirements for social design research, many designers and clients view it as an unnecessary or extravagant part of the building process. Because some principal players do not want their lives "complicated" by new information—even valuable new information—the social design researcher's entry into a project can be difficult.[70] In general, resistance to social design comes primarily from five sources: some designers, some paying clients, some members of the public, government, and even some building users.

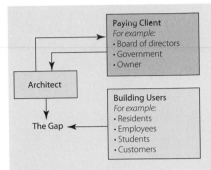

FIGURE 15–4 The gap between architects and building users.

First, designers who are wholly concerned with architecture as a fine art obviously see little need for social design research. They tend to subscribe to some or all of the following views:

- If a building is beautiful, it must also be useful.

- Beauty is so much more valuable than function that social design research on building function is not worth the effort.

- If the building is beautiful, occupants will be so awestruck, impressed, or happy with it that function will somehow take care of itself.

- We architects are capable of placing ourselves in the shoes of occupants, and therefore can create a building that is functional, satisfying, and beautiful for occupants without consulting or studying them.

- People are very adaptive and malleable, so trying to match the building to their needs and activities is unnecessary.

TABLE 15–1 Designer Fallacies

The architect Clovis Heimsath outlined six fallacies that some designers believe. Note that some fallacies are incompatible with others. Different fallacies may be believed by different designers, but, surprisingly, designers often offer a second incompatible fallacy after the weaknesses of the first one has been explained.

1. Designer fallacy.	"The building directly determines behavior in it." This is a form of architectural determinism. Things are just not that simple. Actually, behavior is determined by personal, social, cultural, and economic factors, as well as by the form of the building.
2. Genius fallacy.	"Designs created by great architects have universal value; they may be applied easily in other times and places." Actually, because every set of building users is unique, each new building design should be at least slightly different to take their needs into account.
3. Common-person fallacy.	"Architecture has no important effect on behavior; people will do what they want regardless of building design." After the all the previous chapters, I hope this one requires no further comment!
4. Open-society fallacy.	"Good design is not really necessary because good people will survive and overcome even slums to become successful." But how difficult did that awful building make the life of the few who made it? What about the many who did *not* overcome bad design? Why make life harder for either group?
5. Manipulation fallacy.	"Designing for human behavior is a veiled form of totalitarianism and behavior control." Design already exerts influence on human behavior; we simply do not understand all the mechanisms yet. Also, design can and should be aimed at giving *more* control to building users.
6. Know-nothing fallacy.	"Everything is so complicated that we should just forget about the behavioral implications of design and just get this building built!" The holder of this burned-out position no longer has the energy required for good design. Social design certainly can be complicated, but the situation is not hopeless. Careful adherence to the design process as outlined in this chapter can produce useful information.

A thoughtful architect added several other fallacies to this list (see Table 15-1).[71] Even some designers who appreciate social design nevertheless do not budget for it in their design proposal because they fear the additional initial costs will cause them to lose their contract to a lower bidder. Fortunately, of course, many designers do not subscribe to these views. But resistance does come from designers who are unaware of, or do not understand, social design research.

A second source of resistance to social research comes from some paying clients. The client is paying a substantial fee for the design of a new building; social design research is likely to appear as an unnecessary extra. Some cannot see the long-term benefits of social research, often merely because they still do not know very much about it. Without a clear explanation of how the expenditure may be beneficial to their organization, clients are naturally wary of spending the extra money and time necessary for social research. So far, the most progressive clients appear to be governments and nonprofit service agencies, many of which support social design research in the construction of administration buildings, subsidized housing, prisons, and other public- or service-oriented construction projects.

Third, some members of the public resist social design. When a design proposal, for example, suggests a solution quite different from conventional practice, public resistance sometimes appears. For example, in the suburban neighborhood where I grew up, a house was built with no front picture window and a "stone carpet" instead of a front lawn. Every other house had a picture window and a lawn. Some neighbors actually started a petition to force the owners of the unusual house to install a picture window and a lawn.

The fourth source of resistance to social or innovative design is the government. A San Francisco architect saw the need for shelter among the homeless, so he designed a lockable structure about the size of a small truck camper.[72] It was just large enough to sleep in (in San Francisco's climate, body heat could keep it fairly warm at night) and safely store essentials. But when he supplied shelter to one to two homeless people, the State of California subpoenaed him. As the architect said, "Those are the things that start to happen when you start to play with the prevailing ethic."

Finally, even some building users may resist social design. A standard bathroom is not the most functional bathroom; better-but-nonstandard bathroom designs encounter resistance.[73] In one of the earliest attempts to employ social science to make a setting more habitable, Robert Sommer who was then working in a psychiatric hospital, rearranged the tables and chairs in a ward for elderly women.[74] The chairs were originally placed around the edge of the room in straight rows; this arrangement made it difficult for some of the women to turn to one another for a decent conversation. When he arranged the furniture to resemble a café (four chairs around a table) to facilitate conversation, the women moved the chairs back to their former positions. Apparently, the women could no longer tell "whose chair was whose," and this territorial ownership was very important to them in a setting where residents could lay claim to little else but their own chair. Sommer eventually convinced the women to give his idea a try. They did converse with one another much more than previously. This social interaction may have provided some much-needed stimulation to aging residents. The moral of the story, however, may be that practitioners as well as architects must not forget to consult with users before implementing design changes

Unrealistic Expectations. Some clients and designers are overly optimistic about the power of social design. They naively believe that the right design can solve nearly any problem the organization is experiencing.[75] The common belief in **architectural determinism**—that building design strongly controls behavior—has led listeners in my public talks to ask what color their kitchen should be painted to make people more sociable. Every social design researcher has been asked analogous questions: How big should prison cells be? How loud can a classroom get before students stop learning? Which music should be played to improve office productivity?

The physical environment is important, but it does not directly determine behavior. The social environment is also important for productivity, learning, health, stress, and sociability. Individual characteristics, too, lead occupants to respond differently to the same setting. The social researcher must educate clients and designers to the complexity of environment-behavior relations and remind them that significant but not magical results may be expected from social research in the design process.

Therefore, two alternatives to architectural determinism have been proposed.[76] The first, **environmental possibilism**, began as an extreme anti-determinist point of view, suggesting that people's behavior is *not at all* determined. A more moderate version asserts that the environment

sets certain limits on human behavior, allowing a finite range of behavior. Another alternative is **environmental probabalism**. In many areas of science, from quantum mechanics to human perception, theories have evolved in this century that argue for a statistical point of view. That is, a given combination of circumstances sets up certain odds that an event will occur. Events are never certain and never impossible; their odds are merely very high or very low. Supposedly, a chair can even jump off the ground unassisted—if all

FIGURE 15–5 This thermostat covered with a clear plastic shield tells elderly residents that personal control over their environment is possible, but not by them!

its atoms happen to vibrate in the vertical direction at the same time. Of course, the odds against this actually happening are vanishingly small.

In everyday settings, the various environmental and other factors that operate set up certain odds—according to the environmental probabalist—that an individual will be affected by noise, begin to socialize with a neighbor, or benefit from a negative ion generator. Depending on the number, strength, and direction of these influences, the odds of the individual behaving in these ways vary from quite low to quite high. Social design's goal is to increase the probability of selected activities and feelings.

Conflict. Social design research may bring to light disagreements among the principal players. This may sound like a reason for *not* undertaking design research, but it is not. Sometimes architects and social designers must risk collaboration by questioning some of the basic assumptions that are widely accepted within their own professions in order to develop a shared and improved approach to design problems.[77]

The evaluation of a residence for senior citizens I conducted suggests the value of revealing conflicts. The residence was new, spacious, and lovely. The general quality of construction and furnishings was at least equal to that in most private, middle-class single-family dwellings. Yet a common complaint of residents was that they were too cold. One of the first things I noticed in touring the residence was that every room has its own thermostat, but each one was enclosed in a clear plastic cover (see Figure 15-5). The covers were locked, and only the staff had keys. The staff claimed that residents merely needed to ask, and the setting on their thermostat would be changed. Some residents said this is not true; they were told that their requests were unreasonable. The staff admitted this, claiming that some residents would overheat themselves because they would turn the thermostat up and forget to turn it down later. Residents scoffed at this claim.

Regardless of who was correct, the plastic covers in this residence were a source of conflict between the building's staff and its occupants. That the residents could see the control lever through the plastic but were not allowed to alter it themselves seemed to me a perverse form of torture, although the staff did not see it that way. Energy bills can be a problem, but in this new and presumably well-insulated building, it would seem that slightly higher temperatures would not be financially serious. Perhaps a few residents are endangering themselves, but those who are could be identified. As it was, *no* residents could control their own thermostat.

Conflict may also occur among building users, both as individuals and as groups. Differing preferences among individuals need little description ("different strokes for different folks"). But differences among groups are more serious and more interesting. Consider the design of a hospital.[78] Patients, visitors, physicians, nurses, office, and maintenance staff all use the building differently and therefore want it to look different in many ways. A small example: physicians prefer signs that use medical terminology (e.g., pediatrics), but patients and visitors prefer signs that use everyday words (e.g., children). When building users and architects meet in planning groups, conflict sometimes is suppressed.

In one case, a new psychiatric facility was being designed.[79] A number of design faults that left in-patients at risk were not anticipated by the planning group, and were part of the new building. This happened for six reasons that are very frequently the case when planning groups include no social designer:

- Someone was pressing to finish the building quickly.

- Those who worked hard to identify design problems were viewed as troublemakers who were spoiling the party ("We're lucky to be getting a new building— don't be causing trouble by raising difficult issues!").

- The architects knew little about psychiatry, and the medical staff knew little about architecture.

- Neither side wanted to admit they knew little about the other's profession.

- Both sides subscribed to the leader myth ("They must know what they're doing—they're paid experts!").

- The precise task of the planning group was unclear— were they to merely advise, to pass judgment, or to make final decisions on design features?

Conflict among principal players can be fruitful, but it requires the mediating, neutral role of a good social designer if it is to be turned into an advantage. The conflict was present anyway; the social designer merely brings it to the fore and uses it constructively. Conflicts that are not unearthed remain vague but potent sources of discontent. Conflict cannot be resolved until it is identified. Once identified, conflicts have some chance of resolution.

In another example, a hospital tried to create more space for visiting family members (good idea), but this created the understandable concern that nurses, who already walk a lot, might have to walk even more because beds were therefore farther apart. However, when actual observations were made in smaller and larger units, the nurses in fact did not have to walk more.[80] Careful observational research can resolve speculative conflicts.

However, if conflict fails even to reach the discussion stage, let along the research stage, it may fester and someday become part of a larger eruption. Thus, one problem of social design research is that it often reveals conflicts among principal players. But, with skillful consultation and mediation, this problem becomes one of the key *advantages* of doing social design research. Next, some other advantages offered by social design research are discussed.

The Advantages

To Users. When design research is successful, the occupant receives a more habitable place to live, work, or relax. Three specific benefits of a habitable environment to occupants are that (a) the building mirrors their aesthetic and behavioral tendencies, which (b) thereby reduces their stress, which in turn (c) supports their ability to accomplish their goals.

Mirroring means that the building suits the occupants' customary living or working habits, social patterns, and cultural background. A very simple example is the office building window. Many office employees prefer to work in conditions that are refreshed by the occasional breath of fresh air. Yet many new office buildings do not allow the simple freedom of opening a window. This is a minor irritant that, over time and combined with other failures to mirror, can become a significant source of stress. When occupants are stressed, they must either expend extra energy to overcome the shortcomings of their workspace or simply yield to an unsupportive environmental structure, working less effectively and with less enjoyment.

Participation in the design process gives users a sense of control that has its own intrinsic value. It helps to satisfy the need to create, brings community members together, demonstrates concern by management, and can produce positive public relations.[81] For example, one hospital that asked nurses to participate in the design of a new addition received newspaper coverage that praised the new project as a "nurse's special." Presumably, the opportunity to provide design input and the favorable publicity will make nurses proud and even more ready to care for their patients.

To Designers. Designers can benefit from social design research, too. Evaluation of their work can

- Provide feedback for improvement in the design of the next building.
- Extend and create more contracts.
- Save them undue criticism.[82]
- Save them time.
- Improve communication with other principal players.
- Offer a useful external perspective on the project.[83]

Let's consider these six advantages one at a time. First, many architects specialize in certain types of buildings. The care and consideration that goes into any one of them is enormous. Clearly, much could be learned about how each new building design succeeds and fails by studying the opinions and behavior of the building's users after it is occupied. However, as an early environmental psychologist once said, not very kindly, architects are like cuckoo birds who lay their eggs and then leave the scene.[84] By staying around to learn how the building works in practice, an architect could easily become more skillful (and successful) than competing architects who reinvent the wheel time after time.

Second, some designers turn design research into a more extensive contract. In one case, pedestrian pathways at a certain zoo were imperfectly arranged; some interesting exhibits were missed by zoo visitors who overlooked the walkway leading to them.[85] A study of the problem revealed the reasons for the problem. This research impressed the client, who asked the researchers to do much more design work at the zoo.

Third, in a new headquarters building, the design was generally successful, but there were many complaints about temperature. Most of the blame fell on the architects. Had the architects not followed up their work with an evaluation, they might never have discovered these complaints; meanwhile their reputation was suffering. The evaluation brought these complaints to light and led to an investigation, which found that the heating and ventilation system had been improperly installed. When this was corrected, the temperature problems disappeared and so did the continuing threat to the designer's reputation.

Fourth, social design work can be very inefficient for design professionals who are not trained in social science methods. The interviews with clients and various user groups necessary for fulfillment of the goals espoused in this chapter are not within the time budget, experience, or skill of most designers. In fact, this is true of survey development, behavior mapping, and most other social design methods. Thus, the involvement of an outside research consultant can save the designer much time and effort.

Fifth, designers think and talk in a special way that is strongly oriented toward the pictorial. Some architects are almost mute without a sketch pad. Other principal players, such as clients and building users, are likely to be less visual in their thinking. Some may not be very articulate. A good social design practitioner, with some experience in the visual world of the designer and some in the verbal world of clients and users, may serve as a translator among the principal players.

Finally, most people who spend immense effort on a project feel, near the end of it, that they can no longer see the project objectively. In the design process, endless small and large revisions to floor plans and façades produce this experience. Input from external sources, such as users or the social design researcher, can help place the project into a realistic semblance of how others will perceive it.

To the Paying Client. Social design research can even benefit the paying client, who often is concerned with costs and assumes that research is a net cost to the project. Instead, social research may cost less than other planning methods;

studies have documented direct savings to building projects that may be attributed to social design research.[86] An Australian study suggests that information provided by social design research can help the client avoid mistakes that would cost considerable money indirectly over an extended period of the building's life.[87] These include chronic inefficiency in building maintenance, duplication of effort, user ignorance of building capabilities, overspending, and of course, a design that is inappropriate for the activities housed by the building.

IN SUM *Social design has numerous goals, problems, and advantages. It aims to match settings to their occupants, to satisfy a variety of principal player needs, to promote personal control in the building, and to encourage social support. Under some circumstances, another goal may be to increase productivity or otherwise change behavior. The problems include a frequent lack of communication between those who pay for a building and those who use or occupy it, resistance to the extra effort of involving users and occupants, unrealistic expectations that socially designed buildings will directly cure various evils, and inevitable conflict among principal players. Social design usually means serving the needs of building occupants first, but it also offers benefits to architects and paying clients.*

STAGES IN THE DESIGN PROCESS

CONSTRUCTION FOLLOWS A SERIES OF STAGES that, in general terms, are the same whether the project is a new building, renovation of an older building, or the development of an outdoor setting such as a park. John Zeisel suggested a model of the design process (see Figure 15-6) on which the present discussion is based.[88] Social design can play a role in every stage of this process, but usually it is most prominent in the programming and post-occupancy evaluation phases.

An important feature of Zeisel's model is its cyclical nature. Social designers all agree that knowledge gained from one project ought to be used for the next similar project. This has always occurred, but as noted earlier, to an unfortunately limited extent. In one example of truly cyclical improvement in design, however, behaviorally based evaluations were used to inform the design evolution of three generations of correctional facilities.[89] The complete cycle of participatory planning and subsequent evaluation has been completed in numerous other design projects.[90,91] These studies suggest that participatory planning does increase the likelihood of a positive evaluation later.

Traditionally, when an architectural firm builds numerous structures of a given type, it acquires a store of information. Two problems with these private stores of information are that they come from select and limited sources and that they are not widely shared. The architect's primary feedback comes from the paying client, a few members of the community who make comments in a guest book on opening day, fellow architects, and perhaps an architecture critic. If future designs are to improve, these are necessary but not sufficient sources of information.

However, systematic input from the building's users is conspicuously absent. Whatever information that does get collected may not be widely shared because it constitutes, to some extent, the secrets of the trade. If there are principles of design that are not immediately evident in the actual structure, architects may be understandably reluctant to divulge them. If the building is later found to have serious problems, the architect will not be keen to publicize them. An improved design process would expand the sources of information about each building type and tactfully but widely disseminate knowledge of its strengths and weaknesses.

Designers already act as one-person data banks on the design of various types of buildings.[92] Several observers have called for clearinghouse accumulations of useful design information on successful and unsuccessful social design solutions. These could be stored and retrieved through a computer network. Small-scale clearinghouses already exist in some design circles, but a vastly enlarged system could be extremely useful to prevent design disasters and reduce the time and effort required to produce successful designs.

Robert Sommer and others advocate an **action research** approach, a problem-centered strategy that truly connects theory and practice.[93] In the agricultural world, for example, extension specialists routinely transmit new knowledge from researchers to those who practice (farmers). A similar model would enhance environmental design.

Step one in the design process is the decision to build. This begins with an original plea for space from a group that has outgrown its old space or feels the need for refurbished, expanded, or new facilities. The plea for new space may originate with a formal or informal evaluation of the current setting. The pleading group lobbies the paying client, who may be a board of directors, a government agency, or a wealthy individual. Undoubtedly, other calls for funds will be heard; the group must impress the paying client with its need for new or renovated facilities in competition with other groups.

Programming

ONCE TENTATIVE APPROVAL FOR THE PROJECT is given, the next step is **programming**: that is, the planning of the building that occurs before formal plans are drawn. Programming has both a technical side and a social side. On the technical side, preliminary studies of possible sites, costs, sources of outside funds, and regulations are conducted. In general, it consists of determining the technical and financial constraints to the project.

The social side of programming sometimes is treated very lightly. However, because it is crucial to both matching (congruence and habitability) and to valued outcomes (satisfaction, productivity, personal control, and social support), social design practitioners treat it as one of the most important phases in the design cycle. Social programming involves three steps: understanding building users, involving them in the design process, and setting design guidelines.

Understanding Building Users. The first segment of social programming includes two activities that may occur simultaneously: clarifying the social rationale of the new space and analyzing the needs and wants of its future occupants. Clarifying the social rationale means deciding what the organization's goals are. Prison administrators, for example, should decide whether the institution's goal is to deliver punishment, to offer privacy, to support rehabilitation, to be a warehouse, to encourage integration with

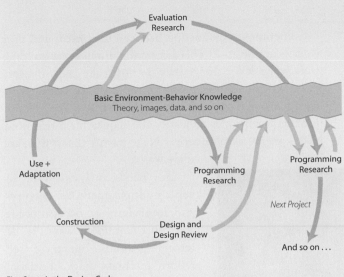

Five Steps in the Design Cycle

1. Programming	(Analysis)	Identifying design objectives, constraints, and criteria
2. Design	(Synthesis)	Making design decisions that satisfy criteria
3. Construction	(Realization)	Building the project and modifying plans under changing constraints
4. Use	(Reality Testing)	Moving in and adapting the environment
5. Evaluation	(Review)	Monitoring the final product in terms of objectives and use—ideally to be translated into future design criteria

FIGURE 15–6 John Zeisel's prominent view of the design cycle.

the outside world, or some combination of these goals.[94] In a new housing complex, is the goal to promote a sense of community or to bolster privacy? Organizations should decide which outcomes they expect the new structure to encourage.

The second activity, analysis of user needs (sometimes called needs assessment), begins with basic questions such as: Who will use the structure? How many people will use it? How many will be visitors, as opposed to eight-hours-per-day users or full-time residents? Which activities will these users be engaged in? Needs assessment also includes more difficult questions such as: How much space is required for each user? How can the customs and values of the occupants be expressed in the building?

The answers may seem obvious when North Americans design buildings for other North Americans, but how should a building look when it is designed for, say, Arabic peoples?[95] This problem can be compounded when such a culture is undergoing rapid change: Arab society has been strongly affected by oil wealth. Cross-cultural researchers have begun to attack this problem, although it is massive. For example, a study of houses in 73 societies found that as sociopolitical complexity or segmentation increases, there is typically more segmentation of house interiors into separate spaces.[96]

Sometimes, a distinction between user *needs* and user *wants* is important.[97] This distinction implies that building users will ask for things they do not really need. If users seem to be doing this, practitioners must ask tactful probing questions that allow users to give answers which permit the practitioner to justify the request as a real need. Needs are much more acceptable to paying clients than are mere wants.[98]

User needs analysis should involve multiple methods. **Surveys** and **interviews** of occupants are the most common ways of determining needs, but these self-report methods have shortcomings. Occupant responses may be inaccurate because of their honest but mistaken memories of their behavior patterns, their lack of knowledge of architectural possibilities, or unfortunate attempts to tell the interviewer what sounds right rather than offer their true opinions.

JOHN ZEISEL's pioneering work on the social science contribution to the design cycle remains important today.

However, interviewing can be useful. One study learned what adolescents prefer when they must be in hospital, for example.[99] In Sweden, the dining room of a geriatric hospital was redecorated based on interviews with patients.[100] The interviews revealed that the sterile hospital environment would best be replaced with one that resembled the patients' homes. The redecorated dining room was constructed to resemble a typical Swedish home from the prime (middle-aged) era of the patients' lives. The redecoration was very popular with the residents, confirming the value of the interviews. Yet, sadly, the hospital administration required the social researchers to return the dining room to its former design after 16 weeks. Apparently, administrators viewed staff needs for efficiency as more important than patient needs for an appealing setting.

Another questionnaire study of the elderly found that their high-priority activities were sleeping, watching TV, preparing food, relaxing, and eating.[101] Once a group's high-priority activities are clarified, the adequacy of the design to meet these needs can be assessed. Some studies focus on one element or another of the design. For example, one research group has concentrated on the kinds of lighting and windows preferred by undergraduates.[102,103]

In the different settings you use (classroom, room at home, library, computer lab), which level of lighting and type of windows (if any) do you prefer?

Four major alternatives to the self-report methods (surveys and interviews) exist.[104] In two of these (**behavior mapping** and **behavior tracking**), researchers systematically observe the daily activities of the occupants. Watching what individuals actually *do* may be a better guide to a useful design program than what occupants *say* they do. For example, one researcher extensively observed the behavior of pedestrians in subways, concert halls, and airports.[105,106] Some of his findings are not surprising; subway patrons usually keep to the right side of walkways, and they tend to seek the shortest path. Other discoveries, however, are less obvious—for example, that 85 percent of parcels are carried in the left hand. This led to the overuse of one vending machine (resulting in high maintenance costs) while another machine was under-used. Subways usually have banks of turnstiles. In one bank of six turnstiles, 43 percent of the subway riders used one of the turnstiles, but only 2 percent used another. Such behavior patterns are unlikely to be uncovered through interviews, yet knowledge of them would be valuable in the design of a new subway station.

In the third alternative to interviews, researchers observe **physical traces** of occupant activities. These include evidence of **erosion** (wear) or **accretion** (something added to the setting). These cues might include worn floor tiles (indicating a heavy traffic path), graffiti and posters (indicating the degree to which occupants want to personalize their own space), or walls built of filing cabinets (indicating a need for more privacy). A major advantage of studying physical traces is that thousands of hours of behavior observation are compressed into a few minutes. The erosion side of physical traces is the environmental psychologist's foray into archeology. On the accretion side is a design oversight in Chandigarh, a modern city in India. The famous architect who designed Chandigarh did not take into account the residents' longstanding practice of hanging clothes out to dry. He was greatly dismayed to find, on a visit to the city, that his beloved design for a highrise residential complex was largely covered up by clothes drying in the wind off nearly every apartment balcony.

The fourth alternative is **simulation**. Researchers may construct a mock-up of a space station, house, or office, and let potential users try it out. Simulation studies do usually include an element of self-report afterward (e.g., "Did you like it this way?"). One study, for example, focused solely on stairs. Some 19 different combinations of stair width and height were built, and 66 people tried them out. [107] (In case you are curious, the most widely satisfying stairs were 18.3 cm/7.25 in. high and 28-30.5 cm/11-12 in. deep.) Of course, simulations are not limited to specific design elements like stairs; they have included full-scale mock-ups of entire dwellings.[108] More advanced forms of simulation—such as holographs, computer imaging, and virtual reality—are in use now.[109,110]

Each of these methods has its advantages and its disadvantages. Interviews allow the social researcher to query the user's opinions, feelings, and perceptions, but they may produce a distorted picture of the user's actual behavior. Behavior mapping and tracking may be time-consuming and expensive, but they can provide an accurate image of user behavior. Physical traces provide a capsule history of building use, but they may be insensitive to the needs or behaviors of individuals who use the building atypically. Simulations offer a way to present several or even many design alternatives without having to construct them, but of course are not directly usable.

The social design practitioner who aims to achieve the best program will employ multiple methods rather than rely solely on any one of them. Two studies of libraries have used multiple methods in this way.[111,112] Both studies found that using all three methods was better than any one method; some things were learned that could *only* have been learned by using all three methods. For example, in a study of a public library, Cheuk Ng and I learned that patrons believed that it did not have enough tables.[113] Yet behavior mapping told us that many tables were unused. Instead of recommending to the library board that more tables be acquired, which would be logical had we merely interviewed the patrons, we recommended that the library furniture be rearranged. The library actually had enough tables, but too many popular activities were located in the same area, so a shortage of tables existed only in that area.

Sometimes the actual occupants of a setting that is being designed are not yet known. During the design phase of a new university residence hall, recreation center, or park, those who will be using it once it is complete are (at present) scattered across the community or nation. In their absence, **surrogate users**[114] or **consumer input**[115] must be studied. The practitioner must find the most nearly equivalent group of accessible individuals. In the case of the residence hall, residents of other dormitories on campus probably are a good approximation of next year's first occupants of the new dormitory.

User needs must be considered within the context of the new setting's social rationale. Knowing the future users and their needs clearly will produce more habitable structures. Knowledge of users' needs is more useful than other kinds of knowledge about them. For example, in Australia, when architects knew future occupants' spatial needs, they designed more appropriate houses for them than when they were armed with knowledge of the future occupants' lifestyles.[116]

Involving Users. Another programming goal is **user activation**. Merely "determining the user's needs and preferences" is to regard them as passive, unable, or unwilling to actively interact with the building. Building users can be involved at different stages of the project.[117] At first, they may protest that they do not know anything about architecture or design, which is true in itself. Some may initially care little about devoting time to the design process. However, part of the social designer's job is to demonstrate to occupants that they need not be professional designers to participate in the planning of the new setting and that good reasons exist for them to become involved in the design of their next work or living space. In one dramatic case, students and principals walked through schools looking for architectural barriers for disabled students.[118] The students found many more barriers than the principals did!

How can user activation be accomplished? The practitioner can present building users with examples of how others participated in the design of their own facilities. Seeing that other lay designers were able to make valuable contributions can be a strong confidence-builder for those who think design is only for the experts. Building users who already believe they can successfully participate become more excited about their own chance to contribute.

Another way to encourage participation is for the practitioner to become an **advocate designer**.[119] In this role, the social designer's goal is to actively serve the educational and political needs of occupants. This means supplying them with technical knowledge, teaching them how they might create their own designs, and representing their interests to the rest of the design team. Some see the advocate designer as a vehicle for diminishing the authoritarian character adopted by certain architects. Ultimately, this would help return the design process to the pre-industrial vernacular model, discussed early in this chapter, in which everyone in the community works together on a project with little role specialization. This is unlikely to occur in technological societies, but it expresses the democratic, user-oriented direction that some designers favor.

Design assistance often is available in inverse proportion to users' need for it. The wealthy, who already occupy less-stressful settings, can afford to hire consultants to improve them. Social design is "in part an attempt to reallocate design services to improve the housing and neighborhood needs of the poor."[120]

Assistance can take the form of **user education**. This does not usually mean classroom-style lectures on design. It may include writing articles that speak directly to users, urging them to actively undertake design projects. One such article, written for office employees describes "the six basic steps in the design process" in straightforward, positive language.[121] Another, presumably aimed at administrators, is titled "Employees Need Role in Design of Work Space."[122] Design education can even be successful with elementary school children. Children aged 8 and 9 were taught enough about design to produce an ideal classroom that was significantly better than those designed by children who did not receive design training.[123] User education may also involve expanding the horizons of users by presenting them with a variety of workable design solutions.

Generally, user-designers find it much easier to provide useful decision information if they are presented with easily understood choices, rather than by being asked "What do you want?"[124] Their contribution also may be through workshops in which they and social designers literally walk through a typical day's activities to experience or re-live the successful and unsuccessful features of the present design. Mock-ups of proposed designs are another possibility. In one such mock-up, social researchers investigating a design for a hospital room discovered a life-threatening flaw.[125] During a drill simulating a cardiac arrest situation, a design research team found that one of two beds in the room could not fit past the other one; a patient who experienced a heart attack might lose valuable time while being transferred to intensive care. As a result of the drill, the designers enlarged the room to prevent the problem.

In Switzerland, a very large laboratory allowed for the full-scale simulation of buildings. Using lightweight blocks, families working with designers could easily construct and revise life-size plans for their houses.[126] Now, of course, future users of a building can be involved by using virtual reality presentations. With special goggles and an interactive device in your hand, a building can be simulated to the extent that a person can walk through it and even look to the left, right, and rear. In fact, a computer lab in North Carolina *was* designed with the help of virtual reality simulation. The architect was convinced to change the position of some walls after experiencing the design in virtual reality.[127]

Another programming activity is facilitation of direct user participation in the design process. User participation varies widely. One view is that common practice includes three kinds of programming.[128] In **traditional planning**, a manager makes a few sketches and tells someone to "draw it up and make it happen," or the organization's architects decide what the users' requirements are *for* them and then work out a design; users themselves are rarely consulted directly. In **direct planning**, corporate managers hire social designers to do the programming. Users are consulted more often, depending on the mandate provided by the corporation and the values and styles of the programmers. In **joint planning**, all phases of programming are accomplished by a coalition of professionals (architects and social designers) and users.

Another view of the range of user participation is as follows:[129]

- Users are not consulted at all.
- Users provide information to a designer, who then creates the design.
- Users choose among already-completed designs.
- Users select and arrange forms provided by the designer.
- Users create the project themselves.

When setting users have pre-existing or newly enhanced enthusiasm for and confidence in the design process, they are ready for something more than the first of these options. Our basic assumption is that informed, motivated occupants can make significant contributions toward solv-

WOLFGANG PREISER has specialized in gathering the insights of many experts on environment–behavior issues into a series of edited volumes.

ing the puzzle of how to translate a social rationale and differing user needs into an actual plan.

One example of direct user participation was the design of a hospital courtyard.[130] A table-sized model of the courtyard was constructed so that it could be taken apart and reassembled in different patterns. After showing many possible variations of the courtyard to over 200 patients and visitors, the social design researchers concluded the courtyard should have densely planted trees, colorful plants, and seating arrangements that allowed for privacy or social interaction. In another project, a landscape architect, a child psychologist, social design researchers, and the staff of a daycare center worked together throughout the programming phase of an outdoor learning environment for preschoolers.[131] Many building users, when offered the opportunity to express their preferences among choices, are pleased that someone cared enough to ask, and even happier when some element of the final design reflects their choices.

In a housing complex in Madison, Wisconsin, low-income residents were guided through a set of procedures for designing their ideal apartment.[132] They were also faced with the necessity of trade-offs ("If the costs of your ideal apartment rose, which features would you sacrifice?"). The notion of trade-offs is central to an approach that emphasizes the user as an active design agent who is capable of adapting to some building features and changing others.[133]

User participation has valuable side effects. Apart from the usefulness of the suggestions and contributions made by users, the *process* itself benefits them. Users who are involved in the design process report more satisfaction than, for example, equivalent users who are not involved.[134] The positive glow from participation even seems to affect perception of the environment. Office employees who received new offices that were smaller than their old ones were so pleased with their participation experience that they believed they had *more* space in their new offices.[135]

In practice, programming takes on a variety of emphases depending on the size and nature of the project and the orientation of the programmer. The focus may be on building users as individuals, as aggregates, or as groupings, or on spaces, individually, aggregate, or groupings, although actual projects often combine some of these approaches.[136] Concentrating on *individuals'* needs or on the design of individual spaces is much easier when few persons or spaces need attention. Programming for *aggregates* occurs when there are many persons or spaces of a given

type, such as secretaries or managers. Programming for *groupings* occurs when the people are not merely the same in some characteristic function, such as their occupation, but also share values, norms, and meaning—as in a cultural group.

Formulating Design Guidelines. The next major part of the programming process, although it overlaps with the activities just described, is the formulation of design guidelines. This phase of the process identifies, based on the foregoing analyses and various constraints, specific objectives that the design should make more likely to achieve. Obviously, these guidelines will apply differently to each design problem, and no comprehensive list will accurately reflect the needs identified by users and designers of any individual building project. Nevertheless, some needs are more frequently identified than others. One list was provided by a pioneer of social design, Fritz Steele.[137]

- *Shelter and security.* Adequate filtering of weather elements (e.g., natural light without too much glare, fresh air without an office gale, etc.), adequate space, territorial control.

- *Social contact.* A balance between too much and too little communication: privacy.

- *Task instrumentality.* Person-machine and micro-spatial arrangements that facilitate work performance.

- *Symbolic identification.* Appropriate workplace symbols to convey employee status in a positive manner.

- *Growth.* The opportunity to explore and to learn.

- *Pleasure.* Comfort, convenience, aesthetic appeal, varied but controllable stimulation.

Steele offered these guidelines as a way to specifically answer questions such as: Is this a quality environment for people? If not, which alterations would help? Many organizations treat physical space only as a factor that *harms* employee morale. Steele's guidelines include some that are concerned with positive outcomes such as personal growth, identification, and social contact. The guidelines were developed from Steele's own observations of many offices and inspired by Abraham Maslow's theory of human needs.

A few examples of projects in which some of these guidelines (and two further ones) have been established may be instructive. In most projects, several to many guidelines are identified, but I will focus on just one guideline for each example. Inadequate privacy is one very common problem. In an earlier chapter, I described the programming for a low-income housing project in Peru that revealed privacy to be the key issue for residents.[138] The architect, Christopher Alexander, designed a **privacy gradient** into the new houses. The long narrow dwellings were arranged so that casual and formal visitors were restricted to the front rooms of the house, leaving the deeper sections of it for family and close friends.

Pleasure is a second guideline illustrated in hospital design. Architects planned to surface parts of the courtyard with brick.[139] Brick is attractive, and other hospitals had used it frequently. However, interviews revealed that patients with recent injuries or surgery found it painful to be wheeled over brick surfaces, which are often bumpy. Although the decision was not popular with aesthetics-minded designers, portions of the courtyard over which wheelchairs were expected to pass were redesigned with a smoother surface. Comfort, physical or psychological, is another guideline. For example, in the Swedish geriatric hospital project discussed earlier, the dining room decor taken from the 1930s and 1940s was familiar and psychologically comforting to the elderly patients.

Clear communication, or **imageability**, is a seventh guideline (in addition to Steele's six; you may recall it from earlier in the chapter). Every building should automatically inform visitors and regular users where all its key elements are. When the building itself cannot or does not do so, signs must be used. But many signs are inadequate or even misleading. The clarity of signs can be studied experimentally. In settings used by people who speak many different languages, the search is on for pictorial representations that communicate well to everyone. In a series of studies in Canada, symbolic representations of public information messages were compared.[140] Pictorial symbols meaning washroom, lost and found, car rental information, and others were presented to participants. Measures of legibility, comprehension of the sign's meaning, and preference were used; because they were highly inter-correlated, an overall measure called *efficiency* was created from them. The efficiency index scores for the various competing signs were computed, allowing the researchers to make recommendations about which symbolic representation of each message was best.

An eighth common guideline, also mentioned earlier, is the **provision of control** to building occupants. One form of control—an important design guideline in some situations—is personalization. An issue in the design of dormitories, for example, is the provision of opportunities for residents to personalize their rooms with pictures, posters, and other personal articles.[141] If control is deemed an important design guideline, dormitories can be designed to facilitate personalization. Nameplates on doors, walls lined with surfaced that can be taped, pasted, or tacked without damage, and movable rather than built-in furniture are a few ways to enhance a resident's sense of control in a dormitory room. Personal control is also important in other settings. For example, even in daycares, children should have the opportunity to change and influence their surroundings, where this is feasible.[142]

Design

IN THE DESIGN PHASE, THE GUIDELINES MUST BE TRANS-FORMED INTO BUILDING PLANS. Because the design stages are not entirely separable, a few examples of design solutions to the problems of creating settings that fulfill design guidelines have already been discussed, in the last section. Building plans must take into account many considerations besides the design guidelines established by the social design process. Constraints imposed by financial limitations, building codes, and siting problems are a few of these challenges.

Some design guidelines fail to survive the political process. Every setting includes a variety of user groups with different and sometimes conflicting needs and goals. To produce a final building plan that successfully integrates design guidelines, constraints, and competing user needs, the social designer needs skill and creativity. The job is to advocate as many design considerations that benefit as many building users as possible. In a large Michigan hospital project, over 500 design and policy changes were recommended.[143] Had these research-based suggestions *not* been made, the architect would have been forced to make many intuitive decisions. As it happened, because of constraints and the political aspect of design, the social design team only managed to get about 60 percent of its recommendations adopted. Nevertheless, this meant that about 300 social design-based improvements to a hospital play a crucial, if brief, role in the lives of thousands of people who must be in that hospital.

Construction

THIS IS THE PHASE IN WHICH SOCIAL DESIGNERS PLAY THEIR SMALLEST ROLE. The architectural plans are turned into wood, concrete, glass, and steel. The architect oversees construction, ensuring that the plans are faithfully executed and that they do not reflect any gross oversights. Legends of rooms with no doors, stairwells with enough headroom for children only, and floors from different sections of the building that do not match keep architects vigilant. Minor problems are often corrected as the building is constructed.

However, the construction phase is not totally without interest from the social designer's point of view. One social design-oriented architect saw an opportunity for participation even in the construction phase.[144] In a medical school project, he insisted that construction workers be given a role in design. Rather than asking the workers to follow the plans in every detail, which can be an alienating, stultifying experience, the architect asked the workers to take a more active role. For instance, they were asked to pick up beautiful rocks or other materials on their way to work and to line the concrete forms with them. Masons were given only a rough idea of the architect's plans for the brickwork and encouraged to do the masonry their own way. Happy, enthusiastic construction workers were even bringing their families to the project on evenings and weekends to show them their personal contributions to its design!

Use and Adaptation

THE BUILDING IS FINALLY OCCUPIED. The smell of new paint and furniture greets curious and optimistic new users. Very often the first days and weeks in the life of a new building are happy ones. The occupants usually have moved from older, perhaps cramped, quarters with cranky heating or cooling systems. The new building is a pleasant novelty.

Gradually, however, strange events occur. A middle manager who moved from small but enclosed offices to a spacious open-plan setting is grouchy. A receptionist who brought in a poster of Greece to put up near her desk is forbidden to do so; the poster does not fit the new image of the organization that the decor is supposed to communicate to clients. A clerk notices that windows do not open; his allergies are acting up inside the building. Cynical graffiti about the wonderful new building begins to appear on the bathroom walls. Top management, sensing problems,

begins to think of the employees as ungrateful for the large expenditure represented by the construction of the new setting (see Figure 15-7).

For the designer, this is a period of reality testing.[145] Building programs are unlikely to anticipate all the needs of all the users. However, the conscientious social design researcher will observe the extent to which the building is used as the program intended, and the unexpected ways users are adapting to the environment. Programs should be sufficiently explicit to be tested, not unlike a hypothesis in a scientific study.[146] If the program was successfully incorporated into the building's plans, patterns of behavior that indicate achievement of the desired goals should be evident.

FIGURE 15–7 When buildings are inadequate because their original designs were unsuitable or because technology has outstripped them, employees must improvise adaptations. For example, this librarian has had to fashion a shield to cut the glare on her computer screen. In the background, an office machine is covered with a blanket to reduce its noise.

The sprouting of odd adaptations of the building reflect a failure of the plans to embody the program goals, or that user needs never were included in the program in the first place. One example would be the teacher who, without training in open-plan education, is placed in an open classroom. The teacher may harness all available materials, such as bookcases, desks, and filing cabinets, to construct makeshift barriers against neighboring classes in the open space. Research in the use-and-adaptation phase is a non-evaluative look at how occupants use their building. However, evaluation is an important next step in social design. We turn now to that phase.

Post-occupancy Evaluation

THE FINAL STAGE OF THE DESIGN PROCESS is post-occupancy evaluation (POE).

What POEs Are and Are Not. A post-occupancy evaluation is "an examination of the effectiveness for human users of occupied designed environments."[147] It must be distinguished from the practice of architectural criticism, which emphasizes aesthetic criteria and is usually done by architectural experts alone or in design juries. The latter are based on the expert's personal reading of the design and views on artistic quality.[148] In contrast, the social design research approach uses the program—remember the programming phase?—as the criterion by which the building is judged, and bases its conclusions on user impressions and behavior in the working setting.

POEs must also be distinguished from the personal appraisals of buildings that each of us makes on an informal basis every day.[149] We dislike this fast-food restaurant's ambiance; we prefer a coffee shop with an atmosphere that we like. The POE, in contrast, is much more careful in that it should include all user groups, all important activities occurring in the building, and rigorous methods of collecting and analyzing data. The POE also differs from most social science experiments, even though both aim for valid results.

GARY MOORE'S work spans childcare centers, space, and architecture. One of the first Ph.Ds in environmental psychology, he is now the Dean of an architectural school.

As POE experts state, "Whereas social science strives to control extraneous factors, evaluation often describes those factors; whereas social science is most concerned with discovering causes for behavior, evaluation looks at influences on behavior...whereas social science aims to reduce the number of factors, evaluation often examines complex systems."[150]

Dimensions. POEs vary along four dimensions:

1. **Size and Scope**. Some POEs are small in the amount of resources invested (one student spends a few hours interviewing a few building users); others are large, involving teams of researchers operating over several years, with six-figure budgets. Others may even encompass an entire neighborhood.

2. **Generality.** Many POEs are designed specifically for one building; the social design researcher does not expect the results to be applicable to any other building. Other POEs are conducted in representative schools, prisons, hospitals, or housing developments with the explicit expectation

that the knowledge gained from the effort will apply to other buildings with similar functions.

3. **Breadth of focus.** Some evaluations aim to study only one or two building characteristics, such as noise, space, privacy, or lighting. Other POEs attempt to study more characteristics of the building or even "all" important ones. These broader POEs often aim to capture the whole complexity of the building as an interrelated system.

4. **Application timing.** The purpose of some POEs is to provide useful information for a renovation scheduled to begin "next month." Others may not know when the results are needed. The POE is performed as part of a program to collect information over the building's lifespan so that one day, when the building needs replacement, a wealth of valuable data is available to guide the designers.

POEs are usually considered tests of *building* effectiveness. For example, is a building that follows "green" design principles good for employees? Although one might think the answer is an automatic "yes," the actual answer in a study of 15 buildings by Lindsay McCunn and me was "not really." Employees in greener buildings were not more engaged in their work than were employees in less-green buildings, and in fact employee impressions of their offices were *negatively* related to the building greenness.[151] This is an important reason for conducting POEs: the results are not always what one would expect, and that leads to asking questions (such as, "Is this true of all green buildings?" "If not, which sorts of green designs are not working for employees?" and "How can offices in green buildings be improved?") which otherwise might not be asked.

POEs may also be tests of *program* effectiveness.[152] When construction follows a clear, testable program, the evaluation is essentially a determination of whether the program successfully identified the needs of users. Sometimes no program was done, or it cannot be found. In this case, the evaluation researcher should try to find the architect and, through an interview, determine what he or she intended to accomplish.[153] If the architect also is unavailable, the social researcher should attempt to discern which values are represented by the building's layout, in order to obtain a very rough idea of the program that guided the designer.

Methods. The focus turns now from the nature of post-occupancy evaluations to methods of doing them. How can we determine whether a building is effective for its users? The major methods are similar to those used in other areas of environmental psychology: surveys, interviews, observations of behavior as it occurs, observations of behavior traces (the physical effects of behavior on the environment, such as worn pathways or posted signs), and analyses of archives (records pertaining to building use). These unobtrusive methods, first discussed in a classic psychology book,[154] have been adapted to environmental psychology.[155-157]

In addition to these general approaches, some environmental psychologists have developed comprehensive assessment instruments designed for specific types of buildings. For example, extensive measures of the physical and social environment of sheltered care environments have been created and used to show how design changes affect the behavior of institutionalized individuals.[158] Others have created standardized sets of evaluation tests for correctional institutions,[159] schizophrenia treatment facilities,[160] or general methods for any building.[161, 162]

Great care, of course, must be taken to ensure that appropriate and valid methods are used. This means that multiple methods should be used rather than just one, that building users should be involved in the development of the methods to ensure that important issues receive attention, that methods imported from other research areas are not used uncritically, and that features of the experimental and quasi-experimental methods, such as control groups, should be used where possible.

Each POE is unique, so when questionnaires, surveys, and other methods are borrowed from elsewhere, they must be scrutinized and revised where necessary to fit the requirements of the current study. One error, for example, might be to use a survey developed for secondary schools in a POE of a new elementary school. Although they may respond in good faith, the younger children may simply be not sufficiently developed to accurately answer some questions about their needs or their behavior in the school.[163]

Of course, when a series of quite similar buildings is to be evaluated, a standardized questionnaire or interview may be used, and these have the added value of helping to build up a bank of easily compared design data. Instruments for this purpose have been developed for hospitals, for example.[164,165] Some POEs are like traditional scientific experiments in that specific goals are identified in the design program, and the POE takes these goals as its

hypotheses. For example, one could redesign a ward for severely disturbed mental patients with the goal of reducing violence and improving patients' self-image,[166] or to reduce the frequency of repetitive behaviors and change where patients hang out.[167] The POE examines the changes in these variables before and after remodeling to evaluate the success of the remodeling.

JACQUELINE VISCHER is one of the field's leading authorities on office design and evaluation.

IN SUM *The design process includes five phases: programming, design, construction, use and adaptation, and post-occupancy evaluation. Programming itself consists of three phases: understanding the needs of building users, involving them in the possibilities of design, and translating their needs into design guidelines—goals the actual design should achieve. The first phase involves discerning user needs through surveys and interviews, observing their behavior, and studying the traces they leave. If the actual users are unavailable, a surrogate group should be studied. The second phase, direct user participation in the design process, increases steadily from traditional to directed to joint planning. It includes encouraging, activating, and educating users, and involving them directly in the planning process. Social researchers often find themselves in a strong advocacy position, arguing for the interests of the average building user against the interests of other principal players. The third phase, formulating design guidelines, requires that specific goals be set. These vary from building to building, but a widely useful group of them includes the provision of shelter and security, appropriate social contact, positive symbolic identification, task instrumentality, pleasure, and the opportunity for growth. Turning these guidelines into plans and reality is the job of architects and construction companies. The* *environmental psychologist returns later to monitor user behavior and adaptation of the new building. Post-occupancy evaluation examines the effectiveness of the program and design, using a variety of social science tools.*

A SELECTION OF
DESIGN PROGRAMS
AND POST—OCCUPANCY
EVALUATIONS

HUNDREDS OF PROGRAMS and POEs have been completed; of course no single example gives a complete sense of programs or POEs. In this section, three programs and POEs have been selected as illustrations because they show the diversity of sites, methods, and results that may be found.

Shelter for Victims of Domestic Violence

TRAGICALLY, HUNDREDS OF SHELTERS for victims of domestic violence have had to be created in recent years. Domestic violence is not new, but buildings to shelter victims are a relatively recent development. If you could start from scratch and design a building especially for this purpose, how would it look? This is a question that Ben Refuerzo and Steve Vanderber tried to answer.[168] Many such shelters are hastily adapted from existing residences and other buildings by well-meaning but underfunded groups. The shelters are often overcrowded, with little privacy.

Refuerzo used a variety of methods to improve the design of shelters. He learned the preferred attributes of shelters by showing pictures of 48 potential shelter buildings to 100 shelter residents and staff members and asking for many different kinds of reactions to each one. After analyzing the answers, Refuerzo and Vanderber produced a set of 11 design guidelines for the ideal shelter. Some of these pertain to the neighborhood in which the shelter is to be located, some are related to the building site and landscaping, and some concern the building itself.

Six design guidelines fell into the first category. They were:

1. Ensure that resources such as stores, schools, parks, and clinics are within walking distance. The trip to these resources should have as safe a path as possible (short and public), to minimize exposure to further violence from angry spouses.

2. The shelter should fit into the neighborhood architecture and reflect the shelter's philosophy, which may tend toward anonymity or toward being a widely recognized landmark.

3. The shelter should not look like an institution, with high walls, no windows or landscaping, etc. The structure should provide a sense of security without looking like a fortress.

4. Shelters should be shielded from urban noise because the residents often are under unusual stress.

Two guidelines pertained to the site and landscaping:

5. Screen the shelter with trees and other vegetation, but do so in a way that avoids the creation of hiding places on the premises.

6. Try to provide safe outdoor places for reflection and privacy. Shelters are often crowded, so such outdoor spots are very useful in the healing process.

Five guidelines for the building and its siting are offered:

1. The entry should be "serialized," that is, created as a series of transitional spaces so that visitors can be observed as they approach the shelter.

2. The entry zone should be arranged so that a receptionist can view visitors as they approach the building, both directly and through a video monitoring system, if possible.

3. Create a courtyard with shelter units surrounding it, if possible. This permits spaces (see guideline 6) that are safe but add space to the shelter as a whole.

4. Include play areas for children that meet the security provisions mentioned in earlier guidelines.

5. Include "viewing stations" indoors that allow parents to watch children outside. Ensure these stations are not vulnerable to invasion by hostile spouses.

Hospital

FRANK BECKER AND DONALD POE were involved in the renovation of a hospital wing.[169] They had helped hospital users of all types (patients, staff, and visitors) to participate in the renovation decision-making. The changes made to the building (see Table 15-2) represented those agreed upon through a consensus-seeking process, although financial and administrative constraints restricted the changes slightly.

The effects of the changes were measured, using three methods, and the renovated hospital wing was compared with two similar but unchanged wings. This is an example of a post-occupancy evaluation rather than a program.

One method of evaluation was to measure changes in **organizational climate,** or attitudes toward the hospital. The mood and morale of the hospital staff on the renovated wing improved dramatically after the design changes, in comparison to the mood and morale of staff who worked on the control wings. The mood and morale of the patients and visitors showed smaller and more variable changes in response to the renovations. The visitors even seemed to dislike the renovations. However, staff opinions may be more important in this case because they must spend the most time on the wing. Readers who are concerned about patient welfare will be glad to hear that their mood and morale also improved, although less so than that of the staff.

A second evaluation method used by Becker and Poe was a questionnaire to directly assess the environment. All user groups were asked to rate various features of the renovated and control wings. The user groups all rated the changed features of the renovated wing as better than comparable features of the unchanged wings, although once again the staff was more favorably affected.

Finally, Becker and Poe observed behavior in the hospital. The ward area receiving the most renovation was the solarium. Behavior mapping showed that on the renovated wing the solarium was used significantly more than before the renovations, but solaria on the control wings were used slightly less than before. Building users were also observed in conversation. Post-renovation conversation increased in the renovated wing, but was essentially unchanged in the control wings.

The post-occupancy evaluation by Becker and Poe is a good example of an intervention that began with programming and ended with evaluation of design changes. The results were enlightening because they showed which user groups seemed to benefit and which did not. Some results were unexpected, such as the negative reaction of visitors after they had been consulted about the changes. This is how one turn of the design cycle goes, and anyone contemplating a hospital renovation should be able to

TABLE 15–2 Changes in the Environment of the Hospital Studied by Becker and Poe

Location	Changes
Corridor	Paint walls and ceilings Wallpaper sections of corridor Remove diffusers from fluorescent lights Signs for nurses' stations and other rooms Railing along corridor
Visitor waiting area	Paint Stretched fabric mural Rearrange seating Different (used) furniture
Solarium (porch)	Remove partition wall Remove equipment stored behind partition Put shelves in existing closet Paint Area rug Rearrange furniture Different (used) furniture Change type of phone booth Stretched fabric murals
Nurses' station	Carpet Shelves Tack board Paint
Nurses' kitchenette	Paint Stretched fabric mural Storage shelves Rearrange furniture Different (used) furniture Remove unused equipment
Alcove outside nursing unit	Directional graphics Paint Relocate phone booth Add (used) chairs and magazine table

benefit from Becker and Poe's work to make the next turn of the cycle even more useful.

Office

ROBERT MARANS AND KENT SPRECKELMEYER evaluated a government office building that won architectural awards for excellence.[170,171] What they learned from questioning three user groups reflects one of the most fundamental findings in environmental psychology: the perceived value of a setting often depends on the evaluator's relation to the building (e.g., employed in it, visitor, or passerby).

Marans and Spreckelmeyer believe that a POE should focus not only on the value of a building's lighting, noise, and parking space, but also on its overall architectural quality or aesthetics. They asked employees to rate the

FIGURE 15–8 The glorious exterior versus one inglorious interior of a famous building. Visitors love the exterior and the building has won several international awards. Its architect was awarded the Gold Medal of the American Institute of Architects in 1985. However, those who actually use the building frequently complain because they experience interiors like this more than the building exterior.

functional aspects of the building, but they also asked employees, visitors, and members of the public to judge its overall architectural quality.

The three groups disagreed on the merits of the office building. Residents of the community and visitors were asked to judge both the interior and the exterior of the building. Their average judgment was that the building was fairly attractive, or about 3 on a scale of 1 to 4. Employee judgments of architectural quality were less positive, averaging about 4 on a scale of 1 to 7. Closer examination of employee judgments showed that lower ratings were given by employees who had worked in the building longer (familiarity seemed to breed contempt) and that ratings of interior features of the building such as spatial arrangements were lower than ratings of general or exterior features.

This pattern of appreciation by judges with weak links to a building (visitors, passersby, and tourists) and dislike by judges with strong links to a building (employees and frequent users) has been found before. My own doctoral dissertation dealt with the architectural merits of a

university campus that had won international awards and fame for its designer.[172] Sunday visitors, strolling through its striking buildings, write adoring comments in the visitors' book. Photos from helicopters on sunny days depict the university's bold exteriors, which remind many viewers of Egyptian or Mayan temples. But students and staff, who frequently endure fog, rain, and drips in the grey concrete edifice, often find the campus cold, inhuman, and depressing (see Figure 15-8).

In addition, as Marans and Spreckelmeyer point out, evaluations of all sorts, including architectural evaluations, are often influenced by external factors. When the local media report that a building has won awards, community residents are likely to believe, *a priori*, that the building must be good. In contrast, employees whose job may be unfulfilling, or worse, may be inclined to negatively evaluate almost anything placed before them. This is unfortunately the case for many office employees, especially in the lower echelons of an organization.

To produce a good POE, the evaluator must be aware of these possible biases. Another possibility is that a building is a chief cause of user dissatisfaction, so the possible existence of biases must not necessarily be interpreted as a reason for ignoring user evaluations. Furthermore, building users usually prefer some features over others, even when a generally negative pall surrounds their evaluations. In the office building studied by Marans and Spreckelmeyer, the single most important predictor of employee satisfaction was the amount of space in the employee's workstation, regardless whether it was open-plan, bullpen, or conventional (walled-in). When workstation size was equivalent, however, employees preferred conventional offices to open-plan offices.

A few problems with social design research do remain. Observers have suggested that social researchers sometimes spend too much effort on data gathering and too little on ways to actually apply the knowledge.[173] Presumably, as design research teams are better supported, more time and effort can be devoted to all phases of the design cycle, including more direct application of research findings. In conclusion, post-occupancy evaluation is a necessary and growing part of the building process. With increasing experience, the methods employed by social researchers are being refined; gradually a knowledge base is accumulating that will be used to create more habitable buildings.

SUMMARY

SOCIAL DESIGN IS AN ESSENTIAL PART of the building-creation process that emphasizes the active involvement of building users, the specification of clear design guidelines, and the evaluation of these guidelines in the finished building. Occupational specialization in modern society has separated designers from occupants; some designers view architecture purely as an art. If buildings are to be very habitable, these tendencies must be overcome. Because it requires some extra effort at the beginning of a building's life and because it calls for input from more principal players, the social design process has met some resistance. Some expect too much in the way of behavior change. The process unavoidably leads to some conflict, although this conflict can be useful as a way to bring different perspectives into an open discussion. Social designers believe the effort is worthwhile; benefits to users, designers, and paying clients outweigh the costs—particularly over the long run. Social design is most active in programming (understanding and involving users and formulating design goals) and in post-occupancy evaluation (examining the program and design in action). Social design research for a shelter for victims of violence, a hospital, and an office are described.

Suggested Supplementary Readings

Gifford, R. (2002). Making a difference: Some ways environmental psychology has improved the world. In R. B. Bechtel & A. Churchman (Eds.), *Handbook of environmental psychology* (pp. 323-334). Hoboken, NJ: Wiley.

Hershberger, R. (2002). Behavioral-based architectural programming. In R. B. Bechtel & A. Churchman (Eds.), *Handbook of environmental psychology* (pp. 292-305). Hoboken, NJ: Wiley.

Preiser, W. F. E., Vischer, J. C., & White, E. T. (Eds.). (1991). *Design intervention: Toward a more humane architecture.* New York: Van Nostrand Reinhold.

Preiser, W. F. E., & Vischer, J. C. (Eds.). (2005). *Assessing building performance.* Amsterdam: Elsevier.

Sommer, R. (1983). *Social design: Creating buildings with people in mind.* Englewood Cliffs, NJ: Prentice-Hall.

Steele, F. I. (1973). *Physical settings and organization development.* Don Mills, ON: Addison-Wesley.

Zeisel, J. (1981). *Inquiry by design: Tools for environment-behavior research.* Monterey, CA: Brooks/Cole.

Zimring, C. (2002). Post-occupancy evaluation: Issues and implementation. In R. B. Bechtel & A. Churchman (Eds.), *Handbook of environmental psychology* (pp. 306-319). Hoboken, NJ: Wiley.

References

1. Izumi, K. (1971). LSD and architectural design. In B. Aaronson & H. Osmond (Eds.). *Psychedelics*. Cambridge, MA: Schenkman.

2. Sommer, R. (1972). *Design awareness*. New York: Holt, Rinehart and Winston.

3. Sommer, R. (1983). *Social design*. Englewood Cliffs, NJ: Prentice-Hall.

4. Sommer, R. (1983). *Social design*. Englewood Cliffs, NJ: Prentice-Hall., p. 7.

5. Sommer, R. (1983). *Social design*. Englewood Cliffs, NJ: Prentice-Hall.

6. Vischer, J. (2008). Towards a user-centred theory of the built environment. *Building Research & Information, 36*, 231-240.

7. Slum surgery in St. Louis. (1951). *Architectural Forum, 94*, 128-136.

8. Douglas, D., & Gifford, R. (2001). Evaluation of the physical classroom by students and professors: A lens model approach. *Educational Research, 43*, 295-309.

9. Devlin, K. (1990). An examination of architectural interpretation: Architects versus non-architects. *Journal of Architectural and Planning Research, 7*, 235-244.

10. Nasar, J. L., & Kang, J. (1989). A post-jury evaluation: The Ohio State University design competition for a center for the visual arts. *Environment and Behavior, 21*, 464-484.

11. Vischer, J. C., & Marcus, C. C. Evaluating evaluation: Analysis of a housing design awards program. *Places, 3*, 66-86.

12. Brown, G. & Gifford, R. (2001). Architects predict lay evaluations of large contemporary buildings: Whose conceptual properties? *Journal of Environmental Psychology, 21*, 93-99.

13. Gifford, R., Hine, D. W., Muller-Clemm, W., & Shaw, K. T. (2002). Why architects and laypersons judge buildings differently: Cognitive properties and physical bases. *Journal of Architectural and Planning Research, 19*, 131-148.

14. Duffy, M., Bailey, S., Beck, B., & Barker, D. G. (1986). Preferences in nursing home design - A comparison of residents, administrators, and designers. *Environment and Behavior, 18*, 246-257.

15. Gifford, R., Hine, D. W., Muller-Clemm, W. & Shaw, K. T. (2000). Decoding modern architecture: Understanding the aesthetic differences of architects and laypersons. *Environment and Behavior, 32*, 163-187.

16. Wilson, M. A., & Canter, D. V. (1990). The development of central concepts during professional education: An example of a multivariate model of the concept of architectural style. *Applied Psychology: An International Review, 39*, 431-455.

17. Goel, V., & Pirolli, P. (1992). The structure of design problem spaces. *Cognitive Science, 16*, 395-429.

18. Downing, F. (1992). The role of place and event imagery in the art of design. *Journal of Architectural and Planning Research, 9*, 64-80.

19. Ahrentzen, S., & Groat, L. N. (1992). Rethinking architectural education: Patriarchal convention and alternative visions from the perspectives of women faculty.

Journal of Architectural and Planning Research, 9, 95-111.

20. Sancar, F. H., & Eyikan, B. (1998). Studio instructors talk about skills, knowledge, and professional roles in architecture and landscape architecture. *Environment and Behavior, 30*, 378-397.

21. Turner, J. F. C. (1987). The enabling practitioner and the recovery of creative work. *Journal of Architectural and Planning Research, 4*, 273-280.

22. Sommer, R. (1983). *Social design*. Englewood Cliffs, NJ: Prentice-Hall, p. 4.

23. Sommer, R. (1983). *Social design*. Englewood Cliffs, NJ: Prentice-Hall.

24. Olwig, K. R. (1990). Designs upon children's special places? *Children's Environments Quarterly, 7*, 47-53.

25. Conway, D. (1973). *Social science and design: A process model for architect and social scientist collaboration*. Washington, DC: American Institute of Architects.

26. Sime, J. D. (1986). Creating places or designing spaces? *Journal of Environmental Psychology, 6*, 49-63.

27. Schneekloth, L. H., & Shibley, R. G. (1993). The practice of placemaking. *Architecture et Comportement/Architecture and Behavior, 9*, 121-144.

28. Stamps, A. (1989). Are environmental aesthetics worth studying? *Journal of Architectural and Planning Research, 6*, 344-356.

29. Dempsey, F. (1914). Nela Park: A novelty in the architectural grouping of industrial buildings. *Architectural Record, 35*, 469-504. (p. 472)

30. Wheeler, L. (1985). Behavior and design: A memoir. *Environment and Behavior, 17*, 133-144.

31. Vischer, J. (2008). Towards a user-centred theory of the built environment. *Building Research & Information, 36*, 231-240.

32. Harrison, A. A. (2010). Humanizing outer space: Architecture, habitability, and behavioral health. *Acta Astronautica, 66*, 890-896.

33. Gifford, R., & Lacombe, C. (2006). *The habitability of spacecraft: Assessments of a virtual reality simulation of the ISS across cultural, personality, and individual differences*. Report to the Canadian Space Agency.

34. Rapoport, Am. (1969). *House form and culture*. Englewood Cliffs, NJ: Prentice Hall.

35. Holahan, C. J. (1983). Interventions to reduce environmental stress: Enhancing social support and personal control. In E. Siedman (Ed.), *Handbook of social interventions*. Beverly Hills, CA: Sage.

36. Holahan, C. J. (1983). Interventions to reduce environmental stress: Enhancing social support and personal control. In E. Siedman (Ed.), *Handbook of social interventions*. Beverly Hills, CA: Sage.

37. Michelson, W. (1976). *Man and his urban environment: A sociological approach*. Don Mills, ON: Addison-Wesley.

38. Preiser, W. P. E., & Taylor, A. (1983). The habitability framework: Linking human behavior and physical environment in a special education. *EEQ: Exceptional Education Quarterly, 4*, 1-15. (p. 6)

39. Lansing, J. B., & Marans, R. W. (1969). Evaluation of neighborhood quality. *Journal of the American Institute of Planners, 35*, 195-199.

40. Rule, B. G., Milke, D. L., & Dobbs, A. R. (1992). Design of institutions: Cognitive functioning and social interactions of the aged resident. *Journal of Applied Gerontology, 11*, 475-488.

41. Christenson, M. A. (1990). Aging in the designed environment. *Physical and Occupational Therapy in Geriatrics, 8*, 3-133.

42. Cohen, U., & Weisman, G. D. (1990). Experimental design to maximize autonomy for older adults with cognitive impairments. *Generations, 14(Suppl)*, 75-78.

43. Hunt, M. E. (1991). The design of supportive environments for older people. Special Issue: Congregate housing for the elderly: Theoretical, policy, and programmatic perspectives. *Journal of Housing for the Elderly, 9*, 127-140.

44. Osmond, H. (1957). Function as the basis of psychiatric ward design. *Mental Hospitals, 8*, 23-30.

45. Gulak, M. B. (1991). Architectural guidelines for state psychiatric hospitals. *Hospital and Community Psychiatry, 42*, 705-707.

46. Remen, S. (1991). Signs, symbols, and the psychiatric environment. *Psychiatric Hospital, 22*, 113-118.

47. Manoleas, P. (1991). Designing mental health facilities: An interactive process. *Hospital and Community Psychiatry, 42*, 305-308.

48. St. Clair, R. (1987). Psychiatric hospital design. *Psychiatric Hospital, 18*, 17-22.

49. Kennedy, D. (1991). The young child's experience of space and child care center design: A practical meditation. *Children's Environments Quarterly, 8*, 37-48.

50. Striniste, N. A., & Moore, R. C. (1989). Early childhood outdoors: A literature review related to the design of childcare environments. *Children's Environments Quarterly, 6*, 25-31.

51. Atlas, R. (1989). Reducing the opportunity for inmate suicide: A design guide. *Psychiatric Quarterly, 60*, 161-171.

52. Christenfeld, R., Wagner, J., Pastva, G., & Acrish, W. P. (1989). How physical settings affect chronic mental patients. *Psychiatric Quarterly, 60*, 253-264.

53. Harvey, M. L., Loomis, R. J., Bell, P. A., & Marino, M. (1998). The influence of museum exhibit design on immersion and psychological flow. *Environment and Behavior, 30*, 601-627.

54. Hooper, J., & Reid, D. H. (1985). A simple environmental re-design for improving classroom performance of profoundly retarded students. *Education and Treatment of Children, 8*, 25-39.

55. van Nieuw-Amerongen, M. E., Kremers, S. P. J., de Vries, N. K., & Kok, G. (2011). The use of prompts, increased accessibility, visibility, and aesthetics of the stairwell to promote stair use in a university building. *Environment and Behavior, 43*, 131-139.

56. Sommer, R. (1983). *Social design*. Englewood Cliffs, NJ: Prentice-Hall.

57. van Hoogdalem, H., van der Voordt, T. J. M., & van Wegen, H. B. R. (1985). Comparative floorplan-analysis as a means to develop

design guidelines. *Journal of Environmental Psychology, 5*, 153-179.

58 Knight, R. C., & Campbell, D. E. (1980). Environmental evaluation research: Evaluator roles and inherent social commitments. *Environment and Behavior, 12*, 502-532.

59 Chapin, D., & Cooper Marcus, C. (1993). Design guidelines: Reflections of experiences passed. *Architecture et Comportement/ Architecture and Behavior, 9*, 99-120.

60 Saegert, S. (1993). Charged contexts: Difference, emotion and power in environmental design research. *Architecture et Comportement/Architecture and Behavior, 9*, 69-84.

61 Sommer, R. (1983). *Social design*. Englewood Cliffs, NJ: Prentice-Hall.

62 Sommer, R. (1983). *Social design*. Englewood Cliffs, NJ: Prentice-Hall, p. 65.

63 Evans, G. W., & McCoy, J. M. (1998). When buildings don't work: The role of architecture in human health. *Journal of Environmental Psychology, 18* 85-94.

64 Holahan, C. J. (1983). Interventions to reduce environmental stress: Enhancing social support and personal control. In E. Siedman (Ed.), *Handbook of social interventions*. Beverly Hills, CA: Sage.

65 Moos, R. H. (1981). A social-ecological perspective on health. In G. Stone et al. (Eds.) *Health psychology*. San Francisco: Jossey-Bass.

66 Mehrabian, A., & Diamond, S. G. (1971). The effects of furniture arrangement, props and personality on social interaction. *Journal of Personality and Social Psychology, 20*, 18-30.

67 Holahan, C. J. (1972). Seating patterns and patient behavior in an experimental dayroom. *Journal of Abnormal Psychology, 80*, 115-124.

68 Refuerzo, B. J., & Verderber, S. (1990). Dimensions of person-environment relationships in shelters for victims of domestic violence. *Journal of Architectural and Planning Research, 7*, 33-52.

69 Hunt, M. E. (1985). Enhancing a building's imageability. *Journal of Architectural and Planning Research, 2*, 151-168.

70 Sommer, R. (1983). *Social design*. Englewood Cliffs, NJ: Prentice-Hall.

71 Heimsath, C. (1977). *Behavioral architecture: Toward an accountable design process*. New York: McGraw-Hill.

72 Barrett, T. (1991, May 11). Thinking small. *Vancouver Sun*, 1, 8-9.

73 Kira, A. (1976). *The bathroom*. New York: Viking.

74 Sommer, R. (1969). *Personal space: The behavioral basis of design*. Englewood Cliffs, NJ: Prentice-Hall.

75 Beal, G., & Keller, R. (1989). Group planning in a psychiatric facility: Problematic group reactions and lessons learned. *International Journal of Therapeutic Communities, 10*, 59-65.

76 Porteous, J. D. (1977). *Environment and behavior: Planning and everyday life*. Don Mills, ON: Addison-Wesley.

77 Shibley, R. G., & Schneekloth, L. H. (1988). Risking collaboration: Professional dilemmas in evaluation and design. *Journal of Architectural and Planning Research, 5*, 304-320.

78 Beck, W. C., & Meyer, R. H. (1982). *The health care environment: The user's viewpoint*. FL: CRC Press.

79 Beal, G., & Keller, R. (1989). Group planning in a psychiatric facility: Problematic group reactions and lessons learned. *International Journal of Therapeutic Communities, 10*, 59-65.

80 Seo, H., & Choi, Y. (2011). Impact of hospital unit design for patient-centered care on nurses' behavior. *Environment and Behavior, 43*, 443-468.

81 Sommer, R. (1983). *Social design*. Englewood Cliffs, NJ: Prentice-Hall.

82 Zimring, C. M., & Reitzenstein, J. E. (1981). A primer on post-occupancy evaluation. *AIA Journal, 70*, 52 58.

83 Sommer, R. (1983). *Social design*. Englewood Cliffs, NJ: Prentice-Hall.

84 Wools, R. (1970). The effects of rooms on behavior. In D. Canter (Ed.), *Architectural psychology*. London: RIBA.

85 Sommer, R. (1983). *Social design*. Englewood Cliffs, NJ: Prentice-Hall.

86 Sommer, R. (1983). *Social design*. Englewood Cliffs, NJ: Prentice-Hall.

87 Reizenstein, J. E. (1982). Hospital design and human behavior: A review of the recent literature. In A. Baum & J. E. Singer (Eds.), *Advances in environmental psychology: Volume 4: Environment and health*. Hillsdale, NJ: Erlbaum.

88 Zeisel, J. (1975). *Sociology and architectural design*. New York: Russell Sage Foundation.

89 Wener, R., Frazier, F. W., & Farbstein, J. (1985). Three generations of evaluation and design of correctional facilities. *Environment and Behavior, 17*, 71-95.

90 Wener, R. E. (1988). Doing it right: Examples of successful application of environment-behavior research. *Journal of Architectural and Planning Research, 5*, 284-303.

91 Gifford, R., & Martin, M. (1991). A multiple sclerosis center program and post-occupancy evaluation. In W. F. E. Preiser, J. C. Vischer, & E. T. White (Eds.), *Design intervention: Toward a more humane architecture*. New York: Van Nostrand Reinhold.

92 Sommer, R. (1972). *Design awareness*. New York: Holt, Rinehart and Winston.

93 Sommer, R. (1997). Utilization issues in environment-behavior research. In G. T. Moore & R. W. Marans (Eds.), *Advances in environment, behavior, and design* (Vol. 4). New York: Plenum.

94 95. Sommer, R. (1976). *Social design: Creating buildings with people in mind*. Englewood Cliffs, NJ: Prentice-Hall.

95 Al-Soliman, T. M. (1991). Societal values and their effect on the built environment in Saudi Arabia: A recent account. *Journal of Architectural and Planning Research, 8*, 235-254.

96 Kent, S. (1991). Partitioning space: Cross-cultural factors influencing domestic spatial segmentation. *Environment and Behavior, 23*, 438-473.

97 Zeisel, J. (1975). *Sociology and architectural design*. New York: Russell Sage Foundation.

98 Sommer, R. (1983). *Social design*. Englewood Cliffs, NJ: Prentice-Hall.

99 Ullan, A. M., Belver, M. H., Fernandez, E., Serrano, I., Delgado, J., & Herrero, C. (2012). Hospital Designs for Patients of Different Ages: Preferences of Hospitalized Adolescents, Nonhospitalized Adolescents, Parents, and Clinical Staff. *Environment and Behavior, 44*, 668-694.

100 Kuller, R., & Mattsson, R. (1984). *The dining room at a geriatric hospital*. Paper presented at International Association for the Study of People and their Surroundings, West Berlin.

101 Nasar, J. L., & Farokhpay, M. (1985). Assessment of activity priorities and design preferences of elderly residents in public housing: A case study. *Gerontologist, 25*, 251-257.

102 Butler, D. L., & Biner, P. M. (1987). Preferred lighting levels: Variability among settings, behaviors, and individuals. *Environment and Behavior, 19*, 695-721.

103 Butler, D. L., & Biner, P. M. (1989). Effects of setting on window preferences and factors associated with those preferences. *Environment and Behavior, 21*, 17-31.

104 Zeisel, J. (1975). *Sociology and architectural design*. New York: Russell Sage Foundation.

105 Barkow, B. (1977). Public transit planning too often ignores people. *Notes from underground*. Long Island City, NY: Committee for Better Transit.

106 Hanlon, M. (1981, November 8). Psychologists used for pedestrian engineering. Toronto *Star*, E5.

107 Irvine, C. H., Snook, S. H., & Sparshatt, J. H. (1990). Stairway risers and treads: Acceptable and preferred dimensions. *Applied Ergonomics, 21*, 215-225.

108 Dalhoum, E. H., & Rydberg-Mitchell, B. (1992). Communicating with laypeople. *Architecture et Comportement/Architecture and Behavior, 8*, 241-251.

109 Martens, B. (1992). Tools for visual simulation of space and their use by students. *Architecture et Comportement/Architecture and Behavior, 8*, 265-272.

110 Rheingold, H. (1990). Travels in virtual reality. *Whole Earth Review, 67*, 80-86.

111 Campbell, D. E., & Schlechter, T. M. (1979). Library design influences on user behavior and satisfaction. *Library Quarterly, 49*, 26-41.

112 Ng, C. F., & Gifford, R. (1986). *Greater Victoria Public Library (Esquimalt Branch): A Post-occupancy report*. Report to the Greater Victoria Public Library Board.

113 Ng, C. F., & Gifford, R. (1986). *Greater Victoria Public Library (Esquimalt Branch): A Post-occupancy report*. Report to the Greater Victoria Public Library Board.

114 Sommer, R. (1976). *Social design: Creating buildings with people in mind*. Englewood Cliffs, NJ: Prentice-Hall.

115 Sommer, R. (1983). *Social design*. Englewood Cliffs, NJ: Prentice-Hall.

116 Mueller, W. S. (1981). Translation of user requirements into house designs: A multidimensional scaling analysis. *Journal of Environmental Psychology, 1*, 97-116.

117 Reis, A. (2000). Assessment of the design participation school of thought. *Journal of Architectural and Planning Research, 17*, 1-15.

118 Pivik, J. R. (2010). The perspective of children and youth: How different stakeholders identify architectural barriers for inclusion in schools. *Journal of Environmental Psychology, 30,* 510-517.

119 Sommer, R. (1972). *Design awareness.* New York: Holt, Rinehart and Winston.

120 Sommer, R. (1983). *Social design.* Englewood Cliffs, NJ: Prentice-Hal, p. 9.

121 Becker, F. D. (1983, July). Creating an office that works. *Xerox Learning Systems.*

122 Becker, F. D. (1980). Employees need role in design of work space. *Hospitals, 54,* 97-105.

123 van Wagenberg, D., Krasner, M., & Krasner, L. (1981). Children planning an ideal classroom: Environmental design in an elementary school. *Environment and Behavior, 13,* 349-359.

124 Kaplan, S. & Kaplan, R. (1982). *Cognition and environment: Functioning in an uncertain world.* New York: Praeger.

125 117. Breu, J. (1984, April 20). Patients, visitors getting chance to help design new hospital. *American Medical News,* 10-11.

126 Lawrence, R. J. (1982). A psychological-spatial approach for architectural design and research. *Journal of Environmental Psychology, 2,* 37-51.

127 Rheingold, H. (1990). Travels in virtual reality. *Whole Earth Review, 67,* 80-86.

128 Davis, G., & Szigeti, F. (1982). Programming, space planning and office design. *Environment and Behavior, 14,* 299-317.

129 Becker, F. D. (1977). *Housing messages.* Stroudsberg, PA: Dowden, Hutchinson and Ross.

130 Carpman, J. R., Grant, M. A., & Simmons, D. A. (1986). *Design that cares: Planning health facilities for patients and visitors.* Chicago: American Hospital Publishing.

131 Busch-Rossnagel, N. A., Nasar, J. L., Campbell, J., & Danish, S. J. (1980). An interdisciplinary approach to designing environments for children. *Journal of Man- Environment Relations, 1,* 1-10.

132 Eisemon, T. (1975). Simulations and requirements for citizen participation in public housing: The Truax technique. *Environment and Behavior, 7,* 99-123.

133 Vischer, J. C. (1985). The adaptation and control model of user needs: A new direction for housing research. *Journal of Environmental Psychology, 5,* 287-298.

134 Reizenstein, J. E. (1982). Hospital design and human behavior: A review of the recent literature. In A. Baum & J. E. Singer (Eds.), *Advances in environmental psychology: Volume 4: Environment and health.* Hillsdale, NJ: Erlbaum.

135 Reizenstein, J. E. (1982). Hospital design and human behavior: A review of the recent literature. In A. Baum & J. E. Singer (Eds.), *Advances in environmental psychology: Volume 4: Environment and health.* Hillsdale, NJ: Erlbaum.

136 Mazumdar, S. (1992). How programming can become counterproductive: An analysis of approaches to programming. *Journal of Environmental Psychology, 12,* 65-91.

137 Steele, F. I. (1973). *Physical settings and organization development.* Don Mills, ON: Addison-Wesley.

138 Zeisel, J. (1975). *Sociology and architectural design.* New York: Russell Sage Foundation.

139 Becker, F. D. (1980). Employees need role in design of work space. *Hospitals, 54,* 97-105.

140 Mackett-Stout, J., & Dewar, R. (1981). Evaluations of symbolic public information signs. *Human Factors, 23,* 139-151.

141 Zeisel, J. (1975). *Sociology and architectural design.* New York: Russell Sage Foundation.

142 Olds, A. R. (1989). Psychological and physiological harmony in child care center design. *Children's Environments Quarterly, 6,* 8-16.

143 Becker, F. D. (1980). Employees need role in design of work space. *Hospitals, 54,* 97-105.

144 Hatch, C. R. (1984). *The scope of social architecture.* Toronto: Van Nostrand Reinhold.

145 Zeisel, J. (1975). *Sociology and architectural design.* New York: Russell Sage Foundation.

146 138. Kaye, S. M. (1975). Psychology in relation to design: An overview. *Canadian Psychological Review, 16,* 104-110.

147 Zimring, C. M., & Reizenstein, J. E. (1980). Post-occupancy evaluation: An overview. *Environment and Behavior, 12,* 429-450.

148 Zimring, C. M., & Reitzenstein, J. E. (1981). A primer on post-occupancy evaluation. *AIA Journal, 70,* 52-58.

149 Friedmann, A., Zimring, C., & Zube, E. (1978). *Environmental design evaluation.* New York: Plenum.

150 Friedmann, A., Zimring, C., & Zube, E. (1978). *Environmental design evaluation.* New York: Plenum.

151 McCunn, L. J., & Gifford, R. (2012). Do green offices affect employee engagement and environmental motivation? *Architectural Science Review, 55,* 128-134.

152 Churchman, A. & Ginosar, O. A theoretical basis for the post-occupancy evaluation of neighborhoods. *Journal f Environmental Psychology, 19,* 267-276.

153 Zimring, C. M., & Reizenstein, J. E. (1980). Post-occupancy evaluation: An overview. *Environment and Behavior, 12,* 429-450.

154 Webb, E. J., Campbell, D. T., Schwartz, R. D., & Sechrest, L. (1966). *Unobtrusive measures: Nonreactive research in the social sciences.* Chicago: Rand-McNally.

155 Zeisel, J. (1981). *Inquiry by design: Tools for environment-behavior research.* Monterey, CA: Brooks/Cole.

156 Sommer, R. (1972). *Design awareness.* New York: Holt, Rinehart and Winston.

157 Zube, E. H. (1980). *Environmental evaluation: Perception and public policy.* Monterey, CA: Brooks/Cole.

158 Lemke, S., & Moos, R. H. (1985). Coping with an intrainstitutional relocation: Behavioral change as a function of residents' personal resources. *Journal of Environmental Psychology, 5,* 137-151.

159 Farbstein, J., & Wener, R. E. (1982). Evaluation of correctional environments. *Environment and Behavior, 14,* 671-694.

160 Gabb, B. S., Speicher, K., & Lodl, K. (1992). Environmental design for individuals with schizophrenia: An assessment tool. *Journal of Applied Rehabilitation Counseling, 23,* 35-40.

161 Davis, G., & Ventre, F. T. (Eds.)(1990). *Performance of buildings and serviceability of facilities.* Philadelphia: ASTM.

162 Preiser, W. F. E., & Vischer, J. C. (Eds.). 2005). *Assessing building performance.* Amsterdam: Elsevier.

163 David, T. G. (1982). Evaluating school environments from a user perspective. *Journal of Man-Environment Relations, 1,* 79-89.

164 Andrade, C., Lima, M. L., Fornara, F., & Bonaiuto, M. (2012). Users' views of hospital environmental quality: Validation of the Perceived Hospital Environment Quality Indicators (PHEQIs). *Journal of Environmental Psychology, 32,* 97-111.

165 Mourshed, M., & Zhao, Y. (2012). Healthcare providers' perception of design factors related to physical environments in hospitals. *Journal of Environmental Psychology, 32,* 362-370.

166 Davis, G., & Ventre, F. T. (Eds.). (1990). *Performance of buildings and serviceability of facilities.* Philadelphia: ASTM.

167 Devlin, A. S. (1992). Psychiatric ward renovation: Staff perception and patient behavior. *Environment and Behavior, 24,* 66-84.

168 Refuerzo, B. J., & Verderber, S. (1988). Creating a safe refuge: The functions of nature in the design of shelters for victims of domestic violence. EDRA: *Environmental Design Research Association, 19,* 63-69.

169 Becker, F. D., & Poe, D. B. (1980). The effects of user-generated design modifications in a general hospital. *Journal of Nonverbal Behavior, 4,* 195-218

170 Marans, R. W., & Spreckelmeyer, K. F. (1982). Evaluating open and conventional office design. *Environment and Behavior, 14,* 333-351.

171 Marans, R. W., & Spreckelmeyer, K. F. (1982). Measuring overall architectural quality: A component of building evaluation. *Environment and Behavior, 14,* 652-670.

172 Gifford, R. (1976). *Personal and situational factors in judgements of typical architecture.* Unpublished doctoral dissertation, Simon Fraser University, Burnaby, British Columbia.

173 Weisman, G. D. (1983). Environmental programming and action research. *Environment and Behavior, 15,* 318-408.

Utopia, Entopia, and You

The Essential, Challenging Discipline

Why Are We Doing This?

HOTEL

THIS HAS BEEN A LONG JOURNEY, an entire term for you and over 25 years for me (if you count all five editions of this book). You have waded through fifteen chapters packed with brief descriptions of environmental psychologists, their ideas, their research projects, and their signposts toward solutions to environmental problems. In this brief look back, I will avoid recounting new studies, more facts. Instead, I would like to attempt a perspective on what this is all about.

THE ESSENTIAL, CHALLENGING DISCIPLINE

IN MY VIEW, TWO FUNDAMENTAL TRUTHS PERVADE ENVIRONMENTAL PSYCHOLOGY, and they underscore the field's crucial importance. The first is that *every* human activity occurs in a physical context. All human activity occurs in residences, offices, schools, parks, streets, studios, retail settings, vehicles, institutions, or factories, and all these settings affect everyone's behavior, interactions, emotions, thoughts, and well-being. Therefore, environmental psychology is essential to every other branch of psychology and, indeed, to *every person*. Environmental psychology matters![1]

The second fundamental truth is that the mutual influence of persons and settings usually is neither sudden nor dramatic (certain natural disasters are exceptions). Because these influences are often cumulative and subtle, because people often adapt even to unhealthy settings, and because in the normal course of daily life people seem to focus on other people and on the task at hand, the physical influences on them and others often go unnoticed. As a result, the vital importance of person-environment transactions sometimes is overlooked. However, if you reflect on the previous fifteen chapters, you will realize that environmental psychology is an essential human endeavor. You may already agree, but remember that not everyone else does, at least so far.

Looking back over the history of scientific psychology, one realizes that in its early days in the 19th century, the discipline focused on mental dynamics (this early fascination has returned in the form of widespread interest in cognitive psychology). Later, in the early 20th century, psychologists began to realize the importance of interpersonal and social forces. Except for the lonely voices of a few pioneers, the role played by the physical environment was only officially recognized less than 50 years ago. Even today, if your experiences are like mine, you must often field questions about what environmental psychology is. Someone hears that you are studying it and says, "That sounds interesting. But what is it?" In fact, on this very day, my barber asked me that question! Try to take great care in giving an answer, because the public at large still is generally unaware of this field; its opinion about environmental psychology depends in part on what it hears from you and me.

Of course, you must develop your own assessment of the field to offer the curious. Years of work have convinced me that environmental psychologists have bravely undertaken a task that is ultimately more difficult than that undertaken by any other branch of science. Understanding the physical world is difficult; sometimes very difficult. But then consider *this* challenge: we humans are the instrument for understanding how we humans transact with all our physical settings! This is like the frog trying to understand the frog, or the microscope trying to understand the microscope, in that we are trying to understand something at the same level of sophistication as ourselves, as opposed to organisms and physical elements that are less sophisticated than ourselves.

In this book, I never promised to provide simple recipes for solutions to practical problems, and I doubt that any simple answers exist for the practical and theoretical problems that environmental psychologists try to solve. Although knowledge is growing so fast that it fairly bulges out of this book, it still provides illumination of theoretical issues and broad research questions more like that offered by the full moon than that offered by the noonday sun.

At this stage, my hope is that you have learned the real strengths of environmental psychology: having the courage to struggle with complex problems, and trying to understand and overcome these problems in local community settings. At present, reading about research and theory in environmental psychology requires more tolerance for uncertainty than a willingness to master a set of established physical or mathematical laws. However, the techniques and procedures needed to conduct applied research that can significantly improve the habitability of the built

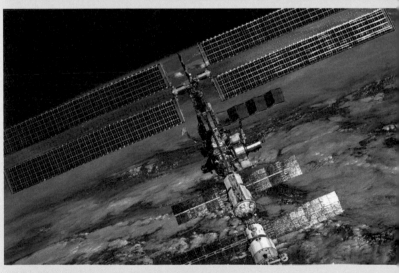

Environmental psychologists work everywhere that humans go in their many physical settings, from encounters with wild animals, to the common but important everyday buildings in our lives, to exotic locations in space, and they have made important contributions to principles and practice in all these domains.

environment, the protection of natural settings, and global sustainability are already well developed and ready for use.

This is all that may reasonably be expected, in my view, after only almost 50 years of sustained effort. Give us another few decades and resources like those allocated to other areas of science for many more decades or even centuries, and the growth of understanding of the individual, social and societal processes involved in environmental psychology will compare very favorably with progress in older disciplines. A primary reason for this lies in the degree of dedication of most environmental psychologists who, in my experience, are even more driven than most others who seek new knowledge as a profession. They seem to derive extra energy from knowing their work forms an integral part of their everyday life; that they can affect the world around them; that they are always in a physical setting that affects them, is affected by them, and might be improved by their efforts.

PETER SUEDFELD has contributed more than anyone to knowledge about what happens to people when they spend time in isolated and confined environments.

WHY ARE WE DOING THIS?

THIS SENSE OF IMPROVING THE COMMUNITY AND CONTRIBUTING TO SUSTAINABILITY creates considerable motivation. Without going into great length, I cannot resist offering a few observations and suggestions about the future, as seen by an environmental psychologist. The topic of utopia is an obvious one for a discipline with a problem-solving mandate,[2] so I offer a few thoughts on that next. Then you can discuss the matter, if you wish, with some friends over a glass of your favorite thirst-quencher. Here is a discussion opener: Are you fundamentally optimistic that communities and the world will improve, that we can reach the goals of quality communities and a sustainable world? Or, are you pessimistic that these goals are not attainable? You

may explore this question further by looking at some of the suggested readings provided later.

Which Topia? Topia is Greek for place. Environmental psychologists hope to help create better places. Utopia is a word coined by Sir Thomas More for his famous 1516 book. It has no precise meaning; "u" is not a Greek prefix. In Greek, *eutopia* translates as "good place" and *outopia* as "no place." Perhaps Thomas More meant *utopia* as a pun or a combination of the two meanings. One way to interpret utopia is as a good place that cannot be realized; this may be why most people think of utopia as nothing but castles in the air. Utopia emphatically is *not* what environmental psychologists aim for. We have a different topia in mind: **entopia**, which means, approximately, *achievable* place.[3] This conveys the important idea that better settings *can*, with effort, be brought into existence. The search for better places is not a hopeless or even foolish search for utopia.

Architectural Entopias. Most utopian visions have a static quality to them: everything should be a certain way, which is presumed to maximally enhance everyone's quality of life; a certain architecture that will support the visionary's philosophy. Yet it seems to me that entopic places must have flexibility, if not guaranteed change. Even a "perfect" place would become deathly boring if it never changed. This raises an ancient paradox: How can an ideal environment remain ideal if we agree that it must change? An architectural entopia should change even if it is constructed for one person, but it would very likely be home for many individuals.

Human personality will always vary from person to person; how should an architectural entopia be designed to fit them all? One major challenge is building settings for different individuals who will use it. Another challenge is to create settings that suit human cognitive, perceptual, and social tendencies that are relatively *similar* across people. Some features of entopia must do the same things for everyone. For example, we need settings that help promote the fulfillment of human potential instead of limiting or even squashing it. To that end, the major physical settings of life, such as homes, schools, and workplaces, must be revamped in an architectural entopia.

All these settings often are saddled with traditions that make them far short of entopic. For instance, classrooms are still hard and set up in rows, many homes have open brick fireplaces that owners rarely use but which are very energy inefficient, and poorly designed offices still plague many employees. Even prison buildings go beyond their purpose of denying freedom; many actually encourage violence and illness. What will it take to change the design process so that user needs are more often taken into account? The process described in Chapter 15 still is not yet in widespread use. One answer is to educate policy makers and the public to the need for humane programming and careful post-occupancy evaluation. For certain kinds of buildings, perhaps those built for members of the public, legislation that ensures consideration of building users is essential.

Space as Entopia. Many people believe that one solution, or perhaps the only long-term solution, is for humanity to head out into the wild black yonder: other bodies in the solar system, such as the moon and Mars. We, as a species, can expand they argue; in fact, human nature dictates that we will expand (witness the mass migrations and "discovery" of the New World in the Americas, for example). We always have pushed outward. Toward this end, some environmental psychologists, like Peter Suedfeld, have put much effort into understand the psychological effects of the isolation and confinement that would be required to make the long journeys in very small vehicles.[4] Others, like Robert Bechtel, have written about Mars as a destination, pointing out the enormous difficulties in such an enterprise, many of which are psychological in nature.[5]

Natural and Sustainable Entopias. What about the natural side of entopia, and entopic sustainability? Some would claim that nature already *is* entopia, but these people probably are not among the millions of victims of nature's awesome dark forces. What *should* we think about nature? At least since Biblical times, when the author of Genesis said that everything was put upon the earth for people to use, humans have almost blindly espoused this utilitarian view. Trees exist for us to make lumber from, some animals exist for eating and hunting, water for washing, stones for building.

However, another view has been recently growing, one that considers nature as a being of its own, with its own independent, intrinsic value. In this view, nature deserves the same sort of love and respect that we would accord a person we love. Ecocentrists see nature as worthy of respect and benign treatment *for its own merits*, as opposed to anthropocentrists, who believe we should treat the earth kindly *so we will have a nice place to live and play*. More radical views envision nature as an entity that is living, breathing, and evolving just like us,[6] one that is even capable of fighting back against human uses and abuses of it.[7]

This difference between viewing nature as a resource pool to enrich human life versus seeing it as worthy of care and respect independent of human needs is a crucial issue. Is "sustainable development" an oxymoron? Should we engage in "de-growth" of the economy? For example, if nature lives and breathes, it could either grow more healthy or less so. As many have pointed out, we humans will not get far on a planet with drastically reduced biodiversity and a ruined atmosphere. One intriguing idea is that nature may be capable of both beneficent love and maleficent destruction. If we treat nature well, will it grow more trees and food for us? If we treat nature poorly, will it respond with natural disasters? Does nature experience a mine shaft as a stab wound? Is a garden like a massage for nature?

ROBERT BECHTEL was the editor of the journal Environment and Behavior for many years, and has made many other contributions to environmental psychology.

In case these philosophic musings are too exotic for you, I turn now to more familiar environmental problems. I believe there are both good and bad trends. One bright spot is that awareness of environmental issues is now extremely widespread. Positive actions may be seen everywhere in anti-litter, conservation, and recycling campaigns. Where curbside recycling is available, over 80% of residents recycle. Although automobile manufacturers always say that new emission control regulations "cannot be achieved" when the laws are enacted, they have never failed to meet those standards by the time the deadline arrives.[8] Acid rain has been cut by 40 to 70 percent, depending on where you live. Contrary to the predictions of opponents, strict air pollution regulations have not hurt the economy, at least not that of the Los Angeles area, where the number of air pollution alerts has declined 86 percent.[9] The Project for Public Spaces (*www.pps.org*), an outgrowth of the pioneering work by William Whyte with New York plazas and squares, has grown and prospered and made many suggestions for improving public spaces. Awareness of climate change is now almost universal, and even leaders whose history suggests they do not support action in that area are at least proclaiming that it is a problem that needs urgent action.

Nevertheless, many more cars are on the roads, the total distance driven around the world keeps increasing at the same time that vehicles kill and injure far too many people and animals, and the amount of greenhouse gases has alarmingly increased in the last century. Not enough neighborhoods are designed to encourage walking, and they contribute to the obesity epidemic. More forests are being made into parks, but at the same time the world's forests are shrinking. Almost no forest is simply left alone: either it becomes a green shrine or it is mowed down.

Nevertheless, the real gap between awareness and reality hurts. Those who try hard are often frustrated by negative trends that seem too strong to change. Environmental depression is a real possibility, yet some therapists tell their clients who have tried to explain that their depression is related to environmental degradation are told to focus on their "real" problems.[10] A previously unknown group of nomads was recently discovered in South America. They were wandering in search of a "painless place" they had heard about. We, too, live in a place that pains many, and needs our help. For now, this is our only home. There's no way out of here. It can, I believe, be turned into an entopia. What are *you* doing to help?

Suggested Readings

Fox, D. R. (1985). Psychology, ideology, utopia, and the commons. *American Psychologist, 40*, 48-58.

Moos, R., & Brownstein, R. (1977). *Environment and utopia: A synthesis.* New York: Plenum.

Porter, P., & Lukerman, R. (1976). The geography of utopia. In D. Lowenthal & M. Bowden (Eds.), *Geographies of the mind.* New York: Oxford, 1976.

Schmuck, P., & Schultz, W. P. (2002). *The psychology of sustainable development.* Norwell, MA: Kluwer Academic.

Zimmerman, M. E., Callicot, J. B., Sessions, G., Warren, K. J., & Clark, J. (1993). *Environmental philosophy: From animal rights to radical ecology.* Englewood Cliffs, NJ: Prentice Hall.

References

1 Gifford, R. (2014). Environmental psychology matters. *Annual Review of Psychology, 65,* 541-580.

2 Moos, R., & Brownstein, R. (1977). *Environment and utopia: A synthesis.* New York: Plenum.

3 Doxiadis, C. A. (1975). *Building entopia.* Athens: Athens Publishing Center.

4 Suedfeld, P. (1987). Extreme and unusual environments. In D. Stokols & I. Altman (Eds.), *Handbook of environmental psychology* (Vol. 1. pp. 863-887). New York: Wiley.

5 Bechtel, R. B. (2002). On to Mars. In R. B. Bechtel & A. Churchman (Eds.), *Handbook of environmental psychology* (2nd ed., pp. 676-685). New York: Wiley.

6 Lovelock, J. (2000). *Gaia: A new look at life on earth.* New York: Oxford University Press.

7 Lovelock, J. (2006). *The revenge of Gaia: Why the earth is fighting back - and how we can still save humanity.* Santa Barbara, CA: Allen Lane.

8 Berg, L. L. (1995, April 24). They always say it can't be done, and it always can. Toronto *Globe and Mail*, p. A-21.

9 Appleby, T. (1995, April 4). Smog rules green in more ways than one. Toronto *Globe and Mail*, p. B-26.

10 Wessan, L. (1994). "What's really bothering you, Lisa?" *The Ecopsychology Newsletter, 1*(2), 4.

Publications, Graduate Schools, and Organizations

STUDENTS AND OTHER READERS frequently ask me where to look for information about particular topics, graduate schools, and organizations for those interested in environmental psychology. This appendix is for those who wish to pursue their interests in environmental psychology and to be aware of the primary institutions in the field. It provides a brief guide to the organizations, journals, publications, graduate schools and their associated websites. It is as accurate as I could make it in mid-2014, but be aware that information in it can change. Probably the best single site for finding everything relevant to this field and links to other useful sites is the American Psychological Association's Population and Environment division: ***www.apa34.org***

Handbooks

THESE ARE MASSIVE COMPENDIA OF KNOWLEDGE ABOUT PERSON–ENVIRONMENT RELATIONS. Handbooks are indispensable for the serious scholar or researcher and, if you are in luck, your library has purchased one or both.

Handbook of Environmental Psychology. Edited by Daniel Stokols and Irwin Altman (1st edition, 1987) and Robert Bechtel and Arza Churchman (2nd edition, 2002).

The Oxford Handbook of Environmental and Conservation Psychology (2012). Edited by Susan D. Clayton. An excellent, more recent, gathering of ideas from across the field, despite (in this author's opinion) the superfluous redundancy in its title.

Journals

Journal of Environmental Psychology. Established in 1981, JEP is the major journal in the field. ***www.journals. elsevier.com/journal-of-environmental-psychology***

Environment and Behavior. Established in 1969, E & B is one of the primary journals in the field. ***eab.sagepub. com***

Annual Review of Psychology. Annual Reviews, Inc., each year publishes volumes that summarize recent developments in psychology (and other fields). Environmental psychology has been the subject of a chapter in the *Annual Review of Psychology* in 1973 (by Kenneth Craik), 1978 (by Daniel Stokols), 1982 (by James Russell and Lawrence Ward), 1986 (by Charles Holahan), 1990 (by Susan Saegert and Gary Winkel), 1992 (by Paul Stern), 1996 (by Eric Sundstrom, Paul Bell, and Paul Busby), 2000 (by Peter Suedfeld and Gary Steel), 2006 (by Gary Evans), and 2014 (by Robert Gifford).

Journal of Architectural and Planning Research. Established in 1984, its emphasis is clear from its title, but it does include a fair amount of behavioral research. ***www.lockescience.com***

Architectural Science Review once focused entirely on technical matters, but it now encourages contributions from the social science approach to environment and behavior. ***http://www.tandfonline.com/toc/tasr20/current#. U4ES1s8U-70***

Journal of Environmental Education focuses on research related to efforts to improve environmental behavior through educational courses and programs. ***http://www.tandfonline.com/toc/vjee20/current#. U4ETCc8U-70***

EDRA Proceedings. These are annual volumes of papers presented at the meetings of the Environmental Design Research Association. See your library's catalog under EDRA.

READERS WILL ALSO FIND SCATTERED ARTICLES OF INTEREST IN MANY OTHER JOURNALS. An indispensable tool for the modern researcher is PsycInfo, the online database. Environmental psychology research is interdisciplinary, so useful articles that one could never otherwise find may be found with this tool in widely scattered journals.

Monographs

EVERY DISCIPLINE NEEDS IN-DEPTH REVIEWS of particular topics at the professional level. There are many such books available; here I will only introduce those that form part of established series. These books consist of chapters reviewing the latest developments in environmental psychology. Some or all should be in your library:

Human Behavior and Environment: Advances in Theory and Research, edited by Irwin Altman and others since 1976, is published by Plenum Press. The first two volumes were on general topics. Since then the volumes have focused on children (3), culture (4), transportation (5), the natural environment (6), the elderly (7), home (8), neighborhood and community (9), public places and spaces (10), emergence of intellectual traditions (11), and place attachment (12).

Advances in Environmental Psychology, published by Lawrence Erlbaum Associates since 1981, has focused on urban life (1), personal control (2), energy conservation (3), health (4), research methods (5), and exposure to hazardous substances (6).

Advances in Environment, Behavior, and Design, from Plenum Press, has published 4 volumes since 1986. Each volume contains chapters on advances in theory, research with building users, and applications.

Community Development Series from the publishers Dowden, Hutchison and Ross contains over two dozen books and the EDRA Proceedings. The emphasis is on community planning and design.

Graduate Schools

STUDENTS WHO WISH TO SPECIALIZE IN ENVIRONMENTAL PSYCHOLOGY will need a Masters or Doctoral degree. Many universities offer formal or informal programs in psychology departments, schools of architecture, and certain other departments. Further details are available by consulting *Graduate Programs in Psychology*, published by the American Psychological Association. The latter may be available in your psychology department office or the campus counselling center. Many of the better programs are listed at: *http://www.apadivisions.org/division-34/about/resources/graduate-programs.aspx* Each one has a slightly different emphasis, so a good idea is to look at each school's website, the interests of the individual professors there, to best match your interests with those of a particular program.

Professional Organizations

The following organizations all play important roles for environmental psychologists, depending on specific interests and where they live.

DIVISION 34 (POPULATION AND ENVIRONMENT)

- The home of environmental psychologists within the American Psychological Association. *http://www.apadivisions.org/division-34/*

INTERNATIONAL ASSOCIATION FOR PEOPLE AND THEIR SURROUNDINGS

- IAPS is the principal home of environmental psychologists in Europe. *http://www.iaps-association. org*

DIVISION OF ENVIRONMENTAL PSYCHOLOGY

- This is the global-level home of environmental psychologists. It is part of the International Association of Applied Psychology. *http://www.iaapsy.org/division4/index. php?page=About-Division4*

ENVIRONMENTAL DESIGN RESEARCH ASSOCIATION

- EDRA is a large association of designers and researchers (mainly designers, but some environmental psychologists) that has held annual meetings since 1969. *www.edra.org*

SECTION ON ENVIRONMENTAL PSYCHOLOGY

- This is the home of environmental psychologists within the Canadian Psychological Association. It is a small hardy group in the Great White North. *http://www.cpa.ca/aboutcpa/cpasections/ environmentalpsychology/*

MAN–ENVIRONMENT RELATIONS ASSOCIATION

- MERA is the home of environmental psychologists in Japan. *http://www.mera-web.jp/index-e.html*

If you notice errors in the Appendix or have any suggestions for it, please contact me:

Robert Gifford
Department of Psychology
University of Victoria
Victoria, British Columbia, Canada V8W 3P5
or *rgifford@uvic.ca*

Index

Environment and Behavior, 6

environment-centered approach, 11-12

equality, commons, 468, 470-71, 472

era effect, environmental concern, 79

ergonomics, 361

Eso, Stephen, 118

ethnicity, environmental concern, 82

ethological approach, territoriality, 154

Euclidean abilities, 36

Euclidean bias, 38

euphony, 345

evacuation, disasters, 401-02

Evans, Gary, 39, 218

evolution, influences, 26, 38, 61, 154, 244, 289, 390

excitation transfer-misattribution model, 385

existential outsideness, 31

expectations, crowding, 174

experience phase, travel model, 367

experiential paradigm, OBEAs, 73

experimental research methods, 426

expert paradigm, 72

expert views, versus laypersons, 67, 396-98, 429

external environmentalism, 77

external locus of control (externals), 110, 111, 118, 173

external proceedings, 106

external validity, 13, 14, 171, 172

extraversion-introversion traits, 105, 108-109, 310, 347

extrinsic motivation, 76

eye contact, 125, 151-52, 170, 187, 258

F

facades, 31, 59, 60-61, 65, 305

fake experts, climate change, 436-37

false consensus, 395-96, 463

false conclusions, 29-30

familiar-context effect, learning, 307

familiarity, perception, 27, 58, 61, 62

familiar strangers, 259-60

fear of crime
communities, 248, 249
defensible space, 251, 263
density, 188, 233
design, 231
residential, 30, 140-41

feedback
climate action, 445, 446
conservation, 476, 481-82, 483
defection, 464
design, 511, 512
recycling, 489

feedback intervention theory, 481

felt responsibility, environmental concerns, 81

field experiments, 13-14, 131-32, 172, 459

field observations, 172

field studies, 13, 132, 140, 171, 203-04, 459

field theory, 5-6, 106-108

file-drawer problem, 384

films, climate change, 431-32, 445

first-order determination, 470

FISH microworld, 459

fittingness, as collative property, 31

floor plans, 37, 39-40, 224, 235

foreign hull, 106-07

formal design, versus social design, 500, 503

formal qualities, environmental design, 61

forms of knowledge, 3-4

fossil fuels, 422-23, 477, 483

Foster, Harold, 405, 406, 407

fourth environment, 258-59

fractals, preference, 61

Freedman, Jonathan, 195, 197

freedom and equality, commons dilemma, 470, 472

Freud, Sigmund, 156

Fried, Marc, 248, 286

friendship, 127, 131, 202, 464, 465, 490

furniture arrangements

behavior, 6, 108-109, 155, 156, 157, 179, 203
classrooms, 318
sense of control, 191
workplaces, 364. *See also* seating arrangements.

functional attachment, place, 275

G

Gallagher, Timothy, 111-12

gangs, 142, 147, 148

gardens,
attitudes, 225, 229, 244, 251
as barriers, 140, 141
design, 371
place attachment, 281, 294

Geller, Scott, 88, 488

gender differences,
crowding, 174-75, 176
density, 186, 231
environmental concern, 79
noise, 310, 347
perception, 26, 58
personal space, 133, 134, 137, 143-44
place attachment, 280
privacy, 180, 324-25
residences, 221-22, 227-28
risk taking, 114
school settings, 307, 330
special cognition, 37-38
territoriality, 138

gender-role orientation, personal space, 143

genealogy, place attachment, 283, 287

general affective model, 385

generalists, 112

generalized environmental ethic, 78

genetics, 151, 154, 390, 470. *See also* evolution.

genius fallacy, 508

geomagnetic forces, 386

Gibson, James, 30, 61

identity-oriented marking, workplace territoriality, 365

ideological communication, environmental meaning, 65

ideologies, inaction, 86, 442

illusion of control, disasters, 403

imageability, 504, 507, 518

Image of the City, The, 34

immigrants, crowding, 188-89, 190

implicit association test, 116

impossible expectations, climate change, 437

inaction. *See* dragons of inaction.

incentives, behavior, 246, 443, 444, 445, 465-66, 480. *See also* rewards.

incongruity, as collative property, 30-31

Inconvenient Truth, An, 432

individual cognitive freedom, 171

individualism, commons behavior, 463

individualistic theories, pro-environmental behavior, 443-44

indoor density, 169, 184, 186, 204, 231, 235. *See also* high-rises.

indoor hazards, 232

inferential mode, looking, 257

information, crowding, 177

information distribution process, 199-200

information-motivation-behavior skills model, 489

information-seeking, hazards, 398

informational overload, crowding, 196

infringement, territory, 129

instrumental-spiritual model, 11

integral neighborhoods, 243

integral theories, 10-11

intellectual growth perspective, 42-43

interactional territories, 129

interactionism, 10

interchangeability, displacement, 287

interest, antiquarian personality, 115

interference, crowding, 176

Intergovernmental Panel on Climate Change (IPCC), 422, 424, 432

interiors, 224-25, 306-08, 319, 324. *See also* color.

internal environmentalism, 77

internal locus of control (internals), 110, 111, 118, 173

internal proceedings, 106

International Association of People-Environment Studies (IAPS), 6

International Modernism, 65

International Space Station, 366

interpersonal attachment, place attachment, 290-91

interpersonal distance
    behavior, 109, 126, 127, 144, 145-46
    children, 133
    equilibrium, 152
    locus of control, 110. *See also* personal space.

interpersonal distance continuum, 152

interpersonal similarity, crowding, 176

interviews, research, 425-26, 514, 515

intimacy, 171, 190, 192, 198, 201

intimate distance, 127

intra-individual responses, climate change, 440

intrinsic motivation, 75-76, 86-87

introversion. *See* extraversion-introversion traits.

invasion, as infringement, 129, 140-41, 143, 144, 145-46

isolation, 171, 176

Issue Investigation and Action Training (IIAT), 83-84

Ittelson, William, 6

J

Jacobs, Jane, 140, 252

Jencks, Charles, 65, 66

job satisfaction, 168, 309, 342, 349, 359, 362, 367-68

Johnson, Philip, 502

joint planning, 516

Journal of Environmental Psychology, 6, 14

judgment formats, Craik's framework, 56, 57

Jung, Carl, 105

just-world belief, 403, 433, 435

K

Kaplan, Rachel, 61-62, 389

Kaplan, Stephen, 61-62, 390

Kelly, I. W., 384

knowledge
    conservation, 478-79
    perception, 26, 37, 87
    surroundings, 326-27, 328

knowledge deficit model, 399

Kormos, Christine, 76, 344

Knowles, Eric, 153, 169, 195

know-nothing fallacy, 508

!Kung, 189

L

Laboratory for Architectural Experimentation (LEA), 235

laboratory research methods, 13, 43, 130, 131, 171-72, 204. *See also* simulations.

Lacombe, Cécile, 232, 250, 366

lamps. *See* lighting.

landfills, 90, 107

landmarks, 34, 36-37, 39, 40, 44

landscapes
    features, 27, 37
    OBEAs, 73, 89-90
    preferences, 26, 31, 58, 63, 109
    simulated, 60
    spatial cognition, 38, 42

language, influence, 25, 44, 137

Lawrence, Roderick, 235

Lawton, M. Powell, 228

layouts, affordances, 30. *See also* floor plans.

learned helplessness, 9, 197

LED lamps, 357

range and commons, 463
scale, 77
multidimensional scaling, 35
multiplace hyperactive urbanites, 244
multiple dispositions, behavior, 109
multiple-unit dwellings, 232, 479-80, 517. *See also* dormitories; high-rises; Pruitt-Igoe apartments.
Murray, Henry, 105-106, 504
music, 262, 348, 349
mystery, Kaplans' framework, 62-63
mystic, III

N

Nadel, Lynn, 44
narcissist, 462
narratives, 283, 431-32
Nasar, Jack, 61
national parks, 70, 73, 196, 369
natural environment awareness test (NEAT), 116
natural hazards, 391-409
naturalistic observation, 34, 131, 172
nature, 81, 246, 281, 285, 288, 387-91, 410. *See also* parks; trees.
Nature on the Way to School, 328
nature orientation, 116-17
nature scale, 116-17
need for privacy, 114
needs assessment, building, 513-14
negative affect escape model, 385
negative ions, workplace, 354-55, 356
neighborhood-confined urbanites, 244
neighborhood satisfaction, 222-23, 243-49, 250
cultural influences, 249
personal influences, 245-46
physical influences, 246-49
social influences, 248-49, 250, 281
neighborhoods
defensible space theory, 140-41
design, 156-57, 224, 248, 264-65

dimensions, 243-244, 248
perception, 42, 59, 243
physical qualities, 243, 250, 251, 390
recycling, 488
schools, 305-06
territoriality, 139
neighborhood work centers (NWCs), 372-73
neutral thwarting, crowding, 176
New Ecological Paradigm (NEP), 75, 77
Newman, Oscar, 140, 263
Newsham, Peter, 360
new urbanism, 257
Ng, Cheuk Fan, 23, 204, 362, 515
noise
feelings, 311-12
health, 349-50
helpfulness, 254-55
neighborhood satisfaction, 246, 247-48
personal influences, 310, 347
personality, 109, 117
place attachment, 282. *See also* educational settings, noise; music; workplace, noise.
noise sensitivity scale, 117
non-attachment, 289
non-rationality, 472-73
non-screeners, 117
non-specialists, 112, 113
nonverbal behavior, 134, 137, 145, 198
norm activation theory (NAM), 75
normal personality, 108-109
norms
behavior, 75, 84, 86, 87, 88, 253
climate action, 442, 445
conservation, 479
crowding, 174
residential satisfaction, 223
Not in My Backyard (NIMBY) syndrome, 67
not neighboring, 171

novelty, collative property, 30-31, 60, 61
nuclear power, perceptions, 67, 68, 78, 107, 394, 395, 401, 403, 405
nursing homes, design, 58, 194, 390, 502

O

objective-subjective dimension, III
object perception, 23
objects, as territories, 128-29
observational research, 277, 426
Observer-based environmental assessments (OBEAs), 70-74, 89-90
observers, Craik's framework, 56, 57
obsessive passion, 463
OCEAN, 108-09
O'Connor, Brian, 144
occupants
collaborators, 503, 504, 511, 515-17
education, 516
matching, 504-05
needs analysis, 514-15, 517
perceptions, 501, 510
physical traces, 514, 515
satisfaction, 504, 510-11, 517, 524
versus designers, 507
office settings
air quality, 355
design and POE, 523-24
infringement, 129, 192
open-plan, 350, 359, 362-63, 364-66, 373
privacy, III, 170, 181, 191, 199, 350, 373
sound levels, 346, 348-50, 373
temperature, 118, 352, 355
windows, 510-11
O'Keefe, John, 44
Olmsted, Frederick Law, 387
Olsen, Helge, 330-31
1/nth personality, 462
open-plan schools, 304, 306, 320-21, 323, 325

influences, 66-68
road climbing, 43
Rokeach Value Survey, 77, 78
Roma, 181
romantic escape scale, 116-17
romantic tourism, 371
Rosenblood, Lorne, 358
Roszak, Theodore, 11
Rotton, James, 384
routine activity theory, 385
rules and pricing, commons choices, 474
Russell, James, 64-65

S

Sacilotto, Paul, 131, 136
Saegert, Susan, 218
safety, 248-49, 360
salient others, commons choices, 474
scale, crowding, 177
Scannell, Leila, 90, 274, 277, 286-87
scenes, preferences, 60-62, 63
scenic beauty estimations (SBEs), 72-73
scenic quality, 89-90
scents, 263, 292, 355-56, 357
schemas, environmental design, 61
schizophrenia, personal space, 134, 156, 174
Schmidt, Faye, 118
scouting, environmental competence, 327
science court, 67
Scott, M.B., 129
screeners, 117, 173
seasonal affective disorder (SAD), 385-86
seasons. See climate, and behavior.
seating arrangements
    educational settings, 317
    place attachment, 293
    reactions, 111-12, 143-44, 146, 155-56, 181
    workplaces, 362, 364

secondary environments, crowding, 174
secondary territories, 128, 150, 188
second-order determinations, 470
seclusion, 171, 181
security, housing, 223
segmentation bias, 38
segments, travelers, 367
selective control, crowding experience, 170
self-actualization, 389
self-control, nature, 388
self-determination theory (SDT), 75-76
self-efficacy, climate change, 428, 440, 442
self-growth, place attachment, 288
self-identity, place attachment, 284
self-interest, commons, 458, 459, 461-62, 464, 471, 472
selfish gene theory, 470
self-protective behavior, hazards, 398-99
self-report methods, 25, 31, 64, 76, 85, 116, 130, 132, 276, 277, 514-15
self-specialists, 113
Selye, Hans, 8
sense of community, 252, 274, 281, 292, 465
sense of control
    hospitals, 410
    place attachment, 288, 293
    privacy, 190, 191-92, 202
    students, 311
    workplaces, 342, 347, 348. See also personalization.
sense of direction, personality, 109
sense of security, 140, 290-91
senses of place, 278
sensory information, 8, 177
Sense of Place Scale, 276
setting claim, workplace, 363
setting congruence, noise, 310
settlement identity, 278
sexual orientation, place attachment, 280

shadow side, place attachment, 289
shelters, design and POE, 522
sick building syndrome, 356
Simon, Julian, 458
simulations
    environmental education, 84, 480
    limitations, 130, 131
    research, 13, 25, 35, 42, 60, 89-90, 130, 135, 459, 473, 514-15, 516
signs, 39-40, 46, 191-92, 262, 482, 518. See also imageability; you-are-here maps.
single-family dwellings, 224, 226, 232-33, 282
single-parent families, 234-35, 289
situational information, crowding, 177
situation modes, crowding, 170
size constancy, 27
sketch maps, 34-35, 37, 38, 40
Skinner, B. F., 469, 472
Smith, Adam, 457
smoke, workplace, 357
sociability, 108-109, 173
social antecedents, crowding, 195
social behavior. See social interaction.
social boundary defense, for territories, 129-30, 139-40
social capital, 281
social climate, 139, 195
social comparison, climate action, 442
social control, 146, 199, 439
social density, 169, 176, 186, 188, 323-24
Social Design, 506
social design, 500-25
    advantages, 510-12
    problems, 507-10
    research, 502, 503, 504-15
    resistance, 507-09
social dilemmas, 10, 458-59, 473-74
social distance, 127
social-environmental processes, relations among, 200-204.
social features, settings, 9

Credits

These pages constitute a continuation of the copyright page.

SOURCE CREDITS (NOTE: All credits appear here, including those for tables, figures, and photographs.)

All photos and figures except those credited below are by the author, © Robert Gifford, copyright renewed 2014.

‡ Indicates use courtesy of the Union of British Columbia Municipalities and the Picture BC initiative.

§ Photos designated with a § appear courtesy of NASA.

ɘ Photos with this symbol appear under licensing terms of Getty Images / Photos.com / Jupiter Images.

All photos of environmental psychologists courtesy of themselves, except where noted below.

TABLE OF CONTENTS PHOTOS: Dedication page: Bob Friesen: blueberry farm, Mission, BC.‡ T.J. Watt: a (former) ancient red cedar in the Klanawa Valley on southwestern Vancouver Island, BC. Kent Kallberg: night dining in White Rock, BC.‡ Phil Best: night in Slocan, BC.‡ Ryan Jensen: Wet'suwet'en fisherman, Smithers, BC.‡

PREFACE: ix: Josh McCulloch. Coast mountains, snow, and skyscrapers; Vancouver, BC.‡ Author photo courtesy of Eva Gifford.

CHAPTER 1: Chapter Pages: Boomer Jerritt, Courtenay, BC, Canada.‡ Marc Christensen, Helliwell Provincial Park, Hornby Island, BC. Brunswik photo courtesy of the University of California, Berkeley. Lewin photo courtesy of Miriam Lewin. Fig 1-6: NASA photo. L-R: Flight Engineer Alexander Misurkin (Russia), Expedition 35 Commander Chris Hadfield (Canada) and Flight Engineer Pavel Vinogradov (Russia) aboard the International Space Station, March 2013.§

CHAPTER 2: Chapter pages: Josh McCulloch. Upana Caves, Nootka, Gold River BC.‡ "Thinker." Photos.com, under license Figure 2-2 courtesy of Kenneth H. Craik. Lynch photo courtesy of Anne B. Lynch. Figure 2-3 adapted from "The perception of traversed distance" by E. K. Sadalla and S. G. Magel, *Environment and Behavior*, 1980, 12, 65-79. Figure 2-7 from "The role of figural organization in city imageability: An information processing analysis" by C. I. Holahan and P. F. Sorenson, *Journal of Environmental Psychology*, 1985, 5, 279-286. © 1985 by Academic Press Inc. Reprinted by permission. Figure 2-8: Marc Christensen. Empress Hotel, Victoria, BC. Figure 2-9 adapted from "Cognitive mapping of largescale environments: The interrelationship of action plans,

acquisition, and orientation" by T. Garling, A. Book, and E. Lindberg, *Environment and Behavior*, 1984, 16, 3-34. Adapted by permission. Table 2-1 adapted from "The elementary spatial functions of the brain" by M. Kritchevsky in *Spatial cognition: Brain bases and development* by I. Stiles-Davis, M. Kritchevsky, and U. Bellugi.

CHAPTER 3: Chapter pages: Marc Christensen. Gulf Islands, BC. Table 3-1 from "The comprehension of the everyday physical environment" by K. H. Craik. Reprinted by permission of the *Journal of the American Institute of Planners*, 34, 1968. Table 3-2 based on "Further toward a set of semantic scales to measure the meaning of designed environments" by R. C. Cass and R. G. Hershberger. Paper presented at the annual meeting of the Environmental Design Research Association, Blacksburg, VA, April, 1973. Used by permission. Figure 3-1: Marc Christensen. Victoria, BC. Table 3-3 based on *Cognition and environment: Functioning in an uncertain world* by S. Kaplan and R. Kaplan, 1982, New York: Praeger. Used by permission. Figure 33 adapted from "A description of the affective quality attributed to environments" by J. A. Russell and G. Pratt, *Journal of Personality and Social Psychology*, 1980, 38, 311-322. ©1980 by the American Psychological Association. Adapted by permission of the author. Figure 3-3 adapted from "Approach-avoidance and affiliation as functions of the emotioneliciting quality of an environment" by J. A. Russell and A. Mehrabian, *Environment and Behavior*, 1978, 10, 355-387.

©1978. Adapted by permission of the author. Figure 3-6: Josh McCulloch, Stair Lake, Gold River, BC.‡ Figure 3-9: Marc Christensen. Figure 3-10: Ian Gould, Waves, Masset, BC.‡

CHAPTER 4: Chapter pages: Wayne Sawchuk, Fort Nelson, BC.‡ The BARREL team at the SANAE IV research station celebrates their final launch in the Antarctica sun. NASA.§ Murray photo courtesy of Caroline C. Murray. Figure 4-1 courtesy of Toby Talbot. Figure 4-4 adapted from "Behavioral responses to air pollution" by G. W. Evans, S. V. Jacobs, and N. B. Frager in *Advances in environmental psychology* by A. Baum and J. E. Singer (Eds.), 1982, Hillsdale, NJ: Erlbaum. Figure 4-5 adapted from *Catastrophe or cornucopia* by S. Cotgrove, 1982, New York: Wiley. Figure 4-7: Jon Pesochin. Farmhouse, Surrey, BC.‡

CHAPTER 5: Chapter pages: Marc Christensen. Fencing, railings and parking lines, Victoria, BC. Office conversation: Getty Images / Photos.com, under license.ə Figure 5-2 (people) courtesy of Nick Cowie; (birds) courtesy of Sistemart. Figure 5-3 based on *The hidden dimension* by E. T. Hall, 1966, Garden City, NY: Doubleday. Figure 5-6 adapted from "Sex, setting and personal space: First grade through college" by G. H. Tennis and J. M. Dabbs, *Sociometry*, 1975, 38, 385-394. Adapted by permission. Figure 55 adapted from "Experiments on orientation and proxemics" by M. Cook, *Human Relations*, 1970, 23, 61-76. ©1970 by Plenum Publishing. Adapted by permission. Figure 5-8 based on "Influence of culture, language, and sex on conversational distance" by N. M. Sussman and H. M. Rosenfeld, *Journal of Personality and Social Psychology*, 1982, 42, 66-74. ©1982 by the American

Psychological Association. Adapted by permission of the author. Figure 5-13 adapted from "The home advantage" by B. Schwartz and S. F. Barsky, *Social Forces*, 1977, 55, 641-661. Figure 5-14 adapted from "A few words about the home field advantage" by B. James, pp. 171-194. Figure 5-15 based on "Personal space in nursery school children" by R. Gifford and J. Price, *Canadian Journal of Behavioural Science*, 1979, 11, 318-326. Figure 5-16 based on "The symbiotic relationship between social psychology and environmental psychology: Implications from crowding, personal space, and intimacy regulation research" by J. R. Aiello, D. E. Thompson, and A. Baum in *Cognition, social behavior, and the environment* by J. H. Harvey (Ed.), 1981, Hillsdale, NJ: Erlbaum. Figure 5-17 from "Discomfort and stop distances from groups and individuals" by E. S. Knowles. Paper presented at the annual meeting of the Midwestern Psychological Association, 1981. Used by permission of the author.

CHAPTER 6: Chapter pages: Crowded ski hill and penguins images, Getty / Photos.com / Jupiter images, under license.ə Figure 6-5 Figure 8-2 courtesy of Fernando Weberich. Figure 6-7 adapted from "Social density and affiliative tendency as determinants of dormitory residential outcomes" by S. Miller, J. Rossbach, and R. Munson, *Journal of Applied Social Psychology*, 1981, 11, 356-365, adapted by permission. Table 6-1 from World Population Profile: 1989 by U.S. Bureau of the Census, 1989, Washington, DC: U.S. Government Printing Office. Figure 6-10 adapted from "Crowding, privacy and coping" by T. A. Walden, P. A. Nelson, and D. E. Smith, *Environment and Behavior*, 1981, 13, 205-224, adapted by permission. Figure 6-11 based on "Physical enclosure, type of job, and privacy in the office" by E. Sundstrom, J. P.

Town, D. W. Brown, A. Forman, and C. McGee, *Environment and Behavior*, 14, 1982, 543-559. Figure 6-13 adapted from "Crowding and the role of interpersonal distance preference" by J. R. Aiello, D. T. DeRisi, Y. M. Epstein, and R.A. Karlin, *Sociometry*, 1977, 40, 271-282. Figure 6-18 adapted from *The human context: Environmental determinants of behavior* by R. H. Moos, 1976, New York: Wiley. Reprinted by permission of John Wiley & Sons, Inc. Figure 6-20 courtesy of Yarik Mission. Figure 6-21 courtesy of Dani Megrelishvili. Figure 6-23 from *The environment and social behavior: Privacy, personal space, territoriality and crowding* by I. Altman, 1975, Monterey, CA: Brooks/Cole. Reprinted by permission of the author. Figure 6-24 from *Houses generated by patterns* by C. Alexander et al., 1969, Berkeley, CA: Center for Environmental Structure. Used by permission. Figure 6-25 based on "The office acoustical environment: A survey of office-workers' attitudes" by C. F. Ng and R. Gifford. Paper presented at the annual meetings of the Canadian Psychological Association, Ottawa, June 1984.

CHAPTER 7: Chapter pages: family mealtime, WavebreakMediaMicro under license from Fotolia.com. Couple looking at house, Andres Rodriguez under license from Fotolia.com. Figure 7-4 based on *Environmental choice, human behavior, and residential satisfaction* by William Michelson. Figure 7-9 based on "Residential mobility and personal wellbeing" by D. Stokols, S. A. Shumaker, and J. Martinez, *Journal of Environmental Psychology*, 1983, 3, 5-19.

CHAPTER 8: Chapter pages: Chapter contents: Jon Pesochin. Coquitlam, Vancouver, BC.‡ Marc Christensen. Warehouse and overpass, Detroit, MI. Figure 8-3. Chicago waterpark and Detroit corner fire hydrant, Marc Christensen. Figure 8-4 adapted from "Ambient temperature and violent crime: Tests of the linear and curvilinear hypotheses" by C. A. Anderson and D. C. Anderson, *Journal of Personality and Social Psychology*, 1984, 46, 91-97. ©1984 by the American Psychological Association, adapted by permission of the author. Figure 8-7: Mall interior, Richmond, BC. Chung Chow.‡ Figure 8-8: Marc Christensen.

CHAPTER 9: Chapter pages: Nick Sanderon Salmon River Valley, Sayward BC.‡ Beachfront joy: Josh McCulloch, Nanaimo, BC.‡ Figure 9-1: Leilia Scannell and Robert Gifford. Defining place attachment: A tripartite organizing framework. *Journal of Environmental Psychology*, 30, 1-10. Figure 9-2: Mike Wakefield. Mountain biking in British Columbia.‡ Figures 9-3 and 9-4: Leila Scannell. Figure 9-5: Josh McCulloch, Abbotsoford, BC.‡ Figure 9-6: Alec Pytlowany.‡ Figures 9-7 and 9-8: Leila Scannell. Figure 9-9: Tony Austin. Cemetery, Metchosin, BC.‡ Figure 9-10, 9-11, and 9-12: Leila Scannell. Fig 9-13: Jared Towers. Kwakwaka'wakw Nation Dancing, Alert Bay, BC.‡ Figure 9-14: Jacqueline Windh. Surfing lessons on Chesterman Beach, Tofino, BC.‡ Figure 9-15: Josh McCulloch. Stawamus Chief, Squamish BC.‡ Figure 9-16: Leila Scannell.

CHAPTER 10: Chapter pages: Schooldesk courtesy of Mark Cacovic. Historical image of Dr. Robert Goddard courtesy of NASA.§ Figure 10-2: Boomer Jerritt. Fossils at Courtenay, BC. Figure 10-4 courtesy of Anissa Thompson. Figure 10-5 adapted from "The effects of classroom noise on adults: Evidence for sex differences" by S. Hykin, 1984, unpublished master's thesis, 1984, University of Victoria,

Victoria, British Columbia, reprinted by permission. Figure 10-6 adapted from "The extra-visual effects of fluorescent illumination on the behavior of school children" by P. Munson and R. Ferguson, unpublished manuscript, 1984, University of Victoria, used by permission. Figure 10-7 adapted from "The effects of varied levels of resources and density on behavior in a day care center" by W. Rohe and A. H. Patterson in *Man-Environment interactions: Evaluations and applications* by D. Carson (Ed.), 1974, Stroudsberg, PA: Dowden, Hutchinson and Ross. Figure 10-8 adapted from "Location and interaction in row and column seating arrangements" by M. Koneya, *Environment and Behavior*, 1976, 8, 265-282. Figure 10-9 adapted from "Individual characteristics and children's performance in 'open' and 'traditional' classroom settings" by D. Solomon and A. J. Kendall, *Journal of Educational Psychology*, 1976, 68, 613-625. Figure 10-10 courtesy of MadMaven/ T. S. Heisele. Figure 10-13, courtesy of Robert Sommer.

CHAPTER 11: Chapter pages: Daniel Casper. Construction at the Kennedy Space Centre.§ Kim Shiflett. Launch Control Center at NASA's Kennedy Space Center in Florida.§ Figure 11-1 courtesy of Leo Cinezi (office) and Carlos Chávez (lift-truck driver). Figure 11-3: Marc Christensen. Figure 11-4 adapted from "Noise from domestic appliances, construction, and industry" by Z. F. Reif and P. J. Vermeulen, and from "A physical description of noise" by H. W. Jones, both from *Noise in the human environment* (Vol. 2), 1979, The Environmental Council of Alberta. Figure 11-6 courtesy of Joseph M. Zlomek. Figure 11-7 adapted from data published by the American Society of Heating, Refrigerating and Air-Conditioning Engineers. Used by permission. Figure 11-8 data from "Estimating oc-

cupant satisfaction from effective Temperature" by F. H. Rohles, Jr., S. Konz, and D. Munson, *Proceedings of the Human Factors Society*, 1980, 24, 223-227. Adapted from *Human factors: Understanding People-System relationships* by B. H. Kantowitz and R. D. Sorkin, 1983, New York: Wiley. ©1983 by John Wiley & Sons. Reprinted by permission of John Wiley & Sons, Inc. Figure 11-10 adapted from "Effects of atmospheric electricity on some substrates of disordered social behavior" by I. M. Charry and F. B. W. Hawkinshire, *Journal of Personal and Social Psychology*, 1981, 41, 185-197, adapted by permission. Figure 11-11 courtesy of Bud Wood. Figure 11-12 courtesy of Robert Sommer. Figure 11-15 courtesy of Walter Rock (hunter) and courtesy of Paco Busteros (diver).

CHAPTER 12: Chapter pages: Larry Doell, Beaver Falls, Montrose, BC.‡ Jillian Votava. A Goddard Space Flight Center intern takes in a view of the Grand Canyon.§ Figure 12-2 adapted from "Stress recovery during exposure to natural and urban environments" by R. S. Ulrich, R. F. Simons, B. D. Losito, E. Fiorito, M. A. Miles, and M. Zelson, *Journal of Environmental Psychology*, 1991, 11, 201-230. Table 12-1 from "Regulation of risk: A psychological perspective" by P. Slovic, B. Fischhoff, and S. Lichtenstein in *Social Science and Regulatory Policy* by R. Noll (Ed.), 1986, Berkeley: University of California Press. Reprinted by permission. Figure 12-3: David Rydevik. Figure 12-6, courtesy of the National Geophysical Data Center. Figure 12-7: US Coast Guard Petty Officer 2nd Class Kyle Niemi. Figure 12-8 adapted from "Coping with natural hazards as stressors: The predictors of activism in a flood disaster" by E. B. Rochford, Jr. and T. I. Blocker, *Environment and Behavior*, 1991, 23, 171-194. Reprinted by permission. Tables 132a and b from "Assessing disaster magnitude: A social science approach" by H. D. Foster, 1979, *The Professional Geographer, 28*, 244-245. Reprinted by permission.

CHAPTER 13: Chapter pages: Ian Routley. Lillooet from Red Rock.‡ Kathryn Hansen. Arctic sea ice inventory.§ Figure 13-1: Peace Photographic. Coal's Resurgence, Tumbler Ridge, BC.‡ Figure 13-2: Stephan Baker, Holstein cows.‡ Figure 13-3: Dezene Huber, courtesy of Simon Fraser University Public Affairs and Media Relations. Figure 13-4: R.L. Schuster. Landslide, La Conchita, CA (U.S. Geological Survey image courtesy of NOAA/NGDC). Figure 13-5: Mike Weeber. Bear Glacier, Stewart, BC.‡ Figure 13-6: Joseph O'Brien, USDA Forest Service, via Bugwood.org. Figure 13-7: Frank Peairs, Colorado State University, via Bugwood.org. Figure 13-8: NASA Goddard/Maryvale Preparatory School, Baltimore, MD.§ Figure 13-9: Honduras, aftermath of Hurricane Mitch. Courtesy of NOAA. Figure 13-10 adapted from Reser, J. P., & Swim, J. K. Adapting to and coping with the threat and impacts of climate change. *American Psychologist*, 2011, *66*, 277-289. Figure 13-11: Aerial views of the damage caused by Hurricane Sandy to the New Jersey coast, Oct. 2012. U.S. Air Force photo by Master Sgt. Mark C. Olsen.

CHAPTER 14: Chapter pages: Marc Roper. Log barge and tug, Port Alice, BC.‡ Cowboys and oil rig, Fort St. John, BC by Andrew Yylosky.‡ Figure 14-5 adapted from "Experimental study of individual vs. group interest" by G. E. Whisk, J. M. Dana, R. H. Doktor, and F. D. Rubenstein, *Acta Sociologica*, 1972, *15*, 366-370, adapted by permission. Figure 14-6 adapted from "Children and the commons dilemma" by R. Gifford, *Journal of Applied Social Psychology*,

1982, *12*, 269-280. Figure 14-8 adapted from "The commons dilemma: A simulation testing resource visibility and territorial division" by R. C. Cass and J. J. Edney, *Human Ecology*, 1978, *6*, 371-386. Adapted by permission. Figure 14-10 courtesy of Claudia Meyer. Figure 14-11 adapted from "Personal and contextual influences on household energy adaptations" by J. S. Black, P. C. Stem, and J. T. Elworth, *Journal of Applied Psychology*, 1985, *70*, 321. Figure 14-12 adapted from "Joint effect of feedback and goal setting on performance: A field study of residential energy conservation" by L. J. Becker, *Journal of Applied Psychology*, 1978, *63*, 428-433, adapted by permission. Figure 14-4: Claudia Meyer.

CHAPTER 15: Chapter pages: Jon Pesochin. Surrey City Centre, Surrey, BC.‡ Phil Taylor. Double-decker transit bus in Langford, BC.‡ Figure 15-2: Jared Towers. Longhouse, Alert Bay, BC.‡ Figure 15-3: Community hall and library, Pouce Coupe, BC. Peace Photographics.‡ Figure 15-4 adapted from *Environmental design evaluation* by A. Friedman, C. Zimring, and E. Zube, 1978, New York: Plenum. Figure 15-6 from *Inquiry by design: Tools for environment-behavior research* by J. Zeisel, 1981, New York: Cambridge University Press. Reprinted by permission. Table 15-2, adapted from "The effects of user-generated design modifications in a general hospital" by F. D. Becker and D. B. Poe, *Journal of Nonverbal Behavior*, 1980, *4*, 195-218. Reprinted by permission. Figure 15-8 (top) courtesy of Simon Fraser University IMC.

EPILOG: Chapter pages: Phil Best. Cityscape, Nelson, BC.‡ Playground of the Gods, Burnaby Mountain, Burnaby, BC. Jon Pesochin.‡ Figure 16-1 courtesy of Dawn Allyn (cougar), and courtesy of NASA (space station).

DESIGN: Design and production by Marc Christensen, GDC, at Emdash Publishing, Canada. Body copy set in Adobe Jenson. Display and accent typography: Leitura family by Dino dos Santos, DSType Foundry, Portugal.

PRINTING: This book printed on 50# Utopia Book Matte, a Forest Stewardship Council-certified paper manufactured in Appleton, WI. The paper is made from 10% post-consumer fibres and 100% sustainable sources in a chlorine-free manufacturing process. Book boards and cover are also 100% FSC-certified. In addition, the power for the printing of this book was generated by hydroeletric means, a renewable carbon-free source of clean energy.